Comprehensive

GO!

Learn | Practice | Succeed

Microsoft®
Office 365®

Excel™ 2019

Shelley Gaskin | Alicia Vargas

Series Editor: Shelley Gaskin

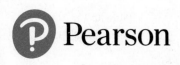

Pearson

VP Courseware Portfolio Management: Andrew Gilfillan
Executive Portfolio Manager: Jenifer Niles
Team Lead, Content Production: Laura Burgess
Content Producer: Shannon LeMay-Finn
Development Editor: Ginny Munroe
Portfolio Management Assistant: Bridget Daly
Director of Product Marketing: Brad Parkins
Director of Field Marketing: Jonathan Cottrell
Product Marketing Manager: Heather Taylor
Field Marketing Manager: Bob Nisbet
Product Marketing Assistant: Liz Bennett
Field Marketing Assistant: Derrica Moser
Senior Operations Specialist: Diane Peirano

Senior Art Director: Mary Seiner
Interior and Cover Design: Pearson CSC
Cover Photo: Jag_cz/Shutterstock, everything possible/Shutterstock
Senior Product Model Manager: Eric Hakanson
Manager, Digital Studio: Heather Darby
Digital Content Producer, MyLab IT: Becca Golden
Course Producer, MyLab IT: Amanda Losonsky
Digital Studio Producer: Tanika Henderson
Full-Service Project Management: Pearson CSC, Katie Ostler
Composition: Pearson CSC
Printer/Binder: LSC Communications, Inc.
Cover Printer: Phoenix Color/Hagerstown

Credits and acknowledgments borrowed from other sources and reproduced, with permission, in this textbook appear on appropriate page within text.

Microsoft and/or its respective suppliers make no representations about the suitability of the information contained in the documents and related graphics published as part of the services for any purpose. all such documents and related graphics are provided "as is" without warranty of any kind. microsoft and/or its respective suppliers hereby disclaim all warranties and conditions with regard to this information, including all warranties and conditions of merchantability, whether express, implied or statutory, fitness for a particular purpose, title and non-infringement. in no event shall Microsoft and/or its respective suppliers be liable for any special, indirect or consequential damages or any damages whatsoever resulting from loss of use, data or profits, whether in an action of contract, negligence or other tortious action, arising out of or in connection with the use or performance of information available from the services.

The documents and related graphics contained herein could include technical inaccuracies or typographical errors. changes are periodically added to the information herein. microsoft and/or its respective suppliers may make improvements and/or changes in the product(s) and/or the program(s) described herein at any time. partial screen shots may be viewed in full within the software version specified.

Microsoft® and Windows® are registered trademarks of the Microsoft Corporation in the U.S.A. and other countries. Screenshots and icons reprinted with permission from the Microsoft Corporation. This book is not sponsored or endorsed by or affiliated with the Microsoft Corporation.

Many of the designations by manufacturers and seller to distinguish their products are claimed as trademarks. Where those designations appear in this book, and the publisher was aware of a trademark claim, the designations have been printed in initial caps or all caps.

Library of Congress Cataloging-in-Publication Data

On file with the Library of Congress.

ISBN-10: 0-13-544268-0
ISBN-13: 978-0-13-544268-5

Brief Contents

Table of Contents

Introducing Microsoft Excel 2019 — 101

About the Authors

Shelley Gaskin, Series Editor, is a professor in the Business and Computer Technology Division at Pasadena City College in Pasadena, California. She holds a bachelor's degree in Business Administration from Robert Morris College (Pennsylvania), a master's degree in Business from Northern Illinois University, and a doctorate in Adult and Community Education from Ball State University (Indiana). Before joining Pasadena City College, she spent 12 years in the computer industry, where she was a systems analyst, sales representative, and director of Customer Education with Unisys Corporation. She also worked for Ernst & Young on the development of large systems applications for their clients. She has written and developed training materials for custom systems applications in both the public and private sector, and has also written and edited numerous computer application textbooks.

This book is dedicated to my husband Fred, and to my students, who inspire me every day.

Alicia Vargas is a faculty member in Business Information Technology at Pasadena City College. She holds a master's and a bachelor's degree in business education from California State University, Los Angeles, and has authored several textbooks and training manuals on Microsoft Word, Microsoft Excel, and Microsoft PowerPoint.

This book is dedicated with all my love to my husband Vic, who makes everything possible; and to my children Victor, Phil, and Emmy, who are an unending source of inspiration and who make everything worthwhile.

GO! with Microsoft Excel 2019 Comprehensive

Introducing seamless digital instruction, practice, and assessment

Using GO! with MyLab IT has never been better! With the integrated etext and pre-built learning modules, instructors can assign learning easily and students can get started quickly.

➤ **Proven content and pedagogical approach of *guided instruction, guided practice*, and *mastery*** is effective for all types of learners and all types of course delivery—face-to-face in the classroom, online, and hybrid.

➤ **Students learn Microsoft Office skills by creating practical projects** they will see in their academic and professional lives.

➤ **With GO! MyLab IT students can learn, practice, and assess live or in authentic simulations of Microsoft Office.**

   • **Microsoft Office autograded Grader** projects for the instructional, mastery, and assessment projects allow students to work live in Excel, Word, Access, or PPT so that during each step of the learning process, they can receive immediate, autograded feedback!

   • **Microsoft Office authentic simulations** allow students to practice what they are learning in a safe environment with learning aids for instant help—*Read*, *Watch*, or *Practice*. Authentic simulations can also be used for assessment without learning aids.

What's New?

* The **book (print or etext) is the student's guide** to completing all autograded Grader projects for instruction, practice, and assessment.

* The **GO! *Learn How* videos**, integrated in the etext, give students an instructor-led, step-by-step guide through the A & B projects.

* **Improved business case connection** throughout the instruction so students always understand the *what* and *why*.

* **Mac tips** 🔲 are woven into the instruction for each project so Mac students can proceed successfully.

   • All text and Grader projects created and tested by the authors on both a Mac and a PC.

   • Content not limited by Mac compatibility! Everything students need to know for MOS exams, Excel, and Access that are not possible on the Mac are still covered!

* **MyLab IT Prebuilt Learning modules** make course setup a snap. The modules are based on research and customer use, and can be easily customized to meet your course requirements.

* **Critical Thinking assessments and badges** expand coverage of Employability Skills.

* **New combined Office Features and Windows chapter** with Grader projects and auto-graded Windows projects for a fast and concise overview of these important features. Shorter and easier to assign.

- **Regular content updates to stay current with Office 365** updates and new features:
  - New *Semester Updates* for the etext and Grader projects through MyLab IT
  - New *Lessons on the GO!* to help you teach new features

What's New for Grader Projects

- **Autograded *Integrated Projects*** covering Word, Excel, Access, and PPT.
- Projects **A & B Grader reports now include *Learning Aids*** for immediate remediation.
- Autograded Critical Thinking Quizzes and Badges
  - Critical Thinking Modules include a Capstone and Quiz that enable students to earn a Critical Thinking Badge
  - Critical Thinking quizzes for the A & B instructional projects
- A **final output image** is provided so students can visualize what their solution should look like.
- **Mac Compatibility:** All Grader projects are built for PC and Mac users, excluding Access. Only projects that have features not supported on the Mac are not 100% compatible.

What's New for Simulations

- Simulations are updated by the authors for improved reinforcement of the software navigation in each instructional project—as always, they are matched one-to-one with the text Activities.
- *Student Action Visualization* provides an immediate playback for review by students and instructors when there's a question about why an action is marked as incorrect.

The Program

The GO! series has been used for over 17 years to teach students Microsoft Office successfully because of the *Quality of Instruction, Ease of Implementation,* and *Excellence in Assessment.* Using the hallmark Microsoft Procedural Syntax and Teachable Moment approach, students understand how to navigate the Microsoft Office ribbon so they don't get lost, and they get additional instruction and tips *when* they need them. Learning by doing is a great approach for skill-based learning, and creating a real-world document, spreadsheet, presentation, or database puts the skills in context for effective learning!

To improve student results, we recommend pairing the text content with **MyLab IT,** which is the teaching and learning platform that empowers you to reach every student. By combining trusted author content with digital tools and a flexible platform, MyLab personalizes the learning experience and will help your students learn and retain key course concepts while developing skills that future employers are seeking in their candidates.

Solving Teaching and Learning Challenges

The GO! series continues to evolve based on author interaction and experience with real students. GO! is written to ensure students know where they are going, how to get there, and why. Today's software is cloud based and changes frequently, so students need to know how the software functions so they can adapt quickly.

Each chapter is written with two instructional projects organized around **student learning outcomes** and **numbered objectives,** so that students understand what they will learn and be able to do when they finish the chapter. The **project approach** clusters the learning objectives around the projects rather than around the software features. This tested pedagogical approach teaches students to solve real problems as they practice and learn the software features. By using the textbook (print or digital), students can complete the A & B instructional projects as autograded Grader projects in MyLab IT. The *Learn How* videos, integrated in the etext or learning modules, give students an instructor-led, step-by-step guide through the project. This unique approach enhances learning and engages students because they receive immediate feedback. Additionally, students can practice the skills they are learning in the MyLab IT simulations, where they also get immediate feedback and help when needed! Both *Graders* and *Simulations* are available in assessment form so that students can demonstrate mastery.

The **Clear Instruction** in the project steps is written following *Microsoft Procedural Syntax* to guide students where to go and *then* what to do, so they never get lost! With the **Teachable Moment** approach, students learn important concepts when they need to as they work through the instructional projects. No long paragraphs of text. And with the integrated etext in MyLab IT, students can access their book anywhere, anytime.

The page design drives effective learning; textbook pages are clean and uncluttered, with screenshots that validate the student's actions and engage visual learners. Important information is boxed within the text so that students won't miss or skip the *Mac Tips, Another Way, By Touch, Note, Alert,* or *More Knowledge* details. **Color-Coded Steps** guide students through the projects with colors coded by project and the **End-of-Project Icon** helps students know when they have completed the project, which is especially useful in self-paced or online environments.

Students can engage in a wide variety of end-of-chapter projects where they apply what they learned in outcomes-based, problem-solving, and critical thinking projects   many of which require students to create a complete project from scratch.

Within the GO! etext and MyLab IT, students also have access to the *GO! Learn How* training videos, the *GO! to Work* videos (which demonstrate how Microsoft Office is used in a variety of jobs), the GO! for Job Success videos (which teach essential employability skills), and the *Where We're Going* videos, which provide a clear and concise overview of the instructional projects to ensure student success!

This complete, highly effective offering ensures students can learn the skills they need to succeed!

Developing Employability Skills

For students to succeed in a rapidly changing job market, they should be aware of their career options and how to go about developing a variety of skills. With MyLab IT and GO! we focus on developing these skills in the following ways:

High-Demand Office Skills are taught to help students gain these skills and prepare for the Microsoft Office Specialist (MOS) certification exams. The MOS objectives are covered throughout the content and highlighted with the MOS icons.

Essential Employability Skills are taught throughout the chapters using GO! for Job Success Videos and discussions, along with the new Critical Thinking badge students can earn by successfully completing the Critical Thinking Modules.

Employability Skills Matrix (ESM)								
	Grader Projects	Project K	Project M	Project O Group Project	Critical Thinking Projects and Badge	GO! To Work and Job Success Videos	MOS Practice Exams	MOS Badges
Critical Thinking	X	X	X		X		X	X
Communication	X			X		X		
Collaboration				X		X		
Knowledge Application and Analysis	X	X	X		X		X	X
Social Responsibility						X		

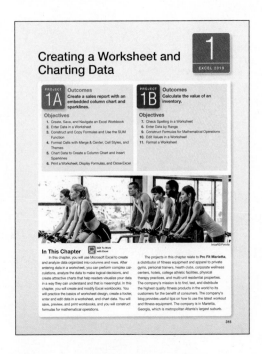

◁ Real-World Projects and GO! To Work Videos

The projects in GO! help you learn skills you'll need in the workforce and everyday life. And the GO! to Work videos give you insight into how people in a variety of jobs put Microsoft Office into action every day.

◁ Projects in GO! are real-world projects you create from start to finish, so that you are using the software features and skills as you will on the job and in everyday life.

GO! to Work videos feature people from a variety of real jobs ◁ explaining how they use Microsoft Office every day to help you see the relevance of learning these programs.

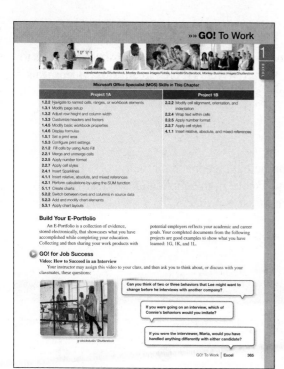

◀ GO! for Job Success Videos and Discussions

Important professional skills you need to succeed in a work environment, such as Accepting Criticism, Customer Service, and Interview Skills, are covered in a video with discussion questions or an overall discussion topic. These are must-have skills.

◀ Skills Badging

Within MyLab IT 2019, you can earn digital badges that demonstrate mastery of specific skills related to Office 2019 or Critical Thinking. These badges can be easily shared across social networks, such as LinkedIn, leading to real opportunities to connect with potential employers.

Applied Learning Opportunities

Throughout the chapters there are two projects for instruction, two for review, and a variety of outcomes-based projects to demonstrate mastery, critical thinking, and problem solving. In addition, within MyLab IT, GO! Learn How videos walk students through the A & B instructional project objectives. Grader projects and simulations provide hands-on instruction, training, and assessment.

▼ Live-in-the-Application Grader Projects

The MyLab IT Grader projects are autograded so students receive immediate feedback on their work. By completing these projects, students gain real-world context as they work live in the application, to learn and demonstrate an understanding of how to perform specific skills to complete a project.

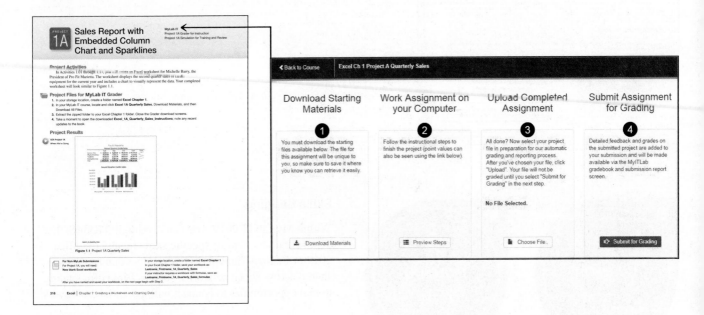

▼ Microsoft Office Simulations

The realistic and hi-fidelity simulations help students feel like they are working in the real Microsoft applications and enable them to explore, use 96% of Microsoft methods, and do so without penalty.

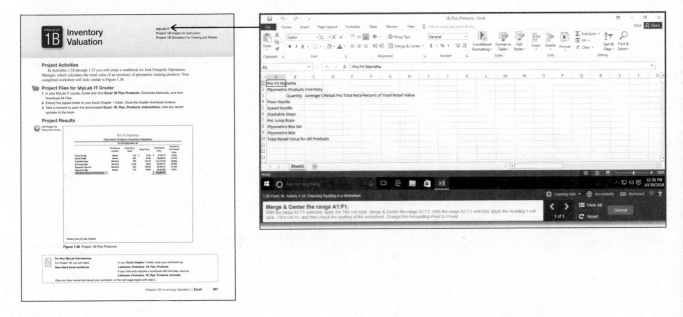

Instructor Teaching Resources

This program comes with the following teaching resources.

Resources available to instructors at www.pearsonhighered.com/go	Features of the Resources
Annotated Instructor Edition Tabs	Available for each chapter and include: • Suggested course implementation strategies and resources for the instructional portion of the chapter • Suggested strategies and resources for the Review, Practice, and Assessment portion of the chapter • Teaching tips
Annotated Solution Files	Annotated solution files in PDF feature callouts to enable easy grading.
Answer Keys for Chapter, MOS, and Critical Thinking Quizzes	Answer keys for each matching and multiple choice question in the chapter.
Application Capstones	Capstone projects for Word, Excel, Access, and PowerPoint that cover the objectives from all three chapters of each application. These are available as autograded Grader projects in MyLab IT, where students can also earn a proficiency badge if they score 90% or higher.
Collaborative Team Project	An optional exercise to assign to students to learn to work in groups.
Content Updates	A living document that features any changes in content based on Microsoft Office 365 changes as well as any errata.
Critical Thinking Quiz and Answers	Additional quiz and answers.
End-of-Chapter Online Projects H-J and M-O	Additional projects that can be assigned at instructor discretion.
Image Library	Every image in the book.
Instructor Manual	Available for each chapter and includes: • Suggested course implementation strategies and resources for the instructional portion of the chapter • Suggested strategies and resources for the Review, Practice, and Assessment portion of the chapter • Objectives • Teaching notes • Discussion questions
List of Objectives and Outcomes	Available for each chapter to help you determine what to assign • Includes every project and identifies which outcomes, objectives, and skills are included from the chapter
Lessons on the GO!	Projects created to teach new features added to Office 365. Available online only.
MOS Mapping and Additional Content	Based on the Office 2019 MOS Objectives • Includes a full guide of where each objective is covered in the textbook. • For any content not covered in the textbook, additional material is available in the Online Appendix document.
PowerPoint Presentations	PowerPoints for each chapter cover key topics, feature key images from the text, and include detailed speaker notes in addition to the slide content. PowerPoints meet accessibility standards for students with disabilities. Features include, but are not limited to: • Keyboard and screen reader access • Alternative text for images • High color contrast between background and foreground colors Audio PPTs contain spoken audio within traditional PowerPoint presentations.
Prepared Exams by Project, Chapter, and Application	An optional exercise that can be used to assess students' ability to perform the skills from each project, chapter, or across all chapters in an application • Each Prepared Exam folder includes the needed data files, instruction file, solution, annotated solution, and scorecard.

Resources available to instructors at www.pearsonhighered.com/go	Features of the Resources
Scorecards and Rubrics	Scorecards allow for easy scoring when hand-grading projects with definitive solutions. Rubrics are for projects without a definitive solution. These are available in Microsoft Word format, enabling instructors to customize the assignments for their classes.
Scripted Lectures	A lecture guide that provides the actions and language to help instructors demonstrate skills from the chapter.
Skills and Procedures Summary Charts	Concise list of key skills, including software icon and keyboard shortcut.
Solution Files, Solution File PDFs, and Solution Files with Formulas (Excel only)	Available for all exercises with definitive solutions.
Student Assignment Trackers	Document with a grid of suggested student deliverables per chapter that can be provided to students with columns for Due Date, Possible Points, and Actual Points.
Student Data Files	Files that students need to complete projects that are not delivered as Grader projects in MyLab IT.
Syllabus Template	Syllabus templates set up for 8-week, 12-week, and 16-week courses.
TestGen and Test Bank	TestGen enables instructors to: • Customize, save, and generate classroom tests • Edit, add, or delete questions from the Test Item Files • Analyze test results • Organize a database of tests and student results. The Test Gen contains approximately 75–100 total questions per chapter, made up of multiple-choice, fill-in-the blank, true/false, and matching. Questions include these annotations: • Correct answer • Difficulty level • Learning objective Alternative versions of the Test Bank are available for the following LMS: Blackboard CE/Vista, Blackboard, Desire2Learn, Moodle, Sakai, and Canvas.
Transition Guide	A detailed spreadsheet that provides a clear mapping of content from GO! Microsoft Office 2016 to GO! Microsoft Office 365, 2019 Edition.

Reviewers of the GO! Series

Carmen Montanez	Allan Hancock College
Jody Derry	Allan Hancock College
Roberta McDonald	Anoka-Ramsey Community College
Paula Ruby	Arkansas State University
Buffie Schmidt	Augusta University
Julie Lewis	Baker College
Melanie Israel	Beal College
Suzanne Marks	Bellevue College
Ellen Glazer	Broward College
Charline Nixon	Calhoun Community College
Joseph Cash	California State University, Stanislaus
Shaun Sides	Catawba Valley Community College
Linda Friedel	Central Arizona College
Vicky Semple	Central Piedmont Community College
Amanda Davis	Chattanooga State Community College
Randall George	Clarion University of Pennsylvania
Beth Zboran	Clarion University of Pennsylvania
Lee Southard	College of Coastal Georgia
Susan Mazzola	College of the Sequoias
Vicki Brooks	Columbia College
Leasa Richards-Mealy	Columbia College
Heidi Eaton	Elgin Community College
Ed Pearson	Friends University
Nancy Woolridge	Fullerton College
Wayne Way	Galveston College
Leslie Martin	Gaston College
Don VanOeveren	Grand Rapids Community College
Therese ONeil	Indiana University of Pennsylvania
Bradley Howard	Itawamba Community College
Edna Tull	Itawamba Community College
Pamela Larkin	Jefferson Community and Technical College
Sonya Shockley	Madisonville Community College
Jeanne Canale	Middlesex Community College
John Meir	Midlands Technical College
Robert Huyck	Mohawk Valley Community College
Mike Maesar	Montana Tech
Julio Cuz	Moreno Valley College
Lynn Wermers	North Shore Community College
Angela Mott	Northeast Mississippi Community College
Connie Johnson	Owensboro Community & Technical College
Kungwen Chu	Purdue University Northwest
Kuan Chen	Purdue University Northwest
Janette Nichols	Randolph Community College
Steven Zhang	Roane State Community College
Elizabeth Drake	Santa Fe College
Sandy Keeter	Seminole State
Pat Dennis	South Plains College
Tamara Dawson	Southern Nazarene University
Richard Celli	SUNY Delhi
Lois Blais	Walters State Community College
Frederick MacCormack	Wilmington University
Jessica Brown	Wilmington University
Doreen Palucci	Wilmington University
Rebecca Anderson	Zane State College

Microsoft Office Features and Windows 10 File Management

1
OFFICE AND
WINDOWS

PROJECT 1A

Outcomes
Use the features common across all Microsoft Office applications to create and save a Microsoft Word document.

Objectives

1. Explore Microsoft Office
2. Create a Folder for File Storage
3. Download and Extract Zipped Files, Enter and Edit Text in an Office Application, and use Editor to Check Documents
4. Perform Office Commands and Apply Office Formatting
5. Finalize an Office Document
6. Use the Office Help Features

PROJECT 1B

Outcomes
Use Windows 10 features and the File Explorer program to manage files and folders.

Objectives

7. Explore Windows 10
8. Prepare to Work with Folders and Files
9. Use File Explorer to Extract Zipped Files and to Display Locations, Folders, and Files
10. Start Programs and Open Data Files
11. Create, Rename, and Copy Files and Folders

Petar Djordjevic/Shutterstock

In This Chapter

GO! To Work
with Office Features

In this chapter, you will practice using the features of Microsoft Office that work similarly across Word, Excel, Access, and PowerPoint. These features include performing commands, adding document properties, applying formatting to text, and searching for Office commands quickly. You will also practice using the file management features of Windows 10 so that you can create folders, save files, and find your documents easily.

The projects in this chapter relate to the **Bell Orchid Hotels**, headquartered in Boston, and which own and operate restaurants, resorts, and business-oriented hotels. Resort property locations are in popular destinations, including Honolulu, Orlando, San Diego, and Santa Barbara. The resorts offer deluxe accommodations and a wide array of dining options. Other Bell Orchid hotels are located in major business centers and offer the latest technology in their meeting facilities. Bell Orchid offers extensive educational opportunities for employees. The company plans to open new properties and update existing properties over the next decade.

PROJECT 1A
Chef Notes

Project Activities

In Activities 1.01 through 1.19, you will create a handout for the Executive Chef at Skyline Metro Grill to give to her staff at a meeting where they will develop new menu ideas for wedding rehearsal dinners. The restaurant is located within Bell Orchid's San Diego resort hotel. Your completed notes will look similar to Figure 1.1.

Project Files for **MyLab IT Grader**

1. For Project 1A, you will start with a blank Word document, and then you will learn how to create a folder for your **MyLab IT** files as you work through the Project instruction. At the appropriate point in the Project, you will be instructed to download your files from your **MyLab IT** course.

Project Results

GO! Project 1A
Where We're Going

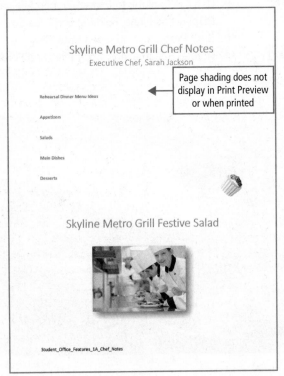

Figure 1.1 (Wavebreakmedia/Shutterstock)

	For Non-MyLab Submissions **Start with a blank Word document** For Project 1A, you will begin with a blank Word document and then learn how to create a folder and save a Word document as you work through the Project instruction.

NOTE   If You Are Using a Touch Screen

Tap an item to click it.

Press and hold for a few seconds to right-click; release when the information or commands display.

Touch the screen with two or more fingers and then pinch together to zoom out or stretch your fingers apart to zoom in.

Slide your finger on the screen to scroll—slide left to scroll right and slide right to scroll left.

Slide to rearrange—similar to dragging with a mouse.

Swipe to select—slide an item a short distance with a quick movement—to select an item and bring up commands, if any.

Objective 1   Explore Microsoft Office

ALERT   Because Office 365 is a cloud-based subscription service that receives continuous updates, you may encounter some variations in what appears on your screen and what is shown in this instruction. Microsoft Office 365 is fully installed on your PC or Mac; no internet access is necessary to create or edit documents. When you *are* connected to the internet, you will receive monthly upgrades and new features, so you always have the latest versions of Office apps as soon as they are available. Your subscription gives you continuous free access to the latest innovations and refinements.

ALERT   **Is Your Screen More Colorful and a Different Size Than the Figures in This Textbook?**

Your installation of Microsoft Office may use the default Colorful theme, where the ribbon in each application is a vibrant color and the title bar displays with white text. In this textbook, figures shown use the White theme, but you can be assured that all the commands are the same. You can keep your Colorful theme, or if you prefer, you can change your theme to White to match the figures here. To do so, open any application and display a new document. On the ribbon, click the File tab, and then on the left, click Options. With General selected on the left, under Personalize your copy of Microsoft Office, click the Office Theme arrow, and then click White. Change the Office Background to No Background. (In macOS, display the menu bar, click the application name—Word, Excel, and so on—click Preferences, and then click General. Under Personalize, click the Office Theme arrow to select either Colorful or Classic.)

Additionally, the figures in this book were captured using a screen resolution of 1280 x 768. If that is not your screen resolution, your screen will closely resemble, but not match, the figures shown. To view or change your screen's resolution, on the desktop, right-click in a blank area, click Display settings, click the Resolution arrow, and then select the resolution you want.

GO! Learn How
Video OF1-1

The term ***desktop application*** or ***desktop app*** refers to a computer program that is installed on your PC and that requires a computer operating system such as Microsoft Windows to run. The programs in Office 365 and in Microsoft Office 2019 are considered to be desktop apps. A desktop app typically has hundreds of features and takes time to learn.

Activity 1.01 | Exploring Microsoft Office

1 On the computer you are using, start Microsoft Word, and then compare your screen with Figure 1.2.

Depending on which operating system you are using and how your computer is set up, you might start Word from the taskbar or from the Start menu. On an Apple Mac computer, you might start the program from the Dock.

On the left, the Home tab is active in this view, referred to as ***Backstage view***, which is a centralized space for all your file management tasks such as opening, saving, printing, publishing, or sharing a file—all the things you can do *with* a file. In macOS the File tab is on the menu bar.

Documents that you have recently opened, if any, display under the Recent tab. You can also click the Pinned tab to see documents you have pinned there, or you can click the Shared with Me tab to see documents that have been shared with you by others.

On the left, you can click New to find a ***template***—a preformatted document that you can use as a starting point and then change to suit your needs. Or you can click Open to navigate to your files and folders. You can also look at Account information, give feedback to Microsoft, or look at the Word Options dialog box.

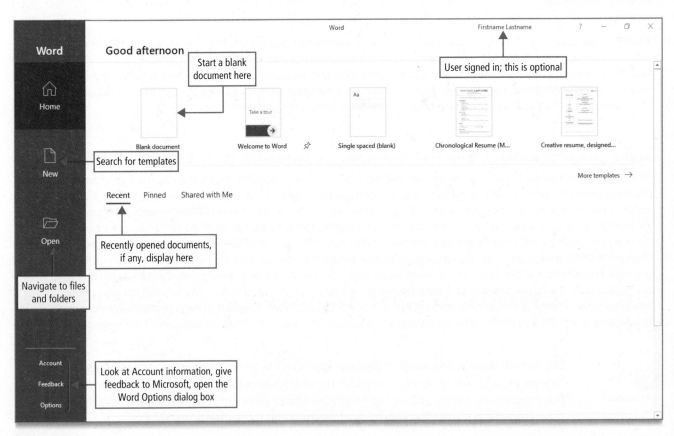

Figure 1.2

2 ▶ Click **Blank document**. Compare your screen with Figure 1.3, and then take a moment to study the description of the screen elements in the table in Figure 1.4.

NOTE **Displaying the Full Ribbon**

If your full ribbon does not display, click any tab, and then at the right end of the ribbon, click 📌 to pin the ribbon to keep it open while you work.

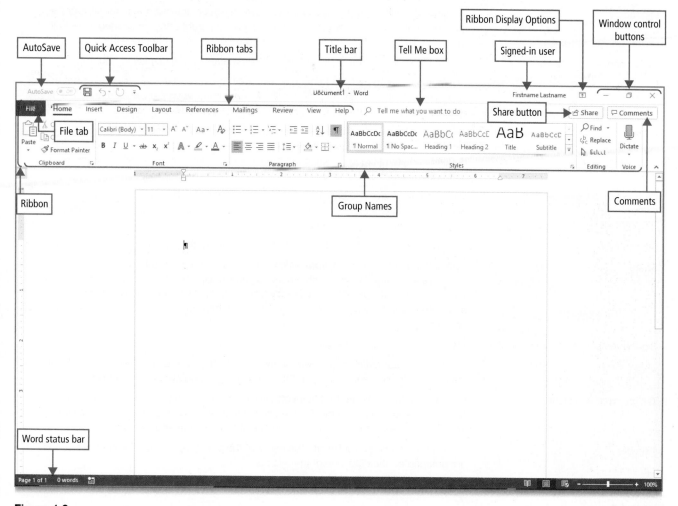

Figure 1.3

Screen Element	Description
AutoSave (off unless your document is saved to OneDrive using an Office 365 subscription)	Saves your document every few seconds so you don't have to. On a Windows system, AutoSave is available in Word, Excel, and PowerPoint for Office 365 subscribers. AutoSave is enabled only when a file is stored on OneDrive, OneDrive for Business, or SharePoint Online. Changes to your document are saved to the cloud as you are working, and if other people are working on the same file, AutoSave lets them see your changes in a matter of seconds.
Comments	Displays a short menu from which you can add a comment to your document or view other comments already in the document.
File tab	Displays Microsoft Office Backstage view, which is a centralized space for all your file management tasks such as opening, saving, printing, publishing, or sharing a file—all the things you can do *with* a file. (In macOS the File tab is on the menu bar.)
Group names	Indicate the name of the groups of related commands on the displayed ribbon tab.
Quick Access Toolbar	Displays buttons to perform frequently used commands and resources with a single click. The default commands include Save, Undo, and Redo. You can add and delete buttons to customize the Quick Access Toolbar for your convenience.
Ribbon	Displays a group of task-oriented tabs that contain the commands, styles, and resources you need to work in Microsoft Office desktop apps. The look of your ribbon depends on your screen resolution. A high resolution will display more individual items and button names on the ribbon.
Ribbon Display Options	Displays three ways you can display the ribbon: Auto-hide Ribbon, Show Tabs, or Show Tabs and Commands; typically, you will want to use Show Tabs and Commands, especially while you are learning Office.
Ribbon tabs	Display the names of the task-oriented tabs relevant to the open document.
Share	Opens the Share dialog box from which you can save your file to the cloud—your OneDrive—and then share it with others so you can collaborate. Here you can also email the Office file or a PDF of the file directly from Outlook if you are using Outlook to view and send email. A *dialog box* enables you to make decisions about an individual object or topic.
Signed-in user	Identifies the user who is signed in to Office.
Status bar	Displays file information on the left; on the right displays buttons for Read Mode, Print Layout, and Web Layout views; on the far right edge, displays Zoom controls.
Tell me what you want to do	Provides a search feature for Microsoft Office commands that you activate by typing what you are looking for in the *Tell me what you want to do* area. As you type, every keystroke refines the results so that you can click the command as soon as it displays.
Title bar	Displays the name of the file and the name of the program; the window control buttons are grouped on the right side of the title bar.
Window control buttons	Displays buttons for commands to Minimize, Restore Down, or Close the window.

Figure 1.4

Create a Folder for File Storage

GO! Learn How
Video OF1-2

A *location* is any disk drive, folder, or other place in which you can store files and folders. A *file* is information stored on a computer under a single name. A *folder* is a container in which you store files. Where you store your files depends on how and where you use your data. For example, for your college classes, you might decide to store your work on a removable USB flash drive so that you can carry your files to different locations and access your files on different computers.

If you do most of your work on a single computer, for example your home desktop system or your laptop computer that you take with you to school or work, then you can store your files in one of the folders on your hard drive provided by your Windows operating system—Documents, Music, Pictures, or Videos.

The best place to store files if you want them to be available anytime, anywhere, from almost any device is on your *OneDrive*, which is Microsoft's free *cloud storage* for anyone with a free Microsoft account. Cloud storage refers to online storage of data so that you can access your data from different places and devices. *Cloud computing* refers to applications and services that are accessed over the internet, rather than to applications that are installed on your local computer.

Besides being able to access your documents from any device or location, OneDrive also offers *AutoSave*, which saves your document every few seconds, so you don't have to. On a Windows system, AutoSave is available in Word, Excel, and PowerPoint for Office 365 subscribers. Changes to your document are saved to the cloud as you are working, and if other people are working on the same file—referred to as *real-time co-authoring*—AutoSave lets them see your changes in a matter of seconds.

If you have an *Office 365* subscription—one of the versions of Microsoft Office to which you subscribe for an annual fee or download for free with your college *.edu* address—your storage capacity on OneDrive is a terabyte or more, which is more than most individuals would ever require. Many colleges provide students with free Office 365 subscriptions. The advantage of subscribing to Office 365 is that you receive monthly updates with new features.

Because many people now have multiple computing devices—desktop, laptop, tablet, smartphone—it is common to store data *in the cloud* so that it is always available. *Synchronization*, also called *syncing*—pronounced SINK-ing—is the process of updating computer files that are in two or more locations according to specific rules. So, if you create and save a Word document on your OneDrive using your laptop, you can open and edit that document on your tablet in OneDrive. When you close the document again, the file is properly updated to reflect your changes. Your OneDrive account will guide you in setting options for syncing files to your specifications. You can open and edit Office files by using Office apps available on a variety of device platforms, including iOS, Android, in a web browser, and in Windows.

MORE KNOWLEDGE | **Creating a Microsoft Account**

Use a free Microsoft account to sign in to Microsoft Office so that you can work on different PCs and use your free OneDrive cloud storage. If you already sign in to a Windows PC or tablet, or you sign in to Xbox Live, Outlook.com, or OneDrive, use that account to sign in to Office. To create a new Microsoft account, in your browser, search for *sign up for a Microsoft account*. You can use any email address as the user name for your new Microsoft account—including addresses from Outlook.com or Gmail.

Activity 1.02 | Creating a Folder for File Storage

Your computer's operating system, either Windows or macOS, helps you to create and maintain a logical folder structure, so always take the time to name your files and folders consistently.

NOTE **This Activity is for Windows PC users. Mac users refer to the document *Creating a Folder for File Storage on a Mac*.**

Mac users can refer to the document Creating a Folder for File Storage on a Mac available within **MyLab IT** or, for non-MyLab users, your instructor can provide this document to you from the Instructor Resource Center.

In this Activity, you will create a folder in the storage location you have chosen to use for your files, and then you will save your file. This example will use the Documents folder on the PC at which you are working. If you prefer to store on your OneDrive or on a USB flash drive, you can use similar steps.

1 Decide where you are going to store your files for this Project.

As the first step in saving a file, determine where you want to save the file, and if necessary, insert a storage device.

2 At the top of your screen, in the title bar, notice that *Document1 – Word* displays.

The Blank option on the opening screen of an Office program displays a new unsaved file with a default name—*Document1, Presentation1*, and so on. As you create your file, your work is temporarily stored in the computer's memory until you initiate a Save command, at which time you must choose a file name and a location in which to save your file.

3 In the upper left corner of your screen, click the **File tab** to display **Backstage** view, and then on the left, if necessary, click **Info**. Compare your screen with Figure 1.5.

Recall that Backstage view is a centralized space that groups commands related to *file* management; that is why the tab is labeled *File*. File management commands include opening, saving, printing, or sharing a file. The ***Backstage tabs***—*Info, New, Open, Save, Save As, Print, Share, Export*, and *Close*—display along the left side. The tabs group file-related tasks together.

Here, the ***Info tab*** displays information—*info*—about the current file, and file management commands display under Info. For example, if you click the Protect Document button, a list of options that you can set for this file that relate to who can open or edit the document displays.

On the right, you can also examine the ***document properties***. Document properties, also known as ***metadata***, are details about a file that describe or identify it, such as the title, author name, subject, and keywords that identify the document's topic or contents.

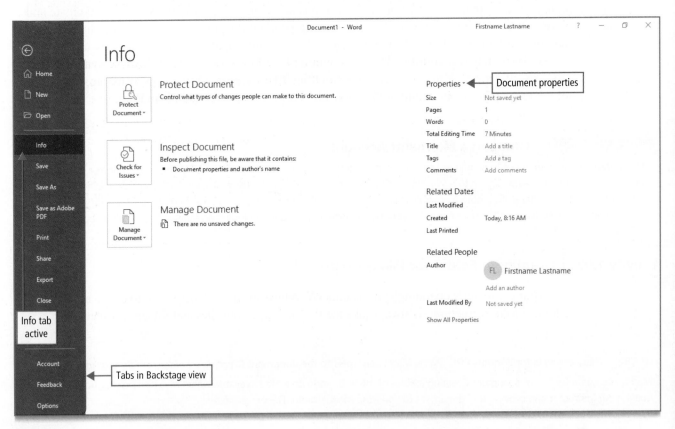

Figure 1.5

4 On the left, click **Save As**, and notice that, if you are signed into Office with a Microsoft account, one option for storing your files is your **OneDrive**. Compare your screen with Figure 1.6.

When you are saving something for the first time, for example a new Word document, the Save and Save As commands are identical. That is, the Save As commands will display if you click Save or if you click Save As.

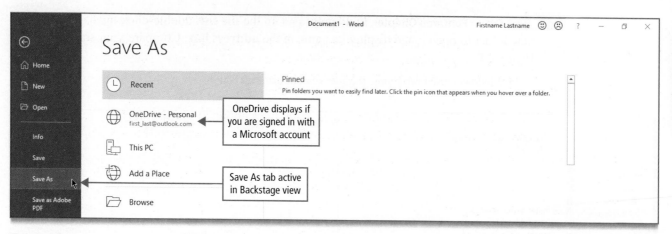

Figure 1.6

NOTE   **Saving After Your File Is Named**

After you name and save a file, the Save command on the Quick Access Toolbar saves any changes you make to the file without displaying Backstage view. The Save As command enables you to name and save a *new* file based on the current one—in a location that you choose. After you name and save the new document, the original document closes, and the new document—based on the original one—displays.

---

5 ▸ To store your Word file in the **Documents** folder on your PC, click **Browse** to display the **Save As** dialog box. On the left, in the **navigation pane**, scroll down; if necessary click > to expand This PC, and then click **Documents**. Compare your screen with Figure 1.7.

In the Save As dialog box, you must indicate the name you want for the file and the location where you want to save the file. When working with your own data, it is good practice to pause at this point and determine the logical name and location for your file.

In the Save As dialog box, a *toolbar* displays, which is a row, column, or block of buttons or icons, that displays across the top of a window and that contains commands for tasks you perform with a single click.

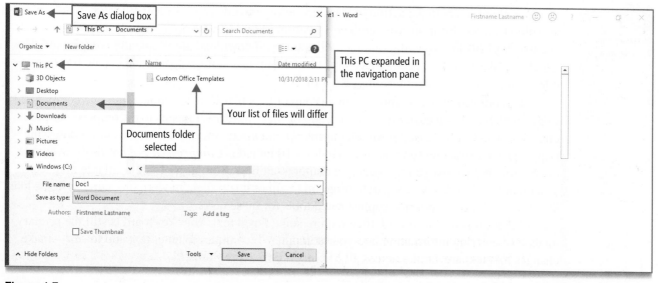

Figure 1.7

6 ▸ On the toolbar, click **New folder**.

In the file list, Windows creates a new folder, and the text *New folder* is selected.

7 Type **Office Features Chapter 1** and press Enter. In the **file list**, double-click the name of your new folder to open it and display its name in the **address bar**. Compare your screen with Figure 1.8.

In Windows-based programs, the Enter key confirms an action.

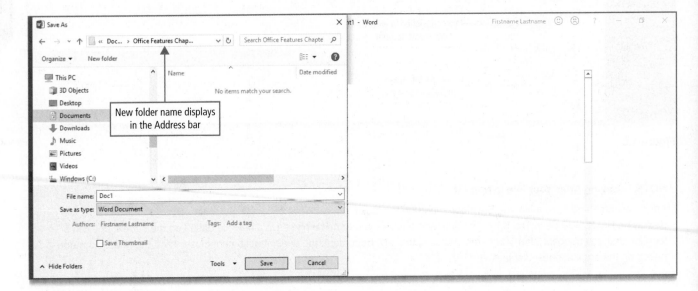

Figure 1.8

8 In the lower right corner of the **Save As** dialog box, click **Cancel**. In the upper left corner of Backstage view, click the **Back** arrow ⊖.

9 In the upper right corner of the Word window, click **Close** ☒. If prompted to save your changes, click Don't Save. Close any other open windows or programs.

Objective 3	**Download and Extract Zipped Files, Enter and Edit Text in an Office Application, and Use Editor to Check Documents**

GO! Learn How
Video OF1-3

Download refers to the action of transferring or copying a file from another location—such as a cloud storage location, your college's Learning Management System, or from an internet site like **MyLab IT**—to your computer. Files that you download are frequently *compressed files*, which are files that have been reduced in size, take up less storage space, and can be transferred to other computers faster than uncompressed files.

A compressed folder might contain a group of files that were combined into one compressed folder, which makes it easier to share a group of files. To *extract* means to decompress, or pull out, files from a compressed form. The terms *zip* and *unzip* refer to the process of compressing (zipping) and extracting (unzipping). Windows 10 includes *Compressed Folder Tools*, available on the ribbon, to assist you in extracting compressed files. Similar tools are available in macOS. You do not need to install a separate program to zip or unzip files; modern operating systems like Windows and macOS provide sophisticated tools for these tasks.

All programs in Microsoft Office require some typed text. Your keyboard is still the primary method of entering information into your computer. Techniques to enter text and to *edit*—make changes to—text are similar across all Microsoft Office programs.

For Non-MyLab Submissions
Start Word and click Blank document. Click the File tab, on the left click Save As, click Browse, and then navigate to your **Office Features Chapter 1 folder**. At the bottom of the **Save As** dialog box, in the **File name** box, using your own name, name the file **Lastname_Firstname_Office_Features_1A_Chef_Notes** and then click Save. Then, move to Step 3 in Activity 1.03.

1 ▶ Sign in to your **MyLab IT** course. Locate and click the Grader project **Office Features 1A Chef Notes**, click **Download Materials**, and then click **Download All Files**. Using the Chrome browser (if you are using a different browser see notes below), extract the zipped folder to your **Office Features Chapter 1 folder** as follows (or use your favorite method to download and extract files):

- In the lower left, next to the downloaded zipped folder, click the small **arrow**, and then click **Show in folder**. The zipped folder displays in *File Explorer*—the Windows program that displays the contents of locations, folders, and files on your computer—in the Downloads folder. (Unless you have changed default settings, downloaded files go to the Downloads folder on your computer.)
- With the zipped folder selected, on the ribbon, under **Compressed Folder Tools**, click the **Extract tab**, and then at the right end of the ribbon, click **Extract all** (you may have to wait a few seconds for the command to become active).
- In the displayed **Extract Compressed (Zipped) Folders** dialog box, click **Browse**. In the **Select a destination** dialog box, use the navigation pane on the left to navigate to your **Office Features Chapter 1 folder**, and double-click its name to open the folder and display its name in the **Address bar**.
- In the lower right, click **Select Folder**, and then in the lower right, click **Extract**; when complete, a new File Explorer window displays showing the extracted files in your chapter folder. Take a moment to open **Office_Features_1A_Chef_Notes_Instructions**; note any recent updates to the book.
- **Close** ⊠ both File Explorer windows, close any open documents, and then close the Grader download screens. You can also close **MyLab IT** and, if open, your Learning Management system.

NOTE   **Using the Edge Browser or Firefox Browser to Extract Files**

Microsoft Edge: At the bottom, click Open, click Extract all, click Browse, navigate to and open your Chapter folder, click Select Folder, click Extract.

Firefox: In the displayed dialog box, click OK, click Extract all, click Browse, navigate to and open your Chapter folder, click Select Folder, and then click Extract.

🖥 **MAC TIP**   Using the Chrome browser, in **MyLab IT**, after you click Download Materials, in the lower left, to the right of the zipped folder, click the arrow. Click Open. Click the blue folder containing the unzipped files. Use Finder commands to move or copy the files to your Office Features Chapter 1 folder.

---

2 ▶ On the Windows taskbar, click **File Explorer** 🗂. Navigate to your **Office Features Chapter 1 folder**, and then double-click the Word file you downloaded from **MyLab IT** that displays your name—**Student_Office_Features_1A_Chef_Notes**. In this empty Word document, if necessary, at the top, click **Enable Editing**.

🖥 **MAC TIP**   When the Word application is not open, on the Dock, use the macOS Finder commands to locate your Word document. When the Word application is open, use the File tab on the menu bar.

---

3 ▶ On the ribbon, on the **Home tab**, in the **Paragraph group**, if necessary, click **Show/Hide** ¶ so that it is active—shaded. On the **View tab**, if necessary, in the **Show group**, select the **Ruler** check box so that rulers display below the ribbon and on the left side of your window, and then redisplay the **Home tab**.

The *insertion point*—a blinking vertical line that indicates where text or graphics will be inserted—displays. In Office programs, the mouse *pointer*—any symbol that displays on your screen in response to moving your mouse device—displays in different shapes depending on the task you are performing and the area of the screen to which you are pointing.

When you press Enter, Spacebar, or Tab on your keyboard, characters display to represent these keystrokes. These screen characters do not print and are referred to as *formatting marks* or *nonprinting characters*.

When working in Word, display the rulers so that you can see how margin settings affect your document and how text and objects align. Additionally, if you set a tab stop or an indent, its location is visible on the ruler.

NOTE   Activating Show/Hide in Word Documents

When Show/Hide is active—the button is shaded—formatting marks display. Because formatting marks guide your eye in a document—like a map and road signs guide you along a highway—these marks will display throughout this instruction. Expert Word users keep these marks displayed while creating documents.

4 Type **Skyline Grille Info** and notice how the insertion point moves to the right as you type. Point slightly to the right of the letter *e* in *Grille* and click to place the insertion point there. Compare your screen with Figure 1.9.

A *paragraph symbol* (¶) indicates the end of a paragraph and displays each time you press Enter. This is a type of formatting mark and does not print.

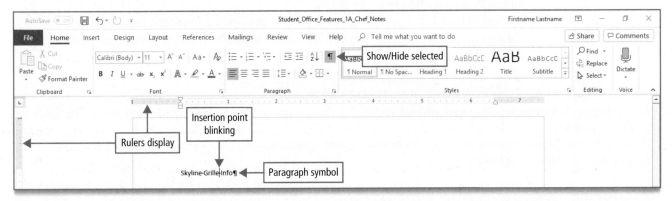

Figure 1.9

5 On your keyboard, locate and then press the Backspace key one time to delete the letter *e*.

Pressing Backspace removes a character to the left of the insertion point.

6 Press → one time to place the insertion point to the left of the *I* in *Info*. Type **Chef** and then press Spacebar one time.

By *default*, when you type text in an Office program, existing text moves to the right to make space for new typing. Default refers to the current selection or setting that is automatically used by a program unless you specify otherwise.

7 Press Del four times to delete *Info* and then type **Notes**

Pressing Del removes a character to the right of the insertion point.

8 With your insertion point blinking after the word *Notes*, on your keyboard, hold down the
Ctrl key. While holding down Ctrl, press ← three times to move the insertion point to the
beginning of the word *Grill*.

> This is a ***keyboard shortcut***—a key or combination of keys that performs a task that would
> otherwise require a mouse. This keyboard shortcut moves the insertion point to the beginning of
> the previous word.
>
> A keyboard shortcut is indicated as Ctrl + ← (or some other combination of keys) to indicate that
> you hold down the first key while pressing the second key. A keyboard shortcut can also include
> three keys, in which case you hold down the first two and then press the third. For example,
> Ctrl + Shift + ← selects one word to the left.

MAC TIP   Press option + ←.

9 With the insertion point blinking at the beginning of the word *Grill*, type **Metro** and press
Spacebar one time.

10 Click to place the insertion point after the letter *s* in *Notes* and then press Enter one time. With
the insertion point blinking, type the following and include the spelling error: **Exective Chef,
Madison Dunham** (If Word autocorrects *Exective* to *Executive*, delete *u* in the word.)

11 With your mouse, point slightly to the left of the *M* in *Madison*, hold down the left mouse
button, and then ***drag***—hold down the left mouse button while moving your mouse—to the
right to select the text *Madison Dunham* but not the paragraph mark following it, and then
release the mouse button. Compare your screen with Figure 1.10.

> The ***mini toolbar*** displays commands that are commonly used with the selected object, which
> places common commands close to your pointer. When you move the pointer away from the mini
> toolbar, it fades from view.
>
> ***Selecting*** refers to highlighting—by dragging or clicking with your mouse—areas of text or data
> or graphics so that the selection can be edited, formatted, copied, or moved. The action of dragging
> includes releasing the left mouse button at the end of the area you want to select.
>
> The Office programs recognize a selected area as one unit to which you can make changes.
> Selecting text may require some practice. If you are not satisfied with your result, click anywhere
> outside of the selection, and then begin again.

MAC TIP   The mini toolbar may not display; use ribbon commands.

BY TOUCH   Tap once on *Madison* to display the gripper—a small circle that acts as a handle—directly below the word.
This establishes the start gripper. If necessary, with your finger, drag the gripper to the beginning of the word. Then drag
the gripper to the end of *Dunham* to select the text and display the end gripper.

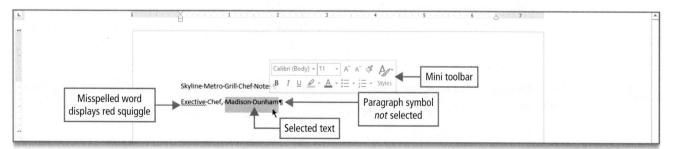

Figure 1.10

12 ▶ With the text *Madison Dunham* selected, type **Sarah Jackson**

In any Windows-based program, such as the Microsoft Office programs, selected text is deleted and then replaced when you begin to type new text. You will save time by developing good techniques for selecting and then editing or replacing selected text, which is easier than pressing [Backspace] or [Del] numerous times to delete text.

Activity 1.04 | Checking Spelling

ALERT   The Display of Spelling Suggestions Varies Among Office Versions

Depending on your version of Office (Office 365 or Office 2019), you may see variations in how the spelling checking displays suggestions for corrections. You will still be able to follow the screen prompts to select the correct spelling.

Microsoft Office has a dictionary of words against which all entered text is checked. In Word and PowerPoint, words that are not in the dictionary display a red squiggle, indicating a possible misspelled word, a proper name, or an unusual word—none of which are in the Office dictionary. In Excel and Access, you can initiate a check of the spelling, but red squiggles do not display.

1 ▶ Notice that the misspelled word *Exective* displays with a red squiggle.

2 ▶ Point to *Exective* and then ***right-click***—click your right mouse button one time.

A ***shortcut menu*** displays, which displays commands and options relevant to the selected text or object. These are ***context-sensitive commands*** because they relate to the item you right-clicked. These are also referred to as ***context menus***. Here, the shortcut menu displays commands related to the misspelled word.

BY TOUCH   Tap and hold a moment—when a square displays around the misspelled word, release your finger to display the shortcut menu.

3 ▶ Press [Esc] two times to cancel the shortcut menus, and then in the lower left corner of your screen, on the status bar, click the **Proofing** icon, which displays an *X* because some errors are detected. In the **Editor** pane that displays on the right, if necessary, click the Results button, and then under **Suggestions**, to the right of *Executive*, click [∨], and then compare your screen with Figure 1.11.

The Editor pane displays on the right. ***Editor***, according to Microsoft, is your digital writing assistant in Word and also in Outlook. Editor displays misspellings, grammatical mistakes, and writing style issues as you type by marking red squiggles for spelling, blue double underlines for grammar, and dotted underlines for writing style issues.

Here you have many more options for checking spelling than you have on the shortcut menu. The suggested correct word, *Executive*, displays under Suggestions. The displayed menu provides additional options for the suggestion. For example, you can have the word read aloud, hear it spelled out, change all occurrences in the document, or add to AutoCorrect options.

In the Editor pane, you can ignore the word one time or in all occurrences, change the word to the suggested word, select a different suggestion, or add a word to the dictionary against which Word checks.

MAC TIP   In the Spelling and Grammar dialog box, click Executive, and then click Change. The Editor pane is not available on a Mac.

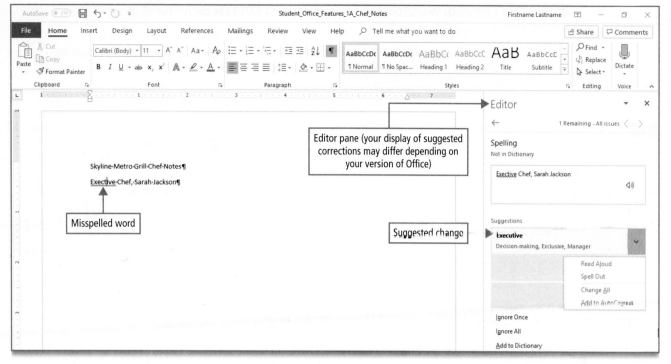

Figure 1.11

 ANOTHER WAY   Press F7 to display the Editor pane; or, on the Review tab, in the Proofing group, you can check your document for Spelling.

4 ▶ In the **Editor** pane, under **Suggestions**, click *Executive* to correct the spelling. In the message box that displays, click **OK**.

5 ▶ If necessary **Close** the **Editor** pane by clicking ⊠ in the upper right corner.

Objective 4   **Perform Office Commands and Apply Office Formatting**

GO! Learn How
Video OF1-4

Formatting refers to applying Office commands to make your document easy to read and to add visual touches and design elements to make your document inviting to the reader. This process establishes the overall appearance of text, graphics, and pages in your document.

Activity 1.05 │ Performing Commands from a Dialog Box

MOS
1.2.4

In a dialog box, you make decisions about an individual object or topic. In some dialog boxes, you can make multiple decisions in one place.

1 ▶ On the ribbon, click the **Design tab**, and then in the **Page Background group**, click **Page Color**.

2 At the bottom of the menu, notice the command **Fill Effects** followed by an **ellipsis** (. . .). Compare your screen with Figure 1.12.

An *ellipsis* is a set of three dots indicating incompleteness. An ellipsis following a command name indicates that a dialog box will display when you click the command.

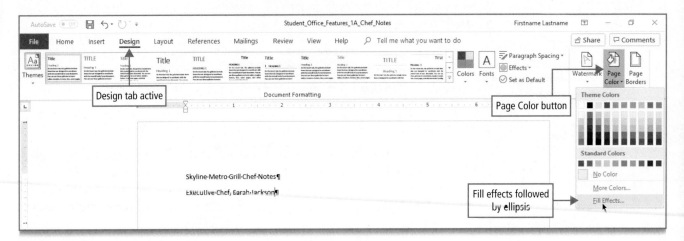

Figure 1.12

3 Click **Fill Effects** to display the **Fill Effects** dialog box. Compare your screen with Figure 1.13.

Fill is the inside color of a page or object. Here, the dialog box displays a set of tabs across the top from which you can display different sets of options. Some dialog boxes display the option group names on the left. The Gradient tab is active. In a *gradient fill*, one color fades into another.

🖥️ **MAC TIP**   Click More Colors to display the Colors dialog box.

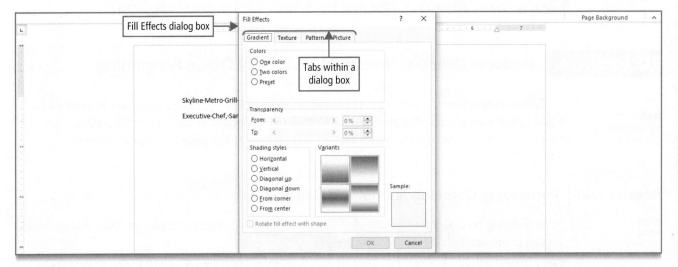

Figure 1.13

4 Under **Colors**, click the **One color** option button.

> The dialog box displays settings related to the *One color* option. An ***option button*** is a round button that enables you to make one choice among two or more options.

5 Click the **Color 1 arrow**—the arrow under the text *Color 1*—and then in the eighth column, point to the second color to display a ScreenTip with the name of the color.

> When you click an arrow in a dialog box, additional options display. A ***ScreenTip*** displays useful information about mouse actions, such as pointing to screen elements or dragging.

6 Click the color, and then notice that the fill color displays in the **Color 1** box. In the **Dark Light** bar, click the **Light arrow** as many times as necessary until the scroll box is all the way to the right—or drag the scroll box all the way to the right. Under **Shading styles**, click the **From corner** option button. Under **Variants**, click the **upper right variant**. Compare your screen with Figure 1.14.

> This dialog box is a good example of the many different elements you may encounter in a dialog box. Here you have option buttons, an arrow that displays a menu, a slider bar, and graphic options that you can select.

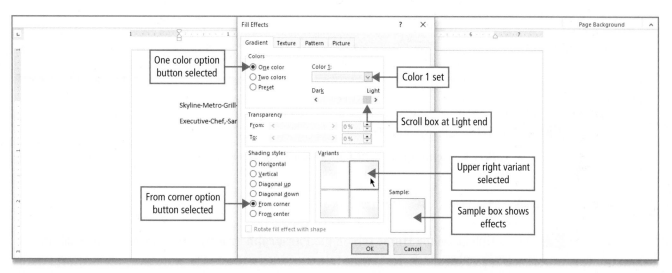

Figure 1.14

7 At the bottom of the dialog box, click **OK**, and notice the subtle page color.

> In Word, the gold shading page color will not print—even on a color printer—unless you set specific options to do so. However, a subtle background page color is effective if people will be reading the document on a screen. Microsoft's research indicates that two-thirds of people who open Word documents on a screen never print or edit them; they only read them.

Activity 1.06 | Using Undo and Applying Text Effects

1 Point to the *S* in *Skyline*, and then drag down and to the right to select both paragraphs of text and include the paragraph marks. On the mini toolbar, click **Styles**, and then *point to* but do not click **Title**. Compare your screen with Figure 1.15.

A *style* is a group of formatting commands, such as font, font size, font color, paragraph alignment, and line spacing that can be applied to a paragraph with one command.

Live Preview is a technology that shows the result of applying an editing or formatting change as you point to possible results—before you actually apply it.

MAC TIP The mini toolbar and Live Preview are not available; use ribbon commands.

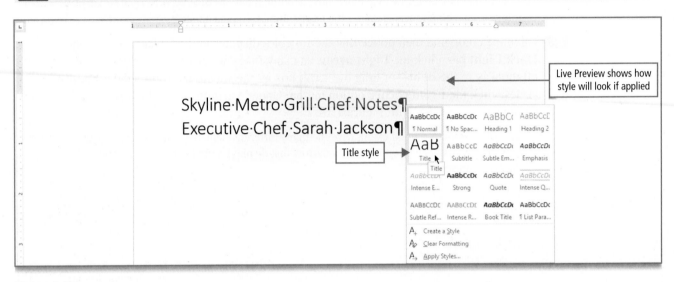

Figure 1.15

2 In the **Styles** gallery, click **Title**.

A *gallery* is an Office feature that displays a list of potential results.

MAC TIP On the Home tab, in the Styles gallery, click Title.

3 On the ribbon, on the **Home tab**, in the **Paragraph group**, click **Center** ☰ to center the two paragraphs.

Alignment refers to the placement of paragraph text relative to the left and right margins. *Center alignment* refers to text that is centered horizontally between the left and right margins. You can also align text at the left margin, which is the default alignment for text in Word, or at the right.

ANOTHER WAY Press [Ctrl] + [E] to use the Center command.

MAC TIP Press [command ⌘] + [E] to use the Center command.

4 With the two paragraphs still selected, on the **Home tab**, in the **Font Group**, click **Text Effects and Typography** [A⁻] to display a gallery.

5 In the second row, click the first effect. Click anywhere to *deselect*—cancel the selection—the text and notice the text effect.

6 ▶ Because this effect might be difficult to read, in the upper left corner of your screen, on the **Quick Access Toolbar**, click **Undo** ↺.

The *Undo* command reverses your last action.

🔄 **ANOTHER WAY**   Press ⌈Ctrl⌉ + ⌈Z⌉ as the keyboard shortcut for the Undo command.

💻 **MAC TIP**   Press ⌈command ⌘⌉ + ⌈Z⌉ as the keyboard shortcut for the Undo command.

7 ▶ Select the two paragraphs of text again, display the **Text Effects and Typography** gallery again, and then in the first row, click the fifth effect. Click anywhere to deselect the text and notice the text effect. Compare your screen with Figure 1.16.

As you progress in your study of Microsoft Office, you will practice using many dialog boxes and commands to apply interesting effects such as this to your Word documents, Excel worksheets, Access database objects, and PowerPoint slides.

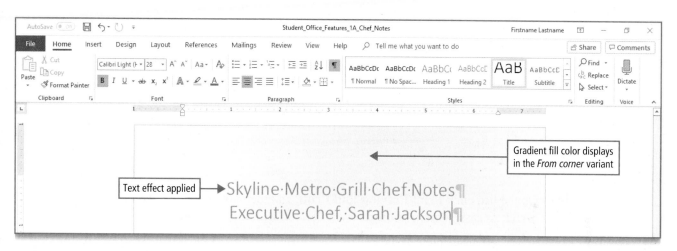

Figure 1.16

Activity 1.07 | Performing Commands from and Customizing the Quick Access Toolbar

The ribbon that displays across the top of the program window groups commands in the way that you would most logically use them. The ribbon in each Office program is slightly different, but all contain the same three elements: *tabs*, *groups*, and *commands*.

Tabs display across the top of the ribbon, and each tab relates to a type of activity; for example, laying out a page. Groups are sets of related commands for specific tasks. Commands— instructions to computer programs—are arranged in groups and might display as a button, a menu, or a box in which you type information.

You can also minimize the ribbon so only the tab names display, which is useful when working on a smaller screen such as a tablet computer where you want to maximize your screen viewing area.

1 ▶ In the upper left corner of your screen, above the ribbon, locate the **Quick Access Toolbar**.

Recall that the Quick Access Toolbar contains commands that you use frequently. By default, only the commands Save, Undo, and Redo display, but you can add and delete commands to suit your needs. Possibly the computer at which you are working already has additional commands added to the Quick Access Toolbar.

2 At the end of the **Quick Access Toolbar**, click the **Customize Quick Access Toolbar** button ⯆, and then compare your screen with Figure 1.17.

A list of commands that Office users commonly add to their Quick Access Toolbar displays, including New, Open, Email, Quick Print, and Print Preview and Print. Commands already on the Quick Access Toolbar display a check mark. Commands that you add to the Quick Access Toolbar are always just one click away.

Here you can also display the More Commands dialog box, from which you can select any command from any tab to add to the Quick Access Toolbar.

👉 **BY TOUCH** Tap once on Quick Access Toolbar commands.

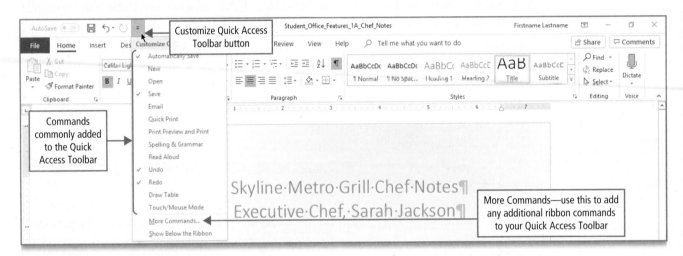

Figure 1.17

3 On the list, click **Print Preview and Print**, and then notice that the icon is added to the **Quick Access Toolbar**. Compare your screen with Figure 1.18.

The icon that represents the Print Preview command displays on the Quick Access Toolbar. Because this is a command that you will use frequently while building Office documents, you might decide to have this command remain on your Quick Access Toolbar.

🔄 **ANOTHER WAY** Right-click any command on the ribbon, and then on the shortcut menu, click Add to Quick Access Toolbar.

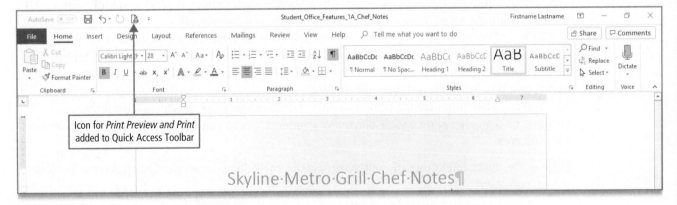

Figure 1.18

Activity 1.08 | Performing Commands from the Ribbon

> **1** In the second line of text, click to place the insertion point to the right of the letter *n* in *Jackson*. Press Enter three times. Compare your screen with Figure 1.19.

Word creates three new blank paragraphs, and no Text Effect is applied.

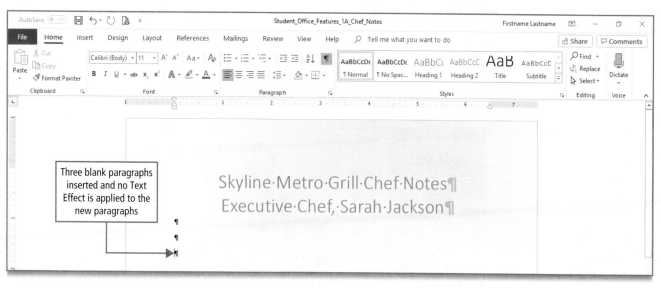

Figure 1.19

> **2** Click to position the insertion point to the left of the **second blank paragraph** that you just inserted. On the ribbon, click the **Insert tab**. In the **Illustrations group**, *point* to **Pictures** to display its ScreenTip.

Many buttons on the ribbon have this type of ***enhanced ScreenTip***, which displays useful descriptive information about the command.

> **3** Click **Pictures**. In the **Insert Picture** dialog box, navigate to your **Office Features Chapter 1 folder**, double-click the **of01A_Chefs** picture, and then compare your screen with Figure 1.20.

The picture displays in your Word document.

MAC TIP Click Picture from File, then navigate to your Office Features Chapter 1 folder.

For Non-MyLab Submissions

The of01A_Chefs picture is included with this chapter's Student Data Files, which you can obtain from your instructor or by downloading the files from www.pearsonhighered.com/go

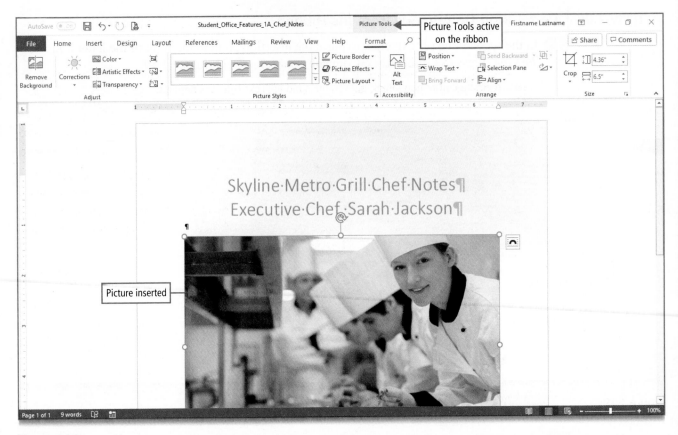

Figure 1.20

> 4 ▷ In the upper right corner of the picture, point to the **Layout Options** button ⬚ to display its
> ScreenTip, and then compare your screen with Figure 1.21.
>
> > *Layout Options* enable you to choose how the *object*—in this instance an inserted picture—
> > interacts with the surrounding text. An object is a picture or other graphic such as a chart or table
> > that you can select and then move and resize.
> >
> > When a picture is selected, the Picture Tools become available on the ribbon. Additionally, *sizing
> > handles*—small circles or squares that indicate an object is selected—surround the selected
> > picture.

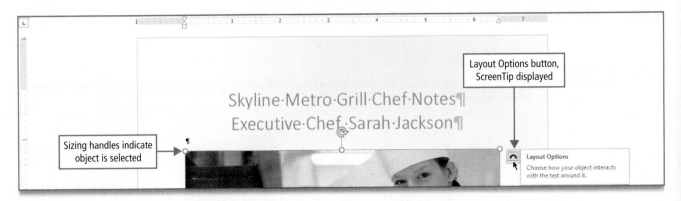

Figure 1.21

> 5 ▷ With the image selected, click **Layout Options** ⬚, and then under **With Text Wrapping**,
> in the second row, click the first layout—**Top and Bottom**. In the upper right corner of the
> **Layout Options** dialog box, click **Close** ☒.

6   On the ribbon, with the **Picture Tools Format tab** active, at the right, in the **Size group**, click in the **Shape Height** box ⬍ 0.29" ↕ to select the existing text. Type **2** and press ⏎.

7   On the **Picture Tools Format tab**, in the **Arrange group**, click **Align**, and then at the bottom of the list, locate **Use Alignment Guides**. If you do not see a checkmark to the left of **Use Alignment Guides**, click the command to enable the guides.

8   If necessary, click the image again to select it. Point to the image to display the 🔩 pointer, hold down the left mouse button and move your mouse slightly to display a green line at the left margin, and then drag the image to the right and down slightly until a green line displays in the center of the image as shown in Figure 1.22, and then release the left mouse button.

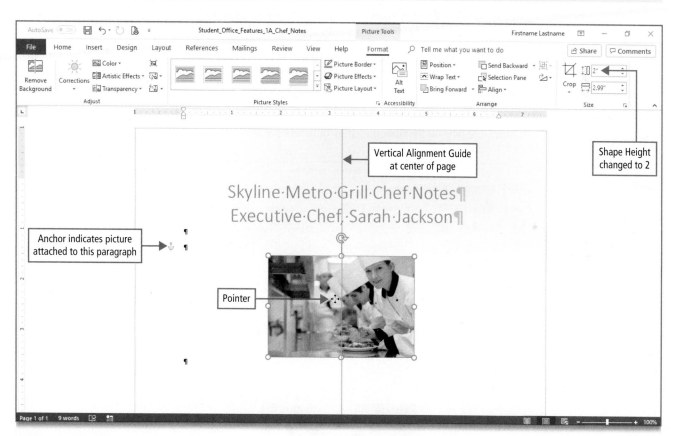

Figure 1.22

9   Be sure that there are two blank paragraphs above the image and that the anchor symbol is attached to the second blank paragraph mark—if necessary, drag the picture up slightly or down slightly. If you are not satisfied with your result, on the Quick Access Toolbar, click Undo ↺ and begin again.

> *Alignment guides* are green lines that display to help you align objects with margins or at the center of a page.

> Inserted pictures anchor—attach to—the paragraph at the insertion point location—as indicated by an anchor symbol.

10 On the ribbon, on the **Picture Tools Format tab**, in the **Picture Styles group**, point to the first style to display the ScreenTip *Simple Frame, White*, and notice that the image displays with a white frame.

NOTE The Size of Groups on the Ribbon Varies with Screen Resolution

Your monitor's screen resolution might be set higher than the resolution used to capture the figures in this book. At a higher resolution, the ribbon expands some groups to show more commands that are available with a single click, such as those in the Picture Styles group. Or, the group expands to add descriptive text to some buttons, such as those in the Arrange group. Regardless of your screen resolution, all Office commands are available to you. In higher resolutions, you will have a more robust view of the ribbon commands.

11 Watch the image as you point to the second picture style, and then to the third, and then to the fourth.

Recall that Live Preview shows the result of applying an editing or formatting change as you point to possible results—*before* you actually apply it.

12 In the **Picture Styles group**, click the fourth style—**Drop Shadow Rectangle**. Reposition the picture up or down so that it is anchored to the second blank paragraph above the image, and then click anywhere outside of the image to deselect it. Notice that the Picture Tools no longer display on the ribbon. Compare your screen with Figure 1.23.

Contextual tabs on the ribbon display only when you need them.

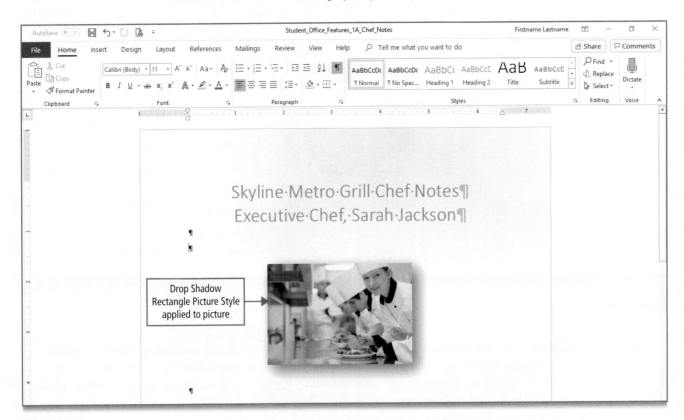

Figure 1.23

13 On the **Quick Access Toolbar**, click Save to save the changes you have made.

Activity 1.09 | Minimizing the Ribbon

1 ▶ Point to any tab on the ribbon and right-click to display a shortcut menu.

Here you can choose to display the Quick Access Toolbar below the ribbon or collapse the ribbon to maximize screen space. You can also customize the ribbon by adding, removing, renaming, or reordering tabs, groups, and commands, although this is not recommended until you become an expert Word user.

2 ▶ Click **Collapse the Ribbon** and notice that only the ribbon tabs display. Click the **Home tab** to display the commands. Click in the last blank paragraph—or anywhere in the document— and notice that the ribbon goes back to the collapsed display.

MAC TIP To minimize the ribbon, click the up arrow on the top right of the screen.

3 ▶ Right-click any ribbon tab, and then click **Collapse the Ribbon** again to remove the check mark from this command.

Most expert Office users prefer the full ribbon display.

4 ▶ Point to any tab on the ribbon, and then on your mouse device, roll the mouse wheel. Notice that different tabs become active as you roll the mouse wheel.

You can make a tab active by using this technique, instead of clicking the tab.

MORE KNOWLEDGE **Displaying KeyTips**

Instead of a mouse, some individuals prefer to navigate the ribbon by using keys on the keyboard. You can do this by activating the *KeyTip* feature where small labels display on the ribbon tabs and also on the individual ribbon commands. Press Alt to display the KeyTips on the ribbon tabs, and then press N to display KeyTips on the ribbon commands. Press Esc to turn the feature off. NOTE: This feature is not yet available on a Mac.

Activity 1.10 | Changing Page Orientation and Zoom Level

1.2.1

1 ▶ On the ribbon, click the **Layout tab**. In the **Page Setup group**, click **Orientation**, and notice that two orientations display—*Portrait* and *Landscape*. Click **Landscape**.

In *portrait orientation*, the paper is taller than it is wide. In *landscape orientation*, the paper is wider than it is tall.

2 ▶ In the lower right corner of the screen, locate the **Zoom slider**.

Recall that to zoom means to increase or decrease the viewing area. You can zoom in to look closely at a section of a document, and then zoom out to see an entire page on the screen. You can also zoom to view multiple pages on the screen.

3 ▶ Drag the **Zoom slider** 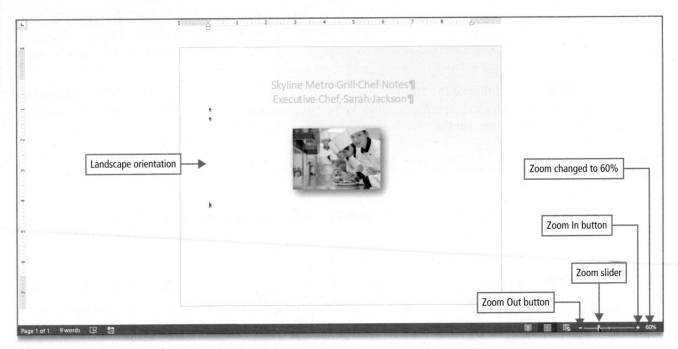 to the left until you have zoomed to approximately *60%*. Compare your screen with Figure 1.24.

Skyline·Metro·Grill·Chef·Notes¶
Executive·Chef,·Sarah·Jackson¶

Landscape orientation

Zoom changed to 60%

Zoom In button

Zoom slider

Zoom Out button

Figure 1.24

👆 **BY TOUCH**   Drag the Zoom slider with your finger.

4 ▶ Use the technique you just practiced to change the **Orientation** back to **Portrait**.

The default orientation in Word is Portrait, which is commonly used for business documents such as letters, reports, and memos.

5 ▶ In the lower right corner, click the **Zoom In** button ➕ as many times as necessary to return to the **100%** zoom setting.

Use the zoom feature to adjust the view of your document for editing and for your viewing comfort.

🔄 **ANOTHER WAY**   You can also control Zoom from the ribbon. On the View tab, in the Zoom group, you can control the Zoom level and also zoom to view multiple pages.

6 ▶ On the **Quick Access Toolbar**, click **Save** 💾.

MORE KNOWLEDGE   **Zooming to Page Width**

Some Office users prefer *Page Width*, which zooms the document so that the width of the page matches the width of the window. Find this command on the View tab, in the Zoom group.

Activity 1.11 | Formatting Text by Using Fonts, Alignment, Font Colors, and Font Styles

MOS
2.2.5

1 If necessary, on the right edge of your screen, drag the vertical scroll box to the top of the scroll bar. To the left of *Executive Chef, Sarah Jackson*, point in the margin area to display the ⟋ pointer and click one time to select the entire paragraph. Compare your screen with Figure 1.25.

Use this technique to select complete paragraphs from the margin area—drag downward to select multiple-line paragraphs—which is faster and more efficient than dragging through text.

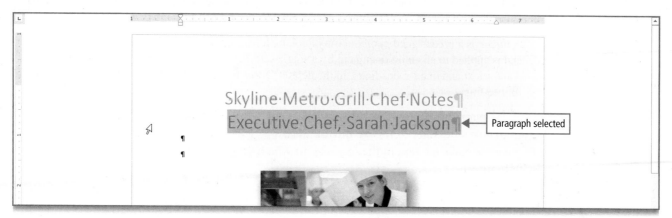

Figure 1.25

2 On the **Home tab**, in the **Font Group**, click **Clear All Formatting** . Compare your screen with Figure 1.26.

This command removes all formatting from the selection, leaving only the normal, unformatted text.

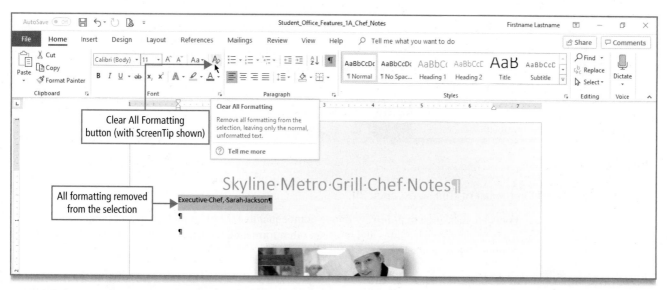

Figure 1.26

3 With the text still selected, on the **Home tab**, in the **Paragraph group**, click **Center** .

4 With the text still selected, on the **Home tab**, in the **Font group**, click the **Font button arrow** Calibri (Body). On the alphabetical list of font names, scroll down and then locate and *point to* **Cambria**.

A *font* is a set of characters with the same design and shape. The default font in a Word document is Calibri, which is a *sans serif font*—a font design with no lines or extensions on the ends of characters.

The Cambria font is a *serif font*—a font design that includes small line extensions on the ends of the letters to guide the eye in reading from left to right.

The list of fonts displays as a gallery showing potential results. For example, in the Font gallery, you can point to see the actual design and format of each font as it would look if applied to text.

5 Point to several other fonts and observe the effect on the selected text. Then, scroll back to the top of the **Font** gallery. Under **Theme Fonts**, click **Calibri Light**.

A *theme* is a predesigned combination of colors, fonts, line, and fill effects that look good together and is applied to an entire document by a single selection. A theme combines two sets of fonts—one for text and one for headings. In the default Office theme, Calibri Light is the suggested font for headings.

6 With the paragraph *Executive Chef, Sarah Jackson* still selected, on the **Home tab**, in the **Font group**, click the **Font Size button arrow** [11 ⌄], point to **20**, and then notice how Live Preview displays the text in the font size to which you are pointing. Compare your screen with Figure 1.27.

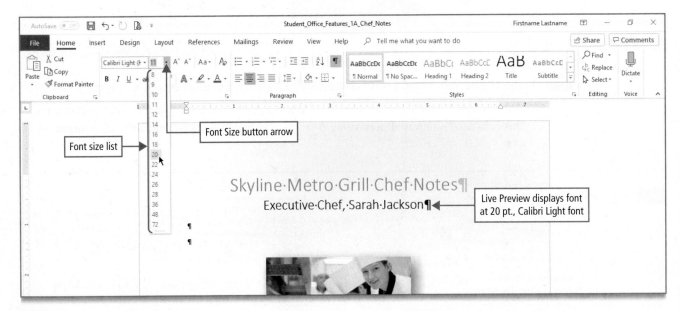

Figure 1.27

7 On the list of font sizes, click **20**.

Fonts are measured in *points*, with one point equal to 1/72 of an inch. A higher point size indicates a larger font size. Headings and titles are often formatted by using a larger font size. The word *point* is abbreviated as *pt*.

8 With *Executive Chef, Sarah Jackson* still selected, on the **Home tab**, in the **Font group**, click the **Font Color button arrow** [A ⌄]. Under **Theme Colors**, in the sixth column, click the fifth (next to last) color, and then click in the last blank paragraph to deselect the text.

9 With your insertion point in the blank paragraph below the picture, type **Rehearsal Dinner Menu Ideas** and then press [Enter] two times.

10 Type **Appetizers** and press ⏎ two times. Type **Salads** and press ⏎ two times. Type **Main Dishes** and press ⏎ two times.

11 Type **Desserts** and press ⏎ four times. Compare your screen with Figure 1.28.

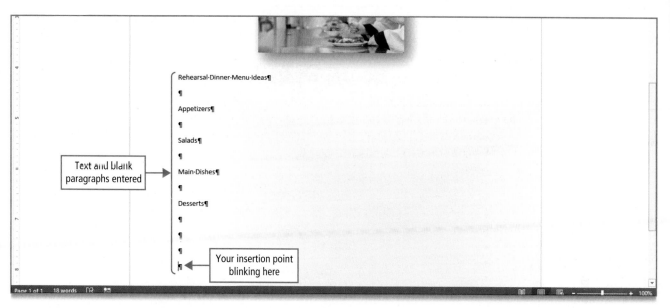

Text and blank paragraphs entered → Rehearsal·Dinner·Menu·Ideas¶ ¶ Appetizers¶ ¶ Salads¶ ¶ Main·Dishes¶ ¶ Desserts¶ ¶ ¶ ¶

Your insertion point blinking here

Page 1 of 1   18 words   100%

Figure1.28

12 Click anywhere in the word *Dinner* and then ***triple-click***—click the left mouse button three times—to select the entire paragraph. If the entire paragraph is not selected, click in the paragraph and begin again.

13 With the paragraph selected, on the mini toolbar, click the **Font Color** button [A ▾], and notice that the text color of the selected paragraph changes.

The font color button retains its most recently used color—the color you used to format *Executive Chef, Sarah Jackson* above. As you progress in your study of Microsoft Office, you will use other commands that behave in this manner; that is, they retain their most recently used format. This is commonly referred to as ***MRU***—most recently used.

Recall that the mini toolbar places commands that are commonly used for the selected text or object close by so that you reduce the distance you must move your mouse to access a command. If you are using a touch screen device, most commands that you need are close and easy to touch.

MAC TIP   Use commands on the ribbon, on the Home tab.

14 With the paragraph *Rehearsal Dinner Menu Ideas* still selected and the mini toolbar displayed, on the mini toolbar, click **Bold** [B] and **Italic** [I].

Font styles include bold, italic, and underline. Font styles emphasize text and are a visual cue to draw the reader's eye to important text.

15 On the mini toolbar, click **Italic** $\boxed{I}$ again to turn off the Italic formatting. Click anywhere to deselect, and then compare your screen with Figure 1.29.

> A *toggle button* is a button that can be turned on by clicking it once, and then turned off by clicking it again.

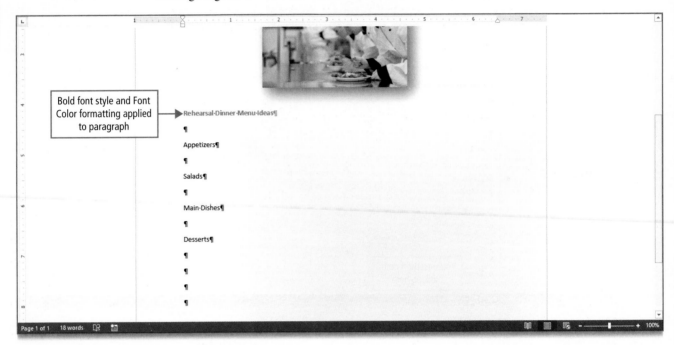

Figure 1.29

Activity 1.12 │ Using Format Painter

> Use the ***Format Painter*** to copy the formatting of specific text or copy the formatting of a paragraph and then apply it in other locations in your document.

1 To the left of *Rehearsal Dinner Menu Ideas*, point in the left margin to display the $\boxed{\cancel{A}}$ pointer, and then click one time to select the entire paragraph. Compare your screen with Figure 1.30.

> Use this technique to select complete paragraphs from the margin area. This is particularly useful if there are many lines of text in the paragraph. You can hold down the left mouse button and drag downward instead of trying to drag through the text.

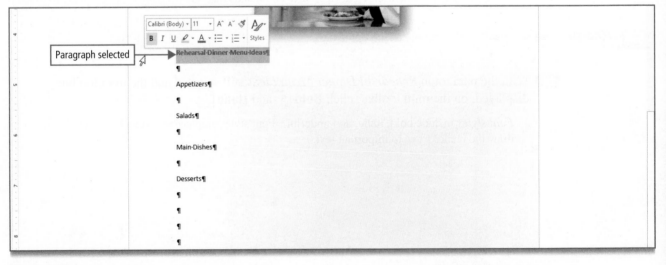

Figure 1.30

2 With *Rehearsal Dinner Menu Ideas* still selected, on the mini toolbar, click **Format Painter** . Then, move your mouse to the right of the word *Appetizers*, and notice the mouse pointer. Compare your screen with Figure 1.31.

> The pointer takes the shape of a paintbrush and contains the formatting information from the paragraph where the insertion point is positioned or from what is selected. Information about the Format Painter and how to turn it off displays in the status bar.

🖥️ **MAC TIP** On the Home tab, in the Clipboard group, click Format Painter.

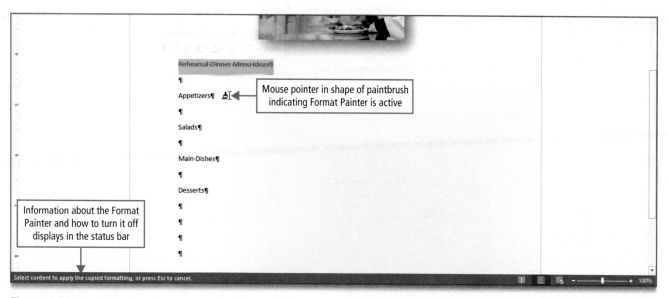

Rehearsal·Dinner·Menu·Ideas¶

Appetizers¶ ← Mouse pointer in shape of paintbrush indicating Format Painter is active

Salads¶

Main·Dishes¶

Desserts¶

Information about the Format Painter and how to turn it off displays in the status bar

Select content to apply the copied formatting, or press Esc to cancel.

Figure 1.31

3 With the pointer, drag to select the paragraph *Appetizers* and notice that the font color and Bold formatting is applied. Then, click anywhere in the word *Appetizers*, right-click to display the mini toolbar, and on the mini toolbar, *double-click* **Format Painter** .

4 Select the paragraph *Salads* to copy the font color and Bold formatting, and notice that the pointer retains the shape. You might have to move the mouse slightly to see the paintbrush shape.

> When you *double-click* the Format Painter button, the Format Painter feature remains active until you either click the Format Painter button again, or press Esc to cancel it—as indicated on the status bar.

5 With Format Painter still active, drag to select the paragraph *Main Dishes*, and then on the ribbon, on the **Home tab**, in the **Clipboard group**, notice that **Format Painter** ✍ is selected, indicating that it is active. Compare your screen with Figure 1.32.

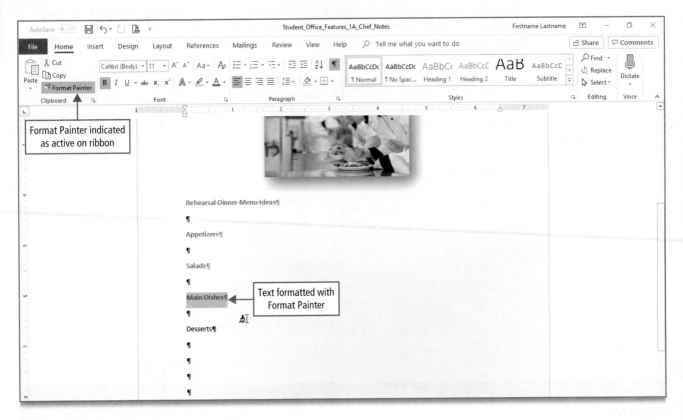

Figure 1.32

6 Select the paragraph *Desserts* to copy the format, and then on the ribbon, click **Format Painter** ✍ to turn the command off.

↻ **ANOTHER WAY** Press [Esc] to turn off Format Painter.

7 On the **Quick Access Toolbar**, click **Save** 🖫 to save the changes you have made to your document.

Activity 1.13 | Using Keyboard Shortcuts and Using the Clipboard to Copy, Cut, and Paste

The **Clipboard** is a temporary storage area that holds text or graphics that you select and then cut or copy. When you **copy** text or graphics, a copy is placed on the Clipboard and the original text or graphic remains in place. When you **cut** text or graphics, a copy is placed on the Clipboard, and the original text or graphic is removed—cut—from the document.

After copying or cutting, the contents of the Clipboard are available for you to **paste**—insert—in a new location in the current document, or into another Office file.

1 ▶ On your keyboard, hold down Ctrl and press Home to move to the beginning of your document, and then take a moment to study the table in Figure 1.33, which describes similar keyboard shortcuts with which you can navigate quickly in a document.

🖥 **MAC TIP** Press command ⌘ + fn + to move to the top of a document.

To Move	On a Windows PC press:	On a Mac press:
To the beginning of a document	Ctrl + Home	command ⌘ + fn + ←
To the end of a document	Ctrl + End	command ⌘ + fn + →
To the beginning of a line	Home	command ⌘ + ←
To the end of a line	End	command ⌘ + →
To the beginning of the previous word	Ctrl + ←	option + ←
To the beginning of the next word	Ctrl + →	option + →
To the beginning of the current word (if insertion point is in the middle of a word)	Ctrl + ←	option + ←
To the beginning of the previous paragraph	Ctrl + ↑	command ⌘ + ↑
To the beginning of the next paragraph	Ctrl + ↓	command ⌘ + ↓
To the beginning of the current paragraph (if insertion point is in the middle of a paragraph)	Ctrl + ↑	command ⌘ + ↑
Up one screen	PgUp	fn + ↑
Down one screen	PgDn	fn + ↓

Figure 1.33

2 ▶ To the left of *Skyline Metro Grill Chef Notes*, point in the left margin area to display the ⌐𝒜 pointer, and then click one time to select the entire paragraph. On the **Home tab**, in the **Clipboard group**, click **Copy** 📋.

Because anything that you select and then copy—or cut—is placed on the Clipboard, the Copy command and the Cut command display in the Clipboard group of commands on the ribbon. There is no visible indication that your copied selection has been placed on the Clipboard.

🔄 **ANOTHER WAY** Right-click the selection, and then click Copy on the shortcut menu; or, use the keyboard shortcut Ctrl + C.

🖥 **MAC TIP** Press command ⌘ + C as a keyboard shortcut for the Copy command.

3 On the **Home tab**, in the **Clipboard group**, to the right of the group name *Clipboard*, click the **Dialog Box Launcher** button ⌐, and then compare your screen with Figure 1.34.

The Clipboard pane displays with your copied text. In any ribbon group, the *Dialog Box Launcher* displays either a dialog box or a pane related to the group of commands. It is not necessary to display the Clipboard in this manner, although sometimes it is useful to do so.

🖳 **MAC TIP**   On a Mac, you cannot view or clear the Clipboard. Use the ribbon commands.

Figure 1.34

4 In the upper right corner of the **Clipboard** pane, click **Close** ☒.

5 Press Ctrl + End to move to the end of your document. On the **Home tab**, in the **Clipboard group**, point to **Paste**, and then click the *upper* portion of this split button.

The Paste command pastes the most recently copied item on the Clipboard at the insertion point location. If you click the lower portion of the Paste button, a gallery of Paste Options displays. A *split button* is divided into two parts; clicking the main part of the button performs a command, and clicking the arrow displays a list or gallery with choices.

🖳 **MAC TIP**   Press command ⌘ + fn + → to move to the end of a document. The Paste button is not split; instead, display the dropdown menu; or use command ⌘ + V to paste.

🔄 **ANOTHER WAY**   Right-click, on the shortcut menu under Paste Options, click the desired option button; or, press Control + V.

---

6 Below the pasted text, click **Paste Options** 📋 as shown in Figure 1.35.

Here you can view and apply various formatting options for pasting your copied or cut text. Typically, you will click Paste on the ribbon and paste the item in its original format. If you want some other format for the pasted item, you can choose another format from the *Paste Options gallery*, which provides a Live Preview of the various options for changing the format of the pasted item with a single click. The Paste Options gallery is available in three places: on the ribbon by clicking the lower portion of the Paste button—the Paste button arrow; from the Paste Options button that displays below the pasted item following the paste operation; or on the shortcut menu if you right-click the pasted item.

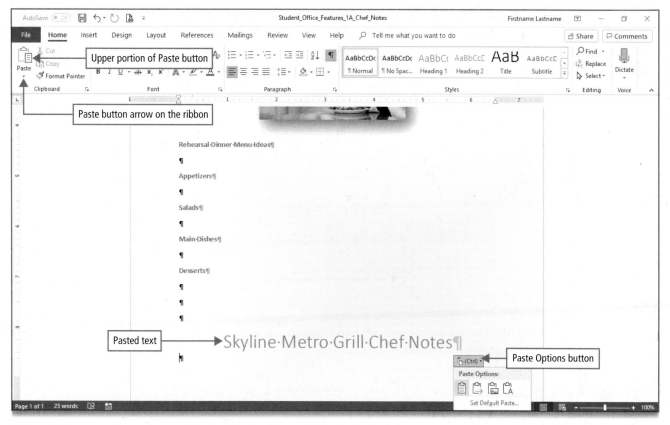

Figure 1.35

> **7** In the **Paste Options** gallery, *point* to each option to see the Live Preview of the format that would be applied if you clicked the button.

> The contents of the Paste Options gallery are contextual; that is, they change based on what you copied and where you are pasting.

> **8** Press ⎋Esc to close the gallery; the button will remain displayed until you take some other screen action.

> **9** On your keyboard, press Ctrl + Home to move to the top of the document, and then click the **chefs image** one time to select it. While pointing to the selected image, right-click, and then on the shortcut menu, click **Cut**.

> Recall that the Cut command cuts—removes—the selection from the document and places it on the Clipboard.

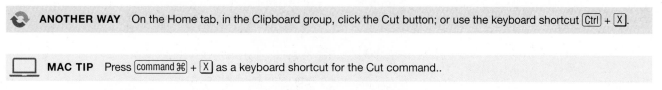

ANOTHER WAY On the Home tab, in the Clipboard group, click the Cut button; or use the keyboard shortcut Ctrl + X.

MAC TIP Press command ⌘ + X as a keyboard shortcut for the Cut command..

> **10** Press Ctrl + End to move to the end of the document.

11 With the insertion point blinking in the blank paragraph at the end of the document, right-click, and notice that the **Paste Options** gallery displays on the shortcut menu. Compare your screen with Figure 1.36.

Figure 1.36

12 On the shortcut menu, under **Paste Options**, click the first button—**Keep Source Formatting**.

MAC TIP On the shortcut menu, click Paste, click the Paste Options button, and then click Keep Source Formatting.

13 Point to the picture to display the [⬚] pointer, and then drag to the right until the center green **Alignment Guide** displays and the blank paragraph is above the picture. Release the left mouse button.

MAC TIP In the Arrange group, on the Picture Format tab, click Align, click Align Center.

14 Above the picture, select the text *Chef Notes*, type **Festive Salad** and then compare your screen with Figure 1.37.

Figure 1.37

15 Click **Save** [💾].

Activity 1.14 | Adding Alternative Text for Accessibility

5.4.3

1 Point to the **chefs picture** and right-click. On the shortcut menu, click **Edit Alt Text** to display the **Alt Text** pane.

Alternative text helps people using a *screen reader*, which is software that enables visually impaired users to read text on a computer screen to understand the content of pictures. *Alt text* is the term commonly used for this feature.

2 In the **Alt Text** pane, notice that Word generates a suggested description of the picture. Click in the box, select the existing text, and then type **Young chefs making salads in a restaurant kitchen** and then compare your screen with Figure 1.38.

Anyone viewing the document with a screen reader will see the alternative text displayed instead of the picture.

Figure 1.38

3 **Close** ☒ the **Alt Text** pane. Press ⌃Ctrl + Home to move to the top of your document. On the Quick Access Toolbar, click **Save** 🖫 to the changes you have made to your document.

Objective 5 | Finalize an Office Document

GO! Learn How
Video OF1-5

There are steps you will want to take to finalize your documents. This typically includes inserting a footer for identifying information and adding Document Properties to facilitate searching. Recall that Document Properties—also known as metadata—are details about a file that describe or identify it, such as the title, author name, subject, and keywords that identify the document's topic or contents. You might also want to take some security measures or mark information to find later.

Activity 1.15 | Inserting a Footer, Inserting Document Info, and Adding Document Properties

MOS
1.3.2

1 On the **Insert tab**, in the **Header & Footer group**, click **Footer**. At the bottom of the list, click **Edit Footer**, and then with the **Header & Footer Tools Design tab** active, in the **Insert group**, click **Document Info**. Click **File Name** to add the file name to the footer.

A *footer* is a reserved area for text and graphics that displays at the bottom of each page in a document. It is common in organizations to add the file name to the footer of documents so that documents are easily identified.

 MAC TIP In the Insert group, click Field. In the dialog box, under Categories, click Document Information. Then under Field names, click FileName. Click OK.

2 On the right end of the ribbon, click **Close Header and Footer**.

3 On the **Quick Access Toolbar**, point to the **Print Preview and Print** button ⎙ you placed there, right-click, and then click **Remove from Quick Access Toolbar**.

> If you are working on your own computer and you want to do so, you can leave the icon on the toolbar; in a college lab, you should return the software to its original settings.

4 Click the **File tab** to display **Backstage** view. With the **Info tab** active, in the lower right corner, click **Show All Properties**. Click in the **Tags** box, and then type **rehearsal dinners, menus**

> *Tags*—also referred to as *keywords*—are custom file properties in the form of words that you associate with a document to give an indication of the document's content. Use tags to assist in searching for and organizing files.

> 🖥 **MAC TIP** On the menu bar, click File, click Properties, click the Summary tab, and then type the tags in the Keywords box. Click OK.

5 Click in the **Subject** box, and then type your course name and number—for example, *CIS 10, #5543*. Under **Related People**, be sure your name displays as the author. (To edit the Author, right-click the name, click Edit Property, type the new name, click in a white area to close the list, and then click OK.)

6 On the left, click **Save** to save your document and return to the Word window.

Activity 1.16 | Inspecting a Document

Word, Excel, and PowerPoint all have the same commands to inspect a file before sharing it.

> 🖥 **MAC TIP** On the menu bar, click Tools. Here you can click Protect Document and Check Accessibility.

MOS
1.4.1, 1.4.2, 1.4.3

1 With your document displayed, click the **File tab**, on the left, if necessary, click **Info**, and then on the right, click **Check for Issues**.

2 On the list, click **Inspect Document**.

> The *Inspect Document* command searches your document for hidden data or personal information that you might not want to share publicly. This information could reveal company details that should not be shared.

3 In the lower right corner of the **Document Inspector** dialog box, click **Inspect**.

> The Document Inspector runs and lists information that was found and that you could choose to remove.

4 In the lower right corner of the dialog box, click **Close**, and then click **Check for Issues** again. On the list, click **Check Accessibility**.

> The *Check Accessibility* command checks the document for content that people with disabilities might find difficult to read. The Accessibility Checker pane displays on the right and lists objects that might require attention.

5 Close ☒ the **Accessibility Checker** pane, and then click the **File tab**.

6 Click **Check for Issues**, and then click **Check Compatibility**.

> The *Check Compatibility* command checks for features in your document that may not be supported by earlier versions of the Office program. This is only a concern if you are sharing documents with individuals with older software.

7 Click **OK**. Leave your Word document displayed for the next Activity.

Activity 1.17 | Inserting a Bookmark and a 3D Model

MOS
1.1.2, 5.2.6

A *bookmark* identifies a word, section, or place in your document so that you can find it quickly without scrolling. This is especially useful in a long document.

3D models are a new kind of shape that you can insert from an online library of ready-to-use three-dimensional graphics. A 3D model is most powerful in a PowerPoint presentation where you can add transitions and animations during your presentation, but you can also insert a 3D model into a Word document for an impactful image that you can position in various ways.

1 In the paragraph *Rehearsal Dinner Menu Items*, select the word *Menu*.

2 On the **Insert tab**, in the **Links group**, click **Bookmark**.

3 In the **Bookmark** name box, type **menu** and then click **Add**.

4 Press Ctrl + Home to move to the top of your document.

5 On the **Home tab**, at the right end of the ribbon, in the **Editing group**, click the **Find button arrow**, and then click **Go To**.

🔄 **ANOTHER WAY**   Press Ctrl + G, which is the keyboard shortcut for the Go To command.

💻 **MAC TIP**   On the menu bar, click Edit, point to Find, click Go To. In the dialog box, click Bookmark.

---

6 Under **Go to what**, click **Bookmark**, and then with *menu* indicated as the bookmark name, click **Go To**. **Close** the **Find and Replace** dialog box, and notice that your bookmarked text is selected for you.

7 Click to position your insertion point at the end of the word *Desserts*. On the **Insert tab**, in the **Illustrations group**, click the upper portion of the **3D Models button** to open the **Online 3D Models** dialog box.

NOTE   3D Models Not Available?

If the 3D Models command is not available on your system, in the **Illustrations group**, click **Pictures**, and then from the files downloaded with this project, click of01A_Cupcake. Change the Height to .75" and then move to Step 12.

---

8 In the search box, type **cupcake** and then press Enter.

9 Click the image of the **cupcake in a pink and white striped wrapper**—or select any other cupcake image. At the bottom, click **Insert**.

10 Point to the **3D control** in the center of the image, hold down the left mouse button, and then rotate the image so the top of the cupcake is pointing toward the upper right corner of the page—your rotation need not be exact. Alternatively, in the 3D Model Views group, click the More button ⌄, and then locate and click Above Front Left.

11 With the cupcake image selected, on the **3D Model Tools Format tab**, in the **Size group**, click in the **Height** box, type **.75"** and press Enter.

12 In the **Arrange group**, click **Wrap Text**, and then click **In Front of Text**. Then, in the **Arrange group**, click **Align**, and click **Align Right** to position the cupcake at the right margin.

13 Press Ctrl + Home to move to the top of your document. On the **Quick Access Toolbar**, click **Save** 🖫.

Activity 1.18 | Printing a File and Closing a Desktop App

1 Click the **File tab** to return to **Backstage** view, on the left click **Print**, and then compare your screen with Figure 1.39.

Here you can select any printer connected to your system and adjust the settings related to how you want to print. On the right, the *Print Preview* displays, which is a view of a document as it will appear on paper when you print it. Your page color effect will not display in Print Preview nor will the shading print. This effect appears only to anyone viewing the document on a screen.

At the bottom of the Print Preview area, in the center, the number of pages and page navigation arrows with which you can move among the pages in Print Preview display. On the right, the Zoom slider enables you to shrink or enlarge the Print Preview. *Zoom* is the action of increasing or decreasing the viewing area of the screen.

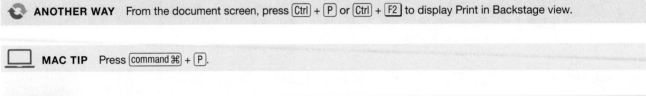

ANOTHER WAY From the document screen, press Ctrl + P or Ctrl + F2 to display Print in Backstage view.

MAC TIP Press command ⌘ + P.

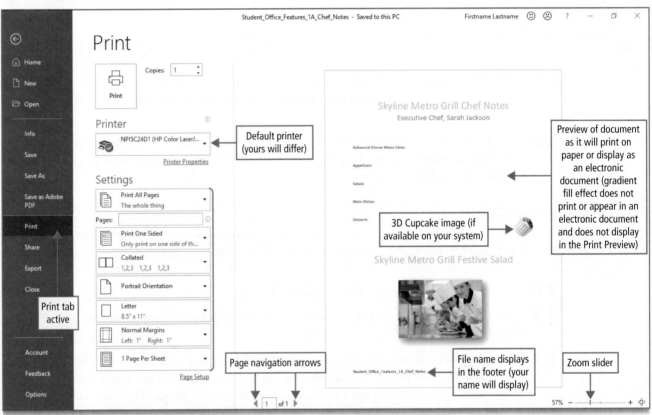

Figure 1.39

2 On the left, click **Save**. In the upper right corner of your screen, click **Close** ☒ to close Word. If a message displays regarding copied items, click No.

MAC TIP On the menu bar, click File, click Close.

3 In **MyLab IT**, locate and click the Grader Project **Office Features 1A Chef Notes**. In **step 3**, under **Upload Completed Assignment**, click **Choose File**. In the **Open** dialog box, navigate to your **Office Features Chapter 1 folder**, and then click your **Student_Office_Features_1A_ Chef_Notes** file one time to select it. In the lower right corner of the **Open** dialog box, click **Open**.

The name of your selected file displays above the Upload button.

4 To submit your file to **MyLab IT** for grading, click **Upload**, wait a moment for a green **Success!** message, and then in **step 4**, click the blue **Submit for Grading** button. Click **Close Assignment** to return to your list of **Course Materials**.

MORE KNOWLEDGE **Creating an Electronic Image of Your Document**

You can create an electronic image of your document that looks like a printed document. To do so, in Backstage view, on the left click Export. On the right, click Create PDF/XPS, and then click the Create PDF/XPS button to display the Publish as PDF or XPS dialog box.

PDF stands for *Portable Document Format*, which is a technology that creates an image that preserves the look of your file. This is a popular format for sending documents electronically, because the document will display on most computers. *XPS* stands for *XML Paper Specification*—a Microsoft file format that also creates an image of your document and that opens in the XPS viewer.

ALERT **The Remaining Activities in This Chapter Are Optional**

The following Activities describing the Office Help features are recommend but are optional to complete.

Objective 6 **Use the Office Help Features**

GO! Learn How
Video OF1-6

Within each Office program, you will see the *Tell Me* feature at the right end of the ribbon— to the right of the Help tab. This is a search feature for Microsoft Office commands that you activate by typing in the *Tell me what you want to do* box. Another way to use this feature is to point to a command on the ribbon, and then at the bottom of the displayed ScreenTip, click *Tell me more*.

Activity 1.19 | **Using Microsoft Office Tell Me, Tell Me More, the Help Tab, and Adding Alt Text to an Excel Chart**

MOS
5.3.3

1 Start Excel and open a **Blank workbook**. With cell **A1** active, type **456789** and press Enter. Click cell **A1** again to make it the active cell.

2 At the top of the screen, click in the *Tell me what you want to do* box, and then type **format as currency** In the displayed list, to the right of **Accounting Number Format**, click the ▶ arrow. Compare your screen with Figure 1.40.

> As you type, every keystroke refines the results so that you can click the command as soon as it displays. This feature helps you apply the command immediately; it does not explain how to locate the command.

🖥 **MAC TIP**   Click the Help tab on the menu bar.

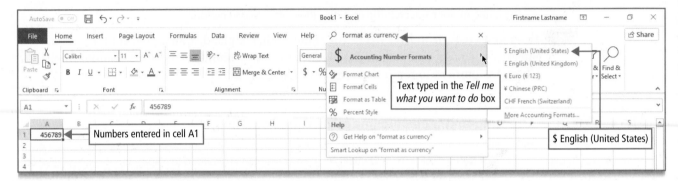

Figure 1.40

3 Click **$ English (United States)**.

4 On the **Home tab**, in the **Font group**, *point* to the **Font Color** button 🅰▾ to display its ScreenTip, and then click **Tell me more**.

> *Tell me more* is a prompt within a ScreenTip that opens the Office online Help system with explanations about how to perform the command referenced in the ScreenTip.

5 In the **Help** pane that displays on the right, if necessary, click **Change the color of text**. Compare your screen with Figure 1.41.

> As you scroll down, you will notice that the Help pane displays extensive information about the topic of changing the color of text, including how to apply a custom color.

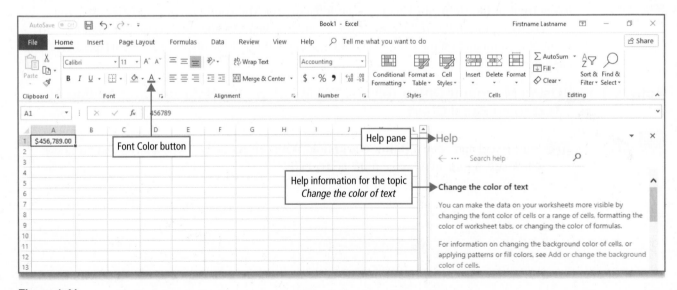

Figure 1.41

6 Close ☒ the **Help** pane.

---

7 On the ribbon, click the **Help tab**. In the **Help** group, click **Help**. In the **Help** pane, type **3D models** and then click the **Search** button 🔍. Click **Get creative with 3D models**, and then compare your screen with Figure 1.42.

Some Help topics include videos like this one to demonstrate and explain the topic.

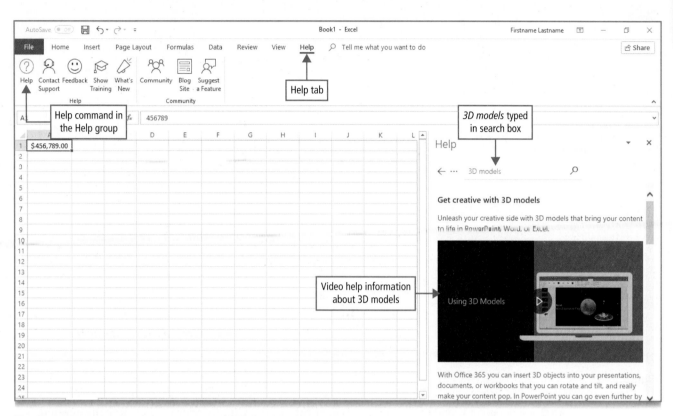

Figure 1.42

8 In the **Help** group and the **Community** group, look at the buttons.

Here you can Contact Support, send Feedback, Show Training developed by Microsoft, and see new features. In the Community group, you can visit the Excel Community, read the Excel Blog, and suggest new features.

9 ▶ Click **Show Training**, and then compare your screen with Figure 1.43.

Here you can view training videos developed by Microsoft.

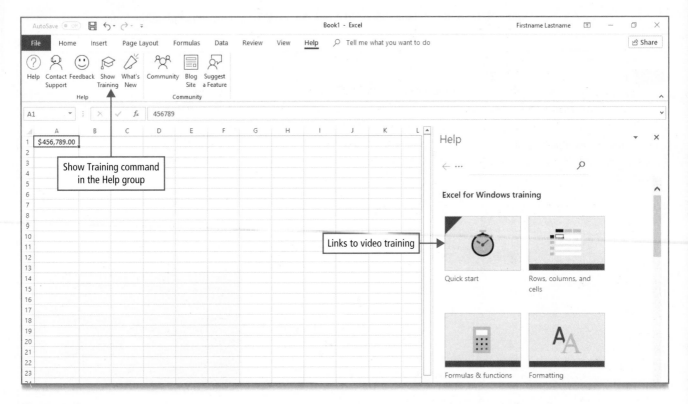

Figure 1.43

10 ▶ Click cell **A1**, and then click the **Insert tab**. In the **Charts group**, click **Recommended Charts**, and then in the **Insert Chart** dialog box, with the first chart selected, click **OK**.

11 ▶ Click the **Chart Tools Format tab**, and then in the **Accessibility group**, click **Alt Text**.

Here you can add text to describe the chart, similar to the Alt Text you added for the chef's image.

12 ▶ **Close** ⊠ the **Help** pane, **Close** ⊠ the **Alt Text** pane, and then in the upper right corner of the Excel window, click **Close** ⊠. Click **Don't Save**.

MORE KNOWLEDGE **Don't Type, Talk! With the New Dictate Feature**

Office 365 subscribers will see the *Dictate* feature in Word, PowerPoint, Outlook, and OneNote for Windows 10. When you enable Dictate, you start talking and as you talk, text appears in your document or slide. Dictate is one of Microsoft's Office Intelligent Services, which adds new cloud-enhanced features to Office. Dictate is especially useful in Outlook when you must write lengthy emails. The Dictate command is on the Home tab in Word and PowerPoint and on the Message tab in Outlook.

You have completed Project 1A **END**

PROJECT 1B Hotel Files

Project Activities

In Activities 1.20 through 1.38, you will assist Barbara Hewitt and Steven Ramos, who work for the Information Technology Department at the Boston headquarters office of the Bell Orchid Hotels. Barbara and Steven must organize some of the files and folders that comprise the corporation's computer data. As you progress through the project, you will insert screenshots of windows that you create into a PowerPoint presentation with five slides that will look similar to Figure 1.44.

Project Files for MyLab IT Grader

For Project 1B, you will start with the Windows 10 desktop displayed, and then learn how to create a folder for your **MyLab IT** files as you work through the project instruction. At the appropriate point in the project, you will be instructed to download your files from your **MyLab IT** course.

Project Results

GO! Project 1B
Where We're Going

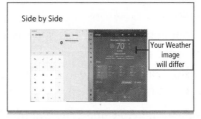

Figure 1.44

📄 **For Non-MyLab Submissions Start with the Windows 10 Desktop Displayed**

For Project 1B, you will start with the Windows 10 desktop displayed and learn how to create a folder and save a new PowerPoint presentation as you work through the project instruction. Additionally, you will need the Student Data Files **win01_1B_Bell_Orchid** from your instructor or from www.pearsonhighered.com/go.

Objective 7   Explore Windows 10

ALERT   Because Windows 10 periodically checks for and then automatically downloads updates, you are assured that your device is up to date with the latest features and security improvements. Therefore, you may encounter some variations in what appears on your screen and what is shown in this instruction. Microsoft Office 365 is fully installed on your PC or Mac; no internet access is necessary to create or edit documents. When you *are* connected to the internet, you will receive monthly upgrades and new features, so you always have the latest versions of Office apps as soon as they are available. Your subscription gives you continuous free access to the latest innovations and refinements.

A *program* is a set of instructions that a computer uses to accomplish a task. A computer program that helps you perform a task for a specific purpose is referred to as an *application*. As an example, there are applications to create a document using word processing software, to play a game, to view the latest weather report, to edit photos or videos, or to manage financial information.

An *operating system* is a specific type of computer program that manages the other programs on a computing device such as a desktop computer, a laptop computer, a smartphone, a tablet computer, or a game console. You need an operating system to:

- Use application programs.
- Coordinate the use of your computer hardware such as a keyboard, mouse, touchpad, touchscreen, game controller, or printer.
- Organize data that you store on your computer and access data that you store on your own computer and in other locations.

Windows 10 is an operating system developed by Microsoft Corporation that works with mobile computing devices and also with traditional desktop and laptop PCs.

The three major tasks of an operating system are to:

- Manage your computer's hardware—the printers, scanners, disk drives, monitors, and other hardware attached to it.
- Manage the application software installed on your computer—programs like those in Microsoft Office and other programs you might install to edit photos and videos, play games, and so on.
- Manage the *data* generated from your application software. Data refers to the documents, worksheets, pictures, songs, and so on that you create and store during the day-to-day use of your computer.

The Windows 10 operating system continues to perform these three tasks, and additionally is optimized for touchscreens; for example, tablets of all sizes and convertible laptop computers. Windows 10 works equally well with any input device, including a mouse, keyboard, touchscreen, and *pen*—a pen-shaped stylus that you tap on a computer screen.

In most instances, when you purchase a computer, the operating system software is already installed. The operating system consists of many smaller programs, stored as system files, which transfer data to and from the disk and transfer data in and out of your computer's memory. Other functions performed by the operating system include hardware-specific tasks such as checking to see if a key has been pressed on the keyboard and, if it has, displaying the appropriate letter or character on the screen.

Windows 10, in the same manner as other operating systems and earlier versions of the Windows operating system, uses a *graphical user interface*—abbreviated as *GUI* and pronounced *GOO-ee*. A graphical user interface uses graphics such as an image of a file folder or wastebasket that you click to activate the item represented. A GUI commonly incorporates the following:

- A *pointer*—any symbol that displays on your screen in response to moving your mouse and with which you can select objects and commands.
- An *insertion point*—a blinking vertical line that indicates where text will be inserted when you type or where an action will take place.
- A *pointing device*, such as a mouse or touchpad, to control the pointer.
- *Icons*—small images that represent commands, files, applications, or other windows.
- A *desktop*—a simulation of a real desk that represents your work area; here you can arrange icons such as shortcuts to programs, files, folders, and various types of documents in the same manner you would arrange physical objects on top of a desk.

In Windows 10, you also have a Start menu with tiles that display when you click the Start button in the lower left corner of your screen. The array of tiles serves as a connected dashboard to all of your important programs, sites, and services. On the Start menu, your view is tailored to your information and activities.

The physical parts of your computer such as the central processing unit (CPU), memory, and any attached devices such as a printer, are collectively known as *resources*. The operating system keeps track of the status of each resource and decides when a resource needs attention and for how long.

Application programs enable you to do work on, and be entertained by, your computer—programs such as Word and Excel found in the Microsoft Office suite of products, Adobe Photoshop, and computer games. No application program, whether a larger desktop app or smaller *Microsoft Store app*—a smaller app that you download from the Store—can run on its own; it must run under the direction of an operating system.

For the everyday use of your computer, the most important and most often used function of the operating system is managing your files and folders—referred to as *data management*. In the same manner that you strive to keep your paper documents and file folders organized so that you can find information when you need it, your goal when organizing your computer files and folders is to group your files so that you can find information easily. Managing your data files so that you can find your information when you need it is one of the most important computing skills you can learn.

Activity 1.20 | Recognizing User Accounts in Windows 10

On a single computer, Windows 10 can have multiple user accounts. This is useful because you can share a computer with other people in your family or organization and each person can have his or her own information and settings—none of which others can see. Each user on a single computer is referred to as a ***user account***. Figure 1.45 shows the Settings screen where you can add additional users to your computer.

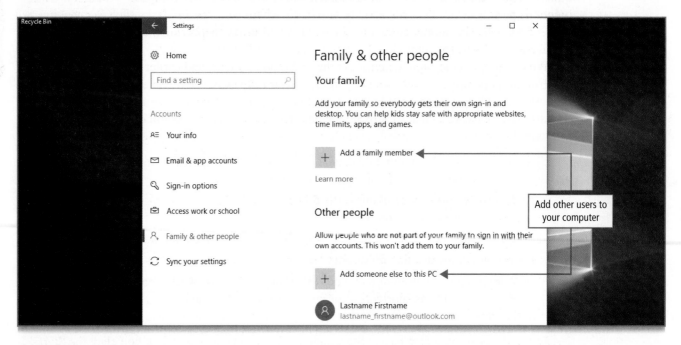

Figure 1.45

ALERT   Variations in Screen Organization, Colors, and Functionality Are Common in Windows 10

Individuals and organizations can determine how Windows 10 displays; therefore, the colors and the organization of various elements on the screen can vary. Your college or organization may customize Windows 10 to display a college picture or company logo or restrict access to certain features. The basic functions and structure of Windows 10 are not changed by such variations. You can be confident that the skills you will practice in this instruction apply to Windows 10 regardless of available functionality or differences between the figures shown and your screen.

NOTE   Comparing Your Screen with the Figures in This Textbook

Your screen will more closely match the figures shown in this textbook if you set your screen resolution to 1280 x 768. At other resolutions, your screen will closely resemble, but not match, the figures shown. To view your screen's resolution, on the desktop, right-click in a blank area, click *Display settings*, and then click the Resolution arrow. To adjust the resolution, select the desired setting, and then click OK.

With Windows 10, you can create a ***Microsoft account***, and then use that account to sign in to *any* Windows 10 computer on which you have, or create, a user account. By signing in with a Microsoft account you can:

- Download apps from the Microsoft Store
- Get your online content—email, social network updates, updated news—automatically displayed in an app when you sign in

Optionally, you can create a local account for use only on a specific PC. On your own Windows 10 computer, you must establish and then sign in with either a local account or a Microsoft account. Regardless of which one you select, you must provide an email address to associate with the user account name. If you create and then sign in with a local account, you can still connect to the internet, but you will not have the advantage of having your personal arrangement of apps displayed on your Start menu every time you sign in to that PC. You can use any email address to create a local account—similar to other online services where an email address is your user ID. You can also use any email address to create a Microsoft account.

To enjoy and get the full benefit of Windows 10, Microsoft Office, Skype, and free OneDrive cloud storage, if you have not already done so, create a Microsoft account. To do so, in your preferred web search engine, search for *create a Microsoft account*.

You can create an account using any email address. By signing in with a Microsoft account, your computer becomes your connected device where *you*—not your files—are the center of activity. At your college or place of employment, sign-in requirements will vary, because those computers are controlled by the organization's IT (Information Technology) professionals who are responsible for maintaining a secure computing environment for the entire organization.

Activity 1.21 | Turning On Your Computer, Signing In, and Exploring the Windows 10 Environment

Before you begin any computer activity, you must, if necessary, turn on your computer. This process is commonly referred to as ***booting the computer***. Because Windows 10 does not require you to completely shut down your computer except to install or repair a hardware device, in most instances moving the mouse or pressing a key will wake your computer in a few seconds. So, most of the time you will skip the lengthier boot process.

In this Activity, you will turn on your computer and sign in to Windows 10. Within an organization, the sign-in process may differ from that of your own computer.

ALERT **The look and features of Windows 10 will differ between your own PC and a PC you might use at your college or workplace.**

The Activities in this project assume that you are working on your own PC and signed in with a Microsoft account, or that you are working on a PC at your college or workplace where you are permitted to sign into Windows 10 with your own Microsoft account.

If you do not have a Microsoft account, or are working at a computer where you are unable to sign in with your Microsoft account, you can still complete the Activities, but some steps will differ.

On your own computer, you created your user account when you installed Windows 10 or when you set up your new computer that came with Windows 10. In a classroom or lab, check with your instructor to see how you will sign in to Windows 10.

NOTE **Create your Microsoft account if you have not already done so.**

To benefit from this instruction and understand your own computer, be sure that you know your Microsoft account login and password and use that to set up your user account. If you need to create a Microsoft account, in your preferred web search engine, search for *create a Microsoft account* and click the appropriate link.

1 If necessary, turn on your computer, and then examine Figure 1.46.

The Windows 10 *lock screen* fills your computer screen with a background—this might be a default picture from Microsoft such as one of the ones shown in the Lock screen settings in Figure 1.46 or a picture that you selected if you have personalized your system already. You can also choose to have a slide show of your own photos display on the lock screen.

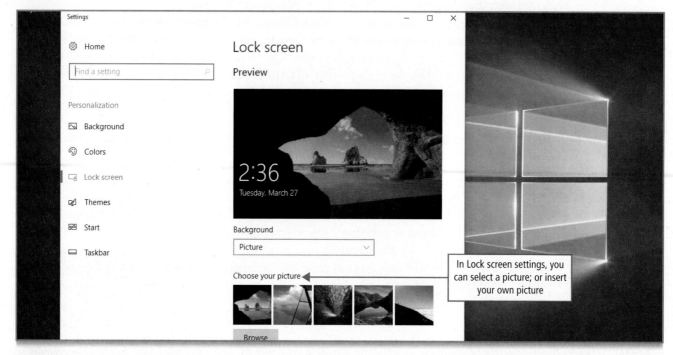

In Lock screen settings, you can select a picture; or insert your own picture

Figure 1.46

2 Determine whether you are working with a mouse and keyboard system or with a touchscreen system. If you are working with a touchscreen, determine whether you will use a stylus pen or the touch of your fingers.

NOTE **This Book Assumes You Are Using a Mouse and Keyboard, but You Can Also Use Touch**

This instruction uses terminology that assumes you are using a mouse and keyboard, but you need only touch gestures (described at the beginning of Project 1A in this chapter) to move through the instruction easily using touch. If a touch gesture needs more clarification, a *By Touch* box will assist you in using the correct gesture. Because more precision is needed for desktop operations, touching with a stylus pen may be preferable to touch using your fingers. When working with Microsoft Store apps, finger gestures are usually precise enough.

---

3 Press Enter to display the Windows 10 sign-in screen. If you are already signed in, go to Step 5.

BY TOUCH On the lock screen, swipe upward to display the sign-in screen. Tap your user image if necessary to display the Password box.

---

4 If you are the displayed user, type your password (if you have established one) and press Enter. If you are not the displayed user, click your user image if it displays or click the Switch user arrow → and then click your user image. Type your password.

The Windows 10 desktop displays with a default desktop background, a background you have selected, or perhaps a background set by your college or workplace.

5 In the lower left corner of your screen, move the mouse pointer over—*point to*—**Start** ⊞ and then *click*—press the left button on your mouse pointing device—to display the **Start menu**. Compare your screen with Figure 1.47, and then take a moment to study the table in Figure 1.48. If your list of programs does not display, in the upper left, click the ▤.

The *mouse pointer* is any symbol that displays on your screen in response to moving your mouse.

The Windows 10 *Start menu* displays a list of installed programs on the left and a customizable group of square and rectangular boxes—referred to as *tiles*—on the right. You can customize the arrangement of tiles from which you can access apps, websites, programs, folders, and tools for using your computer by simply clicking or tapping them.

Think of the right side of the Start menu as your connected *dashboard*—a one-screen view of links to information and programs that matter to *you*—through which you can connect with the people, activities, places, and apps that you care about.

Some tiles are referred to as *live tiles*, because they are constantly updated with fresh information relevant to you—the number of new email messages you have or new sports scores that you are interested in. Live tiles are at the center of your Windows 10 experience.

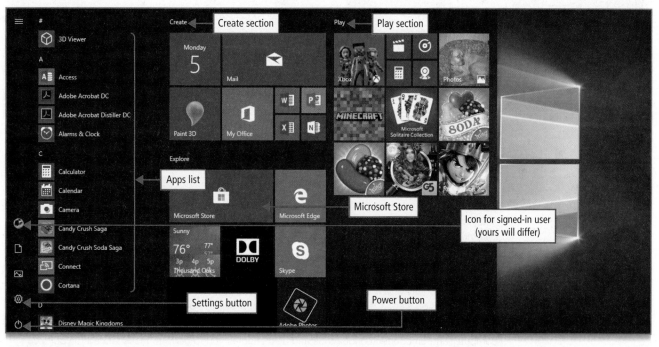

Figure 1.47

Parts of the Windows 10 Start Menu	
Create	Apps pinned to the Start menu that relate to your own information; for example, your Mail, your Calendar, and apps with which you create things; for example, your Office apps.
Apps list	Displays a list of the apps available on your system (yours will differ).
Play and Explore	Apps pinned to the Start menu that relate to games or news apps that you have installed; you can change this heading or delete it.
Power button	Enables you to set your computer to Sleep, Shut down, or Restart.
Settings	Displays the Settings menu to change any Windows 10 setting.
Signed-in User	Displays the icon for the signed-in user.

Figure 1.48

6 Click **Start** ⊞ again to close the Start menu. Compare your screen with Figure 1.49, and then take a moment to study the parts of the Windows desktop as shown in the table in Figure 1.50.

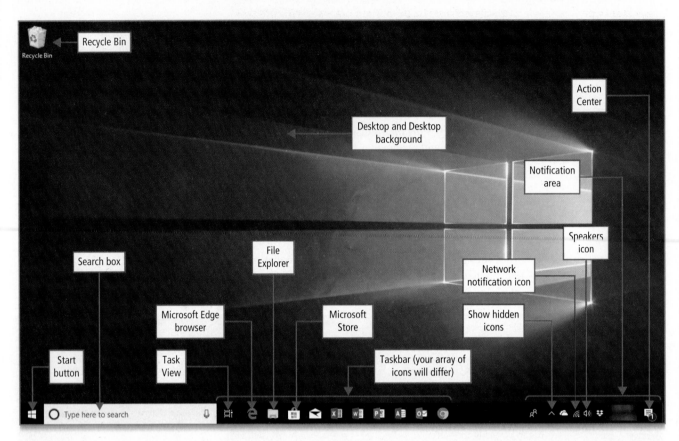

Figure 1.49

Parts of the Windows 10 Desktop	
Action Center	Displays the Action Center in a vertical pane on the right of your screen where you can see notifications—such as new mail or new alerts from social networks—at the top and access commonly used settings at the bottom.
Desktop	Serves as a surface for your work, like the top of an actual desk. Here you can arrange icons—small pictures that represent a file, folder, program, or other object.
Desktop background	Displays the colors and graphics of your desktop; you can change the desktop background to look the way you want it, such as using a picture or a solid color. Also referred to as *wallpaper*.
File Explorer	Launches the File Explorer program, which displays the contents of folders and files on your computer and on connected locations and also enables you to perform tasks related to your files and folders such as copying, moving, and renaming. If your File Explorer icon does not display, search for it, right-click its name in the search results, and then click Pin to taskbar.
Microsoft Edge browser	Launches Microsoft Edge, the web browser program developed by Microsoft that is included with Windows 10.
Microsoft Store	Opens the Microsoft Store where you can select and download Microsoft Store apps.
Network notification icon	Displays the status of your network.
Notification area	Displays notification icons and the system clock and calendar; sometimes referred to as the *system tray*.
Recycle Bin	Contains files and folders that you delete. When you delete a file or folder, it is not actually deleted; it stays in the Recycle Bin if you want it back, until you take an action to empty the Recycle Bin.
Search box	If *Cortana*—Microsoft's intelligent personal assistant—is enabled, a small circle will display on the left edge of the Search box. If Cortana is not enabled, a search icon displays at the left edge.

Parts of the Windows 10 Desktop	
Show hidden icons	Displays additional icons related to your notifications.
Speakers icon	Displays the status of your computer's speakers (if any).
Start button	Displays the Start menu.
Task View	Displays your desktop background with a small image of all open programs and apps. Click once to open, click again to close. May also display the Timeline.
Taskbar	Contains buttons to launch programs and buttons for all open programs; by default, it is located at the bottom of the desktop, but you can move it. You can customize the number and arrangement of buttons.

Figure 1.50

Activity 1.22 | Pinning a Program to the Taskbar

Snipping Tool is a program within Windows 10 that captures an image of all or part of your computer's screen. A ***snip***, as the captured image is called, can be annotated, saved, copied, or shared via email. Any capture of your screen is referred to as a ***screenshot***, and there are many other ways to capture your screen in addition to the Snipping Tool.

> **NOTE   Snip & Sketch Offers Improved Snipping Capabilities**
>
> Although Snipping Tool will be available for several more years, a newer tool for snipping, called Snip & Sketch, will roll out to Windows 10 users. Find it by typing Snip & Sketch in the search box.

1 In the lower left corner of your screen, click in the **Search box**.

Search relies on ***Bing***, Microsoft's search engine, which enables you to conduct a search on your PC, your apps, and the web.

2 With your insertion point in the search box, type **snipping** Compare your screen with Figure 1.51.

> **BY TOUCH**   On a touchscreen, tap in the Search box to display the onscreen keyboard, and then begin to type *snipping*.

Figure 1.51

3 With the **Snipping Tool Desktop app** shaded and displayed at the top of the search results, press Enter one time.

> The Snipping Tool program's *dialog box*—a small window that displays options for completing a task—displays on the desktop, and on the taskbar, the Snipping Tool program button displays underlined and framed in a lighter shade to indicate that the program is open.

BY TOUCH   In the search results, tap the Snipping Tool app.

4 On the taskbar, point to the **Snipping Tool** button and then *right-click*—click the right mouse button one time. On the displayed **Jump List**, click **Pin to taskbar**.

> A *Jump List* displays destinations and tasks from a program's taskbar icon when you right-click the icon.

BY TOUCH   On the taskbar, use the *Swipe to select* technique—swipe upward with a short quick movement—to display the Jump List. On the list, tap *Pin to taskbar*.

5 Point to the upper right corner of the **Snipping Tool** dialog box, and then click **Close** ☒.

> Because Snipping Tool is a useful tool, while completing the Projects in this textbook, it is recommended that you leave Snipping Tool pinned to your taskbar.

Objective 8 | Prepare to Work with Folders and Files

A *file* is a collection of information stored on a computer under a single name. Examples of a file include a Word document, an Excel workbook, a picture, a song, or a program. A *folder* is a container in which you store files. Windows 10 organizes and keeps track of your electronic files by letting you create and label electronic folders into which you can place your files.

Activity 1.23 | Creating a New Folder to Store a File

In this Activity, you will create a new folder and save it in a location of your choice. You might decide to use a *removable storage device*, such as a USB flash drive, which is commonly used to transfer information from one computer to another. Such devices are also useful when you want to work with your files on different computers. For example, you probably have files that you work with at your college, at home, and possibly at your workplace.

A *drive* is an area of storage that is formatted with a file system compatible with your operating system and is identified by a drive letter. For example, your computer's *hard disk drive*—the primary storage device located inside your computer where some of your files and programs are typically stored—is usually designated as drive *C*. Removable storage devices that you insert into your computer will be designated with a drive letter—the letter designation varies depending on how many input ports you have on your computer.

You can also use *cloud storage*—storage space on an internet service that can also display as a drive on your computer. When you create a Microsoft account, free cloud storage called *OneDrive* is provided to you. If you are signed in with your Microsoft account, you can access OneDrive from File Explorer.

Increasingly, the use of removable storage devices for file storage is becoming less common, because having your files stored in the cloud where you can retrieve them from any device is more convenient and efficient.

1 ▶ Be sure your Windows desktop is still displayed. If you want to do so, insert your USB flash drive. If necessary, close any messages.

> Plugging in a device results in a chime sound—if sound is enabled. You might see a message in the taskbar or on the screen that the device software is being installed.

2 ▶ On your taskbar, check to see if the **File Explorer** icon 🗔 displays. If it does, move to Step 3. If not, in the search box, type **file explorer** under **Best match**, point to **File Explorer Desktop app**, right-click, and then click **Pin to taskbar**.

> In an enterprise environment such as a college or business, File Explorer may not be pinned to the taskbar by default, so you might have to pin it there each time you use the computer. Windows 10 Home, the version of Windows that comes on most consumer PCs, typically has File Explorer pinned to the taskbar by default.

3 ▶ On the taskbar, click **File Explorer** 🗔. If necessary, in the upper right corner of the **File Explorer** window, click Expand the Ribbon ⌄.

> *File Explorer* is the program that displays the contents of locations, folders, and files on your computer and also in your OneDrive and other cloud storage locations.

> The *ribbon* is a user interface in Windows 10 that groups commands for performing related tasks on tabs across the upper portion of a window. Commands for common tasks include copying and moving, creating new folders, emailing and zipping items, and changing the view.

> Use the *navigation pane*—the area on the left side of File Explorer window—to get to locations— your OneDrive, folders on your PC, devices and drives connected to your PC, and other PCs on your network.

4 On the ribbon at the top of the window, click the **View tab**, and then in the **Layout group**, click **Tiles**. Compare your screen with Figure 1.52, and then take a moment to study the parts of the File Explorer window as shown in the table in Figure 1.53.

NOTE **Does your ribbon show only the tab names? Does your Quick Access toolbar display below the ribbon?**

By default, the ribbon is minimized and appears as a menu bar, displaying only the ribbon tabs. If your ribbon displays only tabs, click the Expand the Ribbon arrow ⌄ on the right side to display the full ribbon. If your Quick Access toolbar displays below the ribbon, point to it, right-click, and then click Show Quick Access Toolbar above the Ribbon.

The *File Explorer window* displays with the Quick access area selected by default. A File Explorer window displays the contents of the current location and contains helpful parts so you can *navigate*—explore within the file organizing structure of Windows. A *location* is any disk drive, folder, network, or cloud storage area in which you can store files and folders.

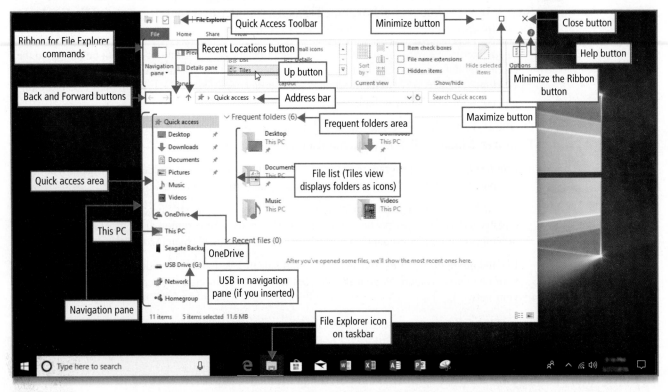

Figure 1.52

Parts of the File Explorer Window

Address bar	Displays your current location in the folder structure as a series of links separated by arrows.
Back and Forward buttons	Provides the ability to navigate to other folders you have already opened without closing the current folder window. These buttons work with the address bar; that is, after you use the address bar to change folders, you can use the Back button to return to the previous folder.
Close button	Closes the window.
File list	Displays the contents of the current folder or location; if you type text into the Search box, only the folders and files that match your search will display here—including files in subfolders.
Frequent folders area	When Quick access is selected in the navigation pane, displays the folders you use frequently.
Help button	Opens a Bing search for Windows 10 help.
Maximize button	Increases the size of a window to fill the entire screen.
Minimize button	Removes the window from the screen without closing it; minimized windows can be reopened by clicking the associated button in the taskbar.

Parts of the File Explorer Window

Minimize the Ribbon button	Collapses the ribbon so that only the tab names display.
Navigation pane	Displays—for the purpose of navigating to locations—the Quick access area, your OneDrive if you have one and are signed in, locations on the PC at which you are working, any connected storage devices, and network locations to which you might be connected.
OneDrive	Provides navigation to your free file storage and file sharing service provided by Microsoft that you get when you sign up for a Microsoft account; this is your personal cloud storage for files.
Quick access area	Displays commonly accessed locations—such as Documents and Desktop—that you want to access quickly.
Quick Access Toolbar	Displays commonly used commands; you can customize this toolbar by adding and deleting commands and by showing it below the ribbon instead of above the ribbon.
Recent Locations button	Displays the path to locations you have visited recently so that you can go back to a previously working directory quickly.
Ribbon for File Explorer commands	Groups common tasks such as copying and moving, creating new folders, emailing and zipping items, and changing views.
Search box	Locates files stored within the current folder when you type a search term.
This PC	Provides navigation to your internal storage and attached storage devices including optical media such as a DVD drive.
Up button	Opens the location where the folder you are viewing is saved—also referred to as the *parent folder*.

Figure 1.53

5 ▶ In the **navigation pane**, click **This PC**. On the right, under **Devices and drives**, locate **Windows (C:)**—or **OS (C:)**—point to the device name to display the ⌨ pointer, and then right-click to display a shortcut menu. Compare your screen with Figure 1.54.

A *shortcut menu* is a context-sensitive menu that displays commands and options relevant to the active object. The Windows logo on the C: drive indicates this is where the Windows 10 operating system is stored.

🖰 **BY TOUCH** Press and hold briefly to display a shaded square and then release.

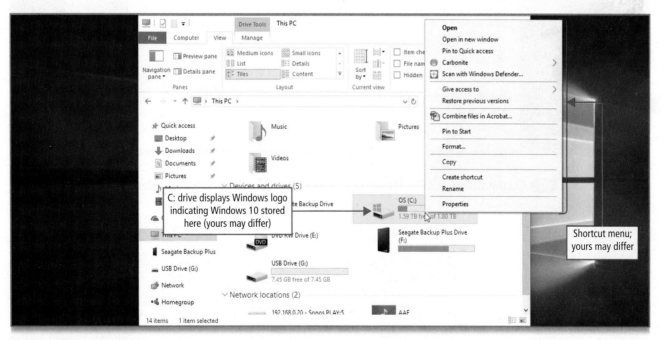

Figure 1.54

6 On the shortcut menu, click **Open** to display the *file list* for this drive.

A file list displays the contents of the current location. This area is also referred to as the ***content pane***. If you enter a search term in the search box, your results will also display here. Here, in the C: drive, Windows 10 stores various files related to your operating system.

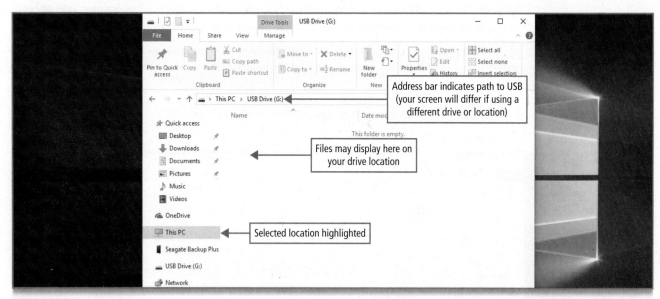

ANOTHER WAY   Point to the device name and double-click to display the file list for the device.

7 On the ribbon, notice that the **Drive Tools** tab displays above the **Manage tab**.

This is a ***contextual tab***, which is a tab added to the ribbon automatically when a specific object is selected and that contains commands relevant to the selected object.

8 To the left of the **address bar**, click **Up** ⬆ to move up one level in the drive hierarchy and close the file list.

The ***address bar*** displays your current location in the folder structure as a series of links separated by arrows. Use the address bar to enter or select a location. You can click a part of the path to go to that level. Or, click at the end of the path to select the path for copying.

9 Under **Devices and drives**, click your **USB flash drive** to select it—or click the folder or location where you want to store your file for this project—and notice that the drive or folder is highlighted in blue, indicating it is selected. At the top of the window, on the ribbon, click the **Computer tab**, and then in the **Location group**, click **Open**. Compare your screen with Figure 1.55.

The file list for the selected location displays. There may be no files or only a few files in the location you have selected. You can open a location by double-clicking its name, using the shortcut menu, or by using this ribbon command.

Figure 1.55

10 On the ribbon, on the **Home tab**, in the **New group**, click **New folder**.

11 With the text *New folder* highlighted, type **Windows 10 Chapter 1** and then press ⏎ to confirm the folder name and select—highlight—the new folder. With the folder selected, press ⏎ again to open the File Explorer window for your **Windows 10 Chapter 1** folder. Compare your screen with Figure 1.56.

> Windows creates a new folder in the location you selected. The address bar indicates the *path* from This PC to your folder. A path is a sequence of folders that leads to a specific file or folder.

> To *select* means to specify, by highlighting, a block of data or text on the screen with the intent of performing some action on the selection.

👉 **BY TOUCH**   You may have to tap the keyboard icon in the lower right corner of the taskbar to display the onscreen keyboard.

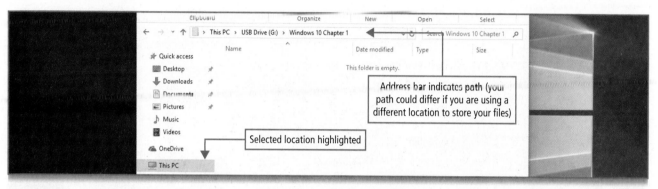

Figure 1.56

MORE KNOWLEDGE   **Use OneDrive as Cloud Storage**

OneDrive is Microsoft's *cloud storage* product. Cloud storage means that your data is stored on a remote server that is maintained by a company so that you can access your files from anywhere and from any device. The idea of having all your data on a single device—your desktop or laptop PC—has become old fashioned. Because cloud storage from large companies like Microsoft are secure, many computer users now store their information on cloud services like OneDrive. Anyone with a Microsoft account has a large amount of free storage on OneDrive, and if you have an Office 365 account—free to most college students—you have 1 terabyte or more of OneDrive storage that you can use across all Microsoft products. That amount of storage is probably all you will ever need—even if you store lots of photos on your OneDrive. OneDrive is integrated into the Windows 10 operating system.

Activity 1.24 | Creating and Saving a File

1 In the upper right corner of your **Windows 10 Chapter 1** folder window, click **Close** ☒.

2 In the lower left corner, click **Start** ⊞.

3 Point to the right side of the **apps list** to display a **scroll bar**, and then drag the **scroll box** down to view apps listed under **T**. Compare your screen with Figure 1.57.

To *drag* is to move something from one location on the screen to another while holding down the left mouse button; the action of dragging includes releasing the mouse button at the desired time or location.

A vertical *scroll bar* displays on the right side of the menu area. A scroll bar displays when the contents of a window or pane are not completely visible. A scroll bar can be vertical as shown or horizontal and displayed at the bottom of a window.

Within the scroll bar, you can move the *scroll box* to bring the contents of the window into view. The position of the scroll box within the scroll bar indicates your relative position within the window's contents. You can click the *scroll arrow* at either end of the scroll bar to move within the window in small increments.

Figure 1.57

MORE KNOWLEDGE **Jump to a Lettered Section of the Apps List Quickly**

To move quickly to an alphabetic section of the apps list, click an alphabetic letter on the list to display an onscreen alphabet, and then click the letter of the alphabet to which you want to jump.

---

4 Click **Tips**. If necessary, in the upper right, click **Maximize** ⬜ so that the **Tips** window fills your entire screen. Then, move your mouse pointer to the right edge of the screen to display the **scroll bar**. Compare your screen with Figure 1.58.

In any window, the *Maximize* button will maximize the size of the window to fill the entire screen.

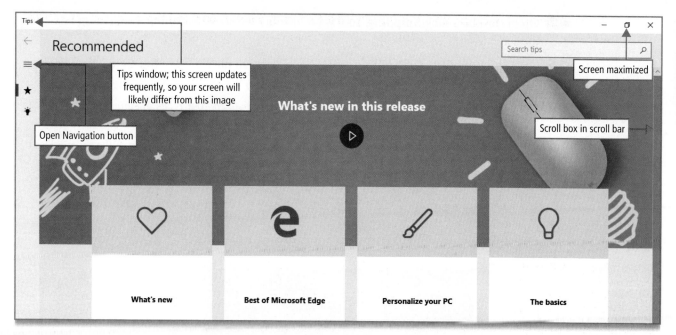

Figure 1.58

5 In the upper left corner, click **Open Navigation** ≡.

This icon is commonly referred to as a *menu icon* or a *hamburger menu* or simply a *hamburger*. The name derives from the three lines that bring to mind a hamburger on a bun. This type of button is commonly used in mobile applications because it is compact to use on smaller screens.

When you click the hamburger icon, a menu expands to identify the icons on the left—Recommended and Collections.

6 Click **Collections**, and then click **Windows**. Click **Get organized**. Move your mouse within the center right side of the screen to display a slideshow arrow ▷, and then click the arrow until you get to the tip **Snap apps side by side**; if this tip is not available, pause at another interesting tip. Compare your screen with Figure 1.59.

To find interesting new things about Windows, Office, Microsoft Mixed Reality, and other topics, take time to explore the Tips app.

Figure 1.59

7 On the taskbar, click **Snipping Tool** 🖾 to display the small **Snipping Tool** dialog box over the screen.

8 On the **menu bar** of the **Snipping Tool** dialog box, to the right of *Mode*, click the **arrow**. Compare your screen with Figure 1.60.

This *menu*—a list of commands within a category—displays four types of snips. A group of menus at the top of a program window is referred to as the *menu bar*.

Use a *free-form snip* to draw an irregular line such as a circle around an area of the screen. Use a *rectangular snip* to draw a precise box by dragging the mouse pointer around an area of the screen to form a rectangle. Use a *window snip* to capture the entire displayed window. Use a *full-screen snip* to capture the entire screen.

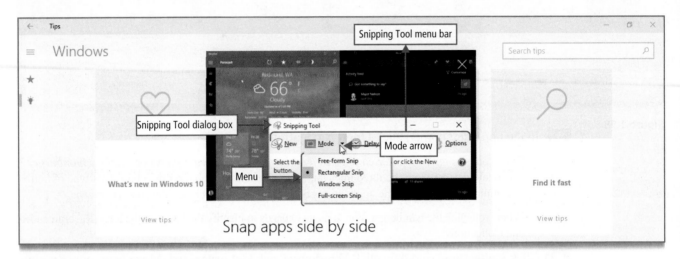

Figure 1.60

9 On the menu, click **Rectangular Snip**, and move your mouse slightly. Notice that the screen dims and your pointer takes the shape of a plus sign ➕.

10 Move the ➕ pointer to the upper left corner of the slide portion of the screen, hold down the left mouse button, and then drag down and to the right until you have captured the slide portion of the screen, as shown in Figure 1.61 and then release the mouse button. If you are not satisfied with your result, close the Snipping Tool window and begin again.

The Snipping Tool mark-up window displays the portion of the screen that you snipped. Here you can annotate—mark or make notes on—save, copy, or share the snip.

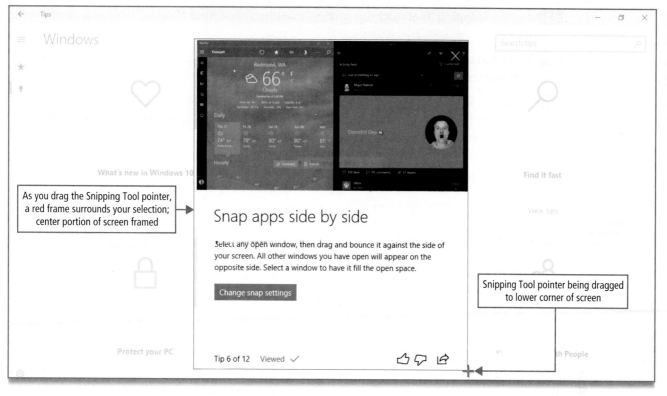

As you drag the Snipping Tool pointer, a red frame surrounds your selection; center portion of screen framed

Snipping Tool pointer being dragged to lower corner of screen

Figure 1.61

11 On the toolbar of the displayed **Snipping Tool** mark-up window, click the **Pen button arrow** [/], and then click **Red Pen**. Notice that your mouse pointer displays as a red dot.

12 On the snip—remember that you are now looking at a picture of the portion of the screen you captured—use the red mouse pointer to draw a circle around the text *Snap apps side by side*—or whatever the name of the tip you selected is. The circle need not be precise. If you are not satisfied with your circle, on the toolbar, click the Eraser button [], point anywhere on the red circle, click to erase, and then begin again. Compare your screen with Figure 1.62.

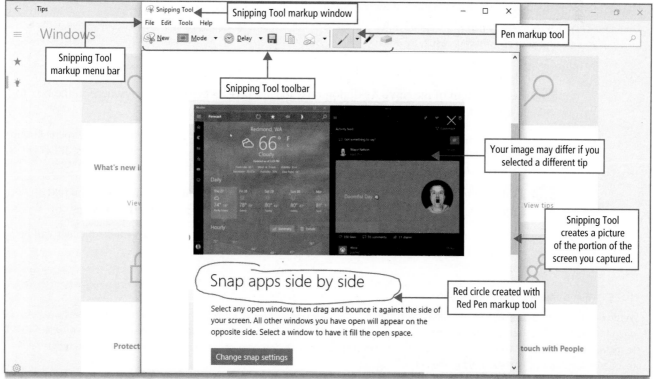

Snipping Tool markup window

Snipping Tool markup menu bar

Snipping Tool toolbar

Pen markup tool

Your image may differ if you selected a different tip

Snipping Tool creates a picture of the portion of the screen you captured.

Red circle created with Red Pen markup tool

Figure 1.62

13 On the **Snipping Tool** mark-up window's toolbar, click **Save Snip** 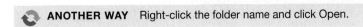 to display the **Save As** dialog box.

14 In the **Save As** dialog box, in the **navigation pane**, drag the scroll box down as necessary to find and then click the location where you created your **Windows 10 Chapter 1** folder.

15 In the **file list**, scroll as necessary, locate and *double-click*—press the left mouse button two times in rapid succession while holding the mouse still—your **Windows 10 Chapter 1** folder. Compare your screen with Figure 1.63.

ANOTHER WAY Right-click the folder name and click Open.

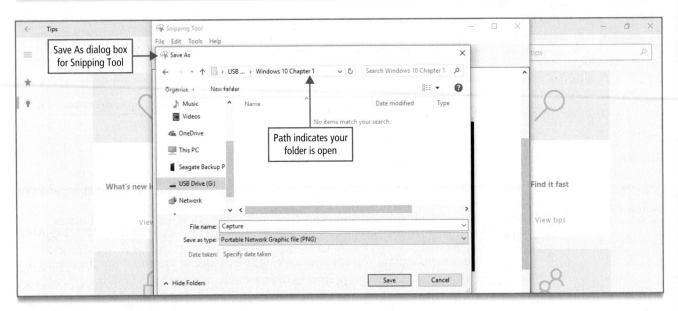

Figure 1.63

NOTE   Successful Double-Clicking Requires a Steady Hand

Double-clicking needs a steady hand. The speed of the two clicks is not as important as holding the mouse still between the two clicks. If you are not satisfied with your result, try again.

---

16 At the bottom of the **Save As** dialog box, locate **Save as type**, click anywhere in the box to display a list, and then on the displayed list click **JPEG file**.

JPEG, which is commonly pronounced *JAY-peg* and stands for Joint Photographic Experts Group, is a common file type used by digital cameras and computers to store digital pictures. JPEG is popular because it can store a high-quality picture in a relatively small file.

17 At the bottom of the **Save As** dialog box, click in the **File name** box to select the text *Capture*, and then using your own name, type **Lastname_Firstname_1B_Tip_Snip**

Within any Windows-based program, text highlighted in blue—selected—in this manner will be replaced by your typing.

NOTE   File Naming in This Textbook

Windows 10 recognizes file names with spaces. You can use spaces in file names, however, some programs, especially when transferring files over the internet, may insert the extra characters %20 in place of a space. In this instruction you will be instructed to save files using an underscore instead of a space. The underscore key is the shift of the ⬚ key—on most keyboards located two or three keys to the left of ⬚Backspace⬚.

---

18 In the lower right corner of the window, click **Save**.

19 **Close** ☒ the **Snipping Tool** mark-up window, and then **Close** ☒ the **Tips** window.

20 Close any open windows and display your Windows desktop.

You have successfully created a folder and saved a file within that folder.

MORE KNOWLEDGE   **The Hamburger**

For a brief history of the hamburger icon, visit http://blog.placeit.net/history-of-the-hamburger-icon

---

For Non-MyLab Submissions

Start PowerPoint and click Blank Presentation. Click the File tab, on the left click Save As, click Browse, and then navigate to your Windows 10 Chapter 1 folder. At the bottom of the Save As dialog box, in the File name box, using your own name, name the file **Lastname_Firstname_Windows_10_1B_Hotel_Files** and then click Save. Move to Activity 1.26.

Activity 1.25 | Downloading and Extracting Zipped Files

1 If the Microsoft PowerPoint application is not pinned to your taskbar, use the same technique you used to search for and pin the Snipping Tool application to search for and pin the PowerPoint application to your taskbar.

2 Sign in to your **MyLab IT** course. In your course, locate and click **Windows 10 1B Hotel Files**, click Download Materials, and then click Download All Files. Using the Chrome browser (if you are using a different browser see notes below), use the steps below to extract the zipped folder to your **Windows 10 Chapter 1** (or use your favorite method to download and extract files):

- In the lower left, next to the downloaded zipped folder, click the small **arrow**, and then click **Show in folder**. The zipped folder displays in *File Explorer*—the Windows program that displays the contents of locations, folders, and files on your computer—in the Downloads folder. (Unless you have changed default settings, downloaded files go to the Downloads folder on your computer.)
- With the zipped folder selected, on the ribbon, under **Compressed Folder Tools**, click the **Extract tab**, and then at the right end of the ribbon, click **Extract all**.
- In the displayed **Extract Compressed (Zipped) Folders** dialog box, click **Browse**. In the **Select a destination** dialog box, use the navigation pane on the left to navigate to your **Windows 10 Chapter 1 folder**, and double-click its name to open the folder and display its name in the **Address bar**.
- In the lower right, click **Select Folder**, and then in the lower right, click **Extract**; when complete, a new File Explorer window displays showing the extracted files in your chapter folder. For this Project, you will see a PowerPoint file with your name and another zipped folder named **win01_1B_Bell_Orchid**, which you will extract later, a result file to check against, and an Instruction file. Take a moment to open **Windows_10_1B_Hotel_Files_Instructions**; note any recent updates to the book.
- **Close** ☒ both File Explorer windows, close the Grader download screens, and close any open documents For this Project, you should close MyLab and any other open windows in your browser.

3 ▶ From the taskbar, click **File Explorer**, navigate to and reopen your **Windows 10 Chapter 1 folder**, and then double-click the PowerPoint file you downloaded from **MyLab IT** that displays your name—**Student_Windows_10_1B_Hotel_Files**. In your blank PowerPoint presentation, if necessary, at the top click **Enable Editing**.

Activity 1.26 | Locating and Inserting a Saved File Into a PowerPoint Presentation

1 ▶ Be sure your PowerPoint presentation with your name is displayed. Then, on the **Home tab**, in the **Slides group,** click **Layout**. In the displayed gallery, click **Title Only**. If necessary, on the right, close the Design Ideas pane. Click anywhere in the text *Click to add title*, and then type **Tip Snip**

2 ▶ Click anywhere in the empty space below the title you just typed. Click the **Insert tab**, and then in the **Images group**, click **Pictures**. In the **navigation pane**, click the location of your **Windows 10 Chapter 1** folder, open the folder, and then in the **Insert Picture** dialog box, click one time to select your **Lastname_Firstname_1B_Tip_Snip** file. In the lower right corner of the dialog box, click **Insert**. If necessary, close the Design Ideas pane on the right. If necessary, drag the image to the right so that your slide title *Tip Snip* displays.

3 ▶ On the Quick Access Toolbar, click **Save** 🖫, and then in the upper right corner of the PowerPoint window, click **Minimize** ⎯ so that PowerPoint remains open but not displayed on your screen; you will need your PowerPoint presentation as you progress through this project.

4 ▶ **Close** ⊠ the File Explorer window and close any other open windows.

Activity 1.27 | Using Snap and Task View

Use *Snap* to arrange two or more open windows on your screen so that you can work with multiple screens at the same time.

Snap with the mouse by dragging the *title bar*—the bar across the top of the window that displays the program, file, or app name—of one app to the left until it snaps into place, and then dragging the title bar of another app to the right until it snaps into place.

Snap with the keyboard by selecting the window you want to snap, and then pressing ⊞ + ⬅. Then select another window and press ⊞ + ➡. This is an example of a *keyboard shortcut*—a combination of two or more keyboard keys used to perform a task that would otherwise require a mouse.

1 From your desktop, click **Start** ▦. In the list of apps, click the letter **A** to display the alphabet, and then click **W**. Under **W**, click **Weather**. If necessary, personalize your weather content by typing your zip code into the Search box, selecting your location, and clicking Start.

2 By using the same technique to display the alphabet, click **C**, and then click **Calculator**. On the taskbar, notice that icons display to show that the Weather app and the Calculator app are open. Notice also that on the desktop, the most recently opened app displays on top and is also framed on the taskbar. Compare your screen with Figure 1.64.

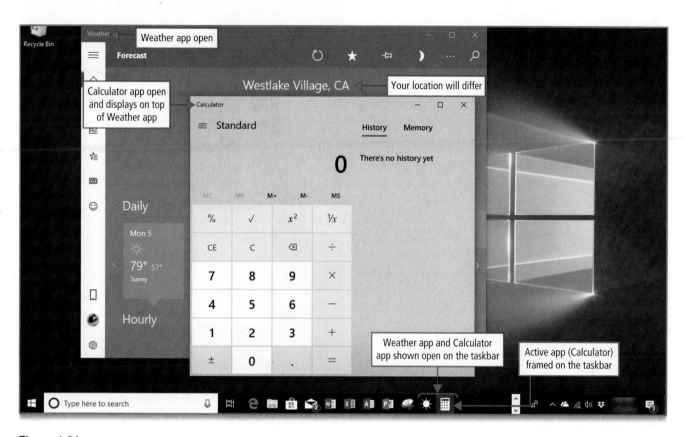

Figure 1.64

3 ▶ Point to the word *Calculator* at the top of this open app, hold down your left mouse button, drag your mouse pointer to the left edge of your screen until an outline displays to show where the window will snap, and then release the mouse button. Compare your screen with Figure 1.65.

> On the right, all open windows display—your PowerPoint presentation and the Weather app. This feature is ***Snap Assist***—after you have snapped a window, all other open windows display as ***thumbnails*** in the remaining space. A thumbnail is a reduced image of a graphic.

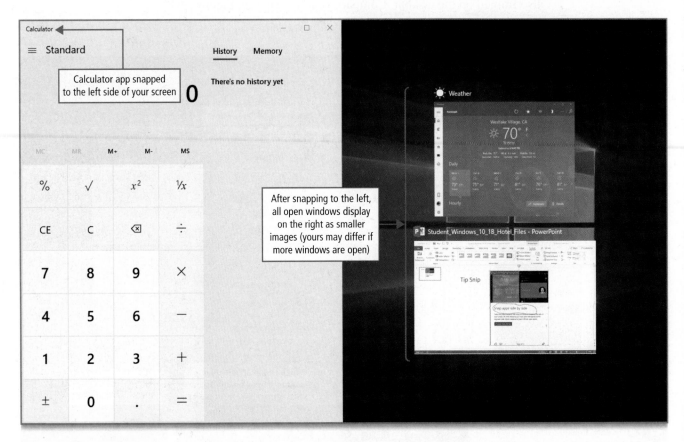

Figure 1.65

4 ▶ Click the **Weather** app to have it fill the right half of your screen.

5 ▶ In the lower left of your keyboard, press and hold down [⊞] and then in upper right of your keyboard, locate and press and release [PrintScrn]. Notice that your screen dims momentarily.

> This is another method to create a screenshot. This screenshot file is automatically stored in the Screenshots folder in the Pictures folder of your hard drive; it is also stored on the Clipboard if you want to copy it immediately.

> A screenshot captured in this manner is saved as a ***.png*** file, which is commonly pronounced PING, and stands for Portable Network Graphic. This is an image file type that can be transferred over the internet.

6 On the taskbar, click **Task View** ▦, point to one of the open apps, and then compare your screen with Figure 1.66.

Use the *Task View* button on the taskbar to see and switch between open apps—including desktop apps. You may see the Windows 10 feature *Timeline*, with which, when you click the Task View button, you can see your activities and files you have recently worked on across your devices. For example, you can find a document, image, or video you worked on yesterday or a week ago.

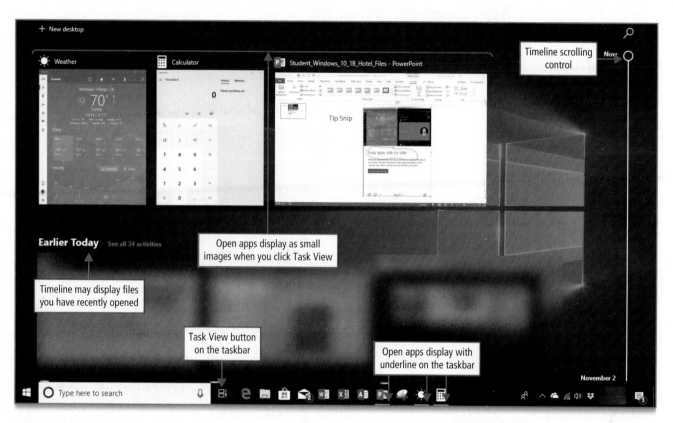

Figure 1.66

7 From **Task View**, click your **PowerPoint** window. On the **Home tab**, in the **Slides group**, click the upper portion of the **New Slide** button to insert a new slide in the same layout as your previous slide.

An arrow attached to a button will display a menu when clicked. Such a button is referred to as a *split button*—clicking the main part of the button performs a command and clicking the arrow opens a menu with choices.

8 As the title type **Side by Side** and then click in the blank space below the title. On the ribbon, on the **Home tab**, in the **Clipboard group**, click the upper portion of the **Paste** button 📋 to paste your screenshot into the slide.

Recall that by creating a screenshot using the ⊞ + PrintScrn command, a copy was placed on the Clipboard. A permanent copy is also stored in the Screenshots folder of your Pictures folder. This is a convenient way to create a quick screenshot.

9 With the image selected, on the ribbon, under **Picture Tools**, click **Format**. In the **Size group**, click in the **Shape Height** box ⬚ 0.05", type 5 and press Enter. Drag the image down and into the center of the space so that your slide title is visible. Compare your screen with Figure 1.67.

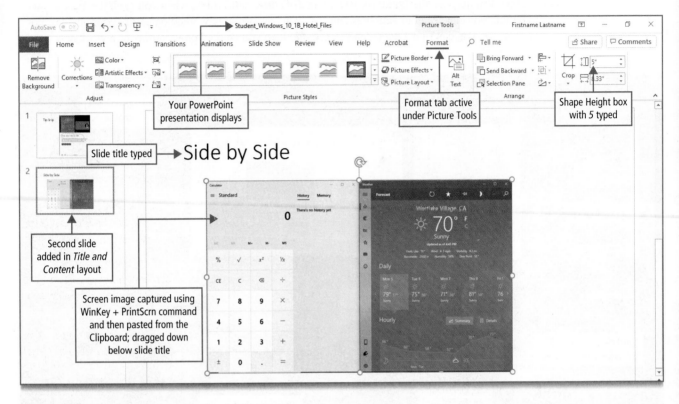

Figure 1.67

10 On the Quick Access Toolbar, click **Save** 🖫, and then in the upper right corner of the PowerPoint window, click **Minimize** ⊟ so that PowerPoint remains open but not displayed on your screen.

11 **Close** ☒ the **Calculator** app and the **Weather** app to display your desktop.

Objective 9	Use File Explorer to Extract Zipped Files and to Display Locations, Folders, and Files

A file is the fundamental unit of storage that enables Windows 10 to distinguish one set of information from another. A folder is the basic organizing tool for files. In a folder, you can store files that are related to one another. You can also place a folder inside of another folder, which is then referred to as a *subfolder*.

Windows 10 arranges folders in a structure that resembles a *hierarchy*—an arrangement where items are ranked and where each level is lower in rank than the item above it. The hierarchy of folders is referred to as the *folder structure*. A sequence of folders in the folder structure that leads to a specific file or folder is a *path*.

Activity 1.28 | Navigating with File Explorer

Recall that File Explorer is the program that displays the contents of locations, folders, and files on your computer and also in your OneDrive and other cloud storage locations. File Explorer also enables you to perform tasks related to your files and folders such as copying, moving, and renaming. When you open a folder or location, a window displays to show its contents. The design of the window helps you navigate—explore within the file structure so you can find your files and folders—and so that you can save and find your files and folders efficiently.

In this Activity, you will open a folder and examine the parts of its window.

1 With your desktop displayed, on the taskbar, *point to* but do not click **File Explorer** , and notice the ScreenTip *File Explorer*.

> A ***ScreenTip*** displays useful information when you perform various mouse actions, such as pointing to screen elements.

2 Click **File Explorer** to display the **File Explorer** window.

> File Explorer is at work anytime you are viewing the contents of a location or the contents of a folder stored in a specific location. By default, the File Explorer button on the taskbar opens with the ***Quick access*** location—a list of files you have been working on and folders you use often—selected in the navigation pane and in the address bar.

> The default list will likely display the Desktop, Downloads, Documents, and Pictures folders, and then folders you worked on recently or work on frequently will be added automatically, although you can change this behavior.

> The benefit of the Quick access list is that you can customize a list of folders that you go to often. To add a folder to the list quickly, you can right-click a folder in the file list and click Pin to Quick Access.

> For example, if you are working on a project, you can pin it—or simply drag it—to the Quick access list. When you are done with the project and not using the folder so often, you can remove it from the list. Removing it from the list does not delete the folder, it simply removes it from the Quick access list.

3 On the left, in the **navigation pane**, scroll down if necessary, and then click **This PC** to display folders, devices, and drives in the **file list** on the right. Compare your screen with Figure 1.68.

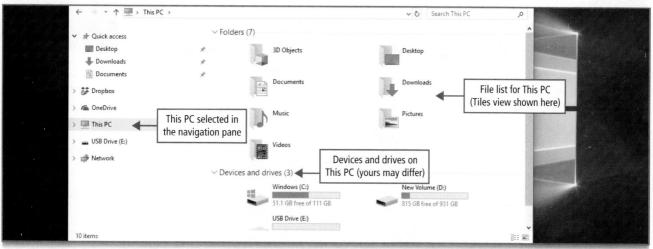

Figure 1.68

4 If necessary, in the upper right corner, click Expand the Ribbon ⌄. In the **file list**, under **Folders**—click **Documents** one time to select it, and then on the ribbon, on the **Computer tab**, in the **Location group**, click **Open**.

5 On the ribbon, click the **View tab**. In the **Show/Hide group**, be sure that **Item check boxes** is selected—select it if necessary, and then in the **Layout group**, if necessary, click **Details**.

The window for the Documents folder displays. You may or may not have files and folders already stored here. Because this window typically displays the file list for a folder, it is also referred to as the *folder window*. Item check boxes make it easier to select items in a file list and also to see which items are selected in a file list.

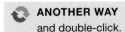 **ANOTHER WAY** Point to Documents, right-click to display a shortcut menu, and then click Open; or, point to Documents and double-click.

6 Compare your screen with Figure 1.69, and then take a moment to study the parts of the window as described in the table in Figure 1.70.

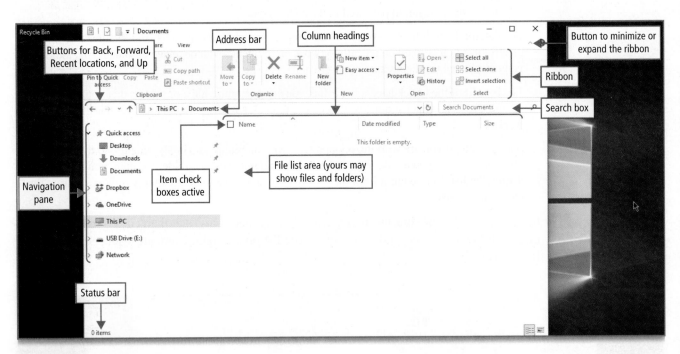

Figure 1.69

Parts of the File Explorer Window	
Window Part	**Function**
Address bar	Displays your current location in the file structure as a series of links separated by arrows. Tap or click a part of the path to go to that level or tap or click at the end to select the path for copying.
Back, Forward, Recent locations, and Up buttons	Enable you to navigate to other folders you have already opened without closing the current window. These buttons work with the address bar; that is, after you use the address bar to change folders, you can use the Back button to return to the previous folder. Use the Up button to open the location where the folder you are viewing is saved—also referred to as the *parent folder*.
Column headings	Identify the columns in Details view. By clicking the column heading name, you can change how the files in the file list are organized; by clicking the arrow on the right, you can select various sort arrangements in the file list. By right-clicking a column heading, you can select other columns to add to the file list.
File list	Displays the contents of the current folder or location. If you type text into the Search box, a search is conducted on the folder or location only, and only the folders and files that match your search will display here—including files in subfolders.
Minimize the Ribbon or Expand the Ribbon button	Changes the display of the ribbon. When minimized, the ribbon shows only the tab names and not the full ribbon.
Navigation pane	Displays locations to which you can navigate; for example, your OneDrive, folders on This PC, devices and drives connected to your PC, folders listed under Quick access, and possibly other PCs on your network. Use Quick access to open your most commonly used folders and searches. If you have a folder that you use frequently, you can drag it to the Quick access area so that it is always available.
Ribbon	Groups common tasks such as copying and moving, creating new folders, emailing and zipping items, and changing views of the items in the file list.
Search box	Enables you to type a word or phrase and then searches for a file or subfolder stored in the current folder that contains matching text. The search begins as soon as you begin typing; for example, if you type G, all the file and folder names that start with the letter G display in the file list.
Status bar	Displays the total number of items in a location, or the number of selected items and their total size.

Figure 1.70

7 Move your pointer anywhere into the **navigation pane**, and notice that a downward pointing arrow ˅ displays to the left of *Quick access* to indicate that this item is expanded, and a right-pointing arrow > displays to the left of items that are collapsed.

You can click these arrows to collapse and expand areas in the navigation pane.

Activity 1.29 | Using File Explorer to Extract Zipped Files

For Non-MyLab Users

From your instructor or from www.pearsonhighered.com/go download the zipped folder **win01_1B_Bell_Orchid** to your **Windows 10 Chapter 1** folder.

1 In the **navigation pane**, if necessary expand **This PC**, scroll down if necessary, and then click your **USB flash drive** (or the location where you have stored your chapter folder) one time to display its contents in the **file list**. Double-click to open your **Windows 10 Chapter 1 folder** and locate the zipped folder **win01_1B_Bell_Orchid**.

2 Use the steps below to extract this zipped folder to your **Windows 10 Chapter 1 folder** as follows (or use your favorite method to unzip):

- On the **Home tab**, click **New folder**, and then name the folder **win01_1B_Bell_Orchid**
- Click the zipped folder **win01_1B_Bell_Orchid** one time to select it.

- With the zipped folder selected, on the ribbon, under **Compressed Folder Tools**, click the **Extract tab**, and then at the right end of the ribbon, click **Extract all**.
- In the displayed **Extract Compressed (Zipped) Folders** dialog box, click **Browse**. In the **Select a destination** dialog box, use the navigation pane on the left to navigate to your **Windows 10 Chapter 1 folder**, and then double-click the name of the new folder you just created to open the folder and display its name in the **Address bar**.
- In the lower right, click **Select Folder**, and then in the lower right, click **Extract**. When complete, click the Up button ⬆ one time. You will see the extracted folder and the zipped folder.
- To delete the unneeded zipped version, click it one time to select it, and then on the **Home tab**, in the **Organize group**, click **Delete**. If necessary, click Yes. Now that the files are extracted, you do not need the zipped copy.

3 ▶ **Close** ☒ all File Explorer windows to display your desktop.

Activity 1.30 | Using File Explorer to Display Locations, Folders, and Files

1 ▶ From the taskbar, open **File Explorer** 📁. In the **navigation pane**, if necessary expand **This PC**, scroll down if necessary, and then click your **USB flash drive** (or the location where you have stored your chapter folder) one time to display its contents in the **file list**. In the **file list**, double-click your **Windows 10 Chapter 1 folder** to display its contents. Compare your screen with Figure 1.71.

In the navigation pane, *This PC* displays all of the drive letter locations attached to your computer, including the internal hard drives, CD or DVD drives, and any connected devices such as a USB flash drive.

Your PowerPoint file, your *Tip_Snip* file, and your extracted folder *win01_1B_Bell_Orchid* folder display if this is your storage location.

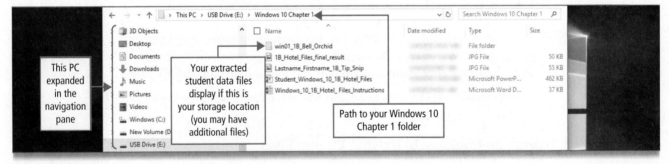

Figure 1.71

> **2** In the **file list**, double-click the **win01_1B_Bell_Orchid** folder to display the subfolders and files.

> Recall that the corporate office of the Bell Orchid Hotels is in Boston. The corporate office maintains subfolders labeled for each of its large hotels in Honolulu, Orlando, San Diego, and Santa Barbara.

ANOTHER WAY   Right-click the folder, and then click Open; or, select the folder and then on the ribbon, on the Home tab, in the Open group, click Open.

> **3** In the **file list**, double-click **Orlando** to display the subfolders, and then look at the **address bar** to view the path. Compare your screen with Figure 1.72.

> Within each city's subfolder, there is a structure of subfolders for the Accounting, Engineering, Food and Beverage, Human Resources, Operations, and Sales and Marketing departments.

> Because folders can be placed inside of other folders, such an arrangement is common when organizing files on a computer.

> In the address bar, the path from the flash drive to the win01_1B_Bell_Orchid folder to the Orlando folder displays as a series of links.

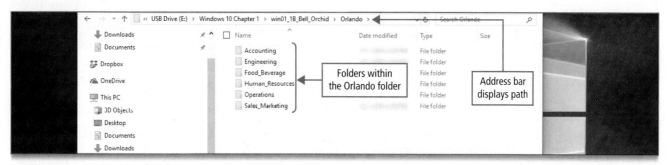

Figure 1.72

> **4** In the **address bar**, to the right of **win01_1B_Bell_Orchid**, click the ⟩ arrow to display a list of the subfolders in the **win01_1B_Bell_Orchid** folder. On the list that displays, notice that **Orlando** displays in bold, indicating it is open in the file list. Then, on the list, click **Honolulu**.

> The subfolders within the Honolulu folder display.

> **5** In the **address bar**, to the right of **win01_1B_Bell_Orchid**, click the ⟩ arrow again to display the subfolders in that folder. Then, on the **address bar**—not on the list—point to **Honolulu** and notice that the list of subfolders in the **Honolulu** folder displays.

> After you display one set of subfolders in the address bar, all of the links are active and you need only point to them to display the list of subfolders.

> Clicking an arrow to the right of a folder name in the address bar displays a list of the subfolders in that folder. You can click a subfolder name to display its contents. In this manner, the address bar is not only a path, but it is also an active control with which you can step from the current folder directly to any other folder above it in the folder structure just by clicking a folder name.

6 On the list of subfolders for **Honolulu**, click **Sales_Marketing** to display its contents in the **file list**. On the **View tab**, in the **Layout group**, if necessary, click **Details**. Compare your screen with Figure 1.73.

ANOTHER WAY   In the file list, double-click the Sales_Marketing folder.

The files in the Sales_Marketing folder for Honolulu display in the Details layout. To the left of each file name, an icon indicates the program that created each file. Here, there is one PowerPoint file, one Excel file, one Word file, and four JPEG images.

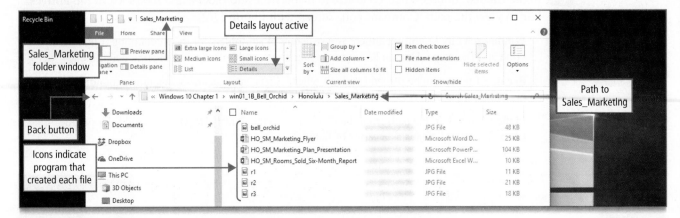

Figure 1.73

7 In the upper left portion of the window, click **Back** ⬅ one time.

The Back button retraces each of your clicks in the same manner as clicking the Back button when you are browsing the internet.

8 In the **file list**, point to the **Human_Resources** folder, and then double-click to open the folder.

9 In the **file list**, click one time to select the PowerPoint file **HO_HR_New_Employee_ Presentation**, and then on the ribbon, click the **View tab**. In the **Panes group**, click **Details pane**, and then compare your screen with Figure 1.74.

The **Details pane** displays the most common **file properties** associated with the selected file. File properties refer to information about a file, such as the author, the date the file was last changed, and any descriptive **tags**—properties that you create to help you find and organize your files.

Additionally, a thumbnail image of the first slide in the presentation displays, and the status bar displays the number of items in the folder.

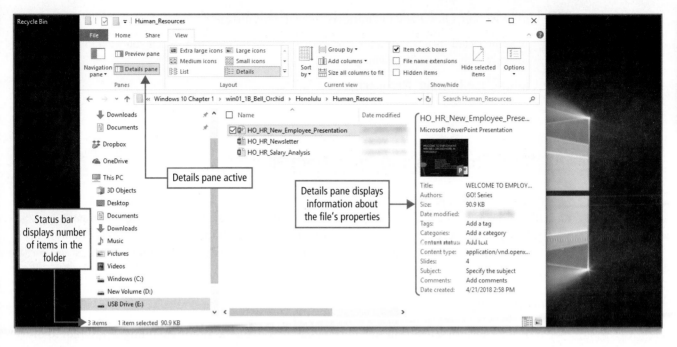

Figure 1.74

> **10** On the right, in the **Details pane**, click **Add a tag**, type **New Employee meeting** and then at the bottom of the pane click **Save**.

> Because you can search for tags, adding tags to files makes them easier to find.

ANOTHER WAY With the file selected, on the Home tab, in the Open group, click Properties to display the Properties dialog box for the file, and then click the Details tab.

> **11** On the ribbon, on the **View tab**, in the **Panes group**, click **Preview pane** to replace the **Details pane** with the **Preview pane**. Compare your screen with Figure 1.75.

> In the Preview pane that displays on the right, you can use the scroll bar to scroll through the slides in the presentation; or, you can click the up or down scroll arrow to view the slides as a miniature presentation.

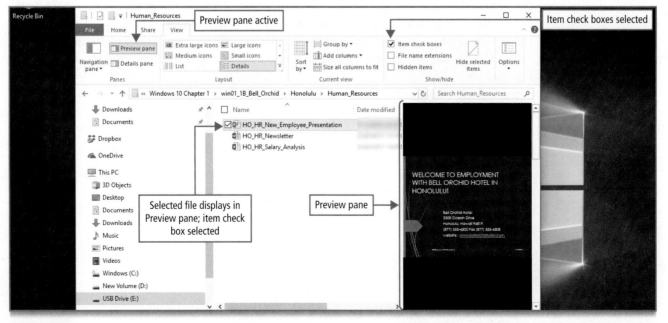

Figure 1.75

12 On the ribbon, click **Preview pane** to close the right pane.

Use the Details pane to see a file's properties and the Preview pane when you want to look at a file quickly without actually opening it.

13 **Close** ☒ the **Human_Resources** window.

Objective 10 **Start Programs and Open Data Files**

When you are using the software programs installed on your computer, you create and save data files—the documents, workbooks, databases, songs, pictures, and so on that you need for your job or personal use. Therefore, most of your work with Windows 10 desktop applications is concerned with locating and starting your programs and locating and opening your files.

Activity 1.31 | Starting Programs

You can start programs from the Start menu or from the taskbar by pinning a program to the taskbar. You can open your data files from within the program in which they were created, or you can open a data file from a window in File Explorer, which will simultaneously start the program and open your file.

1 Be sure your desktop displays and that your PowerPoint presentation is still open but minimized on the taskbar. You can point to the PowerPoint icon to have a small image of the active slide display. Click **Start** ⊞ to place the insertion point in the search box, type **wordpad** and then click the **WordPad Desktop app**.

2 With the insertion point blinking in the document window, type your first and last name.

3 From the taskbar, open your PowerPoint presentation. On the **Home tab**, click the upper portion of the **New Slide** button to insert a blank slide in the Title Only layout. Click anywhere in the text *Click to add title*, and then type **Wordpad**

4 Click anywhere in the lower portion of the slide. On the **Insert tab**, in the **Images group**, click **Screenshot**, and then under **Available Windows**, click the image of the WordPad program with your name typed to insert the image in the PowerPoint slide. Click in a blank area of the slide to deselect the image; if necessary, close the Design Ideas pane on the right. As necessary, drag the image down so that the title displays, and if necessary, use the Shape Height box to decrease the size of the screenshot slightly. Compare your screen with Figure 1.76.

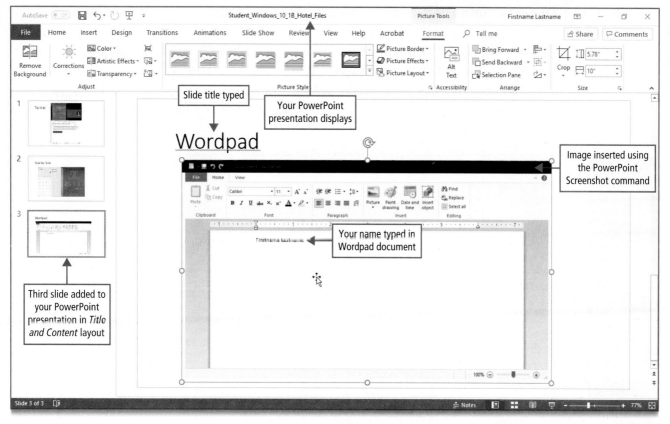

Figure 1.76

> **5** On the Quick Access toolbar, click **Save** 🖫 and then in the upper right corner of the PowerPoint window, click **Minimize** ⎯ so that PowerPoint remains open but not displayed on your screen.

> **6** Close ✕ **WordPad**, and then click **Don't Save**.

Activity 1.32 | Opening Data Files

1 Open **Microsoft Word** from your taskbar, or click **Start** ▦, type **Microsoft word** and then open the **Word** desktop app. Compare your screen with Figure 1.77.

The Word program window has features that are common to other programs you have opened; for example, commands are arranged on tabs. When you create and save data in Word, you create a Word document file.

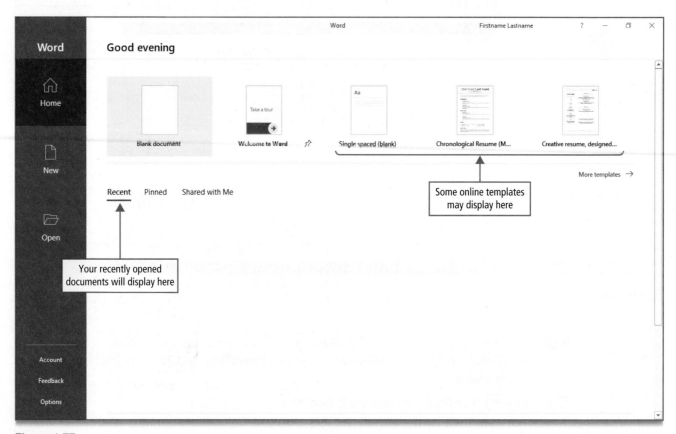

Figure 1.77

2 On the left, click **Open**. Notice the list of places from which you can open a document, including your OneDrive if you are logged in. Click **Browse** to display the **Open** dialog box. Compare your screen with Figure 1.78, and then take a moment to study the table in Figure 1.79.

Recall that a dialog box is a window containing options for completing a task; the layout of the Open dialog box is similar to that of a File Explorer window. When you are working in a desktop application, use the Open dialog box to locate and open existing files that were created in the desktop application.

When you click Browse, typically the Documents folder on This PC displays. You can use the skills you have practiced to navigate to other locations on your computer, such as your removable USB flash drive.

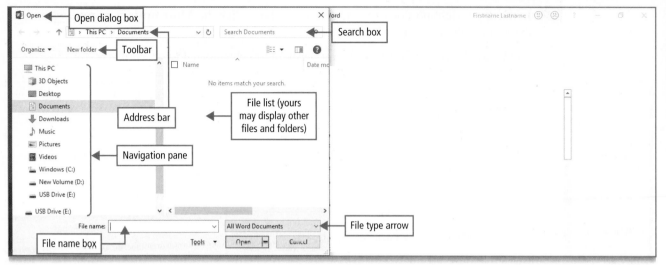

Figure 1.78

Dialog Box Element	Function
Address bar	Displays the path in the folder structure.
File list	Displays the list of files and folders that are available in the folder indicated in the address bar.
File name box	Enables you to type the name of a specific file to locate it—if you know it.
File type arrow	Enables you to restrict the type of files displayed in the file list; for example, the default *All Word Documents* restricts (filters) the type of files displayed to only Word documents. You can click the arrow and adjust the restrictions (filters) to a narrower or wider group of files.
Navigation pane	Navigate to files and folders and get access to Quick access, OneDrive, and This PC.
Search box	Search for files in the current folder. Filters the file list based on text that you type; the search is based on text in the file name (and for files on the hard drive or OneDrive, in the file itself), and on other properties that you can specify. The search takes place in the current folder, as displayed in the address bar, and in any subfolders within that folder.
Toolbar	Displays relevant tasks; for example, creating a new folder.

Figure 1.79

3 In the **navigation pane**, scroll down as necessary, and then under **This PC**, click your **USB flash drive** or whatever location where you have stored your files for this project. In the **file list**, double-click your **win01_1B_Bell_Orchid** folder to open it and display its contents.

4 In the upper right portion of the **Open** dialog box, click the **More options arrow** ▾, and then set the view to **Large icons**. Compare your screen with Figure 1.80.

The Live Preview feature indicates that each folder contains additional subfolders.

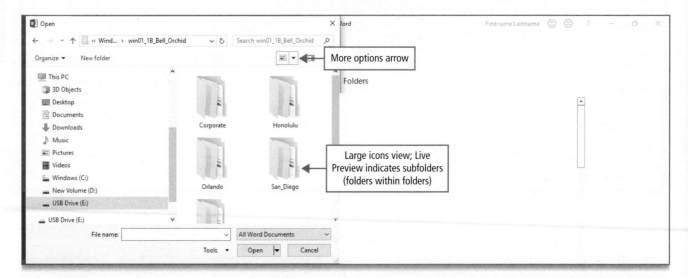

Figure 1.80

5 In the **file list**, double-click the **Corporate** folder, and then double-click the **Accounting** folder.

The view returns to the Details view.

6 In the **file list**, notice that only one document—a Word document—displays. In the lower right corner, locate the **File type** button, and notice that *All Word Documents* displays as the file type. Click the **File type arrow**, and then on the displayed list, click **All Files**. Compare your screen with Figure 1.81.

When you change the file type to *All Files*, you can see that the Word file is not the only file in this folder. By default, the Open dialog box displays only the files created in the active program; however, you can display variations of file types in this manner.

Microsoft Office file types are identified by small icons, which is a convenient way to differentiate one type of file from another. Although you can view all the files in the folder, you can open only the files that were created in the active program, which in this instance is Microsoft Word.

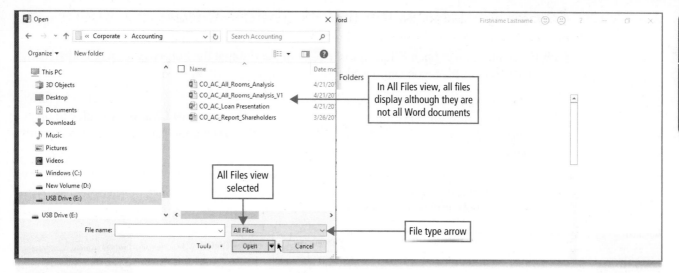

Figure 1.81

7 Change the file type back to **All Word Documents**. Then, in the **file list**, double-click the **CO_AC_Report_Shareholders** Word file to open the document. Take a moment to scroll through the document. If necessary, Maximize ⬜ the window.

8 **Close** ☒ the Word window.

9 Click **Start** ⊞, and then search for **.txt** At the top, click **Filters**, click **Documents**, and then on the list, click **Structure.txt in Future_Hotels**.

The file opens using the Windows 10 *Notepad* desktop app—a basic text-editing program included with Windows 10 that you can use to create simple documents.

In the search box, you can search for files on your computer, and you can search for a file by its *file name extension*—a set of characters at the end of a file name that helps Windows understand what kind of information is in a file and what program should open it. A *.txt file* is a simple file consisting of lines of text with no formatting that almost any computer can open and display.

10 **Close** ☒ the Notepad program.

MORE KNOWLEDGE | **Do Not Clutter Your Desktop by Creating Desktop Shortcuts or Storing Files**

On your desktop, you can add or remove *desktop shortcuts*, which are desktop icons that can link to items accessible on your computer such as a program, file, folder, disk drive, printer, or another computer. In previous versions of Windows, many computer users commonly did this.

Now the Start menu is your personal dashboard for all your programs and online activities, and increasingly you will access programs and your own files in the cloud. So do not clutter your desktop with shortcuts—doing so is more confusing than useful. Placing desktop shortcuts for frequently used programs or folders directly on your desktop may seem convenient, but as you add more icons, your desktop becomes cluttered and the shortcuts are not easy to find. A better organizing method is to use the taskbar for shortcuts to programs. For folders and files, the best organizing structure is to create a logical structure of folders within your Documents folder or your cloud-based OneDrive.

You can also drag frequently-used folders to the Quick access area in the navigation pane so that they are available any time you open File Explorer. As you progress in your use of Windows 10, you will discover techniques for using the taskbar and the Quick access area of the navigation pane to streamline your work instead of cluttering your desktop.

Activity 1.33 | Searching, Pinning, Sorting, and Filtering in File Explorer

1 From the taskbar, open **File Explorer** . On the right, at the bottom, you may notice that under **Recent files**, you can see files that you have recently opened.

2 In the **navigation pane**, click your **USB flash drive**—or click the location where you have stored your files for this project. Double-click your **Windows 10 Chapter 1 folder** to open it. In the upper right, click in the **Search** box, and then type **pool** Compare your screen with Figure 1.82.

> Files that contain the word *pool* in the title display. If you are searching a folder on your hard drive or OneDrive, files that contain the word *pool* within the document will also display. Additionally, Search Tools display on the ribbon.

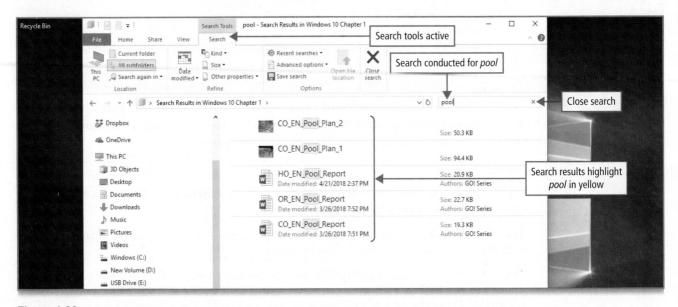

Figure 1.82

3 In the search box, clear the search by clicking ⊠, and then in the search box type **Paris.jpg** Notice that you can also search by using a file extension as part of the search term.

4 **Clear** ⊠ the search. Double-click your **win01_1B_Bell_Orchid** folder to open it.

5 On the **Home tab**, in the **Clipboard group**, click **Pin to Quick access**. If necessary, scroll up in the navigation pane. Compare your screen with Figure 1.83.

> You can pin frequently used folders to the Quick access area, and then unpin them when you no longer need frequent access. Folders that you access frequently will also display in the Quick access area without the pin image. Delete them by right-clicking the name and clicking Unpin from Quick access.

Figure 1.83

> ⟳ **ANOTHER WAY** In the file list, right-click a folder name, and then click Pin to Quick access; or, drag the folder to the Quick access area in the navigation pain and release the mouse button when the ScreenTip displays Pin to Quick access.

6 In the **file list**—double-click the **Corporate** folder and then double-click the **Engineering** folder.

7 On the **View tab**, in the **Current view group**, click **Sort by**, and then click **Type**. Compare your screen with Figure 1.84.

Use this technique to sort files in the file list by type. Here, the JPG files display first, and then the Microsoft Excel files, and so on—in alphabetic order by file type.

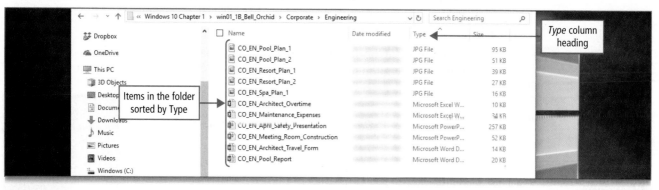

Figure 1.84

8 Point to the column heading **Type**, and then click ^.

9 Point to the column heading **Type** again, and on the right, click ☑. On the displayed list, click **Microsoft PowerPoint Presentation**, and notice that the file list is filtered to show only PowerPoint files.

A *filtered list* is a display of files that is limited based on specified criteria.

10 To the right of the **Type** column heading, click the check mark and then click **Microsoft PowerPoint Presentation** again to clear the Microsoft PowerPoint filter and redisplay all of the files.

11 **Close** ☒ the File Explorer window.

ALERT   **Allow Time to Complete the Remainder of This Project in One Session**

If you are working on a computer that is not your own, for example in a college lab, plan your time to complete the remainder of this project in one working session. Allow 45 to 60 minutes.

Because you will need to store and then delete files on the hard disk drive of the computer at which you are working, it is recommended that you complete this project in one working session—*unless you are working on your own computer or you know that the files will be retained*. In your college lab, files you store on the computer's hard drive will not be retained after you sign off.

Objective 11   Create, Rename, and Copy Files and Folders

File management includes organizing, copying, renaming, moving, and deleting the files and folders you have stored in various locations—both locally and in the cloud.

Activity 1.34 | **Copying Files from a Removable Storage Device to the Documents Folder on the Hard Disk Drive**

Barbara and Steven have the assignment to transfer and then organize some of the corporation's files to a computer that will be connected to the corporate network. Data on such a computer can be accessed by employees at any of the hotel locations through the use of sharing technologies. For example, *SharePoint* is a Microsoft technology that enables employees in an organization to access information across organizational and geographic boundaries.

1 Close any open windows, but leave your open PowerPoint presentation minimized on the taskbar.

2 From the taskbar, open **File Explorer** . In the **navigation pane**, if necessary expand **This PC**, and then click your USB flash drive or the location where you have stored your chapter folder to display its contents in the file list.

> Recall that in the navigation pane, under This PC, you have access to all the storage areas inside your computer, such as your hard disk drives, and to any devices with removable storage, such as CDs, DVDs, or USB flash drives.

3 Open your **Windows 10 Chapter 1** folder, and then in the **file list**, click **win01_1B_Bell_Orchid** one time to select the folder. Compare your screen with Figure 1.85.

Figure 1.85

4 With the **win01_1B_Bell_Orchid** folder selected, on the ribbon, on the **Home tab**, in the **Clipboard group**, click **Copy**.

> The Copy command places a copy of your selected file or folder on the *Clipboard* where it will be stored until you use the Paste command to place the copy somewhere else. The Clipboard is a temporary storage area for information that you have copied or moved from one place and plan to use somewhere else.

> In Windows 10, the Clipboard can hold only one piece of information at a time. Whenever something is copied to the Clipboard, it replaces whatever was there before. In Windows 10, you cannot view the contents of the Clipboard nor place multiple items there in the manner that you can in Microsoft Word.

ANOTHER WAY   With the item selected in the file list, press Ctrl + C to copy the item to the clipboard.

5 To the left of the address bar, click **Up** ⬆ two times. In the **file list**, double-click your **Documents** folder to open it, and then on the **Home tab**, in the **Clipboard group**, click **Paste**.

> A *progress bar* displays in a dialog box and also displays on the taskbar button with green shading. A progress bar indicates visually the progress of a task such as a copy process, a download, or a file transfer.

> The Documents folder is one of several folders within your *personal folder* stored on the hard disk drive. For each user account—even if there is only one user on the computer—Windows 10 creates a personal folder labeled with the account holder's name.

ANOTHER WAY   With the destination location selected, press Ctrl + V to paste the item from the clipboard to the selected location. Or, on the Home tab, in the Organize group, click Copy to, find and then click the location to which you want to copy. If the desired location is not on the list, use the Choose location command at the bottom.

6 Close ✕ the **Documents** window.

Activity 1.35 | Creating Folders, Renaming Folders, and Renaming Files

Barbara and Steven can see that various managers have been placing files related to new European hotels in the *Future_Hotels* folder. They can also see that the files have not been organized into a logical structure. For example, files that are related to each other are not in separate folders; instead they are mixed in with other files that are not related to the topic.

In this Activity, you will create, name, and rename folders to begin a logical structure of folders in which to organize the files related to the European hotels project.

1 From the taskbar, open **File Explorer** ▣, and then use any of the techniques you have practiced to display the contents of the **Documents** folder in the **file list**.

NOTE   Using the Documents Folder and OneDrive Instead of Your USB Drive

In this modern computing era, you should limit your use of USB drives to those times when you want to quickly take some files to another computer without going online. Instead of using a USB drive, use your computer's hard drive, or better yet, your free OneDrive cloud storage that comes with your Microsoft account.

There are two good reasons to stop using USB flash drives. First, searching is limited on a USB drive—search does not look at the content inside a file. When you search files on your hard drive or OneDrive, the search extends to words and phrases actually *inside* the files. Second, if you delete a file or folder from a USB drive, it is gone and cannot be retrieved. Files you delete from your hard drive or OneDrive go to the Recycle Bin where you can retrieve them later.

---

2 In the **file list**, double-click the **win01_1B_Bell_Orchid** folder, double-click the **Corporate** folder, double-click the **Information_Technology** folder, and then double-click the **Future_Hotels** folder to display its contents in the file list; sometimes this navigation is written as *Documents > win01_1B_Bell_Orchid > Corporate > Information_Technology > Future_Hotels*.

Some computer users prefer to navigate a folder structure by double-clicking in this manner. Others prefer using the address bar as described in the following Another Way box. Use whatever method you prefer—double-clicking in the file list, clicking in the address bar, or expanding files in the Navigation pane.

↻ **ANOTHER WAY**   In the navigation pane, click Documents, and expand each folder in the navigation pane. Or, In the address bar, to the right of Documents, click >, and then on the list, click win01_1B_Bell_Orchid. To the right of win01_1B_Bell_Orchid, click the > and then click Corporate. To the right of Corporate, click > and then click Information_ Technology. To the right of Information_Technology, click >, and then click Future_Hotels.

---

3 In the **file list**, be sure the items are in alphabetical order by **Name**. If the items are not in alphabetical order, recall that by clicking the small arrow in the column heading name, you can change how the files in the file list are ordered.

4 On the ribbon, click the **View tab**, and then in the **Layout group**, be sure **Details** is selected.

The *Details view* displays a list of files or folders and their most common properties.

↻ **ANOTHER WAY**   Right-click in a blank area of the file list, point to View, and then click Details.

---

5 On the ribbon, click the **Home tab**, and then in the **New group**, click **New folder**. With the text *New folder* selected, type **Paris** and press ⏎. Click **New folder** again, type **Venice** and then press ⏎. Create a third **New folder** named **London**

In a Windows 10 file list, folders are listed first, in alphabetic order, followed by individual files in alphabetic order.

6 Click the **Venice** folder one time to select it, and then on the ribbon, on the **Home tab**, in the **Organize group**, click **Rename**. Notice that the text *Venice* is selected. Type **Rome** and press ⏎.

ANOTHER WAY Point to a folder or file name, right-click, and then on the shortcut menu, click Rename.

7 In the **file list**, click one time to select the Word file **Architects**. With the file name selected, click the file name again to select all the text. Click the file name again to place the insertion point within the file name, edit the file name to **Architects_Local** and press ⏎. Compare your screen with Figure 1.86.

You can use any of the techniques you just practiced to change the name of a file or folder.

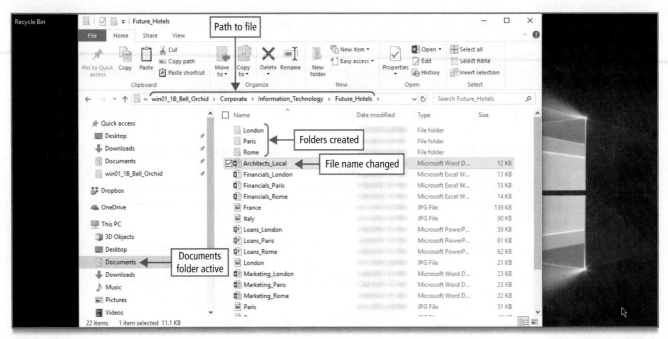

Figure 1.86

8 On the taskbar, click the **PowerPoint** icon to redisplay your **Windows_10_1B_Hotel_Files** presentation, and then on the **Home tab**, click the upper portion of the **New Slide** button to insert a new slide with the Title Only layout.

9 Click anywhere in the text *Click to add title*, type **Europe Folders** and then click anywhere in the empty space below the title.

10 On the **Insert tab**, in the **Images group**, click **Screenshot**, and then under **Available Windows**, click the image of your file list. On the **Picture Tools Format tab**, in the **Size group**, click in the **Shape Height** box, ▯0.05" ▯ type **5** and then press ⏎. As necessary, drag the image down so that the title you typed is visible; your presentation contains four slides.

11 Above the **File tab**, on the Quick Access toolbar, click **Save** ▯, and then in the upper right corner, click **Minimize** ▯ so that PowerPoint remains open but not displayed on your screen.

12 **Close** ☒ the **Future_Hotels** window.

Activity 1.36 | Copying Files

Copying, moving, renaming, and deleting files and folders comprise the most heavily used features within File Explorer. Probably half or more of the steps you complete in File Explorer relate to these tasks, so mastering these techniques will increase your efficiency.

When you *copy* a file or a folder, you make a duplicate of the original item and then store the duplicate in another location. In this Activity, you will assist Barbara and Steven in making copies of the Staffing_Plan file, and then placing the copies in each of the three folders you created—London, Paris, and Rome.

1 From the taskbar, open **File Explorer** 📁, and then by double-clicking in the file list or following the links in the address bar, navigate to **This PC > Documents > win01_1B_Bell_Orchid > Corporate > Information_Technology > Future_Hotels**.

2 In the upper right corner, **Maximize** ⬜ the window. On the **View tab**, if necessary set the **Layout** to **Details**, and then in the **Current view group**, click **Size all columns to fit** 🔲.

3 In the **file list**, click the file **Staffing_Plan** one time to select it, and then on the **Home tab**, in the **Clipboard group**, click **Copy**.

4 At the top of the **file list**, double-click the **London folder** to open it, and then in the **Clipboard group**, click **Paste**. Notice that the copy of the **Staffing_Plan** file displays. Compare your screen with Figure 1.87.

Figure 1.87

> 🔄 **ANOTHER WAY** Right-click the file you want to copy, and on the menu click Copy. Then right-click the folder into which you want to place the copy, and on the menu click Paste. Or, select the file you want to copy, press Ctrl + C to activate the Copy command, open the folder into which you want to paste the file, and then press Ctrl + V to activate the Paste command.

5 With the **London** window open, by using any of the techniques you have practiced, rename this copy of the **Staffing_Plan** file to **London_Staffing_Plan**

6 To the left of the **address bar**, click **Up** ⬆ to move up one level in the folder structure and to redisplay the **file list** for the **Future_Hotels** folder.

> 🔄 **ANOTHER WAY** In the address bar, click Future_Hotels to redisplay this window and move up one level in the folder structure.

7 ▶ Click the **Staffing_Plan** file one time to select it, hold down Ctrl, and then drag the file upward over the **Paris** folder until the ScreenTip + *Copy to Paris* displays, and then release the mouse button and release Ctrl.

> When dragging a file into a folder, holding down Ctrl engages the Copy command and places a *copy* of the file at the location where you release the mouse button. This is another way to copy a file or copy a folder.

8 ▶ Open the **Paris** folder, and then rename the **Staffing_Plan** file **Paris_Staffing_Plan** Then, move up one level in the folder structure to redisplay the **Future_Hotels** window.

9 ▶ Double-click the **Rome** folder to open it. With your mouse pointer anywhere in the **file list**, right-click, and then from the shortcut menu click **Paste**.

> A copy of the Staffing_Plan file is copied to the folder. Because a copy of the Staffing_Plan file is still on the Clipboard, you can continue to paste the item until you copy another item on the Clipboard to replace it.

10 ▶ Rename the file **Rome_Staffing_Plan**

11 ▶ On the **address bar**, click **Future_Hotels** to move up one level and open the **Future_Hotels** window—or click Up ↑ to move up one level. Leave this folder open for the next Activity.

Activity 1.37 | Moving Files

When you **move** a file or folder, you remove it from the original location and store it in a new location. In this Activity, you will move items from the Future_Hotels folder into their appropriate folders.

1 ▶ With the **Future_Hotels** folder open, in the **file list**, click the Excel file **Financials_London** one time to select it. On the **Home tab**, in the **Clipboard group**, click **Cut**.

> The file's Excel icon dims. This action places the item on the Clipboard.

ANOTHER WAY   Right-click the file or folder, and then on the shortcut menu, click Cut; or, select the file or folder, and then press Ctrl + X.

---

2 ▶ Double-click the **London** folder to open it, and then on the **Home tab**, in the **Clipboard group**, click **Paste**.

ANOTHER WAY   Right-click the folder, and then on the shortcut menu, click Paste; or, select the folder, and then press Ctrl + V.

---

3 ▶ Click Up ↑ to move up one level and redisplay the **Future_Hotels** folder window. In the **file list**, point to **Financials_Paris**, hold down the left mouse button, and then drag the file upward over the **Paris** folder until the ScreenTip *Move to Paris* displays, and then release the mouse button.

4 ▶ Open the **Paris** folder, and notice that the file was moved to this folder. Click Up ↑—or on the address bar, click Future_Hotels to return to that folder.

5 In the **file list**, click **Loans_London** one time to select it. hold down Ctrl, and then click the photo image **London** and the Word document **Marketing_London** to select the three files. Release the Ctrl key. Compare your screen with Figure 1.88.

Use this technique to select a group of noncontiguous items in a list.

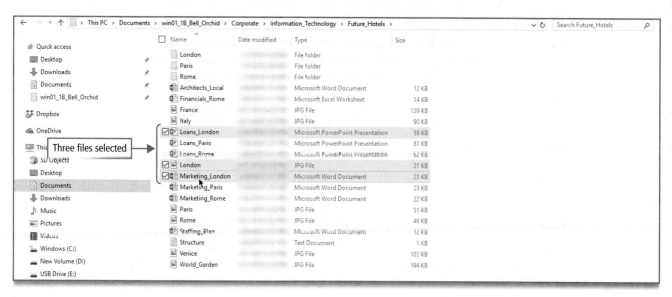

Figure 1.88

6 Point to any of the selected files, hold down the left mouse button, and then drag upward over the **London** folder until the ScreenTip →*Move to London* displays and *3* displays over the files being moved, and then release the mouse button.

You can see that by keeping related files together—for example, all the files that relate to the London hotel—in folders that have an appropriately descriptive name, it will be easier to locate information later.

7 By dragging, move the **Architects_Local** file into the **London** folder.

8 In an empty area of the file list, right-click, and then click **Undo Move**. Leave the **Future_Hotels** window open for the next Activity.

Any action that you make in a file list can be undone in this manner.

ANOTHER WAY   Press Ctrl + Z to undo an action in the file list.

MORE KNOWLEDGE   **Using Shift + Click to Select Files**

If a group of files to be selected are contiguous (next to each other in the file list), click the first file to be selected, hold down Shift and then click the left mouse button on the last file to select all of the files between the top and bottom file selections.

Activity 1.38 | Copying and Moving Files by Snapping Two Windows

Sometimes you will want to open, in a second window, another instance of a program that you are using; that is, two copies of the program will be running simultaneously. This capability is especially useful in the File Explorer program, because you are frequently moving or copying files from one location to another.

In this Activity, you will open two instances of File Explorer, and then use snap, which you have already practiced in this chapter, to display both instances on your screen.

To copy or move files or folders into a different level of a folder structure, or to a different drive location, the most efficient method is to display two windows side by side and then use drag and drop or copy (or cut) and paste commands.

In this Activity, you will assist Barbara and Steven in making copies of the Staffing_Plan files for the corporate office.

1 In the upper right corner, click **Restore Down** ⬀ to restore the **Future_Hotels** window to its previous size and not maximized on the screen.

> Use the *Restore Down* command ⬀ to resize a window to its previous size.

2 Hold down ⊞ and press ← to snap the window so that it occupies the left half of the screen.

3 On the taskbar, *point* to **File Explorer** 🗂 and then right-click. On the jump list, click **File Explorer** to open another instance of the program. With the new window active, hold down ⊞ and press → to snap the window so that it occupies the right half of the screen.

4 In the window on the right, click in a blank area to make the window active. Then navigate to **Documents > win01_1B_Bell_Orchid > Corporate > Human_Resources**. Compare your screen with Figure 1.89.

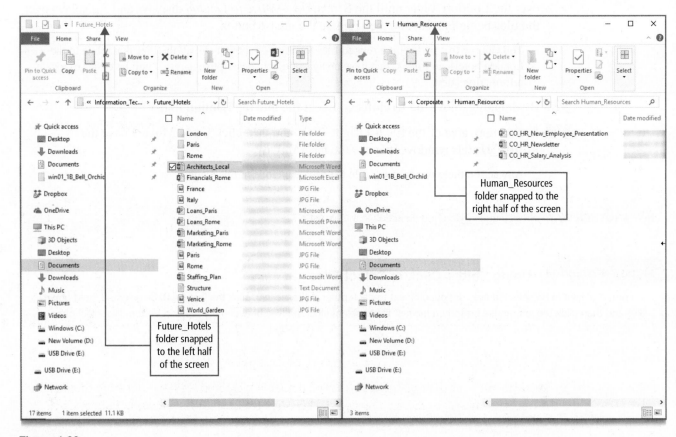

Figure 1.89

5 In the left window, double-click to open the **Rome** folder, and then click one time to select the file **Rome_Staffing_Plan**.

6 Hold down Ctrl, and then drag the file into the right window, into an empty area of the **Human_Resources file list**, until the ScreenTip + *Copy to Human_Resources* displays and then release the mouse button and Ctrl.

7 In the left window, on the **address bar**, click **Future_Hotels** to redisplay that folder. Open the **Paris** folder, point to **Paris_Staffing_Plan** and right-click, and then click **Copy**.

> You can access the Copy command in various ways; for example, from the shortcut menu, on the ribbon, or by using the keyboard shortcut Ctrl + C.

8 In the right window, point anywhere in the **file list**, right-click, and then click **Paste**.

9 On the taskbar, click the PowerPoint icon to redisplay your **Windows_10_1B_Hotel_Files** presentation, and then on the **Home tab**, click the upper portion of the **New Slide** button to insert a new slide with the **Title Only** layout; this will be your fifth slide.

10 Click anywhere in the text *Click to add title*, type **Staffing Plan Files** and then click anywhere in the empty space below the title.

11 On the **Insert tab**, in the **Images group**, click **Screenshot**, and then click **Screen Clipping**. When the dimmed screen displays, move the ⊞ pointer to the upper left corner of the screen, hold down the left mouse button, and drag to the lower right corner but do not include the taskbar. Then release the mouse button.

> Because you have two windows displayed side by side, each window displays under Available Windows. Recall that to capture an entire screen that contains more than one window, use the Screen Clipping tool with which you can capture a snapshot of your screen.

12 If necessary, close the Design Ideas pane on the right. On the **Picture Tools Format tab**, in the **Size group**, click in the **Shape Height** box [↕ 0.05" ↕], type **5** and press Enter. As necessary, drag the image down so that the title you typed is visible.

13 Click outside of the image to deselect it, and then press Ctrl + Home to display the first slide in your presentation; your presentation contains five slides.

14 In the upper right, **Close** ⊠ the **PowerPoint** window, and when prompted, click **Save**.

15 **Close** ⊠ all open windows.

For Non-MyLab Submissions Determine What Your Instructor Requires for Submission
As directed by your instructor, submit your completed PowerPoint file.

---

16 In **MyLab IT**, locate and click the Grader Project **Windows 10 1B Hotel Files**. In **step 3**, under **Upload Completed Assignment**, click **Choose File**. In the **Open** dialog box, navigate to your **Windows 10 Chapter 1 folder**, and then click your **Student_Windows_10_1B_Hotel_Files** file one time to select it. In the lower right corner of the **Open** dialog box, click **Open**.

> The name of your selected file displays above the Upload button.

17 To submit your file to **MyLab IT** for grading, click **Upload**, wait a moment for a green **Success!** message, and then in **step 4**, click the blue **Submit for Grading** button. Click **Close Assignment** to return to your list of **Course Materials**.

| MORE KNOWLEDGE | Deleting Files and Using the Recycle Bin |

It is good practice to delete files and folders that you no longer need from your hard disk drive and removable storage devices. Doing so makes it easier to keep your data organized and also frees up storage space.

When you delete a file or folder from any area of your computer's hard disk drive or from OneDrive, the file or folder is not immediately deleted. Instead, the deleted item is stored in the **Recycle Bin** and remains there until the Recycle Bin is emptied. Thus, you can recover an item deleted from your computer's hard disk drive or OneDrive so long as the Recycle Bin has not been emptied. Items deleted from removable storage devices like a USB flash drive and from some network drives are immediately deleted and cannot be recovered from the Recycle Bin.

To permanently delete a file without first moving it to the Recycle Bin, click the item, hold down [Shift], and then press [Delete]. A message will display indicating *Are you sure you want to permanently delete this file?* Use caution when using [Shift] + [Delete] to permanently delete a file because this action is not reversible.

You can restore items by dragging them from the file list of the Recycle Bin window to the file list of the folder window in which you want to restore. Or, you can restore them to the location they were deleted from by right-clicking the items in the file list of the Recycle Bin window and selecting Restore.

You have completed Project 1B | END

wavebreakmedia/Shutterstock, Monkey Business Images/Fotolia, Ivanko80/Shutterstock, Monkey Business Images/Shutterstock

1 OFFICE AND WINDOWS

Microsoft Office Specialist (MOS) Skills in this Chapter

Project 1A

Microsoft Word

1.1.1 Search for text

1.2.1 Set up document pages

1.2.4 Configure page background elements

1.2.4 Modify basic document properties

1.3.1 Modify basic document properties

1.4.1 Locate and remove hidden properties and personal information

1.4.2 Locate and correct accessibility issues

1.4.3 Locate and correct compatibility issues

2.2.5 Clear formatting

5.2.6 Format 3D models

5.4.3 Add alternative text to objects for accessibility

Microsoft Excel

5.3.3 Add alternative text to charts for accessibility

Build Your E-Portfolio

An E-Portfolio is a collection of evidence, stored electronically, that showcases what you have accomplished while completing your education. Collecting and then sharing your work products with potential employers reflects your academic and career goals. Your completed documents from the following projects are good examples to show what you have learned: 1A and 1B.

GO! for Job Success

Discussion: Managing Your Computer Files

Your instructor may assign this discussion to your class, and then ask you to think about, or discuss with your classmates, these questions:

g-stockstudio/Shutterstock

Why do you think it is important to follow specific guidelines when naming and organizing your files?

Why is it impractical to store files and shortcuts to programs on your desktop?

How are you making the transition from storing all your files on physical media, such as flash drives or the hard drive of your computer, to storing your files in the cloud where you can access them from any computer with an internet connection?

End of Chapter

Summary

Many Office features and commands, such as accessing the Open and Save As dialog boxes, performing commands from the ribbon and from dialog boxes, and using the Clipboard are the same in all Office desktop apps.

A desktop app is installed on your computer and requires a computer operating system such as Microsoft Windows or Apple's macOS to run. The programs in Microsoft Office 365 and Office 2019 are considered to be desktop apps.

The Windows 10 Start menu is your connected dashboard—this is your one-screen view of information that updates continuously with new information and personal communications that are important to you.

File Explorer is at work anytime you are viewing the contents of a location, a folder, or a file. Use File Explorer to navigate your Windows 10 folder structure that stores and organizes the files you create.

GO! Learn It Online

Review the concepts, key terms, and MOS skills in this chapter by completing these online challenges, which you can find at **MyLab IT**.

Chapter Quiz: Answer matching and multiple-choice questions to test what you have learned in this chapter.

Lessons on the GO!: Learn how to use all the new apps and features as they are introduced by Microsoft.

Quiz: Answer questions to review the MOS skills that you practiced in this chapter.

Monkey Business Images/Fotolia

Glossary

Glossary of Chapter Key Terms

.png file An image file type that can be transferred over the internet, an acronym for Portable Network Graphic.

.txt file A simple file consisting of lines of text with no formatting that almost any computer can open and display.

3D models A new kind of shape that you can insert from an online library of ready-to-use three-dimensional graphics.

Address bar In a File Explorer window, the area that displays your current location in the folder structure as a series of links separated by arrows.

Alignment The placement of text or objects relative to the margins.

Alignment guides Green lines that display when you move an object to assist in alignment.

Alt text Text added to a picture or object that helps people using a screen reader understand what the object is; also called *alternative text*.

Alternative text Text added to a picture or object that helps people using a screen reader understand what the object is; also called *alt text*.

Application A computer program that helps you perform a task for a specific purpose.

AutoSave An Office 365 feature that saves your document every few seconds—if saved on OneDrive, OneDrive for Business, or SharePoint Online—and enables you to share the document with others for real-time co-authoring.

Backstage tabs The area along the left side of Backstage view with tabs to display screens with related groups of commands.

Backstage view A centralized space for file management tasks; for example, opening, saving, printing, publishing, or sharing a file.

Bing Microsoft's search engine.

Bookmark A command that marks a word, section, or place in a document so that you can jump to it quickly without scrolling.

Booting the computer The process of turning on the computer.

Center alignment The alignment of text or objects centered horizontally between the left and right margin.

Check Accessibility A command that checks a document for content that people with disabilities might find difficult to read.

Check Compatibility A command that searches your document for features that may not be supported by older versions of Office.

Click The action of pressing the left button of the mouse pointing device.

Clipboard A temporary storage area that holds text or graphics that you select and then cut or copy.

Cloud computing Applications and services that are accessed over the internet.

Cloud storage Online storage of data so that you can access your data from different places and devices.

Commands An instruction to a computer program that causes an action to be carried out.

Compressed Folder Tools A command available in File Explorer with which you can extract compressed files.

Compressed files Files that have been reduced in size, take up less storage space, and can be transferred to other computers faster than uncompressed files.

Content pane In a File Explorer window, another name for the file list.

Context menus Menus that display commands and options relevant to the selected text or object; also called *shortcut menus*.

Context-sensitive commands Commands that display on a shortcut menu that relate to the object or text that is selected.

Contextual tab A tab added to the ribbon automatically when a specific object is selected and that contains commands relevant to the selected object.

Copy A command that duplicates a selection and places it on the Clipboard.

Cortana Microsoft's intelligent personal assistant in Windows 10 and also available on other devices; named for the intelligent female character in the video game Halo.

Cut A command that removes a selection and places it on the Clipboard.

Dashboard The right side of the Start menu that is a one-screen view of links to information and programs that matter to you.

Data The documents, worksheets, pictures, songs, and so on that you create and store during the day-to-day use of your computer.

Data management The process of managing files and folders.

Default The term that refers to the current selection or setting that is automatically used by a computer program unless you specify otherwise.

Deselect The action of canceling the selection of an object or block of text by clicking outside of the selection.

Desktop A simulation of a real desk that represents your work area; here you can arrange icons such as shortcuts to files, folders, and various types of documents in the same manner you would arrange physical objects on top of a desk.

Desktop app A computer program that is installed on your PC and requires a computer operating system such as Microsoft Windows to run; also known as a *desktop application*.

Desktop application A computer program that is installed on your PC and requires a computer operating system such as Microsoft Windows to run; also known as a *desktop app*.

Desktop shortcuts Desktop icons that can link to items accessible on your computer such as a program, file, folder, disk drive, printer, or another computer.

Details pane When activated in a folder window, displays—on the right—the most common file properties associated with the selected file.

Details view A command that displays a list of files or folders and their most common properties.

Dialog box A small window that displays options for completing a task.

Dictate A feature in Word, PowerPoint, Outlook, and OneNote for Windows 10; when you enable Dictate, you start talking and as you talk, text appears in your document or slide.

Dialog Box Launcher A small icon that displays to the right of some group names on the ribbon and that opens a related dialog box or pane providing additional options and commands related to that group.

Document properties Details about a file that describe or identify it, including the title, author name, subject, and keywords that identify the document's topic or contents; also known as *metadata*.

Double-click The action of pressing the left mouse button two times in rapid succession while holding the mouse still.

Glossary

Download The action of transferring or copying a file from another location—such as a cloud storage location, your college's Learning Management System, or from an internet site—to your computer.

Drag The action of holding down the left mouse button while moving your mouse.

Drive An area of storage that is formatted with a file system compatible with your operating system and is identified by a drive letter.

Edit The process of making changes to text or graphics in an Office file.

Editor A digital writing assistant in Word and Outlook that displays misspellings, grammatical mistakes, and writing style issues.

Ellipsis A set of three dots indicating incompleteness; an ellipsis following a command name indicates that a dialog box will display if you click the command.

Enhanced ScreenTip A ScreenTip that displays useful descriptive information about the command.

Extract To decompress, or pull out, files from a compressed form.

File Information stored on a computer under a single name.

File Explorer The Windows program that displays the contents of locations, folders, and files on your computer.

File Explorer window A window that displays the contents of the current location and contains helpful parts so that you can navigate—explore within the file organizing structure of Windows.

File list In a File Explorer window, the area that displays the contents of the current location.

File name extension A set of characters at the end of a file name that helps Windows understand what kind of information is in a file and what program should open it.

File properties Information about a file, such as the author, the date the file was last changed, and any descriptive tags.

Fill The inside color of an object.

Filtered list A display of files that is limited based on specified criteria.

Folder A container in which you can store files.

Folder structure The hierarchy of folders.

Folder window A window that typically displays the File List for a folder.

Font A set of characters with the same design and shape.

Font styles Formatting emphasis such as bold, italic, and underline.

Footer A reserved area for text or graphics that displays at the bottom of each page in a document.

Format Painter The command to copy the formatting of specific text or to copy the formatting of a paragraph and then apply it in other locations in your document; when active, the pointer takes the shape of a paintbrush.

Formatting The process of applying Office commands to make your documents easy to read and to add visual touches and design elements to make your document inviting to the reader; establishes the overall appearance of text, graphics, and pages in an Office file—for example, in a Word document.

Formatting marks Characters that display on the screen, but do not print, indicating where the Enter key, the Spacebar, and the Tab key were pressed; also called *nonprinting characters*.

Free-form snip From the Snipping Tool, a command that draws an irregular line such as a circle around an area of the screen.

Full-screen snip From the Snipping Tool, a command that captures the entire screen.

Gallery An Office feature that displays a list of potential results.

Gradient fill A fill effect in which one color fades into another.

Graphical user interface Graphics such as an image of a file folder or wastebasket that you click to activate the item represented.

Groups On the Office ribbon, the sets of related commands that you might need for a specific type of task.

GUI An abbreviation of the term graphical user interface.

Hamburger Another name for a hamburger menu.

Hamburger menu Another name for a menu icon, deriving from the three lines that bring to mind a hamburger on a bun.

Hard disk drive The primary storage device located inside your computer where some of your files and programs are typically stored, usually designated as drive C.

Hierarchy An arrangement where items are ranked and where each level is lower in rank than the item above it

Icons Small images that represent commands, files, applications, or other windows.

Info tab The tab in Backstage view that displays information about the current file.

Insertion point A blinking vertical line that indicates where text or graphics will be inserted.

Inspect Document A command that searches your document for hidden data of personal information that you might not want to share publicly.

JPEG An acronym that stands for *Joint Photographic Experts Group* and that is a common file type used by digital cameras and computers to store digital pictures.

Jump List A display of destinations and tasks from a program's taskbar icon when you right-click the icon.

Keyboard shortcut A combination of two or more keyboard keys, used to perform a task that would otherwise require a mouse.

KeyTip The letter that displays on a command in the ribbon and that indicates the key you can press to activate the command when keyboard control of the ribbon is activated.

Keywords Custom file properties in the form of words that you associate with a document to give an indication of the document's content.

Landscape orientation A page orientation in which the paper is wider than it is tall.

Layout Options A button that displays when an object is selected and that has commands to choose how the object interacts with surrounding text.

Live Preview A technology that shows the result of applying an editing or formatting change as you point to possible results—*before* you actually apply it.

Live tiles Tiles that are constantly updated with fresh information.

Location Any disk drive, folder, or other place in which you can store files and folders.

Lock screen A background that fills the computer screen when the computer boots up or wakes up from sleep mode.

Maximize A window control button that will enlarge the size of the window to fill the entire screen.

Menu A list of commands within a category.

Menu bar A group of menus at the top of a program window.

Menu icon A button consisting of three lines that, when clicked, expands a menu; often used in mobile applications because it is compact to use on smaller screens—also referred to a *hamburger menu*.

Glossary

Metadata Details about a file that describe or identify it, including the title, author name, subject, and keywords that identify the document's topic or contents; also known as *document properties*.

Microsoft account A user account with which you can sign in to any Windows 10 computer on which you have, or create, an account.

Microsoft Store app A smaller app that you download from the Microsoft Store.

Mini toolbar A small toolbar containing frequently used formatting commands that displays as a result of selecting text or objects.

Minimize A window control button that will keep a program open but will remove it from screen view.

Move In File Explorer, the action of removing a file or folder from its original location and storing it in a new location.

Mouse pointer Any symbol that displays on the screen in response to moving the mouse.

MRU Acronym for *most recently used*, which refers to the state of some commands that retain the characteristic most recently applied; for example, the Font Color button retains the most recently used color until a new color is chosen.

Navigate A process for exploring within the file organizing structure of Windows.

Navigation pane The area on the left side of the File Explorer window to access your OneDrive, folders on your PC, devices and drives connected to your PC, and other PCs on your network.

Nonprinting characters Characters that display on the screen, but do not print, indicating where the Enter key, the Spacebar, and the Tab key were pressed; also called *formatting marks*.

Notepad A basic text-editing program included with Windows 10 that you can use to create simple documents.

Object A text box, picture, table, or shape that you can select and then move and resize.

Office 365 A version of Microsoft Office to which you subscribe for an annual fee.

OneDrive Microsoft's free cloud storage for anyone with a free Microsoft account.

Operating system A specific type of computer program that manages the other programs on a computing device such as a desktop computer, a laptop computer, a smartphone, a tablet computer, or a game console.

Option button In a dialog box, a round button that enables you to make one choice among two or more options.

Page Width A command that zooms the document so that the width of the page matches the width of the window.

Paragraph symbol The symbol ¶ that represents the end of a paragraph.

Parent folder The location in which the folder you are viewing is saved.

Paste The action of placing text or objects that have been copied or cut from one location to another location.

Paste Options gallery A gallery of buttons that provides a Live Preview of all the Paste options available in the current context.

Path A sequence of folders that leads to a specific file or folder

PDF The acronym for Portable Document Format, which is a file format that creates an image that preserves the look of your file, but that cannot be easily changed; a popular format for sending documents electronically, because the document will display on most computers.

Pen A pen-shaped stylus that you tap on a computer screen.

Personal folder The folder created on the hard drive for each Windows 10 user account on a computer; for each user account—even if there is only one user on the computer—Windows 10 creates a personal folder labeled with the account holder's name.

Point to The action of moving the mouse pointer over a specific area.

Pointer Any symbol that displays on your screen in response to moving your mouse.

Pointing device A mouse or touchpad used to control the pointer.

Points A measurement of the size of a font; there are 72 points in an inch.

Portable Document Format A file format that creates an image that preserves the look of your file, but that cannot be easily changed; a popular format for sending documents electronically, because the document will display on most computers.

Portrait orientation A page orientation in which the paper is taller than it is wide.

Print Preview A view of a document as it will appear when you print it.

Program A set of instructions that a computer uses to accomplish a task.

Progress bar A bar that displays in a dialog box—and also on the taskbar button—that indicates visually the progress of a task such as a copy process, a download, or a file transfer.

pt The abbreviation for *point* when referring to a font size.

Quick access In the navigation pane in a File Explorer window, a list of files you have been working on and folders you use often.

Real-time co-authoring A process where two or more people work on the same file at the same time and see changes made by others in seconds.

Rectangular snip From the Snipping Tool, a command that draws a precise box by dragging the mouse pointer around an area of the screen to form a rectangle.

Recycle Bin The area where deleted items are stored until you empty the bin; enables you to recover deleted items until the bin is emptied.

Removable storage device A device such as a USB flash drive used to transfer information from one computer to another.

Resources The collection of the physical parts of your computer such as the central processing unit (CPU), memory, and any attached devices such as a printer.

Restore Down A command that resizes a window to its previous size.

Ribbon In Office applications, displays a group of task-oriented tabs that contain the commands, styles, and resources you need to work in an Office desktop app. In a File Explorer window, the area at the top that groups common tasks on tabs. such as copying and moving, creating new folders, emailing and zipping items, and changing the view on related tabs.

Right-click The action of clicking the right mouse button one time.

Sans serif font A font design with no lines or extensions on the ends of characters.

Screen reader Software that enables visually impaired users to read text on a computer screen to understand the content of pictures.

Screenshot Any captured image of your screen.

ScreenTip A small box that displays useful information when you perform various mouse actions such as pointing to screen elements or dragging.

Glossary

Scroll arrow An arrow found at either end of a scroll bar that can be clicked to move within the window in small increments.

Scroll bar A vertical bar that displays when the contents of a window or pane are not completely visible; a scroll bar can be vertical, displayed at the side of the window, or horizontal, displayed at the bottom of a window.

Scroll box Within a scroll bar, a box that you can move to bring the contents of the window into view.

Select To specify, by highlighting, a block of data or text on the screen with the intent of performing some action on the selection.

Selecting Highlighting, by dragging with your mouse, areas of text or data or graphics, so that the selection can be edited, formatted, copied, or moved.

Serif font A font design that includes small line extensions on the ends of the letters to guide the eye in reading from left to right.

SharePoint A Microsoft technology that enables employees in an organization to access information across organizational and geographic boundaries.

Shortcut menu A menu that displays commands and options relevant to the selected text or object; also called a *context menu*.

Sizing handles Small circles or squares that indicate a picture or object is selected.

Snap An action to arrange two or more open windows on your screen so that you can work with multiple screens at the same time.

Snap Assist A feature that displays all other open windows after one window is snapped.

Snip An image captured by the Snipping tool that can be annotated, saved, copied, or shared via email.

Snipping tool A Windows 10 program that captures an image of all or part of your computer's screen.

Split button A button divided into two parts and in which clicking the main part of the button performs a command and clicking the arrow opens a menu with choices.

Start menu A Windows 10 menu that displays as a result of clicking the Start button and that displays a list of installed programs on the left and a customizable group of tiles on the right that can act as a user dashboard.

Style A group of formatting commands, such as font, font size, font color, paragraph alignment, and line spacing that can be applied to a paragraph with one command.

Subfolder The term for a folder placed within another folder.

Synchronization The process of updating computer files that are in two or more locations according to specific rules—also called *syncing*.

Syncing The process of updating computer files that are in two or more locations according to specific rules—also called *synchronization*.

System tray Another term for the notification area on the taskbar that displays notification icons and the system clock and calendar.

Tabs (ribbon) On the Office ribbon, the name of each activity area.

Tags Custom file properties in the form of words that you associate with a document to give an indication of the document's content; used to help find and organize files. Also called keywords.

Task View A taskbar button that displays your desktop background with small images of all open programs and apps and from which you can see and switch between open apps, including desktop apps.

Taskbar The bar at the bottom of your Windows screen that contains buttons to launch programs and buttons for all open apps.

Tell Me A search feature for Microsoft Office commands that you activate by typing what you are looking for in the Tell Me box.

Tell me more A prompt within a ScreenTip that opens the Office online Help system with explanations about how to perform the command referenced in the ScreenTip.

Template A preformatted document that you can use as a starting point and then change to suit your needs.

Theme A predesigned combination of colors, fonts, and effects that look good together and that is applied to an entire document by a single selection.

Timeline A Windows 10 feature that when you click the Task view button, you can see activities you have worked on across your devices; for example, you can find a document, image, or video you worked on yesterday or a week ago.

Thumbnail A reduced image of a graphic.

Tiles A group of square and rectangular boxes that display on the start menu.

Title bar The bar across the top of the window that displays the program, file, or app name.

Toggle button A button that can be turned on by clicking it once and then turned off by clicking it again.

Toolbar A row, column, or block of buttons or icons that displays across the top of a window and that contains commands for tasks you perform with a single click.

Triple-click The action of clicking the left mouse button three times in rapid succession.

Undo On the Quick Access Toolbar, the command that reverses your last action.

Unzip The process of extracting files that have been compressed.

User account A user on a single computer.

Wallpaper Another term for the Desktop background.

Window snip From the Snipping Tool, a command that captures the entire displayed window.

Windows 10 An operating system developed by Microsoft Corporation that works with mobile computing devices and also with traditional desktop and laptop PCs.

XML Paper Specification A Microsoft file format that creates an image of your document and that opens in the XPS viewer.

XPS The acronym for *XML Paper Specification*—a Microsoft file format that creates an image of your document and that opens in the XPS viewer.

Zip The process of compressing files.

Zoom The action of increasing or decreasing the size of the viewing area on the screen.

Introducing
Microsoft Excel 2019

EXCEL 2019

Kheng Guan Toh/Shutterstock

Excel 2019: Introduction

 Introduction to Excel

Quantitative information! Defined as a type of information that can be counted or that communicates the quantity of something, quantitative information can be either easy or hard to understand—depending on how it is presented. According to Stephen Few, in his book *Show Me the Numbers:* "Quantitative information forms the core of what businesses must know to operate effectively."

Excel 2019 is a tool to communicate quantitative business information effectively. Sometimes you need to communicate quantitative relationships. For example, the number of units sold per geographic region shows a relationship of sales to geography. Sometimes you need to summarize numbers. A list of every student enrolled at your college along with his or her major is not as informative as a summary of the total number of students in each major. In business, the most common quantitative information is some measure of money—costs, sales, payroll, expenses and so on.

Rather than just a tool for making calculations, Excel is also a tool for you to communicate and collaborate with others. When you want to communicate visually with tables and graphs, Excel 2019 has many features to help you do so. If you engage in Business Intelligence activities, you will find rich tools for forecasting and for delivering insights about your organization's data.

Creating a Worksheet and Charting Data

1

EXCEL 2019

PROJECT 1A

Outcomes
Create a sales report with an embedded column chart and sparklines.

Objectives
1. Create, Save, and Navigate an Excel Workbook
2. Enter Data in a Worksheet
3. Construct and Copy Formulas and Use the SUM Function
4. Format Cells with Merge & Center, Cell Styles, and Themes
5. Chart Data to Create a Column Chart and Insert Sparklines
6. Print a Worksheet, Display Formulas, and Close Excel

PROJECT 1B

Outcomes
Calculate the value of an inventory.

Objectives
7. Check Spelling in a Worksheet
8. Enter Data by Range
0. Construct Formulas for Mathematical Operations
10. Edit Values in a Worksheet
11. Format a Worksheet

Wavebreakmedia/Shutterstock

In This Chapter

GO! To Work with Excel

In this chapter, you will use Microsoft Excel to create and analyze data organized into columns and rows. After entering data in a worksheet, you can perform complex calculations, analyze the data to make logical decisions, and create attractive charts that help readers visualize your data in a way they can understand and that is meaningful. In this chapter, you will create and modify Excel workbooks. You will practice the basics of worksheet design, create a footer, enter and edit data in a worksheet, and chart data. You will save, preview, and print workbooks, and you will construct formulas for mathematical operations.

The projects in this chapter relate to **Pro Fit Marietta**, a distributor of fitness equipment and apparel to private gyms, personal trainers, health clubs, corporate wellness centers, hotels, college athletic facilities, physical therapy practices, and multi-unit residential properties. The company's mission is to find, test, and distribute the highest quality fitness products in the world to its customers for the benefit of consumers. The company's blog provides useful tips on how to use the latest workout and fitness equipment. The company is in Marietta, Georgia, which is metropolitan Atlanta's largest suburb.

Sales Report with Embedded Column Chart and Sparklines

Project Activities

In Activities 1.01 through 1.17, you will create an Excel worksheet for Michelle Barry, the President of Pro Fit Marietta. The worksheet displays the second quarter sales of cardio equipment for the current year and includes a chart to visually represent the data. Your completed worksheet will look similar to Figure 1.1.

Project Files for **MyLab IT Grader**

1. In your storage location, create a folder named **Excel Chapter 1**.
2. In your MyLab IT course, locate and click **Excel 1A Quarterly Sales**, Download Materials, and then Download All Files.
3. Extract the zipped folder to your Excel Chapter 1 folder. Close the Grader download screens.
4. Take a moment to open the downloaded **Excel_1A_Quarterly_Sales_Instructions**; note any recent updates to the book.

Project Results

GO! Project 1A
Where We're Going

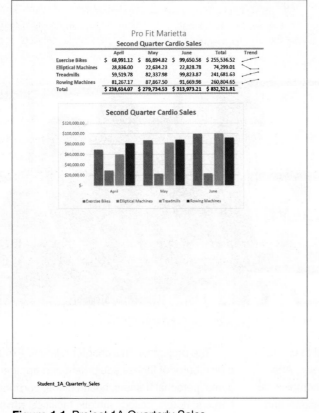

Student_1A_Quarterly_Sales

Figure 1.1 Project 1A Quarterly Sales

For Non-MyLab Submissions
For Project 1A, you will need:
New blank Excel workbook

In your storage location, create a folder named **Excel Chapter 1**
In your Excel Chapter 1 folder, save your workbook as:
Lastname_Firstname_1A_Quarterly_Sales
If your instructor requires a workbook with formulas, save as:
Lastname_Firstname_1A_Quarterly_Sales_formulas

After you have named and saved your workbook, on the next page begin with Step 2.

NOTE   If You Are Using a Touch Screen

Tap an item to click it.

Press and hold for a few seconds to right-click; release when the information or commands display.

Touch the screen with two or more fingers and then pinch together to zoom out or stretch your fingers apart to zoom in.

Slide your finger on the screen to scroll—slide left to scroll right and slide right to scroll left.

Slide to rearrange—similar to dragging with a mouse.

Swipe to select—slide an item a short distance with a quick movement—to select an item and bring up commands, if any.

Objective 1   Create, Save, and Navigate an Excel Workbook

ALERT   Because Office 365 is a cloud-based subscription service that receives continuous updates, you may encounter some variations in what appears on your screen and what is shown in this instruction. Microsoft Office 365 is fully installed on your PC or Mac; no internet access is necessary to create or edit documents. When you *are* connected to the internet, you will receive monthly upgrades and new features, so you always have the latest versions of Office apps as soon as they are available. Your subscription gives you continuous free access to the latest innovations and refinements.

GO Learn How
Video E1-1

On startup, Excel displays a new blank ***workbook***—the Excel document that stores your data—which contains one or more pages called a ***worksheet***. A worksheet—or ***spreadsheet***—is stored in a workbook and is formatted as a pattern of uniformly spaced horizontal rows and vertical columns. The intersection of a column and a row forms a box referred to as a ***cell***.

Activity 1.01 | **Starting Excel, Navigating Excel, and Naming and Saving a Workbook**

> **1** Navigate to your **Excel Chapter 1 folder**, and then double-click the Excel file you downloaded from **MyLab IT** that displays your name—**Student_Excel_1A_Quarterly_Sales**. In your blank workbook, if necessary, at the top click **Enable Editing**.

> **2** In the lower right corner of the window, on the status bar, if necessary, click the **Normal** button ▦, and then to the right, locate the zoom—magnification—level.

Your zoom level should be 100%, although some figures in this textbook may be shown at a higher zoom level. The ***Normal view*** maximizes the number of cells visible on your screen and keeps the column letters and row numbers closer.

3 ▶ Compare your screen with Figure 1.2, and then take a moment to study the Excel window parts in the table in Figure 1.3.

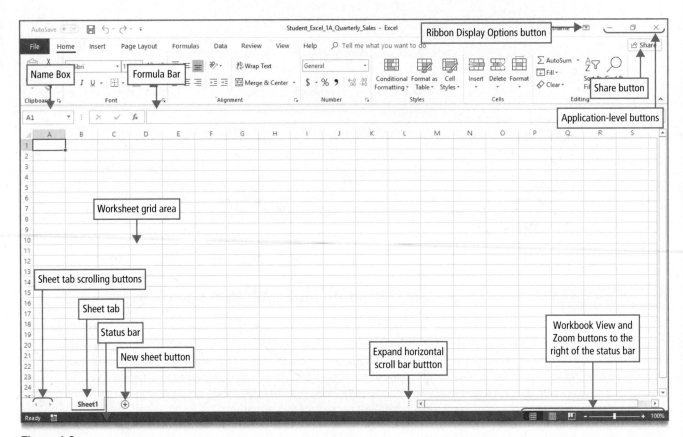

Figure 1.2

Parts of the Excel Window	
Screen Part	**Description**
Application-level buttons	Minimize, close, or restore the previous size of the displayed workbook window.
Expand horizontal scroll bar button	Increases or decreases the width of the horizontal scroll bar by sliding left or right.
Formula Bar	Displays the value or formula contained in the active cell; also permits entry or editing.
Name Box	Displays the name of the selected cell, table, chart, or object.
New sheet button	Inserts an additional worksheet.
Ribbon Display Options button	Displays various ways you can display the ribbon—Show Tabs and Commands is shown here.
Share button	Opens the Share dialog box or the Share pane from which you can save your file to the cloud—for example, your OneDrive—and then share it with others so you can collaborate.
Sheet tab	Identifies the worksheet in the workbook.
Sheet tab scrolling buttons	Display sheet tabs that are not in view when there are numerous sheet tabs.
Status bar	Displays the current cell mode (here in Ready mode) and possibly Macro information as shown here. To the right of the status bar, Workbook View buttons and Zoom buttons display. Here, numerical data and common calculations such as Sum and Average may display.
Worksheet grid area	Displays the columns and rows that intersect to form the worksheet's cells.

Figure 1.3

4 Take a moment to study Figure 1.4 and the table in Figure 1.5 to become familiar with the Excel workbook window.

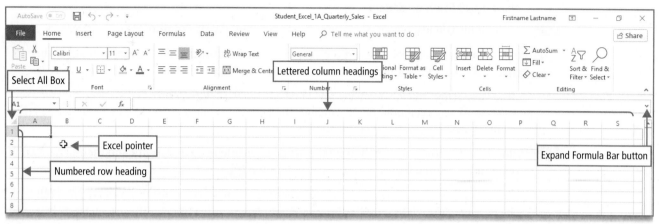

Figure 1.4

Excel Workbook Window Elements	
Workbook Window Element	**Description**
Excel pointer	Displays the location of the pointer.
Expand Formula Bar button	Increases the height of the Formula Bar to display lengthy cell content.
Lettered column headings	Indicate the column letter.
Numbered row headings	Indicate the row number.
Select All box	Selects all the cells in a worksheet.

Figure 1.5

5 In the lower right corner of the screen, in the horizontal scroll bar, click the **right scroll arrow** one time to shift **column A** out of view.

A *column* is a vertical group of cells in a worksheet. Beginning with the first letter of the alphabet, *A*, a unique letter identifies each column—this is called the *column heading*. Clicking one of the horizontal scroll bar arrows shifts the window either left or right one column at a time.

6 Point to the **right scroll arrow**, and then hold down the left mouse button until the columns begin to scroll rapidly to the right; release the mouse button when you begin to see pairs of letters as the column headings.

MAC TIP For rapid scrolling, swipe your finger to the left or right on the mouse or track pad.

BY TOUCH Anywhere on the worksheet, slide your finger to the left to scroll to the right.

7 Slowly drag the horizontal scroll box to the left, and notice that just above the scroll box, ScreenTips with the column letters display as you drag. Drag the horizontal scroll box left or right—or click the left or right scroll arrow—as necessary to position **column Z** near the center of your screen.

Column headings after column Z use two letters starting with AA, AB, and so on through ZZ. After that, columns begin with three letters beginning with AAA. This pattern provides 16,384 columns. The last column is XFD.

MAC TIP Drag the scroll box, there are no ScreenTips.

8 In the vertical scroll bar, click the **down scroll arrow** one time to move **row 1** out of view.

A *row* is a horizontal group of cells. Beginning with number 1, a unique number identifies each row—this is the *row heading*, located at the left side of the worksheet. A single worksheet can have 1,048,576 rows of data.

9 Use the skills you just practiced to scroll horizontally to display **column A**, and if necessary, **row 1**.

10 Point to and then click the cell at the intersection of **column A** and **row 1** to make it the *active cell*—the cell is outlined and ready to accept data.

The intersecting column letter and row number form the *cell reference*—also called the *cell address*. When a cell is active, its column letter and row number are highlighted. The cell reference of the selected cell, *A1*, displays in the Name Box.

11 With cell **A1** as the active cell, type the worksheet title **Pro Fit Marietta** and then press Enter. Compare your screen with Figure 1.6. Click **Save** 🖫 .

Text or numbers in a cell are referred to as *data*. You must confirm the data you type in a cell by pressing Enter or by some other keyboard movement, such as pressing Tab or an arrow key. Pressing Enter moves the active cell to the cell below.

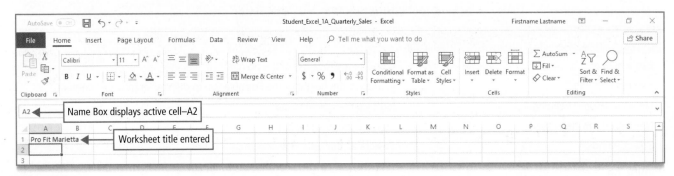

Figure 1.6

Objective 2   Enter Data in a Worksheet

GO! Learn How
Video E1-2

Cell content, which is anything you type in a cell, can be one of two things: either a *constant value*—referred to simply as a *value*—or a *formula*. A formula is an equation that performs mathematical calculations on values in your worksheet. The most commonly used values are *text values* and *number values*, but a value can also include a date or a time of day. A text value is also referred to as a *label*.

Activity 1.02 | Entering Text, Using AutoComplete, and Using the Name Box to Select a Cell

1.2.2

A text value usually provides information about number values in other worksheet cells. In this worksheet for Pro Fit Marietta, the title *Second Quarter Cardio Sales* gives the reader an indication that data in the worksheet relates to information about sales of cardio equipment during the three-month period April through June.

1 In cell **A1**, notice that the text does not fit; the text extends into cell **B1** to the right.

If text is too long for a cell and cells to the right are empty, the text will display. If the cells to the right contain other data, only the text that will fit in the cell displays.

2 In cell **A2**, type the worksheet subtitle **Second Quarter Cardio Sales** and then press Enter. Compare your screen with Figure 1.7.

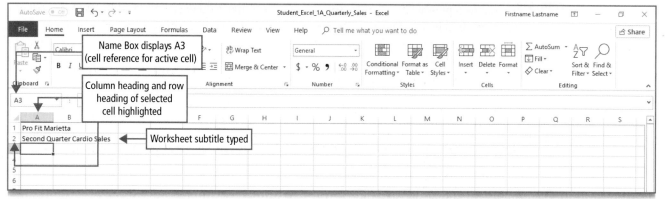

Figure 1.7

3 Above **column A**, click in the **Name Box** to select the cell reference *A3*, and then type **a4** Press Enter to make cell **A4** the active cell. In cell **A4**, type **Exercise Bikes** to form the first row title, and then press Enter.

> The text characters that you typed align at the left edge of the cell—referred to as *left alignment*—and cell A5 becomes the active cell. Left alignment is the default for text values. You can type a cell address in the Name Box and press Enter to move to a specific cell quickly.

4 In cell **A5**, type **E** and notice the text from the previous cell displays.

> If the first characters you type in a cell match an existing entry in the column, Excel fills in the remaining characters for you. This feature, called *AutoComplete*, assists only with alphabetic values.

5 Continue typing the remainder of the row title **lliptical Machines** and press Enter.

> The AutoComplete suggestion is removed when the entry you are typing differs from the previous value.

6 In cell **A6**, type **Treadmills** and press Enter. In cell **A7**, type **Rowing Machines** and press Enter. In cell **A8**, type **Total** and press Enter. On the Quick Access Toolbar, click **Save** 🖫.

🔄 **ANOTHER WAY**   Use the keyboard shortcut Ctrl + S to save changes to your workbook.

💻 **MAC TIP**   Use the keyboard shortcut command ⌘ + S to save changes to your workbook.

Activity 1.03 | Using Auto Fill and Keyboard Shortcuts

MOS
2.1.2

1 Click cell **B3**. Type **A** and notice that when you begin to type in a cell, on the **Formula Bar**, the **Cancel** and **Enter** buttons become active, as shown in Figure 1.8.

Figure 1.8

---

2 Continue to type **pril** On the **Formula Bar**, notice that values you type in a cell also display there, and then on the **Formula Bar**, click **Enter** ☑ to confirm the entry and keep cell **B3** active.

3 With cell **B3** active, locate the small square in the lower right corner of the selected cell.

You can drag this *fill handle*—the small square in the lower right corner of a selected cell—to adjacent cells to fill the cells with values based on the first cell.

4 Point to the **fill handle** until the ⊞ pointer displays, hold down the left mouse button, drag to the right to cell **D3**, and as you drag, notice the ScreenTips *May* and *June*. Release the mouse button.

5 Under the text that you just filled, click the **Auto Fill Options** button 🖳 that displays, and then compare your screen with Figure 1.9.

Auto Fill generates and extends a *series* of values into adjacent cells based on the value of other cells. A series is a group of things that come one after another in succession; for example, *April, May, June.*

The Auto Fill Options button displays options to fill the data; options vary depending on the content and program from which you are filling, and the format of the data you are filling.

Fill Series is selected, indicating the action that was taken. Because the options are related to the current task, the button is referred to as being *context sensitive*.

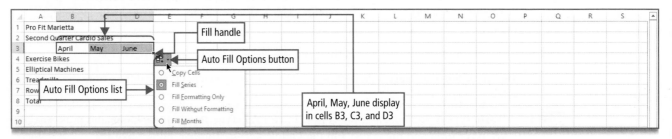

Figure 1.9

6 Click in any cell to cancel the display of the list.

The list no longer displays; the button will display until you perform some other screen action.

7 Press Ctrl + Home, which is the keyboard shortcut to make cell **A1** active.

MAC TIP Press control + fn + ← to make cell A1 active.

8 On the Quick Access Toolbar, click **Save** 🖫 to save the changes you have made to your workbook.

9 Take a moment to study the table in Figure 1.10 to become familiar with keyboard shortcuts with which you can navigate the Excel worksheet.

Keyboard Shortcuts to Navigate the Excel Window		
To Move the Location of the Active Cell:	**On a Windows PC Press:**	**On a Mac Press:**
Up, down, right, or left one cell	↑, ↓, →, ←	↑, ↓, →, ←
Down one cell	Enter	enter
Up one cell	Shift + Enter	shift + enter
Up one full screen	PgUp	fn + ↑
Down one full screen	PgDn	fn + ↓
To column A of the current row	Home	fn + ←
To the last cell on a worksheet, to the lowest used row of the rightmost used column	Ctrl + End	control + fn + →
To cell A1	Ctrl + Home	control + fn + ←
Right one cell	Tab	tab
Left one cell	Shift + Tab	shift + tab
To one screen to the right in a worksheet	Alt + PgDn	fn + option + ↓
To one screen to the left in a worksheet	Alt + PgUp	fn + option + ↑

Figure 1.10

Activity 1.04 | Aligning Text and Adjusting the Size of Columns

MOS
1.3.2

1 In the **column heading area**, point to the vertical line between **column A** and **column B** to display the ⊞ pointer, press and hold down the left mouse button, and then compare your screen with Figure 1.11.

A ScreenTip displays information about the width of the column. The default width of a column is 64 *pixels*. A pixel, short for *picture element*, is a point of light measured in dots per square inch. Sixty-four pixels equal 8.43 characters, which is the average number of characters that will fit in a cell using the default font. The default font in Excel is Calibri and the default font size is 11.

MAC TIP The default font size on a Mac is 12.

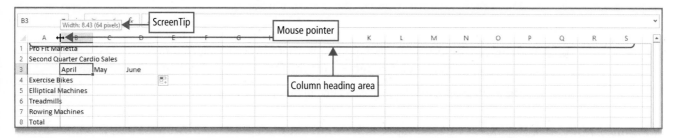

Figure 1.11

2 Drag to the right, and when the number of pixels indicated in the ScreenTip reaches **120 pixels**, release the mouse button. If you are not satisfied with your result, click Undo ↰ on the Quick Access Toolbar and begin again.

This width accommodates the longest row title in cells A4 through A8—*Elliptical Machines*. The worksheet subtitle in cell A2 spans more than one column and still does not fit in column A.

🖥 **MAC TIP**   Change the width to 16.50 (104 pixels).

---

3 Point to cell **B3** and then drag across to select cells **B3**, **C3**, and **D3**. Compare your screen with Figure 1.12; if you are not satisfied with your result, click anywhere and begin again.

The three cells, B3 through D3, are selected and form a ***range***—two or more cells on a worksheet that are adjacent (next to each other) or nonadjacent (not next to each other). This range of cells is referred to as *B3:D3*. When you see a colon (:) between two cell references, the range includes all the cells between the two cell references.

A range of cells you select this way is indicated by a dark border, and Excel treats the range as a single unit so you can make the same changes to more than one cell at a time. The selected cells in the range are highlighted except for the first cell in the range, which displays in the Name Box.

When you select a range of data, the ***Quick Analysis tool*** displays in the lower right corner of the selected range, with which you can analyze your data by using Excel tools such as charts, color-coding, and formulas.

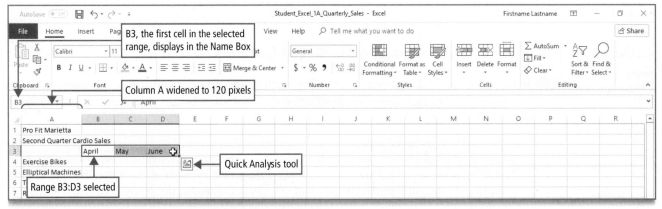

Figure 1.12

👉 **BY TOUCH**   To select a range, tap and hold the first cell, and then when the circular gripper displays, drag it to the right, or to the right and down, to define the beginning and end of a range.

---

4 With the range **B3:D3** selected, point anywhere over the selected range, right-click, and then on the mini toolbar, click **Center** ☰. On the Quick Access Toolbar, click **Save** 🖫.

The column titles *April*, *May*, *June* align in the center of each cell.

🖥 **MAC TIP**   Press ⌘ command + E to center align.

Activity 1.05 | Entering Numbers

To type number values, use either the number keys across the top of your keyboard or the numeric keypad if you have one—laptop computers may not have a numeric keypad.

In this Activity, you will enter the data that Michelle has given you that represents the sales of cardio equipment in the second quarter of the year.

1 ▶ Under *April*, click cell **B4**, type **68991.12** and then on the **Formula Bar**, click **Enter** ☑ to maintain cell **B4** as the active cell. Compare your screen with Figure 1.13.

By default, *number* values align at the right edge of the cell. The default ***number format***—a specific way in which Excel displays numbers—is the ***general format***. In the default general format, whatever you type in the cell will display, with the exception of trailing zeros to the right of a decimal point. For example, in the number 237.50 the *0* following the *5* is a trailing zero and would not display.

Data that displays in a cell is the ***displayed value***. Data that displays in the Formula Bar is the ***underlying value***. The number of digits or characters that display in a cell—the displayed value—depends on the width of the column. Calculations on numbers will always be based on the underlying value, not the displayed value.

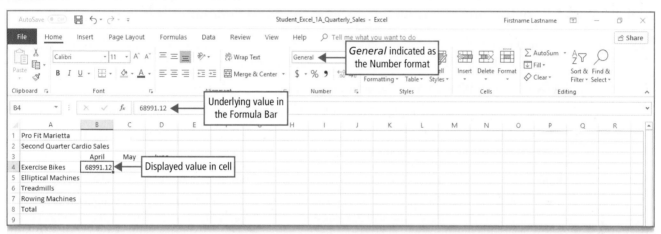

Figure 1.13

2 ▶ Press ⎆Tab to make cell **C4** active. Type **86894.82** and then press ⎆Tab to move to cell **D4**. Type **99650.58** and then press ⏎Enter to move to cell **B5** in the next row. Then, by using the same technique, enter the remaining sales numbers as shown:

	April	May	June
Elliptical Machines	28836	22634.23	22828.78
Treadmills	59519.78	82337.98	99823.87
Rowing Machines	81267.17	87867.50	91669.98

3 ▶ Compare the numbers you entered with Figure 1.14, and then **Save** 🖫 your workbook.

In the default General format, trailing zeros to the right of a decimal point will not display. For example, when you type *87867.50*, the cell displays 87867.5 instead.

Figure 1.14

Objective 3 | Construct and Copy Formulas and Use the SUM Function

GO! Learn How
Video E1-3

A cell contains either a constant value (text or numbers) or a formula. A formula is an equation that performs mathematical calculations on values in other cells, and then places the result in the cell containing the formula. You can create formulas or use a *function*—a prewritten formula that looks at one or more values, performs an operation, and then returns a value.

Activity 1.06 | Constructing a Formula and Using the SUM Function

MOS
4.2.1

In this Activity, you will practice three different ways to sum a group of numbers in Excel so that Michelle can see totals for each month and for each category of equipment sold.

1 Click cell **B8** to make it the active cell and type **=**

The equal sign (=) displays in the cell with the insertion point blinking, ready to accept more data.

All formulas begin with the = sign, which signals Excel to begin a calculation. The Formula Bar displays the = sign, and the Formula Bar Cancel and Enter buttons display.

2 At the insertion point, type **b4** and then compare your screen with Figure 1.15.

A list of Excel functions that begin with the letter *B* may briefly display—as you progress in your study of Excel, you will use functions of this type. A blue border with small corner boxes surrounds cell B4, which indicates that the cell is part of an active formula. The color used in the box matches the color of the cell reference in the formula.

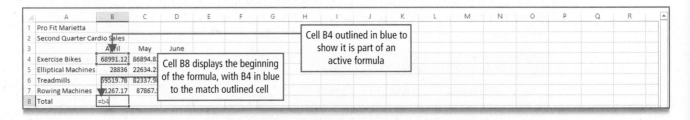

Figure 1.15

3 At the insertion point, type **+** and then type **b5**

A border of another color surrounds cell B5, and the color matches the color of the cell reference in the active formula. When typing cell references, it is not necessary to use uppercase letters.

4 At the insertion point, type **+b6+b7** and then press Enter.

The result of the formula calculation—*238614.1*—displays in the cell. Recall that in the default General format, trailing zeros do not display. (Mac users: yours may display *238614.07*)

---

5 Click cell **B8** again, look at the **Formula Bar**, and then compare your screen with Figure 1.16.

> The formula adds the values in cells B4 through B7, and the result displays in cell B8. In this manner, you can construct a formula by typing. Although cell B8 displays the *result* of the formula, the formula itself displays in the Formula Bar. This is referred to as the ***underlying formula***.

> Always view the Formula Bar to be sure of the exact content of a cell—*a displayed number may actually be a formula.*

Figure 1.16

6 Click cell **C8** and type = to signal the beginning of a formula. Then, point to cell **C4** and click one time.

> The reference to the cell C4 is added to the active formula. A moving border surrounds the referenced cell, and the border color and the color of the cell reference in the formula are color coded to match.

7 At the insertion point, type + and then click cell **C5**. Repeat this process to complete the formula to add cells **C6** and **C7**, and then press Enter.

> The result of the formula calculation—*279734.5*—displays in the cell. This method of constructing a formula is the ***point and click method*** (Mac users: yours may display *279734.53*).

8 Click cell **D8**. On the **Home tab**, in the **Editing group**, click **AutoSum**, and then compare your screen with Figure 1.17.

> SUM is an Excel function—a prewritten formula. A moving border surrounds the range D4:D7 and =*SUM(D4:D7)* displays in cell D8.

> The = sign signals the beginning of a formula, *SUM* indicates the type of calculation that will take place (addition), and *(D4:D7)* indicates the range of cells on which the sum calculation will be performed. A ScreenTip provides additional information about the action.

MAC TIP To display group names on the ribbon, display the menu, click Excel, click Preferences, click View, under In Ribbon, select the Group Titles check box.

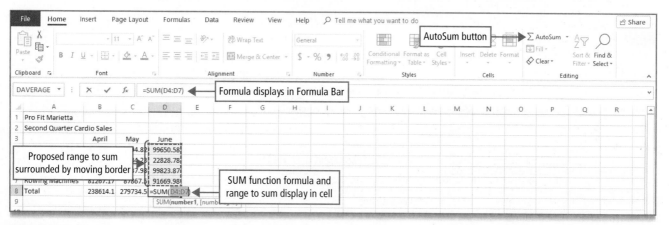

Figure 1.17

9 ▸ Look at the **Formula Bar** and notice that the formula also displays there. Then, look again at the cells surrounded by the moving border.

> When you activate the **Sum function**, Excel first looks *above* the active cell for a range of cells to sum. If no range is above the active cell, Excel will look to the *left* for a range of cells to sum. If the proposed range is not what you want to calculate, you can select a different group of cells.

10 ▸ Press Enter to construct a formula by using the prewritten SUM function.

> Your total is *313973.2*. (Mac users: yours may display *313973.21*) Because the Sum function is frequently used, it has its own button in the Editing group on the Home tab of the ribbon. A larger version of the button also displays on the Formulas tab in the Function Library group. This button is also referred to as **AutoSum**.

11 ▸ Notice that the totals in the range **B8:D8** display only one decimal place. Click **Save** 🖫.

> Number values that are too long to fit in the cell do *not* spill over into the unoccupied cell to the right in the same manner as text values. Rather, Excel rounds the number to fit the space.

> **Rounding** is a procedure that determines which digit at the right of the number will be the last digit displayed and then increases it by one if the next digit to its right is 5, 6, 7, 8, or 9.

💻 **MAC TIP**   The total may display 2 decimal places.

Activity 1.07 | Copying a Formula by Using the Fill Handle

MOS
4.1.1

You have practiced three ways to create a formula—by typing, by using the point and click technique, and by using a Function button from the ribbon. You can also copy formulas. When you copy a formula from one cell to another, Excel adjusts the cell references to fit the new location of the formula.

1 ▸ Click cell **E3**, type **Total** and then press Enter.

> The text in cell E3 is centered because the centered format continues from the adjacent cell.

2 ▸ With cell **E4** as the active cell, hold down Alt, and then press =. Compare your screen with Figure 1.18.

> Alt + = is the keyboard shortcut for the Sum function. Recall that Excel first looks above the selected cell for a proposed range of cells to sum, and if no data is detected, Excel looks to the left and proposes a range of cells to sum.

💻 **MAC TIP**   Press command ⌘ + shift + T as the keyboard shortcut to total.

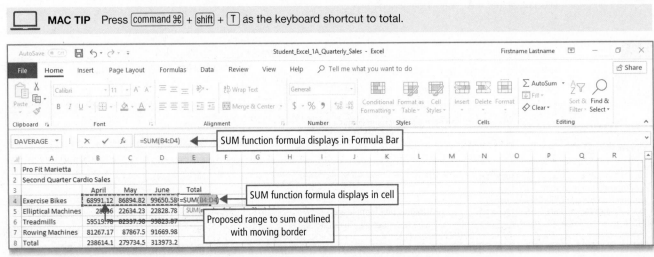

Figure 1.18

3 ▶ On the **Formula Bar**, click **Enter** ☑ to display the result and keep cell **E4** active.

> The total dollar amount of *Exercise Bikes* sold in the quarter is *255536.5*. In cells E5:E8, you can see that you need a formula similar to the one in E4, but formulas that refer to the cells in row 5, row 6, and so on.

4 ▶ With cell **E4** active, point to the fill handle in the lower right corner of the cell until the 🞢 pointer displays. Then, drag down through cell **E8**; if you are not satisfied with your result, on the Quick Access Toolbar, click Undo ↺ and begin again. Compare your screen with Figure 1.19.

E4		✕ ✓ *fx*	=SUM(B4:D4)														

	A	B	C	D	E	F	G	H	I	J	K	L	M	N	O	P	Q	R
1	Pro Fit Marietta																	
2	Second Quarter Cardio Sales																	
3		April	May	June	Total													
4	Exercise Bikes	68991.12	86894.82	99650.5	255536.5													
5	Elliptical Machin	Totals display in		22828.7	74299.01													
6	Treadmills	the selected cells		9982	241681.6													
7	Rowing Machine			91669.9	260804.7		Auto Fill Options button displays											
8	Total	238614.1	279734.5	313973.	832321.8													
9																		

Figure 1.19

5 ▶ Click cell **E5**, look at the **Formula Bar**, and notice the formula *=SUM(B5:D5)*. Click cell **E6**, look at the **Formula Bar**, and then notice the formula *=SUM(B6:D6)*.

> In each row, Excel copied the formula but adjusted the cell references *relative to* the row number. This is called a **relative cell reference**—a cell reference based on the relative position of the cell that contains the formula and the cells referred to in the formula.

> The calculation is the same, but it is performed on the cells in that particular row. Use this method to insert numerous formulas into spreadsheets quickly.

6 ▶ Click cell **F3**, type **Trend** and then press [Enter]. **Save** 💾 your workbook.

Objective 4	**Format Cells with Merge & Center, Cell Styles, and Themes**

GO! Learn How
Video E1-4

> *Format*—change the appearance of—cells to make your worksheet attractive and easy to read.

Activity 1.08 │ Using Merge & Center and Applying Cell Styles

2.2.1

> In this Activity, you will apply formatting to the worksheet so that Michelle and her staff can present a visually attractive worksheet to the company.

1 ▶ Select the range **A1:F1**, and then in the **Alignment group**, click **Merge & Center**. Then, select the range **A2:F2** and click **Merge & Center**.

> The *Merge & Center* command joins selected cells into one larger cell and centers the contents in the merged cell; individual cells in the range B1:F1 and B2:F2 can no longer be selected—they are merged into cells A1 and A2, respectively.

 ANOTHER WAY   Select the range, right-click over the selection, and then on the mini toolbar, click the Merge & Center button.

2 ▶ Click cell **A1**. In the **Styles group**, click **Cell Styles**, and then compare your screen with Figure 1.20.

A *cell style* is a defined set of formatting characteristics, such as font, font size, font color, cell borders, and cell shading.

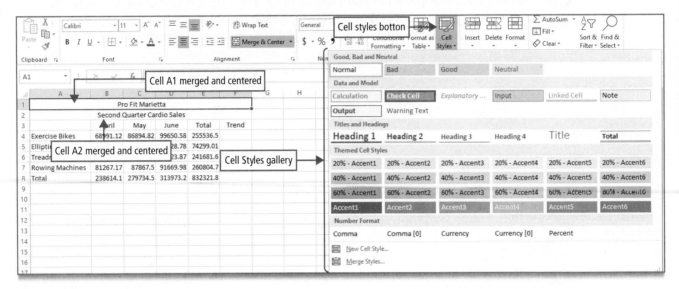

Figure 1.20

3 ▶ In the displayed gallery, under **Titles and Headings**, click **Title** and notice that the row height adjusts to accommodate the larger font size.

4 ▶ Click cell **A2**, display the **Cell Styles** gallery, and then under **Titles and Headings**, click **Heading 1**.

Use cell styles to maintain a consistent look in a worksheet and across worksheets in a workbook.

5 ▶ Select the horizontal range **B3:F3**, hold down Ctrl, and then select the vertical range **A4:A8** to select the column titles and the row titles.

Use this technique to select two or more ranges that are nonadjacent—not next to each other.

🖥 **MAC TIP**   Hold down command ⌘ and then select the vertical range.

---

6 ▶ Display the **Cell Styles** gallery, click **Heading 4** to apply this cell style to the column titles and row titles, and then **Save** 🖫 your workbook.

Activity 1.09 | Formatting Financial Numbers

MOS
2.2.5, 2.2.7

To present a clear and accurate worksheet, Michelle likes to apply appropriate formatting when reporting financial information such as sales.

In this Activity, you will apply formatting to financial numbers.

1 ▶ Select the range **B4:E4**, hold down Ctrl, and then select the range **B8:E8**.

This range is referred to as *b4:e4,b8:e8* with a comma separating the references to the two nonadjacent ranges.

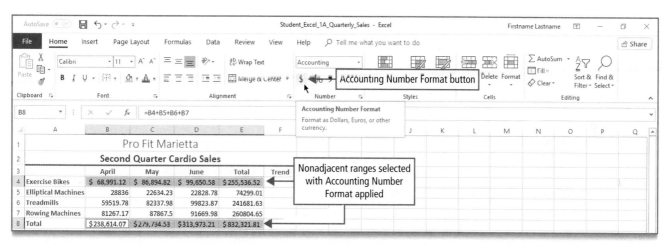**ANOTHER WAY**   In the Name Box type b4:e4,b8:e8 and then press Enter.

2 On the **Home tab**, in the **Number group**, click **Accounting Number Format** $ ▾. Compare your screen with Figure 1.21.

The *Accounting Number Format* applies a thousand comma separator where appropriate, inserts a fixed U.S. dollar sign aligned at the left edge of the cell, applies two decimal places, and leaves a small amount of space at the right edge of the cell to accommodate parentheses when negative numbers are present. Excel widens the columns to accommodate the formatted numbers.

At the bottom of your screen, in the status bar, Excel displays the results for some common calculations that might be made on the range; for example, the Average of the numbers selected and the Count—the number of items selected.

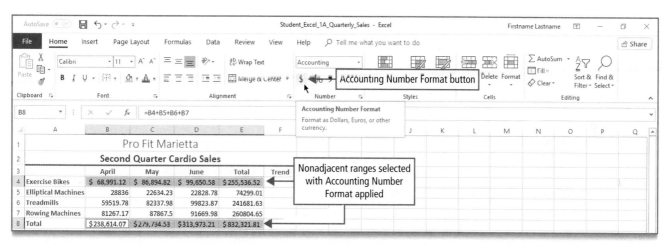

Figure 1.21

ANOTHER WAY   Display the Cell Styles gallery, and under Number Format, click Currency.

3 Select the range **B5:E7**, and then in the **Number group**, click **Comma Style** ▾.

The *Comma Style* inserts a thousand comma separator where appropriate and applies two decimal places. Comma Style also leaves space at the right to accommodate a parenthesis when negative numbers are present.

When preparing worksheets with financial information, the first row of dollar amounts and the total row of dollar amounts are formatted in the Accounting Number Format; that is, with thousand comma separators, dollar signs, two decimal places, and space at the right to accommodate a parenthesis for negative numbers, if any. Rows that are *not* the first row or the total row should be formatted with the Comma Style.

4 Select the range **B8:E8**. In the **Styles group**, display the **Cell Styles** gallery, and then under **Titles and Headings**, click **Total**. Click any blank cell to cancel the selection, and then compare your screen with Figure 1.22.

This is a common way to apply borders to financial information. The single border indicates that calculations were performed on the numbers above, and the double border indicates that the information is complete. Sometimes financial documents do not display values with cents; rather, the values are rounded up. You can do this by selecting the cells, and then clicking the Decrease Decimal button two times.

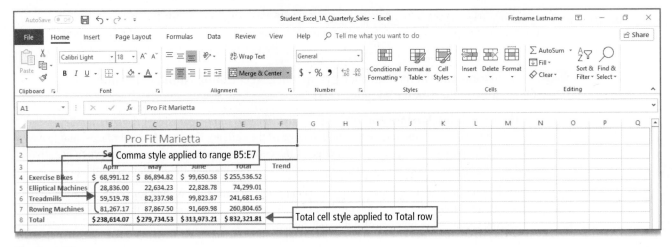

Figure 1.22

Activity 1.10 | Changing the Workbook Theme

A ***theme*** is a predefined set of colors, fonts, lines, and fill effects that coordinate for an attractive look.

1 Click the **Page Layout tab**, and then in the **Themes group**, click **Themes**.

2 Click the **Retrospect** theme, and notice that the cell styles change to match the new theme. Click **Save** 🖫.

MORE KNOWLEDGE **Formatting a Cell's Font, Style, Size, or Color with Individual Commands**

Instead of using Cell Styles, you could use a combination of individual commands to format a cell. For example, on the Home tab, in the Font group, you can change a cell's font by clicking the Font arrow and selecting a different font. You can change the font size by clicking the Font Size arrow and selecting a size. From the same group, you can apply various styles to the cell—such as Bold, Italic, or Underline. To change a cell's font color, in the Font group, click the Font Color arrow and select a different color.

Objective 5 **Chart Data to Create a Column Chart and Insert Sparklines**

GO! Learn How
Video E1-5

A ***chart*** is a graphic representation of data in a worksheet. Data in a chart is easier to understand than a table of numbers. ***Sparklines*** are tiny charts embedded in a cell that give a visual trend summary alongside your data. A sparkline makes a pattern more obvious to the eye.

Activity 1.11 | Charting Data and Using Recommended Charts to Select and Insert a Column Chart

MOS
5.1.1, 5.2.2

Recommended Charts is an Excel feature that displays a customized set of charts that, according to Excel's calculations, will best fit your data based on the range of data that you select.

In this Activity, you will create a **column chart** showing the monthly sales of cardio equipment by category during the second quarter. A column chart is useful for illustrating comparisons among related numbers. The chart will enable the company president, Michelle Barry, to see a pattern of overall monthly sales.

1 ▶ Select the range **A3:D7**.

> When charting data, typically you should *not* include totals—include only the data you want to compare.

2 ▶ With the data that you want to compare selected, click the **Insert tab**, and then in the **Charts group**, click **Recommended Charts**. Compare your screen with Figure 1.23.

> The Insert Chart dialog box displays a list of recommended charts on the left and a preview of the first chart, which is selected, on the right. The second tab of the Insert Chart dialog box includes all chart types—even those that are not recommended by Excel for this type of data
>
> By using different *chart types*, you can display data in a way that is meaningful to the reader—common examples are column charts, pie charts, and line charts.

MAC TIP Instead of an Insert Chart dialog box, you may see a drop-down menu of recommended charts; click the second Clustered Column chart.

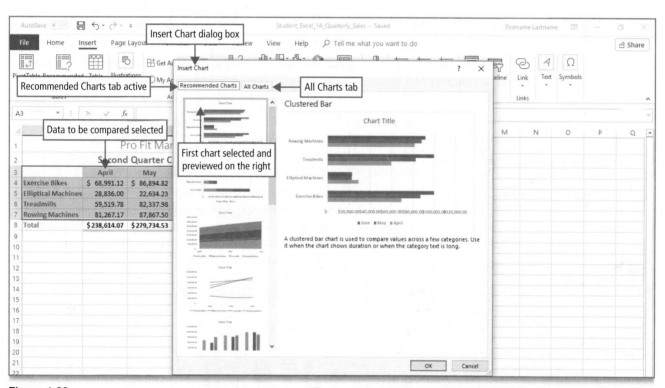

Figure 1.23

3 ▶ In the **Insert Chart** dialog box, use the scroll bar to scroll down about one-third of the way, and then click the second Clustered Column chart to view it in the preview area of the **Insert Chart** dialog box. Compare your screen with Figure 1.24.

> Here, *each type of cardio equipment* displays its *sales for each month*. A clustered column chart is useful to compare values across a few categories, especially if the order of categories is not important.

MAC TIP Because there is no preview, do not click the chart; if you clicked it and it embedded in your worksheet, on the Quick Access toolbar, click Undo.

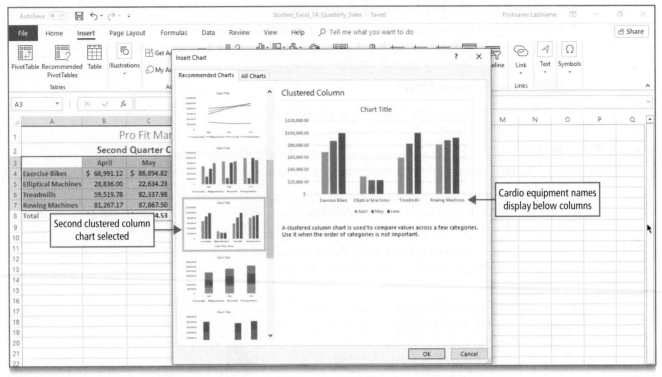

Figure 1.24

> **4** In the **Insert Chart** dialog box, click the chart directly above the selected chart—the first clustered column chart that shows the month names below the columns. Compare your screen with Figure 1.25.

> In this clustered column chart, *each month* displays its *sales for each type of cardio equipment*. When constructing a chart, you can switch the row and column data in this manner to display the data in a way that is most useful to the reader. Here, the president of Pro Fit Marietta wants to compare sales of each type of equipment by month to detect patterns.

> The comparison of data—either by month or by type of equipment—depends on the type of analysis you want to perform. You can select either chart, or, after your chart is complete, you can use the **Switch/Row Column** command on the ribbon to swap the data over the axis; that is, data being charted on the vertical axis will move to the horizontal axis and vice versa.

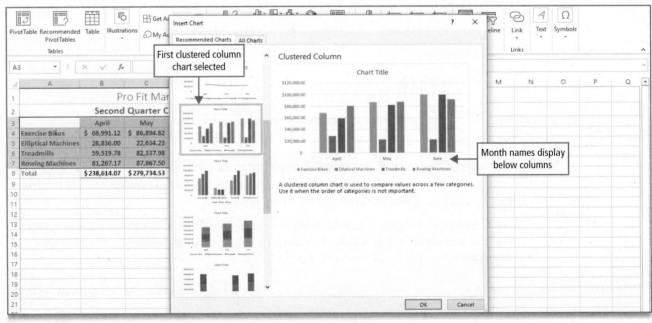

Figure 1.25

5 In the lower right corner of the **Insert Chart** dialog box, click **OK** to insert the selected chart into the worksheet. Compare your screen with Figure 1.26.

Your selected column chart displays in the worksheet, and the charted data is bordered by colored lines. Because the chart object is selected—surrounded by a border and displaying sizing handles—contextual tools named *Chart Tools* display and add contextual tabs next to the standard tabs on the ribbon.

MAC TIP   Click the chart to insert it.

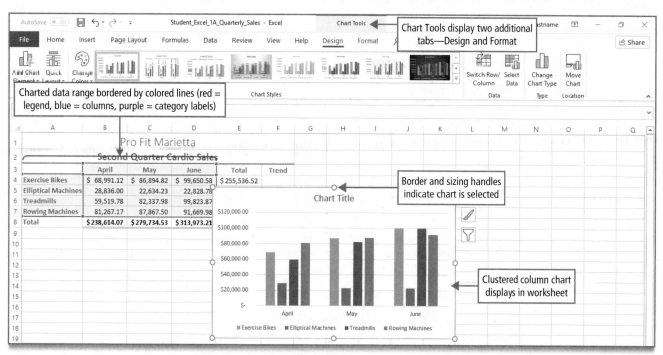

Figure 1.26

Activity 1.12 | Using the Chart Tools to Apply Chart Styles

MOS

5.2.3, 5.3.1

1 On the ribbon, locate the contextual tabs under **Chart Tools—Design** and **Format**.

When a chart is selected, Chart Tools become available and these two tabs provide commands for enhancing the design and format of the chart.

Based on the data you selected in your worksheet and the chart you selected in the Insert Chart dialog box, Excel constructs a column chart and adds *category labels*—the labels that display along the bottom of the chart to identify the category of data. This area is referred to as the *category axis* or the *x-axis*.

Depending on which arrangement of row and column data you select in the Insert Chart dialog box, Excel arranges either the row titles or the column titles as the category names. Here, based on your selection, the column titles that form the category labels are bordered in purple, indicating the cells that contain the category names.

On the left side of the chart, Excel includes a numerical scale on which the charted data is based; this is the *value axis* or the *y-axis*. Along the lower edge of the chart, a *legend*, which is a chart element that identifies the patterns or colors that are assigned to the categories in the chart, displays. Here, the row titles are bordered in red, indicating the cells containing the legend text.

2 To the right of the chart, notice the three buttons, and then point to each button to display its ScreenTip, as shown in Figure 1.27.

The ***Chart Elements button*** enables you to add, remove, or change chart elements such as the title, legend, gridlines, and data labels.

The ***Chart Styles button*** enables you to set a style and color scheme for your chart.

The ***Chart Filters button*** enables you to change which data displays in the chart—for example, to see only the data for *May* and *June* or only the data for *Treadmills* and *Rowing Machines*.

MAC TIP Chart buttons may not display; use menu commands instead.

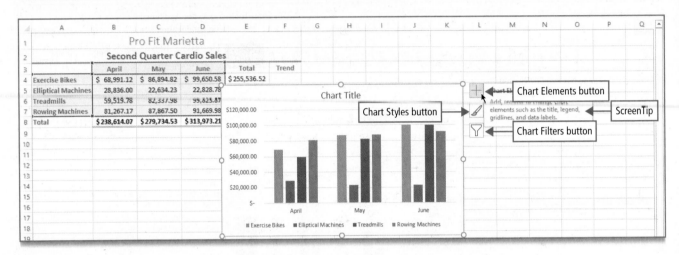

Figure 1.27

3 In the worksheet data, locate the group of cells bordered in blue.

Each of the twelve cells bordered in blue is referred to as a ***data point***—a value that originates in a worksheet cell. Each data point is represented in the chart by a ***data marker***—a column, bar, area, dot, pie slice, or other symbol in a chart that represents a single data point.

Related data points form a ***data series***; for example, there is a data series for *April*, for *May*, and for *June*. Each data series has a unique color or pattern represented in the chart legend.

4 On the **Design tab**, in the **Chart Layouts group**, click **Quick Layout**, and then compare your screen with Figure 1.28.

In the Quick Layout gallery, you can change the overall layout of the chart by selecting a predesigned ***chart layout***—a combination of chart elements, which can include a title, legend, labels for the columns, and the table of charted cells.

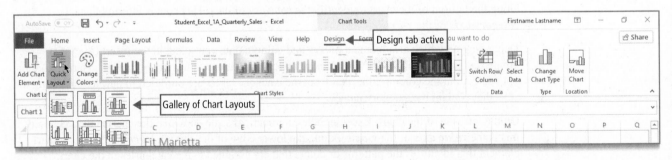

Figure 1.28

5 *Point* to several different layouts to see how Live Preview displays the effect on your chart, and then click the **Quick Layout** button again without changing the layout.

MAC TIP Live Preview may not display.

6 In the chart, click anywhere in the text *Chart Title* to select the title box, watch the **Formula Bar** as you begin to type **Second** and notice that AutoComplete fills in the subtitle for you. Press [Enter] at any point to insert the worksheet subtitle as the chart title.

MAC TIP If necessary, select *Chart Title* and type **Second Quarter Cardio Sales**

7 Click in a white area just slightly *inside* the chart border to deselect the chart title but keep the chart selected. To the right of the chart, click **Chart Styles** ✐, and then at the top of the **Chart Styles** gallery, be sure that **Style** is selected. Compare your screen with Figure 1.29.

The *Chart Styles gallery* displays an array of pre-defined *chart styles*—the overall visual look of the chart in terms of its colors, backgrounds, and graphic effects such as flat or shaded columns. You can also select Chart Styles from the Chart Styles group on the ribbon, but having the gallery closer to the chart makes it easier to use a touch gesture on a touch device to format a chart.

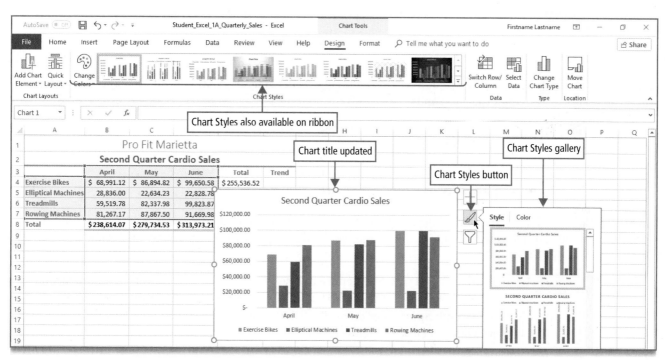

Figure 1.29

8 On the right side of the **Style** gallery, scroll down about halfway, and then by using the ScreenTips as your guide, locate and click **Style 6**.

This style uses a white background, formats the columns with theme colors, and applies a slight shadowed effect to the columns. With this clear visual representation of the data, the president can see the sales of all product categories in each month, and can see that sales of exercise bikes and treadmills have risen markedly during the quarter.

9 At the top of the gallery, click **Color**. Under **Colorful**, point to the third row of colors to display the ScreenTip, and then click to apply this variation of the theme colors.

MAC TIP Click Change Colors

10 Point to the top border of the chart to display the pointer, and then drag the upper left corner of the chart just inside the upper left corner of cell **A10**, approximately as shown in Figure 1.30.

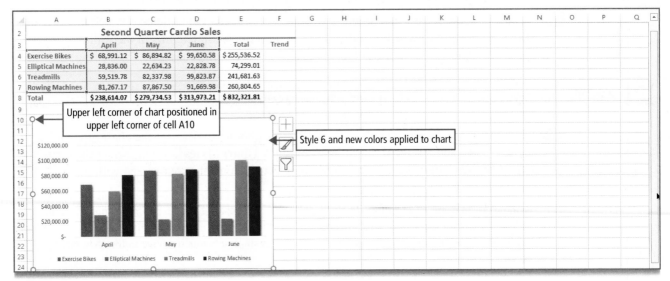

Figure 1.30

11 Click any cell to deselect the chart, and notice that the chart buttons no longer display to the right of the chart and the Chart Tools no longer display on the ribbon. Click **Save** .

Contextual tabs display on the ribbon when an object is selected and then are removed from view when the object is deselected.

Activity 1.13 | Creating and Formatting Sparklines

MOS
2.4.1

By creating sparklines, you provide a context for your numbers. Michelle and her colleagues at Pro Fit Marietta will be able to see the relationship between a sparkline and its underlying data quickly.

1 Select the range **B4:D7**, which represents the monthly sales figures for each product and for each month. Click the **Insert tab**, and then in the **Sparklines group**, click **Line**. In the displayed **Create Sparklines** dialog box, notice that the selected range *B4:D7* displays. Compare your screen with Figure 1.31.

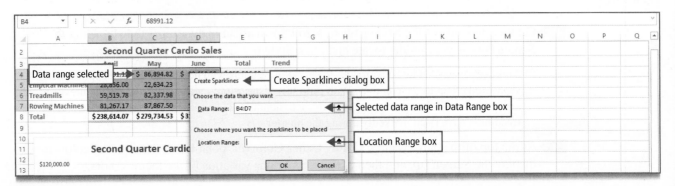

Figure 1.31

2 With the insertion point in the **Location Range** box, type **f4:f7** which is the range of cells where you want the sparklines to display.

 ANOTHER WAY   In the worksheet, select the range F4:F7 to insert it into the Location Range box.

3 Click **OK** to insert the sparklines in the range **F4:F7**, and then on the **Design tab**, in the **Show group**, click the **Markers** check box to select it.

Alongside each row of data, the sparkline provides a quick visual trend summary for sales of each cardio item over the three-month period. For example, you can see instantly that of the four items, only Elliptical Machines had declining sales for the period.

4 On the **Design tab**, in the **Style group**, click **More** ▾. In the first row, click the third style. Press Ctrl + Home to deselect the range and make cell **A1** the active range. Click **Save** 🖫, and then compare your screen with Figure 1.32.

Use markers, colors, and styles in this manner to further enhance your sparklines.

🖵 **MAC TIP**   Select the third style in the first row of the drop-down gallery, not from the row of styles that remain on the toolbar.

| A1 | ▾ : × ✓ fx | Pro Fit Marietta |

	A	B	C	D	E	F
1			Pro Fit Marietta			
2			Second Quarter Cardio Sales			
3		April	May	June	Total	Trend
4	Exercise Bikes	$ 68,991.12	$ 86,894.82	$ 99,650.58	$ 255,536.52	
5	Elliptical Machines	28,836.00	22,634.23	22,828.78	74,299.01	
6	Treadmills	59,519.78	82,337.98	99,823.87	241,681.63	
7	Rowing Machines	81,267.17	87,867.50	91,669.98	260,804.65	
8	Total	$238,614.07	$279,734.53	$313,973.21	$832,321.81	

Sparklines inserted and formatted

Figure 1.32

Objective 6   Print a Worksheet, Display Formulas, and Close Excel

GO! Learn How
Video E1-6

Use the Show Formulas command to display the formula in each cell instead of the resulting value. Use the commands on the Page Layout tab to prepare for printing.

Activity 1.14 │ Creating a Footer and Centering a Worksheet

1.3.1

For each Excel project in this textbook, you will create a footer containing the file name, which includes your name and the project name. You will also center the data horizontally on the page to create an attractive result if your worksheet is shared with others electronically or printed.

1 If necessary, click cell **A1** to deselect the chart. Click the **Page Layout tab**, and then in the **Page Setup group**, click **Margins**. At the bottom of the **Margins** gallery, click **Custom Margins** to display the **Page Setup** dialog box. Compare your screen with Figure 1.33.

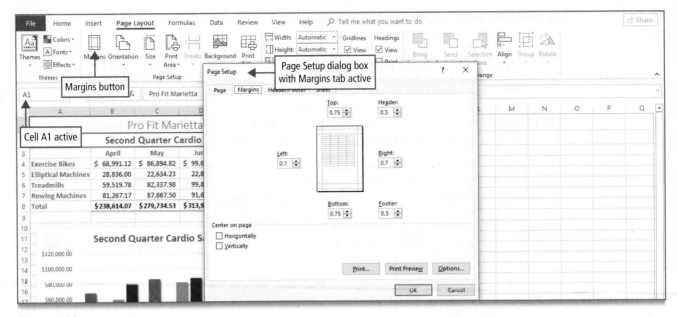

Figure 1.33

2 ▶ On the **Margins tab**, under **Center on page**, select the **Horizontally** check box.

This action will center the data and chart horizontally on the page, as shown in the Preview area.

3 ▶ Click the **Header/Footer tab**, and then in the center of the dialog box, click **Custom Footer**. In the **Footer** dialog box, with your insertion point blinking in the **Left section**, on the row of buttons, click **Insert File Name** 📄. Compare your screen with Figure 1.34.

&[File] displays in the Left section. Here you can type or insert information from the row of buttons into the left, middle, or right section of the footer. The Custom Header button displays a similar screen to enter information in the header of the worksheet.

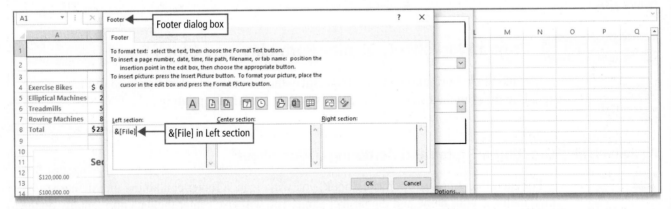

Figure 1.34

4 ▶ Click **OK** two times.

The vertical dotted line between columns indicates that as currently arranged, only the columns to the left of the dotted line will print on the first page. The exact position of the vertical line may depend on your default printer setting.

🔄 **ANOTHER WAY** Deselect the chart. On the Insert tab, in the Text group, click Header & Footer to display Page Layout view. Click in the left section of the displayed footer, and then in the Header & Footer Elements group, click File Name. Click any cell in the workbook to deselect the footer area, and then on the status bar, click the Normal button to return to Normal view.

Activity 1.15 | Adding Document Properties and Printing a Workbook

Michelle likes to add tags and other identifying properties to all company documents so they are easily searchable. In this Activity, you will add searchable document properties to the workbook.

1 In the upper left corner of your screen, click the **File tab** to display **Backstage** view. If necessary, on the left, click the **Info tab**. In the lower right corner, click **Show All Properties**.

> **MAC TIP** Click File, at the bottom of the menu, click Properties, click the Summary tab; for Tags use Keywords.

2 As the **Tags**, type **cardio sales** In the **Subject** box, type your course name and section number. Be sure your name displays in the **Author** box and edit if necessary.

3 On the left, click **Print** to view the **Print Preview**. Compare your screen with Figure 1.35.

> **MAC TIP** Click OK to close Properties dialog box first. Click File, then click Print.

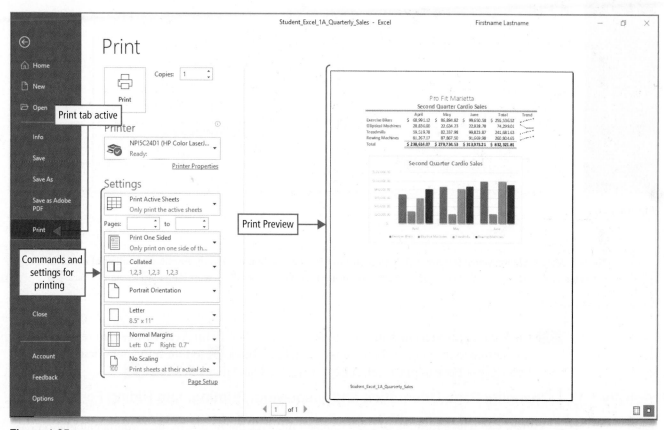

Figure 1.35

4 Note any adjustments that need to be made, and then on the left, click **Save** to save and return to the workbook.

> **MAC TIP** Click Close to close the Print dialog box, then Save your workbook.

Activity 1.16 | Printing a Section of the Worksheet

MOS
1.5.1, 1.5.3

From Backstage view, you can print only the portion of the worksheet that you select, and there are times you might want to do this. For example, sometimes Michelle wants to see data for only one or two types of equipment when she is evaluating various brands of equipment.

1 Select the range **A2:F5** to select only the subtitle and the data for *Exercise Bikes* and *Elliptical Machines* and the column titles.

2 Click the **File tab**, on the left, click **Print** to display **Print Preview**, and then under **Settings**, click the first arrow, which currently displays *Print Active Sheets*. On the list that displays, click **Print Selection**, and then compare your screen with Figure 1.36.

MAC TIP On the File menu, point to Print Area, and then click Set Print Area. When finished, go back to Print Area and click Clear Print Area.

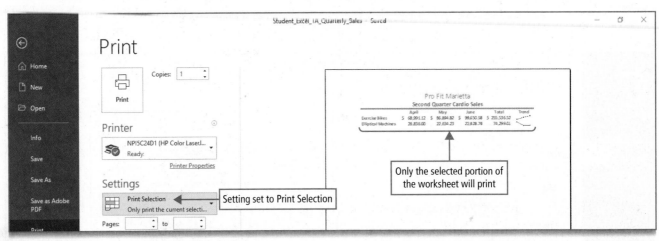

Figure 1.36

For Non-MyLab Submissions: Determine if Your Instructor Requires a Submission for Printing a Section of a Worksheet
If directed by your instructor, print the selection on paper or create an electronic image. Then press [Ctrl] + [Home] and click Save [💾].

3 Click the **Print Selection arrow** again, and then click **Print Active Sheets** to return this setting to the default. In the upper left, click **Back** [←] to return to your document. Press [Ctrl] + [Home] to make cell **A1** the active cell, and then click **Save** [💾].

Activity 1.17 | Changing Page Orientation and Displaying, Printing, and Hiding Formulas

MOS
1.3.1, 1.3.2,
1.4.6, 1.5.3

When you type a formula in a cell, the cell displays the *results* of the formula calculation. Recall that this value is called the displayed value. You can view and print the underlying formulas in the cells. When you do so, a formula often takes more horizontal space to display than the result of the calculation.

1 If necessary, redisplay your worksheet. Because you will make some temporary changes to your workbook, on the Quick Access Toolbar, click **Save** [💾] to be sure your work is saved up to this point.

2 On the **Formulas tab**, in the **Formula Auditing group**, click **Show Formulas**.

ANOTHER WAY Hold down [Ctrl], and then press [~] (usually located below [Esc]).

3 In the **column heading area**, point to the **column A** heading to display the ⬇ pointer, hold down the left mouse button, and then drag to the right to select columns **A:F**. Compare your screen with Figure 1.37.

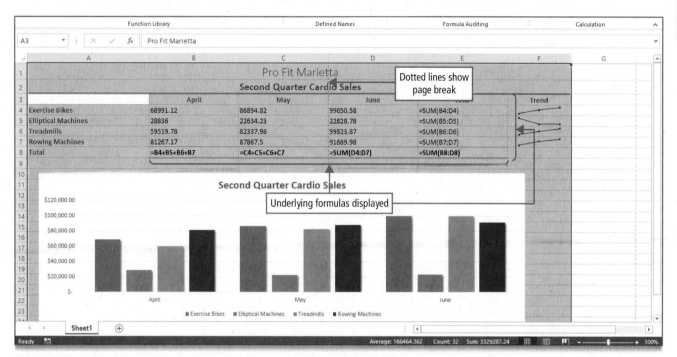

Figure 1.37

NOTE **Turning the Display of Formulas On and Off**

The Show Formulas button is a toggle button. Clicking it once turns the display of formulas on—the button will be shaded. Clicking the button again turns the display of formulas off.

---

4 Point to the column heading boundary between any two of the selected columns to display the ➕ pointer, and then double-click to AutoFit the selected columns.

AutoFit adjusts the width of a column to fit the cell content of the *widest* cell in the column.

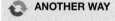 **ANOTHER WAY** With the columns selected, on the Home tab, in the Cells group, click Format, and then click AutoFit Column Width.

---

5 On the **Page Layout tab**, in the **Page Setup group**, click **Orientation**, and then click **Landscape**. In the **Scale to Fit** group, click the **Width arrow**, and then click **1 page** to scale the data to fit onto one page.

Scaling shrinks the width or height of the printed worksheet to fit a maximum number of pages and is convenient for printing formulas. Although it is not always the case, formulas frequently take up more space than the actual data.

ANOTHER WAY In the Scale to Fit group, click the Dialog Box Launcher button to display the Page tab of the Page Setup dialog box. Then, under Scaling, click the Fit to option button.

---

6 In the **Page Setup group**, click **Margins**, click **Custom Margins**, and then on the **Margins tab**, under **Center on page**, be sure the **Horizontally** check box is selected—select it if necessary.

7 ▸ Click **OK** to close the dialog box. Click cell **A1**. Check to be sure your chart is centered below the data and the left and right edges are slightly inside column A and column F—use the pointer to drag a chart edge and then deselect the chart if necessary.

8 ▸ Click the **File tab**, and then on the left click **Print** to display the **Print Preview**. Under **Settings**, if necessary, switch back to the option to **Print Active Sheets**.

9 ▸ On the left, click **Close**, and when prompted, click **Don't Save** so that you do *not* save the changes you made—displaying formulas, changing column widths and orientation, and scaling—to print your formulas.

10 ▸ In the upper right corner of your screen, click **Close** ☒ to close Excel.

For Non-MyLab Submissions: Determine What Your Instructor Requires for Submission

As directed by your instructor, submit your completed Excel workbook.

---

11 ▸ In **MyLab IT**, locate and click the Grader Project **Excel 1A Quarterly Sales**. In **step 3**, under **Upload Completed Assignment**, click **Choose File**. In the **Open** dialog box, navigate to your **Excel Chapter 1 folder**, and then click your **Student_Excel_1A_Quarterly_Sales** file one time to select it. In the lower right corner of the **Open** dialog box, click **Open**.

The name of your selected file displays above the Upload button.

12 ▸ To submit your file to **MyLab IT** for grading, click **Upload**, wait a moment for a green **Success!** message, and then in **step 4**, click the blue **Submit for Grading** button. Click **Close Assignment** to return to your list of **Course Materials**.

You have completed Project 1A ▪ END

Objective	Create a Sales Report with an Embedded Column Chart Using Google Sheets

ALERT   Working with Web-Based Applications and Service

Computer programs and services on the web receive continuous updates and improvements, so the steps to complete this web-based Activity may differ from the ones shown. You can often look at the screens and the information presented to determine how to complete the Activity.

   If you do not already have a Google account, you will need to create one before you begin this Activity. Go to **http://google.com** and in the upper right corner, click Sign In. On the Sign In screen, click Create Account. On the Create your Google Account page, complete the form, read and agree to the Terms of Service and Privacy Policy, and then click Next step. On the Welcome screen, click Get Started.

Activity | Creating a Sales Report with an Embedded Column Chart Using Google Sheets

In this Activity, you will use Google Sheets to create a sales report and chart similar to the one you created in Project 1A.

1 From the desktop, open your browser (use a browser other than Edge), navigate to **https://www.google.com**, and then click the **Google apps** menu ⊞. Click **Drive**, and then if necessary, sign in to your Google account.

2 Open your **GO! Web Projects** folder—or click New to create and then open this folder if necessary.

3 In the upper left corner, click **New**, and then click **Google Sheets**. From your Windows taskbar, open **File Explorer**, navigate to the files you downloaded for this chapter, and then in the **File List**, double-click to open **e01A_Web**.

4 In the displayed Excel worksheet, select the range **A1:E8**, right-click over the selection, click **Copy**, and then **Close** Excel. **Close** the **File Explorer** window.

5 In your blank Google Sheet, with cell **A1** active, point to cell **A1**, right-click, and then click **Paste**; by copying and pasting the data, you can create this Project faster without having to do extra typing. In the column heading area, point to the border between **column A** and **column B** to display the ⟷ pointer, and then widen **column A** slightly so that all of the data displays.

6 Select the range **A1:E1**. On the toolbar, click **Merge cells** ⊞. On the toolbar, click the **Horizontal Align button arrow** ☰ and then click **Center** ☰. Repeat for the range **A2:E2**, and then apply **Bold** Ⓑ to cells **A1** and **A2**.

7 Select the range with the month names, center them, and apply **Bold** Ⓑ. Apply **Bold** Ⓑ to the totals in the range **B8:E8**.

8 Select the range **A3:D7**—the data without the totals and without the titles. On the menu bar, click **Insert**, and then click **Chart**. On the right, in the **Chart editor** pane, be sure the **DATA tab** is active.

9 In the Chart editor pane, scroll down as necessary, and then select the **Switch rows/columns** check box.

10 At the top of the **Chart editor** pane, click the **CUSTOMIZE tab**. Click the **Chart & axis titles arrow**, and then click in the **Chart title** box. Type **Second Quarter Cardio Sales**

11 Click the **Legend arrow**, click the **Position arrow**, and then click **None**. Click the **Chart style arrow**, click the **Background color arrow**, and then in the fourth column, click the third color—**light yellow 3**.

12 Point anywhere inside the selected chart, hold down the left mouse button and begin to drag to display the ⟳ pointer, and then drag the chart slightly below the data. Then using the corner sizing handles, resize and reposition the chart so that it is the width of columns **A:E** and displays below the data.

13 At the top of the worksheet window, click the text *Untitled spreadsheet*, and then using your own name, type **Lastname_Firstname_EX_1A_Web** and press ⏎.

»» **GO!** With Google continues on next page

14 If you are instructed to submit your file to your instructor, you can either share the file through Google Drive, or create a PDF or Excel file. Ask your instructor in what format he or she would like to receive your file.

15 **Close** ☒ the browser tab—a new Google Sheet always opens in a new window in your browser; your work is automatically saved. Notice that your new Google Sheet displays in the file list on your Google Drive. Sign out of your Google account.

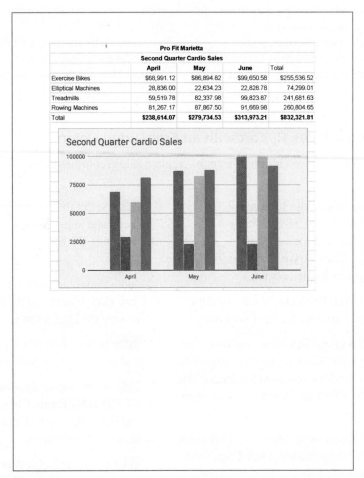

Figure A

Inventory Valuation

Project Activities

In Activities 1.18 through 1.27 you will create a workbook for Josh Feingold, Operations Manager, which calculates the retail value of an inventory of plyometric training products. Your completed worksheet will look similar to Figure 1.38.

Project Files for MyLab IT Grader

1. In your MyLab IT course, locate and click **Excel 1B Plyo Products**, Download Materials, and then Download All Files.
2. Extract the zipped folder to your Excel Chapter 1 folder. Close the Grader download screens.
3. Take a moment to open the downloaded **Excel_1B_Plyo_Products_Instructions**; note any recent updates to the book.

Project Results

GO! Project 1B
Where We're Going

Pro Fit Marietta
Plyometric Products Inventory Valuation

	Warehouse Location	Quantity in Stock	Retail Price	Total Retail Value	Percent of Total Retail Value
As of September 30					
Power Hurdle	Atlanta	125	$ 32.95	$ 4,118.75	1.41%
Speed Hurdle	Atlanta	995	59.95	59,650.25	20.37%
Stackable Steps	Marietta	450	251.59	113,215.50	38.65%
Pro Jump Rope	Marietta	1,105	49.95	55,194.75	18.84%
Plyometric Box Set	Marietta	255	158.05	40,302.75	13.76%
Plyometric Mat	Atlanta	215	94.99	20,422.85	6.97%
Total Retail Value for All Products				$ 292,904.85	

Student_Excel_1B_Plyo_Products

Figure 1.38 Project 1B Plyo Products

For Non-MyLab Submissions

For Project 1B, you will need:
New blank Excel workbook

In your **Excel Chapter 1** folder, save your workbook as:
Lastname_Firstname_1B_Plyo_Products
If your instructor requires a workbook with formulas, save as:
Lastname_Firstname_1B_Plyo_Products_formulas

After you have named and saved your workbook, on the next page begins with step 2.

ALERT Because Office 365 is a cloud-based subscription service that receives continuous updates, you may encounter some variations in what appears on your screen and what is shown in this instruction. Microsoft Office 365 is fully installed on your PC or Mac; no internet access is necessary to create or edit documents. When you *are* connected to the internet, you will receive monthly upgrades and new features, so you always have the latest versions of Office apps as soon as they are available. Your subscription gives you continuous free access to the latest innovations and refinements.

GO! Learn How
Video E1-7

In Excel, the spelling checker performs similarly to the way it behaves in other Microsoft Office programs.

Activity 1.18 │ Checking Spelling in a Worksheet

2.2.7

1 Navigate to your **Excel Chapter 1 folder**, and then double-click the Excel file you downloaded from **MyLab IT** that displays your name—**Student_Excel_1B_Plyo_ Products**. In your blank workbook, if necessary, at the top click **Enable Editing**.

2 In cell **A1**, type **Pro Fit Marietta** and press Enter. In cell **A2**, type **Plyometric Products Inventory** and press Enter.

MAC TIP To display group names on the ribbon, display the menu, click Excel, click Preferences, click View, under In Ribbon, select the Group Titles check box.

3 Press Tab to move to cell **B3**, type **Quantity** and press Tab. In cell **C3**, type **Average Cost** and press Tab. In cell **D3**, type **Retail Price** and press Tab.

4 Click cell **C3**, and then look at the **Formula Bar**. Notice that in the cell, the displayed value is cut off; however, in the **Formula Bar**, the entire text value—the underlying value—displays. Compare your screen with Figure 1.39.

Text that is too long to fit in a cell extends into cells on the right only if they are empty. If the cell to the right contains data, the text in the cell to the left is truncated—cut off. The entire value continues to exist, but it is not completely visible.

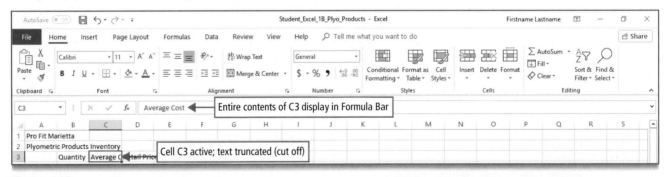

Figure 1.39

5 Click cell **E3**, type **Total Retail Value** and press Tab. In cell **F3**, type **Percent of Total Retail Value** and press Enter.

6 Click cell **A4**. *Without* correcting the spelling error, type **Powr Hurdle** Press Enter. In the range **A5:A10**, type the remaining row titles shown below. Then compare your screen with Figure 1.40.

> **Speed Hurdle**
>
> **Stackable Steps**
>
> **Pro Jump Rope**
>
> **Plyometric Box Set**
>
> **Plyometric Mat**
>
> **Total Retail Value for All Products**

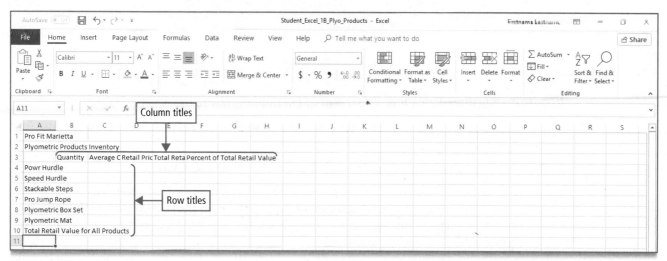

Figure 1.40

7 In the **column heading area**, point to the right boundary of **column A** to display the ⊞ pointer, and then drag to the right to widen **column A** to **215** pixels.

MAC TIP   Change the width to 30 (185 pixels).

8 Select the range **A1:F1**, **Merge & Center** the text, and then from the **Cell Styles** gallery, apply the **Title** style.

9 Select the range **A2:F2**, **Merge & Center** the text, and then from the **Cell Styles** gallery, apply the **Heading 1** style. Press Ctrl + Home to move to cell **A1** at the top of your worksheet.

MAC TIP   Press control + E + ← to move to cell A1.

10 With cell **A1** as the active cell, click the **Review tab**, and then in the **Proofing group**, click **Spelling**. Compare your screen with Figure 1.41.

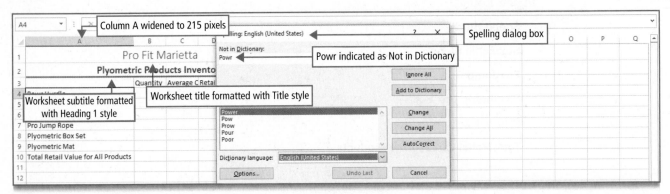

Figure 1.41

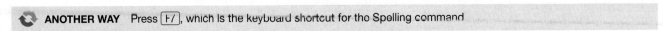

ANOTHER WAY Press F7, which is the keyboard shortcut for the Spelling command

11 In the **Spelling** dialog box, under **Not in Dictionary**, notice the word *Powr*.

The spelling tool does not have this word in its dictionary. Under *Suggestions*, Excel provides a list of suggested spellings.

12 Under **Suggestions**, if necessary click **Power**, and then click **Change**.

Powr, a typing error, is changed to *Power*. A message box displays *Spell check complete. You're good to go!*—unless you have additional unrecognized words. Because the spelling check begins its checking process starting with the currently selected cell, it is good practice to return to cell A1 before starting the Spelling command.

13 Correct any other errors you may have made. When the message displays, *Spell check complete. You're good to go!*, click **OK**. **Save** 💾 your workbook.

| **Objective 8** | **Enter Data by Range** |

GO! Learn How
Video E1-8

You can enter data by first selecting a range of cells. This is a time-saving technique, especially if you use a numeric keypad to enter the numbers.

Activity 1.19 | Entering Data by Range

1 Select the range **B4:D9**, type **125** and then press Enter.

The value displays in cell B4, and cell B5 becomes the active cell.

2 With cell **B5** active in the range, and pressing Enter after each entry, type the following, and then compare your screen with Figure 1.42:

1125

450

1105

255

215

After you enter the last value and press Enter, the active cell moves to the top of the next column within the selected range. Although it is not required to enter data in this manner, you can see that selecting the range before you enter data saves time because it confines the movement of the active cell to the selected range. When you select a range of data, the Quick Analysis button displays. (Mac users: you may not see the Quick Analysis button.)

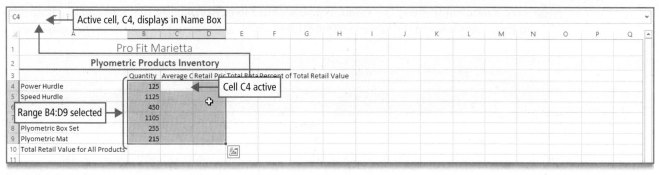

Figure 1.42

> **3** With the selected range still active, from the following table, beginning in cell **C4** and pressing Enter after each entry, enter the data for the **Average Cost** column and then the **Retail Price** column. If you prefer, deselect the range to enter the values—typing in a selected range is optional.

Average Cost	Retail Price
15.50	32.95
29.55	59.95
125.95	251.59
18.75	49.95
85.25	159.05
49.95	94.99

> Recall that the default number format for cells is the *General* number format, in which numbers display exactly as you type them and trailing zeros do not display, even if you type them.

> **4** Click any blank cell, and then compare your screen with Figure 1.43. Correct any errors you may have made while entering data, and then click **Save** .

Figure 1.43

Objective 9 | Construct Formulas for Mathematical Operations

GO! Learn How
Video E1-9

Operators are symbols with which you can specify the type of calculation you want to perform in a formula.

Activity 1.20 | Using Arithmetic Operators

> **1** Click cell **E4**, type **=b4*d4** and notice that the two cells are outlined as part of an active formula. Then, press Enter.

> The *Total Retail Value* of all *Power Hurdle* items in inventory—*4118.75*—equals the *Quantity* (125) times the *Retail Price* (selling price) of 32.95. In Excel, the asterisk (*) indicates multiplication.

2 Take a moment to study the symbols you will use to perform basic mathematical operations in Excel as shown in the table in Figure 1.44, which are referred to as *arithmetic operators*.

Symbols Used in Excel for Arithmetic Operators	
Operator Symbol	**Operation**
+	Addition
-	Subtraction (also negation)
*	Multiplication
/	Division
%	Percent
^	Exponentiation

Figure 1.44

3 Click cell **E4**.

You can see that in cells E5:E9 you need a formula similar to the one in E4, but one that refers to the cells in row 5, row 6, and so on. Recall that you can copy formulas and the cell references will change *relative to* the row number.

4 With cell **E4** selected, position your pointer over the fill handle in the lower right corner of the cell until the + pointer displays. Then, drag down through cell **E9** to copy the formula.

5 Select the range **B4:B9**, and then on the **Home tab**, in the **Number group**, click **Comma Style** . In the **Number group**, click **Decrease Decimal** two times to remove the decimal places from these values.

Comma Style formats a number with two decimal places; because these are whole numbers referring to quantities, no decimal places are necessary.

> **ANOTHER WAY** Select the range, display the Cell Styles gallery, and then under Number Format, click Comma [0].

6 Select the range **E4:E9**, and then at the bottom of your screen, in the status bar, notice the displayed values for **Average**, **Count**, and **Sum**—*50158.89167, 6,* and *300953.35*.

When you select a range of numerical data, Excel's *AutoCalculate* feature displays three calculations in the status bar by default—Average, Count, and Sum. Here, Excel indicates that if you averaged the selected values, the result would be *50158.89167*, there are *6* cells in the selection that contain values, and that if you added the values the result would be *300953.35*.

You can display three additional calculations to this area by right-clicking the status bar and selecting them—Numerical Count, Minimum, and Maximum.

Activity 1.21 | Using the Quick Analysis Tool

2.2.5, 2.2.7

Recall that the Quick Analysis button displays when you select a range of data. Quick Analysis is convenient because it keeps common commands close to your mouse pointer and also displays commands in a format that is easy to touch with your finger if you are using a touchscreen device.

1 With the range **E4:E9** selected, in the lower right corner of the selected range, click **Quick Analysis**. In the displayed gallery, click **Totals**. *Point to*, but do not click, the first **Sum** button, which shows blue cells at the bottom. Compare your screen with Figure 1.45.

Here, the shaded cells on the button indicate what will be summed and where the result will display, and a preview of the result displays in the cell bordered with a gray shadow.

> **MAC TIP** Quick Analysis is not available, use AutoSum.

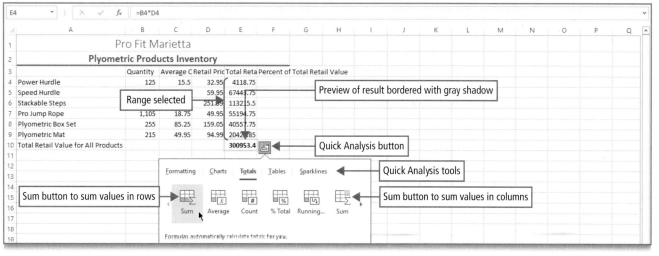

Figure 1.45

> **2** Click the first **Sum** button to display the column total *300953.4* formatted in Bold.
>
> Sums calculated using the Quick Analysis tool are formatted in Bold.

⌨ **MAC TIP**   Select the range E4:E9, and then on the Home tab, click AutoSum. In the Font group, click Bold.

> **3** Select the range **C5:E9** and apply the **Comma Style** ⟨ , ⟩; notice that Excel widens the columns to accommodate the data.
>
> **4** Select the range **C4:E4**, hold down ⟨Ctrl⟩, and then click cell **E10**. Release ⟨Ctrl⟩, and then apply the **Accounting Number Format** ⟨$ ▾⟩. Notice that Excel widens the columns as necessary.
>
> **5** Click cell **E10**, and then from the **Cell Styles** gallery, apply the **Total** style. Click any blank cell, **Save** 💾 your workbook, and then compare your screen with Figure 1.46.

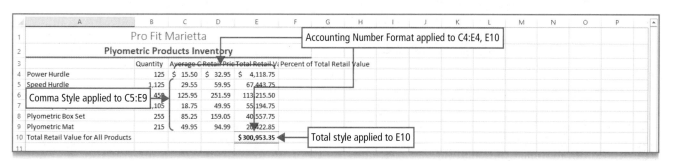

Figure 1.46

Activity 1.22 | Copying Formulas Containing Absolute Cell References

4.1.1

In a formula, a relative cell reference refers to a cell by its position *relative to* the cell that contains the formula. An ***absolute cell reference***, on the other hand, refers to a cell by its *fixed* position in the worksheet, for example, the total in cell E10.

A relative cell reference automatically adjusts when a formula is copied. In some calculations, you do *not* want the cell reference to adjust; rather, you want the cell reference to remain the same when the formula is copied.

1 Click cell **F4**, type = and then click cell **E4**. Type / and then click cell **E10**.

The formula *=E4/E10* indicates that the value in cell E4 will be *divided* by the value in cell E10 because Mr. Feingold wants to know the percentage by which each product's Total Retail Value makes up the Total Retail Value for All Products.

Arithmetically, the percentage is computed by dividing the *Total Retail Value* for each product by the *Total Retail Value for All Products*. The result will be a percentage expressed as a decimal.

2 Press Enter. Click cell **F4** and notice that the formula displays in the **Formula Bar**. Then, point to cell F4 and double-click.

The formula, with the two referenced cells displayed in color and bordered with the same color, displays in the cell. This feature, called the ***range finder***, is useful for verifying formulas because it visually indicates which workbook cells are included in a formula calculation.

3 Press Enter to redisplay the result of the calculation in the cell, and notice that .013686, which is approximately 1% of the total retail value of the inventory, is made up of Power Hurdles.

4 Click cell **F4** again, and then drag the fill handle down through cell **F9**. Compare your screen with Figure 1.47.

Each cell displays an error message—*#DIV/0!* and a green triangle in the upper left corner of each cell indicates that Excel detects an error.

Like a grammar checker, Excel uses rules to check for formula errors and flags errors in this manner. Additionally, the Auto Fill Options button displays, from which you can select formatting options for the copied cells.

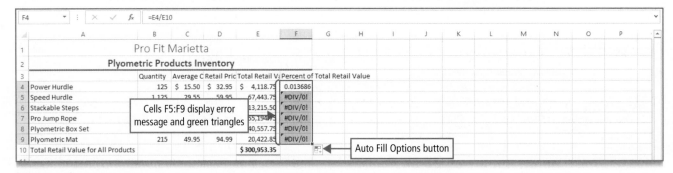

Figure 1.47

5 Click cell **F5**, and then to the left of the cell, point to the **Error Checking** button ▣ to display its ScreenTip—*The formula or function used is dividing by zero or empty cells.*

In this manner, Excel suggests the cause of an error.

MAC TIP On the Formulas tab, click Error Checking.

6 Look at the **Formula Bar** and examine the formula.

The formula is =E5/E11. The cell reference to E5 is correct, but the cell reference following the division operator (/) is *E11*, and E11 is an *empty* cell.

7 Click cell **F6**, point to the **Error Checking** button, and in the **Formula Bar**, examine the formula.

Because the cell references are relative, Excel builds the formulas by increasing the row number for each equation. But in this calculation, the divisor must always be the value in cell E10—the *Total Retail Value for All Products*.

8 Point to cell **F4**, and then double-click to place the insertion point within the cell.

9 Within the cell, use the arrow keys as necessary to position the insertion point to the left of *E10*, and then press F4. Compare your screen with Figure 1.48.

Dollar signs ($) display, which changes the reference to cell E10 to an absolute cell reference. The use of the dollar sign to denote an absolute reference is not related in any way to whether or not the values you are working with are currency values. It is simply the symbol that Excel uses to denote an absolute cell reference.

MAC TIP Press command ⌘ + T to make a cell reference in a formula absolute.

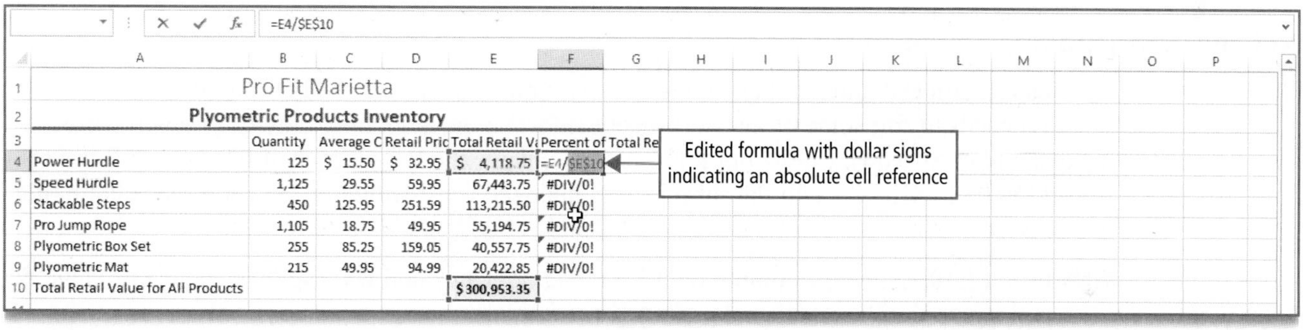

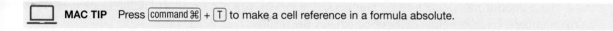

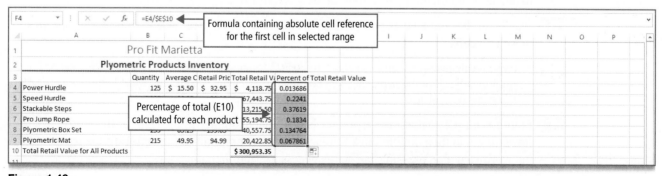

Figure 1.48

ANOTHER WAY Edit the formula so that it indicates =E4/$E$10.

---

10 On the **Formula Bar**, click **Enter** so that **F4** remains the active cell. Then, drag the fill handle to copy the new formula down through cell **F9**. Compare your screen with Figure 1.49.

Figure 1.49

11 ▶ Click cell **F5**, examine the formula in the **Formula Bar**, and then examine the formulas for cells **F6**, **F7**, **F8**, and **F9**.

For each formula, the cell reference for the *Total Retail Value* of each product changed relative to its row; however, the value used as the divisor—*Total Retail Value for All Products* in cell E10—remained absolute. You can see that by using either relative or absolute cell references, it is easy to duplicate formulas without typing them.

12 ▶ **Save** 🖫 your workbook.

MORE KNOWLEDGE **Calculate a Percentage if You Know the Total and the Amount**

Using the equation *amount/total = percentage*, you can calculate the percentage by which a part makes up a total—with the percentage formatted as a decimal. For example, if on a test you score 42 points correctly out of 50, your percentage of correct answers is 42/50 = 0.84 or 84%.

Objective 10 Edit Values in a Worksheet

GO! Learn How
Video E1-10

Excel performs calculations on numbers; that is why you use Excel. If you make changes to the numbers, Excel automatically *re*-calculates the results. This is one of the most powerful and valuable features of Excel.

Activity 1.23 │ Editing Values in a Worksheet

You can edit text and number values directly within a cell or in the Formula Bar.

Josh needs to edit some of the worksheet's information, so in this Activity, you will correct the quantity of Speed Hurdles from 1,125 to 995, change the Retail Price of Plyometric Box Sets from $159.05 to $158.05, edit the subtitle to include the word *Valuation*, and edit the column title in cell B3.

1 ▶ In cell **E10**, notice the column total *$300,953.35*. Click cell **B5**, and then change its value by typing **995** Watch cell **E5** and press Enter.

Excel formulas *re-calculate* if you change the value in a cell that is referenced in a formula. It is not necessary to delete the old value in a cell; selecting the cell and typing a new value replaces the old value with your new typing.

The *Total Retail Value* of all *Speed Hurdle* items recalculates to *59,650.25* and the total in cell E10 recalculates to *$293,159.85*. Additionally, all of the percentages in column F recalculate.

2 ▶ Point to cell **D8**, and then double-click to place the insertion point within the cell. Use the arrow keys to move the insertion point to the left or right of *9*, and use either Del or Backspace to delete *9* and then type **8** so that the new Retail Price is *158.05*.

3 ▶ Watch cell **E8** and **E10** as you press Enter, and then notice the recalculation of the formulas in those two cells.

Excel recalculates the value in cell E8 to *40,302.75* and the value in cell E10 to *$292,904.85*. Additionally, all of the percentages in column F recalculate because the *Total Retail Value for All Products* recalculated.

4 ▶ Point to cell **A2** so that the ⊕ pointer is positioned slightly to the right of the word *Inventory*, and then double-click to place the insertion point in the cell. Edit the text to add the word **Valuation** pressing Spacebar as necessary, and then press Enter.

5 Click cell **B3**, and then in the **Formula Bar**, click to place the insertion point after the letter *y*. Press Spacebar one time, type **in Stock** and then on the **Formula Bar**, click **Enter** ☑. Click **Save** 🖫, and then compare your screen with Figure 1.50.

> Recall that if text is too long to fit in the cell and the cell to the right contains data, the text is truncated—cut off—but the entire value still exists as the underlying value.

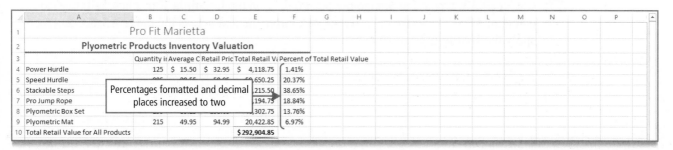

| B3 | fx | Quantity in Stock | ← *in Stock* added to column title |

	A	B	C	D	E	F	G	H	I	J	K	L	M	N	O	P
1		Pro Fit Marietta														
2	Plyometric Products Inventory Valuation ←				*Valuation* added to subtitle										
3		Quantity i	Average C	Retail Pric	Total Retail Va	Percent of Total Retail Value										
4	Power Hurdle	125	$ 15.50	$ 32.95	$ 4,118.75	0.014062										
5	Speed Hurdle	995 ←	29.5	New value in cell B5		0.203651										
6	Stackable Steps	430	125.9	251.55	115,215.50	0.386527										
7	Pro Jump Rope	1,105	18.75	49.95	55,194.75	0.188439										
8	Plyometric Box Set	255	85.25	158.05	40,3	New value in cell D8										
9	Plyometric Mat	215	49.95	94.99	20,422.85	0.069723										
10	Total Retail Value for All Products				$ 292,904.85											

Figure 1.50

Activity 1.24 | Formatting Cells with the Percent Style

MOS
2.2.2

A percentage is part of a whole expressed in hundredths. For example, 75 cents is the same as 75 percent of one dollar. The Percent Style button formats the selected cell as a percentage rounded to the nearest hundredth. In this Activity, you will format the percentage values in column F with the Percent Style.

1 Click cell **F4**, and then in the **Number group**, click **Percent Style** %.

> Your result is 1%, which is *0.014062* rounded to the nearest hundredth and expressed as a percentage. Percent Style displays the value of a cell as a percentage.

2 Select the range **F4:F9**. On the **Home tab**, in the **Number group**, click **Percent Style** %, and then click **Increase Decimal** ⬅.0.00 two times. Then in the **Alignment group**, click **Center** ☰.

MAC TIP   Use commands on the Home tab.

> Percent Style may not offer a percentage precise enough to analyze important financial information—adding additional decimal places to a percentage makes data more precise.

↻ **ANOTHER WAY**   Right-click over the selected range, and then click the commands on the mini toolbar.

3 Click any cell to cancel the selection, **Save** 🖫 your workbook, and then compare your screen with Figure 1.51.

	A	B	C	D	E	F	G	H	I	J	K	L	M	N	O	P
1		Pro Fit Marietta														
2	Plyometric Products Inventory Valuation															
3		Quantity i	Average C	Retail Pric	Total Retail Va	Percent of Total Retail Value										
4	Power Hurdle	125	$ 15.50	$ 32.95	$ 4,118.75	1.41%										
5	Speed Hurdle				650.25	20.37%										
6	Stackable Steps		Percentages formatted and decimal		215.50	38.65%										
7	Pro Jump Rope		places increased to two		194.75	18.84%										
8	Plyometric Box Set				302.75	13.76%										
9	Plyometric Mat	215	49.95	94.99	20,422.85	6.97%										
10	Total Retail Value for All Products				$ 292,904.85											

Figure 1.51

GO! Learn How
Video E1-11

Formatting refers to the process of specifying the appearance of cells and the overall layout of your worksheet. Formatting is accomplished through various commands on the ribbon, for example, applying Cell Styles, and also from commands on shortcut menus, using keyboard shortcuts, and in the Format Cells dialog box.

Activity 1.25 | Inserting and Deleting Rows and Columns

MOS
2.1.3

In the next Activities, you will format the worksheet attractively so that Josh and his staff can view the information easily.

1 In the **row heading area** on the left side of your screen, point to the row heading for **row 3** to display the → pointer, and then right-click to simultaneously select the row and display a shortcut menu.

2 On the shortcut menu, click **Insert** to insert a new **row 3** above the selected row.

The rows below the new row 3 move down one row, and the Insert Options button displays. By default, the new row uses the formatting of the row *above*.

ANOTHER WAY Select the row, on the Home tab, in the Cells group, click the Insert button arrow, and then click Insert Sheet Rows. Or, select the row and click the Insert button—the default setting of the button inserts a new sheet row above the selected row.

3 Click cell **E11**. On the **Formula Bar**, notice that the range changed to sum the new range **E5:E10**. Compare your screen with Figure 1.52.

If you move formulas by inserting additional rows or columns in your worksheet, Excel automatically adjusts the formulas. Here, Excel adjusted all of the formulas in the worksheet that were affected by inserting this new row.

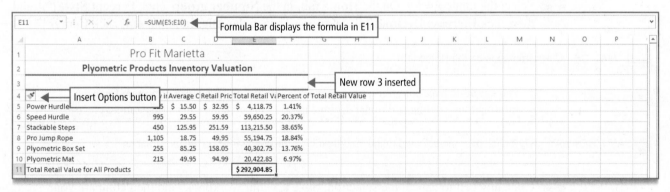

Figure 1.52

4 Click cell **A3**, type **As of September 30** and then on the **Formula Bar**, click **Enter** ✓ to maintain **A3** as the active cell. **Merge & Center** the text across the range **A3:F3**, and then apply the **Heading 2** cell style.

5 In the **column heading area**, point to **column B** to display the ⬇ pointer, right-click, and then click **Insert**.

A column is inserted to the left of column B. By default, the new column uses the formatting of the column to the *left*.

🔄 **ANOTHER WAY** Select the column, on the Home tab, in the Cells group, click the Insert button arrow, and then click Insert Sheet Columns. Or, select the column and click the Insert button—the default setting of the button inserts a new sheet column to the right of the selected column.

6 Click cell **B4**, type **Warehouse Location** and then press Enter.

7 In cell **B5**, type **Atlanta** and then type **Atlanta** again in cells **B6** and **B10**. Use AutoComplete to speed your typing by pressing Enter as soon as the AutoComplete suggestion displays. In cells **B7**, **B8**, and **B9**, type **Marietta**

8 In the **column heading area**, point to **column D**, right-click, and then click **Delete**.

The remaining columns shift to the left, and Excel adjusts all the formulas in the worksheet accordingly. You can use a similar technique to delete a row in a worksheet.

9 Compare your screen with Figure 1.53, and then **Save** 🖫 your workbook.

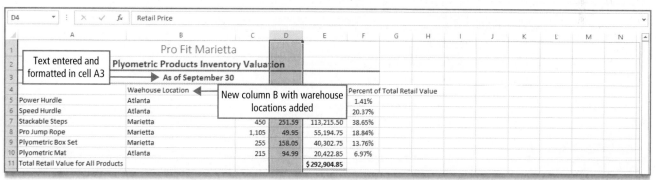

Figure 1.53

Activity 1.26 | Adjusting Column Widths and Wrapping Text

MOS

1.3.2, 2.2.4

Use the Wrap Text command to display the contents of a cell on multiple lines.

1 In the **column heading area**, point to the **column B** heading to display the ⬇ pointer, and then drag to the right to select **columns B:F**.

2 With the columns selected, in the **column heading area**, point to the right boundary of any of the selected columns to display the ✛ pointer, and then drag to set the width to **95 pixels**.

Use this technique to format multiple columns or rows simultaneously.

💻 **MAC TIP** Set the width of columns B:F to 12.83. (82 pixels)

3 Select the range **B4:F4** that comprises the column headings, and then on the **Home tab**, in the **Alignment group**, click **Wrap Text** 🔤. Notice that the row height adjusts to display the column titles on multiple lines.

4 With the range **B4:F4** still selected, in the **Alignment group**, click **Center** ☰ and **Middle Align** ☰. With the range **B4:F4** still selected, apply the **Heading 4** cell style.

The *Middle Align* command aligns text so that it is centered between the top and bottom of the cell.

5 Select the range **B5:B10**, and then in the **Alignment group**, click **Center** ☰. Click cell **A11**, and then from the **Cell Styles** gallery, under **Themed Cell Styles**, click **40% - Accent1**. **Save** 💾 your workbook.

Activity 1.27 | Changing Theme Colors

You can change only the theme *colors* of a workbook—without changing the theme fonts or effects.

1 On the **Page Layout tab**, in the **Themes group**, click **Colors**, and then click **Green** to change the Theme Color. Click any blank cell, and then compare your screen with Figure 1.54.

	A	B	C	D	E	F	G	H	I	J	K	L	M	N
1			Pro Fit Marietta											
2		Plyometric Products Inventory Valuation ◄				Theme colors changed to Green							
3		As of September 30												
4		Waehouse Location	Quantity in Stock	Retail Price	Total Retail Value	Percent of Total Retail Value								
5	Power Hurdle	Atlanta	125	$ 32.95	$ 4,118.75	1.41%								
6	Speed Hurdle	Atlanta	995	59.95	59,650.25	20.37%								
7	Stackable Steps	Marietta	450	251.59	113,215.50	38.65%								
8	Pro Jump Rope	Marietta	1,105	49.95	55,194.75	18.84%								
9	Plyometric Box Set	Marietta	255	158.05	40,302.75	13.76%								
10	Plyometric Mat	Atlanta	215	94.99	20,422.85	6.97%								
11	Total Retail Value for All Products				$ 292,904.85									

Figure 1.54

2 On the **Page Layout tab**, in the **Page Setup group**, click **Margins**, and then click **Custom Margins**.

3 In the **Page Setup** dialog box, on the **Margins tab**, under **Center on page**, select the **Horizontally** check box.

This action will center the data and chart horizontally on the page, as shown in the Preview area.

4 Click the **Header/Footer tab**, and then in the center of the dialog box, click **Custom Footer**. In the **Footer** dialog box, with your insertion point blinking in the **Left section**, on the row of buttons, click **Insert File Name** 🗐.

&[File] displays in the Left section. Here you can type or insert information from the row of buttons into the left, middle, or right section of the footer. The Custom Header button displays a similar screen to enter information in the header of the worksheet.

5 Click **OK** two times.

6 Click the **File tab** to display Backstage view, on the left click the **Info tab**, and then in the lower right corner, click **Show All Properties**.

7 As the **Tags**, type **plyo products, inventory** and as the **Subject**, type your course name and section number. Be sure your name displays in the **Author** box, or edit it if necessary.

8 On the left, click **Print** to view the **Print Preview**. At the bottom of the **Print Preview**, click **Next Page** ▸, and notice that as currently formatted, the worksheet occupies two pages.

9 Under **Settings**, click **Portrait Orientation**, and then click **Landscape Orientation**. Compare your screen with Figure 1.55.

> You can change the orientation on the Page Layout tab, or here, in Print Preview. Because it is in the Print Preview that you will often see adjustments that need to be made, commonly used settings display on the Print tab in Backstage view.

MAC TIP At the bottom of the Print dialog box, click Show Details. Select and click the Landscape Orientation button.

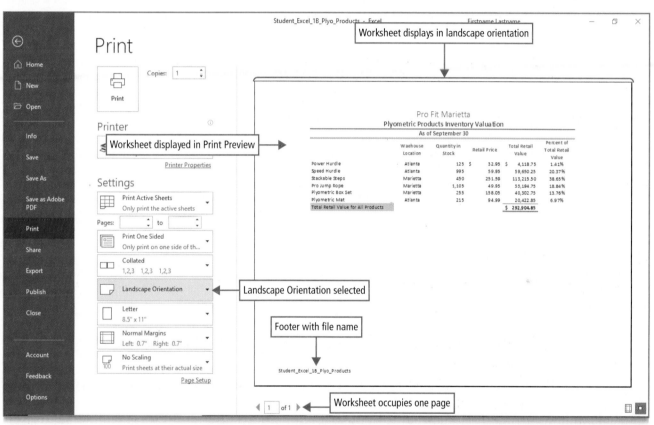

Figure 1.55

10 On the left, click **Save**.

11 In the upper right corner of your screen, click **Close** ✕ to close Excel.

For Non-MyLab Submissions: Determine What Your Instructor Requires for Submission

As directed by your instructor, submit your completed Excel workbook.

---

12 In **MyLab IT**, locate and click the Grader Project **Excel 1B Plyo Products**. In **step 3**, under **Upload Completed Assignment**, click **Choose File**. In the **Open** dialog box, navigate to your **Excel Chapter 1 folder**, and then click your **Student_Excel_1B_Plyo_Products** file one time to select it. In the lower right corner of the **Open** dialog box, click **Open**.

The name of your selected file displays above the Upload button.

13 To submit your file to **MyLab IT** for grading, click **Upload**, wait a moment for a green **Success!** message, and then in **step 4**, click the blue **Submit for Grading** button. Click **Close Assignment** to return to your list of **Course Materials**.

You have completed Project 1B **END**

Objective | Creating an Inventory Valuation Report

ALERT   **Working with Web-Based Applications and Service**

Computer programs and services on the web receive continuous updates and improvements, so the steps to complete this web-based Activity may differ from the ones shown. You can often look at the screens and the information presented to determine how to complete the Activity.

   If you do not already have a Google account, you will need to create one before you being this Activity. Go to **http://google.com** and in the upper right corner, click Sign In. On the Sign In screen, click Create Account. On the Create your Google Account page, complete the form, read and agree to the Terms of Service and Privacy Policy, and then click Next step. On the Welcome screen, click Get Started.

Activity | Creating an Inventory Valuation Report Using Google Sheets

   In this Activity, you will use Google Sheets to create an inventory valuation report similar to the one you created in Project 1B.

1 From the desktop, open your browser (a browser other than Edge), navigate to **https://www.google.com** and then click the **Google Apps** menu ⦀. Click **Drive**, and then if necessary, sign in to your Google account.

2 Open your **GO! Web Projects** folder—or click New to create and then open this folder if necessary.

3 In the upper left, click **New**, and then click **Google Sheets**. From your Windows taskbar, open **File Explorer**, navigate to the files you downloaded for this chapter, and then in the **File List**, double-click the Word document **e01B_Web**. To complete this project quickly and eliminate extra typing, you will copy the data from a Word document.

4 In the displayed Word document, click anywhere in the text, and then in the upper left corner, click to select the **Table Select** icon ⊞ to select the entire Word table. Right-click anywhere over the selection, and then click **Copy**. **Close** Word. **Close** the **File Explorer** window.

5 In your blank Google Sheet, with cell **A1** active, point to cell **A1**, right-click, and then click **Paste**. In the column heading area, point to the border between **column A** and **column B** to display the ⟺ pointer, and then widen **column A** slightly so that all of the data displays.

6 Select the range **A1:E1** and on the toolbar, click **Merge cells**. On the toolbar, click the **Horizontal Align button arrow** ≣ and then click **Center** ≣. Repeat for the range **A2:E2**, and then apply **Bold** B to cells **A1** and **A2**.

7 Select the range **B3:E3**, on the menu bar click **Format**, point to **Text wrapping**, and then click **Wrap**. Center these column titles and apply **Bold** B.

8 Select the range **C4:C9**, on the menu bar click **Format**, point to **Number**, click **Number**, and then on the toolbar, click **Decrease decimal places** ⌐.₀ two times.

9 Click cell **E4**, type = and then click cell **C4**. Type * and then click cell **D4**. Press Enter. Click cell **E4**, point to the fill handle in the lower right corner of the cell, and then drag down to cell **C9**.

10 Select the range **E4:E9**. On the toolbar, click **Functions** Σ ▾, click **SUM**, and then press Enter to total the column and place the result in cell **E10**.

11 Select the range **D4:E4**, hold down Ctrl, and then select cell **D10**. On the menu bar, click **Format**, point to **Number**, and then click **Currency**.

12 Select cell **A10**, hold down Ctrl, and then select cell **E10**. Apply **Bold** B.

13 Click cell **A1**, hold down Ctrl, and then click cell **A2**, cell **A10**, and cell **E10**. With the four cells selected, on the toolbar, click **Fill color** ▾, and then in the fourth column, click the third color—**light yellow 3**.

14 At the top of the worksheet, click the text *Untitled spreadsheet*, and then using your own name, type **Lastname_Firstname_Ex_1B_Web** and press Enter.

»» **GO!** With Google continues on next page

15 If you are instructed to submit your file to your instructor, you can either share the file through Google Drive, or create a PDF or Excel file. Ask your instructor in what format he or she would like to receive your file.

16 Close ⊞ the browser tab—a new Google Sheet always opens in a new window in your browser; your work is automatically saved. Notice that your new Google Sheet displays in the file list on your Google Drive. Sign out of your Google account.

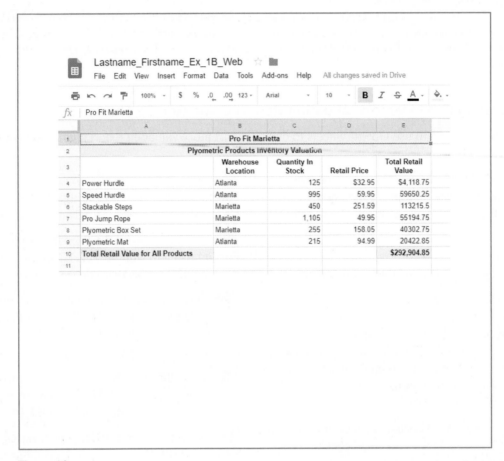

Figure 1A

wavebreakmedia/Shutterstock, Monkey Business Images/Fotolia, Ivanko80/Shutterstock, Monkey Business Images/Shutterstock

Microsoft Office Specialist (MOS) Skills in This Chapter	
Project 1A	**Project 1B**
1.2.2 Navigate to named cells, ranges, or workbook elements	**2.2.2** Modify cell alignment, orientation, and indentation
1.3.1 Modify page setup	**2.2.4** Wrap text within cells
1.3.2 Adjust row height and column width	**2.2.5** Apply number format
1.3.3 Customize headers and footers	**2.2.7** Apply cell styles
1.4.5 Modify basic workbook properties	**4.1.1** Insert relative, absolute, and mixed references
1.4.6 Display formulas	
1.5.1 Set a print area	
1.5.3 Configure print settings	
2.1.2 Fill cells by using Auto Fill	
2.2.1 Merge and unmerge cells	
2.2.5 Apply number format	
2.2.7 Apply cell styles	
2.4.1 Insert Sparklines	
4.1.1 Insert relative, absolute, and mixed references	
4.2.1 Perform calculations by using the SUM function	
5.1.1 Create charts	
5.2.2 Switch between rows and columns in source data	
5.2.3 Add and modify chart elements	
5.3.1 Apply chart layouts	

Build Your E-Portfolio

An E-Portfolio is a collection of evidence, stored electronically, that showcases what you have accomplished while completing your education. Collecting and then sharing your work products with potential employers reflects your academic and career goals. Your completed documents from the following projects are good examples to show what you have learned: 1G, 1K, and 1L.

GO! for Job Success

Video: How to Succeed in an Interview

Your instructor may assign this video to your class, and then ask you to think about, or discuss with your classmates, these questions:

g-stockstudio/ Shutterstock

> Can you think of two or three behaviors that Lee might want to change before he interviews with another company?

> If you were going on an interview, which of Connie's behaviors would you imitate?

> If you were the interviewer, Maria, would you have handled anything differently with either candidate?

End of Chapter

Summary

In Excel, you work with worksheets that are contained in a workbook. A worksheet is formatted as a pattern of uniformly spaced horizontal rows and vertical columns, the intersection of which forms a cell.

A cell can contain a constant value—referred to as a value—or a formula, which is an equation that performs mathematical calculations on the values in your worksheet. Common values are text and numbers.

Charts provide a graphic representation of data in a worksheet. Use the Recommended Charts feature to display customized charts that, according to Excel's calculations, will best represent your data.

You can insert sparklines in an Excel worksheet, which are tiny charts embedded in a cell that give a visual trend summary alongside your data. A sparkline makes a pattern more obvious to the eye.

GO! Learn It Online

Review the concepts, key terms, and MOS skills in this chapter by completing these online challenges, which you can find at **MyLab IT**.

Chapter Quiz: Answer matching and multiple choice questions to test what you learned in this chapter.

Lessons on the GO!: Learn how to use all the new apps and features as they are introduced by Microsoft.

MOS Prep Quiz: Answer questions to review the MOS skills that you practiced in this chapter.

GO! Collaborative Team Project (Available in Instructor Resource Center)

If your instructor assigns this project to your class, you can expect to work with one or more of your classmates—either in person or by using internet tools—to create work products similar to those that you created in this chapter. A team is a group of workers who work together to solve a problem, make a decision, or create a work product. Collaboration is when you work together with others as a team in an intellectual endeavor to complete a shared task or achieve a shared goal.

Monkey Business Images/ Fotolia

Project Guide for Excel Chapter 1

Your instructor will assign Projects from this list to ensure your learning and assess your knowledge.

	Project Guide for Excel Chapter 1		
Project	**Apply Skills from These Chapter Objectives**	**Project Type**	**Project Location**
1A MyLab IT	Objectives 1-6 from Project 1A	**1A Instructional Project (Grader Project)** Instruction Guided instruction to learn the skills in Project 1A.	In **MyLab IT** and in text
1B MyLab IT	Objectives 7–11 from Project 1B	**1B Instructional Project (Grader Project)** Instruction Guided instruction to learn the skills in Project 1B.	In **MyLab IT** and in text
1C	Objectives 1–6 from Project 1A	**1C Skills Review (Scorecard Grading)** Review A guided review of the skills from Project 1A.	In text
1D	Objectives 7–11 from Project 1B	**1D Skills Review (Scorecard Grading)** Review A guided review of the skills from Project 1B.	In text
1E MyLab IT	Objectives 1–6 from Project 1A	**1E Mastery (Grader Project)** Mastery and Transfer of Learning A demonstration of your mastery of the skills in Project 1A with extensive decision-making.	In **MyLab IT** and in text
1F MyLab IT	Objectives 7–11 from Project 1B	**1F Mastery (Grader Project)** Mastery and Transfer of Learning A demonstration of your mastery of the skills in Project 1B with extensive decision-making.	In **MyLab IT** and in text
1G MyLab IT	Objectives 1–11 from Projects 1A and 1B	**1G Mastery (Grader Project)** Mastery and Transfer of Learning A demonstration of your mastery of the skills in Projects 1A and 1B with extensive decision-making.	In **MyLab IT** and in text
1H	Combination of Objectives from Projects 1A and 1B	**1H GO! Fix It (Scorecard Grading)** Critical Thinking A demonstration of your mastery of the skills in Projects 1A and 1B by creating a correct result from a document that contains errors you must find.	IRC
1I	Combination of Objectives from Projects 1A and 1B	**1I GO! Make It (Scorecard Grading)** Critical Thinking A demonstration of your mastery of the skills in Projects 1A and 1B by creating a result from a supplied picture.	IRC
1J	Combination of Objectives from Projects 1A and 1B	**1J GO! Solve It (Rubric Grading)** Critical Thinking A demonstration of your mastery of the skills in Projects 1A and 1B, your decision-making skills, and your critical thinking skills. A task-specific rubric helps you self-assess your result.	IRC
1K	Combination of Objectives from Projects 1A and 1B	**1K GO! Solve It (Rubric Grading)** Critical Thinking A demonstration of your mastery of the skills in Projects 1A and 1B, your decision-making skills, and your critical thinking skills. A task-specific rubric helps you self-assess your result.	In text
1L	Combination of Objectives from Projects 1A and 1B	**1L GO! Think (Rubric Grading)** Critical Thinking A demonstration of your understanding of the Chapter concepts applied in a manner that you would outside of college. An analytic rubric helps you and your instructor grade the quality of your work by comparing it to the work an expert in the discipline would create.	In text
1M	Combination of Objectives from Projects 1A and 1B	**1M GO! Think (Rubric Grading)** Critical Thinking A demonstration of your understanding of the Chapter concepts applied in a manner that you would outside of college. An analytic rubric helps you and your instructor grade the quality of your work by comparing it to the work an expert in the discipline would create.	IRC
1N	Combination of Objectives from Projects 1A and 1B	**1N You and GO! (Rubric Grading)** Critical Thinking A demonstration of your understanding of the Chapter concepts applied in a manner that you would in a personal situation. An analytic rubric helps you and your instructor grade the quality of your work.	IRC
1O	Combination of Objectives from Projects 1A and 1B	**1O Cumulative Group Project for Excel Chapter 1** A demonstration of your understanding of concepts and your ability to work collaboratively in a group role-playing assessment, requiring both collaboration and self-management.	IRC

Glossary

Glossary of Chapter Key Terms

Absolute cell reference A cell reference that refers to cells by their fixed position in a worksheet; an absolute cell reference remains the same when the formula is copied.

Accounting Number Format The Excel number format that applies a thousand comma separator where appropriate, inserts a fixed U.S. dollar sign aligned at the left edge of the cell, applies two decimal places, and leaves a small amount of space at the right edge of the cell to accommodate a parenthesis for negative numbers.

Active cell The cell, surrounded by a black border, ready to receive data or be affected by the next Excel command.

Arithmetic operators The symbols +, -, *, /, %, and ^ used to denote addition, subtraction (or negation), multiplication, division, percentage, and exponentiation in an Excel formula.

Auto Fill An Excel feature that generates and extends values into adjacent cells based on the values of selected cells.

AutoCalculate A feature that displays three calculations in the status bar by default—Average, Count, and Sum—when you select a range of numerical data.

AutoComplete A feature that speeds your typing and lessens the likelihood of errors; if the first few characters you type in a cell match an existing entry in the column, Excel fills in the remaining characters for you.

AutoFit An Excel feature that adjusts the width of a column to fit the cell content of the widest cell in the column.

AutoSum A button that provides quick access to the SUM function.

Category axis The area along the bottom of a chart that identifies the categories of data; also referred to as the x-axis.

Category labels The labels that display along the bottom of a chart to identify the categories of data; Excel uses the row titles as the category names.

Cell The intersection of a column and a row.

Cell address Another name for a cell reference.

Cell content Anything typed into a cell.

Cell reference The identification of a specific cell by its intersecting column letter and row number.

Cell style A defined set of formatting characteristics, such as font, font size, font color, cell borders, and cell shading.

Chart The graphic representation of data in a worksheet; data presented as a chart is usually easier to understand than a table of numbers.

Chart Elements button A button that enables you to add, remove, or change chart elements such as the title, legend, gridlines, and data labels.

Chart Filters button A button that enables you to change which data displays in the chart.

Chart layout The combination of chart elements that can be displayed in a chart such as a title, legend, labels for the columns, and the table of charted cells.

Chart style The overall visual look of a chart in terms of its graphic effects, colors, and backgrounds; for example, you can have flat or beveled columns, colors that are solid or transparent, and backgrounds that are dark or light.

Chart Styles button A button that enables you to set a style and color scheme for your chart.

Chart Styles gallery A group of predesigned chart styles that you can apply to an Excel chart.

Chart types Various chart formats used in a way that is meaningful to the reader; common examples are column charts, pie charts, and line charts.

Column A vertical group of cells in a worksheet.

Column chart A chart in which the data is arranged in columns and that is useful for showing data changes over a period of time or for illustrating comparisons among items.

Column heading The letter that displays at the top of a vertical group of cells in a worksheet; beginning with the first letter of the alphabet, a unique letter or combination of letters identifies each column.

Comma Style The Excel number format that inserts thousand comma separators where appropriate and applies two decimal places; Comma Style also leaves space at the right to accommodate a parenthesis when negative numbers are present.

Constant value Numbers, text, dates, or times of day that you type into a cell.

Context sensitive A command associated with the currently selected or active object; often activated by right-clicking a screen item.

Data Text or numbers in a cell.

Data marker A column, bar, area, dot, pie slice, or other symbol in a chart that represents a single data point; related data points form a data series.

Data point A value that originates in a worksheet cell and that is represented in a chart by a data marker.

Data series Related data points represented by data markers; each data series has a unique color or pattern represented in the chart legend.

Displayed value The data that displays in a cell.

Excel pointer An Excel window element with which you can display the location of the pointer.

Expand Formula Bar button An Excel window element with which you can increase the height of the Formula Bar to display lengthy cell content.

Expand horizontal scroll bar button An Excel window element with which you can increase the width of the horizontal scroll bar.

Fill handle The small square in the lower right corner of a selected cell.

Format Changing the appearance of cells and worksheet elements to make a worksheet attractive and easy to read.

Formula An equation that performs mathematical calculations on values in a worksheet.

Formula Bar An element in the Excel window that displays the value or formula contained in the active cell; here you can also enter or edit values or formulas.

Function A predefined formula—a formula that Excel has already built for you—that performs calculations by using specific values in a particular order.

General format The default format that Excel applies to numbers; this format has no specific characteristics—whatever you type in the cell will display, with the exception that trailing zeros to the right of a decimal point will not display.

Label Another name for a text value, and which usually provides information about number values.

Glossary

Left alignment The cell format in which characters align at the left edge of the cell; this is the default for text entries and is an example of formatting information stored in a cell.

Legend A chart element that identifies the patterns or colors that are assigned to the categories in the chart.

Lettered column headings The area along the top edge of a worksheet that identifies each column with a unique letter or combination of letters.

Merge & Center A command that joins selected cells in an Excel worksheet into one larger cell and centers the contents in the merged cell.

Middle Align An alignment command that centers text between the top and bottom of a cell.

Name Box An element of the Excel window that displays the name of the selected cell, table, chart, or object.

Normal view A screen view that maximizes the number of cells visible on your screen and keeps the column letters and row numbers close to the columns and rows.

Number format A specific way in which Excel displays numbers in a cell.

Number values Constant values consisting of only numbers.

Numbered row headings The area along the left edge of a worksheet that identifies each row with a unique number.

Operators The symbols with which you can specify the type of calculation you want to perform in an Excel formula.

Picture element A point of light measured in dots per square inch on a screen; 64 pixels equals 8.43 characters, which is the average number of characters that will fit in a cell in an Excel worksheet using the default font.

Pixel The abbreviated name for a picture element.

Point and click method The technique of constructing a formula by pointing to and then clicking cells; this method is convenient when the referenced cells are not adjacent to one another.

Quick Analysis Tool A tool that displays in the lower right corner of a selected range, with which you can analyze your data by using Excel tools such as charts, color-coding, and formulas.

Range Two or more selected cells on a worksheet that are adjacent or nonadjacent; because the range is treated as a single unit, you can make the same changes or combination of changes to more than one cell at a time.

Range finder An Excel feature that outlines cells in color to indicate which cells are used in a formula; useful for verifying which cells are referenced in a formula.

Recommended Charts An Excel feature that displays a customized set of charts that, according to Excel's calculations, will best fit your data based on the range of data that you select.

Relative cell reference In a formula, the address of a cell based on the relative positions of the cell that contains the formula and the cell referred to in the formula.

Rounding A procedure in which you determine which digit at the right of the number will be the last digit displayed and then increase it by one if the next digit to its right is 5, 6, 7, 8, or 9.

Row A horizontal group of cells in a worksheet.

Row heading The numbers along the left side of an Excel worksheet that designate the row numbers.

Scaling The process of shrinking the width and/or height of printed output to fit a maximum number of pages.

Select All box A box in the upper left corner of the worksheet grid that, when clicked, selects all the cells in a worksheet.

Series A group of things that come one after another in succession; for example, January, February, March, and so on.

Sheet tab scrolling buttons Buttons to the left of the sheet tabs used to display Excel sheet tabs that are not in view; used when there are more sheet tabs than will display in the space provided.

Sheet tabs The labels along the lower border of the Excel window that identify each worksheet.

Show Formulas A command that displays the formula in each cell instead of the resulting value.

Sparkline A tiny chart in the background of a cell that gives a visual trend summary alongside your data; makes a pattern more obvious.

Spreadsheet Another name for a worksheet.

Status bar The area along the lower edge of the Excel window that displays, on the left side, the current cell mode, page number, and worksheet information; on the right side, when numerical data is selected, common calculations such as Sum and Average display.

SUM function A predefined formula that adds all the numbers in a selected range of cells.

Switch Row/Column A charting command to swap the data over the axis—data being charted on the vertical axis will move to the horizontal axis and vice versa.

Text values Constant values consisting of only text, and which usually provide information about number values; also referred to as labels.

Theme A predefined set of colors, fonts, lines, and fill effects that coordinate with each other.

Underlying formula The formula entered in a cell and visible only on the Formula Bar.

Underlying value The data that displays in the Formula Bar.

Value Another name for a constant value.

Value axis A numerical scale on the left side of a chart that shows the range of numbers for the data points; also referred to as the y-axis.

Workbook An Excel file that contains one or more worksheets.

Worksheet The primary document that you use in Excel to work with and store data, and which is formatted as a pattern of uniformly spaced horizontal and vertical lines.

Worksheet grid area A part of the Excel window that displays the columns and rows that intersect to form the worksheet's cells.

X-axis Another name for the horizontal (category) axis.

Y-axis Another name for the vertical (value) axis.

Chapter Review

Skills Review	Project 1C Step Sales

Apply 1A skills from these Objectives:

1. Create, Save, and Navigate an Excel Workbook
2. Enter Data in a Worksheet
3. Construct and Copy Formulas and Use the SUM Function
4. Format Cells with Merge & Center, Cell Styles, and Themes
5. Chart Data to Create a Column Chart and Insert Sparklines
6. Print a Worksheet, Display Formulas, and Close Excel

In the following Skills Review, you will create a new Excel worksheet with a chart that summarizes the first quarter sales of fitness equipment for step training. Your completed worksheet will look similar to Figure 1.56.

Project Files

For Project 1C, you will need the following file:

New blank Excel workbook

You will save your workbook as:

Lastname_Firstname_1C_Step_Sales

Project Results

Student_Excel_1C_Step_Sales

Figure 1.56

Chapter Review

1 Start Excel and open a new blank workbook. Click the **File tab** to display **Backstage** view, click **Save As**, and then navigate to your **Excel Chapter 1** folder. In the **File name** box, using your own name, type **Lastname_Firstname_1C_Step_Sales** and press Enter.

a. With cell **A1** as the active cell, type the worksheet title **Pro Fit Marietta** and then press Enter. In cell **A2**, type the worksheet subtitle **First Quarter Step Sales** and then press Enter.

b. Click in cell **A4**, type **Basic Step Box** and then press Enter. In cell **A5**, type **Step Storage Box** and then press Enter. In cell **A6**, type **Stackable Steps** and then press Enter. In cell **A7**, type **Step Mats** and then press Enter. In cell **A8**, type **Total** and then press Enter.

c. Click cell **B3**. Type **January** and then in the **Formula Bar**, click **Enter** to keep cell **B3** the active cell. With **B3** as the active cell, point to the fill handle in the lower right corner of the selected cell, drag to the right to cell **D3**, and then release the mouse button to enter the text *February* and *March*.

d. Press Ctrl + Home to make cell **A1** the active cell. In the **column heading area**, point to the vertical line between **column A** and **column B** to display the ⟷ pointer, hold down the left mouse button, and drag to the right to increase the width of **column A** to **130 pixels**.

e. Point to cell **B3**, and then drag across to select cells **B3** and **C3** and **D3**. With the range **B3:D3** selected, on the **Home tab**, in the **Alignment group**, click **Center**.

f. Click cell **B4**, type **75826.99** and press Tab to make cell **C4** active. Enter the remaining values, as shown in **Table 1** below, pressing Tab to move across the rows and pressing Enter to move down the columns.

2 Click cell **B8** to make it the active cell and type **=**

a. At the insertion point, type **b4** and then type **+** Type **b5** and then type **+b6+b7** Press Enter. Your result is *293079.6*.

b. Click in cell **C8**. Type **=** and then click cell **C4**. Type **+** and then click cell **C5**. Repeat this process to complete the formula to add cells **C6** and **C7** to the formula, and then press Enter. Your result is *305016.4*.

c. Click cell **D8**. On the **Home tab**, in the **Editing group**, click **AutoSum**, and then press Enter to construct a formula by using the SUM function. Your result is *307715.3*.

d. In cell **E3** type **Total** and press Enter. With cell **E4** as the active cell, on the **Home tab**, in the **Editing group**, click **AutoSum**. On the **Formula Bar**, click **Enter** to display the result and keep cell **E4** active.

e. With cell **E4** active, point to the fill handle in the lower right corner of the cell. Drag down through cell **E8**, and then release the mouse button to copy the formula with relative cell references down to sum each row.

3 Click cell **F3**. Type **Trend** and then press Enter.

a. Select the range **A1:F1**, and then on the **Home tab**, in the **Alignment group**, click **Merge & Center**. Select the range **A2:F2** and **Merge & Center** the selection.

b. Click cell **A1**. In the **Styles group**, click **Cell Styles**. Under **Titles and Headings**, click **Title**. Click cell **A2**, display the **Cell Styles** gallery, and then click **Heading 1**.

c. Select the range **B3:F3**, hold down Ctrl, and then select the range **A4:A8**. From the **Cell Styles** gallery, click **Heading 4** to apply this cell style to the column and row titles.

d. Select the range **B4:E4**, hold down Ctrl, and then select the range **B8:E8**. On the **Home tab**, in the **Number group**, click **Accounting Number Format**. Select the range **B5:E7**, and then in the **Number group**, click **Comma Style**. Select the range **B8:E8**. From the **Styles group**, display the **Cell Styles** gallery, and then under **Titles and Headings**, click **Total**.

	Table 1		
	January	February	March
Basic Step Box	75826.99	81657.32	72431.22
Step Storage Box	85245.90	92618.95	88337.68
Stackable Steps	68751.64	71997.48	78951.23
Step Mats	63255.10	58742.67	67995.20

Chapter Review

e. On the ribbon, click the **Page Layout tab**, and then in the **Themes group**, click **Themes** to display the **Themes** gallery. Click the **Ion** theme. (This theme widens the columns slightly.) On the Quick Access Toolbar, click **Save**.

4 Select the range **A3:D7**, which includes the row titles, the column titles and the data without the totals. Click the **Insert tab**, and then in the **Charts group**, click **Recommended Charts**. In the **Insert Chart** dialog box, scroll down and click the **Clustered Column** chart in which *each month* displays its *sales for each type of step training equipment*. Click **OK**.

a. In the chart, click anywhere in the text *Chart Title* to select the text box. Watch the **Formula Bar** as you type **First** and then let AutoComplete complete the title by pressing (Enter).

b. Click in a white area just slightly *inside* the chart border to deselect the chart title but keep the chart selected. To the right of the chart, click the second button—the **Chart Styles** button [✏].

Be sure the **Style tab** is active. Use the scroll bar to scroll down, and then by using the ScreenTips, locate and click **Style 6**.

c. At the top of the gallery, click **Color**. Under **Colorful**, click the second row of colors to apply this variation of the theme colors.

d. Point to the top border of the chart to display the [↖] pointer, and then drag the upper left corner of the chart just to the center of cell **A10** to visually center it below the data.

5 Click an empty cell to deselect the chart, and then select the range **B4:D7**. Click the **Insert tab**, and then in the **Sparklines group**, click **Line**. In the **Create Sparklines** dialog box, in the **Location Range** box, type **f4:f7** and then click **OK** to insert the sparklines.

a. On the **Design tab**, in the **Show group**, select the **Markers** check box to display markers in the sparklines.

b. On the **Design tab**, in the **Style group**, click **More** [▾] and then in the first row, click the second style.

6 Click cell **A1** to deselect the chart. Click the **Page Layout tab**, and then in the **Page Setup group**, click **Margins**. Click **Custom Margins**. In the **Page Setup** dialog box, on the **Margins tab**, under **Center on page**, select the **Horizontally** check box.

a. Click the **Header/Footer tab**, and then click **Custom Footer**. With your insertion point in the **Left section**, click **Insert File Name**. Click **OK** two times.

b. Click the **File tab** to display **Backstage** view; if necessary, on the left, click the **Info tab**. In the lower right corner, click **Show All Properties**. As the **Tags**, type **step sales, 1st quarter** In the **Subject** box, type your course name and section number. Be sure your name displays as the author—edit if necessary.

c. On the left, click **Save**.

d. Print or submit your workbook electronically as directed by your instructor. If required by your instructor, print or create an electronic version of your worksheet with formulas displayed by using the instructions at the end of Project 1A. **Close** Excel without saving so that you do not save the changes you made to print formulas. (Mac users: if necessary to fit on one page, on the Page Layout tab, in the Scale to Fit group, set the Width and Height to 1 page.)

You have completed Project 1C **END**

Skills Review Project 1D Band and Tubing Inventory

Apply 1B skills from these Objectives:

7. Check Spelling in a Worksheet
8. Enter Data by Range
9. Construct Formulas for Mathematical Operations
10. Edit Values in a Worksheet
11. Format a Worksheet

In the following Skills Review, you will create a worksheet that summarizes the inventory of band and tubing exercise equipment. Your completed worksheet will look similar to Figure 1.57.

Project Files

For Project 1D, you will need the following file:

New blank Excel workbook

You will save your workbook as:

Lastname_Firstname_1D_Band_Inventory

Project Results

Pro Fit Marietta

Band and Tubing Inventory

As of June 30

	Material	Quantity in Stock	Retail Price	Total Retail Value	Percent of Total Retail Value
Super Strength Bands	Latex	225	$ 48.98	$ 11,020.50	25.16%
Medium Tubing	Rubber	198	27.95	5,534.10	12.64%
Resistance Band, Average	Latex	165	42.95	7,086.75	16.18%
Mini Bands, Medium	Latex	245	25.95	6,357.75	14.52%
Mini Bands, Heavy	Rubber	175	32.95	5,766.25	13.17%
Heavy Tubing	Latex	187	42.95	8,031.65	18.34%
Total Retail Value for All Products				**$ 43,797.00**	

Student_Excel_1D_Band_Inventory

Figure 1.57

Chapter Review

1 Start Excel and display a new blank workbook. **Save** the workbook in your **Excel Chapter 1** folder as **Lastname_Firstname_1D_Band_Inventory** In cell **A1**, type **Pro Fit Marietta** and in cell **A2**, type **Band and Tubing Inventory**

a. Click cell **B3**, type **Quantity in Stock** and press [Tab]. In cell **C3**, type **Average Cost** and press [Tab]. In cell **D3**, type **Retail Price** and press [Tab]. In cell **E3**, type **Total Retail Value** and press [Tab]. In cell **F3**, type **Percent of Total Retail Value** and press [Enter].

b. Click cell **A4**, type **Super Strength Bands** and press [Enter]. In the range **A5:A10**, type the remaining row titles as shown below, including any misspelled words.

Medium Tubing
Resistnce Band, Average
Mini Bands, Medium
Mini Bands, Heavy
Heavy Tubing
Total Retail Value for All Products

c. Press [Ctrl] + [Home] to move to the top of your worksheet. On the **Review tab**, in the **Proofing group**, click **Spelling**. Correct *Resistnce* to **Resistance** and any other spelling errors you may have made, and then when the message displays, *Spell check complete. You're good to go!* click **OK**.

d. In the **column heading area**, point to the right boundary of **column A** to display the [+] pointer, and then drag to the right to widen **column A** to **225 pixels**.

e. In the **column heading area**, point to the **column B** heading to display the [↓] pointer, and then drag to the right to select **columns B:F**. With the columns selected, in the **column heading area**, point to the right boundary of any of the selected columns, and then drag to the right to set the width to **100 pixels**.

f. Select the range **A1:F1**. On the **Home tab**, in the **Alignment group**, click **Merge & Center**, and then from the **Cell Styles** gallery, apply the **Title** style. Select the range **A2:F2**. **Merge & Center** the text across the selection, and then from the **Cell Styles** gallery, apply the **Heading 1** style.

2 On the **Page Layout tab**, in the **Themes group**, change the **Colors** to **Blue Green**. Select the empty range **B4:D9**. With cell **B4** active in the range, type **225** and then press [Enter].

a. With cell **B5** active in the range, and pressing [Enter] after each entry, type the following data in the *Quantity in Stock* column:

198
265
245
175
187

b. With the selected range still active, from the following table, beginning in cell **C4** and pressing [Enter] after each entry, enter the following data for the **Average Cost** column and then the **Retail Price** column. If you prefer, type without selecting the range first; recall that this is optional.

Average Cost	Retail Price
22.75	48.98
15.95	27.95
26.90	42.95
12.95	25.95
18.75	32.95
26.90	42.95

3 In cell **E4**, type **=b4*d4** and then press [Enter] to construct a formula that calculates the *Total Retail Value* of the *Super Strength Bands* (Quantity in Stock X Retail Price).

a. Click cell **E4**, position your pointer over the fill handle, and then drag down through cell **E9** to copy the formula with relative cell references.

b. Select the range **B4:B9**, and then on the **Home tab**, in the **Number group**, click **Comma Style**. Then, in the **Number group**, click **Decrease Decimal** two times to remove the decimal places from these non-currency values.

Chapter Review

c. To calculate the *Total Retail Value for All Products*, select the range **E4:E9**, and then in the lower right corner of the selected range, click the **Quick Analysis** button.

d. In the gallery, click **Totals**, and then click the *first* **Sum** button, which visually indicates that the column will be summed with a result at the bottom of the column.

e. Select the range **C5:E9** and apply the **Comma Style**. Select the range **C4:E4**, hold down [Ctrl], and then click cell **E10**. With the nonadjacent cells selected, apply the **Accounting Number Format**. Click cell **E10**, and then from the **Cell Styles** gallery, apply the **Total** style.

f. Click cell **F4**, type **=** and then click cell **E4**. Type **/** and then click cell **E10**. Press [F4] to make the reference to cell *E10* absolute, and then on the **Formula Bar**, click **Enter** so that cell **F4** remains the active cell. (Mac users: press [command ⌘] + [T].)

g. Drag the fill handle to copy the formula down through cell **F9**. Point to cell **B6**, and then double-click to place the insertion point within the cell. Use the arrow keys to move the insertion point to the left or right of *2*, and use either [Del] or [Backspace] to delete *2*, and then type **1** and press [Enter] so that the new *Quantity in Stock* is *165*. Notice the recalculations in the worksheet.

4 Select the range **F4:F9**, and then in the **Number group**, click **Percent Style**. Click **Increase Decimal** two times, and then **Center** the selection.

a. In the **row heading area** on the left side of your screen, point to **row 3** to display the ➡ pointer, and then right-click to simultaneously select the row and display a shortcut menu. On the shortcut menu, click **Insert** to insert a new **row 3**.

b. Click cell **A3**, type **As of June 30** and then on the **Formula Bar**, click **Enter** to keep cell **A3** as the active cell. **Merge & Center** the text across the range **A3:F3**, and then apply the **Heading 2** cell style.

5 In the **column heading area**, point to **column B**. When the ⬇ pointer displays, right-click, and then click **Insert** to insert a new column.

a. Click cell **B4**, type **Material** and then press [Enter]. In cell **B5**, type **Latex** and then press [Enter]. In cell **B6**, type **Rubber** and then press [Enter].

b. Using AutoComplete to speed your typing by pressing [Enter] as soon as the AutoComplete suggestion displays, in cells **B7**, **B8**, and **B10**, type **Latex** and in cell **B9**, type **Rubber**

c. In the **column heading area**, point to the right boundary of **column B**, and then drag to the left and set the width to **90 pixels**. In the **column heading area**, point to **column D**, right-click, and then click **Delete**.

d. Select the column titles in the range **B4:F4**, and then on the **Home tab**, in the **Alignment group**, click **Wrap Text**, **Center**, and **Middle Align**. With the range still selected, apply the **Heading 4** cell style.

e. Click cell **A11**, and then from the **Cell Styles** gallery, under **Themed Cell Styles**, click **40% - Accent1**.

6 Click the **Page Layout tab**, and then in the **Page Setup group**, click **Margins**. Click **Custom Margins**. In the **Page Setup** dialog box, on the **Margins tab**, under **Center on page**, select the **Horizontally** check box.

a. Click the **Header/Footer tab**, and then click **Custom Footer**. With your insertion point in the **Left section**, click **Insert File Name**. Click **OK** two times.

b. In the **Page Setup group**, click **Orientation**, and then click **Landscape**.

c. Click the **File tab** to display **Backstage** view; if necessary, on the left click the **Info tab**. In the lower right corner, click **Show All Properties**. As the **Tags**, type **bands, tubing, inventory** In the **Subject** box, type your course name and section number. Be sure your name displays as the author—edit if necessary.

d. On the left, click **Save** to be sure that you have saved your work up to this point.

e. Print or submit your workbook electronically as directed by your instructor. (Mac users: if necessary to fit on one page, on the Page Layout tab, in the Scale to Fit group, set the Width and Height to 1 page.)

f. If required by your instructor, print or create an electronic version of your worksheet with formulas displayed by using the instructions at the end of Project 1A. **Close** Excel without saving so that you do not save the changes you made to print formulas.

You have completed Project 1D | **END**

Mastering Excel **Project 1E Gym Sales**

In the following Mastering Excel project, you will create a worksheet comparing the sales of different types of home gym equipment sold in the second quarter. Your completed worksheet will look similar to Figure 1.58.

Project Files for **MyLab IT Grader**

1. In your **MyLab IT** course, locate and click **Excel 1E Gym Sales**, Download Materials, and then Download All Files.
2. Extract the zipped folder to your Excel Chapter 1 folder. Close the Grader download screens.
3. Take a moment to open the downloaded **Excel_1E_Gym_Sales_Instructions**; note any recent updates to the book.

Project Results

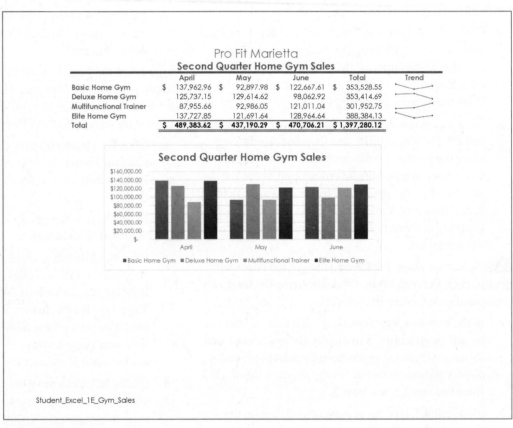

Figure 1.58

For Non-MyLab Submissions

For Project 1E, you will need:
e01E_Gym_Sales

In your Excel Chapter 1 folder, save your workbook as:
Lastname_Firstname_1E_Gym_Sales

If your instructor requires a workbook with formulas, save as:
Lastname_Firstname_1E_Gym_Sales_formulas

After you have named and saved your workbook, on the next page, begin with Step 2.

After Step 16, submit your file as directed by your instructor.

Content-Based Assessments (Mastery and Transfer of Learning)

Mastering Excel: Project 1E Gym Sales (continued)

1 Navigate to your **Excel Chapter 1 folder**, and then double-click the Excel file you downloaded from **MyLab IT** that displays your name—**Student_1E_Gym_Sales**. If necessary, at the top, click **Enable Editing**.

2 Change the workbook theme to **Wisp**. If the Wisp theme is not available on your computer, in the Themes gallery, click Browse for Themes, and then select the theme from your downloaded student files.

3 In cell **B3**, use the fill handle to fill the months *May* and *June* in the range **C3:D3**.

4 **Merge & Center** the title across the range **A1:F1**, and then apply the **Title** cell style. **Merge & Center** the subtitle across the range **A2:F2**, and then apply the **Heading 1** cell style. **Center** the column titles in the range **B3:F3**.

5 Widen **column A** to **180 pixels**, and then widen columns **B:F** to **115 pixels**. (Mac users: set column A to a width of 21.83 or 136 pixels and columns B:F to a width of 13.83 or 88 pixels.) In the range **B7:D7**, enter the monthly sales figures for the Elite Home Gym for April, May, and June as shown in the table below:

	April	May	June
Elite Home Gym	137727.85	121691.64	128964.64

6 In cell **B8**, on the **Home tab**, use the **AutoSum** button to sum the April sales. Copy the resulting formula across to cells **C8:D8** to sum the May monthly sales and the June monthly sales. In cell **E4**, use the **AutoSum** button to sum the *Basic Home Gym* sales. Copy the formula down to cells **E5:E8**.

7 Apply the **Heading 4** cell style to the row titles and the column titles. Apply the **Total** cell style to the totals in the range **B8:E8**.

8 Apply the **Accounting Number Format** to the first row of sales figures and to the total row. Apply the **Comma Style** to the remaining sales figures.

9 To compare the monthly sales of each product visually, select the range that represents the sales figures for the three months, including the month names and the product names—do not include any totals in the range. With this data selected, use the **Recommended Charts** command to insert a **Clustered Column** chart with the month names displayed on the category axis and the product names displayed in the legend.

10 Move the chart so that its upper left corner is positioned in the center of cell **A10**. Then drag the center right sizing handle to the right until the right edge of the chart aligns with the right edge of **column E**; this will display the legend on one row and, after you add the sparklines, center the chart below the data.

11 Apply **Chart Style 6** and change the colors by applying the second row of colors under **Colorful**. Change the **Chart Title** to Second Quarter Home Gym Sales

12 In the range **F4:F7**, insert **Line** sparklines that compare the monthly data. Do not include the totals. Show the sparkline **Markers**. Display the sparkline **Style** gallery, and then in the first row, apply the second style.

13 Center the worksheet **Horizontally** on the page, and then insert a **Footer** with the **File Name** in the **left section**.

14 Change the **Orientation** to **Landscape**. Display the document properties, and then as the **Tags** type **home gym, sales** As the **Subject**, type your course name and section number. Be sure your name displays as the **Author**. Check your worksheet by previewing it in **Print Preview**, and then make any necessary corrections.

15 On the left, click **Save**.

16 In the upper right corner of your screen, click **Close** ☒ to close Excel.

17 In **MyLab IT**, locate and click the Grader Project **Excel 1E Gym Sales**. In **step 3**, under **Upload Completed Assignment**, click **Choose File**. In the **Open** dialog box, navigate to your **Excel Chapter 1 folder**, and then click your **Student_Excel_1E_Gym_Sales** file one time to select it. In the lower right corner of the **Open** dialog box, click **Open**.

The name of your selected file displays above the Upload button.

18 To submit your file to **MyLab IT** for grading, click **Upload**, wait a moment for a green **Success!** message, and then in **step 4**, click the blue **Submit for Grading** button. Click **Close Assignment** to return to your list of **Course Materials**.

You have completed Project 1E | END

Content-Based Assessments (Mastery and Transfer of Learning)

Apply 1B skills from these Objectives:

7. Check Spelling in a Worksheet
8. Enter Data by Range
9. Construct Formulas for Mathematical Operations
10. Edit Values in a Worksheet
11. Format a Worksheet

In the following Mastering Excel project, you will create a worksheet that summarizes the sales of balance and stabilization equipment that Pro Fit Marietta is marketing. Your completed worksheet will look similar to Figure 1.59.

Project Files for **MyLab IT** Grader

1. In your **MyLab IT** course, locate and click **Excel 1F Balance Sales**, Download Materials, and then Download All Files.
2. Extract the zipped folder to your Excel Chapter 1 folder. Close the Grader download screens.
3. Take a moment to open the downloaded **Excel_1F_Balance_Sales_Instructions**; note any recent updates to the book.

Project Results

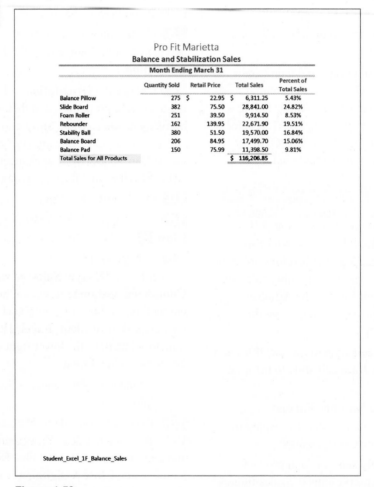

Figure 1.59

For Non-MyLab Submissions

For Project 1F, you will need:
e01F_Gym_Sales

In your Excel Chapter 1 folder, save your workbook as:
Lastname_Firstname_1F_Balance_Sales
If your instructor requires a workbook with formulas, save as:
Lastname_Firstname_1F_Balance_Sales_formulas

After you have named and saved your workbook, on the next page, begin with Step 2.
After Step 18, submit your file as directed by your instructor.

Content-Based Assessments (Mastery and Transfer of Learning)

1 Navigate to your **Excel Chapter 1 folder**, and then double-click the Excel file you downloaded from **MyLab IT** that displays your name—**Student_Excel_1F_Balance_ Sales**. If necessary, at the top, click **Enable Editing**.

2 **Merge & Center** the title and then the subtitle across **columns A:F** and apply the **Title** and **Heading 1** cell styles respectively.

3 Make cell **A1** the active cell, and then check spelling in your worksheet. Correct *Silde* to **Slide**. Widen **column A** to **180 pixels** and widen **columns B:F** to **95 pixels** (Mac users: set column A to 141 pixels and widen columns B:F to 75 pixels.)

4 In cell **E4**, construct a formula to calculate the *Total Sales* of the *Balance Pillow* by multiplying the *Quantity Sold* times the *Retail Price*. Copy the formula down for the remaining products.

5 Select the range **E4:E10**, and then use the **Quick Analysis** tool to **Sum** the *Total Sales for All Products*, which will be formatted in bold. To the total in cell **E11**, apply the **Total** cell style. (Mac users: instead of the Quick Analysis tool, use the Sum button. Complete the step as specified.)

6 Using absolute cell references as necessary so that you can copy the formula, in cell **F4**, construct a formula to calculate the *Percent of Total Sales* for the first product. Copy the formula down for the remaining products.

7 To the computed percentages, apply **Percent Style** with two decimal places, and then **Center** the percentages.

8 Apply the **Comma Style** with no decimal places to the *Quantity Sold* figures. To cells **D4**, **E4**, and **E11** apply the **Accounting Number Format**.

9 To the range **D5:E10**, apply the **Comma Style**.

10 Change the *Retail Price* of the *Slide Board* to **75.50** and the *Quantity Sold* of the *Balance Pad* to **150**.

11 Delete **column B**.

12 Insert a new **row 3**. In cell **A3**, type **Month Ending March 31** and then **Merge & Center** the text across the range **A3:E3**. Apply the **Heading 2** cell style.

13 To cell **A12**, apply the **20%-Accent1** cell style.

14 Select the four column titles. Apply **Wrap Text**, **Middle Align**, and **Center** formatting, and then apply the **Heading 3** cell style.

15 Center the worksheet **Horizontally** on the page, and then insert a **Footer** with the **File Name** in the **left section**.

16 Display the document properties, and then as the **Tags**, type **balance, stability, sales** In the **Subject** box, add your course name and section number. Be sure your name displays as the Author.

17 On the left, click **Save**.

18 In the upper right corner of your screen, click **Close** ☒ to close Excel.

19 In **MyLab IT**, locate and click the Grader Project **Excel 1F Balance Sales**. In **step 3**, under **Upload Completed Assignment**, click **Choose File**. In the **Open** dialog box, navigate to your **Excel Chapter 1 folder**, and then click your **Student_Excel_1F_Balance_Sales** file one time to select it. In the lower right corner of the **Open** dialog box, click **Open**.

The name of your selected file displays above the Upload button.

20 To submit your file to **MyLab IT** for grading, click **Upload**, wait a moment for a green **Success!** message, and then in **step 4**, click the blue **Submit for Grading** button. Click **Close Assignment** to return to your list of **Course Materials**.

You have completed Project 1F | **END**

Content-Based Assessments (Mastery and Transfer of Learning)

Mastering Excel | Project 1G Regional Sales

Apply a combination of 1A and 1B skills:

1. Create, Save, and Navigate an Excel Workbook
2. Enter Data in a Worksheet
3. Construct and Copy Formulas and Use the SUM Function
4. Format Cells with Merge & Center, Cell Styles, and Themes
5. Chart Data to Create a Column Chart and Insert Sparklines
6. Print a Worksheet, Display Formulas, and Close Excel
7. Check Spelling in a Worksheet
8. Enter Data by Range
9. Construct Formulas for Mathematical Operations
10. Edit Values in a Worksheet
11. Format a Worksheet

In the following Mastering Excel project, you will create a new worksheet that compares annual sales by region. Your completed worksheet will look similar to Figure 1.60.

Project Files for **MyLab IT Grader**

1. In your **MyLab IT** course, locate and click **Excel 1G Regional Sales**, Download Materials, and then Download All Files.
2. Extract the zipped folder to your Excel Chapter 1 folder. Close the Grader download screens.
3. Take a moment to open the downloaded **Excel_1G_Regional_Sales_Instructions**; note any recent updates to the book.

Project Results

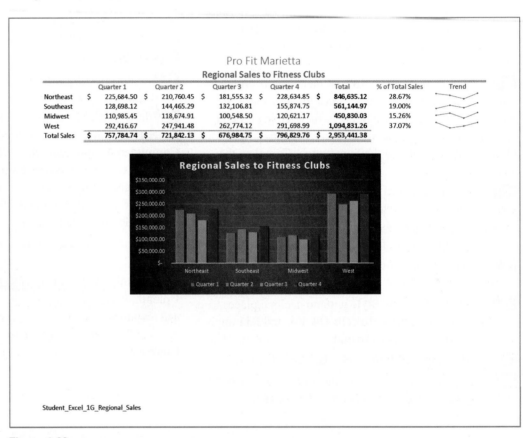

Figure 1.60

For Non-MyLab Submissions

For Project 1G, you will need:
e01G_Regional_Sales

In your Excel Chapter 1 folder, save your workbook as:
Lastname_Firstname_1G_Regional_Sales

If your instructor requires a workbook with formulas, save as:
Lastname_Firstname_1G_Regional_Sales_formulas

After you have named and saved your workbook, on the next page, begin with Step 2.

After Step 18, submit your file as directed by your instructor. (Mac users: if necessary to fit on one page, on the Page Layout tab, in the Scale to Fit group, set the width to 1 page.)

Content-Based Assessments (Mastery and Transfer of Learning)

1 Navigate to your **Excel Chapter 1 folder**, and then double-click the Excel file you downloaded from **MyLab IT** that displays your name—**Student_1G_Regional_Sales**. If necessary, at the top, click **Enable Editing**.

2 Change the **Theme** to **Retrospect**. Set the width of **column A** to **80 pixels** and the width of columns **B:H** to **110 pixels**. (Mac users: Set Column A to 68 pixels and columns B:H to 95 pixels.)

3 **Merge & Center** the title across the range **A1:H1**, and then apply the **Title** cell style. **Merge & Center** the subtitle across the range **A2:H2**, and then apply the **Heading 1** cell style.

4 Select the seven column titles, apply **Center** formatting, and then apply the **Heading 4** cell style.

5 By using the **Quick Analysis** tool, **Sum** the *Quarter 1* sales, and then copy the formula across for the remaining Quarters; the Quick Analysis tool formats totals in bold. (Mac users: use AutoSum and apply bold.)

6 Select the *Northeast* sales for the four quarters, and then display the **Quick Analysis** gallery for **Totals**. Click the second **Sum** option—the sixth item in the gallery—which displays the column selection in yellow. Copy the formula down through cell **F7**; recall that the Quick Analysis tool applies bold formatting to sums. (Mac users: use AutoSum and apply bold.)

7 Apply the **Accounting Number Format** to the first row of sales figures and to the total row, and the **Comma Style** to the remaining sales figures. Format the totals in **row 7** with the **Total** cell style.

8 Insert a new **row 6** with the row title **Midwest** and the following sales figures for each quarter: **110985.45** and **118674.91** and **100548.50** and **120621.17** Copy the formula in cell **F5** down to cell **F6** to sum the new row.

9 Using absolute cell references as necessary so that you can copy the formula, in cell **G4** construct a formula to calculate the *Percent of Total Sales* for the first region. Copy the formula down for the remaining regions.

10 To the computed percentages, apply **Percent Style** with two decimal places, and then **Center** the percentages.

11 Insert **Line** sparklines in the range **H4:H7** that compare the quarterly data. Do not include the totals. Show the sparkline **Markers** and apply a style to the sparklines using the second style in the second row. (Mac users: Select the first color in the second row.)

12 **Save** your workbook. To compare the quarterly sales of each region visually, select the range that represents the sales figures for the four quarters, including the quarter names and each region—do not include any totals in the range. With this data selected, by using the **Recommended Charts** command, insert a **Clustered Column** with the regions as the category axis and the Quarters as the legend.

13 Apply **Chart Style 8**. Change the colors by applying the third row of colors under Colorful. Position the upper middle sizing handle of the chart on the line between **column D** and **column E** and just below **row 9**.

14 Change the **Chart Title** to **Regional Sales to Fitness Clubs**

15 Deselect the chart. Change the page **Orientation** to **Landscape**, center the worksheet **Horizontally** on the page, and then insert a footer with the file name in the left section.

16 Show the document properties. As the **Tags**, type **fitness clubs, regional sales** In the **Subject** box, type your course name and section number. Be sure your name displays as the Author.

17 On the left, click **Save**.

18 In the upper right corner of your screen, click **Close** ☒ to close Excel.

19 In **MyLab IT**, locate and click the Grader Project **Excel 1G Regional Sales**. In **step 3**, under **Upload Completed Assignment**, click **Choose File**. In the **Open** dialog box, navigate to your **Excel Chapter 1 folder**, and then click your **Student_Excel_1G_Regional_Sales** file one time to select it. In the lower right corner of the **Open** dialog box, click **Open**.

The name of your selected file displays above the Upload button.

20 To submit your file to **MyLab IT** for grading, click **Upload**, wait a moment for a green **Success!** message, and then in **step 4**, click the blue **Submit for Grading** button. Click **Close Assignment** to return to your list of **Course Materials**.

You have completed Project 1G | END

Content-Based Assessments (Critical Thinking)

GO! Fix It	Project 1H Team Sales	IRC

GO! Make It	Project 1I Agility Sales	IRC

GO! Solve It	Project 1J Kettlebell Sales	IRC

GO! Solve It	Project 1K Commission	

Project Files

For Project 1K, you will need the following file:

e01K_Commission

You will save your workbook as:

Lastname_Firstname_1K_Commission

Open the file e01K_Commission and save it as **Lastname_Firstname_1K_Commission** Complete the worksheet by using Auto Fill to complete the month headings, and then calculating the Total Commission for each month and for each region. Insert and format appropriate sparklines in the Trend column. Format the worksheet attractively with a title and subtitle, check spelling, adjust column width, and apply appropriate financial formatting. Insert a chart that compares the total sales commission for each region with the months displaying as the categories, and format the chart attractively. Include the file name in the footer, add appropriate properties, and submit as directed.

		Performance Level		
		Exemplary: You consistently applied the relevant skills	**Proficient: You sometimes, but not always, applied the relevant skills**	**Developing: You rarely or never applied the relevant skills**
Performance Criteria	**Create formulas**	All formulas are correct and are efficiently constructed.	Formulas are correct but not always constructed in the most efficient manner.	One or more formulas are missing or incorrect; or only numbers were entered.
	Create a chart	Chart created properly.	Chart was created but incorrect data was selected.	No chart was created.
	Insert and format sparklines	Sparklines inserted and formatted properly.	Sparklines were inserted but incorrect data was selected or sparklines were not formatted.	No sparklines were inserted.
	Format attractively and appropriately	Formatting is attractive and appropriate.	Adequately formatted but difficult to read or unattractive.	Inadequate or no formatting.

You have completed Project 1K | **END**

Outcomes-Based Assessments (Critical Thinking)

Rubric

The following outcomes-based assessments are *open-ended assessments*. That is, there is no specific correct result; your result will depend on your approach to the information provided. Make *Professional Quality* your goal. Use the following scoring rubric to guide you in *how* to approach the problem and then to evaluate *how well* your approach solves the problem.

The *criteria*—Software Mastery, Content, Format and Layout, and Process—represent the knowledge and skills you have gained that you can apply to solving the problem. The *levels of performance*—Professional Quality, Approaching Professional Quality, or Needs Quality Improvements—help you and your instructor evaluate your result.

	Your completed project is of Professional Quality if you:	Your completed project is Approaching Professional Quality if you:	Your completed project Needs Quality Improvements if you:
1-Software Mastery	Choose and apply the most appropriate skills, tools, and features and identify efficient methods to solve the problem.	Choose and apply some appropriate skills, tools, and features, but not in the most efficient manner.	Choose inappropriate skills, tools, or features, or are inefficient in solving the problem.
2-Content	Construct a solution that is clear and well organized, contains content that is accurate, appropriate to the audience and purpose, and is complete. Provide a solution that contains no errors of spelling, grammar, or style.	Construct a solution in which some components are unclear, poorly organized, inconsistent, or incomplete. Misjudge the needs of the audience. Have some errors in spelling, grammar, or style, but the errors do not detract from comprehension.	Construct a solution that is unclear, incomplete, or poorly organized, contains some inaccurate or inappropriate content, and contains many errors of spelling, grammar, or style. Do not solve the problem.
3-Format and Layout	Format and arrange all elements to communicate information and ideas, clarify function, illustrate relationships, and indicate relative importance.	Apply appropriate format and layout features to some elements, but not others. Overuse features, causing minor distraction.	Apply format and layout that does not communicate information or ideas clearly. Do not use format and layout features to clarify function, illustrate relationships, or indicate relative importance. Use available features excessively, causing distraction.
4-Process	Use an organized approach that integrates planning, development, self-assessment, revision, and reflection.	Demonstrate an organized approach in some areas, but not others; or, use an insufficient process of organization throughout.	Do not use an organized approach to solve the problem.

Outcomes-Based Assessments (Critical Thinking)

Apply a combination of the 1A and 1B skills.

GO! Think	Project 1L Video Sales

Project Files

For Project 1L, you will need the following file:

New blank Excel workbook

You will save your workbook as:

Lastname_Firstname_1L_Video_Sales

Michelle Barry, President of Pro Fit Marietta, needs a worksheet that summarizes the following data regarding the first quarter sales of training videos. Michelle would like the worksheet to include a calculation of the total sales for each type of video and a total of the sales of all of the videos. She would also like to know each type of video's percentage of total sales.

	Number Sold	Price
Pilates	156	29.99
Step	392	14.99
Weight Training	147	54.99
Kickboxing	282	29.99
Yoga	165	34.99

Create a worksheet that provides Michelle with the information needed. Include appropriate worksheet, column, and row titles. Using the formatting skills that you practiced in this chapter, format the worksheet in a manner that is professional and easy to read and understand. Insert a footer with the file name and add appropriate document properties. Save the file as **Lastname_Firstname_1L_Video_Sales** and print or submit as directed by your instructor.

You have completed Project 1L | END

GO! Think	Project 1M Planner	IRC

You and GO!	Project 1N Personal Resume	IRC

GO! Collaborative Group Project	Project 1O Bell Orchid Hotels	IRC

Using Functions, Creating Tables, and Managing Large Workbooks

2
EXCEL 2019

PROJECT 2A

Outcomes

Analyze inventory by applying statistical and logical calculations to data and by sorting and filtering data.

Objectives

1. Use Flash Fill and the SUM, AVERAGE, MEDIAN, MIN, and MAX Functions
2. Move Data, Resolve Error Messages, and Rotate Text
3. Use COUNTIF and IF Functions and Apply Conditional Formatting
4. Use Date & Time Functions and Freeze Panes
5. Create, Sort, and Filter an Excel Table
6. View, Format, and Print a Large Worksheet

PROJECT 2B

Outcomes

Summarize the data on multiple worksheets.

Objectives

7. Navigate a Workbook and Rename Worksheets
8. Enter Dates, Clear Contents, and Clear Formats
9. Copy and Paste by Using the Paste Options Gallery
10. Edit and Format Multiple Worksheets at the Same Time
11. Create a Summary Sheet with Column Sparklines
12. Format and Print Multiple Worksheets in a Workbook

joloei/Shutterstock

In This Chapter

 GO! To Work with Excel

In this chapter, you will use the Statistical functions to calculate the average of a group of numbers and perform other summary calculations. You will also use Logical and Date & Time functions. Excel's statistical functions are useful for common calculations that you probably encounter frequently. You will also use Excel's Flash Fill feature to automatically fill in values, use the counting functions, and apply different types of conditional formatting to make data easy to visualize. You will create a table to organize related information and analyze the table's information by sorting and filtering. You will summarize a workbook that contains multiple worksheets.

The projects in this chapter relate to **Rosedale Landscape and Garden**, which grows and sells trees and plants suitable for all areas of North America. Throughout its 75-year history, the company has introduced many new plants for the enjoyment of home gardeners. The company has nurseries and stores in the major metropolitan areas in the United States and Canada. In addition to high-quality plants and trees, Rosedale sells garden tools and outdoor furniture. Rosedale also offers professional landscape design and installation for both commercial and residential clients. The company headquarters is in Pasadena, California.

Inventory Status Report

Project Activities

In Activities 2.01 through 2.20, you will edit a worksheet for Jacob Hill, President of Rosedale Landscape and Garden, detailing the current inventory of trees at the Pasadena nursery. Your completed worksheet will look similar to Figure 2.1.

Project Files for **MyLab IT Grader**

1. In your storage location, create a folder named **Excel Chapter 2**.
2. In your **MyLab IT** course, locate and click **Excel 2A Tree Inventory**, Download Materials, and then Download All Files.
3. Extract the zipped folder to your Excel Chapter 2 folder. Close the Grader download screens.
4. Take a moment to open the downloaded **Excel_2A_Tree_Inventory_Instructions**; note any recent updates to the book.

Project Results

GO! Project 2A

Where We're Going

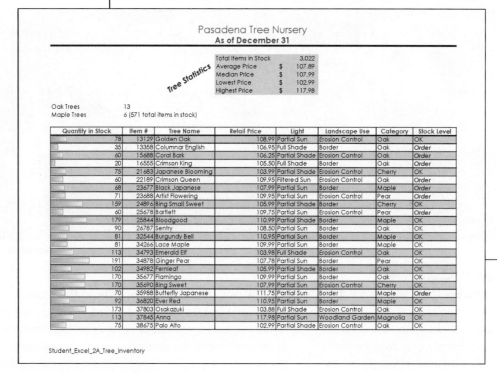

Figure 2.1 Project 2A Tree Inventory

For Non-MyLab Submissions

For Project 2A, you will need:

e02A_Tree_Inventory

In your storage location, create a folder named **Excel Chapter 2**

In your Excel Chapter 2 folder, save your workbook as:

Lastname_Firstname_2A_Tree_Inventory

If your instructor requires a workbook with formulas, save as:

Lastname_Firstname_2A_Tree_Inventory_formulas

After you have named and saved your workbook, on the next page, begin with Step 2.

<table>
<tr>
<td>Objective 1</td>
<td>Use Flash Fill and the SUM, AVERAGE, MEDIAN, MIN, and MAX Functions</td>
</tr>
</table>

ALERT Because Office 365 is a cloud-based subscription service that receives continuous updates, you may encounter some variations in what appears on your screen and what is shown in this instruction. Microsoft Office 365 is fully installed on your PC or Mac; no internet access is necessary to create or edit documents. When you *are* connected to the internet, you will receive monthly upgrades and new features, so you always have the latest versions of Office apps as soon as they are available. Your subscription gives you continuous free access to the latest innovations and refinements.

GO! Learn How

Video E2.1

Flash Fill recognizes a pattern in your data and then automatically fills in values when you enter examples of the output that you want. Use Flash Fill to split data into two or more cells or to combine data from two cells.

A *function* is the name given to a predefined formula—a formula that Excel has already built for you—that performs calculations by using specific values that you insert in a particular order or structure. *Statistical functions*, which include the AVERAGE, MEDIAN, MIN, and MAX functions, are useful to analyze a group of measurements.

Activity 2.01 | Using Flash Fill

2.1.3, Expert 2.1.1

1 Navigate to your **Excel Chapter 2 folder**, and then double-click the Excel file you downloaded from **MyLab IT** that displays your name—**Student_Excel_2A_Tree_Inventory**.

2 Scroll down. Notice that the worksheet contains data related to types of trees in inventory, including information about the *Quantity in Stock*, *Item #/Category*, *Tree Name*, *Retail Price*, *Light*, and *Landscape Use*.

3 In the **column heading area**, point to **column C** to display the ⬇ pointer, and then drag to the right to select **columns C:D**. On the **Home tab**, in the **Cells group**, click the **Insert button arrow**, and then click **Insert Sheet Columns**.

New columns for C and D display and the remaining columns move to the right.

MAC TIP To display group names on the ribbon, display the menu, click Excel, click Preferences, click View, select the Show group titles check box.

ANOTHER WAY Select the columns, right-click anywhere over the selected columns, and then on the shortcut menu, click Insert.

4 Click cell **C11**, type **13129** and then on the **Formula Bar**, click **Enter** ☑ to confirm the entry and keep **C11** as the active cell.

5 On the **Home tab**, in the **Editing group**, click **Fill**, and then click **Flash Fill**. Compare your screen with Figure 2.2.

> Use this technique to split a column of data based on what you type. Flash Fill looks to the left and sees the pattern you have established, and then fills the remaining cells in the column with only the Item #. The Flash Fill Options button displays.

Figure 2.2

6 Near the lower right corner of cell **C11**, click the **Flash Fill Options** button, and notice that here you can *Undo Flash Fill*, *Accept suggestions*, or *Select all 28 changed cells*, for example, to apply specific formatting. Click the button again to close it.

> If Excel is not sure what pattern to use, it suggests a pattern by filling with pale gray characters, and then you can use the Accept suggestions command to accept or start again.

7 Click cell **D11**, type **Oak** and then on the **Formula Bar**, click **Enter** ☑ to confirm the entry and keep **D11** as the active cell. Press Ctrl + E, which is the keyboard shortcut for Flash Fill.

> Flash Fill extracts the text from the *Item#/Category* column and also inserts *Category* as the column name. Now that *Item #* and *Category* are in two separate columns, the data can be sorted and filtered by both Item # and Category.

8 Select **column B**, and then on the **Home tab**, in the **Cells group**, click the **Delete button arrow**. Click **Delete Sheet Columns**. **Save** 🖫 your file.

🔁 **ANOTHER WAY** Select the column, right-click anywhere over the selected column, and then on the shortcut menu, click Delete.

Activity 2.02 | Moving a Column

1 In cell **B10**, type **Item #** and then press Enter. Select **column C**, and then on the **Home tab**, in the **Clipboard group**, click **Cut** ✂. Click cell **H1**, and then in the **Clipboard group**, click the upper portion of the **Paste** button.

🔁 **ANOTHER WAY** Press Ctrl + X to cut and Ctrl + V to paste.

---

2 Select and then delete **column C**. Select **columns A:G**. In the **Cells group**, click **Format**, and then click **AutoFit Column Width**.

🔁 **ANOTHER WAY** Select the columns, in the column heading area, point to any of the selected column borders to display the ⊞ pointer, and then double-click to AutoFit the columns.

---

3 **Merge & Center** cell **A1** across the range **A1:H1**, and then apply the **Title** cell style. **Merge & Center** cell **A2** across the range **A2:H2**, and then apply the **Heading 1** cell style. Compare your screen with Figure 2.3. **Save** 🖫 your workbook.

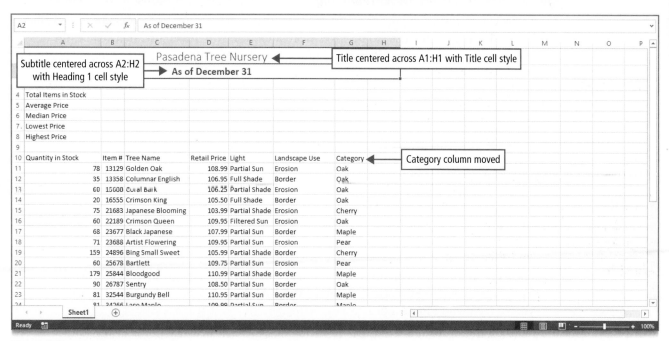

Figure 2.3

Activity 2.03 | Using the SUM and AVERAGE Functions

MOS
4.2.1

In this Activity, you will use the SUM and AVERAGE functions to gather information about the product inventory.

1 Click cell **B4**. Click the **Formulas tab**, and then in the **Function Library group**, click the upper portion of the **AutoSum** button. Compare your screen with Figure 2.4.

The *SUM function* is a predefined formula that adds all the numbers in a selected range of cells. Because it is frequently used, there are several ways to insert the function. For example, you can insert the function from the Home tab's Editing group, or by using the keyboard shortcut [Alt] + [=], or from the Function Library group on the Formulas tab, or from the Math & Trig button in that group.

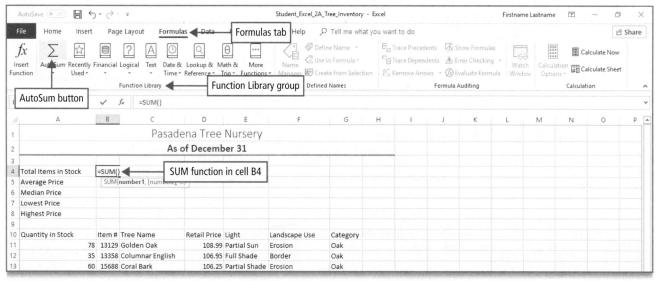

Figure 2.4

Project 2A: Inventory Status Report | **Excel** 177

2 With the insertion point blinking in the function, type the cell range **a11:a39** to sum all the values in the *Quantity in Stock* column, and then press ⏎; your result is *3022*.

3 Click cell **B4**, look at the **Formula Bar**, and then compare your screen with Figure 2.5.

SUM is the name of the function. The values in parentheses are the **arguments**—the values that an Excel function uses to perform calculations or operations. In this instance, the argument consists of the values in the range A11:A39.

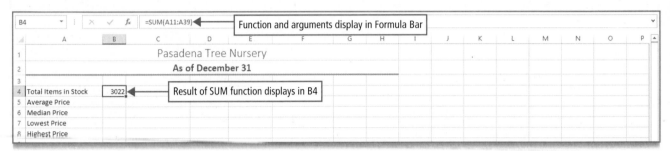

Figure 2.5

4 Click cell **B5**. On the **Formulas tab**, in the **Function Library group**, click **More Functions**, point to **Statistical**, point to **AVERAGE**, and notice the ScreenTip. Compare your screen with Figure 2.6.

The ScreenTip describes how the AVERAGE function will compute the calculation.

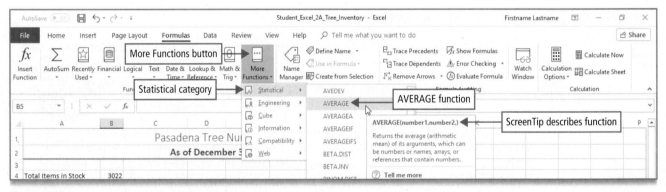

Figure 2.6

5 Click **AVERAGE**, and then if necessary, drag the title bar of the Function Arguments dialog box down and to the right so you can view the Formula Bar and cell B5.

The *AVERAGE function* adds a group of values, and then divides the result by the number of values in the group. In the cell, the Formula Bar, and the dialog box, Excel proposes to average the value in cell B4. Recall that Excel functions will propose a range if there is data above or to the left of a selected cell.

6 In the **Function Arguments** dialog box, notice that *B4* is highlighted. Press ⌦ to delete the existing text, type **d11:d39** and then compare your screen with Figure 2.7.

Because you want to average the retail price values in the range D11:D39—and not cell B4—you must edit the proposed range.

🖥 **MAC TIP** When you click Average, the Formula Builder displays at the right side of the Excel window. In the Formula Builder, under Number1, delete B4, type d11:d39, and then click Done. Leave the Formula Builder open for the next Activity.

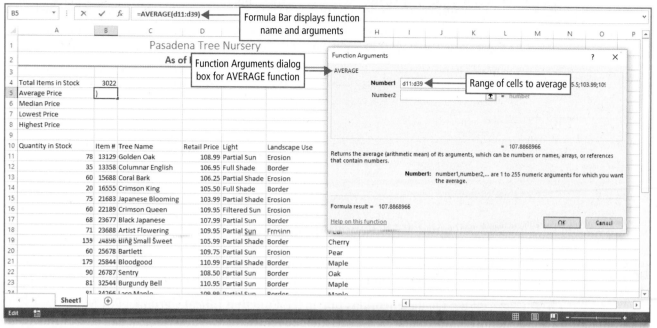

Figure 2.7

7 In the **Function Arguments** dialog box, click **OK**, and then click **Save** 🖫.

The result indicates that the average Retail Price of all products is *107.89.*

Activity 2.04 | Using the MEDIAN Function

The *MEDIAN function* is a statistical function that describes a group of data—it is commonly used to describe the price of houses in a particular geographical area. The MEDIAN function finds the middle value that has as many values above it in the group as are below it. It differs from AVERAGE in that the result is not affected as much by a single value that is greatly different from the others.

1 Click cell **B6**. In the **Function Library group**, click **More Functions**, display the list of **Statistical** functions, scroll down as necessary, and then click **MEDIAN**.

2 Delete the text in the **Number1** box. Type **d11:d39** and then compare your screen with Figure 2.8.

When indicating which cells you want to use in the function's calculation—known as *defining the arguments*—you can either select the values with your mouse or type the range of values, whichever you prefer.

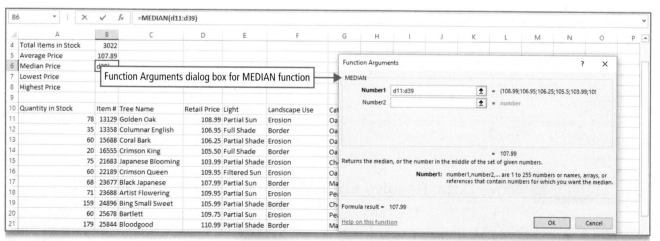

Figure 2.8

3 ▶ Click **OK** to display *107.99* in cell **B6**. Click **Save** 🖫 and compare your screen with Figure 2.9.

In the range of prices, 107.99 is the middle value. Half of all trees in inventory are priced *above* 107.99 and half are priced *below* 107.99.

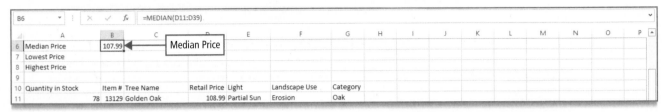

Figure 2.9

Activity 2.05 | Using the MIN and MAX Functions

MOS
4.2.1

The statistical *MIN function* determines the smallest value in a selected range of values. The statistical *MAX function* determines the largest value in a selected range of values.

1 ▶ Click cell **B7**. On the **Formulas tab**, in the **Function Library group**, click **More Functions**, display the list of **Statistical** functions, scroll as necessary, and then click **MIN**.

2 ▶ Delete the text in the **Number1** box. Type **d11:d39** and then click **OK**.

The lowest Retail Price is *102.99*.

3 ▶ Click cell **B8**, and then by using a similar technique, insert the **MAX** function to determine the highest **Retail Price**, and then check to see that your result is *117.98*.

4 ▶ Press Ctrl + Home. Point to cell **B4**, right-click, and then on the mini toolbar, click **Comma Style** ⟨ , ⟩ one time and **Decrease Decimal** ⟨.00→.0⟩ two times.

💻 **MAC TIP** Close the Formula Builder. Press Control + fn + ←. Click cell B4, and then on the Home tab, click Comma Style. Click Decrease Decimal two times.

5 ▶ Select the range **B5:B8**, apply the **Accounting Number Format** ⟨$ ▾⟩, click **Save** 🖫, and then compare your screen with Figure 2.10.

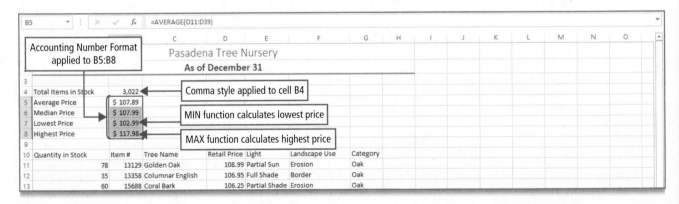

Figure 2.10

Objective 2 | Move Data, Resolve Error Messages, and Rotate Text

GO! Learn How
Video E2-2

When you move a formula, the cell references within the formula do not change, no matter what type of cell reference you use.

If you move cells into a column that is not wide enough to display number values, Excel will display a message so that you can adjust as necessary.

You can reposition data within a cell at an angle by rotating the text.

Activity 2.06 | Moving Data and Resolving a # # # # # Error Message

1 Select **column E** and set the width to **50 pixels**. Select the range **A4:B8**. Point to the right edge of the selected range to display the pointer, and then compare your screen with Figure 2.11.

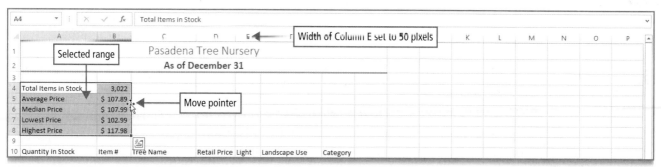

Figure 2.11

2 Drag the selected range to the right until the ScreenTip displays *D4:E8*, release the mouse button, and then notice that a series of *#* symbols displays in **column E**. Point to any of the cells that display *#* symbols, and then compare your screen with Figure 2.12.

Using this technique, cell contents can be moved from one location to another; this is referred to as *drag and drop*.

If a cell width is too narrow to display the entire number, Excel displays the ##### message, because displaying only a portion of a number would be misleading. The underlying values remain unchanged and are displayed in the Formula Bar for the selected cell. An underlying value also displays in the ScreenTip if you point to a cell containing # symbols.

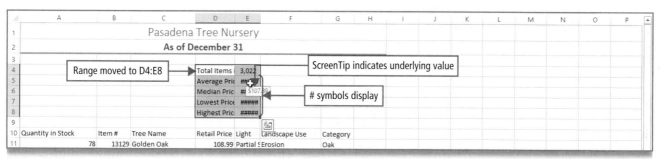

Figure 2.12

3 Select **columns D:E**, and then in the **column heading area**, point to the right boundary of **column E** to display the + pointer. Double-click to AutoFit the columns to accommodate the widest entry in each column.

4 Select the range **D4:E8**. On the **Home tab**, in the **Styles group**, display the **Cell Styles** gallery. Under **Themed Cell Styles**, click **20%-Accent1**. Click **Save** .

Activity 2.07 | Merging Cells and Rotating Text

MOS

2.2.1, 2.2.2, 2.2.6

1 In cell **C6**, type **Tree Statistics** and then press [Enter].

2 Select the range **C4:C8**, right-click over the selection, and then on the shortcut menu, click **Format Cells**.

> **MAC TIP** Hold down [Control] and click the selection. On the shortcut menu, click Format Cells.

3 In the **Format Cells** dialog box, click the **Alignment tab**. Under **Text control**, select the **Merge cells** check box. Under **Orientation**, click in the **Degrees** box to select the value, type **30** and then compare your screen with Figure 2.13.

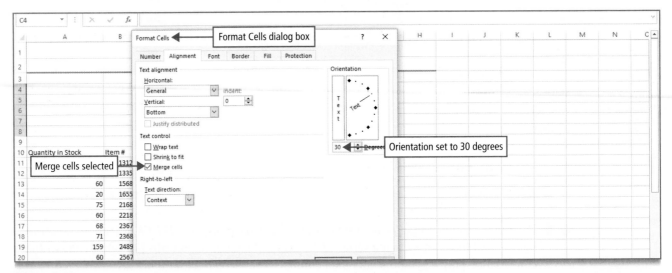

Figure 2.13

> **ANOTHER WAY** In the upper right portion of the dialog box, under Orientation, point to the red diamond, and then drag the diamond upward until the Degrees box indicates 30.

4 In the lower right corner of the **Format Cells** dialog box, click **OK** to apply the merge cell and text rotation settings.

5 On the **Home tab**, in the **Font group**, change the **Font Size** [11 ▾] to 14, and then apply **Bold** [B] and **Italic** [I]. Click the **Font Color arrow** [A ▾], and then in the fifth column, click the first color.

6 In the **Alignment group**, apply **Align Right** [≣]. Move to cell **A1**, and then compare your screen with Figure 2.14.

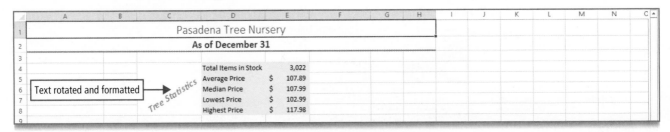

Figure 2.14

7 In the **row heading area**, point to **row 9**, and then right-click to select the row and display the shortcut menu. Click **Insert**, and then press [F4] two times to repeat the last action and insert two additional blank rows.

> [F4] is useful to repeat commands in Microsoft Office programs. Most commands can be repeated in this manner.

> **MAC TIP** To insert rows, from the row heading area, drag to select rows 9:11. On the Home tab, click Insert to insert three rows.

8 From the **row heading area**, select **rows 9:11**. On the **Home tab**, in the **Editing group**, click **Clear** ⬧, and then click **Clear Formats** to remove the blue accent color in columns D and E from the new rows. Click **Save** 🖫.

> When you insert rows or columns, formatting from adjacent rows or columns repeats in the new cells.

9 Click cell **E4**, look at the **Formula Bar**, and then notice that the arguments of the **SUM** function adjusted and refer to the appropriate cells in rows 14:42.

> The referenced range updates to *A14:A42* after you insert the three new rows. In this manner, Excel adjusts the cell references in a formula relative to their new locations.

Objective 3 Use COUNTIF and IF Functions and Apply Conditional Formatting

GO! Learn How
Video E2-3

Recall that statistical functions analyze a group of measurements. Another group of Excel functions, referred to as *logical functions*, test for specific conditions. Logical functions typically use conditional tests to determine whether specified conditions—called *criteria*—are true or false.

Activity 2.08 │ Using the COUNTIF Function

The *COUNT function* counts the number of cells in a range that contain numbers. The *COUNTIF function* is a statistical function that counts the number of cells within a range that meet the given condition—the criteria that you provide. The COUNTIF function has two arguments—the range of cells to check and the criteria.

The trees of Rosedale Landscape and Garden will be featured on an upcoming segment of a TV gardening show. In this Activity, you will use the COUNTIF function to determine the number of *Oak* trees currently available in inventory that can be featured in the TV show.

1 In cell **A10**, type **Oak Trees** and then press Tab.

2 With cell **B10** as the active cell, on the **Formulas tab**, in the **Function Library group**, click **More Functions**, and then display the list of **Statistical** functions. Click **COUNTIF**.

> Recall that the COUNTIF function counts the number of cells within a range that meet the given condition.

3 In the **Range** box, type **g14:g42** and then click in the **Criteria** box. Type **Oak** and then compare your screen with Figure 2.15.

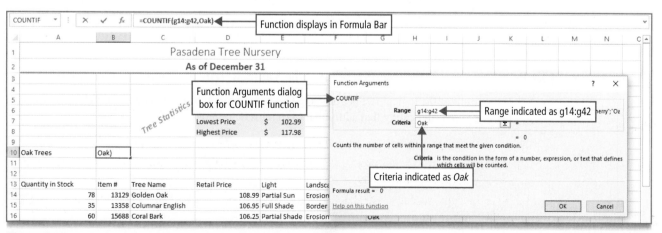

Figure 2.15

4 In the lower right corner of the **Function Arguments** dialog box, click **OK**.

There are *13* different *Oak* trees available to feature on the TV show.

5 On the **Home tab**, in the **Alignment group**, click **Align Left** to place the result closer to the row title. **Save** your workbook.

Activity 2.09 | Using the IF Function

A *logical test* is any value or expression that you can evaluate as being true or false. The *IF function* uses a logical test to check whether a condition is met, and then returns one value if true, and another value if false.

For example, *C14=228* is an expression that can be evaluated as true or false. If the value in cell C14 is equal to 228, the expression is true. If the value in cell C14 is not 228, the expression is false.

In this Activity, you will use the IF function to evaluate the inventory levels and determine if more products should be ordered.

1 Click cell **H13**, type **Stock Level** and then press Enter.

2 In cell **H14**, on the **Formulas tab**, in the **Function Library group**, click **Logical**, and then in the list, click **IF**. Drag the title bar of the **Function Arguments** dialog box up or down to view **row 14** on your screen.

3 With the insertion point in the **Logical_test** box, type **a14<75**

This logical test will look at the value in cell A14, which is *78*, and then determine whether the number is less than 75. The expression *<75* includes the *< comparison operator*, which means *less than*. Comparison operators compare values.

4 Examine the table in Figure 2.16 for a list of comparison operator symbols and their definitions.

Comparison Operators	
Comparison Operators	**Symbol Definition**
=	Equal to
>	Greater than
<	Less than
>=	Greater than or equal to
<=	Less than or equal to
<>	Not equal to

Figure 2.16

5 Press Tab to move the insertion point to the **Value_if_true** box, and then type **Order**

If the result of the logical test is true—the Quantity in Stock is less than 75—cell H14 will display the text *Order*, indicating that additional trees must be ordered.

6 Press `Tab` to move to the **Value_if_false** box, type **OK** and then compare your screen with Figure 2.17.

If the result of the logical test is false—the Quantity in Stock is *not* less than 75—then Excel will display *OK* in the cell, indicating that no order is necessary at this time.

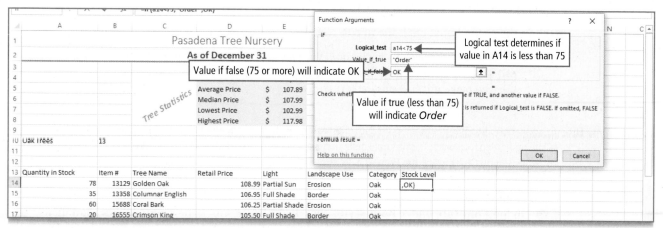

Figure 2.17

7 Click **OK** or press `Enter` to display the result *OK* in cell **H14**.

8 Using the fill handle, copy the function in cell **H14** down through cell **H42**. Then scroll as necessary to view cell **A18**, which contains the value *75*. Look at cell **H18** and notice that the **Stock Level** is indicated as *OK*. **Save** 💾 your workbook. Compare your screen with Figure 2.18.

The comparison operator indicated <75 (less than 75) and therefore a value of *exactly* 75 is indicated as OK.

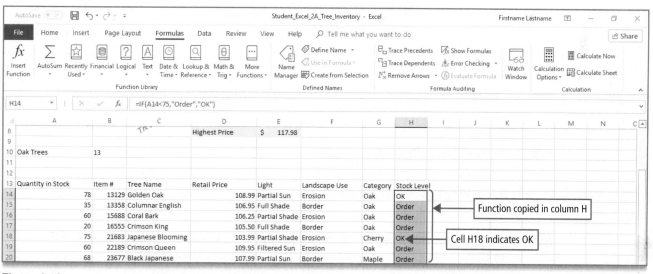

Figure 2.18

Activity 2.10 | Applying Conditional Formatting by Using Highlight Cells Rules and Data Bars

MOS
2.4.2

A ***conditional format*** changes the appearance of a cell based on a condition—a criteria. If the condition is true, the cell is formatted based on that condition; if the condition is false, the cell is *not* formatted. In this Activity, you will use conditional formatting as another way to draw attention to the Stock Level of trees.

1 Be sure the range **H14:H42** is selected. On the **Home tab**, in the **Styles group**, click **Conditional Formatting**. In the list, point to **Highlight Cells Rules**, and then click **Text that Contains**.

2 In the **Text That Contains** dialog box, with the insertion point blinking in the first box, type **Order** and notice that in the selected range, the text *Order* displays with the default format— Light Red Fill with Dark Red Text.

3 In the second box, click the **arrow**, and then in the list, click **Custom Format**.

Here, in the Format Cells dialog box, you can select any combination of formats to apply to the cell if the condition is true. The custom format you specify will be applied to any cell in the selected range if it contains the text *Order*.

MAC TIP To apply conditional formatting, in the New Formatting Rule box, be sure that the dialog box includes the following settings: Classic, Format only cells that contain, Specific Text, and containing. To the right of containing, type Order. Click the Format with arrow, and then click Custom Format.

4 On the **Font tab**, under **Font style**, click **Bold Italic**. Click the **Color arrow**, and then under **Theme Colors**, in the last column, click the first color. Click the **Fill** tab. Under **Background color**, click **No Color**. Click **OK**. Compare your screen with Figure 2.19.

In the range, if the cell meets the condition of containing *Order*, the font color will change to Bold Italic, Green, Accent 6.

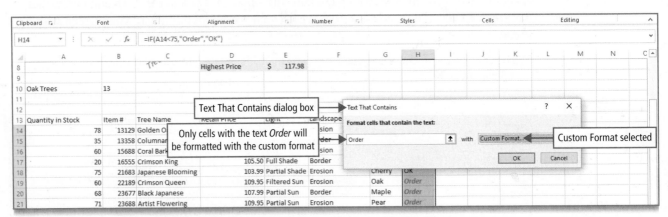

Figure 2.19

5 In the **Text That Contains** dialog box, click **OK**.

MAC TIP In the New Formatting Rule dialog box, click OK.

6 Select the range **A14:A42**. In the **Styles group**, click **Conditional Formatting**. Point to **Data Bars**, and then under **Gradient Fill**, click **Orange Data Bar**. Click anywhere to cancel the selection, click **Save**, and then compare your screen with Figure 2.20.

A *data bar* provides a visual cue to the reader about the value of a cell relative to other cells. The length of the data bar represents the value in the cell. A longer bar represents a higher value and a shorter bar represents a lower value. Data bars are useful for identifying higher and lower numbers quickly within a large group of data, such as very high or very low levels of inventory.

Figure 2.20

Activity 2.11 | Using Find and Replace

1.2.1

The *Find and Replace* feature searches the cells in a worksheet—or in a selected range—for matches, and then replaces each match with a replacement value of your choice.

Comments from customers on the company's blog indicate that using the term *Erosion Control* would be clearer than *Erosion* when describing the best landscape use for specific trees. Therefore, all products of this type will be relabeled accordingly. In this Activity, you will replace all occurrences of *Erosion* with *Erosion Control*.

1 Select the range **F14:F42**. On the **Home tab**, in the **Editing group**, click **Find & Select**, and then click **Replace**.

Restrict the find and replace operation to a specific range in this manner, especially if there is a possibility that the name occurs elsewhere.

MAC TIP Press Control + F to display the Find dialog box, and then click Replace.

2 In the **Find what** box, type **Erosion** and then press Tab. In the **Replace with** box, type **Erosion Control** and then compare your screen with Figure 2.21.

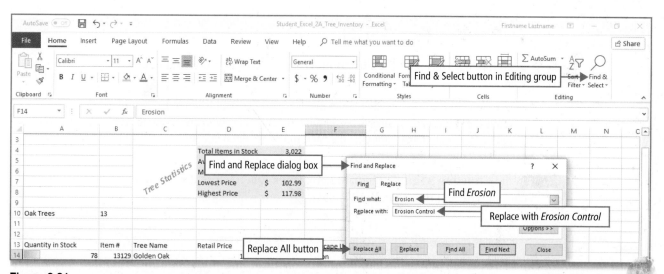

Figure 2.21

3 Click **Replace All**. In the message box, notice that 13 replacements were made, and then click **OK**. In the lower right corner of the **Find and Replace** dialog box, click **Close**, and then click **Save**.

GO! Learn How
Video E2-4

Excel can obtain the date and time from your computer's calendar and clock and display this information on your worksheet.

By freezing or splitting panes, you can view two areas of a worksheet and lock rows and columns in one area. When you freeze panes, you select the specific rows or columns that you want to remain visible when scrolling in your worksheet.

Activity 2.12 | Using the NOW Function to Display a System Date

Expert 3.3.1

The *NOW function* retrieves the date and time from your computer's calendar and clock and inserts the information into the selected cell. The result is formatted as a date and time.

1 To the left of the **Formula Bar**, click in the **Name Box**, type **a44** and then press Enter. Notice that cell A44 is the active cell.

2 With cell **A44** as the active cell, on the **Formulas tab**, in the **Function Library group**, click **Date & Time**. In the list of functions, click **NOW**. Compare your screen with Figure 2.22.

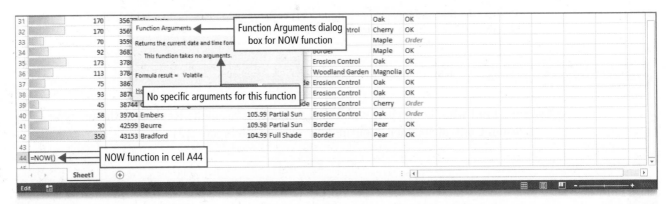

Figure 2.22

3 Read the description in the **Function Arguments** dialog box and notice that this result is *Volatile*.

The Function Arguments dialog box displays a message indicating that this function does not require an argument. It also states that this function is *volatile*, meaning the date and time will not remain as entered, but rather the date and time will automatically update each time you open this workbook.

4 In the **Function Arguments** dialog box, click **OK** to close the dialog box to display the current date and time in cell **A44**. **Save** 🖫 your workbook.

⬜ **MAC TIP**   In the Formula Builder, click Done, and then close the Formula Builder.

MORE KNOWLEDGE   **NOW Function Recalculates Each Time a Workbook Opens**

The NOW function updates each time the workbook is opened. With the workbook open, you can force the NOW function to update by pressing F9 , for example, to update the time.

Activity 2.13 | Freezing and Unfreezing Panes

1.4.3

In a large worksheet, if you scroll down more than 25 rows or scroll beyond column O (the exact row number and column letter varies, depending on your screen size and screen resolution), you will no longer see the top rows or first column of your worksheet where identifying information about the data is usually placed. You will find it easier to work with your data if you can always view the identifying row or column titles.

The **Freeze Panes** command enables you to select one or more rows or columns and then freeze (lock) them into place. The locked rows and columns become separate panes. A **pane** is a portion of a worksheet window bounded by and separated from other portions by vertical or horizontal bars.

1 ▶ Press Ctrl + Home to make cell **A1** the active cell. Scroll down until **row 21** displays at the top of your Excel window, and notice that all of the identifying information in the column titles is out of view.

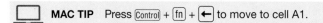
MAC TIP Press Control + fn + ← to move to cell A1.

2 ▶ Press Ctrl + Home again, and then from the **row heading area**, select **row 14**. Click the **View tab**, and then in the **Window group**, click **Freeze Panes**. In the list, click **Freeze Panes**. Click any cell to deselect the row, and then notice that a line displays along the upper border of **row 14**.

> By selecting row 14, the rows above—rows 1–13—are frozen in place and will not move as you scroll down.

3 ▶ Watch the row numbers below **row 13**, and then begin to scroll down to bring **row 21** into view again. Notice that rows 1:13 are frozen in place. Compare your screen with Figure 2.23.

> The remaining rows of data continue to scroll. Use this feature when you have long or wide worksheets.

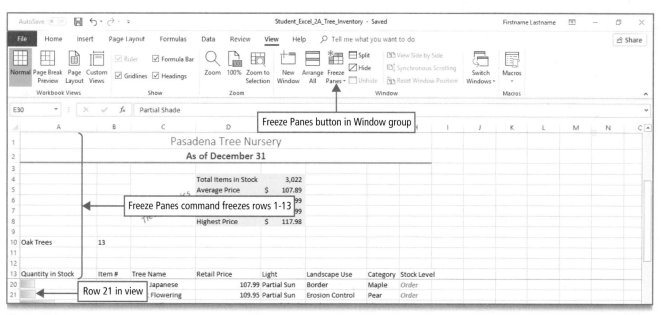

Figure 2.23

4 ▶ In the **Window group**, click **Freeze Panes**, and then click **Unfreeze Panes** to unlock all rows and columns. **Save** 💾 your workbook.

MORE KNOWLEDGE | **Freeze Columns or Freeze Both Rows and Columns**

You can freeze columns that you want to remain in view on the left. Select the column to the right of the column(s) that you want to remain in view while scrolling to the right, and then click the Freeze Panes command. You can also use the command to freeze both rows and columns; click a *cell* to freeze the rows *above* the cell and the columns to the *left* of the cell.

GO! Learn How
Video E2-5

To analyze a group of related data, you can convert a range of cells to an *Excel table*. An Excel table is a series of rows and columns that contains related data that is managed independently from the data in other rows and columns in the worksheet.

Activity 2.14 | Creating an Excel Table and Applying a Table Style

3.1.1 and 3.1.2

1 Be sure that you have applied the Unfreeze Panes command—no rows on your worksheet are locked. Click any cell in the data below **row 13**. Click the **Insert tab**. In the **Tables group**, click **Table**. In the **Create Table** dialog box, if necessary, click to select the My table has headers check box. Verify that in the dialog box, **$A$13:$H$42** displays, and then compare your screen with Figure 2.24.

The column titles in row 13 will form the table headers. By clicking in a range of contiguous data, Excel will suggest the range as the data for the table. You can adjust the range if necessary.

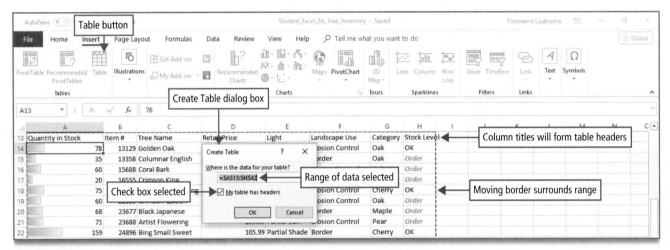

Figure 2.24

ANOTHER WAY   Select the range of cells that make up the table, including the header row, and then click the Table button.

---

2 Click **OK**. With the range still selected, on the ribbon, notice that the **Table Tools** contextual tab is active.

3 On the **Design tab**, in the **Table Styles group**, click **More**, and then under **Light**, locate and click **Light Blue, Table Style Light 16**. If this table style is not available, choose a similar style.

4 Make cell **A1** the active cell. Click **Save**, and then compare your screen with Figure 2.25.

Sorting and filtering arrows display in the table's header row.

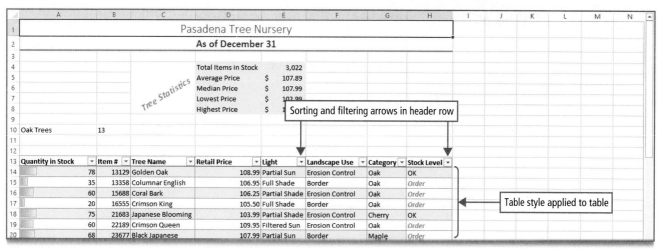

Figure 2.25

Activity 2.15 | Sorting an Excel Table

You can *sort* tables—arrange all the data in a specific order—in ascending or descending order.

1 In the header row of the table, click the **Retail Price arrow**, and then on the menu, click **Sort Smallest to Largest**. Next to the arrow, notice the small **up arrow** indicating an ascending (smallest to largest) sort.

This action sorts the rows in the table from the lowest retail price to highest retail price.

> **MAC TIP** In the Retail Price dialog box, under Sort, click Ascending, and then click Close.

2 In the table's header row, click the **Category arrow**, and then click **Sort Z to A**.

This action sorts the rows in the table in reverse alphabetic order by Category name, and the small arrow points downward, indicating a descending (Z to A) sort. The Retail Price continues to be sorted from smallest to largest within each category.

> **MAC TIP** In the Category dialog box, under Sort, click Descending.

3 Click the **Category arrow**, and then sort from **A to Z**. Next to the arrow, notice the small **up arrow** indicating an ascending (A to Z) sort.

This action sorts the rows in the table alphabetically by Category, and within a Category, it sorts the rows from smallest to largest by Retail Price.

> **MAC TIP** In the Category dialog box, under Sort, click Ascending, and then click Close.

4 In the table header row, click the **Item # arrow**, and then click **Sort Smallest to Largest**, which will apply an ascending sort to the data using the *Item #* column.

> **MAC TIP** In the Item # dialog box, under Sort, click Ascending, and close the dialog box.

Activity 2.16 | Filtering an Excel Table and Displaying a Total Row

3.2.3 and
3.3.1

You can *filter* tables—display only a portion of the data based on matching a specific value—to show only the data that meets the criteria that you specify.

1 Click the **Category arrow**. Click the **(Select All)** check box to clear all the check boxes. Click to select only the **Maple** check box, and then click **OK**. Compare your screen with Figure 2.26.

Only the rows containing *Maple* in the Category column display—the remaining rows are hidden from view. A small funnel—the filter icon—indicates that a filter is applied to the data in the table. Additionally, the row numbers display in blue to indicate that some rows are hidden from view. A filter hides entire rows in the worksheet.

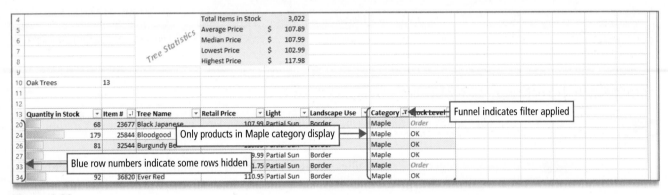

Figure 2.26

2 Point to the right of *Category* and notice that *Equals "Maple"* displays to indicate the filter criteria.

3 Click any cell in the table so that the table is selected. On the **Table Tools Design tab**, in the **Table Style Options group**, select the **Total Row** check box.

Total displays in cell A43. In cell H43, the number *6* indicates that six rows currently display.

4 Click cell **A43**, click the **arrow** that displays to the right of cell **A43**, and then in the list, click **Sum**.

Excel sums only the visible rows in Column A and indicates that 571 products in the Maple category are in stock. In this manner, you can use an Excel table to quickly find information about a group of data.

5 Click cell **A11**, type **Maple Trees** and press Tab. In cell **B11**, type **6 (571 total items in stock)** and then press Enter.

6 In the table header row, click the **Category arrow**, and then click **Clear Filter From "Category"**.

All the rows in the table redisplay.

> **MAC TIP** To clear the filter, click the Category arrow, click Clear Filter, and then click Close.

7 Click the **Landscape Use arrow**, click the **(Select All)** check box to clear all the check boxes, and then click to select the **Erosion Control** check box. Click **OK**.

8 Click the **Category arrow**, click the **(Select All)** check box to clear all the check boxes, and then click the **Oak** check box. Click **OK, Save** 🖫 your workbook, and then compare your screen with Figure 2.27.

By applying multiple filters, you can determine quickly that eight tree names identified with a *Landscape Use* of *Erosion Control* are in the *Oak* tree category with a total of 710 such trees in stock.

	Quantity in Stock	Item #	Tree Name	Retail Price	Light	Landscape Use	Category	Stock Level
10	Oak Trees	13						
11	Maple Trees	6 (571 total items in stock)						
12								
13	Quantity in Stock	Item #	Tree Name	Retail Price	Light	Landscape Use	Category	Stock Level
14	78	13129	Golden Oak	108.99	Partial Sun	Erosion Control	Oak	OK
16	60	15688	Coral Bark	106.25	Partial Shade	Erosion Control	Oak	Order
19	60	22189	Crimson Queen	109.95	Filtered Sun	Erosion Control	Oak	Order
28	113	34793	Emerald Elf	103.98	Full Shade	Erosion Control	Oak	OK
35	173	37803	Osakazuki	103.88	Full Shade	Erosion Control	Oak	OK
37	75	38675	Palo Alto	102.99	Partial Shade	Erosion Control	Oak	OK
38	93	38700	Pacific Fire	103.75	Full Shade	Erosion Control	Oak	OK
40	58	39704	Embers	105.99	Partial Sun	Erosion Control	Oak	Order
43	710							8

8 tree types in Oak category can be used for Erosion Control

Figure 2.27

MORE KNOWLEDGE | **Band Rows and Columns in a Table**

You can band rows to format even rows differently from odd rows, making them easier to read. To band rows or columns, on the Design tab, in the Table Style Options group, select the Banded Rows or Banded Columns check box.

Activity 2.17 | Clearing Filters

When you are finished answering questions about the data in a table, you can clear the filters and remove the total row.

1 Click the **Category arrow**, and then click **Clear Filter From "Category"**. Use the same technique to remove the filter from the **Landscape Use** column.

2 Click anywhere in the table to activate the table. On the **Table Tools Design tab**, in the **Table Style Options group**, click the **Total Row** check box to clear the check mark and remove the Total row from the table.

3 Click **Save** 🖫, and then compare your screen with Figure 2.28.

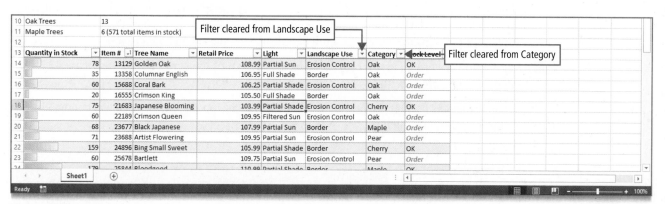

Filter cleared from Landscape Use

Filter cleared from Category

	Quantity in Stock	Item #	Tree Name	Retail Price	Light	Landscape Use	Category	Stock Level
10	Oak Trees	13						
11	Maple Trees	6 (571 total items in stock)						
12								
13	Quantity in Stock	Item #	Tree Name	Retail Price	Light	Landscape Use	Category	Stock Level
14	78	13129	Golden Oak	108.99	Partial Sun	Erosion Control	Oak	OK
15	35	13358	Columnar English	106.95	Full Shade	Border	Oak	Order
16	60	15688	Coral Bark	106.25	Partial Shade	Erosion Control	Oak	Order
17	20	16555	Crimson King	105.50	Full Shade	Border	Oak	Order
18	75	21683	Japanese Blooming	103.99	Partial Shade	Erosion Control	Cherry	OK
19	60	22189	Crimson Queen	109.95	Filtered Sun	Erosion Control	Oak	Order
20	68	23677	Black Japanese	107.99	Partial Sun	Border	Maple	Order
21	71	23688	Artist Flowering	109.95	Partial Sun	Erosion Control	Pear	Order
22	159	24896	Bing Small Sweet	105.99	Partial Shade	Border	Cherry	OK
23	60	25678	Bartlett	109.75	Partial Sun	Erosion Control	Pear	Order
24	170	25844	Bloodgood	110.99	Partial Shade	Border	Maple	OK

Sheet1

Ready

100%

Figure 2.28

MORE KNOWLEDGE | **Converting a Table to a Range**

When you are finished answering questions about the data in a table by sorting, filtering, and totalling, you can convert the table into a normal range. Doing so is useful if you want to use the Table feature only to apply an attractive Table Style to a range of cells. For example, you can insert a table, apply a Table Style, and then convert the table to a normal range of data but keep the formatting. To convert a table to a range, on the Design tab, in the Tools group, click Convert to Range. In the message box, click Yes. Or, with any table cell selected, right-click, point to Table, and then click Convert to Range.

GO! Learn How
Video E2-6

You can magnify or shrink the view of a worksheet on your screen to either zoom in to view specific data or zoom out to see the entire worksheet. You can also split a worksheet window into panes to view different parts of a worksheet at the same time.

A worksheet might be too wide, too long—or both—to print on a single page. Use Excel's *Print Titles* and *Scale to Fit* commands to create pages that are attractive and easy to read.

The Print Titles command enables you to specify rows and columns to repeat on each printed page. Scale to Fit commands enable you to stretch or shrink the width, height, or both, of printed output to fit a maximum number of pages.

Activity 2.18 | Modifying and Shrinking the Worksheet View

1 Press Ctrl + Home to display the top of your worksheet. On the **View tab**, in the **Zoom group**, click **Zoom**.

🖥 **MAC TIP**   Press Control + fn + ←. On the View tab, click the Zoom arrow.

2 In the **Zoom** dialog box, click the **75%** option button, and then click **OK.** Notice that by zooming out in this manner, you can see additional rows of your worksheet on the screen.

3 In the lower right corner of your worksheet, in the status bar, click the **Zoom In** button ➕ until the worksheet redisplays at 100%.

Activity 2.19 | Splitting a Worksheet Window into Panes

MOS
1.4.4

The *Split* command splits the window into multiple resizable panes that contain views of your worksheet. This is useful to view multiple distant parts of your worksheet at one time.

1 Click cell **F9**. On the **View tab**, in the **Window group**, click **Split**.

Horizontal and vertical split bars display. You can drag the split bars to view any four portions of the worksheet. On the right, separate vertical scroll bars display for the upper and lower panes and at the bottom, separate horizontal scroll bars display for the left and right panes.

2 Drag the lower vertical scroll box down to the bottom of the scroll bar to view **row 43.** Compare your screen with Figure 2.29.

Here it could be useful to isolate the Tree Statistics at the top and then scroll to the bottom to browse the inventory items.

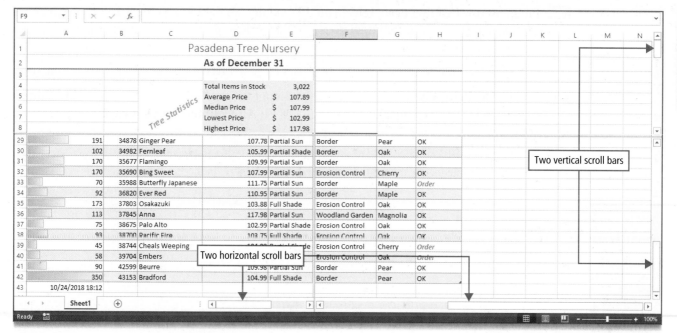

Figure 2.29

3 ▶ Click **Split** again to remove the split bars.

4 ▶ Press ⌃Ctrl + ⌂Home to display the top of your worksheet. On the **Page Layout tab**, in the **Themes group**, click **Themes**, and then click **Slice**.

5 ▶ Select the range **A13:H13**. On the **Home tab**, from the **Styles group**, apply the **Heading 4** cell style, and then apply **Center** ▤. Click cell **A1**.

Activity 2.20 | Printing Titles and Scaling to Fit

1.5.3

1 ▶ Click the **Page Layout tab**, and then in the **Page Setup group**, click **Margins**. At the bottom of the gallery, click **Custom Margins** to display the **Page Setup** dialog box. Under **Center on page**, select the **Horizontally** check box.

2 ▶ Click the **Header/Footer tab**, and then in the center of the dialog box, click **Custom Footer**. In the **Footer** dialog box, with your insertion point blinking in the **Left section**, on the row of buttons, click **Insert File Name** ⊞. Click **OK** two times.

3 ▶ In the **Page Setup group**, click **Orientation**, and then click **Landscape**.

The dotted line indicates that as currently formatted, column H will not fit on the page.

4 ▶ On the **File tab**, click **Print** to display the **Print Preview**. At the bottom of the **Print Preview**, click **Next Page** ▶.

As currently formatted, the worksheet will print on four pages, and the columns will span multiple pages. Additionally, after Page 1, no column titles are visible to identify the data in the columns.

5 ▶ Click **Next Page** ▶ two times to display **Page 4** and notice that one column moves to an additional page.

6 ▶ In the upper left corner of **Backstage** view, click **Back** ⊙ to return to the worksheet. In the **Page Setup group**, click **Print Titles**. Under **Print titles**, click in the **Rows to repeat at top** box, and then at the right, click **Collapse Dialog** ⬆.

7 From the **row heading area**, select **row 13**, and then in the **Page Setup – rows to repeat at top:** dialog box, click **Expand Dialog** 🔲. Click **OK** to print the column titles in row 13 at the top of every page.

> You can collapse and then expand dialog boxes on your screen to enable a better view of your data.

8 Display the **Print Preview** again. At the bottom of the **Settings group**, click the **No Scaling arrow**, and then on the displayed list, point to **Fit All Columns on One Page**. Compare your screen with Figure 2.30.

> This action will shrink the width of the printed output to fit all the columns on one page. You can make adjustments like this on the Page Layout tab, or here, in the Print Preview.

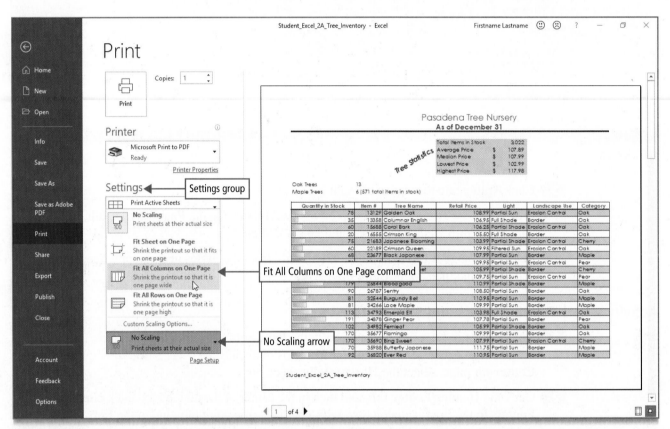

Figure 2.30

🖥 **MAC TIP** To fit the worksheet width on one page, close the Print dialog box. On the Page Layout tab, click the Width button arrow, and then click 1 page.

---

9 Click **Fit All Columns on One Page**. Notice in the **Print Preview** that all the columns display on one page.

🔄 **ANOTHER WAY** With the worksheet displayed, on the Page Layout tab, in the Scale to Fit group, click the Width button arrow, and then click 1 page.

---

10 At the bottom of the **Print Preview**, click **Next Page** ▶ one time. Notice that the output will now print on two pages and that the column titles display at the top of **Page 2**. Compare your screen with Figure 2.31.

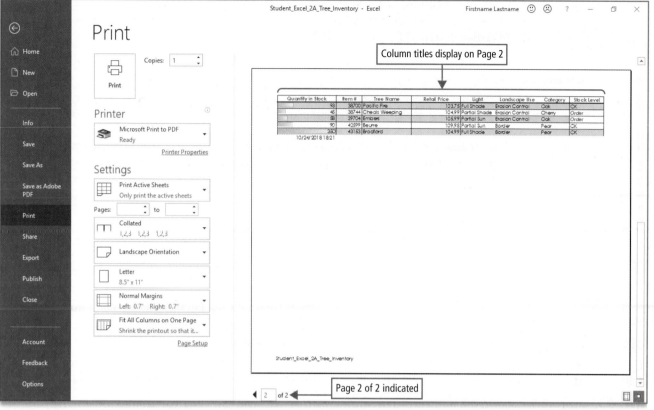

Figure 2.31

11 Display the workbook **Properties**. As the **Tags**, type **tree inventory**, **Pasadena** and as the **Subject**, type your course name and section number. Be sure your name displays as the Author; edit if necessary. **Save** your worksheet and then **Close** Excel.

> **MAC TIP** To edit the document properties, click File, and then click Properties. Click Summary, and then edit the properties as necessary.

MORE KNOWLEDGE **Scaling for Data That Is Slightly Larger Than the Printed Page**

If your data is just a little too large to fit on a printed page, you can scale the worksheet to make it fit. Scaling reduces both the width and height of the printed data to a percentage of its original size or by the number of pages that you specify. On the Page Layout tab, in the Scale to Fit group, click the Scale arrows to select a percentage.

For Non-MyLab Submissions Determine What Your Instructor Requires for Submission
As directed by your instructor, submit your completed Excel workbook.

12 In **MyLab IT**, locate and click the Grader Project **Excel 2A Tree Inventory**. In **step 3**, under **Upload Completed Assignment**, click **Choose File**. In the **Open** dialog box, navigate to your **Excel Chapter 2 folder**, and then click your **Student_Excel_2A_Tree_Inventory** file one time to select it. In the lower right corner of the **Open** dialog box, click **Open**.

The name of your selected file displays above the Upload button.

13 To submit your file to **MyLab IT** for grading, click **Upload**, wait a moment for a green **Success!** message, and then in **step 4**, click the blue **Submit for Grading** button. Click **Close Assignment** to return to your list of **Course Materials**.

You have completed Project 2A | **END**

»» GO! With Google Sheets

Objective	Summarize an Inventory List

ALERT   **Working with Web-Based Applications and Services**

Computer programs and services on the web receive continuous updates and improvements, so the steps to complete this web-based activity may differ from the ones shown. You can often look at the screens and the information presented to determine how to complete the activity.

    If you do not already have a Google account, you will need to create one before you begin this activity. Go to http://google.com and in the upper right corner, click Sign In. On the Sign In screen, click Create Account. On the Create your Google Account page, complete the form, read and agree to the Terms of Service and Privacy Policy, and then click Next step. On the Welcome screen, click Get Started.

Activity | Create SUM, AVERAGE, COUNTIF, and IF functions

1 From the desktop, open your browser, navigate to http://google.com, and then click **Google Apps** . Click **Drive** , and then if necessary, sign in to your Google account.

2 Open your **GO! Web Projects** folder—or click **New** to create and then open this folder if necessary. In the left pane, click **New** and then click **File upload**. Navigate to your student data files, click **e02_2A_Web**, and then click **Open**.

3 Right-click the file you uploaded, point to **Open with**, and then click **Google Sheets**.

4 Select the range **A1:H1**. Click **Merge cells** . Click **Format**, point to **Align**, and then click **Center**. With **A1** selected, click **Paint format** , and then click cell **A2**.

5 Select **A1:A2**, and then click the **Font size arrow** . Click **18**.

6 Click cell **B4**. On the ribbon, click **Functions** , and then click **SUM**. Within the formula's parentheses, type **a11:a33** and press Enter for a result of *2311*. Click **B4**, and then on the ribbon, click **More formats** . Click **Number**, and then click **Decrease decimal places** two times.

7 Click cell **B5**, click **Functions** , and then click **AVERAGE**. Within the parentheses, type **d11:d33** and press Enter. Click **B5**, and then on the ribbon, click **Format as currency** .

8 Click cell **B7**. Type **=countif(g11:g33,"Oak")** and then press Enter to create a function that counts the number of Oak trees in the category column. Compare your screen with Figure A.

	A	B	C	D	E	F	G	H	I	J	K	L	M	N	O	P
1				Austin Tree Nursery												
2				As of March 30												
3																
4	Total Items in Stock	2,311														
5	Average Price	$108.52														
6																
7	Oak Trees:	10														
8																
9																
10	Quantity in Stock	Item #	Tree Name	Retail Price	Light	Landscape Use	Category	Stock Level								
11	78	13129	Golden Oak	108.99	Partial Sun	Erosion	Oak									
12	35	13358	Columnar English	106.95	Full Shade	Border	Oak									
13	60	15688	Coral Bark	106.25	Partial Shade	Erosion	Oak									
14	20	16555	Crimson King	105.5	Full Shade	Border	Oak									
15	75	21683	Japanese Blooming	103.99	Partial Shade	Erosion	Cherry									
16	60	22189	Crimson Queen	109.95	Filtered Sun	Erosion	Oak									
17	68	23677	Black Japanese	107.99	Partial Sun	Border	Maple									

Figure A

9 Click cell **H11**. Type **=if(a11<75,"Order","OK")** and then press Enter. Click cell **H11**, and then drag the fill handle down through cell **H33**.

10 With the range **H11:H33** selected, click **Format**, and then click **Conditional formatting**. On the right side of the window, in the **Apply to range** box, make sure that **H11:H33** displays. Under **Format cells if . . .** , click the displayed box, and then click **Text contains**. Click in the **Value or formula** box, and then type **Order** Under

Formatting style, click **Bold**. Click **Done** to apply the default conditional format and bold to all cells containing the word *Order*.

11 Close the Conditional Format rules pane, click cell **A1** and compare your screen with Figure B.

12 Submit your file as directed by your instructor. Sign out of your Google account and close your browser.

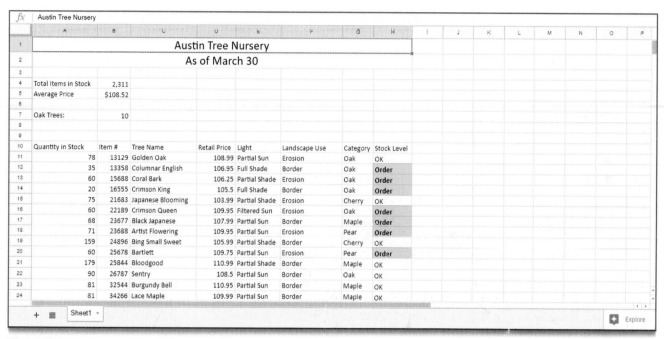

Figure B

Project
2B

Weekly Sales Summary

MyLab IT
Project 2B Grader for Instruction
Project 2B Simulation for Training and Review

Project Activities

In Activities 2.21 through 2.36, you will edit an existing workbook for the Sales Director, Mariam Daly. The workbook summarizes the online and in-store sales of products during a one-week period in May. The worksheets of your completed workbook will look similar to Figure 2.32.

Project Files for MyLab IT Grader

1. In your MyLab IT course, locate and click **Excel 2B Weekly Sales**, Download Materials, and then Download All Files.
2. Extract the zipped folder to your Excel Chapter 2 folder. Close the Grader download screens.
3. Take a moment to open the downloaded **Excel_2B_Weekly_Sales_Instructions**; note any recent updates to the book.

Project Results

 **GO! Project 2B**
Where We're Going

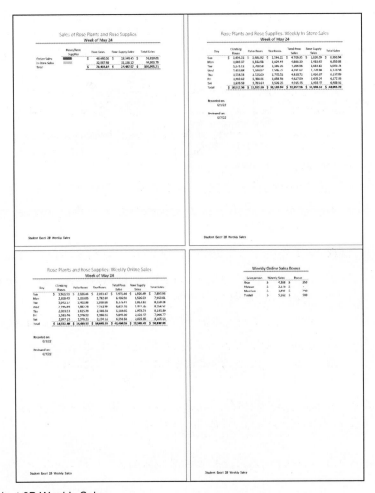

Figure 2.32 Project 2B Weekly Sales

 For Non-MyLab Submissions

For Project 2B, you will need:
e02B_Weekly_Sales

In your Excel Chapter 2 folder, save your workbook as:
Lastname_Firstname_2B_Weekly_Sales
If your instructor requires a workbook with formulas, save as:
Lastname_Firstname_2B_Weekly_Sales_formulas
After you have named and saved your workbook, on the next page, begin with Step 2.

ALERT   Because Office 365 is a cloud-based subscription service that receives continuous updates, you may encounter some variations in what appears on your screen and what is shown in this instruction. Microsoft Office 365 is fully installed on your PC or Mac; no internet access is necessary to create or edit documents. When you *are* connected to the internet, you will receive monthly upgrades and new features, so you always have the latest versions of Office apps as soon as they are available. Your subscription gives you continuous free access to the latest innovations and refinements.

GO! Learn How
Video E2-7

Use multiple worksheets in a workbook to organize data in a logical arrangement. When you have more than one worksheet in a workbook, you can *navigate* (move) among worksheets by clicking the *sheet tabs*. Sheet tabs identify each worksheet in a workbook and display along the lower left edge of the workbook window. When you have more worksheets in the workbook than can display in the sheet tab area, use the sheet tab scrolling buttons to move sheet tabs into and out of view.

Activity 2.21 | Navigating Among Worksheets, Renaming Worksheets, and Changing the Tab Color of Worksheets

Excel names the first worksheet in a workbook *Sheet1* and each additional worksheet that you add in order—*Sheet2*, *Sheet3*, and so on. Most Excel users rename their worksheets with meaningful names. In this Activity, you will navigate among worksheets, rename worksheets, and change the tab color of sheet tabs.

1 Navigate to your **Excel Chapter 2 folder**, and then double-click the Excel file you downloaded from **MyLab IT** that displays your name—**Student_Excel_2B_Weekly_Sales**.

> In this workbook two worksheets display, into which some data has already been entered. For example, on the first worksheet, the days of the week and sales data for the one-week period displays.

2 Along the bottom of the Excel window, point to and then click the **Sheet2 tab**.

> The second worksheet in the workbook displays and becomes the active worksheet. *Sheet2* displays in bold.

3 In cell **A1**, notice the text *In-Store*—this worksheet will contain data for in-store sales.

4 Click the **Sheet1 tab**. Then, point to the **Sheet1 tab**, and double-click to select the sheet tab name. Type **Online Sales** and press Enter.

> The first worksheet becomes the active worksheet, and the sheet tab displays *Online Sales*.

5 Point to the **Online Sales sheet tab** and right-click. Point to **Tab Color**, and then in the next to last column, point to the first color. Compare your screen with Figure 2.33.

🔁 **ANOTHER WAY**   On the Home tab, in the Cells group, click the Format button, and then on the displayed list, point to Tab Color. Mac users may also use this method.

⬜ **MAC TIP**   To display the shortcut menu, point to the Online Sales sheet tab, hold down Control, and then click.

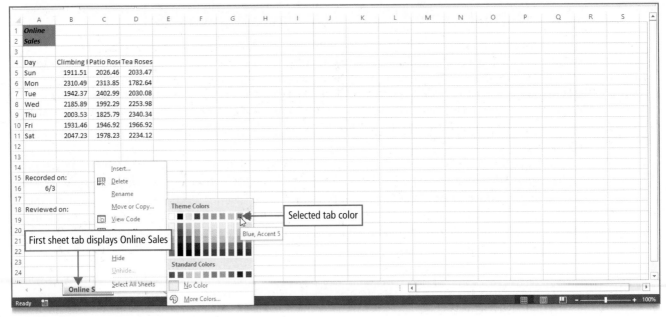

Figure 2.33

6. In the second to last column, click the first color to change the tab color.

7. Point to the **Sheet2 tab**, right-click, and then from the shortcut menu, click **Rename**. Type **In-Store Sales** and press Enter.

   You can either double-click the sheet name or use the shortcut menu to rename a sheet tab.

8. Point to the **In-Store Sales sheet tab** and right-click. Point to **Tab Color**, and then in the last column, click the first color. **Save** 🖫 your workbook.

MORE KNOWLEDGE | **Copying a Worksheet**

To copy a worksheet to the same workbook, right-click the sheet tab, on the shortcut menu click Move or Copy, click the sheet before which you want to insert the copied sheet, select the Create a copy check box, and then click OK. To copy to a different workbook, in the Move or Copy dialog box, click the To book arrow, and then select the workbook into which you want to insert the copy.

Objective 8 | **Enter Dates, Clear Contents, and Clear Formats**

GO! Learn How
Video E2-8

Dates represent a type of value that you can enter in a cell. When you enter a date, Excel assigns a serial value—a number—to the date. This makes it possible to treat dates like other numbers. For example, if two cells contain dates, you can find the number of days between the two dates by subtracting the older date from the more recent date.

Activity 2.22 | **Entering and Formatting Dates**

In this Activity, you will examine the various ways that Excel can format dates in a cell. Date values entered in any of the following formats will be recognized by Excel as a date:

Value Typed	Example
m/d/yy	7/4/2016
d-mmm	4-Jul
d-mmm-yy	4-Jul-16
mmm-yy	Jul-16

On your keyboard, ⊟ (the hyphen key) and ⟋ (the forward slash key) function identically in any of these formats and can be used interchangeably. You can abbreviate the month name to three characters or spell it out. You can enter the year as two digits, four digits, or even leave it off. When left off, the current year is assumed but does not display in the cell.

A two-digit year value of 30 through 99 is interpreted by the Windows operating system as the four-digit years of 1930 through 1999. All other two-digit year values are assumed to be in the 21st century. If you always type year values as four digits, even though only two digits may display in the cell, you can be sure that Excel interprets the year value as you intended. Examples are shown in Figure 2.34.

How Excel Interprets Dates	
Date Typed As:	Completed by Excel As:
7/4/15	7/4/2015
7/4/98	7/4/1998
7/4	4-Jul (current year assumed)
7-4	4-Jul (current year assumed)
July 4	4-Jul (current year assumed)
Jul 4	4-Jul (current year assumed)
Jul/4	4-Jul (current year assumed)
Jul-4	4-Jul (current year assumed)
July 4, 1998	4-Jul-98
July 2012	Jul-12 (first day of month assumed)
July 1998	Jul-98 (first day of month assumed)

Figure 2.34

1 ▶ Click the **Online Sales sheet tab** to make it active. Click cell **A16** and notice that the cell displays *6/3*. In the **Formula Bar**, notice that the full date of June 3, 2022 displays in the format *6/3/2022*.

2 ▶ With cell **A16** selected, on the **Home tab**, in the **Number group**, click the **Number Format arrow**. At the bottom, click **More Number Formats** to display the **Number tab** of the **Format Cells** dialog box.

Under Category, *Date* is selected, and under Type, *3/14* is selected. Cell A16 uses this format type; that is, only the month and day display in the cell.

🖥 **MAC TIP** To display group names on the ribbon, display the menu, click Word, click Preferences, click View, select the Show group titles check box.

3 ▶ In the displayed dialog box, under **Type**, click several other date types and watch the **Sample** area to see how applying the selected date format will format your cell. When you are finished, click the **3/14/12** type, and then compare your screen with Figure 2.35.

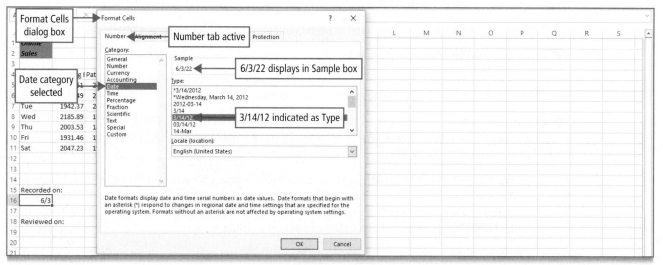

Figure 2.35

4 At the bottom of the dialog box, click **OK**. Click cell **A19**, type **6-7-22** and then press ⏎.

Cell A19 has no special date formatting applied and displays in the default date format *6/7/2022*.

ALERT   **The Date Does Not Display as 6/7/2022?**

Settings in your Windows operating system determine the default format for dates. If your result is different, it is likely that the formatting of the default date was adjusted on the computer at which you are working.

---

5 Click cell **A19** again. Hold down Ctrl and press ⌊;⌋ (semicolon). Press ⏎ to confirm the entry.

Excel enters the current date, obtained from your computer's internal calendar, in the selected cell using the default date format. Ctrl + ⌊;⌋ is a quick method to enter the current date.

6 Click cell **A19** again, type **6/7/22** and then press ⏎.

Because the year *22* is less than 30, Excel assumes a 21st century date and changes *22* to *2022* to complete the four-digit year. Typing *98* would result in *1998*. For two-digit years that you type that are between 30 and 99, Excel assumes a 20th century date.

7 Click cell **A16**, and then on the **Home tab**, in the **Clipboard group**, click **Format Painter** 🖌. Click cell **A19** and notice that the date format from cell **A16** is copied to cell **A19**. **Save** 💾 your workbook.

Activity 2.23 | Clearing Cell Contents and Formats

2.2.8

A cell has *contents*—a value or a formula—and a cell may also have one or more *formats* applied, for example, bold and italic font styles, fill color, font color, and so on. You can choose to clear—delete—the *contents* of a cell, the *formatting* of a cell, or both.

Clearing the contents of a cell deletes the value or formula typed there, but it does *not* clear formatting applied to a cell. In this Activity, you will clear the contents of a cell and then clear the formatting of a cell that contains a date to see its underlying content.

1 In the **Online Sales** worksheet, click cell **A1**. In the **Editing group**, click **Clear** ◇, and then click **Clear Contents**. Notice that the text is cleared, but the green formatting remains.

2 Click cell **A2**, and then press Delete.

You can use either of these two methods to delete the *contents* of a cell. Deleting the contents does not, however, delete the formatting of the cell; you can see that the green fill color format applied to the two cells still displays.

3 In cell **A1**, type **Online Sales** and then on the **Formula Bar**, click **Enter** ✓ so that cell **A1** remains the active cell.

In addition to the green fill color, the bold italic text formatting remains with the cell.

4 In the **Editing group**, click **Clear** ◇, and then click **Clear Formats**.

Clearing the formats deletes formatting from the cell—the green fill color and the bold and italic font styles—but does not delete the cell's contents.

5 Use the same technique to clear the green fill color from cell **A2**. Click cell **A16**, click **Clear** ◇, and then click **Clear Formats**. In the **Number group**, notice that *General* displays as the number format of the cell.

The box in the Number group indicates the current Number format of the selected cell. Clearing the date formatting from the cell displays the date's serial number. The date, June 3, 2022, is stored as a serial number that indicates the number of days since January 1, 1900. This date is the 44,715th day since the reference date of January 1, 1900.

---

6 On the **Quick Access Toolbar**, click **Undo** to restore the date format. **Save** 🖫 your workbook, and then compare your screen with Figure 2.36.

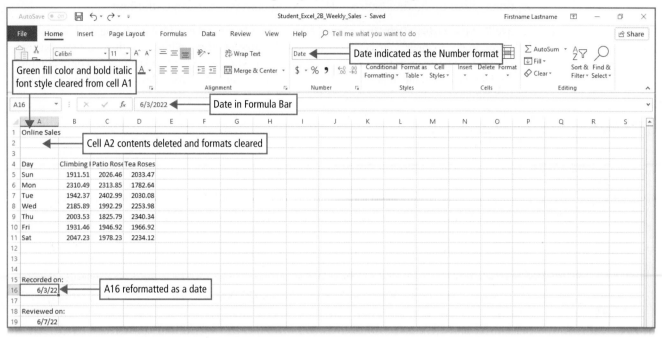

Figure 2.36

> **MORE KNOWLEDGE** **Clearing an Entire Worksheet**
>
> To clear an entire worksheet, in the upper left corner of the worksheet, click the Select All button, and then on the Home tab, in the Editing group, click Clear, and then click Clear All.

Objective 9 | Copy and Paste by Using the Paste Options Gallery

GO! Learn How
Video E2-9

Data in cells can be copied to other cells in the same worksheet, to other sheets in the same workbook, or to sheets in another workbook. The action of placing cell contents that have been copied or moved to the Clipboard into another location is called *paste*.

Activity 2.24 | Copying and Pasting by Using the Paste Options Gallery

MOS
2.1.2

Recall that the Clipboard is a temporary storage area maintained by your Windows operating system. When you select one or more cells, and then perform the Copy command or the Cut command, the selected data is placed on the Clipboard. From the Clipboard storage area, the data is available for pasting into other cells, other worksheets, other workbooks, and even into other Office programs. When you paste, the **Paste Options gallery** displays, which includes Live Preview to preview the Paste formatting that you want.

1 With the **Online Sales** worksheet active, select the range **A4:A19**.

A range of cells identical to this one is required for the *In-Store Sales* worksheet.

2 Right-click over the selection, and then click **Copy** to place a copy of the cells on the Clipboard. The copied cells may display a moving border.

🔄 **ANOTHER WAY** Use the keyboard shortcut for Copy, which is Ctrl + C ; or on the Home tab, click Copy.

⌨ **MAC TIP** On the Home tab, click Copy.

---

3 At the bottom of the workbook window, click the **In-Store Sales sheet tab** to make it the active worksheet. Point to cell **A4**, right-click, and then on the shortcut menu, under **Paste Options**, *point* to the first button—**Paste**. Compare your screen with Figure 2.37.

Live Preview displays how the copied cells will be placed in the worksheet if you click the Paste button. In this manner, you can experiment with different paste options, and then be sure you are selecting the paste operation that you want. When pasting a range of cells, you need only point to or select the cell in the upper left corner of the *paste area*—the target destination for data that has been cut or copied using the Clipboard.

 MAC TIP On the Home tab, click Paste.

Figure 2.37

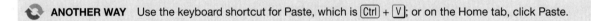 **ANOTHER WAY** Use the keyboard shortcut for Paste, which is Ctrl + V; or on the Home tab, click Paste.

---

4 Click the first button, **Paste**. In the status bar, notice the message that displays, indicating that you can paste your selection to another destination.

5 Display the **Online Sales** worksheet. Press Esc to cancel the moving border. **Save** your workbook.

The status bar no longer displays the message.

Objective 10 Edit and Format Multiple Worksheets at the Same Time

GO! Learn How
Video E2-10

You can enter or edit data on several worksheets at the same time by selecting and grouping multiple worksheets. Data that you enter or edit on the active sheet is reflected in all selected sheets. If the sheet tab displays with a solid background color, you know the sheet is not selected.

Activity 2.25 | Grouping Worksheets for Editing

MOS
2.2.4

In this Activity, you will group the two worksheets, and then format both worksheets at the same time.

1 With the **Online Sales** sheet active, press Ctrl + Home to make cell **A1** the active cell. Point to the **Online Sales sheet tab**, right-click, and then click **Select All Sheets**.

MAC TIP To display the shortcut menu, point to the Online Sales sheet tab, hold down Control, and then click.

---

2 At the top of your screen, notice that *Group* displays in the title bar. Compare your screen with Figure 2.38.

Both worksheets are selected, as indicated by *Group* in the title bar and the sheet tab names underlined. Data that you enter or edit on the active sheet will also be entered or edited in the same manner on all the selected sheets in the same cells.

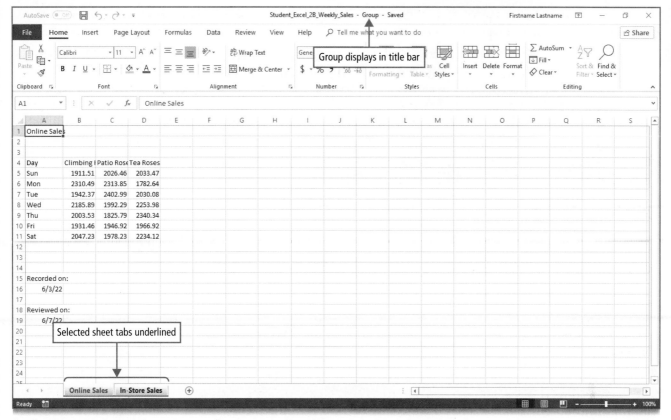

Figure 2.38

3 Select **columns A:G**, and then set their width to **85 pixels**.

4 Click cell **A2**, type **Week of May 24** and then on the **Formula Bar**, click **Enter** ✓ to keep cell **A2** as the active cell. **Merge & Center** 🔲 the text across the range **A2:G2**, and then apply the **Heading 1** cell style.

5 Click cell **E4**, type **Total Rose Sales** and then press Tab. In cell **F4**, type **Rose Supply Sales** and then press Tab. In cell **G4**, type **Total Sales** and then press Enter.

6 Select the range **A4:G4**, and then apply the **Heading 3** cell style. In the **Alignment group**, click **Center** ≡, **Middle Align** ≡, and **Wrap Text**. **Save** 🖫 your workbook.

7 Display the **In-Store Sales** worksheet to cancel the grouping, and then compare your screen with Figure 2.39.

> When you select a single sheet that was not a sheet that was active when you selected all sheets, the grouping of the sheets is cancelled and *Group* no longer displays in the title bar. Because the sheets were grouped, the same new text and formatting were applied to both sheets. In this manner, you can make the same changes to all the sheets in a workbook at one time.

ANOTHER WAY Right-click any sheet tab, and then click Ungroup Sheets.

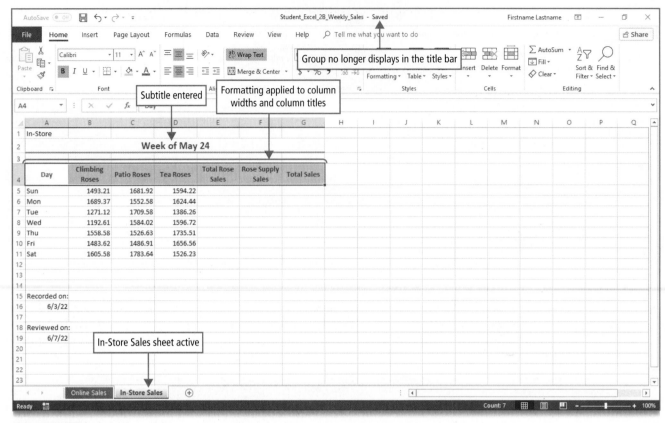

Figure 2.39

MORE KNOWLEDGE **Hide Worksheets**

You can hide any worksheet in a workbook to remove it from view using this technique:

Select the sheet tabs of the worksheets you want to hide, right-click any of the selected sheet tabs, and then click Hide.

Activity 2.26 | Formatting and Constructing Formulas on Grouped Worksheets

Recall that formulas are equations that perform calculations on values in your worksheet and that a formula starts with an equal sign (=). Operators are the symbols with which you specify the type of calculation that you want to perform on the elements of a formula. In this Activity, you will enter sales figures for Rose Supply items from both Online and In-Store sales, and then calculate the total sales.

1 Display the **Online Sales** worksheet. Verify that the sheets are not grouped—*Group* does *not* display in the title bar.

2 Click cell **A1**, replace *Online Sales* by typing **Rose Plants and Rose Supplies: Weekly Online Sales** and then on the **Formula Bar**, click **Enter** ✓ to keep cell **A1** as the active cell. **Merge & Center** 🖽▾ the text across the range **A1:G1**, and then apply the **Title** cell style.

3 In the column titled *Rose Supply Sales*, click cell **F5**. In the range **F5:F11**, type the following data for Rose Supply Sales, and then compare your screen with Figure 2.40.

	Rose Supply Sales
Sun	**1926.49**
Mon	**1526.03**
Tue	**1853.82**
Wed	**1922.36**
Thu	**1973.73**
Fri	**2121.47**
Sat	**2025.55**

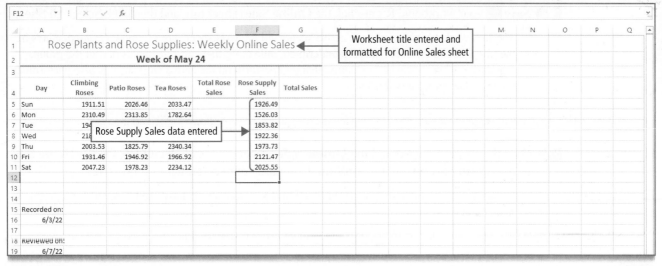

Figure 2.40

4 Display the **In-Store Sales** sheet. In cell **A1**, replace *In-Store* by typing **Rose Plants and Rose Supplies: Weekly In-Store Sales** and then on the **Formula Bar**, click **Enter** ✓ to keep cell **A1** as the active cell. **Merge & Center** the text across the range **A1:G1**, and then apply the **Title** cell style.

5 In the column titled *Rose Supply Sales*, click cell **F5**, in the range **F5:F11**, type the following data for Rose Supply Sales, and then compare your screen with Figure 2.41.

	Rose Supply Sales
Sun	1626.59
Mon	1483.69
Tue	1693.82
Wed	1778.94
Thu	1416.37
Fri	1645.24
Sat	1493.47

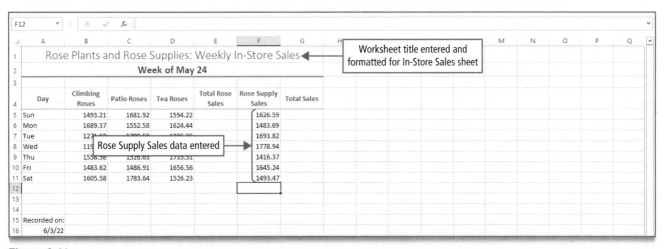

Figure 2.41

6 Save 🖫 your workbook. Right-click the **Online Sales sheet tab**, and then click **Select All Sheets**.

The first worksheet becomes the active sheet, and the worksheets are grouped. *Group* displays in the title bar, and the sheet tabs are underlined, indicating they are selected as part of the group. Recall that when grouped, any action that you perform on the active worksheet is *also* performed on any other selected worksheets.

🖥 **MAC TIP** To display the shortcut menu, point to the Online Sales sheet tab, hold down Control, and then click.

7 With the sheets *grouped* and the **Online Sales** sheet active, click cell **E5**. On the **Home tab**, in the **Editing group**, click **AutoSum**. Compare your screen with Figure 2.42.

Recall that when you enter the SUM function, Excel looks first above and then left for a proposed range of cells to sum.

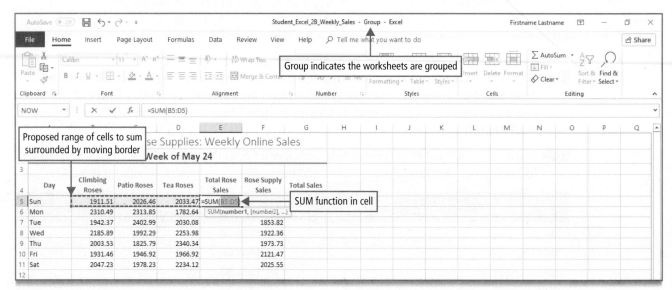

Figure 2.42

8 Press Enter to display Total Rose Sales for Sunday, which is *5971.44*.

9 Click cell **E5**, and then drag the fill handle down to copy the formula through cell **E11**.

10 Click cell **G5**, type = click cell **E5**, type + click cell **F5**, and then compare your screen with Figure 2.43.

Using the point-and-click technique to construct this formula is only one of several techniques you can use. Alternatively, you could use any other method to enter the SUM function to add the values in these two cells.

F5	▾ : × ✓ fx	=E5+F5															
▲	A	B	C	D	E	F	G	H	I	J	K	L	M	N	O	P	Q
1	Rose Plants and Rose Supplies: Weekly Online Sales																
2			Week of May 24														
3																	
4	Day	Climbing Roses	Patio Roses	Tea Roses	Total Rose Sales	Rose Supply Sales	Total Sales										
5	Sun	1911.51	2026.46	2033.47	5971.44	1926.49	=E5+F5		Formula in cell G5								
6	Mon	2310.49	2313.85	1782.64	6406.98	1526.03											
7	Tue	1942.37	2402.99	2030.08	6375.44	1853.82											
8	Wed	2185.89	1992.29	2253.98	6432.16	1922.36											
9	Thu	2003.53	1825.79	2340.34	6169.66	1973.73											
10	Fri	1931.46	1946.92	1966.92	5845.3	2121.47											
11	Sat	2047.23	1978.23	2234.12	6259.58	2025.55											
12																	

Figure 2.43

11 ▶ Press Enter to display the result *7897.93,* and then copy the formula down through cell **G11**. **Save** 💾 your workbook.

Activity 2.27 | Determining Multiple Totals at the Same Time

You can select a contiguous range of cells adjacent to rows or columns of numbers and then click the AutoSum button—or use Alt + =—to enter the SUM function for each row or column.

1 ▶ With the two worksheets still grouped, in cell **A12**, type **Total** and then select the range **B5:G12**, which is all of the sales data and the empty cells at the bottom of each column of sales data.

2 ▶ With the range **B5:G12** selected, hold down Alt and press = to enter the **SUM** function in each empty cell. Click **Save** 💾.

Selecting a range in this manner and then clicking the AutoSum button, or entering the SUM function with the keyboard shortcut Alt + =, places the SUM function in the empty cells at the bottom of each column.

Activity 2.28 | Formatting Grouped Worksheets

1 ▶ With the two worksheets still grouped, select the range **A5:A12**, and then apply the **Heading 4** cell style.

2 ▶ To apply financial formatting to the worksheets, select the range **B5:G5**, hold down Ctrl, and then select the range **B12:G12**. With the nonadjacent ranges selected, apply the **Accounting Number Format** $ ▾.

3 ▶ Select the range **B6:G11** and apply **Comma Style** ,. Select the range **B12:G12** and apply the **Total** cell style. Press Ctrl + Home to move to the top of the worksheet; compare your screen with Figure 2.44.

	A	B	C	D	E	F	G	H	I	J	K	L	M	N	O	P	Q
1			Rose Plants and Rose Supplies: Weekly Online Sales														
		Heading 4 cell style applied to A5:A12		f May 24													
3																	
4	Day	Climbing Roses	Patio Roses	Tea Roses	Total Rose Sales	Rose Supply Sales	Total Sales										
5	Sun	$ 1,911.51	$ 2,026.46	$ 2,033.47	$ 5,971.44	$ 1,926.49	$ 7,897.93										
6	Mon	2,310.49	2,313.85	1,782.64	6,406.98	1,526.03	7,933.01										
7	Tue	1,942.37	2,402.99	2,030.08	6,375.44	1,853.82	8,229.26										
8	Wed	2,185.89	1,992.29	2,253.98	6,432.16	1,922.36	8,354.52		Financial formatting applied to all numbers								
9	Thu	2,003.53	1,825.79	2,340.34	6,169.66	1,973.73	8,143.39										
10	Fri	1,931.46	1,946.92	1,966.92	5,845.30	2,121.47	7,966.77										
11	Sat	2,047.23	1,978.23	2,234.12	6,259.58	2,025.55	8,285.13										
12	Total	$ 14,332.48	$ 14,486.53	$ 14,641.55	$ 43,460.56	$ 13,349.45	$ 56,810.01		Totals calculated in row 12								

Figure 2.44

Activity 2.29 | Ungrouping Worksheets

1 ▶ Right-click the **Online Sales sheet tab**. On the shortcut menu, click **Ungroup Sheets** to cancel the grouping.

2 ▶ Click the **In-store Sales sheet tab**. Click **Save** 💾, and then compare your screen with Figure 2.45.

With your worksheets grouped, the calculations and formatting on the first worksheet were also added on the second worksheet.

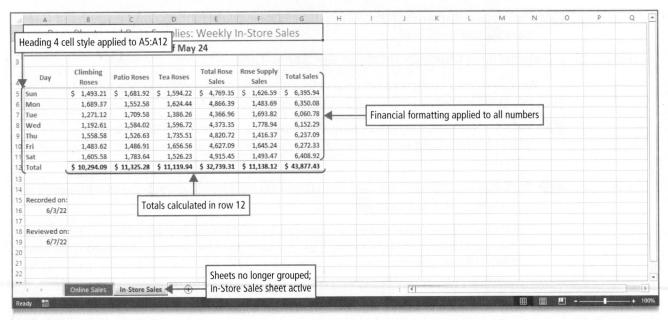

Figure 2.45

Create a Summary Sheet with Column Sparklines

GO! Learn How
Video E2-11

A *summary sheet* is a worksheet where totals from other worksheets are displayed and summarized. Recall that sparklines are tiny charts within a single cell that show a data trend.

Activity 2.30 | Inserting a Worksheet

1 To the right of the **In-Store Sales** sheet tab, click **New sheet** ⊕.

2 Rename the new worksheet tab **Summary** and display the **Tab Color** gallery. In the eighth column, select the first color.

3 Widen **columns A:E** to **110** pixels. In cell **A1**, type **Sales of Rose Plants and Rose Supplies** and then **Merge & Center** the title across the range **A1:E1**. Apply the **Title** cell style.

4 In cell **A2**, type **Week of May 24** and then **Merge & Center** across **A2:E2**; apply the **Heading 1** cell style.

5 Leave **row 3** blank. To form column titles, in cell **B4**, type **Roses/Rose Supplies** and press Tab. In cell **C4**, type **Rose Sales** and press Tab. In cell **D4**, type **Rose Supply Sales** and press Tab. In cell **E4**, type **Total Sales** and press Enter.

6 Select the range **B4:E4**. Apply the **Heading 3** cell style. In the **Alignment group**, click **Center** ☰, **Middle Align** ☰, and **Wrap Text**.

7 To form row titles, in cell **A5**, type **Online Sales** In cell **A6**, type **In-Store Sales**

8 **Save** 🖫, and then compare your screen with Figure 2.46.

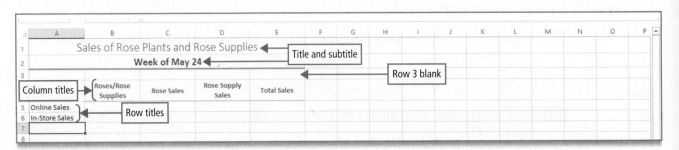

Figure 2.46

Activity 2.31 | Constructing Formulas That Refer to Cells in Another Worksheet

In this Activity, you will construct formulas in the Summary worksheet to display the total sales for both online sales and in-store sales that will update the Summary worksheet whenever changes are made to the other worksheet totals.

1 Click cell **C5**. Type **=** and then click the **Online Sales sheet tab**. On the **Online Sales** worksheet, click cell **E12**, and then press Enter to redisplay the **Summary** worksheet and insert the total **Rose Sales** amount of *$43,460.56*.

2 Click cell **C5** to select it again. Look at the **Formula Bar**, and notice that instead of a value, the cell contains a formula that is equal to the value in another cell in another worksheet. Compare your screen with Figure 2.47.

The value in this cell is equal to the value in cell E12 of the *Online Sales* worksheet. The Accounting Number Format applied to the referenced cell is carried over. By using a formula of this type, changes in cell E12 on the *Online Sales* worksheet will be automatically updated in this *Summary* worksheet.

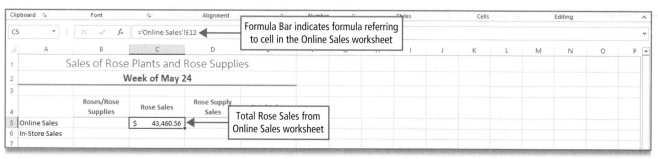

Figure 2.47

3 Click cell **D5**. Type **=** and then click the **Online Sales sheet tab**. Click cell **F12**, and then press Enter to redisplay the **Summary** worksheet and insert the total **Rose Supply Sales** amount of *$13,349.45*.

4 By using the techniques you just practiced, in cells **C6** and **D6** insert the total **Rose Sales** and **Rose Supply Sales** data from the **In-Store Sales** worksheet. Click **Save** 🖫, and then compare your screen with Figure 2.48.

Figure 2.48

Activity 2.32 | Changing Values in a Detail Worksheet to Update a Summary Worksheet

The formulas in cells C5:D6 display the totals from the other two worksheets. Changes made to any of the other two worksheets—sometimes referred to as ***detail sheets*** because the details of the information are contained there—that affect their totals will display on this Summary worksheet. In this manner, the Summary worksheet accurately displays the current totals from the other worksheets.

1 In cell **A7**, type **Total** Select the range **C5:E6**, and then on the **Home tab**, in the **Editing group**, click **AutoSum** to total the two rows.

> This technique is similar to selecting the empty cells at the bottom of columns and then inserting the SUM function for each column. Alternatively, you could use any other method to sum the rows. Recall that cell formatting carries over to adjacent cells unless two cells are left blank.

2 Select the range **C5:E7**, and then click **AutoSum** to total the three columns. Compare your screen with Figure 2.49.

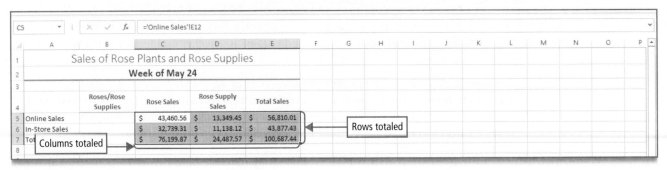

Figure 2.49

3 Notice that in cell **C6**, Rose Sales for In-Store Sales is $32,739.31, and in cell **C7**, the total is $76,199.87. Display the **In-Store Sales** worksheet, click cell **B8**, type **1410.88** and then press Enter. Notice that the formulas in the worksheet recalculate.

4 Display the **Summary** worksheet, and notice that in the **Rose Sales** column, both the total for the *In-Store Sales* and the *Total* were recalculated.

> In this manner, a Summary sheet recalculates any changes made in the other worksheets.

5 On the **Summary** worksheet, select the range **C6:E6** and change the format to **Comma Style** ▾. Select the range **C7:E7**, and then apply the **Total** cell style. Select the range **A5:A7** and apply the **Heading 4** cell style. **Save** 🖫 your workbook. Click cell **A1**, and then compare your screen with Figure 2.50.

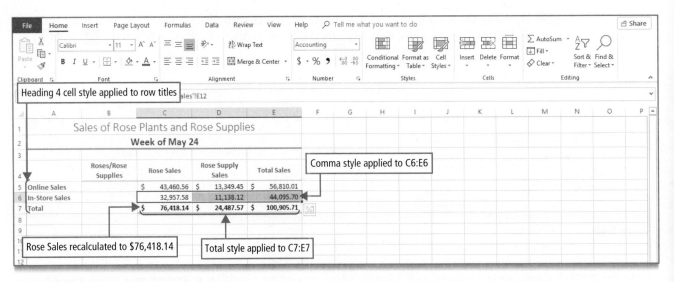

Figure 2.50

Activity 2.33 | Inserting Column Sparklines

In this Activity, you will insert column sparklines to visualize the ratio of Rose sales to Rose Supply sales for both Online and In-Store.

1 On the **Summary** worksheet, click cell **B5**. On the **Insert tab**, in the **Sparklines group**, click **Column**. In the **Create Sparklines** dialog box, with the insertion point blinking in the **Data Range** box, type **c5:d5** and then compare your screen with Figure 2.51.

Figure 2.51

2 Click **OK**. Click cell **B6**, and then **Insert** a **Column Sparkline** for the range **c6:d6**

3 With cell **B6** selected, on the **Design tab**, in the **Style group**, click **More** ⬇, and then in the third row, click the fourth style. Press Ctrl + Home, click **Save** 💾, and then compare your screen with Figure 2.52.

You can see, at a glance, that for both Online and In-Store sales, Rose sales are greater than Rose Supply sales.

💻 **MAC TIP** In the Sparkline Style gallery, use the ScreenTips to locate Gold, Sparkline Style Accent 4, (no dark or light).

Figure 2.52

Activity 2.34 | Determining Bonus Based on Sales Using the IFS Function

The *IFS function* checks whether one or more conditions—logical tests—are met, and then returns a value corresponding to the first TRUE condition.

The salespeople who handle commercial online sales are eligible for bonuses each week based on sales. Weekly sales between $3,000 and $3,999 qualify the salesperson for a $250 bonus. Weekly sales between $4,000 and $4,999 qualify the salesperson for a $350 bonus. Weekly sales greater than $4,999 qualify the salesperson for a $500 bonus. In this Activity, you will use the IFS function to determine the bonus for which each salesperson is eligible.

1 To the right of the **Summary** sheet tab, click **New sheet** ⊕. **Rename** the new worksheet tab **Bonus** and display the **Tab Color** gallery. In the sixth column, select the first color.

2 Widen columns A:C to **95 pixels**. In cell **A1**, type **Weekly Online Sales Bonus** and then **Merge & Center** the title across the range **A1:C1**. Apply the **Heading 1** cell style.

3 In cell **A3**, type **Salesperson** and then press Tab. In cell **B3**, type **Weekly Sales** and then press Tab. In cell **C3**, type **Bonus** and then press Enter. Select **A3:C3**, and then apply the **Heading 3** cell style. **Center** ≡ the headings.

4 In the range **A4:B7**, type the data for each salesperson:

Salesperson	Weekly Sales
Arce	4588
Matsuo	2575
Morrison	3851
Tindall	5162

5 Click cell **C4**. On the **Formulas tab**, in the **Function Library group**, click **Logical**, and then click **IFS**. If necessary, drag the dialog box to the right so that columns A:C are visible.

> **MAC TIP** Skip steps 6–10 and follow these instructions instead. At the right of the Mac window, in the Formula Builder, click in the Logical_test1 box. Type b4>4999 and then below the Logical_test1 box, click +. In the Value_if_true1 box, type 500. Click + and then use this same technique to add three more conditions and TRUE values as follows: b4>3999, 350; b4>2999, 250; b4>0, 0. When you are finished entering the conditions, click Done and then Close the Formula Builder. Then continue with step 11.

6 In the **Logical_test1 box**, type **b4>4999** and then press Tab. In the **Value_if_true1 box**, type **500** and then press Tab. Compare your screen with Figure 2.53.

The first logical test determines whether the Weekly Sales for Arce is greater than $4,999. In this case, the result is FALSE; Weekly Sales of $4,588 are less than $4,999.

When entering the logical tests for the IFS function, begin with the largest value because the IFS function returns a value based on the *first* condition that meets the criteria.

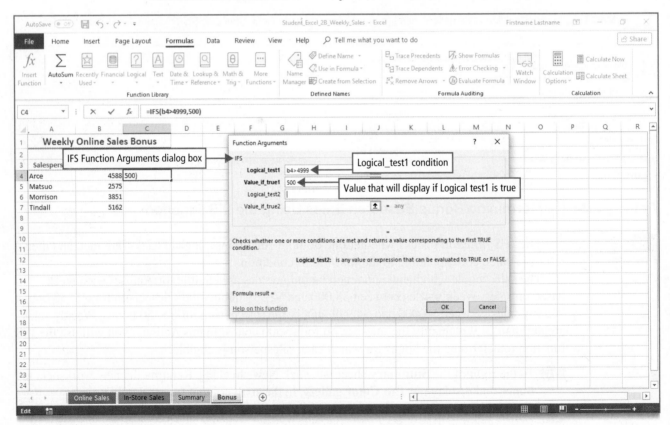

Figure 2.53

7 In the **Logical_test2 box**, type **b4>3999** and then press Tab. In the **Value_if_true2 box**, type **350** and then press Tab.

To the right of the Logical_test2 box, *TRUE* displays, indicating that Weekly Sales for Arce are greater than $3,999. Since this is the first *TRUE* condition, the Value_if_true—*350*—will display in cell C4.

8 In the **Logical_test3 box**, type **b4>2999** and then press (Tab). In the **Value_if_true3 box**, type **250** and then press (Tab).

9 In the **Logical_test4 box**, type **b4>0** and then press (Tab). In the **Value_if_true4 box**, type **0** and then press (Tab).

This IFS function contains four logical tests. It is important to include a default value that displays if none of the conditions are met. When no default value is included, an error message displays if no TRUE conditions are found. In this case, the default value is 0.

10 Click **OK** and notice that in cell **C4**, the IFS function determined that a bonus of 350 was earned.

11 Drag the fill handle down through cell **C7**, and then compare your screen with Figure 2.54.

Based on the conditions specified in the IFS function, three of the four salespersons earned bonuses based on their weekly sales.

In the Formula bar, the IFS statement arguments indicate each of the conditions and the TRUE values.

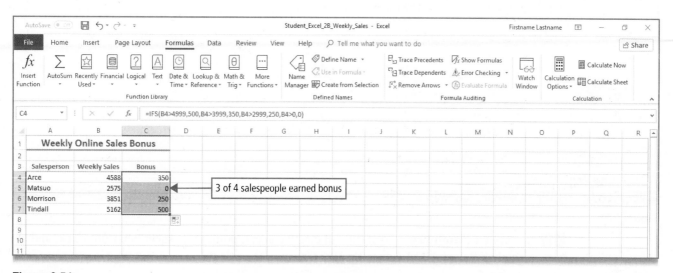

Figure 2.54

12 Select the range **B4:C7**, and then apply **Accounting Number Format** $\boxed{\$ \text{ -}}$. Click **Decrease Decimal** $\boxed{\overset{.00}{\to .0}}$ two times. **Save** $\boxed{\square}$ your workbook.

Objective 12 | Format and Print Multiple Worksheets in a Workbook

GO! Learn How
Video E2-12

Each worksheet within a workbook can have different formatting, for example, different headers or footers. If all the worksheets in the workbook will have the same header or footer, you can select all the worksheets and apply formatting common to all of the worksheets; for example, you can set the same footer in all of the worksheets.

Activity 2.35 | Moving a Worksheet, Repeating Footers, and Formatting Multiple Worksheets in a Workbook

In this Activity, you will move the Summary sheet to become the first worksheet in the workbook. Then you will format and prepare your workbook for printing. The four worksheets can be formatted simultaneously.

1 Point to the **Summary sheet tab**, hold down the left mouse button to display a small black triangle—a caret—and then notice that a small paper icon attaches to the mouse pointer.

2 Drag to the left until the caret and mouse pointer are to the left of the **Online Sales sheet tab**, as shown in Figure 2.55, and then release the left mouse button.

Use this technique to rearrange the order of worksheets within a workbook.

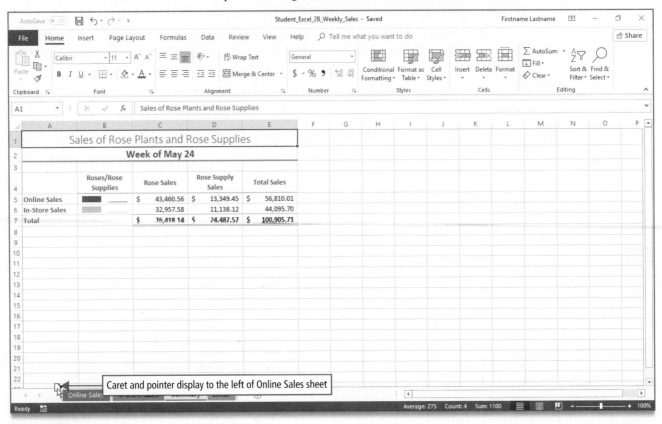

Figure 2.55

3 Be sure the **Summary** worksheet is the active sheet, point to its sheet tab, right-click, and then click **Select All Sheets** to display *Group* in the title bar.

4 Click the **Page Layout tab**. In the **Page Setup group**, click **Margins**, and then at the bottom of the gallery, click **Custom Margins** to display the **Page Setup** dialog box.

5 In the **Page Setup** dialog box, on the **Margins tab**, under **Center on page**, select the **Horizontally** check box.

6 Click the **Header/Footer tab**, and then in the center of the dialog box, click **Custom Footer**. In the **Footer** dialog box, with your insertion point blinking in the **Left section**, on the row of buttons, click **Insert File Name** 🗂.

7 Click **OK** two times.

The dotted line indicates the page break as currently formatted.

8 Press `Ctrl` + `Home`; verify that *Group* still displays in the title bar.

By selecting all sheets, you can apply the same formatting to all the worksheets at the same time, for example to repeat headers or footers.

9 Click the **File tab**, click **Info**, and then display the **Properties**. As the **Tags**, type **weekly sales** and then in the **Subject** box, type your course name and section number. Be sure your name displays as the **Author**; edit if necessary.

10 On the left, click **Print** to display the **Print Preview**, and then compare your screen with Figure 2.56.

> By grouping, you can view all sheets in Print Preview. If you do not see *1 of 4* at the bottom of the Preview, redisplay the workbook, select all the sheets again, and then redisplay Print Preview.

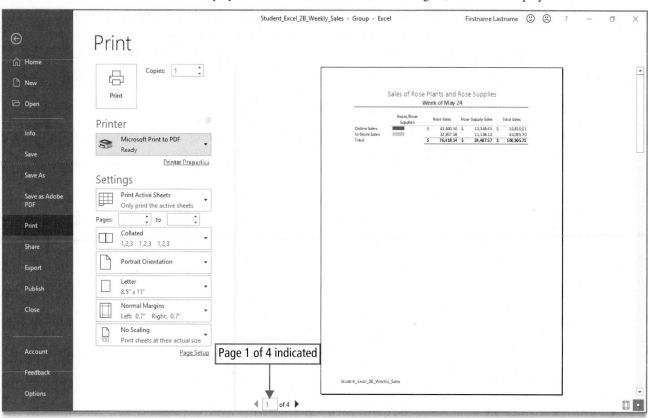

Page 1 of 4 indicated

Figure 2.56

11 At the bottom of the **Print Preview**, click **Next Page** ▶ as necessary and take a moment to view each page of your workbook.

 MAC TIP If the Print Preview indicates more than 4 pages, in the Print dialog box, click Cancel. With the worksheets grouped, on the Page Layout tab, click the Width arrow, and then click 1 page.

Activity 2.36 | Printing All or Individual Worksheets in a Workbook

MOS
1.5.3

1 In **Backstage** view, click **Save** to save your workbook before printing. In the displayed workbook, right-click the **Summary sheet tab**, and then click **Ungroup Sheets**.

2 On the **File tab**, click **Print** to display the **Print Preview**, and then at the bottom of the window, notice that *1 of 1* is indicated.

> Because the worksheets are no longer grouped, only the active sheet is available for printing.

3 On the left, under **Settings**, click **Print Active Sheets**, and then click **Print Entire Workbook**.

> At the bottom of the window, *1 of 4* is indicated. You can use this command to print an entire workbook.

 MAC TIP In the Print dialog box, click the Pages arrow, and then click All to print all sheets, click Single to specify one page, and click Range to specify multiple pages. After you view the Pages options, click Cancel.

4 Click **Save** and then **Close** Excel.

 For Non-MyLab Submissions Determine What Your Instructor Requires for Submission
As directed by your instructor, submit your completed Excel workbook.

5 In **MyLab IT**, locate and click the Grader Project **Excel 2B Weekly Sales**. In **step 3**, under **Upload Completed Assignment**, click **Choose File**. In the **Open** dialog box, navigate to your **Excel Chapter 2 folder**, and then click your **Student_Excel_2B_Weekly_Sales** file one time to select it. In the lower right corner of the **Open** dialog box, click **Open**.

The name of your selected file displays above the Upload button.

6 To submit your file to **MyLab IT** for grading, click **Upload**, wait a moment for a green **Success!** message, and then in **step 4**, click the blue **Submit for Grading** button. Click **Close Assignment** to return to your list of **Course Materials**.

You have completed Project 2B **END**

Objective | Calculate Weekly Sales

ALERT **Working with Web-Based Applications and Services**

Computer programs and services on the web receive continuous updates and improvements, so the steps to complete this web-based activity may differ from the ones shown. You can often look at the screens and the information presented to determine how to complete the activity.

If you do not already have a Google account, you will need to create one before you begin this activity. Go to http://google.com and, in the upper right corner, click Sign In. On the Sign In screen, click Create Account. On the Create your Google Account page, complete the form, read and agree to the Terms of Service and Privacy Policy, and then click Next step. On the Welcome screen, click Get Started.

Activity | Calculating Weekly Sales with Google Sheets

1 From the desktop, open your browser, navigate to http://google.com, and then click **Google Apps**. Click **Drive**, and then if necessary, sign in to your Google account.

2 Open your **GO! Web Projects** folder—or click **New** to create and then open this folder if necessary. Click **New** and then click **File upload**. Navigate to your student data files, click **e02_2B_Web**, and then click **Open**.

3 Right-click the file you uploaded, point to **Open with**, and then click **Google Sheets**.

4 Click cell **E5**. On the ribbon, click **Functions**, and then click **SUM**. Select **B5:D5** and then press Enter to total the rose sales for Sunday. Click cell **E5**, and then drag the fill handle down through cell **E11**. Select **E6:E11**, and then on the ribbon, click **More Formats**. Click **Number**.

5 Click cell **G5** and then enter a formula to add cells **E5** and **F5**. Fill the formula down through cell **G11**, and then format the range **G6:G11** with **Number** format. Click cell **A1** and then compare your screen with Figure A.

6 Select the range **B5:B11**. Click **Functions**, click **SUM**, and then press Enter to sum the selected range and place the result in cell B12. With **B12** selected, fill the formula across to cell **G12**.

7 Click cell **H5**. To calculate the percent that the Sunday sales are of the total sales, type **=g5/g12** and then press F4 to make the cell reference to G12 absolute. Press Enter and then fill the formula down through cell **H11**. With the range **H5:H11** selected, click **Format as percent**.

8 Select the range **B5:G5**. Hold down Ctrl, and then select **B12:G12**. With both ranges selected, click **Format as Currency**.

Day	Climbing Roses	Patio Roses	Tea Roses	Total Rose Sales	Rose Supply Sales	Total Sales	Percent of Sales
Rose Plants and Rose Supplies: Austin Sales							
Week of May 24							
Sun	$911.51	$26.46	$33.47	$971.44	$1,926.49	$2,897.93	
Mon	310.49	313.85	782.64	1,406.98	1,526.03	2,933.01	
Tue	942.37	402.99	30.08	1,375.44	1,853.82	3,229.26	
Wed	185.89	992.29	253.98	1,432.16	1,922.36	3,354.52	
Thu	3.53	825.79	340.34	1,169.66	1,973.73	3,143.39	
Fri	931.46	946.92	966.92	2,845.30	2,121.47	4,966.77	
Sat	47.23	978.23	234.12	1,259.58	2,025.55	3,285.13	
Total Sales							

Figure A

»» **GO!** With Google continues on next page

»» GO! With Google Sheets

9 Click cell **A1** and then compare your screen with Figure B.

10 Submit your file as directed by your instructor. Sign out of your Google account and close your browser.

fx | Rose Plants and Rose Supplies: Austin Sales

Day	Climbing Roses	Patio Roses	Tea Roses	Total Rose Sales	Rose Supply Sales	Total Sales	Percent of Sales
Rose Plants and Rose Supplies: Austin Sales							
Week of May 24							
Sun	$911.51	$26.46	$33.47	$971.44	$1,926.49	$2,897.93	12.17%
Mon	310.49	313.85	782.64	1,406.98	1,526.03	2,933.01	12.32%
Tue	942.37	402.99	30.08	1,375.44	1,853.82	3,229.26	13.56%
Wed	185.89	992.29	253.98	1,432.16	1,922.36	3,354.52	14.09%
Thu	3.53	825.79	340.34	1,169.66	1,973.73	3,143.39	13.20%
Fri	931.46	946.92	966.92	2,845.30	2,121.47	4,966.77	20.86%
Sat	47.23	978.23	234.12	1,259.58	2,025.55	3,285.13	13.80%
Total Sales	$3,332.48	$4,486.53	$2,641.55	$10,460.56	$13,349.45	$23,810.01	

Figure B

wavebreakmedia/Shutterstock, Monkey Business Images/Fotolia, Ivanko80/Shutterstock, Monkey Business Images/Shutterstock

Microsoft Office Specialist (MOS) Skills in This Chapter

Project 2A		Project 2B
1.2.1 Search for data within a workbook		**2.4.1** Insert sparklines
1.4.3 Freeze worksheet rows and columns		**4.1.1** Insert relative, absolute, and
1.4.4 Change window views		mixed references
1.5.3 Configure print settings		
2.1.3 Inoort and delete multiple columns or rows		
2.2.1 Merge and unmerge cells		
2.2.2 Modify cell alignment, orientation, and indentation		
2.2.4 Wrap text within cells		
2.2.6 Apply cell formats from the Format Cells dialog box		
2.2.8 Clear cell formatting		
2.4.2 Apply built-in conditional formatting		
3.1.1 Create Excel tables from cell ranges		
3.1.2 Apply styles to tables		
3.2.3 Insert and configure total rows		
3.3.1 Filter records		
3.3.2 Sort data by multiple columns		
4.2.1 Perform calculations by using the AVERAGE( ), MAX( ), MIN( ), and SUM( ) functions		
4.2.3 Perform conditional operations by using the IF( ) function		
Expert 2.1.1 Fill cells by using Flash Fill		
Expert 3.1.1 Perform logical operations by using nested functions including the IF( ), IFS( ), SWITCH( ), SUMIF( ), AVERAGEIF( ), COUNTIF( ), SUMIFS( ), AVERAGEIFS( ), COUNTIFS( ), MAXIFS( ), MINIFS( ), AND( ), OR( ), and NOT( ) functions		
Expert 3.3.1 Reference date and time by using the NOW( ) and TODAY ( ) functions		

Build Your E-Portfolio

An E-Portfolio is a collection of evidence, stored electronically, that showcases what you have accomplished while completing your education. Collecting and then sharing your work products with potential employers reflects your academic and career goals. Your completed documents from the following projects are good examples to show what you have learned: 2G, 2K, and 2L.

▶ Go! For Job Success

Video: Workplace Goal Setting

Your instructor may assign this video to your class, and then ask you to think about, or discuss with your classmates, these questions:

g-stockstudio/Shutterstock

Is there anything you would change about Theo's behavior at his performance evaluation? Why or Why not?

SMART goals are goals that are specific, measurable, achievable, realistic, and time frame specific. Is Theo's first goal of beating his sales numbers by 10% next year a SMART goal?

How important do you think it is to set career development goals for yourself? Why?

End of Chapter

Summary

Use Flash Fill to recognize a pattern in data and automatically fill in values when you enter examples of desired output. Flash Fill can split data from two or more cells or combine data from two cells.

Functions are formulas that Excel provides and that perform calculations by using specific values in a particular order or structure. Statistical functions are useful to analyze a group of measurements.

You can navigate among worksheets in a workbook by clicking the sheet tabs, which identify each worksheet in a workbook. Use multiple worksheets in a workbook to organize data in a logical arrangement.

Dates are a value you can enter in a cell to which Excel assigns a serial value—a number—so that you can treat dates like other numbers. For example, you can find the number of days between two dates.

GO! Learn It Online

Review the concepts, key terms, and MOS skills in this chapter by completing these online challenges, which you can find at **MyLab IT**.

Chapter Quiz: Answer matching and multiple choice questions to test what you learned in this chapter.

Lessons on the GO!: Learn how to use all the new apps and features as they are introduced by Microsoft.

MOS Prep Quiz: Answer questions to review the MOS skills that you practiced in this chapter.

GO! Collaborative Team Project (Available in Instructor Resource Center)

If your instructor assigns this project to your class, you can expect to work with one or more of your classmates—either in person or by using internet tools—to create work products similar to those that you created in this chapter. A team is a group of workers who work together to solve a problem, make a decision, or create a work product. Collaboration is when you work together with others as a team in an intellectual endeavor to complete a shared task or achieve a shared goal.

Monkey Business Images/Fotolia

Project Guide for Excel Chapter 2

Your instructor will assign Projects from this list to ensure your learning and assess your knowledge.

Project	Apply Skills from These Chapter Objectives	Project Type		Project Location
2A MyLab IT	Objectives 1–6 from Project 2A	**2A Instructional Project (Grader Project)**	Instruction	In **MyLab IT** and in text
		Guided instruction to learn the skills in Project 2A.		
2B MyLab IT	Objectives 7–12 from Project 2B	**2B Instructional Project (Grader Project)**	Instruction	In **MyLab IT** and in text
		Guided instruction to learn the skills in Project 2B.		
2C	Objectives 1–6 from Project 2A	**2C Skills Review (Scorecard Grading)**	Review	In text
		A guided review of the skills from Project 2A.		
2D	Objectives 7–12 from Project 2B	**2D Skills Review (Scorecard Grading)**	Review	In text
		A guided review of the skills from Project 2B.		
2E MyLab IT	Objectives 1–6 from Project 2A	**2E Mastery (Grader Project)**	Mastery and Transfer of Learning	In **MyLab IT** and in text
		A demonstration of your mastery of the skills in Project 2A with extensive decision making.		
2F MyLab IT	Objectives 7–12 from Project 2B	**2F Mastery (Grader Project)**	Mastery and Transfer of Learning	In **MyLab IT** and in text
		A demonstration of your mastery of the skills in Project 2B with extensive decision making.		
2G MyLab IT	Objectives 1–12 from Projects 2A and 2B	**2G Mastery (Grader Project)**	Mastery and Transfer of Learning	In **MyLab IT** and in text
		A demonstration of your mastery of the skills in Projects 2A and 2B with extensive decision making.		
2H	Combination of Objectives from Projects 2A and 2B	**2H GO! Fix It (Scorecard Grading)**	Critical Thinking	IRC
		A demonstration of your mastery of the skills in Projects 2A and 2B by creating a correct result from a document that contains errors you must find.		
2I	Combination of Objectives from Projects 2A and 2B	**2I GO! Make It (Scorecard Grading)**	Critical Thinking	IRC
		A demonstration of your mastery of the skills in Projects 2A and 2B by creating a result from a supplied picture.		
2J	Combination of Objectives from Projects 2A and 2B	**2J GO! Solve It (Rubric Grading)**	Critical Thinking	IRC
		A demonstration of your mastery of the skills in Projects 2A and 2B, your decision-making skills, and your critical thinking skills. A task-specific rubric helps you self-assess your result.		
2K	Combination of Objectives from Projects 2A and 2B	**2K GO! Solve It (Rubric Grading)**	Critical Thinking	In text
		A demonstration of your mastery of the skills in Projects 2A and 2B, your decision-making skills, and your critical thinking skills. A task-specific rubric helps you self-assess your result.		
2L	Combination of Objectives from Projects 2A and 2B	**2L GO! Think (Rubric Grading)**	Critical Thinking	In text
		A demonstration of your understanding of the chapter concepts applied in a manner that you would outside of college. An analytic rubric helps you and your instructor grade the quality of your work by comparing it to the work an expert in the discipline would create.		
2M	Combination of Objectives from Projects 2A and 2B	**2M GO! Think (Rubric Grading)**	Critical Thinking	IRC
		A demonstration of your understanding of the chapter concepts applied in a manner that you would outside of college. An analytic rubric helps you and your instructor grade the quality of your work by comparing it to the work an expert in the discipline would create.		
2N	Combination of Objectives from Projects 2A and 2B	**2N You and GO! (Rubric Grading)**	Critical Thinking	IRC
		A demonstration of your understanding of the chapter concepts applied in a manner that you would in a personal situation. An analytic rubric helps you and your instructor grade the quality of your work.		
2O	Combination of Objectives from Projects 2A and 2B	**2O Collaborative Team Project for EXCEL Chapter 2**	Critical Thinking	IRC
		A demonstration of your understanding of concepts and your ability to work collaboratively in a group role-playing assessment, requiring both collaboration and self-management.		

Glossary

Chapter Key Terms

Arguments The values that an Excel function uses to perform calculations or operations.

AVERAGE function An Excel function that adds a group of values, and then divides the result by the number of values in the group.

Comparison operators Symbols that evaluate each value to determine if it is the same (=), greater than (>), less than (<), or in between a range of values as specified by the criteria.

Conditional format A format that changes the appearance of a cell—for example, by adding cell shading or font color—based on a condition; if the condition is true, the cell is formatted based on that condition, and if the condition is false, the cell is *not* formatted.

COUNT function A statistical function that counts the number of cells in a range that contains numbers.

COUNTIF function A statistical function that counts the number of cells within a range that meet the given condition and that has two arguments—the range of cells to check and the criteria.

Criteria Conditions that you specify in a logical function.

Data bar A cell format consisting of a shaded bar that provides a visual cue to the reader about the value of a cell relative to other cells; the length of the bar represents the value in the cell—a longer bar represents a higher value and a shorter bar represents a lower value.

Detail sheets The worksheets that contain the details of the information summarized on a summary sheet.

Drag and drop The action of moving a selection by dragging it to a new location.

Excel table A series of rows and columns that contains related data that is managed independently from the data in other rows and columns in the worksheet.

Filter The process of displaying only a portion of the data based on matching a specific value to show only the data that meets the criteria that you specify.

Find and Replace A command that searches the cells in a worksheet—or in a selected range—for matches and then replaces each match with a replacement value of your choice.

Flash Fill Recognizes a pattern in your data, and then automatically fills in values when you enter examples of the output that you want. Use it to split data from two or more cells or to combine data from two cells.

Freeze Panes A command that enables you to select one or more rows or columns and freeze (lock) them into place; the locked rows and columns become separate panes.

Function A predefined formula—a formula that Excel has already built for you—that performs calculations by using specific values in a particular order or structure.

IF function A function that uses a logical test to check whether a condition is met, and then returns one value if true, and another value if false.

IFS function A function that checks whether one or more conditions—logical tests—are met, and then returns a value corresponding to the first TRUE condition.

Logical functions A group of functions that test for specific conditions and that typically use conditional tests to determine whether specified conditions are true or false.

Logical test Any value or expression that can be evaluated as being true or false.

MAX function An Excel function that determines the largest value in a selected range of values.

MEDIAN function An Excel function that finds the middle value that has as many values above it in the group as are below it; it differs from AVERAGE in that the result is not affected as much by a single value that is greatly different from the others.

MIN function An Excel function that determines the smallest value in a selected range of values.

Navigate The process of moving within a worksheet or workbook.

NOW function An Excel function that retrieves the date and time from your computer's calendar and clock and inserts the information into the selected cell.

Pane A portion of a worksheet window bounded by and separated from other portions by vertical and horizontal bars.

Paste The action of placing cell contents that have been copied or moved to the Clipboard into another location.

Paste area The target destination for data that has been cut or copied using the Office Clipboard.

Paste Options gallery A gallery of buttons that provides a Live Preview of all the Paste options available in the current context.

Print Titles An Excel command that enables you to specify rows and columns to repeat on each printed page.

Scale to Fit Excel commands that enable you to stretch or shrink the width, height, or both, of printed output to fit a maximum number of pages.

Sheet tabs The labels along the lower border of the workbook window that identify each worksheet.

Sort The process of arranging data in a specific order based on the value in each field.

Split Splits the window into multiple resizable panes that contain views of your worksheet. This is useful to view multiple distant parts of your worksheet at one time.

Statistical functions Excel functions, including the AVERAGE, MEDIAN, MIN, and MAX functions, which are useful to analyze a group of measurements.

SUM function A predefined formula that adds all the numbers in a selected range of cells.

Summary sheet A worksheet where totals from other worksheets are displayed and summarized.

Volatile A term used to describe an Excel function that is subject to change each time the workbook is reopened; for example, the NOW function updates itself to the current date and time each time the workbook is opened.

Chapter Review

Apply 2A skills from these Objectives:

1. Use Flash Fill and the SUM, AVERAGE, MEDIAN, MIN, and MAX Functions
2. Move Data, Resolve Error Messages, and Rotate Text
3. Use COUNTIF and IF Functions and Apply Conditional Formatting
4. Use Date & Time Functions and Freeze Panes
5. Create, Sort, and Filter an Excel Table
6. View, Format, and Print a Large Worksheet

Skills Review Project 2C Roses

2 EXCEL

In the following Skills Review, you will edit a worksheet detailing the current inventory of roses at the Pasadena nursery. Your completed workbook will look similar to Figure 2.57.

Project Files

For Project 2C, you will need the following file:

e02C_Roses

You will save your workbook as:

Lastname_Firstname_2C_Roses

Project Results

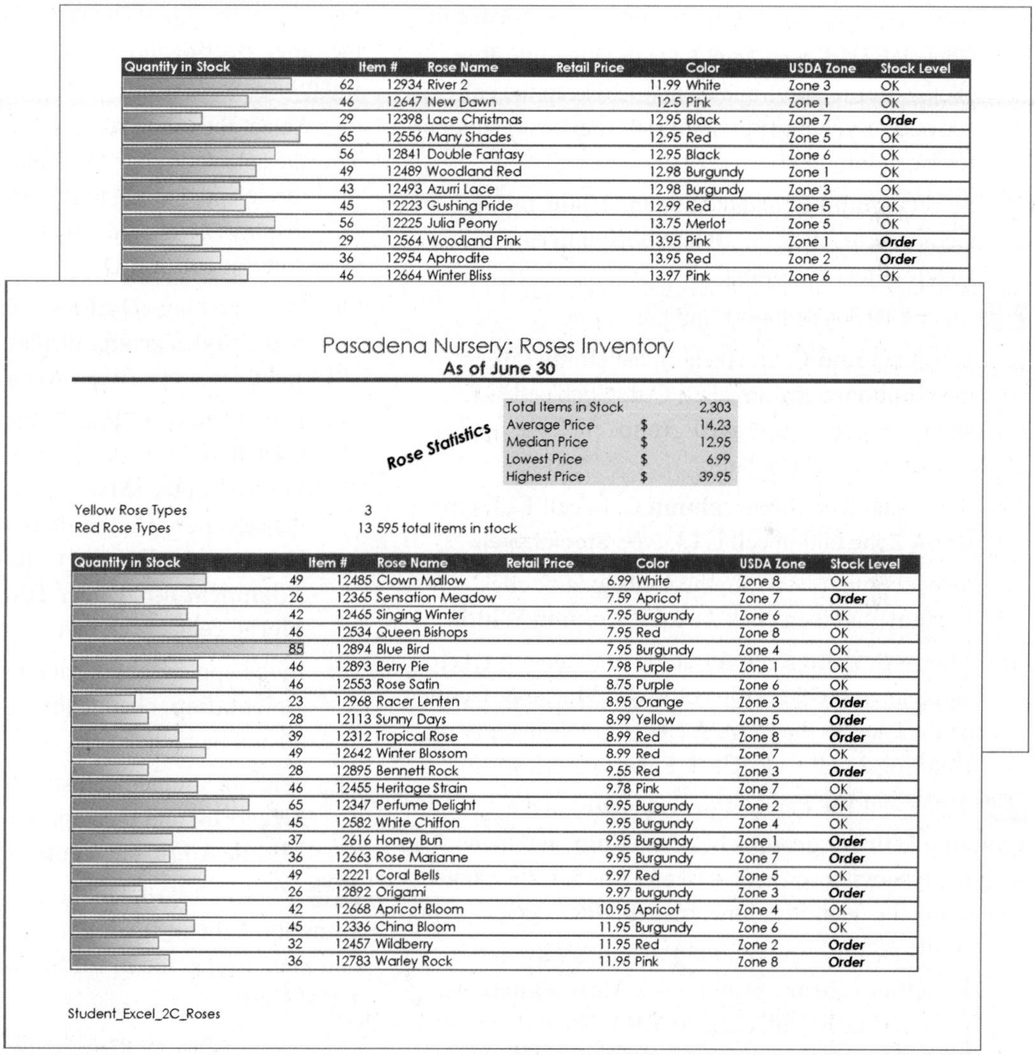

Quantity in Stock	Item #	Rose Name	Retail Price	Color	USDA Zone	Stock Level
62	12934	River 2	11.99	White	Zone 3	OK
46	12647	New Dawn	12.5	Pink	Zone 1	OK
29	12398	Lace Christmas	12.95	Black	Zone 7	**Order**
65	12556	Many Shades	12.95	Red	Zone 5	OK
56	12841	Double Fantasy	12.95	Black	Zone 6	OK
49	12489	Woodland Red	12.98	Burgundy	Zone 1	OK
43	12493	Azurri Lace	12.98	Burgundy	Zone 3	OK
45	12223	Gushing Pride	12.99	Red	Zone 5	OK
56	12225	Julia Peony	13.75	Merlot	Zone 5	OK
29	12564	Woodland Pink	13.95	Pink	Zone 1	**Order**
36	12954	Aphrodite	13.95	Red	Zone 2	**Order**
46	12664	Winter Bliss	13.97	Pink	Zone 6	OK

Pasadena Nursery: Roses Inventory

As of June 30

Rose Statistics		
Total Items in Stock		2,303
Average Price	$	14.23
Median Price	$	12.95
Lowest Price	$	6.99
Highest Price	$	39.95

Yellow Rose Types 3

Red Rose Types 13 595 total items in stock

Quantity in Stock	Item #	Rose Name	Retail Price	Color	USDA Zone	Stock Level
49	12485	Clown Mallow	6.99	White	Zone 8	OK
26	12365	Sensation Meadow	7.59	Apricot	Zone 7	**Order**
42	12465	Singing Winter	7.95	Burgundy	Zone 6	OK
46	12534	Queen Bishops	7.95	Red	Zone 8	OK
85	12894	Blue Bird	7.95	Burgundy	Zone 4	OK
46	12893	Berry Pie	7.98	Purple	Zone 1	OK
46	12553	Rose Satin	8.75	Purple	Zone 6	OK
23	12968	Racer Lenten	8.95	Orange	Zone 3	**Order**
28	12113	Sunny Days	8.99	Yellow	Zone 5	**Order**
39	12312	Tropical Rose	8.99	Red	Zone 8	**Order**
49	12642	Winter Blossom	8.99	Red	Zone 7	OK
28	12895	Bennett Rock	9.55	Red	Zone 3	**Order**
46	12455	Heritage Strain	9.78	Pink	Zone 7	OK
65	12347	Perfume Delight	9.95	Burgundy	Zone 2	OK
45	12582	White Chiffon	9.95	Burgundy	Zone 4	OK
37	2616	Honey Bun	9.95	Burgundy	Zone 1	**Order**
36	12663	Rose Marianne	9.95	Burgundy	Zone 7	**Order**
49	12221	Coral Bells	9.97	Red	Zone 5	OK
26	12892	Origami	9.97	Burgundy	Zone 3	**Order**
42	12668	Apricot Bloom	10.95	Apricot	Zone 4	OK
45	12336	China Bloom	11.95	Burgundy	Zone 6	OK
32	12457	Wildberry	11.95	Red	Zone 2	**Order**
36	12783	Warley Rock	11.95	Pink	Zone 8	**Order**

Student_Excel_2C_Roses

Figure 2.57

(continues on next page)

Chapter Review

1 From the files downloaded with this chapter, locate and open **e02C_Roses**. **Save** the file in your **Excel Chapter 2** folder as **Lastname_Firstname_2C_Roses**

a. In the **column heading area**, point to **column C** to display the ⬇ pointer, and then drag to the right to select **columns C:D**. On the **Home tab**, in the **Cells group**, click the **Insert button arrow**, and then click **Insert Sheet Columns**.

b. Click cell **C14**, type **12113** and then on the **Formula Bar**, click **Enter** to confirm the entry and keep cell **C14** as the active cell. On the **Home tab**, in the **Editing group**, click **Fill**, and then click **Flash Fill**.

c. Click cell **D14**, type **Zone 5** On the **Formula Bar**, click **Enter** to confirm the entry and keep the cell active. Press Ctrl + E, which is the keyboard shortcut for Flash Fill.

d. Select **column B**, and then on the **Home tab**, in the **Cells group**, click the **Delete button arrow**. Click **Delete Sheet Columns**.

2 In cell **B13** type **Item #** and press Enter.

a. Select **column C**, and then on the **Home tab**, in the **Clipboard group**, click **Cut**. Click cell **G1**, and then in the **Clipboard group**, click the upper portion of the **Paste** button.

b. Select and then delete **column C**. In cell **F13**, type **USDA Zone** and in cell **G13**, type **Stock Level**

c. Select columns **A:G**. In the **Cells group**, click **Format**, and then click **AutoFit Column Width**.

d. **Merge & Center** cell **A1** across the range **A1:G1**, and then apply the **Title** cell style. **Merge & Center** cell **A2** across the range **A2:G2**, and then apply the **Heading 1** cell style. Click **Save**.

3 Click cell **B4**. On the **Formulas tab**, in the **Function Library group**, click **AutoSum**, and then within the parentheses, type **a14:a68** which is the range containing the quantities for each item. Press Enter.

a. With cell **B5** active, on the **Formulas tab**, in the **Function Library group**, click **More Functions**. Point to **Statistical**, click **AVERAGE**, and then in the **Number1** box, type **d14:d68** which is the range containing the *Retail Price* for each item. Click **OK**. (Mac users, in the Formula Builder, under Number1, type d14:d68 and then click Done.)

b. Click cell **B6**. In the **Function Library group**, click **More Functions**, point to **Statistical**, and then click **MEDIAN**. In the **Function Arguments** dialog box, type **d14:d68** and then click **OK**. (Mac users, in the Formula Builder, under Number1, type d14:d68, and then click Done.)

c. Click cell **B7**, and then insert the **MIN** function to determine the lowest **Retail Price**. Click cell **B8**, and then insert the **MAX** function to determine the highest **Retail Price**.

4 Select cell **B4**. On the **Home tab**, apply **Comma Style**, and then click **Decrease Decimal** two times. Select the range **B5:B8**, and then apply **Accounting Number Format**.

a. Select the range **A4:B8**. Point to the right edge of the selected range to display the 🔭 pointer. Drag the selected range to the right until the ScreenTip displays *D4:E8*, and then release the mouse button. AutoFit **column D**.

b. With the range **D4:E8** selected, on the **Home tab**, in the **Styles group**, display the **Cell Styles** gallery, and then apply **20% - Accent1**.

c. In cell **C6**, type **Rose Statistics** Select the range **C4:C8**, right-click over the selection, and then click **Format Cells**. (Mac users, hold down Ctrl and click the selection. On the shortcut menu, click Format Cells.) In the **Format Cells** dialog box, click the **Alignment tab**. Under **Text control**, select the **Merge cells** check box.

d. In the upper right portion of the dialog box, under **Orientation**, change the value in the **Degrees** box to **20** and then click **OK**.

e. With the merged cell still selected, change the **Font Size** to **14**, and then apply **Bold** and **Italic**. Apply **Middle Align** and **Center** to the cell.

5 Click cell **B10**. On the **Formulas tab**, in the **Function Library group**, click **More Functions**, and then display the list of **Statistical** functions. Click **COUNTIF**.

a. As the range, type **e14:e68** which is the range with the color of each item. Click in the **Criteria** box, type **Yellow** and then click **OK** to calculate the number of yellow rose types. (Mac users, type the range and criteria in the Formula Builder, and then click Done.)

(continues on next page)

Chapter Review

b. Click cell **G14**. On the **Formulas tab**, in the **Function Library group**, click **Logical**, and then on the list, click **IF**. If necessary, drag the title bar of the **Function Arguments** dialog box up or down so that you can view **row 14** on your screen.

c. With the insertion point in the **Logical_test** box, click cell **A14**, and then type **<40** Press ⓣ Tab to move the insertion point to the **Value_if_true** box, and then type **Order** Press ⓣ Tab to move the insertion point to the **Value_if_false** box, type **OK** and then click **OK**. (Mac users, use the Formula Builder to create the arguments for the IF function, and then click Done. Close the Formula Builder.)

d. Using the fill handle, copy the function in cell **G14** down through cell **G68**.

6 ▶ With the range **G14:G68** selected, on the **Home tab**, in the **Styles group**, click **Conditional Formatting**. In the list, point to **Highlight Cells Rules**, and then click **Text that Contains**. (Mac users, skip steps a and b. Instead, do the following to apply conditional formatting: in the New Formatting Rule box, be sure that the dialog box includes the following settings: Classic, Format only cells that contain, Specific Text, and Containing. To the right of Containing, type Order. Click the Format with arrow, and then click Custom Format. Under Font Style, click Bold Italic, click the Color arrow, and then click Automatic. Click the Fill tab, and then click No Color. Click OK two times.)

a. In the **Text That Contains** dialog box, with the insertion point blinking in the first box, type **Order** and then in the second box, click the **arrow**. On the list, click **Custom Format**.

b. In the **Format Cells** dialog box, on the **Font tab**, under **Font style**, click **Bold Italic**. Click the **Color arrow**, and then click **Automatic**. Click the **Fill tab**, and then click **No Color**. Click **OK** two times to apply bold and italic to the cells that contain the word *Order*.

c. Select the range **A14:A68**. In the **Styles group**, click **Conditional Formatting**. In the list, point to **Data Bars**, and then under **Gradient Fill**, click **Red Data Bar**. Click anywhere to cancel the selection.

d. Select the range **E14:E68**. On the **Home tab**, in the **Editing group**, click **Find & Select**, and then click **Replace**. (Mac users, press ⌃ Ctrl + ⒡ F. In the Find dialog box, click Replace.) In the **Find and Replace** dialog box, in the **Find what** box, type **Deep Burgundy** and then in the **Replace with** box, type **Burgundy** Click **Replace All** and then click **OK**. In the lower right corner of the **Find and Replace** dialog box, click **Close**.

e. Scroll down as necessary, and then click cell **A70**. Type **Edited by Maria Rios** and then press ⏎ Enter. With cell **A71** as the active cell, on the **Formulas tab**, in the **Function Library group**, click **Date & Time**. In the list of functions, click **NOW**, and then click **OK** to enter the current date and time. (Mac users, in the Formula Builder, click Done and then Close the Formula Builder.)

f. **Save** your workbook.

7 ▶ Click any cell in the data below row 13. Click the **Insert tab**, and then in the **Tables group**, click **Table**. In the **Create Table** dialog box, be sure the **My table has headers** check box is selected and that the range **$A$13:$G$68** displays, and then click **OK**. On the **Design tab**, in the **Table Styles group**, click **More**, and then under **Light**, locate and click **Blue, Table Style Light 9**. If the style is not available, choose another style.

a. In the header row of the table, click the **Retail Price arrow**, and then from the menu, click **Sort Smallest to Largest**. (Mac users, click Ascending and then close the Retail Price dialog box.) Click the **Color arrow**. On the menu, click the **(Select All)** check box to clear all the check boxes. Scroll as necessary and then select only the **Red** check box. Click **OK**.

b. Click anywhere in the table. On the **Table Tools Design tab**, in the **Table Style Options group**, select the **Total Row** check box. Click cell **A69**, click the arrow that displays to the right of cell **A69**, and then click **Sum**. In cell **B11**, type the result **13** and then press ⓣ Tab. In cell **C11**, type **595 total items in stock** and then press ⏎ Enter.

c. In the header row of the table, click the **Color arrow** and then click **Clear Filter From "Color"** to redisplay all of the data. (Mac users, click Clear Filter and then Close the Color dialog box.) Click anywhere in the table. Click the **Table Tools Design tab**, in the **Table Style Options group**, clear the **Total Row** check box.

8 ▶ On the **Page Layout tab**, in the **Themes group**, click **Themes** and then click the **Ion** theme. Change the **Orientation** to **Landscape**.

a. In the **Page Setup group**, click **Margins**, and then click **Custom Margins** to display the **Page Setup** dialog box.

(continues on next page)

Chapter Review

b. On the **Margins tab**, under **Center on page**, select the **Horizontally** check box. On the **Header/Footer tab**, display the **Custom Footer**, and then in the **Left section**, insert the file name. Click **OK** two times.

c. In the **Page Setup** group, click **Print Titles** to redisplay the **Page Setup** dialog box. Under **Print titles**, click in the **Rows to repeat at top** box, and then at the right, click **Collapse Dialog**. From the **row heading area**, select **row 13**, and then click **Expand Dialog**. Click **OK** to print the column titles in row 13 at the top of every page.

d. Click the **File tab** and then click **Print**. At the bottom of the **Settings group**, click **No Scaling**, and then on the displayed list, click **Fit All Columns on One Page**. (Mac users, to fit the worksheet width on one page, close the Print dialog box. On the Page Layout tab, click the Width button arrow, and then click 1 page.)

e. Display the **Properties**. As the **Tags**, type **inventory, roses** In the **Subject** box, type your course name and section number. Be sure your name displays as the author. (Mac users, click File, and then click Properties. Click Summary, and then type the Keywords, Subject, and Author name).

9 ▶ **Save** your workbook. Print or submit your workbook electronically as directed by your instructor.

You have completed Project 2C | END

Chapter Review

Skills Review | Project 2D Canada

In the following Skills Review, you will edit a workbook that summarizes sales in the Eastern and Western region of Canada. Your completed workbook will look similar to Figure 2.58.

Project Files

For Project 2D, you will need the following file:

e02D_Canada

You will save your workbook as:

Lastname_Firstname_2D_Canada

Project Results

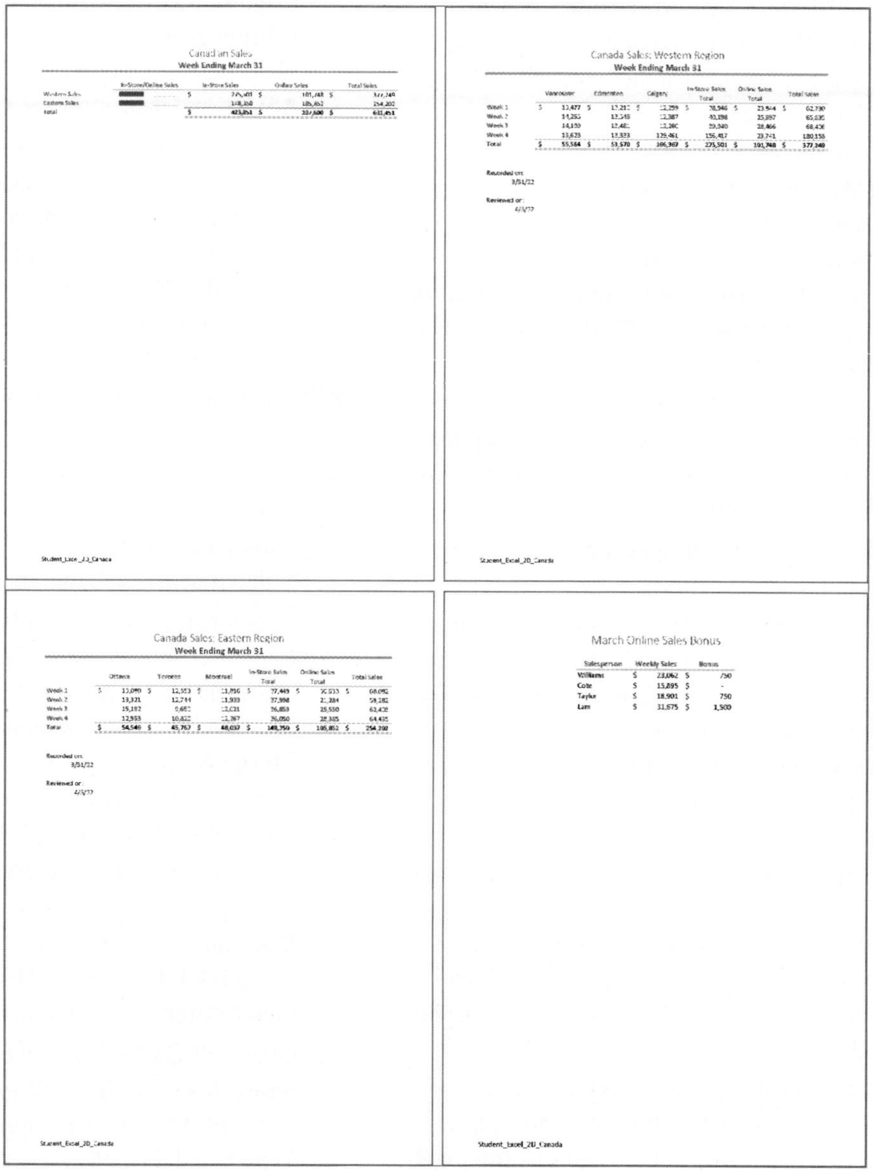

FIGURE 2.58

(continues on next page)

Chapter Review

1 ▶ From the files downloaded with this chapter, locate and open **e02D_Canada**. **Save** the file in your **Excel Chapter 2** folder as **Lastname_Firstname_2D_Canada**

a. Point to the **Sheet1 tab**, and then double-click to select the sheet tab name. Type **Western Sales** and then press Enter.

b. Point to the **Sheet2 tab**, right-click, and then from the shortcut menu, click **Rename**. Type **Eastern Sales** and press Enter. (Mac users, to display the shortcut menu, point to the Sheet2 tab, hold down ctrl, and then click.)

c. Point to the **Western Sales sheet tab** and right-click. On the shortcut menu, point to **Tab Color**, and then in the last column, click the first color. Change the **Tab Color** of the **Eastern Sales sheet tab**—in the fifth column, click the first color.

d. Click the **Western Sales sheet tab**, and then click cell **A13**. On the **Home tab**, in the **Number group**, click the **Number Format arrow**. At the bottom of the list, click **More Number Formats** to display the **Number tab** of the **Format Cells** dialog box. Click the **3/14/12** type, and then click **OK**.

e. Click cell **A16**, type **4/5/22** and then press Enter. Click cell **A13**, and then on the **Home tab**, in the **Clipboard group**, click **Format Painter**. Click cell **A16** to copy the date format from cell **A13** to cell **A16**.

f. Click cell **A1**. In the **Editing group**, click **Clear**, and then click **Clear Formats**.

g. Select the range **A5:A16**. On the **Home tab**, in the **Clipboard group**, click **Copy**. At the bottom of the workbook window, click the **Eastern Sales sheet tab** to make it the active worksheet. Click cell **A5**, and then on the **Home tab**, in the **Clipboard group**, click **Paste**. Display the **Western Sales** sheet. Press Esc to cancel the moving border.

2 ▶ With the **Western Sales** sheet active, make cell **A1** the active cell. Point to the sheet tab, right-click, and then on the shortcut menu, click **Select All Sheets**. Verify that *Group* displays in the title bar. (Mac users, hold down ctrl, and then click the Western Sales sheet tab to display the shortcut menu.)

a. **Merge & Center** the text in cell **A1** across the range **A1:G1**, and then apply the **Title** cell style. Select **columns A:G**, and then set their widths to **100 pixels**.

b. Click cell **A2**, type **Week Ending March 31** and then on the **Formula Bar**, click the **Enter** button to keep cell **A2** as the active cell. **Merge & Center** the text across the range **A2:G2**, and then apply the **Heading 1** cell style.

c. Select the range **B4:G4**, and then apply the **Heading 3** cell style. In the **Alignment group**, click **Center**, **Middle Align**, and **Wrap Text**.

d. With the sheets still grouped and the **Western Sales** sheet active, click cell **E5**. On the **Home tab**, in the **Editing group**, click the **AutoSum** button, and then press Enter. Click cell **E5**, and then drag the fill handle down to copy the formula through cell **E8**.

e. Click cell **G5**, type = click cell **E5**, type + click cell **F5**, and then press Enter. Copy the formula down through cell **G8**. In cell **A9**, type **Total** Select the range **B5:G9**, and then on the **Home tab**, in the **Editing group**, click the **AutoSum** button to enter the SUM function for all the columns. Select the range **A5:A9**, and then apply the **Heading 4** cell style.

f. Select the range **B5:G5**, hold down Ctrl, and then select the range **B9:G9**. (Mac users, hold down command ⌘.) Apply the **Accounting Number Format** and decrease the decimal places to zero. Select the range **B6:G8**, and then apply **Comma Style** with zero decimal places. Select the range **B9:G9**, and then apply the **Total** cell style.

3 ▶ Click the **Eastern Sales sheet tab** to cancel the grouping and display the second worksheet.

a. To the right of the **Eastern Sales sheet tab**, click the **New sheet** button. **Rename** the new worksheet tab **Summary** and then change the **Tab Color**—in the eight column, click the first color.

b. Widen **columns A:E** to **150** pixels. In cell **A1**, type **Canadian Sales** and then **Merge & Center** the title across the range **A1:E1**. Apply the **Title** cell style. In cell **A2**, type **Week Ending March 31** and then **Merge & Center** the text across the range **A2:E2**. Apply the **Heading 1** cell style. In cell **A5**, type **Western Sales** and in cell **A6**, type **Eastern Sales**

c. In cell **B4**, type **In-Store/Online Sales** and in cell **C4**, type **In-Store Sales** In cell **D4**, type **Online Sales** and in cell **E4**, type **Total Sales** Select the range **B4:E4**, apply the **Heading 3** cell style, and then **Center** these column titles.

d. Click cell **C5**. Type = and then click the **Western Sales sheet tab**. In the **Western Sales** worksheet, click cell **E9**, and then press Enter. Click cell **D5**. Type = and then click the **Western Sales sheet tab**. Click cell **F9**, and then press Enter.

(continues on next page)

Chapter Review

e. By using the same technique, in cells **C6** and **D6**, insert the total **In-Store Sales** and **Online Sales** data from the **Eastern Sales** worksheet.

f. Select the range **C5:E6**, and then click **AutoSum** to total the two rows. In cell **A7**, type **Total** and then in **C7** sum the range **C5:C6**. Fill the formula across to **D7:E7**.

g. Select the nonadjacent ranges **C5:E5** and **C7:E7**, and then apply **Accounting Number Format** with zero decimal places. Select the range **C6:E6**, and then apply **Comma Style** with zero decimal places. Select the range **C7:E7**, and then apply the **Total** cell style. Select the range **A5:A7** and apply the **Heading 4** cell style.

h. Click cell **B5**. On the **Insert tab**, in the **Sparklines** group, click **Column**. In the **Create Sparklines** dialog box, with the insertion point blinking in the **Data Range** box, select the range **C5:D5** and then click **OK**.

i. Click cell **B6**, and then insert a **Column Sparkline** for the range **C6:D6**. With the **Eastern Sales** sparkline selected, in the **Style group**, in the first row, apply the second style.

4 ▶ To the right of the **Summary** sheet tab, click **New sheet**. **Rename** the new worksheet tab **Bonus** and display the **Tab Color** gallery. In the sixth column, select the first color. Widen columns **A:C** to **95 pixels**.

a. In cell **A1**, type **March Online Sales Bonus** and then **Merge & Center** the title across the range **A1:C1**. Apply the **Title** cell style. In cell **A3**, type **Salesperson** In cell **B3**, type **Weekly Sales** In cell

Salesperson	Weekly Sales
Williams	23062
Cote	15895
Taylor	18901
Lam	31675

C3, type **Bonus** and then select **A3:C3**. Apply the **Heading 3** cell style and **Center** the headings.

b. In the range **A4:B7**, type the data for each salesperson:

c. Click cell **C4**. On the **Formulas tab**, in the **Function Library group**, click **Logical**, and then click **IFS**.

d. In the **Logical_test1 box**, type **b4>30000** and then press Tab. In the **Value_if_true1 box**, type 1500 and then press Tab. In the **Logical_test2 box**, type

b4>18000 and then press Tab. In the **Value_if_true2 box**, type 750 and then press Tab. In the **Logical_test3 box**, type **b4>0** and then press Tab. In the **Value_if_true3 box**, type **0** and then click **OK**. (Mac users, in the Formula Builder, click in the Logical_test1 box. Type b4>30000 and then below the Logical_test1 box, click +. In the Value_if_true1 box, type 1500. Click + and then use this same technique to add two more conditions and TRUE values as follows: b4>18000, 750; b4>0,0. Click Done and then close the Formula Builder.)

e. Drag the fill handle down through cell **C7**. Select the range **B4:C7**, and then apply **Accounting Number Format**. Click **Decrease Decimal** two times.

5 ▶ Point to the **Summary sheet tab**, hold down the left mouse button to display a small black triangle, drag to the left until the triangle and mouse pointer are to the left of the **Western Sales sheet tab**, and then release the left mouse button to move the sheet to the first position in the workbook.

a. Be sure the **Summary** worksheet is the active sheet and then click cell **A1**. Point to the **Summary sheet tab**, right-click, and then click **Select All Sheets** to display *Group* in the title bar. (Mac users, hold down ctrl, click the Summary sheet tab, and then click Select All Sheets.)

b. On the **Page Layout tab**, in the **Page Setup group**, click **Margins**, and then click **Custom Margins** to display the **Page Setup** dialog box. On the **Margins tab**, center the worksheets **Horizontally**. On the **Header/Footer tab**, insert the file name in the **left section** of the footer.

c. Display the **Print Preview** of the worksheets. Under **Settings**, click **No Scaling**, and then click **Fit All Columns on One Page**. Use the **Next** button to view all four worksheets. (Mac users, on the Page Layout tab, click the Width arrow, and then click 1 page.)

d. Display the **Properties**. As the **Tags**, type **Canada, sales** In the **Subject** box, type your course name and section number. Be sure your name displays as the author. (Mac users, click File, and then click Properties. Click Summary, and then enter the Subject, Keywords, and Author.)

6 ▶ **Save** and **Close** your workbook. Print or submit your workbook electronically as directed by your instructor.

You have completed Project 2D   **END**

Content-Based Assessments (Mastery and Transfer of Learning)

Apply 2A skills from these Objectives:

1. Use Flash Fill and the SUM, AVERAGE, MEDIAN, MIN, and MAX Functions
2. Move Data, Resolve Error Messages, and Rotate Text
3. Use COUNTIF and IF Functions and Apply Conditional Formatting
4. Use Date & Time Functions and Freeze Panes
5. Create, Sort, and Filter an Excel Table
6. View, Format, and Print a Large Worksheet

In the following project, you will edit a worksheet detailing the current inventory of plants at the Pasadena facility. Your completed worksheet will look similar to Figure 2.59.

Project Files for MyLab IT Grader

1. In your **MyLab IT** course, locate and click **Excel 2E Plants**, Download Materials, and then Download All Files.
2. Extract the zipped folder to your Excel Chapter 2 folder. Close the Grader download screens.
3. Take a moment to open the downloaded **Excel_2E_Plants_Instructions**; note any recent updates to the book.

Project Results

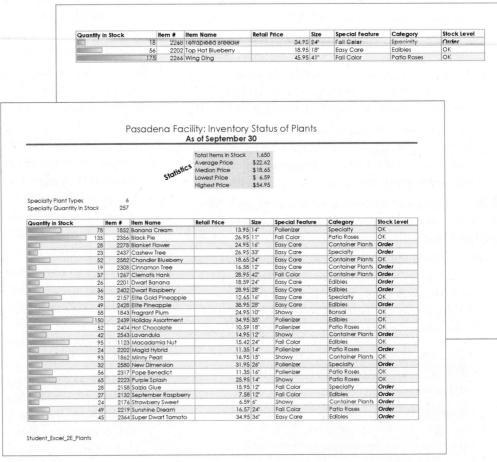

Figure 2.59

For Non-MyLab Submissions

For Project 2E, you will need:

e02E_Plants

In your Excel Chapter 2 folder, save your workbook as:

Lastname_Firstname_2E_Plants

If your instructor requires a workbook with formulas, save as:

Lastname_Firstname_2E_Plants_formulas

After you have named and saved your document, on the next page, begin with Step 2.

After Step 16, save and submit your file as directed by your instructor.

(continues on next page)

Content-Based Assessments (Mastery and Transfer of Learning)

1 Navigate to your **Excel Chapter 2 folder**, and then double-click the Excel file you downloaded from **MyLab IT** that displays your name—**Student_Excel_2E_Plants**.

2 To the right of **column B**, insert two new columns to create **new blank columns C and D**. By using **Flash Fill** in the two new columns, split the data in **column B** into a column for *Item #* in **column C** and *Category* in **column D**. As necessary, type **Item #** as the column title in **column C** and **Category** as the column title in **column D**. Delete **column B**.

3 By using the **Cut** and **Paste** commands, cut **column C**—*Category*—and paste it to **column H**, and then delete the empty **column C**. Apply **AutoFit** to **columns A:G**.

4 In cell **B4**, insert a function to calculate the **Total Items in Stock** by summing the **Quantity in Stock** data, and then apply **Comma Style** with zero decimal places to the result.

5 In each cell in the range **B5:B8**, insert functions to calculate the Average, Median, Lowest, and Highest retail prices, and then apply the **Accounting Number Format** to each result.

6 Move the range **A4:B8** to the range **D4:E8**, apply the **40% - Accent4** cell style to the range, and then select **columns D:E** and **AutoFit**.

7 In cell **C6**, type **Statistics** and then select the range **C4:C8**. Display the **Format Cells** dialog box, merge the selected cells, and change the text **Orientation** to **25 Degrees**. Format the cell with **Bold** and change the **Font Size** to **14 pt**. Apply **Middle Align** and **Align Right**.

8 In the **Category** column, **Replace All** occurrences of **Vine Roses** with **Patio Roses**

9 In cell **B10**, use the **COUNTIF** function to count the number of **Specialty** plant types in the **Category** column.

10 In cell **H13**, type **Stock Level** In cell **H14**, enter an **IF** function to determine the items that must be ordered. If the **Quantity in Stock** is less than **50** the **Value_if_true** is **Order** Otherwise, the **Value_if_false** is **OK** Fill the formula down through cell **H42**.

11 Apply **Conditional Formatting** to the **Stock Level** column so that cells that contain the text **Order** are formatted with **Bold Italic**. Change the font **Color** to **Automatic**, and the **Fill** color to **No Color**. Apply conditional formatting to the **Quantity in Stock** column by applying a **Gradient Fill Green Data Bar**.

12 Format the range **A13:H42** as a **Table** with headers, and apply the style **Light Blue, Table Style Light 20**. If the table style is not available, choose another style. Sort the table from **A to Z** (Ascending order) by **Item Name**, and then filter on the **Category** column to display the **Specialty** types.

13 Display a **Total Row** in the table, and then in cell **A43**, **Sum** the **Quantity in Stock** for the **Specialty** items. Type the result in cell **B11**. Click in the table, and then remove the total row from the table. Clear the **Category** filter.

14 **Merge & Center** the title and subtitle across **columns A:H** and apply **Title** and **Heading 1** styles respectively. Change the theme to **Mesh**, and then **AutoFit** all the columns.

15 Set the orientation to **Landscape**. In the **Page Setup** dialog box, center the worksheet **Horizontally**, insert a custom footer in the **left section** with the file name, and set **row 13** to repeat at the top of each page. Fit all the columns to one page.

16 Display the workbook **Properties**. As the **Tags**, type **plants inventory, Pasadena** As the **Subject**, type your course name and section number. Be sure your name displays as the **Author**. **Save** your workbook and then **Close** Excel.

(continues on next page)

Mastering Excel: Project 2E Plants (continued)

17 In **MyLab IT**, locate and click the Grader Project **Excel 2E Plants**. In **step 3**, under **Upload Completed Assignment**, click **Choose File**. In the **Open** dialog box, navigate to your **Excel Chapter 2 folder**, and then click your **Student_Excel_2E_Plants** file one time to select it. In the lower right corner of the **Open** dialog box, click **Open**.

> The name of your selected file displays above the Upload button.

18 To submit your file to **MyLab IT** for grading, click **Upload**, wait a moment for a green **Success!** message, and then in **step 4**, click the blue **Submit for Grading** button. Click **Close Assignment** to return to your list of **Course Materials**.

You have completed Project 2E **END**

Content-Based Assessments (Mastery and Transfer of Learning)

Apply 2B skills from these Objectives:

7. Navigate a Workbook and Rename Worksheets
8. Enter Dates, Clear Contents, and Clear Formats
9. Copy and Paste by Using the Paste Options Gallery
10. Edit and Format Multiple Worksheets at the Same Time
11. Create a Summary Sheet with Column Sparklines
12. Format and Print Multiple Worksheets in a Workbook

In the following project, you will edit a workbook that summarizes the compensation for the commercial salespersons who qualified for bonuses in Northern and Southern California. Your completed worksheets will look similar to Figure 2.60.

Project Files for MyLab IT Grader

1. In your **MyLab IT** course, locate and click **Excel 2F Bonus**, Download Materials, and then Download All Files.
2. Extract the zipped folder to your Excel Chapter 2 folder. Close the Grader download screens.
3. Take a moment to open the downloaded **Excel_2F_Bonus_Instructions**; note any recent updates to the book.

Project Results

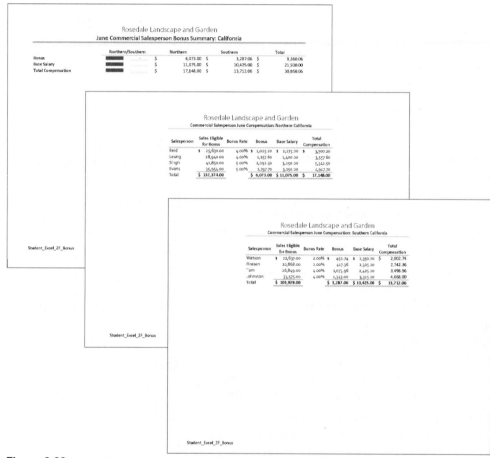

Figure 2.60

For Non-MyLab Submissions

For Project 2F, you will need:
e02F_Bonus

In your Excel Chapter 2 folder, save your workbook as:
Lastname_Firstname_2F_Bonus
If your instructor requires a workbook with formulas, save as:
Lastname_Firstname_2F_Bonus_formulas

After you have named and saved your document, on the next page, begin with Step 2.
After Step 17, save and submit your file as directed by your instructor.

(continues on next page)

Content-Based Assessments (Mastery and Transfer of Learning)

1 Navigate to your **Excel Chapter 2 folder**, and then double-click the Excel file you downloaded from **MyLab IT** that displays your name—**Student_Excel_2F_Bonus**.

2 Rename **Sheet1** as **Northern** and rename **Sheet2** as **Southern**

3 Click the **Northern sheet tab** to make it the active sheet, and then group the worksheets. In cell **A1**, type **Rosedale Landscape and Garden** and then **Merge & Center** the text across the range **A1:F1**. Apply the **Title** cell style. **Merge & Center** the text in cell **A2** across the range **A2:F2**, and then apply the **Heading 3** cell style.

4 The bonus rates for each salesperson are determined by sales amounts using the following scale: Sales **greater than $35,000** earn a bonus rate of **5%**, sales **greater than $25,000** earn a bonus rate of **4%**. All other sales (any amount greater than 0) earn a bonus rate of **2%**. With the sheets still grouped, in cell **C5** use an **IFS** function to determine the bonus rate for the first salesperson whose sales are in cell **B5**. Fill the formula down through cell **C8**.

5 In cell **D5**, calculate **Bonus** for *Reid* by multiplying the **Sales Eligible for Bonus** times the **Bonus Rate**. **Copy** the formula down through cell **D8**.

6 In cell **F5**, calculate **Total Compensation** by summing the **Bonus** and **Base Salary** for *Reid*. Copy the formula down through the cell **F8**.

7 In **row 9**, sum the columns for **Sales Eligible for Bonus**, **Bonus**, **Base Salary**, and **Total Compensation**. Apply the **Accounting Number Format** with two decimal places to the appropriate cells in **row 5** and **row 9** (do not include the percentages).

8 Apply the **Comma Style** with two decimal places to the appropriate cells in **rows 6:8** (do not include the percentages). Apply the **Total** cell style to **B9** and **D9:F9**.

9 **Ungroup** the sheets, and then insert a new worksheet. Change the sheet name to **Summary** and then widen **column A** to **210** pixels and **columns B:E** to **155** pixels.

10 Move the **Summary** sheet so that it is the first sheet in the workbook. In cell **A1** of the **Summary** sheet, type **Rosedale Landscape and Garden** and then **Merge & Center** the title across the range **A1:E1**. Apply the **Title** cell style. In cell **A2**, type **June Commercial Salesperson Bonus Summary: California** and then **Merge & Center** the text across the range **A2:E2**. Apply the **Heading 1** cell style.

11 In the range **A5:A7**, type the following row titles and then apply the **Heading 4** cell style:

Bonus

Base Salary

Total Compensation

12 In the range **B4:E4**, type the following column titles, and then **Center** and apply the **Heading 3** cell style.

Northern/Southern

Northern

Southern

Total

13 In cell **C5**, enter a formula that references cell **D9** in the **Northern** worksheet so that the total bonus amount for the Northern region displays in cell **C5**. Create similar formulas to enter the total **Base Salary** for the **Northern** region in cell **C6**. Using the same technique, enter formulas in the range **D5:D6** so that the **Southern** totals display.

14 Sum the **Bonus** and **Base Salary** rows, and then calculate **Total Compensation** for the **Northern**, **Southern**, and **Total** columns.

15 In cell **B5**, insert a **Column Sparkline** for the range **C5:D5**. In cells **B6** and **B7**, insert **Column** sparklines for the appropriate ranges to compare Northern totals with Southern totals.

16 **Group** the three worksheets, and then center the worksheets **Horizontally** on the page and insert a **Custom Footer** in the **left section** with the file name. Change the **Orientation** to **Landscape** and fit the columns to **1 page**.

17 Display the workbook **Properties**. As the **Tags**, type **June, bonus** As the **Subject**, type your course name and section number. Be sure your name displays as the **Author** and then **Save** the workbook and **Close** Excel.

(continues on next page)

18 In **MyLab IT**, locate and click the Grader Project **Excel 2F Bonus**. In **step 3**, under **Upload Completed Assignment**, click **Choose File**. In the **Open** dialog box, navigate to your **Excel Chapter 2 folder**, and then click your **Student_Excel_2F_Bonus** file one time to select it. In the lower right corner of the **Open** dialog box, click **Open**.

The name of your selected file displays above the Upload button.

19 To submit your file to **MyLab IT** for grading, click **Upload**, wait a moment for a green **Success!** message, and then in **step 4**, click the blue **Submit for Grading** button. Click **Close Assignment** to return to your list of **Course Materials**.

You have completed Project 2F `END`

Content-Based Assessments (Mastery and Transfer of Learning)

| **Mastering Excel**   **Project 2G Inventory**

Apply a combination of 2A and 2B skills:

1. Use Flash Fill and the SUM, AVERAGE, MEDIAN, MIN, and MAX Functions
2. Move Data, Resolve Error Messages, and Rotate Text
3. Use COUNTIF and IF Functions and Apply Conditional Formatting
4. Use Date & Time Functions and Freeze Panes
5. Create, Sort, and Filter an Excel Table
6. View, Format and Print a Large Worksheet
7. Navigate a Workbook and Rename Worksheets
8. Enter Dates, Clear Contents, and Clear Formats
9. Copy and Paste by Using the Paste Options Gallery
10. Edit and Format Multiple Worksheets at the Same Time
11. Create a Summary Sheet with Column Sparklines
12. Format and Print Multiple Worksheets in a Workbook

In the following project, you will edit a worksheet that summarizes the inventory of bulbs and trees at the Pasadena facility. Your completed workbook will look similar to Figure 2.61.

Project Files for **MyLab IT Grader**

1. In your **MyLab IT** course, locate and click **Excel 2G Inventory**, Download Materials, and then Download All Files.
2. Extract the zipped folder to your Excel Chapter 2 folder. Close the Grader download screens.
3. Take a moment to open the downloaded **Excel_2G_Inventory_Instructions** note any recent updates to the book.

Project Results

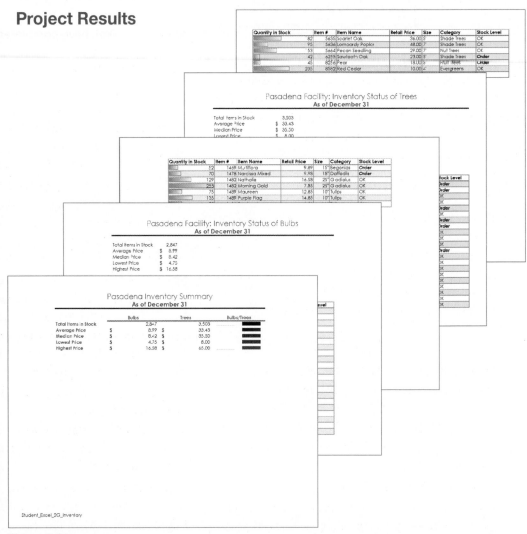

Figure 2.61

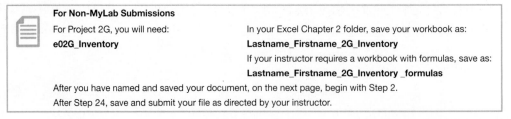

For Non-MyLab Submissions

For Project 2G, you will need:
e02G_Inventory

In your Excel Chapter 2 folder, save your workbook as:
Lastname_Firstname_2G_Inventory

If your instructor requires a workbook with formulas, save as:
Lastname_Firstname_2G_Inventory _formulas

After you have named and saved your document, on the next page, begin with Step 2.

After Step 24, save and submit your file as directed by your instructor.

(continues on next page)

1 Navigate to your **Excel Chapter 2 folder**, and then double-click the Excel file you downloaded from **MyLab IT** that displays your name—**Student_Excel_2G_Inventory**.

2 Change the **Theme** to **Slice**. Rename **Sheet1** as **Bulbs** and **Sheet2** as **Trees** and then make the **Bulbs** sheet the active sheet.

3 To the right of **column B**, insert two new columns to create **new blank columns C and D**. By using **Flash Fill** in the two new columns, split the data in **column B** into a column for *Item #* in **column C** and *Category* in **column D**.

4 Type **Item #** as the column title in **column C** and **Category** as the column title in **column D**. Delete **column B**. By using the **Cut** and **Paste** commands, cut **column C**—*Category*—and paste it to **column G**, and then delete the empty **column C**. Apply **AutoFit** to **columns A:F**.

5 Display the **Trees** worksheet, and then repeat steps 3 and 4 on this worksheet.

6 Make the following calculations in each of the two worksheets *without* grouping the sheets:

- In cell **B4**, enter a function to sum the **Quantity in Stock** data, and then apply **Comma Style** with zero decimal places to the result.

- In cells **B5:B8**, enter formulas to calculate the Average, Median, Lowest, and Highest retail prices, and then apply the **Accounting Number Format**.

7 In each of the two worksheets, make the following calculation *without* grouping the sheets:

- In cell **B10**, enter a COUNTIF function to determine how many different types of **Tulips** are in stock on the **Bulbs** sheet and how many different types of **Evergreens** are in stock on the **Trees** worksheet.

8 Without grouping the worksheets, complete the following in each worksheet:

- In cell **G14**, type **Stock Level**

- In cell **G15**, construct an **IF** function to determine the items that must be ordered. If the **Quantity in Stock** is less than **75** the **Value_if_true** is **Order** Otherwise the **Value_if_false** is **OK** Fill the formula down through all the rows.

9 Without grouping the worksheets, apply conditional formatting as follows to both worksheets:

- Apply **Conditional Formatting** to the **Stock Level** column so that cells that contain the text *Order* are formatted with **Bold Italic,** font **Color** set to **Automatic,** and **Fill** color set to **No color**.

- Apply **Gradient Fill Blue Data Bars** to the **Quantity in Stock** column.

10 In the **Bulbs** sheet, format the range **A14:G42** as a table with headers and apply **Light Orange, Table Style Light 20**. If the style isn't available, choose another style. Insert a **Total Row**, filter by **Category** for **Tulips**, and then **Sum** the **Quantity in Stock** column. Record the result in cell **B11**.

11 Select the table, clear the filter, **Sort** the table on the **Item #** column from **Smallest to Largest** (Ascending) and then remove the **Total Row**. On the **Page Layout tab**, set **Print Titles** so that **row 14** repeats at the top of each page.

12 In the **Trees** sheet, format the range **A14:G42** as a table with headers and apply **Light Green, Table Style Light 19**. If the style isn't available, choose another style. Insert a **Total Row**, filter by **Category** for **Evergreens**, and then **Sum** the **Quantity in Stock** column. Record the result in cell **B11**.

13 Select the table, clear the filter, **Sort** the table on the **Item #** column from **Smallest to Largest** (Ascending), and then remove the **Total Row**. On the **Page Layout tab**, set **Print Titles** so that **row 14** repeats at the top of each page, and then **Save** your workbook.

14 **Group** the two worksheets. **Merge & Center** the title in cell **A1** across the range **A1:G1** and apply the **Title** cell style. **Merge & Center** the subtitle in cell **A2** across the range **A2:G2** and apply the **Heading 1** cell style. **AutoFit** Column A.

15 With the worksheets still grouped, **Center** the worksheets **Horizontally**, change the **Orientation** to **Landscape**, and insert a footer in the left section with the file name. Display the **Print Preview**, and then change the **Settings** to **Fit All Columns on One Page**. (Mac users, on the Page Layout tab, change the Width to 1 page.)

(continues on next page)

Content-Based Assessments (Mastery and Transfer of Learning)

16 **Save** your workbook and then ungroup the sheets. Make the **Trees** sheet the active sheet, and then insert a new worksheet. Change the new sheet name to **Summary** and then widen **columns A:D** to **170** pixels. Move the **Summary** sheet so that it is the first sheet in the workbook.

17 In cell **A1**, type **Pasadena Inventory Summary Merge & Center** the title across the range **A1:D1**, and then apply the **Title** cell style. In cell **A2**, type **As of December 31** and then **Merge & Center** the text across the range **A2:D2**. Apply the **Heading 1** cell style.

18 On the **Bulbs sheet**, **Copy** the range **A4:A8**. Display the **Summary sheet** and **Paste** the selection to cell **A5**. Apply the **Heading 4** cell style to the selection.

19 In the **Summary sheet**, in cell **B4**, type **Bulbs** In cell **C4**, type **Trees** In cell **D4**, type **Bulbs/Trees** and then **Center** the column titles. Apply the **Heading 3** cell style.

20 In cell **B5**, enter a formula that references cell **B4** in the **Bulbs sheet** so that the **Bulbs Total Items in Stock** displays in **B5**. Create similar formulas to enter the **Average Price**, **Median Price**, **Lowest Price**, and **Highest Price** from the **Bulbs sheet** into the **Summary** sheet in the range **B6:B9**.

21 Enter formulas in the range **C5:C9** that reference the Total Items in stock and the Average Price, Median Price, Lowest Price, and Highest Price cells in the **Trees** worksheet.

22 In cells **D5**, **D6**, **D7**, **D8**, and **D9**, insert **Column** sparklines using the values in the *Bulbs* and *Trees* columns. Format each sparkline using the first five Sparkline styles in the first row.

23 To the range **B5:C5**, apply **Comma Style** with zero decimal places, and to the range **B6:C9**, apply **Accounting Number Format**. Center the **Summary** worksheet **Horizontally** and change the **Orientation** to **Landscape**. Insert a footer in the left section with the **File Name**.

24 Display the workbook **Properties**. As the **Tags**, type **Pasadena inventory** As the **Subject**, type your course name and section number. Be sure your name displays as the **Author**. **Save** your workbook and **Close** Excel.

25 In **MyLab IT**, locate and click the Grader Project **Excel 2G Inventory**. In **step 3**, under **Upload Completed Assignment**, click **Choose File**. In the **Open** dialog box, navigate to your **Excel Chapter 2 folder**, and then click your **Student_Excel_2G_Inventory** file one time to select it. In the lower right corner of the **Open** dialog box, click **Open**.

The name of your selected file displays above the Upload button.

26 To submit your file to **MyLab IT** for grading, click **Upload**, wait a moment for a green **Success!** message, and then in **step 4**, click the blue **Submit for Grading** button. Click **Close Assignment** to return to your list of **Course Materials**.

You have completed Project 2G `END`

Content-Based Assessments (Critical Thinking)

GO! Fix It	**Project 2H Planters**	IRC
GO! Make It	**Project 2I Salary**	IRC
GO! Solve It	**Project 2J Sod**	IRC
GO! Solve It	**Project 2K Products**	

Project Files

For Project 2K, you will need the following file:

e02K_Products

You will save your workbook as:

Lastname_Firstname_2K_Products

From your student data files, open the file e02K_Products and save it as **Lastname_Firstname_2K_Products** This workbook contains two worksheets: one for U.S. sales data by product and one for Canadian sales data by product. Complete the two worksheets by calculating totals by product and by month. Then calculate the Percent of Total for all products by dividing the Product Total by the Monthly Total, using absolute cell references as necessary. Format the percentages with two decimal places and center in the cells. Format the worksheets attractively and apply financial formatting. Insert a new worksheet that summarizes the monthly totals for the U.S. and Canada. Enter the months as the column titles and the countries as the row titles. Include a Product Total column and a column for sparklines titled **April/May/June** Format the Summary worksheet attractively with a title and subtitle, insert column sparklines that compare the months, and apply financial formatting. Include the file name in the footer, add appropriate document properties, and submit as directed.

		Performance Level		
		Exemplary: You consistently applied the relevant skills	**Proficient: You sometimes, but not always, applied the relevant skills**	**Developing: You rarely or never applied the relevant skills**
Performance Criteria	**Create formulas**	All formulas are correct and are efficiently constructed.	Formulas are correct but not always constructed in the most efficient manner.	One or more formulas are missing or incorrect; or only numbers were entered.
	Create Summary worksheet	Summary worksheet created properly.	Summary worksheet was created but the data, sparklines, or formulas were incorrect.	No Summary worksheet was created.
	Formatting is attractive and appropriate.	Format attractively and appropriately	Adequately formatted but difficult to read or unattractive.	Inadequate or no formatting.

You have completed Project 2K END

Outcomes-Based Assessments (Critical Thinking)

Rubric

The following outcomes-based assessments are open-ended assessments. That is, there is no specific correct result; your result will depend on your approach to the information provided. Make Professional Quality your goal. Use the following scoring rubric to guide you in how to approach the problem and then to evaluate how well your approach solves the problem.

The *criteria*—Software Mastery, Content, Format and Layout, and Process—represent the knowledge and skills you have gained that you can apply to solving the problem. The *levels of performance*—Professional Quality, Approaching Professional Quality, or Needs Quality Improvements—help you and your instructor evaluate your result.

	Your completed project is of Professional Quality if you:	Your completed project is Approaching Professional Quality if you:	Your completed project Needs Quality Improvements if you:
1-Software Mastery	Choose and apply the most appropriate skills, tools, and features and identify efficient methods to solve the problem.	Choose and apply some appropriate skills, tools, and features, but not in the most efficient manner.	Choose inappropriate skills, tools, or features, or are inefficient in solving the problem.
2-Content	Construct a solution that is clear and well organized, contains content that is accurate, appropriate to the audience and purpose, and is complete. Provide a solution that contains no errors of spelling, grammar, or style.	Construct a solution in which some components are unclear, poorly organized, inconsistent, or incomplete. Misjudge the needs of the audience. Have some errors in spelling, grammar, or style, but the errors do not detract from comprehension.	Construct a solution that is unclear, incomplete, or poorly organized, contains some inaccurate or inappropriate content, and contains many errors of spelling, grammar, or style. Do not solve the problem.
3-Format and Layout	Format and arrange all elements to communicate information and ideas, clarify function, illustrate relationships, and indicate relative importance.	Apply appropriate format and layout features to some elements, but not others. Overuse features, causing minor distraction.	Apply format and layout that does not communicate information or ideas clearly. Do not use format and layout features to clarify function, illustrate relationships, or indicate relative importance. Use available features excessively, causing distraction.
4-Process	Use an organized approach that integrates planning, development, self-assessment, revision, and reflection.	Demonstrate an organized approach in some areas, but not others; or, use an insufficient process of organization throughout.	Do not use an organized approach to solve the problem.

Outcomes-Based Assessments (Critical Thinking)

Apply a combination of the 2A and 2B skills.

GO! Think	2L Palms

Project Files

For Project 2L, you will need the following file:

e02L_Palms

You will save your workbook as:

Lastname_Firstname_2L_Palms

Melanie Castillo, Product Manager for Rosedale Landscape and Garden, has requested a worksheet that summarizes the current palm tree inventory data. Melanie would like the worksheet to include the total Quantity in Stock and Number of Items for each of the four categories of palm trees, and she would like the items to be sorted from lowest to highest retail price. She would also like a separate column for Item # and for Category.

Edit the file e02L_Palms to provide Melanie with the information requested, and use the Table feature to find the data requested. Format the worksheet titles and data and include an appropriately formatted table so that the worksheet is professional and easy to read and understand. Insert a footer with the file name, and add appropriate document properties. Save the file as **Lastname_Firstname_2L_Palms** and print or submit as directed by your instructor.

You have completed Project 2L **END**

GO! Think	Project 2M Contracts	IRC
You and GO!	Project 2N Annual Expenses	IRC
GO! Cumulative Team Project	Project 2O Bell Orchid Hotels	IRC

Analyzing Data with Pie Charts, Line Charts, and What-If Analysis Tools

3

EXCEL 2019

Rob Hainer/Shutterstock

In This Chapter

GO! To Work with Excel

In this chapter, you will work with two different types of commonly used charts that make it easy to visualize data. You will create a pie chart in a separate chart sheet to show how the parts of a fund contribute to a total fund. Pie charts are one type of chart you can use to show part-to-whole relationships. You will also practice using parentheses in a formula, calculate the percentage rate of an increase, answer what-if questions, and then chart data in a line chart to show the flow of data over time. In this chapter, you will also create a map chart and a funnel chart.

The projects in this chapter relate to the city of **Pacifica Bay**, a coastal city south of San Francisco. The city's access to major transportation provides both residents and businesses an opportunity to compete in the global marketplace. The city's mission is to create a more beautiful and more economically viable community for its residents. Each year the city welcomes a large number of tourists who enjoy exploring the rocky coastline and seeing the famous landmarks in San Francisco. The city encourages best environmental practices and partners with cities in other countries to promote sound government at the local level.

PROJECT
3A

Enterprise Fund
Pie Chart

MyLab IT
Project 3A Grader for Instruction
Project 3A Simulation for Training and Review

Project Activities

In Activities 3.01 through 3.12, you will edit a worksheet for Michael Larsen, City Manager, that reports the adjusted figures for Enterprise Fund Expenditures for the next fiscal year, and then present the data in a pie chart. Your completed worksheets will look similar to Figure 3.1.

Project Files for **MyLab IT Grader**

1. In your storage location, create a folder named **Excel Chapter 3**.
2. In your **MyLab IT** course, locate and click **Excel 3A Enterprise Fund**, Download Materials, and then Download All Files.
3. Extract the zipped folder to your Excel Chapter 3 folder. Close the Grader download screens.
4. Take a moment to open the downloaded **Excel_3A_Enterprise_Fund_Instructions**; note any recent updates to the book.

Project Results

GO! Project 3A
Where We're Going

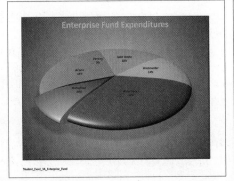

Figure 3.1 Project 3A Enterprise Fund Pie Chart

For Non-MyLab Submissions

For Project 3A, you will need:
e03A_Enterprise_Fund

In your storage location, create a folder named **Excel Chapter 3**
In your Excel Chapter 3 folder, save your workbook as:
Lastname_Firstname_3A_Enterprise_Fund
If your instructor requires a workbook with formulas, save as:
Lastname_Firstname_3A_Enterprise_Fund_formulas

After you have named and saved your workbook, on the next page, begin with Step 2.

ALERT Because Office 365 is a cloud-based subscription service that receives continuous updates, you may encounter some variations in what appears on your screen and what is shown in this instruction. Microsoft Office 365 is fully installed on your PC or Mac; no internet access is necessary to create or edit documents. When you *are* connected to the internet, you will receive monthly upgrades and new features, so you always have the latest versions of Office apps as soon as they are available. Your subscription gives you continuous free access to the latest innovations and refinements.

GO! Learn How
Video E3-1

A *pie chart* shows the relationship of each part to a whole. The size of each pie slice is equal to its value compared to the total value of all the slices. A pie chart displays data that is arranged in a single column or single row and shows the size of items in a single data series proportional to the sum of the items. Whereas a column or bar chart can have two or more data series in the chart, a pie chart can have only one data series.

Consider using a pie chart when you have only one data series to plot; you do not have more than seven categories, and the categories represent parts of a total value.

Activity 3.01 | Calculating Values for a Pie Chart

A *fund* is a sum of money set aside for a specific purpose. In a municipal government like the city of Pacifica Bay, the *general fund* is money set aside for the normal operating activities of the city, such as police, fire, and administering the everyday functions of the city.

Municipal governments also commonly establish an *enterprise fund* to report income and expenditures related to municipal services for which a fee is charged in exchange for goods or services. For example, Pacifica Bay receives income from airport landing fees, parking fees, water usage fees, and rental fees along public beaches, but there are costs—expenditures—related to building and maintaining these facilities and services from which income is received.

1 ▶ Navigate to your **Excel Chapter 3 folder**, and then double-click the Excel file you downloaded from **MyLab IT** that displays your name—**Student_Excel_3A_Enterprise_Fund**.

> The worksheet indicates the originally proposed and adjusted expenditures from the Enterprise Fund for the next fiscal year.

2 ▶ Click cell **D5**, and then type **=** to begin a formula.

3 ▶ Click cell **C5**, which is the first value that is part of the total adjusted Fund Expenditures, to insert it into the formula. Type **/** to indicate division, and then click cell **C11**, which is the total adjusted expenditures.

> Recall that to determine the percentage by which a value makes up a total, you must divide the value by the total. The result will be a percentage expressed as a decimal.

4 ▶ Press F4 to make the reference to the value in cell **C11** absolute, which will enable you to copy the formula. Compare your screen with Figure 3.2.

> Recall that an *absolute cell reference* refers to a cell by its fixed position in the worksheet—the cell reference will not change when you copy the formula. The reference to cell C5 is a *relative cell reference*, because when you copy the formula, you want the reference to change *relative* to its row. In the formula, dollar signs display to indicate that a cell reference is absolute.

🖥 **MAC TIP** Press command ⌘ + T to make a cell reference in a formula absolute.

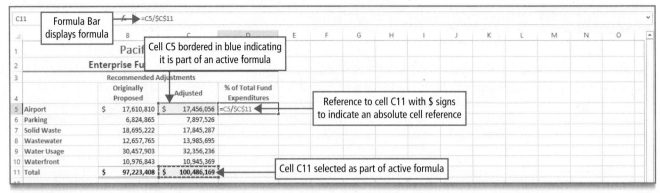

Figure 3.2

> **5** On the **Formula Bar**, click **Enter** ☑ to confirm the entry and to keep cell **D5** the active cell.

> **6** Copy the formula down through cell **D10**, and then compare your screen with Figure 3.3.

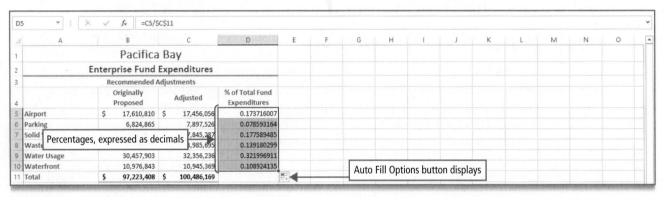

Figure 3.3

> **7** With the range **D5:D10** still selected, apply **Percent Style** %️ and then **Center** ≡ the selection. Click cell **A1** to cancel the selection, and then **Save** 💾 your workbook. Compare your screen with Figure 3.4.

	A	B	C	D
1		Pacifica Bay		
2		Enterprise Fund Expenditures		
3		Recommended Adjustments		
4		Originally Proposed	Adjusted	% of Total Fund Expenditures
5	Airport	$ 17,610,810	$ 17,456,056	17%
6	Parking	6,824,865	7,897,526	8%
7	Solid Waste	18,695,222	17,845,287	18%
8	Wastewater	12,657,765	13,985,695	14%
9	Water Usage	30,457,903	32,356,236	32%
10	Waterfront	10,976,843	10,945,369	11%
11	Total	$ 97,223,408	$ 100,486,169	
12				

Percent of Total for each item calculated, expressed as percentages

Figure 3.4

Activity 3.02 | Creating a Pie Chart and Moving a Chart to a Chart Sheet

MOS

5.1.1 and 5.1.2

> **1** Select the range **A5:A10**, hold down Ctrl, and then select the range **C5:C10** to select the nonadjacent ranges with the item names and the adjusted expenditure for each item.

⌨️ **MAC TIP** With the first range selected, press command ⌘ while selecting the second range.

To create a pie chart, you must select two ranges. One range contains the labels for each slice of the pie chart, and the other range contains the values that add up to a total. The two ranges must have the same number of cells and the range with the values should *not* include the cell with the total.

The item names (Airport, Parking, and so on) are the category names and will identify the slices of the pie chart. Each adjusted expenditure is a ***data point***—a value that originates in a worksheet cell and that is represented in a chart by a ***data marker***. In a pie chart, each pie slice is a data marker. Together, the data points form the ***data series***—related data points represented by data markers—and determine the size of each pie slice.

2 With the nonadjacent ranges selected, click the **Insert tab**, and then in the **Charts group**, click **Insert Pie or Doughnut Chart** 🥧. Under **3-D Pie**, click the chart **3-D Pie** to create the chart on your worksheet and to display the Chart Tools contextual tabs on the ribbon.

MAC TIP To display group names on the ribbon, display the menu, click Excel, click Preferences, click View, select the Group Titles check box.

---

3 On the **Design tab**, at the right end of the ribbon in the **Location group**, click **Move Chart**. In the **Move Chart** dialog box, click the **New sheet** option button.

4 In the **New sheet** box, replace the highlighted text *Chart1* by typing **Expenditures Chart** and then click **OK** to display the chart on a separate worksheet in your workbook. Compare your screen with Figure 3.5.

The pie chart displays on a separate new sheet in your workbook, and a ***legend*** identifies the pie slices. Recall that a legend is a chart element that identifies the patterns or colors assigned to the categories in the chart.

A ***chart sheet*** is a workbook sheet that contains only a chart; it is useful when you want to view a chart separately from the worksheet data. The sheet tab indicates *Expenditures Chart*.

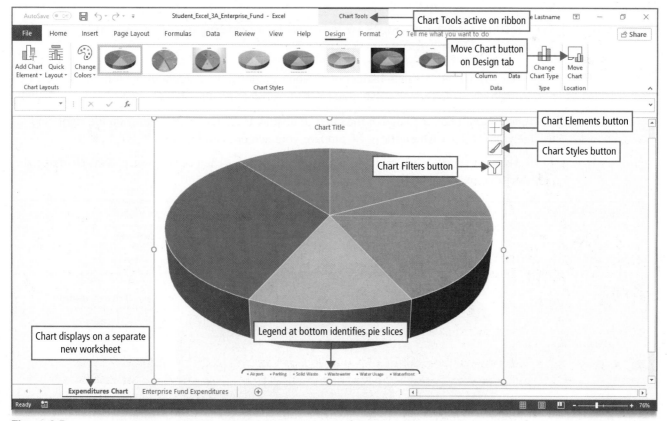

Figure 3.5

GO! Learn How

Video E3-2

Activity 3.03 | Formatting a Chart Title by Applying a WordArt Style and Changing Font Size

1 ▶ Click the text *Chart Title* to surround it with selection handles, and then watch the **Formula Bar** as you type **Enterprise Fund Expenditures** Press ⏎ to create the new chart title in the box.

> **MAC TIP** Select the title text before typing the new chart title. Do not press Enter after typing the new title.

2 ▶ Click the **Format tab**, and then in the **WordArt Styles group**, click **More** ⊟. In the first row, click the last style.

> **MAC TIP** Select the title text and then apply the WordArt style. Be sure to display the entire WordArt Styles gallery to locate the last style in the first row.

3 ▶ Drag to select the chart title text, and then change the **Font Size** to **32**. Click the edge of the chart to deselect the title, and then compare your screen with Figure 3.6.

4 ▶ **Save** 🖫 your workbook.

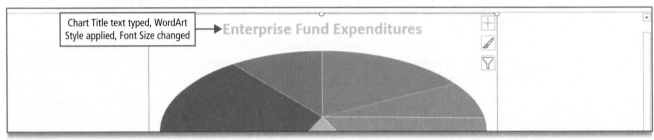

Chart Title text typed, WordArt Style applied, Font Size changed → Enterprise Fund Expenditures

Figure 3.6

Activity 3.04 | Formatting Chart Elements by Removing a Legend and Adding and Formatting Data Labels

5.2.3

In your worksheet, for each budget item, you calculated the percent of the total in column D. These percentages can also be calculated by the Chart feature and added to the pie slices as labels.

1 ▶ If necessary, click the edge of the chart to display the three chart buttons on the right, and then click **Chart Elements** ⊞. Compare your screen with Figure 3.7.

Use the Chart Elements button to add, remove, or change chart elements such as the chart title, the legend, and the data labels.

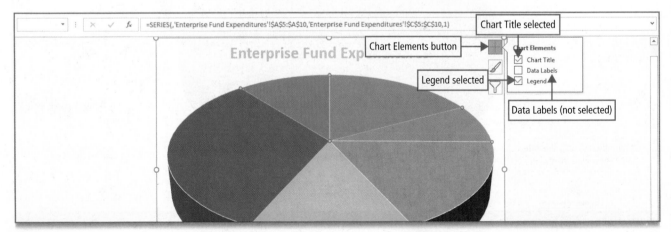

=SERIES(,'Enterprise Fund Expenditures'!$A$5:$A$10,'Enterprise Fund Expenditures'!$C$5:$C$10,1)

Chart Title selected

Enterprise Fund Exp

Chart Elements button

Legend selected

Chart Elements
☑ Chart Title
☐ Data Labels
☑ Legend

Data Labels (not selected)

Figure 3.7

2 Click the **Legend** check box to deselect it and remove the legend from the bottom of the chart.

MAC TIP On the Chart Design tab, click Add Chart Element, point to Legend, and then click None.

3 Point to **Data Labels**, and then click the ▶ **arrow** to display a menu. At the bottom of the menu, click **More Options** to display the **Format Data Labels** pane on the right.

The Format Data Labels pane displays and data labels representing the values display on each pie slice.

MAC TIP On the Chart Design tab, click Add Chart Element, point to Data Labels, and then click More Data Label Options.

4 In the **Format Data Labels** pane, under **Label Options**, click as necessary to select the **Category Name** and **Percentage** check boxes. Click to *clear* any other check boxes in this group. Under **Label Position**, click the **Center** option button. Compare your screen with Figure 3.8.

All of the data labels are selected and display both the category name and the percentage. In the worksheet, you calculated the percent of the total in column D. Here, the percentage will be calculated by the Chart feature and added to the chart as a label.

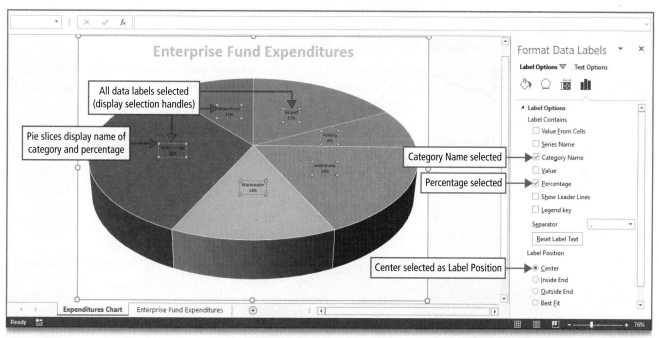

Figure 3.8

5 Point to any of the selected data labels, right-click to display a shortcut menu, and then click **Font** to display the **Font** dialog box.

MAC TIP Press control and then click a data label to display the Shortcut menu.

6 On the **Font tab**, click the **Font style arrow**, and then click **Bold Italic**. In the **Size** box, drag to select *9* and type **11** Compare your screen with Figure 3.9.

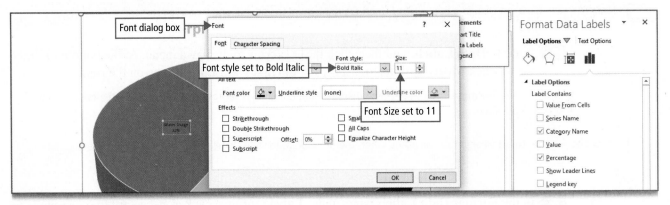

Figure 3.9

7 Click **OK** to close the dialog box and apply the formatting to the data labels. In the upper right corner of the **Format Data Labels** pane, click **Close** ☒. **Save** 🖫 your workbook.

Activity 3.05 │ Formatting a Data Series with 3-D Effects

3-D, which is short for *three-dimensional*, refers to an image that appears to have all three spatial dimensions—length, width, and depth.

1 In any pie slice, point anywhere outside of the selected label, and then double-click to display the **Format Data Series** pane on the right.

> **ANOTHER WAY** Right-click outside the label of any pie slice, and then click Format Data Series to display the Format Data Series pane. Or, on the Format tab, in the Current Selection group, click the Chart Elements arrow, click Series 1, and then click Format Selection.

2 In the **Format Data Series** pane, under **Series Options**, click **Effects** ⬠, and then click **3-D Format**. Compare your screen with Figure 3.10.

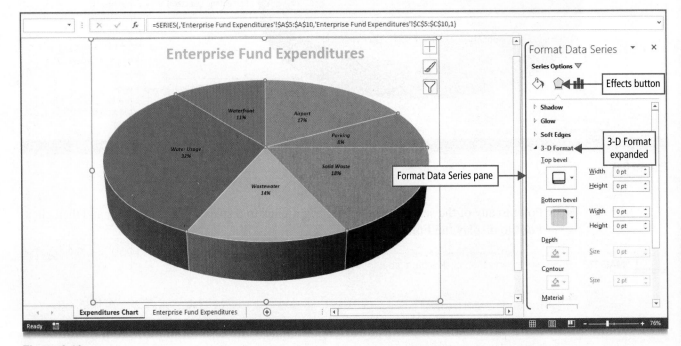

Figure 3.10

3 ▸ Click the **Top bevel arrow**, and then in the gallery, under **Bevel**, click the first bevel, as shown in Figure 3.11.

> **Bevel** is a shape effect that uses shading and shadows to make the edges of a shape appear to be curved or angled.

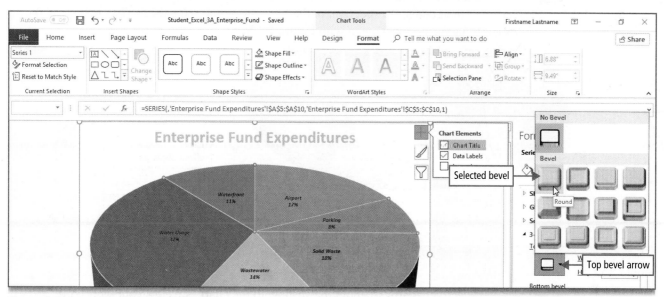

Figure 3.11

4 ▸ Under **Top bevel**, in the **Width** box, select the existing text and type **512** Change the **Height** to **512** and then press Enter.

5 ▸ Under **Bottom bevel**, use the technique you just practiced to apply the first bevel in the first row with a **Width** of **512** and **Height** of **512** Compare your screen with Figure 3.12.

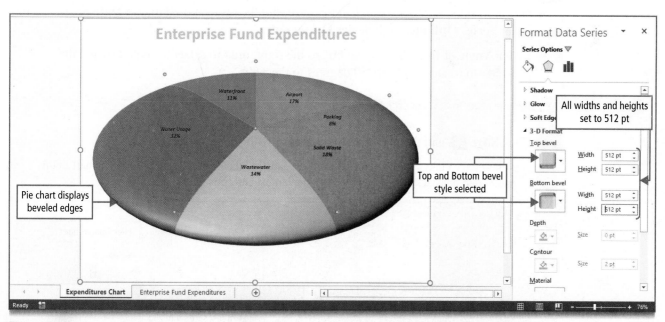

Figure 3.12

6 ▸ In the **Format Data Series** pane, scroll down as necessary, and then click the **Material arrow**. Under **Standard**, click the third material—**Plastic**.

7 ▸ **Save** 🖫 your workbook.

Activity 3.06 | Formatting a Data Series with a Shadow Effect

1 In the **Format Data Series pane**, scroll back to the top of the pane, and then click **Shadow** to expand the options for this effect.

2 Under **Shadow**, click the **Presets arrow**, use the scroll bar to move to the bottom of the gallery, and then under **Perspective**, in the first row, point to the third effect to display the ScreenTip. Compare your screen with Figure 3.13.

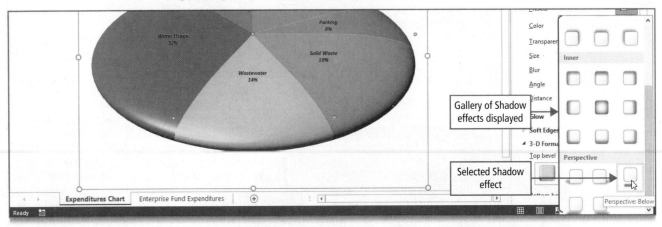

Figure 3.13

3 Click **Perspective: Below** to apply the shadow to the chart. **Save** your workbook.

Activity 3.07 | Rotating a Pie Chart by Changing the Angle of the First Slice

The order in which the data series in pie charts are plotted in Excel is determined by the order of the data on the worksheet. To gain a different view of the chart, you can rotate the chart within the 360 degrees of the circle of the pie shape to present a different visual perspective of the chart.

1 Notice the position of the **Water Usage** and **Waterfront** slices in the chart. Then, with the pie chart still selected—sizing handles surround the pie—in the **Format Data Series** pane, under **Series Options**, click **Series Options**.

2 Under **Angle of first slice**, in the box to the right, drag to select **0°**, type **250** and then press Enter to rotate the chart 250 degrees to the right.

ANOTHER WAY Drag the slider to 250°, or click the spin box up arrow as many times as necessary.

3 Click **Save**, and then compare your screen with Figure 3.14.

Rotating the chart can provide a better perspective to the chart. Here, rotating the chart in this manner emphasizes that Water Usage is the largest enterprise fund expenditure.

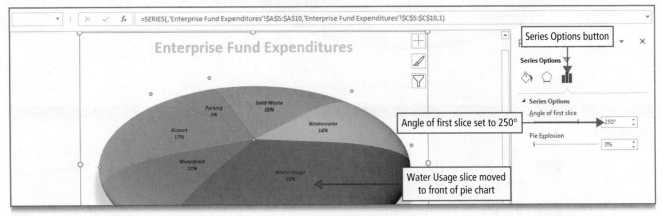

Figure 3.14

Activity 3.08 | Exploding and Coloring a Pie Slice

You can pull out—*explode*—one or more slices of a pie chart to emphasize a specific slice or slices.

1 In the **Format Data Series** pane, under **Series Options**, notice the slider and box for *Pie Explosion*.

When all the pie slices are selected, as they currently are, you can use this command to explode *all* of the pie pieces away from the center by varying degrees to emphasize all the individual slices of the pie chart. An exploded pie chart illustrates the contribution of each value to the total, while at the same time emphasizing individual values.

2 On the pie chart, click the **Waterfront** slice to select only that slice, and then on the right, notice that the **Format Data Point** pane displays.

Excel adjusts the pane, depending on what you have selected, so that the commands you need are available.

3 In the **Format Data Point** pane, in the **Point Explosion** box, select the existing text, type **10%** and then press Enter.

4 With the **Waterfront** slice still selected, in the **Format Data Point** pane, under **Series Options**, click **Fill & Line** ▨, and then click **Fill** to expand its options.

5 Click the **Gradient fill** option button, click the **Preset gradients arrow**, and then in the fourth row, click the last gradient. Click **Save** ▨, and then compare your screen with Figure 3.15.

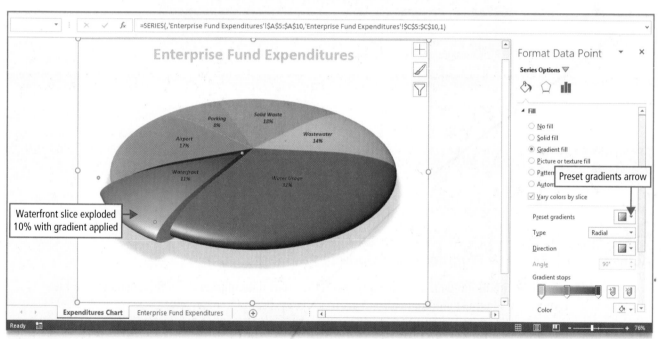

Figure 3.15

Activity 3.09 | Formatting the Chart Area

The entire chart and all of its elements comprise the ***chart area***.

1 Point to the white area just inside the border of the chart to display the ScreenTip *Chart Area*. Click one time, and notice that on the right, the **Format Chart Area** pane displays.

2 Under **Chart Options**, click **Fill & Line** ▨, and be sure the **Fill** options are still displayed.

3 Click the **Gradient fill** option button, click the **Preset gradients arrow**, and then in the fourth row, click the first gradient.

4 In the **Format Chart Area** pane, click **Fill** to collapse the options, and then click **Border** to expand its options.

5 Under **Border**, click **Solid line**, click the **Color arrow** to display the Outline colors, and then in the fourth column, click the first color. In the **Width** box, drag to select the existing width, type **5** and then press Enter.

6 **Close** ☒ the **Format Chart Area** pane, and then click outside of the Chart Area to deselect the chart. Click **Save** 🖫, and then compare your screen with Figure 3.16.

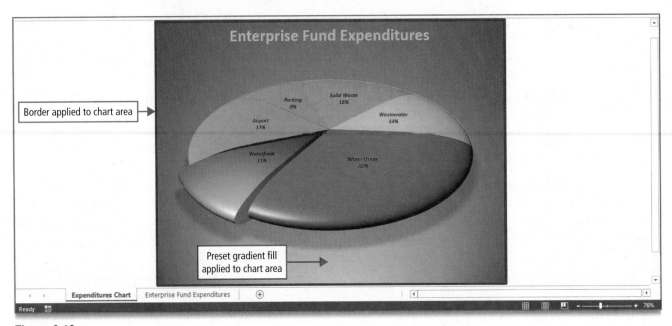

Figure 3.16

Objective 3 | **Edit a Workbook and Update a Chart**

GO! Learn How
Video E3-3

Activity 3.10 | **Editing a Workbook and Updating a Chart**

If you edit the data in your worksheet, the chart data markers—in this instance the pie slices—will adjust automatically to accurately represent the new values.

1 On the pie chart, notice that *Airport* represents 17% of the total projected expenses.

2 In the sheet tab area at the bottom of the workbook, click the **Enterprise Fund Expenditures tab** to redisplay the worksheet.

3 Click cell **C5**, type **18,121,067** and then press Enter. Notice that the Accounting Number Format is retained in the cell.

🔄 **ANOTHER WAY**   Double-click the cell to position the insertion point in the cell and edit.

4 Notice that the total in cell **C11** recalculated to *$101,151,180* and the percentages in **column D** also recalculated.

5 Display the **Expenditures Chart** sheet. Notice that the pie slices adjust to show the recalculation—*Airport* is now *18%* of the adjusted expenditures. Click **Save** 🖫, and then compare your screen with Figure 3.17.

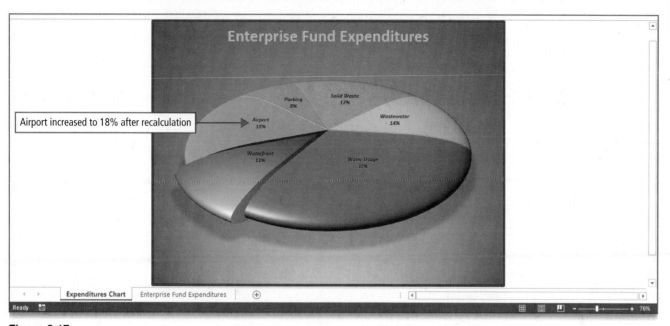

Figure 3.17

Objective 4 | Use Goal Seek to Perform What-If Analysis

GO! Learn How
Video E3-4

Activity 3.11 | Using Goal Seek to Perform What-If Analysis

MOS
Expert 3.4.2

The process of changing the values in cells to see how those changes affect the outcome of formulas in your worksheet is referred to as ***what-if analysis***. One what-if analysis tool in Excel is ***Goal Seek***, which finds the input needed in one cell to arrive at the desired result in another cell.

1 Click the **Enterprise Fund Expenditures sheet tab** to redisplay the worksheet.

2 Select the range **D5:D10**, and then increase the number of decimal places to two. Compare your screen with Figure 3.18.

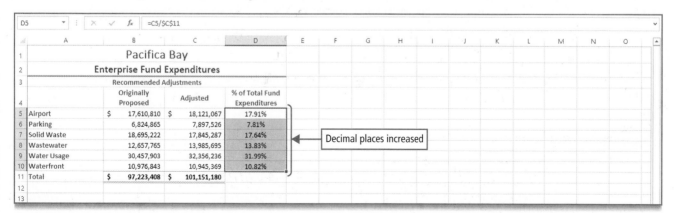

Figure 3.18

3 ▶ Click the cell containing the *Adjusted Total*, cell **C11**. On the **Data tab**, in the **Forecast group**, click **What-If Analysis**, and then click **Goal Seek**.

4 ▶ In the **Goal Seek** dialog box, notice that the active cell, **C11**, is indicated in the **Set cell** box. Press ⎇Tab to move to the **To value** box, and then type **100,000,000**

> C11 is the cell in which you want to set a specific value; $100,000,000 is the total expenditures budgeted for the Enterprise Fund. The Set cell box contains the formula that calculates the information you seek.

5 ▶ Press ⎇Tab to move the insertion point to the **By changing cell** box, and then click cell **C10**. Compare your screen with Figure 3.19.

> Cell C10 contains the value that Excel changes to reach the goal. In the Goal Seek dialog box, Excel formats this cell as an absolute cell reference.

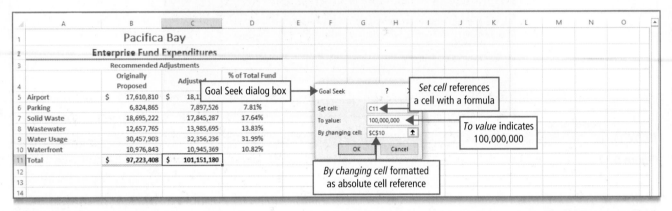

Figure 3.19

6 ▶ Click **OK**. In the displayed **Goal Seek Status** dialog box, click **OK**.

7 ▶ Press ⎈Ctrl + ⌂Home, click **Save** 🖫, and then compare your screen with Figure 3.20.

> Excel calculates that the city must budget for *$9,794,189* in Waterfront expenditures in order to maintain a total Enterprise Fund Expenditure budget of $100,000,000.

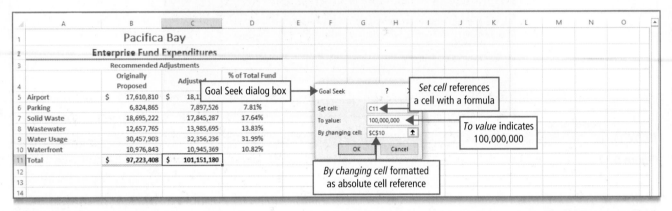

Figure 3.20

Activity 3.12 | Preparing and Printing a Workbook with a Chart Sheet

1 Click the **Page Layout tab**. In the **Page Setup group**, click **Margins**, and then click **Custom Margins**.

2 In the **Page Setup** dialog box, on the **Margins tab**, under **Center on page**, select the **Horizontally** check box.

3 Click the **Header/Footer tab**, and then in the center of the dialog box, click **Custom Footer**. In the **Footer** dialog box, with the insertion point blinking in the **Left section**, on the row of buttons, click **Insert File Name** . Click **OK** two times.

> The dotted line indicates the page break as currently formatted.

4 Display the **Expenditures Chart**, which must have its footer formatted separately. In the **Page Setup group**, click the **Dialog Box Launcher** .

> Chart sheets are automatically centered on the page.

MAC TIP On the Page Layout tab, click Page Setup to display the Page Setup dialog box.

---

5 Click the **Header/Footer tab**, and then in the center of the dialog box, click **Custom Footer**. In the **Footer** dialog box, with the insertion point blinking in the **Left section**, on the row of buttons, click **Insert File Name** . Click **OK** two times.

6 Right-click the **Expenditures Chart sheet tab**, and then click **Select All Sheets**. Verify that *Group* displays in the title bar.

> Recall that by selecting all sheets, you can view all of the workbook pages in Print Preview.

MAC TIP Press control and then click the Expenditures Chart sheet to display the shortcut menu.

---

7 Click **File**, and then click **Print** to display the **Print Preview**. Examine the first page, and then at the bottom of the **Print Preview**, click **Next Page** to view the second page of your workbook.

8 Display the workbook properties. As the **Tags**, type enterprise fund, expenditures As the **Subject**, type your course name and section number. Be sure your name displays as the **Author**. **Save** the workbook and **Close** Excel.

For Non-MyLab Submissions Determine What Your Instructor Requires
As directed by your instructor, submit your completed Excel file.

---

9 In **MyLab IT**, locate and click the Grader Project **Excel 3A Enterprise Fund**. In **step 3**, under **Upload Completed Assignment**, click **Choose File**. In the **Open** dialog box, navigate to your **Excel Chapter 3 folder**, and then click your **Student_Excel_3A_Enterprise_Fund** file one time to select it. In the lower right corner of the **Open** dialog box, click **Open**.

> The name of your selected file displays above the Upload button.

10 To submit your file to **MyLab IT** for grading, click **Upload**, wait a moment for a green **Success!** message, and then in **step 4**, click the blue **Submit for Grading** button. Click **Close Assignment** to return to your list of **Course Materials**.

You have completed Project 3A   **END**

»» GO! With Google Sheets

Objective	Analyze Expenditures with a Pie Chart

ALERT   **Working with Web-Based Applications and Services**

Computer programs and services on the web receive continuous updates and improvements, so the steps to complete this web-based Activity may differ from the ones shown. You can often look at the screens and the information presented to determine how to complete the Activity.

  If you do not already have a Google account, you will need to create one before you begin this Activity. Go to **http://google.com** and, in the upper right corner, click Sign In. On the Sign In screen, click Create Account. On the Create your Google Account page, complete the form, read and agree to the Terms of Service and Privacy Policy, and then click Next step. On the Welcome screen, click Get Started.

Activity | Creating a Pie Chart

1 From the desktop, open your browser, navigate to http://google.com, and then click **Google apps** ▦. Click **Drive** ⬥, and then if necessary, sign in to your Google account.

2 Open your **GO! Web Projects** folder—or click **New** to create and then open this folder if necessary. Click **New**, and then click **File upload**. Navigate to your student data files, click **e03_3A_Web**, and then click **Open**.

3 Right-click the file you uploaded, point to **Open with**, and then click **Google Sheets**.

4 Click cell **D5**. Type = and then click cell **C5**. Type / and then click **C11** and press F4 to make the cell reference absolute. Press Enter to create a formula to calculate % of Total Fund Expenditures.

5 Click cell **D5**, and then apply percent formatting ％. Fill the formula down through cell **D10**. Click the **Format tab**, point to **Align**, and then click **Center.**

6 Select the range **A5:A10**, hold down Ctrl, and then select **C5:C10**. Click the **Insert tab**, and then click **Chart**. In the **Chart editor pane**, click the **Chart type arrow**. To the right of the chart gallery, point to the vertical scroll

bar and drag down to display the Pie charts. Click the third chart—**3D pie chart** to insert the chart in the worksheet.

7 Point to the chart and then drag down and to the left to position the pie chart under the worksheet data so that its left edge aligns with the left edge of cell **A13**. Click the **Chart title** to display a box in which you can type the chart title. Type **Enterprise Fund Expenditures** and then press Enter. In the **Chart editor pane**, click the **Title font size arrow**, and then click **30**. Click anywhere in the chart outside of the title so that the title is not selected.

8 In the **Chart editor pane**, on the **Customize tab**, click **Chart style**. Click the **Background color arrow**, and then in the seventh column, click the third color—**light cornflower blue 3**. Click **Legend**, and then click the **Position arrow**. Click **Right**. Click **Pie Chart**, and then click the **Slice label arrow**. Click **Percentage** and then close the **Chart Editor pane**.

9 Click cell **A1** and then scroll down to view the entire chart. Compare your screen with Figure A.

10 Submit your file as directed by your instructor. Sign out of your Google account and close your browser.

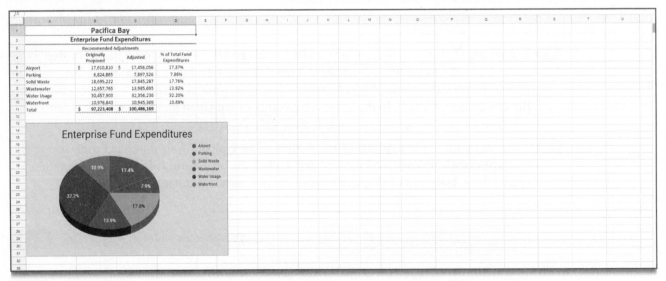

Figure A

Tourism Spending Projection and Analysis

Project Activities

In Activities 3.13 through 3.22, you will assist Michael Larsen, City Manager, in creating a worksheet to estimate future tourism spending based on two possible growth rates. You will also create a line chart to display past visitor spending and a map chart and funnel chart to analyze tourism advertising and event spending. Your resulting worksheet and chart will look similar to Figure 3.21.

Project Files for MyLab IT Grader

1. In your **MyLab IT** course, locate and click **Excel 3B Tourism**, Download Materials, and then Download All Files.
2. Extract the zipped folder to your Excel Chapter 3 folder. Close the Grader download screens.
3. Take a moment to open the downloaded **Excel_3B_Tourism_Instructions**; note any recent updates to the book.

Project Results

GO! Project 3B

Where We're Going

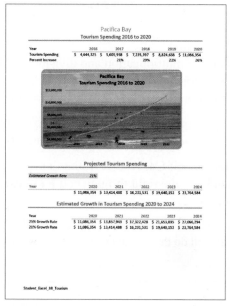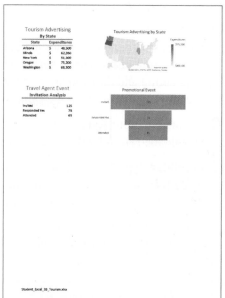

Figure 3.21 Project 3B Tourism Spending Projection and Analysis

GO! Learn How
Video E3-5

If you change the value in a cell referenced in a formula, Excel automatically recalculates the result of the formula. This means that you can change cell values to see what would happen if you tried different values. This process of changing the values in cells to see how those changes affect the outcome of formulas in your worksheet is referred to as what-if analysis.

Activity 3.13 | Using Parentheses in a Formula to Calculate a Percentage Rate of Increase

Mr. Larsen has the city's tourism spending figures for the recent 5-year period. In each year, tourism spending has increased. In this Activity, you will construct a formula to calculate the *percentage rate of increase*—the percent by which one number increases over another number—for each year since 2016. From this information, future tourism spending growth can be estimated.

Excel follows a set of mathematical rules called the *order of operations*, which has four basic parts:

- Expressions within parentheses are processed first.
- Exponentiation, if present, is performed before multiplication and division.
- Multiplication and division are performed before addition and subtraction.
- Consecutive operators with the same level of precedence are calculated from left to right.

1 ▶ Navigate to your **Excel Chapter 3 folder**, and then double-click the Excel file you downloaded from **MyLab IT** that displays your name—**Student_Excel_3B_Tourism**.

2 ▶ In cell **B4**, type **2016** and then press Tab. In cell **C4**, type **2017** and then press Tab. Select the range **B4:C4**, and then drag the fill handle to the right through cell **F4** to extend the series to *2020*. Compare your screen with Figure 3.22.

By establishing a pattern of 1-year intervals with the first two cells, you can use the fill handle to continue the series. The AutoFill feature will do this for any pattern that you establish with two or more cells.

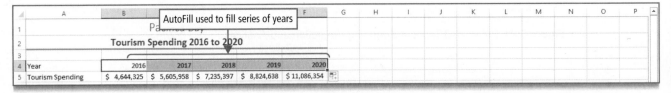

Figure 3.22

3 ▶ Click cell **C6**. Being sure to include the parentheses, type **=(c5-b5)/b5** and then on the **Formula Bar**, click **Enter** ☑ to keep cell **C6** active. Notice that your result displays as *$0.21* because Excel retains the Accounting Number Format of the cells referenced in the formula.

As you type, a list of Excel functions that begin with the letters *C* and *B* may briefly display. This is *Formula AutoComplete*, an Excel feature which, after typing an = (equal sign) and the beginning letter or letters of a function name, displays a list of function names that match the typed letter(s). In this instance, the letters represent cell references, *not* the beginning of a function name.

4 With cell **C6** selected, apply **Percent Style** %, and then compare your screen with Figure 3.23.

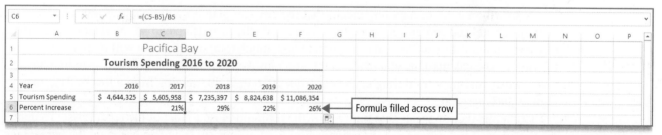

| C6 | ▾ : ✕ ✓ *fx* | =(C5-B5)/B5◄━━━━ | Formula Bar displays formula |

Pacifica Bay
Tourism Spending 2016 to 2020

	A	B	C	D	E	F
4	Year	2016	2017	2018	2019	2020
5	Tourism Spending	$ 4,644,325	$ 5,605,958	$ 7,235,~~307~~	~~8,824,638~~	~~11,086,354~~
6	Percent Increase		21%◄━━━ Formula result in cell C6			

Figure 3.23

5 With cell **C6** selected, drag the fill handle to the right to copy the formula through cell **F6**.

Because this formula uses relative cell references—that is, for each year, the formula is the same but the values used are relative to the formula's location—you can copy the formula in this manner. For example, the result for 2018 uses the 2017 value as the base, the result for 2019 uses the 2018 value as the base, and the result for 2020 uses the 2019 value as the base.

6 Click cell **C6** and look at the **Formula Bar**.

The mathematical formula ***rate = amount of increase/base*** is used to calculate the percentage rate of tourism spending increase from 2016 to 2017. The formula is applied as follows:

First, determine the *amount of increase* by subtracting the ***base***—the starting point represented by the 2016 tourism spending—from the 2017 tourism spending. Therefore, the *amount of increase* = $5,605,958 – $4,644,325 or $961,633. Between 2016 and 2017, tourism spending increased by $961,633. In the formula, this calculation is represented by *C5-B5*.

Second, calculate the *rate*—what the amount of increase ($961,633) represents as a percentage of the base (2016's tourism spending of $4,644,325). Determine this by dividing the amount of increase ($961,633) by the base ($4,644,325). Therefore, $961,633 divided by $4,644,325 is equal to *0.207055492* or, when formatted as a percent and rounded up, 21%.

7 In the **Formula Bar**, locate the parentheses enclosing *C5-B5*.

Recall that Excel follows a set of mathematical rules called the order of operations, in which expressions within parentheses are processed first, multiplication and division are performed before addition and subtraction, and consecutive operators with the same level of precedence are calculated from left to right.

8 **Save** 🖫 your workbook, and then compare your screen with Figure 3.24.

| C6 | ▾ : ✕ ✓ *fx* | =(C5-B5)/B5 | | | | | |

Pacifica Bay
Tourism Spending 2016 to 2020

	A	B	C	D	E	F
4	Year	2016	2017	2018	2019	2020
5	Tourism Spending	$ 4,644,325	$ 5,605,958	$ 7,235,397	$ 8,824,638	$ 11,086,354
6	Percent Increase		21%	29%	22%	26%◄━━ Formula filled across row

Figure 3.24

MORE KNOWLEDGE | **Use of Parentheses in a Formula**

When writing a formula in Excel, use parentheses to specify the order in which the operations should occur. For example, to average three test scores of 100, 50, and 90 that you scored on three different tests, you would add the test scores and then divide by the number of test scores in the list. If you write this formula as = 100 + 50 + 90/3, the result would be 180, because Excel would first divide 90 by 3 and then add 100 + 50 + 30. Excel would do so because the order of operations states that multiplication and division are calculated *before* addition and subtraction.

The correct way to write this formula is = (100 + 50 + 90)/3. Excel will add the three values, and then divide the result by 3, or 240/3 resulting in a correct average of 80. Parentheses play an important role in ensuring that you get the correct result in your formulas.

Activity 3.14 | Using Format Painter

MOS
2.2.3

In this Activity, you will use Format Painter to copy formatting.

1 Click cell **A2**, and then on the **Home tab**, in the **Clipboard group**, click **Format Painter** . Click cell **A8** to copy the format.

The format of cell A2 is *painted*—applied to—cell A8, including the merging and centering of the text across the range A8:F8.

2 Point to cell **F5**, display the shortcut menu, and then click **Copy**. Point to cell **B13**, right-click, and then on the shortcut menu, under **Paste Options**, click **Paste**. Compare your screen with Figure 3.25, and then **Save** your workbook.

🖥 **MAC TIP** Press [control] and then click cell B13. Click Paste.

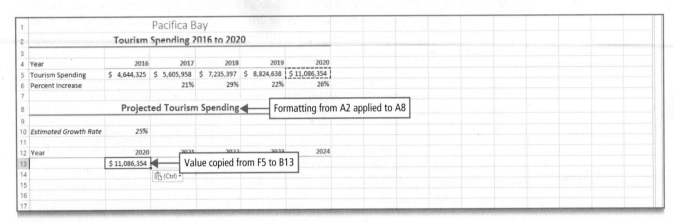

Figure 3.25

MORE KNOWLEDGE **Percentage Calculations**

When you type a percentage into a cell—for example *25%*—the percentage format, without decimal points, displays in both the cell and the Formula Bar. Excel will, however, use the decimal value of *0.25* for actual calculations.

Activity 3.15 | Calculating a Value After an Increase

A growth in tourism spending means that the city can plan for additional revenues and also plan more hotel and conference space to accommodate the increasing number of visitors. Therefore, city planners in Pacifica Bay want to estimate how much tourism spending will increase in the future. The calculations you made in the previous Activity show that tourism spending has increased at varying rates during each year from 2016 to 2020, ranging from a low of 21% to a high of 29% per year.

Economic data suggests that future growth will trend close to that of the recent past. To plan for the future, Mr. Larsen wants to prepare a forecast of tourism spending based on the percentage increase halfway between the high of 29% and the low of 21%; that is, for 25%. In this Activity, you will calculate the tourism spending that would result from a 25% increase.

1 Click cell **C13**. Type **=b13*(100%+b10)** and then on the **Formula Bar**, click **Enter** ✓ to display a result of *13857942.5*.

2 Point to cell **B13**, right-click, click **Format Painter** , and then click cell **C13** to copy the format. Compare your screen with Figure 3.26.

This formula calculates what tourism spending will be in the year 2021 assuming an increase of 25% over 2020's tourism spending. Use the mathematical formula *value after increase = base × percent for new value* to calculate a value after an increase as follows:

First, establish the *percent for new value*. The **percent for new value = base percent + percent of increase**. The *base percent* of 100% represents the base tourism spending and the *percent of increase*—in this instance, 25%. Therefore, the tourism spending will equal 100% of the base year plus 25% of the base year. This can be expressed as 125% or 1.25. In this formula, you will use 100% + the rate in cell B10, which is 25%, to equal 125%.

Second, enter a reference to the cell that contains the *base*—the tourism spending in 2020. The base value resides in cell B13—*$11,086,354*.

Third, calculate the *value after increase*. Because in each future year the increase will be based on 25%—an absolute value located in cell B10—this cell reference can be formatted as absolute by typing dollar signs.

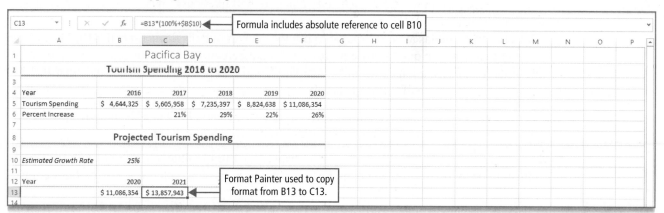

Figure 3.26

3 With cell **C13** as the active cell, drag the fill handle to copy the formula to the range **D13:F13**. Click an empty cell to cancel the selection, click **Save** 🖫 and then compare your screen with Figure 3.27.

The formula in cell C13 uses a relative cell address—B13—for the *base*; the tourism spending in the previous year is used in each of the formulas in cells D13:F13 as the *base* value. Because the reference to the *percent of increase* in cell B10 is an absolute reference, each *value after increase* is calculated with the value from cell B10.

The tourism spending projected for 2021—*$13,857,943*—is an increase of 25% over the spending in 2020. The projected spending in 2022—*$17,322,428*—is an increase of 25% over the spending in 2021, and so on.

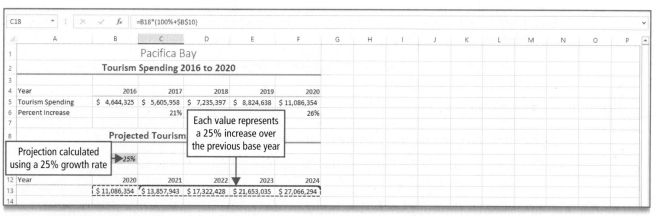

Figure 3.27

MORE KNOWLEDGE **Percent Increase or Decrease**

The basic formula for calculating an increase or decrease can be done in two parts. First determine the percent by which the base value will be increased or decreased, and then add or subtract the results to the base. The formula can be simplified by using (1+amount of increase) or (1–amount of decrease), where 1, rather than 100%, represents the whole. Therefore, the formula used in Step 1 of Activity 3.15 could also be written =b13*(1+b10), or =(b13*b10)+b13.

GO! Learn How
Video E3-6

If a formula depends on the value in a cell, you can see what effect it will have if you change the value in that cell. Then, you can copy the value computed by the formula and paste it into another part of the worksheet where you can compare it to other values.

Activity 3.16 | Answering What-If Questions and Using Paste Special

2.1.1

A growth rate of 25% in tourism spending in each year will result in tourism spending of approximately $27 million by 2018. The city planners will likely ask: *What if* tourism spending grows at the lowest rate of 21%?

Because the formulas are constructed to use the growth rate displayed in cell B10, Mr. Larsen can answer that question quickly by entering a different percentage into that cell. To keep the results of the new calculation so it can be compared, you will paste the results of the what-if question into another area of the worksheet.

1 Click cell **A15**. Type **Estimated Growth in Tourism Spending 2020 to 2024** and then press Enter. Use **Format Painter** to copy the format from cell **A8** to cell **A15**.

2 Select the range **A10:B10**, right-click to display the mini toolbar, click the **Fill Color button arrow**, and then under **Theme Colors**, in the first column, click the third color.

> **MAC TIP** On the Home tab, click the Fill Color button arrow

3 Leave **row 16** blank, and then in the range **A17:A19**, type the following row titles:

Year

25% Growth Rate

21% Growth Rate

4 Select the range **B12:F12**, right-click over the selection, and then on the shortcut menu, click **Copy**.

> **MAC TIP** Press control + C; or, on the Home tab, click Copy.

5 Point to cell **B17**, right-click, and then on the shortcut menu, under **Paste Options**, click **Paste**.

> Recall that when pasting a group of copied cells to a target range, you need only point to or select the first cell of the range.

> **MAC TIP** On the Home tab, click Paste.

6 Select and **Copy** the range **B13:F13**, and then **Paste** it beginning in cell **B18**.

7 Click cell **C18**. On the **Formula Bar**, notice that the *formula* was pasted into the cell, as shown in Figure 3.28.

> This is *not* the desired result. The actual *calculated values*—not the formulas—are needed in the range.

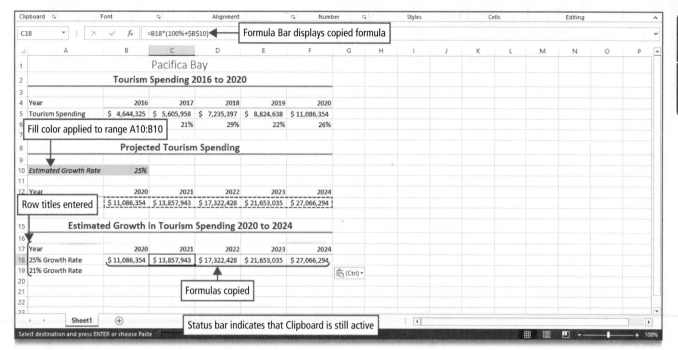

Figure 3.28

8 On the **Quick Access Toolbar**, click **Undo** ↺. With the range **B13:F13** still copied to the Clipboard—as indicated by the message in the status bar and the moving border—point to cell **B18**, and then right-click to display the shortcut menu.

MAC TIP   On the Home tab, click the Paste *arrow*, and then click Values & Number Formatting. Skip to Step 11.

9 Under **Paste Options**, point to **Paste Special** to display another gallery, and then under **Paste Values**, point to **Values & Number Formatting** 📋 to display the ScreenTip as shown in Figure 3.29.

> The ScreenTip *Values & Number Formatting (A)* indicates that you can paste the calculated values that result from the calculation of formulas along with the formatting applied to the copied cells. *(A)* is the keyboard shortcut for this command.

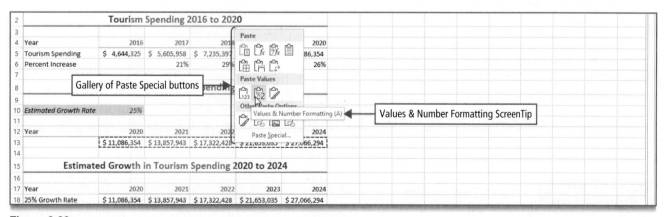

Figure 3.29

10 Click **Values & Number Formatting** 📋.

11 Click cell **C18** and notice on the **Formula Bar** that the cell contains a *value*, not a formula. Press (Esc) to cancel the moving border. Compare your screen with Figure 3.30.

The calculated estimates based on a 25% growth rate are pasted along with their formatting.

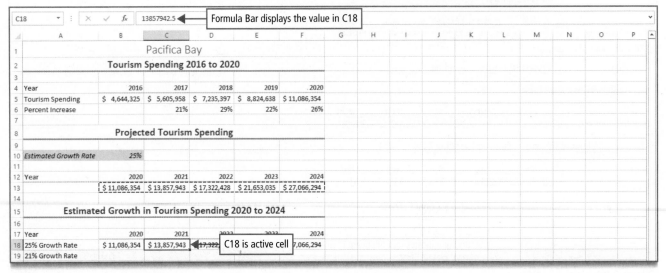

Figure 3.30

12 Click cell **B10**. Type **21** and then watch the values in **C13:F13** *recalculate* as, on the **Formula Bar**, you click **Enter** ☑.

The value *21%* is the lowest percent increase for the past 5-year period.

13 Select and **Copy** the new values in the range **B13:F13**. Point to cell **B19**, right-click, and then on the shortcut menu, point to **Paste Special**. Under **Paste Values**, click **Values & Number Formatting** ☒.

14 Press (Esc) to cancel the moving border, click cell **A1**, click **Save** 🖫, and then compare your screen with Figure 3.31.

With this information, Mr. Larsen can answer what-if questions about the projected increase in tourism spending based on the rates of increase over the past five years.

Figure 3.31

Objective 7 Chart Data with a Line Chart

GO! Learn How
Video E3-7

A *line chart* displays trends over time. Time is displayed along the bottom axis and the data point values connect with a line. The curve and direction of the line make trends obvious to the reader.

The columns in a column chart and the pie slices in a pie chart emphasize the distinct values of each data point. A line chart, on the other hand, emphasizes the flow from one data point value to the next.

Activity 3.17 | Inserting Multiple Rows and Creating a Line Chart

MOS
2.1.3, 5.1.1

So that City Council members can see how tourism spending has increased over a 5-year period, in this Activity, you will chart the actual tourism spending from 2016 to 2020 in a line chart.

1 Click the **Page Layout tab**. In the **Themes group**, click **Colors**, and then change the **Theme Colors** to **Orange**.

2 In the **row header area**, point to **row 8** to display the ➡ pointer, and then drag down to select **rows 8:24**. Right-click over the selection, and then click **Insert** to insert the same number of blank rows as you selected. Compare your screen with Figure 3.32.

Use this technique to insert multiple rows quickly.

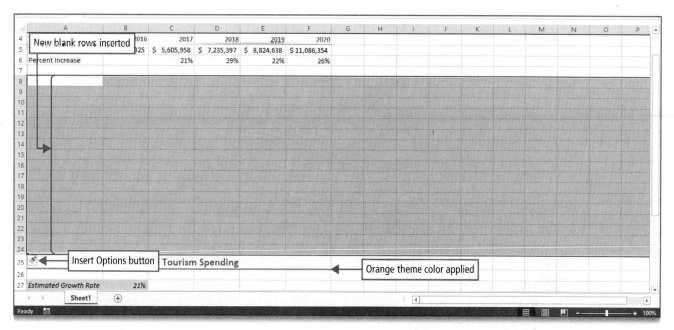

Figure 3.32

3 Near **row 25**, click **Insert Options** 🖼, and then click the **Clear Formatting** option button to clear any formatting from these rows.

You will use this blank area to position your line chart.

💻 **MAC TIP**   On the Home tab, click Clear, and then click Clear Formats.

---

4 Press Ctrl + Home to deselect the rows and move to the top of your worksheet. Select the range **A5:F5**. On the **Insert tab**, in the **Charts group**, click **Insert Line or Area Chart** 📈.

5 In the gallery of line charts, under **2-D Line**, point to the fourth chart type to display the ScreenTip *Line with Markers*. Compare your screen with Figure 3.33.

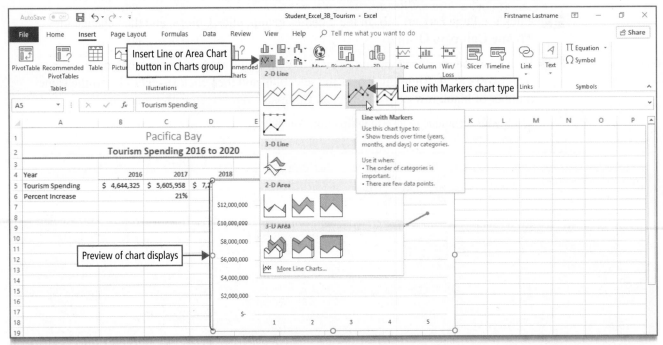

Figure 3.33

6 Click the **Line with Markers** chart type to create the chart in the worksheet.

7 Point to the border of the chart to display the ☐ pointer, and then drag the chart so that its upper left corner is positioned in cell **A8**, aligned approximately under the *t* in the word *Percent* above.

> Excel uses the label in cell A5—*Tourism Spending*—as the suggested chart title.

8 Point to the **Chart Title** *Tourism Spending* and right-click to display the shortcut menu. On the shortcut menu, click **Edit Text** to place the insertion point at the beginning of the title. Type **Pacifica Bay** and press Enter. Press End to move to the end of *Spending*, press Spacebar, and then type **2016 to 2020**

9 ▶ Click the dashed border surrounding the **Chart Title** so that it is a solid line, indicating the entire title is selected. Right-click over the title, and then click **Font**. In the **Font** dialog box, click the **Font style arrow**, and then click **Bold**. Click the **Font color arrow**, and then in the second column, click the first color. Click **OK** and then compare your screen with Figure 3.34.

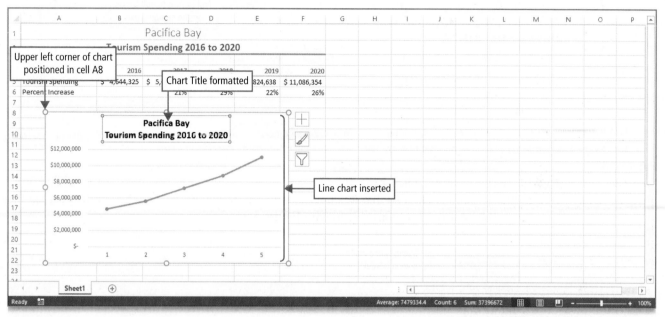

Figure 3.34

Activity 3.18 | Formatting Axes in a Line Chart

MOS
5.2.1

An *axis* is a line that serves as a frame of reference for measurement; it borders the chart *plot area*. The plot area is the area bounded by the axes, including all the data series. In a line chart, the area along the bottom of a chart that identifies the categories of data is referred to as the *category axis* or the *x-axis*. The area along the left side of a chart that shows the range of numbers for the data points is referred to as the *value axis* or the *y-axis*.

In this Activity, you will change the category axis to include the years 2016 to 2020 and adjust the numeric scale of the value axis.

1 ▶ Be sure the chart is still selected. At the bottom of the chart, point to any of the numbers *1* through *5* to display the ScreenTip *Horizontal (Category) Axis*, and then right-click. On the shortcut menu, click **Select Data**.

 MAC TIP   On the Chart Design tab, click Select Data. Click in the Horizontal (Category) axis labels box, and then select the range B4:F4. Click OK. Skip Steps 2, 3, and 4.

ANOTHER WAY   Click the Design tab, and then in the Data group, click Select Data.

On the right side of the **Select Data Source** dialog box, under **Horizontal (Category) Axis Labels**, locate **Edit**, as shown in Figure 3.35.

Here you can change the labels on the category axis to the years that are represented in the chart.

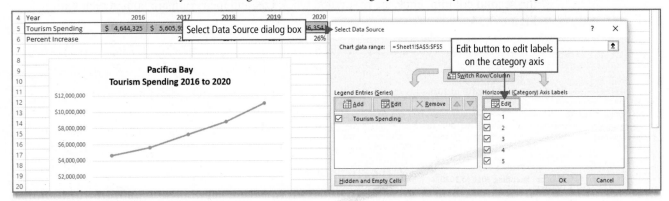

Figure 3.35

In the right column, click **Edit**. If necessary, drag the title bar of the Axis Labels dialog box to the right of the chart so that it is not blocking your view of the data. Select the years in the range **B4:F4**. Compare your screen with Figure 3.36.

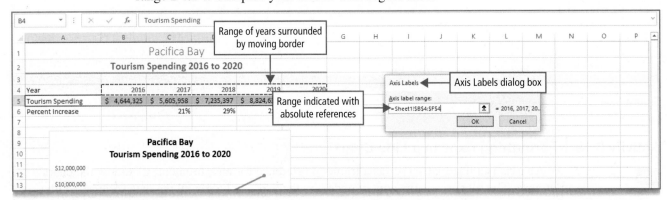

Figure 3.36

In the **Axis Labels** dialog box, click **OK**, and notice that in the right column of the **Select Data Source** dialog box, the years display as the category labels. Click **OK** to close the **Select Data Source** dialog box. Compare your screen with Figure 3.37.

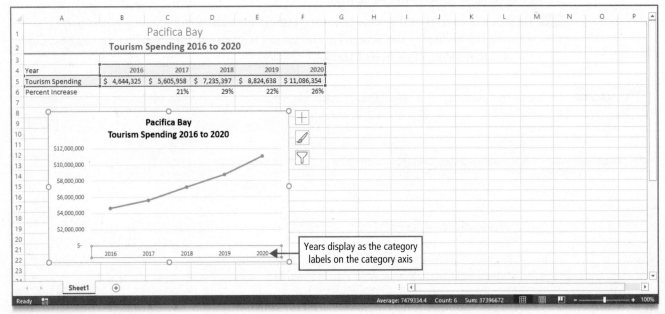

Figure 3.37

5 With the **Horizontal (Category) Axis** selected, click the **Chart Elements** button ⊞, point to **Axes**, click the ▸ **arrow**, and then click **More Options** to display the **Format Axis** pane.

MAC TIP Select the Category Axis. On the Chart Design tab, click Add Chart Element, point to Axes, and then click More Axis Options.

6 Under **Axis Options**, click **Fill & Line** ◇, and then if necessary, click Line to expand the options. Click the **No line** option button and then **Close** ✕ the **Format Axis** pane.

7 On the chart, notice that the orange line—the data series—does not display in the lower portion of the chart. On the left side of the chart, point to any of the dollar values to display the ScreenTip *Vertical (Value) Axis*, and then right-click. On the shortcut menu, click **Format Axis** to display the **Format Axis** pane on the right. Compare your screen with Figure 3.38.

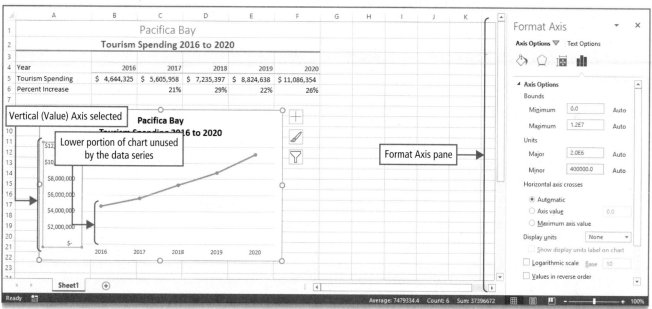

Figure 3.38

ANOTHER WAY On the Format tab, in the Current Selection group, click the Chart Elements arrow, click Vertical (Value) Axis, and then click Format Selection. Or, click the Chart Elements button, point to Axes, click the arrow, click More Options, and then in the Format Axis pane, click the Axis Options arrow. On the displayed list, click Vertical (Value) Axis.

8 In the **Format Axis** pane, under **Bounds**, click in the **Minimum** box, and then select the existing text *0.0*. Type **4000000** and then press Enter.

Because none of the spending figures are under $4,000,000, changing the Minimum number to $4,000,000 will enable the data series to occupy more of the plot area.

9 Under **Units**, in the **Major** box, select the text *1.0E6*, type **2000000** and press Enter. Click **Save** 🖫, and then compare your screen with Figure 3.39.

The *Major unit* value determines the spacing between the gridlines in the plot area. By default, Excel started the values at zero and increased in increments of $2,000,000. By setting the Minimum value on the value axis to $4,000,000, the Major unit is changed to 1.0E6—$1,000,000. Changing the Minimum value to $4,000,000 and setting the Major unit back to $2,000,000 displays a clearer and more pronounced trend in tourism spending.

Numbers that display E + a number are expressed by Excel in the Scientific format, which displays a number in exponential notation.

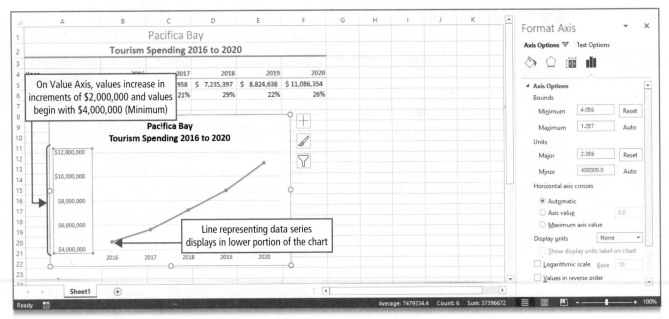

Figure 3.39

Activity 3.19 | Formatting the Chart Area in a Line Chart

An Excel chart has two background elements—the plot area and the chart area—which by default display a single fill color. To add visual appeal to a chart, you can insert a graphic image as the background.

1 Near the top of the **Format Axis** pane, click the **Axis Options arrow**, and then click **Chart Area** to display the **Format Chart Area** pane. Click **Fill & Line** 🖾.

When formatting chart elements, Excel provides multiple ways to display the panes that you need. You can right-click the area you want to format and choose a command on the shortcut menu. You can use an existing pane to move to a different pane, and you can use the Format tab on the ribbon to navigate among various chart elements in the Current Selection group. Use whatever method is easiest for you.

ANOTHER WAY   On the Format tab, in the Current Selection group, click the Chart Elements arrow, click Chart Area, and then click Format Selection. Or, right-click slightly inside the chart to display the shortcut menu, and then click Format Chart Area.

MAC TIP   With the Format Axis pane open, point to a blank area in the upper right corner of the chart until the ScreenTip Chart Area displays, and then click to display the Format Chart Area pane.

2 In the **Format Chart Area** pane, click **Fill** to expand the options, and then click the **Picture or texture fill** option button.

A default texture displays in the chart area.

3 In the **Format Chart Area** pane, under **Insert picture from**, click **File**. In the **Insert Picture** dialog box, navigate to the files you downloaded with this project, and then click **e03B_Surfers**. Click **Insert**, and then compare your screen with Figure 3.40.

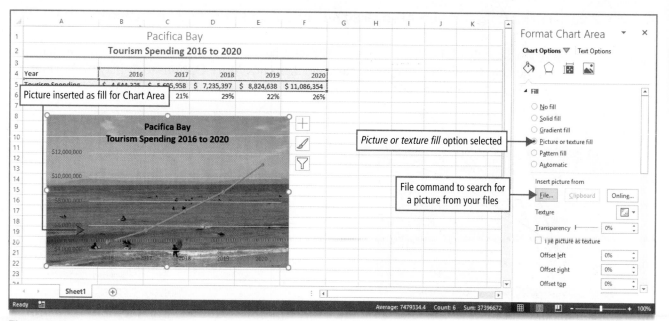

Figure 3.40

4 In the **Format Chart Area** pane, click **Fill** to collapse the options, and then if necessary, click Border to expand the options. Click the **Solid line** option button, click the **Color arrow**, and then under **Theme Colors**, in the fifth column, if necessary, click the first color.

5 Set the **Width** to **4 pt** either by selecting the existing text in the Width box and typing or by clicking the up spin box arrow as necessary.

6 Use the scroll bar on the right side of the Format Chart Area pane if necessary to scroll to the bottom of the pane, and then select the **Rounded corners** check box. On the Quick Access Toolbar, click **Save**, and then compare your screen with Figure 3.41.

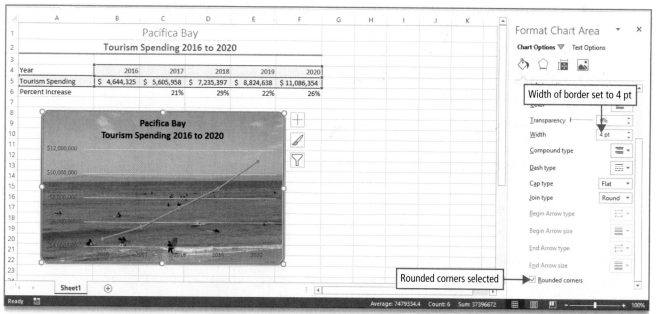

Figure 3.41

Activity 3.20 | Formatting the Plot Area Gridlines and Axis Fonts in a Line Chart

1 To the right of the chart, if necessary, click Chart Elements ⊞ to display the list of elements. Point to **Gridlines**, click the **arrow**, and then click **More Options** to display the **Format Major Gridlines** pane. Compare your screen with Figure 3.42.

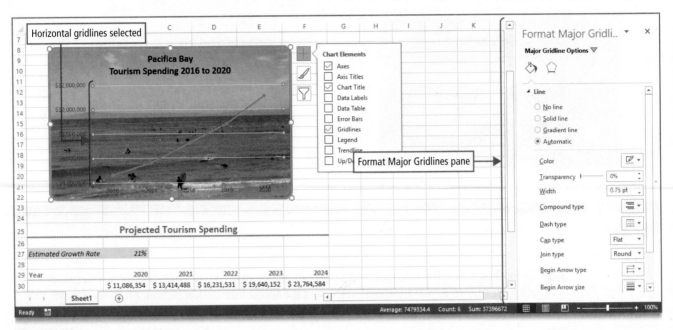

Figure 3.42

🖥 **MAC TIP** On the Chart Design tab, click the Add Chart Element button. Point to Gridlines, and then click More Gridline Options.

---

2 Click the **Solid line** option button. Click the **Color arrow**, and be sure that in the fifth column, the first color is selected.

3 Set the **Width** to **1 pt**.

4 In the chart, point to any of the dollar values on the **Vertical (Value) Axis**, right-click, and then click **Font**.

5 In the **Font** dialog box, change the **Font style** to **Bold**, and then change the **Font color**—in the second column, click the first color. Click **OK**.

6 Use the same technique to format the font of the **Horizontal (Category) Axis** with the same color applied in Step 5. Apply **Bold**.

7 **Close** ☒ the **Format Axis** pane. Click cell **A1** to deselect the chart. Click **Save** 🖫, and then compare your screen with Figure 3.43.

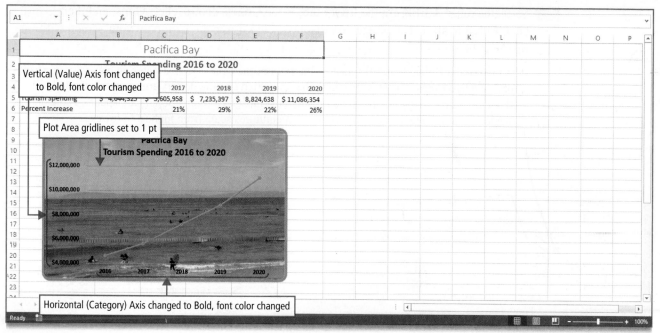

Cell reference: A1 | Pacifica Bay

Pacifica Bay
Tourism Spending 2016 to 2020

Vertical (Value) Axis font changed to Bold, font color changed

	2017	2018	2019	2020
Tourism Spending	$ 4,644,323	$ 5,605,958	$ 7,235,397	$ 8,824,638	$ 11,086,354
Percent Increase		21%	29%	22%	26%

Plot Area gridlines set to 1 pt

Pacifica Bay
Tourism Spending 2016 to 2020

$12,000,000
$10,000,000
$8,000,000
$6,000,000
$4,000,000

2016 2017 2018 2019 2020

Horizontal (Category) Axis changed to Bold, font color changed

Figure 3.43

Objective 8	**Create a Map Chart and a Funnel Chart**

GO! Learn How
Video E3-8

A *map chart* compares values and shows categories across geographical regions; for example, across countries, states, counties, and regions. The charted regions display in map form, and each region displays shading to indicate the values in the data series.

Funnel charts show values across the stages in a process. Typically, the values decrease gradually, allowing the bars to resemble a funnel.

Activity 3.21 | Creating and Sizing a Map Chart

MOS
4.1.2

To encourage visitors to come to the city, the Pacifica Bay Tourism Office conducts advertising campaigns in five states—Oregon, Arizona, Washington, New York, and Illinois. In this Activity, you will create a map chart to depict how the advertising budget is allocated across these five states.

1 Double-click the **Sheet1** tab, type **Expenditures** and then press Enter to rename the sheet. To the right of the **Expenditures** sheet, click **New sheet** ⊕, and then rename the sheet **Advertising**

2 In the **Advertising** sheet, in cell **A1**, type **Tourism Advertising** and then press Enter. In cell **A2**, type **By State** and then press Enter. **Merge & Center** the titles across columns **A:B**. To cell **A1**, apply the **Title** cell style and to cell **A2**, apply the **Heading 1**. Set the width of columns **A:B** to **100 pixels**.

3 In the range **A3:B8**, type the following data:

State	Expenditures
Arizona	48500
Illinois	62350
New York	51300
Oregon	75200
Washington	68500

4 Select the range **B4:B8**, and then apply **Accounting Number Format** with zero decimal places. Select the range **A3:B3**, and then apply the **Heading 2** cell style. **Center** ≡ the range.

5 Select the range **A3:B8**. On the **Insert tab**, in the **Charts group**, click **Maps**, and then click **Filled Map**. If a message box displays, click I Accept. Compare your screen with Figure 3.44.

> A map of the United States displays to the right of the data. The five states display varying shades of orange. Arizona—the state in which the fewest advertising dollars are spent—is the lightest shade of orange. Oregon—the state in which the most advertising dollars are spent—is the darkest shade of orange. The legend displays the Expenditures scale from highest to lowest.

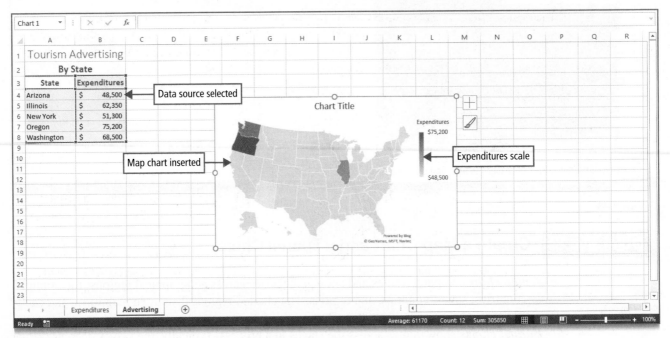

Figure 3.44

6 Click the **Chart Title**, and then select the title text. Type **Tourism Advertising by State** and then click outside of the title so that it is not selected.

7 Point to the map chart to display the [pointer icon] pointer, and then drag the chart so that its upper left corner aligns with the upper left corner of cell **D1**. On the **Format tab**, in the **Height** box [icon], type **2** and then click in the **Width** box [icon]. Type **4** and then press Enter to resize the chart. **Save** [icon], and then compare your screen with Figure 3.45.

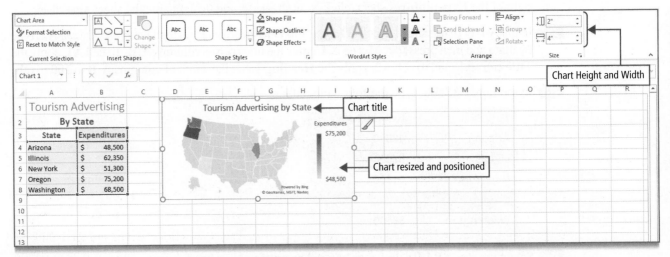

Figure 3.45

Activity 3.22 | Creating and Sizing a Funnel Chart

Expert 4.1.2

As a promotional event, the Pacifica Bay Tourism Office recently invited travel agents, event planners, and wedding planners from the five states in which the city advertises to come to tour the city and see its attractions and venues. The guests were provided with lodging for two days. Invitations were sent to 125 individuals. To track the success of this promotional event, you will create a funnel chart to illustrate the number of invited guests, the number of guests that indicated they would attend, and the number of guests that actually attended.

1 In cell **A12**, type **Travel Agent Event** and then click cell **A1**. On the **Home tab**, in the **Clipboard group**, click **Format Painter** 🖌, and then click cell **A12** to copy the format from cell **A1** to **A12**. Click cell **A13**. Type **Invitation Analysis** and then use **Format Painter** to copy the format from cell **A2** to **A13**.

2 In the range **A15:B17**, type the following data:

Invited	125
Responded Yes	78
Attended	65

3 Select the range **A15:B17**, and then on the **Insert tab**, in the **Charts group**, click **Insert Waterfall, Funnel, Stock, Surface, or Radar Chart** 📊. Click **Funnel** to insert a funnel chart. Compare your screen with Figure 3.46.

The funnel chart displays to the right of the data and slightly overlaps the map chart. Each rectangle in the funnel chart indicates a corresponding value from the data series. The invited guests represent the largest number and the attending guests represent the smallest number.

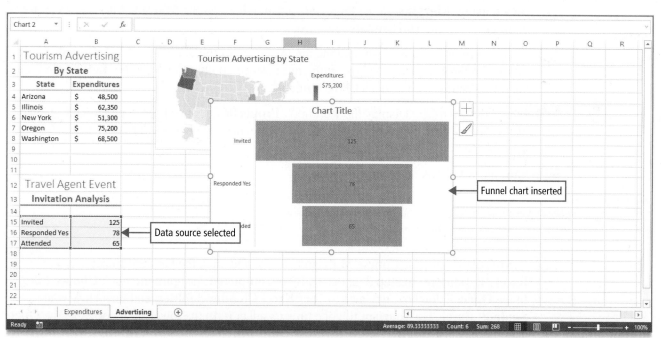

Figure 3.46

4 On the **Format tab**, select the number in the **Height box** 🔳. Type **2.5** and then select the number in the **Width box** 🔲. Type **4** and then press Enter.

5 Click the **Chart Title**, and then select the title text. Type **Promotional Event** and then click outside of the title so that it is not selected.

6 Point to the funnel chart to display the pointer, and then drag the chart so that its upper left corner aligns with the upper left corner of cell **D12**. Compare your screen with Figure 3.47.

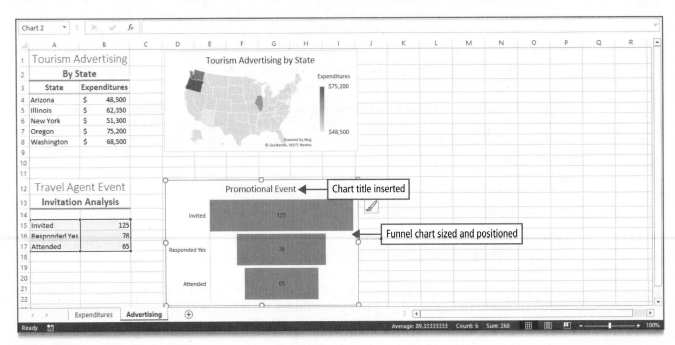

Figure 3.47

7 Group the two worksheets. Click the **Page Layout tab**, and then in the **Scale to Fit group**, click the **Width arrow**. Click **1 page**. In the **Page Setup group**, click **Margins**, and then click **Custom Margins**. In the **Page Setup** dialog box, on the **Margins tab**, under **Center on page**, select the **Horizontally** check box.

8 Click the **Header/Footer tab**, and then in the center of the dialog box, click **Custom Footer**. In the **Footer** dialog box, with your insertion point blinking in the **Left section**, on the row of buttons, click **Insert File Name**.

9 Click **OK** two times. Display the workbook **Properties**. As the **Tags**, type **tourism spending** and as the **Subject**, type your course name and section number. Be sure your name displays as the **Author**.

10 **Save** the workbook and then **Close** Excel.

For Non-MyLab Submissions Determine What Your Instructor Requires
As directed by your instructor, submit your completed Excel file.

---

11 In **MyLab IT**, in your **Course Materials**, locate and click the Grader Project **Excel 3B Tourism**. In **step 3**, under **Upload Completed Assignment**, click **Choose File**. In the **Open** dialog box, navigate to your **Excel Chapter 3 folder**, and then click your **Student_Excel_3B_Tourism** file one time to select it. In the lower right corner of the **Open** dialog box, click **Open**.

The name of your selected file displays above the Upload button.

12 To submit your file to **MyLab IT** for grading, click **Upload**, wait a moment for a green **Success!** message, and then in **step 4**, click the blue **Submit for Grading** button. Click **Close Assignment** to return to your list of **Course Materials**.

You have completed Project 3B **END**

Objective	Analyze Trends with a Line Chart

ALERT   Working with Web-Based Applications and Services

Computer programs and services on the web receive continuous updates and improvements, so the steps to complete this web-based Activity may differ from the ones shown. You can often look at the screens and the information presented to determine how to complete the Activity.

    If you do not already have a Google account, you will need to create one before you begin this Activity. Go to **http://google.com** and, in the upper right corner, click Sign In. On the Sign In screen, click Create Account. On the Create your Google Account page, complete the form, read and agree to the Terms of Service and Privacy Policy, and then click Next step. On the Welcome screen, click Get Started.

Activity | Create a Line Chart

1 1 From the desktop, open your browser, navigate to http://google.com, and then click **Google apps** ⊞. Click **Drive** ⬤, and then if necessary, sign in to your Google account.

2 Open your **GO! Web Projects** folder—or click New to create and then open this folder if necessary. Click **New**, and then click **File upload**. Navigate to your student data files, click **e03_3B_Web**, and then click **Open**.

3 Right-click the file you uploaded, point to **Open with**, and then click **Google Sheets**.

4 Drag to select the years and values in the range **A4:F5**, and then on the menu bar, click the **Insert tab**. Click **Chart** and notice that based on the selected data, a line chart is inserted.

5 Point to the chart, and then drag down and to the left to position the chart so that its upper left corner is aligned with the upper left corner of cell **A21**.

6 Select the existing chart title text. Type **Tourism Spending 2016 to 2020** and then press Enter.

7 In the **Chart editor**, with the **CUSTOMIZE** tab selected, click **Legend**. Click **Auto** and then click **None** to remove the legend. In the **Chart Editor**, click **Vertical Axis**. Click in the **Min** box, type **2500000** and then press Enter so that the lowest value on the Vertical Axis is $2,500,000.

8 In the **Chart Editor**, click **Series**. Click the **Line thickness**, and then click **4px**. Click **Point size**, and then click **10px**. **Close** the **Chart editor**, and then compare your screen with Figure A.

9 Submit your file as directed by your instructor. Sign out of your Google account and close your browser.

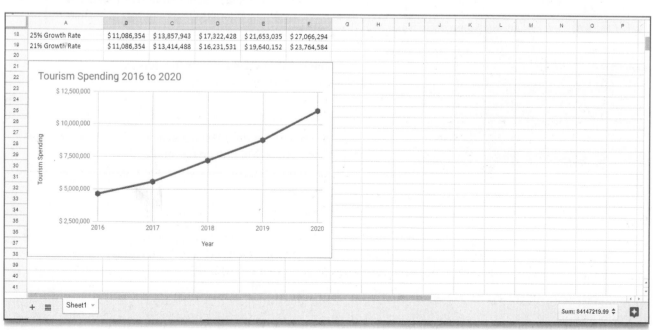

Figure A

»»» GO! To Work

wavebreakmedia/Shutterstock, Monkey Business Images/Fotolia, Ivanko80/Shutterstock, Monkey Business Images/Shutterstock

Microsoft Office Specialist (MOS) Skills in this Chapter	
Project 3A	**Project 3B**
5.1.1 Create charts	**2.1.1** Paste data by using special paste options
5.1.2 Create chart sheets	**2.1.3** Insert and delete multiple columns or rows
5.2.3 Add and modify chart elements	**2.2.3** Format cells by using Format Painter
	5.2.1 Add data series to charts
	Expert 3.4.2 Perform what-if analysis by using Goal Seek and Scenario Manager
	Expert 4.1.2 Create and modify charts including Box & Whisker, Combo, Funnel, Histogram, Map, Sunburst, and Waterfall charts

Build Your E-Portfolio

An E-Portfolio is a collection of evidence, stored electronically, that showcases what you have accomplished while completing your education. Collecting and then sharing your work products with potential employers reflects your academic and career goals. Your completed documents from the following projects are good examples to show what you have learned: 3G, 3K, and 3L.

▶ GO! for Job Success

Video: Workplace Etiquette

Your instructor may assign this video to your class, and then ask you to think about, or discuss with your classmates, these questions:

g-stockstudio/Shutterstock

> Name three specific ways that Rachel demonstrated a lack of professionalism in this video. Be as specific as possible.

> As a manager, what would you do to address Rachel's unprofessional behavior?

> In what ways does Rachel exhibit a lack of respect for the lines of authority in her office?

End of Chapter

Summary

Use pie charts when you want to show the relationship of each part to a whole. Consider using a pie chart when you have only one data series to plot and you do not have more than seven categories.

To create a pie chart, you must select two ranges. One range contains the labels for each pie slice; the other contains the values that add up to a total. Both ranges must have the same number of cells.

In formulas, Excel follows rules called the order of operations; expressions within parentheses are processed first, and multiplication and division are performed before addition and subtraction.

Use a line chart when you want to show trends over time. Time displays along the bottom axis and the data point values connect with a line. The curve and direction of the line make trends obvious.

GO! Learn It Online

Review the concepts, key terms, and MOS skills in this chapter by completing these online challenges, which you can find at **MyLab IT**.

Chapter Quiz: Answer matching and multiple choice questions to test what you learned in this chapter.

Lessons on the GO!: Learn how to use all the new apps and features as they are introduced by Microsoft

MOS Prep Quiz: Answer questions to review the MOS skills that you practiced in this chapter.

GO! Collaborative Team Project (Available in Instructor Resource Center)

If your instructor assigns this project to your class, you can expect to work with one or more of your classmates—either in person or by using internet tools—to create work products similar to those that you created in this chapter. A team is a group of workers who work together to solve a problem, make a decision, or create a work product. Collaboration is when you work together with others as a team in an intellectual endeavor to complete a shared task or achieve a shared goal.

Monkey Business Images/Fotolia

Project Guide for Excel Chapter 3

Your instructor will assign Projects from this list to ensure your learning and assess your knowledge.

Project	Apply Skills from These Chapter Objectives	Project Type		Project Location
3A **MyLab IT**	Objectives 1–4 from Project 3A	**3A Instructional Project (Grader Project)** Guided instruction to learn the skills in Project 3A.	**Instruction**	In **MyLab IT** and in text
3B **MyLab IT**	Objectives 5–8 from Project 3B	**3B Instructional Project (Grader Project)** Guided instruction to learn the skills in Project 3B.	**Instruction**	In **MyLab IT** and in text
3C	Objectives 1–4 from Project 3A	**3C Skills Review (Scorecard Grading)** A guided review of the skills from Project 3A.	**Review**	In text
3D	Objectives 5–8 from Project 3B	**3D Skills Review (Scorecard Grading)** A guided review of the skills from Project 3B.	**Review**	In text
3E **MyLab IT**	Objectives 1–4 from Project 3A	**3E Mastery (Grader Project)** **Mastery and Transfer of Learning** A demonstration of your mastery of the skills in Project 3A with extensive decision making		In **MyLab IT** and in text
3F **MyLab IT**	Objectives 5–8 from Project 3B	**3F Mastery (Grader Project)** **Mastery and Transfer of Learning** A demonstration of your mastery of the skills in Project 3B with extensive decision making.		In **MyLab IT** and in text
3G **MyLab IT**	Objectives 1–8 from Project 3A and 3B	**3G Mastery (Grader Project)** **Mastery and Transfer of Learning** A demonstration of your mastery of the skills in Projects 3A and 3B with extensive decision making.		In **MyLab IT** and in text
3H	Combination of Objectives from Projects 3A and 3B	**3H GO! Fix It (Scorecard Grading)** **Critical Thinking** A demonstration of your mastery of the skills in Projects 3A and 3B by creating a correct result from a document that contains errors you must find.		IRC
3I	Combination of Objectives from Projects 3A and 3B	**3I GO! Make It (Scorecard Grading)** **Critical Thinking** A demonstration of your mastery of the skills in Projects 3A and 3B by creating a result from a supplied picture.		IRC
3J	Combination of Objectives from Projects 3A and 3B	**3J GO! Solve It (Rubric Grading)** **Critical Thinking** A demonstration of your mastery of the skills in Projects 3A and 3B, your decision-making skills, and your critical thinking skills. A task-specific rubric helps you self-assess your result.		IRC
3K	Combination of Objectives from Projects 3A and 3B	**3K GO! Solve It (Rubric Grading)** **Critical Thinking** A demonstration of your mastery of the skills in Projects 3A and 3B, your decision-making skills, and your critical thinking skills. A task-specific rubric helps you self-assess your result.		In text
3L	Combination of Objectives from Projects 3A and 3B	**3L GO! Think (Rubric Grading)** **Critical Thinking** A demonstration of your understanding of the chapter concepts applied in a manner that you would outside of college. An analytic rubric helps you and your instructor grade the quality of your work by comparing it to the work an expert in the discipline would create.		In text
3M	Combination of Objectives from Projects 3A and 3B	**3M GO! Think (Rubric Grading)** **Critical Thinking** A demonstration of your understanding of the chapter concepts applied in a manner that you would outside of college. An analytic rubric helps you and your instructor grade the quality of your work by comparing it to the work an expert in the discipline would create.		IRC
3N	Combination of Objectives from Projects 3A and 3B	**3N You and GO! (Rubric Grading)** **Critical Thinking** A demonstration of your understanding of the chapter concepts applied in a manner that you would in a personal situation. An analytic rubric helps you and your instructor grade the quality of your work.		IRC
3O	Combination of Objectives from Projects 3A and 3B	**3O Collaborative Team Project for EXCEL Chapter 2** **Critical Thinking** A demonstration of your understanding of concepts and your ability to work collaboratively in a group role-playing assessment, requiring both collaboration and self-management.		IRC
Capstone Project for EXCEL Chapters 1-3	Combination of Objectives from Chapters 1-3	A demonstration of your mastery of the skills in Chapters 1-3 with extensive decision making. **(Grader Project)**		In **MyLab IT** and IRC

Glossary

Glossary of Chapter Key Terms

3-D The shortened term for *three-dimensional*, which refers to an image that appears to have all three spatial dimensions—length, width, and depth.

Absolute cell reference A cell reference that refers to cells by their fixed position in a worksheet; an absolute cell reference remains the same when the formula is copied.

Axis A line that serves as a frame of reference for measurement and which borders the chart plot area.

Base The starting point when you divide the amount of increase by it to calculate the rate of increase.

Bevel A shape effect that uses shading and shadows to make the edges of a shape appear to be curved or angled.

Category axis The area along the bottom of a chart that identifies the categories of data; also referred to as the x-axis.

Chart area The entire chart and all of its elements.

Chart sheet A workbook sheet that contains only a chart.

Data marker A column, bar, area, dot, pie slice, or other symbol in a chart that represents a single data point; related data points form a data series.

Data point A value that originates in a worksheet cell and that is represented in a chart by a data marker.

Data series Related data points represented by data markers; each data series has a unique color or pattern represented in the chart legend.

Enterprise fund A municipal government fund that reports income and expenditures related to municipal services for which a fee is charged in exchange for goods or services.

Explode The action of pulling out one or more pie slices from a pie chart for emphasis.

Formula AutoComplete An Excel feature which, after typing an = (equal sign) and the beginning letter or letters of a function name, displays a list of function names that match the typed letter(s).

Fund A sum of money set aside for a specific purpose.

Funnel chart A type of chart that shows values across the stages in a process.

General fund The term used to describe money set aside for the normal operating activities of a government entity such as a city.

Goal Seek A what-if analysis tool that finds the input needed in one cell to arrive at the desired result in another cell.

Legend A chart element that identifies the patterns or colors that are assigned to the categories in the chart.

Line chart A chart type that displays trends over time; time displays along the bottom axis and the data point values are connected with a line.

Major unit The value in a chart's value axis that determines the spacing between tick marks and between the gridlines in the plot area.

Map chart A type of chart that compares values and shows categories across geographical regions; for example, across countries, states, counties, and regions.

Order of operations The mathematical rules for performing multiple calculations within a formula.

Percent for new value = base percent + percent of increase The formula for calculating a percentage by which a value increases by adding the base percentage—usually 100%—to the percent increase.

Percentage rate of increase The percent by which one number increases over another number.

Pie chart A chart that shows the relationship of each part to a whole.

Plot area The area bounded by the axes of a chart, including all the data series.

Rate = amount of increase/base The mathematical formula to calculate a rate of increase.

Relative cell reference In a formula, the address of a cell based on the relative positions of the cell that contains the formula and the cell referred to in the formula.

Value after increase = base x percent for new value The formula for calculating the value after an increase by multiplying the original value—the base—by the percent for new value (see the *Percent for new value* formula).

Value axis A numerical scale on the left side of a chart that shows the range of numbers for the data points; also referred to as the y-axis.

What-if analysis The process of changing the values in cells to see how those changes affect the outcome of formulas in a worksheet.

x-axis Another name for the category axis.

y-axis Another name for the value axis.

Chapter Review

Apply 3A skills from these Objectives:

1. Chart Data with a Pie Chart
2. Format a Pie Chart
3. Edit a Workbook and Update a Chart
4. Use Goal Seek to Perform What-If Analysis

In the following Skills Review, you will edit a worksheet for Jerry Silva, City Parks Manager, which details the revenue generated from city parks and structures. Your completed worksheets will look similar to Figure 3.48.

Project Files

For Project 3C, you will need the following file:

e03C_Parks

You will save your workbook as:

Lastname_Firstname_3C_Parks

Project Results

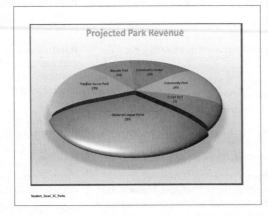

Figure 3.48

(continues on next page)

Chapter Review

1 Start Excel. From your student data files, open the file **e03C_Parks**. Save the file in your **Excel Chapter 3** folder as **Lastname_Firstname_3C_Parks**

a. Click cell **D5**, and then type = to begin a formula. Click cell **C5**, type / and then click cell **C11**. Press F4 to make the reference to the value in cell **C11** absolute. On the **Formula Bar**, click **Enter**, and then fill the formula down through cell **D10**. (Mac users, press command ⌘ + T to make the cell reference absolute.)

b. With the range **D5:D10** selected, on the **Home tab**, click **Percent Style** and **Center**.

2 Select the nonadjacent ranges **A5:A10** and **C5:C10** to select the park names and the projected revenue. Click the **Insert tab**, and then in the **Charts group**, click **Insert Pie or Doughnut Chart**. Under **3-D Pie**, click the chart type **3-D Pie**.

a. On the **Design tab**, in the **Location group**, click **Move Chart**. In the **Move Chart** dialog box, click the **New sheet** option button. In the **New sheet** box, replace the highlighted text *Chart1* by typing **Projected Park Revenue Chart** and then click **OK**.

b. Click the text *Chart Title*. Type **Projected Park Revenue** and then press Enter to create the new chart title. (Mac users, drag to select the title text, type the new text and then click outside of the title.)

c. If necessary, select the title. On the **Format tab**, in the **WordArt Styles group**, click **More** to display the gallery. In the second row, select the fifth style, and then change the **Font Size** to **32**.

d. Click in a white area of the chart to deselect the chart title. Click **Chart Elements**, and then click the **Legend** check box to remove the legend. (Mac users, on the Chart Design tab, click Add Chart Element, point to Legend, and then click None.)

e. In the list of **Chart Elements**, point to **Data Labels**, click the **arrow** that displays, and then click **More Options**. In the **Format Data Labels** pane on the right, under **Label Options**, select the **Category Name** and **Percentage** check boxes, and *clear* all other checkboxes. Under **Label Position**, click **Center**. (Mac users, to display the Format Data Labels Pane, on the Chart Design tab, click Add Chart Element, point to Data Labels, and then click More Options.)

f. With the data labels selected, on the **Home tab**, change the **Font Size** to **11** and then apply **Bold** and **Italic**.

3 In any pie slice, point anywhere outside the selected label, and then double-click to display the **Format Data Series** pane. Under **Series Options**, click **Effects**, and then click **3-D Format**.

a. Click the **Top bevel arrow**, and then under **Bevel**, click the first button. Apply the same bevel to the **Bottom bevel**.

b. Set the **Width** and **Height** of both the **Top bevel** and the **Bottom bevel** to **512 pt**

c. Scroll down, click the **Material arrow**, and then under **Standard**, click the third material—**Plastic**.

d. Scroll to the top of the **Format Data Series** pane, click **Shadow**, and then click the **Presets arrow**. Scroll down, and then under **Perspective**, in the first row, click the third effect—**Perspective: Below**.

e. In the **Format Data Series** pane, under **Series Options**, click the third button—**Series Options**. Set the **Angle of first slice** to **50**

f. On the pie chart, click the **Diamond League Fields** slice to select only that slice, and then in the **Format Data Point** pane, set the **Point Explosion** to **10%**

g. With the **Diamond League Fields** slice still selected, in the **Format Data Point** pane, under **Series Options**, click **Fill & Line**, and then click **Fill** to expand the options.

h. Click the **Gradient fill** option button, click the **Preset gradients arrow**, and then in the fourth row, click the third gradient.

4 Point to the white area just inside the border of the chart to display the ScreenTip *Chart Area*, and then click one time to display the **Format Chart Area** pane.

a. Under **Chart Options**, click **Fill & Line**, and be sure the **Fill** options are still displayed.

b. Click the **Gradient fill** option button, click the **Preset gradients arrow**, and then in the first row, click the fifth gradient.

c. In the **Format Chart Area** pane, click **Fill** to collapse the options, and then click **Border** to expand the options.

d. Click the **Solid line** option button, click the **Color arrow**, and then in the fifth column, click the last color. Set the **Width** of the border to **5 pt** Close the pane, and then **Save** your workbook.

(continues on next page)

Chapter Review

5 In the sheet tab area at the bottom of the workbook, click the **Sheet1 tab**.

a. Click cell **C11**. On the **Data tab**, in the **Forecast group**, click **What-If Analysis**, and then click **Goal Seek**. In the **Goal Seek** dialog box, verify that the Set cell box displays **C11**. press ⌷Tab⌷ to move to the **To value** box, and then type **17,800,000**

b. Press ⌷Tab⌷ to move the insertion point to the **By changing cell** box, and then click cell **C10**. Click **OK**. In the displayed **Goal Seek Status** dialog box, click **OK** to set the total projected revenue to $17,800,000 by changing the projected revenue for the Community Center.

6 With your worksheet displayed, in the sheet tab area, double-click *Sheet1* to select the text, and then type **Projected Park Revenue Data** and press ⌷Enter⌷.

a. Click the **Page Layout tab**. In the **Page Setup Group**, click **Margins**, click **Custom Margins**, and then in the **Page Setup** dialog box, on the **Margins tab**, under **Center on page**, select the **Horizontally** check box.

b. Click the **Header/Footer tab**, click **Custom Footer**, and then with your insertion point in the **Left section**, on the row of buttons, click **Insert File Name**. Click **OK** two times.

c. Display the **Projected Park Revenue Chart**, and then display the **Page Setup** dialog box.

d. Click the **Header/Footer tab**, click **Custom Footer**, and then in the **Left section**, click the **Insert File Name** button. Click **OK** two times.

e. Click the **File tab**, and then display the workbook **Properties**. As the **Tags**, type **park revenue** As the **Subject**, type your course name and section number. Be sure your name displays as the **Author**.

f. **Save** and **Close** your workbook. Print or submit your workbook electronically as directed by your instructor.

You have completed Project 3C ▮END▮

Chapter Review

Skills Review	Project 3D Housing Permits

In the following Skills Review, you will edit a worksheet that forecasts the revenue from new housing permits that the City of Pacifica Bay expects to collect in the five-year period 2020-2024. Your completed worksheet will look similar to Figure 3.49.

Project Files

For Project 3D, you will need the following file:

e03D_Housing_Permits

e03D_Housing

You will save your workbook as:

Lastname_Firstname_3D_Housing_Permits

Project Results

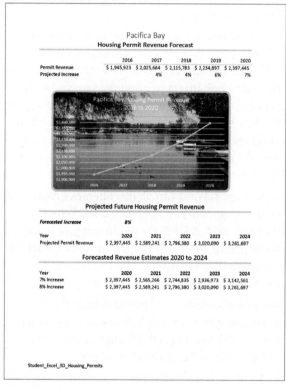

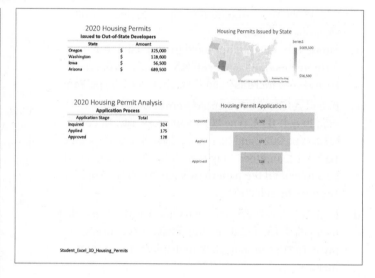

Figure 3.49

(continues on next page)

Chapter Review

1 ▶ Start Excel. From your student data files, open **e03D_Housing_Permits**. Using your own name, save the file in your **Excel Chapter 3** folder as **Lastname_Firstname_3D_Housing_Permits**

a. In cell **B4**, type **2016** and then press Tab. In cell **C4**, type **2017** and then press Enter.

b. Use the fill handle to fill the remaining years through **column F** so that the last year that displays is 2020.

2 ▶ Click cell **C6**. Being sure to include the parentheses, type **=(c5-b5)/b5** and then press Enter. Select cell **C6**, and then apply **Percent Style**.

a. With cell **C6** selected, drag the fill handle to the right through cell **F6**.

b. In cell **A8**, type **Projected Future Housing Permit Revenue** and then press Enter. Click cell **A2**. On the **Home tab**, in the **Clipboard group**, click **Format Painter**, and then click cell **A8**. In cell **A10**, type **Forecasted Increase** and then click **A12**. Type **Year**

c. In cell **A13**, type **Projected Permit Revenue** and then in cell **B12**, type **2020** and press Tab. In cell **C12**, type **2021** and then press Tab. Select the range **B12:C12**, and then drag the fill handle through cell **F12** to extend the pattern of years to *2024*. Apply **Bold** to the selection.

d. Right-click cell **F5**, and then click **Copy**. Right-click over cell **B13**, and then click **Paste**. (Mac users, press control and then click to display the shortcut menu.)

e. In cell **B10**, type **7%** which is the percent of increase from 2019 to 2020. Select the range **A10:B10**, and then apply **Bold** and **Italic**.

3 ▶ Click cell **C13**. Type **=b13*(100%+b10)** and then on the **Formula Bar**, click **Enter** to keep the cell active. With cell **C13** as the active cell, drag the fill handle to copy the formula to the range **D13:F13**.

a. Click cell **B13**. On the **Home tab**, click **Format Painter**, and then select the range **C13:F13**.

b. Click cell **A15**. Type **Forecasted Revenue Estimates 2020 to 2024** and then press Enter. Use **Format Painter** to copy the format from cell **A8** to cell **A15**.

c. In the range **A17:A19**, type the following row titles:

Year
7% Increase
8% Increase

4 ▶ Select the range **B12:F12**, and then on the **Home tab**, in the **Clipboard group**, click **Copy**. **Paste** the selection to the range **B17:F17**.

a. Select the range **B13:F13**, right-click over the selection, and then on the shortcut menu, click **Copy**. Point to cell **B18**, right-click, and then from the shortcut menu, point to **Paste Special**. Under **Paste Values**, click the second button—**Values & Number Formatting**. Press Esc to cancel the moving border. (Mac users, on the Home tab, click the Paste *arrow*, and then click Values & Number Formatting.)

b. Click cell **B10**. Type **8** and then press Enter. Copy the new values in the range **B13:F13**. Point to cell **B19**, right-click, and then point to **Paste Special**. Under **Paste Values**, click **Values & Number Formatting**. **Save** your workbook.

5 ▶ In the **row header area**, point to **row 8** to display the pointer, and then drag down to select **rows 8:24**. Right-click over the selection to display the shortcut menu, and then click **Insert** to insert the same number of blank rows as you selected. Under the selection area near cell **A25**, click **Insert Options**, and then click the **Clear Formatting** option button to clear any formatting from these rows. (Mac users, on the Home tab, click Clear, and then click Clear Formats.)

a. On the **Page Layout tab**, in the **Themes group**, click the **Colors arrow**, and then click **Yellow**. Select the range **A5:F5**. On the **Insert tab**, in the **Charts group**, click **Insert Line or Area Chart**. In the displayed gallery of line charts, click the **Line with Markers** chart type to create the chart.

b. Point to the border of the chart to display the ⛶ pointer, and then drag the chart so that its upper left corner is positioned in cell **A9**, aligned approximately under the *c* in the word *Projected* above.

c. Point to the **Chart Title** *Permit Revenue* and right-click. On the shortcut menu, click **Edit Text**. With the insertion point positioned at the beginning of the title, type **Pacifica Bay Housing** and then press Spacebar. Click at the end of the title after the word *Revenue*, and then press Enter to create a second line. Type **2016 to 2020**

d. Click the dashed border around the chart title to change it to a solid border, right-click over the title, and then on the shortcut menu, click **Font**. In the **Font** dialog box, change the **Font style** to **Bold**, and change the **Size** to **16**. Click **OK**.

(continues on next page)

Chapter Review

Skills Review: Project 3D Housing Permits (continued)

6 At the bottom of the chart, point to any of the numbers *1* through *5*, and then right-click. On the shortcut menu, click **Select Data**. On the right side of the **Select Data Source** dialog box, click **Edit**. In the worksheet, select the years in the range **B4:F4**, and then click **OK** two times to enter the years as the category labels. (Mac users, in the Select Data Source dialog box, click in the Horizontal (Category) axis labels box, and then select the range B4:F4.)

a. With the **Horizontal (Category) Axis** still selected, click **Chart Elements**, point to **Axes**, click the **arrow**, and then click **More Options**. In the **Format Axis** pane, under **Axis Options**, click **Fill & Line**. If necessary, click Line to expand the options. Click the **No line** option button, and then **close** the **Format Axis** pane. (Mac users, on the Chart Design tab, click Add Chart Element, point to Axes, and then click More Axis Options.)

b. On the left side of the chart, point to any of the dollar values, right-click, and then click **Format Axis**. In the **Format Axis** pane, under **Bounds**, select the text in the **Minimum** box, and then type **1900000**

c. Under **Units**, in the **Major** box, select the existing text. Type **50000** and then press Enter.

d. Near the top of the **Format Axis** pane, click the **Axis Options arrow**, and then click **Chart Area** to display the **Format Chart Area** pane. Click **Fill & Line**. (Mac users, point to the upper right corner of the chart to display the Chart Area ScreenTip, and then click to display the Format Chart Area pane.)

e. In the **Format Chart Area** pane, click **Fill** to expand the options, and then click the **Picture or texture fill** option button. Under **Insert picture from**, click **File**. In the **Insert Picture** dialog box, navigate to the student data files, and then click **e03D_Housing**. Click **Insert**.

f. In the **Format Chart Area** pane, click **Fill** to collapse the options, and then if necessary, click Border to expand the Border section. Click the **Solid line** option button. Set the **Width** to **4 pt** Scroll to the bottom of the pane, and then select the **Rounded corners** check box.

g. Select the chart title text, and then on the **Home tab**, click the **Font Color arrow**. In the first column, click the first color.

7 To the right of the chart, click **Chart Elements**, point to **Gridlines**, click the **arrow**, and then click **More Options** to display the **Format Major Gridlines** pane. (Mac users, on the Chart Design tab, click Add Chart Element, point to Gridlines, and then click More Gridline Options.)

a. Under **Line**, click the **Solid line** option button. Set the **Width** to **1 pt**

b. In the chart, point to any of the dollar values on the **Vertical (Value) Axis**, right-click, and then click **Font**. In the **Font** dialog box, change the **Font style** to **Bold**, and the **Font Color** to the first color in the first row.

c. By using the same technique, apply **Bold** to the **Horizontal (Category) Axis** and change the font color to the first color in the first row. **Close** the **Format Axis** pane, and then click cell **A1** to deselect the chart.

d. Click the **Page Layout tab**. In the **Page Setup group**, click **Margins**, and then click **Custom Margins**. On the **Margins tab**, select the **Horizontally** check box. Click the **Header/Footer tab**, click **Custom Footer**, and then in the **Left section**, insert the file name. Click **OK** two times.

8 Click the **Permit Analysis** sheet tab. To create a map chart that shows the revenue from permits issued to out of state developers, select the range **A3:B7**. On the **Insert tab**, in the **Charts group**, click **Maps**, and then click **Filled Map**.

a. Select the chart title and type **Housing Permits Issued by State**

b. Click the **Chart Tools Format tab**, and then in the **Size group**, click in the **Height box**. Type **2** and then click in the **Width box**. Type **4** and then press Enter.

c. Drag the chart so that its upper left corner aligns with the upper left corner of cell **D1**.

9 Select the range **A15:B17**. On the **Insert tab**, in the **Charts group**, click **Insert Waterfall, Funnel, Stock, Surface, or Radar Chart**, and then click **Funnel**. Select the chart title and type **Housing Permit Applications**

a. Click the **Chart Tools Format tab**, and then in the **Size group**, click in the **Height box**. Type **2.5** and then click in the **Width box**. Type **4** and then press Enter.

(continues on next page)

Chapter Review

b. Drag the chart so that its upper left corner aligns with the upper left corner of cell **D12**. Click cell **A1**.

c. On the **Page Layout tab**, in the **Page Setup group**, click **Orientation**, and then click **Landscape**.

d. In the **Page Setup group**, click **Margins**, and then click **Custom Margins**. On the **Margins tab**, select the **Horizontally** check box. Click the **Header/Footer tab**, click **Custom Footer**, and then in the **Left section**, insert the file name. Click **OK** two times.

e. Display the **Properties**. As the **Tags**, type **housing permit revenue** In the **Subject** box, type your course name and section number. Be sure your name displays as the **Author**.

f. **Save** and **Close** your workbook. Print or submit your workbook electronically as directed by your instructor.

You have completed Project 3D | END

MyLab IT Grader

Mastering Excel | **Project 3E Revenue**

Apply 3A skills from these Objectives:

1. Chart Data with a Pie Chart
2. Format a Pie Chart
3. Edit a Workbook and Update a Chart
4. Use Goal Seek to Perform What-If Analysis

In the following project, you will edit a worksheet that summarizes the revenue budget for the City of Pacifica Bay. Your completed worksheets will look similar to Figure 3.50.

Project Files for **MyLab IT Grader**

1. In your **MyLab IT** course, locate and click **Excel 3E Revenue,** Download Materials, and then Download All Files.
2. Extract the zipped folder to your Excel Chapter 3 folder. Close the Grader download screens.
3. Take a moment to open the downloaded **Excel_3E_Revenue_Instructions**; note any recent updates to the book.

Project Results

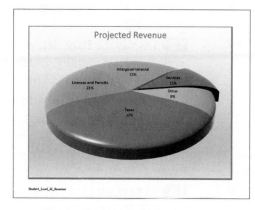
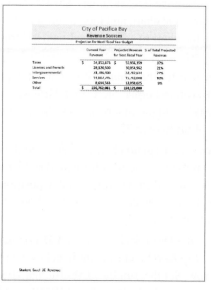

Figure 3.50

For Non-MyLab Submissions

For Project 3E, you will need:

e03E_Revenue

In your Excel Chapter 3 folder, save your workbook as:

Lastname_Firstname_3E_Revenue

If your instructor requires a workbook with formulas, save as:

Lastname_Firstname_3E_Revenue_formulas

After you have named and saved your workbook on the next page, begin with Step 2.

After Step 13, save and submit your file as directed by your instructor.

(continues on next page)

1 Navigate to your **Excel Chapter 3 folder**, and then double-click the Excel file you downloaded from **MyLab IT** that displays your name—**Student_Excel_3E_Revenue**.

2 In cell **D5**, construct a formula to calculate the **% of Total Projected Revenue** from **Taxes** by dividing the **Projected Revenue for Next Fiscal Year** for **Taxes** by the **Total Projected Revenue for Next Fiscal Year**. Use absolute cell references as necessary, format the result in **Percent Style**, and **Center** the percentage. Fill the formula down through cell **D9**.

3 Select the nonadjacent ranges **A5:A9** and **C5:C9** as the data for a pie chart, and then insert a **3-D Pie** chart. Move the chart to a **New sheet** named **Projected Revenue Chart**

4 As the text for the **Chart Title** element, type **Projected Revenue** Format the **Chart Title** with a **WordArt Style**—in the first row, click the second style. Change the **Font Size** to **32**.

5 Remove the **Legend** chart element, and then add the **Data Labels** chart element formatted so that only the **Category Name** and **Percentage** display positioned in the **Center**. Format the data labels with a **Font style** of **Bold** and a **Font Size** of **14**.

6 Format the **Data Series** using a **3-D Format** effect. Change the **Top bevel** and **Bottom bevel** to the first bevel in the first row. Set the **Top bevel Width** and **Height** to **350 pt** and then set the **Bottom bevel Width** and **Height** to **0 pt** Change the **Material** to the second **Special Effect**—**Soft Edge**.

7 Display the **Series Options**, and then set the **Angle of first slice** to **115** so that the **Taxes** slice is in the front of the pie.

8 Select the **Services** slice, and then explode the slice **10%**. Change the **Fill Color** of the **Services** slice to a **Solid fill**—in the eighth column, click the first color.

9 Format the **Chart Area** by applying a **Gradient fill** using the **Preset gradients**—in the first column, click the first gradient style. Format the **Border** of the **Chart Area** by applying a **Solid line** border—in the fifth column, click the first color. Change the **Width** to **5 pt**. Close any panes that are open on the right.

10 Display the **Page Setup** dialog box, and then for this chart sheet, insert a **Custom Footer** in the **left section** with the file name.

11 Display the **Revenue Sources** sheet. Click cell **C10**, and then use **Goal Seek** to determine the projected amount of *Other* revenue in cell **C9** if the value in **C10** is **150,125,000**

12 Display the **Page Setup** dialog box, center the worksheet **Horizontally**, and then insert a custom footer in the **left section** with the file name.

13 Display the workbook **Properties**, and then as the **Tags**, type **revenue sources** As the **Subject**, type your course name and section number. Be sure your name displays as the **Author**. **Save** your workbook and **Close** Excel.

14 In **MyLab IT**, locate and click the Grader Project **Excel 3E Revenue**. In **step 3**, under **Upload Completed Assignment**, click **Choose File**. In the **Open** dialog box, navigate to your **Excel Chapter 3 folder**, and then click your **Student_Excel_3E_Revenue** file one time to select it. In the lower right corner of the **Open** dialog box, click **Open**.

The name of your selected file displays above the Upload button.

15 To submit your file to **MyLab IT** for grading, click **Upload**, wait a moment for a green **Success!** message, and then in **step 4**, click the blue **Submit for Grading** button. Click **Close Assignment** to return to your list of **Course Materials**.

You have completed Project 3E END

Content-Based Assessments (Mastery and Transfer of Learning)

Apply 3B skills from these Objectives:

5. Design a Worksheet for What-If Analysis
6. Answer What-If Questions by Changing Values in a Worksheet
7. Chart Data with a Line Chart
8. Create a Map Chart and a Funnel Chart

In the following project, you will edit a worksheet that the City of Pacifica Bay Facilities Director will use to prepare a five-year forecast of the costs associated with street maintenance. Your completed worksheet will look similar to Figure 3.51.

Project Files for MyLab IT Grader

1. In your **MyLab IT** course, locate and click **Excel 3F Streets,** Download Materials, and then Download All Files.
2. Extract the zipped folder to your Excel Chapter 3 folder. Close the Grader download screens.
3. Take a moment to open the downloaded **Excel_3F_Streets_Instructions**; note any recent updates to the book.

Project Results

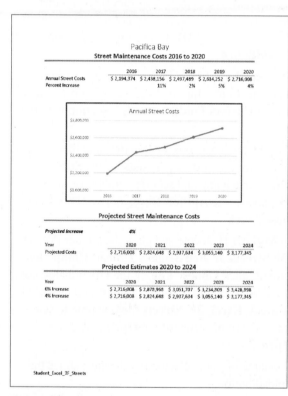

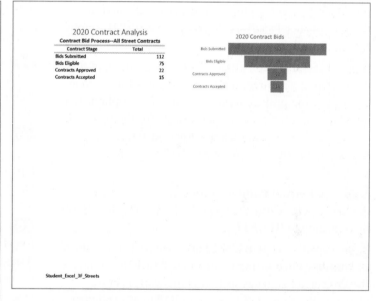

Figure 3.51

For Non-MyLab Submissions

For Project 3F, you will need:
e03F_Streets

In your Excel Chapter 3 folder, save your workbook as:
Lastname_Firstname_3F_Streets
If your instructor requires a workbook with formulas, save as:
Lastname_Firstname_3F_Streets_formulas

After you have named and saved your workbook on the next page, begin with Step 2.
After Step 15, save and submit your file as directed by your instructor.

(continues on next page)

Content-Based Assessments (Mastery and Transfer of Learning)

1 Navigate to your **Excel Chapter 3 folder**, and then double-click the Excel file you downloaded from **MyLab IT** that displays your name—**Student_Excel_3F_Streets**.

2 Change the **Theme Colors** to **Blue Green**. On the **Housing Revenue** sheet, in the range **B4:F4**, fill the year range with the values **2016** through **2020**.

3 In cell **C6**, construct a formula to calculate the percent of increase in annual street maintenance costs from 2016 to 2017. Format the result with the **Percent Style** and then fill the formula through cell **F6** to calculate the percent of increase in each year.

4 In the range **B12:F12**, use the fill handle to enter the years **2020** through **2024**. Use **Format Painter** to apply the format from cell **B4** to the range **B12:F12**.

5 **Copy** the value in cell **F5** to cell **B13**. In cell **B10**, type **6%** which is the projected increase estimated by the City financial analysts. To the range **A10:B10**, apply **Bold** and **Italic**.

6 In cell **C13**, construct a formula to calculate the annual projected street maintenance costs for the year 2021 after the projected increase of 6% is applied. Use absolute cell references as necessary. Fill the formula through cell **F13**, and then use **Format Painter** to copy the formatting from cell **B13** to the range **C13:F13**.

7 Use **Format Painter** to copy the format from cell **A8** to cell **A15**. **Copy** the range **B12:F12**, and then **Paste** the selection to **B17:F17**.

8 Copy the range **B13:F13** and then paste the **Values & Number Formatting** to the range **B18:F18**. Complete the Projected Estimates section of the worksheet by changing the *Projected Increase* in **B10** to **4%** and then copying and pasting the **Values & Number Formatting** to the appropriate range in the worksheet. **Save** your workbook.

9 Select **rows 8:24**, and then **Insert** the same number of blank rows as you selected. **Clear Formatting** from the inserted rows. By using the data in **A5:F5**, insert a **Line with Markers** chart in the worksheet. Move the chart so that its upper left corner is positioned in cell **A9** and visually centered under the data above.

10 Display the **Select Data Source** dialog box, and then edit the **Horizontal (Category) Axis Labels** using the range that contains the years in **B4:F4**. Format the **Bounds** of the **Vertical (Value) Axis** so that the **Minimum** is **2000000** and the **Major unit** is **200000**

11 Format the **Chart Area** with a **Border** by applying a **Solid line**. In the fifth column, click the last color. Change the **Width** of the border to **2 pt**.

12 Click cell **A1** to deselect the chart. Center the worksheet **Horizontally**, and then insert a **Custom Footer** in the **left section** with the file name.

13 Display the **Permit Analysis** worksheet. Select the range **A4:B7** and then insert a **Funnel** chart that depicts the number of bids in each stage of the bid process. Change the chart title to **2020 Contract Bids** and then drag the chart so that the upper left corner aligns with the upper left corner of cell **D1**. Change the chart **Height** to **2** and the **Width** to **4**

14 Deselect the chart, and then change the **Orientation** to **Landscape**. Center the worksheet **Horizontally**, and then insert a **Custom Footer** in the **left section** with the file name.

15 Display the workbook **Properties**, and then as the **Tags**, type **street maintenance costs** As the **Subject**, type your course name and section number. Be sure your name displays as the **Author**. **Save** your workbook and then **Close** Excel.

16 In **MyLab IT**, locate and click the Grader Project **Excel 3F Streets**. In **step 3**, under **Upload Completed Assignment**, click **Choose File**. In the **Open** dialog box, navigate to your **Excel Chapter 3 folder**, and then click your **Student_Excel_3F_Streets** file one time to select it. In the lower right corner of the **Open** dialog box, click **Open**.

The name of your selected file displays above the Upload button.

17 To submit your file to **MyLab IT** for grading, click **Upload**, wait a moment for a green **Success!** message, and then in **step 4**, click the blue **Submit for Grading** button. Click **Close Assignment** to return to your list of **Course Materials**.

You have completed Project 3F **END**

Content-Based Assessments (Mastery and Transfer of Learning)

| MyLab IT Grader | Mastering Excel | Project 3G Expenses |

Apply a combination of 3A and 3B skills:

1. Chart Data with a Pie Chart
2. Format a Pie Chart
3. Edit a Workbook and Update a Chart
4. Use Goal Seek to Perform What-If Analysis
5. Design a Worksheet for What-If Analysis
6. Answer What-If Questions by Changing Values in a Worksheet
7. Chart Data with a Line Chart
8. Create a Map Chart and a Funnel Chart

In the following project, you will you will edit a workbook for Jennifer Carson, City Finance Manager, that analyzes Recreation Department annual expenses, workshop enrollments, and County partnerships in the State of California. Your completed worksheets will look similar to Figure 3.52.

Project Files for **MyLab IT Grader**

1. In your **MyLab IT** course, locate and click **Excel 3G Expenses,** Download Materials, and then Download All Files.
2. Extract the zipped folder to your Excel Chapter 3 folder. Close the Grader download screens.
3. Take a moment to open the downloaded **Excel 3G Expenses Instructions**; note any recent updates to the book.

Project Results

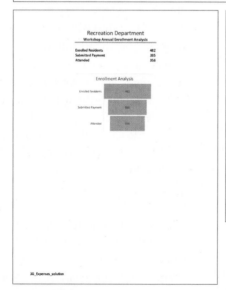

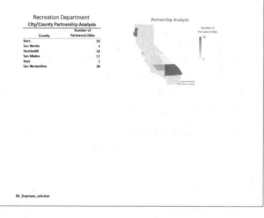

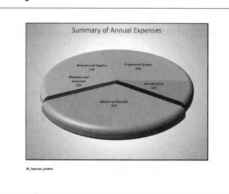

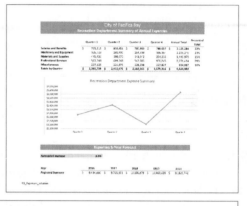

Figure 3.52

For Non-MyLab Submissions

For Project 3G, you will need:
e03G_Expenses

In your Excel Chapter 3 folder, save your workbook as:
Lastname_Firstname_3G_Expenses
If your instructor requires a workbook with formulas, save as:
Lastname_Firstname_3G_Expenses_formulas

After you have named and saved your workbook on the next page, begin with Step 2.
After Step 17, save and submit your file as directed by your instructor.

(continues on next page)

Content-Based Assessments (Mastery and Transfer of Learning)

1 Navigate to your **Excel Chapter 3 folder**, and then double-click the Excel file you downloaded from **MyLab IT** that displays your name—**Student_Excel_3G_Expenses**.

2 In the **Expenses** worksheet, calculate row totals for each Expense item in the range **F5:F9**. Calculate column totals for each quarter and for the Annual Total in the range **B10:F10**. Be sure that **F6:F9** are formatted with **Comma Style** and zero decimal places.

3 In cell **G5**, construct a formula to calculate the **Percent of Total** by dividing the **Annual Total** for **Salaries and Benefits** by the **Annual Total** for all quarters. Use absolute cell references as necessary, format the result in **Percent Style**, and then **Center**. Fill the formula down through cell **G9**.

4 Use a **3-D Pie** chart to chart the **Annual Total** for each item. Move the chart to a **New sheet**; name the sheet **Annual Expenses Chart**

5 As the text for the **Chart Title** element, type **Summary of Annual Expenses** and then change the **Font Size** to **28**.

6 Remove the **Legend** from the chart, and then add **Data Labels** formatted so that only the **Category Name** and **Percentage** display positioned in the **Center**. Format the data labels by applying a **Font style** of **Bold** and **Italic** and a **Font Size** of **12**.

7 Format the **Data Series** using a **3-D Format** effect. Change the **Top bevel** and **Bottom bevel**—under **Bevel**, in the first row, apply the first bevel effect. Set the **Top bevel Width** and **Height** to **50 pt** and then set the **Bottom bevel Width** and **Height** to **256 pt**.

8 Display the **Series Options**, and then set the **Angle of first slice** to **125** so that the **Salaries and Benefits** slice is in the front of the pie. Select the **Salaries and Benefits** slice, and then explode the slice **10%**.

9 Format the **Chart Area** by applying a **Gradient fill** using the **Preset gradients**—in the first column, apply the second gradient. Format the **Border** of the **Chart Area** by adding a **Solid line** border—in the fourth column, apply the first color. Change the **Width** to **3 pt**.

10 Display the **Page Setup** dialog box, and then for this chart sheet, insert a **Custom Footer** in the **left section** with the file name. **Save** your workbook.

11 Display the **Expenses** worksheet, and then by using the Quarter names and the Totals by Quarter, insert a **Line with Markers** chart in the worksheet. Do *not* include the Annual Total. Move the chart so that its upper left corner is positioned slightly inside the upper left corner of cell **A12**. Change the **Width** of the chart to **7.5** and then as the **Chart Title**, type **Recreation Department Expense Summary**

12 Format the **Bounds** of the **Vertical (Value) Axis** so that the **Minimum** is **2100000** and the **Major unit** is **50000** Apply **Bold** to the values on the **Vertical (Value) Axis** and to the labels on the **Horizontal (Category) Axis**. Close any open panes, click cell **A1** to deselect the chart, and then **Save** your workbook.

13 **Copy** the **Annual Total** in cell **F10** and then use **Paste Special** to paste **Values & Number Formatting** in cell **B35**. In cell **C35**, construct a formula to calculate the **Projected Expenses** after the forecasted increase of **3.5%** in cell **B31** is applied. Fill the formula through cell **F35**, and then use **Format Painter** to copy the formatting from cell **B35** to the range **C35:F35**.

14 Change the **Orientation** of this worksheet to **Landscape**, and then use the **Scale to Fit** options to fit the **Height** to **1 page**. In the **Page Setup** dialog box, center this worksheet **Horizontally**, and insert a **Custom Footer** in the **left section** with the file name. **Save** your workbook.

15 Display the **Enrollment** worksheet. Insert a **Funnel chart** that shows resident workshop participation for the year using the range **A4:B6**. Change the **Height** of the chart to **2.5** and the **Width** to **3** and then drag the chart so that the upper left corner aligns with the upper left corner of **A9**. Change the chart title to **Enrollment Analysis** and then click cell **A1**. Center the worksheet **Horizontally** and insert a **Custom Footer** in the left section with the file name.

16 Display the **County Partnership** worksheet. The City of Pacifica Bay is partnering with the County to offer workshops to residents. The Recreation Department staff will visit several cities with similar partnership agreements. Using the range **A3:B9**, insert a **Filled Map chart**. Change the chart title to **Partnership Analysis** and then drag the chart so that the upper left corner aligns with the upper left corner of **D1**. Change the chart **Width** to **4** and then deselect the chart. Change the **Orientation** of this worksheet to **Landscape**.

(continues on next page)

Mastering Excel: Project 3G Expenses (continued)

17 Center this worksheet **Horizontally** and insert a **Custom Footer** in the left section with the file name. Display the workbook **Properties**. As the **Tags**, type **recreation workshops, expenses** and as the **Subject**, type your course name and section number. Be sure your name displays as the **Author**. **Save** your workbook and then **Close** Excel.

18 In **MyLab IT**, locate and click the Grader Project **Excel 3G Expenses**. In **step 3**, under **Upload Completed Assignment**, click **Choose File**. In the **Open** dialog box, navigate to your **Excel Chapter 3 folder**, and then click

your **Student_Excel_3G_Expenses** file one time to select it. In the lower right corner of the **Open** dialog box, click **Open**.

The name of your selected file displays above the Upload button.

19 To submit your file to **MyLab IT** for grading, click **Upload**, wait a moment for a green **Success!** message, and then in **step 4**, click the blue **Submit for Grading** button. Click **Close Assignment** to return to your list of **Course Materials**.

You have completed Project 3G END

Content-Based Assessments (Critical Thinking)

Apply a combination of the 3A and 3B skills.

GO! Fix It	**Project 3H Schools**	IRC
GO! Make It	**Project 3I Tax**	IRC
GO! Solve It	**Project 3J Staffing**	IRC
GO! Solve It	**Project 3K Water Usage**	

Project Files

For Project 3K, you will need the following file:

New blank Excel workbook

You will save your workbook as:

Lastname_Firstname_3K_Water_Usage

Pacifica Bay is a growing community and the City Council has requested an analysis of future resource needs. In this project, you will create a worksheet for the Department of Water and Power that illustrates residential water usage over a five-year period. Create a worksheet with the following data:

	2016	2017	2018	2019	2020
Water Use in Acre Feet	62518	65922	71864	76055	82542

Calculate the percent increase for the years 2017 to 2020. Below the Percent Increase, insert a line chart that illustrates the city's water usage from 2016 to 2020. Format the chart and worksheet attractively with a title and subtitle and apply appropriate formatting. Include the file name in the footer and enter appropriate document properties. Save the workbook as **Lastname_Firstname_3K_Water_Usage** and submit as directed.

		Performance Level		
		Exemplary: You consistently applied the relevant skills	**Proficient: You sometimes, but not always, applied the relevant skills**	**Developing: You rarely or never applied the relevant skills**
Performance Criteria	**Create formulas**	All formulas are correct and are efficiently constructed.	Formulas are correct but not always constructed in the most efficient manner.	One or more formulas are missing or incorrect; or only numbers were entered.
	Insert and format line chart	Line chart created correctly and is attractively formatted.	Line chart was created but the data was incorrect or the chart was not appropriately formatted	No line chart was created.
	Format attractively and appropriately	Formatting is attractive and appropriate.	Adequately formatted but difficult to read or unattractive.	Inadequate or no formatting.

You have completed Project 3K | END

Outcomes-Based Assessments (Critical Thinking)

Rubric

The following outcomes-based assessments are open-ended assessments. That is, there is no specific correct result; your result will depend on your approach to the information provided. Make Professional Quality your goal. Use the following scoring rubric to guide you in how to approach the problem and then to evaluate how well your approach solves the problem.

The *criteria*—Software Mastery, Content, Format and Layout, and Process—represent the knowledge and skills you have gained that you can apply to solving the problem. The *levels of performance*—Professional Quality, Approaching Professional Quality, or Needs Quality Improvements—help you and your instructor evaluate your result.

	Your completed project is of Professional Quality if you:	Your completed project is Approaching Professional Quality if you:	Your completed project Needs Quality Improvements if you:
1-Software Mastery	Choose and apply the most appropriate skills, tools, and features and identify efficient methods to solve the problem.	Choose and apply some appropriate skills, tools, and features, but not in the most efficient manner.	Choose inappropriate skills, tools, or features, or are inefficient in solving the problem.
2-Content	Construct a solution that is clear and well organized, contains content that is accurate, appropriate to the audience and purpose, and is complete. Provide a solution that contains no errors of spelling, grammar, or style.	Construct a solution in which some components are unclear, poorly organized, inconsistent, or incomplete. Misjudge the needs of the audience. Have some errors in spelling, grammar, or style, but the errors do not detract from comprehension.	Construct a solution that is unclear, incomplete, or poorly organized, contains some inaccurate or inappropriate content, and contains many errors of spelling, grammar, or style. Do not solve the problem.
3-Format and Layout	Format and arrange all elements to communicate information and ideas, clarify function, illustrate relationships, and indicate relative importance.	Apply appropriate format and layout features to some elements, but not others. Overuse features, causing minor distraction.	Apply format and layout that does not communicate information or ideas clearly. Do not use format and layout features to clarify function, illustrate relationships, or indicate relative importance. Use available features excessively, causing distraction.
4-Process	Use an organized approach that integrates planning, development, self-assessment, revision, and reflection.	Demonstrate an organized approach in some areas, but not others; or, use an insufficient process of organization throughout.	Do not use an organized approach to solve the problem.

Outcomes-Based Assessments (Critical Thinking)

GO! Think	Project 3L Employment

Project Files

For Project 3L, you will need the following file:

New blank Excel workbook

You will save your workbook as:

Lastname_Firstname_3L_Employment

Sandy Ingram, the Director of the Employment Development Department for the city of Pacifica Bay, has requested an analysis of employment sectors in the city. Employment data for the previous two years is listed below:

Job Sector	2020 Employment	2021 Employment
Government	1,795	1,524
Healthcare	2,832	2,952
Retail	2,524	2,480
Food Service	3,961	3,753
Industrial	1,477	1,595
Professional	2,515	2,802

Create a workbook to provide Sandy with the employment information for each sector and the total employment for each year. Insert a column to calculate the percent change from 2020 to 2021. Note that some of the results will be negative numbers. Format the percentages with two decimal places. Insert a pie chart in its own sheet that illustrates the 2021 employment figures, and format the chart attractively. Format the worksheet so that it is professional and easy to read and understand. Insert a footer with the file name and add appropriate document properties. Save the file as **Lastname_Firstname_3L_Employment** and print or submit as directed by your instructor.

You have completed Project 3L	END

GO! Think!	Project 3M Population	IRC

You and GO!	Project 3N Expense Analysis	IRC

GO! Cumulative Team Project	Project 3O Bell Orchid Hotels	IRC

Creating PivotTables and PivotCharts

4

EXCEL 2019

PROJECT 4A

Outcomes
Query large amounts of data, subtotal and aggregate numeric data, and filter and group data to analyze for relationships and trends.

Objectives

1. Create a PivotTable Report
2. Use Slicers and Search Filters
3. Modify a PivotTable
4. Create a PivotChart

PROJECT 4B

Outcomes
Use a Data Model to analyze data from multiple sources.

Objectives

5. Create a PivotTable from a Data Model
6. Create and Format a 3-D Pie PivotChart
7. Use Power BI to Analyze Data

John_T/Shutterstock

In This Chapter

GO! To Work with Excel

In this chapter, you will create PivotTables and PivotChart reports. Organizations gather large amounts of data, but the data is not useful until it is organized in a manner that reveals patterns or trends. You will use Excel to subtotal, aggregate, and summarize data, and you will extract information from data by organizing the data into groups from which trends, comparisons, patterns, and relationships can be determined. You will also create different views of the data so that more than one pattern or trend can be observed.

The projects in this chapter relate to **Golden Grove**, a growing city located between Los Angeles and San Diego. Just 10 years ago the population was under 100,000; today it has grown to almost 300,000. Community leaders have always focused on quality and economic development in decisions on housing, open space, education, and infrastructure, and encourage best environmental practices, making the city a model for other communities its size around the United States. The city provides many recreational and cultural opportunities with a large park system, thriving arts, and a friendly business atmosphere.

PROJECT
4A

PivotTable and
PivotChart

MyLab IT
Project 4A Grader for Instruction
Project 4A Simulation for Training and Review

Project Activities

In Activities 4.01 through 4.13, you will create a PivotTable and a PivotChart that summarize calls handled at fire department stations and police department precincts during the first quarter of the year for the City of Golden Grove. Your completed worksheets will look similar to Figure 4.1.

Project Files for **MyLab IT** Grader

1. In your storage location, create a folder named **Excel Chapter 4**.
2. In your **MyLab IT** course, locate and click **Excel 4A Fire Police**, Download Materials, and then Download All Files.
3. Extract the zipped folder to your Excel Chapter 4 folder. Close the Grader download screens.
4. Take a moment to open the downloaded **Excel_4A_Fire_Police_Instructions**; note any recent updates to the book.

Project Results

GO! Project 4A
Where We're Going

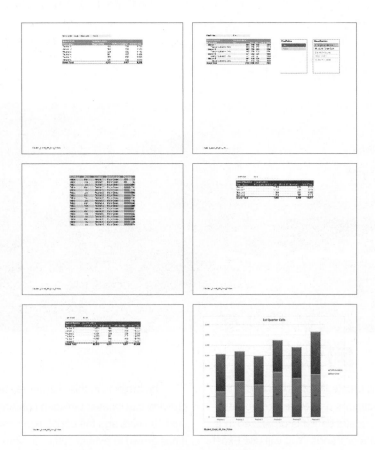

Figure 4.1 Project 4A PivotTable and PivotChart

For Non-MyLab Submissions

For Project 4A, you will need:
e04A_Fire_Police

In your storage location, create a folder named **Excel Chapter 4**
In your Excel Chapter 4 folder, save your workbook as:
Lastname_Firstname_4A_Fire_Police
If your instructor requires a workbook with formulas, save as:
Lastname_Firstname_4A_Fire_Police_formulas
After you have named and saved your workbook, on the next page, begin with Step 2.

Objective 1 | Create a PivotTable Report

GO! Learn How
Video E4-1

A *list* is a series of rows that contains related data with column titles in the first row. A long list of numerical data is not useful until it is organized in a way that is meaningful to the reader. To combine and compare large amounts of data, use Excel's PivotTable report—also called simply a *PivotTable*—which is an interactive Excel report that summarizes and helps you to analyze large amounts of data.

Using a PivotTable, you can show the same data in a table in more than one arrangement. For example, you can manipulate the rows and columns of the table to view or summarize the data from different perspectives. In this manner, you pivot—turn—the information around to get varying views of the data. A PivotTable is especially useful when you want to analyze related totals, such as when you have a long list of numbers to sum and you want to compare several facts about each total. The *source data* for a PivotTable must be formatted in columns and rows and can be located in an Excel worksheet or can be imported from an external source.

Activity 4.01 | Creating a PivotTable Report

> **ALERT** Because Office 365 is a cloud-based subscription service that receives continuous updates, you may encounter some variations in what appears on your screen and what is shown in this instruction. Microsoft Office 365 is fully installed on your PC or Mac; no internet access is necessary to create or edit documents. When you *are* connected to the internet, you will receive monthly upgrades and new features, so you always have the latest versions of Office apps as soon as they are available. Your subscription gives you continuous free access to the latest innovations and refinements.

MOS
4.2.1

The data you use to create your PivotTable should be in the format of a list. Subsequent rows should contain data appropriate to its column title, and there should be no blank rows. Excel will use your column titles as the *field names*—the categories of data. The data in each column should be of the same type. In this Activity, you will use a PivotTable to analyze quarterly fire and police department call and response data.

1 Navigate to your **Excel Chapter 4 folder**, and then double-click the Excel file you downloaded from **MyLab IT** that displays your name—**Student_Excel_4A_Fire_Police**.

> This worksheet displays three months of calls that must be summarized in a PivotTable. There are two classifications for fire department calls and three classifications for police department calls.

2 Click cell **A2**. On the **Insert tab**, in the **Tables group**, click **Recommended PivotTables**. Compare your screen with Figure 4.2.

> The Recommended PivotTables dialog box displays and a moving border surrounds the range of data—this is referred to as the source data. A cell in your data must be active before you create a PivotTable so that you can identify the source of your data.

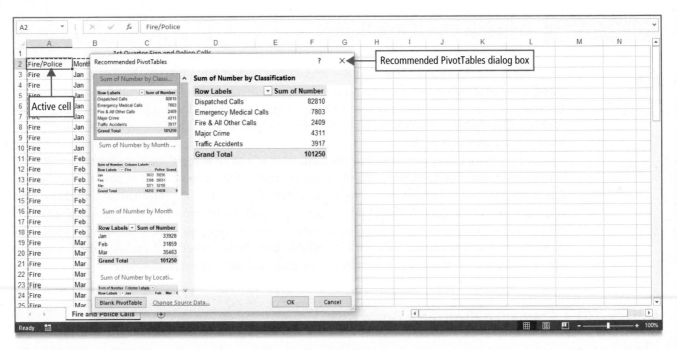

Figure 4.2

🖥️ **MAC TIP** When you click Recommended PivotTables, a PivotTable is inserted in a new sheet. In the PivotTable Fields pane, deselect the Month and Location check boxes. Point to Fire/Police, and then drag it to the Rows area. Point to Location and drag it to the Rows area below Fire/Police. Then skip to Step 5.

---

3 In the **Recommended PivotTables** dialog box, scroll down, point to each preview to display a ScreenTip, and then click the fifth PivotTable—**Sum of Number by Location (+)**. Compare your screen with Figure 4.3.

👆 **BY TOUCH** Select the range A2:E80 and tap Quick Analysis. Tap the Tables tab and point to each PivotTable example to view a preview of the selection, then tap the table you wish to create.

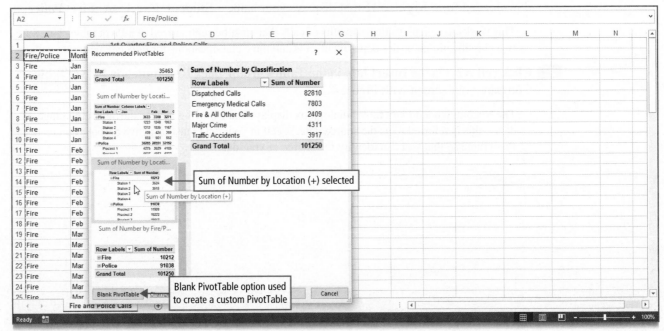

Figure 4.3

Excel suggests PivotTables based on the organization of your data. If the Recommended PivotTables do not provide an appropriate layout for your data, you can create a custom PivotTable by clicking Blank PivotTable. In this case, the Sum of Number by Location (+) layout is a good starting point for your PivotTable.

4 Click **OK**.

Excel adds a new sheet—*Sheet1*—to the workbook. On the left side of the new worksheet, Excel generates a PivotTable report.

On the right side of the window, Excel displays the ***PivotTable Fields pane***—a window in which you can arrange the fields in the PivotTable. The upper portion, referred to as the ***field section***, lists the field names—the column titles from your source data. Use the field section to add fields to and remove fields from the PivotTable. The lower portion, referred to as the ***layout section***, displays four areas where you can build the PivotTable by rearranging and repositioning fields. On the ribbon, the PivotTable Tools include two contextual tabs—Analyze and Design.

MORE KNOWLEDGE | **Create a PivotTable**

If your source data is already formatted as an Excel table, you can create a PivotTable easily by selecting a single cell within the source data, and then on the Table Tools Design tab, in the Tools group, click Summarize with PivotTable.

---

5 **Save** 🖫 your workbook, and then take a moment to study Figure 4.4 and the table in Figure 4.5.

MAC TIP Make sure that the PivotTable displays as shown in the figure. If it does not, in the PivotTable Fields pane, drag the fields so that they are in the correct location and order in the Rows and Values areas.

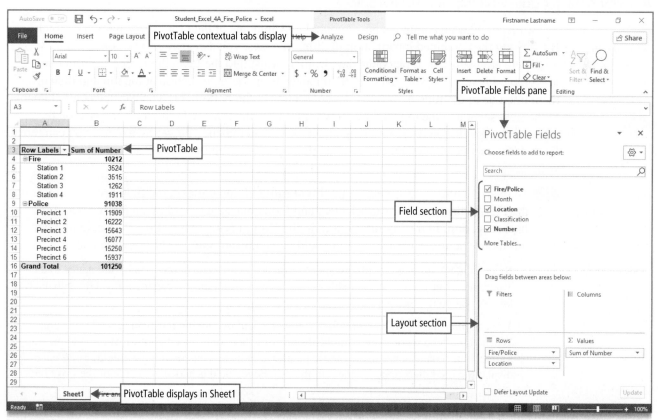

Figure 4.4

PivotTable Screen Elements	
Screen Element	**Description**
PivotTable Fields pane	A window that lists at the top, all of the fields—column titles—from the source data for use in the PivotTable and at the bottom, an area in which you can arrange the fields in the PivotTable.
Filters area	An area to position fields by which you want to filter the PivotTable, enabling you to display a subset of data in the PivotTable report.
Columns area	An area to position fields that you want to display as columns in the PivotTable. Field names placed here become column titles, and the data is grouped in columns by these titles.
Rows area	An area to position fields that you want to display as rows in the PivotTable report. Field names placed here become row titles, and the data is grouped by these row titles.
Values area	An area to position fields that contain data that is summarized in a PivotTable or PivotChart. The data placed here is usually numeric or financial in nature, and the data is summarized—summed. You can also perform other basic calculations such as finding the average, the minimum, or the maximum.
Layout section	The lower portion of the PivotTable Fields pane containing the four areas for layout; use this area to rearrange and reposition fields in the PivotTable.
Field section	The upper portion of the PivotTable Fields pane containing the fields—column titles—from your source data; use this area to add fields to and remove fields from the PivotTable.

Figure 4.5

Activity 4.02 | Adding Fields to a PivotTable

MOS
4.2.2

A PivotTable can combine and compare large amounts of data for analyzing related totals. By viewing the combined information in different ways, you can answer questions.

There are two ways to place the data from your list into the PivotTable report. From the PivotTable Fields pane, you can drag field names from the field section at the top and then drop them into one of the four areas in the layout section at the bottom. Or, you can select a field name in the field section at the top, and Excel will place the field in a default location based on the field's data type. If you want an arrangement other than the one you get by default, you can move fields from one location to another by dragging them between the various areas in the layout section.

1 To the right of the worksheet, in the **PivotTable Fields pane**, in the **field section**, notice that the **Fire/Police** check box is selected, and Excel placed the field in the *Rows area* of the **layout section**. In the **layout section**, in the **Rows area**, point to **Fire/Police**, hold down the left mouse button, and then drag the field name upward into the *Filters area* above.

By default, non-numeric fields are added to the Rows area and numeric fields are added to the Values area, but you can move fields as desired. For example, you can use a PivotTable to analyze the fire and police calls separately.

You can *filter* the report based on the *Fire/Police* field by moving this field to the Filters area. When you filter a report, you limit the display of data to only specific information. As you drag, a small blue icon attaches to the mouse pointer to indicate you are moving a field. *Fire/Police* displays in the Filters area. On the left, the Fire/Police field is added at the top of the PivotTable report.

 ANOTHER WAY   In the Rows area, click the Fire/Police arrow, and then click Move to Report Filter.

2 In the **PivotTable Fields pane**, in the **field section**, verify that the **Location** field check box is selected.

In the layout section, the non-numeric Location field displays in the Rows area. The Location names—Precincts and Stations—display as rows in the PivotTable report. There are six police department precincts and four fire department stations.

3 In the **PivotTable Fields pane**, in the **field section**, select the **Classification** field check box, so that it displays in the **Rows** area. If necessary, drag the Classification field to the Rows area. In the PivotTable, right-click any one of the *Precinct* or *Station* names, point to **Expand/Collapse**, and then click **Expand Entire Field**. Compare your screen with Figure 4.6.

In the layout section, the Classification field displays as the second field in the Rows area. In the PivotTable, the Classification names are added as indented row headings under each police precinct location and under each fire station location. A row that is lower in position in the Rows area is nested within the row immediately above it. Notice that, under each precinct location, only the call classifications related to the police department display. Likewise, as you scroll down, under station locations, only the call classifications related to the fire department display.

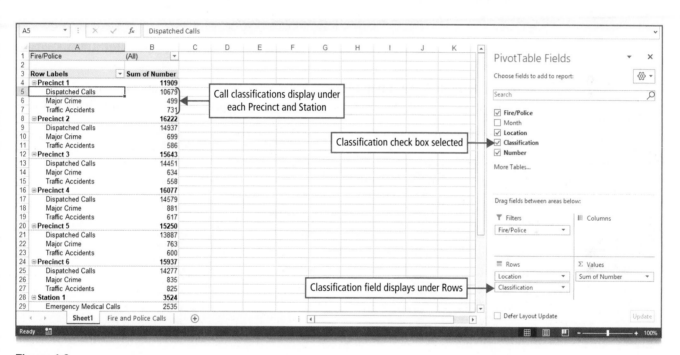

Figure 4.6

4 In the **PivotTable Fields pane**, from the **field section**, drag the **Month** field down to the *Columns area*. Verify that **Sum of Number** displays in the *Values area*. Compare your screen with Figure 4.7.

The PivotTable report is complete; the result is a group of related totals. The arrangement of fields in the layout section reflects the arrangement of the data in the PivotTable report. The long list of figures from the Fire and Police Calls worksheet is summarized, and you can make comparisons among the data. *Sum of Number* displays in cell A3, which refers to the field name *Number*—the number of calls for each call classification has been summed.

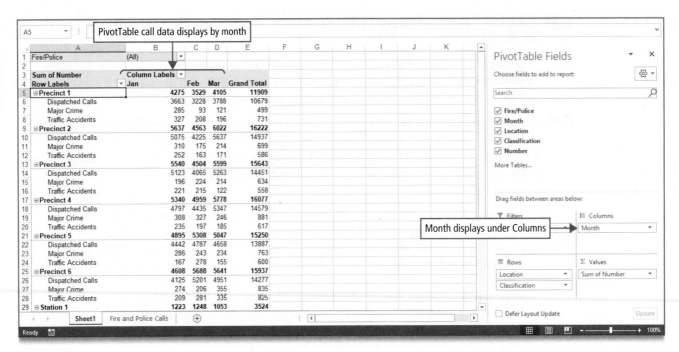

Figure 4.7

5 On the **Design tab**, in the **PivotTable Styles group**, click **More** ⏷, and then under **Medium**, in the second row, click the fourth style. Compare your screen with Figure 4.8.

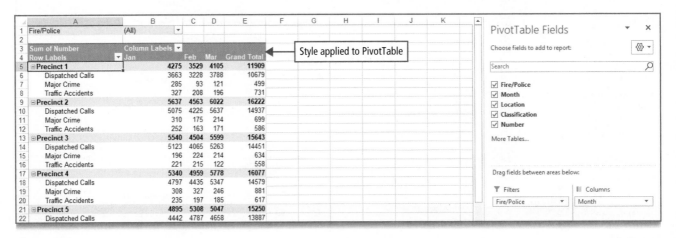

Figure 4.8

6 Click cell **B5**, point to the selected cell, and then notice the ScreenTip that displays.

> Now that the data is organized and the number of calls calculated, you can view and compare various facts about the data. For example, you can see that in January, in Precinct 1, there were a total of 4275 calls, compared with 3529 calls in February. This summary information was not available in the original worksheet. By summarizing and pivoting (turning) data in various ways, you can see different information. Additionally, ScreenTips describe the cell contents.

7 **Close** ⊠ the **PivotTable Fields pane**, and then **Save** 🖫 your workbook.

Objective 2   Use Slicers and Search Filters

GO! Learn How
Video E4-2

You can filter a PivotTable by using a search filter or by using slicers. *Slicers* are filtering controls with buttons that enable you to drill down through large amounts of data. Slicers display as movable objects on your worksheet in the same manner as charts and shapes and make it easy to see what filters are currently applied.

Activity 4.03 | Using a Slicer to Filter a PivotTable

MOS
4.2.3

Limiting the data displayed enables you to focus on parts of the data without the distraction of data you do not need to see. In this Activity, you will limit the data to only the fire department information and then determine which fire department station had the lowest number of emergency medical calls.

> **1** On the **Analyze tab**, in the **Filter group**, click **Insert Slicer**. Compare your screen with Figure 4.9.

The Insert Slicers dialog box displays all the field names from your PivotTable report.

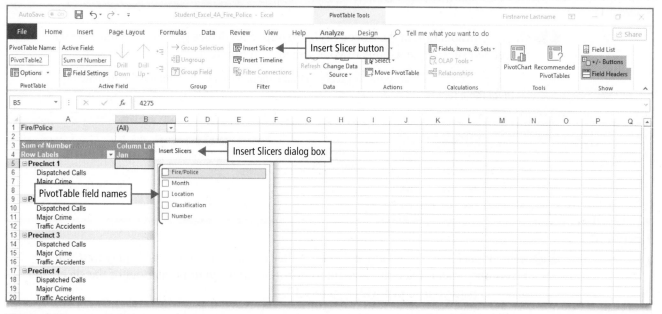

Figure 4.9

> **2** Select the **Fire/Police** check box, and then click **OK**. Compare your screen with Figure 4.10.

The Fire/Police slicer displays.

Figure 4.10

3 ▶ Point to the upper border of the **Fire/Police** slicer to display the pointer, and then drag the slicer up to align with the top of the PivotTable in **Row 3**, and to the right so that it is not blocking your view of the PivotTable. Compare your screen with Figure 4.11.

A slicer includes a ***slicer header*** that indicates the category of the slicer items, ***filtering buttons*** to select the item by which to filter, a Multi-Select button and a Clear Filter button. When a filtering button is selected, the item is included in the filter. The Multi-Select button enables multiple selection of filtering buttons. ***Clear Filter*** removes a filter.

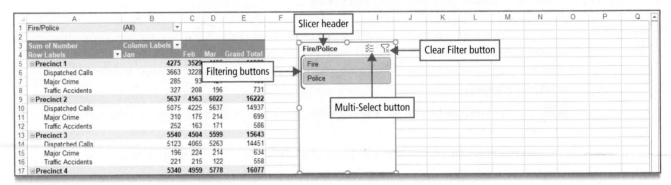

Figure 4.11

4 ▶ On the **Options tab**, in the **Slicer Styles group**, click **More** ⬇, and then under **Dark**, click the second slicer style. Compare your screen with Figure 4.12.

You can apply various styles to slicers to make them easier to differentiate or to match the PivotTable report.

Figure 4.12

5 ▶ In the PivotTable report, notice that the police department precincts display first. On the **Fire/Police slicer**, click the **Fire** filtering button, move your pointer out of the slicer, and then compare your screen with Figure 4.13.

With the data filtered, the records for the police precincts are hidden and only the fire station items display. A filtering button that is not selected indicates that the item is *not* included in the filtered list. By looking at this slicer, you can see that only Fire items are included. Because slicers indicate the current filtering state, it is easy to see exactly what is shown in the PivotTable report—and also to see what is *not* shown.

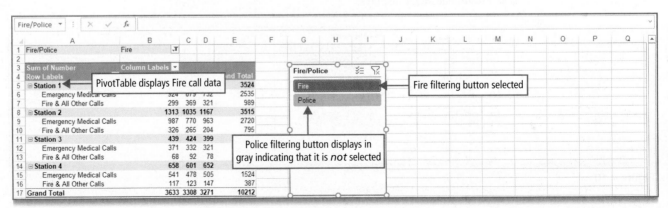

Figure 4.13

6 ▶ Click any cell in the PivotTable. On the **Analyze tab**, in the **Filter group**, click **Insert Slicer**. In the **Insert Slicers** dialog box, select the **Classification** check box, and then click **OK**.

7 ▶ Drag the **Classification** slicer to the right of the Fire/Police slicer in **Row 3**. Notice that call classifications associated with the police department—Dispatched Calls, Major Crime, and Traffic Accidents—are dimmed. Compare your screen with Figure 4.14.

> Because the PivotTable is currently filtered by Fire, no filters related to Police are available.

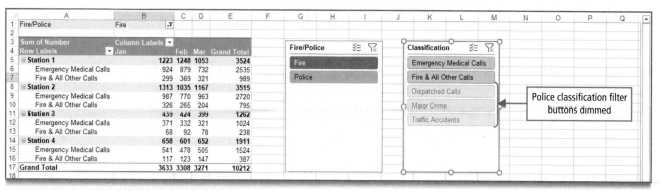

Figure 4.14

8 ▶ On the **Classification slicer**, click the **Emergency Medical Calls** filtering button, and then compare your screen with Figure 4.15.

> Only fire department station items with *Emergency Medical Calls* as the call classification display in the PivotTable report, and you can determine which fire department station had the lowest number of emergency medical calls.

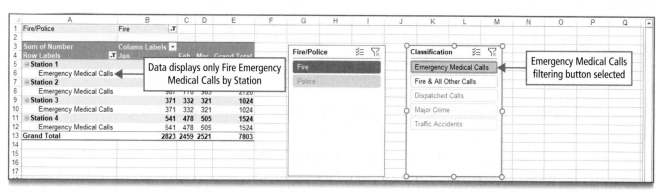

Figure 4.15

9 ▶ Point to the **Sheet1** sheet tab, right-click, and then on the shortcut menu, click **Move or Copy**. In the **Move or Copy** dialog box, at the lower left, select the **Create a copy** check box. Compare your screen with Figure 4.16.

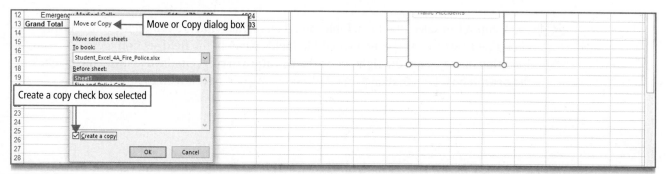

Figure 4.16

10 Click **OK**. Double-click the **Sheet 1 (2)** sheet tab, type **Slicers** and press ⏎.

The sheet is copied and renamed.

11 Save 🖫 your workbook.

Activity 4.04 | Clearing Filters and Filtering by Using the Search Box

Using the Search Filter is another way to filter data in a PivotTable report and find relevant information easily.

1 Display **Sheet1**. In the **Classification slicer**, click the **Fire & All Other Calls** filtering button, and then compare your screen with Figure 4.17.

Clicking a filtering button cancels the selection of another filtering button, unless you hold down the Ctrl key to include multiple filters.

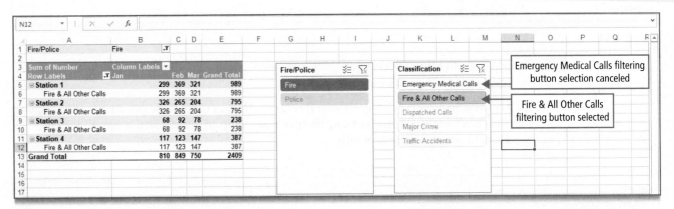

Figure 4.17

2 In the **Classification slicer**, click **Clear Filter** 🗑. In the **Fire/Police** slicer, click **Clear Filter** 🗑.

No filters are applied, and data from both the police department and the fire department displays.

3 Point to the **Fire/Police slicer header** and right-click. On the shortcut menu, click **Remove "Fire/Police"**. By using the same technique, remove the **Classification slicer**.

🖥 **MAC TIP**   Press control and click the slicer header to display the shortcut menu.

4 Click cell **A1** to select the PivotTable, and then on the **Analyze tab**, in the **Show group**, click **Field List** to display the PivotTable Fields pane. In the **field section**, point to **Location**, and then on the right, click the **Location arrow**. On the displayed menu, click in the **Search** box, type **Station 3** and then compare your screen with Figure 4.18.

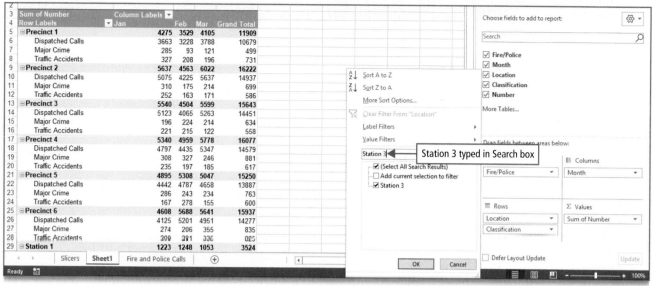

Figure 4.18

5 ▶ Click **OK**. The filter is applied and only Station 3 data displays.

6 ▶ With cell **A1** still active, on the **Analyze tab**, in the **Actions group**, click **Clear**, and then click **Clear Filters**.

You can also clear filters by using this command.

7 ▶ **Save** 🔲 your workbook.

Objective 3   Modify a PivotTable

GO! Learn How
Video E4-3

You have seen how, after adding fields to the PivotTable, you can pivot (turn) the information in various ways, for example, by removing or rearranging the fields. With different views of your data, you can answer different questions. You can display a field as a column rather than a row. You can display parts of the data on separate pages, for example, by creating separate pages for the fire department calls and police department calls. After data is displayed in a useful way, you can format it using any methods you have practiced.

Activity 4.05 │ Rearranging a PivotTable Report

4.2.4

In the Fire/Police PivotTable report, a large amount of detail information displays. Although totals display for both the rows and the columns for each location and for each classification, it is still difficult for a reader to make comparisons across precincts and stations. In this Activity, you will remove and rearrange fields to answer questions regarding the average number of service calls by department, by classification, and by precinct or station.

1 ▶ In the **layout section** of the **PivotTable Fields pane**, from the **Columns area**, drag the **Month** field name upward into the white **field section**—a black X attaches to the pointer as you drag—and then release the mouse button. Compare your screen with Figure 4.19.

The X indicates that the field is being removed from the PivotTable report. When you release the mouse button, the details for each month no longer display in the PivotTable report; only the quarterly totals for the various call classifications at each location display. In the PivotTable Fields pane, *Month* is no longer selected or bold.

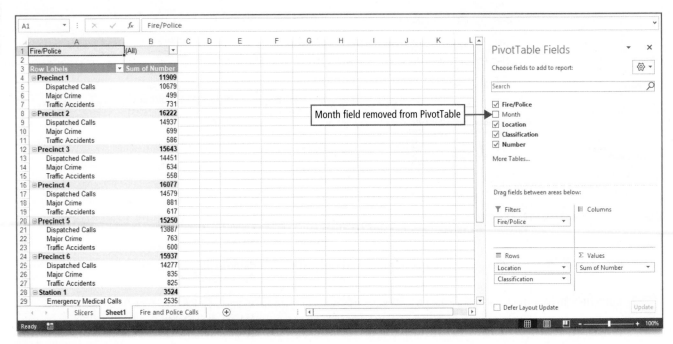

Figure 4.19

2 ▶ In the **layout section** of the **PivotTable Fields pane**, from the **Rows area**, drag the **Classification** field into the **Columns area**. Compare your screen with Figure 4.20.

By moving *Classification* from the Rows area to the Columns area, the various classifications become column titles instead of row titles. The classifications are arranged alphabetically across columns B:F. Now the police-related calls—Dispatched Calls, Major Crime, and Traffic Accidents—display as separate classifications.

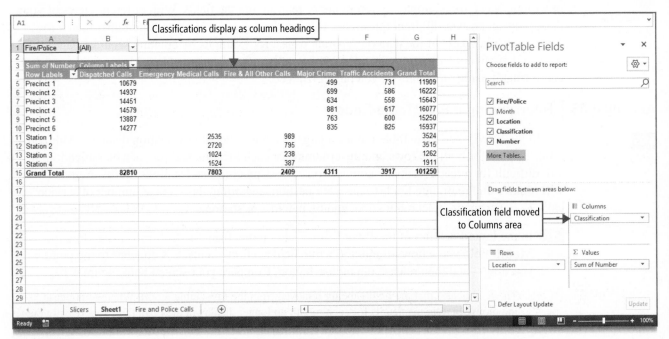

Figure 4.20

3 ▸ **Close** ☒ the **PivotTable Fields pane**. Click cell **B4**—the column title *Dispatched Calls*. Right-click to display a shortcut menu, point to **Move**, and then click **Move "Dispatched Calls" Down**.

> The Dispatched Calls column moves one column to the right.

4 ▸ Click cell **C4**—the column title *Dispatched Calls*—display the shortcut menu, point to **Move**, and then click **Move "Dispatched Calls" Down** again so that it moves one more column to the right.

> The three police-related call classifications are adjacent to one another, and you have a clearer view of the activity by location.

5 ▸ **Save** 🖫 your workbook, and then compare your screen with Figure 4.21.

	A	B				G	H	I	J	K	L	M	N
			Dispatched Calls column moved to column D										
1	Fire/Police	(All)											
2													
3	Sum of Number	Column Labels											
4	Row Labels	Emergency Medical Calls	Fire & All Other Calls	Dispatched Calls	Major Crime	Traffic Accidents	Grand Total						
5	Precinct 1			10679	499	731	11909						
6	Precinct 2			14937	699	586	16222						
7	Precinct 3			14451	634	558	15643						
8	Precinct 4			14579	881	617	16077						
9	Precinct 5			13887	763	600	15250						
10	Precinct 6			14277	835	825	15937						
11	Station 1	2535	989				3524						
12	Station 2	2720	795				3515						
13	Station 3	1024	238				1262						
14	Station 4	1524	387				1911						
15	Grand Total	7803	2409	82810	4311	3917	101250						
16													

Figure 4.21

Activity 4.06 | Displaying PivotTable Report Details in a New Worksheet

From the PivotTable report, you can display details for a particular category of information in a separate worksheet. In this Activity, you will create a separate report showing major crimes reported each month by precinct.

1 ▸ Click cell **E15**—the total for the *Major Crime* classification—and then point to the selected cell to view the ScreenTip.

> To display the Major Crime field as a separate report, first select the total.

2 ▸ Right-click cell **E15**, and then click **Show Details**.

> A new sheet—*Sheet3*—is added to your workbook, and the records for the Major Crime calls display in a table, along with the other fields from the Excel source data. Notice that the *Month* field is included, even though that field is not used in the PivotTable report.

🔁 **ANOTHER WAY** Double-click a total to display the data on a new worksheet.

3 ▸ On **Sheet3**, with the table selected, in the lower right corner, click **Quick Analysis** 📊, and then click **Data Bars**. Click cell **A1**, and then compare your screen with Figure 4.22.

> Conditional formatting is applied to the data in column E.

💻 **MAC TIP** Select the range of data in the Number column—E2:E19. On the Home tab, click Conditional Formatting, point to Data Bars, and then under Solid Fill, click Blue Data Bar.

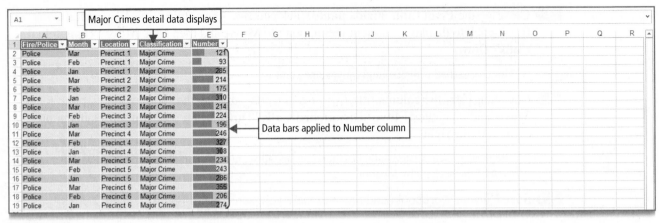

Figure 4.22

> **4** Rename the **Sheet3** tab **Major Crimes** and then **Save** 🖫 your workbook.

Activity 4.07 | Displaying PivotTable Data on Separate Pages

Adding a field to the Filters area is optional, but it enables you to display multiple pages for your PivotTable data. For example, you can display the fire department calls on one page and the police department calls on another page. Doing so will make it easier to answer questions about the calls handled by each Department.

> **1** Click the **Sheet1 tab**, and then rename it **Combined Calls PivotTable**

> **2** Click cell **A1** to select the PivotTable report. On the **Analyze tab**, in the **PivotTable group**, click the **Options arrow**, and then click **Show Report Filter Pages**. Click **OK**.

Because the Fire/Police field was placed in the Filters area, this action adds two new sheets to the workbook, one labeled *Fire* and another labeled *Police*.

> **3** Click the **Police sheet tab**.

The data for the police department calls displays on a separate sheet. The data remains in the form of a PivotTable—you can move fields from a row position to a column position and vice versa.

> **4** Click the **Fire sheet tab**. **Save** 🖫 your workbook, and then compare your screen with Figure 4.23.

The data for the Fire calls displays on a separate sheet.

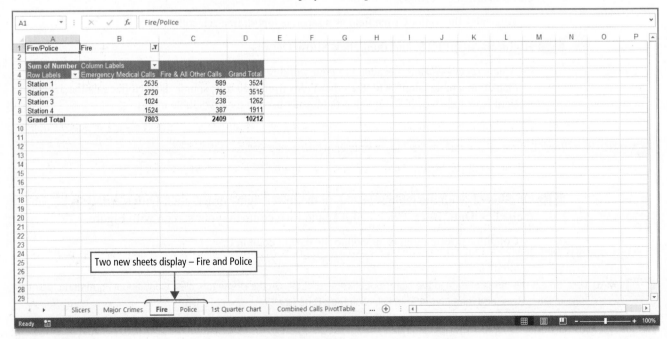

Figure 4.23

Activity 4.08 | Changing Calculations in a PivotTable Report

A PivotTable report combines and compares large amounts of data so that you can analyze related totals. The default calculation in a PivotTable report is to *sum* the numeric data. You can modify the calculation to display an average, minimum, maximum, or some other calculation.

1 Display the **Combined Calls PivotTable** worksheet. Point to any cell containing numerical data, right-click to display the shortcut menu, and then click **Value Field Settings**.

> The Value Field Settings dialog box displays. In the Custom Name box, *Sum of Number* displays; in the Summarize value field by list, *Sum* is selected.

ANOTHER WAY On the Analyze tab, in the Active Field group, click Field Settings.

2 Under **Summarize value field by**, click **Average**. Compare your screen with Figure 4.24.

> The Custom Name box displays *Average of Number*.

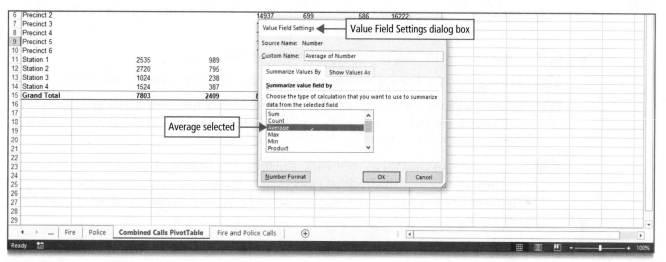

Figure 4.24

3 Click **OK**.

> An average for the three months is calculated and displays with several decimal places in the data cells. Cell A3 indicates *Average of Number*.

4 Right-click any numeric value, and then on the shortcut menu, click **Value Field Settings**. In the lower left corner of the dialog box, click **Number Format**.

> The Format Cells dialog box displays, with only the Number tab included.

5 Under **Category**, click **Number**. Change the **Decimal places** box to **0**. Select the **Use 1000 Separator (,)** check box. Click **OK** two times to close both dialog boxes. Click cell **A1**, and then compare your screen with Figure 4.25.

> The average figures display as whole numbers with the 1000 separator comma appropriately applied.

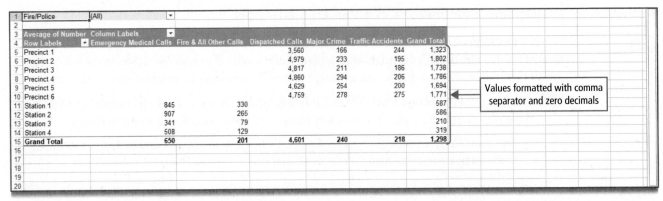

		Emergency Medical Calls	Fire & All Other Calls	Dispatched Calls	Major Crime	Traffic Accidents	Grand Total
1	Fire/Police	(All)					
2							
3	Average of Number	Column Labels					
4	Row Labels						
5	Precinct 1			3,560	166	244	1,323
6	Precinct 2			4,979	233	195	1,802
7	Precinct 3			4,817	211	186	1,738
8	Precinct 4			4,860	294	206	1,786
9	Precinct 5			4,629	254	200	1,694
10	Precinct 6			4,759	278	275	1,771
11	Station 1	845	330				587
12	Station 2	907	265				586
13	Station 3	341	79				210
14	Station 4	508	129				319
15	Grand Total	650	201	4,601	240	218	1,298

Values formatted with comma separator and zero decimals

Figure 4.25

> **6** **Save** 🖫 your workbook.

Activity 4.09 | Formatting a PivotTable Report

You can apply a PivotTable Style to the entire PivotTable report and change field names to make them easier to understand. For example, the field name *Average of Number* would be easier to understand as *Average Number of Calls*.

> **1** In cell **A1**, type **1st Quarter Fire & Police Calls** and then press Enter.

> **2** Click cell **A3**, type **Average Number of Calls** and then press Enter. **AutoFit column A**.

> **3** Display the **Police** worksheet. On the **Design tab**, in the **PivotTable Styles group**, display the **PivotTable Styles** gallery, and then under **Medium**, in the first row apply the second style.

> **4** Point to any numerical value, right-click, and then click **Number Format**. Under **Category**, click **Number**. Change the **Decimal places** box to **0**, and then select the **Use 1000 Separator (,)** check box. Click **OK**. Click cell **A1**, and then compare your screen with Figure 4.26.

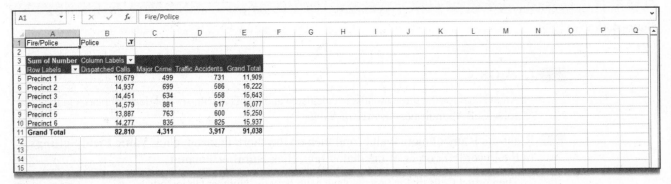

	A	B	C	D	E
1	Fire/Police	Police			
2					
3	Sum of Number	Column Labels			
4	Row Labels	Dispatched Calls	Major Crime	Traffic Accidents	Grand Total
5	Precinct 1	10,679	499	731	11,909
6	Precinct 2	14,937	699	586	16,222
7	Precinct 3	14,451	634	558	15,643
8	Precinct 4	14,579	881	617	16,077
9	Precinct 5	13,887	763	600	15,250
10	Precinct 6	14,277	835	825	15,937
11	Grand Total	82,810	4,311	3,917	91,038

Figure 4.26

> **5** Display the **Fire** worksheet. Using the techniques you just practiced, display the **PivotTable Styles** gallery, and then under **Medium** in the first row, apply the third style. Format the numbers to display using the 1000 comma separator with no decimal places.

> **6** **Save** 🖫 your workbook.

Activity 4.10 | Updating PivotTable Report Data

In this Activity, you will update some of the data. If you change the underlying data on which the PivotTable report is based, you must also *refresh*—update—the PivotTable to reflect the new data.

1 ▶ On the **Fire** worksheet, in cell **B5**, notice that the total **Emergency Medical Calls** for **Station 1** is *2,535*.

2 ▶ Display the **Combined Calls PivotTable** worksheet, and then click cell **B11**. Notice that the *average* number of **Emergency Medical Calls** for **Station 1** is *845*.

3 ▶ Display the **Fire and Police Calls** worksheet—your original source data. Click cell **E3** and change the number from *924* to **824** and then press Enter. In cell **E11**, change the number from *879* to **778** and then press Enter.

4 ▶ Display the **Combined Calls PivotTable** worksheet. Although you adjusted the underlying data, notice that in cell **B11**, the average number of Emergency Medical Calls for Station 1 has not changed—it still indicates *845*.

5 ▶ On the **Analyze tab**, in the **Data group**, click the **Refresh arrow**, and then click **Refresh**. Compare your screen with Figure 4.27.

The average number of Emergency Medical Calls for Station 1 updates to *778*, and the average for this type of call from all stations changes to *634*.

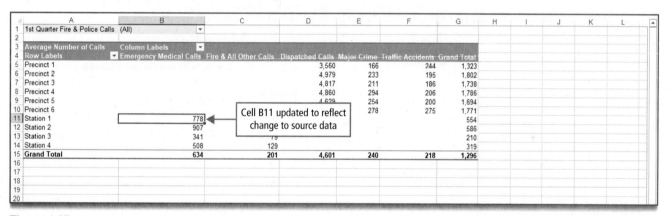

Figure 4.27

6 ▶ Display the **Fire** worksheet, and then click cell **B5**. Notice that the total number of Emergency Medical Calls for Station 1 has been updated to *2,334*. **Save** 🖫 your workbook.

Objective 4   Create a PivotChart

GO! Learn How
Video E4-4

A *PivotChart* is a graphical representation of the data in a PivotTable—referred to as the *associated PivotTable report*. A PivotChart usually has an associated PivotTable, and the two are interactive; that is, if you change the field layout or data in the associated PivotTable, the changes are immediately reflected in the PivotChart. A PivotChart and its associated PivotTable must be in the same workbook.

Most of the formatting that you have practiced in standard charts works the same way in a PivotChart. A PivotChart displays data series, categories, data markers, and axes in the same manner as a standard chart. There are some differences. For example, whereas standard charts are linked directly to a range of worksheet cells, PivotCharts are based on the data source of the associated PivotTable.

Activity 4.11 | Creating a PivotChart Report from a PivotTable Report

MOS
4.3.1

In this Activity you will create a PivotChart to analyze the police Major Crime and Traffic Accident calls.

1 Display the **Combined Calls PivotTable** worksheet, and then make cell **A1** the active cell so that the PivotTable is selected.

2 On the **Analyze tab**, in the **Tools group**, click **PivotChart**. In the **Insert Chart** dialog box, on the left side, if necessary, click **Column**, and then click **OK** to accept the default chart—**Clustered Column**. Compare your screen with Figure 4.28.

The PivotChart displays *field buttons*. You can click on any button with an arrow to choose a filter and change the data that is displayed in the chart. Filters you apply will be reflected in the PivotTable and vice versa. After your chart is complete, you can hide the field buttons from view. Here, the Classification field items form the legend, and the Location field items form the category axis.

💻 **MAC TIP** A clustered column chart is inserted when you click PivotChart.

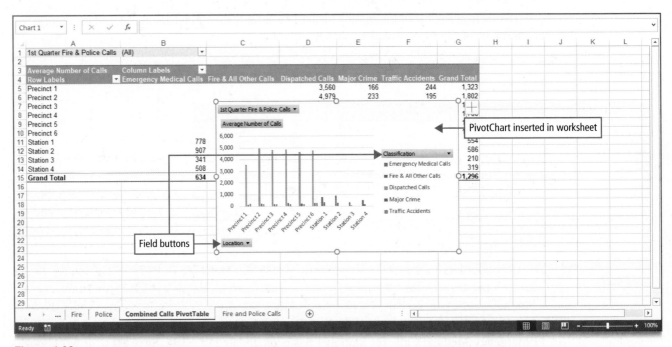

Figure 4.28

3 On the **Design tab**, in the **Location group**, click **Move Chart**. In the **Move Chart** dialog box, click the **New sheet** option, replace the highlighted text *Chart1* by typing **1st Quarter Chart** and then click **OK**.

4 In the **1st Quarter Chart** sheet, on the **Design tab**, in the **Chart Layouts group**, click **Quick Layout**, and then click the first chart layout—**Layout 1**. In the **Chart Styles group**, click **More** ⤓, and then apply **Style 14**.

5 ▸ Click the **Chart Title**. Replace it with **1st Quarter Calls** and then insert a Custom Footer with the file name on the left.

6 ▸ Compare your screen with Figure 4.29, and then **Save** 🖫 your workbook.

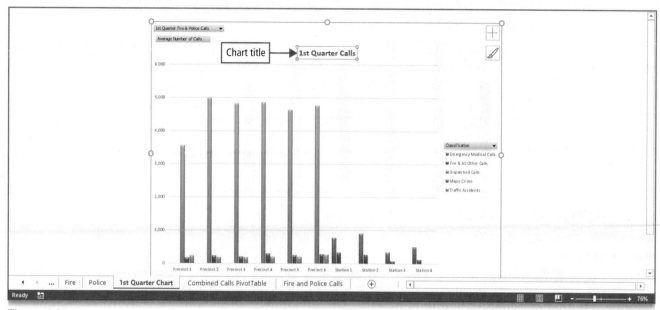

Figure 4.29

Activity 4.12 | Modifying a PivotChart Report

4.3.2 and 4.3.4

You can filter and change the values of the data in the PivotChart report by using the gray field buttons that display on the chart. For example, most of the calls number in the hundreds, but the Dispatched Calls number in the thousands, resulting in a larger vertical scale. To make the data easier to analyze, you will filter the data to show only Police calls in the Major Crime and Traffic Accidents classifications. You will also change the summary data back to total number of calls rather than the average.

1 ▸ In the upper left corner of the chart, click the **1st Quarter Fire & Police Calls** button. In the lower left corner of the list, select (place a check mark in) the **Select Multiple Items** check box. Click to clear the **(All)** check box, and then select the **Police** check box. Click **OK**, and then compare your screen with Figure 4.30.

Only the Police precinct calls display.

MAC TIP Display the Combined Calls PivotTable sheet, and then in cell B4, click the Column Labels Filter button (down-pointing arrow). Click Select All so that none of the Classifications are selected, and then click Major Crime and Traffic Accidents to select them. Close the Classification dialog box. Display the 1st Quarter Chart sheet, and then skip to step 3.

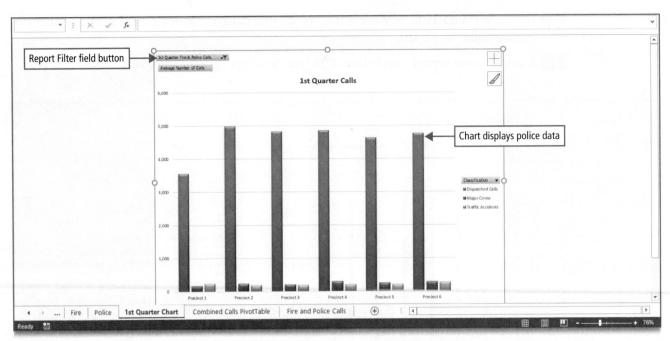

Figure 4.30

2 To the right of the PivotChart, click the **Classification** button above the chart legend. Click to *clear* the check box for **Dispatched Calls**, and then click **OK**.

> This action removes the Dispatched Calls classification; only the two remaining call classifications for Police precincts display. The Legend field button displays a funnel icon to indicate that a filter is applied. Because the number of dispatched calls is in the thousands, compared to hundreds for the other call types, removing this classification allows for a clearer comparison of the other call classifications.

3 On the **Design tab**, in the **Type group**, click **Change Chart Type**. In the **Change Chart Type** dialog box, with **Column** selected, click the second chart type—**Stacked Column**—and then click **OK**. Compare your screen with Figure 4.31.

> Stacked columns display the two call classifications by location. Within each location, the stacked column shows the amount of Activity as part of a whole.

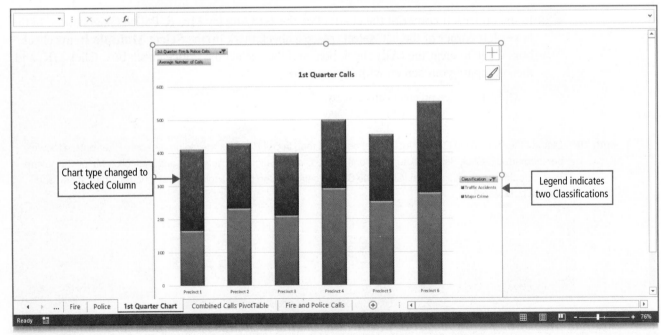

Figure 4.31

4 ▸ Display the **Combined Calls PivotTable** worksheet, and then compare your screen with Figure 4.32.

The data is rearranged and only the precinct calls display. Each time you change the PivotChart, the underlying PivotTable changes to reflect the new display of the data.

	A	B	C	D	E	F	G	H	I	J	K	L	M	N
1	1st Quarter Fire & Police Calls	Police												
2														
3	Average Number of Calls	Column Labels												
4	Row Labels	Major Crime	Traffic Accidents	Grand Total										
5	Precinct 1	166	244	205										
6	Precinct 2	233	195	214										
7	Precinct 3	211	186	199										
8	Precinct 4	294	206	250										
9	Precinct 5	254	200	227										
10	Precinct 6	278	275	277										
11	Grand Total	240	218	229										

PivotTable displays Police data for two classifications

Figure 4.32

5 ▸ Click the **1st Quarter Chart sheet tab,** and then click in the chart title to make the chart active. On the **Design tab**, in the **Chart Layouts group**, click **Add Chart Element**, point to **Data Labels**, and then click **Center**.

Labels display on each segment of the columns showing the value for that portion of the column. For the call classification at a particular station, the number represents the *average* number of calls per month in the three months that comprise the first quarter.

6 ▸ On the **Analyze tab**, in the **Show/Hide group**, click **Field List**.

The PivotChart Fields pane displays. Here you can change the way the data is summarized.

7 ▸ In the **PivotChart Fields pane**, in the **Values area**, click **Average Number of Calls**, and then click **Value Field Settings**. In the dialog box, click **Sum**, and then click **OK**. Compare your screen with Figure 4.33.

The chart changes to display the total number of calls rather than the average number of calls.

MAC TIP Display the Combined Calls PivotTable sheet, and then click any numeric value in the PivotTable. On the PivotTable Analyze tab, click Field Settings. Click Sum, and then click OK. Close the PivotTable Fields pane, save the workbook, and then continue with Activity 4.13.

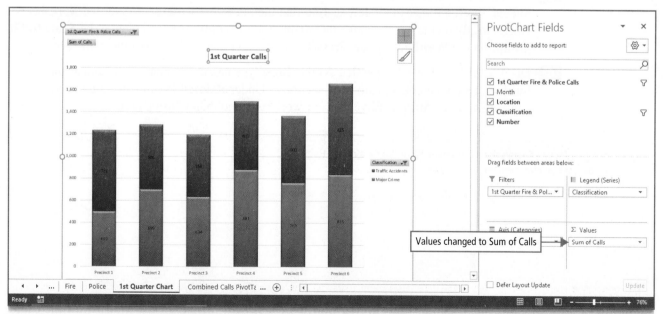

Figure 4.33

8 On the **Analyze tab**, in the **Show/Hide group**, click the **Field Buttons arrow**, and then click **Hide All** so that the field buttons do not display in the chart.

9 **Close** ☒ the **PivotChart Fields** pane, and then **Save** 🖫 your workbook.

Activity 4.13 | Arranging and Hiding Worksheets in a Multi-sheet Workbook

1 At the bottom of the Excel window, to the left of the sheet tabs, click the **left arrow** as necessary so that the **Slicers** worksheet displays, and then click the **Slicers sheet tab** to make it the active sheet.

2 To the right of the sheet tabs, locate the horizontal scroll bar. At the left end of the scroll bar, point to the three vertical dots to display the ⬌ pointer, and then drag to the right to decrease the width of the scroll bar to display all seven worksheets in this workbook. Compare your screen with Figure 4.34.

MAC TIP Skip step 2 and continue with step 3.

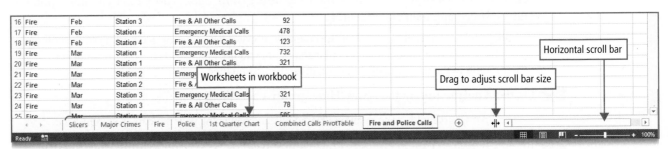

Figure 4.34

3 Drag the **Combined Calls PivotTable sheet tab** to the left until it is the first worksheet.

4 Right-click the **Fire and Police Calls sheet tab** to display the shortcut menu, and then click **Hide**.

In this manner you can hide a worksheet to prevent a user from altering the data.

5 Point to the **Combined Calls PivotTable sheet tab**, right-click, and then click **Select All Sheets**. Insert a footer in the **left section** that includes the **file name**. Center the worksheets **Horizontally** on the page, change the orientation to **Landscape**, and then in the **Scale to Fit group**, set the **Width** to **1 page**. Press Ctrl + Home to move to the top of the worksheet.

6 Display the workbook **Properties**. As the **Tags**, type **fire, police call activity** and as the **Subject**, type your course name and section #. Under **Related People**, be sure that your name displays as **Author**. **Save** 🖫 your workbook and then **Close** Excel.

For Non-MyLab Submissions Determine What Your Instructor Requires
As directed by your instructor, submit your completed Excel file.

---

7 In **MyLab IT**, locate and click the Grader Project **Excel 4A Fire Police**. In **step 3**, under **Upload Completed Assignment**, click **Choose File**. In the **Open** dialog box, navigate to your **Excel Chapter 4 folder**, and then click your **Student_Excel_4A_Fire_Police** file one time to select it. In the lower right corner of the **Open** dialog box, click **Open**.

The name of your selected file displays above the Upload button.

8 To submit your file to **MyLab IT** for grading, click **Upload**, wait a moment for a green **Success!** message, and then in **step 4**, click the blue **Submit for Grading** button. Click **Close Assignment** to return to your list of **Course Materials**.

You have completed Project 4A   **END**

PROJECT
4B

Supply Expenditure Analysis

MyLab IT
Project 4B Grader for Instruction
Project 4B Simulation for Training and Review

Project Activities

In Activities 4.14 through 4.17, you will create a PivotTable and PivotChart using two related lists of data from Microsoft Access. Your completed worksheets will look similar to Figure 4.35.

Project Files for MyLab IT Grader

1. In your **MyLab IT** course, locate and click **Excel 4B First Aid**, Download Materials, and then Download All Files.
2. Extract the zipped folder to your Excel Chapter 4 folder. Close the Grader download screens.
3. Take a moment to open the downloaded **Excel_4B_First_Aid_Instructions**; note any recent updates to the book.

Project Results

GO! Project 4B
Where We're Going

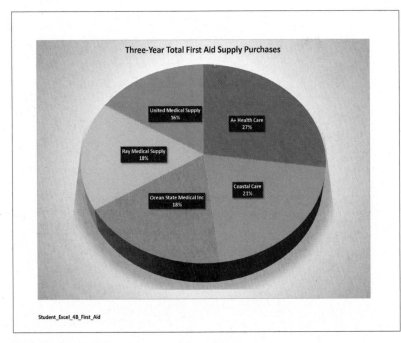

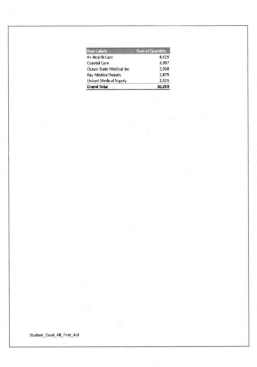

Figure 4.35 Project 4B Supply Expenditure Analysis

For Non-MyLab Submissions

For Project 4B, you will need:
New blank Excel workbook
e04B_Medical_Supplies

In your Excel Chapter 4 folder, save your workbook as:
Lastname_Firstname_4B_First_Aid
If your instructor requires a workbook with formulas, save as:
Lastname_Firstname_4B_First_Aid_formulas

After you have named and saved your workbook, on the next page, begin with step 2.

Objective 5 | Create a PivotTable from a Data Model

A **data model** is a method of incorporating data from multiple, related tables into an Excel worksheet. The data can be in an Excel workbook, imported from an Access database, or imported from an external source such as a corporate database, a public data feed, or an analysis service.

A Microsoft Access table stores data in rows and columns. Each row is a **record**—each category of data pertaining to one person, place, event, thing, or idea. Each column is a **field**—a single piece of information for every record. An Access database can contain multiple, related tables, and you can use these related tables to create PivotTables and PivotCharts.

Activity 4.14 | Creating a Data Model by Getting External Data from Microsoft Access

ALERT Because Office 365 is a cloud-based subscription service that receives continuous updates, you may encounter some variations in what appears on your screen and what is shown in this instruction. Microsoft Office 365 is fully installed on your PC or Mac; no internet access is necessary to create or edit documents. When you *are* connected to the internet, you will receive monthly upgrades and new features, so you always have the latest versions of Office apps as soon as they are available. Your subscription gives you continuous free access to the latest innovations and refinements.

When you import Access tables into an Excel data model, you can establish a **relationship**—an association between the tables of data that share a common field. When the connection is established, you can use fields from each of the imported tables to create a PivotTable. In this Activity, you will get external data from two Microsoft Access tables so that you can analyze the purchase of first aid supplies.

1 Take a moment to view Figures 4.36 and 4.37, which display the data in the two Access tables that you will be working with in your PivotTable. By importing the data from the two tables into one PivotTable, you can use Excel's PivotTable tools to conduct your analysis.

In Figure 4.36, the Suppliers table contains the contact information for each supplier, and each supplier is assigned a unique Supplier ID. In Microsoft Access, the field used to uniquely identify a record is the **primary key**.

In Figure 4.37, the Supply Order Summary table includes the first aid supply purchases made by the Golden Grove fire department from each supplier for a three-year period. The supplier name and contact information is not part of the table. Instead, the Supplier ID field identifies the supplier and is the common field that connects the two databases.

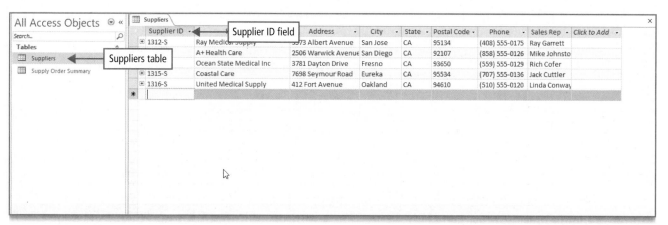

Figure 4.36

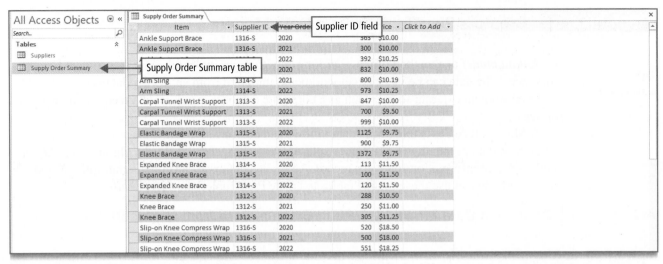

Figure 4.37

2 Navigate to your **Excel Chapter 4 folder**, and then double-click the Excel file you downloaded from **MyLab IT** that displays your name—**Student_Excel_4B_First_Aid**.

3 Click the **Data tab**, and then at the left end of the ribbon, click **Get Data**. Point to **From Database**, and then click **From Microsoft Access Database**. Navigate to your downloaded files for this project, click **e04B_Medical_Supplies**, and then click **Import**. Compare your screen with Figure 4.38.

The Navigator dialog box displays the database name and the two tables shown in Figures 4.36 and 4.37—Suppliers and Supply Order Summary.

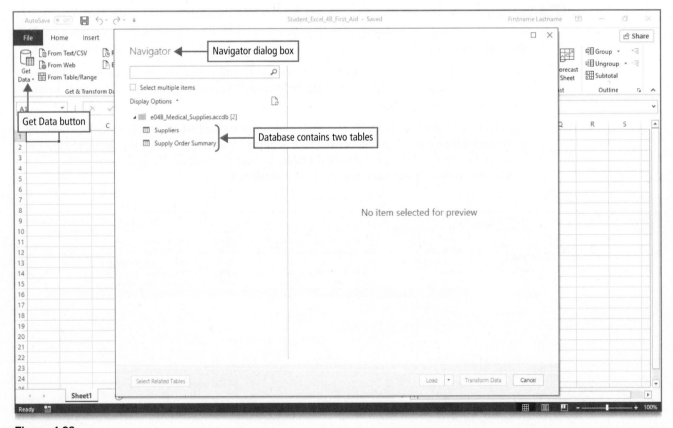

Figure 4.38

4 ▶ In the **Navigator** dialog box, select the **Select multiple items** check box, and then select the **Suppliers** and **Supply Order Summary** check boxes so that both tables are selected. Compare your screen with Figure 4.39.

> You can select all of the tables in the database or you can select individual tables to be included in your data model. On the right side of the Navigator dialog box, a preview of one of the tables displays.

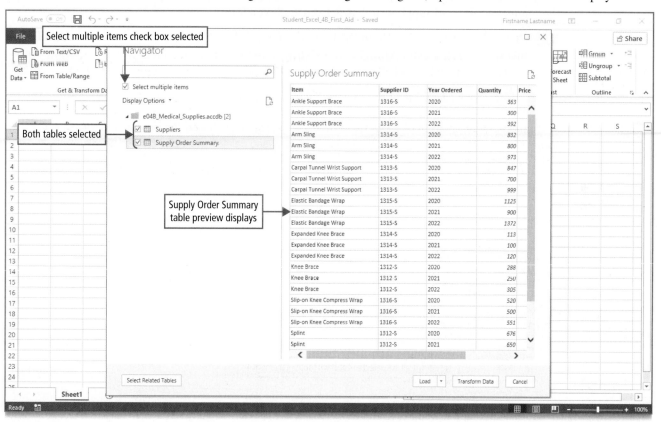

Figure 4.39

5 ▶ Click **Load** and then compare your screen with Figure 4.40.

> The Queries & Connections pane displays the two selected tables that are added to the data model. It may take a few moments for the tables to load.

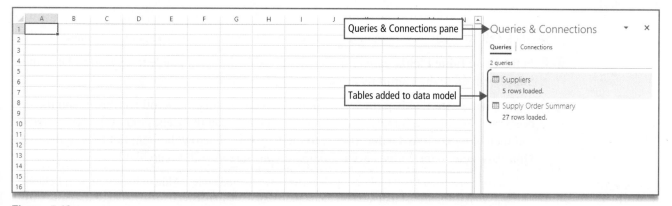

Figure 4.40

6 ▶ **Close** the **Queries & Connections pane**, and then **Save** 🖫 your workbook.

Activity 4.15 | Creating a PivotTable Using Multiple Tables

MOS
4.2.1

The data model enables you to create PivotTables by using the data from multiple, related tables. The Suppliers table contains the contact information for each supplier, and each supplier is assigned a unique Supplier ID. Recall that in Microsoft Access, the field that uniquely identifies a record is the primary key.

The Supply Order Summary table includes the purchases made by the fire department from each supplier. The supplier name and contact information is not part of the table. Instead, the Supplier ID field identifies the supplier and is the common field that connects the two tables.

In this Activity, you will generate a PivotTable report using fields from both tables to analyze the number of first aid supply purchases from each vendor.

1 On the **Insert tab**, click **PivotTable**. In the **Create PivotTable** dialog box, verify that **Use this workbook's Data Model** and **Existing Worksheet** are selected. In the **Location box**, verify that **Sheet1!$A$1** displays, and then compare your screen with Figure 4.41.

The source data for the PivotTable will come from the two tables in the data model.

> **MAC TIP** Click the Insert tab, and then click PivotTable. With the data selected, under Choose where to place the PivotTable, click New worksheet, and then click OK. Select and delete rows 1 and 2 which are blank. Skip step 2 and continue with step 3.

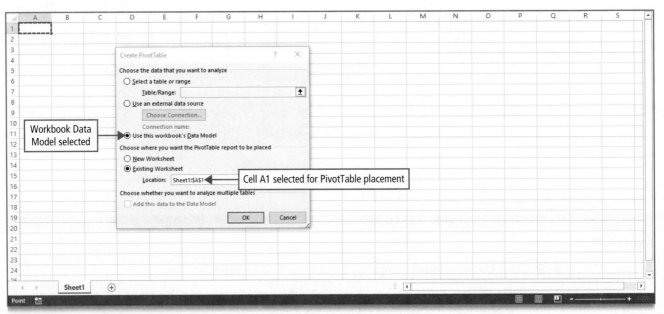

Figure 4.41

2 Click **OK** to insert a PivotTable placeholder and to open the PivotTable Fields pane.

3 In the **PivotTable Fields pane**, if necessary click the Suppliers table to expand it. Drag the **Supplier** field to the **Columns area**.

4 In the **PivotTable Fields pane**, in the field list section, drag the scroll bar down, and if necessary, expand the Supply Order Summary table. Drag the **Item** field to the **Rows area**, and then drag the **Year Ordered** field to the **Rows area** below the Item field. Drag the **Quantity** field to the **Values area**. Compare your screen with Figure 4.42.

You have created a PivotTable using data from two related tables. Although the common field—*Supplier ID*—is not used in the PivotTable, the relationship between the two tables that was created in the Access database enables Excel to use the common field to locate the data necessary from each table.

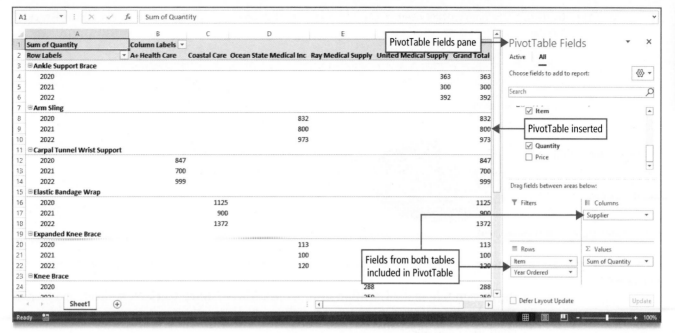

Figure 4.42

 Point to cell **F4** and right-click. On the shortcut menu, click **Number Format**. Under **Category**, click **Number**, change the **Decimal places** to **0**, and then select the **Use 1000 Separator (,)** check box. Click **OK** to apply the format to all of the values in the PivotTable.

 On the **Design tab**, in the **PivotTables Styles group**, click **More** ⊡, and then under **Medium**, in the second row, click the sixth style.

 Double-click the **Sheet1** sheet tab, and then rename the sheet **Supply PivotTable**

MAC TIP Rename Sheet2 since this is the sheet in which your PivotTable is located.

 Close ⊠ the **PivotTable Fields** pane and **Save** 🖫 your workbook.

| Objective 6 | Create and Format a 3-D Pie PivotChart |

GO! Learn How
Video E4-6

Recall that a pie chart is used to illustrate the relationship of each part to a whole. You can create a PivotChart from the data in a data model, and then filter the PivotChart to best represent your data.

Activity 4.16 | Creating a 3-D Pie PivotChart

MOS
4.3.1

In this Activity, you will create a 3-D pie chart that identifies which vendors supply the fire department with the most first aid supplies.

 If necessary, click anywhere in the PivotTable so that the PivotTable Tools are active. On the **Analyze tab**, in the **Tools group**, click **PivotChart**. Click **Pie**, and then click **3-D Pie**. Click **OK**, and then compare your screen with Figure 4.43.

A 3-D pie chart based on the PivotTable displays. The field buttons correspond to the fields used in the PivotTable.

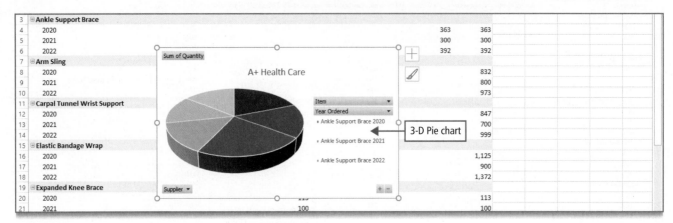

Figure 4.43

2 On the **Design tab**, in the **Location group**, click **Move Chart**. Click **New sheet**, and then in the **New sheet** box, select the existing text. Type **Suppliers Chart** and then click **OK** to move the chart to a chart sheet.

3 On the **Analyze tab**, in the **Show/Hide group**, click **Field List** to display the PivotChart Fields pane.

You can modify the data that displays in the PivotChart by dragging the fields between areas in the PivotChart Fields pane.

4 In the **Axis (Categories) area**, click **Item** and then click **Remove Field**. Use the same technique to remove the **Year Ordered** field.

5 In the **Legend (Series)** area, point to **Supplier**, and then drag the **Supplier** field to the **Axis (Categories)** area. Compare your screen with Figure 4.44.

The Axis (Categories) area corresponds to the legend in a pie chart.

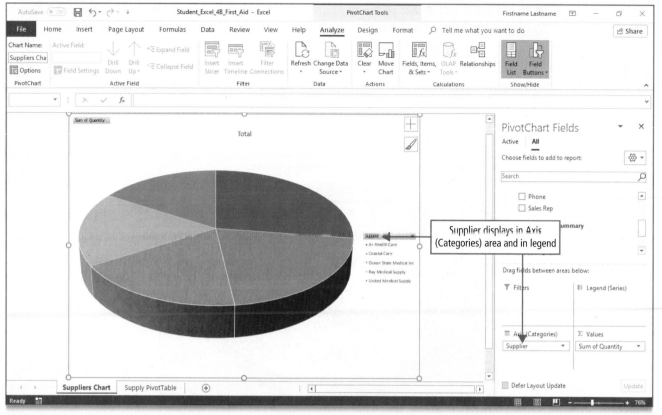

Figure 4.44

> **6** Close ⊠ the **PivotChart Fields** pane, and then **Save** 🖫 your workbook.

Activity 4.17 | Formatting a 3-D Pie PivotChart

MOS
4.3.3

You can format a PivotChart using the same techniques that you use to format a chart.

> **1** On the **Design tab**, in the **Chart Styles group**, click **Style 3**.

> **2** In the upper right corner of the Chart Area, click **Chart Elements** ⊞, and then clear the **Legend** check box.

💻 **MAC TIP**   Hold down control and then click the Legend. On the shortcut menu, click Delete to remove the legend.

> **3** With the **Chart Elements** list displayed, point to **Data Labels**, click the **arrow**, and then click **More Options**. In the **Format Data Labels** pane, select and clear check boxes as necessary so that only the **Category Name** and **Percentage** check boxes are selected. **Close** ⊠ the **Format Data Labels** pane.

💻 **MAC TIP**   Point to any data label and double-click to display the Format Data Labels pane. Select and clear check boxes as necessary so that only the Category Name and Percentage check boxes are selected, and then close the Format Data Labels pane.

> **4** With all of the data labels selected, right-click one of the selected data labels, and then click **Font**. In the **Font** dialog box, select the value in the **Size box**, type **11** and then click **OK**.

> **5** Replace the chart title, *Total*, with **Three-Year Total First Aid Supply Purchases**

6 In the upper left corner of the chart area, right-click the **Sum of Quantity** button, and then click **Hide Value Field Buttons on Chart**. Compare your screen with Figure 4.45.

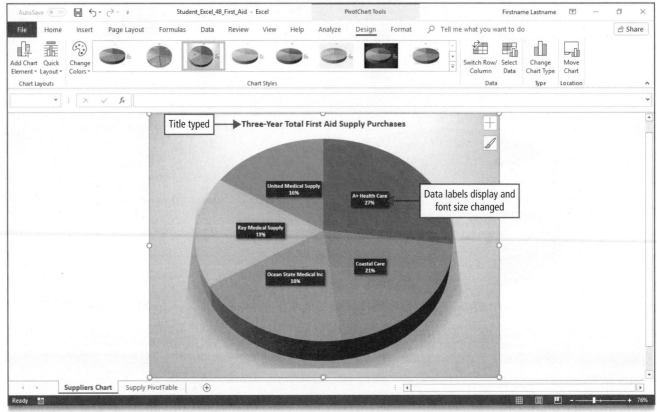

Figure 4.45

7 Display the **Page Setup** dialog box, and then click the **Header/Footer tab**. Click **Custom Footer**, and then in the **Left section**, insert the file name. Click **OK** two times.

8 Display the **Supply PivotTable** sheet and notice that the PivotTable is arranged to match the data in the pie chart. Insert a footer in the **left section** that includes the **file name**, and then center the worksheet **Horizontally** on the page.

9 Display the file **Properties**. As the **Tags**, type **first aid supplies** and as the **Subject**, type your course name and section #. Under **Related People**, be sure that your name displays as **Author**. **Save** 🖫 your workbook and **Close** ✕ Excel.

 For Non-MyLab Submissions Determine What Your Instructor Requires
As directed by your instructor, submit your completed Excel file.

---

10 In **MyLab IT**, locate and click the Grader Project **Excel 4B First Aid**. In **step 3**, under **Upload Completed Assignment**, click **Choose File**. In the **Open** dialog box, navigate to your **Excel Chapter 4 folder**, and then click your **Student_Excel_4B_First_Aid** file one time to select it. In the lower right corner of the **Open** dialog box, click **Open**.

The name of your selected file displays above the Upload button.

11 To submit your file to **MyLab IT** for grading, click **Upload**, wait a moment for a green **Success!** message, and then in **step 4**, click the blue **Submit for Grading** button. Click **Close Assignment** to return to your list of **Course Materials**.

You have completed Project 4B **END**

Power BI (BI is an acronym for Business Intelligence) is a business analytics service that organizations use to transform and analyze data by creating visually impactful interactive reports. The tools in Power BI enable you to discover new stories in your data and then display the data on pre-built dashboards. By using Power BI, organizations can connect and prepare multiple data sources, keep data secure, develop data models, and deliver compelling reports.

Activity 4.18 | Installing Power BI and Creating Visualizations

During the month of October, the city develops plans for adjustments to staffing levels at each of the Golden Grove fire stations. The City Fire Commissioner, Jason Ramirez, is requesting an analysis of the number of calls that each of the four city fire stations responded to during the first three quarters of the year. In this Activity, you will download the Power BI Desktop app, sign in, load data, and create several visualizations to assist the commissioner with this decision.

MAC TIP If Power BI is not available for your Mac, complete this activity on a Windows system.

1 Open your browser. In the address bar, type https://powerbi.microsoft.com and then press Enter.

2 Point to **Products**, and then click **Power BI Desktop**. Click **Download Free**. If necessary, click Open Microsoft Store. In the **Microsoft Store** window, with **Power BI Desktop** displayed, click **Get**.

The application will take several minutes to install. When complete, a message indicates that the product is installed and the Launch button displays.

3 Click **Launch**, and then if the Power BI Desktop sign up screen displays, fill in each required field. Otherwise, skip to Step 4. In the **Email address field**, type your college email address. In the **Enter your phone number field**, type the main phone number for your college—the number is probably on the homepage of your college's website. In the **Company name field**, type the name of your college. In the **Company Size field**, click **250-999**. In the **Job Title field**, click **Other**, and then click **Done**.

4 In the **Power BI Desktop** window, click **Get data**, or on the **Power BI Desktop** ribbon, in the **External data group**, click **Get Data**. Compare your screen with Figure 4.46.

Here you can choose the type of file that you want to import into Power BI.

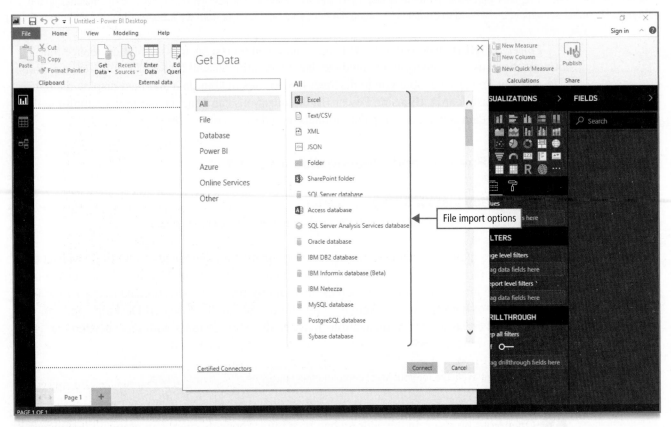

Figure 4.46

5 Click **Excel**, and then click **Connect**. In the **Open** dialog box, navigate to the files you downloaded with this chapter, click **e04B_Power_BI**, and then click **Open**.

Excel data that you want to use in Power BI should be formatted as a table with column headings and should not include formulas or totals.

6 In the **Navigator window**, select the **Table1** check box, and then in the lower right, click **Load**. Compare your screen with Figure 4.47.

On the right side of your Power BI window, the FIELDS pane displays the table fields. The VISUALIZATIONS pane displays the interactive visuals that you can include in your report. The blank layout area is the area where you will arrange your visuals.

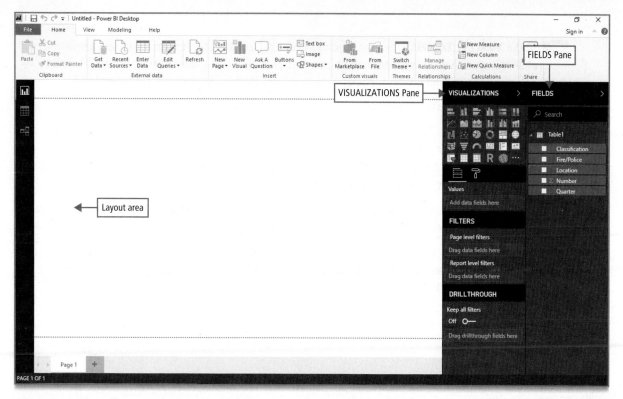

Figure 4.47

7 Under **VISUALIZATIONS**, use the ScreenTips to locate and click the **Clustered bar chart** ▤.

A sample bar chart displays in the layout area of the window. You can size the chart by dragging the sizing handles.

8 In the **FIELDS** pane, select the **Classification** and **Number** check boxes. In the **VISUALIZATIONS** pane, under **FILTERS**, click **Classification**, and then select the **Emergency Medical Calls** and **Fire & All Other Calls** check boxes. Compare your screen with Figure 4.48.

You can add and remove Fields from the chart by clicking the check boxes in the FIELDS pane and then view precise data by modifying the filters.

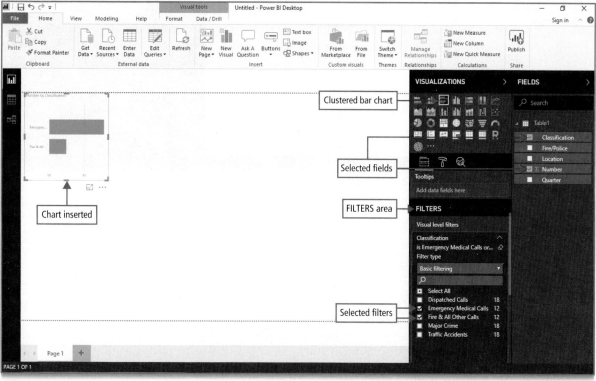

Figure 4.48

9 ▶ In the **VISUALIZATIONS** pane, click **Format** 🖌 to display the formatting options for the chart. Click **Y-Axis** to expand the options, and then click the **Color arrow**. Under **Theme colors**, in the second column, click the first color—**Black**. Change the **Text size** to **13**.

10 ▶ Point to the center-right sizing handle, and then drag to the right until *Emergency Medical Calls* fully displays.

11 ▶ In the **VISUALIZATIONS** pane, click **Y-Axis** to collapse the options, and then click **X-Axis**. Change the **Color** to **Black** and the **Text size** to **13**. Scroll down and change the second **Color** box to **Black** to display the chart gridlines.

12 ▶ Scroll down and click **Title**. In the **Title Text** box, type **Fire Calls by Classification** and then change the **Font color** to **Black**. Change the **Text size** to **14**.

13 ▶ If necessary, scroll down, and then to the right of **Border**, click **Off** to toggle the setting to **On**. Click anywhere in the layout area so that the chart is not selected, and then compare your screen with Figure 4.49.

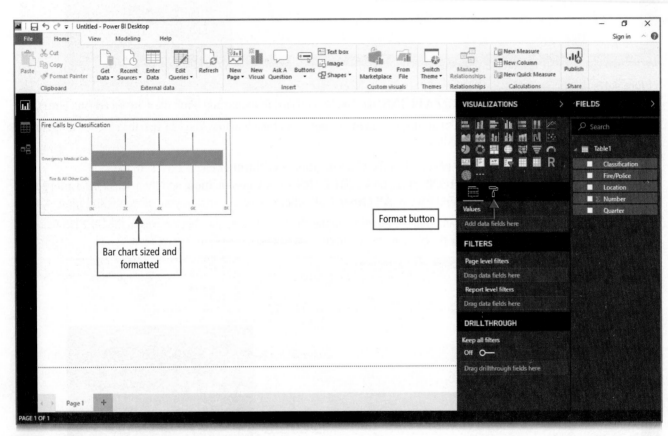

Figure 4.49

14 Under **VISUALIZATIONS**, use the ScreenTips to locate and then click **Multi-row card** 🔲. In the **FIELDS** pane, in the following order, select the check boxes for **Classification**, **Quarter**, and then **Number**. In the **VISUALIZATIONS** pane, under **FILTERS**, click **Classification**, and then select the check boxes for **Emergency Medical Calls** and **Fire & Other Calls**. Compare your screen with Figure 4.50.

Use a multi-row card to display important information about your data in text format.

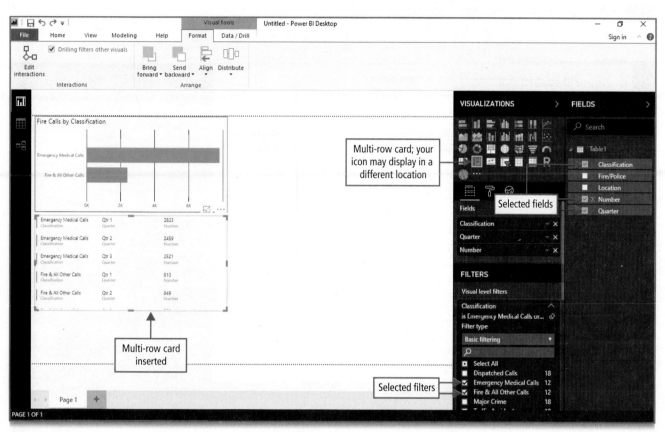

Figure 4.50

15 Point to the bottom center sizing handle, and then drag down until all the data displays— three quarters for Emergency Medical Calls and three quarters for Fire & All Other Calls. In the **VIZUALIZATIONS** pane, click **Format** 🖌, and then to the right of **Border**, click **Off** to toggle it to *On*.

16 In the bar chart, point to the **Emergency Medical Calls bar**, and then click the bar. Notice that the *Fire & All Other Calls* bar is dimmed and only the Emergency Medical Calls display in the Card below the chart.

You can use this technique to focus on relevant data.

17 In the chart, click the **Emergency Medical Calls bar** again to redisplay all the data in the card.

18 Right-click anywhere in the bar chart and then click **Show Data**. Compare your screen with Figure 4.51.

A table displays below the chart indicating the values for each chart data series. Above the bar chart, in the upper left, a *Back to Report* button displays that when clicked, returns you to the chart and card.

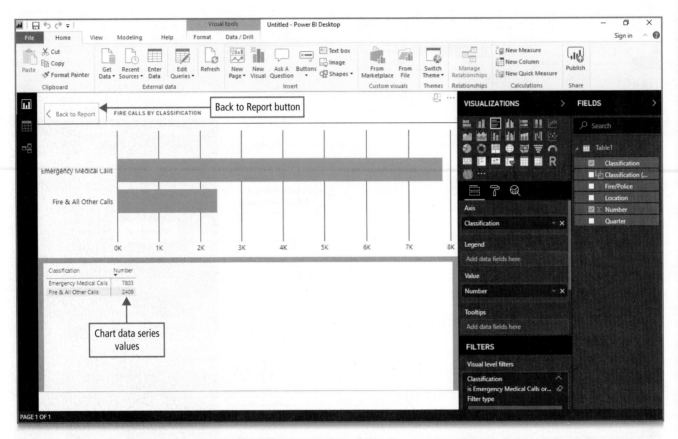

Figure 4.51

19 Click **Back to Report**, and then click anywhere in the layout area so that neither the chart nor the card are selected. In the **VISUALIZATIONS** pane, use the ScreenTips to locate and then click **Pie chart** . In the **FIELDS** pane, select the **Location** and **Number** fields.

20 In the **VISUALIZATIONS** pane, at the bottom, locate **Report level filters** and below it, notice the box **Drag data fields here**—in the next step you will drag a field here.

21 In the **FIELDS** pane, *point* to the **Classification** field, hold down the left mouse button, and then drag this field to the lower portion of the **VISUALIZATIONS** pane and drop it under the **Report level filters** area. With the **Report Level Filters** area expanded, select the **Emergency Medical Calls** and **Fire & All Other Calls** check boxes. Compare your screen with Figure 4.52.

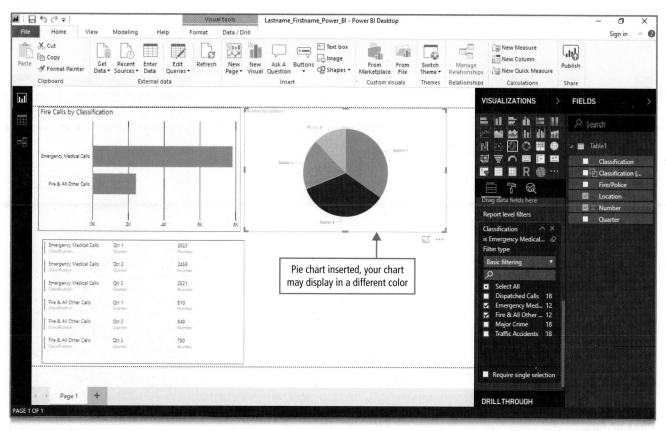

Figure 4.52

22 With the pie chart selected, click **Format** 🎨. Click **Detail labels**, click **Label style**, and then click **Category, percent of total**. Click the **Label position arrow**, and then click **Inside**.

By including the percentages in the pie chart, Commissioner Ramirez can clearly see that Stations 1 and 2 handle most of the fire calls and may need additional staffing.

23 At the bottom of the **VISUALIZATIONS** pane, click **Title**, and then change the **Title Text** to **Number of Calls by Station** Change the **Font color** to **Black** and the **Text size** to **14**. Scroll down and click to toggle the **Border** on. Click anywhere in the layout area so that none of your three visualizations are selected, and then compare your screen with Figure 4.53.

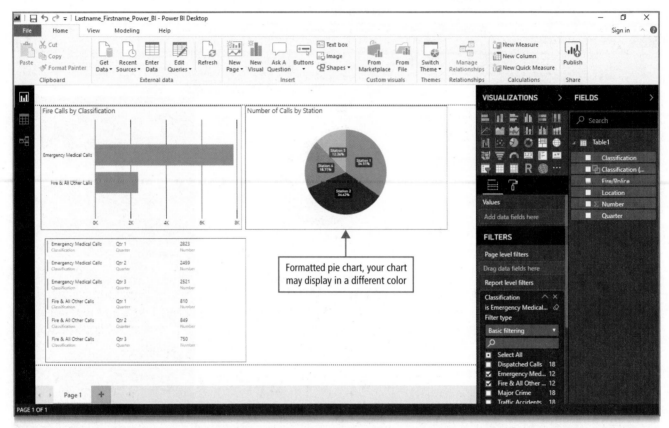

Figure 4.53

24 Click **File**, and then click **Save As**. Navigate to your **Excel Chapter 4 folder**, and then in the **File name** box, using your own name, type **Lastname_Firstname_Power_BI** and press Enter.

25 In the upper right, click the **File tab**, and then click **Exit**. **Close** your browser window. Submit your file as directed by your instructor.

You have completed the optional portion of this project **END**

wavebreakmedia/Shutterstock, Monkey Business Images/Fotolia, Ivanko80/Shutterstock, Monkey Business Images/Shutterstock

Microsoft Office Specialist (MOS) Skills in This Chapter	
Project 4A	**Project 4B**
Expert **4.2.1** Create a new PivotTable	Expert **4.2.1** Create a new PivotTable
Expert **4.2.2** Modify field selections and options	Expert **4.3.1** Create PivotCharts
Expert **4.2.3** Create a slicer	Expert **4.3.3** Apply styles to PivotCharts
Expert **4.2.4** Group PivotTable data	
Expert **4.2.5** Add calculated fields	
Expert **4.2.6** Format data	
Expert **4.3.1** Create PivotCharts	
Expert **4.3.2** Manipulate options in existing PivotCharts	
Expert **4.3.4** Drill down into PivotChart details	

Build Your E-Portfolio

An E-Portfolio is a collection of evidence, stored electronically, that showcases what you have accomplished while completing your education. Collecting and then sharing your work products with potential employers reflects your academic and career goals. Your completed documents from the following projects are good examples to show what you have learned: 4G, 4K, and 4L.

GO! For Job Success

Discussion: Agile Business Culture

Your instructor may assign these questions to your class, and then ask you to think about them or discuss them with your classmates:

Markets and technologies move fast in today's high-tech environment. Companies that need to adapt to changes quickly are adopting an agile business culture. Evolved from a software development technique, agile businesses put their focus on customer needs and welcome the changes to products or services that customers request. Constant innovation toward more effective strategies is seen as the norm.

g-stockstudio/Shutterstock

> What are some businesses that you interact with, either at a physical location or online, that might benefit from the quicker innovation and response to customer input provided by an agile culture?

> Do you see areas at your college that you think would benefit from a more agile culture?

> Are there areas of your personal or professional life where an agile approach to change and innovation might be beneficial?

End of Chapter

Summary

PivotTables and PivotCharts are used to organize and display data. PivotTables are useful for summarizing and analyzing large amounts of data. PivotCharts graphically represent the data in PivotTables.

By manipulating data in PivotTables and PivotCharts, you can present and organize information into groups from which trends, comparisons, patterns, and relationships can be determined.

Excel uses the Data Model to incorporate data from multiple sources into related tables in Excel. The data can come from an Excel worksheet or an external source such as databases and data feeds.

A PivotChart can be formatted in much the same way as any other chart in Excel. You can apply chart styles and layouts, and add, remove, and format chart elements. When you rearrange the fields in a PivotChart, the associated PivotTable is rearranged to reflect the same data.

GO! Learn It Online

Review the concepts, key terms, and MOS skills in this chapter by completing these online challenges, which you can find at **MyLab IT**.

Chapter Quiz: Answer matching and multiple choice questions to test what you learned in this chapter.

Lessons on the GO!: Learn how to use all the new apps and features as they are introduced by Microsoft.

MOS Prep Quiz: Answer questions to review the MOS skills that you practiced in this chapter.

Project Guide for Excel Chapter 4

Your instructor will assign Projects from this list to ensure your learning and assess your knowledge.

Project	Apply Skills from These Chapter Objectives	Project Type	Project Location
4A MyLab IT	Objectives 1–4 from Project 4A	**4A Instructional Project (Grader Project)** **Instruction** Guided instruction to learn the skills in Project 4A.	In **MyLab IT** and in text
4B MyLab IT	Objectives 5–6 from Project 4B	**4B Instructional Project (Grader Project)** **Instruction** Guided instruction to learn the skills in Project 4B.	In **MyLab IT** and in text
4C	Objectives 1–4 from Project 4A	**4C Skills Review (Scorecard Grading)** **Review** A guided review of the skills from Project 4A.	In text
4D	Objectives 5–6 from Project 4B	**4D Skills Review (Scorecard Grading)** **Review** A guided review of the skills from Project 4B.	In text
4E MyLab IT	Objectives 1–4 from Project 4A	**4E Mastery (Grader Project)** **Mastery and Transfer of Learning** A demonstration of your mastery of the skills in Project 4A with extensive decision making.	In **MyLab IT** and in text
4F MyLab IT	Objectives 5–6 from Project 4B	**4F Mastery (Grader Project)** **Mastery and Transfer of Learning** A demonstration of your mastery of the skills in Project 4B with extensive decision making.	In **MyLab IT** and in text
4G MyLab IT	Objectives 1–6 from Project 4A and 4B	**4G Mastery (Grader Project)** **Mastery and Transfer of Learning** A demonstration of your mastery of the skills in Projects 4A and 4B with extensive decision making.	In **MyLab IT** and in text
4H	Combination of Objectives from Projects 4A and 4B	**4H GO! Fix It (Scorecard Grading)** **Critical Thinking** A demonstration of your mastery of the skills in Projects 4A and 4B by creating a correct result from a document that contains errors you must find.	IRC
4I	Combination of Objectives from Projects 4A and 4B	**4I GO! Make It (Scorecard Grading)** **Critical Thinking** A demonstration of your mastery of the skills in Projects 4A and 4B by creating a result from a supplied picture.	IRC
4J	Combination of Objectives from Projects 4A and 4B	**4J GO! Solve It (Rubric Grading)** **Critical Thinking** A demonstration of your mastery of the skills in Projects 4A and 4B, your decision-making skills, and your critical thinking skills. A task-specific rubric helps you self-assess your result.	IRC
4K	Combination of Objectives from Projects 4A and 4B	**4K GO! Solve It (Rubric Grading)** **Critical Thinking** A demonstration of your mastery of the skills in Projects 4A and 4B, your decision-making skills, and your critical thinking skills. A task-specific rubric helps you self-assess your result.	In text
4L	Combination of Objectives from Projects 4A and 4B	**4L GO! Think (Rubric Grading)** **Critical Thinking** A demonstration of your understanding of the chapter concepts applied in a manner that you would outside of college. An analytic rubric helps you and your instructor grade the quality of your work by comparing it to the work an expert in the discipline would create.	In text
4M	Combination of Objectives from Projects 4A and 4B	**4M GO! Think (Rubric Grading)** **Critical Thinking** A demonstration of your understanding of the chapter concepts applied in a manner that you would outside of college. An analytic rubric helps you and your instructor grade the quality of your work by comparing it to the work an expert in the discipline would create.	IRC
4N	Combination of Objectives from Projects 4A and 4B	**4N You and GO! (Rubric Grading)** **Critical Thinking** A demonstration of your understanding of the chapter concepts applied in a manner that you would in a personal situation. An analytic rubric helps you and your instructor grade the quality of your work.	IRC

Glossary

Chapter Key Terms

Associated PivotTable report The PivotTable report in a workbook that is graphically represented in a PivotChart.

Clear Filter A button that removes a filter.

Columns area An area to position fields that you want to display as columns in the PivotTable report. Field names placed here become column titles, and the data is grouped in columns by these titles.

Data Model A method of incorporating data from multiple, related tables into an Excel worksheet.

Field A single piece of information for every record.

Field button A button on a PivotChart with an arrow to choose a filter and thus change the data that is displayed in the chart.

Field names The column titles from source data that form the categories of data for a PivotTable.

Field section The upper portion of the PivotTable Fields pane containing the fields—column titles—from your source data; use this area to add fields to and remove fields from the PivotTable.

Filter To limit the display of data to only specific information.

Filtering button A button on a slicer used to select the item by which to filter.

Filters area An area in the lower portion of the PivotTable Fields pane to position fields by which you want to filter the PivotTable report, enabling you to display a subset of data in the PivotTable report.

Layout section The lower portion of the PivotTable Fields pane containing the four areas for layout; use this area to rearrange and reposition fields in the PivotTable.

List A series of rows that contains related data with column titles in the first row.

PivotChart A graphical representation of the data in a PivotTable report.

PivotTable An interactive Excel report that summarizes and analyzes large amounts of data.

PivotTable Fields pane A window that lists at the top, all of the fields—column titles—from the source data for use in the PivotTable and at the bottom, an area in which you can arrange the fields in the PivotTable.

Power BI A business analytics service that organizations use to transform and analyze data by creating visually impactful interactive reports.

Primary key The field used to uniquely identify a record in an Access table.

Record All of the categories of data pertaining to one person, place, event, thing, or idea.

Refresh The command to update a PivotTable to reflect the new data.

Relationship An association between tables that share a common field.

Rows area An area to position fields that you want to display as rows in the PivotTable report. Field names placed here become row titles, and the data is grouped by these row titles.

Slicer Easy-to-use filtering control with buttons that enable you to drill down through large amounts of data.

Slicer header The top of a slicer that indicates the category of the slicer items.

Source data The data for a PivotTable, formatted in columns and rows, that can be located in an Excel worksheet or an external source.

Values area An area to position fields that contain data that is summarized in a PivotTable report or PivotChart report. The data placed here is usually numeric or financial in nature and the data is summarized—summed. You can also perform other basic calculations such as finding the average, the minimum, or the maximum.

Chapter Review

Skills Review	Project 4C Parks and Pools Calls

Apply 4A skills from these Objectives:

1. Create a PivotTable Report
2. Use Slicers and Search Filters
3. Modify a PivotTable
4. Create a PivotChart

In the following Skills Review, you will assist Lindsay Johnson, Director of Parks and Recreation, in preparing a comparative report for phone calls received by the various park and pool facilities in the city. You will create and modify a PivotTable and PivotChart. The first six worksheets in your workbook will look similar to Figure 4.54.

Project Files

For Project 4C, you will need the following file:

e04C_Parks_Pools

You will save your workbook as:

Lastname_Firstname_4C_Parks_Pools

Project Results

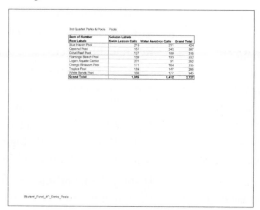

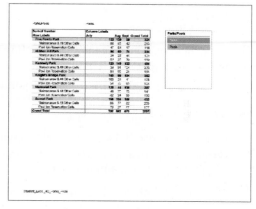

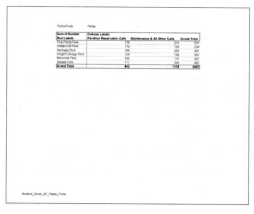

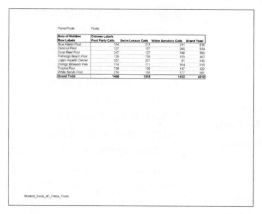

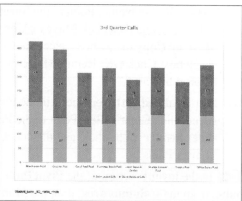

Figure 4.54

(continues on next page)

Chapter Review

1 Start Excel. From your student files, open **e04C_ Parks_Pools**. **Save** the file in your **Excel Chapter 4** folder as **Lastname_Firstname_4C_Parks_Pools**

a. Click cell **A2**. On the **Insert tab**, in the **Tables group**, click **Recommended PivotTables**, and then, in the **Recommended PivotTables** dialog box, click **Sum of Number by Location (+)**. Click **OK**.

b. In the **PivotTable Fields pane**, in the **layout section**, verify that **Parks/Pools** and **Location** are listed in the **Rows area**, and **Sum of Number** is listed in the **Values area**. Remove any other fields from the Layout section.

c. Drag the **Parks/Pools field** from the **Rows area** up to the **Filters area**.

d. In the field section, drag the **Classification field** to the **Rows area** so that it is positioned below **Location**. Right-click **A4**, point to **Expand/Collapse**, and then click **Expand Entire Field**. (Mac users, the field should expand when Classification is dragged to the Rows area. If it is not expanded, point to A4, display the shortcut menu, point to Expand/Collapse, and then click Expand Entire Field.)

e. In the **PivotTable Fields pane**, from the **field section**, drag the **Month** field down to the **Columns area**.

f. On the **Design tab**, in the **PivotTable Styles group**, click **More**, and then under **Light**, in the second row, click the second style.

2 On the **Analyze tab**, in the **Filter group**, click **Insert Slicer**. Select the **Parks/Pools** check box, and then click **OK**. Drag the **Parks/Pools slicer** to the right of the PivotTable.

a. On the **Options tab**, in the **Slicer Styles group**, click **More**, and then under **Dark**, click the last style.

b. Click cell **A1**. On the **Parks/Pools slicer**, click the **Parks** filtering button. Point to the **Sheet1** sheet tab, right-click, and then click **Move or Copy**. In the **Move or Copy** dialog box, select the **Create a copy** check box. Click **OK**. **Rename** the copied sheet **Filtered by Parks**

c. Display the **Sheet1** worksheet. In the **Parks/Pools slicer**, click **Clear Filter**. Point to the **Parks/Pools slicer header**, right-click, and then click **Remove "Parks/Pools"**.

3 In the **layout section** of the **PivotTable Fields pane**, from the **Columns area**, drag the **Month** field name upward into the **field section** and then release the

mouse button. In the **layout section**, from the **Rows area**, drag the **Classification** field into the **Columns area**. **Close** the PivotTable Fields pane.

a. Click cell **B4**. Right-click, point to **Move**, and then click **Move "Maintenance & All Other Calls" Down**. Point to cell **E19**, right-click, and then click **Show Details** to create a worksheet with the details of cell **E19**—the swim lesson calls.

b. In the lower right corner of the selected table, click **Quick Analysis**, and then click **Data Bars**. (Mac users, select E2:E25. On the Home tab, click Conditional Formatting, and then apply the Solid Fill Blue Data Bar.)

c. **AutoFit** columns **C** and **D** and then click cell **A1**. Rename the **Sheet3** tab **Swim Lesson Calls**

d. Click the **Sheet1 tab**. Rename the sheet **Combined Calls PivotTable** and then click cell **A1**. On the **Analyze tab**, in the **PivotTable group**, click the **Options arrow**, and then click **Show Report Filter Pages**. In the dialog box, click **OK** to create worksheets for Parks and for Pools.

e. Display the **Combined Calls PivotTable** worksheet. Point to any cell with numerical data, right-click, and then click **Value Field Settings**. Click **Number Format**, click **Number**, and then set the **Decimal places** to **0** and select the **Use 1000 Separator (,)** check box. Click **OK** two times.

f. Click cell **A1**. Type **3rd Quarter Parks & Pools** and then press [Enter]. **AutoFit column A**.

g. Display the **Parks and Pools Calls** worksheet, which is your source data. Change the value in cell **E3** from *95* to **85** and then press [Enter]. Display the **Combined Calls PivotTable** worksheet. Click cell **A1**. On the **Analyze tab**, in the **Data group**, click the **Refresh arrow**, and then click **Refresh**.

4 With the **Combined Calls PivotTable** sheet displayed, on the **Analyze tab**, in the **Tools group**, click **PivotChart**. On the **Insert Chart** dialog box, on the left verify that **Column** is selected, on the right, verify the first chart—**Clustered Column** is selected, and then click **OK**. On the **Design tab**, in the **Location group**, click **Move Chart**. In the **Move Chart** dialog box, click the **New sheet** option, replace the highlighted text *Chart1* by typing **3rd Quarter Chart** and then click **OK**. In the new chart sheet, on the **Design tab**, in the **Chart Layouts group**, click **Quick Layout**, and then click **Layout 3**. In the **Chart Styles group**, click **More**, and then apply **Style 13**.

(continues on next page)

Chapter Review

Skills Review: Project 4C Parks and Pools Calls (continued)

a. Replace the **Chart Title** text with **3rd Quarter Calls** and then insert a **Custom Footer** with the file name in the **left section**.

b. In the upper left corner of the chart, click **3rd Quarter Parks & Pools Calls**. In the lower left corner of the list, select the **Select Multiple Items** check box. Click to clear the **(All)** check box, select the **Pools** check box, and then click **OK**. At the bottom of the PivotChart, click the **Classification** filter arrow, and then *clear* the check box for **Pool Party Calls**. Click **OK**. (Mac users, display the Combined Calls PivotTable sheet, and then in cell B4, click the Column Labels Filter button, the down-pointing arrow). Click Select All so that none of the Classifications are selected, and then click Major Crime and Traffic Accidents to select them. Close the Classification dialog box. Display the 3rd Quarter Chart sheet.)

c. On the **Design tab**, in the **Type group**, click **Change Chart Type**. In the **Change Chart Type** dialog box, click **Stacked Column,** and then click **OK**. On the **Design tab**, in the **Chart Layouts group**, click **Add Chart Element**, point to **Data Labels**, and then click **Center**.

d. On the **Analyze tab**, in the **Show/Hide group**, click the **Field Buttons arrow**, and then click **Hide All**.

e. Drag the **Combined Calls PivotTable sheet tab** to the left until it is the first worksheet. Right-click the **Parks and Pools Calls** sheet and then click **Hide** to hide the source data.

f. Point to the **Combined Calls PivotTable sheet tab**, right-click, and then click **Select All Sheets**. Insert a footer in the **left section** that includes the **file name**. Center the worksheets **Horizontally** on the page, change the orientation to **Landscape**, and then in the **Scale to Fit group**, set the **Width** to **1 page**.

g. Display the workbook **Properties**. As the **Tags**, type **parks, pools** and as the **Subject**, type your course name and section #. Under **Related People**, be sure that your name displays as Author.

h. **Save** and **Close** your workbook. Print or submit your workbook electronically as directed by your instructor.

You have completed Project 4C | END

Chapter Review

Skills Review	Project 4D Office Supplies

Apply 4B skills from these Objectives

5. Create a PivotTable from a Data Model
6. Create and Format a 3-D Pie PivotChart

In the following Skills Review, you will assist City Council Office Manager Jake Curley in creating a Data Model, PivotTable, and 3-D Pie PivotChart. Your results will look similar to those in Figure 4.55.

Project Files

For Project 4D, you will need the following files:

New blank workbook

e04D_Office_Supplies

You will save your workbook as:

Lastname_Firstname_4D_Office_Supplies

Project Results

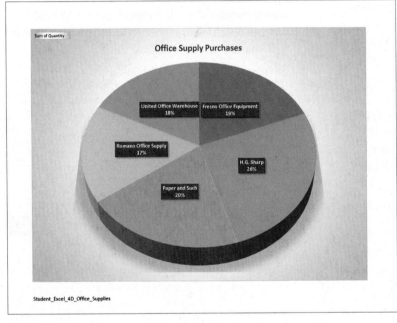

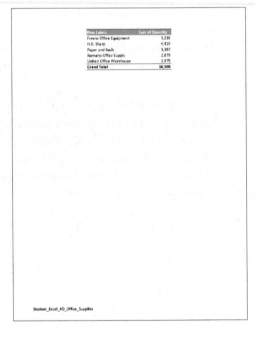

Figure 4.55

(continues on next page)

Chapter Review

Skills Review: Project 4D Office Supplies (continued)

1 Start Excel and open a new blank workbook. **Save** the workbook in your **Excel Chapter 4** folder as **Lastname_Firstname_4D_Office_Supplies**

a. Click the **Data tab**, and then click **Get Data**. Point to **From Database**, and then click **From Microsoft Access Database**. Navigate to your student data files, click **e04D_Office_Supplies,** and then click **Import**. (Mac users, on the Data tab, click From text. From your downloaded files, click e04D_Office_csv, and then click Get Data. With Delimited selected, click Next. Under Delimiters, click Comma and clear all other Delimiters. Click Next. Under Column data format, click General, and then click Finish. Put the data in the Existing sheet in A1, and then skip steps b and c and continue with step 2.)

b. In the **Navigator** dialog box, select the **Select multiple items** check box, and then select the **Suppliers** and **Supply Order Summary** check boxes so that both tables are selected.

c. Click **Load** and then once the two tables are loaded, **Close** the **Queries & Connections pane**.

2 On the **Insert tab**, click **PivotTable**. In the **Create PivotTable** dialog box, verify that **Use this workbook's Data Model** and **Existing Worksheet** are selected. In the **Location box**, verify that **Sheet1!$A$1** displays, and then click **OK**. (Mac users, click the Insert tab, and then click PivotTable. With the data selected, under Choose where to place the PivotTable, click New worksheet, and then click OK. Select and delete rows 1 and 2 which are blank.)

a. In the **PivotTable Fields pane**, expand the **Suppliers** table. Drag the **Supplier** field to the **Columns area**.

b. In the **PivotTable Fields pane**, drag the vertical scroll bar down to display the **Supply Order Summary** table and if necessary, expand the table. Drag the **Item** field to the **Rows area**, and then drag the **Year Ordered** field to the **Rows area** below Item. Drag the **Quantity** field to the **Values area**.

c. Point to any of the values in the PivotTable, right-click, and then click **Number Format**. Under **Category**, click **Number**, change the **Decimal places** to **0**, and then select the **Use 1000 Separator (,)** check box. Click **OK** to apply the format to all of the values in the PivotTable.

d. On the **Design tab**, in the **PivotTables Styles group**, click **More**, and then under **Medium**, in the second row, click the sixth style. **Close** the PivotTable Fields pane.

e. **Rename** the sheet **Office PivotTable**

3 If necessary, click anywhere in the PivotTable so that the PivotTable Tools are active. On the **Analyze tab**, in the **Tools group**, click **PivotChart**. Click **Pie**, and then click **3-D Pie**. Click **OK**. (Mac users, after inserting the chart, click the Design tab, and then click Change Chart Type. Point to Pie, and then click 3-D Pie.)

a. On the **Design tab**, in the **Location group**, click **Move Chart**. Click **New sheet**, and then in the New sheet box, select the existing text. Type **Suppliers Chart** and then click **OK** to move the chart to a chart sheet.

b. On the **Analyze tab**, in the **Show/Hide group**, click **Field List** to display the PivotChart Fields pane. In the **Axis (Categories)** area, click **Item** and then click **Remove Field**. Use the same technique to remove the **Year Ordered** field. (Mac users, drag the fields that you want to remove up to the FIELD NAME area.)

c. In the **Legend (Series)** area, point to **Supplier**, and then drag the **Supplier** field to the **Axis (Categories)** area. **Close** the PivotChart Fields pane.

d. On the **Design tab**, in the **Chart Styles group**, click **Style 3**.

e. In the upper right corner of the **Chart Area**, click **Chart Elements**, and then *clear* the **Legend** check box to remove the legend from the chart. (Mac users, click the legend, and then press Delete.)

f. On the **Design tab**, click **Add Chart Element**, point to **Data Labels**, and then click **More Data Label Options**. In the **Format Data Labels** pane, select and clear check boxes as necessary so that only the **Category Name** and **Percentage** check boxes are selected. **Close** the Format Data Labels pane.

g. With all of the data labels selected, right-click one of the selected data labels, and then click **Font**. In the **Font dialog box**, select the value in the **Size** box, type **11** and then click **OK**.

(continues on next page)

Chapter Review

Skills Review: Project 4D Office Supplies (continued)

4 Select the chart title, and then type **Office Supply Purchases**

a. Display the **Page Setup** dialog box, and then click the **Header/Footer tab**. Click **Custom Footer**, and then in the **Left section**, insert the file name. Click **OK** two times.

b. Display the **Office PivotTable** sheet and notice that the PivotTable is arranged to match the data in the pie chart. Insert a footer in the left section that includes the file name, and then center the worksheet **Horizontally** on the page.

c. Display the workbook **Properties**. As the **Tags**, type **office supplies** and as the **Subject**, type your course name and section #. Under **Related People**, be sure that your name displays as Author.

d. **Save** and **Close** your workbook. Print or submit your workbook electronically as directed by your instructor.

You have completed Project 4D   **END**

Content-Based Assessments (Mastery and Transfer of Learning)

Mastering Excel Project 4E Concessions

In the following Mastering Excel project, you will help Lindsay Johnson, the Director of Parks and Recreation, create and modify a PivotTable and PivotChart to analyze revenue from park concessions such as food, boat rentals, and golf fees. Your completed workbook will look similar to Figure 4.56.

Apply 4A skills from these Objectives:

1. Create a PivotTable Report
2. Use Slicers and Search Filters
3. Modify a PivotTable
4. Create a PivotChart

Project Files for MyLab IT Grader

1. In your **MyLab IT** course, locate and click **Excel 4E Concessions**, Download Materials, and then Download All Files.
2. Extract the zipped folder to your Excel Chapter 4 folder. Close the Grader download screens.
3. Take a moment to open the downloaded **Excel_4E_Concessions_Instructions**; note any recent updates to the book.

Project Results

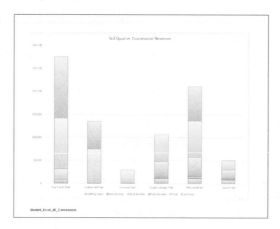

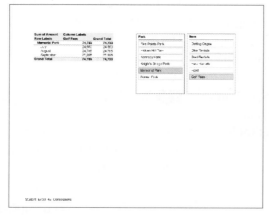

Figure 4.56

For Non-MyLab Submissions

For Project 4E, you will need:
e04E_Concessions

In your Excel Chapter 4 folder, save your workbook as:
Lastname_Firstname_4E_Concessions
If your instructor requires a workbook with formulas, save as:
Lastname_Firstname_4E_Concessions_formulas

After you have named and saved your workbook, on the next page, begin with step 2.
After step 11, save and submit your file as directed by your instructor.

(continues on next page)

Content-Based Assessments (Mastery and Transfer of Learning)

1 Navigate to your **Excel Chapter 4 folder**, and then double-click the Excel file you downloaded from **MyLab IT** that displays your name—**Student_Excel_4E_Concessions**.

2 Click cell **A2**. Insert the last **Recommend PivotTable—Sum of Amount by Park**. Add the **Month** field to the **Rows area** below Park, and the **Item** field in the **Columns area**, and then **Close** the **PivotTable Fields pane**. (Mac users, be sure that Park displays above Month.)

3 Insert two slicers, one for the **Park** field and one for the **Item** field. Move the slicers so that they are to the right of the PivotTable. Apply **Lavender, Slicer Style Light 4** to the **Park** slicer and **Light Orange, Slicer Style Light 6** to the **Item** slicer.

4 Use the slicers to filter the PivotTable by **Memorial Park**, and then by **Golf Fees**. Change the **Number Format** to the **Number** category and display zero decimal places and the 1000 Separator. Move the **Park** slicer so that its upper left corner aligns with the upper left corner of cell **E3**. Move the **Item** slicer so that its upper left corner aligns with the upper left corner of cell **H3**.

5 Make a copy of this worksheet and **Rename** the copied worksheet **Memorial Golf Fees** Insert a footer with the file name in the **left section**. Change the **Orientation** to **Landscape**, set the **Width** to **1 page**, and center the sheet **Horizontally**.

6 Rename **Sheet1 Concessions Revenue** and then clear the filters and remove the slicers. In cell **A1**, type **Third Quarter Park Concessions Revenue** and apply the **Title** cell style.

7 Display the **Field List**, and then *remove* the **Month** field from the **Rows area** to display the Grand totals for each park and for each item. **Close** the **PivotTable Fields pane**.

8 Insert a **PivotChart** using the **Stacked Column** chart type. (Mac users, click the Design tab, click Change Chart Type, point to Column, and then click Stacked Column.) Move the chart to a new worksheet named **Concessions Chart**

9 Apply the **Layout 3** chart layout and **Chart Style 5**. As the **Chart Title**, type **3rd Quarter Concessions Revenue** and then insert a custom footer with the file name in the left section. Hide all of the field buttons on the chart.

10 Hide the **Park Concessions** worksheet. Display the **Concessions Revenue** sheet, and then insert a footer with the file name in the **left section**. Change the **Orientation** to **Landscape**, set the **Width** to **1 page**, and center the sheet **Horizontally**.

11 Display the properties. As the **Tags**, type **concession revenue** and as the **Subject**, type your course name and section number. Under **Related People**, be sure that your name displays as **Author**. **Save** your workbook and **Close** Excel.

12 In **MyLab IT**, locate and click the Grader Project **Excel 4E Concessions**. In **step 3**, under **Upload Completed Assignment**, click **Choose File**. In the **Open** dialog box, navigate to your **Excel Chapter 4 folder**, and then click your **Student_Excel_4E_Concessions** file one time to select it. In the lower right corner of the **Open** dialog box, click **Open**.

The name of your selected file displays above the Upload button.

13 To submit your file to **MyLab IT** for grading, click **Upload**, wait a moment for a green **Success!** message, and then in **step 4**, click the blue **Submit for Grading** button. Click **Close Assignment** to return to your list of **Course Materials**.

You have completed Project 4E | END

Content-Based Assessments (Mastery and Transfer of Learning)

| MyLab IT Grader | Mastering Excel | Project 4F Vehicles |

Apply 4B skills from these Objectives:

5. Create a PivotTable from a Data Model
6. Create and Format a 3-D Pie PivotChart

In the following Mastering Excel project, you will assist Caryn Black, the Vehicle Fleet Manager, to create a Data Model, PivotTable, and PivotChart. Your results will look similar to those in Figure 4.57.

Project Files for **MyLab IT Grader**

1. In your **MyLab IT** course, locate and click **Excel 4F Vehicles**, Download Materials, and then Download All Files.
2. Extract the zipped folder to your Excel Chapter 4 folder. Close the Grader download screens.
3. Take a moment to open the downloaded **Excel_4F_Vehicles_Instructions**; note any recent updates to the book.

Project Results

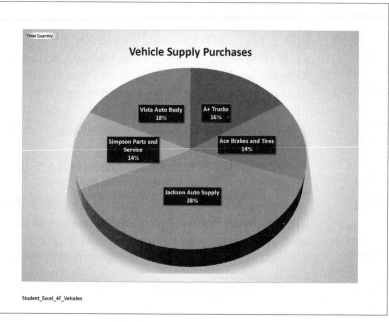

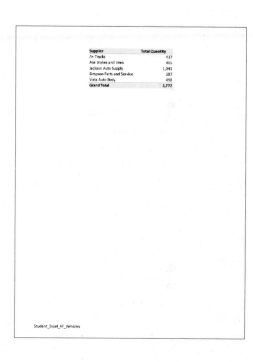

Student_Excel_4F_Vehicles

Figure 4.57

For Non-MyLab Submissions

For Project 4F, you will need:
New blank Excel workbook
e04F_Vehicle_Parts

In your Excel Chapter 4 folder, save your workbook as:
Lastname_Firstname_4F_Vehicles
If your instructor requires a workbook with formulas, save as:
Lastname_Firstname_4F_Vehicles_formulas

After you have named and saved your workbook, on the next page, begin with step 2.
After step 11, save and submit your file as directed by your instructor.

(continues on next page)

Mastering Excel: Project 4F Vehicles (continued)

1 Navigate to your **Excel Chapter 4 folder**, and then double-click the Excel file you downloaded from **MyLab IT** that displays your name—**Student_Excel_4F_Vehicles**.

2 On the **Data tab**, click **Get Data** and then from your downloaded files, import the **Microsoft Access Database e04F_Vehicle_Parts**. Load both of the tables in the database. (Mac users, on the Data tab, click From text. From your downloaded files, click e04F_Vehicle_Parts_csv, and then click Get Data. Use Comma delimiters and General column data format. Put the data in the Existing sheet in A1.)

3 Insert a PivotTable in the **Existing Worksheet** and verify that **Use this workbook's Data Model** is selected. In the **Location box**, verify that **Sheet1!$A$1** displays, and then click **OK**. (Mac users, insert a PivotTable in a New worksheet. Select and delete rows 1 and 2 which are blank.)

4 In the **PivotTable Fields pane**, add the **Supplier** field to the **Columns area**, the **Item** field to the **Rows area**, and the **Year Ordered** field to the **Rows area** below Item. Add the **Quantity** field to the **Values area**.

5 Change the **Number Format** to **Number**, change the **Decimal places** to **0**, and then select the **Use 1000 Separator (,)** check box. **Rename** the sheet **Vehicle Supplies**

6 Insert a **3-D Pie PivotChart** and then move the chart to a **New sheet** and name the new sheet **Vehicle Supplies Chart**

7 Display the **Field List** and then modify the chart so that only the **Supplier** field displays in the **Axis (Categories)** area. Remove any fields that display in the **Legend (Series)** area. Apply **Style 3** to the chart.

8 Remove the **Legend** and add the **Category Name** and **Percentage Data Labels**. Format the **Data Labels** by changing the **Font Size** to **13**.

9 Change the **Chart Title** to **Vehicle Supply Purchases** and then change the title font size to **24**. Insert a footer with the file name in the left section.

10 Display the **Vehicle Supplies** sheet. In cell **A1** type **Supplier** and in **B1** type **Total Quantity** Insert a footer in the left section that includes the file name, and then center the worksheet **Horizontally** on the page.

11 Display the file **Properties**. As the **Tags**, type **vehicle supplies** and as the **Subject**, type your course name and section number. Under **Related People**, be sure that your name displays as Author. **Save** your workbook and **Close** Excel.

12 In **MyLab IT**, locate and click the Grader Project **Excel 4F Vehicles**. In **step 3**, under **Upload Completed Assignment**, click **Choose File**. In the **Open** dialog box, navigate to your **Excel Chapter 4 folder**, and then click your **Student_Excel_4F_Vehicles** file one time to select it. In the lower right corner of the **Open** dialog box, click **Open**.

The name of your selected file displays above the Upload button.

13 To submit your file to **MyLab IT** for grading, click **Upload**, wait a moment for a green **Success!** message, and then in **step 4**, click the blue **Submit for Grading** button. Click **Close Assignment** to return to your list of **Course Materials**.

You have completed Project 4F END

Content-Based Assessments (Mastery and Transfer of Learning)

Apply 4A and 4B skills from these Objectives:

1. Create a PivotTable Report
2. Use Slicers and Search Filters
3. Modify a PivotTable
4. Create a PivotChart
5. Create a PivotTable from a Data Model
6. Create and Format a 3-D Pie PivotChart

In the following Mastering Excel project, you will assist Lindsay Johnson, the Director of Pools and Recreation, in creating and modifying a PivotTable report and a PivotChart report to analyze revenue and expenses from the Aquatics Program. Your completed workbook will look similar to Figure 4.58.

Project Files for MyLab IT Grader

1. In your **MyLab IT** course, locate and click **Excel 4G Aquatics**, Download Materials, and then Download All Files.
2. Extract the zipped folder to your Excel Chapter 4 folder. Close the Grader download screens.
3. Take a moment to open the downloaded **Excel_4B_Aquatics_Instructions**; note any recent updates to the book.

Project Results

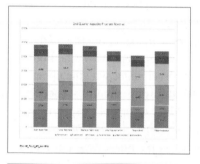

Figure 4.58

For Non-MyLab Submissions

For Project 4G, you will need:
e04G_Aquatics
e04G_Pool_Supplies

In your Excel Chapter 4 folder, save your workbook as:
Lastname_Firstname_4G_Aquatics
If your instructor requires a workbook with formulas, save as:
Lastname_Firstname_4G_Aquatics_formulas

After you have named and saved your workbook, on the next page, begin with step 2.

After step 17, save and submit your file as directed by your instructor.

Content-Based Assessments (Mastery and Transfer of Learning)

1 Navigate to your **Excel Chapter 4 folder**, and then double-click the Excel file you downloaded from **MyLab IT** that displays your name—**Student_Excel_4G_Aquatics**.

2 Click cell **A2**, and then insert a **Recommended PivotTable** by choosing the **Blank PivotTable** option in the lower left corner of the dialog box. Add the **Month** field to the **Filters** area, add the **Pool** field to the **Rows** area and the **Item** field to the **Columns area**. Place the **Amount** field in the **Values area** and then **Close** the **PivotTable Fields pane**. (Mac users, move fields as necessary so that they are placed in the correct areas of the layout section.)

3 Format the values in the PivotTable using the **Number** category to display zero decimal places and the 1000 Separator.

4 Insert slicers for the **Pool** and **Item** fields, and then filter by the **Tropics Pool** and **Spa Fees**. Move the **Pool** slicer so that it's upper left corner aligns with the upper left corner of **E3**. Move the **Item** slicer so that its upper left corner aligns with **G3**. Make a copy of this worksheet, and then name the copied worksheet **Tropics Pool**

5 Display **Sheet1** and clear the filters from the slicers and remove the slicers from the worksheet. **Rename** the sheet **2Q Revenue**

6 Insert a **PivotChart** using the **Stacked Column** chart type. Move the chart to a new worksheet named **2Q Revenue Chart**

7 Apply the **Layout 3** chart layout. Add centered data labels, and then hide all of the field buttons on the chart. As the **Chart Title**, type **2nd Quarter Aquatics Program Revenue** and then insert a custom footer with the file name in the **left section**.

8 Add a new worksheet to the workbook. On the **Data tab**, click **Get Data** and then from your downloaded files, import the **Microsoft Access Database e04G_Pool_Supplies**. Load both of the tables in the database. (Mac users, on the Data tab, click From Text. From your downloaded files, click e04G_Pool_Supplies_csv, and then click Get Data. Use Comma delimiters and General column data format. Put the data in the Existing sheet in A1.)

9 Insert a **PivotTable** in the **Existing Worksheet** and verify that **Use this workbook's Data Model** is selected. (Mac users, insert a PivotTable, in a New worksheet. Select and delete rows 1 and 2 which are blank.)

10 To create the PivotTable, place the **Supplier** field from the **Suppliers** table in the **Columns** area. From the **Supply Order Summary table**, place the **Item** field in the **Rows area**, and the **Quantity** field in the **Values area**. Apply the **Number** format to the values in the PivotTable with zero decimals and the **1000 separator**.

11 **Insert** a row above the PivotTable, and in cell **A1**, type **Aquatics Program Purchases** and then apply the **Title** cell style. **Rename** the sheet **Aquatics Purchases**

12 Click in the PivotTable, and then insert a **3-D Pie PivotChart**. Move the chart to a new sheet with the name **Aquatic Supplies Chart**

13 Display the **Field List** and then modify the chart so that only the **Supplier** field displays in the **Axis (Categories)** area. Remove any fields that display in the **Legend (Series) area**.

14 Apply **Style 3**, remove the legend from the chart, and display only the **Category Name** and **Percentage** data labels positioned in the **Center**. Format the data labels by changing the font size to **11**.

15 Change the chart title to **Aquatic Supply Purchases** and then change the font size to **24**. Hide all of the field buttons on the chart, and then insert a footer with the file name.

16 **Hide** the **Aquatics Revenue** sheet. Select all the sheets and insert a footer in the left section that includes the file name, and then center the worksheets **Horizontally** on the page. Change the **Orientation** to **Landscape** and scale the **Width** to fit to **1 page**.

17 Display the properties. As the **Tags**, type **aquatic revenue, supplies** and as the **Subject**, type your course name and section #. Under **Related People**, be sure that your name displays as Author. **Save** your workbook and then **Close** Excel.

18 In **MyLab IT**, locate and click the Grader Project Excel 4G Aquatics. In **step 3**, under **Upload Completed Assignment**, click **Choose File**. In the **Open** dialog box, navigate to your **Excel Chapter 4 folder**, and then click your **Student_Excel_4G_Aquatics** file one time to select it. In the lower right corner of the **Open** dialog box, click **Open**.

The name of your selected file displays above the Upload button.

19 To submit your file to **MyLab IT** for grading, click **Upload**, wait a moment for a green **Success!** message, and then in **step 4**, click the blue **Submit for Grading** button. Click **Close Assignment** to return to your list of **Course Materials**.

You have completed Project 4G END

Content-Based Assessments (Critical Thinking)

Apply a combination of the 4A and 4B skills.	**GO! Fix It**	**Project 4H Park Revenue**	IRC
	GO! Make It	**Project 4I City Services Revenue**	IRC
	GO! Solve It	**Project 4J Fixed Assets**	IRC
	GO! Solve It	**Project 4K Park Expenses**	

Project Files

For Project 4K, you will need the following file:

e04K_Park_Expenses

You will save your workbook as:

Lastname_Firstname_4K_Park_Expenses

Open the file **e04K_Park_Expenses** and save it as **Lastname_Firstname_4K_Park_Expenses** From the source data, create a PivotTable. Use the Month and Park fields as row labels. Use the Expense Item field as column labels. Place the Amount field in the Values area. Format the numbers to display zero decimal places and the 1000 separator. Format the PivotTable with an attractive style. Create a PivotChart on a separate sheet using the column chart style, and then use the report filters on the chart to show only the June data for Knight's Bridge, Five Points, and Sunset Parks, and only the expenses for Equipment, Grounds & Maintenance, and Utilities. Format the chart attractively. Hide the Park Expenses worksheet. On all sheets, insert the file name in the footer in the left section. Set the orientation to landscape and center horizontally. Add appropriate information to the document properties including the tags **park grounds** and submit as directed by your instructor.

		Performance Level		
		Exemplary	**Proficient**	**Developing**
Performance Criteria	**Create a PivotTable Report**	The PivotTable Report displays Month and Park row labels, Expense Item in Columns area, and Amount field in the Values area.	The PivotTable Report displays some of the items from the field list, but not all according to the directions.	The PivotTable was not created.
	Format a PivotTable Report	The PivotTable is formatted with the numbers displaying zero decimal places, the 1000 separator, and an attractive style.	The PivotTable is formatted with some but not all of the formatting, numbers displaying zero decimal places, the 1000 separator, and some attractive formatting.	The PivotTable was not formatted.
	Create and Format a PivotChart	A PivotChart displays on a separate sheet using the column chart style. The chart is filtered showing the data for June, only for Knight's Bridge, Five Points, and Sunset Parks, and only the expenses for Equipment, Grounds & Maintenance, and Utilities. The chart is formatted attractively.	A PivotChart displays on a separate sheet using the column chart style. The chart is filtered showing some but not all of the data for June, only for Knight's Bridge, Five Points, and Sunset Parks, and only the expenses for Equipment, Grounds & Maintenance, and Utilities. Some of the chart is formatted attractively.	The PivotChart was not created.

You have completed Project 4K | END

Rubric

The following outcomes-based assessments are open-ended assessments. That is, there is no specific correct result; your result will depend on your approach to the information provided. Make Professional Quality your goal. Use the following scoring rubric to guide you in how to approach the problem and then to evaluate how well your approach solves the problem.

The *criteria*—Software Mastery, Content, Format and Layout, and Process—represent the knowledge and skills you have gained that you can apply to solving the problem. The *levels of performance*—Professional Quality, Approaching Professional Quality, or Needs Quality Improvements—help you and your instructor evaluate your result.

	Your completed project is of Professional Quality if you:	Your completed project is Approaching Professional Quality if you:	Your completed project Needs Quality Improvements if you:
1-Software Mastery	Choose and apply the most appropriate skills, tools, and features and identify efficient methods to solve the problem.	Choose and apply some appropriate skills, tools, and features, but not in the most efficient manner.	Choose inappropriate skills, tools, or features, or are inefficient in solving the problem.
2-Content	Construct a solution that is clear and well organized, contains content that is accurate, appropriate to the audience and purpose, and is complete. Provide a solution that contains no errors of spelling, grammar, or style.	Construct a solution in which some components are unclear, poorly organized, inconsistent, or incomplete. Misjudge the needs of the audience. Have some errors in spelling, grammar, or style, but the errors do not detract from comprehension.	Construct a solution that is unclear, incomplete, or poorly organized, contains some inaccurate or inappropriate content, and contains many errors of spelling, grammar, or style. Do not solve the problem.
3-Format and Layout	Format and arrange all elements to communicate information and ideas, clarify function, illustrate relationships, and indicate relative importance.	Apply appropriate format and layout features to some elements, but not others. Overuse features, causing minor distraction.	Apply format and layout that does not communicate information or ideas clearly. Do not use format and layout features to clarify function, illustrate relationships, or indicate relative importance. Use available features excessively, causing distraction.
4-Process	Use an organized approach that integrates planning, development, self-assessment, revision, and reflection.	Demonstrate an organized approach in some areas, but not others; or, use an insufficient process of organization throughout.	Do not use an organized approach to solve the problem.

Outcomes-Based Assessments (Critical Thinking)

GO! Think	Project 4L Golf Course Revenue

Project Files

For Project 4L, you will need the following file:

e04L_Golf_Courses

You will save your workbook as:

Lastname_Firstname_4L_Golf_Courses

Open the file **e04L_Golf_Courses**, and then save it in your Excel Chapter 4 folder as **Lastname_Firstname_4L_Golf_Courses** From the source data, create a PivotTable and filter the report on Month. Use Course as the row labels and Item as the column labels. Sum the amounts and apply appropriate number formatting. Create a PivotChart report on a separate sheet for the 3rd Quarter Revenue. Exclude Logo Shirts and Golf Balls from the PivotChart, and then apply appropriate formatting. Hide the source data worksheet. Insert the file name in the left section of the footer on each page, center horizontally, set the orientation to landscape, add appropriate information to the document properties, including the tags **golf course revenue** and submit as directed by your instructor.

You have completed Project 4L | END

GO! Think	Project 4M Pool Expenses	IRC

You and GO!	Project 4N Inventory	IRC

Managing Large Workbooks and Using Advanced Sorting and Filtering

5

EXCEL 2019

PROJECT 5A

Outcomes
Manage and format large workbooks and save workbooks to share with others.

Objectives
1. Navigate and Manage Large Worksheets
2. Enhance Worksheets with Themes and Styles
3. Format a Worksheet to Share with Others
4. Save Excel Data in Other File Formats

PROJECT 5B

Outcomes
Analyze information in a database format using advanced sort, filter, subtotaling, and outlining.

Objectives
5. Use Advanced Sort Techniques
6. Use Custom and Advanced Filters
7. Subtotal, Outline, and Group a List of Data

Roman Samborskyi/Shutterstock

In This Chapter

 GO! To Work with Excel

In this chapter, you will navigate within a worksheet, insert a hyperlink in a worksheet, and save a worksheet as a webpage or other file format that you can share with others. You will practice applying and modifying themes, styles, lines, and borders to enhance the format of your worksheets. You will use Excel's advanced table features and database capabilities to organize data in a useful manner. You will use advanced sorting, sorting on multiple columns, and custom filtering to compare subsets of data. You will also limit data to display records that meet one or more specific conditions, add subtotals, and outline data.

The projects in this chapter relate to **Laurel College**. The college offers this diverse geographic area in Pennsylvania a wide range of academic and career programs, including associate degrees, certificate programs, and noncredit continuing education courses. Over 2,100 faculty and staff make student success a top priority. The college makes positive contributions to the community through cultural and athletic programs and partnerships with businesses and nonprofit organizations. The college also provides industry-specific training programs for local businesses through its Economic Development Center.

Project Activities

In Activities 5.01 through 5.13, you will assist Michael Schaeffler, Vice President of Instruction, in formatting and navigating a worksheet that lists the class schedule for three departments at Laurel College. You will also save Excel data in other file formats. The worksheets in your completed workbook will look similar to Figure 5.1.

Project Files for **MyLab IT Grader**

1. In your storage location, create a folder named **Excel Chapter 5**.
2. In your **MyLab IT** course, locate and click **Excel 5A Class Schedule**, Download Materials, and then Download All Files.
3. Extract the zipped folder to your Excel Chapter 5 folder. Close the Grader download screens.
4. Take a moment to open the downloaded **Excel_5A_Class_Schedule_Instructions**; note any recent updates to the book.

Project Results

GO! Project 5A

Where We're Going

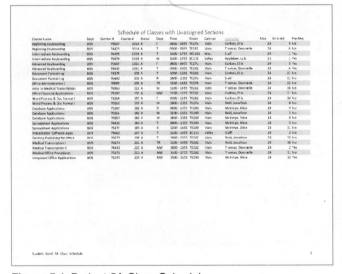

Figure 5.1 Project 5A Class Schedule

For Non-MyLab Submissions

For Project 5A, you will need:

e05A_Class_Schedule

e05A_Faculty_Contacts

e05A_Teaching_Requests

In your storage location, create a folder named **Excel Chapter 5**

In your Excel Chapter 5 folder, save your workbook as:

Lastname_Firstname_5A_Class_Schedule

If your instructor requires a workbook with formulas, save as:

Lastname_Firstname_5A_Class_Schedule_formulas

After you have named and saved your workbook, on the next page, begin with Step 2.

5
EXCEL

ALERT Because Office 365 is a cloud-based subscription service that receives continuous updates, you may encounter some variations in what appears on your screen and what is shown in this instruction. Microsoft Office 365 is fully installed on your PC or Mac; no internet access is necessary to create or edit documents. When you are connected to the internet, you will receive monthly upgrades and new features, so you always have the latest versions of Office apps as soon as they are available. Your subscription gives you continuous free access to the latest innovations and refinements.

GO! Learn How
Video E5-1

Because you may not be able to view all the columns and rows of a large worksheet on your screen at one time, Excel provides features that help you control the screen display and navigate the worksheet so you can locate information quickly. For example, you can hide columns or use the *Freeze Panes* command, which sets the column and row titles so that they remain on the screen while you scroll. The locked rows and columns become separate *panes*—portions of a worksheet window bounded by and separated from other portions by vertical or horizontal lines.

You can also use the *Find* command to find and select specific text, formatting, or a type of information within the workbook quickly.

Activity 5.01 | Using the Go To Special Command

Use the *Go To Special* command to move to cells that have special characteristics, for example, to cells that are blank or to cells that contain constants as opposed to formulas.

1 Navigate to your **Excel Chapter 5 folder**, and then double-click the Excel file you downloaded from **MyLab IT** that displays your name—**Student_Excel_5A_Class_Schedule**.

This worksheet lists the computer courses that are available for the upcoming semester in three college departments.

2 On the **Home tab,** in the **Editing group**, click **Find & Select**, and then click **Go To Special**. Compare your screen with Figure 5.2.

In the Go To Special dialog box, you can click an option button to move to cells that contain the special options listed.

MAC TIP Press ⌃control + G, and then click Special.

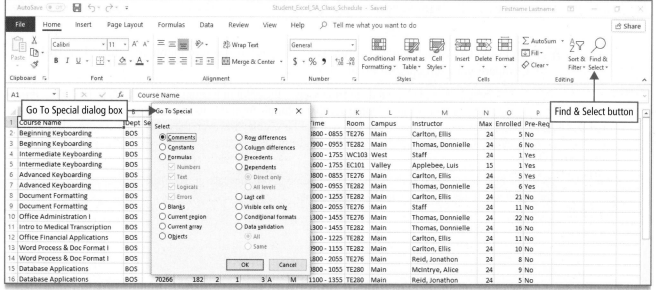

Figure 5.2

3 In the first column, click **Blanks**, and then click **OK**.

The blank cell—J33—in the *active area* of the worksheet is located and selected. The active area is the area of the worksheet that contains data or has contained data—it does not include any empty cells that have not been used in this worksheet. Cell J33 is missing the time for a Linux/UNIX Fundamentals class held on Wednesday.

4 On the **Home tab**, in the **Font group**, click the **Fill Color arrow** 🎨▾ and then under **Standard Colors**, click **Yellow** to highlight the blank cell.

This missing information must be researched before a time can be entered, and the yellow fill color will help locate this cell later, when the correct time for the class is determined.

5 Save 💾 your workbook and compare your screen with Figure 5.3.

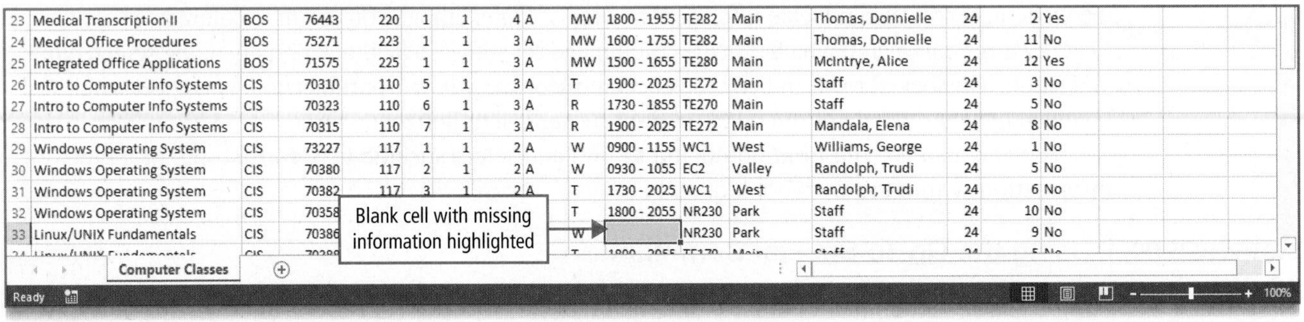

23	Medical Transcription II	BOS	76443	220	1	1	4 A	MW	1800 - 1955	TE282	Main	Thomas, Donnielle	24	2 Yes
24	Medical Office Procedures	BOS	75271	223	1	1	3 A	MW	1600 - 1755	TE282	Main	Thomas, Donnielle	24	11 No
25	Integrated Office Applications	BOS	71575	225	1	1	3 A	MW	1500 - 1655	TE280	Main	McIntrye, Alice	24	12 Yes
26	Intro to Computer Info Systems	CIS	70310	110	5	1	3 A	T	1900 - 2025	TE272	Main	Staff	24	3 No
27	Intro to Computer Info Systems	CIS	70323	110	6	1	3 A	R	1730 - 1855	TE270	Main	Staff	24	5 No
28	Intro to Computer Info Systems	CIS	70315	110	7	1	3 A	R	1900 - 2025	TE272	Main	Mandala, Elena	24	8 No
29	Windows Operating System	CIS	73227	117	1	1	2 A	W	0900 - 1155	WC1	West	Williams, George	24	1 No
30	Windows Operating System	CIS	70380	117	2	1	2 A	W	0930 - 1055	EC2	Valley	Randolph, Trudi	24	5 No
31	Windows Operating System	CIS	70382	117	3	1	2 A	T	1730 - 2025	WC1	West	Randolph, Trudi	24	6 No
32	Windows Operating System	CIS	70358					T	1800 - 2055	NR230	Park	Staff	24	10 No
33	Linux/UNIX Fundamentals	CIS	70386					W		NR230	Park	Staff	24	9 No
34	Linux/UNIX Fundamentals	CIS	70389					T	1800 - 2055	TE170	Main	Staff	24	5 No

Blank cell with missing information highlighted →

Computer Classes   ⊕

Ready

100%

Figure 5.3

Activity 5.02 | Hiding Columns

In a large worksheet, you can hide columns that are not necessary for the immediate task, and then unhide them later. You can also hide columns or rows to control the data that will print or to remove confidential information from view—hidden data does not print. For example, to create a summary report, you can hide the columns between the row titles and the totals column, and the hidden columns would not display on the printed worksheet, resulting in a summary report.

1 Press Ctrl + Home to make cell **A1** the active cell. From the column heading area, select **columns E:G**.

💻 **MAC TIP** Press control + fn + ← to make cell A1 the active cell.

2 Right-click over the selected columns to display the shortcut menu, and then click **Hide**. Compare your screen with Figure 5.4.

Columns E, F, and G are hidden from view—the column headings skip from D to H. A dark line between columns D and H indicates that columns from this location are hidden from view. After you click in another cell, this line will not be visible; however, the column letters provide a visual indication that some columns are hidden from view.

💻 **MAC TIP** Select the columns that you want to hide. On the Home tab, in the Cells group, click Format. Under Visibility, point to Hide & Unhide, and then click Hide Columns.

	A	B	C	D	H	I	J	K	L	M	N	O	P	Q	R	S	T	U
	Course Name	Dept	Section #	Course #	Status	Days	Time	Room	Campus	Instructor	Max	Enrolled	Pre-Req					
1	Course Name	Dept	Section #	Course #	Status	Days	Time	Room	Campus	Instructor	Max	Enrolled	Pre-Req					
2	Beginning Keyboarding	BOS	75007	101	A	F	0800 - 0855	TE276	Main	Carlton, Ellis	24	5	No					
3	Beginning Keyboarding	BOS	74423	101A	A	T	0900 - 0955	TE282	Main	Thomas, Donnielle	24	6	No					
4	Intermediate Keyboarding	BOS	76455	101B	A	T	1600 - 1755	WC103	West	Staff	24	1	Yes					
5	Intermediate Keyboarding	BOS					00 - 1755	EC101	Valley	Applebee, Luis	15	1	Yes					
6	Advanced Keyboarding	BOS					00 - 0855	TE276	Main	Carlton, Ellis	24	5	Yes					
7	Advanced Keyboarding	BOS					00 - 0955	TE282	Main	Thomas, Donnielle	24	6	Yes					
8	Document Formatting	BOS	74376	102	A	T	1000 - 1255	TE282	Main	Carlton, Ellis	24	21	No					
9	Document Formatting	BOS	76442	102	A	R	1800 - 2055	TE276	Main	Staff	24	11	No					
10	Office Administration I	BOS	70685	105	A	TR	1300 - 1455	TE276	Main	Thomas, Donnielle	24	22	No					
11	Intro to Medical Transcription	BOS	76563	112	A	M	1300 - 1455	TE282	Main	Thomas, Donnielle	24	16	No					

Columns E, F, and G are hidden from view

E1 — ID #

Figure 5.4

🔄 **ANOTHER WAY** Select the columns that you want to hide. On the Home tab, in the Cells group, click Format. Under Visibility, point to Hide & Unhide, and then click Hide Columns.

3 Notice that the line between the **column D heading** and the **column H heading** is slightly wider, indicating hidden columns. Make cell **A1** the active cell, and then **Save** 💾 your workbook.

MORE KNOWLEDGE **Unhiding Columns**

To unhide columns, drag to select the columns on both sides of the hidden columns. Right-click over the selection, and then click Unhide.

Activity 5.03 | Using the Go To Command and the COUNTIF Function

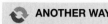

1.2.2

Use the *Go To* command to move to a specific cell or range of cells in a large worksheet.

1 On the **Home tab**, in the **Editing group**, click **Find & Select**, and then click **Go To**. In the **Go To** dialog box, with the insertion point blinking in the **Reference** box, type **m50** and then click **OK**.

💻 **MAC TIP** Press [control] + [G], and then click in the Reference box. Type m50 and click OK.

2 With cell **M50** active, on the **Formulas tab**, in the **Functions Library group**, click **More Functions**, point to **Statistical**, scroll down the list, and then click **COUNTIF**. As the **Range**, type **m2:m49** and as the **Criteria**, type **Staff** to count the number of courses that are assigned to Staff and still need an instructor assignment. Click **OK**. Compare your screen with Figure 5.5.

Your result is 13, indicating that 13 courses still need an instructor assigned.

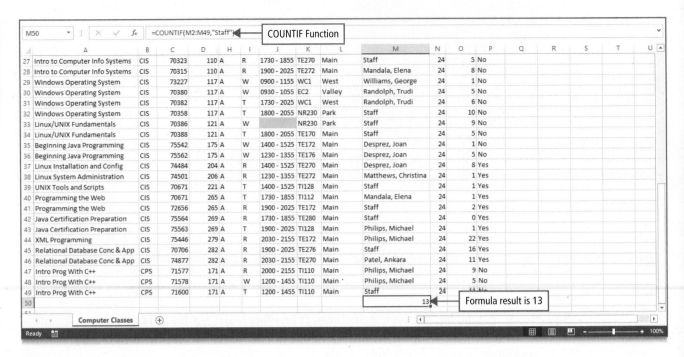

Figure 5.5

3 In cell **J50**, type **Unassigned classes** and press Enter.

4 Press Ctrl + Home to make cell **A1** the active cell, and then **Save** 💾 your workbook.

Activity 5.04 | Arranging Multiple Workbooks and Splitting Worksheets

MOS
1.4.4

If you need to refer to information in one workbook while you have another workbook open, you can arrange the window to display sheets from more than one workbook—instead of jumping back and forth between the two workbooks from the taskbar. This is accomplished by using the ***Arrange All*** command, which tiles all open Excel windows on the screen. Additionally, you can view separate parts of the *same* worksheet on your screen by using the ***Split*** command, which splits the window into multiple resizable panes to view distant parts of your worksheet at once.

1 Click **File** and then click **Open**. Click **Browse** and then navigate to the files you downloaded for this project. Click **e05A_Teaching_Requests**, and then click **Open**.

This worksheet contains a list of instructors who submitted requests for classes they would like to teach. You do not need to save this file; it is for reference only.

2 On the **View tab**, in the **Window group**, click **Switch Windows**, and then click your **5A_Class_Schedule** file to make it the active worksheet.

🖥 **MAC TIP**   In the e05A_Teaching_Requests file, notice that in row 3, Martin Clark would like to teach section 71600. Close the e05A_Teaching Requests workbook. In your 5A_Class_Schedule worksheet, press control + fn + → to move to the last cell in the workbook—P50. Skip to step 6.

---

3 On the **View tab**, in the **Window group**, click **Arrange All**. Click **Horizontal** and then compare your screen with Figure 5.6.

Here, in the Arrange Windows dialog box, you can control how two or more worksheets from multiple open workbooks are arranged on the screen.

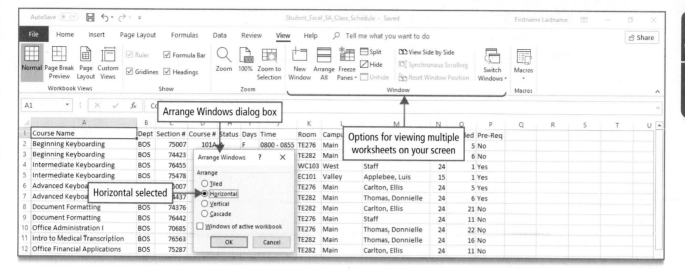

Figure 5.6

4 Click **OK**. Compare your screen with Figure 5.7.

The screen is split horizontally, and the **e05A_Teaching_Requests** worksheet displays below your Lastname_Firstname_5A_Class_Schedule worksheet. The active window title bar displays the file name in a darker shade of gray, and the row and column headings are shaded to indicate active cells. When multiple worksheets are open on the screen, only one is active at a time. To activate a worksheet, click anywhere on the worksheet or click the worksheet's title bar.

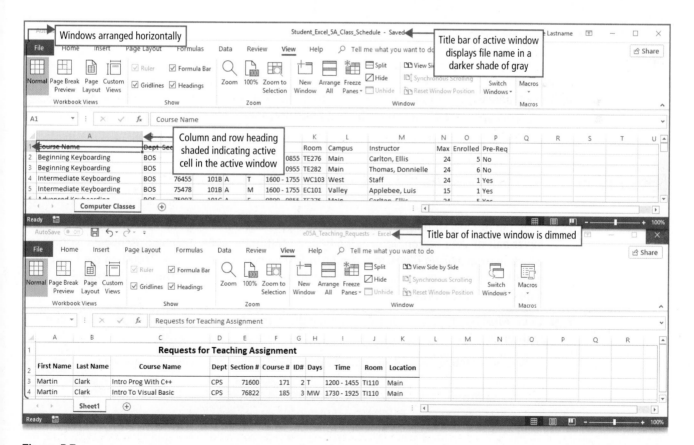

Figure 5.7

5 Press `Ctrl` + `End` to move to cell **P50**, which is now the end of the active area of the worksheet.

6 Click cell **A50**. On the **View tab**, in the **Window group**, click **Split** to split this upper window horizontally at row 50. Compare your screen with Figure 5.8.

A light gray horizontal bar displays at the top of row 50, and two sets of vertical scroll bars display in the Lastname_Firstname_5A_Class_Schedule worksheet—one in each of the two worksheet panes displayed in this window. You can drag the horizontal bar up slightly to make the lower pane easier to see.

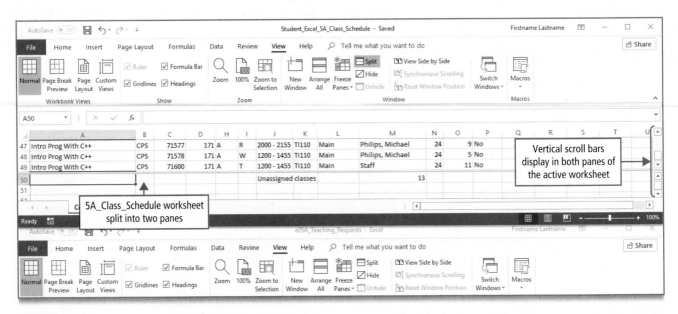

Figure 5.8

7 Click above the **split bar**, press `Ctrl` + `Home` and then click in any cell in **column C**. Press `Ctrl` + `F` to display the **Find tab** of the **Find and Replace** dialog box.

Column C lists the Section # for each class. This is a unique number that identifies each class.

BY TOUCH On the Home tab, in the Editing group, tap Find.

---

8 Drag the title bar of the dialog box into the upper right area of your screen. Then, in the lower half of your screen, look at the first request in the **e05A_Teaching_Requests** worksheet, which is from *Martin Clark* to teach *Intro Prog with C++, Section # 71600*. In the **Find what** box, type **71600** so that you can locate the course in the **Lastname_Firstname_5A_ Class_Schedule** worksheet.

9 Click **Find Next**, be sure that you can see the **Name Box**, and then compare your screen with Figure 5.9.

Section # 71600 is located and selected in cell C49 of the Class Schedule worksheet.

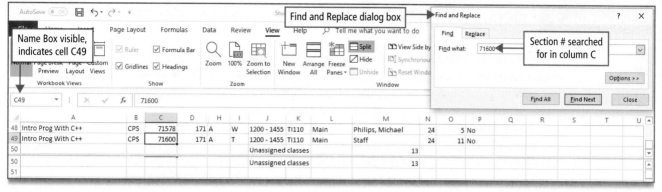

Figure 5.9

10 In your **Lastname_Firstname_5A_Class_Schedule** worksheet, click in cell **M49**, type **Clark, Martin** to replace *Staff* and assign the class to Mr. Clark. Press Enter.

> The class is assigned to Mr. Clark, and the number of unassigned classes, which you can view below the split bar, decreases by one, to 12. Use the Split command when you need to see two distant parts of the same worksheet simultaneously.

MAC TIP Close the Find dialog box, and then in cell M49, type Clark, Martin.

11 In the **Find and Replace** dialog box, click **Close**, and then compare your screen with Figure 5.10.

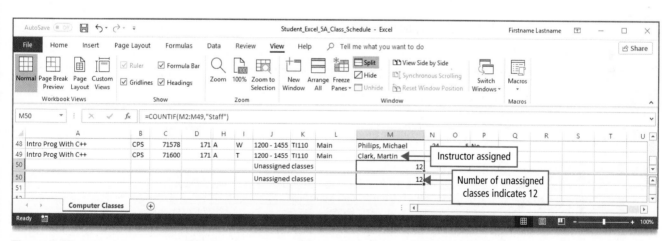

Figure 5.10

12 Click anywhere in the **e05A_Teaching_Requests** workbook, and then click **Close** ✕ to close the workbook. On the title bar of your **Lastname_Firstname_5A_Class_Schedule** workbook, click **Maximize** ☐ to restore the size of the worksheet to its full size.

13 On the **View tab**, in the **Window group**, click **Split** to remove the split.

14 Press Ctrl + Home, and then **Save** 🖫 your workbook.

Individuals commonly use worksheets to communicate information both within an organization and to the public. A worksheet might be seen by individuals in an email, in a PowerPoint presentation, or in public blogs and publications. Accordingly, you will want to use some creative elements when preparing your worksheets.

Recall that a theme is a predesigned set of colors, fonts, lines, and fill effects that look good together and that can be applied to your workbook. A theme combines two sets of fonts—one for text and one for headings. In the default Office theme, Calibri Light is the font for headings and Calibri is the font for body text.

Activity 5.05 | Changing and Customizing a Workbook Theme

In Excel, the applied theme has a set of complementary *cell styles*—a defined set of formatting characteristics, such as fonts, font sizes, font colors, cell borders, and cell shading. The applied theme also has a set of complementary table styles for data that you format as a table.

1 Point to the **row 1 heading** to display the ➡ pointer, right-click, and then click **Insert** to insert a new blank row.

MAC TIP   Hold down (control), and then click the row 1 heading to display the shortcut menu. Then click Insert.

2 In cell **A1**, type **Schedule of Classes with Unassigned Sections** and press (Enter). **Merge & Center** this title across the range **A1:P1**, and then apply the **Title** cell style.

3 On the **Page Layout tab**, in the **Themes group**, click **Themes**. Compare your screen with Figure 5.11.

A gallery of predesigned themes displays.

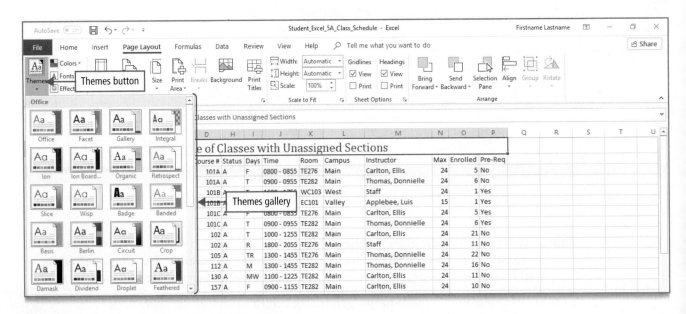

Figure 5.11

4 Point to several of the themes and notice how Live Preview displays the colors and fonts associated with each theme. Then, click the **Ion** theme.

5 In the **Themes group**, click **Fonts**.

The font associated with the Ion theme for both headings and body text is Century Gothic, but you can customize a theme by mixing the Colors, Fonts, and Effects from any of the supplied themes.

6 At the top of the Fonts list, click **Office** to change the Theme Fonts for this workbook. **Save** 🖫 your workbook.

Activity 5.06 | Creating and Applying a Custom Table Style

Excel comes with many predefined table styles, but if none of these meets your needs, you can create and apply a custom table style of your own design. Custom table styles that you create are stored only in the current workbook, so they are not available in other workbooks.

1 On the **Home tab**, in the **Styles group**, click **Format as Table**. At the bottom, click **New Table Style**.

2 In the **New Table Style** dialog box, in the **Name** box, replace the existing text by typing **Class Schedule**

3 In the list under **Table Element**, click **First Row Stripe**, and then compare your screen with Figure 5.12.

Here you can select one or more elements of the table, and then customize the format for each element.

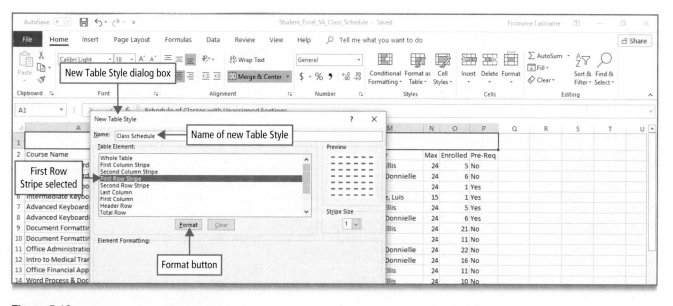

Figure 5.12

4 Below the list of table elements, click **Format**. In the **Format Cells** dialog box, click the **Fill tab**. In the fourth column of colors, click the second color, and notice that the **Sample** area previews the color you selected. Compare your screen with Figure 5.13.

MAC TIP Click the Background color arrow to display the color palette.

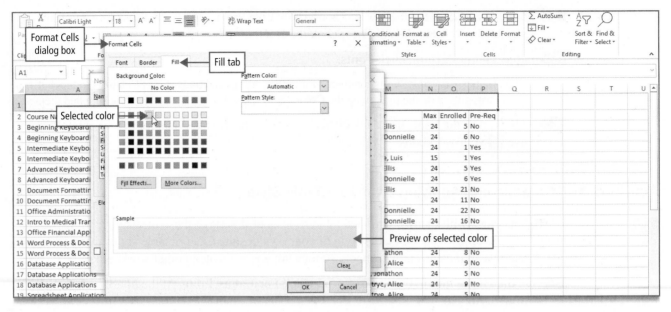

Figure 5.13

5 Click **OK**, notice the **Preview**, and then in the lower left corner of the dialog box, click to select the check box **Set as default table style for this document**. Click **OK**.

You must select this check box to make your table style available in the gallery of table styles.

6 Select the range **A2:P50**—do *not* include rows 1 and 51 in your selection. In the **Styles group**, click **Format as Table**. At the top of the gallery, under **Custom**, point to your custom table style to display the ScreenTip *Class Schedule*. Compare your screen with Figure 5.14.

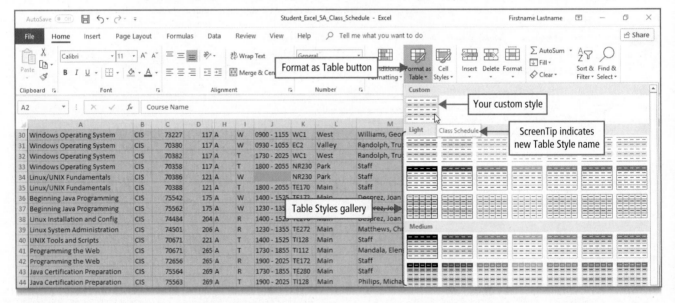

Figure 5.14

7 Click your **Class Schedule** table style, and then in the **Format As Table** dialog box, click **OK**.

8 Press Ctrl + Home to deselect and move to cell **A1**, and then **Save** 💾 your workbook.

Objective 3 Format a Worksheet to Share with Others

GO! Learn How

Video E5-3

You can share a worksheet with others by printing and distributing paper copies, sending it electronically as an Excel file or some other file format, or posting it to the web or to a shared workspace. Regardless of how you distribute the information, a large worksheet will be easier for others to view if you insert appropriate page breaks and repeat column or row titles at the top of each page.

You can also add a *hyperlink* to a worksheet, which, when clicked, takes you to another location in the worksheet, to another file, or to a webpage on the internet or on your organization's intranet.

Activity 5.07 | Previewing and Modifying Page Breaks

1.4.2

Before you print or electronically distribute a large worksheet, preview it to see where the pages will break across the columns and rows. You can move the page breaks to a column or row that groups the data logically, and you can change the orientation between portrait and landscape if you want to display more rows on the page (portrait) or more columns on the page (landscape). You can also apply *scaling* to the data to force the worksheet into a selected number of pages. Scaling adjusts the horizontal and vertical size of the printed data by a percentage or by the number of pages that you specify.

1 Click **File** and then click **Print** to display the **Print Preview**. Notice that as currently formatted, the worksheet will print on 4 pages.

2 At the bottom of the **Print Preview**, click **Next Page** ▶ three times to view the four pages required to print this worksheet.

As you view each page, notice that pages 3 and 4 display the Room, Campus, Instructor, Max, Enrolled, and Pre-Req columns that relate to the first two pages of the printout. You can see that the printed worksheet will be easier to read if all the information related to a class is on the same page.

3 Click **Back** ◉ to return to the worksheet. Click the **View tab**, and then in the **Workbook Views group**, click **Page Break Preview**. Compare your screen with Figure 5.15.

The Page Break Preview window displays blue dashed lines to show where the page breaks are in the current page layout for this worksheet.

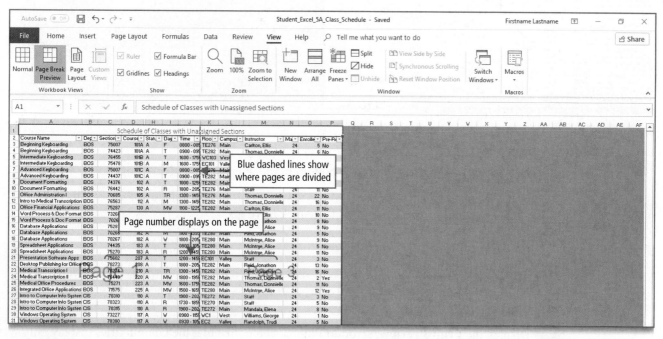

Figure 5.15

4 Scroll down to view the other pages and see where the page breaks are indicated. Then, in the **Workbook Views group**, click **Normal** to redisplay the worksheet in Normal view.

Dashed lines display at the page break locations on the worksheet.

5 On the **Page Layout tab**, in the **Page Setup group**, set the **Orientation** to **Landscape**. In the **Scale to Fit group**, click the **Width arrow**, and then click **1 page**.

In the Scale to Fit group, there are two ways to override the default printout size. In the Scale box, you can specify a scaling factor from between 10 and 400 percent. Or, you can use the Width and Height arrows to fit the printout to a specified number of pages.

6 Display the **Page Setup** dialog box. Click **Header/Footer**, and then click **Custom Footer**. In the **Left section**, insert the **file name**, and then click in the **Right section**. Click **Insert Page Number** 🔢, and then click **OK** two times.

It is good practice to insert any headers or footers *before* making the final page break decisions on your worksheet.

7 Display the **Print Preview**, and at the bottom, notice that the worksheet is now a total of two pages.

By applying the scaling, each complete row of data will fit on one page.

8 Return to the worksheet. On the **View tab**, click **Page Break Preview**. Scroll to view the page break between **Page 1** and **Page 2**.

9 Point to the horizontal page break line between **Page 1** and **Page 2**. When the resize pointer ↕ displays, drag the line up between **row 26** and **row 27**; this will break the pages between the BOS courses and the CIS courses. Compare your screen with Figure 5.16.

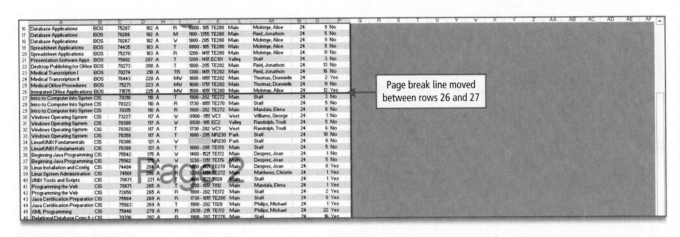

Figure 5.16

10 Display the **Print Preview**. At the bottom of the window, click **Next Page** to view **Page 2**.

11 Return to the worksheet. On the list of view buttons on the right side of the **Status bar**, click **Normal** ▦. Press Ctrl + Home, and then click **Save** 💾.

Activity 5.08 | Repeating Column or Row Titles

Recall that when your worksheet layout spans multiple pages, you will typically want to repeat the column titles on each page. If your worksheet is wider than one page, you will also want to repeat the row titles on each page.

1 Display the **Print Preview**, scroll to **Page 2**, and notice that the column titles display only on the first page. Return to the worksheet.

Repeating the column titles on each page will make it easier to understand and read the information on the pages.

2 On the **Page Layout tab**, in the **Page Setup group**, click **Print Titles** to display the **Sheet tab** of the **Page Setup** dialog box.

Here you can select rows to repeat at the top of each page and columns to repeat at the left of each page.

3 Under **Print titles**, click in the **Rows to repeat at top** box, and then from the **row heading area**, select **row 2**. Compare your screen with Figure 5.17.

A moving border surrounds row 2, and the mouse pointer displays as a black, select-row arrow. The absolute reference $2:$2 displays in the Rows to repeat at top box.

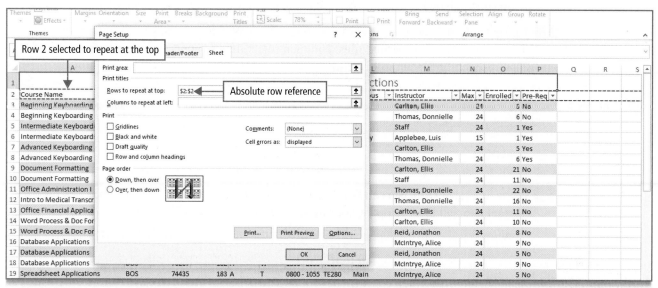

Figure 5.17

4 Click **OK**. Display the **Print Preview**, display **Page 2**, and notice that the column titles display at the top of the page. Compare your screen with Figure 5.18. **Save** your workbook.

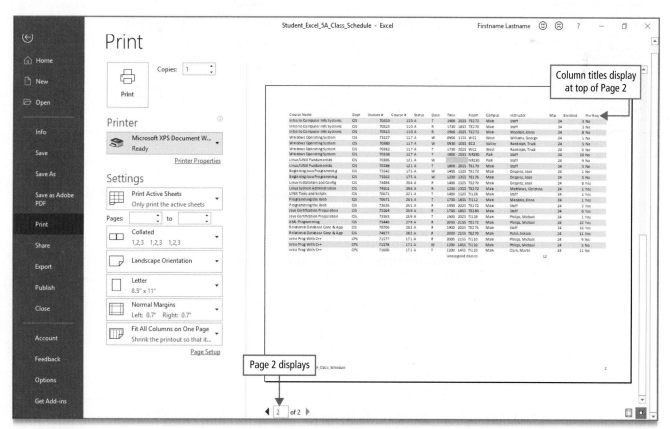

Figure 5.18

Activity 5.09 | Inserting a Hyperlink in a Worksheet

1.2.3

Recall that a hyperlink is colored and underlined text that you can click to go to a file, a location in a file, a webpage on the internet, or a webpage on your organization's intranet. Hyperlinks can be attached to text or to graphics. In this Activity, you will add a hyperlink that will open a file containing the contact information for instructors.

1 Click cell **M2**. On the **Insert tab**, in the **Links group**, click **Link** to display the **Insert Hyperlink** dialog box.

2 Under **Link to**, if necessary, click Existing File or Web Page. Click the **Look in arrow**, navigate to your downloaded files, and then select the file **e05A_Faculty_Contacts**, which contains faculty contact information.

> **MAC TIP** With Web Page or File selected, to the right of Address, click Select. Navigate to your downloaded files, click **e05A_Faculty_Contacts**, and then click Open.

3 In the upper right corner of the **Insert Hyperlink** dialog box, click **ScreenTip**.

4 In the **Set Hyperlink ScreenTip** dialog box, in the **ScreenTip text** box, type **Click here for contact info** and then compare your dialog box with Figure 5.19.

When you point to the hyperlink on the worksheet, this is the text of the ScreenTip that will display.

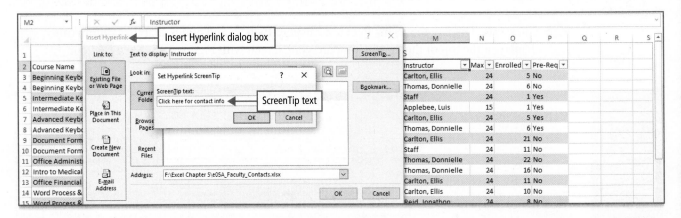

Figure 5.19

5 In the **Set Hyperlink ScreenTip** dialog box, click **OK** and then in the **Insert Hyperlink** dialog box, click **OK**.

In the Ion theme, the color for a hyperlink is light blue.

6 Point to the **Instructor hyperlink** and read the ScreenTip that displays. Compare your screen with Figure 5.20.

When you point to the hyperlink, the Link Select pointer 🖑 displays and the ScreenTip text displays.

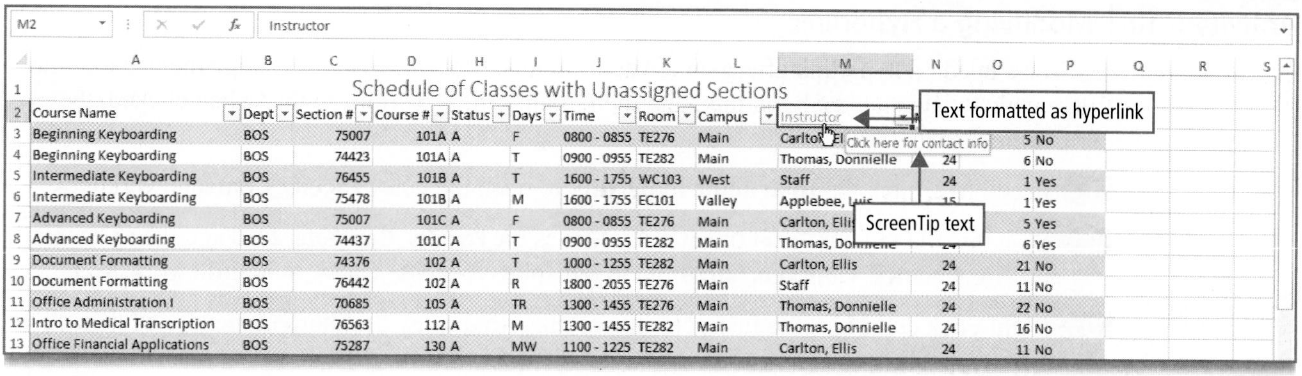

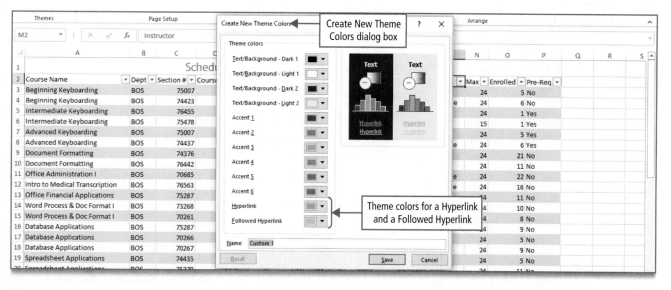

Figure 5.20

7 Click the **Instructor hyperlink**.

The **e05A_Faculty_Contacts** file opens in a new window and displays the contact information.

8 Close ⊠ the **e05A_Faculty_Contacts** file and redisplay your **5A_Class_Schedule** worksheet.

MAC TIP   Skip steps 9 and 10 and continue with Activity 5.10.

---

9 On the **Page Layout** tab, in the **Themes group**, click the **Colors arrow**. At the bottom of the gallery, click **Customize Colors**. Locate the colors for **Hyperlink** and **Followed Hyperlink**, and then compare your screen with Figure 5.21.

Each color scheme uses a set of colors for a hyperlink and for a hyperlink that has been clicked (followed) one time. Now that you have followed your inserted hyperlink one time, the text displays in the Followed Hyperlink color. Here you can also change the colors for any of the colors associated with a theme.

Figure 5.21

10 In the lower right corner of the dialog box, click **Cancel**, and then **Save** 🖫 your workbook.

Activity 5.10 | Modifying a Hyperlink

You can edit a hyperlink after you create it. In this Activity, you will change the name of the file to which you created a hyperlink, and then modify the hyperlink so that when clicked, the correct file displays.

1 In cell **M2**, click the **Instructor hyperlink** to open the **e05A_Faculty_Contacts** workbook.

2 Save this file in your **Excel Chapter 5** folder as **5A_Faculty_Contacts_2020** and then **Close** ⊠ the **5A_Faculty_Contacts_2020** file to redisplay your **5A_Class_Schedule** worksheet.

3 Right-click cell **M2**—the Instructor hyperlink—to display the shortcut menu, and then click **Edit Hyperlink**.

4 In the **Edit Hyperlink** dialog box, click the **Look in arrow**, navigate to your **Excel Chapter 5 folder**, and then select **5A_Faculty_Contacts_2020**. Compare your screen with Figure 5.22.

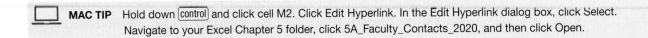
MAC TIP Hold down `control` and click cell M2. Click Edit Hyperlink. In the Edit Hyperlink dialog box, click Select. Navigate to your Excel Chapter 5 folder, click 5A_Faculty_Contacts_2020, and then click Open.

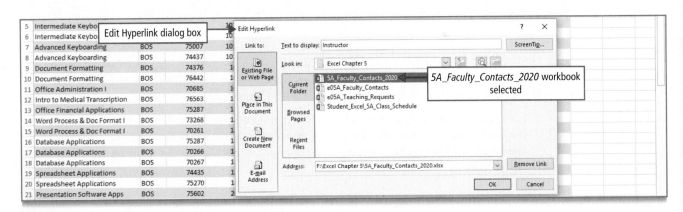

Figure 5.22

5 Click **OK**. In cell **M2**, click the hyperlinked text—**Instructor**.

6 Click **Close** ⊠ to close **5A_Faculty_Contacts_2020**.

7 Display the workbook **Properties**. As the **Tags**, type **class schedule** and as the **Subject**, type your course name and section number. Under **Related People**, be sure that your name displays as **Author**. **Save** the workbook and **Close** Excel.

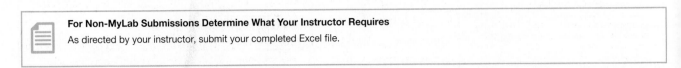
For Non-MyLab Submissions Determine What Your Instructor Requires
As directed by your instructor, submit your completed Excel file.

8 In **MyLab IT**, locate and click the Grader Project **Excel 5A Class Schedule**. In **step 3**, under **Upload Completed Assignment**, click **Choose File**. In the **Open** dialog box, navigate to your **Excel Chapter 5 folder**, and then click your **Student_Excel_5A_Class_Schedule** file one time to select it. In the lower right corner of the **Open** dialog box, click **Open**.

The name of your selected file displays above the Upload button.

> **9** To submit your file to **MyLab IT** for grading, click **Upload**, wait a moment for a green **Success!** message, and then in **step 4**, click the blue **Submit for Grading** button. Click **Close Assignment** to return to your list of **Course Materials**.

You have completed Project 5A | **END**

Objective 4 | Save Excel Data in Other File Formats

ALERT **Activities 5.11, 5.12, and 5.13 are Optional**

Activities 5.11, 5.12, and 5.13, in which you save your Excel workbook in various file formats, are optional. Check with your instructor to see if you should complete these three Activities. These Activities are not included in the **MyLab IT** Grader system.

GO! Learn How
Video E5-4

By default, Excel files are saved in the Excel Workbook file format with the *.xlsx file name extension*, which is a set of characters that helps your Windows operating system understand what kind of information is in a file and what program should open it.

Using the Save As command, you can choose to save an Excel file in another file format from the Save as type list. Some frequently used file formats are: Excel 97-2003 Workbook, Excel Template, Single File Web Page, Web Page, Excel Macro-Enabled Workbook, Text (Tab delimited), and CSV (Comma delimited).

For the purpose of posting Excel data to a website or transferring data to other applications, you can save your Excel file in a variety of other file formats. For example, saving an Excel worksheet as a *tab delimited text file* separates the cells of each row with tab characters. Saving an Excel worksheet as a *CSV (comma separated values) file* separates the cells of each row with commas. This type of file is also referred to as a *comma delimited file*. Text formats are commonly used to import data into a database program.

You can also save an Excel file in an electronic format that is easy to read for the viewer of the workbook. Such files are not easily modified and are an electronic printed version of the worksheet.

Activity 5.11 | Viewing and Saving a Workbook as a Web Page

1.5.2

Before you save a worksheet as a webpage, it is a good idea to view it as a webpage to see how it will display. When saving a multiple-page workbook as a webpage, all of the worksheets are available and can be accessed. You can also save a single worksheet as a webpage. Excel changes the contents of the worksheet into *HTML (Hypertext Markup Language)*, which is a language web browsers can interpret, when you save a worksheet as a webpage. In this Activity, you will save and publish a worksheet as a webpage.

> **1** Open your **Student_Excel_5A_Class_Schedule** workbook. Click **File**, and then click **Save As**. Click **Browse**, and then in the lower portion of the dialog box, click the **Save as type arrow**, and click **Web Page**.

> Your Excel files no longer display in the dialog box, because only files with the type Web Page are visible. The file type changes to Web Page, and additional web-based options display below.

> **2** In the lower portion of the dialog box, click **Change Title**.

> The text that you type here will become the title when the file displays as a webpage.

> **3** In the **Enter Text** dialog box, in the **Page title** box, using your own name, type **Computer Courses Lastname Firstname** and then compare your screen with Figure 5.23.

🖥 **MAC TIP** Click Web Options. On the General tab, click in the Web page title box, and type the title. Click OK, and then skip to Step 8.

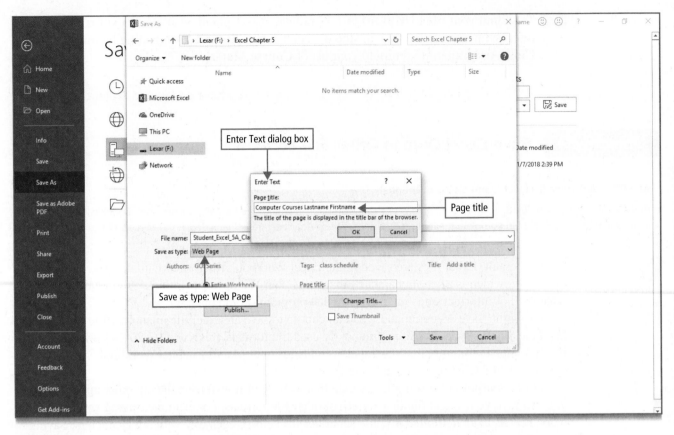

Figure 5.23

> **4** In the **Enter Text** dialog box, click **OK**, and notice that in the **Page title** box, your typed text displays.

> **5** In the **Save As** dialog box, click **Publish**.

> **6** In the **Publish as Web Page** dialog box, click the **Choose arrow**, notice the objects that can be published as a webpage, and then click **Items on Computer Classes** to select the *Computer Classes* sheet. In the lower left corner, select the **Open published web page in browser** check box. Compare your screen with Figure 5.24.

> Under Item to publish, you can choose which elements to include. You can select the entire workbook, a specific worksheet in the workbook, a range of cells, or previously published items that you are modifying. The Open published web page in browser selection ensures that the internet browser software will automatically start and display the page.

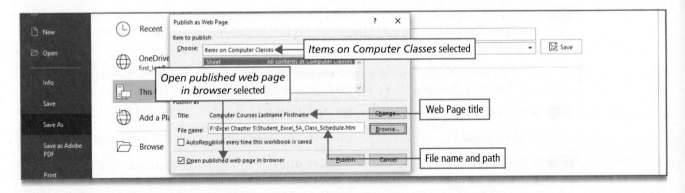

Figure 5.24

7 Click **Browse** to display the **Publish As** dialog box.

8 Navigate to your **Excel Chapter 5 folder**. In the **File name** box, using your own name, type **Lastname_Firstname_Excel_5A_Schedule_Webpage** and then compare your screen with Figure 5.25.

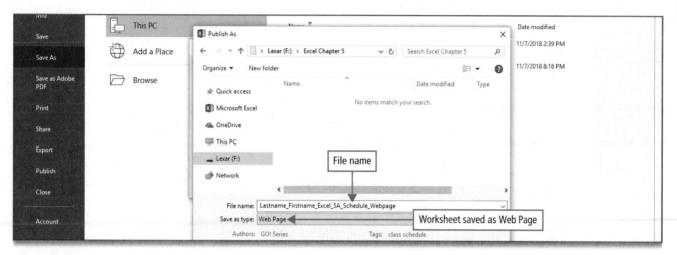

Figure 5.25

9 Click **OK**, and then in the **Publish as Web Page** dialog box, click **Publish**. Compare your screen with Figure 5.26.

The webpage is saved in your selected folder, and the Class Schedule file opens in your default internet browser. The browser tab displays the text you typed in the Enter Text dialog box.

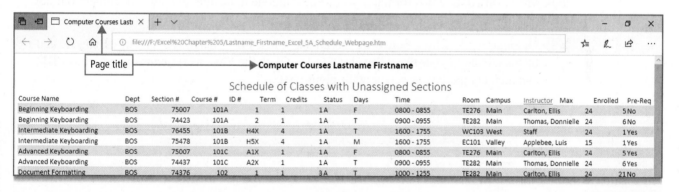

Figure 5.26

10 If you are instructed to print your webpage on paper, consult the instructions to print from your specific browser software.

Your printed results will vary depending on which browser software you are using. Do not be concerned about the printout; webpages are intended for viewing, not printing.

11 On the browser title bar, click **Close**, and then redisplay your **5A_Class_Schedule** Excel workbook.

Activity 5.12 | Saving Excel Data in CSV File Format

MOS
1.5.2

You can save an Excel worksheet as a comma separated values (CSV) file, which saves the contents of the cells by placing commas between them and an end-of-paragraph mark at the end of each row.

1 With your **5A_Class_Schedule** workbook open, display the **Save As** dialog box, click the **Save as type arrow**, and then click **CSV (Comma delimited)**. Be sure you save the file in your **Excel Chapter 5** folder. In the **File name** box, using your own name, type **Lastname_ Firstname_5A_Schedule_CSV** and then compare your screen with Figure 5.27.

Your Excel files no longer display, because only CSV files are displayed.

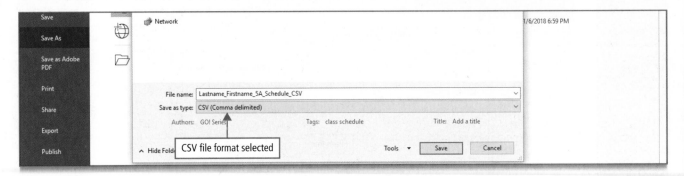

Figure 5.27

2 Click **Save** and then **Close** ☒ your file.

Activity 5.13 | Saving Excel Data as a PDF File

1.5.2

You can create portable documents to share across applications and platforms with accurate visual representations. To publish a document and ensure that the appearance of the document is the same no matter what computer it is displayed on, save the document in **PDF (Portable Document Format)**. PDF is a widely used format developed by Adobe Systems that lets you create a representation of *electronic paper* that displays your data on the screen as it would look when printed. Use this format if you want someone to be able to view a document but not change it.

1 **Open** your **5A_Class_Schedule** workbook. Click **File**, click **Save As**, click **Browse**, and then navigate to your **Excel Chapter 5** folder. Click the **Save as type arrow**, point to **PDF**, and then compare your screen with Figure 5.28.

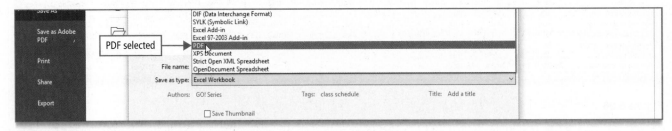

Figure 5.28

2 Click **PDF**, and then in the lower right section of the dialog box, if necessary, select the Open file after publishing check box. As the file name, using your own name, type **Lastname_Firstname_5A_Schedule_PDF** and then compare your screen with Figure 5.29.

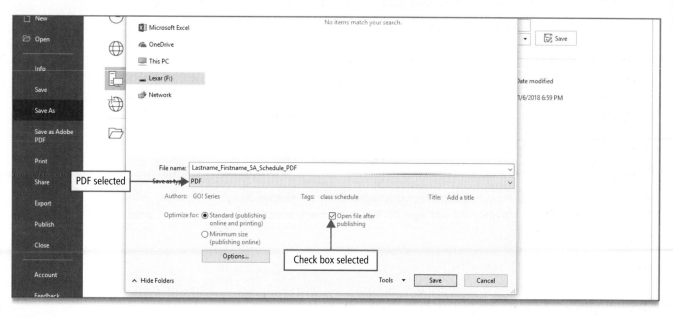

Figure 5.29

3 Click **Save**.

The file is saved in PDF format, and then opens as a PDF document using the default PDF program on your computer.

4 **Close** ☒ the **PDF** document. **Close** Excel and then submit your files from this project as directed by your instructor.

CONVERTING A TAB **Delimited Text File to a Word Table**

By choosing Text File as the file type, you can save an Excel worksheet as a text file, which saves the contents of the cells by placing a tab character, rather than commas, between the cells and an end-of-paragraph mark at the end of each row. This type of file can be readily exchanged with various database programs, in which it is referred to as a tab-delimited text file. A text file can be converted from tab-delimited text to a Word table. Word has a *Convert Text to Table* command that can easily convert a tabbed file into a table. A table displays in a row and column format, like an Excel spreadsheet.

You have completed the optional portion of this project **END**

Sorted, Filtered, and Outlined Database

Project Activities

In Activities 5.14 through 5.20, you will use advanced table features to provide Dr. Kesia Toomer, the Dean of the Computer and Business Systems Division, information about the Fall course sections and assigned faculty in the Division. Your completed worksheets will look similar to Figure 5.30.

Project Files for MyLab IT Grader

5. In your **MyLab IT** course, locate and click **Excel 5B Fall Sections**, Download Materials, and then Download All Files.

6. Extract the zipped folder to your Excel Chapter 5 folder. Close the Grader download screens.

7. Take a moment to open the downloaded **Excel_5B_Fall_Sections_Instructions**; note any recent updates to the book.

Project Results

GO! Project 5B
Where We're Going

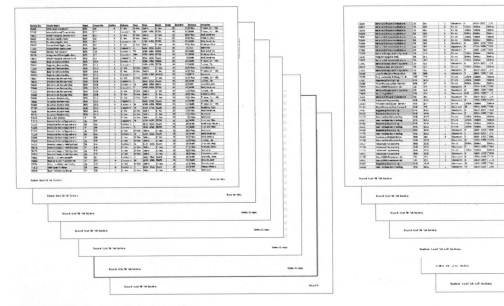

Figure 5.30 Project 5B Fall Sections

For Non-MyLab Submissions

For Project 5B, you will need:

e05B_Fall_Sections

In your Excel Chapter 5 folder, save your workbook as:

Lastname_Firstname_5B_Fall_Sections

If your instructor requires a workbook with formulas, save as:

Lastname_Firstname_5B_Fall_Sections_formulas

After you have named and saved your workbook, on the next page, begin with step 2.

Objective 5 Use Advanced Sort Techniques

Sort means to organize data in a particular order; for example, alphabetizing a list of names. An **ascending** sort refers to text that is sorted alphabetically from A to Z, numbers sorted from lowest to highest, or dates and times sorted from earliest to latest. A **descending** sort refers to text that is sorted alphabetically from Z to A, numbers sorted from highest to lowest, or dates and times sorted from latest to earliest.

Sorting helps you to visualize your data. By sorting in various ways, you can find the data that you want, and then use your data to make good decisions. You can sort data in one column or in multiple columns. Most sort operations are column sorts, but you can also sort by rows.

Activity 5.14 | Sorting on Multiple Columns

ALERT Because Office 365 is a cloud-based subscription service that receives continuous updates, you may encounter some variations in what appears on your screen and what is shown in this instruction. Microsoft Office 365 is fully installed on your PC or Mac; no internet access is necessary to create or edit documents. When you are connected to the internet, you will receive monthly upgrades and new features, so you always have the latest versions of Office apps as soon as they are available. Your subscription gives you continuous free access to the latest innovations and refinements.

3.3.2

To sort data based on several criteria at once, use the **Sort dialog box**, which enables you to sort by more than one column or row. In this Activity, you will convert the data into an Excel table, and then use the Sort dialog box to arrange the data.

1▶ Navigate to your **Excel Chapter 5 folder**, and then double-click the Excel file you downloaded from **MyLab IT** that displays your name—**Student_Excel_5B_Fall_Sections**.

2▶ Be sure that the first worksheet, **Room Conflicts**, is the active sheet. In the **Name Box**, type **a1:m50** and press Enter to select this range. On the **Insert tab**, in the **Tables group**, click **Table**. In the **Create Table** dialog box, be sure that the **My table has headers** check box is selected, and then click **OK**.

 ANOTHER WAY With cell A1 active, on the Insert tab, in the Tables group, click Table, and Excel will select all the contiguous data as the range.

3▶ On the **Design tab**, in the **Table Styles group**, click **More**, and then under **Light**, in the third row, click the third style. Click any cell to deselect the table, and then compare your screen with Figure 5.31.

A table of data like this one forms a **database**—an organized collection of facts related to a specific topic. In this table, the topic relates to the Fall course sections for this division of the college.

Each table row forms a **record**—all of the categories of data pertaining to one person, place, thing, event, or idea. In this table, each course section is a record. Each table column forms a **field**—a single piece of information that is stored in every record, such as a name or course number.

When information is arranged as records in rows and fields in columns, then you can **query**—ask a question of—the data. A query restricts records through the use of criteria conditions that display records that answer a question about the data.

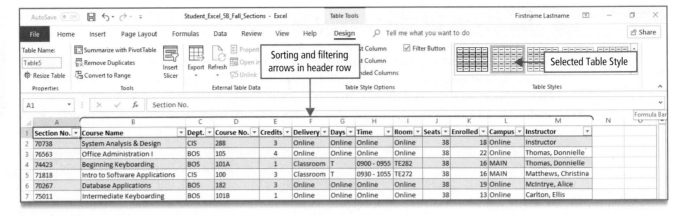

Figure 5.31

> **4** ▶ On the **Data tab**, in the **Sort & Filter group**, click **Sort**.
>
> In the Sort dialog box, you can sort up to 64 columns (levels) of data.

NOTE **Defining data as a table prior to sort operations is optional.**

Defining your range of data as an Excel table is not required to perform sort operations. Doing so, however, is convenient if you plan to perform sorts on all of the data, because any sort commands will be performed on the entire table. Defining the data as a table also freezes the column titles automatically, so they will not move out of view as you scroll down a worksheet that contains many rows. If you want to sort only part of a list of data, do not convert the data to a table. Instead, select the range, and then click the Sort button.

> **5** ▶ In the **Sort** dialog box, under **Column**, click the **Sort by arrow**. Notice that the list displays in the order of the field names—the column titles. On the list, click **Dept**.
>
> **6** ▶ Under **Sort On**, verify that *Cell Values* displays and that under **Order**, *A to Z* displays. Compare your screen with Figure 5.32.
>
> The default Sort On option *Cell Values* indicates that the sort will be based on the values in the cells of the Sort by column—the Dept. column. The default sort Order *A to Z* indicates that the values in the column will be sorted in ascending alphabetic order.

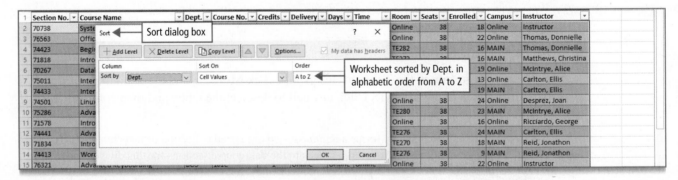

Figure 5.32

> **7** ▶ In the upper left corner of the **Sort** dialog box, click **Add Level**. In the second level row, click the **Then by arrow**, and then click **Course No**. Be sure that **Sort On** indicates *Cell Values* and **Order** indicates *Smallest to Largest*.
>
> When you initiate the sort operation, these numeric values will be sorted from the smallest number to the largest.

⌨ **MAC TIP** The Add Level button is located in the lower left corner of the dialog box and is indicated by a + sign.

---

8 Click **Add Level** again. In the new row, under **Column**, click the **Then by arrow**, and then click **Section No**. Sort on the default options **Cell Values**, from **Smallest to Largest**. Compare your screen with Figure 5.33.

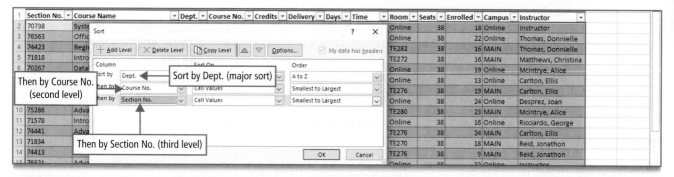

Figure 5.33

9 Click **OK**. Scroll down until **row 25** is at the top of the worksheet, take a moment to examine the arrangement of the data, and then compare your screen with Figure 5.34.

The first sort level, sometimes referred to as the *major sort*, is by the Dept. field in alphabetic order, so after the BOS department, the CIS department sections are listed, and then the CPS department sections.

The second sort level is by the Course No. field in ascending order, so within each department, the courses are sorted in ascending order by course number.

The third sort level is by the Section No. field in ascending order, so within each Course No. the section numbers display in ascending order.

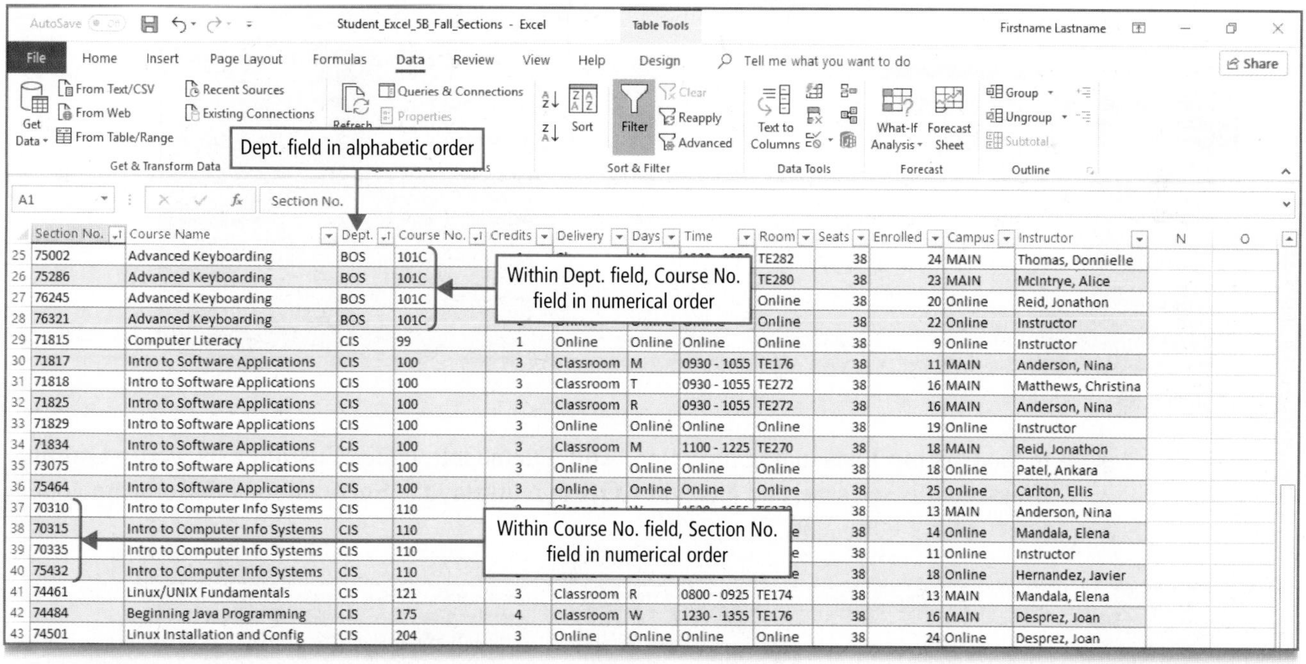

Figure 5.34

10 Press [Ctrl] + [Home] to make cell **A1** the active cell. On the **Page Layout tab**, in the **Page Setup group**, click **Print Titles**. On the **Sheet tab** of the **Page Setup** dialog box, click in the **Rows to repeat at top** box, point to the **row 1** heading to display the pointer, and click to select **row 1** so that the column titles will print on each sheet. In the dialog box, click **OK**.

11 **Save** your workbook.

Activity 5.15 | Sorting by Using a Custom List

You can use a *custom list* to sort in an order that you define. Excel includes a day-of-the-week and month-of-the-year custom list, so that you can sort chronologically by the days of the week or by the months of the year from January to December.

Optionally, you can create your own custom list by typing the values you want to sort by, in the order you want to sort them, from top to bottom; for example, *High, Medium, Low*. A custom list that you define must be based on a value—text, number, date, or time.

In this Activity, you will create a custom list showing all the Fall sections sorted by Delivery, with all online courses listed first.

1 In the **sheet tab area**, click **Online-Campus** to display the second worksheet in the workbook.

MAC TIP On the menu, click Excel, and then click Preferences. Under Formulas and Lists, click Custom Lists. Under List entries, type Online, Classroom and then click Add. Close the Custom Lists dialog box. On the Data tab, click Sort. Sort by Delivery and then click the Order arrow. Click Custom List, and then click Online, Classroom. Click OK two times and then continue with step 6.

2 On the **Data tab**, in the **Sort & Filter group**, click **Sort** to display the **Sort** dialog box. Set the first (major) level to sort by **Delivery** and to sort on **Cell Values**. Then, click the **Order arrow** for this sort level, and click **Custom List** to display the **Custom Lists** dialog box.

3 Under **Custom lists**, be sure **NEW LIST** is selected. Under **List entries**, click in the empty box, type **Online** and then press [Enter]. Type **Classroom** and then compare your screen with Figure 5.35.

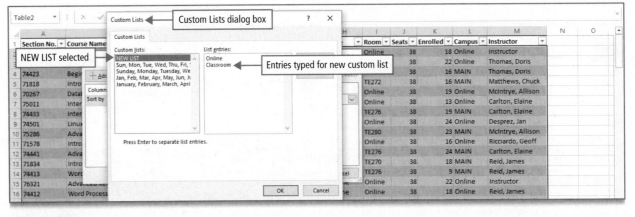

Figure 5.35

4 In the **Custom Lists** dialog box, click **Add**. On the left, under **Custom lists**, verify **Online, Classroom** is selected, and then click **OK** to redisplay the **Sort** dialog box. Compare your screen with Figure 5.36.

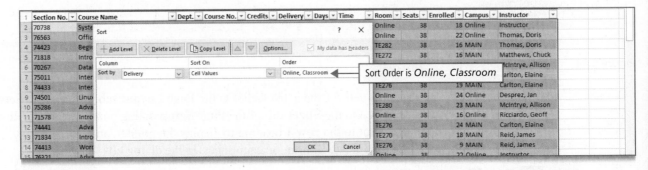

Figure 5.36

5 Click **OK** and then click any cell to deselect the table. Scroll down the worksheet, and notice that all of the online courses are listed first, and then scroll down so that **row 82** displays at the top of the worksheet. Notice the **Classroom** sections begin in **row 92**. Compare your screen with Figure 5.37.

	Section No.	Course Name	Dept.	Course No.	Credits	Delivery	Days	Time	Room	Seats	Enrolled	Campus	Instructor	N	O
82	70445	Linux/UNIX Fundamentals	CIS	121	3	Online	Online	Online	Online	38	17	Online	Instructor		
83	76243	Beginning Keyboarding	BOS	101A	1	Online	Online	Online	Online	38	11	Online	Reid, James		
84	71821	Intro to Software Applications	CIS	100	3	Online	Online	Online	Online	38	13	Online	Instructor		
85	76875	Intro To Visual Basic	CPS	185	4	Online	Online	Online	Online	38	21	Online	Philips, Matt		
86	75457	Intro to Software Applications	CIS	100	3	Online	Online	Online	Online	38	21	Online	Carlton, Elaine		
87	70388	Linux/UNIX Fundamentals	CIS	121	3	Online	Online	Online	Online	38	13	Online	Instructor		
88	75605	Advanced Keyboarding	BOS	101C	1	Online	Online	Online	Online	38	21	Online	Applebee, Linda		
89	75430	Intro to Computer Info Systems	CIS	110	3	Online	Online	Online	Online	38	16	Online	Hernandez, Jose		
90	75271	Medical Transcription II	BOS	220	4	Online	Online	Online	Online	38	0	Online	Thomas, Doris		
91	75126	Intro to Software Applications	CIS	100	3	Online	Online					Online	Anderson, Nancy		
92	74423	Beginning Keyboarding	BOS	101A	1	Classroom	T					MAIN	Thomas, Doris		
93	71818	Intro to Software Applications	CIS	100	3	Classroom	T					MAIN	Matthews, Chuck		
94	74433	Intermediate Keyboarding	BOS	101B	1	Classroom	F	1200 - 1255	TE276	38	19	MAIN	Carlton, Elaine		
95	75286	Advanced Keyboarding	BOS	101C	1	Classroom	M	1700 - 1755	TE280	38	23	MAIN	McIntrye, Allison		
96	74441	Advanced Keyboarding	BOS	101C	1	Classroom	F	1200 - 1255	TE276	38	24	MAIN	Carlton, Elaine		
97	71834	Intro to Software Applications	CIS	100	3	Classroom	M	1100 - 1225	TE270	38	18	MAIN	Reid, James		

> All Online sections display followed by Classroom sections

Figure 5.37

6 Press Ctrl + Home to move to cell **A1**. On the **Page Layout tab**, in the **Page Setup group**, click **Print Titles.** On the **Sheet tab** of the **Page Setup** dialog box, click in the **Rows to repeat at top** box, point to the **row 1** heading to display the pointer, click to select **row 1**, and then click **OK**. Save your workbook.

MORE KNOWLEDGE **A Custom List Remains Available for All Workbooks in Excel**

When you create a custom list, the list remains available for all Excel workbooks on the computer on which you created the list. To delete a custom list, display the Sort dialog box, and then display the Custom Lists dialog box. Click the custom list that you want to remove, and then click Delete.

Objective 6 **Use Custom and Advanced Filters**

GO! Learn How
Video E5-6

Filtering displays only the rows that meet the *criteria*—conditions that you specify to limit which records are included in the results—and hides the rows that do not meet your criteria.

When you format a range of data as a table, or select a range and click the Filter command, Excel displays filter arrows in the column headings, from which you can display the *AutoFilter menu* for a column—a drop-down menu from which you can filter a column by a list of values, by a format, or by criteria.

Use a *custom filter* to apply complex criteria to a single column. Use an *advanced filter* to specify three or more criteria for a particular column, to apply complex criteria to two or more columns, or to specify computed criteria. You can also use an advanced filter for extracting—copying the selected rows to another part of the worksheet, instead of displaying the filtered list.

Activity 5.16 | **Filtering by Format and Value Using AutoFilter**

MOS
3.3.1

There are three types of filters that you can create with AutoFilter. You can filter by one or more values, for example *CIS* for the CIS department. You can filter by a format, such as cell color. Or, you can filter by criteria; for example, course sections that are greater than 2 credits, which would display courses that have 3 or more credits. Each of these filter types is mutually exclusive for the column; that is, you can use only one at a time.

1 Click the **CIS & CPS sheet tab** to display the third worksheet in the workbook.

2 Click the **Data tab**. In the **Sort & Filter group**, notice that **Filter** is active. In **row 1**, notice the **filter arrows** in each column title.

The data in this worksheet is formatted as an Excel table, and filter arrows are automatically added in the header row of the table. A filter arrow, when clicked, displays the AutoFilter menu. On the ribbon, the active Filter button indicates that the data is formatted to use filters.

3 In **column B**, notice that some courses are formatted with a yellow fill color, which indicates courses that have been designated as introductory courses recommended for high school seniors who want to take a college class.

4 In cell **B1**, click the **Course Name filter arrow** ▾. On the **AutoFilter** menu, point to **Filter by Color**, and then compare your screen with Figure 5.38.

Two options display—Filter by Cell Color and Filter by Font Color. Under each option, color blocks display the colors available in the filtered column.

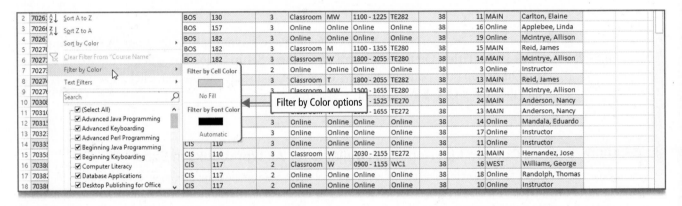

Figure 5.38

🖥 **MAC TIP**   Click the By color arrow, point to Cell color, and then click Yellow.

---

5 Under **Filter by Cell Color**, click the **yellow block**.

Only courses with a yellow fill color in column B display; the status bar indicates that 79 of the 169 records display.

6 Point to the **filter arrow** ▼ in cell **B1**, and notice the ScreenTip *Course Name: Equals a Yellow cell color*. Notice also that a small funnel displays to the right of the arrow. Compare your screen with Figure 5.39.

The funnel indicates that a filter is applied, and the ScreenTip indicates how the records are filtered. The Status bar indicates the number of records that display out of the total number of records.

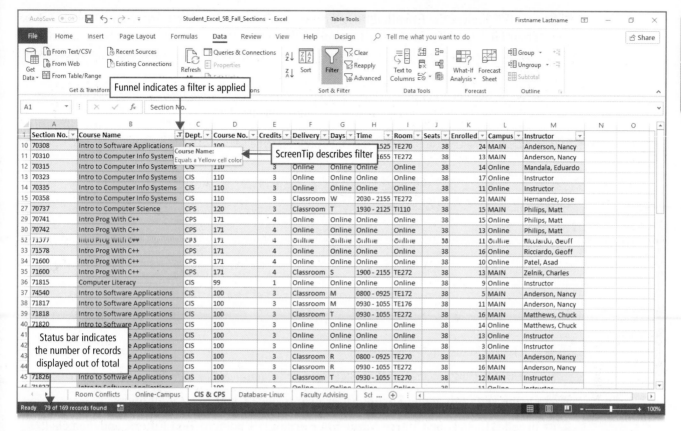

Figure 5.39

7 In cell **B1**, click the **Course Name filter arrow** [filter icon], and then click **Clear Filter From "Course Name"**. Then, in cell **B1**, point to the **Course Name filter arrow**, and notice that *(Showing All)* displays.

> The funnel no longer displays. The status bar no longer indicates that a filter is active. A filter arrow without a funnel means that the filtering feature is enabled but not applied; if you point to the arrow, the ScreenTip will display (Showing All).

8 Click cell **I5**, which contains the value *TE280*. Right-click over the selected cell to display the shortcut menu, point to **Filter**, and then click **Filter by Selected Cell's Value**. Notice that only the courses that meet in Room TE280 display; all the other records are hidden.

> Excel filters the records by the selected value—TE280—and indicates in the status bar that 10 of the 169 records are displayed. This is a quick way to filter a set of records.

9 On the **Data tab**, in the **Sort & Filter group**, click **Clear** to clear all of the filters.

> Use this command to clear all filters from a group of records. This command also clears any sorts that were applied.

10 **Save** [save icon] your workbook.

Activity 5.17 | Filtering by Custom Criteria Using AutoFilter

MOS
3.3.1

By using a custom filter, you can apply complex criteria to a single column. For example, you can use comparison criteria to compare two values by using the *comparison operators* such as Equals (=) Greater Than (>) or Less Than (<) singly or in combinations. When you compare two values by using these operators, your result is a logical value that is either true or false.

1 Click the **Database-Linux sheet tab** to display the fourth worksheet in the workbook.

2 In cell **K1**, click the **Enrolled filter arrow** ⏷, point to **Number Filters**, and then click **Less Than Or Equal To**. In the **Custom AutoFilter** dialog box, in the first box, be sure that *is less than or equal to* displays. In the second box type **12** and then compare your screen with Figure 5.40.

In the Custom AutoFilter dialog box, you can create a *compound filter*—a filter that uses more than one condition—and one that uses comparison operators.

MAC TIP Under Filter, click the Choose One arrow, and then click Less Than Or Equal To. In the box to the right, type 12.

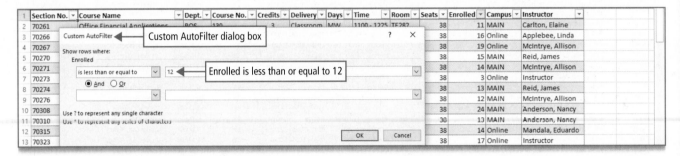

Figure 5.40

3 Click **OK** to display 49 records.

This filter answers the question, *Which course sections have 12 or fewer students enrolled?*

4 On the **Data tab**, in the **Sort & Filter group**, click **Clear** to clear all filters.

5 In cell **B1**, click the **Course Name filter arrow** ⏷, point to **Text Filters**, and then click **Contains**.

MAC TIP Under Filter, click the Choose One arrow, and then click Contains.

6 In the **Custom AutoFilter** dialog box, under **Course Name**, in the first box, be sure that *contains* displays. In the box to the right, type **database**

7 Between the two rows of boxes, click the **Or** option button. For the second filter, in the first box, click the arrow, scroll down as necessary, and then click **contains**. In the second box, type **linux** and then compare your screen with Figure 5.41.

For the *Or comparison operator*, only one of the two comparison criteria that you specify must be true. By applying this filter, only courses that contain the word *database* or *linux* will display.

For the *And comparison operator*, each and every one of the comparison criteria that you specify must be true.

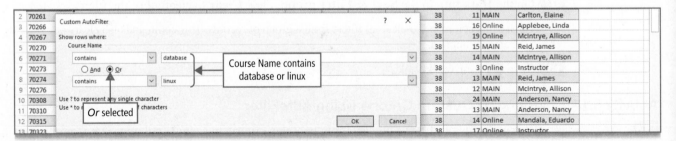

Figure 5.41

8 Click **OK** to display 14 records. Compare your screen with Figure 5.42 and then **Save** 🖫 your workbook.

This filter answers the question, *Which course sections relate to either databases or the Linux operating system?*.

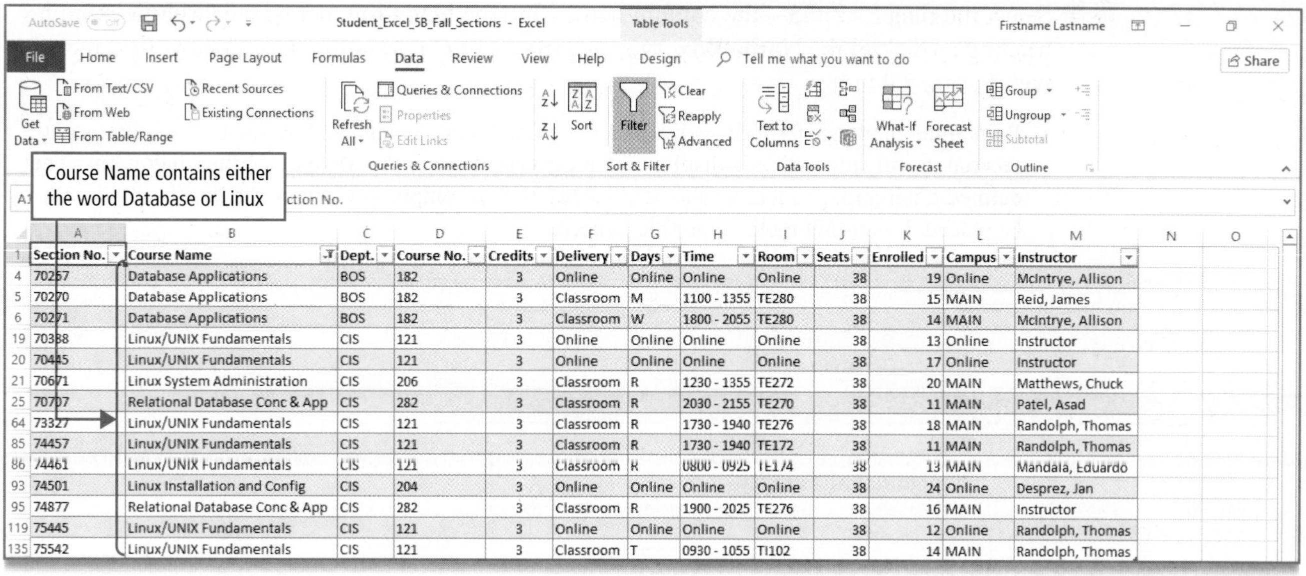

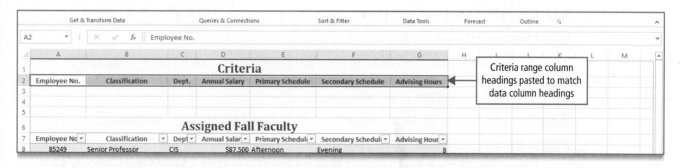

Figure 5.42

Activity 5.18 | Using the Name Manager and Filtering by Using Advanced Criteria

Use an advanced filter when the data you want to filter requires complex criteria, for example, to specify three or more criteria for a particular column, to apply complex criteria to two or more columns, or to specify computed criteria. When you use the Advanced Filter command, the Advanced dialog box displays, rather than the AutoFilter menu, and you type the criteria on the worksheet above the range you want to filter.

In this Activity, you will create an advanced filter to determine faculty members whose classification includes Professor and that have an annual salary of $70,000 or more, and who have 8 or more hours of assigned advising hours.

1 Display the **Faculty Advising** sheet.

2 Select and **Copy** the range **A7:G7**. **Paste** the selection to cell **A2**, and then press Esc to cancel the moving border. Compare your screen with Figure 5.43.

The first step in filtering by using advanced criteria is to create a *criteria range*—an area on your worksheet where you define the criteria for the filter. The criteria range indicates how the displayed records are filtered.

Typically, the criteria range is placed *above* the data. The criteria range includes a row for the column headings that must match the column headings in the data range exactly. The criteria range must also include at least one row for the criteria—you will need additional rows if you have multiple criteria for a column. You can also add a title row. Separate the criteria range from the data by a blank row.

Figure 5.43

3 Select the range **A2:G3**—the column names and the blank row below the Criteria column headings. Click in the **Name Box**, type **Criteria** and then press Enter. Compare your screen with Figure 5.44.

> By naming the range Criteria, which is a predefined name recognized by Excel, the reference to this range will automatically display as the Criteria range in the Advanced Filter dialog box. This defined criteria range includes the field names and one empty row, where the limiting criteria will be placed. It does not include the title Criteria.

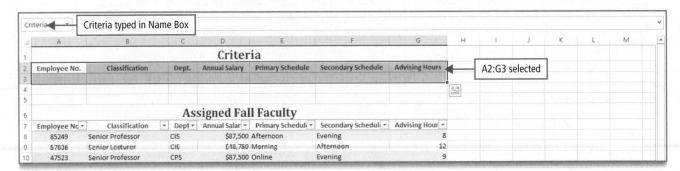

Figure 5.44

4 On the **Formulas tab**, in the **Defined Names** group, click **Name Manager**, and then compare your screen with Figure 5.45.

> In this workbook, in addition to the Criteria name that you defined, there are several named tables—Excel automatically assigns defined tables with names. Additionally, the Print Titles ranges defined in previous worksheets are listed.

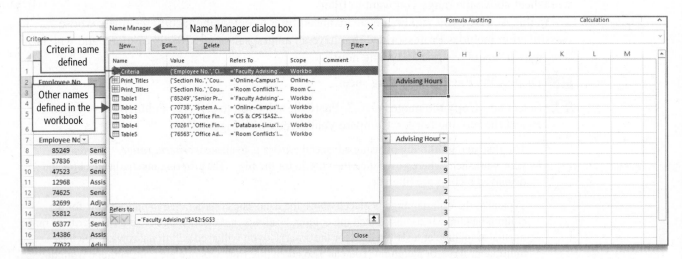

Figure 5.45

5 **Close** the **Name Manager** dialog box.

6 Click cell **D3**, type **>=70000** and then press Enter.

> This action creates a criteria using a comparison operator to look for salary values that are greater than or equal to $70,000. Do not include a comma when you type this value, because the comma is a cell format, not part of the value.

7 Click cell **A7**. On the **Data tab**, in the **Sort & Filter group**, click **Advanced**.

8 In the **Advanced Filter** dialog box, in the **List range** box, type **$A$7:$G$34** which is your Excel table. Be sure the **Criteria range** is identified as cells **$A$2:$G$3**. Compare your screen with Figure 5.46.

Both the List and the Criteria ranges use absolute cell references. Under Action, you can choose to display the results in the table—in-place—or copy the results to another location.

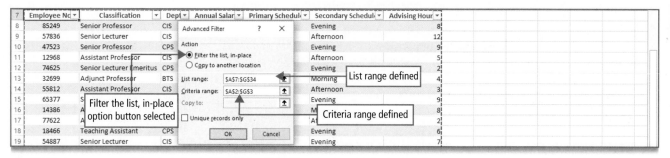

Figure 5.46

9 Click **OK** to have the filter results display in-place—in the table. Press Ctrl + Home and compare your screen with Figure 5.47.

Only the records for faculty members whose salary is $70,000 or more display. The row numbers for the records that meet the criteria display in blue. The Advanced command disables the AutoFilter command and removes the AutoFilter arrows from the column headings.

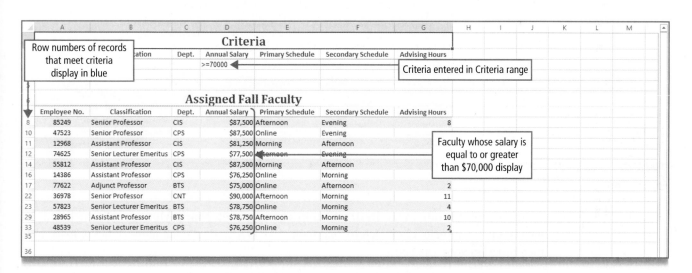

Figure 5.47

10 Click cell **B3**, type ***Professor** and then press Enter.

The asterisk (*) is a wildcard. Use a *wildcard* to search a field when you are uncertain of the exact value or you want to widen the search to include more records. The use of a wildcard enables you to include faculty whose classification ends with the word *Professor*. It directs Excel to find Professor and anything before it. The criterion in the Salary field still applies.

The use of two or more criteria on the same row is known as *compound criteria*—all conditions must be met for the records to be included in the results.

11 Click cell **A7**. On the **Data tab**, in the **Sort & Filter group**, click **Advanced**. Verify that the database range is correctly identified in the **List range** box and that the **Criteria range** still indicates *$A$2:$G$3*. Click **OK**. Compare your screen with Figure 5.48.

Only the eight faculty members with a classification containing *Professor* and a salary of $70,000 or more display.

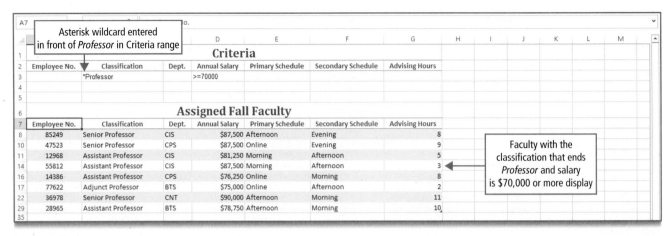

Figure 5.48

> **12** Using the techniques you just practiced, filter the data further by adding additional criteria—faculty who are assigned 8 hours or more of advising. Compare your result with Figure 5.49.

> Five faculty members meet all three of the criteria in the Criteria range.

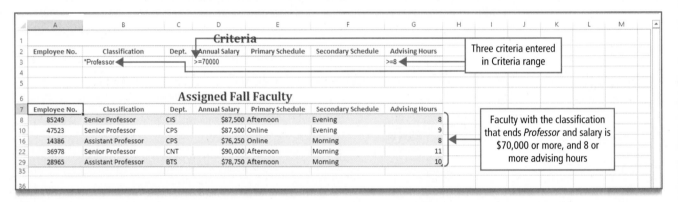

Figure 5.49

> **13** On the **Formulas tab**, in the **Defined Names group**, click **Name Manager**. In the list of names, click **Criteria**, click **Delete**, and then click **OK** to delete the name. Click **Close**, and then **Save** 🖫 your workbook.

> It is good practice to delete a Criteria name if you plan to filter data in another worksheet within the same workbook. If you do not delete the Criteria name, the Advanced Filter feature will continue to use the named Criteria range in future filters.

💻 **MAC TIP** On the Formulas tab, click Define Name. Under Names in workbook, click Criteria. Below the list of names, click the minus (–) sign, and then click OK to delete the name.

MORE KNOWLEDGE | **Using Wildcards**

A wildcard can help you locate information when you are uncertain how the information might be displayed in your records. The placement of the asterisk in relationship to the known value determines the result. If it is placed first, the variable will be in the beginning of the string of characters. For example, in a list of names if you used *son as the criteria, it will look for any name that ends in son. The results might display Peterson, Michelson, and Samuelson. If the asterisk is at the end of the known value in the criteria, then the variable will be at the end. You can also include the asterisk wildcard at the beginning and at the end of a known value. You can also use an asterisk wildcard in the middle, so searching for m*t will result in both mat and moist.

A question mark (?) can also be used as part of your search criteria. Each question mark used in the criteria represents a single position or character that is unknown in a group of specified values. Searching for *m?n* would find, for example, *min*, *men*, and *man*; whereas searching for *m??d* would find, for example, *mind*, *mend*, *mold*.

Activity 5.19 | Naming Ranges and Extracting Filtered Rows

MOS
2.3.1

You can *extract*—pull out the results of a filter to another area of your worksheet—instead of displaying a filtered list as you did in the previous activity. The location to which you copy the records is the **Extract area** and is commonly placed below the table of data.

In this Activity, you will extract data to create a report showing how many faculty have a Morning-Evening schedule.

1 ▶ Display the **Schedule Comparison** sheet and notice that a Criteria range has been created at the top of the worksheet.

2 ▶ **Copy** the range **A2:G2**, and then **Paste** the selection in cell **A37**. Compare your screen with Figure 5.50.

	A	B	C	D	E	F	G	H	I	J	K	L	M	N	O	P
31	26136	Associate Lecturer	CNT	$51,250	Afternoon	Morning	3									
32	54896	Lecturer	BTS	$50,000	Online	Evening	12									
33	48539	Senior Lecturer Emeritus	CPS	$76,250	Online	Morning	2									
34	19375	Senior Lecturer	CIS	$58,750	Evening	Morning	9									
35																
36		**Morning-Evening Schedule**														
37	Employee No.	Classification	Dept.	Annual Salary	Primary Schedule	Secondary Schedule	Advising Hours									
38																
39																
40																

Extract area created to match Data and Criteria range column headings

Figure 5.50

3 ▶ With the range **A37:G37** selected, in the **Name Box**, type **Extract** and press [Enter].

This action defines the Extract area so that the range will display automatically in the Copy to box of the Advanced Filter dialog box. Excel recognizes *Extract* as the location in which to place the results of an advanced filter.

4 ▶ Select the range **A7:G34** and then in the **Name Box**, type **Database** and press [Enter].

This action defines the list area. Excel recognizes *Database* as the range to be filtered.

5 ▶ At the top of your worksheet, in cell **E3**, type **Morning** and then in cell **F3**, type **Evening**

When applied, the filter will display only those records where the Primary Schedule is Morning and the Secondary Schedule is Evening.

6 ▶ On the **Data tab**, in the **Sort & Filter group**, click **Advanced**. Verify that the **List range** is **$A$7:$G$34**.

7 ▶ Click in the **Criteria range** box, and then scroll the worksheet to display the criteria range. Select the range **A2:G3**.

8 ▶ Under **Action**, click **Copy to another location**. Verify that in the **Copy to** box, the absolute reference to the Extract area—*$A$37:$G$37*—displays. Compare your screen with Figure 5.51.

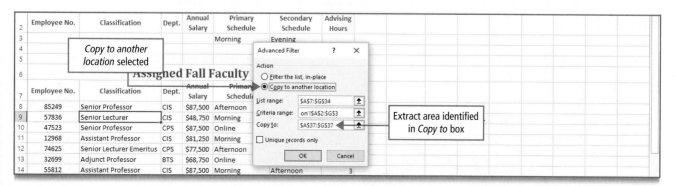

Figure 5.51

9 Click **OK**, and then scroll to view the lower portion of your worksheet. Compare your screen with Figure 5.52 and then **Save** 💾 your workbook.

Two records meet the criteria and are copied to the extract area on your worksheet. When you use an extract area in this manner, instead of reformatting the table to display the qualifying records, Excel places a copy of the qualifying records in the Extract area.

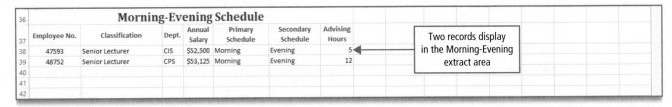

Figure 5.52

Objective 7   Subtotal, Outline, and Group a List of Data

GO! Learn How
Video E5-7

You can group and summarize a *list*—a series of rows that contains related data—by adding subtotals. The first step in adding subtotals is to sort the data by the field for which you want to create a subtotal.

Activity 5.20   Subtotaling, Outlining, and Grouping a List of Data

MOS
Expert 2.2.4

In this Activity, you will use Excel subtotal and outline features to summarize the faculty salaries by department.

1 Display the **Salaries by Department** sheet.

2 Select the range **A2:G29**. On the **Data tab**, in the **Sort & Filter group**, click **Sort**. In the **Sort** dialog box, click the **Sort by arrow**, and then click **Dept**. Click **Add Level**, click the **Then by arrow**, and then click **Annual Salary**. Compare your **Sort** dialog box with Figure 5.53.

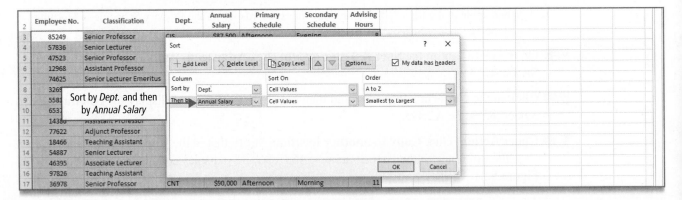

Figure 5.53

3 Click **OK**. With the range still selected, on the **Data tab**, in the **Outline group**, click **Subtotal**.

The *Subtotal command* totals several rows of related data together by automatically inserting subtotals and totals for the selected cells.

4 In the **Subtotal** dialog box, in the **At each change in** box, click the **arrow** to display the list, and then click **Dept**. In the **Use function** box, display the list and click **Sum**. In the **Add subtotal to** list, select the **Annual Salary** check box, and then scroll the list and *deselect* any other check boxes that are selected. Compare your screen with Figure 5.54.

These actions direct Excel to create a group for each change in value in the Dept. field. Excel will then use the Sum function to add a subtotal in the Annual Salary field. The check boxes at the bottom of the dialog box indicate how the subtotals will display.

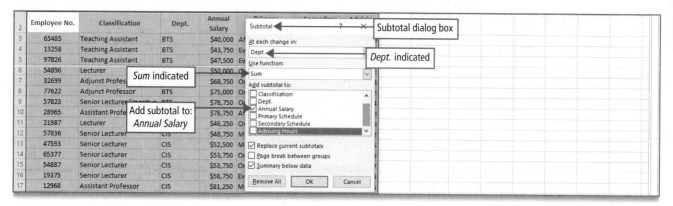

Figure 5.54

5 ▶ Click **OK**, press Ctrl + Home, **AutoFit column C**, and then compare your screen with Figure 5.55.

The Dept. sort applied earlier in this Activity placed the data for each department together so that at each change in Dept., subtotals for the department salaries display.

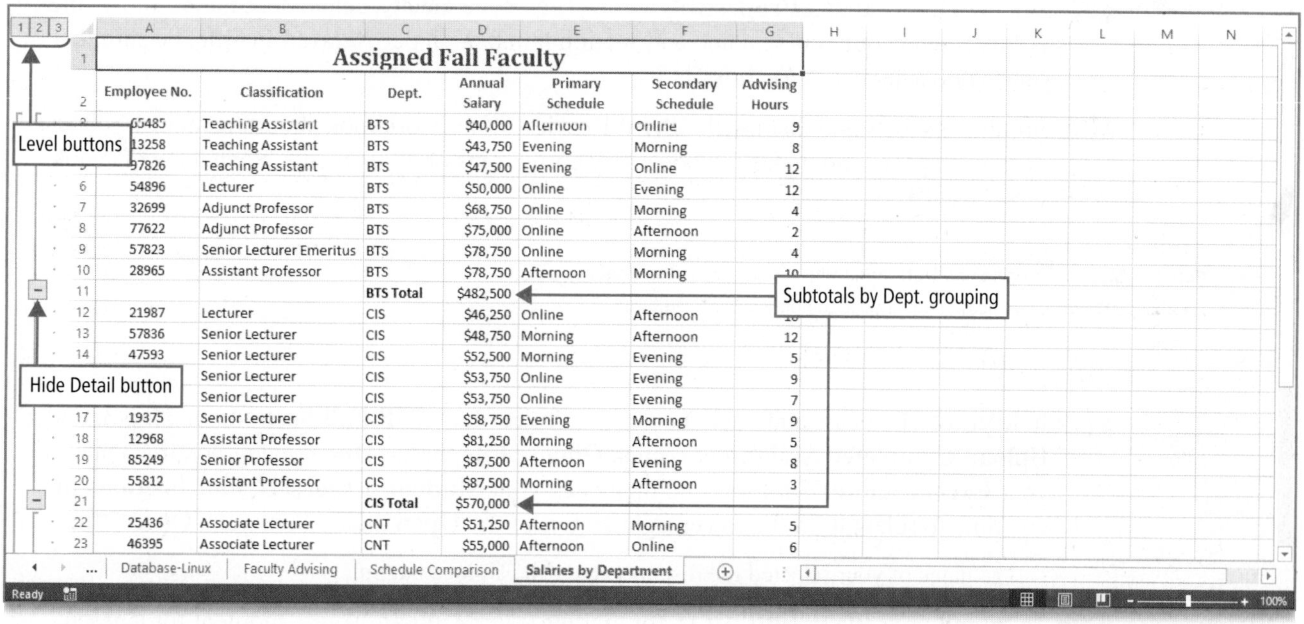

Figure 5.55

6 ▶ Along the left edge of your workbook, locate the outline.

When you add subtotals, Excel defines groups based on the rows used to calculate a subtotal. The groupings form an outline of your worksheet based on the criteria you indicated in the Subtotal dialog box, and the outline displays along the left side of your worksheet.

The outline bar along the left side of the worksheet enables you to show and hide levels of detail with a single mouse click. For example, you can show details with the totals, which is the default view. Or, you can show only the summary totals or only the grand total.

There are three types of controls in the outline. Hide Detail (−) collapses a group of cells, Show Detail (+) expands a collapsed group of cells, and the level buttons (1, 2, 3) can hide all levels of detail below the number clicked.

7 To the left of **row 25**, click **Hide Detail** (−) to collapse the detail for the **CNT** department.

> *Detail data* refers to the subtotaled rows that are totaled and summarized. Detail data is typically adjacent to and either above or to the left of the summary data.

8 At the top of the outline area, click the **Level 2** button to hide all Level 3 details and display only the Level 2 summary information and the Level 1 Grand Total. Compare your screen with Figure 5.56.

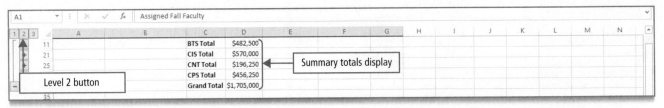

	A	B	C	D
11			BTS Total	$482,500
21			CIS Total	$570,000
25			CNT Total	$196,250
			CPS Total	$456,250
			Grand Total	$1,705,000

Summary totals display

Level 2 button

Figure 5.56

9 Group all the worksheets and change the **Orientation** to **Landscape**. Center the sheets **Horizontally** on the page and insert a footer that includes the file name in the **left section**, and in the **right section**, insert the **Sheet Name** . On the **Page Layout tab**, set the **Width** to **1 page**.

10 **Ungroup** the worksheets, and then display the **Schedule Comparison** sheet. On the **Page Layout tab**, set the **Height** to **1 page**.

11 Display the workbook **Properties**. As the **Tags**, type **faculty, schedule, salaries** and as the **Subject**, type your course name and section number. Under **Related People**, be sure that your name displays as **Author**.

12 Group the sheets and display the **Print Preview**. Your workbook should contain 14 pages. View each page, and make any necessary corrections or adjustments. **Save** the workbook and **Close** Excel.

For Non-MyLab Submissions Determine What Your Instructor Requires
As directed by your instructor, submit your completed Excel file.

---

13 In **MyLab IT**, locate and click the Grader Project **Excel 5B Fall Sections**. In **step 3**, under **Upload Completed Assignment**, click **Choose File**. In the **Open** dialog box, navigate to your **Excel Chapter 5 folder**, and then click your **Student_Excel_5B_Fall_Sections** file one time to select it. In the lower right corner of the **Open** dialog box, click **Open**.

> The name of your selected file displays above the Upload button.

14 To submit your file to **MyLab IT** for grading, click **Upload**, wait a moment for a green **Success!** message, and then in **step 4**, click the blue **Submit for Grading** button. Click **Close Assignment** to return to your list of **Course Materials**.

MORE KNOWLEDGE **Outlining a Worksheet**

A horizontal outline bar can be created for data that is summarized by row, rather than summarized by column as it was in this activity. In addition, if the data is not organized so that Excel can outline it automatically, you can create an outline manually. To do so, on the Data tab, in the Outline group, click the Group button arrow, and then click Auto Outline.

You have completed Project 5B **END**

Microsoft Office Specialist (MOS) Skills in This Chapter	
Project 5A	**Project 5B**
1.2.2 Navigate to a named cell, range, or workbook element	**2.3.1** Define and name ranges
1.2.3 Insert and remove hyperlinks	**3.3.1** Filter records
1.4.2 Change workbook views	**3.3.2** Sort data by multiple columns
1.4.4 Change window views	**Expert 2.2.4** Calculate data by inserting subtotals and totals
1.5.2 Save workbooks in alternative file formats	
3.2.2 Configure table style options	

Build Your E-Portfolio

An E-Portfolio is a collection of evidence, stored electronically, that showcases what you have accomplished while completing your education. Collecting and then sharing your work products with potential employers reflects your academic and career goals. Your completed documents from the following projects are good examples to show what you have learned: 5G, 5K, and 5L.

GO! For Job Success

Discussion: Organizational Decisions

Your instructor may assign these questions to your class, and then ask you to think about them or discuss them with your classmates:

Organizational decisions like new products or global expansion have historically been made after lengthy analysis of available information and risk. Today, though, organizations of every kind operate in an environment where decisions need to be made quickly, even as the amount of data available on which to base them has reached unprecedented levels. Business people at all levels are being trained to accelerate their decision making. Accelerated decision making requires the ability to quickly understand the situation, identify possible options, evaluate the risk, and then take action, without having all the data or time to consider every alternative.

g-stockstudio/Shutterstock

What are some situations in your career, in your personal life, or education where you have had to make a decision under these circumstances?

Think about your own decision style. Do you think you would easily adapt to an accelerated decision situation? Why or why not?

Some situations are more suited to an accelerated decision than others. What are some factors that could require a business to make an accelerated decision?

End of Chapter

Summary

You can navigate a large worksheet using the Freeze Panes, Go To, and Find commands. Control the screen display by hiding rows and columns, and work with multiple workbooks using the Arrange All command.

A theme is a set of formatting characteristics, such as fonts, number formats, borders, and shading. Insert page breaks, repeat column or row titles, and use Landscape orientation for worksheets with many columns.

By default, Excel files are saved in the Excel Workbook file format with the .xlsx file name extension. Excel data can also be saved in other file formats such as HTML, CSV, and PDF.

Sorting organizes data in a particular order. Filtering displays only the rows that meet specific criteria. Sorting and filtering along with subtotaling, outlining, and grouping are used for data analysis.

GO! Learn It Online

Review the concepts, key terms, and MOS skills in this chapter by completing these online challenges, which you can find at **MyLab IT**.

Chapter Quiz: Answer matching and multiple choice questions to test what you learned in this chapter.

Lessons on the GO!: Learn how to use all the new apps and features as they are introduced by Microsoft.

MOS Prep Quiz: Answer questions to review the MOS skills that you practiced in this chapter.

Project Guide for Excel Chapter 5

Your instructor will assign Projects from this list to ensure your learning and assess your knowledge.

Project	Apply Skills from These Chapter Objectives	Project Type	Project Location
5A **MyLab IT**	Objectives 1–4 from Project 5A	**5A Instructional Project (Grader Project)** **Instruction** Guided instruction to learn the skills in Project 5A.	In **MyLab IT** and in text
5B **MyLab IT**	Objectives 5–7 from Project 5B	**5B Instructional Project (Grader Project)** **Instruction** Guided instruction to learn the skills in Project 5B.	In **MyLab IT** and in text
5C	Objectives 1–4 from Project 5A	**5C Skills Review (Scorecard Grading)** **Review** A guided review of the skills from Project 5A.	In text
5D	Objectives 5–7 from Project 5B	**5D Skills Review (Scorecard Grading)** **Review** A guided review of the skills from Project 5B.	In text
5E **MyLab IT**	Objectives 1–4 from Project 5A	**5E Mastery (Grader Project)** **Mastery and Transfer of Learning** A demonstration of your mastery of the skills in Project 5A with extensive decision making.	In **MyLab IT** and in text
5F **MyLab IT**	Objectives 5–7 from Project 5B	**5F Mastery (Grader Project)** **Mastery and Transfer of Learning** A demonstration of your mastery of the skills in Project 5B with extensive decision making.	In **MyLab IT** and in text
5G **MyLab IT**	Objectives 1–7 from Projects 5A and 5B	**5G Mastery (Grader Project)** **Mastery and Transfer of Learning** A demonstration of your mastery of the skills in Projects 5A and 5B with extensive decision making.	In **MyLab IT** and in text
5H	Combination of Objectives from Projects 5A and 5B	**5H GO! Fix It (Scorecard Grading)** **Critical Thinking** A demonstration of your mastery of the skills in Projects 5A and 5B by creating a correct result from a document that contains errors you must find.	IRC
5I	Combination of Objectives from Projects 5A and 5B	**5I GO! Make It (Scorecard Grading)** **Critical Thinking** A demonstration of your mastery of the skills in Projects 5A and 5B by creating a result from a supplied picture.	IRC
5J	Combination of Objectives from Projects 5A and 5B	**5J GO! Solve It (Rubric Grading)** **Critical Thinking** A demonstration of your mastery of the skills in Projects 5A and 5B, your decision-making skills, and your critical thinking skills. A task-specific rubric helps you self-assess your result.	IRC
5K	Combination of Objectives from Projects 5A and 5B	**5K GO! Solve It (Rubric Grading)** **Critical Thinking** A demonstration of your mastery of the skills in Projects 5A and 5B, your decision-making skills, and your critical thinking skills. A task-specific rubric helps you self-assess your result.	In text
5L	Combination of Objectives from Projects 5A and 5B	**5L GO! Think (Rubric Grading)** **Critical Thinking** A demonstration of your understanding of the chapter concepts applied in a manner that you would outside of college. An analytic rubric helps you and your instructor grade the quality of your work by comparing it to the work an expert in the discipline would create.	In text
5M	Combination of Objectives from Projects 5A and 5B	**5M GO! Think (Rubric Grading)** **Critical Thinking** A demonstration of your understanding of the chapter concepts applied in a manner that you would outside of college. An analytic rubric helps you and your instructor grade the quality of your work by comparing it to the work an expert in the discipline would create.	IRC
5N	Combination of Objectives from Projects 5A and 5B	**5N You and GO! (Rubric Grading)** **Critical Thinking** A demonstration of your understanding of the chapter concepts applied in a manner that you would in a personal situation. An analytic rubric helps you and your instructor grade the quality of your work.	IRC

Glossary

Glossary of Chapter Key Terms

Active area The area of the worksheet that contains data or has contained data.

Advanced filter A filter that can specify three or more criteria for a particular column, apply complex criteria to two or more columns, or specify computed criteria.

And comparison operator The comparison operator that requires each and every one of the comparison criteria to be true.

Arrange All The command that tiles all open program windows on the screen.

Ascending The term that refers to the arrangement of text that is sorted alphabetically from A to Z, numbers sorted from lowest to highest, or dates and times sorted from earliest to latest.

AutoFilter menu A drop-down menu from which you can filter a column by a list of values, by a format, or by criteria.

Cell style A defined set of formatting characteristics, such as font, font size, font color, cell borders, and cell shading.

Comma delimited file A file type that saves the contents of the cells by placing commas between them and an end-of-paragraph mark at the end of each row; also referred to as a CSV (comma separated values) file.

Comparison operators Symbols that evaluate each value to determine if it is the same (=) greater than (>) less than (<) or in between a range of values as specified by the criteria.

Compound criteria The use of two or more criteria on the same row— all conditions must be met for the records to be included in the results.

Compound filter A filter that uses more than one condition—and one that uses comparison operators.

Criteria Conditions that you specify in a logical function or filter.

Criteria range An area on your worksheet where you define the criteria for the filter and that indicates how the displayed records are filtered.

CSV (comma separated values) file A file type in which the cells in each row are separated by commas and an end-of-paragraph mark at the end of each row; also referred to as a comma delimited file.

Custom filter A filter with which you can apply complex criteria to a single column.

Custom list A sort order that you can define.

Database An organized collection of facts related to a specific topic.

Descending The term that refers to the arrangement of text that is sorted alphabetically from Z to A, numbers sorted from highest to lowest, or dates and times sorted from latest to earliest.

Detail data The subtotaled rows that are totaled and summarized; typically adjacent to and either above or to the left of the summary data.

Extract The process of pulling out multiple sets of data for comparison purposes.

Extract area The location to which you copy records when extracting filtered rows.

Field A specific type of data such as name, employee number, or social security number that is stored in columns.

Filtering A process in which only the rows that meet the criteria display; rows that do not meet the criteria are hidden.

Find A command that locates and selects specific text or formatting.

Freeze Panes A command that enables you to select one or more rows or columns and freeze (lock) them into place so that they remain on the screen while you scroll; the locked rows and columns become separate panes.

Go To A command that moves to a specific cell or range of cells that you specify.

Go To Special A command that moves to cells that have special characteristics, for example, to cells that are blank or to cells that contain constants, as opposed to formulas.

HTML (Hypertext Markup Language) A language web browsers can interpret.

Hyperlink Text or graphics that, when clicked, take you to another location in the worksheet, to another file, or to a webpage on the internet or on your organization's intranet.

List A series of rows that contains related data that you can group by adding subtotals.

Major sort A term sometimes used to refer to the first sort level in the Sort dialog box.

Or comparison operator The comparison operator that requires only one of the two comparison criteria that you specify to be true.

Pane A portion of a worksheet window bounded by and separated from other portions by vertical and horizontal bars.

PDF (Portable Document Format) A file format developed by Adobe Systems that creates a representation of electronic paper that displays your data on the screen as it would look when printed, but that cannot be easily changed.

Query A process of restricting records through the use of criteria conditions that will display records that will answer a question about the data.

Record All the categories of data pertaining to one person, place, thing, event, or idea.

Scaling The group of commands by which you can reduce the horizontal and vertical size of the printed data by a percentage or by the number of pages that you specify.

Sort The process of arranging data in a specific order.

Sort dialog box A dialog box in which you can sort data based on several criteria at once, and that enables a sort by more than one column or row.

Split The command that enables you to view separate parts of the same worksheet on your screen; it splits the window into multiple resizable panes to allow you to view distant parts of the worksheet at one time.

Subtotal command The command that totals several rows of related data together by automatically inserting subtotals and totals for the selected cells.

Tab delimited text file A file type in which cells are separated by tabs; this type of file can be readily exchanged with various database programs.

Wildcard A character, for example the asterisk or question mark, used to search a field when you are uncertain of the exact value or when you want to widen the search to include more records.

.xlsx file name extension The default file format used by Excel to save an Excel workbook.

Chapter Review

Skills Review | Project 5C Science Schedule

Apply **5A** skills from
these Objectives:

1. Navigate and
   Manage Large
   Worksheets
2. Enhance
   Worksheets with
   Themes and
   Styles
3. Format a
   Worksheet to
   Share with Others
4. Save Excel Data
   in Other File
   Formats

In the following Skills Review, you will assist Susanne Black, Program Chair for Science, in formatting and navigating a large worksheet that lists the class schedule for the Science departments at Laurel College. You will also save Excel data in other file formats. Your completed workbook will look similar to Figure 5.57.

Project Files

For Project 5C, you will need the following files:

e05C_Science_Faculty

e05C_Science_Requests

e05C_Science_Sohcdule

You will save your workbooks as:

Lastname_Firstname_5C_Science_CSV (not shown)

Lastname_Firstname_5C_Science_Schedule

Project Results

Figure 5.57

(continues on next page)

Chapter Review

1 Start Excel. From your student files, open the file **e05C_Science_Schedule**. Display the **Save As** dialog box, navigate to your **Excel Chapter 5** folder, and then **Save** the workbook as **Lastname_Firstname_5C_Science_Schedule**

a. On the **Home tab**, in the **Editing group**, click **Find & Select**, and then click **Go To Special**. (Mac users, press [control] + [G], and then click Special.) In the first column, click **Blanks**, and then click **OK** to select all blank cells in the worksheet's active area. On the **Home tab**, in the **Font group**, click the **Fill Color button arrow**, and then under **Standard Colors**, click the fourth color—**Yellow**—to fill all the selected blank cells. These cells still require Room assignments.

b. Press [Ctrl] + [Home] to make cell **A1** the active cell. From the column heading area, select **columns E:H**. Right-click over the selected area to display the shortcut menu, and then click **Hide**. (Mac users, press [control] and then click the selected area.)

c. On the **Home tab**, in the **Editing group**, click **Find & Select**, and then click **Go To**. In the **Go To** dialog box, in the **Reference** box, type **m172** and then click **OK**. (Mac users, press [control] + [G], and then click in the Reference box.) With cell **M172** active, on the **Formulas tab**, in the **Function Library** group, click **More Functions**, point to **Statistical**, and then click **COUNTIF**. As the **Range**, type **m2:m170** and as the **Criteria**, type **Staff** Click **OK**. Your result is *27*, indicating that 27 courses still indicate *Staff* and need an instructor assigned. In cell **I172**, type **Still need instructor assigned** and press [Enter]. Press [Ctrl] + [Home] and click **Save**.

2 From your student files, open **e05C_Science_Requests**. (Mac users, do *not* open the file, or if you have opened the e05C_Science_Requests workbook, close the file. In your Lastname_Firstname_5C_Science_Schedule file, click cell M38, type Marshall, Eric and then make cell A1 the active cell. Skip steps a – f and continue with step 3.)

a. On the **View tab**, in the **Window group**, click **Switch Windows**, and then on the list, click your **Lastname_Firstname_5C_Science_Schedule** file to make it the active worksheet. On the **View tab**, in the **Window group**, click **Arrange All**. Click **Horizontal**, and then click **OK**.

b. Click cell **A172**. In the **Window group**, click **Split**. Above the split bar, click any cell in **column C**. Press [Ctrl] + [F] to display the **Find and Replace** dialog box. Locate the first request in the e05C_Science_Requests worksheet, which is from *Eric Marshall* to teach *Survey of Astronomy Section # 76822*. In the **Find what** box, type **76822** so that you can locate the course in the worksheet.

c. Click **Find Next**. Drag the title bar of the dialog box into the upper right area of your screen so that you can see the **Name Box**. In your **Lastname_Firstname_5C_Science_Schedule** worksheet, click in cell **M38**, type **Marshall, Eric** to delete *Staff* and assign the class to Mr. Marshall. Press [Enter].

d. **Close** the **Find and Replace** dialog box. In cell **M172**, notice that *26* classes remain unassigned.

e. Click any cell in the **e05C_Science_Requests** worksheet, and then on this worksheet's title bar, click **Close**. On the title bar of your **Lastname_Firstname_5C_Science_Schedule** worksheet, click **Maximize** to restore the size of the worksheet to its full size. On the **View tab**, in the **Window group**, click **Split** to remove the split.

f. Press [Ctrl] + [Home], and then **Save** your workbook.

3 Point to the **row 1 heading**, right-click, and then click **Insert**. (Mac users, hold down [control], and then click the row 1 heading to display the shortcut menu. Then click Insert.) In cell **A1**, type **Schedule of Classes with Unassigned Sections Merge & Center** this title across the range **A1:P1**, and then apply the **Title** cell style.

a. On the **Page Layout tab**, in the **Themes group**, click **Themes**, and then, click **Slice**. In the **Themes group**, click **Fonts**. Scroll to the top if necessary, and then click **Office**.

b. On the **Home tab**, in the **Styles group**, click **Format as Table**. At the bottom, click **New Table Style**. In the **New Table Style** dialog box, in the **Name** box, replace the existing text by typing **Science Schedule** In the list under **Table Element**, click **First Row Stripe**, and then click **Format**. In the **Format Cells** dialog box, click the **Fill tab**. (Mac users, click the Background color arrow to display the color palette.) In the fifth column of colors, click the second color, and then click **OK**.

(continues on next page)

Chapter Review

c. In the lower left corner of the dialog box, click to select the check box **Set as default table style for this document**, and then click **OK**.

d. Select the range **A2:P171**, and then in the **Styles group**, click **Format as Table**. At the top of the gallery, under **Custom**, locate and then click your custom **Science Schedule** table style. In the **Format As Table** dialog box, click **OK**. Press Ctrl + Home to deselect and move to cell **A1**. Click **Save**.

4 On the **Page Layout tab**, in the **Page Setup group**, set the **Orientation** to **Landscape**. Then, in the **Scale to Fit group**, click the **Width arrow**, and then click **1 page**.

a. Insert a footer that includes the file name in the **left section**.

b. On the **View tab**, in the **Workbook Views group**, click **Page Break Preview**. Scroll down to view pages 4 and 5, and then position the break between **Page 4** and **Page 5** between **row 152** and **row 153**.

c. On the **View tab**, in the **Workbook Views group**, click **Normal**, and then press Ctrl + Home.

d. Click the **Page Layout tab**, in the **Page Setup group**, click **Print Titles** to display the **Sheet tab** of the **Page Setup** dialog box.

e. Under **Print titles**, click in the **Rows to repeat at top** box, and then in the worksheet, select **row 2**. Click **OK**.

5 Click cell **M2**. On the **Insert tab**, in the **Links group**, click **Link**. Under **Link to**, click **Existing File or Web Page**. Click the **Look in arrow**, navigate to your student data files, and then select the **e05C_Science_ Faculty** workbook. Click **OK**. (Mac users, with Web Page or File selected, to the right of Address, click Select. Navigate to your downloaded files, click e05C_Science_ Faculty, click Open, and then click OK.)

a. Point to cell **M2** to display the 🖑 pointer, and then click to confirm that the link opens the workbook containing the contact information. **Close** the workbook with the faculty contacts.

b. Point to cell **M2**, right-click, and then click **Edit Hyperlink**. In the upper right corner of the **Edit Hyperlink** dialog box, click **ScreenTip**. In the **ScreenTip text** box, type **Click here for contact information** and then click **OK** two times. Point to cell **M2** and confirm that your **ScreenTip** displays.

c. Display the workbook **Properties**. As the **Tags**, type **science schedule** and as the **Subject**, type your course name and section number. Under **Related People**, be sure that your name displays as **Author**.

d. **Save** and **Close** your workbook. Print or submit your workbook electronically as directed by your instructor.

You have completed Project 5C   **END**

Chapter Review

c. In the lower left corner of the dialog box, click to select the check box **Set as default table style for this document**, and then click **OK**.

d. Select the range **A2:P171**, and then in the **Styles group**, click **Format as Table**. At the top of the gallery, under **Custom**, locate and then click your custom **Science Schedule** table style. In the **Format As Table** dialog box, click **OK**. Press Ctrl + Home to deselect and move to cell **A1**. Click **Save**.

4 On the **Page Layout tab**, in the **Page Setup group**, set the **Orientation** to **Landscape**. Then, in the **Scale to Fit group**, click the **Width arrow**, and then click **1 page.**

a. Insert a footer that includes the file name in the **left section**.

b. On the **View tab**, in the **Workbook Views group**, click **Page Break Preview**. Scroll down to view pages 4 and 5, and then position the break between **Page 4** and **Page 5** between **row 152** and **row 153**.

c. On the **View tab**, in the **Workbook Views group**, click **Normal**, and then press Ctrl + Home.

d. Click the **Page Layout tab**, in the **Page Setup group**, click **Print Titles** to display the **Sheet tab** of the **Page Setup** dialog box.

e. Under **Print titles**, click in the **Rows to repeat at top** box, and then in the worksheet, select **row 2**. Click **OK**.

5 Click cell **M2**. On the **Insert tab**, in the **Links group**, click **Link**. Under **Link to**, click **Existing File or Web Page**. Click the **Look in arrow**, navigate to your student data files, and then select the **e05C_Science_ Faculty** workbook. Click **OK**. (Mac users, with Web Page or File selected, to the right of Address, click Select. Navigate to your downloaded files, click e05C_Science_ Faculty, click Open, and then click OK.)

a. Point to cell **M2** to display the 🖑 pointer, and then click to confirm that the link opens the workbook containing the contact information. **Close** the workbook with the faculty contacts.

b. Point to cell **M2**, right-click, and then click **Edit Hyperlink**. In the upper right corner of the **Edit Hyperlink** dialog box, click **ScreenTip**. In the **ScreenTip text** box, type **Click here for contact information** and then click **OK** two times. Point to cell **M2** and confirm that your **ScreenTip** displays.

c. Display the workbook **Properties**. As the **Tags**, type **science schedule** and as the **Subject**, type your course name and section number. Under **Related People**, be sure that your name displays as **Author**.

d. **Save** and **Close** your workbook. Print or submit your workbook electronically as directed by your instructor.

You have completed Project 5C | END

Chapter Review

Apply 5B skills from these Objectives:

5. Use Advanced Sort Techniques
6. Use Custom and Advanced Filters
7. Subtotal, Outline, and Group a List of Data

In the following Skills Review, you will use advanced table features to provide Dr. Marshall Eaton, the Dean of the Arts Division, information about the Spring course sections and assigned faculty in the Division. Your completed worksheets will look similar to Figure 5.58.

Project Files

For Project 5D, you will need the following file:

e05D_Spring_Sections

You will save your workbook as:

Lastname_Firstname_5D_Spring_Sections

Project Results

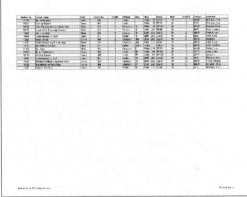

Figure 5.58

(continues on next page)

Chapter Review

1 Start Excel. From your student files, open the file **e05D_Spring_Sections**, and then **Save** the file in your **Excel Chapter 5** folder as **Lastname_Firstname_5D_Spring_Sections**

a. Make sure the **Online-Campus-Studio** worksheet displays. On the **Data tab**, in the **Sort & Filter group**, click **Sort**. In the **Sort** dialog box, under **Column**, click the **Sort by arrow**, and then click **Delivery**. Under **Sort On**, click the **arrow**, and then click **Cell Values**. Under **Order**, click the **Order arrow** for this sort level, and then click **Custom List**. In the dialog box, under **Custom lists**, be sure **NEW LIST** is selected. Then, under **List entries**, click in the empty box and type **Studio** Press [Enter], type **Classroom** Press [Enter], type **Online** and then in the **Custom Lists** dialog box, click **Add**. Click **OK**. (Mac users, on the menu, click Excel, and then click Preferences. Under Formulas and Lists, click Custom Lists. Under List entries, type Studio, Online, Classroom and then click Add. Close the Custom Lists dialog box. On the Data tab, click Sort. Sort by Delivery and then click the Order arrow. Click Custom List, and then click Studio, Online, Classroom. Click OK.)

b. Click **Add Level**, and then as the second level sort, click **Dept**. Click **Add Level** again, and as the third level sort, click **Course Name**. Click **OK**. (Mac users, in the lower left corner of the Sort dialog box, click the plus sign (+) to add a level.)

2 Click the **Music & Dance sheet tab** to display the second worksheet. In cell **C1**, click the **Dept. filter arrow**. Click the **(Select All)** check box to clear all the check boxes, and then select the **Drama** and the **Music** check boxes. Click **OK**.

a. In cell **E1**, click the **Credits filter arrow**, and then filter the list further by selecting **3**. In cell **F1**, click the **Delivery filter arrow**, and filter the list further by selecting **Online**. The status bar information indicates that *4 of the 39* course sections meet the filter criteria.

b. On the **Data tab**, in the **Sort & Filter group**, **Clear** all filters. In cell **K1**, click the **Enrolled filter arrow**, point to **Number Filters**, and then click **Less Than Or Equal To**. In the first box, be sure that *is less than or equal to* displays, and then in the second box, type **15** Click **OK** to display *16* records. (Mac users, under Filter, click the Choose One arrow, and then click Less Than Or Equal To. In the box to the right, type 15.) **Save** the workbook.

3 Display the **Schedule Comparison** worksheet. **Copy** the range **A6:G7**, **Paste** it in cell **A1**, and then change the title in cell **A1** to **Criteria**

a. Select the range **A2:G3**, and then in the **Name Box**, name this range **Criteria**

b. **Copy** the range **A1:G2**, scroll down to view **row 34**, point to cell **A34**, right-click, and then click **Paste**. Click cell **A34**, and then change the title to **Morning-Evening Schedule** and then press [Enter]. Select the range **A35:G35** and then in the **Name Box**, name this range **Extract**

c. Select the range **A7:G32** and then in the **Name Box**, name this range **Database**

d. At the top of your worksheet, in cell **E3**, type **Morning** and in cell **F3**, type **Evening**

e. On the **Data tab**, in the **Sort & Filter group**, click **Advanced**. Under **Action**, click **Copy to another location**. Verify that in the **Copy to** box—*$A$35:$G$35*—displays. Click **OK**, and then scroll to view the lower portion of your worksheet. Two records meet the criteria. **Save** the workbook.

4 Display the **Salaries by Department** worksheet. Select the range **A2:G30**. On the **Data tab**, in the **Sort & Filter group**, click **Sort**. In the **Sort** dialog box, sort by the **Dept.** column, and then add a level and sort by the **Annual Salary** column. Click **OK**.

a. With the range still selected, on the **Data tab**, in the **Outline group**, click **Subtotal**. In the **Subtotal** dialog box, in the **At each change in** box, display the list, and then click **Dept**. In the **Use function** box, display the list and click **Sum**. In the **Add subtotal to** list, select the **Annual Salary** check box, and then deselect any other check boxes. Click **OK**.

b. At the top of the outline area, click the **Level 2** button to hide all Level 3 details and display only the Level 2 summary information, and the Level 1 Grand Total.

c. Group the four worksheets. Insert a footer in the **left section** that includes the file name, and in the **right section**, insert the **Sheet Name**. On the **Page Layout tab**, set the **Width** to **1 page** and set the **Height** to **1 page**—this will scale each worksheet to fit on a single page. **Ungroup** the worksheets.

(continues on next page)

Chapter Review

d. Click the **Online-Campus-Studio** sheet, hold down Shift, and then click the **Music & Dance** sheet to select both sheets. Change the **Orientation** to **Landscape**, and then **Ungroup** the sheets.

e. Display the workbook **Properties**. As the **Tags**, type **sections, schedule, salaries** and as the **Subject**, type your course name and section number. Under **Related People**, be sure that your name displays as **Author**.

f. **Save** and **Close** your workbook. Print or submit your workbook electronically as directed by your instructor.

You have completed Project 5D | END

MyLab IT Grader | **Mastering Excel** | **Project 5E Sports Schedule**

Apply 5A skills from these Objectives:

1. Navigate and Manage Large Worksheets
2. Enhance Worksheets with Themes and Styles
3. Format a Worksheet to Share with Others
4. Save Excel Data in Other File Formats

In the following Mastering Excel project, you will assist Damian Howard, Athletic Director at Laurel College, in formatting and navigating a large worksheet that lists the sports events schedule for spring sports. Your completed worksheets will look similar to Figure 5.59.

Project Files for **MyLab IT Grader**

1. In your **MyLab IT** course, locate and click **Excel 5E Sports Schedule**, Download Materials, and then Download All Files.
2. Extract the zipped folder to your Excel Chapter 5 folder, and then close the Grader download screens.
3. Take a moment to open the downloaded **Excel_5E_Sports_Schedule_Instructions**; note any recent updates to the book.

Project Results

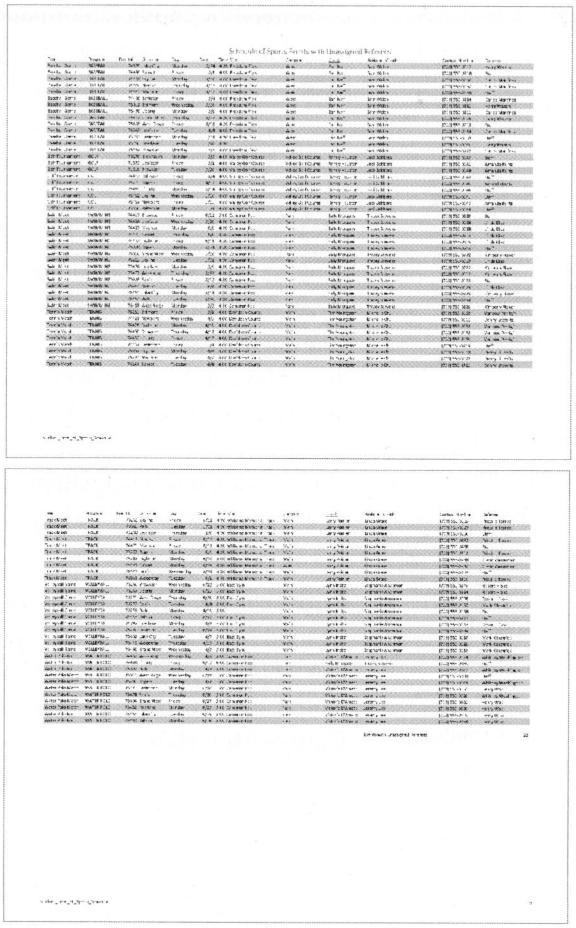

Figure 5.59

For Non-MyLab Submissions

For Project 5E, you will need:

e05E_Sports_Schedule

e05E_Sports_Coaches

e05E_Referee_Requests

In your Excel Chapter 5 folder, save your workbook as:

Lastname_Firstname_5E_Sports_Schedule

If your instructor requires a workbook with formulas, save as:

Lastname_Firstname_5E_Sports_Schedule_formulas

After you have named and saved your workbook, on the next page, begin with step 2.

After step 12, save and submit your file as directed by your instructor.

Content-Based Assessments (Mastery and Transfer of Learning)

1 ▶ Navigate to your **Excel Chapter 5 folder**, and then double-click the Excel file you downloaded from **MyLab IT** that displays your name—**Student_Excel_5E_Sports_Schedule**.

2 ▶ **Go To** cell **M82**, and then insert a **COUNTIF** function to count the number of **Staff** referees using the range **M1:M80** in the formula. In cell **K82**, type **Events with Unassigned Referees**

3 ▶ Move to cell **A1**, and then from the files you downloaded for this project, **Open** the file **e05E_Referee_Requests**. Switch windows, and then make your **5E_Sports_Schedule** the active window. Arrange the two files horizontally. (Mac users, do *not* open the file, or if you have opened the e05E_Referee_Requests workbook, close the file. In your 5E_Sports_Schedule file, click cell M48, type Danny Litowitz and then make cell A1 the active cell. Skip steps 4 and 5, and then continue with step 6.)

4 ▶ In your **5E_Sports_Schedule** workbook, **Go To** cell **A82**, **Split** the window, and then click in any cell above the split in **column C**. Use **Find** to locate the first **Event #** request from the **e05E_Referee_Requests** worksheet, and then in cell **M48** in your **5E_Sports_Schedule** workbook, type **Danny Litowitz** to assign him as the *Referee*.

5 ▶ **Close** the **Find and Replace** dialog box, and then **Close** the **e05E_Referee_Requests** workbook. **Maximize** your **5E_Sports_Schedule** worksheet, and then remove the **Split**.

6 ▶ Insert a new blank **row 1**. In cell **A1**, type **Schedule of Sports Events with Unassigned Referees** and then **Merge & Center** the title across the range **A1:M1**. Apply the **Title** cell style.

7 ▶ Create a **New Table Style** named **Sports Schedule** and format the **First Row Stripe** with a **Fill**—in the last column, the third color. Set the style you created as the default table style for this workbook.

8 ▶ Select the range **A2:M81** and apply the **Custom table style**—**Sports Schedule**.

9 ▶ **AutoFit columns A:M**. Set the **Orientation** to **Landscape**, set the **Width** to **1 page**, and center the worksheet **Horizontally**. Insert a footer in the **left section** that includes the file name, and in the **right section**, insert a page number.

10 ▶ In **Page Break Preview**, break **Page 1** after **row 49** to end Page 1 with *TENNIS* and begin **Page 2** with *TRACK*. Return to **Normal** view. Set **Print Titles** to repeat **row 2** at the top of each page.

11 ▶ In cell **J2**, **Insert** a **Hyperlink** to your student data file **e05E_Sports_Coaches**. Create the **ScreenTip Click here for contact information** and then test your hyperlink. **Close** the **e05E_Sports_Coaches** file.

12 ▶ Display the workbook **Properties**, and then as the **Tags**, type **sports schedule** As the **Subject**, type your course name and section number. Be sure your name displays as the **Author** and then **Save** your workbook and **Close** Excel.

13 ▶ In **MyLab IT**, locate and click the Grader Project Excel 5E Sports Schedule. In **step 3**, under **Upload Completed Assignment**, click **Choose File**. In the **Open** dialog box, navigate to your **Excel Chapter 5 folder**, and then click your **Student_Excel_5E_Sports_Schedule** file one time to select it. In the lower right corner of the **Open** dialog box, click **Open**.

The name of your selected file displays above the Upload button.

14 ▶ To submit your file to **MyLab IT** for grading, click **Upload**, wait a moment for a green **Success!** message, and then in **step 4**, click the blue **Submit for Grading** button. Click **Close Assignment** to return to your list of **Course Materials**.

You have completed Project 5E `END`

MyLab IT Grader	Mastering	Project 5F Career Programs

Apply 5B skills from these Objectives:

5. Use Advanced Sort Techniques
6. Use Custom and Advanced Filters
7. Subtotal, Outline, and Group a List of Data

In the following Mastering Excel project, you will edit a worksheet for Michael Schaeffler, Vice President of Instruction, with data that has been sorted, filtered, and grouped that analyzes Career Tech programs at Laurel College. The worksheets of your workbook will look similar to Figure 5.60.

Project Files for **MyLab IT Grader**

1. In your **MyLab IT** course, locate and click **Excel 5F Career Programs**, Download Materials, and then Download All Files.
2. Extract the zipped folder to your Excel Chapter 5 folder, and then close the Grader download screens.
3. Take a moment to open the downloaded **Excel_5F_Career_Programs_Instructions**; note any recent updates to the book.

Project Results

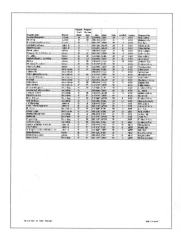
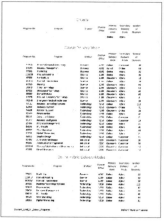
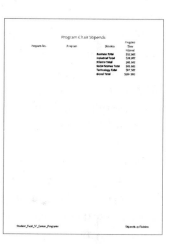

Figure 5.60

For Non-MyLab Submissions

For Project 5F, you will need:
e05F_Career Programs

In your Excel Chapter 5 folder, save your workbook as:
Lastname_Firstname_5F_Career_Programs

If your instructor requires a workbook with formulas, save as:
Lastname_Firstname_5F_Career_Programs_formulas

After you have named and saved your workbook, on the next page, begin with step 2.

After step 10, save and submit your file as directed by your instructor.

(continues on next page)

Content-Based Assessments (Mastery and Transfer of Learning)

1 Navigate to your **Excel Chapter 5 folder**, and then double-click the Excel file you downloaded from **MyLab IT** that displays your name—**Student_Excel_5F_Career_Programs**.

2 On the **Main-East-West** worksheet, insert a table using the range **A1:J40**. Display the **Table Styles** gallery, and then under **Light**, in the last row, apply the first style.

3 **Sort** the table by **Campus** using a **Custom List** in the following order: **MAIN, EAST, WEST**. (Mac users, create the custom list in the Excel, Preferences, Custom Lists dialog box.) Add a second level sort by **Division** and a third level sort by **Program Name** both in ascending order.

4 Display the second worksheet, **Delivery Mode Comparison**. **Copy** the range **A6:G7**, and then **Paste** the range to cell **A1**. Change the title in cell **A1** to **Criteria** and then select the range **A2:G3** and name it **Criteria**

5 **Copy** the range **A1:G2**, and then **Paste** the range to cell **A36**. Change the title in cell **A36** to **Online-Hybrid Delivery Modes** and then select the range **A37:G37** and name it **Extract** Select the range **A7:G34**, and then name this range **Database**

6 Create an advanced filter that will place in the **Extract** area the records from the **Database** range in which **Online** is the primary delivery mode and **Hybrid** is the secondary delivery mode.

7 Display the **Stipends by Division** worksheet. Sort the data in ascending order first by **Division** and then by **Program Chair Stipend**.

8 Apply subtotals to the **Program Chair Stipend** column at each change in **Division**. AutoFit columns **C:D** and then collapse the outline so that the **Level 2** summary information is displayed.

9 Group all three worksheets. Insert a footer in the **left section** that includes the file name, and in the **right section**, insert the **Sheet Name**. Center the worksheets **Horizontally**, and then set the **Width** and **Height** to **1 page**.

10 Display the workbook **Properties**, and then as the **Tags**, type **career programs** As the **Subject**, type your course name and section number. Be sure your name displays as the **Author**, and then **Save** your workbook and **Close** Excel.

11 In **MyLab IT**, locate and click the Grader Project **Excel 5F Career Programs**. In **step 3**, under **Upload Completed Assignment**, click **Choose File**. In the **Open** dialog box, navigate to your **Excel Chapter 5 folder**, and then click your **Student_Excel_5F_Career_Programs** file one time to select it. In the lower right corner of the **Open** dialog box, click **Open**.

The name of your selected file displays above the Upload button.

12 To submit your file to **MyLab IT** for grading, click **Upload**, wait a moment for a green **Success!** message, and then in **step 4**, click the blue **Submit for Grading** button. Click **Close Assignment** to return to your list of **Course Materials**.

You have completed Project 5F END

Content-Based Assessments (Mastery and Transfer of Learning)

MyLab IT Grader	**Mastering**	**Project 5G Sports Programs**

Apply 5A and 5B skills from these Objectives:

1. Navigate and Manage Large Worksheets
2. Enhance Worksheets with Themes and Styles
3. Format a Worksheet to Share with Others
4. Save Excel Data in Other File Formats
5. Use Advanced Sort Techniques
6. Use Custom and Advanced Filters
7. Subtotal, Outline, and Group a List of Data

In the following Mastering Excel project, you will create a worksheet for Sandy Chase, Assistant Director of Athletics, with data that has been sorted, filtered, and grouped and that analyzes sports programs at Laurel College. The worksheets of your workbook will look similar to Figure 5.61.

Project Files for **MyLab IT Grader**

1. In your **MyLab IT** course, locate and click **Excel 5G Sports Programs**, Download Materials, and then Download All Files.
2. Extract the zipped folder to your Excel Chapter 5 folder, and then close the Grader download screens.
3. Take a moment to open the downloaded **Excel_5G_Sports_Programs_Instructions**; note any recent updates to the book.

Project Results

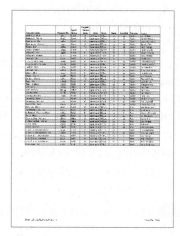

Figure 5.61

For Non-MyLab Submissions

For Project 5G, you will need:
e05G_Sports_Programs
e05G_Coach_Information

In your Excel Chapter 5 folder, save your workbook as:
Lastname_Firstname_5G_Sports_Programs
If your instructor requires a workbook with formulas, save as:
Lastname_Firstname_5G_Sports_Programs_formulas

After you have named and saved your workbook, on the next page, begin with step 2.
After step 11, save and submit your file as directed by your instructor.

(continues on next page)

Content-Based Assessments (Mastery and Transfer of Learning)

1 Navigate to your **Excel Chapter 5 folder**, and then double-click the Excel file you downloaded from **MyLab IT** that displays your name—**Student_Excel_5G_Sports_Programs**.

2 Display the **Valley-Park-West** worksheet. Select the range **A1:J40**, insert a table, and then display the **Table Styles** gallery. In the third row, apply the fourth style or choose another style.

3 **Sort** the table on the **Campus** column using a **Custom List** in the following order: **Valley, Park, West**. (Mac users, create the custom list in the Excel, Preferences, Custom Lists dialog box.) Add a second level sort by **Sport Group** and a third level sort by **Program Name** both in ascending order.

4 Display the **Sports Season Comparison** worksheet. **Copy** the range **A6:G7**, **Paste** it in cell **A1**, and then change the title in cell **A1** to **Criteria** Select the range **A2:G3**, and then name this range **Criteria**

5 **Copy** the range **A1:G2**, and then **Paste** the copied range in cell **A36**. Change the title in cell **A36** to **Fall-Summer Sports Season** Name the range **A37:G37 Extract** and then name the range **A7:G34 Database**

6 Create an advanced filter that will place in the **Extract** area the records from the Database range in which **Fall** is the primary season and **Summer** is the secondary season.

7 Display the **Stipends by Group** worksheet. **Sort** the data in ascending order by **Group**, then by the **Coach Stipend**.

8 Apply subtotals to the **Coach Stipend** column at each change in **Group**. **AutoFit columns C:D** and then collapse the outline so that the Level 2 summary information is displayed.

9 On the **Valley-Park-West** worksheet, in cell **J1**, insert a **Hyperlink** to the file you downloaded with this project, **e05G_Coach_Information**. Display the **ScreenTip**, type **Click here for contact information** and then test your hyperlink. **Close** the **e05G_Coach_Information** file.

10 Select all three worksheets. Insert a footer in the **left section** that includes the file name, and in the **right section**, insert the **Sheet Name**. Set the **Width** and **Height** to **1 page**, and **Center** the worksheets horizontally. Change the **Theme** to **Slice**, and then change the **Fonts** theme to **Corbel**.

11 Display the workbook **Properties**, and then as the **Tags**, type **sports programs** As the **Subject**, type your course name and section number. Be sure your name displays as the **Author**, and then **Save** your workbook and **Close** Excel.

12 In **MyLab IT**, locate and click the Grader Project **Excel 5G Sports Programs**. In **step 3**, under **Upload Completed Assignment**, click **Choose File**. In the **Open** dialog box, navigate to your **Excel Chapter 5 folder**, and then click your **Student_Excel_5G_Sports_Programs** file one time to select it. In the lower right corner of the **Open** dialog box, click **Open**.

The name of your selected file displays above the Upload button.

13 To submit your file to **MyLab IT** for grading, click **Upload**, wait a moment for a green **Success!** message, and then in **step 4**, click the blue **Submit for Grading** button. Click **Close Assignment** to return to your list of **Course Materials**.

You have completed Project 5G **END**

Content-Based Assessments (Critical Thinking)

Apply a combination of the 5A and 5B skills.

GO! Fix It	Project 5H Programs	IRC
GO! Make It	Project 5I Arts Faculty	IRC
GO! Solve It	Project 5J Organizations	IRC
GO! Solve It	Project 5K Dept Tutors	

Project Files

For Project 5K, you will need the following file:

e05K_Dept_Tutors

You will save your workbook as:

Lastname_Firstname_5K_Dept_Tutors

Open the file **e05K_Dept_Tours** and save it in your Excel Chapter 5 folder as **Lastname_Firstname_5K_Dept_Tours**

The Director of the Tutoring Center wants to know which tutors are available to tutor online from the CPS department. Create and name Criteria, Extract, and Database ranges, and then use the Advanced filtering feature to copy the requested information to the extract range. Include the file name in the footer, add appropriate properties, and then save your workbook. Submit as directed.

		Performance Level		
		Exemplary	**Proficient**	**Developing**
Performance Criteria	Range names created	All range names are created.	Some, but not all range names are created.	Range names are not created.
	Data filtered correctly	Data is filtered according to both criteria and copied to extract range.	Not all criteria are applied or the data is filtered in place and is not copied to the extract range.	The data is not filtered.

You have completed Project 5K END

Outcomes-Based Assessments (Critical Thinking)

Rubric

The following outcomes-based assessments are *open-ended assessments*. That is, there is no specific correct result; your result will depend on your approach to the information provided. Make *Professional Quality* your goal. Use the following scoring rubric to guide you in *how* to approach the problem and then to evaluate *how well* your approach solves the problem.

The *criteria*—Software Mastery, Content, Format and Layout, and Process—represent the knowledge and skills you have gained that you can apply to solving the problem. The *levels of performance*—Professional Quality, Approaching Professional Quality, or Needs Quality Improvements—help you and your instructor evaluate your result.

	Your completed project is of Professional Quality if you:	Your completed project is Approaching Professional Quality if you:	Your completed project Needs Quality Improvements if you:
1-Software Mastery	Choose and apply the most appropriate skills, tools, and features and identify efficient methods to solve the problem.	Choose and apply some appropriate skills, tools, and features, but not in the most efficient manner.	Choose inappropriate skills, tools, or features, or are inefficient in solving the problem.
2-Content	Construct a solution that is clear and well organized, contains content that is accurate, appropriate to the audience and purpose, and is complete. Provide a solution that contains no errors of spelling, grammar, or style.	Construct a solution in which some components are unclear, poorly organized, inconsistent, or incomplete. Misjudge the needs of the audience. Have some errors in spelling, grammar, or style, but the errors do not detract from comprehension.	Construct a solution that is unclear, incomplete, or poorly organized, contains some inaccurate or inappropriate content, and contains many errors of spelling, grammar, or style. Do not solve the problem.
3-Format and Layout	Format and arrange all elements to communicate information and ideas, clarify function, illustrate relationships, and indicate relative importance.	Apply appropriate format and layout features to some elements, but not others. Overuse features, causing minor distraction.	Apply format and layout that does not communicate information or ideas clearly. Do not use format and layout features to clarify function, illustrate relationships, or indicate relative importance. Use available features excessively, causing distraction.
4-Process	Use an organized approach that integrates planning, development, self-assessment, revision, and reflection.	Demonstrate an organized approach in some areas, but not others; or, use an insufficient process of organization throughout.	Do not use an organized approach to solve the problem.

Outcomes-Based Assessments (Critical Thinking)

GO! Think	Project 5L Summer Sections

Project Files

For Project 5L, you will need the following file:

e05L_Summer_Sections

You will save your workbook as:

Lastname_Firstname_5L_Summer_Sections

From your student files, open the file e05L_Summer_Sections, and then save it in your Excel Chapter 5 folder as **Lastname_Firstname_5L_Summer_Sections** Create a custom table style, name it **Summer Sections** and then create a table using the Summer Sections style. Sort the table on the Campus field using the following order: Online, Valley, Park, West. Add a second sort level by Dept. and a third sort level by Course Name. Include the file name in the footer, set the orientation to landscape and the width to 1 page, and repeat rows as necessary at the top of each page. Add appropriate properties with the tags **summer sections** and then submit as directed.

	You have completed Project 5L	END

GO! Think	Project 5M Social Science	IRC

You and GO!	Project 5N Personal Expenses	IRC

Creating Charts, Diagrams, and Templates

EXCEL 2019

Azhar Hassan/Shutterstock

In This Chapter

GO! To Work with Excel

In this chapter, you will create charts and diagrams to communicate data visually. Charts make a set of numbers easier to understand by displaying data in a graphical format. Excel's SmartArt illustrations make diagrams, like an organizational chart or process cycle, easy to comprehend.

In this chapter, you will also work with templates. Templates have built-in formulas for performing calculations and are used for standardization and protection of data. You will create a template for an order form.

The projects in this chapter relate to **The Dallas–Ft. Worth Job Fair**, which is a nonprofit organization that

brings together employers and job seekers in the Dallas–Ft. Worth metropolitan area. Each year the organization holds targeted Job Fairs and the annual Dallas–Ft. Worth fair draws over 900 employers in more than 75 industries and registers more than 30,000 candidates. Candidate registration is free; employers pay a nominal fee to display and present at the fairs. Candidate resumes and employer postings are managed by a state-of-the-art database system, allowing participants quick and accurate access to job data and candidate qualifications.

PROJECT

6A

Attendance Charts
and Diagrams

MyLab IT
Project 6A Grader for Instruction
Project 6A Simulation for Training and Review

Project Activities

In Activities 6.01 through 6.17, you will create and format column and line charts for The Dallas–Ft. Worth Job Fair that display attendance patterns at the fairs over a five-year period. You will also create a process diagram and a funnel chart. Your completed worksheets will look similar to Figure 6.1.

Project Files for MyLab IT Grader

1. In your storage location, create a folder named **Excel Chapter 6**.
2. In your **MyLab IT** course, locate and click **Excel 6A Attendance**, Download Materials, and then Download All Files.
3. Extract the zipped folder to your Excel Chapter 6 folder. Close the Grader download screens.
4. Take a moment to open the downloaded **Excel_6A_Attendance_Instructions**; note any recent updates to the book.

Project Results

GO! Project 6A

Where We're Going

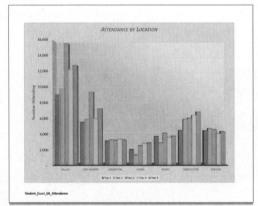

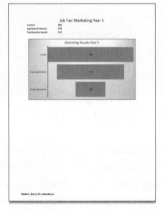

Figure 6.1 Project 6A Attendance Charts and Diagrams

For Non-MyLab Submissions	In your storage location, create a folder named **Excel Chapter 6**
For Project 6A, you will need: **e06A_Attendance**	In your Excel Chapter 6 folder, save your workbook as: **Lastname_Firstname_6A_Attendance** If your instructor requires a workbook with formulas, save as: **Lastname_Firstname_6A_Attendance_formulas**

After you have named and saved your workbook, on the next page, begin with Step 2.

Objective 1 | Create and Format Sparklines and a Column Chart

ALERT Because Office 365 is a cloud-based subscription service that receives continuous updates, you may encounter some variations in what appears on your screen and what is shown in this instruction. Microsoft Office 365 is fully installed on your PC or Mac; no internet access is necessary to create or edit documents. When you are connected to the internet, you will receive monthly upgrades and new features, so you always have the latest versions of Office apps as soon as they are available. Your subscription gives you continuous free access to the latest innovations and refinements.

GO! Learn How
Video E6-1

Recall that *sparklines* are tiny charts that fit within a cell and give a visual trend summary alongside your data. For example, sparklines are useful to show trends in a series of values such as seasonal increases or decreases in sales. Also recall that a *column chart*, which presents data graphically in vertical columns, is useful to make comparisons among related data.

Activity 6.01 | Creating and Formatting Sparklines

2.4.1

To create sparklines, first select the data you want to plot—represent graphically—and then select the range of cells alongside each row of data where you want to display the sparklines. Positioning a sparkline close to its data will have the greatest impact on the reader of your spreadsheet.

In this Activity, you will create sparklines to show each city's Job Fair attendance trend over the past five years.

1 Navigate to your **Excel Chapter 6 folder**, and then double-click the Excel file you downloaded from **MyLab IT** that displays your name—**Student_Excel_6A_Attendance**. If necessary, at the top click **Enable Editing**.

2 In your worksheet, notice that the data shows the number of applicants who have attended Job Fairs held over a five-year period at various locations in the greater Dallas–Ft. Worth area.

3 Select the range **B4:F10**, which represents the attendance numbers. In the lower right corner of the selected range, click **Quick Analysis** 📊, and then click **Sparklines**. Compare your screen with Figure 6.2.

MAC TIP On the Insert tab, in the Sparklines group, click Sparklines, and then click Line. When the Create Sparklines dialog box opens, select the range G4:G10 and click OK.

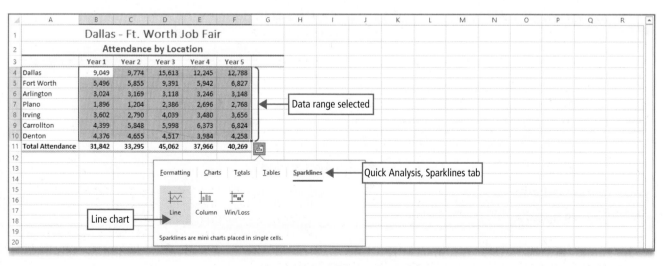

Figure 6.2

4 With **Sparklines** selected in the **Quick Analysis** tool, click **Line**. Compare your screen with Figure 6.3.

Sparklines display alongside each row of data and provide a quick visual trend summary for each city's Job Fair attendance. The sparklines provide a quick indication that—for most locations—attendance has had an overall upward trend over the five-year period.

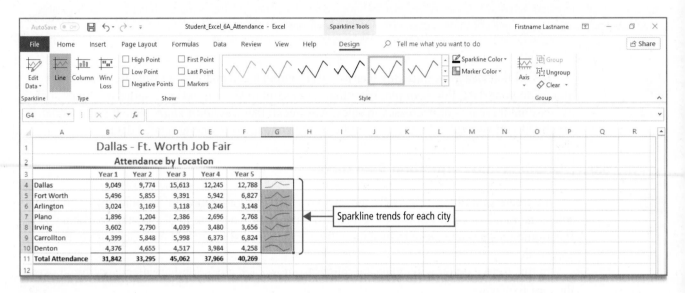

Figure 6.3

5 With the range containing the sparklines selected, click the **Sparkline Tools Design tab**. In the **Show group**, select the **High Point** check box and the **Last Point** check box.

By showing the High Point and the Last Point, you further emphasize the visual story that sparklines depict.

6 On the **Design tab**, in the **Style group**, click **More** ☑, and then in the first row, click the first style—**Sparkline Style Accent 1**.

7 In cell **G3**, type **Trend** and press Enter. Click cell **A1** to make it the active cell. **Save** 🖫 your workbook, and then compare your screen with Figure 6.4.

Use styles in this manner to further enhance your sparklines.

🖵 **MAC TIP** Use the first row of the drop-down Style group box, not the Styles still on the ribbon.

	A	B	C	D	E	F	G
A1	Dallas - Ft. Worth Job Fair						
1		Dallas - Ft. Worth Job Fair					
2		Attendance by Location					
3		Year 1	Year 2	Year 3	Year 4	Year 5	Trend
4	Dallas	9,049	9,774	15,613	12,245	12,788	
5	Fort Worth	5,496	5,855	9,391	5,942	6,827	
6	Arlington	3,024	3,169	3,118	3,246	3,148	
7	Plano	1,896	1,204	2,386	2,696	2,768	
8	Irving	3,602	2,790	4,039	3,480	3,656	
9	Carrollton	4,399	5,848	5,998	6,373	6,824	
10	Denton	4,376	4,655	4,517	3,984	4,258	
11	Total Attendance	31,842	33,295	45,062	37,966	40,269	

Formatted sparklines

Figure 6.4

Activity 6.02 | Creating a Column Chart

MOS
5.1.1, 5.1.2,
5.2.3, 5.3.2

A chart is a graphic representation of data. When you create a chart, first decide whether you are going to plot the values representing *totals* or the values representing *details*—you cannot plot both in the same chart.

Excel's ***Recommended Charts*** feature can help you make this decision by previewing suggested charts based upon patterns in your data. In this Activity, you will select the details—the number of attendees at each location each year. To help the reader understand the chart, you will also select the ***labels*** for the data—the column and row headings that describe the values. Here, the labels are the location names and the years.

1 Take a moment to study the data elements shown in Figure 6.5.

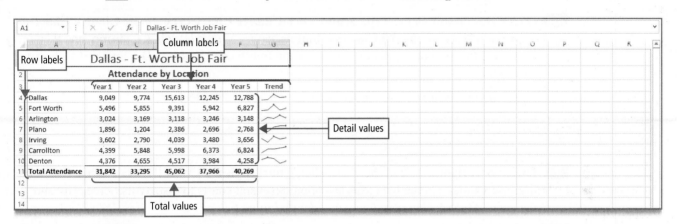

Figure 6.5

2 Select the range **A3:F10**. On the **Insert tab**, in the **Charts group**, click **Recommended Charts**. Compare your screen with Figure 6.6.

Excel recommends several charts based on the data you selected. The Clustered Column chart displays in the preview window.

ANOTHER WAY Click Quick Analysis, click Charts, and then click More Charts to open the Insert Chart dialog box.

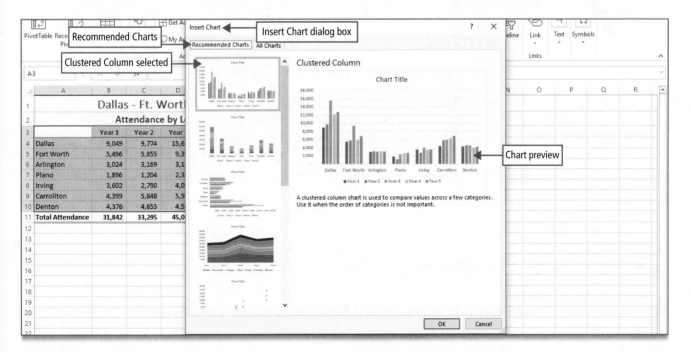

Figure 6.6

3 In the **Insert Chart** dialog box, with the **Clustered Column** chart selected, click **OK**.

MAC TIP Click the Clustered Column chart in the drop-down menu.

4 On the **Chart Tools Design tab**, in the **Location group**, click **Move Chart**.

The Move Chart dialog box displays. You can accept the default to display the chart as an object within the worksheet, which is an *embedded chart*. Or, you can place the chart on a separate sheet, referred to as a *chart sheet*, in which the chart fills the entire page. A chart sheet is useful when you want to view a chart separately from the worksheet data.

5 In the **Move Chart** dialog box, click **New sheet**. In the **New sheet** box, type **Attendance Chart** and then click **OK**.

6 On the **Design tab**, in the **Type group**, click **Change Chart Type**. In the **Change Chart Type** dialog box, on the **All Charts tab**, if necessary, on the left click **Column**, and then on the right, at the top of the dialog box, click the fourth chart icon—**3-D Clustered Column**. Click **OK**.

Use this technique to change the chart type.

MAC TIP In the drop-down menu, point to Column. Under 3-D Column, click the first style.

7 In the upper right corner of the chart, click **Chart Styles** 🖌. With the **Style tab** active in the displayed gallery, in the list of Styles, point to several charts to display its ScreenTip, and then click **Style 3**. Compare your screen with Figure 6.7.

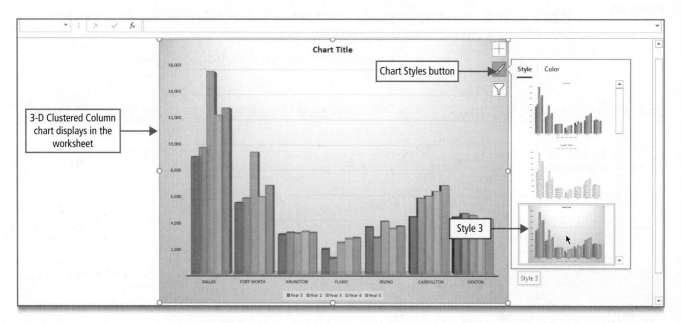

Figure 6.7

MAC TIP On the Chart Design ribbon, using the ScreenTips, click Style 3.

ANOTHER WAY On the Design tab, in the Chart Styles group, click More ▾, and then click Style 3.

8 ▶ Click **Chart Styles** ✐ to close the **Chart Styles** gallery. On the ribbon, in the **Chart Layouts group**, click **Add Chart Element** to display the **Chart Elements** list. Compare your screen with Figure 6.8, and then take a moment to study the table in Figure 6.9, which lists the elements that are typically found in a chart.

The Chart Elements list displays. *Chart elements* are the objects that make up a chart. From the Chart Elements list, you can select a chart element to format it.

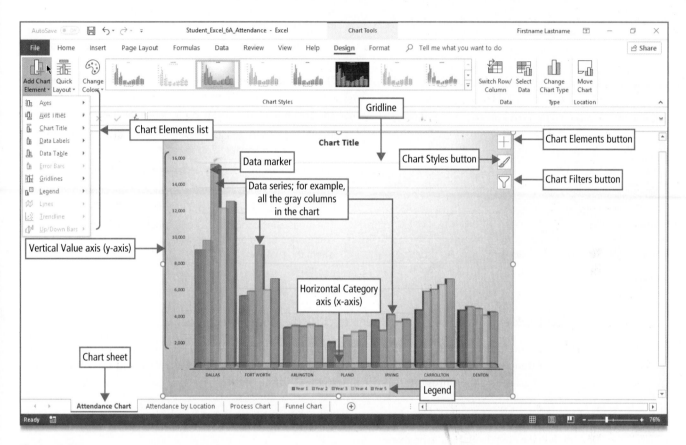

Figure 6.8

Microsoft Excel Chart Elements	
Chart Element	**Description**
Axis	A line that serves as a frame of reference for measurement and that borders the chart plot area.
Category labels	The labels that display along the bottom of the chart to identify the category of data.
Chart area	The entire chart and all its elements.
Data labels	Labels that display the value, percentage, and/or category of each particular data point and can contain one or more of the choices listed—Series name, Category name, Value, or Percentage.
Data marker	A column, bar, area, dot, pie slice, or other symbol in a chart that represents a single data point.
Data points	The numeric values of the selected worksheet.

(chart continues on next page)

Microsoft Excel Chart Elements	
Chart Element	**Description**
Data series	A group of related data points that are plotted in a chart.
Gridlines	Lines in the plot area that aid the eye in determining the plotted values.
Horizontal Category axis (x-axis)	The axis that displays along the bottom of the chart to identify the category of data. Excel uses the row titles as the category names.
Legend	A key that identifies patterns or colors that are assigned to the categories in the chart.
Major unit value	The value that determines the spacing between tick marks and between the gridlines in the plot area.
Plot area	The area bounded by the axes, including all the data series.
Tick mark labels	Identifying information for a tick mark generated from the cells on the worksheet used to create the chart.
Tick marks	The short lines that display on an axis at regular intervals.
Vertical Value axis (y-axis)	The axis that displays along the left side of the chart to identify the numerical scale on which the charted data is based.
Walls and floor	The areas surrounding a 3-D chart that give dimension and boundaries to the chart. Two walls and one floor display within the plot area.

Figure 6.9

9 Click in a blank area of the screen to close the **Chart Elements** list.

10 In the **Chart Area**, click the text *Chart Title* to select it. Watch the **Formula Bar** as you type **Attendance** as the chart title—your typing displays in the **Formula Bar** and not on the chart—and then press Enter to display the text in the chart.

MAC TIP Select the text *Chart Title* and then type *Attendance*. Your typing will not display in the Formula Bar unless you click in the Formula Bar and type there.

11 Click the tallest column displayed, which is in the **Dallas** category. Compare your screen with Figure 6.10.

All the columns representing the Series *Year 3* are selected—selection handles display at the corners of each column in the series—and a ScreenTip displays the value for the column you are pointing to. Recall that a data series is a group of related data—in this instance, the attendees at all the Job Fairs that were held in Year 3. Also notice that the Formula Bar displays the address for the selected data series.

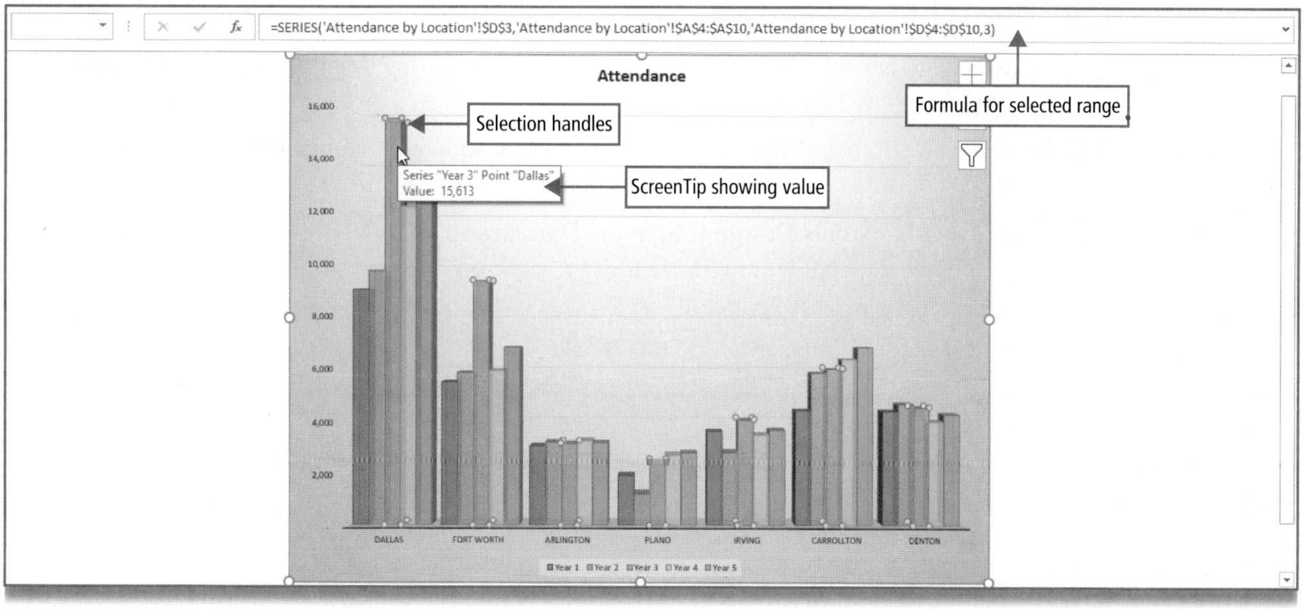

Attendance

Selection handles

Formula for selected range

Series "Year 3" Point "Dallas"
Value: 15,613

ScreenTip showing value

Figure 6.10

12 Locate the **Plano** category, and then click the shortest column in that group.

The selected series changes to those columns that represent the attendees at the Job Fairs in Year 2. The Formula Bar changes to indicate the selected series and a new ScreenTip displays when you point to the column.

13 Click outside the chart area to deselect the chart.

MORE KNOWLEDGE | **Sizing Handles and Selection Handles**

Sizing handles and selection handles look the same, and the terms are often used interchangeably. If a two-headed resize arrow—

⬍, ↔, ⬊, ⬈—displays when you point to boxes surrounding an object, it is a sizing handle; otherwise, it is a selection handle. Some objects in a chart cannot be resized, such as the category axis or the value axis, but they can be selected and then reformatted.

Activity 6.03 | Changing the Display of Chart Data

5.2.2

As you create a chart, you make choices about what data to include, the chart type, chart titles, and location. You can change the chart type, change the way the data displays, add or change titles, select different colors, and modify the background, scale, and chart location.

In the column chart you created, the attendance numbers are displayed along the value axis—the vertical axis—and the locations for each Job Fair are displayed along the category axis—the horizontal axis. The cells you select for a chart include the row and column labels from your worksheet. In a column or line chart, Excel selects whichever has more items—either the rows or the columns—and uses those labels to plot the data series, in this instance, the locations.

After plotting the data series, Excel uses the remaining labels—in this example, the years identified in the row headings—to create the data series labels on the legend. The legend is the key that defines the colors used in the chart; here it identifies the data series for the years. A different color is used for each year in the data series. The chart, as currently displayed, compares the change in attendance year to year grouped by location category. You can change the chart to display the years on the category axis and the locations as the data series identified in the legend.

1 In the **Dallas** category, click the fourth column.

All columns with the same color are selected. The ScreenTip displays *Series "Year 4" Point "Dallas" Value: 12,245.*

2 Point to each of the other gold columns that are selected and notice that the ScreenTip that displays identifies each gold column as being in the *Series "Year 4."*

3 Click the **Chart Tools Design tab**, in the **Data group**, click **Switch Row/Column**. Compare your screen with Figure 6.11.

The chart changes to display the locations as the data series. The locations are the row headings in the worksheet and are now identified in the legend. The years display as the category labels on the horizontal axis.

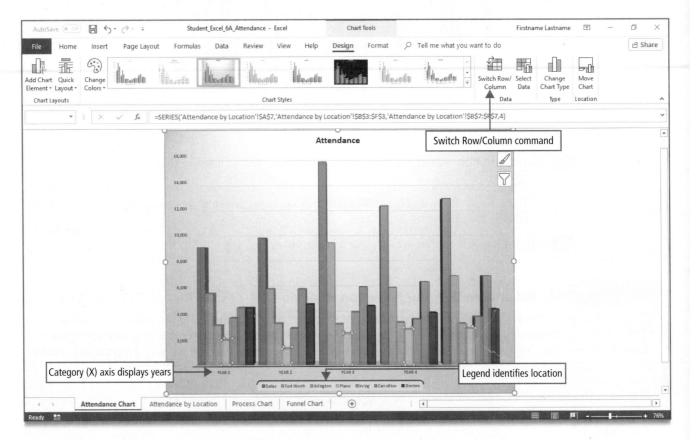

Figure 6.11

4 Click one of the gold columns. Point to each gold column and read the ScreenTip.

The ScreenTips for the gold columns now identify these columns as the *Plano* series.

5 On the **Design tab**, in the **Data group**, click **Switch Row/Column** again, and then **Save** 🖫 your workbook.

The chart changes back to the more useful arrangement with the years identified in the legend and the locations displayed as the category labels.

MORE KNOWLEDGE | **Changing the Range of Data in a Chart**

After creating a chart, you can adjust the range of data that displays in the chart. To do so, on the Design tab, in the Data group, click Select Data. Edit the source address displayed in the Chart data range box; or, drag over the data in the worksheet to adjust the range as needed.

Activity 6.04 | Editing and Formatting the Chart Title

The data displayed in the chart focuses on the attendance by location. It is good practice to create a chart title to reflect your charted data.

1 Click the text of the **Chart Title**—*Attendance*—to select it, and then click to position the mouse pointer to the right of *Attendance*.

> To edit a title, click once to select the chart object, and then click a second time to position the insertion point in the title and change to editing mode.

2 Press Spacebar one time, and then type **by Location**

3 Click the border surrounding the text *Attendance by Location* to change it to a solid line, point to the title text and right-click, and then on the shortcut menu, click **Font** to display the **Font** dialog box.

4 Set the **Font style** to **Bold Italic** and change the **Font Size** to **20**. Click the **Font color arrow**, and then under **Theme Colors**, in the first column, click the last color. Apply the **Small Caps** effect. Click **OK**, and then **Save** your workbook.

> Use the Font dialog box in this manner to apply multiple formats to a chart title or to other text.

Activity 6.05 | Adding, Formatting, and Aligning Axis Titles

You can add a title to display with both the value axis and the category axis.

1 With the chart selected, on the **Design tab**, in the **Chart Layouts group**, click **Add Chart Element**. Point to **Axis Titles**, and then click **Primary Vertical**.

> On the left side of the chart, *Axis Title* displays and is selected.

2 Click in the **Formula Bar**, type **Number Attending** as the **Vertical Axis Title**, and then press Enter to display the axis title text in the chart.

3 On the left side of the chart, point to the solid line surrounding the vertical axis title to display the pointer, right-click, and then on the shortcut menu, click **Font** to display the **Font** dialog box.

4 In the dialog box, change the **Font Size** to **14**. Click the **Font color arrow**, and then in the first column, click the last color. Be sure the **Font style** is set to **Bold**, and then click **OK**.

5 Click the **Chart Tools Format tab**, in the **Current Selection group**, click the **Chart Elements arrow**, click **Horizontal (Category) Axis**, and then at the bottom of the chart, notice that the **Category axis** containing the city names is selected.

6 Point to the border of the selected axis to display the pointer, right-click, and then on the shortcut menu, click **Font**. In the **Font dialog box**, click the **Font style arrow**, and then click **Bold**. Click the **Font color arrow**, and then in the first column, click the last color. Click **OK**.

7 On the left side of the chart, point to any number in the **Vertical (Value) Axis**, and then click one time to select the axis. Click the **Home tab**, and then in the **Font group**, change the **Font Size** to **12**.

> You can use multiple techniques to change font characteristics.

8 **Save** your workbook, and then compare your screen with Figure 6.12.

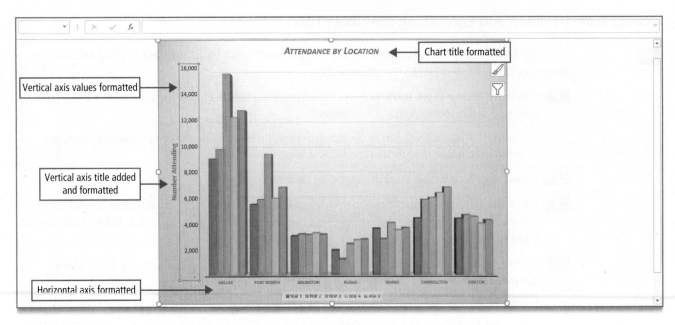

Figure 6.12

Activity 6.06 | Editing Source Data

One of the characteristics of an Excel chart is that it reflects changes made to the underlying data.

1 In the **Fort Worth** column cluster, point to the last column—**Year 5**. Notice that the *Value* for this column is *6,827*.

MAC TIP On the Chart Tools Tab on the right of the ribbon, click Format Pane.

2 At the bottom of your workbook, click the **Attendance by Location sheet tab**, and then in cell **F5**, type **7261** and press Enter.

3 Redisplay the **Attendance Chart** worksheet, **Save** 🖫 your workbook, and then point to the **Fort Worth** column for Year 5. Compare your screen with Figure 6.13.

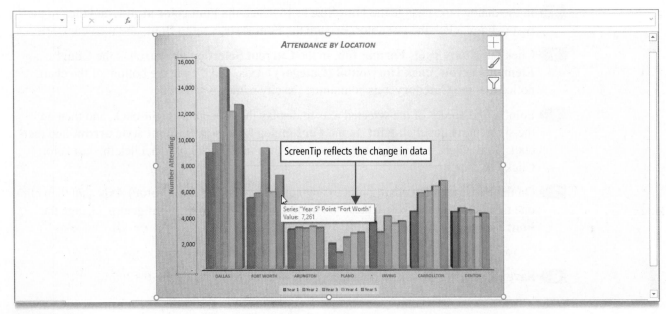

Figure 6.13

Activity 6.07 | Formatting the Chart Floor and Chart Walls

5.2.3

If your chart style includes shaded walls and a floor, you can format these elements.

1 Click the **Chart Tools Format tab**. In the **Current Selection group**, click the **Chart Elements arrow**, and then click **Back Wall**. Then in the same group, click **Format Selection**.

2 On the right, in the **Format Wall** pane, if necessary, expand **Fill**, click **Solid fill**, and then click the **Color arrow**. Under **Theme Colors**, in the fourth column, click the fourth color. Drag the slider to set the **Transparency** to **75%**.

3 At the top of the **Format Wall** pane, click the arrow to the right of **Wall Options** to display the **Chart Elements** list. Click **Side Wall**, and then apply the same fill, but with a **Transparency** of **60%**.

💻 **MAC TIP**   On the Format tab, in the Current Selection group, click the Chart Elements arrow, click Side Wall, click Format Pane.

---

4 At the top of the pane, click the **Wall Options arrow** again to display the list, click **Floor**, and then apply a **Solid fill**. Click the **Color arrow**, and then in the first column, click the last color. Leave the **Transparency** set to **0%**.

5 On the ribbon, in the **Current Selection group**, click to display the **Chart Elements** list, click the **Chart Area**, and then in the **Format Chart Area** pane on the right, click **Solid fill**. Click the **Color arrow**, and then in the seventh column, click the third color. **Close** ⊠ the **Format Chart Area** pane, click **Save** 🖫, and then compare your screen with Figure 6.14.

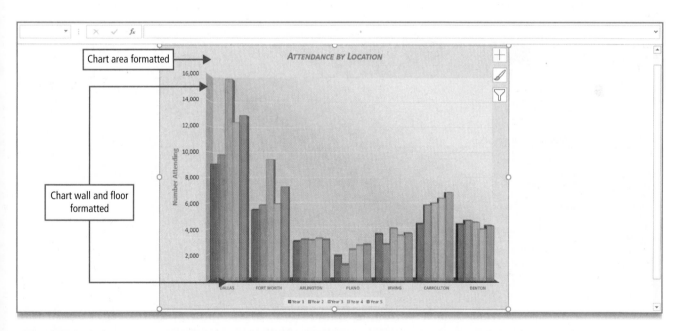

Figure 6.14

GO! Learn How

Video E6-2

Line charts show trends over time. A line chart can consist of one line, such as the price of a single company's stock over time, or it can display more than one line to show a comparison of related numbers over time. For example, charts tracking stock or mutual fund performance often display the price of the mutual fund on one line and an industry standard for that type of fund on a different line.

Activity 6.08 | Creating a Line Chart

5.1.1

In this Activity, you will create a line chart showing the change in attendance at the Dallas Job Fair over the five-year period.

1 In your **Attendance Chart** chart sheet, click in a white area outside the chart to deselect it, and then at the lower edge of your workbook, click the **Attendance by Location sheet tab**.

2 In the **Attendance by Location** worksheet, select the range **A3:F4**—the column titles and the data for Dallas. Click the **Insert tab**, in the **Charts group**, click **Insert Line or Area Chart** . In the first row, click the fourth chart type—**Line with Markers**. Compare your screen with Figure 6.15.

Cell A3 must be included in the selection, despite being empty, because the same number of cells must be equal in each selected row. Excel identifies the first row as a category because of the empty first cell.

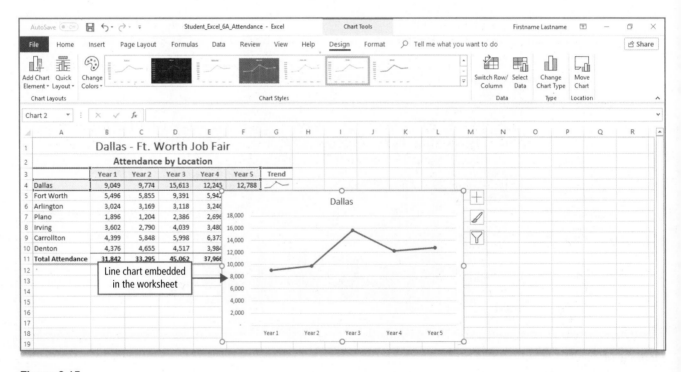

Figure 6.15

3 Point to the upper left chart border to display the pointer, and then drag the upper left corner of the chart slightly inside the upper left corner of cell **A13**.

4 Scroll down to view **row 30**. Point to the lower right corner of the chart to display the pointer, and then drag the lower right corner of the chart inside the lower right corner of cell **G29**. Click anywhere outside the chart to deselect. **Save** your workbook. Compare your screen with Figure 6.16.

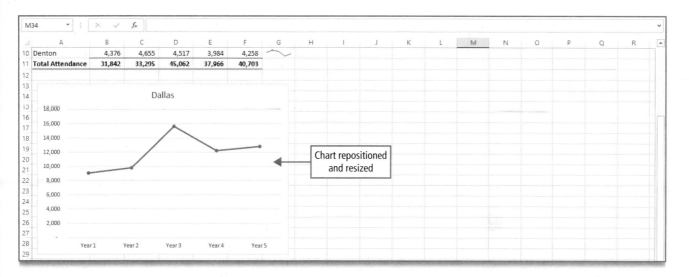

Figure 6.16

Activity 6.09 | Changing a Chart Title

When you select the chart type, the resulting chart might contain elements that you want to delete or change. For example, you might want to edit the chart title to be more specific.

1 Click the text of the **Chart Title**—*Dallas*. Type **Attendance at Dallas Job Fairs** as the chart title, which will display in the Formula Bar, and then press Enter to display the title text in the chart.

2 Point to the **Chart Title**, right-click, and then click **Font**. Change the **Font Size** to **16** and the **Font style** to **Bold Italic**. Click **OK**. Click outside of the chart to deselect it, **Save** your workbook, and then compare your chart with Figure 6.17.

The size of the title increases, and the plot area decreases slightly.

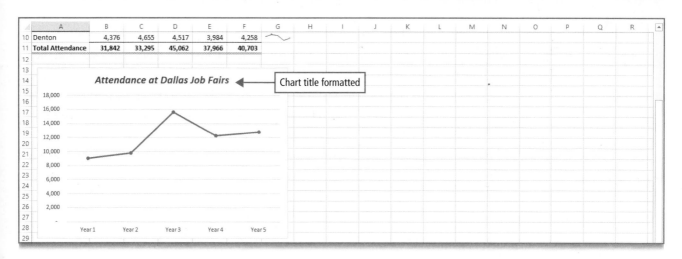

Figure 6.17

Activity 6.10 | Changing the Values on the Value Axis

You can change the values on the value axis to increase or decrease the variation among the numbers displayed. The *scale* is the range of numbers in the data series; the scale controls the minimum, maximum, and incremental values on the value axis. In the line chart, the attendance figures for Dallas are all higher than 8,000, but the scale begins at zero, so the line occupies only the upper area of the chart. In this Activity, you will adjust the scale to make your charts more meaningful to the reader.

1 ▶ On the left side of the line chart, point to any number, and then when the ScreenTip displays *Vertical (Value) Axis*, right-click, and then click **Format Axis**.

2 ▶ On the right, in the **Format Axis** pane, if necessary, expand **Axis Options**. Under **Bounds**, in the **Minimum** box, select the existing text and type **5000** Under **Units**, change the **Major unit** to **1000** and then press Enter. Compare your screen with Figure 6.18.

Here you can change the beginning and ending numbers displayed on the chart, and you can also change the unit by which the major gridlines display.

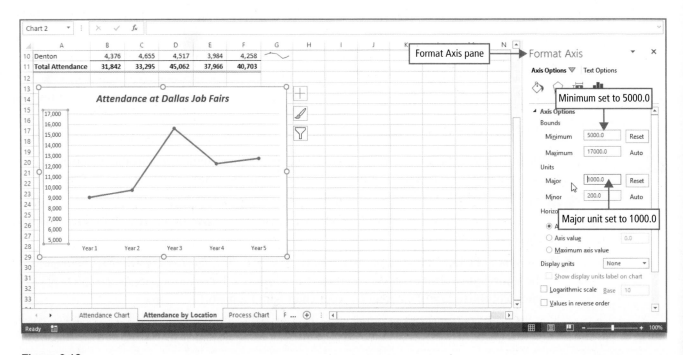

Figure 6.18

3 ▶ In the upper right corner of the **Format Axis** pane, click **Close** ☒. Click **Save** 🖫, and then compare your screen with Figure 6.19.

The Value Axis begins at 5,000 with major gridlines at intervals of 1,000. This will emphasize the change in attendance over the five years by starting the chart at a higher number and decreasing the interval for gridlines.

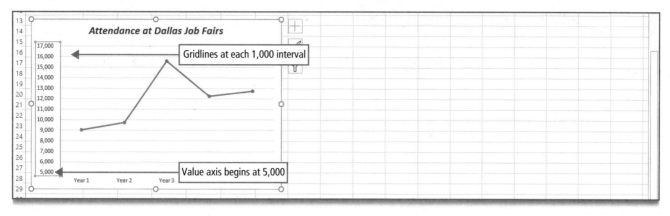

Figure 6.19

MOS
5.2.3

Activity 6.11 | Formatting the Plot Area and the Data Series

1 Right-click anywhere *within*, but not directly *on* a line, in the lined **Plot Area**, and then click **Format Plot Area**.

> The Format Plot Area pane displays. Here you can change the border of the plot area or the background color.

2 In the **Format Plot Area** pane, if necessary, expand **Fill**. Click **Solid fill**. Click the **Color arrow**, and then under **Theme Colors**, in the first column, click the fourth color.

3 Point to the blue chart line, right-click, and then click **Format Data Series**.

> In the Format Data Series pane, you can change the data markers—the indicators for a data point value, which on the line chart is represented by a circle shape. You can also change the line connecting the data markers.

4 In the **Format Data Series** pane, click **Fill & Line** ⬦. Under **Line**, click **Solid line**. Use the spin box arrows to set the **Width** to **4 pt**.

5 Under the **Fill & Line** icon, click **Marker**. If necessary, expand the **Marker Options**. Click **Built-in**, click the **Type arrow**, and then click the **triangle**—the third symbol in the list. Set the **Size** of the **Marker Type** to **12**.

6 Under **Fill**, click **Solid fill**. Scroll down to view the lower portion of the pane, click the **Color arrow**, and then in the first column, click the last color.

7 Under **Border**, click **No line**, and then **Close** ☒ the **Format Data Series** pane.

8 Click the **Chart Tools Format tab**. In the **Current Selection group**, click the **Chart Elements arrow**, and then click **Chart Area**. In the same group, click **Format Selection** to display the **Format Chart Area** pane.

💻 **MAC TIP** Click Format Pane.

9 In the **Format Chart Area** pane, under **Border**, apply a **Solid line**. Click the **Color arrow**, and then in the first column, click the third color. **Close** ⊠ the **Format Chart Area** pane.

10 Click in any cell outside of the chart, **Save** 🖫 your workbook, and then compare your screen with Figure 6.20.

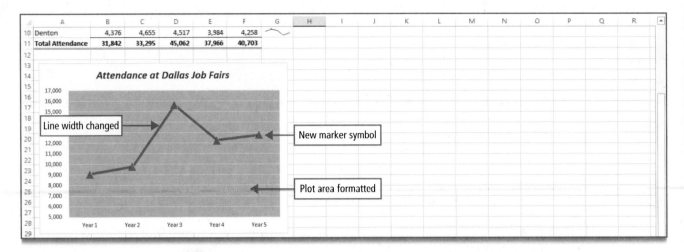

Figure 6.20

Activity 6.12 │ Inserting a Trendline

MOS

5.2.3

A **_trendline_** is a graphic representation of trends in a data series, such as a line sloping upward to represent increased sales over a period of months. A trendline is always associated with a data series, but it does not represent the data of that data series. Rather, a trendline depicts trends in the existing data.

1 Click in the white area slightly inside the chart border to select the entire chart. Next to the chart, click **Chart Elements** ⊞, click **Trendline**, click the **arrow**, and then click **Linear**. Click in any cell outside of the chart. **Save** 🖫 your workbook, and then compare your screen with Figure 6.21.

A linear trendline displays in the chart. The chart shows a significant increase in attendance for Year 3 and a drop in attendance in Year 4, but the trendline indicates an overall increasing trend in attendance over the past five years.

 MAC TIP On the Chart Design tab, in the Chart Locations group, click Add Chart Element. Point to Trendline, click Linear.

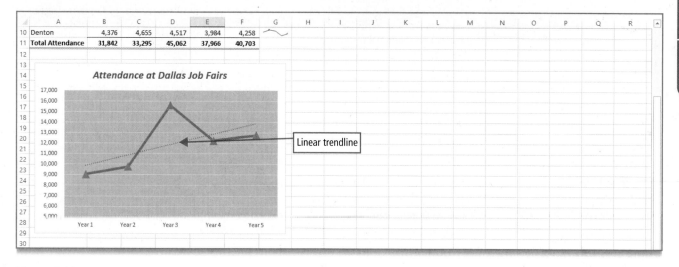

Figure 6.21

| Objective 3 | Create and Modify a SmartArt Graphic |

GO! Learn How

Video E6-3

A ***SmartArt graphic*** is a visual representation of your information and ideas. You can create SmartArt graphics by choosing from among many different layouts to communicate complex messages and relationships easily and effectively.

Unlike charts, a SmartArt graphic does not depend on any underlying data in a worksheet; rather, it is a graphical tool that depicts ideas or associations. In the following Activities, you will create a process diagram to illustrate how an employer can register to have a booth at the Job Fair.

Activity 6.13 | Creating a Process SmartArt Graphic

In this Activity, you will use a Process SmartArt graphic, which shows steps in a process or timeline.

1 In your **Attendance by Location** worksheet, click cell **A1** to make it the active cell, and then, at the lower edge of your workbook, click the **Process Chart sheet tab**.

2 With the **Process Chart** worksheet displayed, on the **Insert tab**, in the **Illustrations group**, click **SmartArt** 🔲.

3 On the left, notice the types of SmartArt graphics that are available, and then take a moment to examine the table in Figure 6.22.

SmartArt	
Use this SmartArt type:	**To do this:**
List	Show nonsequential information
Process	Show steps in a process or timeline
Cycle	Show a continual process
Hierarchy	Create an organization chart or show a decision tree
Relationship	Illustrate connections
Matrix	Show how parts relate to a whole
Pyramid	Use a series of pictures to show relationships
Picture	Display pictures in a diagram
Office.com	Displays additional layouts available from Office.com; this type will be periodically updated with new layouts. For example, the Architecture Layout shows a hierarchical relationship that builds from the bottom up. (Not available on a Mac.)

Figure 6.22

4 On the left, click **Process**, and then in the center section of the dialog box, *point* to the graphics to display their ScreenTips. By using the ScreenTips, locate and then click **Step Down Process**. Click **OK**.

5 If necessary, on the **Design tab**, in the **Create Graphic group**, click **Text Pane** to display the Text Pane on the left side of the graphic. Then, as necessary, click to place your insertion point in the first bullet of the **Text Pane**. Type **Apply**

The text *Apply* displays in the Text Pane and in the first box in the diagram. Use the **Text Pane**, which displays to the left of the graphic, to input and organize the text in your graphic. The Text Pane is populated with placeholder text that you replace with your information. If you prefer, close the Text Pane and type directly into the graphic.

6 In the **Text Pane**, click the next bullet, which is indented, and then type **Register for Booth** Compare your screen with Figure 6.23.

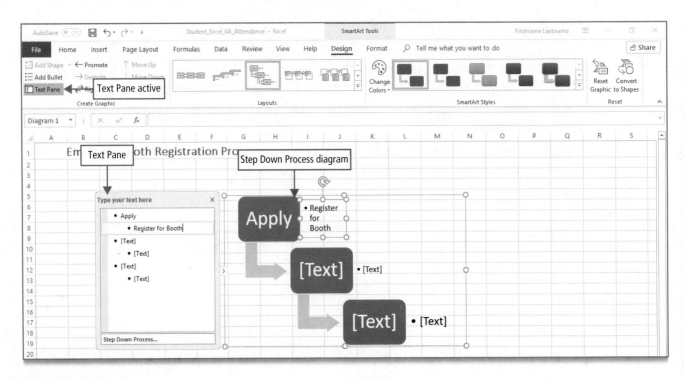

Figure 6.23

7 In the **Text Pane**, click the next bullet, and then type **Prepare** Under *Prepare* click the indented bullet and type **Booth Number Assigned**

8 Click the next bullet and type **Attend** Click the next bullet, and then type **Set Up Job Fair Booth** Compare your diagram with Figure 6.24.

The Text Pane entries display on the left in the Text Pane, and the process diagram with entries displays on the right in the process diagram.

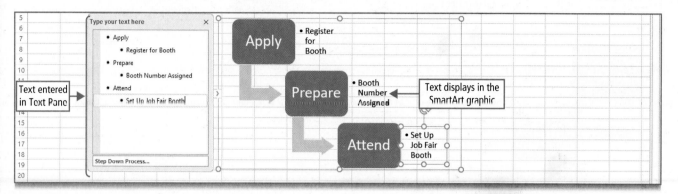

Figure 6.24

9 **Close** ⊠ the **Text Pane**, and then **Save** 🖫 your workbook.

Activity 6.14 | Modifying the Diagram Style

Excel provides preformatted SmartArt styles that you can apply to your diagram. This gives an overall visual style for your SmartArt graphic.

1 With the SmartArt still selected, on the **Design tab**, in the **SmartArt Styles group**, click **More** ⊡. Under **3-D**, click the first style—**Polished**.

2 In the **SmartArt Styles group**, click **Change Colors**, and then under **Colorful**, click the fifth option—**Colorful Range – Accent Colors 5 to 6**.

3 By using the ⊡ pointer, drag the upper left corner of the graphic border inside the upper left corner of cell **A4**. Point to the lower right corner of the graphic's border to display the ⊡ pointer, and then drag to resize the graphic and position the lower right corner inside the lower right corner of cell **H22**.

4 **Save** 🖫 your workbook, and then compare your screen with Figure 6.25.

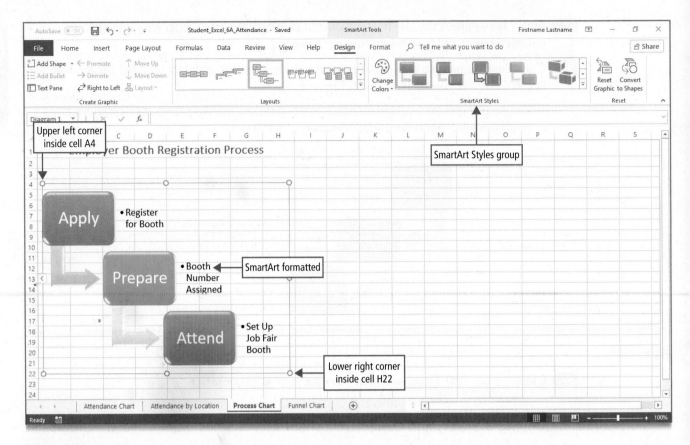

Figure 6.25

Objective 4 | Create and Modify a Funnel Chart

GO! Learn How
Video E6-4

A *funnel chart* shows values across the stages in a process. Typically, the values decrease gradually, and so the bars resemble a funnel. One common use for a funnel chart is the representation of a sales process; the chart can identify potential problem areas in the sales process of an organization.

Activity 6.15 | Creating and Formatting a Funnel Chart

MOS
Expert 4.1.2

In Year 5, the Dallas–Ft. Worth Job Fair launched a marketing campaign to increase the number of hiring companies that purchase booths at their Job Fairs.

To visualize this information, you will create a funnel chart to illustrate the number of companies invited to purchase a booth, the number of companies that expressed interest in purchasing a booth, and the number of companies that actually purchased a booth.

1 In your **Process Chart** worksheet, click cell **A1**, and then display the **Funnel Chart** worksheet.

2 In the **Funnel Chart** worksheet, in the range **A2:B4**, type the following data:

Invited	352
Expressed Interest	275
Purchased a Booth	122

3 ▶ Select the range **A2:A4**, and then from the **Home tab**, apply the **Heading 4** cell style.

4 ▶ Select the range **A2:B4**, and then on the **Insert tab**, in the **Charts group**, click **Insert Waterfall or Stock Chart**. Click **Funnel** to insert a funnel chart.

> The funnel chart displays to the right of the data. Each rectangle in the funnel chart indicates a corresponding value from the data series. The invited companies represent the largest number and those that purchased a booth represent the smallest number.

5 ▶ Drag the upper left corner of the chart into the upper left corner of cell **A6**.

6 ▶ On the **Chart Tools Format tab**, change the **Shape Height** to **3.5"** and the **Shape Width** to **5.75"** and press Enter.

7 ▶ Click the **Chart Title**. Type **Marketing Results Year 5** and then click outside of the title so that it is not selected. Compare your screen with Figure 6.26.

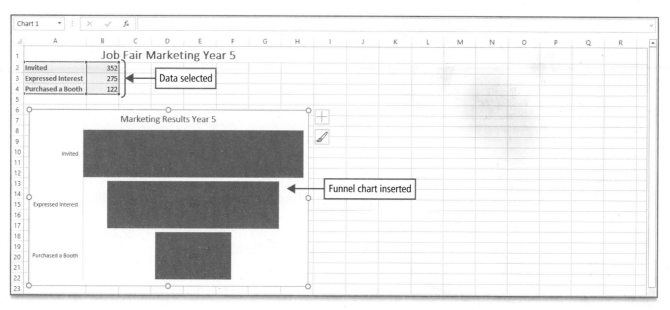

Figure 6.26

Activity 6.16 │ Formatting a Funnel Chart

MOS

Expert 4.1.2

In this Activity, you will format the funnel chart.

1 ▶ With the funnel chart still selected, click the **Chart Tools Design tab**. In the **Chart Styles group**, click the third style.

2 ▶ In the **Chart Styles group**, click **Change Colors**, scroll to the bottom of the gallery, and then click the last group of colors, which are shades of green.

MAC TIP ScreenTip indicates Monochromatic Palette 13.

3 ▶ Click the **Chart Tools Format tab**. In the **Current Selection group**, click the **Chart Elements arrow**, and then click **Chart Area**. In the same group, click **Format Selection**.

MAC TIP Click Format Pane.

4 In the **Format Chart Area** pane, if necessary expand the **Border** category. Click **Solid line**. Click the **Color arrow**, and then in the last column under **Theme Colors**, click the last color. Set the **Width** to **2 pt** and then **Close** ☒ the **Format Chart Area** pane.

5 Click cell **A1**, and then **Save** 🖫 your workbook. Compare your screen with Figure 6.27.

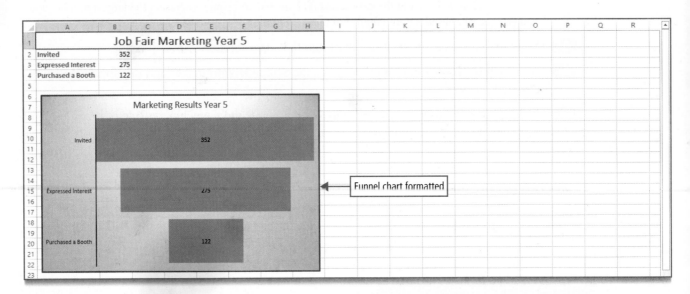

Figure 6.27

Activity 6.17 | Preparing Worksheets Containing Charts and Diagrams for Printing

MOS
1.5.3

1 Display the **Attendance Chart** worksheet. On the ribbon, click the **Page Layout tab**, and then in the **Page Setup group**, click the **Dialog Box Launcher** 🖼.

💻 **MAC TIP**   In the Page Setup group, click Page Setup.

2 In the **Page Setup** dialog box, click the **Header/Footer tab**, and then click **Custom Footer**. With the insertion point in the **Left section**, in the small toolbar in the center of the dialog box, click **Insert File Name** 🖳, and then click **OK** two times.

3 Click the **Attendance by Location sheet tab**, hold down ⌃Ctrl, and then click the **Process Chart sheet tab** and the **Funnel Chart sheet tab** to select the remaining three worksheets and group them. Release the ⌃Ctrl key. Compare your screen with Figure 6.28.

💻 **MAC TIP**   Hold down command ⌘.

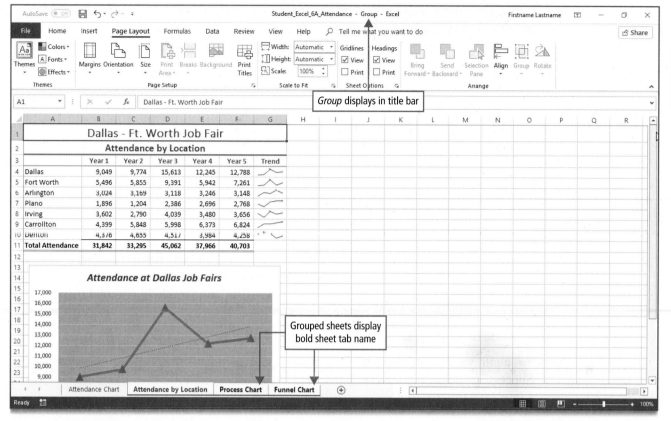

Figure 6.28

> **4** On the **Page Layout tab**, in the **Page Setup group**, click **Margins**, and then at the bottom click **Custom Margins**.

> **5** On the **Margins tab**, below **Center on page**, click to select the **Horizontally** check box.

> **6** In the dialog box, click the **Header/Footer tab**, click **Custom Footer**, and then in the **Left section**, click **Insert File Name** ⊞. Click **OK** two times.

> **7** Click the **File tab** to display **Backstage** view. On the right, at the bottom of the **Properties** list, click **Show All Properties**. On the list of **Properties**, in the **Tags** box, type **attendance statistics** In the **Subject** box, type your course name and section #. Under **Related People**, be sure that your name displays as the author. If necessary, right-click the author name, click **Edit Property**, type your name, click outside of the **Edit person** dialog box, and then click **OK**.

🖵 **MAC TIP** Display the toolbar, click File, click Properties, click the Summary tab.

> **8** On the left, click **Print**. Under **Settings**, click the **Print Active Sheets arrow**, and then click **Print Entire Workbook**. At the bottom of the window, click **Next Page** ▶ to scroll through the worksheets.

🖵 **MAC TIP** Display the toolbar, click File, click Print. Click Cancel to return to your workbook.

9 On the left, click **Save** to save your workbook and redisplay the workbook window. Click the **Attendance Chart sheet tab** to ungroup the sheets.

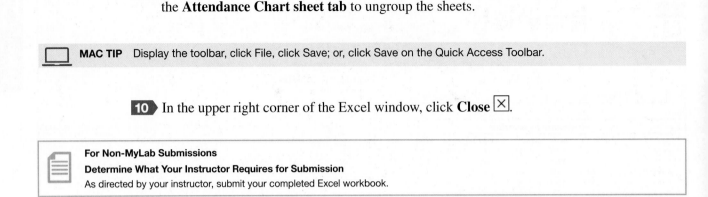

MAC TIP   Display the toolbar, click File, click Save; or, click Save on the Quick Access Toolbar.

10 In the upper right corner of the Excel window, click **Close** ⊠.

For Non-MyLab Submissions
Determine What Your Instructor Requires for Submission
As directed by your instructor, submit your completed Excel workbook.

11 In **MyLab IT**, locate and click the Grader Project **Excel 6A Attendance**. In **step 3**, under **Upload Completed Assignment**, click **Choose File**. In the **Open** dialog box, navigate to your **Excel Chapter 6 folder**, and then click your **Student_Excel_6A_Attendance** file one time to select it. In the lower right corner of the **Open** dialog box, click **Open**.

The name of your selected file displays above the Upload button.

12 To submit your file to **MyLab IT** for grading, click **Upload**, wait a moment for a green **Success!** message, and then in **step 4**, click the blue **Submit for Grading** button. Click **Close Assignment** to return to your list of **Course Materials**.

You have completed Project 6A   **END**

Project Activities

In Activities 6.18 through 6.25, you will create a booth registration order template for use by the Job Fair staff to ensure that totals for items ordered are calculated accurately. Then you will use the template to complete a booth order. Your completed worksheet will look similar to Figure 6.29.

Project Files for MyLab IT Grader

1. In your **MyLab IT** course, locate and click **Excel 6B Booth Order**, Download Materials, and then Download All Files.

2. Extract the zipped folder to your Excel Chapter 6 folder. Close the Grader download screens.

3. Take a moment to open the downloaded **Excel_6B_Booth_Order_Instructions**; note any recent updates to the book.

Project Results

GO! Project 6B

Where We're Going

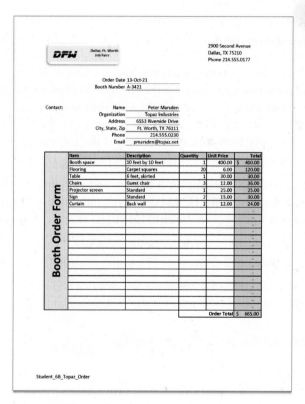

Figure 6.29 Project 6B Booth Order Form

For Non-MyLab Submissions

For Project 6B, you will need:
e06B_Booth_Order
e06B_Logo

In your Excel Chapter 6 folder, you will save workbooks as:
Lastname_Firstname_6B_Booth_Order (do not submit)
Lastname_Firstname_6B_Order_Template (do not submit)
Lastname_Firstname_6B_Topaz_Order (submit this file)
If your instructor requires a workbook with formulas, save as:
Lastname_Firstname_6B_Topaz_Order_fomulas

Open e06B_Booth_Order, save it in your Chapter 6 folder as **Lastname_Firstname_6B_Booth_Order** and then on the next page, begin with Step 2.

ALERT   Because Office 365 is a cloud-based subscription service that receives continuous updates, you may encounter some variations in what appears on your screen and what is shown in this instruction. Microsoft Office 365 is fully installed on your PC or Mac; no internet access is necessary to create or edit documents. When you are connected to the internet, you will receive monthly upgrades and new features, so you always have the latest versions of Office apps as soon as they are available. Your subscription gives you continuous free access to the latest innovations and refinements.

GO! Learn How
Video E6-5

A *template* is a workbook that you create and use as the basis for other similar workbooks. Excel also has predesigned templates that include, among others, financial forms to record expenses, time worked, balance sheet items, and other common financial reports.

Standardization and *protection* are the two main reasons for creating templates for commonly used forms in an organization. Standardization means that all forms created within the organization will have a uniform appearance; the data will always be organized in the same manner. Protection means that individuals entering data cannot change areas of the worksheet that are protected, and therefore cannot alter important formulas and formats that you build in to a template.

Activity 6.18 │ Entering Template Text

To create a template, you can start with a new blank workbook. Then, enter the text, formatting, and formulas necessary for the specific worksheet purpose and save the file as a template. Saving a workbook as a template adds the extension *.xltx* to the file name. In this Activity, you will format a workbook for the purpose of creating a template for a purchase order.

As employers apply for booth space at one of the Job Fairs, the order taker can enter in the details of what the employer's requirements are for the booth they want to have at the Job Fair.

1 ▶ Navigate to your **Excel Chapter 6 folder**, and then double-click the Excel file you downloaded from **MyLab IT** that displays your name—**Student_Excel_6B_Booth_Order**. If necessary, at the top click **Enable Editing**.

2 ▶ Click the **File tab**, and then on the left, click **New**. Click in the **Search for online templates** box, type **business** and then press Enter. Compare your screen with Figure 6.30.

From the *Search for online templates* box, you can find and download many different predesigned templates from Microsoft's site. Microsoft updates this list frequently.

MAC Tip   Display the toolbar, click File, click New from Template.

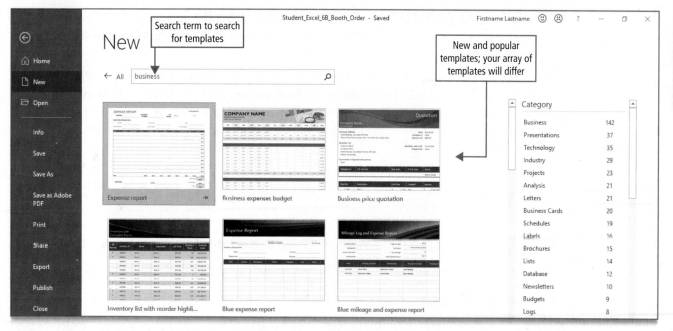

Figure 6.30

> **3** In the upper left corner, click **Back** ⊕ to redisplay your workbook. In cell **A1**, type **Dallas–Ft. Worth Job Fair** and press Enter. Compare your screen with Figure 6.31.
>
> > Some formatting is already applied. Until the format and design of the order form is complete, you will save your work as a normal workbook—not as a template.

MAC Tip Click Close.

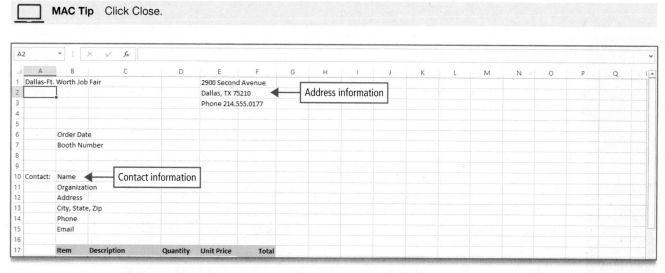

Figure 6.31

Activity 6.19 | Formatting a Template

> One of the goals in designing a template is to make it easy for others to complete. It should be obvious to the person completing the form what information is necessary and where to place the information. For example, when order takers work with employers to reserve a booth at one of the Job Fairs, the order takers will not have to guess where to put the necessary information.

> **1** Select column **B**. On the **Home tab**, in the **Cells group**, click **Format**, and then click **Column Width**.

> **2** In the **Column Width** dialog box, type **21.5** and then click **OK**.

3 Select the range **B6:B15**, hold down Ctrl, and then select the range **C10:C15**. Release Ctrl, and then with the two ranges selected, on the **Home tab**, in the **Alignment group**, click **Align Right** ▤.

4 Select the range **C6:C7**. Hold down Ctrl, and then select the range **C10:C15**. With the two ranges selected, on the **Home tab**, in the **Font group**, click the **Borders button arrow** ⊞ ▾, and then at the bottom, click **More Borders**. In the **Format Cells** dialog box, on the **Border tab**, under **Line**, in the **Style** list, click the second line in the first column—**the dotted line**.

💻 **MAC Tip** Hold down command ⌘.

---

5 Under **Border**, click **Middle Border** ⊞, and **Bottom Border** ⊞. Click **OK**.

Inserting borders on cells in a template creates lines as a place to record information when the form is filled out. This provides a good visual cue to the person filling out the form as to where information should be placed.

6 Select the range **B17:F40**. Right-click over the selected area and click **Format Cells**. In the **Format Cells** dialog box, if necessary, click the **Border tab**. Under **Presets**, click **Outline** and **Inside**, and then click **OK**.

This action applies a visible grid of columns and rows, which is helpful to those individuals completing the form.

7 Click cell **A1** to make it the active cell. Click the **File tab**, and then on the left, click **Print** to view the Print Preview. Compare your screen with Figure 6.32.

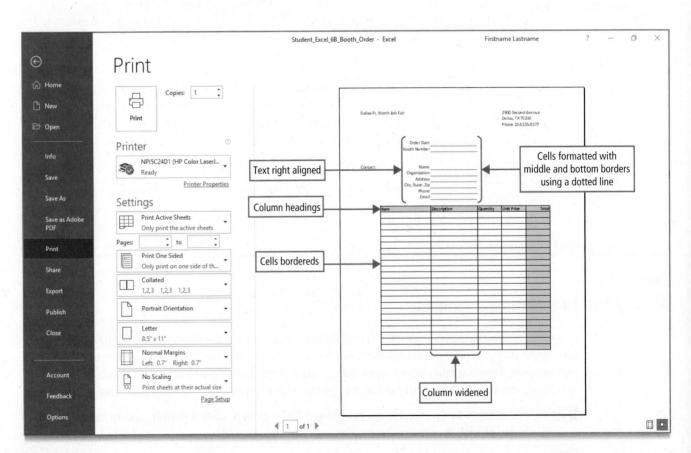

Figure 6.32

8 On the left, click **Save** to save and return to your workbook.

A vertical dotted line on the worksheet indicates where the first page would end if the worksheet were printed as it is currently set up. As you develop your template, use the Print Preview to check your progress.

MAC Tip Click Cancel, then save your workbook.

Activity 6.20 | Entering Template Formulas

MOS
2.1.2

After the text is entered and formatted in your template, add formulas to the cells where you want the result of the calculations to display. In this Activity, you will create a formula in the Total column to determine the dollar value for the quantity of each item ordered, and then create another formula to sum the Total column.

1 In cell **F18**, type **=d18*e18** and then on the **Formula Bar**, click **Enter** ☑.

No value displays in cell F18. However, when the person entering information into the worksheet types the Quantity in cell D18 and the Unit Price in cell E18, the formula will multiply the two values to calculate a total for the item.

2 Use the fill handle to copy the formula in cell **F18** down through cell **F39**. Select the range **F19:F39**, and then on the **Home tab**, in the **Number group**, click **Comma Style** ☐.

When copying a formula, the format of the copied cell carries into the cells. This action changes the Number format of the cells in the range F19:F39 to the Comma Style.

3 Click cell **F40**. On the **Home tab**, in the **Editing group**, click **AutoSum** Σ AutoSum ▾. In the **Formula Bar**, be sure the range displays as *F18:F39*, and then press Enter.

4 Select the range **D40:E40**. In the **Alignment group**, click **Merge & Center**. Type **Order Total** and then on the **Formula Bar**, click **Enter** ☑. In the **Alignment group**, click **Align Right** ☰. In the **Font** group, click **Bold** B.

A label is added and formatted to identify the total for the entire order.

5 Select the range **B40:C40**, right-click, and then click **Format Cells**. In the **Format Cells** dialog box, if necessary, click the **Border tab**, and then in the **Border preview** area, click **Left Border**, **Middle Border** ☐, and **Bottom Border** ☐ to *remove* these borders from the preview—be sure the right and top borders remain in the preview area. Compare your dialog box with Figure 6.33.

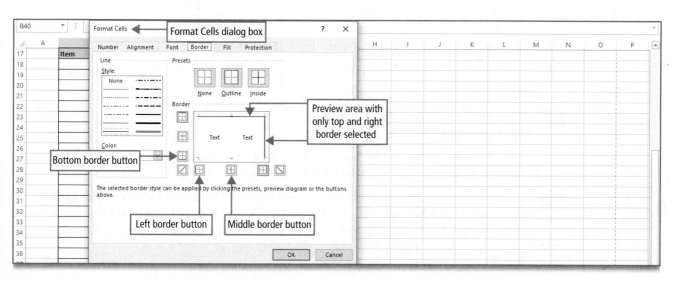

Figure 6.33

6 Click **OK**. Click the **File tab**, and then click **Print** to view the Print Preview. Compare your screen with Figure 6.34.

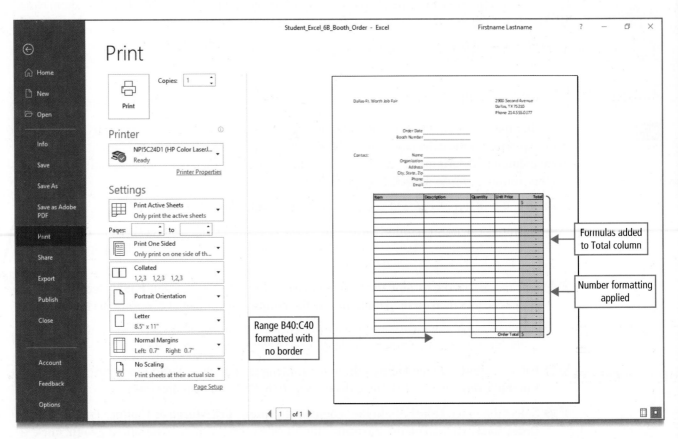

Figure 6.34

7 In **Backstage** view, on the left, click **Save** to save and return to your workbook.

MAC Tip   Click Cancel and click Save on the Quick Access Toolbar.

Activity 6.21 │ Inserting and Modifying an Image

In the following Activity, you will add a logo image to the form.

1 Click cell **A1** and press Delete to remove the Job Fair name. On the **Insert tab**, in the **Illustrations group**, click **Pictures**.

2 In the **Insert Picture** dialog box, navigate to the downloaded files that accompany this project, and then insert the file **e06B_Logo**.

The Dallas–Ft. Worth Job Fair logo displays in the upper left corner of the worksheet. The Picture Tools contextual tab displays when the object is selected.

3 With the image selected, on the **Picture Tools Format tab**, in the **Picture Styles group**, click **More**, and then by using the ScreenTips, locate and click the **Bevel Rectangle** style. Point to the image to display the pointer, and then drag the image down and to the right slightly, as shown in Figure 6.35. **Save** your workbook.

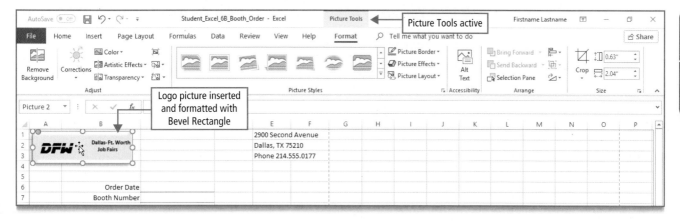

Figure 6.35

Activity 6.22 | Changing the Orientation of Text in a Cell

2.2.2

Orientation is a feature with which you can rotate text diagonally or vertically in a cell and is useful when you need to create a label in a narrow column. In this Activity, you will merge cells in column A and then change the orientation of the text in the merged cell to create a vertical label.

1 Scroll so that **row 16** is at the top of the Excel window, and then click cell **A17**.

2 Select the range **A17:A39**, and then on the **Home tab**, in the **Alignment group**, click **Merge & Center**.

3 In the **Alignment group**, click **Orientation** ⟨ ⟩, and then compare your screen with Figure 6.36.

> Here you can change the orientation of text in the cell. The illustrations on the left show how each command will orient the text in the cell. For additional options, at the bottom of the list, you can display the Alignment tab of the Format Cells dialog box.

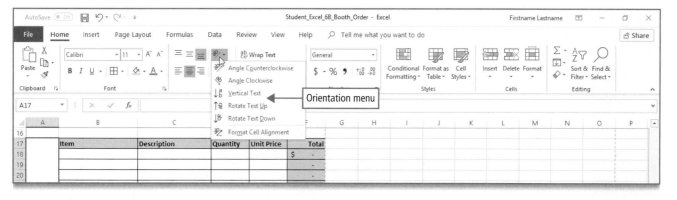

Figure 6.36

4 On the list, click **Rotate Text Up**, type **Booth Order Form** and then press Enter. Click the merged cell again to select it, and then in the **Alignment group**, click **Middle Align** ☰.

5 With the merged cell still selected, in the **Font group**, apply **Bold**, and then change the **Font size** to **26**. Click the **Fill Color arrow** ⟨ ⟩, and then in the eighth column, click the third color. Compare your screen with Figure 6.37.

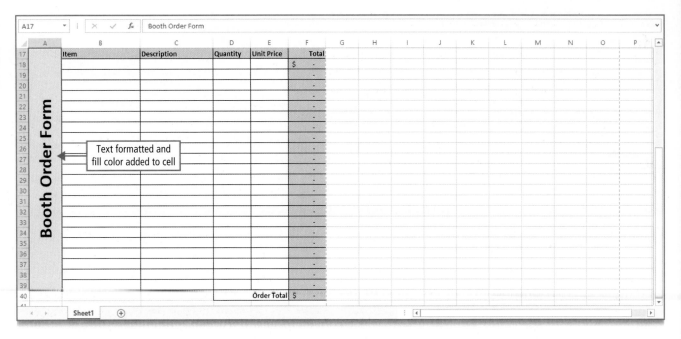

Figure 6.37

> **6** In the **Font group**, click the **Borders button arrow** ⊞ ▾, and then on the list, click **Bottom Border**. Display the list again and click **Top Border**. Display the list again and click **Left Border**.

> **7** Click the **File tab**, and then on the left, click **Print** to view the Print Preview. Compare your screen with Figure 6.38.

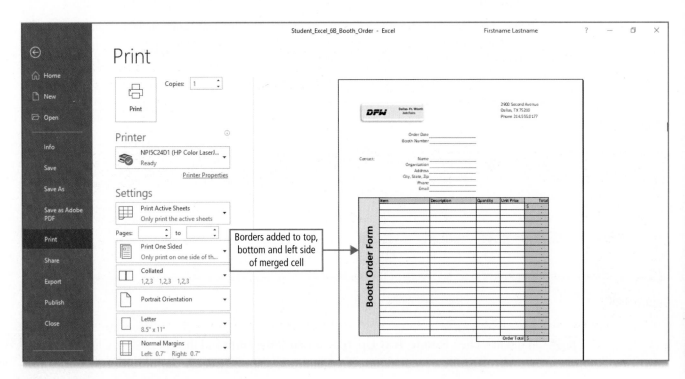

Figure 6.38

> **8** On the left, click **Save** to save and redisplay your workbook.

Activity 6.23 | Saving a File as a Template

After you complete the formatting and design of a worksheet that you would like to reuse many times, you can save it as a template file. When saved as a template file, the *.xltx* file extension is added to the file name instead of *.xlsx*.

If a template is saved in the Custom Office Templates folder on the hard drive of your computer, or the network location where the Excel software resides, the template will be available to other people who have access to the same system from the New tab in Backstage view.

Regardless of where the template file is saved, when the template is opened, a new *copy* of the workbook opens, preserving the original template for future use.

Instead of the Custom Office Templates folder, which might be restricted in a college lab, you will save the template in your chapter folder.

1 Click the **File tab**, and then on the left, click **Save As**. Click **Browse** to display the **Save As** dialog box.

2 Click the **Save as type arrow**, and then on the list, click **Excel Template**. At the top of the **Save As** dialog box, notice that the path changes to the **Custom Office Templates** folder in the **Documents** folder of your hard drive; or, in a college lab, the path may display another location.

MAC Tip Path may not change to Documents folder.

3 Navigate to your **Excel Chapter 6** folder so that it displays in the **Address bar** at the top of the dialog box. In the **File name** box, using your own name, change the **File name** to **Lastname_Firstname_6B_Order_Template** and then click **Save**.

A copy of the template is saved with your other files.

4 **Close** the file and **Close** Excel.

5 From the taskbar, click **File Explorer**. Navigate to your **Excel Chapter 6** folder, and then notice that for your *Lastname_Firstname_6B_Order_Template* file, the **Type** is listed as *Microsoft Excel Template*. Compare your screen with Figure 6.39. **Close** ✕ the **File Explorer** window.

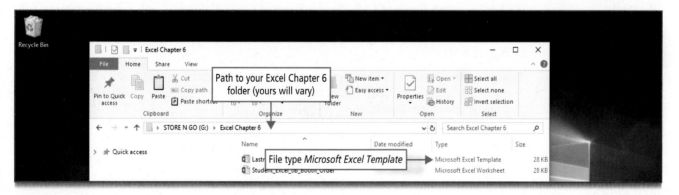

Figure 6.39

GO! Learn How
Video E6-6

When the template design is complete, you can enable the protection of the worksheet. Protection prevents anyone from changing the worksheet—they cannot insert, modify, delete, or format data in any locked cells.

For purposes of creating a form that you want someone else to complete, you can protect the worksheet, and then unlock specific areas where you *do* want the person completing the form to enter data.

By default, all cells in Excel are *locked*—data cannot be typed into them. However, the locked feature is disabled until you protect the worksheet. After protection is enabled, the locked cells cannot be changed. Of course, you will want to designate some cells to be *unlocked*, so that individuals completing your form can type data into those cells.

The basic process is to first determine the cells that you will allow people to change, unlock those cells, and then protect the worksheet. Only the cells that you designate as unlocked will be available to any person using the template. You may want to add an optional *password* to prevent someone from disabling the worksheet protection. The password can be any combination of numbers, letters, or symbols up to 15 characters long. The password should be shared only with people who have permission to change the template.

Activity 6.24 | Protecting a Worksheet

Expert 1.2.1
Expert 1.2.2
Expert 1.2.3

1 Start Excel, and then on the left, click **Open**. Click **Browse**, navigate to your **Excel Chapter 6** folder, click one time to select your **Lastname_Firstname_6B_Order_Template** file, and then click **Open**.

2 Select the range **C6:C7**, hold down Ctrl, and then select the nonadjacent ranges **C10:C15** and **B18:E39**.

> The selected cells are the ones that you want individuals placing booth orders to be able to fill in—they should *not* be locked when protection is applied.

⌨ **MAC Tip** Hold down command ⌘.

---

3 With the three ranges selected, on the **Home tab**, in the **Cells group**, click **Format**, and then at the bottom, click **Format Cells**. In the **Format Cells** dialog box, click the **Protection tab**.

4 Click to *clear* the check mark from the **Locked** check box, and then compare your screen with Figure 6.40.

> Recall that all cells are locked by default, but the locking feature is enabled only when protection is applied. Therefore, you must *unlock* the cells you want to have available for use in this manner *before* you protect the worksheet.

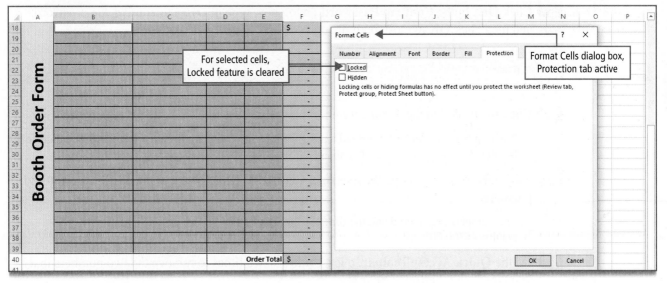

Figure 6.40

5 Click **OK** to close the **Format Cells** dialog box.

6 In the **Cells group**, click **Format**, and then under **Protection**, click **Protect Sheet**.

> The Protect Sheet dialog box displays. Under *Allow all users of this worksheet to*, the *Select locked cells* and *Select unlocked cells* check boxes are selected by default. The *Select locked cells* option allows the user to click the locked cells and *view* the formulas, but because the cells are locked, they cannot *change* the content or format of the locked cells. If you deselect this option, the user cannot view or even click in a locked cell.

> For the remaining check boxes, you can see that, because they are not selected, users are restricted from performing all other actions on the worksheet.

7 Leave the first two check boxes selected. At the top of the dialog box, be sure the **Protect worksheet and contents of locked cells** check box is selected. In the **Password to unprotect sheet** box, type **goseries** Compare your screen with Figure 6.41.

> The password does not display—rather bullets display as placeholders for each letter or character that is typed. Passwords are case sensitive; therefore, *GOSeries* is different from *goseries*.

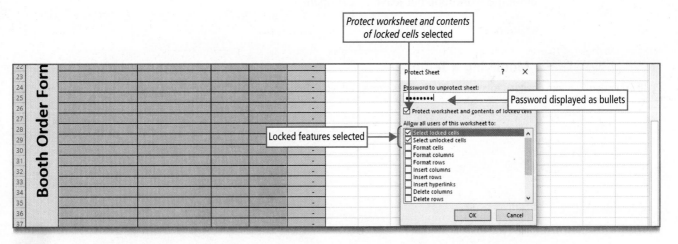

Figure 6.41

8 Click **OK**. In the **Confirm Password** dialog box, type **goseries** to confirm the password, and then click **OK** to close both dialog boxes.

MAC Tip Confirm password appears in the Protect Sheet dialog box.

9 Click in any cell in the **Total** column, type **123** and observe what happens.

> The number is not entered; instead a message informs you that the cell you are trying to change is protected—you cannot enter data there.

10 Click **OK** to acknowledge the message. Click cell **D18**, type **2** and press ⎋Tab⎋, type **150** and press ⎋Enter⎋.

> The numbers are entered and the formulas in cells F18 and F40 calculate and display the results—$300.00

11 On the **Quick Access Toolbar**, click **Undo** ↶ two times to remove the two numbers that you typed, and then click **Save** ⊟.

> You have tested your template, and it is protected and saved.

12 Display the **Document Properties** and under **Related People**, be sure that your name displays as the author. If necessary, right-click the author name, click **Edit Property**, and then type your name. In the **Subject** box, type your course name and section #, and in the **Tags** box, type **booth order form, template**

MAC Tip Display the toolbar, click File, click Properties, click the Summary tab.

13 Display the **Print Preview**, and then on the left click **Save** to save and redisplay the workbook.

MAC Tip Click Cancel.

14 You will not submit this workbook for grading; rather, you will use it to create a workbook based on this template in the next Activity. Click the **File tab**. On the left click **Close** to close the workbook but leave Excel open.

MORE KNOWLEDGE **Modifying a Template**

If you need to make changes to a template after it is protected, you must first remove the protection.

Objective 7 | Create a Worksheet Based on a Template

GO! Learn How
Video E6-7

After you protect your template, it is ready for use. If the template is stored in the Custom Office Templates folder, anyone using the system or network on which it is stored can open it from the New tab in Backstage view. When opened from this location, Excel opens a new copy of the template as a workbook. Then you can enter information in the unlocked cells and save it as a new file. You can provide templates to coworkers by storing them on a company intranet; or, templates can be made available to customers through a website.

Activity 6.25 | Creating a Worksheet Based on a Template

1 Click the **File tab**, on the left click **Open**, click **Browse**, navigate to your **Excel Chapter 6** folder, and then click one time to select your **Lastname_Firstname_6B_Order_Template** file. Click **Open**.

2 Click the **File tab**, on the left click **Save As**, and then click **Browse** to display the **Save As** dialog box. Navigate to your **Excel Chapter 6** folder, and then set the **Save as type box** to **Excel Workbook**—the first choice at the top of the list. In the **File name** box, using your own name, type **Lastname_Firstname_6B_Topaz_Order** Compare your screen with Figure 6.42.

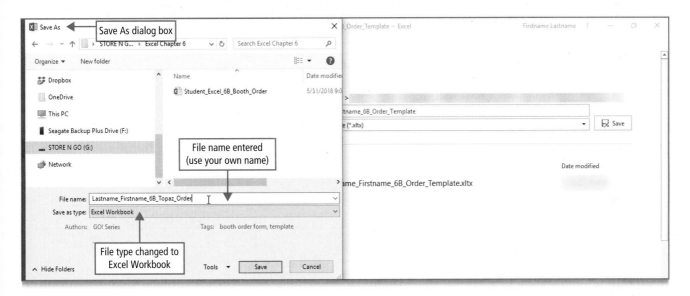

Figure 6.42

NOTE **Creating a Workbook from a Template in the Custom Office Templates Folder in Backstage View**

When you are able to open a template from the Custom Office Templates folder in Backstage view, a new copy of the template opens as a workbook, not as a template, and displays the number *1* at the end of the file name in the title bar. The number *1* indicates a new workbook. If you are able to work from the Custom Office Templates folder, the Save operation will automatically set the file type to Excel Workbook.

3 Click **Save**. Click cell **C6**, type **October 13, 2021** press $\boxed{\text{Enter}}$, and notice that Excel applies the default date format. As the booth number, type **A-3421** and then press $\boxed{\text{Tab}}$ to move to cell **C10**—the next unprotected cell.

4 Starting in cell **C10**, enter the company information as follows:

Name	**Peter Marsden**
Organization	**Topaz Industries**
Address	**6553 Riverside Drive**
City, State, Zip	**Ft. Worth, TX 76111**
Phone	**214.555.0230**
Email	**pmarsden@topaz.net**

5 In cell **B18**, type **Booth space** and press $\boxed{\text{Tab}}$, type **10 feet by 10 feet** and press $\boxed{\text{Tab}}$, type **1** and press $\boxed{\text{Tab}}$, type **400.00** and then press $\boxed{\text{Tab}}$.

6 Beginning in cell **B19**, complete the order by entering the following items, pressing $\boxed{\text{Tab}}$ to move from cell to cell. When you are finished, scroll to display **row 17** at the top of your screen, and then compare your screen with Figure 6.43.

Item	Description	Quantity	Unit Price
Booth space	10 feet by 10 feet	1	400
Flooring	**Carpet squares**	**20**	**6**
Table	**6 feet, skirted**	**1**	**30**
Chairs	**Guest chair**	**3**	**12**
Projector screen	**Standard**	**1**	**25**
Sign	**Standard**	**2**	**15**
Curtain	**Back wall**	**2**	**12**

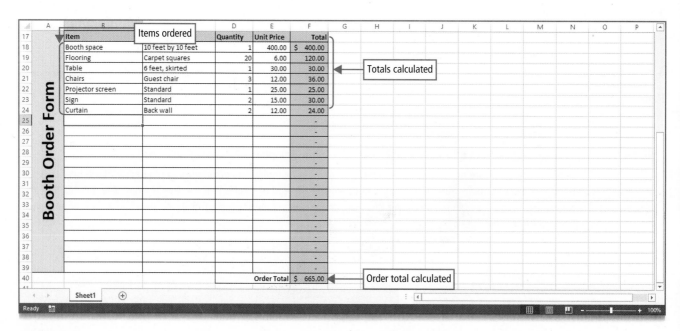

Figure 6.43

7 From the **Page Layout tab**, display the **Page Setup** dialog box. In the **Page Setup** dialog box, click the **Header/Footer tab**, click **Custom Footer**, and then in the **Left section**, insert the **File name**. Click **OK**. Click the **Margins tab**, and then center the worksheet horizontally on the page. Click **OK**.

8 Display the **Document Properties**. Be sure your name displays as the **Author** and your course name and section # displays in the **Subject** box. Change the **Tags** box to **Topaz booth order**

9 Display the **Print Preview** to review your worksheet, and then on the left, click **Save** to save your workbook and redisplay the Excel window. In the upper right corner of the Excel window, click **Close** ☒.

MAC Tip   Click Cancel to return to the Excel window.

For Non-MyLab Submissions
Determine What Your Instructor Requires for Submission
As directed by your instructor, submit your completed Lastname_Firstname_6B_Topaz_Order Excel workbook.

---

10 In **MyLab IT**, locate and click the Grader Project **Excel 6B Booth Order**. In **step 3**, under **Upload Completed Assignment**, click **Choose File**. In the **Open** dialog box, navigate to your **Excel Chapter 6 folder**, and then click your **Lastname_Firstname_6B_Topaz_Order** file one time to select it. In the lower right corner of the **Open** dialog box, click **Open**.

The name of your selected file displays above the Upload button.

11 To submit your file to **MyLab IT** for grading, click **Upload**, wait a moment for a green **Success!** message, and then in **step 4**, click the blue **Submit for Grading** button. Click **Close Assignment** to return to your list of **Course Materials**.

You have completed Project 6B   **END**

»»» GO! To Work

wavebreakmedia/Shutterstock, Monkey Business Images/Fotolia, Ivanko80/Shutterstock, Monkey Business Images/Shutterstock

Microsoft Office Specialist (MOS) Skills in This Chapter	
Project 6A	**Project 6B**
2.4.1 Insert sparklines	**2.1.2** Fill cells by using Auto Fill
5.1.1 Create charts	**2.2.2** Modify cell alignment, orientation, and indentation
5.1.2 Create chart sheets	**1.2.1** Expert: Restrict editing
5.2.2 Switch between rows and columns in source data	**1.2.2** Expert: Protect worksheets and cell ranges
5.2.3 Add and modify chart elements	**1.2.3** Expert: Protect workbook structure
5.3.2 Apply chart styles	
4.1.2 Expert: Create and modify funnel charts	

Build Your E-Portfolio

An E-Portfolio is a collection of evidence, stored electronically, that showcases what you have accomplished while completing your education. Collecting and then sharing your work products with potential employers reflects your academic and career goals. Your completed documents from the following projects are good examples to show what you have learned: 6G, 6K, and 6L.

GO! For Job Success

Discussion: Multichannel Marketing

Your instructor may assign this discussion to your class and then ask you to think about, or discuss with your classmates, these questions.

Mobile devices, unlimited data plans, public Wi-Fi networks, streaming video and music services, and social media provide many more ways for companies to reach their customers than in the past. Years ago, companies focused on only a few advertising outlets—radio, TV, newspapers, and magazines—to reach consumers. Now companies use multichannel marketing to reach current and potential customers. In addition to traditional commercials on television or radio, products must be advertised on websites, in YouTube videos, on social media sites, by direct mail and email, in retail stores, and through catalogs.

Multichannel marketing enables customers to do more than just passively view ads. Multichannel marketing encourages consumers to become part of the marketing experience. For example, a television show can display a Twitter hashtag so that viewers can simultaneously discuss the show on social media.

g-stockstudio/ Shutterstock

> What are some other multichannel marketing tools you have seen companies use to generate interest in their products or services?

> Some studies show that consumers who are exposed to multiple marketing channels spend up to four times more on a company's products than those who see only traditional advertising. Are there products you have become interested in or purchased because you saw their social media accounts or videos or perhaps a photo on Instagram?

> Multichannel marketing is not always useful for all products or services. What products or services might reach more customers through traditional marketing channels or direct sales instead of multichannel marketing?

End of Chapter

Summary

Excel's Recommended Charts feature displays suggested charts based on your data and helps you to decide the best chart type to use. You can easily modify, create, and format various chart elements.

Excel includes many different chart types, including column and line charts. A column chart shows a comparison among related numbers and a line chart displays a trend over time.

A SmartArt graphic is a visual representation of your information and ideas. SmartArt diagrams are not linked to the underlying worksheet data but float on top of the worksheet like other images.

Templates have built-in formulas and are used for standardization and protection of data. You can create a template using text, formatting, formulas, locked and unlocked cells, and password protection.

GO! Learn It Online

Review the concepts, key terms, and MOS skills in this chapter by completing these online challenges, which you can find at **MyLab IT**.

Chapter Quiz: Answer matching and multiple choice questions to test what you learned in this chapter.

Lessons on the GO!: Learn how to use all the new apps and features as they are introduced by Microsoft.

MOS Prep Quiz: Answer questions to review the MOS skills that you practiced in this chapter.

Project Guide for Excel Chapter 6

Your instructor may assign one or more of these projects to help you review the chapter and assess your mastery and understanding of its contents.

	Project Guide for Excel Chapter 6		
Project	**Apply Skills from These Chapter Objectives**	**Project Type**	**Project Location**
6A MyLab IT	Objectives 1–4 from Project 6A	**6A Instructional Project (Grader Project)** **Instruction** Guided instruction to learn the skills in Project 6A.	In **MyLab IT** and in text
6B MyLab IT	Objectives 5–7 from Project 6B	**6B Instructional Project (Grader Project)** **Instruction** Guided instruction to learn the skills in Project 6B.	In **MyLab IT** and in text
6C	Objectives 1–4 from Project 6A	**6C Skills Review (Scorecard Grading)** **Review** A guided review of the skills from Project 6A.	In text
6D	Objectives 5–7 from Project 6B	**6D Skills Review (Scorecard Grading)** **Review** A guided review of the skills from Project 6B.	In text
6E MyLab IT	Objectives 1–4 from Project 6A	**6E Mastery (Grader Project)** **Mastery and Transfer of Learning** A demonstration of your mastery of the skills in Project 6A with extensive decision-making.	In **MyLab IT** and in text
6F MyLab IT	Objectives 5–7 from Project 6B	**6F Mastery (Grader Project)** **Mastery and Transfer of Learning** A demonstration of your mastery of the skills in Project 6B with extensive decision-making.	In **MyLab IT** and in text
6G MyLab IT	Combination of Objectives from Projects 6A and 6B	**6G Mastery (Grader Project)** **Mastery and Transfer of Learning** A demonstration of your mastery of the skills in Projects 6A and 6B with extensive decision-making.	In **MyLab IT** and in text
6H	Combination of Objectives from Projects 6A and 6B	**6H GO! Fix It (Scorecard Grading)** **Critical Thinking** A demonstration of your mastery of the skills in Projects 6A and 6B by creating a correct result from a document that contains errors you must find.	IRC
6I	Combination of Objectives from Projects 6A and 6B	**6I GO! Make It (Scorecard Grading)** **Critical Thinking** A demonstration of your mastery of the skills in Projects 6A and 6B by creating a result from a supplied picture.	IRC
6J	Combination of Objectives from Projects 6A and 6B	**6J GO! Solve It (Rubric Grading)** **Critical Thinking** A demonstration of your mastery of the skills in Projects 6A and 6B, your decision-making skills, and your critical thinking skills. A task-specific rubric helps you self-assess your result.	IRC
6K	Combination of Objectives from Projects 6A and 6B	**6K GO! Solve It (Rubric Grading)** **Critical Thinking** A demonstration of your mastery of the skills in Projects 6A and 6B, your decision-making skills, and your critical thinking skills. A task-specific rubric helps you self-assess your result.	In text
6L	Combination of Objectives from Projects 6A and 6B	**6L GO! Think (Rubric Grading)** **Critical Thinking** A demonstration of your understanding of the Chapter concepts applied in a manner that you would outside of college. An analytic rubric helps you and your instructor grade the quality of your work by comparing it to the work an expert in the discipline would create.	In text
6M	Combination of Objectives from Projects 6A and 6B	**6M GO! Think (Rubric Grading)** **Critical Thinking** A demonstration of your understanding of the Chapter concepts applied in a manner that you would outside of college. An analytic rubric helps you and your instructor grade the quality of your work by comparing it to the work an expert in the discipline would create.	IRC
6N	Combination of Objectives from Projects 6A and 6B	**6N You and GO! (Rubric Grading)** **Critical Thinking** A demonstration of your understanding of the Chapter concepts applied in a manner that you would in a personal situation. An analytic rubric helps you and your instructor grade the quality of your work.	IRC

Glossary

Glossary of Chapter Key Terms

Axis A line that serves as a frame of reference for measurement and that borders the chart plot area.

Category labels The labels that display along the bottom of a chart to identify the categories of data.

Chart area The entire chart and all of its elements.

Chart elements Objects that make up a chart.

Chart sheet A workbook sheet that contains only a chart.

Column chart A chart in which the data is arranged in vertical columns and that is useful for showing data changes over a period of time or for illustrating comparisons among items.

Cycle A category of SmartArt graphics that illustrates a continual process.

Data labels Labels that display the value, percentage, and/or category of each particular data point and can contain one or more of the choices listed—Series name, Category name, Value, or Percentage.

Data marker A column, bar, area, dot, pie slice, or other symbol in a chart that represents a single data point; related data points form a data series.

Data point A value that originates in a worksheet cell and that is represented in a chart by a data marker.

Data series Related data points represented by data markers; each data series has a unique color or pattern represented in the chart legend.

Embedded chart A chart that is inserted into the same worksheet that contains the data used to create the chart.

Gridlines Lines in the plot area that aid the eye in determining the plotted values.

Hierarchy A category of SmartArt graphics used to create an organization chart or show a decision tree.

Horizontal Category axis (x-axis) The area along the bottom of a chart that identifies the categories of data; also referred to as the x-axis.

Labels Column and row headings that describe the values and help the reader understand the chart.

Legend A chart element that identifies the patterns or colors that are assigned to the categories in the chart.

Line chart A chart type that is useful to display trends over time; time displays along the bottom axis and the data point values are connected with a line.

List A category of SmartArt graphics used to show nonsequential information.

Locked [cells] In a protected worksheet, data cannot be inserted, modified, deleted, or formatted in these cells.

Major unit value A number that determines the spacing between tick marks and between the gridlines in the plot area.

Matrix A category of SmartArt graphics used to show how parts relate to a whole.

Organization chart A type of graphic that is useful to depict reporting relationships within an organization.

Orientation A feature with which you can rotate text diagonally or vertically in a cell and is useful when you need to label a narrow column.

Password An optional element of a template added to prevent someone from disabling a worksheet's protection.

Picture A category of SmartArt graphics that is used to display pictures in a diagram.

Plot area The area bounded by the axes of a chart, including all the data series.

Process A category of SmartArt graphics that is used to show steps in a process or timeline.

Protection A feature that prevents anyone from altering the formulas or changing other template components.

Pyramid A category of SmartArt graphics that uses a series of pictures to show relationships.

Recommended Charts An Excel feature that helps you choose a chart type by previewing suggested charts based on patterns in your data.

Relationship A category of SmartArt graphics that is used to illustrate connections.

Scale The range of numbers in the data series that controls the minimum, maximum, and incremental values on the value axis.

SmartArt graphic A visual representation of information and ideas.

Sparklines Tiny charts that fit within a cell and give a visual trend summary alongside data.

Standardization All forms created within the organization will have a uniform appearance; the data will always be organized in the same manner.

Template A special workbook that may include formatting, formulas, and other elements and is used as a pattern for creating other workbooks.

Text Pane A window that displays to the left of a SmartArt graphic, is populated with placeholder text, and is used to build a graphic by entering and editing text.

Tick mark labels Identifying information for a tick mark generated from the cells on the worksheet used to create the chart.

Tick marks The short lines that display on an axis at regular intervals.

Trendline A graphic representation of trends in a data series, such as a line sloping upward to represent increased sales over a period of months.

Unlocked [cells] Cells in a protected worksheet that may be filled in.

Vertical Value axis (y-axis) A numerical scale on the left side of a chart that shows the range of numbers for the data points; also referred to as the y-axis.

Walls and floor The areas surrounding a 3-D chart that give dimension and boundaries to the chart.

Chapter Review

In the following Skills Review, you will assist Linda Wong, Employer Relations Manager, in displaying the employer participation for the Dallas–Ft. Worth Job Fair in charts and diagrams. Your completed workbook will look similar to Figure 6.44.

Apply 6A skills from these Objectives:

1. Create and Format Sparklines and a Column Chart
2. Create and Format a Line Chart
3. Create and Modify a SmartArt Graphic
4. Create and Modify a Funnel Chart

Project Files

For Project 6C, you will need the following file:
e06C_Employer_Participation
You will save your workbook as:
Lastname_Firstname_6C_Employer_Participation

Project Results

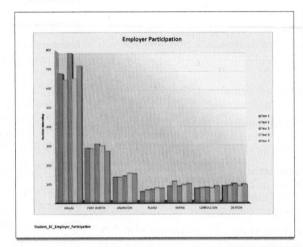

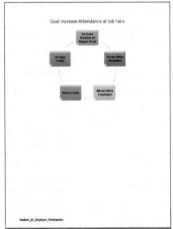

Figure 6.44

(continues on next page)

Chapter Review

1 From the files downloaded for this chapter, open the file **e06C_Employer_Participation**. Using your own name, save the file in your **Excel Chapter 6** folder as **Lastname_Firstname_6C_Employer_Participation**

a. On the **Participation by Location** worksheet, select the range **B4:F10**. Click the **Quick Analysis** button, click **Sparklines**, and then click **Line**. (Mac users: On the Insert tab, in the Sparklines group, click Sparklines, click Line. In the dialog box, select G4:G10; click OK.)

b. On the **Design tab**, in the **Show group**, select the **High Point** check box and the **Last Point** check box. On the **Design tab**, in the **Style group**, click **More**, and then in the first row, click the second style. In cell **G3**, type **Trend** and press **Enter**.

c. Select the range **A3:F10**. On the **Insert tab**, in the **Charts group**, click **Recommended Charts**. With the **Clustered Column** chart selected, click **OK**. On the **Design tab**, in the **Location group**, click **Move Chart**. Click **New sheet**, name the new sheet **Participation Chart** and then click **OK**. (Mac users: click Clustered Column.)

d. With the new **Participation Chart** worksheet displayed, on the **Design tab**, in the **Type group**, click **Change Chart Type**. In the **Change Chart Type** dialog box, if necessary, click the **All Charts** tab. On the left, be sure **Column** is selected, and then on the right, at the top of the dialog box, click the fourth chart type—**3-D Clustered Column**. Click **OK**. (Mac users: on the menu, point to Column; under 3-D Column, click the first style.)

e. In the upper right corner of the chart, click **Chart Styles** ✎. Scroll down if necessary, and then click **Style 3**. (Mac users: on the Chart Design ribbon, using ScreenTips, click Style 3.)

f. On the **Design tab**, in the **Chart Layouts group**, click **Add Chart Element**. In the **Chart Elements** list, point to **Legend**, and then click **Right**. Click **Add Chart Element** again, point to **Axis Titles**, and then click **Primary Vertical**. With the **Axis Title** box selected on the left, in the **Formula Bar**, type **Number Attending** and then press **Enter**.

g. In the chart, click the text *Chart Title*. In the **Formula Bar**, type **Employer Participation** as the chart title, and then press **Enter**. **Save** your workbook.

h. In the **Fort Worth** column cluster, point to the last column—**Year 5**. Notice that the Value for this column is 306. Display the **Participation by Location** worksheet, and then in cell **F5**, type **270** and press **Enter**. Display the **Participation Chart** worksheet and verify the value for the column has changed.

i. Click the **Chart Tools Format tab**, in the **Current Selection group**, click the **Chart Elements arrow**, and then click **Back Wall**. Then in the same group, click **Format Selection**. In the **Format Wall** pane on the right, if necessary expand **Fill**, click **Solid fill**, and then click the **Color arrow**. Under **Theme Colors**, in the fourth column, click the fourth color. Set the **Transparency** to **75%**. (Mac users: on the Chart Tools Format tab click Format Pane.)

j. At the top of the **Format Wall** pane, click the arrow to the right of *Wall Options* to display the **Chart Elements** list. (Mac users: On the Format tab, in the Current Selection group, click the Chart Elements arrow, and then click Side Wall; click Format Pane.)

k. Click **Side Wall**, and then apply the same fill, but with a **Transparency** of **60%**. To the **Floor**, apply a **Solid fill** using the last color in the first column with **0% Transparency**. To the **Chart Area**, apply a **Solid fill**—in the eighth column, click the second color. **Close** the **Format Chart Area** pane. Click outside of the chart to deselect it.

2 Display the **Participation by Location** worksheet. Select the range **A3:F4**—the data for Dallas—and then on the **Insert tab**, in the **Charts group**, click **Insert Line or Area Chart**. Click the **Line with Markers** chart type. Drag the upper left corner of the chart inside the upper left corner of cell **A13**. Drag the lower right corner of the chart inside the lower right corner of cell **G29**.

a. In the embedded chart, click the **Chart Title** text *Dallas*, in the **Formula Bar** type **Employer Participation at Dallas Job Fairs** and press **Enter**. Point to the chart title that you just typed, right-click, click **Font**, and then change the font **Size** to **16**. Click **OK**.

(continues on next page)

Chapter Review

b. On the left side of the line chart, point to any value in the **Vertical (Value) axis**, right-click, and then click **Format Axis**. In the **Format Axis** pane, if necessary, expand **Axis Options**. Under **Bounds**, in the **Minimum** box, type **500** Under **Units**, change the **Major unit** to **25** and press Enter. **Close** the **Format Axis** pane.

c. On the **Format tab**, in the **Current Selection group**, click the **Chart Elements arrow**, and then click **Plot Area**. In the same group, click **Format Selection**. (Mac users: click Format Pane.)

d. In the **Format Plot Area** pane, if necessary, expand **Fill**. Under **Fill**, click **Solid fill**, click the **Color arrow**, and then under **Theme Colors**, in the first column, click the fourth color.

e. Point to the chart line, right-click, and then click **Format Data Series**. In the pane on the right, under **Series Options**, click **Fill & Line**. Under **Line**, click **Solid line**. Use the spin box arrows to set the **Width** to **4 pt**. Under the **Fill & Line** icon, click **Marker**. Expand **Marker Options**. Click **Built-in**, click the **Type arrow**, and then click the **triangle**—the third symbol in the list. Set the **Size** of the **Marker Type** to **14**.

f. Under **Fill**, click **Solid fill**, and then click the **Color arrow**. Under **Theme Colors**, in the first column, click the last color. Under **Border**, click **No Line**.

g. Click in the white area just inside the chart border to open the **Format Chart Area** pane. Under **Fill**, apply a **Solid fill**—as the color, in the first column, click the third color. Under **Border**, click **Solid Line**, click the **Color arrow**, and then under **Theme Colors**, in the fifth column, click the first color. Be sure the **Width** is **0.75 pt**. **Close** the **Format Chart Area** pane. Click in any cell outside of the chart.

h. Click slightly inside the chart border to select the entire chart. On the **Design tab**, in the **Charts Layouts group**, click **Add Chart Element**, point to **Trendline**, and then click **Linear**. Click cell **A1**. **Save** your workbook.

3 Display the **Process Chart** worksheet. On the **Insert tab**, in the **Illustrations group**, click **SmartArt**. On the left, click **Cycle**, and then by using the ScreenTips, locate and click **Block Cycle**. Click **OK**. (Mac users: Point to Cycle.)

a. On the **Design tab**, in the **Create Graphic group**, if necessary, click **Text Pane**. In the **Text Pane**, as the first bullet, type **Increase Number of People Hired** Click the next bullet, and then type **Attract More Attendees** As the third bullet, type **Attract More Employers** As the fourth bullet, type **Reduce Costs** As the last bullet, type **Increase Profits Close** the **Text Pane**.

b. If necessary, click the edge of the SmartArt graphic to select it. On the **Design tab**, in the **SmartArt Styles group**, click **More**. Under **3-D**, locate and click the **Polished** style. Click **Change Colors**, and then under **Colorful,** click the first option—**Colorful—Accent Colors**. Drag the upper left corner of the graphic into the upper left corner of cell **A3**. Drag the lower right corner inside the lower right corner of cell **H20**. Click the **Format tab**, and then in the **WordArt Styles group**, click **Text Fill**. In the second column, click the first color. Click cell **A1**, and then click **Save**.

4 Display the **Funnel Chart** worksheet. Select the range **A3:B5**. On the **Insert tab**, in the **Charts group**, click **Insert Waterfall, Funnel, Stock, Surface, or Radar Chart** and then click **Funnel**.

a. In the chart, click **Chart Title**, and then type **HR Directors Seminar Participation**

b. Click the outside border of the chart to select only the chart. Click the **Chart Tools Design tab**, and then in the **Chart Styles group**, click the third style. Click **Change Colors**, and then under **Monochromatic**, click **Monochromatic Palette 4**.

c. Click the **Chart Tools Format tab**. In the **Current Selection group**, click the **Chart Elements arrow**, and then click **Chart Area**. In the same group, click **Format Selection**. (Mac users: click Format Pane.)

d. In the **Format Chart Area** pane, if necessary, expand **Border**. Click **Solid line**, and then click the **Color arrow**. In the eighth column, click the next to last color. Set the **Width** to **2 pt** and then close the **Format Chart Area** pane.

e. Drag the upper left corner of the chart into cell **A6**, positioned slightly below the *D* in *Directors*. Then click cell **A1**.

(continues on next page)

Chapter Review

5 Click the **Participation Chart sheet tab**, and if necessary, click in a white area of the screen to deselect the chart. Display the **Page Setup** dialog box, click the **Header/Footer tab**, and then click **Custom Footer**. With the insertion point in the **Left section**, in the small toolbar in the center of the dialog box, click **Insert File Name** , and then click **OK** two times.

a. Click the **Participation by Location sheet tab**, hold down Ctrl, and then click the **Process Chart sheet tab** and the **Funnel Chart sheet tab** to select the remaining worksheets and group them. On the **Page Layout tab**, in the **Page Setup group**, click **Margins**, and then at the bottom click **Custom Margins**. On the **Margins tab**, below **Center on page**, select the **Horizontally** check box. Click the **Header/Footer tab**, click **Custom Footer**, and then in the **Left section**, click **Insert File Name** . Click **OK** two times.

b. Click the **File tab** to display **Backstage** view. If necessary, click the **Info tab**. On the right, at the bottom of the **Properties** list, click **Show All Properties**. On the list of **Properties**, in the **Tags** box, type **participation statistics** In the **Subject** box, type your course name and section #. Under **Related People**, be sure that your name displays as the author. If necessary, right-click the author name, click **Edit Property**, type your name, click outside of the **Edit person** dialog box, and then click **OK**.

c. On the left, click **Print**. Under **Settings**, click the **Print Active Sheets arrow**, and then click **Print Entire Workbook.** At the bottom of the window, click **Next Page** to scroll through the worksheets. On the left, click **Save**. Click the **Participation Chart** sheet tab to ungroup the sheets.

d. In the upper right corner of the Excel window, click **Close**. Submit your file as directed by your instructor.

You have completed Project 6C END

Chapter Review

Apply 6B skills from these Objectives:

5. Create an Excel Template
6. Protect a Worksheet
7. Create a Worksheet Based on a Template

In the following Skills Review, you will assist Job Fair Director, Amanda Shay, in creating a template for a Purchase Order. Then you will create a new purchase order by using the template. Your completed workbook will look similar to Figure 6.45.

Project Files

For Project 6D, you will need the following files:

e06D_Purchase_Order

e06D_Logo

You will save your workbooks as:

Lastname_Firstname_6D_Purchase_Order_Template (will not be submitted for grading)

Lastname_Firstname_6D_Hancock_PO

Project Results

| 2900 Second Avenue |
| Dallas, TX 75210 |
| 214.555.0177 |

Date	18-Oct-21
Purchase Order Number	S-6255
Vendor Name	Hancock Industries
Address	191 Oak Avenue
City, State, Zip	Plano, TX 75074
Phone	214.555.0222
Email	orders@hancock.net

Purchase Order Form

Item	Description	Quantity	Unit Price	Total
Mugs	Green logo coffee mugs	125	3.25	$ 406.25
Pens	Black logo fine tip	700	0.65	455.00
Notepads	Green logo, lined	200	1.50	300.00
				-
				-
				-
				-
				-
				-
				-
				-
				-
			Order Total	$ 1,161.25

Student_Excel_6D_Hancock_PO

Figure 6.45

(continues on next page)

Chapter Review

Skills Review: Project 6D Purchase Order (continued)

1 From your downloaded files for this project, open **e06D_Purchase_Order**. Click the **File tab**, on the left click **Save As**, and then click **Browse**. In the lower portion of the **Save As** dialog box, click the **Save as type arrow**, and then click **Excel Template**. Navigate to your **Excel Chapter 6** folder. As the file name, using your own name, type **Lastname_Firstname_6D_Purchase_Order_Template** and then click **Save**.

a. Select **column B**. On the **Home tab**, in the **Cells group**, click **Format**, and then by using the **Column Width** command, set the width of **column B** to **13.5** Use the same technique to set the width of **column C** to **22.8** and the width of **column D** to **20** Select **columns E:F** and set the width to **10**

b. Select the range **C8:C9**, hold down Ctrl and select the nonadjacent range **C11:C15**, and then on the **Home tab**, in the **Alignment group**, click **Align Right**. (Mac users: hold down command ⌘.)

c. Select the range **D8:D9**. In the **Font group**, click the **Borders button arrow**, and then click **More Borders**. In the **Format Cells** dialog box, on the **Border tab**, under **Line**, in the **Style** list, click the second line in the first column—a dotted line. Click the **Color arrow**, and then under **Theme Colors**, in the sixth column, click the last color. In the Preview area, under **Border**, click **Middle Border** and **Bottom Border**. Click **OK**.

d. With the range **D8:D9** still selected, in the **Alignment group**, click **Align Right**. Right-click over the selected range, on the mini toolbar, click the **Format Painter**, and then select the range **D11:D15** to copy the format. (Mac users: On the Home tab, in the Clipboard group, click Format.)

e. Select the range **B18:F32**. Right-click over the selected range and click **Format Cells**. In the **Format Cells** dialog box, click the **Border tab**. Under **Presets**, click **Outline** and **Inside**, and then click **OK**. Select the range **B18:F18**, hold down Ctrl and select the range **F19:F32**. In the **Font group**, click the **Fill Color arrow**, and then under **Theme Colors**, in the sixth column, click the third color.

f. Click cell **A1**. Click the **File tab**, on the left click **Print** to view the Print Preview. On the left, click **Save** to save and return to your workbook.

2 To construct a formula to multiply the Quantity times the Unit Price, in cell **F19**, type **=d19*e19** and then on the **Formula Bar**, click **Enter**. Use the fill handle to copy the formula in cell **F19** down through cell **F31**. Click cell **F32**. On the **Home tab**, in the **Editing group**, click **AutoSum**. In the **Formula Bar**, be sure the range displays as **F19:F31**, and then press Enter. Select the range **E19:E31**. In the **Number group**, click **Comma Style**. Click cell **F19**, hold down Ctrl, and then click cell **F32**. In the **Number group**, click **Accounting Number Format**. Select the range **F20:F31**, and then click **Comma Style**. Select the range **D19:D31**, and then in the **Styles group**, click **Cell Styles**, and then under **Number Format**, click **Comma [0]**.

a. Select the range **D32:E32**. In the **Alignment group**, click **Merge & Center**. Type **Order Total** and press Enter. Click cell **D32** again, and then in the **Alignment group**, click **Align Right**. Apply **Bold**.

b. Select the range **B32:C32**, right-click, and then click **Format Cells**. On the **Border tab**, in the **Border** preview area, click **Left Border**, **Middle Border**, and **Bottom Border** to remove these borders from the preview—be sure the right and top border lines remain in the preview area. Click **OK**.

c. Click cell **A1** to make it the active cell. On the **Insert tab**, in the **Illustrations group**, click **Pictures**. In the **Insert Picture** dialog box, navigate to the files downloaded with this project, and then insert the file **e06D_Logo**. With the image selected, click the **Picture Tools Format tab**, in the **Picture Styles group**, click **More**, and then locate and click the **Simple Frame, Black** style. **Save** your workbook.

d. Scroll so that **row 16** is at the top of the Excel window. Select the range **A18:A31**, and then on the **Home tab**, in the **Alignment group**, click **Merge & Center**. In the **Alignment group**, click **Orientation**, and then click **Rotate Text Up**. Type **Purchase Order Form** and then press Enter.

e. Click the merged cell again to select it, and then in the **Alignment group**, click **Middle Align**. With the merged cell still selected, in the **Font group**, apply **Bold**, and then change the **Font size** to **22**. Click the **Fill color arrow**, and then in the third column, click the second color.

(continues on next page)

Chapter Review

f. In the **Font group**, click the **Borders button arrow**, and then on the list, click **Bottom Border**. Display the list again and click **Top Border**. Display the list again and click **Left Border**.

3 ▶ Select the range **D8:D9**, hold down ⌃Ctrl, select the range **D11:D15** and the range **B19:E31**. With the three ranges selected, on the **Home tab**, in the **Cells group**, click **Format**, and then click **Format Cells**. In the **Format Cells** dialog box, click the **Protection tab**. Click to clear the check mark from the **Locked** check box. Click **OK**.

a. In the **Cells group**, click **Format**, and then under **Protection**, click **Protect Sheet**. Under **Allow all users of this worksheet to:** leave the first two check boxes selected. At the top of the dialog box, be sure the **Protect worksheet and contents of locked cells** check box is selected. In the **Password to unprotect sheet** box, type **goseries** (Mac users: confirm password in the same dialog box.)

b. Click **OK**. In the displayed **Confirm Password** dialog box, type **goseries** to confirm the password, and then click **OK** to close both dialog boxes. Click **Save**.

c. Display the **document properties**. As the **Tags**, type **purchase order form, template**

d. On the left click **Print** to view the Print Preview, and then on the left, click **Save** to save your template and return to the worksheet window.

4 ▶ To create a purchase order from your template, display the **Save As** dialog box, and then set the **Save as type** box to **Excel Workbook**—the first choice at the top of the list. Navigate to your **Excel Chapter 6** folder, and then in the **File name** box, using your own name, type **Lastname_Firstname_6D_Hancock_PO** Click **Save**.

a. Click cell **D8**, type **October 18, 2021** and press Enter —Excel applies the default date format. As the **Purchase Order Number**, type **S-6255** and then press Enter two times to move to cell **D11**. Beginning in cell **D11**, enter the vendor information as follows:

Vendor Name	**Hancock Industries**
Address	**191 Oak Avenue**
City, State, Zip	**Plano, TX 75074**
Phone	**214.555.0222**
Email	**orders@hancock.net**

b. Click cell **B19**, and then complete the order by entering the following items as shown in the following table, pressing Tab to move from cell to cell.

Item	Description	Quantity	Unit Price
Mugs	**Green logo coffee mugs**	125	3.25
Pens	**Black logo fine tip**	700	0.65
Notepads	**Green logo, lined**	200	1.50

c. Click the **Page Layout tab**, display the **Page Setup** dialog box, click the **Header/Footer tab**, click **Custom Footer**, and then in the **Left section**, insert the **File name**. (Mac users: On the Page Layout tab, in the Scale to Fit group, click the Width arrow, and then click 1 page.)

d. Display the **document properties**. Be sure your name displays in the **Author** box. As the **Subject**, type your course name and section #. Change the **Tags** to **Hancock, promotional items** On the left, click **Save**.

e. In the upper right corner of the Excel window, click **Close**. As directed by your instructor, submit your **Lastname_Firstname_6D_Hancock_PO workbook**.

You have completed Project 6D | END

Content-Based Assessments (Mastery and Transfer of Learning)

| MyLab IT Grader | Mastering Excel | Project 6E Hires |

Apply 6A skills from these Objectives:

1. Create and Format Sparklines and a Column Chart
2. Create and Format a Line Chart
3. Create and Modify a SmartArt Graphic
4. Create and Modify a Funnel Chart

In this project, you will assist Linda Wong, Employer Relations Manager, in tracking the number of people who get hired by an employer at each fair. You will create and format a chart to display the number of job candidates hired at the fairs over a five-year period, create a diagram of the communities served, and create a funnel chart to visualize the number of candidates hired as a result of the Job Fairs in Year 5. Your completed worksheets will look similar to Figure 6.46.

Project Files for MyLab IT Grader

1. In your **MyLab IT** course, locate and click **Excel 6E Hires**, Download Materials, and then Download All Files.
2. Extract the zipped folder to your Excel Chapter 6 folder. Close the Grader download screens.
3. Take a moment to open the downloaded **Excel_6E_Hires_Instructions** document; note any recent updates to the book.

Project Results

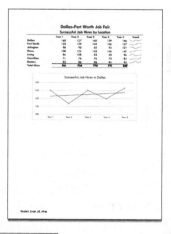
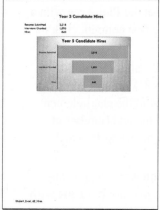
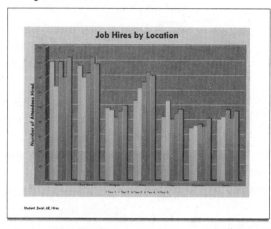

Figure 6.46

For Non-MyLab Submissions

For Project 6E, you will need: In your Excel Chapter 6 folder, save your workbook as:
e06E_Hires   **Lastname_Firstname_6E_Hires**

After you have named and saved your workbook, on the next page, begin with Step 2.
After Step 21, submit your file as directed by your instructor.

(continues on next page)

1 Navigate to your **Excel Chapter 6 folder**, and then double-click the Excel file you downloaded from **MyLab IT** that displays your name— **Student_Excel_6E_Hires**. If necessary, at the top, click Enable Editing.

2 On the first worksheet, select the data in the range **B4:F10**, and then use the **Quick Analysis** tool to insert **Sparklines** using the **Line** format. Place the sparklines in the range adjacent to the **Year 5** column, show the **High Point** and **Last Point**. Apply a sparkline style using the first sparkline style in the first row. (Mac users: use the Insert Line Sparkline command on the Insert tab.)

3 Type **Trend** in the cell above the sparklines.

4 Using the data for the years and for each location (not the totals) and the **Recommended Charts** command, create a **Clustered Column** chart on a separate chart sheet named **Hires by Location Chart**

5 Display the **Change Chart Type** dialog box. On the **All Charts tab**, if necessary, on the left click **Column**, and then on the right, at the top of the dialog box, click **3-D Clustered Column**. Click **OK**.

6 Apply **Chart Style 5** to the chart, and then add a chart title above the chart with the text **Job Hires by Location** Set the title's font size to **28**.

7 Format the **Chart Area** with a solid fill—in the first column, click the third color. Format the **Plot Area** with a solid fill two shades darker—in the first column, click the fifth color.

8 Format the floor and the side wall with a solid color—in the next to last column, click the last color. Set the transparency for both at **60%**. Add the chart element **Axis Title** to the vertical axis with the text **Number of Attendees Hired** and change the font size to **16**. Click outside of the chart to deselect it.

9 On the **Job Hires by Location** worksheet, using the data for **Dallas** *including the years*, insert a **Line with Markers** line chart. Resize the chart to position the upper left corner within cell **A13** and the lower right corner within cell **G26**.

10 Change the chart title to **Successful Job Hires in Dallas** and set the title's font size to **14**. Format the **Vertical (Value) Axis** so that the **Minimum** value is **100** and the **Major unit** is **20**

11 Add a **Linear Trendline**. Format the trendline by applying a color—in the sixth column, click the last color. Set the **Width** of the line to **2 pt**. Click cell **A1**.

12 Display the **List Chart** worksheet. In cell **A1**, type **Three Largest Communities We Serve** Merge and center this title across the range **A1:G1** and apply the **Title** cell style.

13 Insert a **SmartArt** graphic using the **Vertical Box List**. In the three boxes type, in order, **Dallas** and **Fort Worth** and **Carrollton**

14 Resize the graphic to position the upper left corner in cell **A3** and the lower right corner in cell **G16**. Apply the **3-D Inset** style and change the colors to **Colorful Range – Accent Colors 4 to 5**. Click cell **A1** to deselect the graphic.

15 Display the **Funnel Chart** worksheet. By using the data in the range **A3:B5**, insert a funnel chart. Apply the third Chart Style. As the **Chart Title**, type **Year 5 Candidate Hires**

16 Display the **Format Axis** pane, and then click the **Fill & Line** icon. Format the **Line** using a solid line and then in the Color gallery, in the sixth column, click the last color. Set the line **Width** to **2 pt** and then close the pane.

17 Display the **Format Chart Area** pane, and then apply a **2 pt Solid line** border using the same color as the axis line. Close the pane. Drag the upper left corner of the chart into cell **A6**, positioned slightly below the *G* in *Granted*. Click cell **A1** to deselect the chart.

18 Display the **Hires by Location chart sheet**. From the **Page Layout tab**, use the Dialog Box Launcher to display the **Page Setup** dialog box. Insert a **Custom Footer** with the **File Name** in the **Left section**.

19 Display the **Job Hires by Location** sheet. Hold down Ctrl and select the remaining two worksheets to group the three sheets. Insert a **Custom Footer** with the **File Name** in the **Left section**, and then center the sheets horizontally.

20 Click the **File tab** to display **Backstage** view. On the left, click **Print**. Under **Settings**, click the **Print Active Sheets arrow**, and then click **Print Entire Workbook**. At the bottom of the window, click **Next Page** to scroll through the worksheets to check your worksheets. On the left, click **Save**.

21 **Close** Excel.

(continues on next page)

Mastering Excel: Project 6E Hires (continued)

22 In **MyLab IT**, locate and click the Grader Project **Excel 6E Hires**. In **step 3**, under **Upload Completed Assignment**, click **Choose File**. In the **Open** dialog box, navigate to your **Excel Chapter 6 folder**, and then click your **Student_Excel_6E_Hires** file one time to select it. In the lower right corner of the **Open** dialog box, click **Open**.

23 The name of your selected file displays above the Upload button.

24 To submit your file to **MyLab IT** for grading, click **Upload**, wait a moment for a green **Success!** message, and then in **step 4**, click the blue **Submit for Grading** button. Click **Close Assignment** to return to your list of **Course Materials**.

You have completed Project 6E | END

| **Mastering Excel** | **Project 6F Event Budget**

In the following Mastering Excel Project, you will create a budget template for Job Fair events. Then you will create a worksheet based on the budget template for review by Milton Hyken, Dallas Job Fair Director. Your completed worksheet will look similar to Figure 6.47.

Project Files for **MyLab IT Grader**

1. In your **MyLab IT** course, locate and click **Excel 6F Event Budget**, Download Materials, and then Download All Files.
2. Extract the zipped folder to your Excel Chapter 6 folder. Close the Grader download screens.
3. Take a moment to open the downloaded **Excel_6F_Event_Budget_Instructions** document; note any recent updates to the book.

Project Results

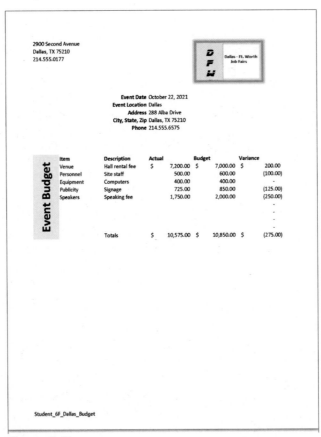

Figure 6.47

For Non-MyLab Submissions

For Project 6F, you will need:

e06F_Event_Budget

e06F_Logo

In your Excel Chapter 6 folder, you will save workbooks as:

Lastname_Firstname_6F_Event_Budget (do not submit)

Lastname_Firstname_6F_Event_Budget_Template (do not submit)

Lastname_Firstname_6F_Dallas_Budget (submit this file)

Open e06F_Event_Budget and save it in your Chapter 6 folder as Lastname_Firstname_6F_Event_Budget and then on the next page, begin with Step 2.

After Step 13, save and submit your file Lastname_Firstname_6F_Dallas_Budget as directed by your instructor.

(continues on next page)

Content-Based Assessments (Mastery and Transfer of Learning)

1 Navigate to your **Excel Chapter 6 folder**, and then double-click the Excel file you downloaded from **MyLab IT** that displays your name— **Student_Excel_6F_Event_Budget**. If necessary, at the top, click **Enable Editing**.

2 In cell **B16**, type **Item** and press Tab. In cell **C16**, type **Description** In cell **D16**, type **Actual** In cell **E16**, type **Budget** In cell **F16**, type **Variance** Click cell **C26** and type **Totals**

3 To the ranges **C8:C12** and **B16:F16**, apply **Bold**. To the range **C8:C12**, apply **Align Right**. To the range **D8:D12**, apply **Align Left**. Select columns **B:F**, display the **Column Width** dialog box, and then set the width of columns **B:F** to **15** (Mac users: Set the width to 13)

4 To construct a formula to compute the Variance (Variance = Actual - Budget) for each budget item, in cell **F17**, type **=d17-e17** and copy the formula through cell **F25**.

5 In the range **D26:F26**, insert appropriate formulas to sum these columns. To the range **D18:F25**, apply **Comma Style**. To the ranges **D17:F17** and **D26:F26**, apply **Accounting Number Format**. (Remember that you are creating a template, so there is no data entered yet.)

6 Click cell **E1**, insert the picture **e06F_Logo**. Select the range **A16:A26**, and then apply **Merge & Center**. Change the **Orientation** to **Rotate Text Up**, type **Event Budget** and press Enter. Select the merged cell, apply **Middle Align**, apply **Bold**, and change the **Font Size** to **24**.

7 To the merged cell, apply a **Fill Color**—in the fifth column click the second color.

8 Select the ranges **D8:D12** and **B17:E25**. Remove the **Locked** formatting from the selected cells, and then protect the worksheet. Be sure the check box at the top and the first two check boxes in the list are selected, and as the password type **goseries**

9 Display the **Page Setup** dialog box, insert a footer in the **left section** with the file name, and center the worksheet horizontally on the page. Display the **Save As** dialog box. Change the **Save as type** to **Excel Template**. Navigate to your **Excel Chapter 6** folder, and then using your own name, save the file as **Lastname_Firstname_6F_Event_Budget_Template**

10 To create a new budget report using the template as your model, display the **Save As** dialog box again,

navigate to your **Excel Chapter 6** folder, change the **Save as type** to **Excel Workbook**, and then using your own name, save the file as **Lastname_Firstname_6F_Dallas_Budget** This is the workbook you will submit for grading. In the new workbook, enter the following data in column D:

Event Date	**October 22, 2021**
Event Location	**Dallas**
Address	**288 Alba Drive**
City, State, Zip	**Dallas, TX 75210**
Phone	**214.555.6575**

11 Beginning in cell **B17**, complete the order by entering the following items:

Item	Description	Actual	Budget
Venue	**Hall rental fee**	**7200**	**7000**
Personnel	**Site staff**	**500**	**600**
Equipment	**Computers**	**400**	**400**
Publicity	**Signage**	**725**	**850**
Speakers	**Speaking fee**	**1750**	**2000**

12 Display the document properties. Be sure your name displays in the Author box. As the **Subject**, type your course name and section number. As the **Tags**, type **Dallas, event budget** Check the Print Preview to be sure the file name updated and displays in the left section of the footer. On the left, click **Save**.

13 In the upper right corner of the Excel window, click Close ☒.

14 In **MyLab IT**, locate and click the Grader Project **Excel 6F Event Budget**. In **step 3**, under **Upload Completed Assignment**, click **Choose File**. In the **Open** dialog box, navigate to your **Excel Chapter 6 folder**, and then click your **Student_Excel_6F_Dallas_Budget** file one time to select it. In the lower right corner of the **Open** dialog box, click **Open**.

The name of your selected file displays above the Upload button.

15 To submit your file to **MyLab IT** for grading, click **Upload**, wait a moment for a green **Success!** message, and then in **step 4**, click the blue **Submit for Grading** button. Click **Close Assignment** to return to your list of **Course Materials**.

You have completed Project 6F | END

Content-Based Assessments (Mastery and Transfer of Learning)

Apply 6A and 6B skills from these Objectives:

1. Create and Format Sparklines and a Column Chart
2. Create and Format a Line Chart
3. Create and Modify a SmartArt Graphic
4. Create and Modify a Funnel Chart
5. Create an Excel Template
6. Protect a Worksheet
7. Create a Worksheet Based on a Template

In this project, you will assist Ann Takei, Internship Coordinator, in tracking the number of internships by industry at each Job Fair. You will insert and format sparklines, a line chart, a SmartArt graphic, and a funnel chart. You will also create a template to use for travel expenses. Your completed worksheets will look similar to Figure 6.48.

Project Files for **MyLab IT Grader**

1. In your Course Materials, locate and click **Excel 6G Internships Travel**, Download Materials, and then Download All Files.
2. Extract the zipped folder to your Excel Chapter 6 folder. Close the Grader download screens.
3. Take a moment to open the downloaded **Excel_6G_Internships_Travel_Instructions** document; note any recent updates to the book.

Project Results

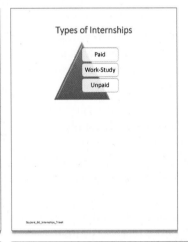

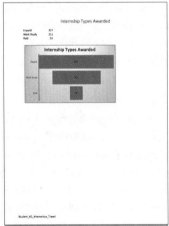

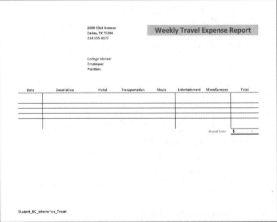

Figure 6.48

For Non-MyLab Submissions

For Project 6G, you will need:
e06G_Internships_Travel

In your Excel Chapter 6 folder, save your workbook as:
Lastname_Firstname_6G_Internships_Travel

After you have named and saved your workbook, on the next page, begin with Step 2.

After step 18, save and submit your file as directed by your instructor.

(continues on next page)

Content-Based Assessments (Mastery and Transfer of Learning)

1 Navigate to your **Excel Chapter 6 folder**, and then double-click the Excel file you downloaded from **MyLab IT** that displays your name—**Student_Excel_6G_Internships_Travel**. If necessary, at the top, click **Enable Editing**.

2 On the **Internships by Industry** worksheet, select the range **B4:F10**, and then use the **Quick Analysis** tool to insert **Line Sparklines** in the range **G4:G10**. (Mac users: Use the Insert Line Sparklines command on the Insert tab.)

3 Format the Sparklines to show the **High Point** and the **Last Point**. From the sparkline **Style** gallery, in the first row, apply the second style.

4 By using the data in the ranges **A3:F3** and **A7:F7**, insert a **Line with Markers** chart for the internships available in the **Technology** industry. Position the chart so that the upper left corner of the chart aligns with the upper left corner of cell **A13** and the bottom right corner aligns with the lower right corner of cell **G27**.

5 Change the chart title to **Internships Available in Technology**

6 Edit the **Vertical (Value) Axis** to set the **Minimum** to **35** and the **Major unit** to **5**

7 Format the **Plot Area** with a **Solid fill**—in the last column click the second color. Format the **Chart Area** with a **Solid fill**—in the last column, click the fourth color.

8 Insert a **Linear Trendline** and change the width of the line to **2.5 pt**. Click cell **A1** to deselect the chart. **Close** any displayed Format panes.

9 On the **List Chart** worksheet, insert a SmartArt graphic using the **Pyramid List** style. Position the SmartArt so that the upper left corner of the graphic aligns with the upper left corner of cell **A3**.

10 In the SmartArt, type **Paid** in the top text box. Type **Work-Study** in the second text box, and type **Unpaid** in the last text box.

11 Apply the **Inset 3-D** SmartArt style to the graphic. Change the colors to **Colored Fill – Accent 1**. Click cell **A1** to deselect the graphic.

12 On the **Funnel Chart** worksheet, by using the data in the range **A3:B5**, insert a **Funnel** chart. Apply the third chart style. Change the **Chart Title** to **Internship Types Awarded** Position the upper left corner of the chart in the upper left corner of cell **A7**.

13 Change the **Shape Width** of the chart to **4.5"** Apply a **Solid line 3 pt** border—as the color, in the Color gallery, in the fifth column, click the first color. Click cell **A1** to deselect the chart.

14 Display the **Save As** dialog box. In the **Save as type** box, click the arrow, and then change the file type to **Excel Template**. Navigate to your **Excel Chapter 6** folder. Using your own name, as the **File name** type **Lastname_Firstname_6G_Internships_Travel_Template** and click **Save**. Display the **Travel Expenses** worksheet. In cell **H22** enter a formula that will add the contents of the range **H15:H21**. Apply the **Total** cell style to cell **H22**.

15 Select the ranges **D8:D10** and **A15:G21**, and then remove the Locked formatting from the selected ranges. Protect the worksheet using the default selections and the password **goseries** Click cell **A1**.

16 Display the **Save As** dialog box, navigate to your **Excel Chapter 6** folder, change the file type to **Excel Workbook**, and then using your own name, as the **File name** type **Lastname_Firstname_6G_Internships_Travel** This is the file you will submit for grading.

17 Select all of the sheets, display the **Page Setup** dialog box, and then insert a **Custom Footer** with the file name in the left section. Center the sheets horizontally. Display the document properties; as the **Tags** type **travel template** and as the **Subject**, type your course name and section number. Be sure your name displays as the author. Display the print preview, examine your worksheets for any errors or changes. On the left, click **Save** to save your workbook and redisplay the Excel window.

18 In the upper right corner of the Excel window, click **Close** ☒.

19 In **MyLab IT**, locate and click the Grader Project **Excel 6G Internships Travel**. In **step 3**, under **Upload Completed Assignment**, click **Choose File**. In the **Open** dialog box, navigate to your **Excel Chapter 6 folder**, and then click your **Lastname_Firstname_Excel_6G_Internships_Travel** file one time to select it. In the lower right corner of the **Open** dialog box, click **Open**.

The name of your selected file displays above the Upload button.

20 To submit your file to **MyLab IT** for grading, click **Upload**, wait a moment for a green **Success!** message, and then in **step 4**, click the blue **Submit for Grading** button. Click **Close Assignment** to return to your list of **Course Materials**.

You have completed Project 6G | **END**

Apply a combination of the 6A and 6B skills.	**GO! Fix It**	**Project 6H Operations Chart**	**IRC**
	GO! Make It	**Project 6I Advertisers**	**IRC**
	GO! Solve It	**Project 6J Sponsors**	**IRC**
	GO! Solve It	**Project 6K Time Card**	

Project Files

For Project 6K, you will need the following file:

e06K_Time_Card

You will save your workbook as:

Lastname_Firstname_6K_Time_Template

Open the file e06K_Time_Card and save it as a template in your chapter folder with the name **Lastname_Firstname_6K_Time_Template** Insert a formula to calculate daily pay (Regular Hours x Rate Per Hour using an absolute cell reference), a formula to total the hours for the week, and a formula to calculate the total pay. Apply appropriate number and financial formatting. Reposition the WordArt above the Time Card chart. Unlock the cells in which an individual would enter variable data, and then protect the sheet with the password **goseries** Insert the file name in the footer, add appropriate information to the document properties including the tags **timecard, payroll** and submit as directed by your instructor.

		Performance Level		
		Exemplary	**Proficient**	**Developing**
Performance Criteria	**Place WordArt Object and Apply Financial Formatting**	Appropriate formulas, cell formatting, and WordArt placement are applied.	Appropriate formulas, cell formatting, and WordArt placement are partially applied.	Appropriate formulas, cell formatting, and WordArt placement are not applied.
	Lock Formulas	Formula cells are locked and variable data cells are unlocked.	Only one of the formula cells or variable data cells has the locked or unlocked feature applied appropriately.	Formula cells are unlocked and variable data cells are locked.
	Protect Worksheet	The worksheet is protected with the password goseries.	The worksheet is protected but not with the password goseries.	The worksheet is not protected with a password.

You have completed Project 6K | **END**

Outcomes-Based Assessments (Critical Thinking)

Rubric

The following outcomes-based assessments are open-ended assessments. That is, there is no specific correct result; your result will depend on your approach to the information provided. Make Professional Quality your goal. Use the following scoring rubric to guide you in how to approach the problem and then to evaluate how well your approach solves the problem.

The *criteria*—Software Mastery, Content, Format and Layout, and Process—represent the knowledge and skills you have gained that you can apply to solving the problem. The *levels of performance*—Professional Quality, Approaching Professional Quality, or Needs Quality Improvements—help you and your instructor evaluate your result.

	Your completed project is of Professional Quality if you:	Your completed project is Approaching Professional Quality if you:	Your completed project Needs Quality Improvements if you:
1-Software Mastery	Choose and apply the most appropriate skills, tools, and features and identify efficient methods to solve the problem.	Choose and apply some appropriate skills, tools, and features, but not in the most efficient manner.	Choose inappropriate skills, tools, or features, or are inefficient in solving the problem.
2-Content	Construct a solution that is clear and well organized, contains content that is accurate, appropriate to the audience and purpose, and is complete. Provide a solution that contains no errors of spelling, grammar, or style.	Construct a solution in which some components are unclear, poorly organized, inconsistent, or incomplete. Misjudge the needs of the audience. Have some errors in spelling, grammar, or style, but the errors do not detract from comprehension.	Construct a solution that is unclear, incomplete, or poorly organized, contains some inaccurate or inappropriate content, and contains many errors of spelling, grammar, or style. Do not solve the problem.
3-Format and Layout	Format and arrange all elements to communicate information and ideas, clarify function, illustrate relationships, and indicate relative importance.	Apply appropriate format and layout features to some elements, but not others. Overuse features, causing minor distraction.	Apply format and layout that does not communicate information or ideas clearly. Do not use format and layout features to clarify function, illustrate relationships, or indicate relative importance. Use available features excessively, causing distraction.
4-Process	Use an organized approach that integrates planning, development, self-assessment, revision, and reflection.	Demonstrate an organized approach in some areas, but not others; or, use an insufficient process of organization throughout.	Do not use an organized approach to solve the problem.

Content-Based Assessments (Mastery and Transfer of Learning)

GO! Think	**Project 6L Tech Industry**

Project Files

For Project 6L, you will need the following file:

e06L_Tech_Industry

You will save your workbook as:

Lastname_Firstname_6L_Tech_Industry

From your student files, open the file e06L_Tech_Industry, and then save it in your chapter folder as **Lastname_Firstname_6L_Tech_Industry** Format the data attractively, add appropriate formulas, add sparklines, and insert a line chart in the sheet that tracks the data for the Irving location. Create a 3-D chart on a separate page based on the data in the worksheet, and format it attractively. Change the Fort Worth 2016 data point from 84 to 96. Insert the file name in the footer on each page, format each sheet for printing, add appropriate information to the document properties including the tags **technology employers** and submit as directed by your instructor.

	You have completed Project 6L	END

GO! Think	**Project 6M Location List**	IRC

You and GO!	**Project 6N Job Finding**	IRC

Use Financial and Lookup Functions, Define Names, Validate Data, and Audit Worksheets

7
EXCEL 2019

AlenD/Shutterstock

In This Chapter

GO! To Work with Excel

In this chapter, you will use Financial functions and What-If Analysis tools to make your worksheets more valuable for analyzing data and making financial decisions. In addition, you will define names and use them in a formula. You will use the Lookup functions to locate information that is needed in a form and create a validation list to ensure that only accurate data is entered. In this chapter, you will also use Excel's auditing features to help you understand the construction of formulas in a worksheet and to locate and correct any errors. For example, by tracing relationships you will be able to test your formulas for accuracy.

The projects in this chapter relate to **Jesse Jewelers**, a Toronto-based retailer of jewelry and accessories for men and women. Jesse sells unique and beautiful items at a great price. Products include necklaces, bracelets, key chains, business cases, jewelry boxes, handmade bags, and personalized items. Founded in 2011 by two college friends, this growing company has several retail locations and an online store. The company distributes its products to department and specialty stores throughout the United States and Canada. Jesse Jewelers provides exceptional customer service from a well-trained staff of product experts.

Amortization Schedule and Merchandise Costs

Project Activities

In Activities 7.01 through 7.09, you will create a worksheet for Alaina Dubois, International Sales Director for Jesse Jewelers, that details the loan information to purchase furniture and fixtures for a new store in Houston. You will also define names for ranges of cells in a workbook containing quarterly and annual merchandise costs for the new store. Your completed worksheets will look similar to Figure 7.1.

Project Files for **MyLab IT Grader**

1. In your storage location, create a folder named **Excel Chapter 7.**
2. In your **MyLab IT** course, locate and click **Excel 7A Loan and Costs**, Download Materials, and then Download All Files.
3. Extract the zipped folder to your Excel Chapter 7 folder. Close the Grader download screens.
4. Take a moment to open the downloaded **Excel_7A_Loan_and_Costs_Instructions**; note any recent updates to the book.

Project Results

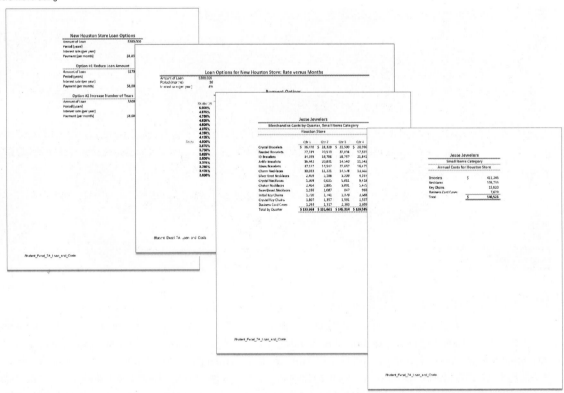

GO! Project 7A
Where We're Going

Figure 7.1 Project 7A Amortization Schedule and Merchandise Costs

---

For Non-MyLab Submissions

For Project 7A, you will need:
e07A_Loan_and_Costs

In your storage location, create a folder named **Excel Chapter 7**
In your Excel Chapter 7 folder, save your workbook as:
Lastname_Firstname_7A_Loan_and_Costs

After you have named and saved your workbook, on the next page, begin with Step 2.

ALERT Because Office 365 is a cloud-based subscription service that receives continuous updates, you may encounter some variations in what appears on your screen and what is shown in this instruction. Microsoft Office 365 is fully installed on your PC or Mac; no Internet access is necessary to create or edit documents. When you *are* connected to the Internet, you will receive monthly upgrades and new features, so you always have the latest versions of Office apps as soon as they are available. Your subscription gives you continuous free access to the latest innovations and refinements.

GO! Learn How
Video E7-1

Financial functions are prebuilt formulas that make common business calculations such as calculating a loan payment on a vehicle or calculating how much to save each month to buy something. Financial functions commonly involve a period of time such as months or years.

When you borrow money from a bank or other lender, the amount charged to you for your use of the borrowed money is called *interest*. Loans are typically made for a period of years, and the interest that must be paid is a percentage of the loan amount that is still owed. In Excel, this interest percentage is called the *rate*.

The initial amount of the loan is called the ***Present value (Pv)***, which is the total amount that a series of future payments is worth now and is also known as the ***principal***. When you borrow money, the loan amount is the present value to the lender. The number of time periods—number of payments—is abbreviated ***Nper***. The value at the end of the time periods is the ***Future value (Fv)***—the cash balance you want to attain after the last payment is made. The future value is usually zero for loans, because you will have paid off the full amount at the end of the term.

Activity 7.01 | Inserting the PMT Financial Function

MOS
Expert 3.4.3,
Expert 3.4.4

In this Activity, you will calculate the monthly payments that Jesse Jewelers must make to finance the purchase of the furniture and fixtures for a new store in Houston, the total cost of which is $300,000. You will calculate the monthly payments, including interest, for a three-year loan at an annual interest rate of 4.0%. To stay within Alaina's budget, the monthly payment must be approximately $8,000.

1 Navigate to your **Excel Chapter 7 folder**, and then double-click the Excel file you downloaded from **MyLab IT** that displays your name—**Student_Excel_7A_Loan_and_Costs**. If necessary, at the top click **Enable Editing**.

2 Be sure that the **Houston New Store Loan** worksheet is active, and then compare your screen with Figure 7.2.

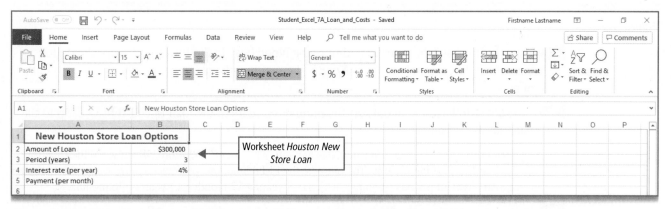

Figure 7.2

3 On the **Houston New Store Loan** worksheet, click cell **B5**. On the **Formulas tab**, in the **Function Library group**, click **Financial**. In the list, scroll down as necessary, and then click **PMT**.

> The Function Arguments dialog box displays. Recall that *arguments* are the values that an Excel function uses to perform calculations or operations.

4 If necessary, drag the **Function Arguments** dialog box to the right side of your screen so you can view columns A:B.

> The *PMT function* calculates the payment for a loan based on constant payments and at a constant interest rate.

🖥 **MAC TIP**   The Formula Builder pane opens on the right.

5 With your insertion point positioned in the **Rate** box, type **b4/12** and then compare your screen with Figure 7.3.

> Excel will divide the annual interest rate of 4%, which is 0.04 in decimal notation, located in cell B4 by 12 (months), which will result in a *monthly* interest rate.

> When borrowing money, the interest rate and number of periods are quoted in years. The payments on a loan, however, are usually made monthly. Therefore, the number of periods, which is stated in years, and the *annual* interest rate must be changed to a monthly equivalent in order to calculate the monthly payment amount. You can see that calculations like these can be made as part of the argument in a function.

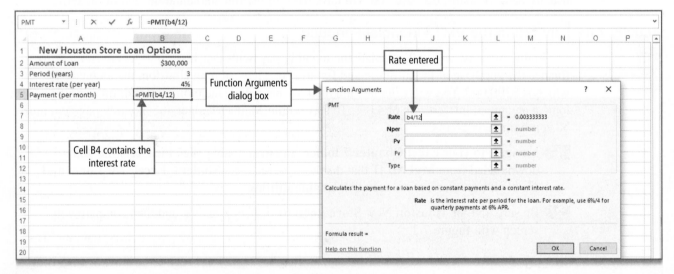

Figure 7.3

6 Press `Tab` to move the insertion point to the **Nper** box. In the lower portion of the dialog box, notice Excel points out that *Nper is the total number of payments for the loan* (number of periods).

7 Type **b3*12** to have Excel convert the number of years in the loan in cell **B3** (3 years) to the total number of months.

> Recall that the PMT function calculates a *monthly* payment. Therefore, all values in the function must be expressed in months. To complete the PMT function, you must determine the total number of loan payment periods (months), which is 3 years x 12 months per year, or 36 months.

8 Press `Tab` to move to the **Pv** box, and then type **b2** to indicate the cell that contains the amount of the loan.

> Pv represents the present value—the amount of the loan before any payments are made. In this instance, the Pv is $300,000.

9 In cell **B5** and on the **Formula Bar**, notice that the arguments that comprise the PMT function are separated by commas. Notice also, in the **Function Arguments** dialog box, that the value of each argument displays to the right of the argument box. Compare your screen with Figure 7.4.

NOTE   Optional Arguments

The PMT function has two arguments not indicated by bold; these are optional. The Future value (Fv) argument assumes that the unpaid portion of the loan should be zero at the end of the last period. The *Type argument* indicates when the loan payment is due. If not specified, the Type argument assumes that the payment will be made at the end of each period. These default values are typical of most loans and may be left blank.

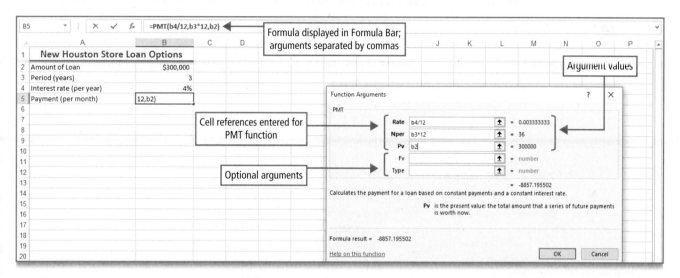

Figure 7.4

10 In the lower right corner of the **Function Arguments** dialog box, click **OK**.

The monthly payment amount—($8,857.20)—displays in cell B5. The amount displays in red and in parentheses to show that it is a negative number, a number that will be paid out. This monthly payment of $8,857.20 is larger than the $8,000 per month that Alaina has budgeted for her payments.

MAC TIP   Click Done and close the Formula Builder pane.

11 Click in the **Formula Bar**, and then using the arrow keys on the keyboard, position the insertion point between the equal sign and *PMT*. Type – (minus sign) to insert a minus sign into the formula, and then press Enter.

By placing a minus sign in the formula, the monthly payment amount of $8,857.20 displays in cell B5 as a *positive* number, which is more familiar and simpler to work with.

12 Save your workbook.

Objective 2   Use Goal Seek

GO! Learn How

Video E7-2

What-If Analysis is a process of changing the values in cells to determine how those changes affect the outcome of formulas on the worksheet; for example, you might vary the interest rate to determine the amount of loan payments.

Goal Seek is part of a suite of data tools used for What-If Analysis. It is a method to find a specific value for a cell by adjusting the value of another cell. With Goal Seek, you can work backward from the desired outcome to find the number necessary to achieve your goal. If you have a result in mind, you can try different numbers in one of the cells used as an argument in the function until you get close to the result you want.

Activity 7.02 | Using Goal Seek to Produce a Desired Result

2.1.1, Expert 3.4.2

Alaina knows that her budget cannot exceed $8,000 per month for the new store loan. The amount of $300,000 is necessary to purchase the furniture and fixtures to open the new store. Now she has two options: borrow less money and reduce the amount or quality of the furniture and fixtures in the store or extend the time to repay the loan. To find out how much she can borrow for three years to stay within the budget or how much to increase the repayment period, you will use the Goal Seek tool.

1 Click cell **B5**. On the **Data tab**, in the **Forecast group**, click **What-If Analysis**, and then on the list, click **Goal Seek**. In the **Goal Seek** dialog box, in the **Set cell** box, confirm that *B5* displays.

The cell address in this box is the cell that will display the desired result.

2 Press Tab. In the **To value** box, type the payment goal of **8000** and press Tab. In the **By changing cell** box, type **b2** which is the amount of the loan, and then compare your screen with Figure 7.5.

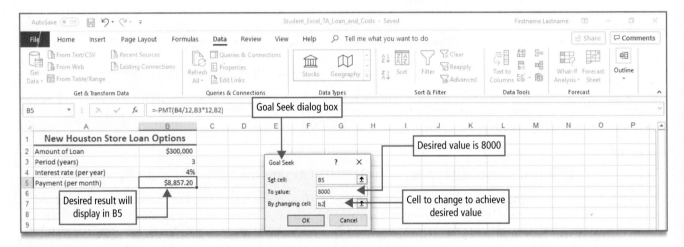

Figure 7.5

3 Click **OK**, and then in the **Goal Seek Status** dialog box, click **OK**.

Excel's calculations indicate that to achieve a monthly payment of $8,000.00 using a 3-year loan, Alaina can borrow only *$270,966*—not $300,000.

4 Click cell **A7**. Type **Option #1 Reduce Loan Amount** and then on the **Formula Bar**, click **Enter** ✓ to keep the cell active. Select the range **A7:B7**, and then from the **Home tab**, click **Merge & Center** ⊞▾ to center this heading across the two cells. Display the **Cell Styles** gallery, and then under **Titles and Headings**, click the **Heading 2** cell style.

5 Select the range **A2:B5**, right-click, and then click **Copy**. Point to cell **A8**, right-click, on the shortcut menu, click the **Paste Special arrow**, and then under **Paste Values**, click the **second** button—**Values & Number Formatting (A)** 🗐. Press Esc to cancel the moving border.

💻 **MAC TIP** Click cell A8, right-click, and then click Paste Special. In the Paste Special dialog box, under Paste, click the Values and Number Formats option button, and then click OK.

6 ▸ **Save** 🖫 your workbook, and then compare your worksheet with Figure 7.6.

By using the Paste Special command, you can copy the *value* in a cell, rather than the formula, and the cell formats are retained—cell B5 contains the PMT function formula, but here you need only the value that *results* from that formula.

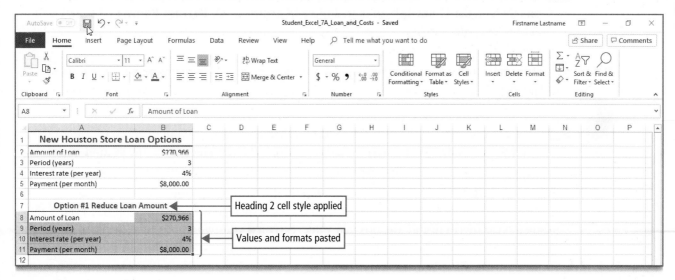

Figure 7.6

7 ▸ Click cell **B2**, replace the existing value by typing **300000** and then press **Enter** to restore the original loan amount.

Activity 7.03 | Using Goal Seek to Find an Increased Payment Period

For Alaina's purchase of furniture and fixtures for the new store in Houston, an alternative to borrowing less money—which would mean buying fewer items or items of lesser quality—would be to increase the number of years of payments.

1 ▸ Be sure that you have restored cell **B2** to $300,000, and then click cell **B5**. On the **Data tab**, in the **Forecast group**, click **What-If Analysis**, and then click **Goal Seek**.

2 ▸ In the **Set cell** box, confirm that *B5* displays. Press **Tab**. In the **To value** box, type **8000** Press **Tab**. In the **By changing cell** box, type **b3** which is the number of years for the loan. Compare your screen with Figure 7.7.

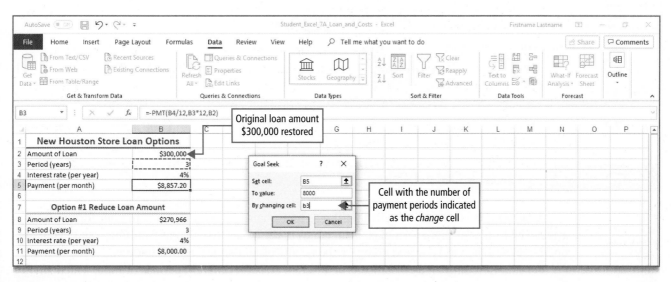

Figure 7.7

3 ▶ Click **OK** two times.

Excel's calculations indicate that by making payments for 3.3 years—*3.343845511*—the monthly payment is the desired amount of $8,000.00.

4 ▶ Click cell **A13**. Type **Option #2 Increase Number of Years** and then press Enter. Click cell **A7**, and then on the **Home tab**, in the **Clipboard group**, click **Format Painter** 🖌. Click cell **A13** to copy the format.

> 🔄 **ANOTHER WAY**   Right-click over cell A7, on the mini toolbar click Format Painter, and then click cell A13 to copy the format.

5 ▶ Select the range **A2:B5** and right-click, and then click **Copy**. Point to cell **A14**, right-click, point to the **Paste Special arrow**, and then under **Paste Values**, click the **second** button—**Values & Number Formatting (A)** 📋. Press Esc to cancel the moving border.

6 ▶ Click cell **B15**, and then on the **Home tab**, in the **Number group**, click **Decrease Decimal** 🔽 until the number of decimal places displayed is two. Click cell **B3**. Type **3** and then press Enter to restore the original value. **Save** 💾 your workbook, and then compare your screen with Figure 7.8.

> 🔄 **ANOTHER WAY**   Right-click over cell B15, and then click Decrease Decimal on the mini toolbar.

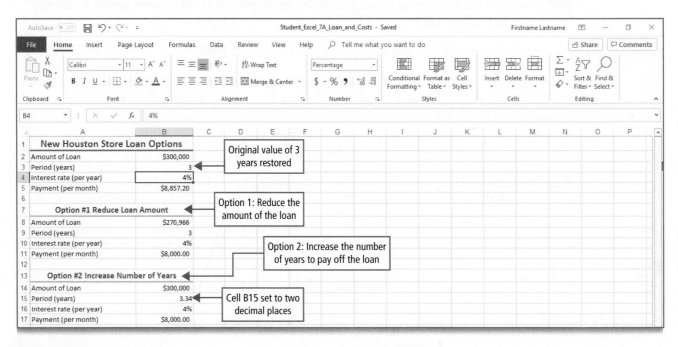

Figure 7.8

Objective 3	Create a Data Table

GO! Learn How
Video E7-3

A ***Data table*** is a range of cells that shows how changing certain values in your formulas affects the results of those formulas. Data tables make it easy to calculate multiple versions in one operation, and then to view and compare the results of all the different variations.

For example, banks may offer loans at different rates for different periods of time, which require different payments. By using a data table, you can calculate the possible values for each argument.

A *one-variable data table* changes the value in only one cell. For example, use a one-variable data table if you want to see how different interest rates affect a monthly payment. A *two-variable data table* changes the values in two cells—for example, if you want to see how different interest rates *and* different payment periods will affect a monthly payment.

Activity 7.04 | Designing a Two-Variable Data Table

2.1.2

Recall that the PMT function has three required arguments: Present value (Pv), Rate, and Number of periods (Nper). Because Alaina would still like to borrow $300,000 and purchase the fixtures and furniture that she has selected for the new store, in this data table, the present value will *not* change. The two values that *will* change are the Rate and Number of periods. Possible periods will range from 24 months (2 years) to 60 months (5 years) and the rate will vary from 5% to 3%.

1 In your **Houston New Store Loan** worksheet, click cell **A1**, and then at the lower edge of the worksheet, click the **Payment Table sheet**.

2 In the range **B2:B4**, enter the following data:

$300,000

36

4%

3 In cell **C7**, type **24** and then press Tab. Type **30** and then press Tab. Select the range **C7:D7**, point to the fill handle, and then drag to the right through cell **I7** to use Auto Fill to fill in a pattern of months from 24 to 60 in increments of six months.

Recall that the Auto Fill feature will duplicate a pattern of values that you set in the beginning cells.

4 In cell **B8**, type **5.000%** and then press Enter. In cell **B9**, type **4.875%** and then press Enter. Compare your screen with Figure 7.9.

Excel rounds both values to two decimal places.

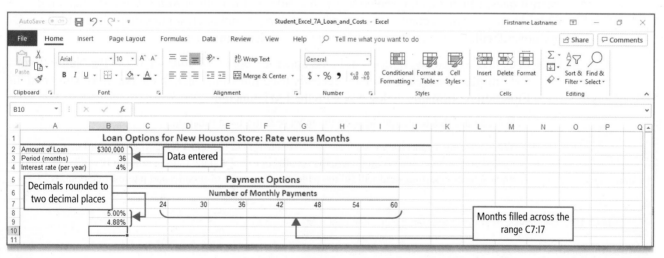

Figure 7.9

5 Select the range **B8:B9**. Point to the fill handle, and then drag down through cell **B24** to fill a pattern of interest rates in increments of .125 from 5.00% down to 3.00%.

6 With the range selected, on the **Home tab**, in the **Number group**, click **Increase Decimal** one time. Press Ctrl + Home to make cell **A1** the active cell.

7 **Save** 🖫 your workbook, and then compare your screen with Figure 7.10.

Row 7 represents the number of monthly payments, and the range B8:B24 in column B represents a range of possible annual interest rates. These two arguments will be used to calculate varying payment arrangements for a loan of $300,000.

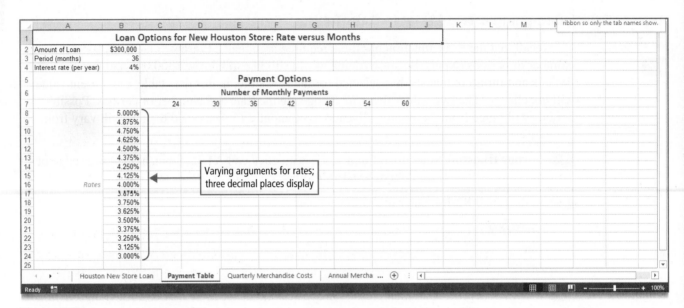

Figure 7.10

Activity 7.05 | Using a Data Table to Calculate Options

MOS
Expert 3.4.3

Recall that a data table is a range of cells that shows how changing certain values in your formulas affects the results of those formulas.

In this Activity, you will create a table of payments for every combination of payment periods, which are represented by the column titles under *Number of Monthly Payments*, and interest rates, which are represented by the row titles to the right of *Rates*. From the resulting table, Alaina can find a combination of payment periods and interest rates that will enable her to go forward with her plan to borrow $300,000 to purchase furniture and fixtures.

1 In cell **B7**, type = and notice that in the upper left corner of your screen, in the **Name Box**, *PMT* displays indicating the most recently used function. Click in the **Name Box** to open the **Function Arguments** dialog box with the PMT function.

You can use this technique to open the most recently used function.

When creating a data table, you enter the PMT function in the upper left corner of your range of data, so that when the data table is completed, the months in row 7 and the rates in column B will be substituted into each cell's formula and will fill the table with the range of months and interest rate options.

🖳 **MAC TIP** Click the spin arrow in the Name Box, then click PMT.

2 In the **Rate** box, type **b4/12** to divide the interest rate per year shown in cell **B4** by *12* and convert it to a monthly interest rate.

3 Press ⎆Tab to move the insertion point to the **Nper** box. Type **b3** which is the cell that contains the number of months, and then press ⎆Tab.

The periods in cell B3 are already stated in months and do not need to be changed.

4 In the **Pv** box, type **-b2** to enter the amount of the loan as a negative number. Compare your dialog box with Figure 7.11.

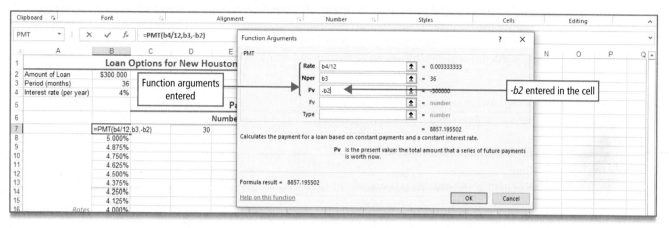

Figure 7.11

5 Click **OK** to close the **Function Arguments** dialog box and display the result in cell **B7**.

The payment—*$8,857.20*—is calculated by using the values in cells B2, B3, and B4. This is the same payment that you calculated on the first worksheet. Now it displays as a positive number because you entered the loan amount in cell B2 as a negative number.

6 Select the range **B7:I24**, which encompasses all of the months and all of the rates. With the range **B7:I24** selected, on the **Data tab**, in the **Forecast group**, click **What-If Analysis**, and then click **Data Table**.

7 In the **Data Table** dialog box, in the **Row input cell** box, type **b3** and then press Tab. In the **Column input cell** box, type **b4** and then compare your screen with Figure 7.12.

The row of months will be substituted for the value in cell B3, and the column of interest rates will be substituted for the value in cell B4.

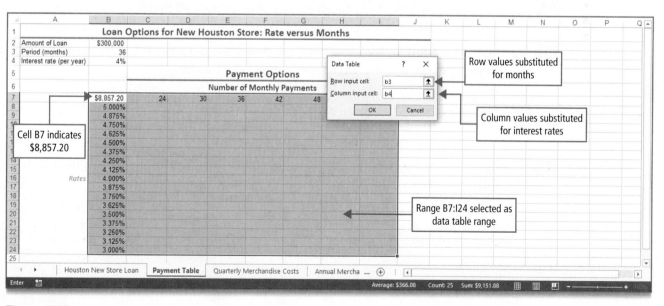

Figure 7.12

8 Click **OK**. Click cell **F8**, and then examine the formula in the **Formula Bar**. Compare your screen with Figure 7.13.

The table is filled with payment options that use the month and interest rate corresponding to the position in the table. So, if Alaina chooses a combination of 42 months at an interest rate of 5.000%, the monthly payment will be $7,800.91, which is slightly under the monthly payment she wanted. The data table is one of a group of Excel's What-If Analysis tools.

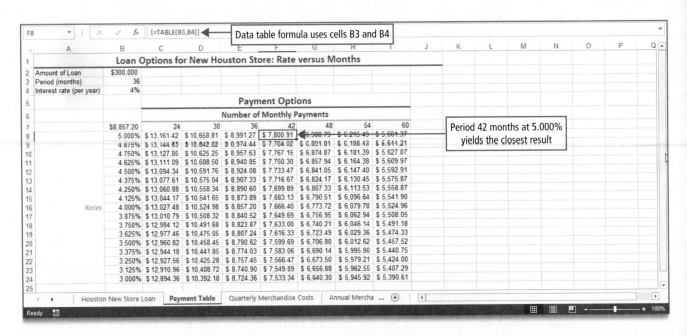

Figure 7.13

9 Select the range **F8:F19**. From the **Home tab**, display the **Cell Styles** gallery, and then under **Data and Model**, click the **Note** cell style to highlight the desired payment options.

10 Select the range **B8:B24**, hold down Ctrl, and then select the range **C7:I7**. In the Font group, click **Bold** B and then in the **Alignment group**, click **Center** ≡.

ANOTHER WAY Right-click over the selected range, and then on the mini toolbar, click Bold and Center.

11 Click cell **A1** to deselect the range, click **Save** 🖫, and then compare your worksheet with Figure 7.14.

By using a data table of payment options, you can see that Alaina can get a loan for at least 42 months (3.5 years) for any of the interest rates between 5.000% and 3.000% in order to purchase the furniture and fixtures she wants and still keep the monthly payment under $8,000.

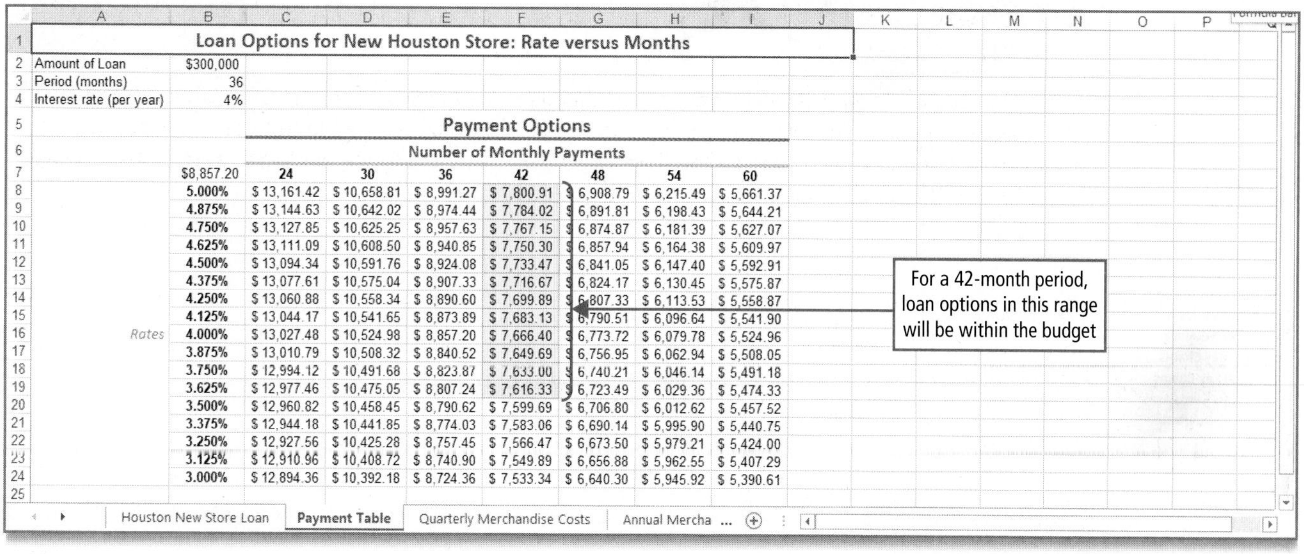

Loan Options for New Houston Store: Rate versus Months

				Payment Options				
Amount of Loan	$300,000							
Period (months)	36							
Interest rate (per year)	4%							
				Payment Options				
				Number of Monthly Payments				
	$8,857.20	24	30	36	42	48	54	60
	5.000%	$ 13,161.42	$ 10,658.81	$ 8,991.27	$ 7,800.91	$ 6,908.79	$ 6,215.49	$ 5,661.37
	4.875%	$ 13,144.63	$ 10,642.02	$ 8,974.44	$ 7,784.02	$ 6,891.81	$ 6,198.43	$ 5,644.21
	4.750%	$ 13,127.85	$ 10,625.25	$ 8,957.63	$ 7,767.15	$ 6,874.87	$ 6,181.39	$ 5,627.07
	4.625%	$ 13,111.09	$ 10,608.50	$ 8,940.85	$ 7,750.30	$ 6,857.94	$ 6,164.38	$ 5,609.97
	4.500%	$ 13,094.34	$ 10,591.76	$ 8,924.08	$ 7,733.47	$ 6,841.05	$ 6,147.40	$ 5,592.91
	4.375%	$ 13,077.61	$ 10,575.04	$ 8,907.33	$ 7,716.67	$ 6,824.17	$ 6,130.45	$ 5,575.87
	4.250%	$ 13,060.88	$ 10,558.34	$ 8,890.60	$ 7,699.89	$ 6,807.33	$ 6,113.53	$ 5,558.87
	4.125%	$ 13,044.17	$ 10,541.65	$ 8,873.89	$ 7,683.13	$ 6,790.51	$ 6,096.64	$ 5,541.90
Rates	4.000%	$ 13,027.48	$ 10,524.98	$ 8,857.20	$ 7,666.40	$ 6,773.72	$ 6,079.78	$ 5,524.96
	3.875%	$ 13,010.79	$ 10,508.32	$ 8,840.52	$ 7,649.69	$ 6,756.95	$ 6,062.94	$ 5,508.05
	3.750%	$ 12,994.12	$ 10,491.68	$ 8,823.87	$ 7,633.00	$ 6,740.21	$ 6,046.14	$ 5,491.18
	3.625%	$ 12,977.46	$ 10,475.05	$ 8,807.24	$ 7,616.33	$ 6,723.49	$ 6,029.36	$ 5,474.33
	3.500%	$ 12,960.82	$ 10,458.45	$ 8,790.62	$ 7,599.69	$ 6,706.80	$ 6,012.62	$ 5,457.52
	3.375%	$ 12,944.18	$ 10,441.85	$ 8,774.03	$ 7,583.06	$ 6,690.14	$ 5,995.90	$ 5,440.75
	3.250%	$ 12,927.56	$ 10,425.28	$ 8,757.45	$ 7,566.47	$ 6,673.50	$ 5,979.21	$ 5,424.00
	3.125%	$ 12,910.96	$ 10,408.72	$ 8,740.90	$ 7,549.89	$ 6,656.88	$ 5,962.55	$ 5,407.29
	3.000%	$ 12,894.36	$ 10,392.18	$ 8,724.36	$ 7,533.34	$ 6,640.30	$ 5,945.92	$ 5,390.61

For a 42-month period, loan options in this range will be within the budget

Houston New Store Loan | **Payment Table** | Quarterly Merchandise Costs | Annual Mercha ...

Figure 7.14

Objective 4 Use Defined Names in a Formula

GO! Learn How
Video E7-4

A ***name***, also referred to as a ***defined name***, is a word or string of characters in Excel that represents a cell, a range of cells, a formula, or a constant value. A defined name that is distinctive and easy to remember typically defines the *purpose* of the selected cells. When creating a formula, the defined name may be used instead of the cell reference.

All names have a ***scope***, which is the location within which the name is recognized without qualification. The name's scope usually refers either to a specific worksheet or to an entire workbook.

Activity 7.06 Defining a Name

MOS
2.3.1

In this Activity, you will practice three ways to define a name for a cell or group of cells. After defining a name, you can use the name in a formula to refer to the cell or cells. Names make it easier for you and others to understand the meaning of formulas in a worksheet.

1 At the bottom of your workbook, click the **Quarterly Merchandise Costs** worksheet, and then compare your screen with Figure 7.15.

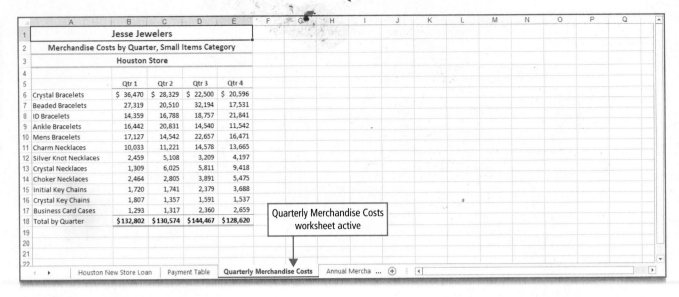

Figure 7.15

> **2** Select the range **B6:E10**. On the **Formulas tab**, in the **Defined Names group**, click **Define Name**. Compare your screen with Figure 7.16.

The New Name dialog box displays—some text may display in the Name Box as a suggested name for the range.

MAC TIP   Define Name dialog box displays.

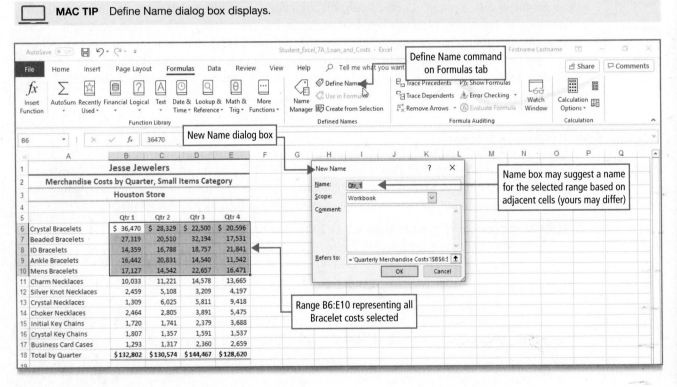

Figure 7.16

> **3** In the **Name Box**, delete any existing text, and then type **Bracelet_Costs** as the name. Compare your screen with Figure 7.17.

Naming cells has no effect on the displayed or underlying values; it simply creates an easy-to-remember name that you can use when creating formulas that refer to this range of cells. A named range cannot contain spaces.

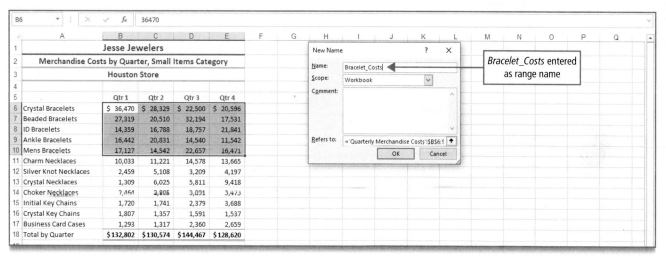

Figure 7.17

4 At the bottom of the dialog box, at the right edge of the **Refers to** box, point to and click **Collapse Dialog Box** ⬆. Compare your screen with Figure 7.18.

The dialog box collapses (shrinks) so that only the *Refers to* box is visible, and the selected range is surrounded by a moving border. When you define a name, the stored definition is an absolute cell reference and includes the worksheet name.

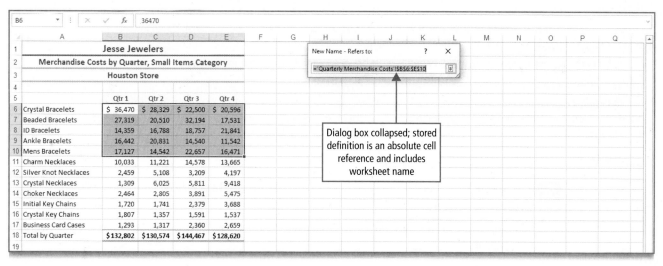

Figure 7.18

5 Click **Expand Dialog Box** ⬇ to redisplay the entire **New Name** dialog box, and then click **OK**.

6 Select the range **B11:E14**. In the upper left corner of the Excel window, to the left of the **Formula Bar**, click in the **Name Box**, and notice that the cell reference *B11* is highlighted in blue. Type **Necklace_Costs** as shown in Figure 7.19.

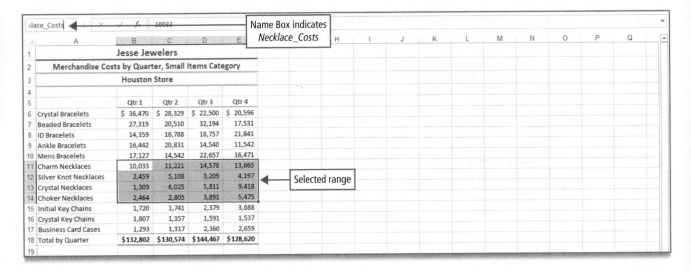

Figure 7.19

> **7** Press Enter, and then take a moment to study the rules for defining names, as described in the table in Figure 7.20.

Rules for Defining Names
The first character of the defined name must be a letter, an underscore (_), or a backslash (\).
After the first character, the remaining characters in the defined name can be letters, numbers, periods, and underscore characters.
Spaces are not valid in a defined name; use a period or the underscore character as a word separator, for example, 1st.Quarter or 1st_Qtr.
The single letter C or R in either uppercase or lowercase cannot be defined as a name, because these letters are used by Excel for selecting a row or column when you enter them in a Name or a Go To text box.
A defined name can be no longer than 255 characters; short, meaningful names are the most useful.
Defined names cannot be the same as a cell reference, for example M$10 or QTR1.
Defined names can contain uppercase and lowercase letters; however, Excel does not distinguish between them. So, for example, if you create the name Sales and then create another name SALES in the same workbook, Excel considers the names to be the same and prompts you for a unique name.

Figure 7.20

> **8** Click **cell A1** to cancel the selection. Click the **Name Box arrow**, and then compare your screen with Figure 7.21.
>
> Your two defined names display in alphabetical order. You can drag the edge of the Name Box to resize it.

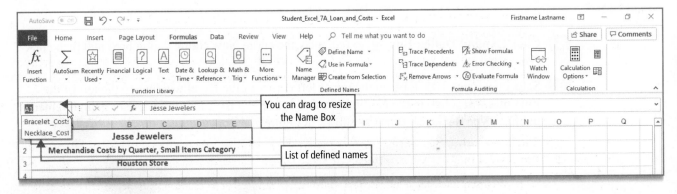

Figure 7.21

9 From the list, click **Bracelet_Costs** and notice that Excel selects the range of values that comprise the cost of various Bracelet styles.

10 Click the **Name Box arrow** again, and then click **Necklace_Costs** to select the range of values that comprise the Necklace costs.

11 Select the range **B15:E16**. On the **Formulas tab**, in the **Defined Names group**, click **Name Manager**, and then notice that the two names that you have defined display in a list.

12 In the upper left corner of the **Name Manager** dialog box, click **New**. With the text *Initial_Key_Chains* selected, type **Key_Chain_Costs** and then click **OK**. Compare your screen with Figure 7.22.

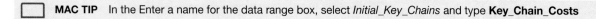

MAC TIP In the Enter a name for the data range box, select *Initial_Key_Chains* and type **Key_Chain_Costs**

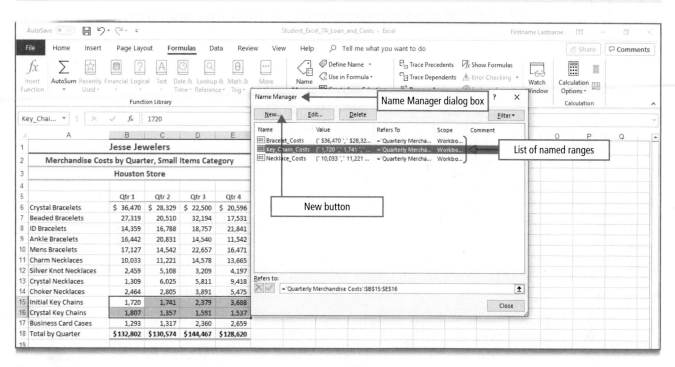

Figure 7.22

13 **Close** the **Name Manager** dialog box and **Save** your workbook.

This is another method to define a name—by creating a new name in the Name Manager dialog box. The Name Manager dialog box displays the three range names that you have created, in alphabetical order.

Activity 7.07 | Inserting New Data into a Named Range

2.3.2

You can insert new data into the range of cells that a name represents. In this Activity, you will modify the range named *Necklace_Costs* to include new data.

1 On the left side of your window, point to the **row 15** heading and right-click to select the entire row and display a shortcut menu. On the menu, click **Insert** to insert a new blank row above.

A new row 15 is inserted, and the remaining rows move down one row. Recall that when new rows are inserted in this manner, Excel adjusts formulas accordingly.

2 Click the **Name Box arrow**, and then click **Key_Chain_Costs**. Notice that Excel highlights the correct range of cells, adjusting for the newly inserted row.

If you insert rows, the defined name adjusts to the new cell addresses to represent the cells that were originally defined. Likewise, if you move the cells, the defined name goes with them to the new location.

3 ▶ In cell **A15**, type **Sweetheart Necklaces** and then press [Tab]. In cell **B15**, type **1166** and press [Tab]. In cell **C15**, type **1087** and press [Tab]. In cell **D15**, type **847** and press [Tab]. In cell **E15**, type **965** and press [Enter].

The cells in the newly inserted row adopt the format from the cells above.

4 ▶ On the **Formulas tab**, in the **Defined Names group**, click **Name Manager**.

⬜ **MAC TIP** Remember, Name Manager is found in the Define Name dialog box.

5 ▶ In the **Name Manager** dialog box, in the **Name** column, click **Necklace_Costs**. At the bottom of the dialog box, click in the **Refers to** box and edit the reference, changing **$E$14** to **$E$15** as shown in Figure 7.23.

This action will include the Sweetheart Necklaces values in the named range.

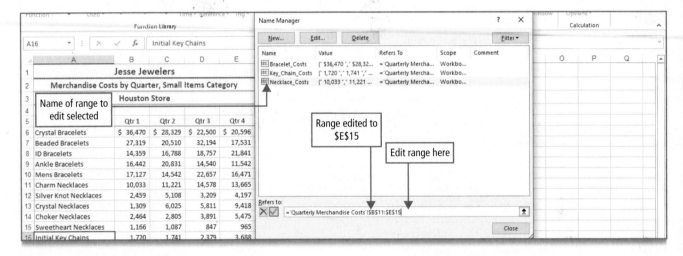

Figure 7.23

6 ▶ In the **Name Manager** dialog box, click **Close**, and then click **Yes** to save the changes you made to the name reference. In the upper left corner of the window, click the **Name Box arrow** and then click the range name **Necklace_Costs**. Notice that the selected range now includes the new row 15. **Save** 🖫 your workbook.

⬜ **MAC TIP** You may not be prompted to save.

NOTE   Changing a Defined Name

If you create a defined name and then decide to change it, you can use the Name Manager to edit the name. Display the Name Manager dialog box, select the defined name, and then at the top of the dialog box, click Edit. If the defined name is used in a formula, the new name is automatically changed in any affected formulas.

Activity 7.08 | Creating a Defined Name by Using Row and Column Titles

MOS

2.3.1

You can use the Create from Selection command to use existing row or column titles as the name for a range of cells.

1 ▶ Select the range **A18:E18**. On the **Formulas tab**, in the **Defined Names group**, click **Create from Selection**. Compare your screen with Figure 7.24.

The Create Names from Selection dialog box displays. A check mark displays in the *Left column* check box, which indicates that Excel will use the value of the cell in the leftmost column of the selection as the range name, unless you specify otherwise.

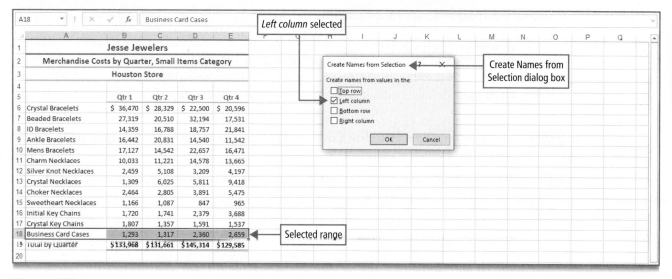

Figure 7.24

> **2** In the **Create Names from Selection** dialog box, click **OK**, and then click anywhere to cancel the selection.

> **3** Click the **Name Box arrow**, and then click the name **Business_Card_Cases**, and notice that in the new range name, Excel inserts the underscores necessary to fill a blank space in the range name. Also notice that the actual range consists of only the numeric values, as shown in Figure 7.25. **Save** 💾 your workbook.

> This method is convenient for naming a range of cells without having to actually type a name—Excel uses the text of the first cell to the left of the selected range as the range name and then formats the name properly.

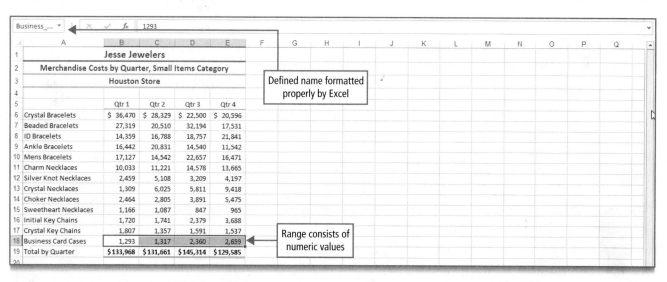

Figure 7.25

NOTE **Deleting a Defined Name**

If you create a defined name and then decide that you no longer need it, you can delete the name and its accompanying range reference. Display the Name Manager dialog box, select the defined name, and then at the top of the dialog box, click Delete. Deleting a defined name does not modify the cell contents or formatting of the cells. Deleting a defined name does not delete any cells or any values. It deletes only the name that you have applied to a group of cells. However, any formula that contains the range name will display the #NAME? error message, and will have to be adjusted manually.

Activity 7.09 | Using Defined Names in a Formula

4.1.2, 4.2.1

The advantage to naming a range of cells is that you can use the name in a formula in other parts of your workbook. The defined name provides a logical reference to data. For example, referring to data as *Bracelet_Costs* is easier to understand than referring to data as *B6:E10*.

When you use a defined name in a formula, the result is the same as if you typed the cell references.

> **1** In your **Quarterly Merchandise Costs** worksheet, click cell **A1**. Then, display the **Annual Merchandise Costs** worksheet.

> **2** In cell **B5**, type **=sum(B** and then scroll to the bottom of the AutoComplete list; compare your screen with Figure 7.26.

> The Formula AutoComplete list displays, containing all of Excel's built-in functions that begin with the letter B and any defined names in this workbook that begin with the letter B. To the left of your defined name *Bracelet_Costs*, a defined name icon displays.

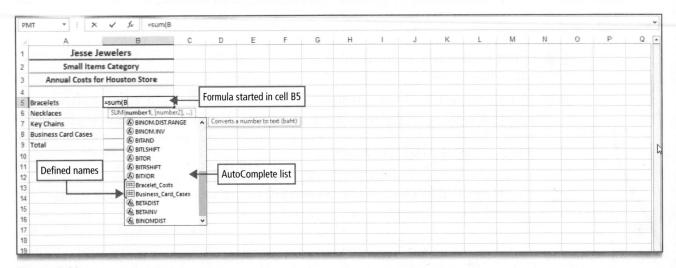

Figure 7.26

> **3** Double-click **Bracelet_Costs**, and then press Enter.

> Your result is *$411,346*—cell styles are already applied in the worksheet. Recall that SUM is a function—a formula already built by Excel—that adds all the cells in a selected range. Therefore, Excel sums all the cells in the range you defined as Bracelet_Costs on the third worksheet in the workbook, and then places the result in cell B5 of this worksheet.

> **MAC TIP** Click *Bracelet_Costs* one time, then add a parenthesis to the end of the formula.

> **ANOTHER WAY** You can simply type the defined name in the formula.

> **4** In cell **B6**, type **=sum(N** and then on the **Formula AutoComplete** list, double-click **Necklace_Costs** to insert the defined name. Press Enter to display the result *105,733*.

> **5** In cell **B7**, type **=sum(** and then on the **Formulas tab**, in the **Defined Names group**, click **Use in Formula**. On the list, click **Key_Chain_Costs**, and then press Enter to display the total *15,820*.

> **MAC TIP** *Use in Formula* may not be available; continue typing K, click *Key_Chain_Costs* and add a parenthesis to the end of the formula. Press ENTER.

6 In cell **B8**, use any of the techniques you just practiced to sum the cells containing the costs for **Business Card Cases** and to display a result of *7,629*. In cell **B9**, in the **Function Library group**, click **AutoSum** $\boxed{\Sigma \text{ AutoSum } \cdot}$ to sum **column B** and press Enter to display a result of *$540,528*. Compare your screen with Figure 7.27.

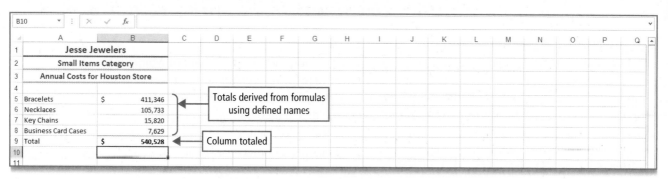

Figure 7.27

7 Click cell **A1**. At the bottom of the workbook window, right-click any sheet tab name, and then click **Select All Sheets**.

8 With the four worksheets grouped, from the **Page Layout tab**, display the **Page Setup** dialog box, and then insert a **Custom Footer** in the **Left section** that includes the file name. Click the **Margins tab**, and then center the worksheets **Horizontally** on the page.

9 Click the **Payment Table** worksheet, and then on the **Page Layout tab**, in the **Page Setup group**, change the **Orientation** to **Landscape**.

10 Click the **File tab** to display **Backstage** view. Click the **Info tab.** On the right, at the bottom of the **Properties** list, click **Show All Properties**. Under **Related People**, be sure that your name displays as the author. If necessary, right-click the author name, click **Edit Property**, type your name, and then click OK. In the **Subject** box, type your course name and section number, and in the **Tags** box, type **store loan, merchandise costs** On the left, click **Save**.

11 In the upper right corner of the Excel window, click **Close** $\boxed{\times}$.

For Non-MyLab Submissions
Determine What Your Instructor Requires for Submission
As directed by your instructor, submit your completed Excel workbook.

---

12 In **MyLab IT**, locate and click the Grader Project **Excel 7A Loan and Costs**. In **step 3**, under **Upload Completed Assignment**, click **Choose File**. In the **Open** dialog box, navigate to your **Excel Chapter 7 folder**, and then click your **Student_Excel_7A_Loan_and_Costs** file one time to select it. In the lower right corner of the **Open** dialog box, click **Open**.

   The name of your selected file displays above the Upload button.

13 To submit your file to **MyLab IT** for grading, click **Upload**, wait a moment for a green **Success!** message, and then in **step 4**, click the blue **Submit for Grading** button. Click **Close Assignment** to return to your list of **Course Materials**.

You have completed Project 7A | END

PROJECT

7B

Lookup Form and
Revenue Report

MyLab IT
Project 7B Grader for Instruction
Project 7B Simulation for Training and Review

Project Activities

In Activities 7.10 through 7.19, you will assist Mike Connor, the Vice President of Marketing at Jesse Jewelers, by adding lookup functions to a phone order form so that an order taker can complete the form quickly. You will use the Formula Auditing features to review a revenue worksheet and to resolve the errors, and you will use the Watch Window to monitor changes in sales worksheets. Your completed worksheets will look similar to Figure 7.28.

Project Files for MyLab IT Grader

1. In your **MyLab IT** course, locate and click **Excel 7B Lookup Revenue Report**, Download Materials, and then Download All Files.
2. Extract the zipped folder to your Excel Chapter 7 folder. Close the Grader download screens.
3. Take a moment to open the downloaded **Excel_7B_Lookup_Revenue_Report_Instructions**; note any recent updates to the book.

Project Results

GO! Project 7B

Where We're Going

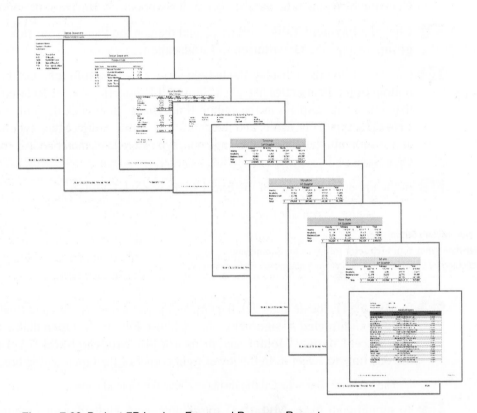

Figure 7.28 Project 7B Lookup Form and Revenue Report

For Non-MyLab Submissions

For Project 7B, you will need:

e07B_Lookup_Revenue_Report

In your Excel Chapter 7 folder, save your workbook as:

Lastname_Firstname_7B_Lookup_Revenue_Report

After you have named and saved your workbook, on the next page, begin with Step 2.

GO! Learn How

Video E7-5

Objective 5 | Use Lookup Functions

ALERT Because Office 365 is a cloud-based subscription service that receives continuous updates, you may encounter some variations in what appears on your screen and what is shown in this instruction. Microsoft Office 365 is fully installed on your PC or Mac; no Internet access is necessary to create or edit documents. When you *are* connected to the Internet, you will receive monthly upgrades and new features, so you always have the latest versions of Office apps as soon as they are available. Your subscription gives you continuous free access to the latest innovations and refinements.

Lookup functions look up a value in a defined range of cells located in another part of the workbook to find a corresponding value. For example, you can define a two-column range of cells containing names and phone numbers. Then, when you type a name in the cell referred to by the lookup formula, Excel fills in the phone number by looking it up in the defined range. In the lookup formula, the defined range is referred to as the *table array*.

The *VLOOKUP* function looks up values in a table array arranged as vertical columns. The function searches the first column of the table array for a corresponding value, and then returns a value from any cell on the same row. The *HLOOKUP* function looks up values in a table array arranged in horizontal rows. The function searches the top row of the table array for a corresponding value, and then returns a value from any cell in the same column.

There is one requirement for the lookup functions to work properly. The data in the table array, which can be numbers or text, must be sorted in ascending order. For the VLOOKUP function, the values must be sorted on the first column in ascending order. For the HLOOKUP function, the values must be sorted on the first row in ascending order.

Activity 7.10 | Defining a Range of Cells for a Lookup Function

The first step in using a lookup function is to define the range of cells that will serve as the table array. In the Jesse Jewelers Phone Order form, after an Item Number is entered on the form, Mr. Connors wants the description of the item to display automatically in the Description column. This will improve accuracy, because the order taker will not have to look up the information each time. To accomplish this, you will define a table array that includes the item number in one column and a description of the item in the second column.

1 Navigate to your **Excel Chapter 7 folder**, and then double-click the Excel file you downloaded from **MyLab IT** that displays your name—**Student_Excel_7B_Lookup_Revenue_Report**. If necessary, at the top click **Enable Editing**.

2 At the bottom of the screen, in the sheet tab row, be sure that the **Phone Order** worksheet is active. Compare your screen with Figure 7.29.

When store managers call Jesse Jewelers headquarters to place an order, the order taker uses this type of worksheet to record the information.

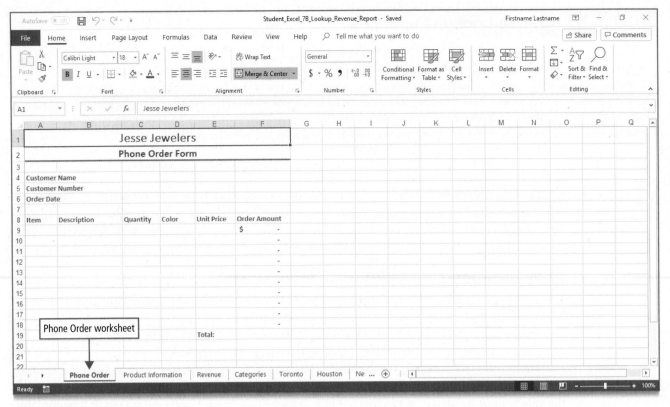

Figure 7.29

> **3** Click the **Product Information sheet tab** to display the second worksheet.

The Product Information worksheet contains the Style Code, Description, and Unit Price of specific bracelets and necklaces.

> **4** On the **Product Information** worksheet, select the range **A4:C11**. On the **Data tab**, in the **Sort & Filter group**, click **Sort**. If necessary, drag the **Sort** dialog box to the right side of your screen so you can view **columns A:C**.

To use this list to look up information with the Excel VLOOKUP function, you must sort the list in ascending order by Style Code, which is the column that will be used to look up the matching information.

> **5** In the **Sort** dialog box, under **Column**, click the **Sort by arrow**. Notice that the selected range is now **A5:C11** and that the column titles in the range **A4:C4** display in the **Sort by** list. Compare your screen with Figure 7.30.

When the selected range includes a header row that should remain in place while the remaining rows are sorted, Excel usually recognizes those column headings, selects the *My data has headers* check box, and then displays the column headings in the Sort by list.

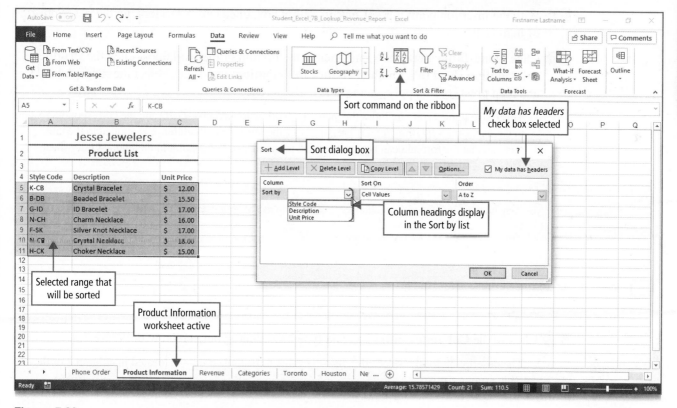

Figure 7.30

6 ▸ On the **Sort by** list, click **Style Code**, which is the first column heading and the column heading that Excel selects by default.

7 ▸ Under **Sort On**, verify that *Cell Values* displays, and under **Order**, verify that *A to Z* displays.

Cell Values indicates that the sort will be based on the values in the cells of the first column, rather than cell color or some other cell characteristic. *A to Z* indicates that the cells will be sorted in ascending order.

8 ▸ Click **OK** to sort the data by *Style Code* in ascending order.

Excel sorts the data alphabetically by Style Code; *B-DB* is first in the list and *N-CH* is last.

9 ▸ **Save** 🖫 your workbook.

Activity 7.11 | Inserting the VLOOKUP Function

MOS

4.1.1, Expert 3.2.1

Recall that the VLOOKUP function looks up values in a range of cells arranged as vertical columns. The arguments for this function include *lookup_value*—the value to search in the first column of the table array, *table_array*—the range that contains the data, and *col_index_num*—the column number (1, 2, 3, 4, and so on) in the table array that contains the result you want to retrieve from the table, which in this instance is the Description.

1 ▸ Display the **Phone Order** worksheet. In cell **A9**, type **G-ID** and press Tab.

2 ▸ With cell **B9** as the active cell, on the **Formulas tab**, in the **Function Library group**, click **Lookup & Reference**, and then click **VLOOKUP**.

The Function Arguments dialog box for VLOOKUP displays.

⎕ **MAC TIP** Formula Builder pane opens on right.

3 With the insertion point in the **Lookup_value** box, click cell **A9** to look up the description of Item G-ID.

4 Click in the **Table_array** box, and then at the bottom of the workbook, click the **Product Information sheet tab**. On the **Product Information** worksheet, select the range **A4:C11**, and then press F4 to apply an absolute cell reference.

This range (table array) includes the value that will be looked up—*G-ID* and the corresponding value to be displayed—*ID Bracelet*. By pressing F4, the absolute cell reference is applied to the table array so that the formula can be copied to the remainder of the column in the Phone Order sheet.

NOTE

On a laptop computer, you may have to enable the F function keys across the top of your keyboard by pressing the FN key on your keyboard.

MAC TIP   Edit the reference to $A$4:$C$11

5 Click in the **Col_index_num** box and type **2** Compare your screen with Figure 7.31.

The description for the selected item—the value to be looked up—is located in column 2 of the table array.

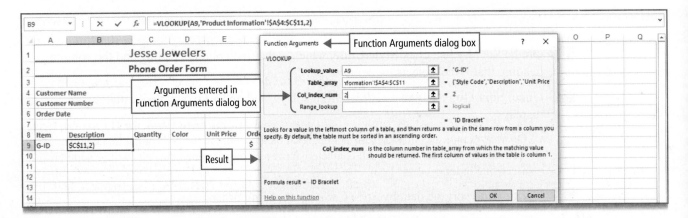

Figure 7.31

6 Click **OK**.

In the Phone Order form, the description for Item G-ID displays in cell B9.

MAC TIP   Click Done and close the Formula Builder pane.

---

7 If necessary, click cell **B9** so that it is the active cell. In the **Formula Bar**, notice that this cell contains the VLOOKUP formula. Point to the fill handle in the lower right corner of the cell, and then drag to fill the VLOOKUP formula down through cell **B18**. Compare your screen with Figure 7.32.

> The *#N/A* error notation displays in the cells where you copied the formula. Excel displays this error when a function or formula exists in a cell but has no value available with which to perform a calculation; values have not yet been entered in column A in those rows.

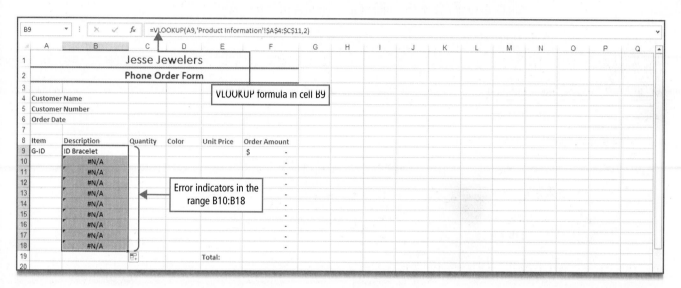

Figure 7.32

8 Click cell **C9**, type **12** as the quantity ordered and press Tab. In cell **D9**, type **Silver** and press Tab.

9 With cell **E9** as the active cell, on the **Formulas tab**, in the **Function Library group**, click **Lookup & Reference**, and then click **VLOOKUP**.

10 With the insertion point in the **Lookup_value** box, click cell **A9** to look up information for Item G-ID. Click in the **Table_array** box, display the **Product Information** sheet, and then select the range **A4:C11**. Press F4 to make the values in the range absolute.

11 In the **Col_index_num** box, type **3** to look up the price in the third column of the range, and then click **OK**.

> The Phone Order worksheet redisplays, and the Unit Price for the ID Bracelet—*$17.00*—displays in cell E9.

MAC TIP Click Done and close the Formula Builder pane.

12 Click cell **F9**, and notice in the **Formula Bar** that a formula to calculate the total for the item, Quantity times Unit Price, has already been entered in the worksheet.

This formula has also been copied to the range F10:F18.

13 Click cell **E9**, and then copy the VLOOKUP formula down through cell **E18**. Compare your screen with Figure 7.33.

The *#N/A* error notation displays in the cells where you copied the formula, and also in cells F10:F18, because the formulas there have no values yet with which to perform a calculation—values have not yet been entered in column A in those rows.

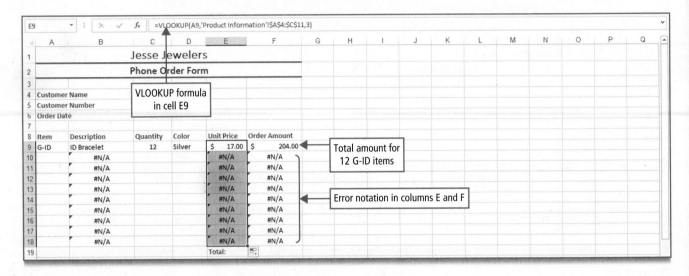

Figure 7.33

14 Click cell **A10**, type **N-CB** and press Tab two times.

Excel looks up the product description and the product price in the vertical table array on the Product Information sheet, and then displays the results in cells B10 and E10.

15 In cell **C10**, type **24** as the Quantity and press Tab. Notice that Excel calculates the total for this item in cell **F10**—*432.00*.

16 In cell **D10**, type **White** and then press Enter. Notice that after data is entered in the row, the error notations no longer display. **Save** 💾 your workbook. Compare your screen with Figure 7.34.

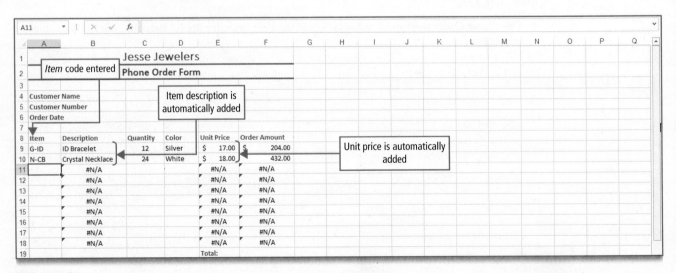

Figure 7.34

Objective 6 | Validate Data

GO! Learn How
Video E7-6

Another technique to improve accuracy when completing a worksheet is ***data validation***—a technique in which you control the type of data or the values that are entered into a cell. This technique improves accuracy because it limits and controls the type of data an individual, such as an order taker, can enter into the form.

One way to control the type of data entered is to create a ***validation list***—a list of values that are acceptable for a group of cells. Only values on the list are valid; any value *not* on the list is considered *invalid*. For example, in the Phone Order sheet, it would be useful if in the Item column, only valid Style Codes could be entered.

Activity 7.12 | Creating a Validation List

MOS
Expert 2.2.2

A list of valid values must either be on the same worksheet as the destination cell, or if the list is in another worksheet, the cell range must be named. In this Activity, you will create a defined name for the Style Codes, and then create a validation list for column A of the Phone Order worksheet.

1 Display the **Product Information** worksheet. Select the range **A4:A11**. On the **Formulas tab**, in the **Defined Names group**, click **Create from Selection**.

Recall that by using the Create from Selection command, you can automatically generate a name from the selected cells that uses the text in the top row or the leftmost column of a selection.

2 In the **Create Names from Selection** dialog box, be sure the **Top row** check box is selected, and then click **OK** to use *Style Code* as the range name.

3 In the **Defined Names group**, click **Name Manager**, and then notice that the new defined name is listed with the name *Style_Code*.

Style_Code displays as the defined name for the selected cells. Recall that Excel replaces spaces with an underscore when it creates a range name.

💻 **MAC TIP** Click Yes in the message box; click Define Name to see the Names in the Workbook box.

---

4 **Close** the **Name Manager** dialog box. Display the **Phone Order** sheet, and then select the range **A9:A18**.

Before you set the validation requirement, you must first select the cells that you want to restrict to only valid entries from the list.

5 On the **Data tab**, in the **Data Tools group**, click **Data Validation** 🔲. In the **Data Validation** dialog box, be sure the **Settings tab** is selected.

6 Under **Validation criteria**, click the **Allow arrow**, and then click **List**.

A Source box displays as the third box in the Data Validation dialog box. Here you select or type the source data.

7 Click to position the insertion point in the **Source** box, type **=Style_Code** and then compare your screen with Figure 7.35.

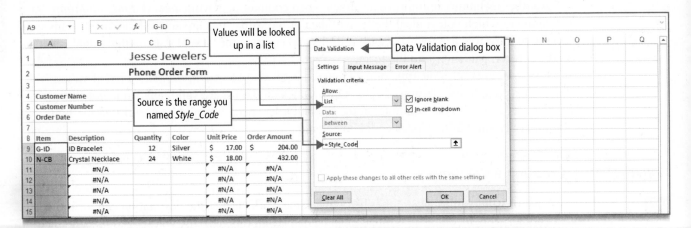

Figure 7.35

8 Click **OK**. Click cell **A11**, and notice that a list arrow displays at the right edge of the cell.

9 In cell **A11**, click the **list arrow** to display the list, and then compare your screen with Figure 7.36.

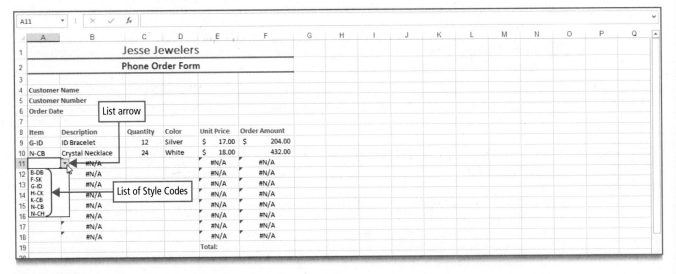

Figure 7.36

10 From the list, click **B-DB**.

The Style Code is selected from the list and the Item, Description, and Unit Price cells are filled in for row 11.

11 Press Tab two times, type **24** as the **Quantity**, press Tab, type **Multi** as the **Color**, and then press Enter to return to the beginning of the next row. Compare your screen with Figure 7.37.

You can see that when taking orders by phone, it will speed the process if all of the necessary information can be filled in automatically. Furthermore, accuracy will be improved if item codes are restricted to only valid data.

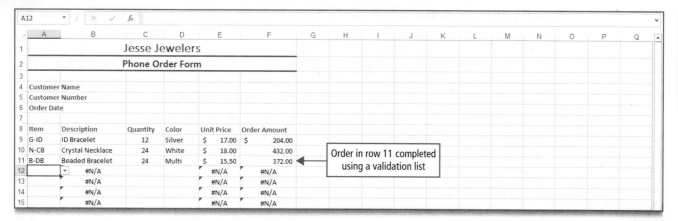

Figure 7.37

12 With cell **A12** active, click the **list arrow**, and then click **F-SK**. As the **Quantity**, type **18** and as the **Color**, type **Antique** and then press [Enter].

13 In cell **A13**, type **G-W** and press [Tab].

An error message displays indicating that you entered a value that is not valid; that is, it is not on the validation list you created. If the order taker mistakenly types an invalid value into the cell, this message will display.

Restricting the values that an order taker can enter will greatly improve the accuracy of orders. Also, encouraging order takers to select from the list, rather than typing, will reduce the time it takes to fill in the order form.

14 In the error message, click **Cancel**. Click the **list arrow** again, click **H-CK,** and press [Tab] two times. As the **Quantity**, type **18** and for the **Color**, type **Ivory** and then press [Enter].

15 Select the unused rows **14:18**, right-click over the selection, and then click **Delete**.

16 Click cell **F14**, on the **Home tab**, in the **Editing group**, click **AutoSum** and press [Enter]. Apply the **Total** cell style to cell **F14**.

17 Click cell **A1**, and then **Save** 🖫 your workbook.

MORE KNOWLEDGE | **Creating Validation Messages**

In the Data Validation dialog box, you can use the Input Message tab to create a ScreenTip that will display when the cell is selected. The message can be an instruction that tells the user what to do. You can also use the Error Alert tab to create a warning message that displays if invalid data is entered in the cell.

Objective 7 | **Audit Worksheet Formulas**

GO! Learn How
Video E7-7

Auditing is the process of examining a worksheet for errors in *formulas*. Formulas are equations that perform calculations on values in your worksheet. A formula consists of a sequence of values cell references, cynces, names, functions, or operators in a cell, which together produce a new value. Recall that a formula always begins with an equal sign.

Excel includes a group of *Formula Auditing* features, which consists of tools and commands accessible from the Formulas tab that help you to check your worksheet for errors. In complex worksheets, use these Formula Auditing features to show relationships between cells and formulas to ensure that formulas are logical and correct and also to resolve error messages. Although sometimes it is appropriate to hide the error message, at other times error notations can indicate a problem that should be corrected.

Activity 7.13 | Tracing Precedents

MOS
Expert 3.5.1

Precedent cells are cells that are referred to by a formula in another cell. The ***Trace Precedents command*** displays arrows that indicate what cells affect the values of the cell that is selected. By using the Trace Precedents command, you can see the relationships between formulas and cells. As an auditing tool, the process of tracing a formula is a way to ensure that you constructed the formula correctly.

1 Display the **Revenue** worksheet, and then compare your screen with Figure 7.38.

The worksheet details the revenue and expenses related to the Miami store over a six-month period. Several error notations are present (#VALUE!, #REF!, #DIV/0!), green triangles display in the top left corners of several cells indicating a potential error, and two columns are too narrow to fit the data, which Excel indicates by displaying pound signs—####.

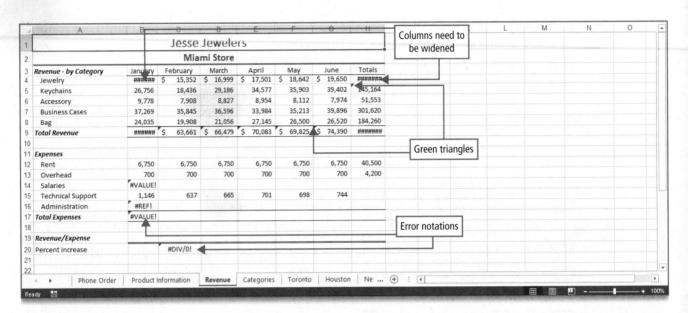

Figure 7.38

2 Display **Backstage** view, and then on the left, click **Options**. In the **Excel Options** dialog box, on the left, click **Formulas**. Under **Error checking rules**, point to the small information icon after the first Error checking rule to display the ScreenTip. Compare your screen with Figure 7.39.

Here you can control which error checking rules you want to activate, and you can get information about each of the rules by clicking the small blue information icon at the end of each rule. By default, all but the next to last rule are selected, and it is recommended that you maintain these default settings. This textbook assumes these default settings.

MAC TIP   Display the menu bar, click Excel, click Preferences. In the Formulas and Lists group, click Error Checking.

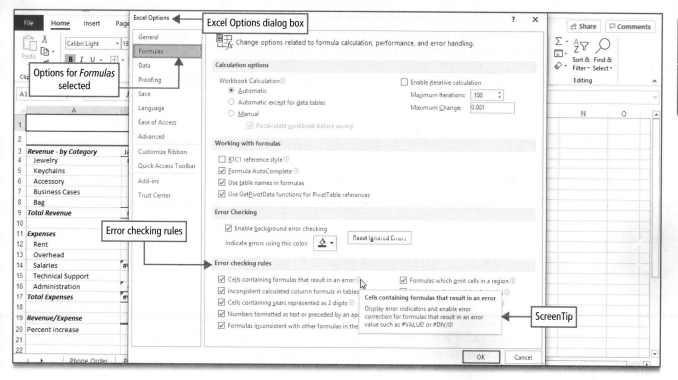

Figure 7.39

> **3** In the lower right corner of the dialog box, click **Cancel** to close the dialog box.

> **4** Take a moment to study the table in Figure 7.40, which details some common error values that might display on your worksheet.

An **error value** is the result of a formula that Excel cannot evaluate correctly.

Microsoft Excel Error Values		
Error Value	**Meaning**	**Possible Cause**
#####	Cannot see data.	The column is not wide enough to display the entire value.
#DIV/0!	Cannot divide by zero.	The divisor in a formula refers to a blank cell or a cell that contains zero.
#NAME?	Does not recognize a name you used in a formula.	A function or a named range may be misspelled or does not exist.
#VALUE!	Cannot use a text field in a formula.	A formula refers to a cell that contains a text value rather than a numeric value or a formula.
#REF!	Cannot locate the reference.	A cell that is referenced in a formula may have been deleted or moved.
#N/A	No value is available.	No information is available for the calculation you want to perform.
#NUM!	Invalid argument in a worksheet function.	An unacceptable argument may have been used in a function. Or, a formula result could be too large or too small.
#NULL!	No common cells.	A space was entered between two ranges in a formula to indicate an intersection, but the ranges have no common cells.

Figure 7.40

5 On your worksheet, in the **column heading area**, select **column B**, hold down `Ctrl`, and then select **column H**. Point to the right edge of either of the selected column headings to display the ⊞ pointer, and then double-click to apply AutoFit.

AutoFit widens the columns to accommodate the longest values in each column; the ##### errors no longer display.

MAC TIP   Use COMMAND instead of CTRL.

---

6 Click cell **C9**, and then notice the **green triangle** in the upper left corner of the cell.

A green triangle in the upper left corner of a cell indicates that the formula in the cell is suspect for some reason. Typically, this is because the formula does not match the formula in the cells next to it, or because it does not include all of the adjacent cells.

7 In cell **C9**, to the left of the cell, point to **Error Checking** ⚠, and then read the **ScreenTip** that displays. Compare your screen with Figure 7.41.

The ScreenTip indicates that adjacent cells containing numbers are not included in the formula. It is possible that the formula purposely consists of a group of cells that excludes some of the cells adjacent to it. However, because that is not as common as including *all* of the cells that are adjacent to one another, Excel flags this as a potential error.

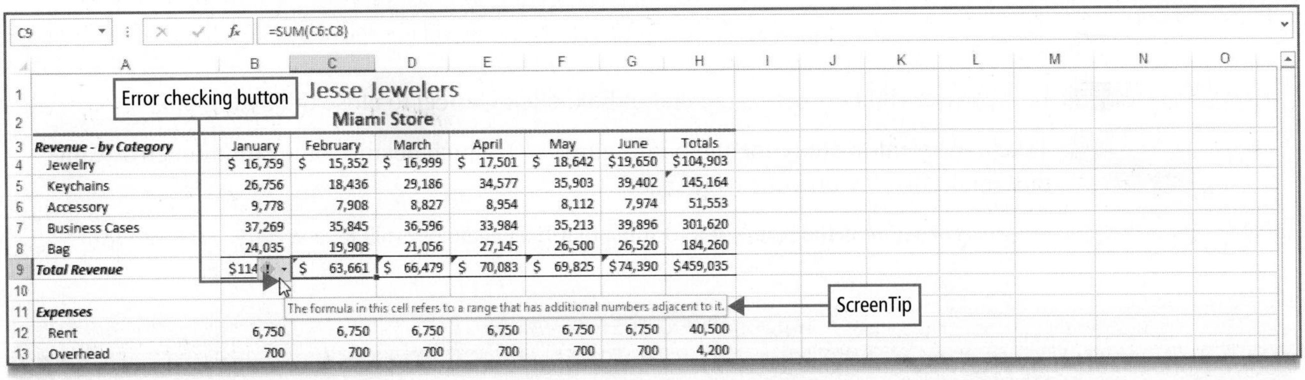

| C9 | ▾ | : | × | ✓ | *fx* | =SUM(C6:C8) |

	A	B	C	D	E	F	G	H
1			Jesse Jewelers					
2			Miami Store					
3	*Revenue - by Category*	January	February	March	April	May	June	Totals
4	Jewelry	$ 16,759	$ 15,352	$ 16,999	$ 17,501	$ 18,642	$19,650	$104,903
5	Keychains	26,756	18,436	29,186	34,577	35,903	39,402	145,164
6	Accessory	9,778	7,908	8,827	8,954	8,112	7,974	51,553
7	Business Cases	37,269	35,845	36,596	33,984	35,213	39,896	301,620
8	Bag	24,035	19,908	21,056	27,145	26,500	26,520	184,260
9	Total Revenue	$114	$ 63,661	$ 66,479	$ 70,083	$ 69,825	$74,390	$459,035
10								
11	Expenses							
12	Rent	6,750	6,750	6,750	6,750	6,750	6,750	40,500
13	Overhead	700	700	700	700	700	700	4,200

Error checking button

The formula in this cell refers to a range that has additional numbers adjacent to it.   ScreenTip

Figure 7.41

---

8 On the **Formulas tab**, in the **Formula Auditing group**, click **Trace Precedents**. Notice that the range **C6:C8** is bordered in blue and a blue arrow points to cell **C9**.

Recall that precedent cells are cells that are referred to by a formula in another cell. Here, the precedent cells are bordered in blue. A blue arrow, called a *tracer arrow*, displays from C6:C8, pointing to the selected cell C9. A tracer arrow shows the relationship between the active cell and its related cells. Tracer arrows are blue when pointing from a cell that provides data to another cell.

Because this total should include *all* of the revenue categories for February, this is an error in the formula—the formula should include the range C4:C8. By tracing the precedents, you can see that two cells were mistakenly left out of the formula.

9 To the left of cell **C9**, click **Error Checking** ![icon] to display a list of error checking options. Compare your screen with Figure 7.42.

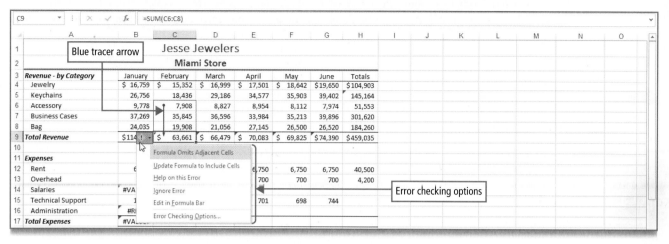

Figure 7.42

10 On the list, notice that Excel indicates the potential error highlighted—*Formula Omits Adjacent Cells*. Notice also that you can update the formula, seek help with the error, ignore the error, edit the formula in the Formula Bar, or display the Error Checking Options in the Excel Options dialog box. Click **Update Formula to Include Cells**, and then look at the formula in the **Formula Bar**.

> As shown in the Formula Bar, the formula is updated to include the range C4:C8; the green triangle no longer displays in the cell.

MAC TIP The blue tracer arrow no longer displays.

11 Click cell **D9**, which also displays a green triangle, and then point to **Error Checking** ![icon] to display the **ScreenTip**.

> The same error exists in cell D9—not all adjacent cells in the column were included in the formula. This error also exists in the range E9:G9. You can click in each cell and use the Error Checking button's options list to correct each formula, or you can use the fill handle to copy the corrected formula in cell C9 to the remaining cells.

12 Click cell **C9,** drag the fill handle to the right to copy the corrected formula to the range **D9:G9**, and then notice that all the green triangles are removed from the range. If necessary, apply AutoFit to column **G**.

13 Click cell **H5**, point to **Error Checking** ![icon], and read the **ScreenTip**.

> The formula in this cell is not the same as the formula in the other cells in this area of the worksheet.

14 On the **Formulas tab**, in the **Formula Auditing group**, click **Trace Precedents**. Compare your screen with Figure 7.43.

A blue border surrounds the range B8:G8, and a blue tracer arrow displays from the cell B8 to cell H5. This indicates that the formula in cell H5 is summing the values in row 8 rather than the values in row 5.

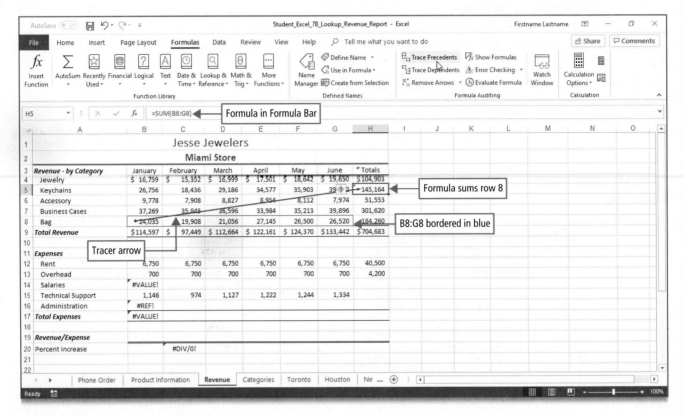

Figure 7.43

15 To the left of cell **H5**, click **Error Checking** 🛈 to display the list of error checking options, notice the explanation *Inconsistent Formula*, examine the formula in the Formula Bar, and then click **Copy Formula from Above**. If necessary, AutoFit **column H** to display the values correctly.

16 Look at the **Formula Bar** to verify that the formula is summing the numbers in **row 5**—the range **B5:G5**. With cell **H5** still selected, from the **Home tab**, display the **Cell Styles gallery**, and then, under **Number Format**, click the **Comma [0]** number format.

The blue tracer arrow no longer displays, the formula sums row 5, and the proper number format is applied.

17 Click cell **H4**. On the **Formulas tab**, in the **Formula Auditing group**, click **Trace Precedents**. Notice the tracer arrow indicates that the appropriate cells are included in the formula, as shown in Figure 7.44.

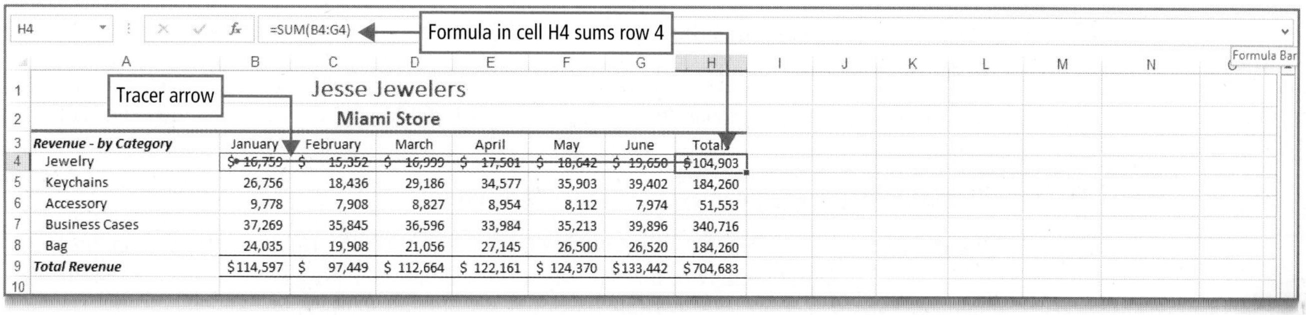

Figure 7.44

18 Click cell **H5**, click **Trace Precedents**, notice the **tracer arrow**, and then click cell **H6**. Click **Trace Precedents**, notice the tracer arrow, and verify that the correct cells are included in the formula.

19 Click cell **H7**, click **Trace Precedents**, and then click cell **H8**. Click **Trace Precedents**. Compare your screen with Figure 7.45.

Cells H7 and H8 display blue tracer arrows that are inconsistent with the other formulas in this column. However, green triangle indicators do not display in either of these cells. When auditing a worksheet, you cannot rely on the error notations and triangle indicators alone. To ensure the accuracy of a worksheet, you should use the tracer arrows to verify that all of the formulas are logical and correct.

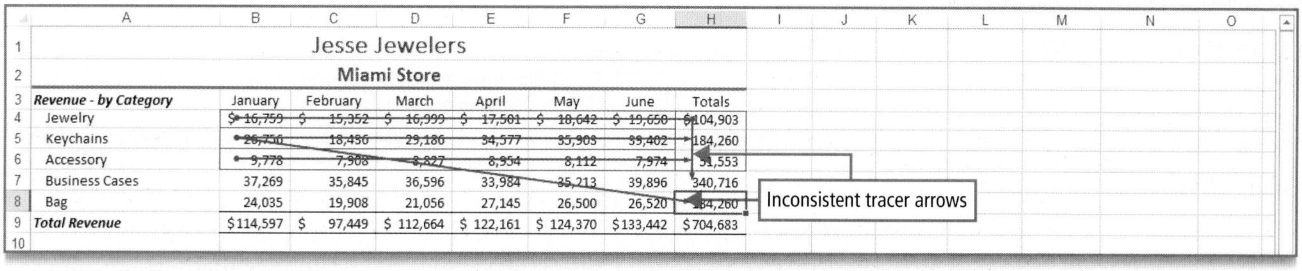

Figure 7.45

20 In the **Formula Auditing group**, click **Remove Arrows**. Click cell **H6** and then use the fill handle to copy the correct formula down to cells **H7:H8**.

21 Save 🖫 your workbook.

Activity 7.14 | Tracing Dependents

Expert 3.5.1

Dependent cells are cells that contain formulas that refer to other cells—they *depend* on the values of other cells to display a result. The ***Trace Dependents command*** displays arrows that indicate what cells are affected by the value of the currently selected cell.

1 ▶ Click cell **B14**, which displays the error *#VALUE!*. To the left of the cell, point to **Error Checking** 🔳 and read the ScreenTip.

This formula contains a reference to a cell that is the wrong data type—a cell that does not contain a number.

2 ▶ In the **Formula Auditing group**, click **Trace Precedents**.

A blue tracer arrow indicates that cell B3 is included in the formula. Because cell B3 contains text—*January*—and not a number, no mathematical calculation is possible. The salaries should be calculated as 5 percent of *Total Revenue*, plus the constant amount of 36,000.

3 ▶ In the **Formula Auditing group**, click **Trace Dependents**. Compare your screen with Figure 7.46.

A red tracer arrow displays, showing that the formula in cell B17 depends on the result of the formula in cell B14. Tracer arrows are red if a cell contains an error value, such as #VALUE!.

	A	B	C	D	E	F	G	H
1				Jesse Jewelers				
2				Miami Store				
3	*Revenue - by Category*	January	February	March	April	May	June	Totals
4	Jewelry	$ 16,759	$ 15,352	$ 16,999	$ 17,501	$ 18,642	$ 19,650	$104,903
5	Keychains	26,756	18,436	29,186	34,577	35,903	39,402	184,260
6	Accessory	9,778	7,908	8,827	8,954	8,112	7,974	51,553
7	Business Cases	37,269	35,845	36,596	33,984	35,213	39,896	218,803
8	Bag	24,035	19,908	21,056	27,145	26,500	26,520	145,164
9	*Total Revenue*	$114,597	$ 97,449	$ 112,664	$ 122,161	$ 124,370	$133,442	$704,683
10								
11	*Expenses*							
12	Rent	6,750	6,750	6,750	6,750	6,750	6,750	40,500
13	Overhead	700	700	700	700	700	700	4,200
14	Salaries	#VALUE!						
15	Technical Support	1,146	974	1,127	1,222	1,244	1,334	
16	Administration	#REF!						
17	*Total Expenses*	#VALUE!						
18								
19	*Revenue/Expense*							
20	Percent increase		#DIV/0!					

Blue tracer arrow (pointing from a cell that provides data to another cell)

Figure 7.46

4 ▶ To the left of cell **B14**, click **Error Checking** 🔳 and then click **Show Calculation Steps**.

The Evaluate Formula dialog box displays and indicates the formula as =*"January"**0.05+36000. January is not a number, nor is it a range name that refers to a group of numbers; so, it cannot be used in a mathematical formula. At the bottom of the dialog box, Excel indicates that the next evaluation will result in an error.

MAC TIP   The Evaluate Formula dialog box may not be available.

5 ▶ At the bottom of the dialog box, click **Evaluate**.

The formula in the Evaluation box indicates *#Value!+36000*. You can use this box to evaluate each step of the formula. With complex formulas, this can be helpful in examining each piece of a formula to see where the error has occurred.

> **6** Close the **Evaluate Formula** dialog box. With cell **B14** still the active cell, click in the **Formula Bar**, edit the formula to change cell **B3** to **B9**, and then press Enter. If necessary, AutoFit **column B**.

The error is removed and the result—41,730—displays in cell B14.

> **7** Click cell **B14**. Drag the fill handle to copy the corrected formula in cell **B14** across the row to cells **C14:G14**.

> **8** Click cell **B9**. In the **Formula Auditing group**, click **Trace Dependents**. Compare your screen with Figure 7.47.

Each cell where an arrowhead displays indicates a dependent relationship.

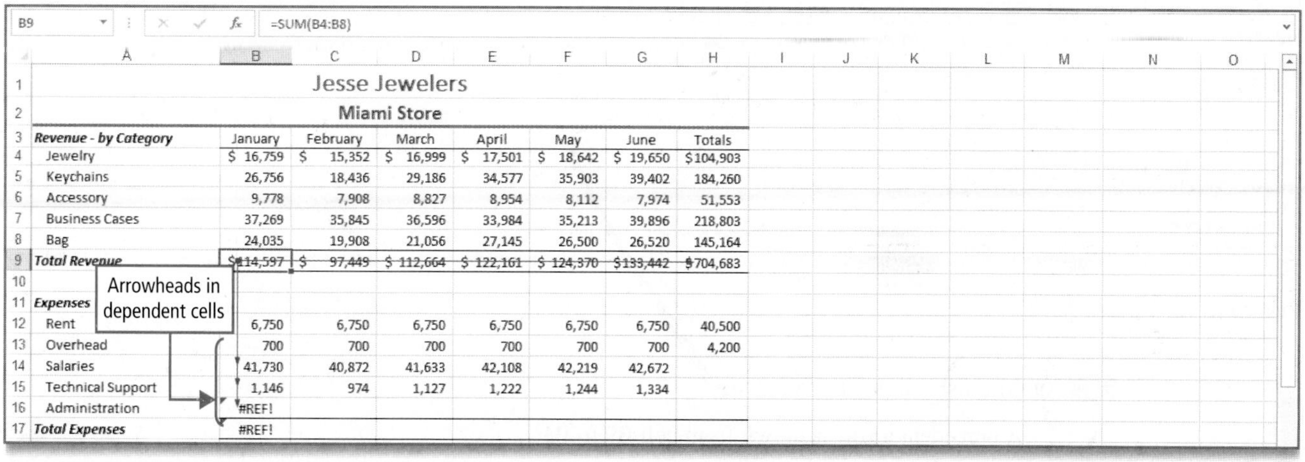

B9	▼ : ✕ ✓ fx	=SUM(B4:B8)													
	A	B	C	D	E	F	G	H	I	J	K	L	M	N	O
1				Jesse Jewelers											
2				Miami Store											
3	*Revenue - by Category*	January	February	March	April	May	June	Totals							
4	Jewelry	$ 16,759	$ 15,352	$ 16,999	$ 17,501	$ 18,642	$ 19,650	$104,903							
5	Keychains	26,756	18,436	29,186	34,577	35,903	39,402	184,260							
6	Accessory	9,778	7,908	8,827	8,954	8,112	7,974	51,553							
7	Business Cases	37,269	35,845	36,596	33,984	35,213	39,896	218,803							
8	Bag	24,035	19,908	21,056	27,145	26,500	26,520	145,164							
9	*Total Revenue*	$114,597	$ 97,449	$ 112,664	$ 122,161	$ 124,370	$133,442	$704,683							
10															
11	*Expenses*														
12	Rent	6,750	6,750	6,750	6,750	6,750	6,750	40,500							
13	Overhead	700	700	700	700	700	700	4,200							
14	Salaries	41,730	40,872	41,633	42,108	42,219	42,672								
15	Technical Support	1,146	974	1,127	1,222	1,244	1,334								
16	Administration	#REF!													
17	*Total Expenses*	#REF!													

Arrowheads in dependent cells

Figure 7.47

> **9** In the **Formula Auditing group**, click **Remove Arrows**. **Save** 🖫 your workbook.

Activity 7.15 │ Tracing Formula Errors

Another tool you can use to help locate and resolve an error is the ***Trace Error command***. Use this command to trace a selected error value such as #VALUE!, #REF!, #NAME?, or #DIV/0!.

> **1** Click cell **B16**, which indicates the error *#REF!*, point to **Error Checking** 🛈 and read the ScreenTip.

The error message indicates that a cell that was referenced in the formula has been moved or deleted, or the function is causing an invalid reference error. In other words, Excel does not know where to look to get the value that should be used in the formula.

> **2** On the ribbon, on the **Formulas tab**, in the **Formula Auditing group**, click the **Error Checking arrow** to display a list, and then compare your screen with Figure 7.48.

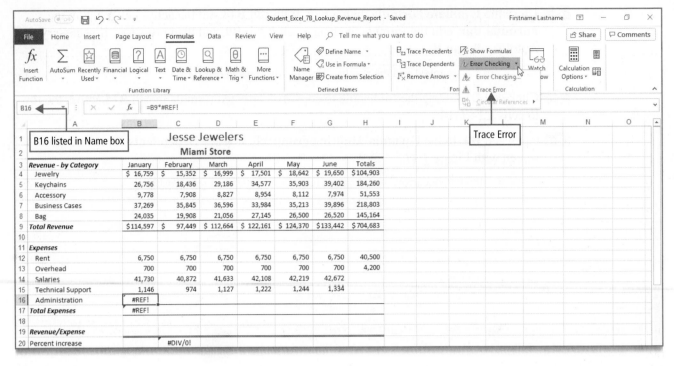

Figure 7.48

3 On the list, click **Trace Error**.

A precedent arrow is drawn from cell B9 to B16.

4 In the **Formula Auditing group**, click the **Error Checking arrow** again, and then click **Trace Error** again.

An arrow is drawn between cells B4 and B9 and the range B4:B8 is bordered in blue. The blue border indicates that this range is used in the formula in cell B9, which sums the values.

5 Click in cell **A24**. Type **Admin Percent** press Tab, type **2** and then press Enter.

The percent used to calculate administrative expenses was moved or deleted from the worksheet causing the #REF! error. You must re-enter the value so that it can be referenced in the formula in cell B16.

6 Click **B16**. Next to the cell, click **Error Checking** 🗈 to display the list of error checking options, and then click **Edit in Formula Bar**.

The insertion point displays in the Formula Bar so that you can edit the formula.

7 Delete *#REF!*. Type **b24** Press F4 to make the cell reference absolute, and then press Enter.

The error notation in cell B16 is replaced with *2,292*. The corrected formula needs to be copied across row 16, and the corrected formula also needs to use an absolute reference so that the 2% Admin Percent will be applied for each month.

🖥 **MAC TIP**   Press COMMAND + T to make the cell reference absolute.

---

8 Click cell **B16** and then drag the fill handle to copy the formula to the right to cells **C16:G16**.

Save 🖫 your workbook, click cell **A1**, and then compare your screen with Figure 7.49.

	A	B	C	D	E	F	G	H
3	**Revenue - by Category**	January	February	March	April	May	June	Totals
4	Jewelry	$ 16,759	$ 15,352	$ 16,999	$ 17,501	$ 18,642	$ 19,650	$104,903
5	Keychains	26,756	18,436	29,186	34,577	35,903	39,402	184,260
6	Accessory	9,778	7,908	8,827	8,954	8,112	7,974	51,553
7	Business Cases	37,269	35,845	36,596	33,984	35,213	39,896	218,803
8	Bag	24,035	19,908	21,056	27,145	26,500	26,520	145,164
9	**Total Revenue**	$114,597	$ 97,449	$ 112,664	$ 122,161	$ 124,370	$133,442	$704,683
10								
11	**Expenses**							
12	Rent	6,750	6,750	6,750	6,750	6,750	6,750	40,500
13	Overhead	700	700	700	700	700	700	4,200
14	Salaries	41,730	40,872	41,633	42,108	42,219	42,672	
15	Technical Support	1,146	974	1,127	1,222	1,244	1,334	
16	Administration	2,292	1,949	2,253	2,443	2,487	2,669	
17	**Total Expenses**	$ 52,618						
18								
19	**Revenue/Expense**							
20	Percent increase		#DIV/0!					
21								
22								
23	Technical Support Percent	1%						
24	Admin Percent	2%						
25								

Formula copied from B16 to C16:G16

Admin Percent added

Phone Order | Product Information | **Revenue** | Categories | Toronto | Houston | Ne ...

Ready

Figure 7.49

Activity 7.16 | Using Error Checking

Expert 3.5.4

The ***Error Checking command*** checks for common errors that occur in formulas. The behavior is similar to checking for spelling; that is, the command uses a set of rules to check for errors in formulas. The command opens the Error Checking dialog box, which provides an explanation about the error and enables you to move from one error to the next. Therefore, you can review all of the errors on a worksheet.

1 Be sure that cell **A1** is the active cell. In the **Formula Auditing group**, click the **Error Checking arrow**, and then click **Error Checking**.

The Error Checking dialog box displays, and indicates the first error—in cell C20. Here the error notation *#DIV/0!* displays. The Error Checking dialog box provides an explanation of this error—a formula or function is trying to divide by zero or divide by an empty cell.

2 In the **Error Checking** dialog box, click **Show Calculation Steps**.

The Evaluate Formula dialog box displays, and in the Evaluation box, **0/0** displays.

MAC TIP   Show Calculation Steps and Evaluate Formula may not be available. In the Error Checking dialog box, click Trace Error to see where errors are located.

3 In the **Evaluate Formula** dialog box, click **Evaluate**.

The Evaluation box displays the error *#DIV/0!* and the Evaluate button changes to Restart.

4 Click **Restart**.

The formula *(C19-B19)/C19* displays; the first reference to C19 is underlined. The underline indicates that this is the part of the formula that is being evaluated. Each time you click the Evaluate button, it moves to the next cell reference or value in the formula.

5 In the **Evaluate Formula** dialog box, click **Step In**. Compare your screen with Figure 7.50.

A second box displays, which normally displays the value in the referenced cell. In this instance, the cell that is referenced is empty, as indicated in the message in the lower part of the dialog box. In a complex formula, this dialog box can help you examine and understand each part of the formula and identify exactly where the error is located.

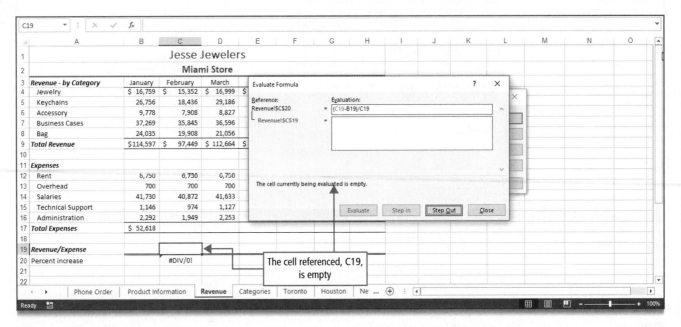

Figure 7.50

6 Click **Step Out**.

The cell evaluation box closes and the underline moves to the next cell in the formula—B19—which you can visually verify is empty by looking at the worksheet. To remove this error, you must complete the remainder of the worksheet.

7 **Close** the **Evaluate Formula** dialog box. In the **Error Checking** dialog box, click **Next**.

A message box displays stating that the error checking is complete for the entire sheet.

8 Click **OK**.

Both the message box and the Error Checking dialog box close.

9 Click cell **H13** and then use the fill handle to copy this formula down to cells **H14:H16**. Click cell **B17** and use the fill handle to copy this formula to the right into cells **C17:H17**. **AutoFit** any columns, if necessary, to display all of the data.

The formulas in the rows and columns are completed.

10 Click cell **B19** and type **=b9-b17** In the **Formula Bar**, click **Enter** ✓ to keep cell **B19** active, and then copy the formula to the right into cells **C19:H19**.

The revenue/expense for each month is calculated. Notice that the *#DIV/0!* error in cell C20 is removed, but the formatting of the cell needs to be changed from dollars to percent.

11 Click cell **C20**, and then on the **Home tab**, in the **Number group**, click **Percent Style** %. Copy the formula to the right into cells **D20:G20**.

This formula calculates the percent change in revenue versus expenses, month to month.

12 Click cell **A1**. Save 🖫 your workbook. Compare your screen with Figure 7.51.

	A	B	C	D	E	F	G	H
1			Jesse Jewelers					
2			Miami Store					
3	*Revenue - by Category*	January	February	March	April	May	June	Totals
4	Jewelry	$ 16,759	$ 15,352	$ 16,999	$ 17,501	$ 18,642	$ 19,650	$104,903
5	Keychains	26,756	18,436	29,186	34,577	35,903	39,402	184,260
6	Accessory	9,778	7,908	8,827	8,954	8,112	7,974	51,553
7	Business Cases	37,269	35,845	36,596	33,984	35,213	39,896	218,803
8	Bag	24,035	19,908	21,056	27,145	26,500	26,520	145,164
9	Total Revenue	$114,597	$ 97,449	$ 112,664	$ 122,161	$ 124,370	$133,442	$704,683
10								
11	*Expenses*							
12	Rent	6,750	6,750	6,750	6,750	6,750	6,750	40,500
13	Overhead	700	700	700	700	700	700	4,200
14	Salaries	41,730	40,872	41,633	42,108	42,219	42,672	251,234
15	Technical Support	1,146	974	1,127	1,222	1,244	1,334	7,047
16	Administration	2,292	1,949	2,253	2,443	2,487	2,669	14,094
17	Total Expenses	$ 52,618	$ 51,246	$ 52,463	$ 53,223	$ 53,400	$ 54,125	$317,075
18								
19	Revenue/Expense	$ 61,979	$ 46,203	$ 60,201	$ 68,938	$ 70,970	$ 79,317	$387,608
20	Percent increase		-34%	23%	13%	3%	11%	

Formula entered in cell B19 and copied across row

Formulas copied across row 17 and down column H

Percent style applied and formula copied

Figure 7.51

Activity 7.17 | Circling Invalid Data

Expert 2.2.2

If you use validation lists in a worksheet, you can apply data validation and instruct Excel to circle invalid data. In this manner you can verify that valid values—values from the list—have been entered on the worksheet.

1 Click the **Categories sheet tab**.

This worksheet lists the merchandise types included in each category; only merchandise types from these categories are valid.

2 In the upper left corner, click the **Name Box arrow**, and then click **Items**. Compare your screen with Figure 7.52.

The named range in row 2 is highlighted.

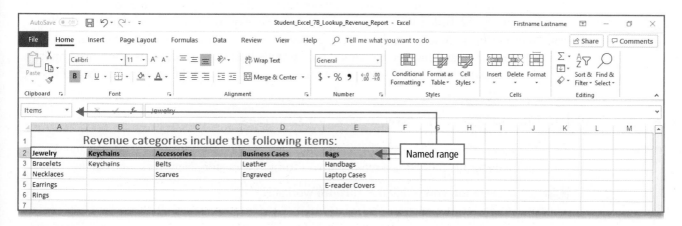

Figure 7.52

3 Display the **Revenue** worksheet. On the **Data tab**, in the **Data Tools group**, click the **Data Validation arrow** ⊞▾ and then click **Circle Invalid Data**. Compare your screen with Figure 7.53.

Red circles display around Accessory and Bag.

	A	B	C	D	E	F	G	H	I	J	K	L	M	N	O
1	Cells with invalid data circled			Jesse Jewelers											
2				Miami Store											
3	*Revenue - by Category*	January	February	March	April	May	June	Totals							
4	Jewelry	$ 16,759	$ 15,352	$ 16,999	$ 17,501	$ 18,642	$ 19,650	$104,903							
5	Keychains	26,756	18,436	29,186	34,577	35,903	39,402	184,260							
6	Accessory	9,778	7,908	8,827	8,954	8,112	7,974	51,553							
7	Business Cases	37,269	35,845	36,596	33,984	35,213	39,896	218,803							
8	Bag	24,035	19,908	21,056	27,145	26,500	26,520	145,164							
9	*Total Revenue*	$114,597	$ 97,449	$ 112,664	$ 122,161	$ 124,370	$ 133,442	$704,683							
10															

Figure 7.53

4 Click cell **A6** and click the **list arrow** that displays at the right side of the cell.

The validation list displays.

5 On the list, click **Accessories**.

The item is corrected but the red circle is not removed.

6 Click cell **A8**, click the **list arrow**, and then on the list, click **Bags**.

7 In the **Data Tools group**, click the **Data Validation arrow** ⊞▾, and then click **Clear Validation Circles** to remove the circles.

8 In the **Data Tools group**, click the **Data Validation arrow** ⊞▾, and then click **Circle Invalid Data**.

No circles are applied, which confirms that the data is now valid against the validation list.

9 Click cell **A1**. Display the **Categories** worksheet, click cell **A1**, and then **Save** 💾 your workbook.

Objective 8 | Use the Watch Window to Monitor Cell Values

GO! Learn How
Video E7-8

You can monitor cells in one part of a workbook while working on another part of the workbook using the *Watch Window*—a window that displays the results of specified cells. You can monitor cells on other worksheets and see the results as soon as formulas are calculated or changes are made that affect the outcome of the watched cells. This feature is also useful on large worksheets for which the total rows and columns are not visible on the screen with the details.

Activity 7.18 | Using the Watch Window to Monitor Changes

MOS
Expert 3.5.2

Mike Connor's assistant is preparing the 1st Quarter sales worksheets using the Watch Window for sales totals for the four largest retail stores—Toronto, Houston, New York, and Miami.

1 In the **sheet tab row**, click the **Toronto** worksheet.

🖥 **MAC TIP**   The Watch Window may not be available on a Mac; move to Step 7.

2 Click cell **E8**. On the **Formulas tab**, in the **Formula Auditing group**, click **Watch Window**.

The Watch Window displays on your screen. As you create totals for the columns and rows on each worksheet in this Activity, you will be able to use the Watch Window to view the results for all the worksheets at once.

3 In the upper left corner of the **Watch Window**, click **Add Watch**. Point to the title bar of the **Add Watch** dialog box, and then drag it below your data. Compare your screen with Figure 7.54.

The Add Watch dialog box displays the address for the selected cell—Toronto!$E$8

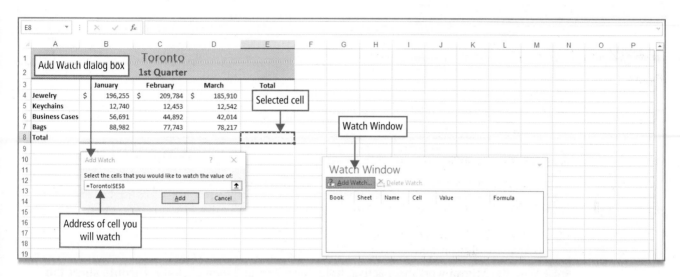

Figure 7.54

4 In the **Add Watch** dialog box, click **Add**.

Because there is no value or formula in the cell at this time, the Name, Value, and Formula columns are empty in the Watch Window.

5 Display the **Houston** worksheet and then click cell **E8**. In the **Watch Window**, click **Add Watch**, and then in the **Add Watch** dialog box, click **Add**. Compare your screen with Figure 7.55.

A second cell is added to the Watch Window.

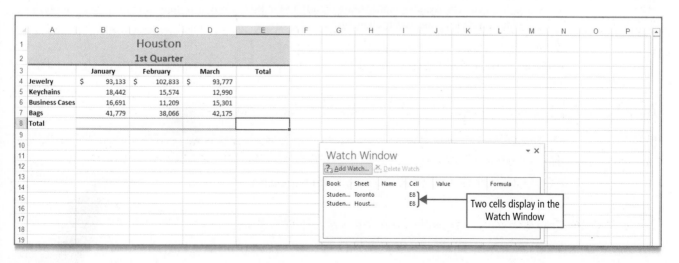

Figure 7.55

6 Using the technique you just practiced, add cell **E8** from the **New York** sheet and cell **E8** from the **Miami** sheet to the **Watch Window**. Adjust the size of the Watch Window columns as necessary to view all four sheets. Compare your screen with Figure 7.56, and verify cell **E8** is listed for each of the four worksheets.

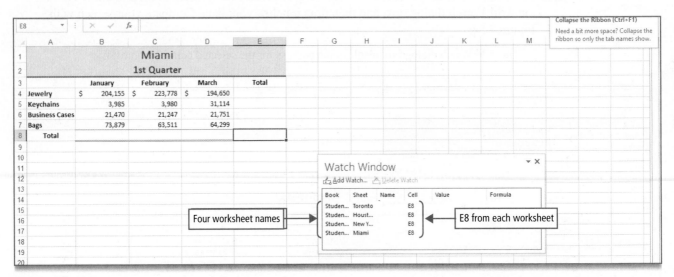

Figure 7.56

7 With the **Miami** worksheet active, hold down Shift, and then click the **Toronto sheet tab**.

The four store worksheets are selected and *Group* displays in the title bar.

8 In the **Miami** worksheet, select the range **B4:E8**.

This includes the data and the empty row and column immediately adjacent to the data. Because the sheets are grouped, this action is taking place on all four worksheets.

9 On the **Formulas tab**, in the **Function Library group**, click **AutoSum** ∑ AutoSum ▾. Select the range **B8:E8**, and then from the **Home tab**, display the **Cell Styles gallery**. At the bottom, click **Currency [0]**. Compare your screen with Figure 7.57.

The totals for the rows and columns in this worksheet, as well as in the other three worksheets, are calculated. The results display immediately in the Watch Window, indicating that calculations took place on all four sheets simultaneously.

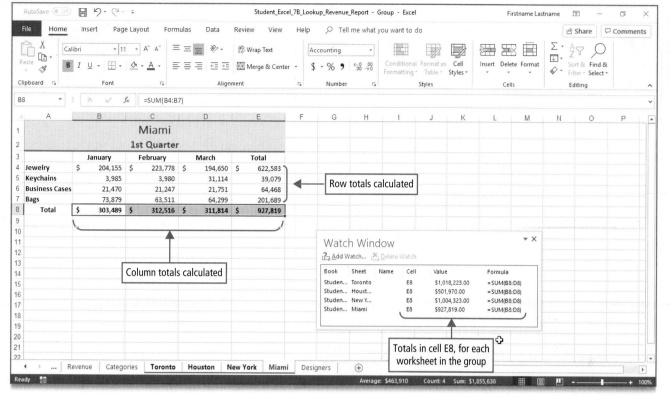

Figure 7.57

10 Close ☒ the **Watch Window**, click cell **A1**, and then **Save** 🖫 your workbook.

GO! Learn How
Video E7-9

Objective 9 | Use the MATCH and INDEX Functions

Use the *MATCH function* instead of one of the LOOKUP functions when you need the *position* of an item in a range of cells instead of the item itself. By providing search parameters, the MATCH function indicates *where* in the list you can find what you are looking for. The MATCH function searches for a specified item in a range of cells, and if the value is found, the result is the relative position of the match in the row or column.

Use the *INDEX function* in Excel to find a value within a table or range based on a relative row and column.

The MATCH function is commonly combined with the INDEX function. Combining the two functions enables you to find the row number and/or column number, and then use INDEX to display the value you are looking for.

There are times when these functions are a better choice than VLOOKUP; for example, when you need to insert or delete a column in your lookup table or if your worksheet has many hundreds of rows.

MOS
Expert 3.2.1

In this Activity, you will use the MATCH and INDEX functions to answer the questions *At what position in the Specialty column is Jade rings?* and *What is the name of the designer of Jade rings?*

1 In the **sheet tab row**, click the **Designers** worksheet. In cell **B1**, notice the **Specialty** *Jade Rings* is indicated.

2 Click cell **B2**. Type **=M** and then compare your screen with Figure 7.58.

The list of Excel functions that begin with M displays and the ScreenTip for the MATCH function also displays.

MAC TIP ScreenTip may not display.

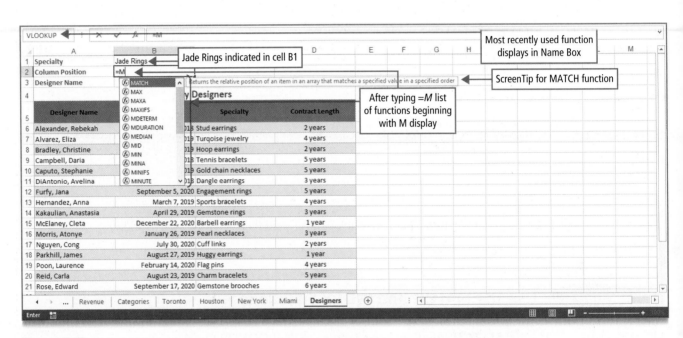

Figure 7.58

3 Being sure to include the comma, continue typing **ATCH(b1,c6:c27,** and then compare your screen with Figure 7.59.

As you type the formula, Excel borders the range you typed—the range c6:c27 which includes the value *Jade rings*—and displays options that are useful if you are looking for a specific number. Here, you want to find an exact match to the value in cell B1, which is *Jade Rings*.

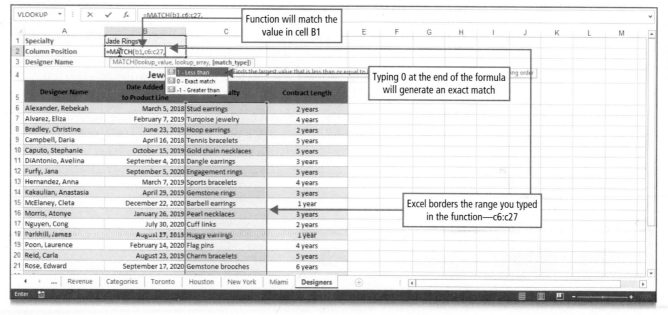

Figure 7.59

4 Continue typing **0)** to search for an exact match, and then compare your screen with Figure 7.60. Be sure your typing matches what is in the figure and make any corrections.

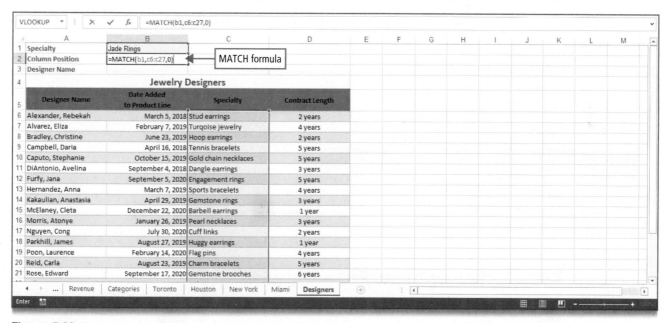

Figure 7.60

5 Press [Enter]; your result is *17*.

The number *17* indicates that within the range c6:c27, the item *Jade Rings* is the 17th item in the range.

6 Click cell **B3**. Type the following formula and notice at the end you will type) two times: **=INDEX(a6:a27,MATCH(b1,c6:c27,0))** and then compare your screen with Figure 7.61.

Here, to find the name of the designer, Excel must first index the column where the designer names are—the range a6:a27 in column A—and then complete the match portion of the formula.

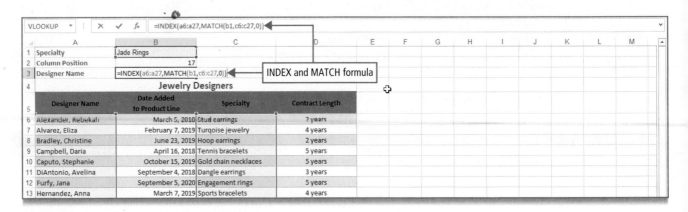

Figure 7.61

7 Press [Enter], and then compare your screen with Figure 7.62.

Your result is *Soltan, Reza* the name of the designer for Jade Rings.

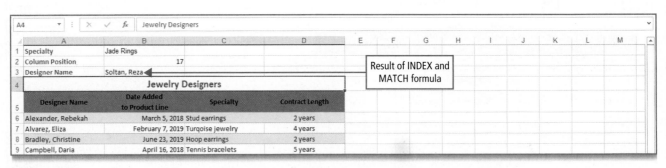

Figure 7.62

8 Click cell **A1**, and then **Save** 🖫 your workbook.

9 In the **sheet tab row**, right-click any sheet tab, and then click **Select All Sheets**.

10 On the **Page Layout tab**, in the **Page Setup group**, click the **Dialog Box Launcher** 🖳 to display the **Page Setup** dialog box.

🖥 **MAC TIP** In the Page Setup group, click Page Setup.

11 In the **Page Setup** dialog box, click the **Margins tab**, and then under **Center on page**, click **Horizontally**. Click the **Header/Footer tab**, click **Custom Footer**, and then in the **Left section**, insert the **File Name** ⬛. Because this workbook has nine worksheets, click in the **Right section**, and then click **Insert Sheet Name** ⊞. Notice that *&[Tab]* displays. Click **OK** two times.

> Because this workbook has nine worksheets in the workbook, it will be useful to display each worksheet's name in the right section of the footer.

12 Right-click any sheet tab, and then click **Ungroup Sheets**. Click the **Revenue sheet tab**, hold down Ctrl, and then click the **Categories sheet tab** and the **Designers sheet tab**.

MAC TIP   Use COMMAND instead of CTRL.

---

13 With these three worksheets selected, on the **Page Layout tab**, in the **Page Setup group**, click **Orientation**, and then click **Landscape**.

14 Click the **Phone Order** worksheet, which will ungroup the sheets. Display **Backstage** view, click the **Info tab,** click **Show All Properties**. On the list of **Properties**, in the **Tags** box, type **revenue by category and phone order form** In the **Subject** box, type your course name and section number. Under **Related People**, be sure that your name displays as the author. If necessary, right-click the author name, click **Edit Property**, type your name, click outside of the **Edit person** dialog box, and then click **OK**.

15 On the left, click **Print**. Under **Settings**, click the **Print Active Sheets arrow**, and then click **Print Entire Workbook**. At the bottom of the window, click **Next Page** ▶ to scroll through the worksheets.

16 On the left, click **Save**. In the upper right corner of the Excel window, click **Close** ✕.

For Non-MyLab Submissions
Determine What Your Instructor Requires for Submission
As directed by your instructor, submit your completed Lastname_Firstname_7B_Lookup_Revenue_Report Excel workbook.

---

17 In **MyLab IT**, locate and click the Grader Project **Excel 7B Lookup Revenue Report**. In **step 3**, under **Upload Completed Assignment**, click **Choose File**. In the **Open** dialog box, navigate to your **Excel Chapter 7 folder**, and then click your **Excel_Student_7B_Lookup_Revenue_Report** file one time to select it. In the lower right corner of the **Open** dialog box, click **Open**.

> The name of your selected file displays above the Upload button.

18 To submit your file to **MyLab IT** for grading, click **Upload**, wait a moment for a green **Success!** message, and then in **step 4**, click the blue **Submit for Grading** button. Click **Close Assignment** to return to your list of **Course Materials**.

You have completed Project 7B   **END**

»» GO! To Work

wavebreakmedia/Shutterstock, Monkey Business Images/Fotolia, Ivanko80/Shutterstock, Monkey Business Images/Shutterstock

Microsoft Office Specialist (MOS) Skills in This Chapter

Project 7A	Project 7B
2.1.1 Paste data by using special paste options	**4.1.1** Insert relative, absolute, and mixed references
2.1.2 Fill cells by using Auto Fill	**Expert 2.2.2** Configure data validation
2.3.1 Define a named range	**Expert 3.2.1** Look up data by using VLOOKUP function
4.1.2 Reference named ranges in formulas	**Expert 3.5.1** Trace precedence and dependence
4.2.1 Perform calculations by using the SUM() function	**Expert 3.5.2** Monitor cells and formulas by using the Watch Window
Expert 3.4.4 Calculate financial data by using the PMT function	**Expert 3.5.3** Validate formulas by using error checking rules
	Expert 3.5.4 Evaluate formulas

Build Your E-Portfolio

An E-Portfolio is a collection of evidence, stored electronically, that showcases what you have accomplished while completing your education. Collecting and then sharing your work products with potential employers reflects your academic and career goals. Your completed workbooks from the following projects are good examples to show what you have learned: 7G, 7K, and 7L.

GO! For Job Success

Discussion: Mobile Devices

Your instructor may assign these questions to your class, and then ask you to think about them, or discuss them with your classmates:

Mobile devices that can do more at low cost are popular for employers and employees. Employers who provide a smartphone or tablet to employees benefit by having employees available to handle customer or production issues quickly from any location. Employees like not being tied to a desk and a phone. A downside, however, is that many employees feel they have to be available 24 hours a day and are constantly tempted to check their work emails even when they are on personal time.

g-stockstudio/Shutterstock

Do you think employers should expect employees to be available during non-work hours if they are issued an employer-paid mobile device?

What are two reasons an employee might prefer having mobile access to work rather than being at a desk in the office?

What are two strategies an employee can implement to avoid looking at work emails during non-work hours?

End of Chapter

Summary

The PMT function calculates the payment for a loan. The PMT function has three required arguments: Rate (interest), Nper (number of payments), and Pv (present value), and two optional arguments.

Two of Excel's What-If Analysis tools are Goal Seek—to find a specific value for a cell by adjusting the value of another cell—and Data Tables, which display the results of different inputs into a formula.

A defined name can represent a cell, range of cells, formula, or constant value and can be used in a formula. A Lookup function looks up data located in another part of a workbook to find a corresponding value.

Data validation can control the type of data or the values that are entered into a cell. Formula auditing improves the accuracy of data entry and checks a worksheet for various types of errors.

GO! Learn It Online

Review the concepts, key terms, and MOS skills in this chapter by completing these online challenges, which you can find at **MyLab IT**.

Chapter Quiz: Answer matching and multiple-choice questions to test what you learned in this chapter.

Lessons on the GO!: Learn how to use all the new apps and features as they are introduced by Microsoft.

MOS Prep Quiz: Answer questions to review the MOS skills that you practiced in this chapter.

Project Guide for Excel Chapter 7

Your instructor will assign Projects from this list to ensure your learning and assess your knowledge.

		Project Guide for Excel Chapter 7		
Project	**Apply Skills from These Chapter Objectives**	**Project Type**		**Project Location**
7A MyLab IT	Objectives 1–4 from Project 7A	**7A Instructional Project (Grader Project)** Guided instruction to learn the skills in Project 7A.	Instruction	In **MyLab IT** and in text
7B MyLab IT	Objectives 5–9 from Project 7B	**7B Instructional Project (Grader Project)** Guided instruction to learn the skills in Project 7B.	Instruction	In **MyLab IT** and in text
7C	Objectives 1–4 from Project 7A	**7C Skills Review (Scorecard Grading)** A guided review of the skills from Project 7A.	Review	In text
7D	Objectives 5–9 from Project 7B	**7D Skills Review (Scorecard Grading)** A guided review of the skills from Project 7B.	Review	In text
7E MyLab IT	Objectives 1–4 from Project 7A	**7E Mastery (Grader Project)** A demonstration of your mastery of the skills in Project 7A with extensive decision-making.	Mastery and Transfer of Learning	In **MyLab IT** and in text
7F MyLab IT	Objectives 5–9 from Project 7B	**7F Mastery (Grader Project)** A demonstration of your mastery of the skills in Project 7B with extensive decision-making.	Mastery and Transfer of Learning	In **MyLab IT** and in text
7G MyLab IT	Combination of Objectives from Projects 7A and 7B	**7G Mastery (Grader Project)** A demonstration of your mastery of the skills in Projects 7A and 7B with extensive decision-making.	Mastery and Transfer of Learning	In **MyLab IT** and in text
7H	Combination of Objectives from Projects 7A and 7B	**7H GO! Fix It (Scorecard Grading)** A demonstration of your mastery of the skills in Projects 7A and 7B by creating a correct result from a document that contains errors you must find.	Critical Thinking	IRC
7I	Combination of Objectives from Projects 7A and 7B	**7I GO! Make It (Scorecard Grading)** A demonstration of your mastery of the skills in Projects 7A and 7B by creating a result from a supplied picture.	Critical Thinking	IRC
7J	Combination of Objectives from Projects 7A and 7B	**7J GO! Solve It (Rubric Grading)** A demonstration of your mastery of the skills in Projects 7A and 7B, your decision-making skills, and your critical thinking skills. A task-specific rubric helps you self-assess your result.	Critical Thinking	IRC
7K	Combination of Objectives from Projects 7A and 7B	**7K GO! Solve It (Rubric Grading)** A demonstration of your mastery of the skills in Projects 7A and 7B, your decision-making skills, and your critical thinking skills. A task-specific rubric helps you self-assess your result.	Critical Thinking	In text
7L	Combination of Objectives from Projects 7A and 7B	**7L GO! Think (Rubric Grading)** A demonstration of your understanding of the Chapter concepts applied in a manner that you would outside of college. An analytic rubric helps you and your instructor grade the quality of your work by comparing it to the work an expert in the discipline would create.	Critical Thinking	In text
7M	Combination of Objectives from Projects 7A and 7B	**7M GO! Think (Rubric Grading)** A demonstration of your understanding of the Chapter concepts applied in a manner that you would outside of college. An analytic rubric helps you and your instructor grade the quality of your work by comparing it to the work an expert in the discipline would create.	Critical Thinking	IRC
7N	Combination of Objectives from Projects 7A and 7B	**7N You and GO! (Rubric Grading)** A demonstration of your understanding of the Chapter concepts applied in a manner that you would in a personal situation. An analytic rubric helps you and your instructor grade the quality of your work.	Critical Thinking	IRC

Glossary

Glossary of Chapter Key Terms

Arguments The values that an Excel function uses to perform calculations or operations.

Auditing The process of examining a worksheet for errors in formulas.

Data table A range of cells that shows how changing certain values in your formulas affects the results of those formulas and that makes it easy to calculate multiple versions in one operation.

Data validation A technique by which you can control the type of data or the values that are entered into a cell by limiting the acceptable values to a defined list.

Defined name A word or string of characters in Excel that represents a cell, a range of cells, a formula, or a constant value; also referred to as simply a *name*.

Dependent cells Cells that contain formulas that refer to other cells.

Error Checking command A command that checks for common errors that occur in formulas.

Error value The result of a formula that Excel cannot evaluate correctly.

Financial functions Prebuilt formulas that perform common business calculations such as calculating a loan payment on a vehicle or calculating how much to save each month to buy something; financial functions commonly involve a period of time such as months or years.

Formula An equation that performs mathematical calculations on values in a worksheet.

Formula Auditing Tools and commands accessible from the Formulas tab that help you check your worksheet for errors.

Future value (Fv) The value at the end of the time period in an Excel function; the cash balance you want to attain after the last payment is made—usually zero for loans.

Goal Seek One of Excel's What-If Analysis tools that provides a method to find a specific value for a cell by adjusting the value of one other cell—find the right input when you know the result you want.

HLOOKUP An Excel function that looks up values that are displayed horizontally in a row.

INDEX function An Excel function that finds a value within a table or range based on a relative row and column; commonly combined with the MATCH function to find the row number and/or column number, and then use INDEX to display the value you are looking for.

Interest The amount charged for the use of borrowed money.

Lookup functions A group of Excel functions that look up a value in a defined range of cells located in another part of the workbook to find a corresponding value.

MATCH function An Excel function that finds the *position* of an item in a range of cells instead of the item itself; by providing search parameters, the MATCH function indicates *where* in the list you can find what you are looking for.

Name A word or string of characters in Excel that represents a cell, a range of cells, a formula, or a constant value; also referred to as a *defined name*.

Nper The abbreviation for *number of time periods* in various Excel functions.

One-variable Data table A data table that changes the value in only one cell.

PMT function An Excel function that calculates the payment for a loan based on constant payments and a constant interest rate.

Precedent cells Cells that are referred to by a formula in another cell.

Present value (Pv) The total amount that a series of future payments is worth now; also known as the *principal*.

Principal The total amount that a series of future payments is worth now; also known as the *Present value (Pv)*.

Rate In the Excel PMT function, the term used to indicate the interest rate for a loan.

Scope The location within which a defined name is recognized without qualification—usually either to a specific worksheet or to the entire workbook.

Table array A defined range of cells, arranged in columns or rows, used in a VLOOKUP or HLOOKUP function.

Trace Dependents command A command that displays arrows that indicate what cells are affected by the value of the currently selected cell.

Trace Error command A tool that helps locate and resolve an error by tracing the selected error value.

Trace Precedents command A command that displays arrows to indicate what cells affect the value of the cell that is selected.

Tracer arrow An indicator that shows the relationship between the active cell and its related cell.

Two-variable Data table A data table that changes the values in two cells.

Type argument An optional argument in the PMT function that assumes that the payment will be made at the end of each time period.

Validation list A list of values that are acceptable for a group of cells; only values on the list are valid and any value *not* on the list is considered invalid.

VLOOKUP An Excel function that looks up values that are displayed vertically in a column.

Watch Window A window that displays the results of specified cells.

What-If Analysis The process of changing the values in cells to see how those changes affect the outcome of formulas in a worksheet.

Chapter Review

Apply 7A skills from these Objectives:

1. Use Financial Functions
2. Use Goal Seek
3. Create a Data Table
4. Use Defined Names in a Formula

In the following Skills Review, you will create a worksheet for Patricia Murphy, U.S. Sales Director, which details loan information for purchasing seven automobiles for Jesse Jewelers sales representatives. The monthly payment for the seven automobiles cannot exceed $3,500. You will also help Ms. Murphy calculate quarterly Store Supply costs using defined names. Your four completed worksheets will look similar to Figure 7.63.

Project Files

For Project 7C, you will need the following file:

e07C_Loan_Supply_Costs

You will save your workbook as:

Lastname_Firstname_7C_Loan_Supply_Costs

Project Results

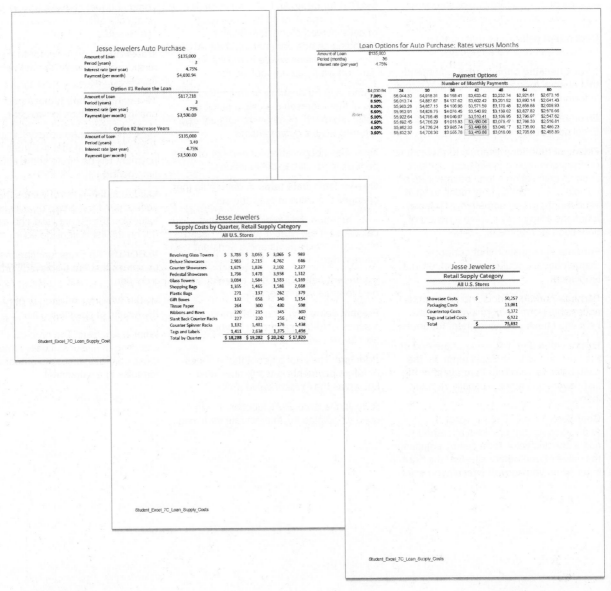

Figure 7.63

(continues on next page)

Chapter Review

Skills Review: Project 7C Auto Loan (continued)

1 ▶ From the files downloaded for this project, open the file **e07C_Loan_Supply_Costs**, and then, using your own name, **Save** the file in your **Excel Chapter 7** folder as **Lastname_Firstname_7C_Loan_Supply_Costs**

a. In the **Auto Loan** worksheet, in the range **A2:B5**, enter the following row titles and data.

Amount of Loan	$135,000
Period (years)	3
Interest rate (per year)	4.75%
Payment (per month)	

b. Click cell **B5**. On the **Formulas tab**, in the **Function Library group**, click **Financial**, and then scroll down and click **PMT**. If necessary, drag the **Function Arguments** dialog box to the right side of your screen so you can view **columns A:B**.

c. In the **Rate** box, type **b4/12** to convert the annual interest rate to a monthly interest rate. Press [Tab], and then in the **Nper** box, type **b3*12** to have Excel convert the number of years in the loan (3) to the total number of months. Press [Tab], and then in the **Pv** box, type **b2** to enter the present value of the loan. Click **OK** to create the function. (Mac users: click Done and close the Formula Builder.)

d. In the **Formula Bar**, between the equal sign and PMT, type – (minus sign) to insert a minus sign into the formula, and then press [Enter] to display the loan payment as a positive number.

2 ▶ Click cell **B5**. On the **Data tab**, in the **Forecast group**, click **What-If Analysis**, and then in the list, click **Goal Seek**. In the **Goal Seek** dialog box, in the **Set cell** box, confirm that *B5* displays.

a. Press [Tab]. In the **To value** box, type the payment goal of **3500** and then press [Tab]. In the **By changing cell** box, type **b2** which is the amount of the loan. Click **OK** two times. For three years at 4.75%, Patricia can borrow only $117,218 if she maintains a monthly payment of $3,500.

b. Click cell **A7**. Type **Option #1 Reduce the Loan** and then on the **Formula Bar**, click **Enter** ✓. **Merge & Center** the title across the range **A7:B7**, from the **Home tab**, display the **Cell Styles** gallery, and then apply the **Heading 2** cell style.

c. Select the range **A2:B5**, right-click, and then click **Copy**. Point to cell **A8**, right-click, click the **Paste Special arrow**, and then under **Paste Values**, click the second button—**Values & Number Formatting (A)**. Press [Esc] to cancel the moving border.

d. In cell **B2**, type **135000** and then press [Enter] to restore the original loan amount. Click cell **B5**. On the **Data tab**, in the **Forecast group**, click **What-If Analysis**, and then click **Goal Seek**.

e. In the **Set cell** box, confirm that *B5* displays. Press [Tab]. In the **To value** box, type **3500** Press [Tab]. In the **By changing cell** box, type **b3** which is the number of years for the loan. Click **OK** two times.

f. Click **A13**. Type **Option #2 Increase Years** and then press [Enter]. Use the **Format Painter** to copy the format from cell **A7** to cell **A13**. Select the range **A2:B5**, right-click, and then click **Copy**. Point to cell **A14**, right-click, click the **Paste Special arrow**, and then under **Paste Values**, click the second button—**Values & Number Formatting (A)**. Press [Esc] to cancel the moving border.

g. Select cell **B15**, from the **Home tab**, in the **Number group**, click **Decrease Decimal** until the number of decimal places is two. Click cell **B3**. Type **3** and then press [Enter] to restore the original value. Click cell **A1**. **Save** your workbook.

(continues on next page)

Chapter Review

3 To determine how variable interest rates and a varying number of payments affect the payment amount, Patricia will set up a two-variable data table. Click the **Payment Table** worksheet.

a. In the range **B2:B4**, enter the following data.

$135,000
36
4.75%

b. Click cell **C8**. Type **24** and then press [Tab]. Type **30** and then press [Tab]. Select the range **C8:D8**. Drag the fill handle to the right through cell **I8** to fill a pattern of months from 24 to 60 in increments of six months.

c. In cell **B9**, type **7.0%** and press [Enter]. Type **6.5%** and press [Enter]. Select the range **B9:B10**, and then drag the fill handle down through cell **B16** to fill a pattern of interest rates in increments of 0.5% from 7.00% down to 3.50%. If necessary, adjust to display two decimal places.

d. Click cell **B8**. On the **Formulas tab**, in the **Function Library group**, click **Financial**, and then click **PMT**. In the **Rate** box, type **b4/12** to divide the interest rate per year by 12 to convert it to a monthly interest rate. Press [Tab], and then in the **Nper** box, type **b3** Press [Tab]. In the **Pv** box, type **-b2** and then click **OK**. (Mac users: Click Done and close the Formula Builder pane.)

e. Select the range **B8:I16**. On the **Data tab**, in the **Forecast group**, click **What-If Analysis**, and then in the list, click **Data Table**. In the **Data Table** dialog box, in the **Row input cell** box, type **b3** and then press [Tab]. In the **Column input cell** box, type **b4** and then in the **Data Table** dialog box, click **OK** to create the data table. Click in any cell outside of the table to deselect.

f. Use the **Format Painter** to copy the format from cell **B8** to the range **C9:I16**.

g. Select the range **F14:F16** and apply the **Note** cell style to highlight the desired payment option. Select the nonadjacent ranges **C8:I8** and **B9:B16**, apply **Bold** and **Center**. Click cell **A1**.

4 Display the **Quarterly Supply Costs** worksheet.

a. Select the range **B6:E9**. On the **Formulas tab**, in the **Defined Names group**, click **Define Name**. With *Revolving_Glass_Towers* selected, type **Showcase_Costs** as the name. At the bottom of the dialog box, at the right edge of the **Refers to** box, point to and click the **Collapse Dialog Box** arrow. Change the range by selecting the range **B6:E10**.

b. Click the **Expand Dialog Box** arrow to redisplay the **New Name** dialog box, and then click **OK**.

c. Select the range **B11:E14**. In the upper left corner of the Excel window, to the left of the **Formula Bar**, click in the **Name Box**. Type **Wrapping_Costs** and press [Enter].

d. Select the range **B15:E16**. On the **Formulas tab**, in the **Defined Names group**, click **Name Manager**. In the upper left corner of the **Name Manager** dialog box, click **New**. With *Slant_Back_Counter_Racks* selected, type **Countertop_Costs** and then click **OK**. **Close** the **Name Manager** dialog box. (Mac tip: Click Define Name and change *Slant_Back_Counter_Racks* to *Countertop_Costs*)

e. On the left side of your window, in the **row heading area**, point to the **row 15** heading and right-click to select the entire row and display a shortcut menu. Click **Insert** to insert a new blank row above. Click cell **A15**, type **Ribbons and Bows** and then press [Tab]. In cell **B15**, type **220** and press [Tab]. In cell **C15**, type **215** and press [Tab]. In cell **D15**, type **345** and press [Tab]. In cell **E15**, type **300** and press [Enter].

f. On the **Formulas tab**, from the **Defined Names group**, display the **Name Manager** dialog box. In the **Name Manager** dialog box, in the **Name** column, click **Wrapping_Costs**. (Mac users: Click Define Name) At the bottom of the dialog box, click in the **Refers to** box and edit the reference, changing *$E$14* to **$E$15** to include the new row in the range. **Close** the **Name Manager** dialog box, and click **Yes** to save the changes you made to the name reference.

(continues on next page)

Chapter Review

g. On the **Formulas tab**, from the **Defined Names group**, display the **Name Manager** dialog box. (Mac users: Click Define Name) Click **Wrapping_Costs**, and then click **Edit**. In the **Edit Name** dialog box, with *Wrapping_Costs* selected, type **Packaging_Costs** Click **OK**, and then **Close** the **Name Manager** dialog box.

h. Select the range **A18:E18**. On the **Formulas tab**, in the **Defined Names group**, click **Create from Selection**. In the **Create Names from Selection** dialog box, be sure the **Left column** check box is selected, and then click **OK**. Click the **Name Box arrow**, and then click the name **Tags_and_Labels**. Notice that in the new range name, Excel inserted the underscores necessary to fill blank spaces in the range name. Click cell **A1**, and then **Save** your workbook.

5 Display the **Annual Supply Costs** worksheet.

a. In cell **B5**, type **=sum(S** Continue typing **howcase_Costs** and then press Enter. Your result is 50257. In cell **B6**, type **=sum(P** and then on the **Formula AutoComplete list**, double-click **Packaging_Costs** to insert the formula. Press Enter to display the result 13081.

b. In cell **B7**, type **=sum(** and then on the **Formulas tab**, in the **Defined Names group**, click **Use in Formula**. On the list, click **Countertop_Costs** and then press Enter to display the total 5372. (Mac users: Use in Formula may not be available.)

c. In cell **B8**, use any of the techniques you just practiced to sum the cells containing the costs for **Tags_and_Labels** and to display a result of 6922. Click cell **B9**, and then on the **Formulas tab**, in the **Function Library group**, click **AutoSum** and press Enter to display a total of *75632*. From the **Home tab**, by using the commands at the bottom of the **Cell Styles** gallery, apply **Currency [0]** style to cell **B5** and cell **B9**. Apply **Comma [0]** style to the range **B6:B8**. Apply the **Total** cell style to cell **B9**. Click cell **A1** and **Save** your workbook.

6 At the bottom of the workbook window, right-click any sheet tab name, and then click **Select All Sheets**.

a. With the four worksheets grouped, from the **Page Layout tab**, display the **Page Setup** dialog box, and then insert a **Custom Footer** in the **left section** that includes the file name. Click the **Margins tab**, and then center the worksheets **Horizontally** on the page. Click **OK**.

b. Click the **Payment Table** worksheet, and then on the **Page Layout tab**, in the **Page Setup group**, change the **Orientation** to **Landscape**.

c. Click the **File tab** to display **Backstage** view. Click the **Info tab**. On the right, at the bottom of the **Properties** list, click **Show All Properties**. In the **Subject** box, type your course name and section number, and in the **Tags** box, type **auto loan, supply costs** On the left, click **Save**.

d. As directed by your instructor, submit your Excel file. If required by your instructor, create a version of your worksheets with formulas displayed. In the upper right corner of the Excel window, click **Close**.

You have completed Project 7C | **END**

Chapter Review

Project 7D Quarterly Cost Report and Lookup Form

Apply 7B skills from these Objectives:

5. Use Lookup Functions
6. Validate Data
7. Audit Worksheet Formulas
8. Use the Watch Window to Monitor Cell Values
9. Use the MATCH and INDEX Functions

In the following Skills Review, you will assist Mike Connor, the Vice President of Marketing at Jesse Jewelers, by adding lookup functions to a Packing Slip form so that an order taker can complete the form quickly. You will use the Formula Auditing tools to review a revenue worksheet for the Houston store, you will use the Watch Window to edit the store's utility cost worksheets, and you will use the MATCH and INDEX functions. Your completed worksheets will look similar to Figure 7.64.

Project Files

For Project 7D, you will need the following file:

e07D_Form_Cost_Report

You will save your workbook as:

Lastname_Firstname_7D_Form_Cost_Report

Project Results

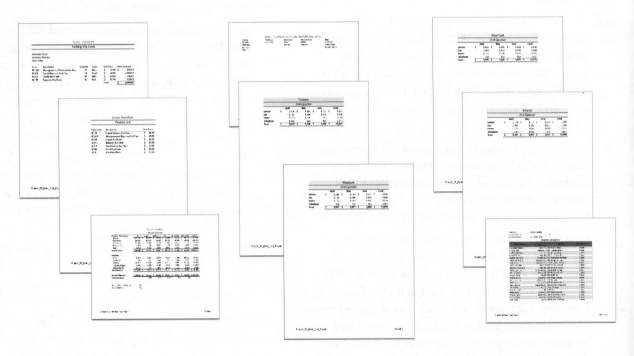

Figure 7.64

(continues on next page)

Chapter Review

1 From the files that accompany this project, open the file **e07D_Form_Cost_Report**, and then using your own name, **Save** the file in your **Excel Chapter 7** folder as **Lastname_Firstname_7D_Form_Cost_Report**

a. Display the **Product Information** worksheet. Select the range **A4:C11**. On the **Data tab**, in the **Sort & Filter group**, click **Sort**. If necessary, drag the Sort dialog box to the right side of your screen so you can view **columns A:C**.

b. In the **Sort** dialog box, under **Column**, click the **Sort by arrow**. Notice that the selected range is now **A5:C11** and that the column titles in the range **A4:C4** display in the **Sort by** list. In the **Sort by** list, click **Style Code**. Under **Sort On**, verify that *Cell Values* displays, and under **Order**, verify that **A to Z** displays. Click **OK** to sort the data by Style Code in ascending order. Click cell **A1** and **Save** your workbook.

c. Display the **Packing Slip** worksheet. In cell **A9**, type **BC-MO** and press [Tab]. With cell **B9** as the active cell, on the **Formulas tab**, in the **Function Library group**, click **Lookup & Reference**, and then click **VLOOKUP**.

d. With the insertion point in the **Lookup_value** box, click cell **A9** to look up the description of Item BC-MO. Click in the **Table_array** box, and then at the bottom of the workbook, click the **Product Information sheet tab**. On the **Product Information** sheet, select the range **A4:C11**, and then press [F4]. Click in the **Col_index_num** box, type **2** and then click **OK**.

e. With cell **B9** as the active cell and containing the VLOOKUP formula, point to the fill handle in the lower right corner of the cell, and then drag to fill the VLOOKUP formula down through cell **B18**.

f. Click cell **C9**, type **12** as the quantity ordered, and then press [Tab]. In cell **D9**, type **Black** and press [Tab]. With cell **E9** as the active cell, on the **Formulas tab**, in the **Function Library group**, click **Lookup & Reference**, and then click **VLOOKUP**.

g. With the insertion point in the **Lookup_value** box, click cell **A9** to look up information for Item BC-MO. Click in the **Table_array** box, display the **Product Information** sheet, and then select the range **A4:C11**. Press [F4] to make the values in the range absolute. (Mac users: Add $ as necessary.)

h. In the **Col_index_num** box, type **3** to look up the price in the third column of the range, and then click **OK**. The Unit Price for the Monogrammed Business Card Case displays in cell **E9**. Click cell **F9**, and notice that a formula to calculate the total for the item, Quantity times Unit Price, was already entered in the worksheet.

i. Click cell **E9**, and then copy the VLOOKUP formula down through cell **E18**.

j. Click cell **A10**, type **BC-CB** and press [Tab] two times. In cell **C10**, type **24** and press [Tab]. Notice that Excel calculates the total for this item in cell **F10**—1,104.00. In cell **D10**, type **Pearl** and then press [Enter]. **Save** your workbook.

2 Display the **Product Information** sheet. Select the range **A4:A11**. On the **Formulas** tab, in the **Defined Names** group, click **Create from Selection**.

a. In the **Create Names from Selection** dialog box, be sure only the **Top row** check box is selected, and then click **OK**.

b. Display the **Packing Slip** worksheet, and then select the range **A9:A18**. On the **Data tab**, in the **Data Tools group**, click **Data Validation**. In the **Data Validation** dialog box, be sure the **Settings tab** is selected.

c. Under **Validation criteria**, click the **Allow arrow**, and then click **List**. Click to position the insertion point in the **Source** box, type **=Style_Code** and then click **OK**.

d. Click cell **A11**, and then click the **list arrow** to display the list. In the list, click **KC-CB**. Press [Tab] two times, type **24** and press [Tab], type **Blue** and then press [Enter] to return to the beginning of the next row.

e. With cell **A12** active, click the **list arrow**, and then click **KC-EN**. As the **Quantity**, type **18** and as the **Color**, type **Red** Press [Enter]. In cell **A13**, type **B-W** and press [Tab]. An error message displays indicating that you entered a value that is not valid; that is, it is not on the validation list you created. In the error message, click **Cancel**.

f. Select the unused **rows 13:18**, right-click over the selected rows, and then click **Delete**. In cell **F13**, **Sum** the order amounts and then apply the **Total** cell style. Click cell **A1**, and then **Save** your workbook.

(continues on next page)

Chapter Review

3 ▶ Display the **Revenue** worksheet.

a. In the **column heading area**, select **column B**, hold down Ctrl, and then select **column H**. Point to the *right* edge of either of the selected column headings to display the pointer, and then double-click to AutoFit the columns. (Mac users: Hold down COMMAND.)

b. Click cell **C9**. On the **Formulas tab**, in the **Formula Auditing group**, click **Trace Precedents**. To the left of the cell, click **Error Checking**, and then click **Update Formula to Include Cells**. Drag the fill handle to copy the corrected formula in cell **C9** to the range **D9:G9**.

c. Click cell **H5**, and then point to the **Error Checking** button to read the ScreenTip. On the **Formulas tab**, in the **Formula Auditing group**, click **Trace Precedents**. To the left of cell **H5**, click **Error Checking** to display the list of error checking options, click **Copy Formula from Above**, and then look at the **Formula Bar** to verify that the formula is summing the numbers in **row 5**. With cell **H5** still selected, from the **Home tab**, display the **Cell Styles gallery**, and then click the **Comma [0]** number format.

d. Click cell **H6**, on the **Formulas tab**, click **Trace Precedents**, and then verify that the row is correctly summed. Click cell **H7**, and then click **Trace Precedents**. Notice that the formula is not correct. Click cell **H8**, and then click **Trace Precedents**. Notice that the formula is not correct. In the **Formula Auditing group**, click **Remove Arrows**. Click cell **H6**, and then use the fill handle to copy the correct formula down to cells **H7:H8**.

4 ▶ Click cell **B14**, which displays the error *#VALUE!*. To the left of the cell, point to **Error Checking** and read the ScreenTip. In the **Formula Auditing group**, click **Trace Precedents**.

a. To the left of the cell, click **Error Checking**, and then on the list, click **Show Calculation Steps**. Notice that the formula is multiplying by a text value. (Mac users: Show Calculation Steps may not be available.)

b. **Close** the **Evaluate Formula** dialog box. With cell **B14** still the active cell, click in the **Formula Bar**, and then edit the formula to change the reference to cell **B3** to **B9** and press Enter. Click cell **B14**, and then drag the fill handle to copy the corrected formula across the row to cells **C14:G14**.

5 ▶ Click cell **B16**, point to **Error Checking**, and read the ScreenTip. In the **Formula Auditing group**, click the **Error Checking arrow** to display a list. On the list, click **Trace Error**. In the **Formula Auditing group**, click the **Error Checking arrow**, and then click **Trace Error** again to view the precedent cells. Click in cell **A24**. Type **Admin Percent** and press Tab, and then type **2** to fill in the missing data.

a. Click **B16**. Remove the arrows. To the left of the cell, click **Error Checking** to display the list of error checking options, and then click **Edit in Formula Bar**. Delete *#REF!*. Type **b24** and press F4 to make the cell reference absolute. Press Enter. Click cell **B16**, and then use the fill handle to copy the formula to the right to cells **C16:G16**. (Mac users: Press COMMAND + T to make the cell reference absolute.)

6 ▶ Click cell **A1**. In the **Formula Auditing group**, click the **Error Checking arrow**, and then click **Error Checking**—cell **C20** is selected. In the **Error Checking** dialog box, click **Show Calculation Steps**; notice that the divisor is an empty cell. In the **Evaluate Formula** dialog box, click **Evaluate**. Click **Restart**. (Mac users: Evaluate Formula dialog box may not be available. Move to Step b. and click cell H13.)

a. In the **Evaluate Formula** dialog box, click **Step In** to examine the formula. Click **Step Out**. Close the **Evaluate Formula** dialog box.

b. In the **Error Checking** dialog box, click **Next**. Click **OK**. Click cell **H13**, and then use the fill handle to copy this formula down to cells **H14:H16**. Click cell **B17** and drag the fill handle to copy this formula to the right into cells **C17:H17**.

c. Click cell **B19** and type **=b9-b17** Press Enter, and then copy the formula to the right into cells **C19:H19**. Click cell **C20**, and then on the **Home tab**, in the **Number group**, click **Percent Style**. Copy the formula to the right into cells **D20:G20**. Click cell **A1**, and then **Save** your workbook.

7 ▶ Display the **Categories** worksheet. To the left of the **Formula Bar**, click the **Name Box** arrow, and then click **Items**. Examine the selected range.

a. Redisplay the **Revenue** worksheet. On the **Data tab**, in the **Data Tools group**, click the **Data Validation arrow**, and then click **Circle Invalid Data**.

(continues on next page)

Chapter Review

b. Click cell **A8**, and then click the **list arrow** at the right side of the cell. From the list, click **Bags**. In the **Data Tools group**, click the **Data Validation arrow**, and then click **Clear Validation Circles**. Click cell **A1**, and then **Save** your workbook.

8 Display the **Toronto** worksheet, and then click cell **E8**. On the **Formulas tab**, in the **Formula Auditing group**, click **Watch Window**. In the upper left corner of the **Watch Window**, click **Add Watch**. In the **Add Watch** dialog box, click **Add**. (Mac users: Watch Window may not be available, move to Step b.)

a. Display the **Houston** worksheet, and using the same technique, add cell **E8** from the **Houston** worksheet. Repeat this for the **New York** worksheet and for the **Miami** worksheet. Adjust the size of the **Watch Window** and columns as necessary to view all four sheets, and verify that cell **E8** is listed for each of the four worksheets.

b. With the **Miami** worksheet active, hold down Shift and click the **Toronto** sheet tab to select all four worksheets. In the **Miami** worksheet, select the range **B4:E8**. On the **Formulas tab**, in the **Function Library group**, click **AutoSum**. **Close** the **Watch Window**. With the four worksheets still selected as a group, select the range **E5:E7**, and then apply **Comma Style** with zero decimal places. Select cell **E4**, and then from the **Cell Styles** gallery, apply the **Currency [0]** format. Click cell **A1**, and then **Save** your workbook.

9 Display the **Designers** worksheet. In cell **B1**, notice the **Specialty** *Sports bracelets* is indicated.

a. Click cell **B2**. Type **=MATCH(b1,c6:c27,0)** to search for an exact match for *Sports bracelets*, and then press Enter. This item occupies the 8th position in the list.

b. Click cell **B3**. Type **=INDEX(a6:a27,MATCH(b1, c6:c27,0))** and press Enter. The designer of Sports bracelets is *Anna Hernandez*. Click cell **A1**, and then **Save** your workbook.

10 In the **sheet tab row**, right-click any sheet tab, and then click **Select All Sheets**.

a. On the **Page Layout tab**, in the **Page Setup group**, click the **Dialog Box Launcher** to display the **Page Setup** dialog box. (Mac users: Click Page Setup.)

b. Click the **Margins tab**, and then under **Center on page**, click **Horizontally**. Click the **Header/ Footer tab**, click **Custom Footer**, and then in the **Left section**, insert the **File Name**. Click in the **Right section**, and then click **Insert Sheet Name** to display *&[Tab]*. Click **OK** two times.

c. Right-click any sheet tab, and then click **Ungroup Sheets**. Click the **Revenue sheet tab**, hold down Ctrl and then click the **Categories sheet tab** and the **Designers sheet tab**. (Mac users: Do not group; change the orientation to Landscape one sheet at a time.)

d. With these three worksheets selected, on the **Page Layout tab**, in the **Page Setup group**, click **Orientation**, and then click **Landscape**.

e. Display the **Packing Slip** worksheet, which will ungroup the sheets. Display **Backstage** view, click the **Info tab**, click **Show All Properties**. On the list of **Properties**, in the **Tags** box, type **order form, cost report** In the **Subject** box, type your course name and section number. Under **Related People**, be sure that your name displays as the author. If necessary, right-click the author name, click **Edit Property**, type your name, click outside of the **Edit person** dialog box, and then click **OK**.

f. On the left, click **Print**. Under **Settings**, click the **Print Active Sheets arrow**, and then click **Print Entire Workbook**. At the bottom of the window, click **Next Page** to scroll through the worksheets. On the left, click **Save**.

g. Submit your Excel workbook as directed by your instructor. If required by your instructor, print or create an electronic version of your worksheet with formulas displayed. In the upper right corner of the Excel window, click **Close**.

You have completed Project 7D **END**

Content-Based Assessments (Mastery and Transfer of Learning)

MyLab IT Grader	Mastering Excel	Project 7E Condo Loan and Quarterly Cost Report

Apply 7A skills from these Objectives:

1. Use Financial Functions
2. Use Goal Seek
3. Create a Data Table
4. Use Defined Names in a Formula

In the following Mastering Excel project, you will create a worksheet for Jacques Celestine, President of Jesse Jewelers, which analyzes loan options for a condo in Toronto that the company is considering purchasing. Jacques wants to provide a lodging facility for company visitors, but would like to keep the monthly loan payment below $6,250. You will also define names for ranges of cells in a worksheet containing quarterly advertising costs. The worksheets of your workbook will look similar to Figure 7.65.

Project Files for MyLab IT Grader

1. In your **MyLab IT** course, locate and click **Excel 7E Condo Loan Advertising**, Download Materials, and then Download All Files.
2. Extract the zipped folder to your Excel Chapter 7 folder. Close the Grader download screens.
3. Take a moment to open the downloaded **Excel_7E_Condo_Loan_Advertising_Instructions** document; note any recent updates to the book.

Project Results

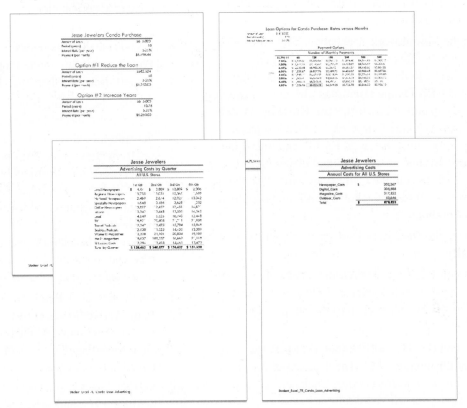

Figure 7.65

For Non-MyLab Submissions

For Project 7E, you will need this file:
e07E_Condo_Loan_Advertising

In your Excel Chapter 7 folder, save your workbook as:
Lastname_Firstname_7E_Condo_Loan_Advertising

After you have named and saved your workbook, on the next page, begin with Step 2.
After Step 14, submit your file as directed by your instructor.

(continues on next page)

1 Navigate to your **Excel Chapter 7 folder**, and then double-click the Excel file you downloaded from **MyLab IT** that displays your name—**Student_Excel_7E_ Condo_Loan_Advertising**. If necessary, at the top, click **Enable Editing**.

2 Display the **Condo Purchase** worksheet. In cell **B5**, insert the **PMT** function using the data from the range **B2:B4**—be sure to divide the interest rate by **12** multiply the years by **12** and display the payment as a positive number. The result, *$6,598.44*, is larger than the maximum payment of $6,250.

3 Click cell **B5**, and then use **Goal Seek** to change the amount of the loan so that the payment goal is **6250** Then, in cell **A7**, type **Option #1 Reduce the Loan** Use the **Format Painter** to apply the cell style from cell **A1** to cell **A7**. **Copy** the range **A2:B5**, and then **Paste** the **Values & Number Formatting** to cell **A8**. In cell **B2**, type **615000** to restore the original loan amount. If necessary, press ⎋ to cancel the moving border.

4 Click cell **B5**, and then use **Goal Seek** to change the period of the loan (of the original data) so that the payment is **6250** Then, in cell **A13**, type **Option #2 Increase Years** Format the cell the same as cell **A7**. **Copy** the range **A2:B5**, and then **Paste** the **Values & Number Formatting** to cell **A14**. Display the value in cell **B15** with two decimal places, and then in cell **B3**, type **10** to restore the original value. If necessary, press ⎋ to cancel the moving border. Click cell **A1**, and then **Save** your workbook.

5 Display the **Payment Table** worksheet, in the range **A2:B4**, enter the following row titles and data. (The Currency [0] cell style is already applied to cell **B2**.)

Amount of Loan	615,000
Period (months)	120
Interest Rate (per year)	5.25%

6 In cell **C8**, type **60**—the number of months in a 5-year loan. In **D8**, type **120**—the number of months in a 10-year loan. Fill the series through cell **H8**. Apply **Bold** and **Center** to the range **C8:H8**.

7 Beginning in cell **B9**, enter varying interest rates in decrements of 0.5% beginning with **7.5%** and ending with **4.0%** If necessary, format all the interest rates with two decimal places, and then apply **Bold** and **Center** to the range **B9:B16**.

8 In cell **B8**, enter a **PMT** function using the information in cells **B2:B4**. Be sure that you convert the interest rate to a monthly rate and that the result displays as a positive number.

9 Create a **Data table** in the range **B8:H16** using the information in cells **B2:B4** in which the **Row input cell** is the **Period** and the **Column input cell** is the **Interest rate**. **Copy** the format from cell **B8** to the results in the data table. Format cell **D16** with the **Note** cell style as the payment option that is close to but less than $6,250 per month. Click cell **A1**.

10 Display the **Advertising Costs by Quarter** sheet. Name the following ranges: **B6:E10 Newspaper_Costs B11:E14 Digital_Costs B15:E16 Magazine_Costs B17:E17 Billboard_Costs** Insert a new **row 15**. In cell **A15**, type **Business Podcasts** In cell **B15**, type **12500** In cell **C15**, type **11525** In cell **D15**, type **14455** In cell **E15**, type **13009**

11 Display the **Name Manager**, click **Digital_Costs**, and then in the **Refers to** box, edit as necessary so that the end of the range is cell **E15**. Select the **Billboard_ Costs** and then **Edit** the name to **Outdoor_Costs** Click cell **A1**, and then **Save** your workbook.

12 Display the **Annual Advertising Costs** sheet. In cell **B5**, type **=sum(N** and sum the values using the appropriate range name in the displayed list of functions. Repeat for the other named ranges. From the **Formulas tab**, in the **Function Library group**, use **AutoSum** to sum all the costs. Apply the **Total** cell style to cell **B9**. Click cell **A1**, and then click **Save**.

13 At the bottom of the workbook window, right-click any sheet tab name, and then click **Select All Sheets**. With the four worksheets grouped, from the **Page Layout tab**, display the **Page Setup** dialog box, and then insert a **Custom Footer** in the **left section** that includes the file name. Click the **Margins tab**, and then center the worksheets **Horizontally** on the page. Click the **Payment Table** worksheet, and then set the **Orientation** of this sheet to **Landscape**.

(continues on next page)

14 Display **Backstage** view, click the **Info tab**, click **Show All Properties**. On the list of **Properties**, in the **Tags** box, type **payment table, advertising costs** In the **Subject** box, type your course name and section number. On the left, click **Save. Close** Excel.

15 In **MyLab IT**, locate and click the Grader Project **Excel 7E Condo Loan Advertising**. In **step 3**, under **Upload Completed Assignment**, click **Choose File**. In the **Open** dialog box, navigate to your **Excel Chapter 7 folder**, and then click your **Student_Excel_7E_Condo_ Loan_Advertising** file one time to select it. In the lower right corner of the **Open** dialog box, click **Open**.

The name of your selected file displays above the Upload button.

16 To submit your file to **MyLab IT** for grading, click **Upload**, wait a moment for a green **Success!** message, and then in **step 4**, click the blue **Submit for Grading** button. Click **Close Assignment** to return to your list of **Course Materials**.

You have completed Project 7E **END**

Apply 7B skills from these Objectives:

5. Use Lookup Functions
6. Validate Data
7. Audit Worksheet Formulas
8. Use the Watch Window to Monitor Cell Values
9. Use the MATCH and INDEX Functions

In the following Mastering Excel project, you will assist Mike Connor, the Vice President of Marketing at Jesse Jewelers, by adding lookup functions to an Advertising Order form so that an order taker can complete the form quickly. You will also use the Formula Auditing features and visual inspection to find and correct several types of errors and use the MATCH and INDEX functions. Your completed worksheets will look similar to Figure 7.66.

Project Files for MyLab IT Grader

1. In your **MyLab IT** course, locate and click **Excel 7F Ad Form NY Revenue**, Download Materials, and then Download All Files.
2. Extract the zipped folder to your Excel Chapter 7 folder. Close the Grader download screens.
3. Take a moment to open the downloaded **Excel_7F_Ad_Form_NY_Revenue_Instructions** document; note any recent updates to the book.

Project Results

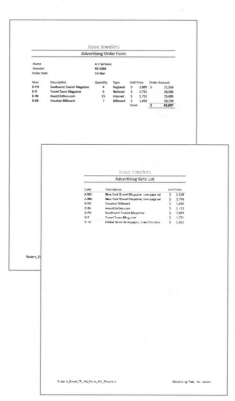
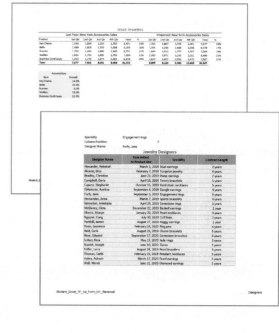

Figure 7.66

For Non-MyLab Submissions

For Project 7F, you will need:
e07F_Ad_Form_NY_Revnue

In your Excel Chapter 7 folder, you will save your workbook as:
Lastname_Firstname_7F_Ad_Form_NY_Revenue

Begin with Step 2. After Step 12, save and submit your file Lastname_Firstname_7F_Ad_Form_NY_Revenue as directed by you instructor.

(continues on next page)

Content-Based Assessments (Mastery and Transfer of Learning)

1 Navigate to your **Excel Chapter 7 folder**, and then double-click the Excel file you downloaded from **MyLab IT** that displays your name—**Student_Excel_7F_Ad_Form_NY_Revenue**. If necessary, at the top, click **Enable Editing**.

2 Display the second worksheet—**Advertising Rate Information**. Select the range **A4:C11**, and then sort by **Code**. Name the range **A4:A11** by using the **Create from Selection** command and using the top row as the name. Click cell **A1**.

3 Display the first worksheet—**Advertising Order Form**. In the range **A9:A18**, create a data validation list using the defined name equal to **Code**

4 Click cell **A9**, click the **list arrow**, and then click **D-PH**. Click cell **B9** to make it the active cell, and then insert a **VLOOKUP** function that will look up the **Description** of the item in cell **A9** using the information in the **Advertising Rate Information** sheet as the table array. After selecting the table array, be sure to press F4 to make it an absolute reference. The Description to be looked up is in **column 2** of the table array. (Mac users: Add $ as necessary to create an absolute reference.)

5 With cell **B9** as the active cell, fill the VLOOKUP formula through cell **B18**. In cell **C9**, type **4** as the **Quantity** ordered and in cell **D9**, type **Regional** In cell **E9**, insert a **VLOOKUP** function to look up **Unit Price** of the item in cell **A9** of the **Advertising Order Form**; the **Unit Price** is in **column 3** of the table array. Copy the **VLOOKUP** formula down through cell **E18**. Add the following orders beginning in **row 10**:

Item	Quantity	Type
D-R	6	National
D-IN	15	Internet
B-BB	7	Billboard

6 Delete the unused rows. Sum the **Order Amount**, and then apply the **Total** cell style. Click cell **A1**.

7 Display the **Sales Data** sheet. Click cell **I5**, which displays a green triangle indicating a potential error, and then on the **Formulas tab**, click **Trace Precedents**. To the left of the cell, click **Error Checking**, and then click **Edit in Formula Bar**. Change *$B$14* to **$B$15** so that the formula is using the Growth Assumption for *Belts*, not for Key Chains, and then press Enter.

8 On the **Formulas tab**, in the **Formula Auditing group**, click **Error Checking** to begin checking for errors from this point in the worksheet. In cell **M6**, the flagged error, notice the formula is trying to divide by cell **L10**, which is empty. Click **Edit in Formula Bar**, change **10** to **9** and then in the **Error Checking** dialog box, click **Resume**.

9 In cell **F7**, examine the error information, and then click **Copy Formula from Above**. Examine the error in cell **J8**, and then click **Copy Formula from Left**. Click **OK**, and then use **Format Painter** to copy the format in cell **M5** to cell **M6**. Click cell **A1**. (Mac users: If necessary, use the Error Checking command on the ribbon.)

10 Display the **Designers** worksheet. In cell **B2**, insert a **MATCH** function to find the position of *Engagement rings* in the range **c6:c27**. In cell **B3**, insert a combined **INDEX** and **MATCH** function to display the name of the designer for Engagement rings. Click cell **A1**, and then **Save** your workbook.

11 In the **sheet tab row**, right-click any sheet tab, and then click **Select All Sheets**. Display the **Page Setup** dialog box, click the **Margins tab**, and then under **Center on page**, click **Horizontally**. Click the **Header/Footer tab**, click **Custom Footer**, and then in the **Left section**, insert the **File Name**. In the **Right section**, insert the **Sheet Name**. Click **OK** two times. Display the **Sales Data** sheet. For this sheet, set the **Orientation** to **Landscape**, and in the **Scale to Fit** group, set the **Scale** to **85%** Set the **Orientation** of the **Designers** worksheet to **Landscape**.

(continues on next page)

12 12Display **Backstage** view, click the **Info tab**, click **Show All Properties**. On the list of **Properties**, in the **Tags** box, type **advertising costs, New York revenue** In the **Subject** box, type your course name and section number. Under **Related People**, be sure that your name displays. On the left, click **Print**. Under **Settings**, click the **Print Active Sheets arrow**, and then click **Print Entire Workbook**. At the bottom of the window, click **Next Page** [▶] to scroll through the worksheets. On the left, click **Save**. **Close** Excel.

13 In **MyLab IT**, locate and click Grader Project **Excel 7F Ad Form NY Revenue**. In **step 3**, under **Upload Completed Assignment**, click **Choose File**. In the **Open** dialog box, navigate to your **Excel Chapter 7 folder**, and then click your **Student_Excel_7F_Ad_Form_NY_Revenue** file one time to select it. In the lower right corner of the **Open** dialog box, click **Open**. The name of your selected file displays above the Upload button.

14 To submit your file to **MyLab IT** for grading, click **Upload**, wait a moment for a green **Success!** message, and then in **step 4**, click the blue **Submit for Grading** button. Click **Close Assignment** to return to your list of Course Materials.

You have completed Project 7F | END

Content-Based Assessments (Mastery and Transfer of Learning)

Mastering Excel

Project 7G Warehouse Loan and Staff Lookup Form

Apply 7A and 7B skills from these Objectives:

1. Use Financial Functions
2. Use Goal Seek
3. Create a Data Table
4. Use Defined Names in a Formula
5. Use Lookup Functions
6. Validate Data
7. Audit Worksheet Formulas
8. Use the Watch Window to Monitor Cell Values
9. Use the MATCH and INDEX Functions

In the following Mastering Excel project, you will create a worksheet for Jacques Celestine, President of Jesse Jewelers, which analyzes loan options for a warehouse that the company is considering purchasing. Jacques wants to establish an additional storage facility in the United States, but would like to keep the monthly loan payment below $10,000 using a 15-year loan. You will also assist Mike Connor, the Vice President of Marketing at Jesse Jewelers by adding lookup functions to a Staff Planning form so that a manager can complete the form quickly. You will also use Formula Auditing to check a worksheet for errors and use the MATCH and INDEX functions. Your completed worksheets will look similar to Figure 7.67.

Project Files for MyLab IT Grader

1. In your Course Materials, locate and click **Excel 7G Loan Staff Revenue**, Download Materials, and then Download All Files.
2. Extract the zipped folder to your Excel Chapter 7 folder. Close the Grader download screens.
3. Take a moment to open the downloaded **Excel_7G_Loan_Staff_Revenue_Instructions** document; note any recent updates to the book.

Project Results

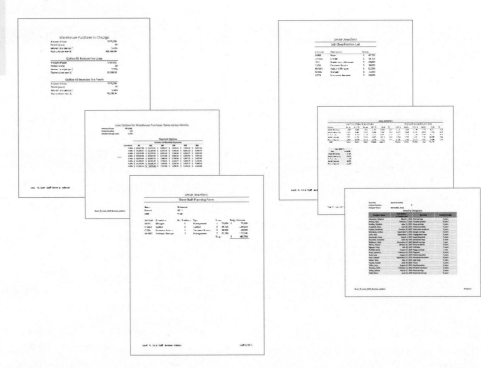

Figure 7.67

For Non-MyLab Submissions

For Project 7G, you will need:
e07G_Loan_Staff_Revenue

In your Excel Chapter 7 folder, save your workbook as:
Lastname_Firstname_7G_Loan_Staff_Revenue

After you have named and saved your workbook, on the next page, begin with Step 2.
After step 16, save and submit your file as directed by your instructor.

(continues on next page)

1 Navigate to your **Excel Chapter 7 folder**, and then double-click the Excel file you downloaded from **MyLab IT** that displays your name-**Student_Excel_7G_Loan_Staff_Revenue**. If necessary, at the top, click **Enable Editing**.

2 Display the second worksheet named **Warehouse Payment Table**. In cell **B8**, enter a **PMT** function using cell **B4** divided by **12** as the rate, cell **B3** as the number of payment periods, and cell **B2** as the present value of the loan. Display the result as a positive number.

3 Create a two-variable data table in the range **B8:H16**. Set cell **B3** as the row input cell, and cell **B4** as the column input cell. From the **Cell Styles** gallery, apply the **Currency** cell style to the range **C9:H16**. Select the payment option closest to but less than $10,000 per month for a 120-month loan—cell **D16**—and format the option with the **Note** cell style. Click cell **A1**. **Save** your workbook.

4 Display the fourth worksheet named **Job Information**, select the range **A4:C11**, and then sort the range by **Job Code** in ascending order. Create a range named **Job_Code** using the data in cells **A5:A11**. Click cell **A1**.

5 Display the **Staffing Plan** worksheet, and then select the range **A9:A18**. Display the **Data Validation** dialog box, and validate from a **List** using the **Source =Job_Code**

6 Click cell **A9**, click the **list arrow**, and then click **M-MG**. Click cell **B9** to make it the active cell, and then insert a **VLOOKUP** function that will look up the **Description** of the **Job Code** in cell **A9** using the information in the **Job Information** worksheet as the table array. After selecting the table array, be sure to press F4 to make it an absolute cell reference. The **Description** to be looked up is in **column 2** of the table array.

7 With cell **B9** as the active cell, copy the VLOOKUP formula down through cell **B18**. In cell **C9**, type **1** as the **# of Positions** and in cell **D9**, type **Management** as the **Type**.

8 In cell **E9**, insert the **VLOOKUP** function to look up the **Salary** of the **Job Code** in cell **A9** by using the information in the **Job Information** sheet as the table array; the **Salary** is in **column 3** of the table array. Copy the VLOOKUP formula in cell **E9** down through cell **E18**.

9 Beginning in cell **A10**, add these staff positions:

Item	# of Positions	Type
C-CASH	3	Cashier
C-CSA	1	Customer Service
M-AMG	3	Management

10 Delete any unused rows between the last item and the Total row. Sum the **Budget Amount** column and apply the **Total** cell style. Click cell **A1**. **Save** your workbook.

11 Display the **Bracelet Revenue** worksheet. Click cell **I5**, and then on the **Formulas tab**, click **Trace Precedents**. On the ribbon, in the **Formula Auditing group**, click **Error Checking**, and then click **Edit in Formula Bar**. Edit the formula so that the formula is using the Growth Assumption for *Beaded Bracelets*, not for *Crystal Bracelets*.

12 In the **Error Checking** dialog box, click **Resume**. In cell **M6**, notice the formula is trying to divide by cell **L10**, which is empty. Click **Edit in Formula Bar**, change **10** to **9** Ensure that the reference to L9 is an absolute reference, and then in the **Error Checking** dialog box, click **Resume**.

13 In cell **F7**, examine the error information, and then click **Copy Formula from Above**. Examine the error in cell **J8**, and then click **Copy Formula from Left**. Click **OK**. Use **Format Painter** to copy the format in cell **M5** to cell **M6**. Click cell **A1**. **Save** your workbook.

14 Display the **Designers** worksheet. In cell **B2**, insert a **MATCH** function to find the position of *Sports bracelets* in the range **c6:c27**. In cell **B3**, insert a combined **INDEX** and **MATCH** function to display the name of the designer for *Sports bracelets*. Click cell **A1**, and then **Save** your workbook.

15 In the **sheet tab row**, right-click any sheet tab, and then click **Select All Sheets**. Display the **Page Setup** dialog box, click the **Margins tab**, and then under **Center on page**, click **Horizontally**. Click the **Header/Footer tab**, click **Custom Footer**, and then in the **Left section**, insert the **File Name**. Insert the sheet name in the **Right section**. Click **OK** two times. Ungroup the sheets, and then for these three worksheets—**Warehouse Payment Table**, **Staffing Plan**, and **Bracelet Revenue**—set the **Orientation** to **Landscape**. Select only the **Bracelet Revenue** sheet, and on the **Page Layout tab**, set the **Scale** to **90%**.

16 Display **Backstage** view, click the **Info tab**, click **Show All Properties**. On the list of **Properties**, in the **Tags** box, type **New York revenue** In the **Subject** box, type your course name and section number. Under **Related People**, be sure that your name displays as the Author. On the left, click **Print**. Under **Settings**, click the **Print Active Sheets arrow**, and then click **Print Entire Workbook**. At the bottom of the window, click **Next Page** ▶ to scroll through the six worksheets. On the left, click **Save**. **Close** Excel.

(continues on next page)

Mastering Excel: Project 7G Warehouse Loan and Staff Lookup Form (continued)

17 In **MyLab IT**, locate and click Grader Project **Excel 7G Loan Staff Revenue**. In **step 3**, under U**pload Completed Assignment**, click **Choose File**. In the **Open** dialog box, navigate to your **Excel Chapter 7 folder**, and then click your **Student_Excel_7G_Loan_Staff_ Revenue** file one time to select it. In the lower right corner of the **Open** dialog box, click **Open**. The name of your selected file displays above the Upload button.

18 To submit your file to **MyLab IT** for grading, click **Upload**, wait a moment for a green **Success!** message, and then in **step 4**, click the blue **Submit for Grading** button. Click **Close Assignment** to return to your list of Course Materials.

You have completed Project 7G END

Content-Based Assessments (Critical Thinking)

Apply a combination of the 7A and 7B skills.

GO! Fix It	**Project 7H Bag Costs by Quarter**	IRC
GO! Make It	**Project 7I Arizona Store Loan**	IRC
GO! Solve It	**Project 7J Store Furnishings**	IRC
GO! Solve It	**Project 7K Order Form**	

Project Files

For Project 7K, you will need the following file:

e07K_Order_Form

You will save your workbook as:

Lastname_Firstname_7K_Order_Form

Open the file **e07K_Order_Form** and save it as **Lastname_Firstname_7K_Order_Form** Prepare the Product Information worksheet for a VLOOKUP function by sorting the items by Style Code, and then create a named range for the Style Code information. On the Order Form worksheet, using the named range, set data validation for the Item column. Insert the VLOOKUP function in column B and column E, referencing the appropriate data in the Product Information worksheet. Then enter the data below.

Item	Description	Quantity	Color
C-S		12	White
C-T		15	Natural
M-MC		25	Assorted
M-CF		50	Green

Delete the unused row. Construct formulas to total the order, and then apply appropriate financial formatting. On both sheets, include your file name in the footer, add appropriate properties, and then submit them as directed.

		Performance Level		
		Exemplary: You consistently applied the relevant skills	**Proficient: You sometimes, but not always, applied the relevant skills**	**Developing: You rarely or never applied the relevant skills**
Performance Criteria	**Use Lookup Functions**	The VLOOKUP function correctly looks up data on the validation list.	The VLOOKUP function looks up some but not all data on the validation list.	The VLOOKUP function does not look up any of the correct information.
	Validate Data	The Validation List is sorted correctly and used on the order form.	The Validation List was sorted, but not used on the order form.	The Validation List is not sorted and not used on the order form.
	Calculate and Format the Order Amount	The Order Amount and financial information is properly calculated and formatted	Some, but not all, of the Order Amount and financial information is properly calculated and formatted.	Incorrect formulas and/or incorrect financial formatting were applied in most of the cells.

You have completed Project 7K | END

Outcome-Based Assessments (Critical Thinking)

Rubric

The following outcomes-based assessments are open-ended assessments. That is, there is no specific correct result; your result will depend on your approach to the information provided. Make Professional Quality your goal. Use the following scoring rubric to guide you in how to approach the problem and then to evaluate how well your approach solves the problem.

The criteria—Software Mastery, Content, Format and Layout, and Process—represent the knowledge and skills you have gained that you can apply to solving the problem. The levels of performance—Professional Quality, Approaching Professional Quality, or Needs Quality Improvements—help you and your instructor evaluate your result.

	Your completed project is of Professional Quality if you:	Your completed project is Approaching Professional Quality if you:	Your completed project Needs Quality Improvements if you:
1-Software Mastery	Choose and apply the most appropriate skills, tools, and features and identify efficient methods to solve the problem.	Choose and apply some appropriate skills, tools, and features, but not in the most efficient manner.	Choose inappropriate skills, tools, or features, or are inefficient in solving the problem.
2-Content	Construct a solution that is clear and well organized, contains content that is accurate, appropriate to the audience and purpose, and is complete. Provide a solution that contains no errors of spelling, grammar, or style.	Construct a solution in which some components are unclear, poorly organized, inconsistent, or incomplete. Misjudge the needs of the audience. Have some errors in spelling, grammar, or style, but the errors do not detract from comprehension.	Construct a solution that is unclear, incomplete, or poorly organized, contains some inaccurate or inappropriate content, and contains many errors of spelling, grammar, or style. Do not solve the problem.
3-Format and Layout	Format and arrange all elements to communicate information and ideas, clarify function, illustrate relationships, and indicate relative importance.	Apply appropriate format and layout features to some elements, but not others. Overuse features, causing minor distraction.	Apply format and layout that does not communicate information or ideas clearly. Do not use format and layout features to clarify function, illustrate relationships, or indicate relative importance. Use available features excessively, causing distraction.
4-Process	Use an organized approach that integrates planning, development, self-assessment, revision, and reflection.	Demonstrate an organized approach in some areas, but not others; or, use an insufficient process of organization throughout.	Do not use an organized approach to solve the problem.

Outcomes-Based Assessments (Critical Thinking)

GO! Think	Project 7L Key Chains

Project Files

For Project 7L, you will need the following file:

e07L_Key_Chains

You will save your workbook as:

Lastname_Firstname_7L_Key_Chains

From your student files, open the file **e07L_Key_Chains**, and then save it in your chapter folder as **Lastname_Firstname_7L_Key_Chains** So that order takers do not have to type the Style Code, Description, and Unit Price in the Order Form worksheet, use the information on the Product Information sheet to create a validation list for the Item and then insert a VLOOKUP function in the Description and Unit Price columns. Then create an order for two of the Plush Animal Key Chains (K-S) and two of the Classic Key Chains (M-TF). Delete unused rows, create appropriate totals, apply financial formatting, and then save and submit it as directed.

	You have completed Project 7L	END

GO! Think	Project 7M Delivery Van Purchase	IRC

You and GO!	Project 7N Vehicle Loan	IRC

Using the Data Analysis, Solver, and Scenario Features, and Building Complex Formulas

8

EXCEL 2019

theskaman306/Shutterstock

In This Chapter

GO! To Work with Excel

Organizations forecast future results based on current trends. In this chapter, you will use Excel tools to analyze data, project values, determine the moving average of sales, project sales based on an expected growth rate, and determine a break-even point.

You will use the Solver and Scenario Manager tools to search for solutions to problems. Solver can analyze financial planning problems that involve a quantity that changes over time. By using a scenario, you can look at a set of values and project forward to focus on possible results. Finally, you will create complex formulas to determine which employees meet specific performance criteria.

The Projects in this chapter relate to **Brina's Bistro**, which is a chain of 25 casual, full-service restaurants based in Ft. Lauderdale, Florida. The Brina's Bistro owners plan an aggressive expansion program. To expand by 15 additional restaurants in Tennessee, Florida, Georgia, North Carolina, and South Carolina by 2025, the company must attract new investors, develop new menus, and recruit new employees, all while adhering to the company's quality guidelines and maintaining its reputation for excellent service. To succeed, the company plans to build on its past success and maintain its quality elements.

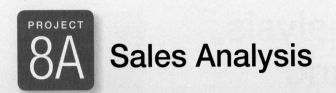
Project Activities

In Activities 8.01 through 8.06, you will use Excel's data analysis tools to determine the moving average of sales for the first six weeks at the new Brina's Bistro restaurant in Charlotte, North Carolina. Then you will project sales based on an expected growth rate and determine the break-even point for the restaurant. Your completed worksheets will look similar to Figure 8.1.

Project Files for MyLab IT Grader

1. In your storage location, create a folder named **Excel Chapter 8**.
2. In your **MyLab IT** course, locate and click **Excel 8A Charlotte Sales**, Download Materials, and then Download All Files.
3. Extract the zipped folder to your Excel Chapter 8 folder. Close the Grader download screens.
4. Take a moment to open the downloaded **Excel_8A_Charlotte_Sales_Instructions**; note any recent updates to the book.

Project Results

GO! Project 8A
Where We're Going

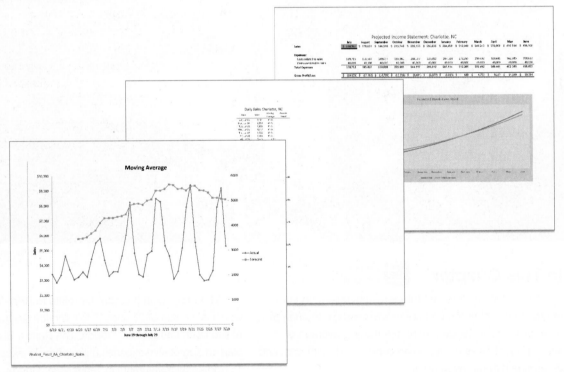

Figure 8.1 Project 8A Sales Analysis

For Non-MyLab Submissions

For Project 8A, you will need: In your storage location, create a folder named **Excel Chapter 8**
e08A_Charlotte_Sales   In your Excel Chapter 8 folder, save your workbook as:
                                        Lastname_Firstname_8A_Charlotte_Sales

After you have named and saved your workbook, on the next page, begin with Step 2.

ALERT   Because Office 365 is a cloud-based subscription service that receives continuous updates, you may encounter some variations in what appears on your screen and what is shown in this instruction. Microsoft Office 365 is fully installed on your PC or Mac; no internet access is necessary to create or edit documents. When you *are* connected to the internet, you will receive monthly upgrades and new features, so you always have the latest versions of Office apps as soon as they are available. Your subscription gives you continuous free access to the latest innovations and refinements.

GO! Learn How
Video E8-1

Start-up businesses usually operate at a loss while the business grows with an expectation that at some future point the business will become profitable. Owners and investors want to know if the business is on track to become profitable and when the point of profitability is likely to occur.

Excel offers Data Analysis tools, which range from basic to very sophisticated, to help you project future results based on past performance. One of the basic tools is a ***moving average***. A moving average is a sequence of averages computed from parts of a data series. In a chart, a moving average evens out the fluctuations in data, showing a pattern or trend more clearly. When you use a moving average, you choose how many preceding intervals to include in the average. A series of averages is calculated by moving—or changing—the range of cells used to calculate each average.

Activity 8.01 | Transposing Numbers and Creating a Custom Number Format

MOS

2.1.3, 2.2.6,
Expert 2.2.1

Kelsey Tanner, the Chief Financial Officer for the Brina's Bistro restaurant chain, wants to see how sales have grown in the first six weeks at the new restaurant in Charlotte, North Carolina. Because there is a wide variation in sales at restaurants between weekday and weekend sales, Kelsey first needs to add the day of the week to the Charlotte sales report. To accomplish this, you will customize the format applied to the date. You can customize numbers or dates when the available options do not match your needs.

1 Navigate to your **Excel Chapter 8 folder**, and then double-click the Excel file you downloaded from **MyLab IT** that displays your name—**Student_Excel_8A_Charlotte_Sales**. If necessary, at the top click **Enable Editing**.

2 Select the horizontal range **A3:AV4**. On the **Home tab**, in the **Clipboard group**, click **Copy**, which displays a moving border around the range. Click cell **A5**. In the **Clipboard group**, click the **Paste button arrow** 📋, and then under **Paste**, click **Transpose (T)** 📋. Compare your screen with Figure 8.2.

If data in a worksheet is arranged in rows but you want to work with columns instead, you can use this method to *transpose*, or switch, the rows and columns.

 ANOTHER WAY   Point to the selected range, right-click, and then use the Copy and Paste commands from the shortcut menu.

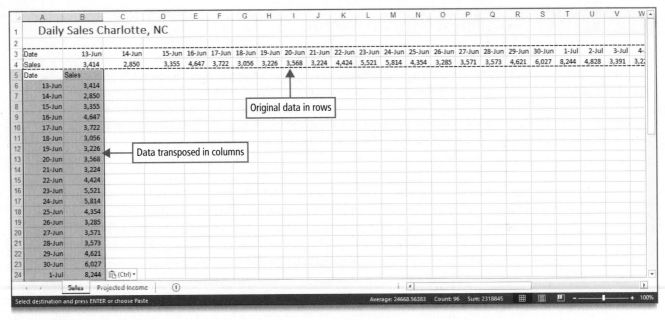

Figure 8.2

3 ▶ Delete **rows 2:4**. In cell **C2**, type **Moving Average** and press Tab. In cell **D2**, type **Growth Trend** Select the range **A2:D2**, apply the **Heading 3** cell style, and then in the **Alignment group**, click **Wrap Text**, **Center** ≡, and **Middle Align** ≡.

4 ▶ Click cell **A3**. On the **Home tab**, in the **Number group**, click the **Dialog Box Launcher** ⌐. In the **Format Cells** dialog box, be sure the **Number tab** is selected. Under **Category**, click **Custom**. Examine the table in Figure 8.3 to familiarize yourself with the codes you can use to create a custom date format.

In the displayed Format Cells dialog box, custom codes display under Type, and the code for the selected date in cell A3 displays in the Type box. You can use this format as a starting point and then modify it, or you can type a new code in the Type box.

▭ **MAC TIP**   Click the Number Format arrow, click More Number Formats.

Date Codes	
To Display	**Use This Code**
Months as 1–12	m
Months as 01–12	mm
Months as Jan–Dec	mmm
Months as January–December	mmmm
Months as the first letter of the month	mmmmm
Days as 1–31	d
Days as 01–31	dd
Days as Sun–Sat	ddd
Days as Sunday–Saturday	dddd
Years as 00–99	yy
Years as 1900–9999	yyyy

Figure 8.3

5 In the **Type** box, select the existing text and replace it by typing **ddd, mmm dd** Compare your screen with Figure 8.4.

As you type, you can see the date displayed in the new format in the Sample box. This code creates a date that displays as *Sun, Jun 13*. The comma displays as a comma.

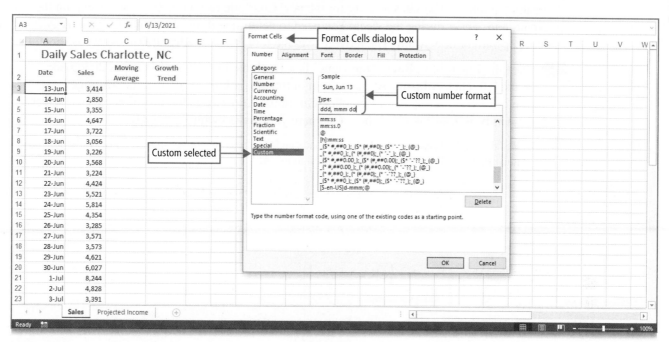

Figure 8.4

6 Click **OK** and notice the new date format in cell **A3**. Drag the fill handle to copy the new format down through cell **A49**.

7 Click cell **A50** and type **Total** Press Tab to move to cell **B50**, and then in the **Editing group**, click **AutoSum**. Verify the range to be summed is **B3:B49** and then on the **Formula Bar**, click **Enter** ✓.

8 From the **Cell Styles** gallery, apply the **Currency [0]** cell style to cell **B50**. Your total equals *$232,844*. Apply the **Total** cell style to the range **A50:B50**. Click cell **A1**, click **Save** 🖫, and then compare your screen with Figure 8.5.

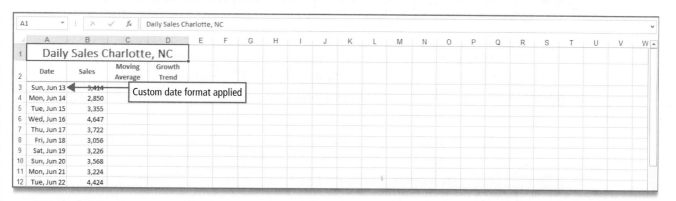

Figure 8.5

MORE KNOWLEDGE **The TRANSPOSE Function**

You can use the TRANSPOSE function to swap rows and columns. TRANSPOSE is an array function. The advantage to using the TRANSPOSE function is that a link is maintained between the original and transposed data.

Recall that a moving average calculates an average for a group of numbers over a specified interval. The number range that is averaged is constantly changing, dropping off the first number in the range and adding on the most recent number. In this manner, you can see a trend for widely fluctuating numbers. The sales activity for the new Charlotte restaurant has been strong on the weekends and slower during the week. You need to determine if, overall, the sales activity is trending upward or downward. The moving average tool is one of several Data Analysis tools.

1 Click the **File tab**. In **Backstage** view, click **Options**. In the **Excel Options** dialog box, on the left, click **Add-ins**. At the bottom of the dialog box, verify that the **Manage** box displays *Excel Add-ins*, and then click **Go**. In the **Add-Ins** dialog box, if necessary, select the **Analysis ToolPak** check box. Compare your screen with Figure 8.6.

Recall that *Add-ins* are optional commands and features that are not immediately available; you must first install and/or activate an add-in to use it.

MAC TIP   Display the menu bar, click Tools, click Excel Add-ins, select the Analysis ToolPak check box, click OK.

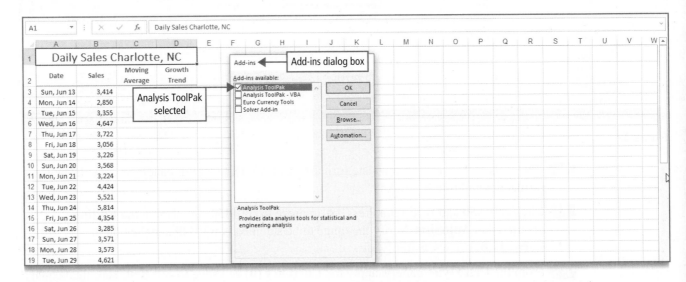

Figure 8.6

2 Click **OK**, and then click cell **A2** to make it the active cell. On the **Data tab**, in the **Analyze group**, click **Data Analysis**. Scroll the list as necessary, and then click **Moving Average**. Click **OK**.

The Moving Average dialog box displays. Here you define the input range, the *interval*—the number of cells to include in the average—and the output range.

3 With the insertion point blinking in the **Input Range** box, type **b2:b49** and then click the **Labels in First Row** check box.

The input range consists of the sales figures for the first six weeks, from Jun 13 through Jul 29. The first cell in the range, B2, contains the label *Sales*.

4 Click in the **Interval** box, and then type **7**

The moving average will be a weekly (7-day) average of sales. The first average will be from Sun, Jun 13 through Sat, Jun 19. The next average will be from Mon, Jun 14 through Sun, Jun 20. This pattern—dropping the oldest date and adding in the next date—will continue for the entire range.

5 ▶ Click in the **Output Range** box, type **c3** and then select the **Chart Output** check box. Compare your **Moving Average** dialog box with Figure 8.7.

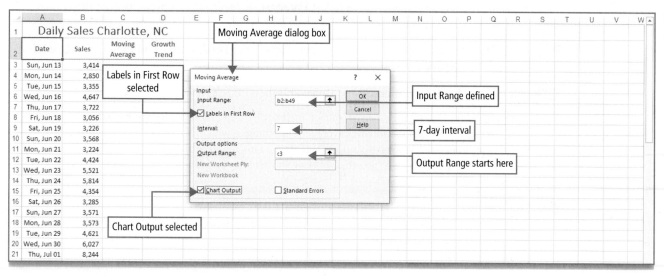

Figure 8.7

6 ▶ Click **OK**. **Save** 🖫 your workbook, and then compare your screen with Figure 8.8.

The moving averages display in column C and a chart is added to the worksheet. The first six cells in column C display the error code *#N/A* because there were not seven numbers available to use in the average. Green triangles display because the formulas in these cells refer to a range that has additional numbers adjacent. The first average—for Sun, Jun 13 through Sat, Jun 19—is *3,467*.

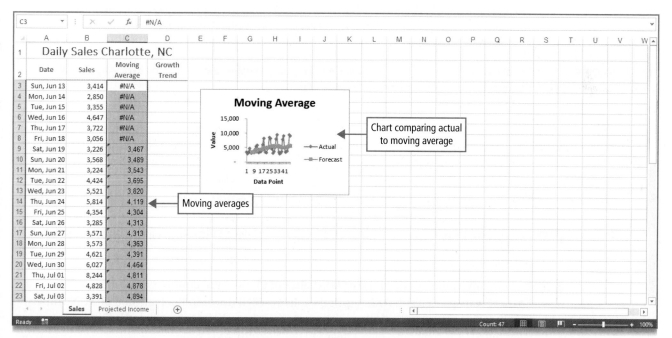

Figure 8.8

Activity 8.03 | Modifying the Moving Average Chart and Creating a Dual-Axis Chart

5.1.2, 5.2.1,
Expert 4.1.1

To gain a clearer image of a trend, you can modify the moving average chart. In the moving average chart, the moving average is labeled Forecast. A *forecast* is a prediction of the future, often based on past performances.

1 Click the outer edge of the chart to select it, click the **Design tab**, and then in the **Location group**, click **Move Chart**.

2 Click **New sheet**, type **Sales Trend Chart** and then click **OK**.

By displaying this chart on a separate chart sheet, you can more easily see the actual data points—in dark blue—versus the moving average—in orange—which is labeled *Forecast*. The horizontal category axis—the X-axis—is titled *Data Point*. This represents the dates for each sales figure. You can see by the orange line that, overall, the sales activity for the first six weeks is trending slightly upward.

3 At the bottom of the chart, point to any of the data points to display the ScreenTip *Horizontal (Category) Axis*, and then click to select the axis. On the **Design tab**, in the **Data group**, click **Select Data**.

In the Select Data Source dialog box, you can change the category axis labels to display the range of dates that correspond to the sales figures. You can also use this method to add or edit the data series used in a chart.

> **ANOTHER WAY** Right-click the axis, and then click Select Data.

4 In the **Select Data Source** dialog box, on the right under **Horizontal (Category) Axis Labels**, click **Edit**. Click the **Sales sheet tab** to display the *Sales* worksheet, and then select the range **A9:A49**. Compare your screen with Figure 8.9.

The selected range displays in the dialog box. You can select the range of cells to use as labels for the category axis. Start with cell A9 because that is the first row for which there is a moving average calculation.

> **MAC TIP** In the Select Data Source dialog box, click in the Horizontal (Category) axis labels box to display the Sales sheet where you can select the range A9:A49. Click OK.

37	Sat, Jul 17	3,348	5.419
38	Sun, Jul 18	2,954	5.404
39	Mon, Jul 19	3,018	5.323
40	Tue, Jul 20	3,631	5.107
41	Wed, Jul 21	7,896	5.105
42	Thu, Jul 22	9,174	5.077
43	Fri, Jul 23	5,266	5.041
44	Sat, Jul 24	3,408	5.050

Axis Labels ? × ← **Axis Labels dialog box**
Axis label range:
=Sales!$A$9:$A$49 ↑ = Sat, Jun 19, S...
OK Cancel

Axis label range defined

Figure 8.9

5 In the **Axis Labels** dialog box, click **OK**. In the **Select Data Source** dialog box, click **OK**.

Dates display along the category axis at the bottom of the chart.

6 Point to any value on the **Horizontal (Category) Axis** and double-click to display the **Format Axis** pane. With **Axis Options** active, scroll down in the pane and click **Number**. Scroll down and click the **Category arrow**, and then click **Date**. Click the **Type arrow**, click the **3/14** format, and then **Close** ☒ the **Format Axis** pane.

This action shortens the date format displayed on the axis.

> **ANOTHER WAY** Click anywhere on the axis one time to select it. On the Format tab, in the Current Selection group, click Format Selection to display the Format Axis pane

7 ▶ Click the **Horizontal (Category) Axis Title**—*Data Point*—one time to select it. Type **June 19 through July 29** (your typing displays on the Formula Bar) and then press Enter.

⌨ **MAC TIP**   Click in the Formula Bar before typing; or select the words *Data Point* and then type the new title.

---

8 ▶ Click the **Vertical (Value) Axis Title**—*Value*—one time to select it. Type **Sales** (your typing displays on the Formula Bar) and then press Enter.

9 ▶ Point to any value on the **Vertical (Value) Axis** and double-click to select the axis and display the **Format Axis** pane.

10 ▶ Scroll to the bottom of the **Format Axis** pane, if necessary expand **Number**. Scroll down and click the **Category arrow**, and then click **Currency**. If necessary, set **Decimal places** to **0**, and then **Close** ⊠ the **Format Axis** pane.

> This action changes the values to Currency with 0 decimal places.

11 ▶ On the chart, point anywhere on the orange **Series "Forecast" line** and double-click to display the **Format Data Series** pane. In the pane, if necessary, click the **Series Options** icon 📊. Under **Plot Series On**, click **Secondary Axis**. **Close** ⊠ the **Format Data Series** pane. Click outside of the chart to deselect it. **Save** your workbook, and then compare your chart with Figure 8.10.

> Plotting the Forecast series on the secondary axis makes the trend easier to visualize because the scale is adjusted to reflect the smaller differences in the Forecast series values. A *dual-axis chart* is useful when comparing data series that use different scales or different types of measurements.

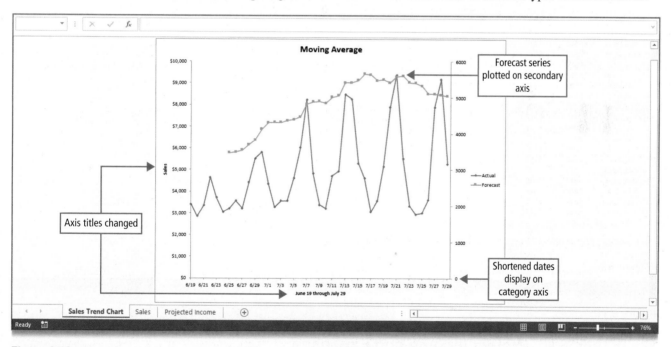

Figure 8.10

MORE KNOWLEDGE   **Using a Moving Average to Forecast Trends**

It is common to see moving averages presented to calculate stock or mutual fund performance, where fluctuations in value may be frequent, but the overall trend is what is important. You can also use moving averages as a tool to help predict how much inventory will be needed to meet demand. Although this is a forecasting tool, it is important to recognize its limitations. A moving average is based on historical data, and it is not necessarily a good prediction of what will occur in the future. Changes in the economy, competition, or other factors can affect sales dramatically, causing the moving average trend to change.

Activity 8.04 | Calculating Growth Based on a Moving Average

You can also use a moving average to calculate the growth rate at different intervals.

1 ▶ Display the **Sales** worksheet. Scroll to position **row 21** near the top of your screen. Click cell **D21**, type **=(c21-c14)/c14** and then on the **Formula Bar**, click **Enter** ✓.

This formula calculates a weekly sales growth percentage from one Thursday to the next, based on the moving average.

2 ▶ With cell **D21** active, on the **Home tab**, in the **Number group**, click **Percent Style** %. Click **Increase Decimal** one time to display one decimal place—your result is *16.8%*.

3 ▶ With cell **D21** still selected, in the **Clipboard group**, click **Copy**. Click cell **D28**, click the **Paste button arrow**, and then click **Paste (P)**.

This action copies the formula to the next date that is a Thursday.

↻ ANOTHER WAY Right-click cells and use the shortcut menus to copy and paste.

---

4 ▶ Click cell **D35**, and then paste the formula into the cell—recall that the copied cell remains on the Clipboard so you can continue to paste into additional cells. Continue in the same manner to paste the formula into cells **D42** and **D49**—the next two Thursday dates. Press Esc to cancel the moving border. Click **Save** 🖫, and then compare your screen with Figure 8.11.

The formula results show that the trend has moved up and down over five weeks of business operation.

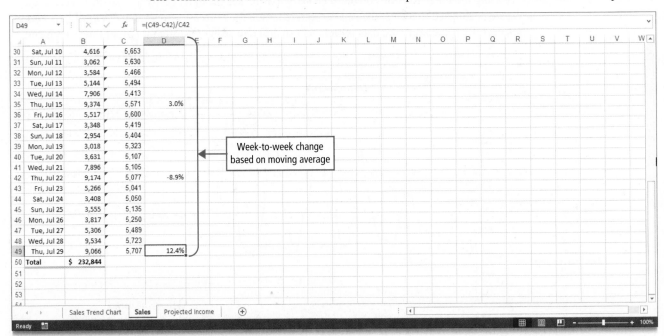

Figure 8.11

Objective 2 | Project Income and Expenses

GO! Learn How
Video E8-2

Income generally consists of money received from the sales of products and services. In a restaurant, this includes the sale of food and beverages. Expenses can be classified according to two broad categories: fixed expenses and variable expenses. *Fixed expenses* remain the same each month regardless of the amount of activity. They include items such as rent, utilities, insurance, and general overhead. *Variable expenses* change depending on the amount of sales. In a restaurant, the cost of the food—otherwise known as cost of goods sold—and wages are the two most common variable expenses. In this Activity, you will work with a worksheet that uses these two broad categories of expenses.

Activity 8.05 | Projecting Income and Expenses

1 On the **Sales** worksheet, click cell **A51**, type **July Sales** Press ⇥, and then in cell **B51**, type **=sum(b21:b49)** and then press Enter. Display the **Projected Income** worksheet. Click cell **B3**. Type **=** click the **Sales sheet tab**, click cell **B51**, which represents the July sales total, on the **Formula Bar**, click **Enter** ✓, and then compare your screen with Figure 8.12.

This sheet contains the first portion of an income statement for the Charlotte restaurant. Now that you have referenced the July total from the Sales worksheet, you will use that value to project sales and expenses through June of next year.

Figure 8.12

2 Click cell **B2**, and then use the fill handle to fill the months for a year—from July to June—across to **column M**. With the range **B2:M2** selected, apply **Center** ▤.

3 Click cell **C3**, type **=b3*(1+b12)** and then on the **Formula Bar**, click **Enter** ✓. From the **Cell Styles** gallery, apply the **Currency [0]** cell style.

This formula takes the previous month's sales in cell B3 and multiplies it by 110% to determine a growth rate of 10 percent (in cell B12) over the previous month—*$176,651*. Cell B12 indicates the Required Sales Growth rate of 10%, and the absolute cell reference is used so this formula can be copied across the row.

4 With cell **C3** as the active cell, use the fill handle to copy the formula and the formatting across to **column M**. Compare your screen with Figure 8.13.

Based on this projection, by June of next year, the Charlotte restaurant should have *$458,188* in monthly sales.

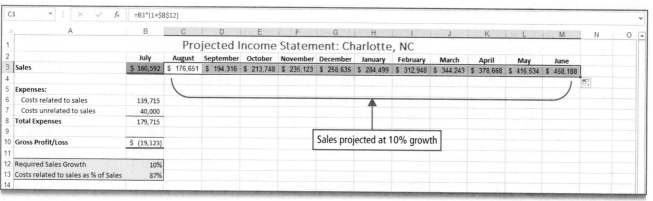

Figure 8.13

5 Click cell **B6** and examine the formula.

This formula multiplies the sales for July by the value in cell B13—*87%*. It is estimated that variable expenses for the first year will be 87 percent of sales. So that you can copy this formula across the worksheet, it is formatted as an absolute reference.

6 Use the fill handle to copy the formula from cell **B6** across the row to **column M**.

The variable expenses, which are based on sales, are projected for the next year. Variable expenses for June are calculated to be *398,623*.

7 Click cell **B7**. Use the fill handle to copy the value from cell **B7** across the row to **column M**.

These are fixed costs—costs such as rent and insurance that are not directly tied to sales—which total 40,000.

8 Select the range **C8:M8**, and then on the **Home tab**, in the **Editing group**, click **AutoSum**.

This action calculates the total expenses for each month.

9 Click cell **B10**.

This formula calculates the gross profit or loss for a month—sales minus expenses.

10 Use the fill handle to copy the formula from cell **B10** across to **column M**. Compare your screen with Figure 8.14.

	B10		✕ ✓ *fx*	=B3-B8										
	A	B	C	D	E	F	G	H	I	J	K	L	M	N	O
1				Projected Income Statement: Charlotte, NC										
2		July	August	September	October	November	December	January	February	March	April	May	June	
3	Sales	$ 160,592	$ 176,651	$ 194,316	$ 213,748	$ 235,123	$ 258,635	$ 284,499	$ 312,948	$ 344,243	$ 378,668	$ 416,534	$ 458,188	
4														
5	Expenses:													
6	Costs related to sales	139,715	153,687	169,055	185,961	204,557	225,012	247,514	272,265	299,492	329,441	362,385	398,623	
7	Costs unrelated to sales	40,000	40,000	40,000	40,000	40,000	40,000	40,000	40,000	40,000	40,000	40,000	40,000	
8	Total Expenses	179,715	193,687	209,055	225,961	244,557	265,012	287,514	312,265	339,492	369,441	402,385	438,623	
9														
10	Gross Profit/Loss	$ (19,123)	$ (17,035)	$ (14,739)	$ (12,213)	$ (9,434)	$ (6,377)	$ (3,015)	$ 683	$ 4,752	$ 9,227	$ 14,149	$ 19,564	
11														
12	Required Sales Growth	10%												
13	Costs related to sales as % of Sales	87%												
14														
15														

Profit or loss

Break-even point

Figure 8.14

Objective 3   Determine a Break-Even Point

GO! Learn How
Video E8-3

The goal of a business is to make a profit. However, a new business often operates at a loss for a period of time before becoming profitable. The point at which a company starts to make a profit is known as the ***break-even point***. A break-even point can be calculated for a product, a branch office, a division, or an entire company. The Brina's Bistro restaurants use a model for new restaurants that projects 10 percent growth, month-to-month, in the first year, with the expectation that sometime during the first year the restaurant will start to make a profit. Ms. Tanner wants to estimate when the new Charlotte restaurant will become profitable, based on sales for its first full month of business.

Activity 8.06 | Charting the Break-Even Point With a Line Chart

5.1.1, 5.3.1

You can chart the results of the estimated income statement to create a visual image of the income and expenses and the projected break-even point.

Recall that a line chart displays trends over time. Time is displayed along the bottom axis and the data point values are connected with a line. If you want to compare more than one set of values, each group is connected by a different line. The curves and directions of the lines make trends noticeable to the reader.

1 Be sure that **columns A:M** display on your screen—if necessary, in the lower right corner of your screen, set the Zoom to 80% to that you can see the entire range.

2 Select the range **A2:M3**. On the **Insert tab**, in the **Charts group**, click **Recommended Charts**. In the **Insert Chart** dialog box, with the **Line chart** selected, click **OK**.

By including the months in row 2 and the labels in column A in the selection, the chart will be properly labeled.

3 On the **Design tab**, in the **Data group**, click **Select Data**. In the **Select Data Source** dialog box, under **Legend Entries (Series)**, click **Add**. With the Insertion point in the **Series name** box, click cell **A8**. Press Tab, select the range **B8:M8** and then click **OK**. Compare your screen with Figure 8.15.

By selecting the income totals and the expense totals, you will be able to see where they cross on a graph when you chart the break-even point. The Chart data range box displays the selected range—including the sheet name—using absolute references.

MAC TIP Click + to Add a series, then click Series 2 to make it active. Click in the Series name box.

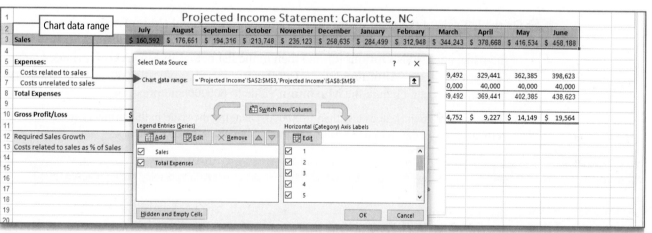

Figure 8.15

4 Click **OK**. On the **Design tab**, in the **Chart Layouts group**, click **Quick Layout**, and then click **Layout 3**. In the chart, click the text *Chart Title*, and then watch the **Formula Bar** as you type **Expected Break-Even Point** Press Enter.

5 By using the ⬚ pointer, drag to position the upper left corner of the chart inside the upper left corner of cell **B15**.

6 Scroll to position **row 13** at the top of your screen. Drag the lower right sizing handle of the chart inside the lower right corner of cell **M36**. Compare your chart with Figure 8.16.

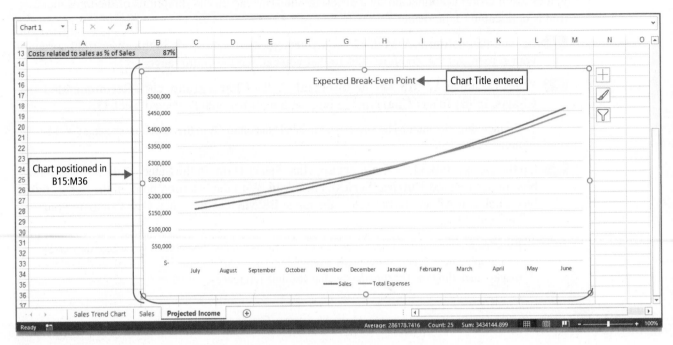

Figure 8.16

7 On the left side of the chart, point to any value on the **Vertical (Value) Axis** and double-click to select the axis and display the **Format Axis** pane. If necessary, at the top of the pane, click **Axis Options** and then in the list below, expand **Axis Options**. Under **Axis Options**, in the **Minimum** box, select the existing text, type **100000** and then press Enter. In the same manner, change the **Maximum** value to **500000** and press Enter.

Because there are no values less than $100,000, changing the scale in this manner provides more vertical space on the chart and results in a more dramatic slope on the line.

ANOTHER WAY Right-click a value, and then on the shortcut menu, click Format Axis to display the Format Axis pane.

---

8 At the top of the **Format Axis** pane, click the **Axis Options arrow**, and then click **Chart Area** to display the **Format Chart Area** pane. Click **Fill & Line**. If necessary, expand **Fill**, and then click **Solid fill**. Click the **Color arrow**, and then under **Theme Colors**, in the third column, click the second color.

MAC TIP On the Format tab, in the Current Selection group, click the Chart Elements arrow and select Chart Area. On the right of the ribbon, click Format Pane.

---

9 At the top of the **Format Chart Area** pane, click the **Chart Options arrow**, and then click **Plot Area**. Format the **Plot Area** with a **Solid fill**—in the fourth column, click the second color. **Close** ⊠ the **Format Plot Area** pane. Compare your screen with Figure 8.17.

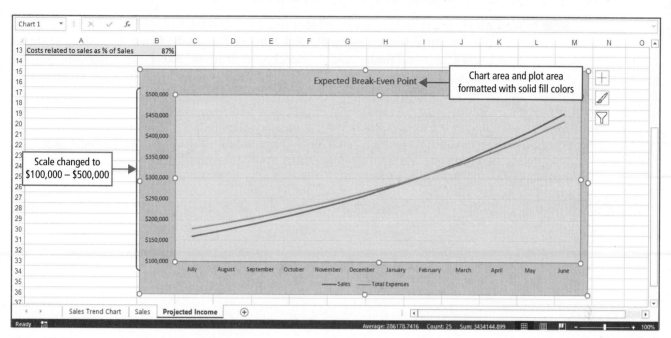

Figure 8.17

10 Click cell **A1** to deselect the chart and make cell **A1** the active cell. Display the **Sales Trend Chart** worksheet. On the **Page Layout tab**, in the **Page Setup group**, click the **Dialog Box Launcher** button 🔲 to display the **Page Setup** dialog box. Insert a **Custom Footer** with the file name in the **left section**.

11 Display the **Projected Income** worksheet. If necessary, set the **Zoom** ➕ back to **100%**. Right-click the **sheet tab**, and then click **Select All Sheets** so that *Group* displays in the title bar. Insert a footer in the **left section** that includes the file name and center the worksheets horizontally on the page.

12 With all the sheets still selected, on the **Page Layout tab**, set the **Orientation** to **Landscape**, and then in the **Scale to Fit group**, set the **Width** to **1 page** and the **Height** to **1 page**. Be sure that cell **A1** is still the active cell.

13 Display the **document properties** and under **Related People**, be sure that your name displays as the author. If necessary, right-click the author name, click **Edit Property**, and then type your name. In the **Subject** box, type your course name and section number, and in the **Tags** box, type moving average, break-even point Display the grouped worksheets in **Print Preview**.

14 Under **Settings**, click the **Print Active Sheets arrow**, and then click **Print Entire Workbook**. At the bottom of the window, click **Next Page** ▶ to scroll through the worksheets.

15 On the left, click **Save**. Click the **Sales Trend Chart** worksheet to ungroup the sheets.

🖥 **MAC TIP**   Click Cancel in the Print dialog box; click Save.

---

16 In the upper right corner of the Excel window, click **Close** ⊠.

17 In **MyLab IT**, locate and click the Grader Project **Excel 8A Charlotte Sales**. In **step 3**, under **Upload Completed Assignment**, click **Choose File**. In the **Open** dialog box, navigate to your **Excel Chapter 8 folder**, and then click your **Student_Excel_8A_Charlotte_Sales** file one time to select it. In the lower right corner of the **Open** dialog box, click **Open**.

The name of your selected file displays above the Upload button.

18 To submit your file to **MyLab IT** for grading, click **Upload**, wait a moment for a green **Success!** message, and then in **step 4**, click the blue **Submit for Grading** button. Click **Close Assignment** to return to your list of **Course Materials**.

You have completed Project 8A   **END**

Project Activities

In Activities 8.07 through 8.19, you will assist Jillian Zachary, manager of the Ft. Lauderdale restaurant, in determining the most efficient work schedule for the server staff. You will also evaluate sales to determine which servers are eligible for Employee of the Week status. Your completed worksheets will look similar to Figure 8.18.

Project Files for MyLab IT Grader

1. In your **MyLab IT** course, locate and click **Excel 8B Staffing Analysis**, Download Materials, and then Download All Files.
2. Extract the zipped folder to your Excel Chapter 8 folder. Close the Grader download screens.
3. Take a moment to open the downloaded **Excel_8B_Staffing_Analysis_Instructions**; note any recent updates to the book.

Project Results

GO! Project 8B

Where We're Going

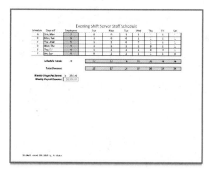
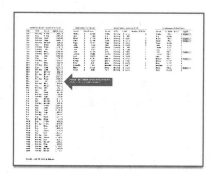

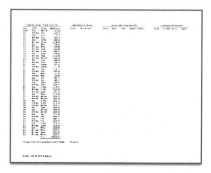
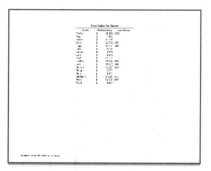

Figure 8.18 Project 8B Staffing Analysis

Objective 4 | Use Solver

GO! Learn How
Video E8-4

Solver is an Excel what-if analysis tool with which you can find an optimal (maximum or minimum) value for a formula in one cell subject to constraints, or limits, on the values of other formula cells on a worksheet.

Use Solver when you need to make a decision that involves more than one variable. For example, the manager of the Ft. Lauderdale restaurant needs to determine the number of servers to assign to each evening shift so there are enough servers to handle customer demand, but not too many servers for the work required. Additionally, the schedule must allow each server to have two or more consecutive days off. Solver can help determine values like these—values that result in minimums, maximums, or specific results.

When you use Solver, the focus is on the *objective cell*—the cell that contains a formula for the results you are trying to determine, such as minimum weekly payroll expense. Your worksheet will have *decision variables*—also referred to as *variable cells*—that are cells in which the values will change to achieve the desired results. Your worksheet will also have *constraint cells*—cells that contain values that limit or restrict the outcome. As an example of a constraint, in determining a work schedule, you cannot schedule more than the total number of employees on the payroll.

Activity 8.07 | Installing Solver

Recall that add-ins are optional commands and features that are not immediately available; you must first install and/or activate an add-in to use it. Solver is an add-in.

1 Navigate to your **Excel Chapter 8 folder**, and then double-click the Excel file you downloaded from **MyLab IT** that displays your name—**Student_Excel_8B_Staffing_Analysis**. If necessary, at the top click **Enable Editing**.

2 Click the **Data tab**, and then at the right end of the **Data tab**, in the **Analyze group**, check to see if **Solver** displays. Compare your screen with Figure 8.19.

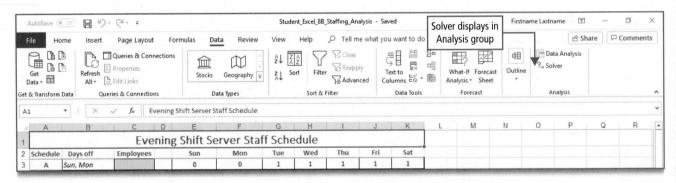

Figure 8.19

3 If **Solver** displays, Solver has been installed on your computer and you can move to Activity 8.08. If Solver does *not* display, complete the remaining steps in this Activity to install it.

4 From **Backstage** view, display **Options**. On the left, click **Add-ins**, and then at the bottom of the screen, in the **Manage** box, if necessary, select **Excel Add-ins**. Compare your screen with Figure 8.20.

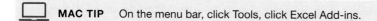 **MAC TIP**   On the menu bar, click Tools, click Excel Add-ins.

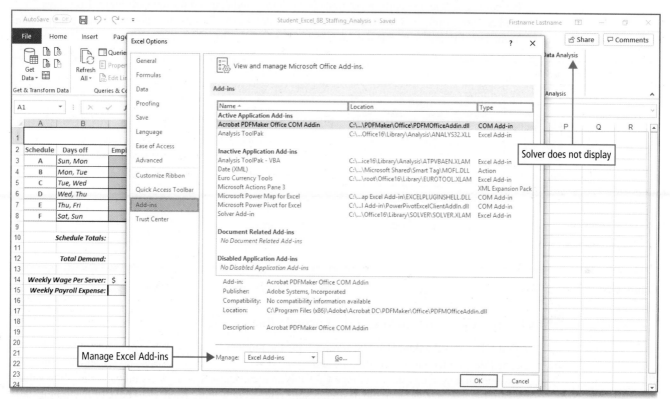

Figure 8.20

5 Click **Go**.

The Add-Ins dialog box displays.

6 In the **Add-ins** dialog box, select the **Solver Add-in** check box, and then click **OK**.

The Solver Add-in is installed. On the Data tab, in the Analyze group, Solver displays.

Activity 8.08 | Understanding a Solver Worksheet

The manager of the Ft. Lauderdale restaurant wants to minimize the weekly payroll expense by scheduling only enough servers to handle established customer activity. She has reviewed customer activity for the past three months and determined how many servers are needed for the evening schedule on each day of the week. For example, more servers are needed on Friday and Saturday evenings than on Tuesday and Wednesday evenings. You will use Solver to determine the number of servers to schedule for each evening shift to meet the demand while minimizing the payroll expense. Before you can solve the problem of minimizing payroll expenses, familiarize yourself with the components of the worksheet.

1 > On the **Evening Shift** worksheet, click in cell **E4**, type **1** and press `Enter` to complete the information for **Schedule B**. Examine the range **A2:K8**, and then compare your screen with Figure 8.21.

Six possible schedules are labeled—A through F. Column B lists the consecutive days off for each schedule. For example, servers who work Schedule C have Tuesday and Wednesday off. Servers who work Schedule D have Wednesday and Thursday off.

For each schedule, the cells in columns E through K indicate a 0 for days off and a 1 for days worked. For example, Schedule C indicates 0 under Tue and Wed—the days off—and 1 under Sun, Mon, Thu, Fri, and Sat—the days worked.

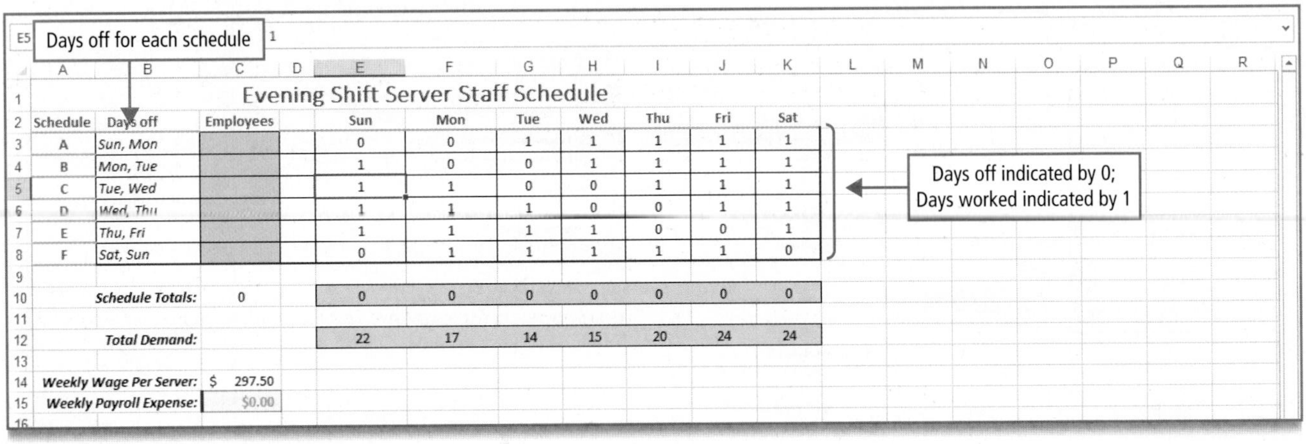

Figure 8.21

2 > Click cell **C10**, and then look at the **Formula Bar**.

Cell C10 sums the range C3:C8. It represents the number of servers who are assigned to each schedule—Schedule A, Schedule B, and so on. It is currently zero because no servers have been assigned to any schedule. The range C3:C8 is shaded. These are the decision variables—the values that will change to achieve the desired results. Here, the desired result is to have only enough staff assigned to meet customer demand and therefore minimize payroll expense.

3 > Click cell **C14** and examine the formula.

This formula calculates the weekly wage, based on $8.50 per hour, multiplied by seven hours worked each day, multiplied by five days worked per week. The proposed schedule shows all servers working five days each week.

4 > Click cell **C15**, which is formatted using the Calculation cell style, and examine the formula.

The formula in this cell calculates the total weekly payroll expense by multiplying the number of servers scheduled to work—cell C10—by the Weekly Wage Per Server—cell C14. Cell C15 is the objective cell. Recall that the objective cell contains the result that you are trying to achieve. In this instance, you are trying to achieve the minimum payroll expense that must be paid while maintaining enough servers on duty to meet established customer demand.

5 > Select the range **E12:K12**.

These cells represent the minimum number of servers required to serve the number of customers expected each day of the week. The cells in this row will be one of the constraints used to determine the minimum weekly payroll expense. Recall that *constraints* are conditions or restrictions that must be met. Here the number of servers scheduled must be equal to or greater than the number required for each day.

6 > Click cell **E10**.

The formulas in this row multiply the number of servers assigned to work each schedule, arriving at a total number available each day of the week.

7 ▸ Click cell **C3**, and then click the **Name Box arrow**. Notice that cell **C3** has been named *Sun_Mon*. Compare your screen with Figure 8.22 and take a moment to review each of the cells you will work with in this project.

The cells in the range C3:C8, the decision variables, have been named with their corresponding days off. For example, if an employee is assigned the B Schedule, he or she will have Mondays and Tuesdays off.

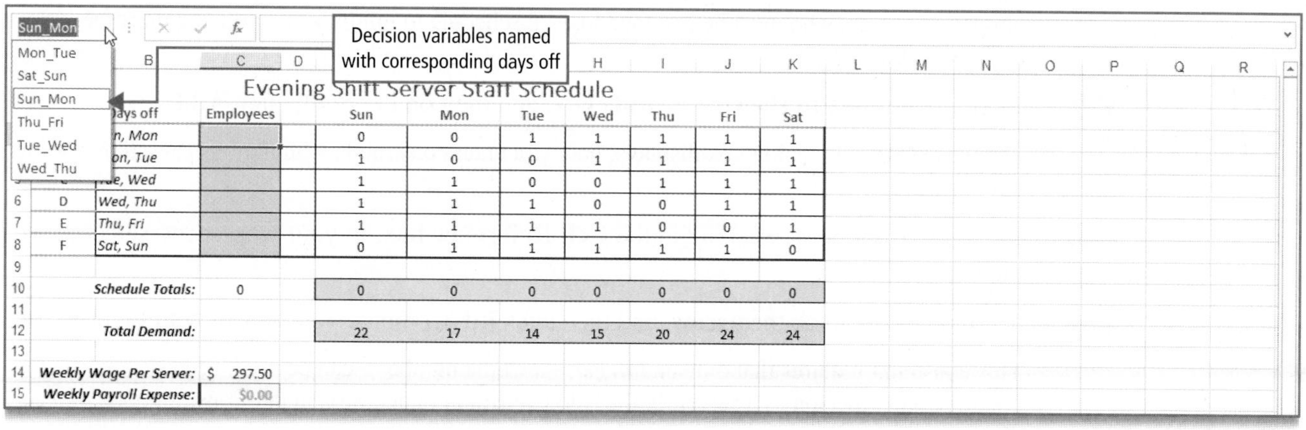

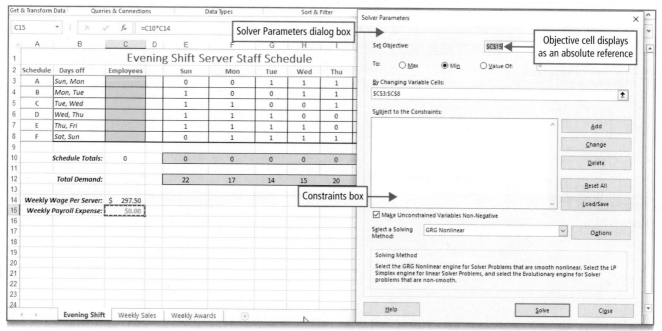

Figure 8.22

Activity 8.09 | Using Solver

In this Activity, you will use Solver to determine the minimum payroll expense, that is, the minimum number of servers who can be on duty and still meet expected customer demand. This process involves identifying the objective cell, the decision variable cells, and the constraint cells.

1 ▸ Click cell **C15**—the objective cell. On the **Data tab**, in the **Analyze group**, click **Solver**. If necessary, drag the **Solver Parameters** dialog box to the right side of your worksheet. In the **Set Objective** box, be sure that *$C$15* displays. Compare your screen with Figure 8.23.

The Solver Parameters dialog box displays and cell C15 displays as an absolute reference in the Set Objective box.

Figure 8.23

2 In the **Solver Parameters** dialog box, under **Set Objective**, if necessary, click the **Min** option button.

The three option buttons here enable you to use the Solver tool to maximize, minimize, or solve for a specific value.

3 Click in the **By Changing Variable Cells** box, and then in your worksheet, select the range **C3:C8**.

The range displays as an absolute reference. In this cell range, Solver will place the optimum number of servers who must be assigned to each schedule to minimize payroll and meet the constraints that are set.

4 Click in the **Subject to the Constraints** box, and then on the right, click **Add**.

The Add Constraint dialog box displays; here you enter constraints—limitations caused by various circumstances.

5 With the insertion point blinking in the **Cell Reference** box, in your worksheet, select the shaded range **C3:C8**.

6 In the middle box, click the **arrow**, and then click **Int**. Compare your screen with Figure 8.24.

This constraint requires that only an *integer*—a whole number—can be used, because you cannot assign part of a person as a server. In the Add Constraint dialog box, in the Constraint box, *integer* displays.

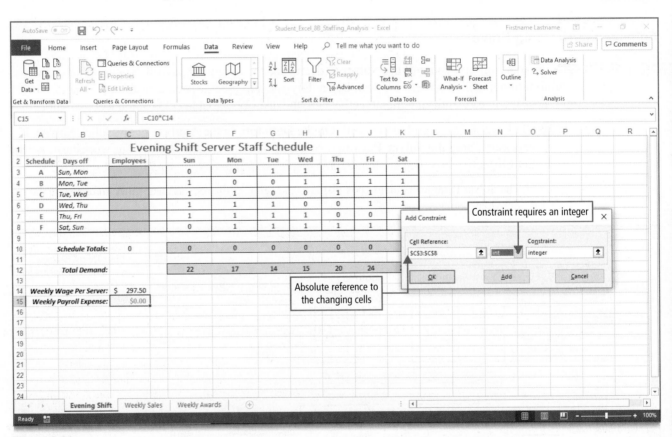

Figure 8.24

7 Click **OK**.

The Add Constraint dialog box closes and the first constraint is added to the Solver Parameters dialog box.

8 Click **Add** again. With the insertion point in the **Cell Reference** box, in your worksheet, select the shaded range **C3:C8**. In the middle box, click the **arrow**, and then click **>=**. In the **Constraint** box, type **0** (zero) and then compare your dialog box with Figure 8.25.

This constraint (limitation) requires that the number of servers assigned to each schedule be a positive number—a negative number of servers cannot be assigned. The number must be equal to or greater than zero.

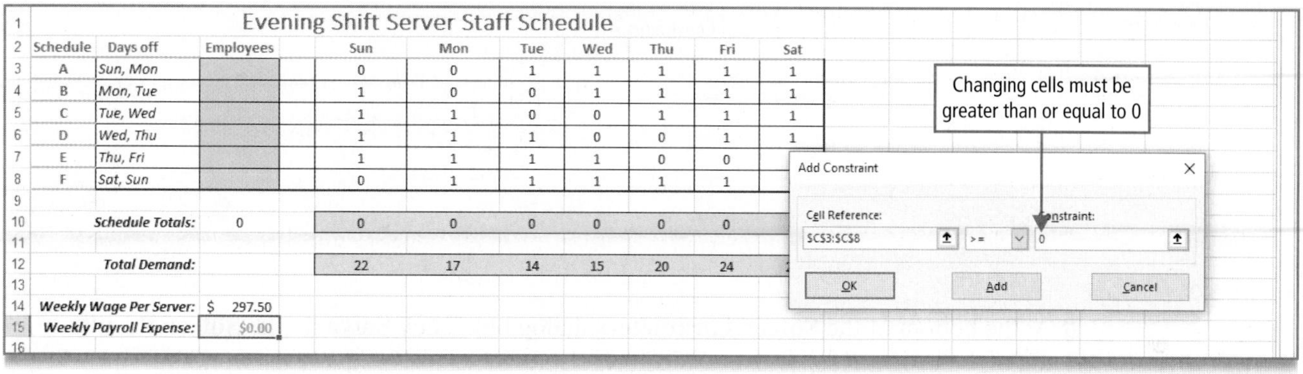

Figure 8.25

9 Click **OK**.

The second constraint is added to the Solver Parameters dialog box.

10 Click **Add**. With the insertion point blinking in the **Cell Reference** box, in your worksheet, select the range **E10:K10**. In the middle box, click the **arrow**, and then click **>=**. With the insertion point blinking in the **Constraint** box, in your worksheet, select the range **E12:K12**.

This constraint requires that the number of servers assigned to each shift be greater than or equal to the number of servers required each day to meet the projected demand. For example, on Saturday, the number of servers assigned must be at least 24.

11 Click **OK**. Compare your **Solver Parameters** dialog box with Figure 8.26.

Three constraints display in the Solver Parameters dialog box. First, the number of servers assigned to any given Schedule—C3:C8—must be a whole number. Second, the number of servers—C3:C8—assigned to any given Schedule must be a positive number equal to or greater than zero. Third, the number of servers—E10:K10—assigned to each day's shift must be equal to or greater than the number of servers needed to meet the established demand in cells E12:K12. With the constraints established, you can solve for—calculate—the minimum payroll expense.

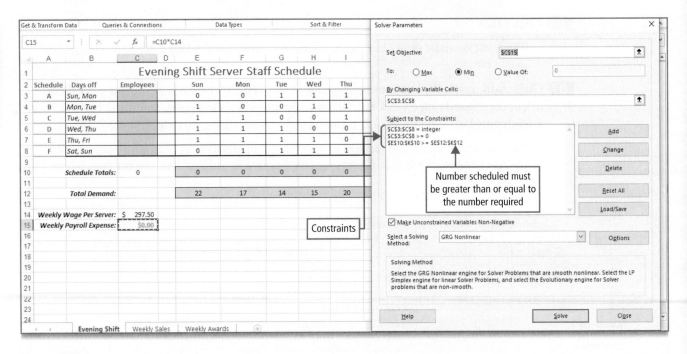

Figure 8.26

> **12** At the bottom of the **Solver Parameters** dialog box, click **Solve**. In the **Solver Results** dialog box, with **Keep Solver Solution** selected, click **OK**. **Save** your workbook, and then compare your screen with Figure 8.27.

The decision variables—the shaded cell range C3:C8—displays the number of servers who should be assigned to each Schedule to meet the demand while minimizing payroll. Cell C15—the objective cell—shows the Weekly Payroll Expense as *$8,330.00*, and the number of servers who will work each schedule displays in cells E10:K10. Thus, to adequately staff the evening shifts and to give servers two consecutive days off requires a total of 28 servers each working 5 days a week and 7 hours each day—cell C10. The minimum payroll expense for 28 servers is $8,330.00—28 servers times $297.50.

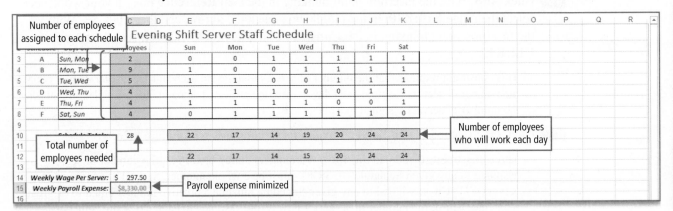

Figure 8.27

> **13** This is one possible solution. Later, you will consider alternatives with a different distribution of staff over the week.

MORE KNOWLEDGE | **Solver Reports**

The Solver Results dialog box offers three reports—Answer, Sensitivity, and Limits—that you can create to help you understand the results. The Answer Report displays the original and final values for the objective cell and the decision variables. It also shows the impact of the constraints on determining values for the decision variables and whether the result for each cell is binding or nonbinding. It helps you understand where there may be some flexibility in the results if you want to do further analysis or consider other alternatives. The Sensitivity and Limits reports are not meaningful in the current example because of the integer constraints that have been applied.

Objective 5 Create Scenarios

GO! Learn How
Video E8-5

The current solution indicates nine servers assigned to *Schedule B, Mon and Tue off*, and only two servers assigned to *Schedule A, Sun and Mon off*. Ms. Zachary wants to see what would happen if she assigned more servers to Schedule A. You can create several possible solutions to a problem and then use Excel's ***Scenario Manager*** What-If Analysis tool to compare the alternatives. A ***scenario*** is a set of values that Excel saves and can substitute automatically in your worksheet.

Activity 8.10 | Creating a Scenario Using the Scenario Manager

Expert 3.4.2

You can create a scenario from the Solver dialog box, or you can open the Scenario Manager dialog box and create a scenario. Here, you will use the Scenario Manager dialog box to save the existing solution for minimizing the weekly server staff payroll.

1 Select the green-shaded range **C3:C8**.

These are the decision variable cells defined in Solver that are used to calculate the minimum payroll expense while matching the staffing requirements that are shown in row 12.

2 On the **Data tab**, in the **Forecast group**, click **What-If Analysis**, and then click **Scenario Manager**. Compare your screen with Figure 8.28.

The Scenario Manager dialog box displays. It shows that no scenarios have been defined.

2	Schedule	Days off	Employees		Sun	Mon	Tue	Wed	Thu	Fri	Sat
3	A	Sun, Mon	2		0	0	1	1	1	1	1
4	B	Mon, Tue	9		1	0	0	1	1	1	1
5	C	Tue, Wed	5		1	1	0	0	1	1	1
6	D	Wed, Thu	4		1	1	1	0	0	1	1
7	E	Thu, Fri	4		1	1	1	1	0	0	1
8	F	Sat, Sun	4		0	1	1	1	1	1	0
9											
10		Schedule Totals:	28		22	17	14	19			
11											
12		Total Demand:			22	17	14	15	20	24	24
13											
14		Weekly Wage Per Server:	$ 297.50								
15		Weekly Payroll Expense:	$8,330.00								

Figure 8.28

3 In the **Scenario Manager** dialog box, click **Add**.

The Add Scenario dialog box displays. Here you name the scenario and identify the decision variable cells.

MAC TIP Click +.

4 In the **Scenario name** box, type **Option 1** Verify that the **Changing cells** box displays *C3:C8*.

You will save the existing solution as your first scenario.

The Scenario Values dialog box displays and the current value in each of the decision variable cells is listed. You will accept the values that are displayed.

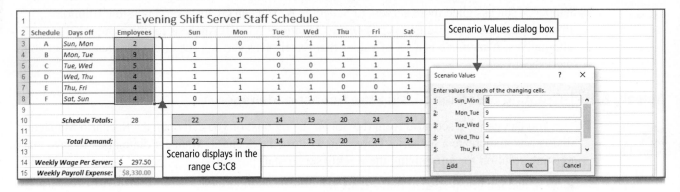

Figure 8.29

6 In the **Scenario Values** dialog box, click **OK**.

The Scenario Manager dialog box redisplays, and the first scenario is listed in the Scenarios box as *Option 1*.

7 In the **Scenario Manager** dialog box, click **Close**. **Save** 🖫 your workbook.

Activity 8.11 | Creating a Scenario Using Solver

3.4.2

You can also create a scenario using the Solver Parameters dialog box. Ms. Zachary wants to add another schedule option that would assign more servers to Schedule A so more people could be off on Sunday, a more traditional day off, and to help balance the numbers of shifts among employees.

1 Click cell **C15**—the objective cell. On the **Data tab**, in the **Analyze group**, click **Solver**. In the **Solver Parameters** dialog box, verify that the **Set Objective** box displays *$C$15* and the **By Changing Variable Cells** box displays *$C$3:$C$8*.

The values from the first solution display in the Solver Parameters dialog box.

2 To the right of the **Subject to the Constraints** box, click **Add**.

3 In the **Add Constraint** dialog box, click in the **Cell Reference** box, and then click cell **C3**. In the middle box, click the **arrow**, and then click **=**. In the **Constraint** box, type **4**

This constraint will assign four servers to *Schedule A—Sun and Mon off*.

4 Click **OK**.

A fourth constraint is added to the Solver Parameters dialog box. Recall that because each of the cells in the range C3:C8 were named, the constraint displays as *Sun_Mon = 4*. The range name displays when you summarize the alternatives you are creating.

5 In the lower right corner of the dialog box, click **Solve**. Drag the **Solver Results** dialog box to the right side of the screen and compare your screen with Figure 8.30.

A new solution is found and the Solver Results dialog box displays. The Weekly Payroll Expense remains at $8,330.00, but the servers are more evenly distributed across the schedules, with more servers scheduled on Friday and Saturday when the restaurant is the busiest. This provides a better distribution of staff on the busiest weekend days, while giving more people Sunday off. This shows that there may be more than one acceptable solution to the problem of minimizing the payroll.

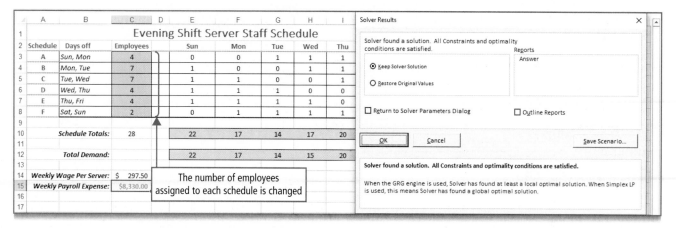

Figure 8.30

6 Click **Save Scenario** to display the **Save Scenario** dialog box.

7 In the **Scenario Name** box, type **Option 2** and then click **OK**.

A second scenario is saved and the Solver Results dialog box displays.

8 In the **Solver Results** dialog box, click **Restore Original Values**, and then click **OK**. Save 🖫 your workbook.

The dialog box closes and the previous solution redisplays on the worksheet.

Activity 8.12 | Creating a Scenario Summary

Ms. Zachary wants to see what would happen if she schedules six servers to have Saturday off. Schedule F includes both Saturday and Sunday off, which would give more employees a traditional weekend off. After the third scenario is created, you will view a summary of the results of all three alternatives.

1 Verify that cell **C15** is still the active cell. On the **Data tab**, in the **Analyze group**, click **Solver**.

In the Solver Parameters dialog box, all four constraints (from Option 2) display, even though the currently displayed solution—Option 1—does not use the constraint that requires four servers be assigned to schedule A—*Sun_Mon = 4*.

2 In the **Subject to the Constraints** box, select the fourth constraint—**Sun_Mon = 4**—and then on the right side of the dialog box, click **Delete**.

3 Click **Add**.

4 In the **Add Constraint** dialog box, click in the **Cell Reference** box, and then click cell **C8**. Change the middle box to **=**. In the **Constraint** box, type **6** and then click **OK**. Compare your screen with Figure 8.31.

Four constraints are listed in the Solver Parameters dialog box.

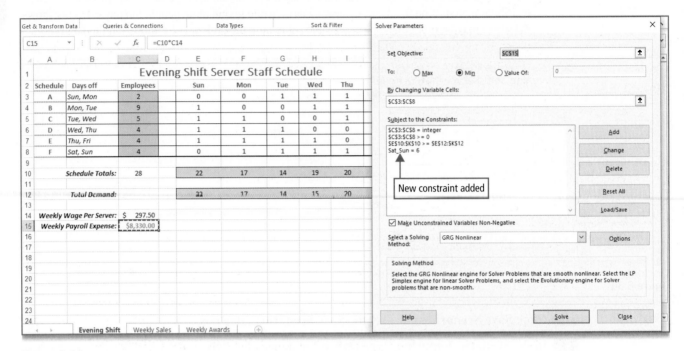

Figure 8.31

5 Click **Solve**.

A new solution is found; however, the Weekly Payroll Expense in cell C15 increases to *$8,925.00*, and the number of servers required to meet this scenario in cell C10 increases to 30.

6 Click **Save Scenario**. In the **Save Scenario** dialog box, type **Option 3** and then click **OK**.

The third scenario is saved and the Solver Results dialog box displays.

7 Click **Restore Original Values**, and then click **OK**.

The previous solution is restored to the worksheet.

8 On the **Data tab**, in the **Forecast group**, click **What-If Analysis**, and then click **Scenario Manager**. Compare your screen with Figure 8.32.

The Scenario Manager dialog box displays the three scenario names that you created.

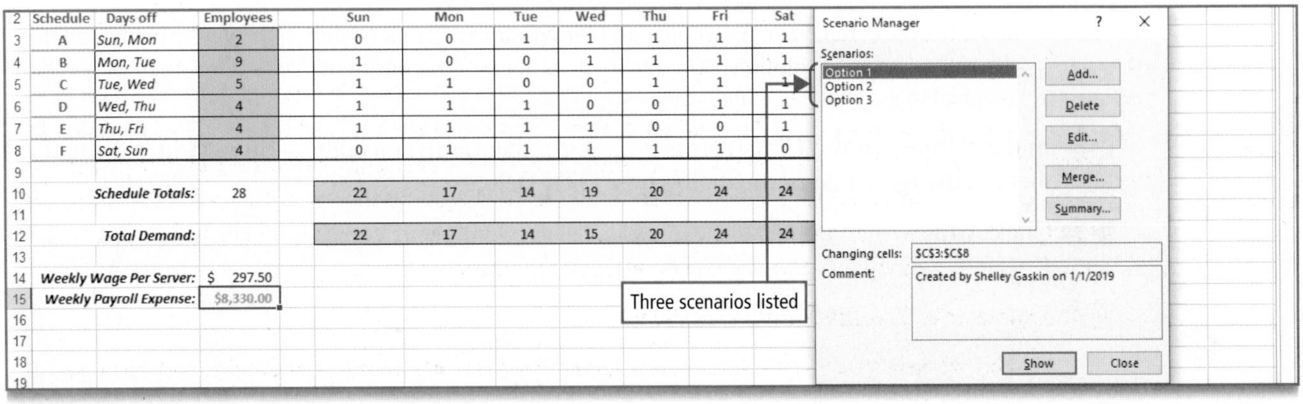

Figure 8.32

9 In the **Scenario Manager** dialog box, click **Summary**.

The Scenario Summary dialog box displays. Here you can choose between a Scenario summary, which displays the data in a table, or a Scenario PivotTable report.

10 Be sure **Scenario summary** is selected, and then click **OK**. Compare your screen with Figure 8.33.

Excel inserts a new worksheet in your workbook—the *Scenario Summary* sheet, which compares the three options side by side. The results for Option 1 and Option 2 indicate the same amount in the results cell—$8,330.00—and Option 3 indicates *$8,925.00* in payroll expenses. The outline pane displays along the top and left side of the worksheet.

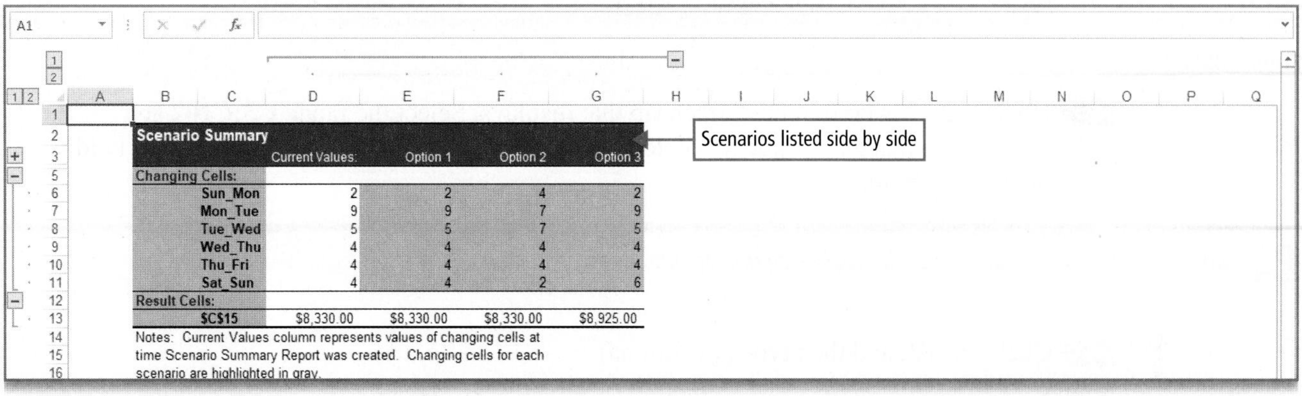

Figure 8.33

11 Select the range **D12:G12** and then on the **Home tab**, in the **Editing group**, click **AutoSum** | Σ AutoSum ▾ |. **Save** 🖫 your workbook.

The total number of servers required for each scenario is added to the Scenario Summary sheet. Options 1 and 2 require 28 servers to fill the schedule and Option 3 requires 30 servers.

Objective 6 Use Logical Functions

GO! Learn How
Video E8-6

There are a number of *logical functions* you can use to test for specific conditions. The results of a logical test are either TRUE or FALSE. Recall the SUM function adds values in a specified range of cells. The *SUMIF function* contains a logic test—it will add values in a specified range that meet a certain condition or criteria. The *SUMIFS function* is similar to the SUMIF function, but allows you to specify multiple ranges and multiple criteria to test. The *COUNTIF function* and *COUNTIFS function* work in the same way, counting cells that meet specific criteria in specified ranges. The *syntax*, or arrangement of the arguments in a function, displays in a ScreenTip as you begin to build the function.

Activity 8.13 | Using the SUMIF Function

MOS

4.1.1,
Expert 3.1.1

Ms. Zachary wants to see the total each server has sold over the past week. This can provide information about how well servers are encouraging diners to promote new and higher priced "specials" or to order desserts or beverages to increase the total amount of the bill. SUMIF can be used to add values in a range that meet a specific condition or criteria. In this Activity, you will use SUMIF to calculate the total weekly sales for each server.

1 Display the **Weekly Sales** worksheet.

This worksheet lists the sales for each server that has worked the day or evening shift the week of January 1–8.

2 Click cell **G3**, and then type **=sumif(** and then compare your screen with Figure 8.34.

The syntax displays for the SUMIF function. It has two required arguments: *range* and *criteria*, and one optional argument: *sum_range*.

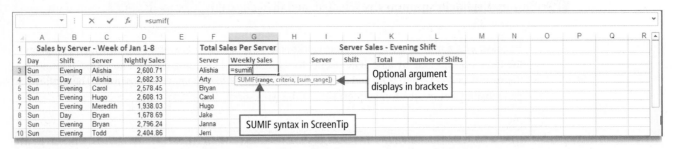

Figure 8.34

3 Notice *range* is bold in the ScreenTip that displays. Select the range **C3:C102** and press F4 to make the value absolute. Type **,** (a comma) and notice *criteria* is now bold in the ScreenTip.

MAC TIP To make a value absolute, press COMMAND + T

4 Click cell **F3**, and then type **,** (a comma).

5 Notice *[sum_range]* is now bold. Select the range **D3:D102** and press F4. Type **)** and then, on the **Formula Bar**, click **Enter** ✓.

The brackets around *sum_range* indicate it is an optional argument. If you do not include it, Excel will attempt to determine what range to use for the calculation.

6 Drag the fill handle to copy the formula down through cell **G19**. Format the range **G3:G19** using cell style **Currency [0]**. **Save** 🖫 your workbook and compare your screen with Figure 8.35.

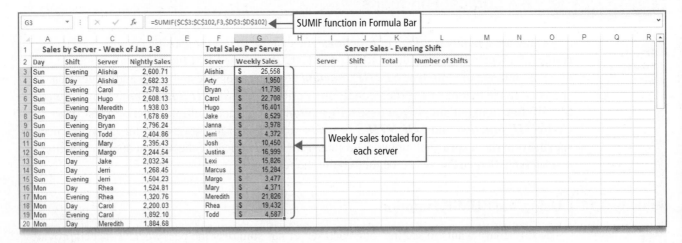

Figure 8.35

Activity 8.14 | Using the SUMIFS Function

Because each server may work multiple shifts, you can use the SUMIFS function to include a second criteria—Shift—to SUM. In this Activity, you will use SUMIFS to calculate sales for each server for only the *evening* shift.

1 Select the range **F3:F19**, which contains the server names. **Copy** the selection, and then **Paste (P)** the copied selection into cell **I3**. Click cell **J3**, type **Evening** and then copy the cell down through **J19**.

2 Click cell **K3** and type **=sumifs(** Compare your screen with Figure 8.36.

In the SUMIFS function, the *sum_range* argument is specified first, followed by the first *criteria_range1* and *criteria1*. Additional *criteria_range* and *criteria* arguments can follow, up to a maximum of 127.

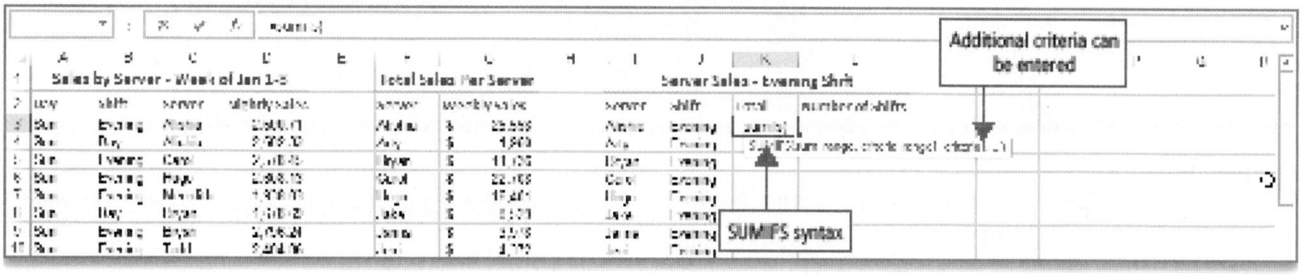

Figure 8.36

3 Select the range **D3:D102** and press F4 to make the value absolute. Type **,** (a comma), select the range **C3:C102**, and press F4. Type **,** (a comma). Click cell **I3**, and then type **,** (a comma).

The optional arguments [criteria_range2, criteria2] display in brackets in the ScreenTip.

4 Select the range **B3:B102** and then press F4. Type **,** and then click cell **J3**. Type **)** and then click **Enter**.

5 Drag the fill handle to copy the formula down through cell **K19**. Format the range **K3:K19** using cell style **Currency [0]**. **Save** your workbook and compare your screen with Figure 8.37.

In this SUMIFS function, you used the Nightly Sales as the sum_range, the Server as the first criteria, and the Shift as the second criteria.

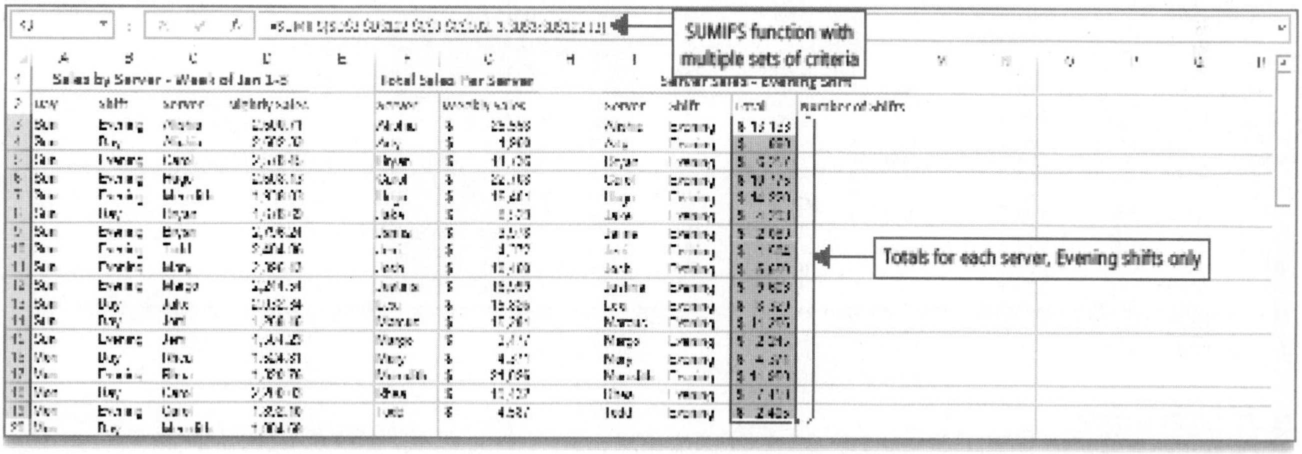

Figure 8.37

Activity 8.15 | Using the COUNTIFS Function

MOS
Expert 3.1.1

Ms. Zachary wants to see the number of Evening shifts each server has worked over the past week. Use the COUNTIFS function to count items that meet multiple conditions—in this instance, the server and the shift worked. This information is useful to see if some servers may be getting more favored assignments than other servers. For example, tips are typically higher in the Evening shifts than in the Day shifts because diners are selecting more expensive entrees and adding higher-priced beverages.

1 ▶ Click cell **L3** and type **=countifs(** and then compare your screen with Figure 8.38.

The COUNTIFS function has two required arguments: *criteria_range1* and *criteria1*. Additional *criteria_range* and *criteria* arguments can follow.

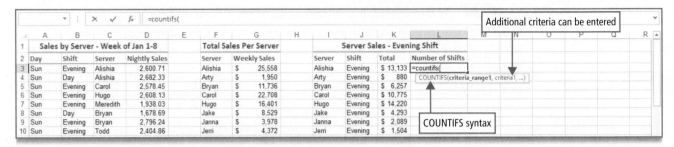

Figure 8.38

2 ▶ Select the range **C3:C102** and press F4 to make the value absolute. Type **,** (a comma), click cell **I3**, and then type **,** (a comma).

The optional arguments [criteria_range2, criteria2] display in brackets in the ScreenTip.

3 ▶ Select the range **B3:B102** and then press F4. Type **,** and then click cell **J3**. Type **)** and then click **Enter** ✓.

4 ▶ Drag the fill handle to copy the formula down through cell **L19**. **Save** 🖫 your workbook and compare your screen with Figure 8.39.

In this COUNTIFS function, you used the Servers as the criteria_range1 and the Server name as criteria1, then you used the Shift as criteria_range2 and "Evening" shift as criteria 2. Using the COUNTIFS function, Ms. Zachary is able to see how many evening shifts each server worked this week.

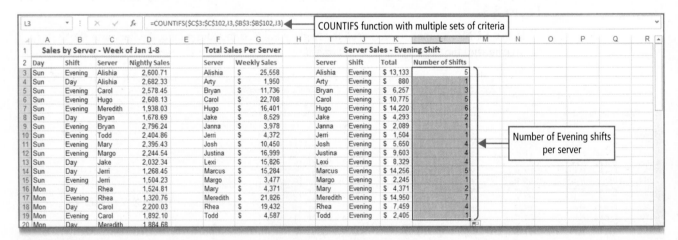

Figure 8.39

Objective 7 | **Create Complex Formulas**

GO! Learn How
Video E8-7

Use the logical functions AND and OR to develop compound logical tests using up to 255 arguments. The **AND function** returns a result of TRUE if *ALL* of the conditions are met. The **OR function** returns a value of TRUE if *ANY* of the conditions are met. The similar **NOT function** takes only one argument and tests one condition. If the condition is true, NOT returns the logical opposite FALSE. If the condition is false, then TRUE is returned.

Activity 8.16 | Building Compound Conditional Tests Using the AND Function

MOS

2.3.1, 4.1.2,
Expert 3.4.3

To determine the Employee of the Week, Ms. Zachary needs to determine the server with the best sales that worked at least three Evening shifts but no more than five Evening shifts during the week, and worked at least one shift during the slower days Monday and Tuesday. To do this, she needs to use a compound conditional test.

1 ▶ Click cell **N1** and type **Employees of the Week** and press Enter. **Merge & Center** the text over the range **N1:Q1** and apply the **Heading 2** cell style. In cell **N2**, type **Server** and press Tab. In cell **O2**, type **3-5 Shifts** and press Tab. In cell **P2**, type **M or T** and press Enter. Copy the server names from the range **I3:I19** and then paste them into the range **N3:N19**.

2 ▶ Select the range **A3:A102**. Click in the **Name Box** to select the existing text *A3*, type **DAY** and then press Enter. Select the range **B3:B102**, in the **Name Box**, type **SHIFT** and then press Enter. Select the range **C3:C102**, in the **Name Box**, type **SERVER** and then press Enter.

By naming the ranges, it will be easier to construct and understand these complex formulas.

3 ▶ In cell **O3**, type **=and(** Compare your screen with Figure 8.40.

The AND function takes the argument *logical1*, followed by optional additional logical tests.

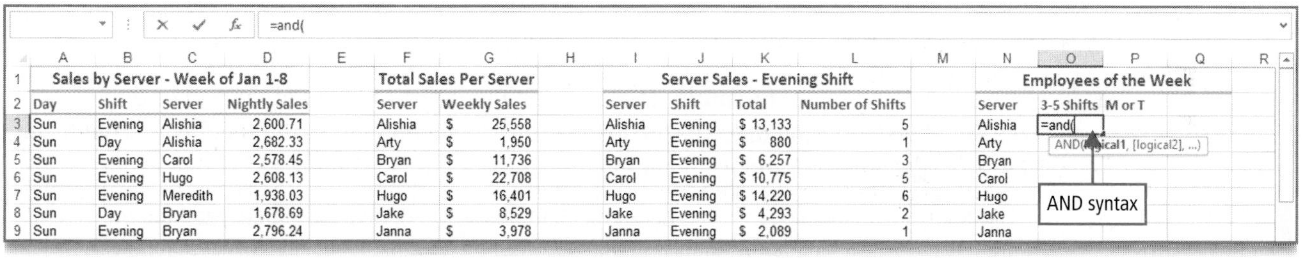

Figure 8.40

4 ▶ Click cell **L3**, type **>=3,** (include the comma). Click cell **L3**, and type **<=5)** Click **Enter** ✓ and copy the formula down through cell **O19**. Compare your screen with Figure 8.41.

The AND function performs two logical tests *L3>=3* and *L3<=5*. Both of the tests must be true for the function to return TRUE. If either or both tests fail, the function returns the result FALSE.

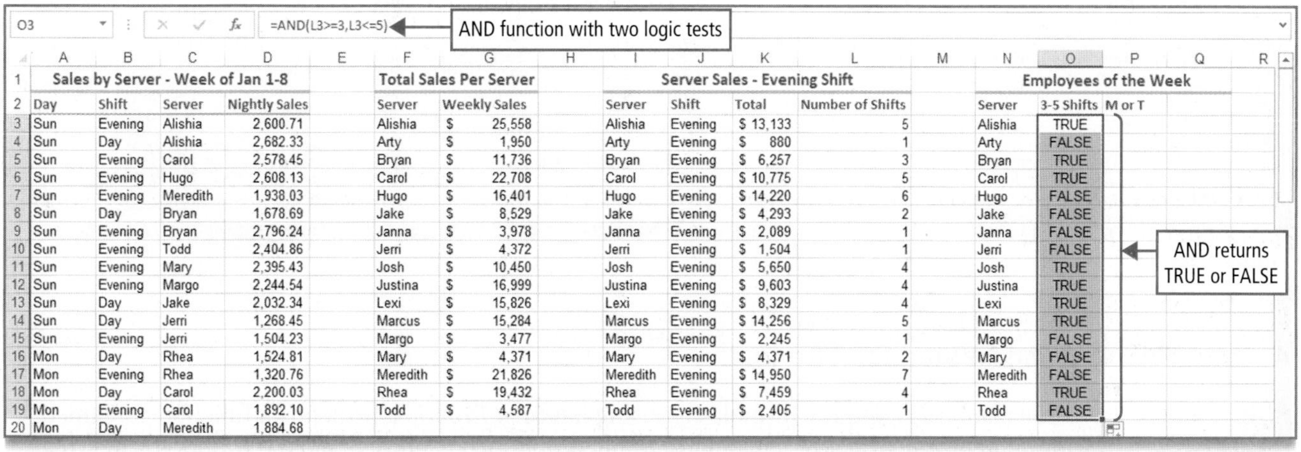

Figure 8.41

5 Click cell **P3**, and then type the formula **=countifs(server,n3,day,"Mon")** Click **Enter** ☑ and copy the formula down through cell **P19**. Compare your screen with Figure 8.42.

This formula uses the named ranges SERVER and DAY as the criteria ranges to determine the number of Monday shifts each server has worked.

| P3 | ▼ : × ✓ *fx* | =COUNTIFS(SERVER,N3,DAY,"Mon") | COUNTIFS function using named ranges SERVER and DAY |

	A	B	C	D	E	F	G	L	M	N	O	P	Q	R
1	Sales by Server - Week of Jan 1-8					Total Sales Per Server		Server Sales - Evening Shift				Employees of the Week		
2	Day	Shift	Server	Nightly Sales		Server	Weekly Sales	Server	Shift	Total	Number of Shifts	Server	3-5 Shifts	M or T
3	Sun	Evening	Alishia	2,600.71		Alishia	$ 25,558	Alishia	Evening	$ 13,133	5	Alishia	TRUE	0
4	Sun	Day	Alishia	2,682.33		Arty	$ 1,950	Arty	Evening	$ 880	1	Arty	FALSE	0
5	Sun	Evening	Carol	2,578.45		Bryan	$ 11,736	Bryan	Evening	$ 6,257	3	Bryan	TRUE	2
6	Sun	Evening	Hugo	2,608.13		Carol	$ 22,708	Carol	Evening	$ 10,775	5	Carol	TRUE	2
7	Sun	Evening	Meredith	1,938.03		Hugo	$ 16,401	Hugo	Evening	$ 14,220	6	Hugo	FALSE	0
8	Sun	Day	Bryan	1,678.69		Jake	$ 8,529	Jake	Evening	$ 4,293	2	Jake	FALSE	1
9	Sun	Evening	Bryan	2,796.24		Janna	$ 3,978	Janna	Evening	$ 2,089	1	Janna	FALSE	0
10	Sun	Evening	Todd	2,404.86		Jerri	$ 4,372	Jerri	Evening	$ 1,504	1	Jerri	FALSE	0
11	Sun	Evening	Mary	2,395.43		Josh	$ 10,450	Josh	Evening	$ 5,650	4	Josh	TRUE	0
12	Sun	Evening	Margo	2,244.54		Justina	$ 16,999	Justina	Evening	$ 9,603	4	Justina	TRUE	0
13	Sun	Day	Jake	2,032.34		Lexi	$ 15,826	Lexi	Evening	$ 8,329	4	Lexi	TRUE	0
14	Sun	Day	Jerri	1,268.45		Marcus	$ 15,284	Marcus	Evening	$ 14,256	5	Marcus	TRUE	0
15	Sun	Evening	Jerri	1,504.23		Margo	$ 3,477	Margo	Evening	$ 2,245	1	Margo	FALSE	1
16	Mon	Day	Rhea	1,524.81		Mary	$ 4,371	Mary	Evening	$ 4,371	2	Mary	FALSE	1
17	Mon	Evening	Rhea	1,320.76		Meredith	$ 21,826	Meredith	Evening	$ 14,950	7	Meredith	FALSE	2
18	Mon	Day	Carol	2,200.03		Rhea	$ 19,432	Rhea	Evening	$ 7,459	4	Rhea	TRUE	2
19	Mon	Evening	Carol	1,892.10		Todd	$ 4,587	Todd	Evening	$ 2,405	1	Todd	FALSE	1
20	Mon	Day	Meredith	1,884.68										

Number of Monday shifts worked by each server

Figure 8.42

6 Click cell **P3** and in the **Formula Bar**, position the insertion point at the end of the formula. Type **+countifs(server,n3,day,"Tue")** Click **Enter** ☑ and copy the formula down through cell **P19**. **Save** 🖫 your workbook and compare your screen with Figure 8.43.

Use the mathematical operators, plus sign (+), minus sign (−), division sign (/), and multiplication sign (*), to build complex formulas; in this instance, by adding the results of two functions.

| P3 | ▼ : × ✓ *fx* | =COUNTIFS(SERVER,N3,DAY,"Mon")+COUNTIFS(SERVER,N3,DAY,"Tue") | Mathematical operator + used to add another COUNTIFS function | Number of Monday + Tuesday shifts worked by each server |

	A	B	C	D	E	F	G	H	I	J			
1	Sales by Server - Week of Jan 1-8					Total Sales Per Server			Server Sales - Evening Shift			Employees of the Week	
2	Day	Shift	Server	Nightly Sales		Server	Weekly Sales		Server	Shift	Total	Number of Shifts	Server	3-5 Shifts	M or T
3	Sun	Evening	Alishia	2,600.71		Alishia	$ 25,558		Alishia	Evening	$ 13,133	5	Alishia	TRUE	1
4	Sun	Day	Alishia	2,682.33		Arty	$ 1,950		Arty	Evening	$ 880	1	Arty	FALSE	0
5	Sun	Evening	Carol	2,578.45		Bryan	$ 11,736		Bryan	Evening	$ 6,257	3	Bryan	TRUE	4
6	Sun	Evening	Hugo	2,608.13		Carol	$ 22,708		Carol	Evening	$ 10,775	5	Carol	TRUE	5
7	Sun	Evening	Meredith	1,938.03		Hugo	$ 16,401		Hugo	Evening	$ 14,220	6	Hugo	FALSE	3
8	Sun	Day	Bryan	1,678.69		Jake	$ 8,529		Jake	Evening	$ 4,293	2	Jake	FALSE	1
9	Sun	Evening	Bryan	2,796.24		Janna	$ 3,978		Janna	Evening	$ 2,089	1	Janna	FALSE	0
10	Sun	Evening	Todd	2,404.86		Jerri	$ 4,372		Jerri	Evening	$ 1,504	1	Jerri	FALSE	1
11	Sun	Evening	Mary	2,395.43		Josh	$ 10,450		Josh	Evening	$ 5,650	4	Josh	TRUE	1
12	Sun	Evening	Margo	2,244.54		Justina	$ 16,999		Justina	Evening	$ 9,603	4	Justina	TRUE	0
13	Sun	Day	Jake	2,032.34		Lexi	$ 15,826		Lexi	Evening	$ 8,329	4	Lexi	TRUE	0
14	Sun	Day	Jerri	1,268.45		Marcus	$ 15,284		Marcus	Evening	$ 14,256	5	Marcus	TRUE	1
15	Sun	Evening	Jerri	1,504.23		Margo	$ 3,477		Margo	Evening	$ 2,245	1	Margo	FALSE	1
16	Mon	Day	Rhea	1,524.81		Mary	$ 4,371		Mary	Evening	$ 4,371	2	Mary	FALSE	1
17	Mon	Evening	Rhea	1,320.76		Meredith	$ 21,826		Meredith	Evening	$ 14,950	7	Meredith	FALSE	4
18	Mon	Day	Carol	2,200.03		Rhea	$ 19,432		Rhea	Evening	$ 7,459	4	Rhea	TRUE	2
19	Mon	Evening	Carol	1,892.10		Todd	$ 4,587		Todd	Evening	$ 2,405	1	Todd	FALSE	1
20	Mon	Day	Meredith	1,884.68										

Figure 8.43

Activity 8.17 | Using Nested Functions

2.4.2, Expert 3.1.1

You can build complex formulas by using a ***nested function***, which is a function contained inside another function. The inner, nested function is evaluated first and the result becomes the argument for the outer function. Recall that the IF function uses a single logic test and returns one value if true and another value if false. In this Activity, you will use an IF function with a nested AND function to determine which servers are eligible for Employee of the Week status.

1 ▶ Click cell **Q2**, type **Eligible** and then press Enter.

2 ▶ In cell **Q3**, type the following formula and be sure you use the letter o and not the number 0: **=if(and(o3,p3>=1),"Eligible","")** Click **Enter** ☑ and copy the formula down through cell **Q19**. **Save** 🖫 your workbook and compare your screen with Figure 8.44.

There are six servers that meet both criteria—O3 is true and P3 is greater than or equal to 1— and are listed as *Eligible*. The double quotes make the cell blank rather than displaying the word FALSE if the result is false.

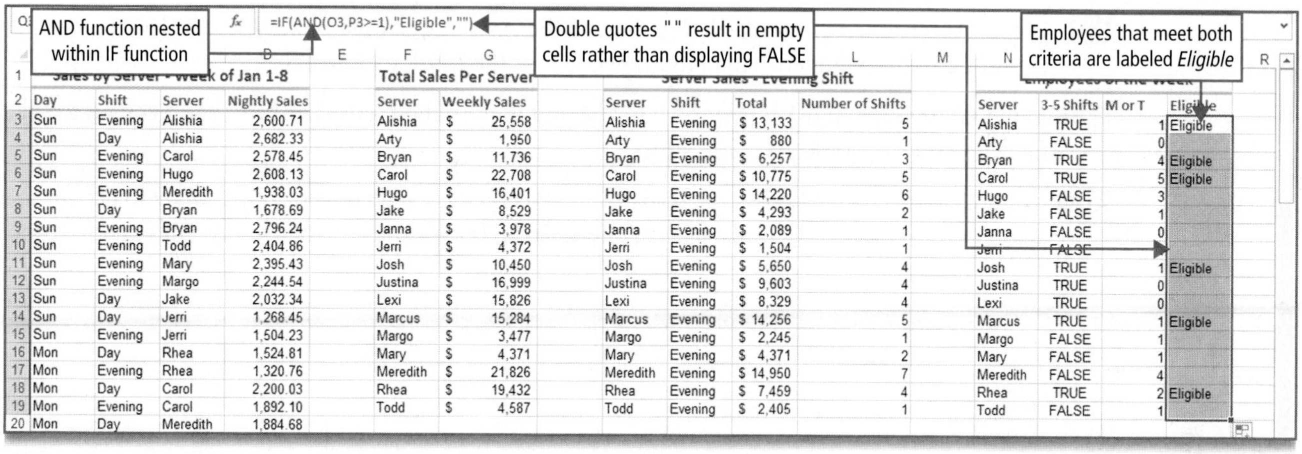

Figure 8.44

3 ▶ With the range **Q3:Q19** still selected, press Ctrl + Q to open **Quick Analysis** at the bottom of the selection, and then click the first option—**Text Contains**. In the **Text That Contains** dialog box, verify **Format cells that contain the text** displays *Eligible*. Click the **with arrow**, and then click **Green Fill with Dark Green Text**. Compare your screen with Figure 8.45.

This action applies conditional formatting to the cells in the selected range that contain text, which makes it easy for Ms. Zachary to see which employees are eligible.

💻 **MAC TIP**   On the Home tab, in the Styles group, click Conditional Formatting; point to Highlight Cells Rules and click Text that Contains.

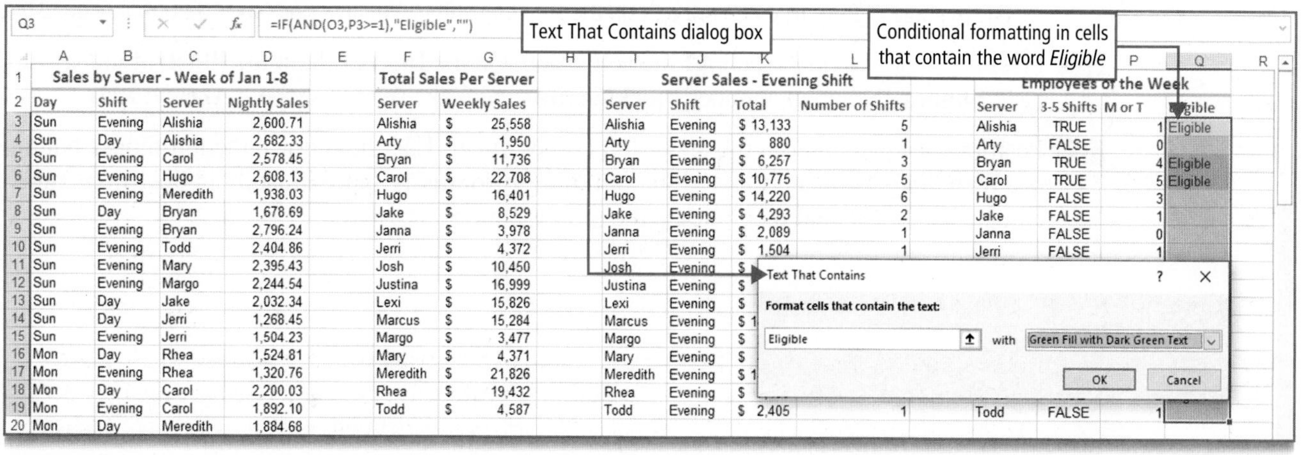

Figure 8.45

4 ▶ Click **OK**.

Activity 8.18 | Using the AVERAGEIFS Function and Inserting a Shape Containing Text

Ms. Zachary is interested to know what is the average nightly sales for servers working the Evening shift who have sales over $2,000. To compute this, she can use Excel's *AVERAGEIFS function*, which enables you to specify multiple criteria when computing an average.

1 Click cell **A105,** type **Average if Shift = Evening and Nightly Sales > $2,000** and then press Enter.

2 Click cell **F105**. On the **Formulas tab**, in the **Function Library group**, click **More Functions**, point to **Statistical**, and then click **AVERAGEIFS**.

3 In the **Function Arguments** dialog box, in the **Average_range** box, type **d3:d102** to define the range to be averaged—the Nightly Sales for the week of Jan 1-8.

4 In the **Criteria_range1** box, type **b3:b102** and then in the **Criteria1** box type **Evening** to set the first criteria—only Evening shifts.

5 In the **Criteria_range2** box, type **d3:d102** and then in the **Criteria2** box, type **>2000** to narrow the amounts to be averaged to only sales greater than $2,000. Compare your screen with Figure 8.46.

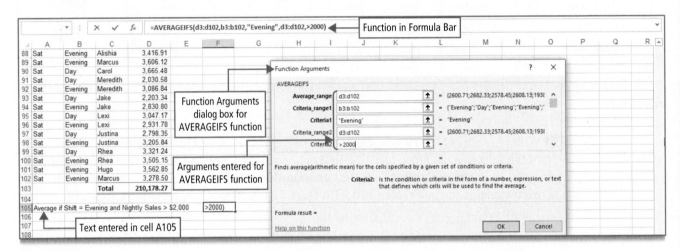

Figure 8.46

6 Click **OK**, with cell **F105** selected, on the **Home tab**, in the **Number group**, click **Accounting Number Format** $ ▾.

The average nightly sales for servers on the Evening shift who have sales over $2,000 is $2,652.78.

7 Press Ctrl + Home to make cell **A1** the active cell. On the **Insert tab**, in the **Illustrations group**, click **Shapes** ▾, and then under **Block Arrows**, click the second shape—**Arrow: Left**.

8 Position the ✛ pointer in the upper left corner of cell **E21**, hold down the left mouse button, and then drag down and to the right until the ✛ pointer is approximately in the lower right corner of cell **I28**, and then release the mouse button.

9 Click any cell to deselect the shape. Then, point to the shape and double-click to position an insertion point within the shape. Type **Average nightly sales for servers on the Evening shift who have sales over $2,000 is $2,652.78** Compare your screen with Figure 8.47.

	A	B	C	D	E	F	G	H	I	J	K	L	M	N	O	P	Q
1	Sales by Server - Week of Jan 1-8					Total Sales Per Server			Server Sales - Evening Shift					Employees of the Week			
2	Day	Shift	Server	Nightly Sales		Server	Weekly Sales		Server	Shift	Total	Number of Shifts		Server	3-5 Shifts	M or T	Eligible
3	Sun	Evening	Alishia	2,600.71		Alishia	$ 25,558		Alishia	Evening	$ 13,133	5		Alishia	TRUE	1	Eligible
4	Sun	Day	Alishia	2,682.33		Arty	$ 1,950		Arty	Evening	$ 880	1		Arty	FALSE	0	
5	Sun	Evening	Carol	2,578.45		Bryan	$ 11,736		Bryan	Evening	$ 6,257	3		Bryan	TRUE	4	Eligible
6	Sun	Evening	Hugo	2,608.13		Carol	$ 22,708		Carol	Evening	$ 10,775	5		Carol	TRUE	5	Eligible
7	Sun	Evening	Meredith	1,938.03		Hugo	$ 16,401		Hugo	Evening	$ 14,220	6		Hugo	FALSE	3	
8	Sun	Day	Bryan	1,678.69		Jake	$ 8,529		Jake	Evening	$ 4,293	2		Jake	FALSE	1	
9	Sun	Evening	Bryan	2,796.24		Janna	$ 3,978		Janna	Evening	$ 2,089	1		Janna	FALSE	0	
10	Sun	Evening	Todd	2,404.86		Jerri	$ 4,372		Jerri	Evening	$ 1,504	1		Jerri	FALSE	1	
11	Sun	Evening	Mary	2,395.43		Josh	$ 10,450		Josh	Evening	$ 5,650	4		Josh	TRUE	1	Eligible
12	Sun	Evening	Margo	2,244.54		Justina	$ 16,999		Justina	Evening	$ 9,603	4		Justina	TRUE	0	
13	Sun	Day	Jake	2,032.34		Lexi	$ 15,826		Lexi	Evening	$ 8,329	4		Lexi	TRUE	0	
14	Sun	Day	Jerri	1,268.45		Marcus	$ 15,284		Marcus	Evening	$ 14,256	5		Marcus	TRUE	1	Eligible
15	Sun	Evening	Jerri	1,504.23		Margo	$ 3,477		Margo	Evening	$ 2,245	1		Margo	FALSE	1	
16	Mon	Day	Rhea	1,524.81		Mary	$ 4,371		Mary	Evening	$ 4,371	2		Mary	FALSE	1	
17	Mon	Evening	Rhea	1,320.76		Meredith	$ 21,826		Meredith	Evening	$ 14,950	7		Meredith	FALSE	4	
18	Mon	Day	Carol	2,200.03		Rhea	$ 19,432		Rhea	Evening	$ 7,459	4		Rhea	TRUE	2	Eligible
19	Mon	Evening	Carol	1,892.10		Todd	$ 4,587		Todd	Evening	$ 2,405	1		Todd	FALSE	1	
20	Mon	Day	Meredith	1,884.68													
21	Mon	Evening	Meredith	1,765.96													
22	Mon	Day	Bryan	2,337.52													
23	Mon	Evening	Bryan	2,328.36		Average nightly sales for servers on the Evening shift who have sales over $2,000 is $2,652.78				Left Arrow shape inserted with text							
24	Mon	Day	Todd	2,181.69													
25	Mon	Evening	Mary	1,975.43													
26	Mon	Day	Margo	1,232.93													
27	Mon	Evening	Jake	1,462.11													
28	Tue	Day	Jerri	1,599.01													

Scenario Summary   Evening Shift   **Weekly Sales**   Weekly Awards

Ready   100%

Figure 8.47

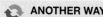 **ANOTHER WAY**   Point to the shape, right-click, and then on the shortcut menu, click Edit Text.

10 Click any cell to deselect the shape. On the **Page Layout tab**, click **Print Titles**. Under **Print titles**, click in the **Rows to repeat at top** box, and then from the **row heading area**, select **rows 1:2**. Click **OK**.

> This worksheet will print on two pages so adding column titles will make it easier to understand the information on the second page.

11 Press Ctrl + Home to make cell **A1** active. **Save** your workbook.

Activity 8.19 | Using the IFS Function

Expert 3.1.1

The *IFS function* checks whether one or more conditions are met and then returns a value that corresponds to the *first* TRUE condition. The benefit of using the IFS function is that it can take the place of multiple nested IF statements, which can be confusing to construct and read. The IFS function is much easier to read when you have multiple conditions. You can test up to 127 different conditions.

Each week, servers can earn an extra cash bonus based on their weekly sales. Weekly sales of $25,000 or more earns a cash bonus of $100. Weekly sales of $20,000 or more—but under $25,000—earns a cash bonus of $75. And weekly sales of $15,000 or more—but under $20,000—earns a cash bonus of $50.

1 ▸ Display the **Weekly Awards** worksheet.

2 ▸ Click in cell **C3**. Click the **Formulas tab**, in the **Function Library group** click **Logical**, and then click **IFS**. In the **Logical_test1** box type **b3> = 25000** and press ⌷Tab⌷. In the **Value_if_true1** box, type **$100** and then compare your screen with Figure 8.48.

If the value in cell B3 is greater than or equal to 25000 then display *$100*.

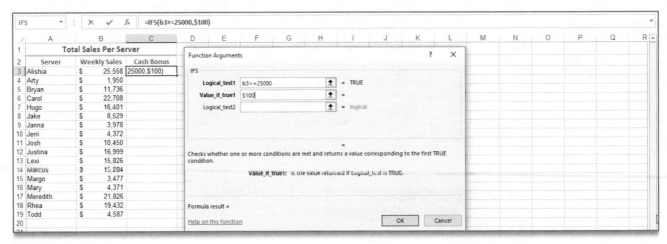

Figure 8.48

3 ▸ Press ⌷Tab⌷. Notice that quote marks display in the second box—Excel will add the quote marks automatically. In the **Logical_test2** box type **b3>=20000** and press ⌷Tab⌷. Type **$75** and press ⌷Tab⌷. Compare your screen with Figure 8.49.

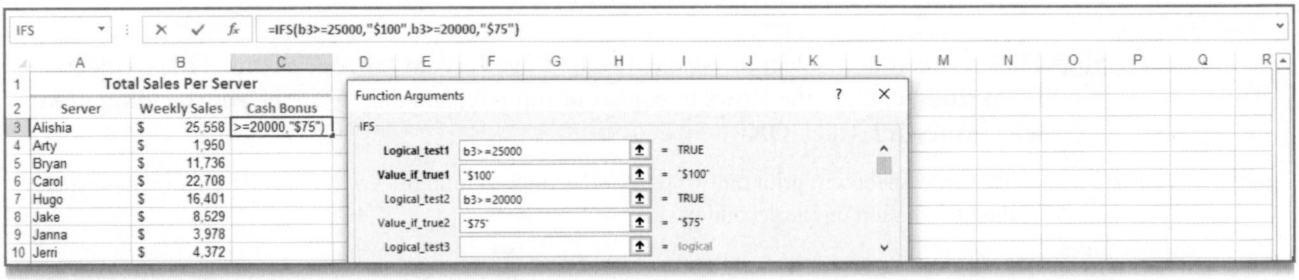

Figure 8.49

4 ▸ In the **Logical_test3** box, type **b3>=15000** and press ⌷Tab⌋. In the **Value_if_true3** box, type **$50** and press ⌷Tab⌋.

5 ▸ In the **Logical_test4** box, type **b3<15000** and press ⌷Tab⌋. In the **Value_if_true4** box, type **""** (two quote marks with no space between). Look at the **Formula Bar**, and then compare your screen with Figure 8.50.

The double quotes make the cell blank rather than displaying an error message.

The entire formula indicates:

- *if the value in cell B3 is greater than or equal to 25000 then display $100 in the cell,*
- *if the value in cell B3 is greater than or equal to 20000 then display $75 in the cell,*
- *if the value in cell B3 is greater than or equal to 15000 then display $50 in the cell,*
- *if the value in cell B3 is less than 15000, then display nothing in the cell.*

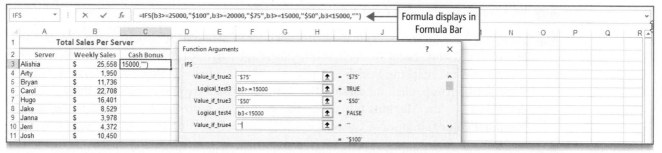

Figure 8.50

6 ▶ Click **OK** to display *$100* in cell **B3**, and then copy the formula down through cell **C19**. Compare your screen with Figure 8.51.

Eight servers will earn a cash bonus for the week. Alishia will earn a $100 cash bonus, Carol and Meredith will each earn a $75 cash bonus, and Hugo, Justina, Lexi, Marcus, and Rhea will each earn a $50 cash bonus.

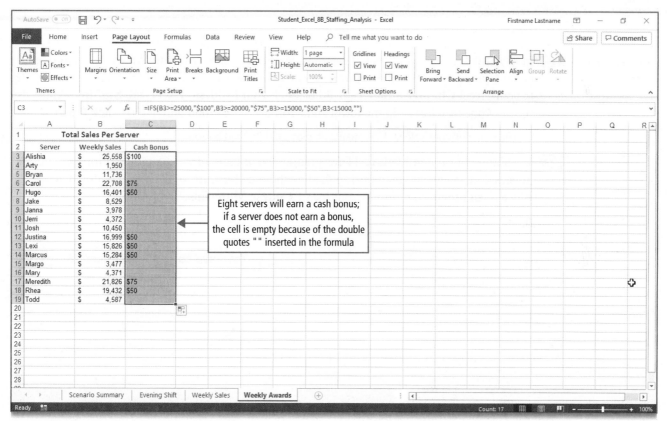

Figure 8.51

7 Press (Ctrl) + (Home) to make cell **A1** active. **Save** 🖫 your workbook.

8 Right-click the sheet tab and then click **Select All Sheets** so that *Group* displays in the title bar. With the worksheets grouped, display the **Page Layout tab**, set the **Orientation** to **Landscape** and scale the **Width** to **1 page**. Click **Margins**, and then click **Normal**. In the **Page Setup group**, click the **Dialog Box Launcher** button 🖼 to display the **Page Setup** dialog box. On the **Margins tab**, center the worksheets horizontally on the page. On the **Header/Footer tab**, insert a **Custom Footer** in the **left section** that includes the file name.

9 Display the **document properties** and if necessary, right-click the author name, click Edit Property, and then type your name. In the **Subject** box, type your course name and section #, and in the **Tags** box, type **staff schedule** Display the grouped worksheets in **Print Preview**—you will have five total pages.

10 On the left, click **Save** to save your workbook and redisplay the Excel window. In the upper right corner of the Excel window, click **Close** ☒.

For Non-MyLab Submissions   **Determine What Your Instructor Requires for Submission**
As directed by your instructor, submit your completed Lastname_Firstname_8B_Staffing_Analysis Excel workbook.

11 In **MyLab IT**, locate and click the Grader Project **Excel 8B Staffing Analysis**. In **step 3**, under **Upload Completed Assignment**, click **Choose File**. In the **Open** dialog box, navigate to your **Excel Chapter 8 folder**, and then click your **Student_Excel_8B_Staffing_Analysis** file one time to select it. In the lower right corner of the **Open** dialog box, click **Open**.

The name of your selected file displays above the Upload button.

12 To submit your file to **MyLab IT** for grading, click **Upload**, wait a moment for a green **Success!** message, and then in **step 4**, click the blue **Submit for Grading** button. Click **Close Assignment** to return to your list of **Course Materials**.

You have completed Project 8B   **END**

Microsoft Office Specialist (MOS) Skills in This Chapter

Project 8A	Project 8B
2.1.3 Insert and delete multiple rows and columns	**2.3.1** Define a named range
2.2.6 Apply cell formats from the Format Cells dialog box	**2.4.2** Apply built-in conditional formatting
2.2.7 Apply cell styles	**4.1.1** Insert relative, absolute, and mixed references
5.1.1 Create charts	**4.1.2** Reference named ranges and named tables in formulas
5.1.2 Create chart sheets	**Expert 3.1.1:** Perform logical operations by using nested functions including IFS, SUMIF, SUMIFS, AND, COUNTIFS, AVERAGEIFS
5.2.1 Add data series to charts	**Expert 3.4.2:** Perform what-if analysis by using Goal Seek and Scenario Manager
5.3.1 Apply chart layouts	**Expert 3.4.3:** Forecast data by using the AND function
Expert 2.2.1: Create custom number formats	
Expert 4.1.1: Create and modify dual axis charts	

Build Your E-Portfolio

An E-Portfolio is a collection of evidence, stored electronically, that showcases what you have accomplished while completing your education. Collecting and then sharing your work products with potential employers reflects your academic and career goals. Your completed documents from the following projects are good examples to show what you have learned: 8G, 8K, and 8L.

GO! For Job Success

Project Management

Your instructor may assign this topic to your class, and then ask you to think about, or discuss with your classmates, these questions:

Project management is a discipline that identifies and plans for the resources required to complete a defined set of tasks to achieve a stated goal. Project managers develop timelines, coordinate resources, organize and motivate cross-functional groups working on the project, and forecast and monitor costs. Size and complexity of projects vary: Construction and architecture projects might entail building a new highway or skyscraper; software projects develop new software products or upgrades of existing products. Administrative projects might include meeting and event planning. To ensure that the corporate strategy translates into projects actually being implemented, many organizations have implemented a Project Management Office, which ensures alignment between strategy and projects so that the right projects move forward at the right time and right budget.

g-stockstudio/ Shutterstock

Project managers must have skills in a variety of areas including accounting, management, forecasting, and writing. What are some other skills that would be valuable in project management?

What "soft" skills do you think are required to be a successful project manager?

What do you think are some other benefits to both executives and project managers of using a Project Management Office?

End of Chapter

Summary

A moving average is a sequence of averages computed from parts of a data series. It evens out the data to show a pattern or trend. The break-even point is the point at which a company starts to make a profit.

Solver is a what-if analysis tool used to find an optimal value for a formula in one cell—referred to as the objective cell—subject to constraints, on the values of other formula cells in a worksheet.

You can create several possible solutions to a problem and use Scenario Manager to compare the alternatives. A scenario is a set of values that Excel saves and that you can substitute automatically in your worksheet.

Build complex formulas by nesting functions. A nested function is contained inside another function. The inner function is evaluated first and the result becomes the argument for the outer function. The IFS function can eliminate the need for nested functions.

GO! Learn It Online

Review the concepts, key terms, and MOS skills in this chapter by completing these online challenges, which you can find at **MyLab IT**.

Chapter Quiz: Answer matching and multiple choice questions to test what you learned in this chapter.

Lessons on the GO!: Learn how to use all the new apps and features as they are introduced by Microsoft.

MOS Prep Quiz: Answer questions to review the MOS skills that you practiced in this chapter.

Project Guide for Excel Chapter 8

Your instructor will assign Projects from this list to ensure your learning and assess your knowledge.

Project	Apply Skills from These Chapter Objectives	Project Type		Project Location
8A MyLab IT	Objectives 1–4 from Project 8A	**8A Instructional Project (Grader Project)** Guided instruction to learn the skills in Project 8A.	**Instruction**	In **MyLab IT** and in text
8B MyLab IT	Objectives 5-8 from Project 8B	**8B Instructional Project (Grader Project)** Guided instruction to learn the skills in Project 8B.	**Instruction**	In **MyLab IT** and in text
8C	Objectives 1–4 from Project 8A	**8C Skills Review (Scorecard Grading)** A guided review of the skills from Project 8A.	**Review**	In text
8D	Objectives 5-8 from Project 8B	**8D Skills Review (Scorecard Grading)** A guided review of the skills from Project 8B.	**Review**	In text
8E MyLab IT	Objectives 1–4 from Project 8A	**8E Mastery (Grader Project)** A demonstration of your mastery of the skills in Project 8A with extensive decision-making.	**Mastery and Transfer of Learning**	In **MyLab IT** and in text
8F MyLab IT	Objectives 5–8 from Project 8B	**8F Mastery (Grader Project)** A demonstration of your mastery of the skills in Project 8B with extensive decision-making.	**Mastery and Transfer of Learning**	In **MyLab IT** and in text
8G MyLab IT	Objectives 1–8 from Projects 8A and 8B	**8G Mastery (Grader Project)** A demonstration of your mastery of the skills in Projects 8A and 8B with extensive decision-making.	**Mastery and Transfer of Learning**	In **MyLab IT** and in text
8H	Combination of Objectives from Projects 8A and 8B	**8H GO! Fix It (Scorecard Grading)** A demonstration of your mastery of the skills in Projects 8A and 8B by creating a correct result from a document that contains errors you must find.	**Critical Thinking**	IRC
8I	Combination of Objectives from Projects 8A and 8B	**8I GO! Make It (Scorecard Grading)** A demonstration of your mastery of the skills in Projects 8A and 8B by creating a result from a supplied picture.	**Critical Thinking**	IRC
8J	Combination of Objectives from Projects 8A and 8B	**8J GO! Solve It (Rubric Grading)** A demonstration of your mastery of the skills in Projects 8A and 8B, your decision-making skills, and your critical thinking skills. A task-specific rubric helps you self-assess your result.	**Critical Thinking**	IRC
8K	Combination of Objectives from Projects 8A and 8B	**8K GO! Solve It (Rubric Grading)** A demonstration of your mastery of the skills in Projects 8A and 8B, your decision-making skills, and your critical thinking skills. A task-specific rubric helps you self-assess your result.	**Critical Thinking**	In text
8L	Combination of Objectives from Projects 8A and 8B	**8L GO! Think (Rubric Grading)** A demonstration of your understanding of the Chapter concepts applied in a manner that you would outside of college. An analytic rubric helps you and your instructor grade the quality of your work by comparing it to the work an expert in the discipline would create.	**Critical Thinking**	In text
8M	Combination of Objectives from Projects 8A and 8B	**8M GO! Think (Rubric Grading)** A demonstration of your understanding of the Chapter concepts applied in a manner that you would outside of college. An analytic rubric helps you and your instructor grade the quality of your work by comparing it to the work an expert in the discipline would create.	**Critical Thinking**	IRC
8N	Combination of Objectives from Projects 8A and 8B	**8N You and GO! Rubric Grading** A demonstration of your understanding of the Chapter concepts applied in a manner that you would in a personal situation. An analytic rubric helps you and your instructor grade the quality of your work.	**Critical Thinking**	IRC

Glossary

Glossary of Chapter Key Terms

Add-in Optional command or feature that is not immediately available; you must first install and/or activate it to use it.

AND function A logical function that can be used to develop compound logical tests using up to 255 arguments. The function returns a result of TRUE if ALL of the conditions are met.

AVERAGEIFS function A statistical function that enables you to specify multiple criteria when computing an average.

Break-even point The point at which a company starts to make a profit.

Constraint In Solver, a condition or restriction that must be met.

Constraint cell In Solver, a cell that contains a value that limits or restricts the outcome.

COUNTIF function A logical function that counts the cells that meet specific criteria in a specified range.

COUNTIFS function A logical function that counts the cells that meet specific criteria in multiple ranges.

Decision variable In Solver, cell in which the value will change to achieve the desired results.

Dual-axis chart A chart that has one series plotted on a secondary axis. Useful when comparing data series that use different scales or different types of measurements.

Fixed expense Expense that remains the same each month regardless of the amount of activity.

Forecast A prediction of the future, often based on past performances.

IFS function A logical function that checks whether one or more conditions are met and returns a value corresponding to the first TRUE condition.

Integer A whole number.

Interval The number of cells to include in a moving average.

Logical function A function that tests for specific conditions.

Moving average A sequence of averages computed from parts of a data series.

Nested function A function that is contained inside another function. The inner function is evaluated first and the result becomes the argument for the outer function.

NOT function A logical function that takes only one argument and is used to test one condition. If the condition is true, the function returns the logical opposite FALSE. If the condition is false, then TRUE is returned.

Objective cell In Solver, a cell that contains a formula for the results you are trying to determine.

OR function A logical function that can be used to develop compound logical tests using up to 255 arguments. The function returns a value of TRUE if ANY of the conditions are met.

Scenario A set of values that Excel saves and can substitute automatically in your worksheet.

Scenario Manager A what-if analysis tool that compares alternatives.

Solver A what-if analysis tool with which you can find an optimal (maximum or minimum) value for a formula in one cell—referred to as the objective cell—subject to constraints, or limits, on the values of other formula cells on a worksheet.

SUMIF function A logical function that contains one logic test—it will add values in a specified range that meet certain conditions or criteria.

SUMIFS function A logical function that will add values in multiple ranges that meet multiple criteria.

Syntax The arrangement of the arguments in a function.

Transpose To switch the data in rows and columns.

Variable cell In Solver, a cell in which the value will change to achieve the desired results.

Variable expense Expense that varies depending on the amount of sales.

Chapter Review

Skills Review Project 8C Orlando Sales

Apply 8A skills from these Objectives:

1. Calculate a Moving Average
2. Project Income and Expenses
3. Determine a Break-Even Point

In the following Skills Review, you will create a worksheet for Kelsey Tanner, the Chief Financial Officer of Brina's Bistro, who wants to see how sales have grown in the first six weeks at the new restaurant in Orlando, Florida. Your completed worksheets will look similar to Figure 8.52.

Project Files

For Project 8C, you will need the following file:

e08C_Orlando_Sales

You will save your workbook as:

Lastname_Firstname_8C_Orlando_Sales

Project Results

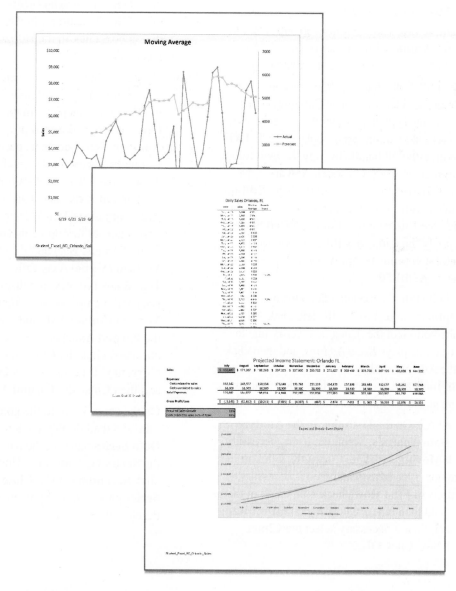

Figure 8.52

(continues on next page)

Chapter Review

1 From the files that accompany this project, open the file **e08C_Orlando_Sales**, and then in your **Excel Chapter 8** folder, using your own name, **Save** the file as **Lastname_Firstname_8C_Orlando_Sales**

a. Select the range **A3:AV4**. On the **Home tab**, in the **Clipboard group**, click **Copy**. Click cell **A5**. In the **Clipboard group**, click the **Paste button arrow**, and then under **Paste**, click **Transpose (T)**. Delete **rows 2:4**. In cell **C2** type **Moving Average** In cell **D2** type **Growth Trend** Select the range **A2:D2** and apply the **Heading 3** cell style, and then in the **Alignment group**, click **Wrap Text**, **Center**, and **Middle Align**. Click cell **A3**.

b. On the **Home tab**, in the **Number group**, click the **Dialog Box Launcher**. (Mac users: Select More Number Formats in the Number Format box.)

c. In the **Format Cells** dialog box, be sure the **Number tab** is selected. Under **Category**, click **Custom**. In the **Type** box, select the existing text, and then type **ddd, mmm dd** to replace it. Click **OK**, and then drag the fill handle to copy the new format down through cell **A49**. Click cell **A50** and type **Total** Press ⎡Tab⎤ to move to cell **B50**, in the **Editing group**, click **AutoSum**, and then on the **Formula Bar**, click the **Enter** button. From the **Cell Styles** gallery, apply the **Currency [0]** cell style to cell **B50**. AutoFit **column B**. Apply the **Total** cell style to the range **A50:B50**.

d. Click the **File tab**. On the left, click **Options**. In the **Excel Options** dialog box, on the left, click **Add-ins**. At the bottom of the dialog box, verify that the **Manage** box displays *Excel Add-ins*, and then click **Go**. In the **Add-ins** dialog box, if necessary, select the **Analysis ToolPak** check box. Click **OK**. (Mac users: On the menu bar, click Tools, click Excel Add-ins.)

2 Click cell **A2**. On the **Data tab**, in the **Analyze group**, click **Data Analysis**. Scroll the list as necessary, and then click **Moving Average**. Click **OK**. Click in the **Input Range** box, type **b2:b49** and then if necessary, select the **Labels in First Row** check box. Click in the **Interval** box, and then type **7** Click in the **Output Range** box, type **c3** and then if necessary select the **Chart Output** check box. Click **OK**.

a. Click the outer edge of the chart to select it, and then on the **Design tab**, in the **Location group**, click **Move Chart**. Click **New sheet**, type **Sales Trend Chart** and then click **OK**. At the bottom of the chart, point to any of the data points to display the ScreenTip *Horizontal (Category) Axis*, and then click one time to select the axis. On the **Design tab**, in the **Data group**, click **Select Data**. In the **Select Data Source** dialog box, on the right, under **Horizontal (Category) Axis Labels**, click **Edit**. Display the **Sales** worksheet, and then select the range **A9:A49**. In the **Axis Labels** dialog box, click **OK**. In the **Select Data Source** dialog box, click **OK**. (Mac users: In the Select Data Source dialog box, click in the Horizontal (Category) axis labels box.)

b. Point anywhere on the selected **Horizontal (Category) Axis** and double-click to display the **Format Axis** pane. In the pane, with **Axis Options** selected, scroll down and click to expand **Number**. Scroll down as necessary, click the **Category arrow**, and then click **Date**. Click the **Type** arrow, click the **3/14** format, and then **Close** the **Format Axis** pane. Click the **Horizontal (Category)Axis Title**—*Data Point*—to select it. Type **June 26 through July 28** (your typing displays in the Formula Bar) and then press ⎡Enter⎤. Click the **Vertical (Value) Axis Title**—*Value*—to select it. Type **Sales** (your typing displays in the Formula Bar) and then press ⎡Enter⎤. Point to any value on the **Vertical (Value) Axis** and double-click to display the **Format Axis** pane. In the pane, scroll down to **Number**, click the **Category arrow**, and then click **Currency**. If necessary, set **Decimal places** to **0**, and then **Close** the **Format Axis** pane.

c. On the chart, point to the gold **Series "Forecast"** line, and then double-click to display the **Format Data Series** pane. In the pane, if necessary, click the **Series Options** icon. Under **Plot Series On**, click **Secondary Axis**. **Close** the **Format Data Series** pane. Click anywhere outside the chart to deselect it.

(continues on next page)

Chapter Review

d. Display the **Sales** worksheet. Click cell **D21**, and then type **=(c21-c14)/c14** Press Enter. Scroll to position **row 21** near the top of your screen. Click cell **D21**, and then on the **Home tab**, in the **Number group**, click **Percent Style**. Click **Increase Decimal** one time to display one decimal. With cell **D21** still selected, in the **Clipboard group**, click **Copy**. Click cell **D28**, and then in the **Clipboard group**, click **Paste**. In the same manner, paste the copied cell into cells **D35, D42,** and **D49.** Press Esc to cancel the moving border.

3 Click cell **A51**, type **July Sales** press Tab, and then in cell **B51**, type **=sum(b21:b49)** and then press Enter. Display the **Projected Income** worksheet. Click cell **B3**. Type **=** click the **Sales sheet tab**, click cell **B51**—the July sales total—and then to the left of the **Formula Bar**, click the **Enter** button. On the **Projected Income** worksheet, click cell **B2**, and then use the fill handle to fill the months for a year—from July to June—across to **column M**. With the range **B2:M2** selected, apply **Center**.

a. Click cell **B3**; in the **Formula Bar**, notice the cell reference. Click cell **C3**, type **=b3*(1+b12)** and then on the **Formula Bar**, click **Enter**. From the **Cell Styles** gallery, apply the **Currency [0]** cell style. Use the fill handle to copy the formula in cell **C3** across the row to cell **M3**.

b. Click cell **B6** and examine the formula. Use the fill handle to copy the formula from cell **B6** across the row to cell **M6**. Drag the fill handle to **Copy** the value in cell **B7** across the row to cell **M7**. Select the range **C8:M8**, and then on the **Home tab**, in the **Editing group**, click **AutoSum**. Drag the fill handle to **Copy** the formula in cell **B10** across the row to cell **M10**.

4 In the lower right corner of your screen, if necessary, set the Zoom to **80%** so that **columns A:M** display on your screen. Select the range **A2:M3**. On the **Insert tab**, in the **Charts group**, click **Recommended Charts**. In the **Insert Chart** dialog box, with the **Line** chart selected, click **OK**.

a. On the **Design tab**, in the **Data group**, click **Select Data**. In the **Select Data Source** dialog box, under **Legend Entries (Series)**, click **Add**. With the insertion point in the **Series name** box, click cell **A8**. Press Tab, select the range **B8:M8**, and then click **OK**. Verify that the **Chart data range** is *$A$2:$M$3* and *$A$8:$M$8*. Click **OK**. On the **Design tab**, in the **Chart Layouts group**, click **Quick Layout**, and then click **Layout 3**. In the chart, click the text *Chart Title*, and then watch the **Formula Bar** as you type **Expected Break-Even Point** Press Enter. (Mac users: Click in the Formula Bar to type.)

b. Drag to position the upper left corner of the chart inside the upper left corner of cell **B15**. Scroll to position **row 13** near the top of your screen. Drag the lower right corner of the chart inside the lower right corner of cell **M36**.

c. On the left side of the chart, point to any value in the **Vertical (Value) Axis** and double-click to display the **Format Axis** pane. In the pane, verify that **Axis Options** is selected. Under **Axis Options**, in the **Minimum** box, replace the existing text with **150000** and press Enter. In the same manner, change the **Maximum** value to **500000** and press Enter.

d. At the top of the pane, click the **Axis Options arrow**, and then click **Chart Area**. Click the **Fill & Line** button. Format the **Chart Area** with a **Solid fill**—as the color, in the third column click the first color. **Close** the **Format Chart Area** pane, and then click cell **A1** to deselect the chart. (Mac users: On the Chart Format tab, in the Current Selection group, click the Chart Elements arrow, click Chart Area. Click Format Pane on the right of the ribbon.)

e. Display the **Sales Trend Chart** worksheet. On this chart sheet, from the **Page Layout tab**, display the **Page Setup** dialog box, and then insert a custom footer with the file name in the **left section**. **Close** the dialog boxes.

(continues on next page)

Chapter Review

5 Display the **Projected Income** worksheet; if necessary, set the **Zoom** back to **100%**. Right-click the sheet tab, and then click **Select All Sheets** so that *Group* displays in the title bar. With the worksheets grouped, display the **Page Setup** dialog box. Insert a custom footer in the **left section** that includes the file name, and center the worksheets horizontally on the page.

a. On the **Page Layout tab**, set the **Orientation** to **Landscape**, and then in the **Scale to Fit group**, set the **Width** to **1 page**, and the **Height** to **1 page**.

b. Display the **document properties**, and under **Related People**, be sure that your name displays as the author. If necessary, right-click the author name, click **Edit Property**, and then type your name. In the **Subject** box, type your course name and section number, and in the **Tags** box, type **Orlando, break-even** On the left, click **Print** to display the grouped worksheets in **Print Preview** and scroll to view the pages.

c. On the left, click **Save**. Click any sheet tab to ungroup the sheets. In the upper right corner of the Excel window, click **Close**. Submit your completed workbook as directed by your instructor.

You have completed Project 8C | END

Chapter Review

Skills Review | Project 8D Charlotte Staffing

Apply 8B skills from these Objectives:

4. Use Solver
5. Create Scenarios
6. Use Logical Functions
7. Create Complex Formulas

In the following Skills Review, you will assist Stephanie Wheaton, manager of the Charlotte restaurant, in determining the most efficient work schedule for the evening server staff. Your completed worksheets will look similar to Figure 8.53.

Project Files

For Project 8D, you will need the following file:

e08D_Charlotte_Staffing

You will save your workbook as:

Lastname_Firstname_8D_Charlotte_Staffing

Project Results

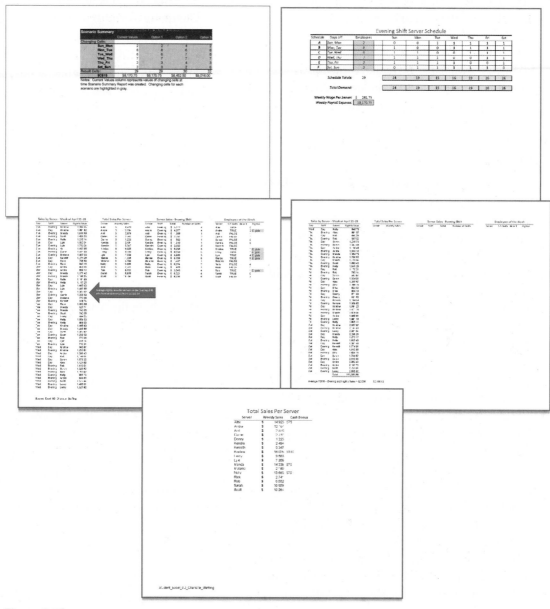

Figure 8.53

(continues on next page)

Chapter Review

1 ▶ Start Excel and display a blank workbook. Click the **Data tab**, and then at the right end of the **Data tab**, check to see if, in the **Analyze group**, **Solver** displays. If Solver displays, Solver is installed, and you can move to Step a. If Solver does *not* display, from **Backstage** view, click **Options**. On the left, click **Add-Ins**, and then at the bottom of the screen, in the **Manage** box, if necessary, select **Excel Add-ins**. Click **Go**. Select the **Solver Add-in** check box, and then click **OK**. On the **File tab**, click **Close** and move to Step a.

a. From the files downloaded with this project, open the file **e08D_Charlotte_Staffing**. Display the **Save As** dialog box, navigate to your **Excel Chapter 8** folder, and then using your own name, **Save** the workbook as **Lastname_Firstname_8D_Charlotte_Staffing**

b. Examine the formulas in cells **C10**, **C14**, and **C15**. Click cell **C3**, and then click the **Name Box arrow**; notice that cell **C3** is named *Sun_Mon* and the other schedules also have been named.

c. Click cell **C15**—the objective cell. On the **Data tab**, in the **Analyze group**, click **Solver**.

d. To the right of **To**, click **Min**. Click in the **By Changing Variable Cells** box, and then select the range **C3:C8**. Click in the **Subject to the Constraints** box, and then on the right click **Add** to add the first constraint. With the insertion point blinking in the **Cell Reference** box, select the range **C3:C8**. In the middle box, click the arrow, and then click **int**. Click **OK**—the result must be a whole number.

e. Click **Add** to add the second constraint. With the insertion point in the **Cell Reference** box, select the range **C3:C8**. In the middle box, click the arrow, and then click **>=**. In the **Constraint** box, type **0** Click **OK**.

f. Click **Add** to add the third constraint. In the **Cell Reference** box, select the range **E10:K10**. In the middle box, click the arrow, and then click **>=**. In the **Constraint** box, select the range **E12:K12**. Click **OK**; the result must be equal to or greater than the demand for each day. At the bottom of the **Solver Parameters** dialog box, click **Solve**. With **Keep Solver Solution** selected, click **OK**. Cell **C15** indicates *$8,170.75*.

2 ▶ Select the range **C3:C8**. On the **Data tab**, in the **Forecast group**, click **What-If Analysis**, and then click **Scenario Manager**. In the **Scenario Manager** dialog box, click **Add**. In the **Scenario name** box, type **Option 1** Verify that the **Changing cells** box displays *C3:C8*. Click **OK**. In the **Scenario Values** dialog box, click **OK**. In the **Scenario Manager** dialog box, click **Close**.

a. Click cell **C15**—the objective cell. On the **Data tab**, in the **Analyze group**, click **Solver**. In the **Solver Parameters** dialog box, verify that the **Set Objective** box displays *$C$15* and the **By Changing Variable Cells** box displays *$C$3:$C$8*.

b. To the right of the **Subject to the Constraints** box, click **Add** to add an additional constraint. In the **Add Constraint** dialog box, click the **Cell Reference** box, and then click cell **C3**. In the middle box, click the arrow, and then click **=**. In the **Constraint** box, type **4** Click **OK**; this constraint will raise the number of employees who have Sunday and Monday off to 4.

c. In the lower right corner of the dialog box, click **Solve**. Click **Save Scenario** to display the **Save Scenario** dialog box. In the **Scenario Name** box, type **Option 2** and then click **OK**. In the **Solver Results** dialog box, click **Restore Original Values**, and then click **OK**.

d. Verify that cell **C15** is still the active cell. On the **Data tab**, in the **Analyze group**, click **Solver**. In the **Subject to the Constraints** box, select the fourth constraint—*Sun_Mon = 4*—and then on the right click **Delete** to delete this constraint.

e. Click **Add**. In the **Add Constraint** dialog box, click in the **Cell Reference** box, and then select cell **C8**. Change the middle box to **=**. In the **Constraint** box, type **6** and then click **OK**; this constraint will raise the number of employees who have Saturday and Sunday off to 6.

f. Click **Solve**. Click **Save Scenario**. In the **Save Scenario** dialog box, type **Option 3** and then click **OK**. Click **Restore Original Values**, and then click **OK**.

(continues on next page)

Chapter Review

g. On the **Data tab**, in the **Forecast group**, click **What-If Analysis**, and then click **Scenario Manager**. In the **Scenario Manager** dialog box, click **Summary**. Be sure **Scenario summary** is selected, and then click **OK** to summarize the three Options on a new worksheet. Select the range **D12:G12** and then on the **Home tab**, in the **Editing group**, click **AutoSum**. **Save** your workbook.

3 ▶ Display the **Weekly Sales** worksheet. Click cell **G3**, and then type **=sumif(** Select the range **C3:C102** and press [F4] to make the value absolute. Type **,** (a comma). Click cell **F3**, and then type **,** (a comma). Select the range **D3:D102** and press [F4]. Type **)** and then on the **Formula Bar**, click **Enter**. (Mac users: Press COMMAND + T to make a value absolute.)

a. Drag the fill handle to copy the formula down through cell **G19**. Format the range **G3:G19** using cell style **Currency [0]**.

b. Select the range **F3:F19**. **Copy** the selection, and then in cell **I3**, **Paste (P)** the copied cells. Click cell **J3**, and then type **Evening** and then copy the cell down through **J19**.

c. Click cell **K3** and type **=sumifs(** Select the range **D3:D102** and press [F4] to make the value absolute. Type **,** (a comma), select the range **C3:C102**, and press [F4]. Type **,** (a comma). Click cell **I3**, and then type **,** (a comma). Select the range **B3:B102** and then press [F4]. Type **,** and then click cell **J3**. Type **)** and then click **Enter**. Drag the fill-handle to copy the formula down through cell **K19**. Format the range **K3:K19** using cell style **Currency [0]**.

d. Click cell **L3** and type **=countifs(** Select the range **C3:C102** and press [F4] to make the value absolute. Type **,** (a comma), click cell **I3**, and then type **,** (a comma). Select the range **B3:B102**, and then press [F4]. Type **,** and then click cell **J3**. Type **)** and then click **Enter**. Drag the fill handle to copy the formula down through cell **L19**.

4 ▶ Click cell **N1** and type **Employees of the Week** and press [Enter]. **Merge & Center** the text over the range **N1:Q1** and apply the **Heading 2** cell style. In cell **N2**, type **Server** and press [Tab]. In cell **O2**, type **3-5 Shifts** and press [Tab]. In cell **P2**, type **M or T** and press [Enter]. Copy the server names from the range **I3:I19** to the range **N3:N19**.

a. Select the range **A3:A102**, in the **Name Box** type **DAY** and then press [Enter]. Select the range **B3:B102**, in the **Name Box** type **SHIFT** and then press [Enter]. Select the range **C3:C102**, in the **Name Box** type **SERVER** and then press [Enter].

b. In cell **O3**, type **=and(** Click cell **L3**, type **>=3,** (include the comma). Click cell **L3** and type **<=5)** Click **Enter** and copy the formula down through cell **O19**.

c. Click cell **P3**, and then type the formula **=countifs(server,n3,day,"Mon")** Click **Enter** and copy the formula down through cell **P19**. Click cell **P3** and in the **Formula Bar**, position the insertion point at the end of the formula. Type **+countifs(server,n3,day,"Tue")** Click **Enter** and copy the formula down through cell **P19**.

d. Click cell **Q2**, type **Eligible** and then press [Enter]. In cell **Q3**, type **=if(and(o3,p3>=1),"Eligible","")** Click **Enter** and copy the formula down through cell **Q19**. Note that cell Q3 results in an empty cell, but the formula still exists to copy.

e. With the range still selected, press [Ctrl] + [Q] to open **Quick Analysis** at the bottom of the selection, and then click the first option—**Text Contains**. In the **Text That Contains** dialog box, in the **Format cells that contain the text** box type **Eligible** Click the **with arrow**, and then click **Green Fill with Dark Green Text**. Click **OK**. Press [Ctrl] + [Home] to make cell **A1** the active cell. On the **Page Layout tab**, in the **Page Setup group**, click **Print Titles**. Under **Print titles**, click in the **Rows to repeat at top** box, and then from the **row heading area**, select **rows 1:2**. Click **OK**. (Mac tip: Use the ribbon instead of Quick Analysis.)

5 ▶ To find servers who have average nightly sales of over $2,000, click in cell **A105** and type **Average if Shift = Evening and Nightly Sales > $2,000** and press [Enter].

a. Click cell **F105**. On the **Formulas tab**, in the **Function Library group**, click **More Functions**, point to **Statistical**, and then click **AVERAGEIFS**. As the **Average_range** type **d3:d102** and in the **Criteria_range1** box type **b3:b102** In the **Criteria1** box type **Evening** and in the **Criteria_range2** box type **d3:d102** In the **Criteria2** box, type **>2000**

b. Click **OK**. Format cell **F105** with the **Accounting Number Format**.

(continues on next page)

Chapter Review

c. Press Ctrl + Home to make cell **A1** the active cell. On the **Insert tab**, in the **Illustrations group**, click **Shapes**, and then under **Block Arrows**, click the second shape—**Arrow: Left**.

d. Position the ⊞ pointer in the upper left corner of cell **E21**, hold down the left mouse button, and then drag down and to the right until the ⊞ pointer is approximately in the lower right corner of cell **I27**, and then release the mouse button.

e. Click any cell to deselect the shape. Then, point to the shape and double-click to position an insertion point within the shape. Type **Average nightly sales for servers on the Evening shift who have sales over $2,000 is $2,150.13**

6 Click cell **A1**. Display the **Weekly Awards** worksheet. To identify servers who can earn a weekly cash bonus, click cell **C3**.

a. On the **Formulas tab**, click in the **Function Library group**, click **Logical** and then click **IFS**. As **Logical_test1** type **b3>=15000** and as the **Value_if_true1** type **$100** As the **Logical_test2** type **b3>=12275** and as the **Value_if_true2** type **$75** As the **Logical_test3** type **b3<12275** and as the **Value_if_true** type **""** Click **OK**, and then copy the formula down through cell **B19**; three servers earned a cash bonus of $75 and one server earned a cash bonus of $100.

7 Click cell **A1**. Right-click the sheet tab and then click **Select All Sheets** so that *Group* displays in the title bar. With the worksheets grouped, on the **Page Layout tab**, in the **Page Setup group**, click **Margins**, and then click **Normal**, set the **Orientation** to **Landscape** and scale the **Width** to **1 page**. Display the **Page Setup** dialog box. On the **Margins tab**, center the worksheets horizontally on the page. On the **Header/Footer tab**, insert a **Custom Footer** in the **left section** that includes the file name.

a. Display the document properties and if necessary, right-click the author name, click **Edit Property**, and then type your name. In the **Subject** box, type your course name and section #, and in the **Tags** box, type **Charlotte, server schedule** Display and then review the grouped worksheets in Print Preview—you will have five total pages.

b. On the left, click **Save**. Click any sheet tab to ungroup the sheets.

c. In the upper right corner of the Excel window, click **Close**. Submit your file as directed by your instructor.

You have completed Project 8D | END

Content-Based Assessments (Mastery and Transfer of Learning)

MyLab IT Grader	Mastering Excel	Project 8E Seafood Inventory

Apply 8A skills from these Objectives:

1. Calculate a Moving Average
2. Project Income and Expenses
3. Determine a Break-Even Point

In this Project, you will create a worksheet for Joe Flores, manager of the Dallas region, who wants to analyze the fluctuation in the quantity of shrimp that is used at the four Dallas restaurants. You will use the moving average tool to help identify the variation in shrimp usage in recipes over a four-week period. Your completed worksheets will look similar to Figure 8.54.

Project Files for MyLab IT Grader

1. In your **MyLab IT** course, locate and click **Excel 8E Seafood Inventory**, Download Materials, and then Download All Files.
2. Extract the zipped folder to your Excel Chapter 8 folder. Close the Grader download screens.
3. Take a moment to open the downloaded **Excel_8E_Seafood_Inventory_Instructions**; note any recent updates to the book.

Project Results

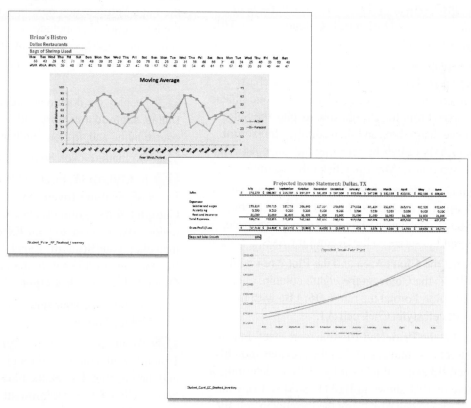

Figure 8.54

For Non-MyLab Submissions

For Project 8E, you will need:
e08E_Seafood_Inventory

In your Excel Chapter 8 folder, save your workbook as:
Lastname_Firstname_8E_Seafood_Inventory

After you have named and saved your workbook, on the next page, begin with Step 2.
After Step 16, submit your file as directed by your instructor.

(continues on next page)

Content-Based Assessments (Mastery and Transfer of Learning)

1 Navigate to your **Excel Chapter 8 folder**, and then double-click the Excel file you downloaded from **MyLab IT** that displays your name—**Student_Excel_8E_Seafood_Inventory**. If necessary, at the top, click **Enable Editing**.

2 Ensure that the **Analysis ToolPak** is enabled. On the **Moving Average** worksheet, insert a **Moving Average** using the range **A5:AB5** as the **Input Range**. Type **4** as the **Interval** and use cell **A6** as the **Output Range**. Select *only* the **Chart Output** check box; do NOT select the Labels in First Row check box.

3 Position the chart between cells **C8** and **Z29**, keeping the chart slightly inside the cell borders.

4 Edit the **Vertical (Value) Axis Title** to **Bags of Shrimp Used** Edit the **Horizontal (Category) Axis Title** to **Four-Week Period**

5 To display the days of the week as the **Horizontal (Category) Axis Labels**, at the bottom of the chart, point to any of the data points, and then click one time to select the axis. From the **Design tab**, display the **Select Data Source** dialog box, and then edit the **Horizontal (Category) Axis Labels** by selecting the range **A4:AB4**; click **OK** two times. (Mac tip: Click OK one time.)

6 To plot the **Forecast series** on a secondary axis, on the chart, point to the **Series "Forecast" line**, double-click the line to display the **Format Data Series** pane, and then plot the series on the **Secondary Axis**.

7 Format the **Chart Area** and the **Plot Area** with a **Solid fill**. As the **Color**, in the eighth column, click the second color. Format the range **D6:AB6** with the **Comma [0]** cell style. Click cell **A1**.

8 Display the **Projected Income** worksheet. In cell **C3**, construct a formula that takes the previous month's sales in cell **B3** and multiplies it by 110% to determine a growth rate of 10% shown in **B13** (1+b13). Copy the formula across to cell **M3**. Copy the formula in cell **B9** across to cell **M9**.

9 To create a line chart with a second series, select the nonadjacent ranges **A2:M3** and **A9:M9**, and then insert the first Line chart style.

10 Change the **Chart Title** to **Expected Break-Even Point**

11 Position the chart between cells **B15** and **M36**, keeping the chart slightly inside the cell borders.

12 Double-click a value on the vertical axis, and then in the **Format Axis** pane, display the **Axis Options**. Set the **Minimum** bounds to **150000** and the **Maximum** to **550000** to provide more vertical space on the chart to show a more dramatic slope.

13 Format both the **Plot Area** and the **Chart Area** with a **Solid fill**. As the **Color**, in the fifth column, click the second color.

14 Click cell **A1**. Select all the sheets, and then display the **Page Setup** dialog box. Insert a custom footer in the left section that includes the file name, and then center the worksheets horizontally. On the ribbon, set the **Orientation** to **Landscape**, and scale the **Width** to **1 page**.

15 Display the document properties. As the **Tags**, type **Dallas, seafood inventory** and as the **Subject**, type your course name and section number.

16 On the left, click **Save**. **Close** ☒ Excel.

17 In **MyLab IT**, locate and click the Grader Project **Excel 8E Seafood Inventory**. In **step 3**, under **Upload Completed Assignment**, click **Choose File**. In the **Open** dialog box, navigate to your **Excel Chapter 8 folder**, and then click your **Student_Excel_8E_Seafood_Inventory** file one time to select it. In the lower right corner of the **Open** dialog box, click **Open**.

> The name of your selected file displays above the Upload button.

18 To submit your file to **MyLab IT** for grading, click **Upload**, wait a moment for a green **Success!** message, and then in **step 4**, click the blue **Submit for Grading** button. Click **Close Assignment** to return to your list of **Course Materials**.

You have completed Project 8E | END

Content-Based Assessments (Mastery and Transfer of Learning)

| MyLab IT Grader | Mastering Excel | Project 8F Seafood Chowder |

Apply 8B skills from these Objectives:

4. Use Solver
5. Create Scenarios
6. Use Logical Functions
7. Create Complex Formulas

In this Mastering Excel project, you will assist Jillian Zachary, manager of the Ft. Lauderdale East restaurant, by using Solver to create several scenarios for how much of each of the three seafood ingredients—scallops, shrimp, and fish—to include in the chowder at the new seasonal prices to maintain a profit margin of 35 percent on a serving of chowder at the current wholesale seafood costs. Your completed worksheets will look similar to Figure 8.55.

Project Files for MyLab IT Grader

1. In your **MyLab IT** course, locate and click **Excel 8F Seafood Chowder**, Download Materials, and then Download All Files.
2. Extract the zipped folder to your Excel Chapter 8 folder. Close the Grader download screens.
3. Take a moment to open the downloaded **Excel_8F_Seafood_Chowder_Instructions**; note any recent updates to the book.

Project Results

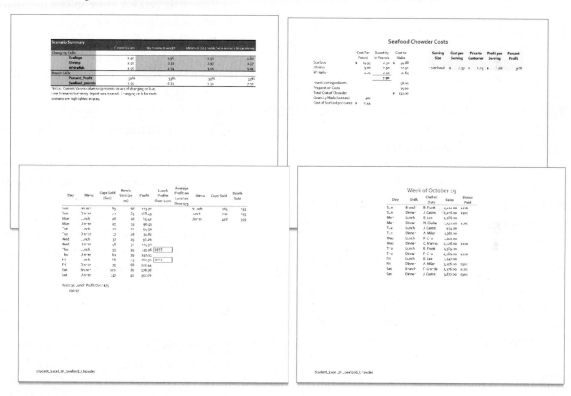

Figure 8.55

For Non-MyLab Submissions

For Project 8F, you will need:

e08F_Seafood_Chowder

In your Excel Chapter 8 folder, save your workbook as:

Lastname_Firstname_8F_Seafood_Chowder

After you have named and saved your workbook, on the next page, begin with Step 2.

After Step 15, save and submit your file as directed by your instructor.

(continues on next page)

Content-Based Assessments (Mastery and Transfer of Learning)

1 Navigate to your **Excel Chapter 8 folder**, and then double-click the Excel file you downloaded from **MyLab IT** that displays your name—**Student_Excel_8F_Seafood_Chowder**. If necessary, at the top, click **Enable Editing**.

2 Ensure that **Solver** is installed. With the **Seafood Chowder Costs** worksheet displayed, in the upper left, click the **Name Box arrow**, and then click **Percent_Profit** to select cell **J5**. Open **Solver**. Set the objective cell, **Percent_Profit** (cell J5) to the **Value Of 35%** and set the variable cells by selecting the range **C4:C6**. Click **Solve**.

3 Save the scenario as **No minimum weight** and then restore the original values.

4 Open **Solver**. Add a constraint where cell **C7 >= 7.5** and then click **Solve**.

5 Save the scenario as **Minimum 7.5 pounds** and restore the original values.

6 Add a constraint where cell **C6 = c5*2** and then click **Solve**.

7 Save the scenario as **Twice as much fish as shrimp** and restore the original values.

8 Open the **Scenario Manager** and create a scenario summary. As the **Result cells** type **=j5,c7** to summarize results from cells **J5** and **C7**.

9 Display the **Weekly Sales** worksheet. Recall that the SUMIF function begins =*sumif(* and then—separated by commas—requires a *range*, then a *criteria* cell, and then a *sum range* within the parentheses. In cell **I2** using the ScreenTip to guide you, enter a **SUMIF** function that looks at the range **B2:B15**, which has the defined name **MENU** for the criteria *Menu* type in cell **H2** and then sums the number of cups of soup sold in the range **C2:C15**, which has the defined name **CUPS** Then copy the formula down through cell **I4** to average the cups of soups sold for Lunch and for Dinner.

10 Using the same technique, in cell **J2** enter the SUMIF function that uses the Named Ranges **MENU** and **BOWLS** to count the number of bowls of soup sold for each menu in column H (use the cell reference **H2** as the criteria). Copy the formula down through cell **J4**.

11 In cell **F2**, enter an **IF** function with a nested **AND** function to test for lunch profits (in cell B2) greater than or equal to $100 (cell E2), that returns the word **BEST** when both conditions are met, and that leaves the cell blank if conditions are not met. Begin the formula **=IF(AND(b2="lunch",** and then complete the formula. You will not see a result in cell F2 because if does not meet the conditions. Copy the formula down through cell **F15**—only two cells will meet the conditions. Use the conditional formatting rule Text that Contains to format the cells with a red border for those days that meet both conditions.

12 In cell **A17** type **Average Lunch Profit Over $75** Click cell **A18** and then on the **Formulas tab**, in the **Function Library**, click **More Functions**, point to **Statistical**, and then click **AVERAGEIFS**. Average the range **E2:E15** using the Criteria range **MENU** with the **Criteria1** equal to **Lunch** The second criteria range is **E2:E15** and the second criteria is greater than **75** Format the result with two decimal places.

13 Display the **Chef Awards** worksheet. Chefs earn a bonus based on the Sales during their shift—Lunch, Dinner, or Brunch. In cell **E3**, enter an **IFS** function by using the **Function Arguments** dialog box to compute a bonus based on the following: Sales over $3,000 earn a bonus of $300, Sales over $2,000 earn a bonus of $200, Sales over $1,500 earn a bonus of $100, and if conditions are not met, leave the cell blank. Copy the formula down through cell **E16**. Eight bonuses display as the result.

14 **Select All Sheets**, click the **Page Layout tab**, set the **Orientation** to **Landscape** and scale the **Width** to **1 page**. Display the **Page Setup** dialog box, center the worksheets horizontally, and insert a **Custom Footer** with the file name in the **left section**. Make cell **A1** active and then right-click any sheet tab and click **Ungroup Sheets**. Display the **document properties**, if necessary add your name as the author, type your course name and section # in the **Subject** box, and as the **Tags**, type **seafood chowder, recipe costs** On the left, click **Save**.

15 In the upper right corner of the Excel window, click **Close**.

16 In **MyLab IT**, locate and click the Grader Project **Excel 8F Seafood Chowder**. In **step 3**, under **Upload Completed Assignment**, click **Choose File**. In the **Open** dialog box, navigate to your **Excel Chapter 8 folder**, and then click your **Student_Excel_8F_Seafood_Chowder** file one time to select it. In the lower right corner of the **Open** dialog box, click **Open**.

The name of your selected file displays above the Upload button.

17 To submit your file to **MyLab IT** for grading, click **Upload**, wait a moment for a green **Success!** message, and then in **step 4**, click the blue **Submit for Grading** button. Click **Close Assignment** to return to your list of **Course Materials**.

You have completed Project 8F | END

Content-Based Assessments (Mastery and Transfer of Learning)

| MyLab IT Grader | **Mastering Excel** | **Project 8G Income Model** |

Apply 8A and 8B skills from these Objectives:

1. Calculate a Moving Average
2. Project Income and Expenses
3. Determine a Break-Even Point
4. Use Solver
5. Create Scenarios
6. Use Logical Functions
7. Create Complex Formulas

In this Mastering Excel project, you will assist Kelsey Tanner, CFO of Brina's Bistro, to use a worksheet model and Solver to create several scenarios that would result in breaking even six months after opening. In this model for projecting the income, a new restaurant is expected to break even eight months after opening. Management wants to examine the assumptions and see what changes are needed to shorten the time it takes to break even. Month 0 is the first month of operation and it assumes that a new restaurant will gross $156,250 in sales in the opening month. The costs related to sales are assumed to be 87%; fixed costs are $40,000; and the anticipated growth rate in the first year, month-to-month, is 10%. The worksheet extends these assumptions out to month 11, which is the end of the first year of operation. Your completed worksheets will look similar to Figure 8.56.

Project Files for MyLab IT Grader

1. In your Course Materials, locate and click **Excel 8G Income Model**, Download Materials, and then Download All Files.
2. Extract the zipped folder to your Excel Chapter 8 folder. Close the Grader download screens.
1. Take a moment to open the downloaded **Excel_8G_Income_Model_Instructions** document; note any recent updates to the book.

Project Results

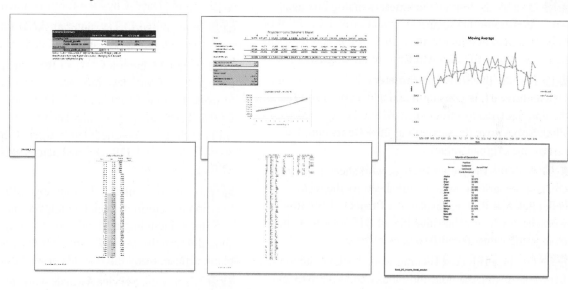

Figure 8.56

For Non-MyLab Submissions

For Project 8G, you will need: In your Excel Chapter 8 folder, save your workbook as:

e08G_Income_Model   **Lastname_Firstname_8G_Income_Model**

After you have named and saved your workbook, on the next page, begin with Step 2.

After step 19, save and submit your file as directed by your instructor.

(continues on next page)

1 Navigate to your **Excel Chapter 8 folder**, and then double-click the Excel file you downloaded from **MyLab IT** that displays your name—**Student_Excel_8G_Income_Model**. If necessary, at the top, click **Enable Editing**.

2 On the **Projected Income** worksheet, change the value in cell **B15** to **6** and press Enter—in the green shaded area, *Sales* now indicates *$276,806* and the *Gross Profit/Loss* indicates *($4,015)*. Note that these match the figures under Month 6 in cells H3 and H10 respectively. Management wants to create several scenarios that would result in breaking even six months after opening.

3 Ensure that the Solver add-in is installed. Change the value in cell **B16** to **11%** and press Enter. Open **Solver**. Set the objective cell as **b20** to a **Value Of 0** and set the **Variable Cells** to **b16,b18** (be sure to type the comma between the two cell references) to change both the growth rate in cell **B16** and the costs related to Sales % in cell **B18**. Click **Solve**. Save this scenario as **11% Growth** and then restore the original values.

4 Display the **Solver Parameters** dialog box again. Add a constraint that requires Percent growth in cell **B16** to be less than or equal to **10%** Click **Solve**, and then save this scenario as **10% Growth** Restore the original values.

5 Display the **Solver Parameters** dialog box again. Delete the existing constraint and add a constraint for the Costs related to sales in cell **B18** to be equal to **85%** Click **Solve**, save the scenario as **85% Costs** and then restore the original values.

6 With the **Projected Income** worksheet displayed, create a scenario summary worksheet. As the result cell, click cell **B20**. Redisplay the **Projected Income** worksheet. Change the value in cell **B15** back to **1** and change the value in cell **B16** back to **10%**

7 On the **Projected Income** worksheet, create a **Line** chart using the noncontiguous ranges **A2:M3** and **A8:M8**.

8 Change the **Chart Title** to **Expected Break-Even Point** Position the chart so that the upper left corner of the chart aligns with the upper left corner of cell **B22**. Click cell **A1** to deselect the chart and move to the top of the worksheet.

9 Ensure that the Analysis ToolPak add-in is installed. Display the **Sales** worksheet. Create a **Moving Average** using the sales **B2:B49** as the input range, **7** as the **Interval**, **C3** as the **Output Range**, and selecting the **Labels in First Row** and **Chart Output** check boxes.

10 Select the chart, and then move the chart to a new sheet named **Sales Trend Chart**

11 On the **Sales Trend Chart** worksheet, click one time to select the **Horizontal (Category) Axis Labels**, display the **Select Data Source** dialog box, click to **Edit** the **Horizontal (Category) Axis Labels**, if necessary display the **Sales** worksheet, and then select the range **A9:A49** from the **Sales** worksheet. On the **Sales Trend Chart** worksheet, change the date format used for the **Horizontal (Category) Axis** labels to the **3/14 Date** format.

12 On the **Sales Trend Chart** worksheet, change the **Horizontal (Category) Axis** title to **Date** On the **Vertical (Value) Axis**, set the **Minimum** to **3500** Click outside of the chart to deselect it. On this chart sheet, insert a custom footer with the file name in the **left section**.

13 On the **Schedules** worksheet, in cell **F3**, enter a **COUNTIFS** function to count the number of Day shifts each server is scheduled to work. Defined names exist for SERVER and SHIFT and the order is SERVER, cell E3, SHIFT, and "Day." Copy the formula down to cell **F19**.

14 In the range **I3:I19**, enter an **AND** function to determine which servers are scheduled for 2-5 day shifts.

15 In cell **J3**, enter a **COUNTIFS** function to calculate the number of Monday shifts each server is scheduled to work. Edit the formula in cell **J3** by adding a second **COUNTIFS** function to calculate the number of Tuesday shifts each server is scheduled to work. Copy the formula down through cell **J19**. Defined names exist for the range SERVER and DAY.

16 In cell **K3**, enter an **IF** function with a nested **AND** function to determine which employees are scheduled for 2–5 shifts, including a Monday or Tuesday. The function should return the world **Eligible** if true and leave the cell blank if false. Copy the formula down through cell **K19**.

17 Display the **Service Awards** worksheet. Servers earn a cash award when the number of Comment Cards from customers with a positive comment is 20 or more per month. In cell **C3**, enter an **IFS** function by using the Function Arguments dialog box to compute the cash award based on the following: Comments of 30 or more earn a bonus of $75; Comments of 25 or more but less than 30 earn a bonus of $50; Comments of 20 or more but less than 25 earn a bonus of $25; if conditions are not met, leave the cell blank. Copy the formula down through cell **C19**. Ten awards display as the result.

(continues on next page)

Mastering Excel: Project 8G Income Model (continued)

18 Right-click the **Service Awards** sheet tab, and then click **Select All Sheets**. Click the **Page Layout tab**, set the **Orientation** to **Landscape**. Scale both the **Width** and the **Height** to **1 page**. Display the **Page Setup** dialog box, center the worksheets horizontally, and insert a **Custom Footer** with the file name in the **left section**. Make cell **A1** active. Right-click any sheet tab and then click **Ungroup Sheets**.

19 Display the **document properties**, if necessary add your name as the author, type your course name and section # in the **Subject** box, and as the **Tags**, type **income, sales model** On the left, click **Save**. **Close** Excel.

20 In **MyLab IT**, locate and click the Grader Project **Excel 8G Income Model**. In **step 3**, under **Upload Completed Assignment**, click **Choose File**. In the **Open** dialog box, navigate to your **Excel Chapter 8 folder**, and then click your **Student_Excel_8G_Income_Model** file one time to select it. In the lower right corner of the **Open** dialog box, click **Open**. The name of your selected file displays above the Upload button.

21 To submit your file to **MyLab IT** for grading, click **Upload**, wait a moment for a green **Success!** message, and then in **step 4**, click the blue **Submit for Grading** button. Click **Close Assignment** to return to your list of **Course Materials**.

You have completed Project 8G   END

Content-Based Assessments (Critical Thinking)

GO! Fix It	**Project 8H Maintenance Expenses**	IRC
GO! Make It	**Project 8I Oyster Usage**	IRC
GO! Solve It	**Project 8J Tampa Income**	IRC
GO! Solve It	**Project 8K Ahi Salad**	

Project Files

For Project 8K, you will need the following file:

e08K_Ahi_Salad

You will save your workbook as:

Lastname_Firstname_8K_Ahi_Salad

Open the file e08K_Ahi_Salad and using your own name, save it as **Lastname_Firstname_8K_Ahi_Salad** Be sure that Solver is installed. Create three scenarios and a summary. Set the objective cell to J5, value of 60%. Solve for **No minimum weight of vegetables** by changing variable cells to the range C4:C6. Solve for **Minimum 5 pounds of vegetables** by using the constraints cell C5, >=, and 5. Solve for **Twice as many vegetables as greens** by using the constraints cell C5, =, C6*2. Create a Scenario Summary. On all sheets, insert the file name in the footer in the left section. Set the orientation to Landscape, width to 1 page, and center horizontally. Add appropriate information to the document properties including the tag **Ahi salad** and submit as directed by your instructor.

		Performance Level		
		Exemplary	**Proficient**	**Developing**
Performance Criteria	**Use Solver to Create Scenarios**	Three scenarios were created using Solver based on the instructions.	Two scenarios were created using Solver based on the instructions.	None or one scenario was created using Solver based on the instructions.
	Create a Scenario Summary	A Scenario Summary listing three scenarios was created.	A Scenario Summary listing two scenarios was created.	A Scenario Summary was not created.

You have completed Project 8K | END

Outcomes-Based Assessments (Critical Thinking)

Rubric

The following outcomes-based assessments are open-ended assessments. That is, there is no specific correct result; your result will depend on your approach to the information provided. Make Professional Quality your goal. Use the following scoring rubric to guide you in how to approach the problem and then to evaluate how well your approach solves the problem.

The *criteria*—Software Mastery, Content, Format and Layout, and Process—represent the knowledge and skills you have gained that you can apply to solving the problem. The *levels of performance*—Professional Quality, Approaching Professional Quality, or Needs Quality Improvements—help you and your instructor evaluate your result.

	Your completed project is of Professional Quality if you:	Your completed project is Approaching Professional Quality if you:	Your completed project Needs Quality Improvements if you:
1-Software Mastery	Choose and apply the most appropriate skills, tools, and features and identify efficient methods to solve the problem.	Choose and apply some appropriate skills, tools, and features, but not in the most efficient manner.	Choose inappropriate skills, tools, or features, or are inefficient in solving the problem.
2-Content	Construct a solution that is clear and well organized, contains content that is accurate, appropriate to the audience and purpose, and is complete. Provide a solution that contains no errors of spelling, grammar, or style.	Construct a solution in which some components are unclear, poorly organized, inconsistent, or incomplete. Misjudge the needs of the audience. Have some errors in spelling, grammar, or style, but the errors do not detract from comprehension.	Construct a solution that is unclear, incomplete, or poorly organized, contains some inaccurate or inappropriate content, and contains many errors of spelling, grammar, or style. Do not solve the problem.
3-Format and Layout	Format and arrange all elements to communicate information and ideas, clarify function, illustrate relationships, and indicate relative importance.	Apply appropriate format and layout features to some elements, but not others. Overuse features, causing minor distraction.	Apply format and layout that does not communicate information or ideas clearly. Do not use format and layout features to clarify function, illustrate relationships, or indicate relative importance. Use available features excessively, causing distraction.
4-Process	Use an organized approach that integrates planning, development, self-assessment, revision, and reflection.	Demonstrate an organized approach in some areas, but not others; or, use an insufficient process of organization throughout.	Do not use an organized approach to solve the problem.

Outcomes-Based Assessments (Critical Thinking)

Apply a combination of the 8A and 8B skills

GO! Think	**Project 8L Seasonings Inventory**

Project Files

For Project 8L, you will need the following file:

e08L_Seasonings_Inventory

You will save your workbook as:

Lastname_Firstname_8L_Seasonings_Inventory

Open the file e08L_Seasonings_Inventory, and then using your own name save it in your chapter folder as **Lastname_Firstname_8L_Seasonings_Inventory** From the source data, create a Moving Average chart to help identify the variation in seafood seasoning used over a four-week period using a 7-day interval. Begin the output range in cell A6. Move the chart to a new sheet. Format the chart attractively. Insert the file name in the left section of the footer on each page, center horizontally, set the orientation to Landscape, add appropriate information to the document properties, including the tag **seasonings inventory** and submit as directed by your instructor.

	You have completed Project 8L	END

GO! Think	**Project 8M PT Staff**	IRC

You and GO!	**Project 8N Entertainment**	IRC

Using Macros and Visual Basic for Applications

EXCEL 2019

Rob/Shutterstock

In This Chapter

**GO! To Work
with Excel**

In this chapter, you will automate Excel worksheets to make it easier and faster to perform complex or repetitive tasks. Because individuals who do the same type of work each day may use a specific sequence of Excel commands repeatedly, Excel enables you to record a sequence of commands in a macro and then activate the sequence with a single button or keystroke. A button can be attached to the macro and placed on the worksheet or ribbon. You can also program Excel to perform tasks that are not represented by existing commands or to validate data against complex criteria that requires more than a simple comparison.

Westland Plains Human Resources Consulting provides its customers with services such as Employee Benefits Administration, Recruitment Services, Payroll Processing, Computer Technology Training, Employee Assistance Programs, and Corporate Health and Wellness Programs. Customers are typically small and midsize companies who, for cost savings and efficiency, use an outside source for such services. Westland has a staff of 35 full-time employees in five regional offices throughout the metropolitan area. Westland's knowledgeable consultants help companies remain compliant with federal and state laws and regulations.

Travel Expenses

Project Activities

In Activities 9.01 through 9.07, you will set a macro security level, remove file protection, record a macro, and assign a macro to the Quick Access Toolbar. You will test and modify a macro to fill in employee information for a Travel Expense Report and protect the worksheet. Your completed project will look similar to Figure 9.1.

Project Files for **MyLab IT Grader**

1. In your storage location, create a folder named **Excel Chapter 9**.
2. In your **MyLab IT** course, locate and click **Excel 9A Travel Macro**, Download Materials, and then Download All Files.
3. Extract the zipped folder to your Excel Chapter 9 folder. Close the Grader download screens.
4. Take a moment to open the downloaded **Excel_9A_Travel_Macro_Instructions**; note any recent updates to the book.

Project Results

GO! Project 9A
Where We're Going

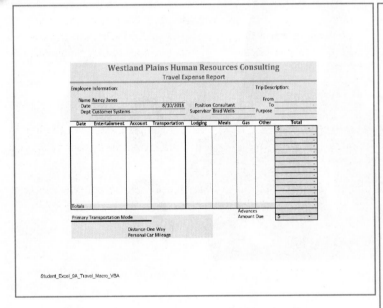

Figure 9.1 Project 9A Travel Expenses

For Non-MyLab Submissions	In your storage location, create a folder named **Excel Chapter 9**
For Project 9A, you will need:	In your Excel Chapter 9 folder, save your workbook as a Macro-Enabled Workbook:
e09A_Travel_Macro	**Lastname_Firstname_9A_Travel_Macro**
	If your instructor requires a workbook with formulas, save as:
	Lastname_Firstname_9A_Travel_Macro_Formulas

Complete Activity 9.01. In Activity 9.02, Step 3, open e09A_Travel_Macro and then continue with the project.

Objective 1 Record a Macro

GO! Learn How

Video E9-1

A ***macro*** is an action or a set of actions with which you can automate tasks by grouping a series of commands into a single command. You can perform the command with a single mouse click, a keyboard shortcut, or when a workbook opens.

For example, you could record a macro that automatically enters employee names in the first column, alphabetizes the names, and then applies a fill color to the cells containing the names. When you have a sequence of actions that you perform frequently, record the actions as a macro to automate the task.

Macros are recorded in the ***Visual Basic for Applications*** programming language—also referred to as ***VBA***—which is the language used to write computer programs within the Microsoft Windows environment.

To work with macros, you must:

- Add the Developer tab to the ribbon, which displays the commands you will need to work with macros.
- Select a macro security setting to enable macros when using Excel.
- Save the workbook that includes macros as an Excel Macro-Enabled Workbook file type.

Activity 9.01 | Adding the Developer Tab to the Ribbon

ALERT   Because Office 365 is a cloud-based subscription service that receives continuous updates, you may encounter some variations in what appears on your screen and what is shown in this instruction. Microsoft Office 365 is fully installed on your PC or Mac; no internet access is necessary to create or edit documents. When you *are* connected to the internet, you will receive monthly upgrades and new features, so you always have the latest versions of Office apps as soon as they are available. Your subscription gives you continuous free access to the latest innovations and refinements.

The macro commands are located on the Developer tab, which, by default, does not display in Excel. You must enable the Developer tab from the Excel Options dialog box. In this Activity, you will add the Developer tab to the ribbon.

1 Start Excel and open a new blank workbook. Click the **File** tab to display **Backstage** view, and then click **Options**. In the **Excel Options** dialog box, on the left, click **Customize Ribbon**.

MAC TIP   Click the Excel menu, and then click Preferences. Under Authoring, click Ribbon & Toolbar.

2 On the right, under **Customize Ribbon**, verify that **Main Tabs** is selected, select the **Developer** check box, and then compare your screen with Figure 9.2.

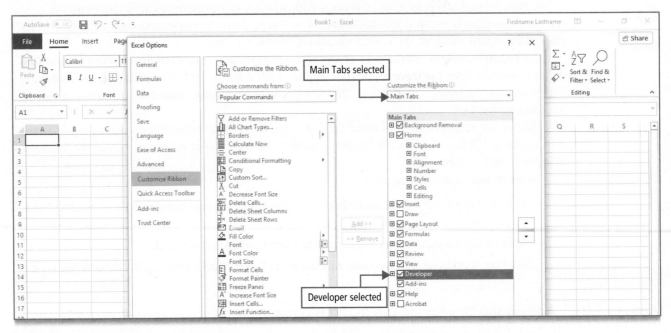

Figure 9.2

3 In the lower right corner, click **OK**. On the ribbon, click the **Developer tab**, and then compare your screen with Figure 9.3.

The *Developer tab* displays on the ribbon. The *Code group* contains the commands you will need to work with macros.

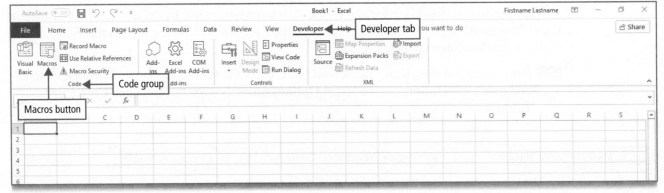

Figure 9.3

Activity 9.02 | Changing the Macro Security Settings in Excel

Expert 1.1.3

Opening an Excel workbook that has a macro attached to it might cause a message to display, indicating that macros are disabled. This is a precautionary measure because macros may contain viruses. Because a macro is a computer program, programming code that erases or damages files can be inserted by the person creating the macro. This unauthorized code is called a *macro virus*. In this Activity, you will change the security setting so that you can choose to enable macros when you open a workbook that contains a macro.

1 On the **Developer tab**, in the **Code group**, click **Macro Security**. Compare your screen with Figure 9.4, and then take a moment to study the table in Figure 9.5.

The Trust Center dialog box displays. On the left, Macro Settings is selected. The Macro Settings enable you to decide, each time you open a workbook, how or whether to run the macros that are contained in the workbook. The table in Figure 9.5 summarizes how macro virus protection works under each setting. Regardless of which option you choose, any installed antivirus software that works with your Microsoft Office software will scan the workbook for known viruses before it is opened. In an organization, you may not be permitted to change these settings without permission from your System Administrator. Any macro setting changes that you make in Excel in the Macro Settings category apply only to Excel and do not affect any other Office program.

MAC TIP   Click the Excel menu. Click Preferences and then click Security & Privacy.

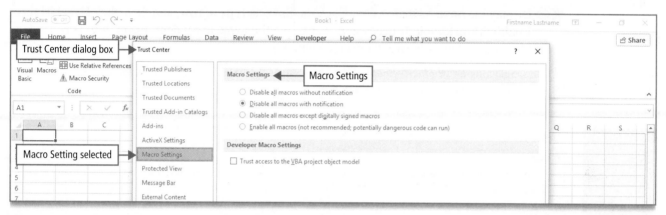

Figure 9.4

Macro Settings and Their Effects	
Macro Setting	**Description**
Disable all macros without notification	This setting disables all macros and security alerts unless the Excel workbook is in a trusted location.
Disable all macros with notification	This setting is enabled by default. You are alerted if macros are present in the workbook. This setting enables you to choose each time you open a workbook whether or not to run the macros that are contained in the workbook.
Disable all macros except digitally signed macros	This setting enables macros from trusted publishers to run; otherwise, this setting is the same as the *Disable all macros with notification* setting.
Enable all macros (not recommended; potentially dangerous code can run)	Use this setting when you want to enable all macros to run on a temporary basis. It is not recommended as a permanent setting because it makes your computer vulnerable to potential malicious code.

Figure 9.5

2 ▶ Under **Macro Settings**, verify that the default option—**Disable all macros with notification**—is selected, and then click **OK**.

By selecting the security level *Disable all macros with notification*, you have the option of enabling macros on a file-by-file basis. This security level causes a Security Warning to display, indicating that macros have been disabled, and gives you the option to enable or disable macros.

Excel provides safeguards that help protect against viruses that can be transmitted by macros. If you share macros with others, you can certify that the macro is from a trustworthy source by using a ***digital signature***—an electronic, encryption-based, secure stamp of authentication on a macro or document. The digital signature confirms that the macro or document originated from the signer and has not been altered. If a file has been digitally signed, a certificate that identifies the source displays; then you can decide whether this is a trusted source before you activate the macros.

3 From the files you downloaded with this project, open **Student_Excel_9A_Travel_Macro**.

4 Display the **Save As** dialog box. Click the **Save as type arrow**, and then click **Excel Macro-Enabled Workbook**. If necessary, change the file name to Student_Excel_9A_Travel_ Macro, and then compare your screen with Figure 9.6.

Selecting *Excel Macro-Enabled Workbook* saves the Excel file in the XML-based format, allowing macros to be saved to the workbook.

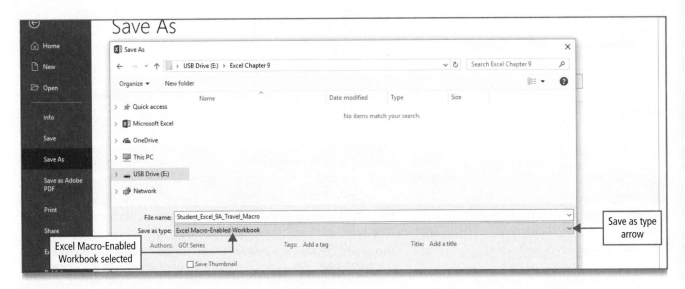

Figure 9.6

5 Click **Save**. Insert a footer in the **left section** that includes the file name. Return to **Normal** view and scroll to view the top of the worksheet.

6 **Save** 💾 your workbook.

Activity 9.03 | Unprotecting a Workbook

This workbook is a form that employees of Westland Plains Human Resources Consulting use to report travel expenses. A *form* is a worksheet or Excel object that contains fields and controls that enable a user to easily enter or edit data. The worksheet is protected so that employees can fill in their travel expense information only in the unlocked cells. A worksheet must be *unprotected* to record a macro.

1 On the **Review tab**, in the **Protect group**, click **Protect Workbook**.

2 In the **Unprotect Workbook** dialog box, type **travel** which is the password applied to this form, and then click **OK**.

Activity 9.04 | Recording a Macro

MOS
Expert 3.6.1, 3.6.2

The macro recorder records all the steps (keystrokes and mouse clicks) that you require to complete the actions you want your macro to perform—*except* for navigation on the ribbon, which is not included in the recorded steps. When you record a macro, assign it a name so that you can refer to the macro name later. In this Activity, you will record a macro that will fill in employee information for a specific employee on a Travel Expense form.

1 With cell **B6** active, click the **Developer tab**, and then, in the **Code group**, click **Record Macro**.

In the Record Macro dialog box, you can name the macro, assign a shortcut key, and start the recording. The *Record Macro* command records your actions in Visual Basic for Applications (VBA).

ANOTHER WAY On the View tab, in the Macros group, click the Macros button arrow, and then click Record Macro.

2 In the **Macro name** box, delete the existing text, and then type **Employee_Info**

The first character of the macro name must be a letter. Following characters can be letters, numbers, or underscore characters. Spaces are not permitted in a macro name; an underscore character works well as a word separator. Do not use a macro name that could be a cell reference—you will get an error message that the macro name is not valid.

3 In the **Shortcut key** box, type **r**

You can create a shortcut key to execute the macro, in this instance *Ctrl + r*. If you do not specify a shortcut key at the time you create the macro, you can add it later. Shortcut keys are case sensitive.

MAC TIP In the Shortcut key box, type e. Note that the shortcut key on a Mac will be ⌥option + ⌘command ⌘ + E.

NOTE   Assigning Shortcut Keys to a Macro

The Excel program uses shortcut keys for common commands, such as Ctrl + S for saving a file or Ctrl + P for printing a file. When you assign a shortcut key to a macro, it takes precedence over the shortcut keys that are built into Excel. For this reason, use caution when you assign a shortcut key so that you do not override an existing shortcut. To see a list of Excel shortcut keys, in the Excel Help files, in the Search help box, type *keyboard shortcuts*, and then examine the topic *Keyboard shortcuts in Excel for Windows*.

4 Click the **Store macro in arrow** to see the available options.

You can store a macro in *This Workbook*—the default setting—in *New Workbook*, or in a *Personal Macro Workbook*. The *New Workbook* option opens a new workbook and adds the macro to that workbook. The *Personal Macro Workbook* is a workbook where you can store macros that you want to be able to use in other workbooks.

Be sure **This Workbook** is selected, and then click the **Store macro in arrow** to close the list. Click in the **Description** box. Type **Fills in the Employee Information** and then compare your screen with Figure 9.7.

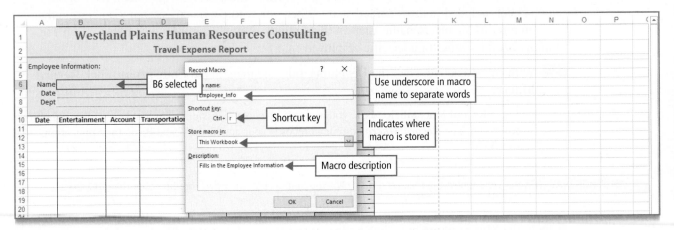

Figure 9. 7

6 Click **OK**, and in the Status bar in the lower left corner of your screen, notice the white square button indicating that a macro is recording.

The macro recorder is turned on. From this point forward, every action you take will be recorded as part of the macro. The amount of time you take between actions is not being recorded, so there is no need to rush. If you make an error, take the appropriate steps to correct it; the corrective steps will simply become part of the macro, and you can edit the mistakes out of the macro later.

7 In cell **B6**, type **Nancy Jones** and then press Enter. With cell **B7** active, hold down Ctrl and press ; (semicolon), which will insert the current date. Press Enter.

8 With cell **B8** active, type **Customer Systems** and then press Enter. Click cell **F7**, type **Consultant** and then press Enter. In cell **F8**, type **Brad Wells** and then click cell **A11**, so that when the macro completes, the first cell in the data area is active to begin filling in the travel information.

9 On the **Developer tab**, in the **Code group**, click **Stop Recording**. Compare your screen with Figure 9.8.

The macro stops recording and cell A11 is selected. The Stop Recording button returns to a Record Macro button on the ribbon. In the status bar, if you point to the button to the right of *Ready*, the ScreenTip indicates *No macros are currently recording. Click to begin recording a new macro.*

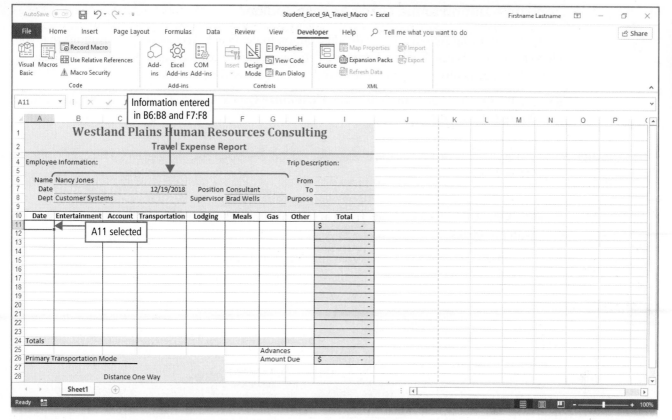

Figure 9.8

10 Delete the text you just typed in the five cells—**B6**, **B7**, **B8**, **F7**, **F8**—and then click cell **B6**. Press Ctrl + R to test your macro.

The shortcut key activates the macro, the employee information is filled in, and cell A11 is selected.

 MAC TIP Press option + command ⌘ + E to run the macro.

11 Save 🖫 your workbook.

Objective 2 Assign a Macro to a Button on the Quick Access Toolbar

GO! Learn How
Video E9-2

You have practiced activating a macro with a keyboard shortcut, but another option is to activate a macro by clicking a button on the Quick Access Toolbar. To do so, you must create a new toolbar button.

Activity 9.05 | Adding a Button to the Quick Access Toolbar

MOS
1.4.1

In the following Activity, you will add a button to the Quick Access Toolbar. Buttons that you add to the Quick Access Toolbar become a permanent part of the toolbar to which it was added unless you specifically remove it or reset the Quick Access Toolbar.

1 On the **Quick Access Toolbar**, click **Customize Quick Access Toolbar** ⬇, and then click **More Commands**.

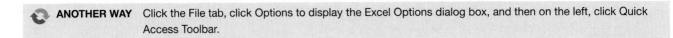

ANOTHER WAY Click the File tab, click Options to display the Excel Options dialog box, and then on the left, click Quick Access Toolbar.

2 Click the **Choose commands from arrow**, and then click **Macros**. Compare your screen with Figure 9.9.

Under <Separator>, your Employee_Info macro and a default icon display.

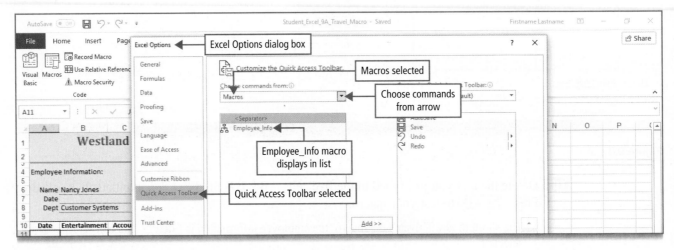

Figure 9.9

3 Click your **Employee_Info** macro, and then in the center of the dialog box click **Add**. Compare your screen with Figure 9.10.

The Employee_Info macro displays on the right in the panel that contains buttons that currently display on the Quick Access Toolbar.

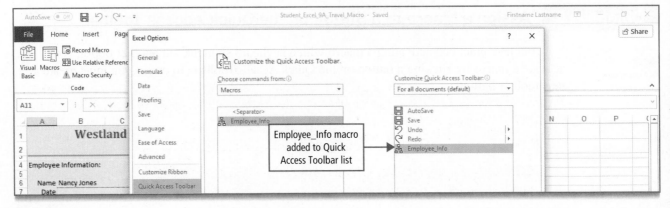

Figure 9.10

4 With your **Employee_Info** command selected on the right, click **Modify**. Compare your screen with Figure 9.11.

The Modify Button dialog box displays. The first symbol is selected and at the bottom of the dialog box, Display name indicates *Employee_Info*.

MAC TIP Skip Steps 4 and 5. Click Save. Your Quick Access Toolbar displays a small circle icon.

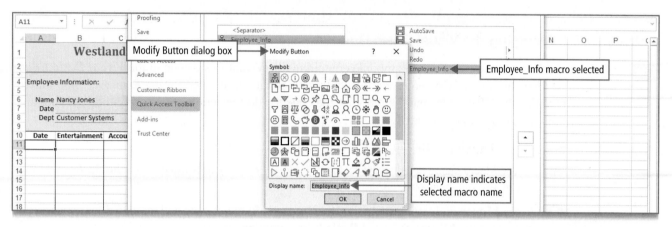

Figure 9.11

5 Under **Symbol**, in the fourth row, click the last icon—the **Smiley Face**—and then click **OK** two times. **Save** your workbook, and then compare your screen with Figure 9.12.

The Smiley Face icon displays on the Quick Access Toolbar.

Figure 9.12

Activity 9.06 | Testing the Macro Button

After you add the button, test it to verify that the button performs as you intended. When you point to the button, the ScreenTip indicates the name of the button. The action that causes your macro to run is called an *event* and might be a combination of keystrokes or the click of a button on the Quick Access Toolbar.

1 Select and delete the cell contents in the nonadjacent ranges **B6:B8** and **F7:F8**.

2 Click cell **B6**, and then on the **Quick Access Toolbar**, click your new **Employee_Info** button—the Smiley Face.

The employee information is filled in, and cell A11 is selected.

MAC TIP On the Quick Access Toolbar, click the circle icon.

Objective 3 Modify a Macro

GO! Learn How
Video E9-3

When you record a macro, a **module** is the place where the Visual Basic for Applications (VBA) programming code is stored. A module consists of one or more **procedures**—a unit of computer code that performs an action. Procedures are commonly referred to as **sub procedures**, or simply **subs**. If you want to modify the way your macro performs, you can modify the actual code that was created by the macro.

Activity 9.07 | Changing the Visual Basic Code

MOS
Expert 3.6.3

You can view and edit the module containing the Visual Basic code in the **Visual Basic Editor** window. In this Activity, you will open the module that was created for the *Employee_Info* macro, examine the VBA code, and then modify the code to add the action of centering the worksheet both horizontally and vertically.

1 On the **Developer tab**, in the **Code group**, click **Macros**.

The Macro dialog box displays and the *Employee_Info* macro is listed. From this dialog box, you can also run the macro.

2 In the **Macro** dialog box, with the **Employee_Info** macro selected, click **Edit**. If necessary, maximize the Microsoft Visual Basic Editor window and the Code window.

The Microsoft Visual Basic Editor window displays. This window has several panes that can be displayed, and some of the available panes may be opened or closed.

3 In the **Code window** on the right, locate the green and black lines of text that comprise the comments and code for the Employee_Info macro. Compare your screen with Figure 9.13.

Your window may be configured differently than the one shown in Figure 9.13. The first section, displayed in green and in lines preceded by an apostrophe ('), consists of comments that describe the macro. These comments are not part of the macro procedure. In this module, the comments include the data you entered when you created the macro—the macro name and description and the shortcut key that was assigned.

The VBA code that follows, in black type, includes the instructions to select the cell ranges and enter data. *Sub* indicates the beginning of the sub procedure. *End Sub* indicates the end of the sub procedure.

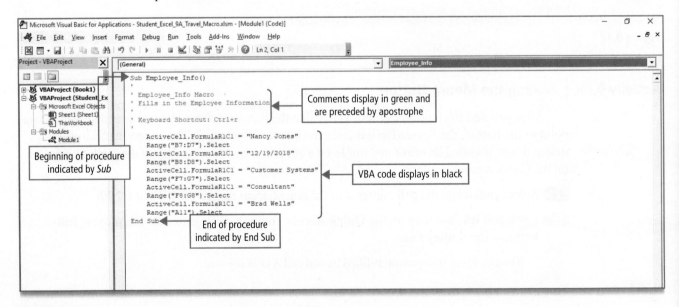

Figure 9.13

4 At the end of the *last* line of code—*Range("A11").Select*—click to place the insertion point after *Select*, and then press Enter.

In this manner, you can insert a blank line to type new code.

5 On the new, empty line, type **With ActiveSheet.PageSetup** and then press Enter.

The word *With* notes the beginning of a **VBA construct**—an instruction that enables the macro to perform multiple operations on a single object. The remainder of the code—*ActiveSheet. PageSetup*—is the equivalent of displaying the Page Setup dialog box.

6 Press Tab to indent and type **.CenterHorizontally = True** Press Enter and type **.CenterVertically = True** and then press Enter. Verify that you typed the period preceding each line of code.

The period identifies the command that follows. In this case, the two commands that you typed following each period instruct Excel to center the worksheet horizontally and vertically on the page. The commands are indented using Tab to make it easier to read the code. When you press Enter, the text will continue to wrap to that same level of indentation.

7 Press Shift + Tab. Type **End With** and then compare your screen with Figure 9.14.

Instructions that have a beginning and ending statement, such as *With* and *End With*, should be indented at the same level. To decrease the level of indentation, press Shift + Tab, which will move the indentation toward the left margin.

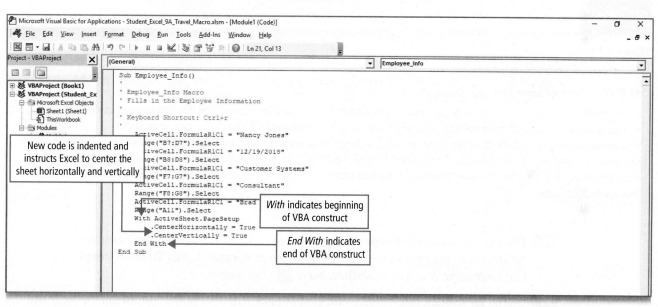

Figure 9.14

8 On the menu bar, click **File**, and then click **Close and Return to Microsoft Excel**.

⌨ **MAC TIP**   In the upper left corner of the Microsoft Visual Basic window, click Close to return to your Excel worksheet.

9 Select the nonadjacent ranges **B6:B8** and **F7:F8** and press ⎯Del⎯ so that these cells are empty again. Select cell **B6**. On the **Quick Access Toolbar**, click the **Employee_Info** button that you created, and then display the **Print Preview**. Compare your screen with Figure 9.15.

The worksheet is centered horizontally and vertically on the page.

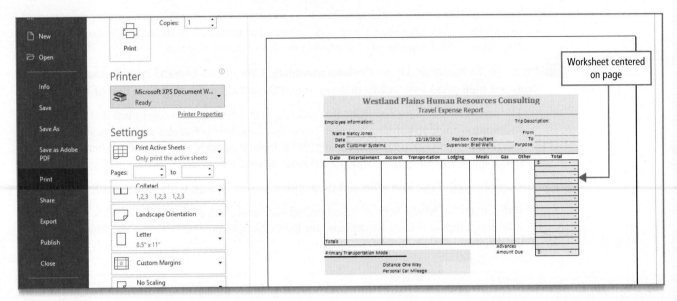

Figure 9.15

ALERT   Does an Error Message Display?

If you made a mistake in entering the code, you will see a Microsoft Visual Basic dialog box informing you of the error. The message will vary, depending on the error that you have made. If this happens, in the dialog box, click Debug. This action will return you to the Microsoft Visual Basic Editor window and the line of code with the error will be highlighted in yellow. Examine the code and compare it with the instructions. Look for a typing error, a missing period, or a missing line of code. Correct the error and then, on the File menu, click Close and Return to Microsoft Excel. In the message box, click OK to stop the debugger. Test the button again.

---

10 Display the document **Properties**. In the **Tags** box, type **travel expense form** and in the **Subject** box, type your course name and section number. Under **Related People**, be sure that your name displays as **Author**. **Save** 🖫 your workbook.

11 On the **Developer tab**, in the **Code group**, click **Macros**. In the **Macro** dialog box, with the **Employee_Info** macro selected, click **Edit** to display the Microsoft Visual Basic Editor window.

12 In the Microsoft Visual Basic Editor window, press ⎯Ctrl⎯ + ⎯A⎯ to select all of the code. Press ⎯Ctrl⎯ + ⎯C⎯ to copy the code to the clipboard. On the menu bar, click **File**, and then click **Close and Return to Microsoft Excel**.

13 In the sheet tab area, click **New sheet** ⊕ to insert a new worksheet. **Rename** the inserted sheet **VBA Code**

14 In the **VBA Code** sheet, with cell **A1** active, on the **Home tab**, in the **Clipboard group**, click **Paste** to paste the VBA code to the new worksheet so that it can be verified. **AutoFit** column A.

15 Click the **File tab**, and then click **Save As**. Navigate to your **Excel Chapter 9 folder**, and then click the **Save as type arrow**. Click **Excel workbook**. In the **File name** box, type **Student_Excel_9A_Travel_Macro_VBA** and then click **Save**. In the message box, click **Yes**.

For Non-MyLab Submissions Determine What Your Instructor Requires
As directed by your instructor, submit your completed Excel file.

16 In **MyLab IT**, locate and click the Grader Project **Excel 9A Travel Macro**. In **step 3**, under **Upload Completed Assignment**, click **Choose File**. In the **Open** dialog box, navigate to your **Excel Chapter 9 folder**. Click your **Student_Excel_9A_Travel_Macro_VBA** file one time to select it. In the lower right corner of the **Open** dialog box, click **Open**.

The name of your selected file displays above the Upload button. *Be sure that you select the file with the copied VBA code.* If you selected the macro-enabled file, it may not be accepted by **MyLab IT**.

17 To submit your file to **MyLab IT** for grading, click **Upload**, wait a moment for a green **Success!** message, and then in **step 4**, click the blue **Submit for Grading** button. Click **Close Assignment** to return to your list of **Course Materials**.

MORE KNOWLEDGE

To copy a macro to another workbook, be sure that both Excel files are open, and then open the VBA Editor for the macro that you wish to copy. On the left, in the Project Explorer pane of the editor, both worksheets will be listed. Simply drag the selected module to the destination worksheet.

You have completed Project 9A | END

Project Activities

In Activities 9.08 through 9.13, you will assist Edward Salisbury, Controller at Westland Plains Human Resources Consulting, by writing a set of commands in the VBA programming language using ActiveX Control buttons to automate the travel policy guidelines for expense reports. Your completed workbook will look similar to Figure 9.16.

Project Files for MyLab IT Grader

1. In your **MyLab IT** course, locate and click **Excel 9B Expense Report**, Download Materials, and then Download All Files.
2. Extract the zipped folder to your Excel Chapter 9 folder. Close the Grader download screens.
3. Take a moment to open the downloaded **Excel_9B_Expense_Report_Instructions**; note any recent updates to the book.

Project Results

GO! Project 9B
Where We're Going

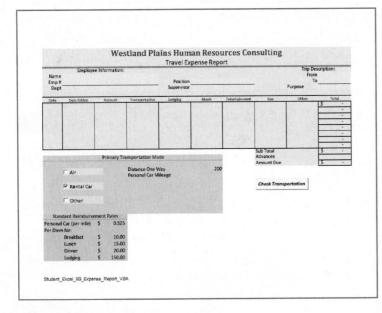

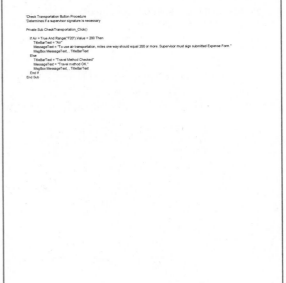

Figure 9.16 Project 9B Expense Report

For Non-MyLab Submissions

For Project 9B, you will need:
e09B_Expense_Report

In your Excel Chapter 9 folder, save your workbook as:
Lastname_Firstname_9B_Expense_Report
If your instructor requires a workbook with formulas, save as:
Lastname_Firstname_9B_Expense_Report_Formulas

Save your document as directed on the next page in Step 2.

GO! Learn How

Video E9-4

Recall that within VBA, you can write a procedure—a named sequence of statements in a computer program that performs an action or task. A procedure can include an ***ActiveX control***—a graphic object such as a check box or a button that can be placed on a worksheet or form to display or enter data, to perform an action, or to make the form easier to read. When the person filling in the form clicks the ActiveX control, VBA code runs that automates a task or offers options.

A ***Form control*** is a simpler object that does not require VBA code (therefore it works on other versions of Excel that do not support ActiveX). You can assign a macro directly to a Form control without using the VBA Editor. Unlike ActiveX controls, you can put a Form control on a chart sheet. A Form control is formatted by right-clicking it to open a Format dialog box. ActiveX controls are more flexible and customizable than Form controls.

Activity 9.08 | Inserting ActiveX Controls

ActiveX controls are especially useful for forms that individuals complete online, because you can control different events that occur when the control is used. In the following Activity, you will insert check boxes. A ***check box*** is a type of ActiveX control that the person filling in the form can select to indicate a choice.

Westland Plains Human Resources Consulting has a policy that requires employees to use ground transportation—company car, company van, rental car, or personal car—for trips under 200 miles. In this project, you will design a travel expense report that will verify that when an employee submits an expense report that lists air as the mode of travel, that the one-way distance is over 200 miles, and if it is not, a message will display indicating that a supervisor signature is required.

1 ▸ Navigate to your **Excel Chapter 9 folder**, and then double-click the Excel file you downloaded from **MyLab IT** that displays your name—**Student_Excel_9B_Expense_Report**.

MAC TIP   This project covers ActiveX controls, which are a MOS skill, but cannot be completed on a Mac. Please consult with your instructor. Complete Activity 9.13 to restore your system to its original settings.

2 ▸ Display the **Save As** dialog box. Navigate to your **Excel Chapter 9** folder. Click the **Save as type arrow**, and then click **Excel Macro-Enabled Workbook**. Click **Save**.

3 On the **Developer tab**, in the **Controls group**, click **Insert**.

A gallery of Form Controls and ActiveX Controls displays.

4 Under **ActiveX Controls**, point to each button to display the ScreenTip. Take a moment to study the description of the ActiveX controls in the table in Figure 9.17.

ActiveX Controls		
Button	**ScreenTip**	**Description**
☐	Command Button	Inserts a command button control to which code can be attached, initiating an action when clicked.
	Combo Box	Inserts a combo box control, which displays a list of choices from another source; the user can either select a choice from the list or type his or her own entry in the box.
☑	Check Box	Inserts a check box control that can be turned on (selected) or turned off (cleared).
	Image	Inserts an image control to embed a picture.
A	Label	Inserts a text label to provide information about a control.
	List Box	Inserts a list box control, which displays a list of choices.
	More Controls	Displays a list of additional controls.
⦿	Option Button	Inserts an option button control to indicate an on/off choice.
	Scroll Bar	Inserts a scroll bar control, which scrolls through a range of values.
	Spin Button	Inserts a spin button control, which displays a range of numbers from which the user can increase or decrease a value.
abl	Text Box	Inserts a text box control in which the user can type text.
	Toggle Button	Inserts a toggle button control, which remains pressed in when clicked, and then releases when clicked again.

Figure 9.17

5 Under **ActiveX Controls**, click **Check Box** ☑ and notice that the mouse pointer changes to the ✛ shape.

6 Point to the upper left corner of cell **B20** and drag to insert a check box object that is approximately the height of the cell and the width of columns **B:C**. Compare your screen with Figure 9.18. The size and placement need not be exact—you will adjust the size and placement later. If you are not satisfied with your result, click **Undo** and begin again, or use the sizing handles to adjust the size.

The object name—*CheckBox1*—displays in the check box and also displays in the Name Box. An EMBED formula displays on the Formula Bar.

The formula defines the object as an embedded object and includes the name of the object source. Recall that to **embed** means to insert something created in one program into another program. ActiveX controls are not part of Excel but may be added to it. This provides other software vendors and individuals the opportunity to write ActiveX controls to handle a wide variety of desired actions. The More Controls button at the end of the ActiveX Controls gallery lists many additional ActiveX controls, and there are more available for download from the internet.

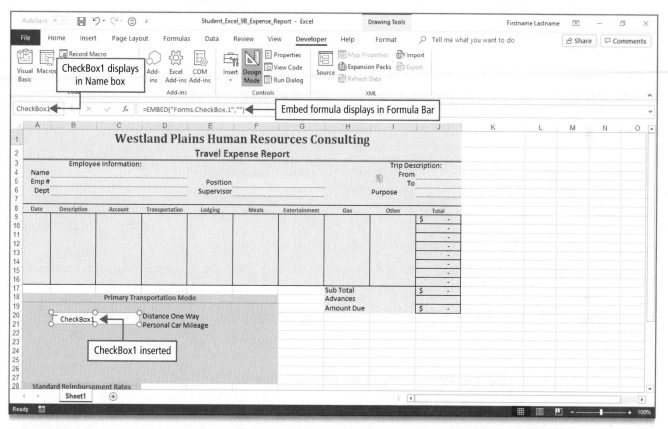

Figure 9.18

7 Repeat this process to add two more check boxes of the same approximate size under **CheckBox1**. Verify that the boxes do not overlap—leave a slight space between each box. Use any technique for moving and sizing objects that you have practiced, and then compare your screen with Figure 9.19.

> ActiveX controls are not attached to cells—rather, they float on the worksheet like inserted Shapes or SmartArt.

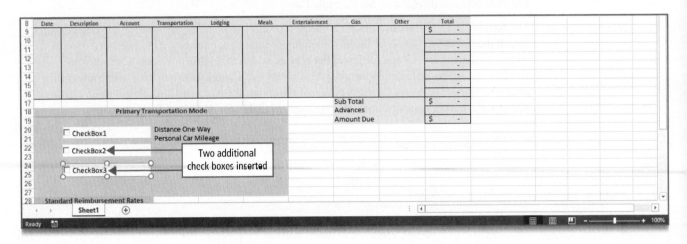

Figure 9.19

8 Click **CheckBox1**, and then on the **Developer tab**, in the **Controls group**, notice that *Design Mode*—a feature in which you can add and modify ActiveX controls—is active.

> When you are finished creating and editing the ActiveX controls in your worksheet, you can click Design Mode to toggle it off. When you add controls, Design Mode is activated. Use the Design Mode button to move in and out of Design Mode.

9 With **CheckBox1** selected, hold down Ctrl, and click each of the remaining check boxes so that all three check boxes are selected.

10 On the **Page Layout tab**, in the **Arrange group**, click **Align**, and then click **Align Left** to align the check boxes on the left. **Save** your workbook.

Activity 9.09 | Changing the Properties of an ActiveX Control

Each ActiveX control has a set of *properties*—characteristics—that you can change. This is similar to formatting a shape by changing its color, font, or some other property. There are many properties associated with ActiveX controls, and the properties vary depending on the type of control. In this Activity, you will change the name of each of the check boxes, change the caption that displays in each check box, and change the height and width of each check box.

1 Click the **Developer tab**. In the **Controls group**, verify that **Design Mode** is active.

2 Click another area of the worksheet to deselect the group of check boxes, and then click **CheckBox1** to select the check box. In the **Controls group**, click **Properties** to display the Properties pane.

3 ▶ Drag the **Properties** pane near the upper right of your screen. Point to the lower left sizing handle to display the [🖈] pointer and then drag down and to the left as necessary so that you can see the entire list of properties, as shown in Figure 9.20.

The properties are organized in alphabetical order on the *Alphabetic* tab. On the *Categorized* tab, the same properties are listed, but they are organized by logical groups. You can click the arrow at the top of the Properties pane to display a list from which you can select the object whose properties you want to modify.

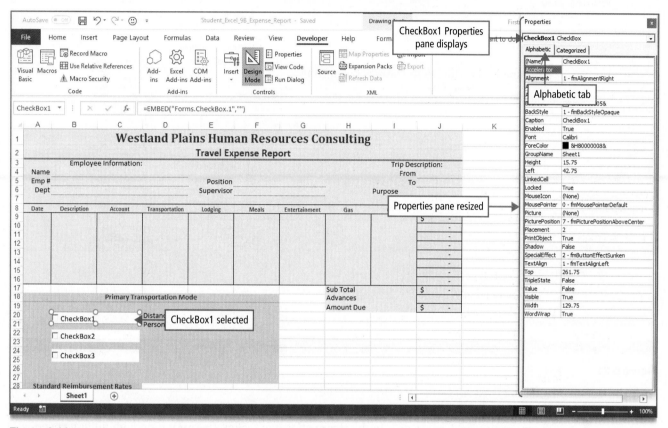

Figure 9.20

ALERT   The CheckBox1 Properties Pane

If your Properties pane does not display the properties for CheckBox1, you may have inserted a Form control, rather than an ActiveX control. Delete your check boxes and then create them again, being sure to choose the ActiveX control from the Controls gallery.

---

4 ▶ At the top of the **Alphabetic** list, in the first column, click **(Name)**, and then type **Air** Notice that your typing displays in the column to the right. Press Enter, and notice that *Air* displays in the **Name Box**.

Use the (Name) field when you need to refer to an object in a program. The naming convention is the same for naming cells in Excel; that is, the name cannot include spaces or punctuation marks.

5 ▶ In the first column, click the **Caption** property, type **Air** and then press Enter.

The text in the check box changes to *Air*.

6 Under **Alphabetic**, click **Height**. Type **15.75** and then click **Width**. Type **84.75** and then press Enter. Compare your screen with Figure 9.21.

The check box resizes to a height of 15.75 pixels and a width of 84.75 pixels.

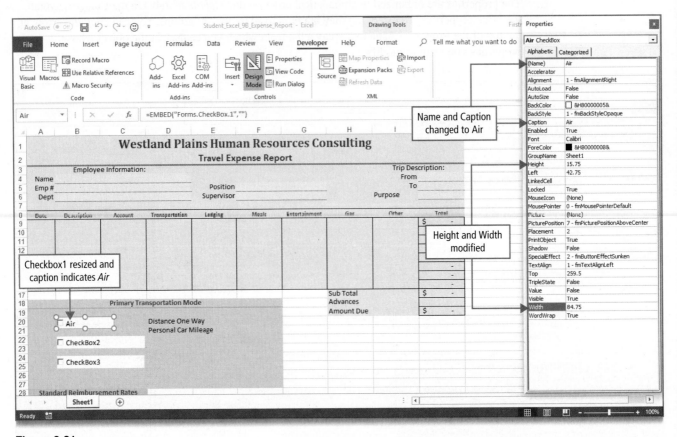

Figure 9.21

7 Click **CheckBox2** to select the check box and notice that the **Properties** pane displays the properties for *CheckBox2*. In the **Properties** pane, click **(Name)**, type without any spaces **RentalCar** and then press Enter. Click the **Caption** property. Including the space, type **Rental Car** and then press Enter.

8 Using the technique you just practiced, change the **(Name)** and **Caption** for the remaining check box to **Other**

9 Select the **Rental Car** check box, hold down Ctrl, and then select the **Other** check box so that both check boxes are selected.

If you want to change the same property for a group of objects, you can press Ctrl to select multiple objects and then change the property. You must change the Name and Caption of each check box individually.

10 With both check boxes selected, in the **Properties** pane, change the **Height** to **15.75** and the **Width** to **84.75**

The Rental Car and Other check boxes are resized and are the same height and width as the Air check box.

11 With both check boxes selected, hold down Ctrl, and then click the **Air** check box so that all three check boxes are selected. In the **Properties** pane, click **BackColor**, and notice that an arrow displays at the right edge of the BackColor box. Click the **BackColor arrow**, click the **System tab**, scroll down, and then click **Button Light Shadow**.

12 **Close** the **Properties** pane. If necessary, select the three check boxes. On the **Page Layout tab**, in the **Arrange group**, click **Align**, and then click **Distribute Vertically**. Click cell **A1** to deselect the group of check boxes. **Save** 🖫 your workbook, and then compare your screen with Figure 9.22.

The space between each of the check boxes is equal.

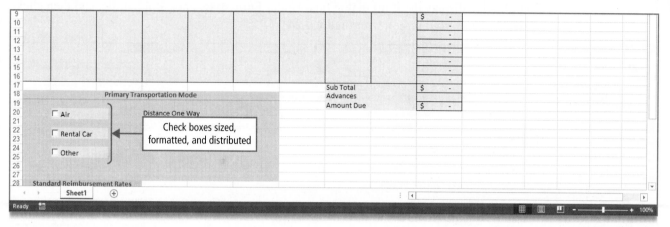

Figure 9.22

Activity 9.10 | Writing a VBA Procedure for a Command Button

Recall that a Command Button runs a macro that performs an action when a user clicks it. In this Activity, you will insert a Command Button and then write a VBA procedure to test whether the *Distance One Way* cell is less than 200 and whether *Air* transportation was used. If both conditions are true, a warning message will display indicating that a supervisor's signature is required in the Supervisor box.

1 Click cell **H22** to identify the location where you will place the Command Button.

2 On the **Developer tab**, in the **Controls group**, click **Insert**, and then under **ActiveX Controls**, click **Command Button** ▭. Point to the upper left corner of cell **H22**, and then click one time to insert a Command Button. Compare your screen with Figure 9.23.

The Command Button is added and a portion of the text *CommandButton1* displays as the caption on the button. By selecting cell H22, you have a visual cue as to where to place the Command Button. Recall, however, that ActiveX objects are not actually attached to a cell—the cell address is only a guide to direct you to the location where the control will be placed.

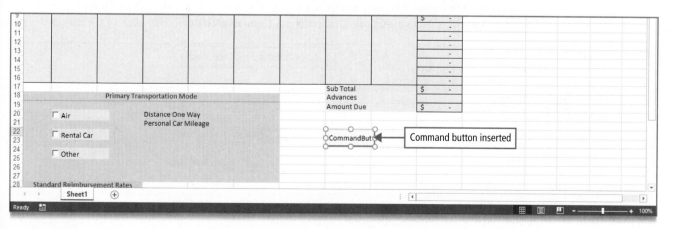

Figure 9.23

3 In the **Controls group**, click **Properties**. In the **Properties** pane, click **(Name)**. Type **CheckTransportation** and then press ⏎. Click the **Caption** property. Type **Check Transportation** and then press ⏎. Click **AutoSize**, click the **AutoSize arrow**, and then click **True**.

When AutoSize is set to True, the button resizes to accommodate the new caption.

4 In the **Properties** pane, click **Font**, and then at the right of the second column click **Font build ...** to display the **Font** dialog box. Under **Font style**, click **Bold Italic**, and then click **OK**. Compare your screen with Figure 9.24.

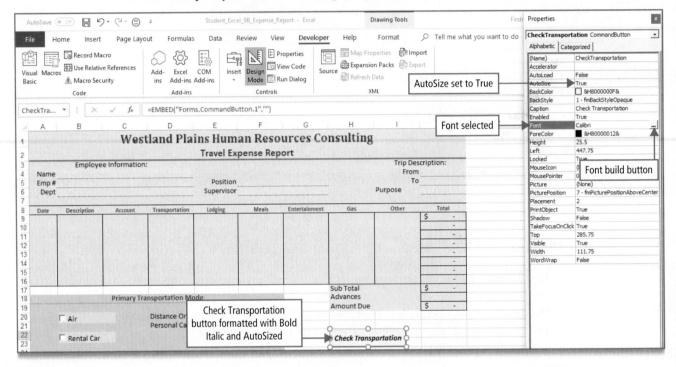

Figure 9.24

5 **Close** ☒ the **Properties** pane.

6 Select the **Check Transportation** control, if necessary. On the **Developer tab**, in the **Controls group**, click **View Code**. At the top of the **Code window**, click the **Object arrow**, and then on the list, click **CheckTransportation**. Compare your screen with Figure 9.25.

The Microsoft Visual Basic Code window displays and *CheckTransportation* displays in the Object box at the top of the window. This is the name of the selected ActiveX control. The beginning of this VBA procedure is indicated by *Private Sub CheckTransportation_Click()*. *Private* indicates that this procedure can be used only in this workbook. *End Sub* indicates the end of the procedure. The event that will activate the Check Transportation Command Button is one click of the button.

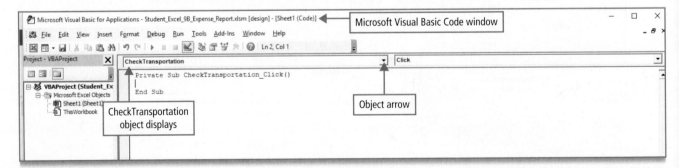

Figure 9.25

🔄 **ANOTHER WAY** In Design Mode, right-click the command button, and then click View Code, or in Design Mode, double-click the command button.

7 ▶ Click to the left of *Private Sub CheckTransportation_Click( )* to place the insertion point there, and then press Enter to insert a blank line. Press ↑ to move to the blank line. Including the apostrophe, type **'Check Transportation Button Procedure** and then press Enter. Be sure that you included the apostrophe at the beginning of the line. Type **'Determines if a supervisor signature is necessary** and then press Enter. Compare your screen with Figure 9.26.

Comments display in green and are preceded by an apostrophe ('). A line separates the comments from the VBA code. When writing a VBA procedure, it is recommended that you document the procedure with comments. Comments do not affect the running of the procedure.

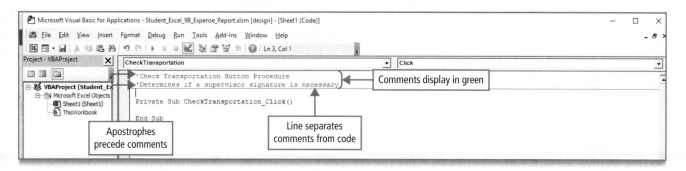

Figure 9.26

NOTE   Writing VBA Documentation

For purposes of this instruction, the documentation you entered is brief. When you create documentation in your own worksheets, you may want to include additional information about your VBA procedures.

8 ▶ Click to position the insertion point in the blank line above *End Sub*. Press Enter, and then press Tab. Type the lines of VBA code spaced as shown below. Use the Tab key to indent the middle three lines and Shift + Tab to reduce the indent by one tab for the last line. Compare your screen with Figure 9.27.

```
If Air = True Then
    TitleBarText = "Air"
    MessageText = "To use air transportation, miles one way should equal 200 or more."
    MsgBox MessageText, , TitleBarText
End If
```

The VBA code tests to see if the Air check box is selected, indicating that it is true. If the check box is selected, a message box will display the Message Text.

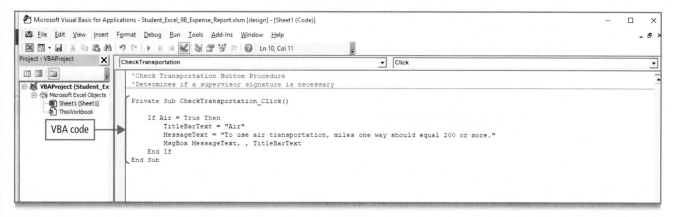

Figure 9.27

9 On the menu bar, click **File**, and then click **Close and Return to Microsoft Excel**.

10 In the **Controls group**, click **Design Mode** to exit Design Mode.

11 In the tan shaded section, select the **Air** check box, and then click the **Check Transportation** Command Button. If an error message displays, see the Alert box that follows for instructions on how to resolve the error. Compare your screen with Figure 9.28.

A check mark displays in the Air check box, and the Air message box displays.

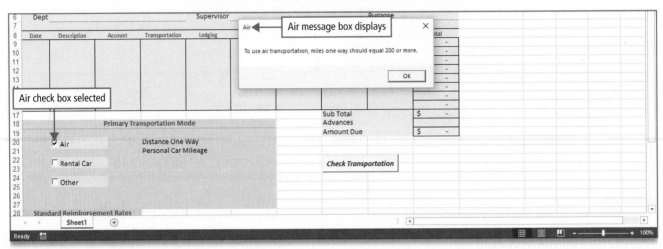

Figure 9.28

12 In the **Air** message box, click **OK**. **Save** your workbook.

ALERT   If an Error Message Displays

If you made a mistake in entering the code, you will see a Microsoft Visual Basic dialog box informing you of the error. The message varies depending on the error that you have made. If this happens, in the dialog box, click Debug. This action returns you to the Microsoft Visual Basic Editor window, and the line of code with the error will be highlighted in yellow. Examine the code and compare it with the instructions. Look for a typing error, a missing dot, or a missing line of code. Correct the error, and then on the File menu, click Close and Return to Microsoft Excel. In the message box, click OK to stop the debugger. Test the button again. If you are unable to resolve the error, seek assistance from your instructor or lab assistant.

Activity 9.11 | Modifying a VBA Procedure

You can modify a VBA procedure in the same manner that you modified the VBA code that was created when you used a macro. In this Activity, you will add a second condition—the distance one way must be 200 miles or more—and a second message box regarding the supervisor signature. To do this, you will use an If, Then, Else statement.

1 In the **Controls group**, click **Design Mode**, and then click **View Code**.

2 In the line of code beginning with *If Air*, click to place the insertion point to the *left* of the word *Then*. Type the following line of code, pressing Spacebar one time at the end:

And Range("F20").Value < 200

3 ▶ Verify the first line of code: *If Air = True And Range("F20").Value < 200 Then*

4 ▶ In the *MessageText* line, click to the left of the closing quotation mark, press [Spacebar], and then type a second sentence as follows: **Supervisor must sign submitted Expense Form.**

If the travel method is Air and the mileage is less than 200, the following message displays: *"To use air transportation, miles one way should equal 200 or more. Supervisor must sign submitted Expense Form."* The line of text extends across the Visual Basic Editor window, and the screen scrolls to the right.

5 ▶ Scroll to the left. At the end of the *MsgBox* line, place the insertion point after *TitleBarText.* Press [Enter], and then press [Shift] + [Tab]. Type the following code spaced as shown below:

Else

    TitleBarText = "Travel Method Checked"
    MessageText = "Travel method OK."
    MsgBox MessageText, , TitleBarText

6 ▶ Compare your VBA code with Figure 9.29.

If the Air check box is selected and the mileage is 200 or more, or if the Air check box is not selected, a message box indicating that the travel method is OK will display.

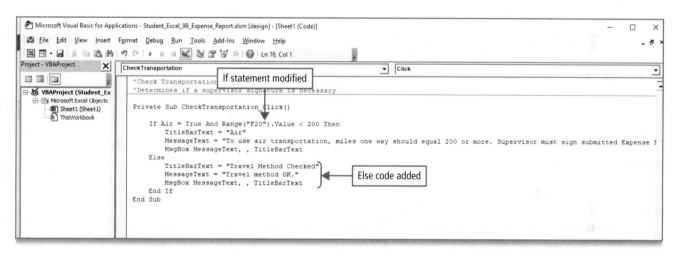

Figure 9.29

7 ▶ Click **File**, and then click **Close and Return to Microsoft Excel**. On the **Developer tab**, in the **Controls group**, click **Design Mode** to exit Design Mode. **Save** 🖫 your workbook.

Activity 9.12 | Testing the VBA Procedure and the ActiveX Control

After you create a VBA procedure, you should test it to verify that it works as you intended.

1 Be sure the **Air** check box is still selected—it displays a check mark. Be sure **Design Mode** is not selected. In cell **F20**, type **150** and then press Enter. Click the **Check Transportation** button. Compare your screen with Figure 9.30.

The first message box displays and informs you that a supervisor's signature is required.

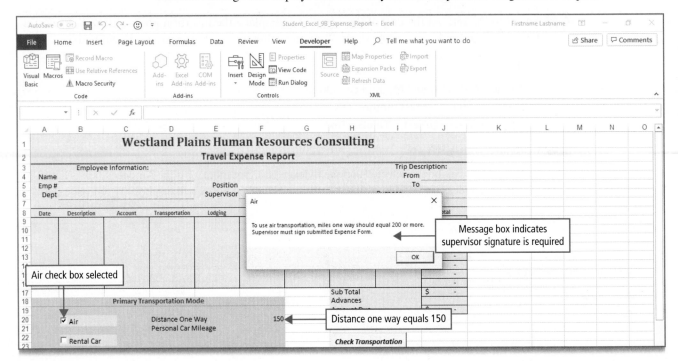

Figure 9.30

ALERT   Does an Error Message Display?

If an error message displays, in the message box, click Debug to return to the Visual Basic Editor window and correct the error that is highlighted in yellow. After correcting the highlighted error, on the File menu, click Close and Return to Microsoft Excel. Repeat Step 1 to continue.

---

2 In the **Air** message box, click **OK**. Click cell **F20**, type **200** and then press Enter. Click the **Check Transportation** button.

The second message box displays indicating *Travel method OK*. If you get the first message box, return to the code and correct the cell reference to F20.

3 In the **Travel Method Checked** message box, click **OK**.

You have tested both conditions for using air transportation—when the miles are 200 or more, and when the miles are less than 200. You also need to test the Command Button when other modes of transportation are used.

4 Clear the check mark from the **Air** check box. Select the **Rental Car** check box, and then click the **Check Transportation** Command Button.

The second message box displays indicating *Travel method OK*.

5 Click **OK** to acknowledge the message.

6 ▶ Insert a footer in the **left section** that includes the file name. Return to **Normal** view, and then press Ctrl + Home to move to the top of the worksheet. Display the workbook **Properties**. In the **Tags** box, type **expense report** and in the **Subject** box type your course name and section number. In the **Author** box, replace the existing text with your first and last name. Display the worksheet in **Print Preview**, return to the workbook and make any necessary corrections or adjustments.

7 ▶ Click the **Review tab**. In the **Protect group**, click **Protect Workbook**. In the **Protect Structure and Windows** dialog box, verify that **Structure** is selected and then type **1234** in the **Password** box. Compare your screen with Figure 9.31.

It is good practice to protect a workbook that contains a form so that users do not modify the ActiveX controls.

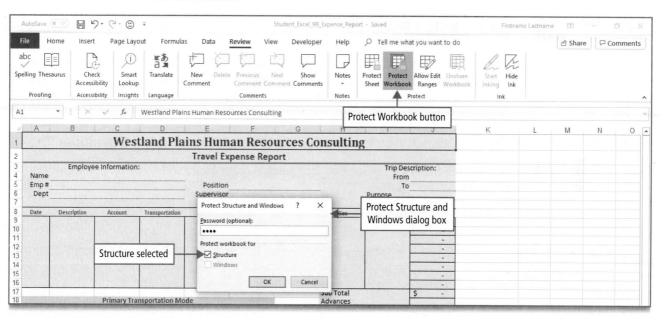

Figure 9.31

8 ▶ Click **OK**. In the **Confirm Password** dialog box, type **1234** and click **OK**. Save 💾 your workbook.For Non-MyLab Submissions Determine What Your Instructor Requires

9 ▶ On the **Developer tab**, in the **Controls group**, click **View Code**. In the Microsoft Visual Basic Editor window, press Ctrl + A to select all of the code. On the toolbar, click **Copy** 🖹. On the menu bar, click **File**, and then click **Close and Return to Microsoft Excel**.

10 ▶ On the **Review tab**, in the **Protect group**, click **Protect Workbook**. In the **Password** box, type **1234** and then click **OK**.

11 ▶ In the sheet tab area, click **New sheet** ⊕ to insert a new worksheet. **Rename** the inserted sheet **VBA Code**

12 ▶ In the **VBA Code** sheet, with cell **A1** active, on the **Home tab**, in the **Clipboard group**, click **Paste** to paste the VBA code to the new worksheet so that it can be verified. **AutoFit** column A. On the **Page Layout tab**, in the **Scale to Fit group**, change the **Width** to **1 page**.

13 ▶ Click the **File tab**, and then click **Save As**. Navigate to your **Excel Chapter 9 folder**, and then click the **Save as type arrow**. Click **Excel Workbook**. In the **File name** box, type **Student_Excel_9B_Expense_Report_VBA** and then click **Save**. In the message box, click **Yes**. **Close** your workbook.

For Non-MyLab Submissions Determine What Your Instructor Requires
As directed by your instructor, submit your completed Excel file.

14 In **MyLab IT**, locate and click the Grader Project **Excel 9B Expense Report**. In **step 3**, under **Upload Completed Assignment**, click **Choose File**. In the **Open** dialog box, navigate to your **Excel Chapter 9 folder**, and then click your **Student_Excel_9B_Expense_Report_VBA** file one time to select it. In the lower right corner of the **Open** dialog box, click **Open**.

> The name of your selected file displays above the Upload button. *Be sure that you select the file with the copied VBA code.* If you selected the macro-enabled file, it may not be accepted by **MyLab IT**.

15 To submit your file to **MyLab IT** for grading, click **Upload**, wait a moment for a green **Success!** message, and then in **step 4**, click the blue **Submit for Grading** button. Click **Close Assignment** to return to your list of **Course Materials**.

Objective 5 | Restore Initial Settings

GO! Learn How
Video E9-5

When you use a computer in a public location such as a college computer lab, or when you use someone else's computer, it is proper computer etiquette to return it to the condition in which you found it. In this chapter, you created a macro and then placed a button on the Quick Access Toolbar.

Activity 9.13 | Removing the Quick Access Toolbar Button, Macro, and the Developer Tab

1 Right-click the **Smiley Face** icon on the **Quick Access Toolbar**, and then click **Remove from Quick Access Toolbar**.

The Employee_Info button is removed from the Quick Access Toolbar.

> **MAC TIP** On the Quick Access Toolbar, click Customize Quick Access Toolbar, and then click More Commands. Make sure that Quick Access Toolbar is selected. In the Customize Quick Access Toolbar list, click <<No label>>. In the center of the dialog box, click the Remove arrow and then click Save.

2 On the **Developer tab**, in the **Code group**, click **Macros**.

3 Verify that the Macro dialog box is empty. If the Employee_Info macro you created is displayed, select the macro name, and then click **Delete**.

> **MAC TIP** In the Macro name list, click Employee_Info. Below the list, click – (the minus sign). In the Alert box click yes.

> The Employee_Info macro is part of the 9A_Travel_Macro workbook and will not be deleted from that file. If you accidentally saved the macro in another place and it displays in this list, it should now be deleted.

4 Click **Cancel**.

5 Right-click the **Developer tab**, and then click **Customize the Ribbon**. In the right pane, click **Developer** to deselect it, and then click **OK** to remove the **Developer tab**. **Close** Excel.

You have completed Project 9B **END**

wavebreakmedia/Shutterstock, Monkey Business Images/Fotolia, Ivanko80/Shutterstock, Monkey Business Images/Shutterstock

Microsoft Office Specialist (MOS) Skills in This Chapter	
Project 9A	**Project 9B**
1.4.1 Customize the Quick Access toolbar **Expert 1.1.3** Enable macros in a workbook **Expert 3.6.1** Record simple macros **Expert 3.6.2** Name simple macros **Expert 3.6.3** Edit simple macros	**Expert 1.2.3** Protect workbook structure

Build Your E-Portfolio

An E-Portfolio is a collection of evidence, stored electronically, that showcases what you have accomplished while completing your education. Collecting and then sharing your work products with potential employers reflects your academic and career goals. Your completed documents from the following projects are good examples to show what you have learned: 9G, 9K, and 9L.

GO! For Job Success

Discussion: Cyber Security

Your instructor may assign these questions to your class, and then ask you to think about them or discuss them with your classmates:

The U.S. Homeland Security Department describes cyber incidents (hacking) as actions where there is an attempt to gain unauthorized access to a system or its data, unwanted disruption to service, unauthorized use of a system, or change to a system without the owner's permission. As companies store and process more and more data at centralized, offsite "cloud" data centers, the opportunities for criminals to hack data are growing. Cyber security is an important part of every organization's information systems protocols, and many companies now employ a senior executive with the title Chief Information Security Officer.

g-stockstudio/ Shutterstock

What cyber incidents have you heard of in the news over the last year?

What precautions have you taken with your personal data to prevent a hack?

What would you do if you learned that a company you do business with, such as your bank or college, had been the subject of a cyber incident?

End of Chapter

Summary

You can automate an Excel worksheet to perform complex tasks faster and to perform repetitive actions using macros and the programming language called Visual Basic for Applications (VBA).

In the Visual Basic Editor window, comments that describe the macro are displayed in green and in lines preceded by an apostrophe ('). The VBA code that follows displays in black type.

A set of instructions that accomplishes a specific task is called a sub procedure, or simply sub. In the VBA code, Sub indicates the beginning of the sub procedure and End Sub indicates the end.

An ActiveX control is a graphic object, such as a check box or button, that can be placed on a worksheet or form. When the ActiveX control is clicked, a macro or code runs that automates a task or offers options.

GO! Learn It Online

Review the concepts, key terms, and MOS skills in this chapter by completing these online challenges, which you can find at **MyLab IT**.

Chapter Quiz: Answer matching and multiple-choice questions to test what you learned in this chapter.

Lessons on the GO!: Learn how to use all the new apps and features as they are introduced by Microsoft.

MOS Prep Quiz: Answer questions to review the MOS skills that you practiced in this chapter.

Project Guide for Excel Chapter 9

Your instructor will assign Projects from this list to ensure your learning and assess your knowledge.

	Project Guide for Excel Chapter 9		
Project	**Apply Skills from These Chapter Objectives**	**Project Type**	**Project Location**
9A MyLab IT	Objectives 1–3 from Project 9A	**9A Instructional Project (Grader Project)** **Instruction** Guided instruction to learn the skills in Project 9A.	In **MyLab IT** and in text
9B MyLab IT	Objectives 4–5 from Project 9B	**9B Instructional Project (Grader Project)** **Instruction** Guided instruction to learn the skills in Project 9B.	In **MyLab IT** and in text
9C	Objectives 1–3 from Project 9A	**9C Skills Review (Scorecard Grading)** **Review** A guided review of the skills from Project 9A.	In text
9D	Objectives 4–5 from Project 9B	**9D Skills Review (Scorecard Grading)** **Review** A guided review of the skills from Project 9B.	In text
9E MyLab IT	Objectives 1–3 from Project 9A	**9E Mastery (Grader Project)** **Mastery and Transfer of Learning** A demonstration of your mastery of the skills in Project 9A with extensive decision making.	In **MyLab IT** and in text
9F MyLab IT	Objectives 4–5 from Project 9B	**9F Mastery (Grader Project)** **Mastery and Transfer of Learning** A demonstration of your mastery of the skills in Project 9B with extensive decision making.	In **MyLab IT** and in text
9G MyLab IT	Objectives 1–5 from Projects 9A and 9B	**9G Mastery (Grader Project)** **Mastery and Transfer of Learning** A demonstration of your mastery of the skills in Projects 9A and 9B with extensive decision making.	In **MyLab IT** and in text
9H	Combination of Objectives from Projects 9A and 9B	**9H GO! Fix It (Scorecard Grading)** **Critical Thinking** A demonstration of your mastery of the skills in Projects 9A and 9B by creating a correct result from a document that contains errors you must find.	IRC
9I	Combination of Objectives from Projects 9A and 9B	**9I GO! Make It (Scorecard Grading)** **Critical Thinking** A demonstration of your mastery of the skills in Projects 9A and 9B by creating a result from a supplied picture.	IRC
9J	Combination of Objectives from Projects 9A and 9B	**9J GO! Solve It (Rubric Grading)** **Critical Thinking** A demonstration of your mastery of the skills in Projects 9A and 9B, your decision-making skills, and your critical thinking skills. A task-specific rubric helps you self-assess your result.	IRC
9K	Combination of Objectives from Projects 9A and 9B	**9K GO! Solve It (Rubric Grading)** **Critical Thinking** A demonstration of your mastery of the skills in Projects 9A and 9B, your decision-making skills, and your critical thinking skills. A task-specific rubric helps you self-assess your result.	In text
9L	Combination of Objectives from Projects 9A and 9B	**9L GO! Think (Rubric Grading)** **Critical Thinking** A demonstration of your understanding of the chapter concepts applied in a manner that you would outside of college. An analytic rubric helps you and your instructor grade the quality of your work by comparing it to the work an expert in the discipline would create.	In text
9M	Combination of Objectives from Projects 9A and 9B	**9M GO! Think (Rubric Grading)** **Critical Thinking** A demonstration of your understanding of the chapter concepts applied in a manner that you would outside of college. An analytic rubric helps you and your instructor grade the quality of your work by comparing it to the work an expert in the discipline would create.	IRC
9N	Combination of Objectives from Projects 9A and 9B	**9N You and GO! (Rubric Grading)** **Critical Thinking** A demonstration of your understanding of the chapter concepts applied in a manner that you would in a personal situation. An analytic rubric helps you and your instructor grade the quality of your work.	IRC

Glossary

Glossary of Chapter Key Terms

ActiveX control A graphic object, such as a check box or button that you place on a form to display or enter data, perform an action, or make the form easier to read. When the person filling in the form clicks the ActiveX control, VBA code runs that automates a task or offers options.

Check box A type of ActiveX control that the person filling in the form can select to indicate a choice.

Design Mode An Excel feature in which you can add and modify ActiveX controls.

Digital signature An electronic, encryption-based, secure stamp of authentication on a macro or document.

Embed The action of inserting something created in one program into another program.

Event The action that causes a program or macro to run, such as clicking a button or a command or pressing a combination of keys.

Form An Excel worksheet or object containing fields and controls that enable a user to easily enter or edit data.

Form control A graphic object that does not require VBA code. A Form control is compatible with versions of Excel that do not support ActiveX.

Macro An action or a set of actions with which you can automate tasks by grouping a series of commands into a single command.

Macro virus Unauthorized programming code in a macro that erases or damages files.

Module The place where the Visual Basic for Applications (VBA) programming code is stored.

Procedure A unit of computer code that performs an action.

Property A characteristic of an object that can be changed.

Record Macro A command that records your actions in Visual Basic for Applications (VBA).

Sub Short for a sub procedure.

Sub procedure A unit of computer code that performs an action.

VBA The abbreviation for the Visual Basic for Applications programming language.

VBA construct An instruction that enables a macro to perform multiple operations on a single object.

Visual Basic Editor The window in which you can view and edit Visual Basic code.

Visual Basic for Applications The programming language used to write computer programs in the Microsoft Windows environment.

Chapter Review

Skills Review	Project 9C Training

Apply 9A skills from these Objectives:

1. Record a Macro
2. Assign a Macro to a Button on the Quick Access Toolbar
3. Modify a Macro

In the following Skills Review, you will assist Matt Gallagher, Training Director, in creating a macro that will make it easier for staff members to include the required information in their training department expense reports. You will assign the macro to a button on the Quick Access Toolbar, and then modify the macro by changing the Visual Basic Code. Your completed worksheet will look similar to Figure 9.32.

Project Files

For Project 9C, you will need the following file:

e09C_Training

You will save your workbook as:

Lastname_Firstname_9C_Training

Project Results

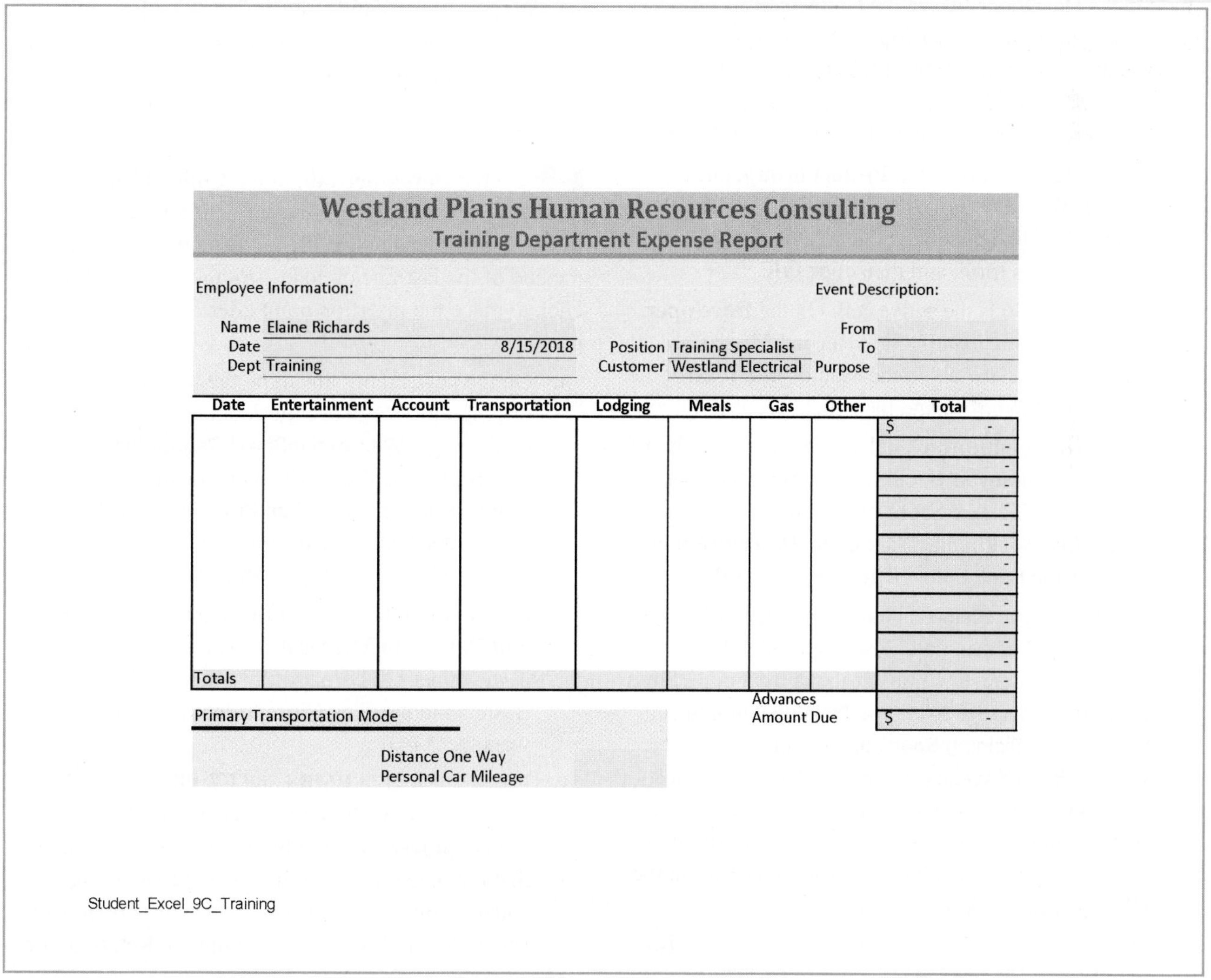

Student_Excel_9C_Training

Figure 9.32

(continues on next page)

Chapter Review

1 **Start** Excel. From your student files, open the file **e09C_Training**. Display the **Save As** dialog box, navigate to your **Excel Chapter 9** folder, click the **Save as type arrow**, and then click **Excel Macro-Enabled Workbook**. In the **File name** box, type **Lastname_Firstname_9C_Training** and then click **Save**.

a. To display the **Developer** tab, click **File** to display Backstage view. Click **Options**. In the **Excel Options** dialog box, on the left, click **Customize Ribbon**. Under **Customize Ribbon**, verify that **Main Tabs** is selected, select the **Developer** check box, and then click **OK**. (Mac users, click the Excel menu, and then click Preferences. Under Authoring, click Ribbon &Toolbar.)

b. On the **Developer tab**, in the **Code group**, click **Macro Security**. Under **Macro Settings**, verify that **Disable all macros with notification** is selected, and then click **OK**. (Mac users, click the Excel menu. Click Preferences and then click Security & Privacy.)

c. On the **Review tab**, in the **Protect group**, click **Protect Workbook**. In the **Unprotect Workbook** dialog box, type **goseries** which is the password applied to this form, and then click **OK**.

d. Be sure cell **B6** is the active cell. On the **Developer tab**, in the **Code group**, click **Record Macro**. (Mac users, on the View tab, in the Macros group, click the Macros button arrow, and then click Record Macro.)

e. In the **Macro name** box, delete the existing text, and then type **Employee_Section** In the **Shortcut key** box, type **t** Click the **Store macro in arrow**, then click **This Workbook**. Click in the **Description** box. Type **Fills in the Employee section** Click **OK**.

f. In cell **B6**, type **Elaine Richards** and then press (Enter). With cell **B7** active, hold down (Ctrl) and press (;) (semicolon), which will insert the current date. Press (Enter). With cell **B8** active, type **Training** Click in cell **F7** and type **Training Specialist** and then press (Enter). In cell **F8**, type **Westland Electrical** and then click cell **A11**, so that when the macro completes, the first cell in the data area is active to begin filling in the travel information. On the **Developer tab**, in the **Code group**, click **Stop Recording**.

g. Delete the text you just typed in the five cells—**B6, B7, B8, F7, F8**—and then click cell **B6**. Then, to test that your macro will fill in the employee information and the date, run the macro by pressing the shortcut key (Ctrl) + (T). **Save** your workbook. (Mac users, press (option) + (command ⌘) + (T).)

2 On the **Quick Access Toolbar**, click **Customize Quick Access Toolbar**, and then click **More Commands**.

a. Click the **Choose commands from arrow**, and then click **Macros**. Click your **Employee_Section** macro, and then, in the center of the dialog box, click **Add**.

b. With your **Employee_Section** command selected on the right, click **Modify**. Under **Symbol**, in the seventh row, click the seventh icon—**Checkered Square**—and then click **OK** two times. (Mac users, skip this step.)

c. **Save** your workbook. Select the nonadjacent ranges **B6:B8** and **F7:F8** and press (Del) so that these cells are empty again. Click cell **B6**, and then on the **Quick Access Toolbar**, click your new **Employee_Section** button—the Checkered Square. (Mac users, on the Quick Access Toolbar, click the circle icon.)

3 On the **Developer tab**, in the **Code group**, click **Macros**. Be sure the **Employee_Section** macro is selected, and then click **Edit**. In the **Code window**, at the end of the last line of code—*Range("A11").Select*—click to place the insertion point after *Select*, and then press (Enter).

a. On the new, empty line, type the following code to center the worksheet horizontally and vertically on the page: **With ActiveSheet.PageSetup** and then press (Enter). Press (Tab) to indent and type **.CenterHorizontally = True** Press (Enter) and type **.CenterVertically = True** and then press (Enter). Press (Shift) + (Tab), and then type **End With**

b. On the **menu bar**, click **File**, and then click **Close and Return to Microsoft Excel**. (Mac users, in the upper left corner of the Microsoft Visual Basic window, click Close to return to your Excel worksheet.)

c. Delete the text in **B6:B8** and **F7:F8**. Click cell **B6**, and then on the **Quick Access Toolbar**, click the **Employee_Section** button that you created, so that the macro runs and includes the centering you added to the macro. Display the **Print Preview** to verify that the worksheet is centered. Return to the worksheet.

(continues on next page)

Chapter Review

d. Right-click the **Checkered Square** icon on the **Quick Access Toolbar**, and then click **Remove from Quick Access Toolbar**. If you are directed to remove the Developer tab, follow the directions in Activity 9.13. (Mac users, On the Quick Access Toolbar, click Customize Quick Access Toolbar, and then click More Commands. Make sure that Quick Access Toolbar is selected. In the Customize Quick Access Toolbar list, click <<No label>>. In the center of the dialog box, click the Remove arrow and then click Save.)

e. Insert a footer in the **left section** that includes the file name. Display the file properties. As the **Tags**, type **training expense** and as the **Subject**, type your course name and section number. Under **Related People**, be sure that your name displays as **Author**.

f. **Save** and **Close** your workbook. Submit as directed by your instructor.

You have completed Project 9C **END**

Chapter Review

Skills Review **Project 9D Spring Sections**

Apply 9B skills from these Objectives:

4. Write a VBA Procedure to Use an ActiveX Control
5. Restore Initial Settings

In the following Skills Review, you will assist Matt Gallagher, Training Director at Westland Plains Human Resources Consulting, by writing a set of commands in the VBA programming language, using ActiveX Control buttons to automate the Recruitment Department policy guidelines for expense reports. Your completed workbook will look similar to Figure 9.33.

Project Files

For Project 9D, you will need the following file:

e09D_Recruitment

You will save your workbook as:

Lastname_Firstname_9D_Recruitment

Project Results

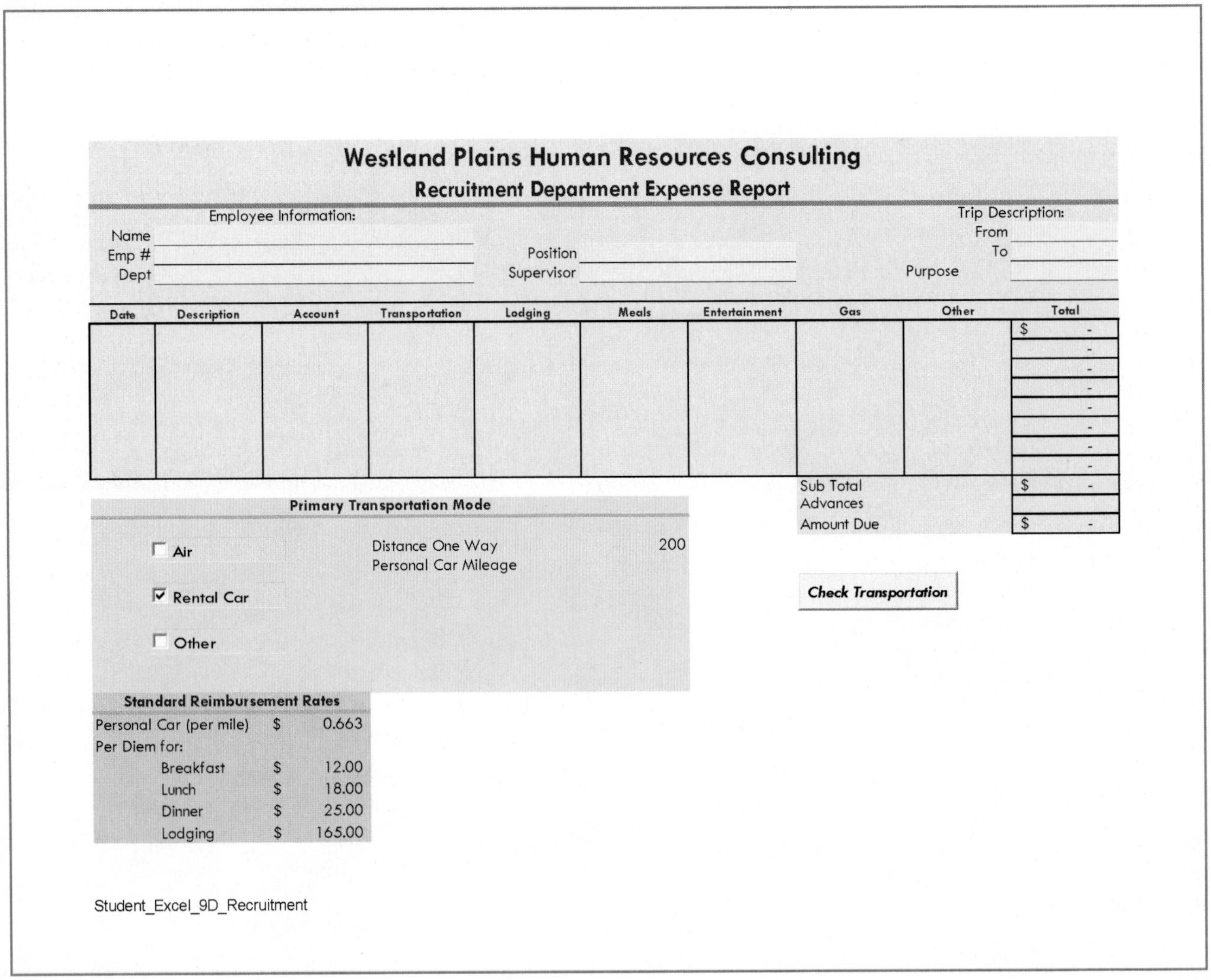

Figure 9.33

(continues on next page)

Chapter Review

Skills Review: Project 9D Spring Sections (continued)

1 **Start** Excel. From your student files, locate and open the file **e09D_Recruitment**. If necessary, on the Security Warning bar, click Enable Content. **Save** the workbook in your **Excel Chapter 9** folder as an **Excel Macro-Enabled Workbook** with the file name **Lastname_Firstname_9D_Recruitment** (Mac users, this project covers ActiveX controls, which are a MOS skill, but cannot be completed on a Mac. Please consult with your instructor.)

a. On the **Developer tab**, in the **Controls group**, click **Insert**. Under **ActiveX Controls**, click **Check Box**. Point to the upper left corner of cell **B20** and drag to insert a check box object that is approximately the height of the cell and the width of columns **B:C**. Repeat this process to add two more check boxes of the same approximate size under **CheckBox1**.

b. Click **CheckBox1**, hold down Ctrl and then click each of the remaining check boxes so that all three check boxes are selected. On the **Page Layout tab**, in the **Arrange group**, click **Align**, and then click **Align Left** to align the check boxes on the left.

2 Click the **Developer tab**. In the **Controls group**, verify that **Design Mode** is active. Click another area of the worksheet to deselect the group of check boxes, and then click **CheckBox1** to select the check box. In the **Controls group**, click **Properties**. Drag the **Properties** pane near the upper right of your screen, and then expand its lower edge so that you can see the entire list of properties.

a. At the top of the **Alphabetic** list, in the first column, click **(Name)**. Type **Air** and then press Enter to display *Air* in the **Name Box**. In the first column, click the **Caption** property, type **Air** and then press Enter. Click **Height**. Type **15.75** and then click **Width**. Type **84.75** and then press Enter.

b. Using the technique you just practiced, change the properties for the remaining two check boxes as shown in the table below.

c. In the yellow shaded area of the worksheet, select the **Air** check box, hold down Ctrl, and then click each of the other check boxes to select all three check boxes. In the **Properties** pane, click **BackColor**, click the **BackColor arrow**, click the **System tab**, scroll down and click **Button Light Shadow**. **Close** the **Properties** pane.

d. On the **Page Layout tab**, in the **Arrange group**, click **Align**, and then click **Distribute Vertically**. Click cell **A1** to deselect the group of check boxes, and then click **Save**.

3 Click cell **H22** to identify the location where you will place a Command Button. On the **Developer tab**, in the **Controls group**, click **Insert**, and then under **ActiveX Controls**, click **Command Button**. Point to the upper left corner of cell **H22**, and then click one time to insert the button.

a. In the **Controls group**, click **Properties**, and then in the **Properties** pane, click **(Name)**. Type **CheckTransportation** and then click the **Caption** property. Type **Check Transportation** and then click **AutoSize**. Click the **AutoSize arrow**, and then click **True**. In the **Properties** pane, click **Font**, and then click **Font build** to display the **Font** dialog box. Under **Font style**, click **Bold Italic**, and then click **OK**. **Close** the **Properties** pane.

b. Be sure the **Check Transportation** command button is selected. On the **Developer tab**, in the **Controls group**, click **View Code**. Click the **Object arrow**, and then on the list, click **CheckTransportation**.

c. Click to the left of *Private Sub* to place the insertion point there, and then press Enter to insert a blank line. Press ↑ to move to the blank line, and then type the following comments. Be sure to type the apostrophe at the beginning of each line, and at the end of both lines, press Enter.

'Check Transportation Button Procedure
'Function: Validates transportation mode

	Name	Caption	Height	Width
CheckBox2	**RentalCar**	**RentalCar**	**15.75**	**84.75**
CheckBox3	**Other**	**Other**	**15.75**	**84.75**

(continues on next page)

Chapter Review

d. Click to position the insertion point on the blank line under *Private Sub*. Press Enter, and then press Tab. Type the following lines of VBA code, spaced as shown, to test the mileage. Use the Tab key to indent the middle lines and Shift + Tab to reduce the indent by one tab for the last line. As you type, a prompt box may display to assist you with the VBA syntax. Ignore the prompts and type the code as shown.

> **If Air = True Then**
>   **TitleBarText = "Air"**
>   **MessageText = "To use air transportation, miles one way should equal 200 or more."**
>   **MsgBox MessageText, , TitleBarText**
> **End If**

e. On the menu bar, click **File**, and then click **Close and Return to Microsoft Excel**. In the **Controls group**, click **Design Mode** to exit Design Mode. In the yellow shaded section, select the **Air** check box, and then click the **Check Transportation** Command Button. Click **OK** to acknowledge the message.

4 ▶ In the **Controls group**, click **Design Mode**, and then click **View Code**. At the end of the first line of the If statement, click to place the insertion point to the left of the word *Then*. Type the following line of code, pressing Spacebar at the end:

And Range("F20").Value < 200

a. Verify that the first line of code now reads: *If Air = True And Range("F20").Value < 200 Then*. In the *MessageText* line, click to the left of the closing quotation mark and after the period. Press Spacebar, and then type **Supervisor must sign this Expense Form.**

b. Scroll to the left. At the end of the *MsgBox* line of code, place the insertion point after TitleBarText and press Enter. Then press Shift + Tab. Type the following code spaced as shown:

> **Else**
>   **TitleBarText = "Travel Method Checked"**
>   **MessageText = "Travel method OK."**
>   **MsgBox MessageText, , TitleBarText**

c. On the menu bar, click **File**, and then click **Close and Return to Microsoft Excel**. In the **Controls group**, click **Design Mode** to return to the active worksheet.

d. Be sure the **Air** check box is still selected—it displays a check mark. In cell **F20**, type **150** and then press Enter. Click the **Check Transportation** button. In the **Air** message box, click **OK**. Click cell **F20**, type **200** and then press Enter. Click the **Check Transportation** button.

e. In the **Travel Method Checked** message box, click **OK**. Clear the check mark from the **Air** check box. Select the **Rental Car** check box, and then click the **Check Transportation** Command Button. Click **OK** to acknowledge the message.

5 ▶ Insert a footer in the **left section** that includes the file name. Display the file properties. As the **Tags**, type **recruitment department expense report** and as the **Subject**, type your course name and section number. Under **Related People**, be sure that your name displays as **Author**. **Save** your workbook.

a. Click the **Review tab**. In the **Protect group**, click **Protect Workbook**. In the **Protect Structure and Windows** dialog box, verify **Structure** is selected and then type **1234** in the **Password** box. Confirm the password, and then **Save** your workbook. If you are directed to remove the **Developer tab**, follow the directions in Activity 9.13.

b. **Save** and **Close** your workbook. Submit as directed by your instructor.

You have completed Project 9D   **END**

Content-Based Assessments (Mastery and Transfer of Learning)

MyLab IT Grader	Mastering Excel	Project 9E Operations

Apply 9A skills from these Objectives:

1. Record a Macro
2. Assign a Macro to a Button on the Quick Access Toolbar
3. Modify a Macro

In the following Mastering Excel project, you will assist Bill Roman, Project Director, in creating a macro that will assign an operations department heading required on all reports. You will modify the macro by changing the Visual Basic Code. Your completed worksheet will look similar to Figure 9.34.

Project Files for MyLab IT Grader

1. In your **MyLab IT** course, locate and click **Excel 9E Operations**, Download Materials, and then Download All Files.
2. Extract the zipped folder to your Excel Chapter 9 folder, and then close the Grader download screens.
3. Take a moment to open the downloaded **Excel_9E_Operations_Instructions**; note any recent updates to the book.

Project Results

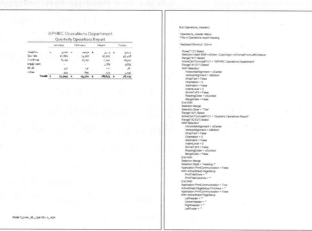

Figure 9.34

For Non-MyLab Submissions

For Project 9E, you will need:
e09E_Operations

In your Excel Chapter 9 folder, save your workbook as an Excel Macro-Enabled Workbook:
Lastname_Firstname_9E_Operations
If your instructor requires a workbook with formulas, save as:
Lastname_Firstname_9E_Operations_Formulas

After you have named and saved your workbook, on the next page, begin with Step 2.
After Step 8, save and submit your file as directed by your instructor.

Content-Based Assessments (Mastery and Transfer of Learning)

1 Navigate to your **Excel Chapter 9 folder**, and then double-click the Excel file you downloaded from **MyLab IT** that displays your name—**Student_Excel_9E_Operations**.

2 Verify that the **Developer tab** is enabled and the **Macro Settings** are set to **Disable all macros with notification**. Display the **Save As** dialog box, navigate to your **Excel Chapter 9** folder, set the **Save as type** to **Excel Macro-Enabled Workbook**, and then save your file.

3 With cell **A1** active, record a macro with the name **Operations_Header** and the shortcut key Ctrl + M . (Mac users, use option + command ⌘ + M .) Store the macro in **This Workbook**. As the description, type **Fills in Operations report heading** and then click **OK** to begin recording the macro.

4 **Insert** two blank rows at the top of the worksheet, and then click cell **A1**. Type **WPHRC Operations Department** and then **Merge & Center** the text you typed across the range **A1:E1**. Apply the **Title** cell style. In cell **A2**, type **Quarterly Report** and then **Merge & Center** the text you typed across the range **A2:E2**. Apply the **Heading 1** cell style. Center the worksheet **Horizontally**, click cell **A1**, and then stop recording the macro.

5 Delete **rows 1:2**, click cell **A1**, and then use the shortcut key to test the macro.

6 On the **Developer tab**, in the **Code group**, click **Macros**. Verify that the **Operations_Header** macro is selected, and then click **Edit**. Scroll down and locate the first instance of *End With*, and then in the fourth line following End With, edit *"Quarterly Report"* to indicate **"Quarterly Operations Report"**

7 Close the VBA window and return to your Excel worksheet. Delete **rows 1:2**, click cell **A1**, and then use the keyboard shortcut to run the macro to test that *Quarterly Operations Report* displays as the subtitle of the report.

8 Insert a footer with the file name in the left section, and then display the worksheet in **Print Preview** to verify that the worksheet is centered horizontally. Display the file properties. As the **Tags**, type **operations department report** and as the **Subject**, type your course name and section number. Under **Related People**, be sure that your name displays as **Author**. **Save** your workbook.

9 On the **Developer tab**, in the **Code group**, click **Macros**. Select your **Operations_Header** macro, and then click **Edit**. Select and **Copy** all of the code. **Close and Return to Microsoft Excel**. In the sheet tab area, click **New sheet** to insert a new worksheet. **Rename** the inserted sheet **Macro Code** and then with cell **A1** active, **Paste** the code to the new worksheet. **AutoFit** column A.

10 Click the **File tab**, and then click **Save As**. Navigate to your **Excel Chapter 9 folder**, and then click the **Save as type arrow**. Click **Excel workbook**. In the **File name** box, type **Student_Excel_9E_Operations_VBA** and then click **Save**. In the displayed message box, click **Yes**. **Close** your workbook.

11 In **MyLab IT**, locate and click the Grader Project **Excel 9E Operations**. In step 3, under **Upload Completed Assignment**, click **Choose File**. In the **Open** dialog box, navigate to your **Excel Chapter 9** folder, and then click your **Student_Excel_9E_Operations_VBA** file one time to select it. In the lower right corner of the **Open** dialog box, click **Open**.

The name of your selected file displays above the Upload button.

12 To submit your file to **MyLab IT** for grading, click **Upload**, wait a moment for a green **Success!** message, and then in step 4, click the blue **Submit for Grading** button. Click **Close Assignment** to return to your list of **Course Materials**.

You have completed Project 9E | END

Content-Based Assessments (Mastery and Transfer of Learning)

MyLab IT Grader

Mastering Excel | **Project 9F Evaluation**

Apply 9B skills from these Objectives:

4. Write a VBA Procedure to Use an ActiveX Control
5. Restore Initial Settings

In the following Mastering Excel project, you will assist Matt Gallagher, Training Director, by adding ActiveX controls to an evaluation form to gather feedback about training seminars. You will write VBA code to create input boxes that the respondent will use to enter information about the seminar. Your completed worksheet will look similar to Figure 9.35.

Project Files for **MyLab IT Grader**

1. In your **MyLab IT** course, locate and click **Excel 9F Evaluation**, Download Materials, and then Download All Files.
2. Extract the zipped folder to your Excel Chapter 9 folder, and then close the Grader download screens.
3. Take a moment to open the downloaded **Excel_9F_Evaluation_Instructions**; note any recent updates to the book.

Project Results

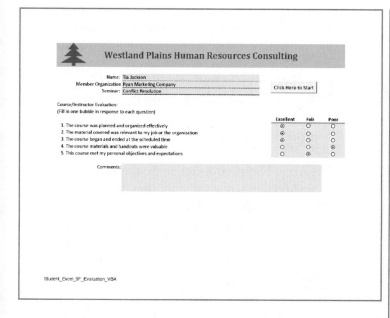

Figure 9.35

	For Non-MyLab Submissions

For Non-MyLab Submissions

For Project 9F, you will need:
e09F_Evaluation

In your Excel Chapter 9 folder, save your workbook as an Excel Macro-Enabled Workbook:
Lastname_Firstname_9F_Evaluation
If your instructor requires a workbook with formulas, save as:
Lastname_Firstname_9F_Evaluation_Formulas

After you have named and saved your workbook, on the next page, begin with Step 3.
After Step 12, save and submit your file as directed by your instructor.

(continues on next page)

1 ▶ Navigate to your **Excel Chapter 9 folder**, and then double-click the Excel file you downloaded from **MyLab IT** that displays your name—**Student_Excel_9F_Evaluation**. (Mac users, this project covers ActiveX controls, which are a MOS skill, but cannot be completed on a Mac. Please consult with your instructor.)

2 ▶ Display the **Save As** dialog box, navigate to your **Excel Chapter 9** folder, set the **Save as type** to **Excel Macro-Enabled Workbook**, and then save your file.

3 ▶ Click cell **G17** and insert an **ActiveX Controls Option Button** in this location, and then display the **Properties** pane. Click (**Name**), type **Q5E** and then select the **Caption** property text—*OptionButton1*. Delete the caption text. Click **GroupName**, and then type **Question5**

4 ▶ Change the **Height** property to **9.75** Change the **Left** property to **465** Change **Top** to **234.75** and **Width** to **9.75** Change the SpecialEffect to the first effect **0 – fmButtonEffectFlat**.

5 ▶ Using the same technique, add two more option buttons in **row 17** and set the properties shown in the table at the bottom of this page, being sure to delete the **Caption** text.

6 ▶ Insert a **Command Button ActiveX Control** at cell **G7**. Change the property **Name** to **Start** and the **Caption** to **Click Here to Start** Set the **AutoSize** property to *True*.

7 ▶ **Close** the **Properties** pane, and then view the code. Click the **Object arrow**, scroll down, and then click **Start**. In the **Code window**, click to the left of *Private Sub Start_Click( )* and press ⏎. In the blank line, type the following comments, pressing ⏎ after each line.

' Start Button Procedure

' Function: Complete seminar information

8 ▶ Click in the empty line following *Private Sub Start_Click( )*, press ⭾, and then type the following VBA code on three lines to create a procedure instructing seminar attendees to fill in the requested information.

Range("B6").Value = InputBox("Enter your name", "Name")

Range("B7").Value = InputBox("Enter the name of your organization", "Organization")

Range("B8").Value = InputBox("Enter the seminar title", "Seminar")

9 ▶ Return to Microsoft Excel, and then exit Design Mode.

10 ▶ Test your **Command Button** and type the following in each of the input boxes that display; click **OK** to close each box:

Name: **Tia Jackson**

Organization: **Ryan Marketing Company**

Seminar: **Conflict Resolution**

11 ▶ Click the **Excellent** option button for each of the five questions. Now, test to see what happens when you change your mind. For **Question 4**, click **Poor** and for **Question 5** click **Fair**. The original option buttons are cleared for both questions, and only the new option buttons are selected.

12 ▶ Click **A1**, and then insert a footer in the **left section** that includes the file name. Display the workbook **Properties**. As the **Tags**, type **evaluation report** and as the **Subject**, type your course name and section number. Under **Related People**, be sure that your name displays as **Author**. **Save** the workbook.

13 ▶ On the **Developer tab**, in the **Controls group**, click **View Code**. In the Microsoft Visual Basic Editor window, press Ctrl + A to select all of the code. Press Ctrl + C to copy the code to the clipboard. **Close and Return to Microsoft Excel**. In the sheet tab area, click **New sheet** to insert a new worksheet. **Rename** the inserted sheet **Evaluation Code**

14 ▶ In the **Evaluation Code** sheet, with cell **A1** active, **Paste** the code to the new worksheet. Be sure that the code displays in **A1:A8**. **AutoFit** column A.

15 ▶ Click the **File tab**, and then click **Save As**. Navigate to your **Excel Chapter 9 folder**, and then click the **Save as type arrow**. Click **Excel workbook**. In the **File name** box, type **Student_Excel_9F_Evaluation_VBA** and then click **Save**. In the displayed message box, click **Yes**. **Close** your workbook.

(continues on next page)

Location/ Property	Name	Caption	GroupName	Height	Left	Top	Width	SpecialEffect
Cell H17	**Q5F**	Delete	**Question5**	**9.75**	**519**	**234.75**	**9.75**	0 – fmButtonEffectFlat
Cell I17	**Q5P**	Delete	**Question5**	**9.75**	**570**	**234.75**	**9.75**	0 – fmButtonEffectFlat

(return to Step 6)

Content-Based Assessments (Mastery and Transfer of Learning)

Mastering Excel: Project 9F Evaluation (continued)

16 In **MyLab IT**, locate and click the Grader Project **Excel 9F Evaluation**. In step 3, under **Upload Completed Assignment**, click **Choose File**. In the **Open** dialog box, navigate to your **Excel Chapter 9** folder, and then click your **Student_Excel_9F_Evaluation_VBA** file one time to select it. In the lower right corner of the **Open** dialog box, click **Open**.

The name of your selected file displays above the Upload button.

17 To submit your file to **MyLab IT** for grading, click **Upload**, wait a moment for a green **Success!** message, and then in step 4, click the blue **Submit for Grading** button. Click **Close Assignment** to return to your list of **Course Materials**.

You have completed Project 9F   **END**

Content-Based Assessments (Mastery and Transfer of Learning)

MyLab IT Grader		**Mastering Excel** **Project 9G Billing**

Apply 9A and 9B skills from these Objectives:

1. Record a Macro
2. Assign a Macro to a Button on the Quick Access Toolbar
3. Modify a Macro
4. Write a VBA Procedure to Use an ActiveX Control
5. Restore Initial Settings

In this project you will assist Erica Ramirez, Sales Manager, to create a macro that enters footer information on chart sheets. You will also create several check boxes to indicate manager approval on sales bonuses. Your completed worksheets will look similar to Figure 9.36.

Project Files for **MyLab IT Grader**

1. In your **MyLab IT** course, locate and click **Excel 9G Billing**, Download Materials, and then Download All Files.
2. Extract the zipped folder to your Excel Chapter 9 folder, and then close the Grader download screens.
3. Take a moment to open the downloaded **Excel_9G_Billing_Instructions**; note any recent updates to the book.

Project Results

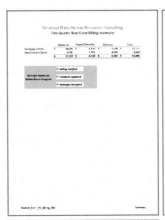

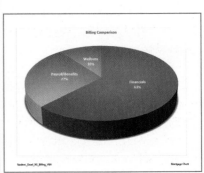

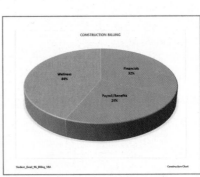

Figure 9.36

For Non-MyLab Submissions

For Project 9G, you will need:
e09G_Billing

In your Excel Chapter 9 folder, save your workbook as a Macro-Enabled workbook:
Lastname_Firstname_9G_Billing
If your instructor requires a workbook with formulas, save as:
Lastname_Firstname_9G_Billing_Formulas

After you have named and saved your workbook, on the next page, begin with Step 3.
After Step 10, save and submit your file as directed by your instructor.

(continues on next page)

Content-Based Assessments (Mastery and Transfer of Learning)

Mastering Excel: Project 9G Billing (continued)

1 Navigate to your **Excel Chapter 9 folder**, and then double-click the Excel file you downloaded from **MyLab IT** that displays your name—**Student_Excel_9G_Billing**. (Mac users, this project covers ActiveX controls, which are a MOS skill, but cannot be completed on a Mac. Please consult with your instructor.)

2 Display the **Save As** dialog box, navigate to your **Excel Chapter 9** folder, set the **Save as type** to **Excel Macro-Enabled Workbook**, and then save your file.

3 Display the **Mortgage Chart** sheet. Record a macro named **Chart_Setup** and assign **J** as the **Shortcut key**. Store the macro in **This Workbook**. As the description, type **Create footers in chart sheets** and then click **OK** to begin recording the macro.

4 On the **Page Layout tab**, click **Margins**, and then click **Custom Margins**. Display the **Header/Footer tab**, and then insert a **Custom Footer** on the **Mortgage Chart** sheet that includes the **File name** in the left section and the **Sheet name** in the right section, and then **Stop Recording** the macro.

5 Display the **Macro** dialog box and then **Edit** the macro code. Click after the apostrophe in the line below the second comment—*Create footers in chart sheets*—press Spacebar, and then type **Inserts file name and sheet name**

6 **Close and Return to Microsoft Excel**. Add the **Chart_Setup** macro to the **Quick Access Toolbar**. **Modify** the button by changing it to the **pie chart**. If the pie chart button is not available, choose another button.

7 Display the **Construction Chart** sheet, and then use the button you assigned to the Quick Access Toolbar to insert the footer. View the **Print Preview** to verify that the footer was inserted.

8 Display the **Summary** sheet. Insert three **ActiveX Check Box** controls positioned at cells **B10**, **B12**, and **B14** and assign the following properties:

Property	Name	Caption
CheckBox1	**Billing**	**Billing Verified**
CheckBox2	**Contact**	**Contacts Updated**
CheckBox3	**Manager**	**Manager Assigned**

9 Select all three check box controls so that you can modify the following properties at the same time. Change the **Height** to **18** and the **Width** to **105** and then change the **Font** to **Bold Italic**. With all three check boxes still selected, **Distribute Vertically** and then **Align Left**. Turn off **Design Mode** and then select each check box.

10 Remove the pie chart icon from the **Quick Access Toolbar**. Display the file properties. As the **Tags**, type **billing summary** and as the **Subject**, type your course name and section number. Under **Related People**, be sure that your name displays as **Author**. **Save** your workbook.

11 On the **Developer tab**, in the **Code group**, click **Macros**, and then with the **Chart_Setup** macro selected, click **Edit**. Select and **Copy** the four green comment lines beginning with the *Chart_Setup Macro* line and ending with the *Keyboard Shortcut* line. Be sure to include the apostrophe at the beginning of the first selected line. **Close and Return to Microsoft Excel**.

12 Insert a new worksheet. **Rename** the sheet **Macro Code** and then **Paste** the comment code to cell **A1**. **AutoFit** column A and then move the **Macro Code** sheet to the end of the workbook after the **Construction Chart** sheet. Make the **Summary** sheet the active sheet.

13 Click the **File tab**, and then click **Save As**. Navigate to your **Excel Chapter 9 folder**, and then click the **Save as type arrow**. Click **Excel workbook**. In the **File name** box, type **Student_Excel_9G_Billing_VBA** and then click **Save**. In the displayed message box, click **Yes**. **Close** your workbook.

14 In **MyLab IT**, locate and click the Grader Project **Excel 9G Billing**. In step 3, under **Upload Completed Assignment**, click **Choose File**. In the **Open** dialog box, navigate to your **Excel Chapter 9** folder, and then click your **Student_Excel_9G_Billing_VBA** file one time to select it. In the lower right corner of the **Open** dialog box, click **Open**.

The name of your selected file displays above the Upload button.

15 To submit your file to **MyLab IT** for grading, click **Upload**, wait a moment for a green **Success!** message, and then in step 4, click the blue **Submit for Grading** button. Click **Close Assignment** to return to your list of **Course Materials**.

You have completed Project 9G | END

Content-Based Assessments (Critical Thinking)

GO! Fix It	Project 9H Finance Macro	IRC
GO! Make It	Project 9I Timecard	IRC
GO! Solve It	Project 9J Filename Macro	IRC
GO! Solve It	Project 9K Book	

Project Files

For Project 9K, you will need the following file:

e09K_Book

You will save your workbook as:

Lastname_Firstname_9K_Book

Open the file e09K_Book and save it as an Excel Macro-Enabled Workbook **Lastname_Firstname_9K_Book** In the following Mastering Excel project, you will assist Matt Gallagher, Training Director, by adding an ActiveX Control Command Button to an evaluation form to gather feedback from the consultants about a new book that will be used at customer seminars. In cell H7, add an ActiveX Control Command Button to the worksheet. In the properties, change the name to **Start** and the caption to **Click Here to Start** and AutoSize to *True*. Add the following comments to the VBA code:

> ' **Start Button Procedure**
> ' **Function: When clicked, the Start button will display four input boxes**

Add the following VBA code:

Range("B6").Value = InputBox("Enter your name", "Name")
Range("B7").Value = InputBox("Enter the name of your position", "Position")
Range("B8").Value = InputBox("Enter the name of your department", "Department")
Range("B9").Value = InputBox("Enter your email", "Email")

Add the file name in the footer and appropriate name and course information to the document properties including the tags **book evaluation, VBA** and then submit as directed by your instructor.

		Performance Level		
		Exemplary	**Proficient**	**Developing**
Performance Criteria	**Insert an ActiveX Control Command Button and Change Properties**	An ActiveX Control Command Button was inserted and appropriate name, caption, and AutoSize properties were assigned.	An ActiveX Control Command Button was inserted but not all name, caption, and AutoSize properties were assigned.	An ActiveX Control Command Button was not inserted.
	Write a VBA Procedure for a Command Button	The VBA Procedure for a Start Command Button was correctly written.	The VBA Procedure for a Start Command Button was only partially written.	The VBA Procedure for a Start Command Button was not written.

You have completed Project 9K | END

Outcomes-Based Assessments (Critical Thinking)

Rubric

The following outcomes-based assessments are open-ended assessments. That is, there is no specific correct result; your result will depend on your approach to the information provided. Make Professional Quality your goal. Use the following scoring rubric to guide you in how to approach the problem and then to evaluate how well your approach solves the problem.

The *criteria*—Software Mastery, Content, Format and Layout, and Process—represent the knowledge and skills you have gained that you can apply to solving the problem. The *levels of performance*—Professional Quality, Approaching Professional Quality, or Needs Quality Improvements—help you and your instructor evaluate your result.

	Your completed project is of Professional Quality if you:	Your completed project is Approaching Professional Quality if you:	Your completed project Needs Quality Improvements if you:
1-Software Mastery	Choose and apply the most appropriate skills, tools, and features and identify efficient methods to solve the problem.	Choose and apply some appropriate skills, tools, and features, but not in the most efficient manner.	Choose inappropriate skills, tools, or features, or are inefficient in solving the problem.
2-Content	Construct a solution that is clear and well organized, contains content that is accurate, appropriate to the audience and purpose, and is complete. Provide a solution that contains no errors of spelling, grammar, or style.	Construct a solution in which some components are unclear, poorly organized, inconsistent, or incomplete. Misjudge the needs of the audience. Have some errors in spelling, grammar, or style, but the errors do not detract from comprehension.	Construct a solution that is unclear, incomplete, or poorly organized, contains some inaccurate or inappropriate content, and contains many errors of spelling, grammar, or style. Do not solve the problem.
3-Format and Layout	Format and arrange all elements to communicate information and ideas, clarify function, illustrate relationships, and indicate relative importance.	Apply appropriate format and layout features to some elements, but not others. Overuse features, causing minor distraction.	Apply format and layout that does not communicate information or ideas clearly. Do not use format and layout features to clarify function, illustrate relationships, or indicate relative importance. Use available features excessively, causing distraction.
4-Process	Use an organized approach that integrates planning, development, self-assessment, revision, and reflection.	Demonstrate an organized approach in some areas, but not others; or, use an insufficient process of organization throughout.	Do not use an organized approach to solve the problem.

Outcomes-Based Assessments (Critical Thinking)

| GO! Think | Project 9L Accounting Department |

Project Files

For Project 9L, you will need the following file:

e09L_Accounting

You will save your workbook as:

Lastname_Firstname_9L_Accounting

Open the file e09L_Accounting, and then save it in your chapter 9 folder as a Macro-Enabled workbook with the name **Lastname_Firstname_9L_Accounting**

Record a macro with the shortcut key Ctrl + r, that will insert a header that is required on all reports—Westland Plains Human Resources Consulting in the left section and Accounting Department in the right section. Edit the macro to change the left header to WPHR Consulting. Insert a new worksheet, type a title in cell A1, and test your macro.

Insert the file name in the left section of the footer, add appropriate information to the document properties including the tags **accounting, macro** and submit as directed by your instructor.

| You have completed Project 9L | END |

| GO! Think | Project 9M Sign | IRC |

| You and GO! | Project 9N Personal Footer | IRC |

External Data, Database Functions, Side-by-Side Tables, and Workbook Distribution and Collaboration

10

EXCEL 2019

PROJECT 10A

Outcomes
Import and manage external data and use database functions in Excel.

Objectives
1. Get External Data into Excel
2. Clean Up and Manage Imported Data
3. Use Database Functions

PROJECT 10B

Outcomes
Create a side-by-side table with conditional formatting and customized headers and footers, and then prepare a workbook for sharing and collaboration.

Objectives
4. Insert a Second Table into a Worksheet
5. Manage and Use Formulas in Conditional Formatting Rules
6. Create Custom Headers and Footers
7. Inspect a Workbook
8. Use Co-Authoring and Prepare a Final Workbook for Distribution

Rido/Shutterstock

In This Chapter

GO! To Work with Excel

In this chapter, you will use Excel's database capabilities to organize data. You will import and manage data from other sources, including from an Access database and a text file. You will use database functions to summarize information and analyze data. You will insert a second table in a worksheet and sort data in side-by-side tables. You will also apply conditional formatting to data using icon sets, by creating a conditional formatting rule by using a formula, and by managing the conditional formatting rules. Finally, you will prepare a workbook for sharing and collaboration.

The projects in this chapter relate to **Sunshine Health System**, which is the premier patient care and research institution serving the metropolitan area of Miami, Florida. Because of its outstanding reputation in the medical community and around the world, Sunshine Health System is able to attract top physicians, scientists, and researchers in all fields of medicine and achieve a level of funding that allows it to build and operate state-of-the-art facilities and provide the newest, innovative treatment options. Individuals throughout the area travel to Sunshine Health System for world-class diagnosis and care.

Medical Center
Information

Project Activities

In Activities 10.01 through 10.11, you will import data about medical center nurses, doctors, and supplies into Excel, and use Excel functions including database functions. Your completed worksheets will look similar to Figure 10.1.

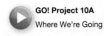

Project Files for **MyLab IT Grader**

1. In your storage location, create a folder named **Excel Chapter 10**.
2. In your **MyLab IT** course, locate and click **Excel 10A Medical Center**, Download Materials, and then Download All Files.
3. Extract the zipped folder to your Excel Chapter 10 folder. Close the Grader download screens.
4. Take a moment to open the downloaded **Excel_10A_Medical_Center_Instructions**; note any recent updates to the book.

Project Results

GO! Project 10A
Where We're Going

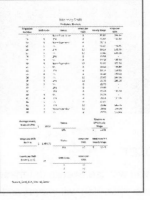
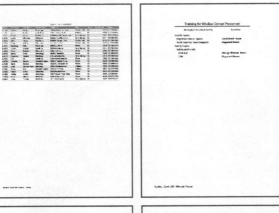

Figure 10.1 Project 10A Medical Center Information

For Non-MyLab Submissions

For Project 10A, you will need:

e10A_Medical_Center (Excel Workbook)
e10A_Nurse_Information (Access Database)
e10A_Orthopedic_Supplies (XML Document)
e10A_Physician_Information (Text Document)

Additional files supplied for Mac users as indicated in the instruction.

After you have named and saved your document, on the next page, begin with Step 2.

In your storage location, create a folder named **Excel Chapter 10**
In your Excel Chapter 10 folder, save your workbook as:
Lastname_Firstname_10A_Medical_Center

Objective 1 | Get External Data into Excel

GO! Learn How
Video E10-1

You have used many of Excel's powerful tools for analyzing data, but what if the data you want to analyze is not in Excel? You can get data that resides outside of Excel into Excel by using the commands in the ***Get & Transform Data*** group located on the Data tab. This group of commands enables you to bring data from an Access database, from the Web, from a text file, from an XML file, and from other sources such as a database on a SharePoint or SQL server, or an external data feed, into Excel without repeatedly copying the data. Then you can apply Excel's data analysis tools to the data. You can also establish links, or ***data connections***, to the external data so that you can automatically update your Excel workbook from the original data whenever the original data source gets new information.

NOTE   To Maintain Connections to External Data

To connect to external data when you open a workbook, you must enable data connections by using the Trust Center bar or by putting the workbook in a trusted location.

Activity 10.01 | Importing Data into Excel from an Access Database

Data in an Access database is organized in a format of horizontal rows and vertical columns—just like an Excel worksheet. Each horizontal row stores all of the data about one database item and is referred to as a ***record***. Each vertical column stores information that describes the record and is referred to as a ***field***. Data stored in a format of rows and columns is referred to as a ***table***. In this Activity, you will import data into Excel from an Access database.

1 Navigate to your **Excel Chapter 10 folder**, and then double-click the Excel file you downloaded from **MyLab IT** that displays your name—**Student_Excel_10A_Medical_Center**. If necessary, at the top click **Enable Editing**.

MAC TIP   Office 365 for Mac does not include the Access application, but Mac users can complete the projects in this chapter by importing CSV files for Mac users that are included with the files downloaded for each project. Move to Step 4.

2 Click the **File tab**, on the left click **Options**, and then in the **Excel Options** dialog box, on the left, click **Trust Center**. Under **Microsoft Excel Trust Center**, click **Trust Center Settings**. In the **Trust Center** dialog box, on the left, click **External Content**. Verify that the default selections *Prompt user about Data Connections* and *Prompt user on automatic update for Workbook Links* are selected, and then click **OK**. In the **Excel Options** dialog box, click **OK**.

Here you can make decisions about enabling connections. By default, both settings are set to *Prompt user*, and it is recommended that you maintain these default settings. This instruction assumes the default settings.

3 At the bottom of the Excel window, in the row of sheet tabs, locate the horizontal scroll bar. At the left end of the scroll bar, point to the three vertical dots to display the ⟨╫⟩ pointer, and then drag to the right to decrease the width of the scroll bar to display all five worksheets in this workbook as shown in Figure 10.2.

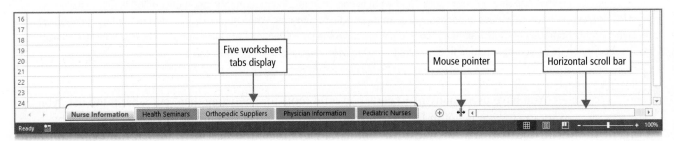

Figure 10.2

4 On the **Nurse Information** worksheet, click cell **A2**. On the **Data tab**, at the left end of the ribbon, in the **Get & Transform Data group**, click **Get Data**. *Point* to **From Database**, and then click **From Microsoft Access Database**.

Get Data commands enable you to bring data from many different sources into your Excel worksheet in a manner that lets you transform the data. That is, you can modify the data in a way that meets your needs and is useful to you; for example, you could remove a column of data. Such an action is referred to as a ***data transformation***.

Microsoft Access is a database program that manages database files. Use this technique to import data from Access or from other database programs.

5 In the **Import Data** dialog box, navigate to the files downloaded with this project in your **Excel Chapter 10 folder**. Click the Access file **e10A_Nurse_Information**, and then in the lower right corner of the dialog box, click **Import** to display the **Navigator** window.

Excel uses a dedicated Query Editor to facilitate and display data transformations. After you select the data source—in this instance an Access database—the ***Navigator window*** displays so you can select which table or tables you want to use in your query.

> **MAC TIP** From the File menu, click Import, click CSV. Select the comma-delimited file e10A_Nurses_CSV_for_Mac_users file. In Step 2 of the wizard, select Comma as the delimiter and start at cell A2. Format the imported data as a table (in the Alert, click Yes) and apply Green, Table Style Medium 7. Autofit all columns, save, and move to Activity 10.02.

6 In the **Navigator** window, on the left, click the **Nurses** table one time to select it.

When you select a table, a preview of its data displays in the right pane of the Navigator window.

7 In the lower right corner, click the **Load button arrow**, and then click **Load To**.

8 In the **Import Data** dialog box, under **Where do you want to put the data?**, click the **Existing worksheet** option button.

The selected option buttons indicate that the information will be imported as a table and into the existing worksheet in cell A2—the active cell.

9 In the **Import Data** dialog box, click **OK**, and then compare your screen with Figure 10.3.

Excel imports the table of nurse information. Beside each column title, an arrow displays for easy sorting and filtering. The field names display in row 2 and the records display in rows 3 to 22.

On the Table Tools Design tab, the External Table Data group includes commands to *Unlink* and *Refresh* the data from the external table. If you unlink the table, then your Excel data will not be updated when the external data is changed.

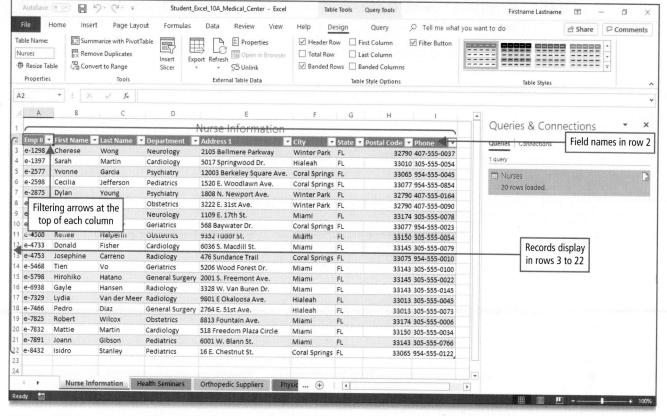

Figure 10.3

> **10** ▶ **Close** ☒ the **Queries & Connections** pane.

> **11** ▶ **Save** 🖫 your workbook.

Activity 10.02 | Hide Worksheets, Hide Rows and Columns, and Modify Cell Alignment and Indentation

MOS
2.2.2

To indent data in a cell, use the Increase Indent command. To remove an indent, use the Decrease Indent command. Use caution not to type spaces to achieve an indent—doing so can affect sorting and searching.

When you have many worksheets in a workbook, you may want to hide some from view so you have fewer worksheet tabs to manage. If necessary, you can continue to reference the data in a hidden worksheet.

> **1** ▶ Make the next worksheet—**Health Seminars**—the active sheet.

> **2** ▶ Select the range **A2:B2**. On the **Home tab**, in the **Alignment group**, click **Center** ☰ and then click **Middle Align** ☰ so that the text is centered both horizontally and vertically in the cell.

🔄 **ANOTHER WAY**　Right-click over the selection, click Format Cells, click the Alignment tab, and then under Text alignment, set Horizontal to Center and set Vertical to Center.

> **3** ▶ Select the range **A4:A5**. On the **Home tab**, in the **Alignment group**, click **Increase Indent** ☰ one time. Click cell **A7**, hold down Ctrl, and then click cell **A10**. Click **Increase Indent** ☰ one time.

🖥 **MAC TIP**　Hold down COMMAND.

4 ▶ Select the range **A8:A9**, hold down Ctrl, select the range **A11:A12**, and then click **Increase Indent** ▤ two times.

5 ▶ Press Ctrl + Home to make cell **A1** the active cell, and then compare your screen with Figure 10.4.

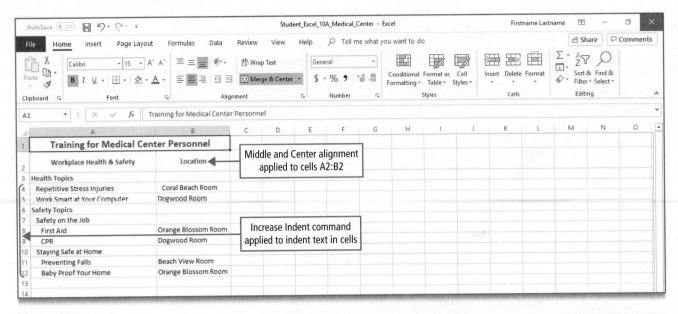

Figure 10.4

6 ▶ Because the *Staying Safe at Home* training meetings are still tentative, select **rows 10:12**, and then on the **Home tab**, in the **Cells group**, click **Format**. Under **Visibility**, point to **Hide & Unhide**, and then click **Hide Rows**. Compare your screen with Figure 10.5.

A green line indicates that some rows are hidden from view, and the row numbers jump from row 9 to row 13 to show which row numbers are hidden.

🔄 **ANOTHER WAY**   Select the rows, right-click over the selection, and then on the shortcut menu, click Hide.

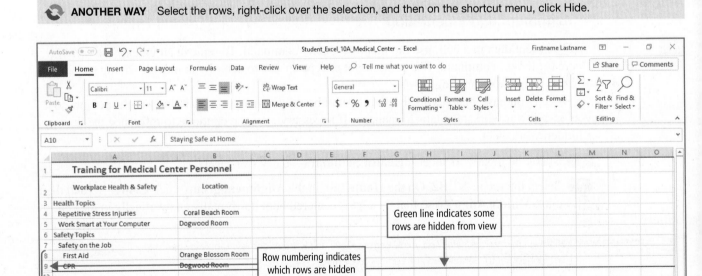

Figure 10.5

7 To hide the entire worksheet, on the **Home tab**, in the **Cells group**, click **Format**. Under **Visibility**, point to **Hide & Unhide**, and then click **Hide Sheet**.

⟳ **ANOTHER WAY** Right-click the sheet tab, and then on the shortcut menu, click Hide.

8 Now Unhide the worksheet: on the **Home tab**, in the **Cells group**, click **Format**. Under **Visibility**, point to **Hide & Unhide**, click **Unhide Sheet**, and then compare your screen with Figure 10.6.

You can select multiple worksheets and then hide them as a group; however, you can unhide only one worksheet at a time.

⟳ **ANOTHER WAY** Right-click any sheet tab, and then on the shortcut menu, click Unhide.

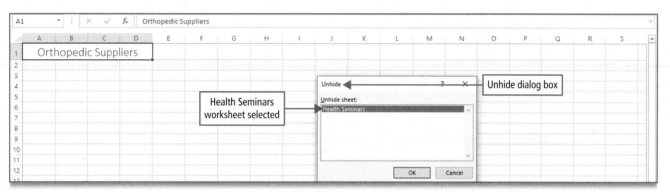

Figure 10.6

9 Click **OK** to redisplay the worksheet, click cell **A1**, **Save** 💾 your workbook, and then compare your screen with Figure 10.7.

Rows 10:12 remain hidden, indicated by a small break in the row numbers.

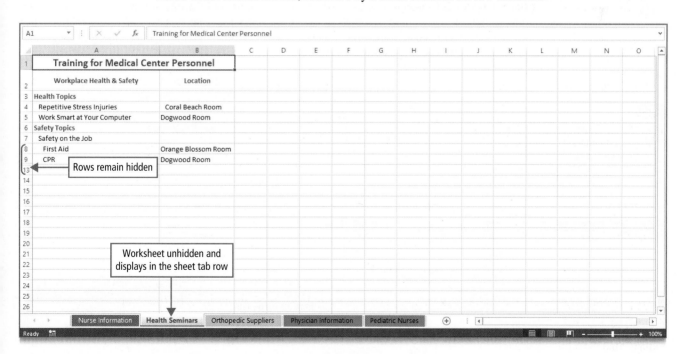

Figure 10.7

Activity 10.03 | Importing Data into Excel from an XML File, Adding and Removing Table Rows and Columns, and Converting a Table to a Cell Range

3.1.3, 3.2.1

In this Activity, you will import data into Excel from an XML file. ***Extensible Markup Language (XML)*** is a language that structures data in text files so that it can be read by other systems, regardless of the hardware platform or operating system. Such portability is why XML has become a popular technology for exchanging data.

1 Display the next worksheet—**Orthopedic Suppliers**.

2 Click cell **A2**. On the **Data tab**, in the **Get & Transform Data group**, click **Get Data**. Point to **From File**, and then click **From XML**.

3 In the **Import Data** dialog box, navigate to the files downloaded with this project in your **Excel Chapter 10 folder**, and then click the XML file **e10A_Orthopedic_Supplies**. At the bottom of the dialog box, notice that the file type is *XML Files*.

> The Orthopedic Supplies file contains supplier information for orthopedic supplies at the Medical Center. In this manner, you can import data from an XML file.

MAC TIP From the File menu, click Import, click CSV. Select the comma-delimited file e10A_Supplies_CSV_for_Mac_users file. In Step 2 of the wizard, select Comma as the delimiter and start at cell A2. Format the imported data as a table (in the Alert, click Yes) and apply Green, Table Style Medium 7. Autofit all columns and move to Step 8.

---

4 With the **e10A_Orthopedic_Supplies** file selected, in the lower right, click **Import**.

5 In the **Navigator** window, on the left, click the **supply** table. In the lower right corner, click the **Load arrow**, and then click **Load To**.

6 In the **Import Data** dialog box, under **Where do you want to put the data?**, click the **Existing worksheet** option button, and then click **OK**. Compare your screen with Figure 10.8.

> The table of orthopedic suppliers is imported as an Excel table with filter arrows in the column titles. The field names display in row 2 and the records display in rows 3 to 10.

> In the Queries & Connections pane, you can see a summary of the tables of data you have brought into your workbook using the Get & Transform commands. You can also point to any of the table in the Queries & Connections pane to see a summary of the data, how many columns of data were brought in, and the source of the data.

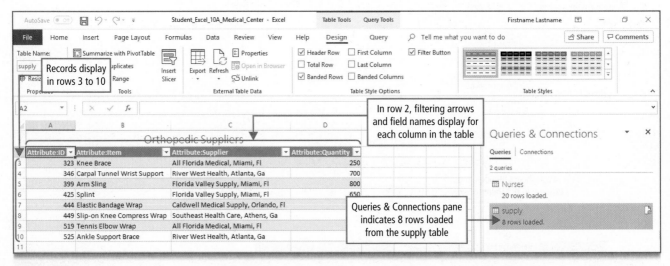

Figure 10.8

7 Close ☒ the **Queries & Connections** pane.

8 Click cell **B8**. On the **Home tab**, in the **Cells group**, click the **Delete button arrow**, and then click **Delete Table Rows**.

> To delete a table row or column, you need only click in a cell, and then use the appropriate command. Similarly, you can insert a table row or column by clicking the Insert button arrow in the Cells group.

🔁 **ANOTHER WAY**   Click in the cell, right-click to display a shortcut menu, point to Delete (or Insert), and then click Table Rows or Table Columns—depending on what you want to delete or insert.

9 To convert the table back to a normal range, click the **Table Tools Design tab**, and then in the **Tools group**, click **Convert to Range.** In the displayed message, click **OK** Compare your screen with Figure 10.9.

> When you convert your table back to a range of normal cells, all the functionality of the table, such as filters and the data connections, are removed, but the style, like colors and bold, will remain.

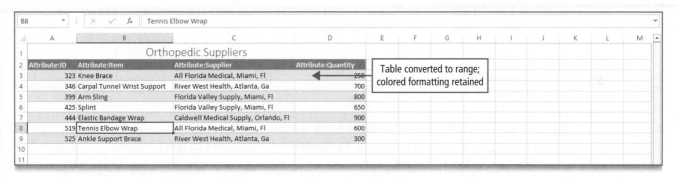

Figure 10.9

🔁 **ANOTHER WAY**   Click in any cell, right-click, and then on the shortcut menu, point to Table, and then click Convert to Range.

MORE KNOWLEDGE   **Viewing or Modifying Queries & Connections**

To view or modify external data connections, on the Data tab, in the Queries & Connections group, click Queries & Connections to display the Queries & Connections pane.

Activity 10.04 | Importing Data into Excel from a Delimited Text File

In this Activity, you will import information into Excel from a delimited text file.

MOS
1.1.1, 1.1.2

1 Make the next worksheet—**Physician Information**—active.

2 Click cell **A2**. On the **Data tab**, in the **Get & Transform Data group**, click **Get Data**. Point to **From File**, and then click **From Text/CSV**.

3 In the **Import Data** dialog box, navigate to the files downloaded with this project in your **Excel Chapter 10 folder**, and then click the Text file **e10A_Physician_Information**. Click **Import**, and then compare your screen with Figure 10.10.

> The Physician Information file contains contact information for doctors at the Medical Center. Use this technique to import data from a text file.

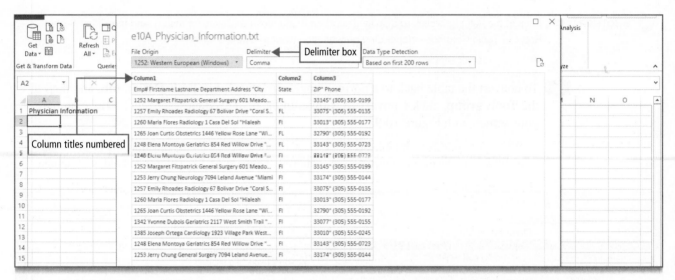

Figure 10.10

4 At the top of the window, notice that the column headings are indicated as *Column1*, *Column2*, and so on, and that the **Delimiter** box indicates *Comma*.

> The Get & Transform command determines that the Physician Information file is *delimited*—separated by commas or tabs—and indicates *Comma* as the delimiter. Data might also be delimited by colons or spaces, and so on.

5 Click the **Delimiter arrow**, and then on the list, click **Tab**. Compare your screen with Figure 10.11.

> The data in the text file is separated by tabs, and there are column names within the text. By selecting Tab, you can import the column names.

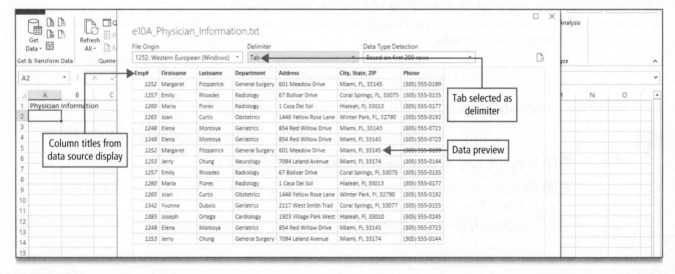

Figure 10.11

6 In the lower right, click the **Load arrow**, and then click **Load To**. In the **Import Data** dialog box, under **Where do you want to put the data?**, click the **Existing worksheet** option button, and then compare your screen with Figure 10.12.

The Import Data dialog box displays similarly to the other data imports you have performed. Under *Where do you want to put the data?*, the Import Data dialog box indicates that the table will be imported into the existing worksheet in cell $A$2—the active cell.

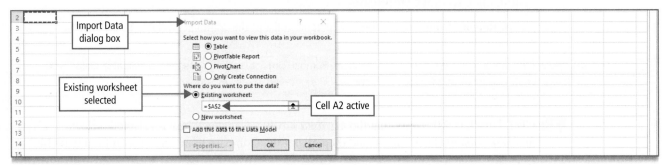

Figure 10.12

7 In the **Import Data** dialog box, click **OK**. Compare your screen with Figure 10.13.

The data displays as a table with the column headings included. In the Queries & Connections pane, your three imports display. For the current data, *15 rows loaded* displays, because you brought in 15 rows of data plus the column headings. Because you converted the Orthopedic Supplier data back to a range, it indicates *Connection only*.

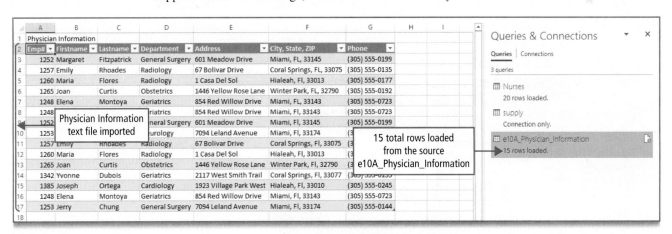

Figure 10.13

8 If necessary, click cell **A2**, and then on the **Table Tools Design tab**, in the **Tools group**, click **Convert to Range**. In the message, click **OK**.

🖥 **MAC TIP** Format the imported data as a table (in the Alert, click Yes) and apply Green, Table Style Medium 7. Autofit all columns.

9 **Close** ⊠ the **Queries & Connections** pane, and then **Save** 🖫 your workbook.

Objective 2 **Clean Up and Manage Data**

GO! Learn How
Video E10-2

Data in a worksheet is not always formatted in a way you can use it. The data may be in the wrong columns, duplicate records may be imported, and even the case of the letters may be incorrect. In addition to standard formatting tools such as cell styles, Excel includes several tools to help you clean up the data automatically, including text functions and ribbon commands.

Activity 10.05 | Removing Duplicates

In a worksheet with many records, it can be difficult to locate duplicate records by eye. In this Activity, you will remove duplicate records from the Physician Information worksheet automatically.

1 With the **Physician Information** worksheet active, on the **Data tab**, in the **Data Tools group**, click **Remove Duplicates** ▣.

The Remove Duplicates dialog box includes a list of the columns available in the data.

 MAC TIP Select the range A3:G17. On the Data tab, click Remove Duplicates. In the Remove Duplicates dialog box, select only Column A and Column D (Emp# and Department). Click OK.

2 Click **Unselect All**, verify that the *My data has headers* check box is selected, select the *Emp#* and *Department* check boxes, and then click **OK**. Compare your screen with Figure 10.14.

By removing duplicate records, you ensure that an employee will only appear one time for each department. Six duplicate records were found and deleted. In this manner you can clean up duplicate data automatically.

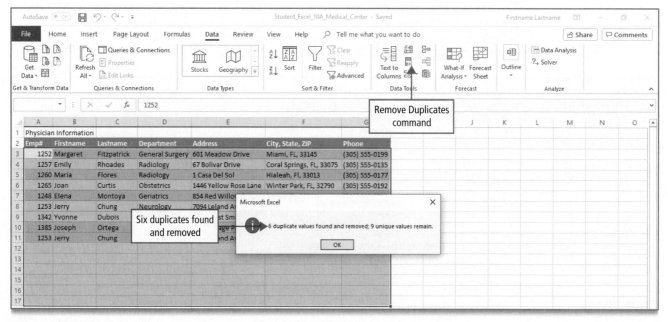

Figure 10.14

3 Click **OK**, and then **Save** 🖫 your workbook.

Activity 10.06 | Using Flash Fill to Expand Data

Excel can format text data. For example, to make sorting and filtering easier, you can separate data into separate fields using *Flash Fill*—an Excel feature that predicts how to alter data based on the pattern you enter into the cell at the beginning of the column. To use Flash Fill, the data must be in the adjacent column. In this Activity, you will use Flash Fill to clean up imported data.

1 On the **Physician Information** worksheet, notice the *City*, *State*, and *ZIP* are all in the same field in **column F**.

2 Click the **column G** header to select the column. On the **Home tab**, in the **Cells group**, click the **Insert button arrow**, and then click **Insert Sheet Columns**.

ANOTHER WAY Select the column, right-click over the selection, and then click Insert.

3 Use the same method to insert two additional columns.

Three new columns are added between the *City, State, Zip* and *Phone* fields.

ANOTHER WAY Press F4 to repeat the most recent command.

4 Click cell **G2**, type **City** and then press Tab. In cell **H2** type **State** press Tab, in cell **I2** type **ZIP** and then press Enter.

5 In cell **G3**, type **Miami** and press Enter. In cell **G4** type **Co** and compare your screen with Figure 10.15.

Based on your entries in cell G3 and G4, Flash Fill suggests entries for the remaining cells in the column.

MAC TIP After inserting the columns and entering the column headings, select the range F3:F11. On the Data tab, click Text to Columns. Select Comma as the delimiter. Select G3 as the destination. Click Finish. Delete the contents of cells H3:I11.

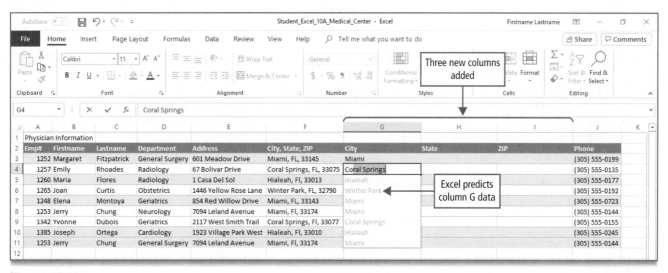

Figure 10.15

6 Press Enter to have Flash Fill complete the column. Click cell **H3**, type **Fl** press Enter, and then use the **fill handle** to copy the text down through **H11**. **Save** your workbook.

Excel's Flash Fill feature automatically completes column G using the pattern. Because all employees live in Florida, you can simply drag to fill column H.

Activity 10.07 | Using Text Functions

4.3.1, 4.3.2, 4.3.2

Among Excel's *Text functions*, which are functions that assist in formatting text, you will find functions to combine or separate data, change case, and apply formatting to a string of characters. The text function *RIGHT* will return the specified number of characters from the end (right) of a string of characters. The similar *LEFT* function returns the specified number of characters from the beginning (left) of a string, and the *MID* function extracts a series of characters from a text string given the location of the beginning character.

The *CONCAT* text function (known as the CONCATENATE function in older versions of Excel) can join up to 255 strings of characters. The *TRIM* function can remove extra blank spaces from a string. This is especially useful for removing leading blank spaces, which are difficult to see by eye, but can cause problems with sorting and filtering. The *UPPER* and *LOWER* functions will change the case of the characters in a string, making all characters uppercase or lowercase, and the *PROPER* function will capitalize the first letter of each word; for example, all proper nouns such as the names of cities. In this Activity, you will use text functions to clean up imported data.

1 ▶ Click cell **I3**. On the **Formulas tab**, in the **Function Library group**, click **Text**, and then click **RIGHT**.

2 ▶ If necessary, drag the **Function Arguments** dialog box down so **row 3** is visible. With the insertion point in the **Text** box, click cell **F3**. Press Tab, in the **Num_chars** box, type **5** and then compare your dialog box with Figure 10.16.

> **MAC TIP**   Formula Builder pane opens on the right. Click Done when finished.

| I3 | ▼ | : | × | ✓ | *fx* | =RIGHT(F3,5) | | | | | | ▾ |

	A	B	C	D	E	F	G	H	I	J	K
1	Physician Information										
2	Emp#	Firstname	Lastname	Department	Address	City, State, ZIP	City	State	ZIP	Phone	
3	1252	Margaret	Fitzpatrick	General Surgery	601 Meadow Drive	Miami, FL, 33145	Miami	Fl	=RIGHT(F3,5)	(305) 555-0199	
4	1257	Emily	Rhoades	Radiology	67 Bolivar Drive	Coral Springs, FL, 33075	Coral Springs	Fl		(305) 555-0135	
5	1260	Maria	Flores	Radiology	1 Casa Del Sol	Hialeah, Fl, 33013	Hialeah	Fl		(305) 555-0177	
6	1265	Joan	Curtis	Obstetrics	1446 Yellow Rose Lane	Winter Park, FL, 32790	Winter Park	Fl		(305) 555-0192	
7	1248	Elena	Mon					Fl		(305) 555-0723	
8	1253	Jerry	Chu					Fl		(305) 555-0144	
9								Fl		(305) 555-0155	
10								Fl		(305) 555-0245	
11								Fl		(305) 555-0144	

Function Arguments dialog box:
- Text: F3 = "Miami, FL, 33145"
- Num_chars: 5 = 5
- = "33145"
- Returns the specified number of characters from the end of a text string.
- Num_chars specifies how many characters you want to extract, 1 if omitted.
- Formula result = 33145
- Help on this function   OK   Cancel

Text and Num_chars arguments entered

RIGHT function

Results preview

Figure 10.16

3 ▶ Click **OK**. Drag the **fill handle** to copy the function down through cell **I11**.

The text function RIGHT displays the last 5 characters of the text in column F.

4 ▶ Click cell **H3**. In the **Function Library group**, click **Text**, scroll down as necessary, and then click **UPPER**. In the **Function Arguments** dialog box, in the **Text** box, type **Fl** and then click **OK**.

5 ▶ Drag the **fill handle** to copy the function down through cell **H11**. **Save** 🖫 your workbook.

6 ▶ Click cell **K2**, type **Full Name** and press Enter. With cell **K3** active, on the **Formulas tab**, in the **Function Library group**, click **Text**, and then click **CONCAT**.

7 ▶ If necessary, drag the **Function Arguments** dialog box so **columns B:C** are visible. With the insertion point in the **Text1** box, click cell **B3**. Press `Tab`. In the **Text2** box type " and then press `Space` and then type " Press `Tab` and in the **Text3** box, click **C3**. Compare your dialog box with Figure 10.17.

> **MAC TIP** Click + in the CONCAT Formula Builder box to add Text2 and Text3.

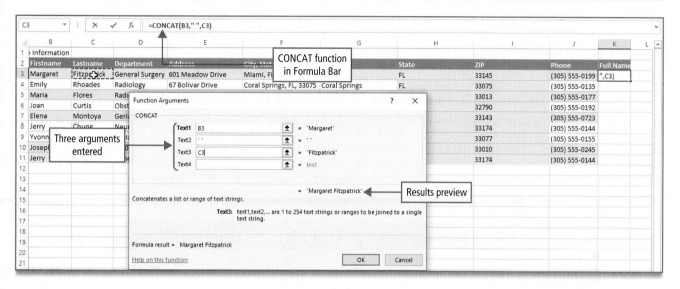

Figure 10.17

8 ▶ Click **OK**. Use the **fill handle** to copy the function down through cell **K11**.

> The CONCAT function combined the text entered in the function argument boxes into a single cell.

9 ▶ Click cell **A1**. **Merge & Center** the text across the range **A1:K1** and apply the **Title** cell style. Select **columns A:K** and apply **AutoFit**. Click the **column F** heading to select the column. On the **Home tab**, in the **Cells group**, click **Format**, point to **Hide & Unhide**, and then click **Hide Columns**.

10 ▶ Select **rows 3:11**, and then on the **Home tab** in the **Font group**, click the **Fill Color arrow** ⬛▾, and then click **No Fill**.

> 🔄 **ANOTHER WAY** Right-click over the selected column, and then on the shortcut menu, click Hide.

11 ▶ Click cell **A1**, and then **Save** 💾 your workbook.

Objective 3   Use Database Functions

GO! Learn How
Video E10-3

In Excel, not only can you track and manage financial and numerical data, but you can also create simple databases. A ***database*** is a collection of data related to a particular topic or purpose. ***Data*** refers to facts about people, events, things, or ideas. Data that is organized in a useful manner is referred to as ***information***. An example of information at the Sunshine Health System is the list of nurses who work in various departments or who work various shifts.

Recall that a ***function*** is a predefined formula that performs calculations by using specific values, called ***arguments***. Database functions are identified by the letter *D*—each function starts with a D, for example, DSUM, DAVERAGE, and DCOUNT. The initial letter *D* identifies to Excel that a database range will be used in the formula, rather than a single column or row of numbers.

Activity 10.08 | Using the DAVERAGE Database Function

The *syntax*—arrangement of arguments in a function—for the majority of database functions is: DFunction Name(database, field, criteria), where *database* identifies the range of cells where the data is displayed, *field* is the field name to be considered, and *criteria* is the range of cells where the search criteria has been defined.

The criteria is defined in a separate area on the worksheet. In this Activity, you will use the DAVERAGE function to determine the average hourly wage for LPNs (Licensed Practical Nurses) in the pediatric wing of the hospital. The **DAVERAGE function** determines an average in a database that is limited by criteria set for one or more cells.

1 In your workbook, display the next worksheet—**Pediatric Nurses**.

This worksheet lists the Employee Number, Shift Code, Status, Hours per Shift, Hourly Wage, and Wage per Shift for pediatric nurses who work on Mondays. The Wage per Shift field contains a formula that multiplies the Hours per Shift in column D times the Hourly Wage in column E. The number in the Shift Code field is a code for the shift. Not all nurses work on Mondays; so, some rows indicate 0 hours per shift. Additionally, some nurses prefer 12-hour shifts instead of 8-hour shifts so they can reduce the number of days worked per week.

The Shift Codes represent the following hours:

Shift	Code
Day (6a–2p)	1
Evening (7p–3a)	2
Afternoon (12p–8p)	3
Night (10p–6a)	4
Day 12-hr (6a–6p)	5
Night 12-hr (6p–6a)	6

2 Click cell **B28**, and then to the left of the **Formula Bar**, click **Insert Function** [fx].

You can use the Insert Function dialog box to locate any function in Excel. Cell C28 will form the first cell in the criteria range for the DAVERAGE function, which must consist of at least two vertical cells. The top cell is the field name that is to be searched, and the cell immediately below it is the criteria used in the function search. The value—LPN—is the search criteria.

ANOTHER WAY On the Formulas tab, in the Function Library group, click Insert Function.

3 In the **Insert Function** dialog box, click the **Or select a category arrow**, and then click **Database**. In the **Select a function** box, click **DAVERAGE**, and then click **OK**. Compare your screen with Figure 10.18.

The Function Arguments dialog box for DAVERAGE displays. Recall that *arguments* are the values that an Excel function uses to perform calculations or operations.

MAC TIP In the Formula Builder pane, search for DAVERAGE, select it, and then click Insert Function.

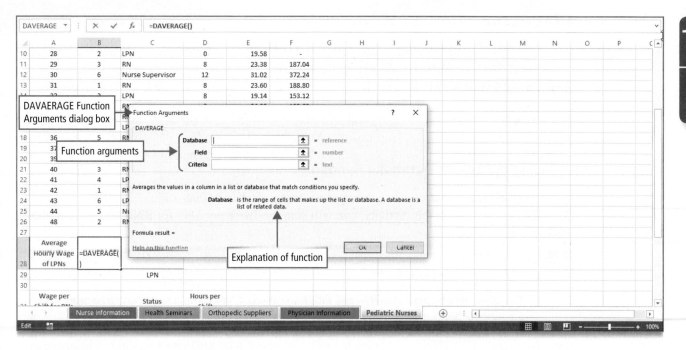

Figure 10.18

> **4** In the **Database** box, click **Collapse Dialog Box** ⬆, and then select the range **A3:F26**. Then, in the collapsed dialog box, click **Expand Dialog Box** ⬇.
>
> This action defines the database range in the first argument box.

💻 **MAC TIP** It is not necessary to collapse the dialog box.

> **5** In the **Field** box, type **Hourly Wage** and press Tab.
>
> This action identifies the field or column in the database that you want to average; the insertion point moves to the Criteria box. Excel adds quotation marks around the Field name, which identifies it as a string of characters to use in the search.

> **6** With the insertion point in the **Criteria** box, select the vertical range **C28:C29**—the criteria range that was previously defined. Compare your screen with Figure 10.19.
>
> The two cells in the criteria range will limit the DAVERAGE calculation to only those records where *Status* is equal to *LPN*—RNs and Nurse Supervisors will not be included.

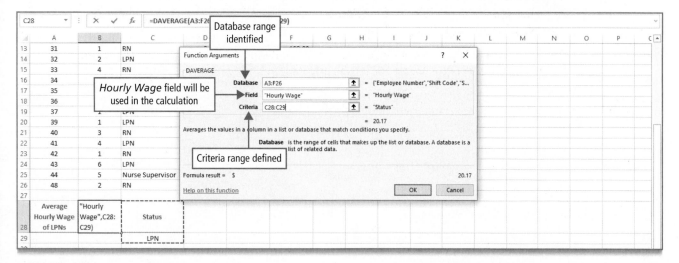

Figure 10.19

7 Click **OK**.

The result, *$20.17*, displays in cell B28. This is the average hourly wage for LPNs who work in the pediatric wing of the hospital on Mondays.

8 **Save** 🖫 your workbook.

💻 **MAC TIP**   Click Done.

Activity 10.09 | Using the DSUM Database Function

The ***DSUM function*** sums a column of values in a database that is limited by criteria set for one or more cells. In this Activity, you will sum the *Wage per Shift* for RNs who work in the Pediatric wing on Mondays.

1 Click cell **B31**, and then type **=dsum(** to begin the formula for the DSUM function. Compare your screen with Figure 10.20.

The *Status* will be limited to RN, and the *Hours Worked* will be limited to those RNs who worked a number of hours greater than zero. This is a ***compound criteria***—use of two or more criteria on the same row—all conditions must be met for the records to be included in the results.

Recall that you can type the function arguments directly into the cell instead of using the *Function Argument* dialog box. A ScreenTip displays the parts of the argument that must be included, which guides you through the process of entering all of the arguments necessary for this function.

💻 **MAC TIP**   As you type you will need to click DSUM when it appears below your typing.

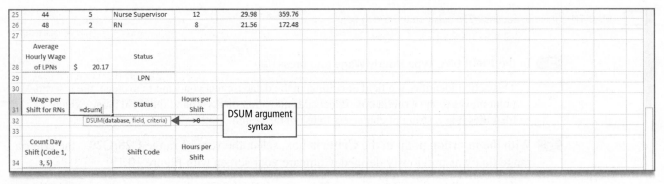

25	44	5	Nurse Supervisor	12	29.98	359.76		
26	48	2	RN	8	21.56	172.48		
27								
28	Average Hourly Wage of LPNs	$ 20.17	Status					
29			LPN					
30								
31	Wage per Shift for RNs	=dsum(	Status	Hours per Shift				
32		DSUM(database, field, criteria)		0		DSUM argument syntax		
33								
34	Count Day Shift (Code 1, 3, 5)		Shift Code	Hours per Shift				

Figure 10.20

2 Notice that in the function ScreenTip, *database* displays in bold, indicating that you must select a range that is the database. Select the range **A3:F26**, and then type **,** (a comma). You can look at the **Formula Bar** to see your typing and correct as necessary. Compare your screen with Figure 10.21.

The database range is defined, and the *field* argument displays in bold.

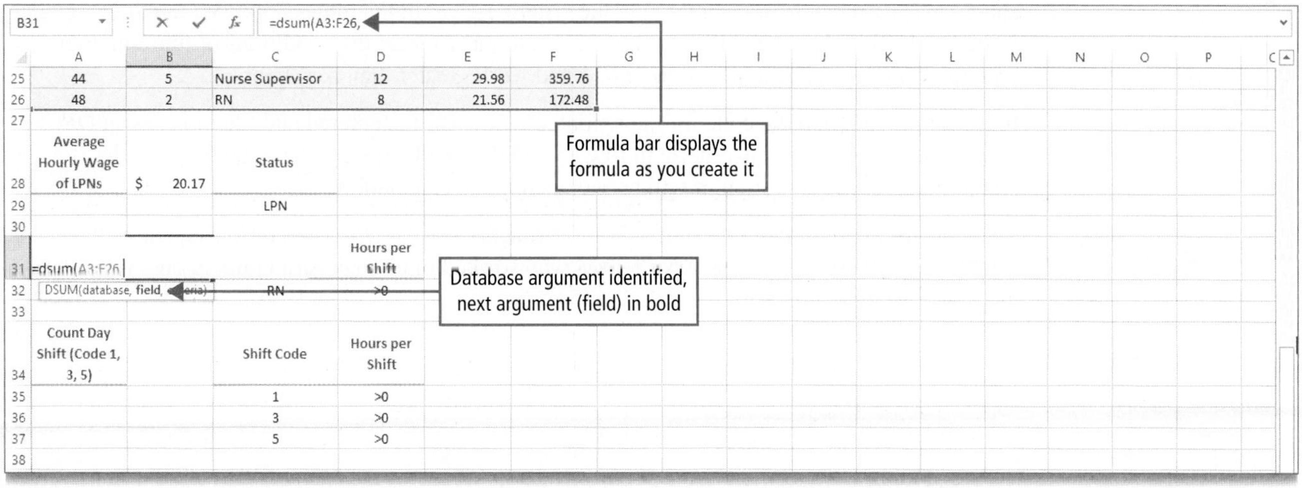

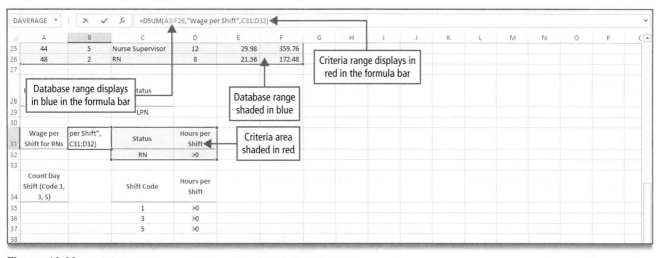

Figure 10.21

3 Notice that in the function ScreenTip, *field* displays in bold, indicating that you must type the name of the field. Being sure to include the comma at the end, type **"Wage per Shift",** to enter the second part of the argument; you can look at the **Formula Bar** to see your typing and correct as necessary.

The field that you want to sum is the *Wage per Shift* field, so the field name is entered as the second argument. The quotation marks define this as a string of characters; it must match the field name exactly. The comma separates this argument from the next argument.

4 As indicated by *criteria* in the ScreenTip, type the criteria as **c31:d32** and then press Enter.

After you type the criteria range, Excel automatically adds a closing parenthesis. The final result of the formula—$1,455.72—displays in cell B31. The total cost to pay all the RNs who work in the Pediatric wing on Mondays is $1,455.72.

5 Click cell **B31**, click in the **Formula Bar** and examine the parts of the DSUM function. Compare your screen with Figure 10.22.

Figure 10.22

6 Click cell **A1**, and then **Save** your workbook.

Activity 10.10 | Using the DCOUNT Function

In this Activity, you will count the number of nurses who work the day shift.

1 Scroll down as necessary to view **rows 34:37**, and then compare your screen with Figure 10.23.

Cell A34 forms the label for the function. Three shifts include daytime hours—Shift Codes 1, 3, and 5—so you must include all three in the criteria range. In the range C35:D35, the Shift Code value for the first daytime shift, which is *1*, is entered. To meet the conditions of this compound criteria, a nurse must be assigned to Shift 1 and work greater than zero hours.

In the range C36:D36 the code for the second daytime shift is entered and functions as an *OR* criteria. Excel evaluates the criteria in row 35 and then will consider the criteria in row 36. If a record meets either condition, it will be included in the calculation.

The code for the third daytime shift—*5*—also functions as an *OR* criteria. Consequently, the calculation will count the number of nurses who worked more than zero hours in one of the three day shifts, whether it is Shift Code 1, 3, or 5.

Figure 10.23

2 Click cell **B34**. To the left of the **Formula Bar**, click **Insert Function** 𝑓ₓ.

> 🖥 **MAC TIP**   In the Formula Builder pane, search for DCOUNT, select it, and then click Insert Function.

3 If necessary, click the **Or select a category arrow**, and then click **Database**. In the **Select a function** box, click *DCOUNT*, and then click **OK**.

The Function Arguments dialog box for DCOUNT displays.

4 In the **Database** box, click **Collapse Dialog Box** ⬆. Move the collapsed box to the upper right corner of your screen. Scroll as necessary, and then select the range **A3:F26**.

> 🖥 **MAC TIP**   It is not necessary to collapse the dialog box.

5 In the collapsed dialog box, click **Expand Dialog Box** ⬇.

The database range is defined and displays in the first argument box.

6 In the **Field** box, type **Employee Number** and then press ⟮Tab⟯.

The *Employee Number* field will be counted.

7 With the insertion point in the **Criteria** box, click **Collapse Dialog Box** ⬆, scroll as necessary, and then select the range **C34:D37**—the criteria area that was previously defined. In the collapsed dialog box, click **Expand Dialog Box** ⬇. Compare your **Function Arguments** dialog box with Figure 10.24.

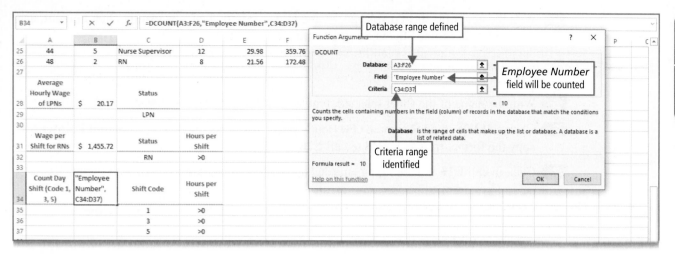

Figure 10.24

8 Click **OK**.

> The result, *10*, displays in cell B34. This is the total number of nurses assigned to work the day shift in the pediatric wing of the hospital on Mondays.

9 Press Ctrl + Home to make cell **A1** the active cell, and then **Save** 🖫 your workbook.

🖳 **MAC TIP**   Close the Formula Builder pane.

Activity 10.11 | Copying a Worksheet and Using the MAXIFS Function

MOS
2.2.3, Expert 3.1.1

In this Activity, you will copy a worksheet to create an additional worksheet in your 10A_Medical_Center workbook. You will also use the *MAXIFS function*, which returns the maximum value among cells specified by a given set of conditions or criteria. There is also a *MINIFS function*, which returns the minimum value among cells specified by a given set of conditions or criteria.

1 With the **Pediatric Nurses** worksheet displayed, on the **Home tab**, in the **Cells group**, click **Format**, and then under **Organize Sheets**, click **Move or Copy Sheet**.

🔄 **ANOTHER WAY**   Right-click over the sheet tab name and click Move or Copy to display the Move or Copy dialog box.

---

2 In the **Move or Copy** dialog box, under **Before sheet**, click **(move to end)**, and then click to select the **Create a copy** check box. Compare your screen with Figure 10.25.

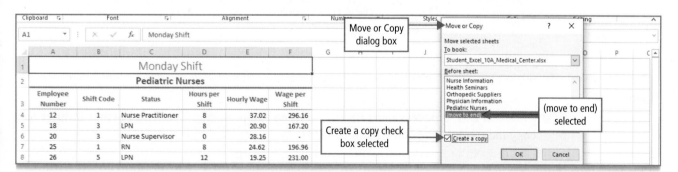

Figure 10.25

3 Click **OK**, and notice that a new worksheet is added as the last worksheet and is named *Pediatric Nurses (2)*.

4 With the new worksheet displayed, on the **Home tab**, in the **Cells group**, click **Format**, and then under **Organize Sheets**, click **Rename Sheet**.

ANOTHER WAY Right-click over the new sheet tab name, click Rename, and then type the new name.

5 With the name of the sheet selected, type **Hourly Wages** and press Enter.

6 Click cell **E28**, type **Maximum LPN Hourly Wage** and press Enter. Use the **Format Painter** to copy the format from cell **C28** to cell **E28**.

7 Click in cell **E29** and then type **=maxifs(** and then compare your screen with Figure 10.26.

MAC TIP As you type, click MAXIFS when it displays below your typing.

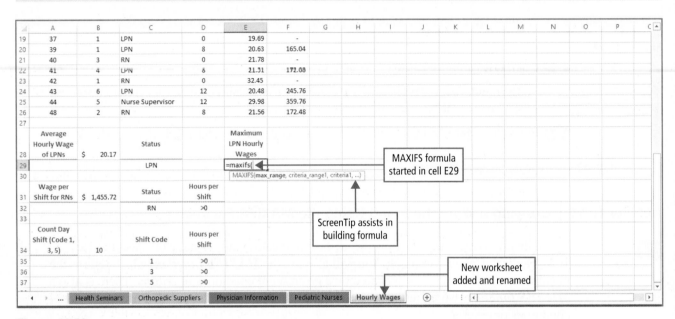

Figure 10.26

8 Select the range **E4:E26**, which represents the Hourly Wage for all Pediatric Nurses. Type a comma **,** and then select the range **C4:C26** and type a comma **,** and then click cell **C29**— LPN. Press Enter, and then compare your screen with Figure 10.27.

The highest Hourly Wage for an LPN in this group is $21.51.

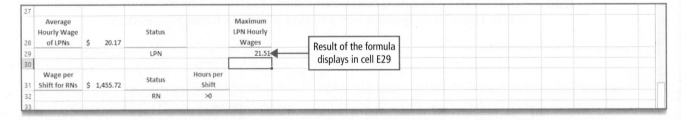

Figure 10.27

9 Click cell **E31**, type **Maximum RN Hourly Wage** and press Enter. Then use **Format Painter** to copy the format from cell **C31** to cell **E31**.

10 Click cell **E32**. By using the technique you just practiced, create a **MAXIFS** function using the range **E4:E26** as the **max_range**, the range **C4:C26** as the **criteria_range1**, and cell **C32**—RN—as **criteria1**. Press Enter.

The highest Hourly Wage for an RN in this group is $32.45.

11 Apply **Accounting Number Format** to cell **E29** and **E32**. Compare your screen with Figure 10.28.

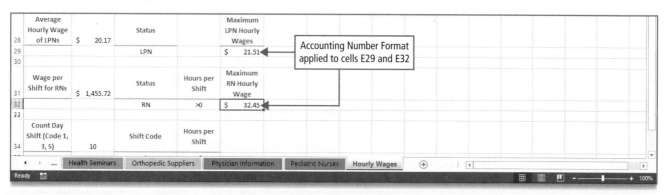

Figure 10.28

12 Group the worksheets. On the **Page Layout tab**, click **Margins**, at the bottom click **Custom Margins** to display the **Page Setup** dialog box, and then center the worksheets horizontally on the page. Click the **Header/Footer tab**, and then create a **Custom Footer** with the **File Name** in the **left section**. Click **OK** two times.

13 With all the sheets still grouped, press Ctrl + Home to make cell **A1** the active cell. In the **Scale to Fit group**, set the **Width** to **1 page** and the **Height** to **1 page**. Display the **document properties**. As the **Tags**, type **medical center information** In the **Subject** box, type your course name and section number. Be sure your name displays as the author.

14 On the left, click **Print** to display the **Print Preview**. Scroll through the six worksheets. On the left, click **Save** to save your workbook and return to the workbook window. Right-click any sheet tab and then click **Ungroup Sheets**.

MAC TIP On the File tab, click Print.

15 In the upper right corner of the Excel window, click **Close** ☒.

> **For Non-MyLab Submissions Determine What Your Instructor Requires for Submission**
> As directed by your instructor, submit your completed **Lastname_Firstname_10A_Medical_Center** Excel workbook.

16 In **MyLab IT**, locate and click the Grader Project **Excel 10A Medical Center**. In **step 3**, under **Upload Completed Assignment**, click **Choose File**. In the **Open** dialog box, navigate to your **Excel Chapter 10 folder**, and then click your **Student_Excel_10A_Medical_Center** file one time to select it. In the lower right corner of the **Open** dialog box, click **Open**.

The name of your selected file displays above the Upload button.

17 To submit your file to **MyLab IT** for grading, click **Upload**, wait a moment for a green **Success!** message, and then in **step 4**, click the blue **Submit for Grading** button. Click **Close Assignment** to return to your list of **Course Materials**.

You have completed Project 10A   **END**

PROJECT 10B — Office Equipment Inventory

MyLab IT
Project 10B Grader for Instruction
Project 10B Simulation for Training and Review

Project Activities

In Activities 10.12 through 10.18, you will edit a worksheet for Pat Shepard, Vice President of Operations, detailing the current inventory of two office equipment types—Office Equipment Nursing Station and Office Equipment Administrative. Your completed worksheets will look similar to Figure 10.29.

Project Files for MyLab IT Grader

1. In your **MyLab IT** course, locate and click **Excel 10B Equipment Inventory**, Download Materials, and then Download All Files.
2. Extract the zipped folder to your Excel Chapter 10 folder. Close the Grader download screens.
3. Take a moment to open the downloaded **Excel_10B_Equipment_Inventory_Instructions**, note any recent updates to the book.

Project Results

GO! Project 10B
Where We're Going

 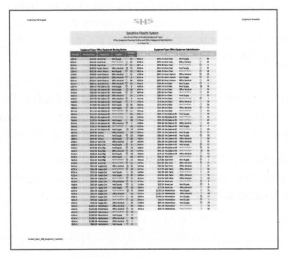 

Figure 10.29 Project 10B Equipment Inventory

For Non-MyLab Submissions

For Project 10B, you will need:
e10B_Equipment_Inventory
e10B_Logo

In your Excel Chapter 10 folder, save your workbook as:
Lastname_Firstname_10B_Equipment_Inventory

After you have named and saved your document, on the next page, begin with Step 2.

ALERT Because Office 365 is a cloud-based subscription service that receives continuous updates, you may encounter some variations in what appears on your screen and what is shown in this instruction. Microsoft Office 365 is fully installed on your PC or Mac; no internet access is necessary to create or edit documents. When you *are* connected to the internet, you will receive monthly upgrades and new features, so you always have the latest versions of Office apps as soon as they are available. Your subscription gives you continuous free access to the latest innovations and refinements.

GO! Learn How
Video E10-4

In Excel, you can insert a table beside another table in the *same* worksheet, and then work with the data in each table separately. This enables you to view and compare similar sets of data.

Activity 10.12 | Inserting a Second Table into a Worksheet

3.1.1

1 Navigate to your **Excel Chapter 10 folder**, and then double-click the Excel file you downloaded from **MyLab IT** that displays your name—**Student_Excel_10B_Equipment_Inventory**. If necessary, at the top click **Enable Editing**.

2 On the **Equipment Inventory** worksheet, select the range **A7:E62**, and then on the **Insert tab**, in the **Tables group**, click **Table**. In the **Create Table** dialog box, verify that =$A$7:$E$62 displays as the data range and that the **My table has headers** check box is selected. Click **OK**.

> The Office Equipment Nursing Station data converts to a table, a table style is applied, and the headings display filter arrows.

3 Click the **Administrative** sheet tab, select the range **A1:E52**, right-click over the selection, and then, click **Copy**.

BY TOUCH Press and hold to display the right-click menu.

4 Display the **Equipment Inventory** worksheet. Scroll up as necessary, point to cell **F6** and right-click. On the shortcut menu, under **Paste Options**, click **Paste (P)**. Click any cell to deselect. Compare your screen with Figure 10.30.

> The data regarding Office Equipment Administrative is added to the right of the Office Equipment Nursing Station table.

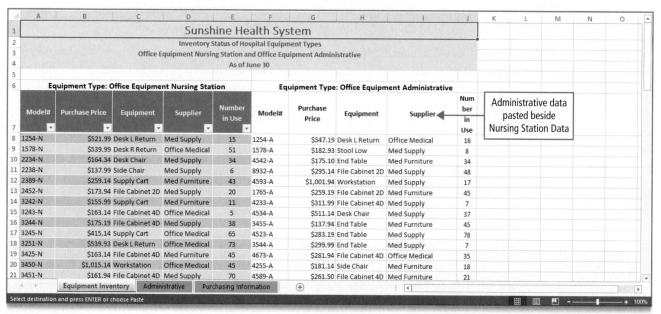

Figure 10.30

5 Select the range **F7:J57**. In the lower right corner of the selection click **Quick Analysis** [icon], click **Tables**, and then click **Table**.

[computer icon] **MAC TIP** On the Insert tab, in the Table group, click Table.

This is another method to convert data to a table in Excel. Here you see that side-by-side tables do *not* have to contain the same number of rows or columns.

6 On the **Table Tools Design tab**, in the **Table Styles group**, click **More** [icon], and then in the gallery, under **Medium**, click the gold colored **Table Style Medium 12**—you can use the ScreenTips to view the table names.

7 Click cell **A1** to deselect the table. **Save** [icon] your workbook, and then compare your screen with Figure 10.31.

The data for *Office Equipment Administrative* is converted to a table, a style is applied, and the headings display filtering arrows—also referred to as *filtering controls*.

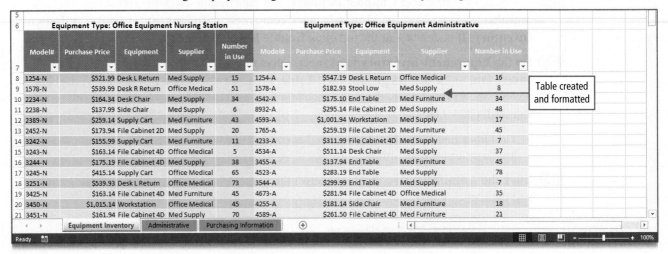

Figure 10.31

Activity 10.13 | Sorting Side-by-Side Tables

MOS
3.3.2

1 On the left, click in any cell in the **Office Equipment Nursing Station** table. On the **Data tab**, click **Sort** to display the **Sort** dialog box.

2 In the **Sort** dialog box, under **Column**, click the **Sort by arrow**, and then click **Equipment**. Verify that **Sort On** indicates *Cell Values* and **Order** indicates *A to Z*.

3 Click **Add Level**. Under **Column**, click the **Then by arrow**, and then click **Purchase Price**. In the same row, click the **Order arrow**, and then set the sort order to **Largest to Smallest**. Compare your screen with Figure 10.32.

[computer icon] **MAC TIP** Click + to add level.

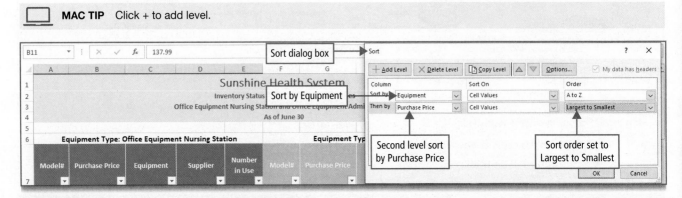

Figure 10.32

4 Click **OK**, and then compare your screen with Figure 10.33.

The Equipment column is sorted alphabetically, and within each equipment type, the items are sorted by Purchase Price from the highest to lowest.

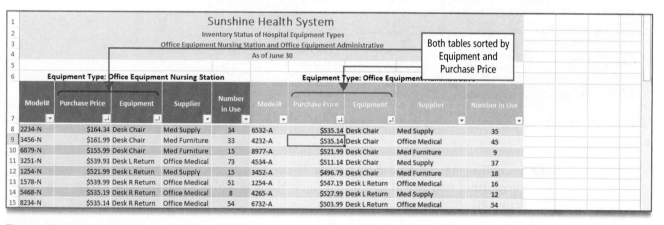

Figure 10.33

5 By using the same technique and the same sort orders, sort the **Office Equipment Administrative** table. **Save** your workbook, and then compare your screen with Figure 10.34.

By having the two tables side-by-side in the same worksheet, you can sort similar sets of data to make comparisons. For example, you can see that the Administrative desk chairs are more expensive than the Nursing Station desk chairs.

Figure 10.34

Objective 5 | **Manage and Use Formulas in Conditional Formatting Rules**

GO! Learn How
Video E10-5

Recall that *conditional formatting* makes your data easier to interpret by changing the appearance of your data based on a condition; if the condition is true, the cell is formatted based on that condition, and if the condition is false, the cell is not formatted.

Excel provides built-in conditional formatting rules, but sometimes you will need to create your own rules by using a formula. You can also manage—change—either built-in rules or rules that you have created.

Icon sets are sets of three, four, or five small graphic images that make your data visually easier to interpret. The icons are placed inside the cells. Their shape or color indicates the values in the cells relative to all other adjacent cells formatted using the same condition.

Activity 10.14 | Managing and Using Formulas in Conditional Formatting Rules

MOS

2.4.2, Expert 2.3.1,
Expert 2.3.2,
Expert 2.3.3

Mr. Shepard is planning a remodel and needs an inventory of nursing station equipment. Additionally, the company *Med Furniture* is going out of business, and Mr. Shepard needs to know which items have been purchased from this company so that he can check on any warranties or parts that might be needed before the company closes.

In this Activity, you will use icon sets as the conditional formatting to distinguish visually the Number in Use of equipment items. You will also create a conditional formatting rule using a formula and change—manage—a rule.

1 Select the range **E8:E62**. On the **Home tab**, in the **Styles group**, click **Conditional Formatting**.

2 Point to **Icon Sets**, and then under **Directional**, in the first row, click the first icon set—**3 Arrows (Colored)**. Click cell **E63** to deselect, and then compare your screen with Figure 10.35.

In this icon set, a colored arrow provides the visual cue about the value of a cell relative to other cells. A green upward pointing arrow represents a higher value, a yellow sideways pointing arrow represents a mid-level value, and a red downward pointing arrow represents a lower value. Icon sets are useful to quickly identify higher and lower numbers within a large group of data, such as very high or very low levels of inventory.

	A	B	C	D		E	F	G	H	I	J	K	L	M	N
42	3566-N	$161.99	Stool Low	Med Furniture	⬇	11	5478-A	$167.99	Side Chair	Office Medical	21				
43	3245-N	$415.14	Supply Cart	Office Medica	⬆	65	5678-A	$161.94	Side Chair	Office Medical	37				
44	4233-N	$381.59	Supply Cart	Med Furniture	⬇	10	4573-A	$172.26	Sofa Table	Office Medical	46				
45	6234-N	$319.14	Med Supply		➡	54	4590-A	$167.99	Sofa Table	Med Furniture	55				
46	6121-N	$211.99	Supply Cart	Med Supply	⬆	85	5489-A	$161.94	Sofa Table	Office Medical	34				
47	5677-N	Conditional formatting	Med Furniture	⬇	27	6121-A	$141.54	Sofa Table	Office Medical	48				
48	3452-N	indicates inventory level	Office Medica	⬇	6	8755-A	$497.94	Stool Low	Med Furniture	8				
49	7988-N			Med Supply	⬇	8	1578-A	$182.93	Stool Low	Med Supply	8				
50	5378-N	$271.14	Supply Cart	Med Supply	⬇	16	6845-A	$173.99	Stool Low	Office Medical	55				
51	4235-N	$261.59	Supply Cart	Med Furniture	⬆	73	7654-A	$1,015.19	Workstation	Med Supply	35				
52	3578-N	$261.55	Supply Cart	Office Medica	➡	53	4258-A	$1,013.99	Workstation	Office Medical	48				
53	2389-N	$259.14	Supply Cart	Med Furniture	⬇	43	4593-A	$1,001.94	Workstation	Med Supply	17				
54	3242-N	$155.99	Supply Cart	Med Furniture	⬇	11	6455-A	$979.19	Workstation	Med Supply	7				

Figure 10.35

3 Select the range **E8:E62** again. On the **Home tab**, in the **Styles group**, click **Conditional Formatting**, and then at the bottom, click **Manage Rules**. Compare your screen with Figure 10.36.

Here you can edit or delete the conditional formatting rule applied to the selected cells.

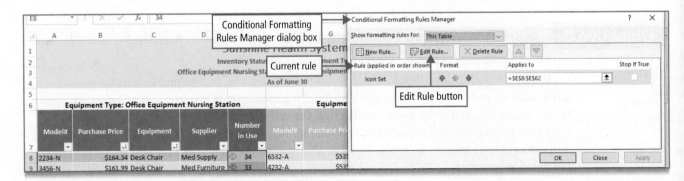

Figure 10.36

4 In the **Conditional Formatting Rules Manager** dialog box, click **Edit Rule**, and then in the **Edit Formatting Rule** dialog box, in the lower portion of the dialog box, click the **Icon Style arrow**, scroll down about half way, and then point to the three circles with the symbols X, !, and ✓, as shown in Figure 10.37.

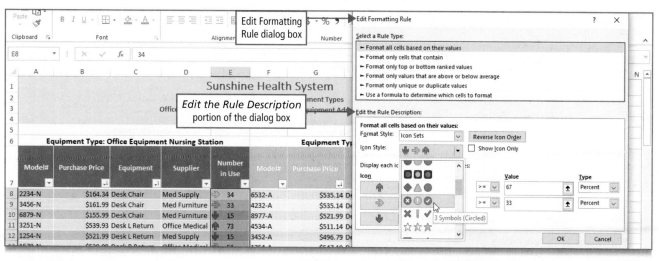

Figure 10.37

5 Click the **3 Symbols (Circled)** icon style, and then click **OK** two times to change the icon style.

Mr. Shepard thinks these symbols are more descriptive of the information he wants to see at a glance regarding the number of equipment types in use.

6 In the second table, select the range **J8:J57**. On the **Home tab**, in the **Styles group**, click **Conditional Formatting**, point to **Icon Sets**, and then under **Indicators**, click **3 Symbols (Circled)** to apply the same icon set to the second table.

7 In the first table, select the range **D8:D62**. On the **Home tab**, in the **Styles group**, click **Conditional Formatting**, and then at the bottom click **New Rule**. In the **New Formatting Rule** dialog box, under **Select a Rule Type**, click the last rule type—**Use a formula to determine which cells to format**.

🖥 **MAC TIP** Click Formula.

8 In the lower portion of the dialog box, in the **Format values where this formula is true** box, type **=d8="Med Furniture"** and then compare your screen with Figure 10.38.

🖥 **MAC TIP** In the Style box, click Classic.

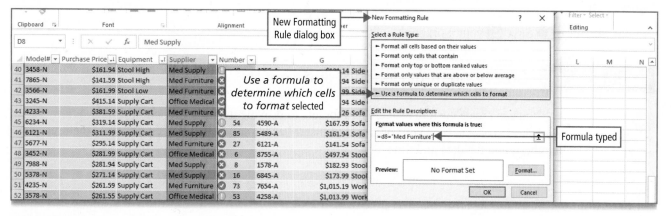

Figure 10.38

9 In the lower right corner of the dialog box, click **Format**. In the **Format Cells** dialog box, under **Font style**, click **Bold Italic**. Click the **Color arrow**, and then under **Standard Colors**, click the second color—**Red**. Compare your screen with Figure 10.39.

When the conditional formatting is applied, the text will be formatted in red bold italic.

> 🖥 **MAC TIP** In the Format with box, select Red Text (to remove the cell fill color). Then in the Format with box, click Custom Format.

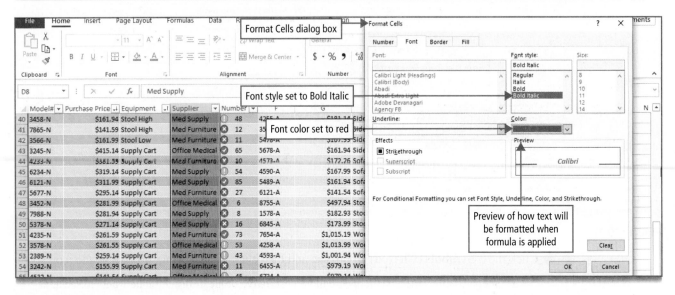

Figure 10.39

10 Click **OK** two times. In the second table, select the range **I8:I57**, and then create the same conditional formatting rule using the formula **=i8="Med Furniture"** and apply it to the selection. Press Ctrl + Home, and then compare your screen with Figure 10.40.

Figure 10.40

11 **Save** 🖫 your workbook.

Objective 6   Create Custom Headers and Footers

GO! Learn How
Video E10-6

You can create custom headers and footers to provide useful information about your worksheet. You can type your own text or insert header and footer elements such as pictures, page numbers, and the date and time.

Activity 10.15 | Creating Custom Headers and Footers

In this Activity, you will create a custom header by inserting a logo, text, and the date and time. You will create a custom footer by inserting Header & Footer Elements.

1 Point to the **Administrative** sheet tab, right-click, and then click **Delete**. In the warning box, click **Delete**.

2 Click the **Equipment Inventory** sheet tab to display the worksheet, and then right-click the **Equipment Inventory** sheet tab. On the shortcut menu, click **Select All Sheets**.

3 With the worksheets grouped, on the **View tab**, in the **Workbook Views group**, click **Page Layout**, and then compare your screen with Figure 10.41.

> Use Page Layout view to fine-tune your pages before printing. As in Normal view, you can change the layout and format of your data, but here you can also use the rulers to measure and get a better visual view of your headers and footers.

ANOTHER WAY On the status bar, on the right, click the Page Layout button.

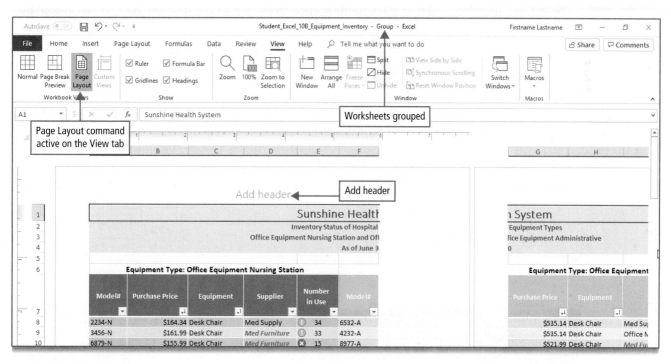

Figure 10.41

4 Scroll up as necessary and then click the text *Add header*. Click the **Header & Footer Tools Design tab**, and then in the **Header & Footer Elements group**, click **Picture**.

5 In the **Insert Pictures** dialog box, click **From a file**. In the **Insert Picture** dialog box, navigate to the files you downloaded with this project, click the file **e10B_Logo**, and then click **Insert**.

6 Click above *&[Picture]* outside of the box, and then compare your screen with Figure 10.42.

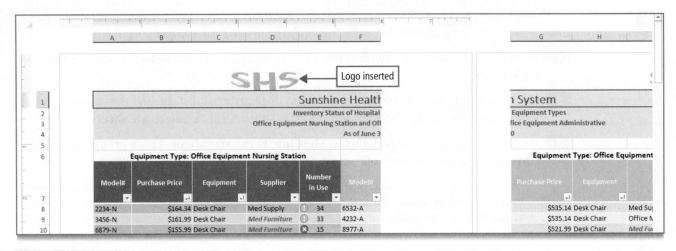

Figure 10.42

7 Click the logo, and then click in the section to the left of the inserted logo. Type **Created by Pat Shepard**

8 Press ⟨Tab⟩ two times to move to the right section. Click the **Header & Footer Tools Design tab**, and then in the **Header & Footer Elements group**, click **Sheet Name**. Click above the header, and then compare your screen with Figure 10.43.

In the header, the logo displays in the center section, text displays in the left section, and the sheet name displays in the right section.

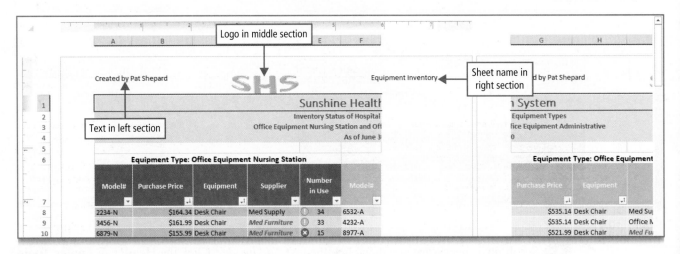

Figure 10.43

9 Click anywhere in the header, click the **Header & Footer Design tab**, and then in the **Navigation group**, click **Go to Footer**.

10 ▶ Click in the left section, and then in the **Header & Hooter Elements group**, click **File Name**. Click a cell just above the footer area to deselect, and then compare your screen with Figure 10.44.

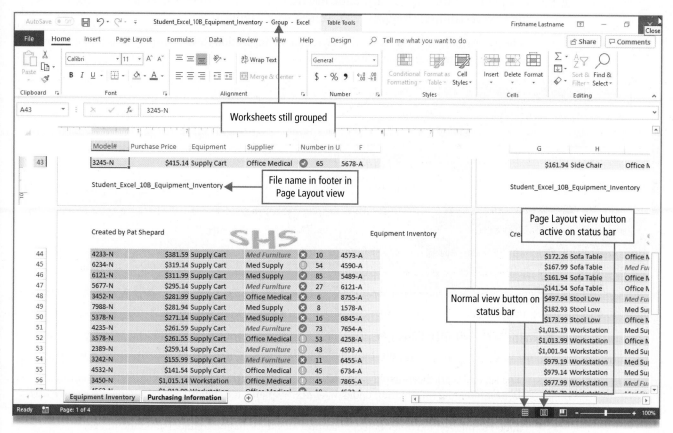

Figure 10.44

11 ▶ In the lower right corner of your screen, in the status bar, click **Normal** ▦ to return to **Normal** view, and then press Ctrl + Home to display the top of your worksheet.

12 ▶ With the worksheets still grouped, on the **Page Layout tab**, click **Margins**, click **Custom Margins**, and then under **Center on page**, click the **Horizontally** check box. Click **OK**.

13 ▶ Set the **Orientation** to **Landscape**. In the **Scale to Fit group**, set the **Width** to **1 page** and the **Height** to **1 page**. Display the **document properties**. As the **Tags**, type **equipment inventory** In the **Subject** box, type your course name and section number. Be sure your name displays as the author.

14 ▶ On the left, click **Save**.

Objective 7 | Inspect a Workbook

GO! Learn How
Video E10-7

When you finish editing a workbook, you may want to review its contents to ensure that it is accessible to individuals with disabilities, that it does not contain sensitive or personal information that you do not want to share with other people, and that it is compatible with earlier versions of Excel.

Activity 10.16 | Ensuring Accessibility in a Workbook

MOS
1.5.4

To ensure that an Excel workbook is accessible and can be read by individuals with disabilities, you can run the *Accessibility Checker*, which finds any potential accessibility issues and creates a report so that you can resolve the issues to make your file easier for those with disabilities to use.

1 ▶ Click the **File tab**, if necessary, click the **Info tab**, click **Check for Issues**, and then click **Check Accessibility**. Compare your screen with Figure 10.45.

The Accessibility Checker pane displays, and the Inspection Results display an error and warnings. Errors are more severe than warnings.

▭ **MAC TIP** On the Review tab, in the Document group, click Check Accessibility.

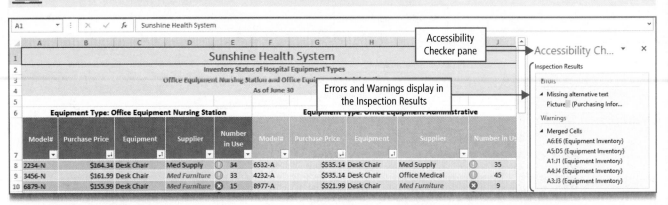

Figure 10.45

2 ▶ In the **Accessibility Checker** pane, under **Errors**, point to the text below *Missing alternative text* to display an arrow, and then click the **arrow**. Compare your screen with Figure 10.46.

The second worksheet displays, and the image of an office chair is selected. Under *Additional Information*, the information under *Why Fix?* explains the importance of adding *alternative text* to images for people who can't see the screen. Also referred to as *alt text*, alternative text is text added to images and other objects that provides information to understand the image.

▭ **MAC TIP** Click Picture 3 (Purchasing Information...)

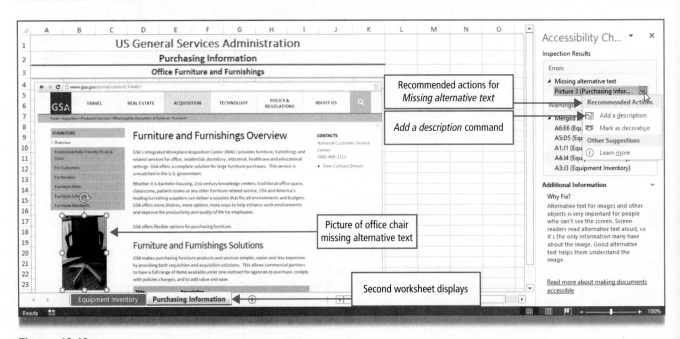

Figure 10.46

3 On the left, click to select the image, right-click, and then on the shortcut menu, click **Edit Alt Text**.

4 In the **Alt Text** pane that displays on the right, click in the box, type **Black office chair on rolling castors** and then compare your screen with Figure 10.47.

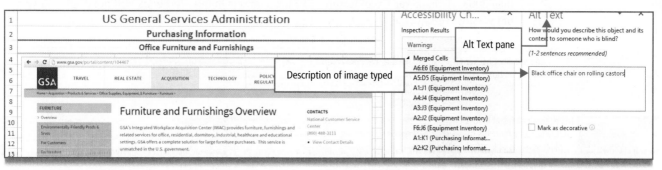

Figure 10.47

5 **Close** ⊠ the **Alt Text** pane, and notice that the error no longer displays in the Accessibility Checker pane.

6 In the **Accessibility Checker** pane, under **Merged Cells**, point to the first item to display an arrow, and then click the **arrow**. Under *Why Fix?* notice the information regarding merged cells. Compare your screen with Figures 10.48.

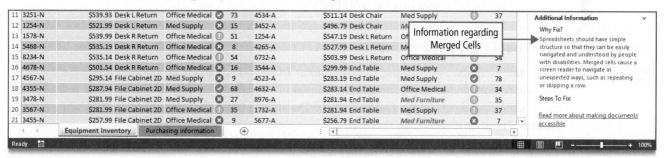

Figure 10.48

7 **Save** 🖫 your workbook, and then **Close** ⊠ the **Accessibility Checker** pane.

Activity 10.17 │ Ensuring Backward-Compatibility in a Workbook

MOS
1.5.4

To ensure that an Excel workbook does not have compatibility issues that cause a significant loss of functionality or a minor loss of fidelity in an earlier version of Excel, you can run the ***Compatibility Checker***, which finds any potential compatibility issues and creates a report so that you can resolve the issues.

When you work on a workbook in ***Compatibility Mode***, where the workbook is in Excel 97-2003 file format (.xls) instead of the newer file format (.xlsx), the Compatibility Checker runs automatically when you save a workbook. In this Activity, you will run the Compatibility Checker to identify features in the workbook that cannot be transferred to earlier versions of Excel.

> **MAC TIP** Check for Issues and Check Compatibility may not be available. Per Microsoft's Help "A Compatibility function can be added to the Mac ribbon." Read the information in the steps below to gain an understanding of these features.

Click the **File tab**, click the **Info tab**, click **Check for Issues**, and then click **Check Compatibility**. Compare your screen with Figure 10.49.

The Microsoft Excel - Compatibility Checker dialog box displays. The Compatibility Checker displays issues that can result in loss of functionality if someone is using a version of Excel earlier than 2003. Here, newer Excel features like the icon sets in this workbook will not display in very old versions of Excel.

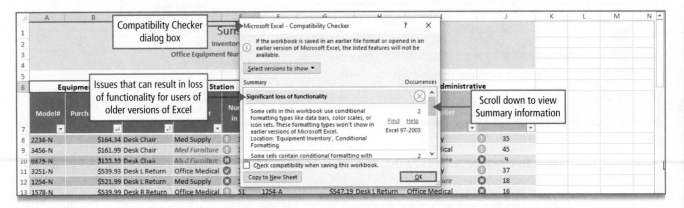

Figure 10.49

 Scroll down to view the remainder of the **Summary** information, and then click **OK** without making any changes to your workbook.

Activity 10.18 | Inspecting a Document

MOS
1.5.6

In this Activity, you will use the *Document Inspector*, which is an Excel feature that can find and remove hidden properties and personal information in a workbook. You will inspect the workbook and review the results that the Document Inspector finds to determine what information, if any, should be removed.

MAC TIP Check for Issues and Inspect Document may not be available. Read the steps to gain an understanding of these features. In the Excel Preferences dialog box, a Mac user can click Security & Privacy. Under Office Intelligent Services, there is a choice to *Remove personal information from this file on save.*

 Save 🖫 your workbook.

Before inspecting a document, be sure you have saved your workbook.

 Click the **File tab**, click the **Info tab**, click **Check for Issues**, and then click **Inspect Document**. Compare your screen with Figure 10.50.

The Document Inspector dialog box displays and lists the various types of content that will be checked. By default, all the check boxes are selected.

Figure 10.50

3 In the lower right corner of the dialog box, click **Inspect**.

> The Document Inspector indicates categories that contain personal information. A red exclamation point and a Remove All button display in the inspection results for this category. In this workbook, the Document Inspector found document properties, author, and other information. When sending a workbook to others, it is a good idea to remove identifying information that you don't want to share—such as the author name.

4 **Close** the **Document Inspector** dialog box without taking any action.

MORE KNOWLEDGE **Removing Document Properties and Personal Information**

When you remove document properties and personal information using the Document Inspector, it applies a setting that automatically removes properties and personal information whenever you save the document. To add properties such as author or tags to such a file, on the File tab, enter the properties and then, under Inspect Workbook, click Allow this information to be saved in your file.

---

5 On the left, click **Print** to display the **Print Preview**. Scroll through the two worksheets. On the left, click **Save** to save your workbook and return to the workbook window.

6 In the upper right corner of the Excel window, click **Close** ⊠.

 For Non-MyLab Submissions Determine What Your Instructor Requires for Submission
As directed by your instructor, submit your completed **Lastname_Firstname_10B_Equipment_Inventory** Excel workbook.

---

7 In **MyLab IT**, in your **Course Materials**, locate and click the Grader Project **Excel 10B Equipment Inventory**. In **step 3**, under **Upload Completed Assignment**, click **Choose File**. In the **Open** dialog box, navigate to your **Excel Chapter 10 folder**, and then click your **Student_Excel_10B_Equipment_Inventory** file one time to select it. In the lower right corner of the **Open** dialog box, click **Open**.

> The name of your selected file displays above the Upload button.

8 To submit your file to **MyLab IT** for grading, click **Upload**, wait a moment for a green **Success!** message, and then in **step 4**, click the blue **Submit for Grading** button. Click **Close Assignment** to return to your list of **Course Materials**.

You have completed Project 10B **END**

Activities 10.19–10.20 in Objective 8 are optional. Check with your instructor to see if you should complete these Activities. These Activities are *not* included in the **MyLab IT** Grader system; you will need to obtain the starting file from your instructor or from www. pearsonhighered.com/go.

Objective 8	Use Co-Authoring and Prepare a Workbook for Final Distribution

GO! Learn How

Video E10-8

You can share a workbook and work on it with others at the same time. Before distributing Excel workbooks to others, you may need to protect it with a password and mark it as final so that others do not change it.

Activity 10.19 | Sharing a Workbook for Co-Authoring

You and your colleagues can open and work on the same Excel workbook. This is referred to as *co-authoring* and replaces the Track Changes features in earlier versions of Excel.

As you co-author, you can see the changes of others in a few seconds, and in some versions of Excel, the work of others will display in different colors.

1 From the files downloaded with this Project, open the workbook **e10B_Imaging_Facilities**, and then display the **Save As** dialog box. Using your own name, **Save** the file in your **Excel Chapter 10** folder as **Lastname_Firstname_10B_Imaging_Facilities_Encrypted**

2 In the upper right corner, click the **Share** button, as shown in Figure 10.51. If you don't have the Share button, just read the following information.

You must store the shared file in Microsoft OneDrive, Microsoft OneDrive for Business, or in a Microsoft SharePoint Online library.

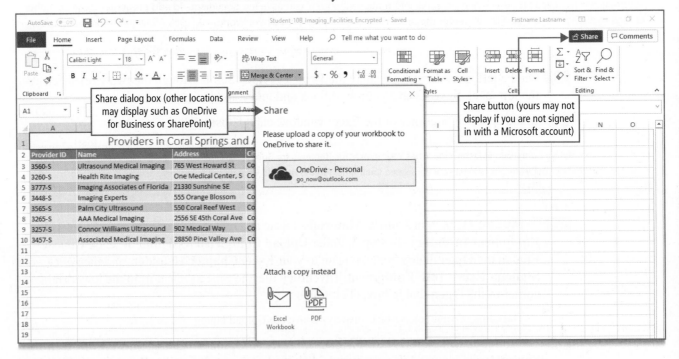

Figure 10.51

3 If you have displayed the **Share** dialog box, in the upper right corner, click **Close** ☒.

🖥 **MAC TIP**   Click somewhere outside the box.

Activity 10.20 | Encrypting a Workbook and Protecting Workbook Structure

Expert 1.2.3

You can provide a level of security for your workbook by adding *encryption*, which is the process by which a file is encoded so that it cannot be opened without the proper password. Encryption is more than simple password protection—the process digitally obscures information to make it unreadable without a proper key to decode it. Passwords prevent users from *editing* a worksheet or the entire workbook. Encryption is different—it prevents users from *opening* the file. In this Activity, you will protect the workbook structure and apply encryption to a workbook.

1 With your **Lastname_Firstname_10B_Imaging_Facilities_Encrypted** workbook open, display the **document properties**, and then in the **Tags** box, **encrypted**

2 While still in **Backstage view**, on the **Info tab**, click **Protect Workbook**, and then click **Protect Workbook Structure**. Click **OK**.

> Protecting the workbook structure prevents changes at the workbook level such as the addition of new worksheets.

3 Click the **File tab**, and then click **Protect Workbook** again. Click **Encrypt with Password**.

> The Encrypt Document dialog box displays. A box in which to type the password and a note of caution about entering passwords displays.

MAC TIP Display the menu bar, click File, click Passwords. Enter goseries in the Password to open box.

---

4 In the **Encrypt Document** dialog box, with the insertion point blinking in the **Password** box, type **goseries** and then click **OK**. In the **Reenter password** box, type **goseries** and then click **OK**.

5 On the left, click **Close**, and in the message box, click **Save**.

> The workbook closes but Excel remains open.

6 Use any method to navigate to your **Excel** Chapter 10 folder, and then reopen your **Lastname_Firstname_10B_Imaging_Facilities_Encrypted** file.

> The Password dialog box displays. The workbook cannot be opened without the password.

7 Type **goseries** and then click **OK**.

> Your Lastname_Firstname_10B_Imaging_Facilities_Encrypted workbook opens.

ALERT   **Does the Workbook Not Open?**

If the workbook does not open, you may have mistyped the password; try typing the password again. If the workbook still does not open, you may have mistyped the password and the reenter password when you encrypted the workbook. There is no simple way to recover a mistyped password from an encrypted document. Open the e10B_Imaging_Facilities file, and repeat Steps 1 through 5.

MORE KNOWLEDGE   **Making Passwords More Secure**

Microsoft has the following suggestions for secure passwords: "A more secure or strong password is one that's difficult for others to determine by guessing or by using automated programs. Strong passwords contain 7–16 characters, do not include common words or names, and combine uppercase letters, lowercase letters, numbers, and symbols."

Activity 10.21 | Marking a Workbook as Final

Before you share a workbook, you can apply the Mark as Final command, which makes the document read-only. The *Mark as Final* command prevents additional changes to the document and disables typing and editing commands. When the document is opened by others, the user will be notified by Microsoft Excel that the document has been *Marked as Final*. (Mac users: on the File tab, click Always Open Read-Only.)

1 With your **Lastname_Firstname_10B_Imaging_Facilities_Encrypted** workbook open, display **Backstage view**, click the **Info tab**, and then click **Protect Workbook**. Click **Mark as Final**.

The Microsoft Excel dialog box displays and indicates that the workbook will be marked as final and then saved.

2 Click **OK**. Read the message box, and then click **OK**.

The workbook is marked as final. The title bar displays *Read-Only* to indicate the file can be read but not edited. A yellow bar displays below the ribbon tabs, indicating that *An author has marked this workbook as final to discourage editing*. If someone opening the file clicks Edit Anyway, the workbook will no longer be *Marked as Final* and will not be a Read-Only file.

3 Click any cell and type a number or text to confirm the workbook cannot be edited.

The Mark as Final command is not a security feature. Anyone can edit a document that has been marked as final by removing the Mark as Final status from the document, editing the file, and then reapplying the Mark as Final status. To ensure that a workbook cannot be edited, you must password protect the workbook. Mark as Final signifies the intent of the author that the document is final in content.

4 If directed by your instructor to do so, submit your Excel file. In the upper right corner of the Excel window, click **Close** ☒.

You have completed the optional portion of this project **END**

wavebreakmedia/Shutterstock, Monkey Business Images/Fotolia, Ivanko80/Shutterstock, Monkey Business Images/Shutterstock

Microsoft Office Specialist (MOS) Skills in This Chapter

Project 10A	Project 10B
1.1.1 Import data from .txt files	**1.3.3** Customize headers and footers
1.1.2 Import data from .csv files	**1.4.2** Display and modify workbook content in different views
2.1.3 Insert and delete multiple columns or rows	**1.5.4** Inspect workbooks for issues
2.2.2 Modify cell alignment, orientation, and indentation	**2.4.2** Apply built-in conditional formatting
2.2.3 Format cells by using Format Painter	**3.1.1** Create Excel tables from cell ranges
3.1.3 Convert tables to cell ranges	**3.3.2** Sort data by multiple columns
3.2.1 Add or remove table rows and columns	**Expert 1.2.3** Protect workbook structure
4.3.1 Format text by using RIGHT and LEFT functions	**Expert 2.3.1** Create custom conditional formatting rules
4.3.2 Format text by using UPPER function	**Expert 2.3.2** Create conditional formatting rules that use formulas
4.3.3 Format text by using CONCAT function	**Expert 2.3.3** Manage conditional formatting rules
Expert 2.1.1 Fill cells by using Flash Fill	
Expert 2.2.5 Remove duplicate records	
Expert 3.1.1 Perform logical operations by using MAXIFS function	

Build Your E-Portfolio

An E-Portfolio is a collection of evidence, stored electronically, that showcases what you have accomplished while completing your education. Collecting and then sharing your work products with potential employers reflects your academic and career goals. Your completed workbooks from the following projects are good examples to show what you have learned: 10G, 10K, and 10L.

GO! For Job Success

Career Passion

Your instructor may assign this topic to your class, and then ask you to think about, or discuss with your classmates, these questions:

When students talk about career plans, they inevitably hear advice like, "Follow your passion!" or "Do what you love and you'll be successful." But is that really true? Should everyone expect that following their dreams will lead to a successful career? Are you a failure if you don't follow your passion?

With millions of people unemployed but millions of jobs going unfilled, many career experts believe a new way of thinking about "passion" is needed. More realistic advice might be to find a passion for the job you have rather than struggling to find a job that fits your passion. A particular skill or area of knowledge will result in a successful career only if there is a need for it in the market—employers and customers must be willing to pay you to do it.

FotolEdhar / Fotolia

> Do you think doing what you love is a requirement for a rewarding and successful career?

> If you have a passion for an activity or cause, do you think it's realistic that you could make a living devoted to it, and do you think you would continue to be passionate about it if you had to do it for a living every day?

> Do you think it's possible to be happy in a job or career that you are not passionate about, but that you like or are good at?

End of Chapter

Summary

Data can be imported into Excel from external sources such as webpages, databases, or text files. Cleaning up data includes removing duplicates, fixing spacing and case, and separating or merging fields.

A database is an organized collection of facts related to a specific topic or purpose. Excel's database functions such as DSUM, DAVERAGE, and DCOUNT can be used to perform calculations on the database.

You can insert a second table in a worksheet and sort data in side-by-side tables to compare data. Apply conditional formatting using icon sets to add visual emphasis to the conditional format of a list.

You can create custom headers and footers that include pictures; for example, a logo or a product picture. You can also insert elements such as the sheet name, the date, and text that you type.

GO! Learn It Online

Review the concepts, key terms, and MOS skills in this chapter by completing these online challenges, which you can find in **MyLab IT**.

Chapter Quiz: Answer matching and multiple-choice questions to test what you learned in this chapter.

Lessons on the GO!: Learn how to use all the new apps and features as they are introduced by Microsoft.

MOS Prep Quiz: Answer questions to review the MOS skills you practiced in this chapter.

Project Guide for Excel Chapter 10

Your instructor will assign Projects from this list to ensure your learning and assess your knowledge.

	Project Guide for Excel Chapter 10		
Project	**Apply Skills from These Chapter Objectives**	**Project Type**	**Project Location**
10A MyLab IT	Objectives 1–3 from Project 10A	**10A Instructional Project (Grader Project)** **Instruction** Guided instruction to learn the skills in Project 10A	In **MyLab IT** and in text
10B MyLab IT	Objectives 4–8 from Project 10B	**10B Instructional Project (Grader Project)** **Instruction** Guided instruction to learn the skills in Project 10B	In **MyLab IT** and in text
10C	Objectives 1–3 from Project 10A	**10C Skills Review (Scorecard Grading)** **Review** A guided review of the skills from Project 10A.	In text
10D	Objectives 4–8 from Project 10B	**10D Skills Review (Scorecard Grading)** **Review** A guided review of the skills from Project 10B.	In text
10E MyLab IT	Objectives 1–3 from Project 10A	**10E Mastery (Grader Project)** **Mastery and Transfer of Learning** A demonstration of your mastery of the skills in Project 10A with extensive decision making.	In **MyLab IT** and in text
10F MyLab IT	Objectives 4–8 from Project 10B	**10F Mastery (Grader Project)** **Mastery and Transfer of Learning** A demonstration of your mastery of the skills in Project 10B with extensive decision making.	In **MyLab IT** and in text
10G MyLab IT	Objectives 1–8 from Projects 10A and 10B	**10G Mastery (Grader Project)** **Mastery and Transfer of Learning** A demonstration of your mastery of the skills in Projects 10A and 10B with extensive decision making.	In **MyLab IT** and in text
10H	Combination of Objectives from Projects 10A and 10B	**10H GO! Fix It (Scorecard Grading)** **Critical Thinking** A demonstration of your mastery of the skills in Projects 10A and 10B by creating a correct result from a document that contains errors you must find.	IRC
10I	Combination of Objectives from Projects 10A and 10B	**10I GO! Make It (Scorecard Grading)** **Critical Thinking** A demonstration of your mastery of the skills in Projects 10A and 10B by creating a result from a supplied picture.	IRC
10J	Combination of Objectives from Projects 10A and 10B	**10J GO! Solve It (Rubric Grading)** **Critical Thinking** A demonstration of your mastery of the skills in Projects 10A and 10B, your decision-making skills, and your critical thinking skills. A task-specific rubric helps you self-assess your result.	IRC
10K	Combination of Objectives from Projects 10A and 10B	**10K GO! Solve It (Rubric Grading)** **Critical Thinking** A demonstration of your mastery of the skills in Projects 10A and 10B, your decision-making skills, and your critical thinking skills. A task-specific rubric helps you self-assess your result.	In text
10L	Combination of Objectives from Projects 10A and 10B	**10L GO! Think (Rubric Grading)** **Critical Thinking** A demonstration of your understanding of the Chapter concepts applied in a manner that you would outside of college. An analytic rubric helps you and your instructor grade the quality of your work by comparing it to the work an expert in the discipline would create.	In text
10M	Combination of Objectives from Projects 10A and 10B	**10M GO! Think (Rubric Grading)** **Critical Thinking** A demonstration of your understanding of the Chapter concepts applied in a manner that you would outside of college. An analytic rubric helps you and your instructor grade the quality of your work by comparing it to the work an expert in the discipline would create.	IRC
10N	Combination of Objectives from Projects 10A and 10B	**10N You and GO! (Rubric Grading)** **Critical Thinking** A demonstration of your understanding of the Chapter concepts applied in a manner that you would in a personal situation. An analytic rubric helps you and your instructor grade the quality of your work.	IRC
Capstone Project for Excel Chapters 1-10	Combination of Objectives from Chapters 1-10	Excel Capstone (Grader Project) **Mastery and Transfer of Learning** A demonstration of your mastery of the skills in Chapters 1-10 with extensive decision making.	In **MyLab IT**

Glossary

Glossary of Chapter Key Terms

Accessibility Checker An Excel feature that finds any potential accessibility issues and creates a report so that you can resolve the issues to make your file easier for those with disabilities to use.

Alt text A shortened version of the term alternative text, which is text added to images and other objects that provides information to understand the image or object.

Alternative text Text added to images and other objects that provides information to understand the image or object.

Arguments The values that an Excel function uses to perform calculations or operations.

Co-authoring The process by which you and your colleagues can open and work on the same Excel workbook and see each other's changes.

Compatibility Checker An Excel feature that finds any potential compatibility issues and creates a report so that you can resolve the issues.

Compatibility Mode A mode where the workbook is in Excel 97-2003 file format (.xls) instead of the newer file format (.xlsx).

CONCAT A text function used to join up to 255 strings of characters. In older versions of Excel, known as CONCATENATE.

Conditional formatting A format that changes the appearance of a cell— for example, by adding cell shading or font color—based on a condition; if the condition is true, the cell is formatted based on that condition, and if the condition is false, the cell is not formatted.

Data Facts about people, events, things, or ideas.

Data connection A link to external data that automatically updates an Excel workbook from the original data whenever the original data source gets new information.

Data transformation Using Excel tools to modify the arrangement of the data you brought into Excel from another source to make the data more useful.

Database An organized collection of facts related to a specific topic or purpose.

DAVERAGE function A function that determines an average in a database that is limited by criteria set for one or more cells.

DCOUNT function A function that counts the number of occurrences of a specified condition in a database.

Delimited A text file in which the text is separated by commas or tabs.

Document Inspector An Excel feature that can find and remove hidden properties and personal information in a workbook.

DSUM function A function that sums a column of values in a database that is limited by criteria set for one or more cells.

Encryption The process by which a file is encoded so that it cannot be opened without the proper password.

Extensible Markup Language (XML) A language that structures data in text files so it can be read by other systems, regardless of the hardware platform or operating system.

Field A specific type of data such as name, employee number, or social security number that is stored in columns.

Filtering controls The arrows that display in the column titles of Excel data when the data is converted to a table that enable you to sort and filter the data.

Flash Fill An Excel feature that predicts how to alter data based upon the pattern you enter into the cell at the beginning of the column; the data must be in the adjacent column.

Function A predefined formula that performs calculations by using specific values, called arguments, in a particular order or structure.

Get & Transform Data A group of commands that enables you to bring data from an Access database, from the web, from a text file, from an XML file, and from many other sources, into Excel in a manner that lets you transform—modify— the data.

Icon set A set of three, four, or five small graphic images that make your data visually easier to interpret.

Information Data that has been organized in a useful manner.

LEFT A text function that returns the specified number of characters from the beginning (left) of a string of characters.

LOWER A text function that changes the case of the characters in a string, making all characters lowercase.

Mark as Final A command that prevents additional changes to the file and disables typing and editing commands.

MAXIFS function An Excel function that returns the maximum value among cells specified by a given set of conditions or criteria.

MINIFS function An Excel function that returns the minimum value among cells specified by a given set of conditions or criteria.

Microsoft Access A database program used to manage database files.

MID A text function that extracts a series of characters from a text string given the location of the beginning character.

Navigator window The window that displays the table or tables from the data source selected using the Get & Transform commands.

PROPER A text function that capitalizes the first letter of each word.

Record All of the data about one item in a database stored in a horizontal row.

RIGHT A text function that returns the specified number of characters from the end (right) of a string of characters.

Syntax The arrangement of the arguments in a function.

Table Data stored in a format of rows and columns.

Text function A function that can be used to combine or separate data, change case, and apply formatting to a string of characters.

TRIM A text function that removes extra blank spaces from a string of characters.

UPPER A text function that changes the case of the characters in a string, making all characters uppercase.

Chapter Review

Skills Review	Project 10C Lab Information

Apply 10A skills from these Objectives:

1. Get External Data into Excel
2. Clean Up and Manage Imported Data
3. Use Database Functions

In the following Skills Review, you will get data about lab department technicians, hematologists, blood bank services, and lab suppliers into Excel. Your completed worksheets will look similar to Figure 10.52.

Project Files

For Project 10C, you will need the following files:

e10C_Hematologist_Information (Text Document)
e10C_Lab_Dept (Excel Workbook)
e10C_Lab_Supplies (XML Document)
e10C_Lab_Supplies_CSV_for_Mac_users (only for Mac users)
e10C_Technician_Information (Access Database)
e10C_Technician_Information_CSV_for_Mac_users (only for Mac users)

You will save your workbook as:

Lastname_Firstname_10C_Lab_Dept

Project Results

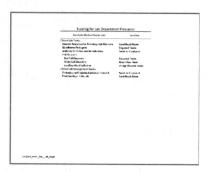
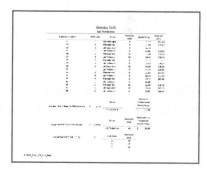

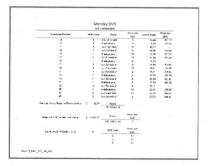

Figure 10.52

(continues on next page)

Chapter Review

1 ▶ Navigate to the files that accompany this project. Open the Excel file **e10C_Lab_Dept**. Click the **File tab**, on the left click **Save As**, click **Browse**, and then in the **Save As** dialog box, navigate to your **Excel Chapter 10 folder**. Using your own name, save the file as **Lastname_Firstname_10C_Lab_Dept**

a. On the **Lab Tech Information** worksheet, click cell **A2**. On the **Data tab**, in the **Get & Transform Data group**, click **Get Data**. Point to **From Database**, and then click **From Microsoft Access Database**. In the **Import Data** dialog box, navigate to the files that accompany this project in your **Excel Chapter 10 folder**, click the Access file **e10C_Technician Information**, and then click **Import**.

(Mac users: From the File menu, click Import, click CSV. Select the comma-delimited file *e10C_Technician_Information_CSV_for_Mac_users* file. In Step 2 of the wizard, select Comma as the delimiter and start at cell A2. Format the imported data as a table (in the Alert, click Yes) and apply Dark Red, Table Style Medium 7. Move to step 1c.)

b. In the **Navigator** window, on the left, click the **Lab Technicians** table. In the lower right corner, click the **Load arrow**, click **Load To**, and then in the **Import Data** dialog box, under **Where do you want to put the data?**, click the **Existing worksheet** option button. Click **OK**.

c. **Merge & Center** the text in cell **A1** across the range **A1:I1**, and then apply the **Title** cell style. **Close** the **Queries & Connections** pane. **Save** your workbook.

2 ▶ Display the **Lab Seminars** worksheet. Select the range **A2:B2**. On the **Home tab**, in the **Alignment group**, click **Center**, and then click **Middle Align**.

a. Select the range **A4:A7**. On the **Home tab**, in the **Alignment group**, click **Increase Indent** one time. Select the range **A8:A10**, and then click **Increase Indent** two times.

b. Select the range **A12:A13** and click **Increase Indent** one time. Click cell **A1**. **Save** your workbook.

3 ▶ Display the **Hematologist Information** worksheet. Click in cell **A2**. On the **Data tab**, in the **Get & Transform Data group**, click **Get Data**. Point to **From File**, and then click **From Text/CSV**. In the **Import Data** dialog box, navigate to the files that accompany this project. Select the Text file **e10C_Hematologist_Information**, and then click **Import**. (Mac users: Click From Text. Be sure the Delimiter is set to Tab. On the Insert tab click Table. Move to Step 4.)

a. Be sure that **Delimiter** is set to **Tab**. In the lower right, click the **Load arrow**, and then click **Load To**.

b. In the **Import Data** dialog box, under **Where do you want to put the data?**, click the **Existing worksheet** option button. Click **OK**.

c. **Close** the **Queries & Connections** dialog box.

4 ▶ With the **Hematologist Information** worksheet active, on the **Data tab**, in the **Data Tools group**, click **Remove Duplicates**.

a. In the **Remove Duplicates** dialog box, click **Unselect All**, verify that the *My data has headers* check box is selected, and then select the **Doctor ID** and **Department** check boxes. Click **OK**, and then click **OK** again.

b. Click in any cell in the table, and then on the **Table Tools Design tab**, in the **Tools group**, click **Convert to Range**. Click **OK**.

5 ▶ Notice the *City, State, and ZIP* are all in the same field in **column F**. Click the **column G** header to select the column. On the **Home tab**, in the **Cells group**, click the **Insert button arrow**, and then click, **Insert Sheet Columns**. Use the same method to insert two additional columns.

a. Click cell **G2**, type **City** and then press Tab. In cell **H2** type **State** press Tab, in cell **I2** type **ZIP** and then press Enter.

b. In cell **G3**, type **Miami** and press Enter. In cell **G4** type **W** and then press Enter to have Flash Fill complete the column.

c. Click cell **H3** and type **FI** Use the fill handle to copy the text down through **H11**. (Mac users: After inserting columns and column headings, select F3:F11. On the Data tab, click Text to Columns. Select Comma as the delimiter. Select G3 as the destination. Click Finish. Delete the contents of cells H3:I11.)

6 ▶ Click cell **I3**. On the **Formulas tab**, in the **Function Library group**, click **Text**, and then click **RIGHT**.

a. With the insertion point in the **Text** box, click cell **F3**. Press Tab, and then, in the **Num_chars** box, type **5** Click **OK**. Drag the **fill handle** to copy the function down through cell **I11**.

b. Click cell **H3**, in the **Function Library**, click **Text**, scroll down as necessary and then click **UPPER**. With the insertion point in the **Text** box, type **FL** and then click **OK**. Drag the fill handle to copy the function down through cell **H11**.

(continues on next page)

Chapter Review

c. Click cell **K2**, type **Full Name** and press Enter. With cell **K3** active, on the **Formulas tab**, in the **Function Library group**, click **Text**, and then click **CONCAT**. With the insertion point in the **Text1** box, click cell **B3**. Press Tab, in the **Text2** box type **"** and then press Space. Type **"** and then press Tab. In the **Text3** box, click **C3**. Click **OK**. Use the **fill handle** to copy the function down through cell **K11**.

d. Select **rows 2:11**, and then on the **Home tab**, in the **Editing group**, click **Clear**, and then click **Clear Formats**.

e. Click cell **A1**. **Merge & Center** the text across the range **A1:K1** and apply the **Title** cell style. **AutoFit columns A:K**. Click the **column F** heading. On the **Home tab**, in the **Cells group**, click **Format**. Point to **Hide & Unhide**, and then click **Hide Columns**. Select the range **A2:K2**, apply **Bold**, apply **Center**, and then from the **Cell Styles** gallery, apply **Accent6**. Click cell **A1** and **Save** your workbook.

7 Display the **Lab Suppliers** worksheet. Click in cell **A2**. On the **Data tab**, in the **Get & Transform Data group**, click **Get Data**. Point to **From File**, and then click **From XML**. In the **Import Data** dialog box, navigate to the files that accompany this project in your **Excel Chapter 10 folder**, and then click **e10C_Lab_Supplies**. Click **Import**. (Mac users: From the File menu, click Import, click CSV, select comma-delimited file e10C_Lab_Supplies_CSV_for Mac_users. In Step 2 of the wizard, select Comma as the delimiter and start at cell A2. Format the imported data as a table (in the Alert, click Yes). Apply Dark Red, Table Style Medium 7. Move to step 7b.)

a. In the **Navigator** window, click the **supply** table. In the lower right, click the **Load arrow**, click **Load To**, and then in the **Import Data** dialog box, under **Where do you want to put the data?**, click the **Existing worksheet** option button. Click **OK**.

b. **Close** the **Queries & Connections** pane. **Merge & Center** the title in cell **A1** across the range **A1:D1**, and then apply the **Title** cell style. **Save** your workbook.

8 Display the **Lab Technicians** worksheet. In cell **A22**, type **Average Hourly Wage for Phlebotomists** and press Tab. **AutoFit column A**. Click cell **C3**, **Copy** the cell, and then paste it, using **Paste (P)** into cell **C22**.

a. In cell **C23**, type **Phlebotomist** and press Tab. Click cell **B22**, and then to the left of the **Formula Bar**, click **Insert Function**. In the **Insert Function** dialog box, click the **Or select a category arrow**, and then on the list, click **Database**. In the **Select a function** box, click **DAVERAGE**, and then click **OK**. (Mac users: In the Formula Builder pane, select DAVERAGE and click Insert Function.)

b. In the **Function Arguments** dialog box, in the **Database** box, click **Collapse Dialog Box**, and then select the range **A3:F20**. Then, in the collapsed dialog box, click **Expand Dialog Box**. In the **Field** box, type **Hourly Wage** and press Tab. With the insertion point in the **Criteria** box, select the vertical range **C22:C23**. Click **OK**. To cell **B22**, apply **Accounting Number Format**. Your result is $21.77.

9 In cell **A25**, type **Wage per Shift for Lab Technicians** and press Tab. Select and then copy the range **C3:D3**. Paste the selection into cell **C25** to fill the range C25:D25. Press Esc to cancel the moving border.

a. In cell **C26**, type **Lab Technician** and press Tab. In cell **D26**, type **>0** and then press Enter.

b. Click cell **B25**, and then type **=dsum(** to begin the formula for the DSUM function. Select the range **A3:F20**, and then type **,** (a comma). Being sure to include the comma at the end, type **"Wage per Shift",** to enter the second part of the argument. As indicated by *criteria* in the ScreenTip, type the criteria as **c25:d26** and then press Enter. To cell **B25**, apply **Accounting Number Format**.

10 In cell **A28**, type **Count Day Shift (Code 1, 3, 5)** and press Tab. Click cell **B3**, hold down Ctrl and click cell **D3**. **Copy** the selection, and then paste into cell **C28**. Press Esc to cancel the moving border.

a. In cell **C29**, type **1** and press Tab. In cell **D29**, type **>0** and press Enter. In cell **C30**, type **3** and press Tab. In cell **D30**, type **>0** and press Enter. In cell **C31**, type **5** and press Tab. In cell **D31**, type **>0** and press Enter.

b. Click cell **B28**. To the left of the **Formula Bar**, click **Insert Function**. In the **Select a function** box, click **DCOUNT**, and then click **OK**. (Mac users: In the Formula Builder pane, select DCOUNT and click Insert Function.)

c. In the **Function Arguments** dialog box, in the **Database** box, click **Collapse Dialog Box**. Move the collapsed box to the upper right corner of your screen. Scroll as necessary, and then select the range **A3:F20**. In the collapsed dialog box, click **Expand Dialog Box**.

(continues on next page)

Chapter Review

d. In the **Field** box, type **Employee Number** and then press Tab. With the insertion point in the **Criteria** box, click **Collapse Dialog Box**, scroll as necessary, and then select the range **C28:D31**. In the collapsed dialog box, click **Expand Dialog**. Click **OK**.

e. Click cell **A1**.

11 On the **Home tab**, in the **Cells group**, click **Format**, and then under **Organize Sheets**, click **Move or Copy Sheet**.

a. In the **Move or Copy** dialog box, under **Before sheet**, click (**move to end**), and select the **Create a copy** check box. Click **OK**.

b. With the new worksheet displayed, on the **Home tab**, in the **Cells group**, click **Format**, and then under **Organize Sheets**, click **Rename Sheet**. With the name of the sheet selected, type **Hourly Wages** and press Enter.

c. Click cell **E22**, and type **Maximum Phlebotomist Hourly Wage** and press Enter. Use **Format Painter** to copy the format from cell **C22** to cell **E22**, and then widen **column E** as necessary so that *Phlebotomist* displays on one line.

d. Click in cell **E23**, Type **=maxifs(** and then select the range **E4:E20**. Type a comma **,** and then select the range **C4:C20**. Type a comma **,** and then click cell **C23**. Press Enter. The highest Hourly Wage for a Phlebotomist in this group is $23.46.

e. Click cell **E25**, and type **Maximum Lab Technician Hourly Wage** and press Enter. Use **Format Painter** to copy the format from cell **D25** to cell **E25**.

f. Click in cell **E26**, Type **=maxifs(** and then select the range **E4:E20**. Type a comma **,** and then select the range **C4:C20**. Type a comma **,** and then click cell **C26**. Press Enter. The highest Hourly Wage for a Lab Technician in this group is $35.40.

g. Apply **Accounting Number Format** to cell **E23** and **E26**. Click Cell **A1** to make it the active cell.

12 Display the first worksheet—**Lab Tech Information**. In the sheet tab area, point to any sheet tab, right-click, and then click **Select All Sheets** to group the worksheets. On the **Page Layout tab**, click **Margins**, click **Custom Margins**, and then in the **Page Setup** dialog box, under **Center on page**, center the worksheets **Horizontally**. Click the **Header/Footer tab**, click **Custom Footer**, and then in the **left section**, insert the **File Name**. Click **OK** two times.

a. With all the sheets still grouped, press Ctrl + Home to make cell **A1** the active cell. In the **Page Setup group**, set the **Orientation** to **Landscape**. In the **Scale to Fit group**, set the **Width** to **1 page** and the **Height** to **1 page**. Display the **document properties**. As the **Tags**, type **lab department information** In the **Subject** box, type your course name and section number. Be sure your name displays as the author.

b. On the left, click **Print** to display the **Print Preview**. Scroll through the six worksheets to check for placement. On the left, click **Save** to save your workbook and return to the workbook window.

c. Ungroup the worksheets. In the upper right corner of the Excel window, click **Close**. Submit your Excel file as directed by your instructor.

You have completed Project 10C **END**

Chapter Review

Skills Review | Project 10D Medical Supplies

In the following Skills Review, you will edit a worksheet for Pat Shepard, Vice President of Operations, detailing the current inventory of two medical supply types. Your completed worksheets will look similar to Figure 10.53.

Project Files

For Project 10D, you will need the following files:

e10D_Logo

e10D_Medical_Supplies

You will save your workbook as:

Lastname_Firstname_10D_Medical_Supplies

Project Results

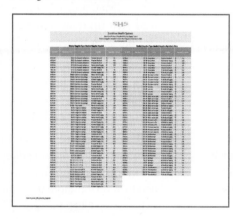 

Figure 10.53

(continues on next page)

Chapter Review

1 From the files that you downloaded for this project, open the Excel file **e10D_Medical_Supplies**. Using your own name, in your **Excel Chapter 10 folder**, save the file as **Lastname_Firstname_10D_Medical_Supplies**

a. On the **Medical Supplies Inventory** worksheet, select the range **A7:E62**, and then on the **Insert tab**, in the **Tables group**, click **Table**. In the **Create Table** dialog box, verify that *=$A$7:$E$62* displays as the data range and that the **My table has headers** check box is selected. Click **OK**.

b. Display the **Physician's Clinic** worksheet, select the range **A1:E52**, right-click over the selection, and then, click **Copy**. Display the **Medical Supplies Inventory** worksheet, scroll up as necessary, point to cell **F6** and right-click, and then, under **Paste Options**, click **Paste (P)**. Click any cell to deselect.

c. Select the range **F7:J57**. In the lower right corner of the selection, click **Quick Analysis**, click **Tables**, and then click **Table**. On the **Table Tools Design tab**, in the **Table Styles group**, click **More** and then under **Medium**, use the ScreenTips to locate and click **Green, Table Style Medium 12**. (Mac users: On the Insert tab click table.)

2 Click any cell in the **Medical Supplies Hospital** table on the left. On the **Data tab**, click **Sort** to display the **Sort** dialog box.

a. In the **Sort** dialog box, under **Column**, click the **Sort by arrow**, and then click **Item**. Be sure **Sort On** indicates *Cell Values* and **Order** indicates *A to Z*. In the upper left corner, click **Add Level**. Under **Column**, click the **Then by arrow**, and then click **Purchase Price**. On the same row, click the **Order arrow**, and then set the sort order to **Largest to Smallest**. Click **OK**.

b. Using the same technique and sort orders, sort the **Medical Supplies Physician's Clinic** table. AutoFit columns A:J.

3 Select the range **E8:E62**. On the **Home tab**, in the **Styles group**, click **Conditional Formatting**. Point to **Icon Sets**, and then under **Directional**, in the first row, click the first icon set—**3 Arrows (Colored)**. Click any cell to deselect.

a. Select the range **J8:J57** and then in the lower right corner of the selection click **Quick Analysis**. Click **Icon Set**. (Mac users: use ribbon commands.)

b. Select the range **C8:C62**. On the **Home tab**, in the **Styles group**, click **Conditional Formatting**, and then at the bottom click **New Rule**. Under **Select a Rule Type**, click **Use a formula to determine which cells to format**. (Mac users: In the New Formatting Rule dialog box, in the Style box, select Classic; then select Use a formula to determine which cells to format.)

c. In the **Format values where this formula is true** box type **=c8="Latex tubing"** and then in the lower right, click **Format**. Under **Font style** click **Bold italic**. Click the **color arrow**, and at the bottom under **Standard Colors**, click **Red**. Click **OK** two times. (Mac users: In the Format with box, select Red Text (to remove the cell fill color). Then in the Format with box, select Custom Format.)

4 Display **Backstage view**, click the **Info tab**, and then click **Check for Issues**. On the list, click **Check Accessibility**. (Mac users: On the Review tab, in the Document group, click Check Accessibility.)

a. In the **Accessibility Checker** pane, under **Errors**, point to the text below *Missing alternative text*, and then click the **arrow**. On the left, right-click to the selected image, and then on the shortcut menu, click **Edit Alt Text**. (Mac users: Click Picture 3 Medical Equipment Info).

b. In the **Alt Text** pane, click in the box, type **Blood pressure monitor** and then close the two panes.

5 Point to the **Physician's Clinic** sheet tab, right-click, and then click **Delete**. Click **Delete** a second time to confirm the deletion. Right-click the **Medical Supplies Inventory sheet tab**, and then click **Select All Sheets**. Click the **View tab**, and then in the **Workbook Views group**, click **Page Layout**. Scroll up if necessary, click the text *Add header*. On the **Header & Footer Tools Design tab**, in the **Header & Footer Elements group**, click **Picture**.

a. In the **Insert Pictures** dialog box, click **From a file**. In the **Insert Picture** dialog box, navigate to the files you downloaded with this project, click the file **e10D_Logo**, and then click **Insert**.

b. On the **Design tab**, in the **Navigation group**, click **Go to Footer**. Click in the **left section**, and then in the **Header & Footer Elements group**, click **File Name**. Click in any worksheet cell to deselect the footer. In the lower right corner of your screen, in the status bar, click **Normal** to return to **Normal** view, and then press ⌃ **Ctrl** + **Home** to display the top of your worksheet.

(continues on next page)

Chapter Review

6 With the worksheets still grouped, on the **Page Layout tab**, click **Margins**, click **Custom Margins**, and then under **Center on page**, select the **Horizontally** check box. Click **OK.**

a. Set the **Orientation** to **Landscape**. In the **Scale to Fit group**, set the **Width** to **1 page** and the **Height** to **1 page**. Display the document properties. As the Tags, type **medical supplies inventory** In the **Subject** box, type your course name and section number. Be sure your name displays as the author.

b. On the left, click **Print** to display the **Print Preview**. Scroll through the two worksheets. On the left, click **Save** to save your workbook and return to the workbook window.

c. In the upper right corner of the Excel window, click **Close**. Submit your Excel file as directed by your instructor.

You have completed Project 10D | **END**

Content-Based Assessments (Mastery and Transfer of Learning)

Apply 10A skills from these Objectives:

1. Get External Data into Excel
2. Clean Up and Manage Imported Data
3. Use Database Functions

In the following Mastering Excel project, you will import data about Emergency Department technicians, ER doctors, paramedic services, and emergency suppliers into Excel. Your completed worksheet will look similar to Figure 10.54.

Project Files for MyLab IT Grader

1. In your **MyLab IT** course, locate and click **Excel 10E ER Department**, Download Materials, and then Download All Files.
2. Extract the zipped folder to your Excel Chapter 10 folder. Close the Grader download screens.
3. Take a moment to open the downloaded **Excel_10E_ER_Departent_Instructions**; note any recent updates to the book.

Project Results

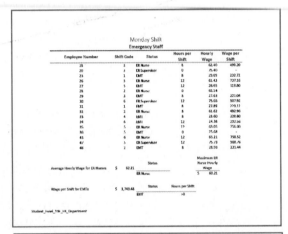

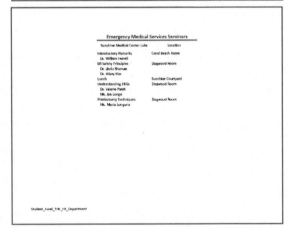

Figure 10.54

For Non-MyLab Submissions

For Project 10E, you will need:

e10E_ER_Department
e10E_ER_Doctors (Text document)
e10E_ER_Staff (Access database)
e10E_ER_Staff_CSV_for_Mac_users (CSV file only for Mac users)

In your Excel Chapter 10 folder, save your workbook as:

Lastname_Firstname_10E_ER_Department

After you have named and saved your workbook, on the next page, begin with Step 2.
After Step 13, submit your file as directed by your instructor.

(continues on next page)

Content-Based Assessments (Mastery and Transfer of Learning)

1 Navigate to your **Excel** Chapter 10 **folder**, and then double-click the Excel file you downloaded from **MyLab IT** that displays your name—**Student_Excel_10E_ER_Department**. If necessary, at the top, click **Enable Editing**.

2 On the **Emergency Staff** worksheet, in cell **B22**, insert a **DAVERAGE** function. As the **Database**, use the range **A3:F20** and as the **Field**, type **"Hourly Wage"** and as the **Criteria**, use the range **C22:C23**

3 In cell **B25**, enter a **DSUM** function using the database range **A3:F20**, type **"Wage per Shift"** as the field, and **C25:D26** as the criteria.

4 Apply **Accounting Number Format** to the results in cells **B22** and **B25**. Click cell **A1**.

5 Display the **ER Staff Information** worksheet, and then click cell **A2**. From the **Data tab**, use the **Get Data** command to get data from the Microsoft Access Database downloaded with this project—**e10E_ER_Staff**. Select the **ER Staff** table and load it into the existing worksheet. **Close** the **Queries & Connections** pane. Click cell **A1**, and then **Save** your workbook.

(Mac users: From the File menu, click Import, click CSV. Select the comma-delimited file *e10E_ER_Staff_CSV_for_Mac_users* file. In Step 2 of the wizard, select Comma as the delimiter and start at cell A2. Format the imported data as a table (in the Alert, click Yes) and apply Green, Table Style Medium 7.)

6 Display the **ER Doctors** worksheet, and then click cell **A2**. Import the text file **e10E_ER_Doctors** downloaded with this project. Be sure the **Delimiter** is set to **Tab**, and then load the data into the existing worksheet. Convert the table to a range, click **OK**, and then close the **Queries & Connections** pane. (Mac users: format the imported data as a table (in the Alert, click Yes) and apply Green, Table Style Medium 7, and then convert the table to a range.)

7 Select the table range **A2:G11**. Remove duplicate doctors (**ER Doctor ID**) from each unit (**ER Unit**). One duplicate value is found and removed.

8 Insert three new columns between columns **F:G**. In cell **G3**, use **Flash Fill** to fill the cities down through cell **G10**. In cell **H3**, type **FL** and copy this abbreviation down through cell **H10**. Capture the **ZIP** field from **column F** by using the **RIGHT** function in cell **I3**, and then copy the function down through cell **I10**.

Select **rows 2:10**, and then from the **Home tab**, in the **Editing group**, clear formats. In cell **G2**, type **City** and in cell **H2**, type **State** and in cell **I2** type **ZIP AutoFit** columns **A:J**, and then hide **column F**. Select the range **A2:K2**, apply **Bold** and **Center**, and then apply the **Accent6** cell style. Click cell **A1**.

(Mac users: Insert three columns between F:G. Select the range F2:F10. With F2:F10 selected, on the Data tab, click Text to Columns, and use Comma as the delimiter. Delete the contents in the range F2:F10. In cell H3, type FL and fill down. Extract the Zip field from column F by using the RIGHT function in column I. AutoFit columns A:J, and then hide column F.)

9 In cell **K2**, type **Full Name** and then in cell **K3**, insert the **CONCAT** function to combine the text in cell **B3** and **C3**, separated by a space. Copy the formula down through cell **K10**, and then apply **AutoFit** to **column K**. Click cell **A1**.

10 Display the **ER Seminars** worksheet. Center the titles in cells **A2** and **B2** vertically and horizontally. Indent the names of the presenters. Click cell **A1**.

11 Display the **Emergency Staff** worksheet. Click cell **E22**, type **Maximum ER Nurse Hourly Wage** and press Enter. Use **Format Painter** to copy the format from cell **C22** to cell **E22**. Click cell **E23**. By using the **MAXIFS** function, determine the highest hourly wage for an ER nurse on the Monday shift. Use the *Hourly Wages* in the range **E4:E20** as the max range, the *Status* in the range **C4:C20** as the criteria range, and cell **C23**—*ER Nurse*—as the criteria. Apply **Accounting Number Format** to your result—*63.21*—in cell **E23**.

12 Select all the sheets, display the **Page Setup** dialog box, center the worksheets horizontally, create a **Custom Footer** and insert the file name in the left section of the footer. **Close** the **Page Setup** dialog box. Set the **Orientation** to **Landscape**, set the **Width** to **1 page** and the **Height** to **1 page**. Make cell **A1** the active cell. Display the document properties, add your Course and Section # as the Subject and as the **Tags** type **ER information**

13 On the left, click **Print** to display the **Print Preview**. Scroll through the four worksheets. On the left, click **Save** to save your workbook and return to the workbook window. **Close** ☒ Excel.

(continues on next page)

Mastering Excel: Project 10E ER Department (continued)

14 In **MyLab IT**, locate and click the Grader Project **Excel 10E ER Department**. In **step 3**, under **Upload Completed Assignment**, click **Choose File**. In the **Open** dialog box, navigate to your **Excel Chapter 10 folder**, and then click your **Student_Excel_10E_ER_Department** file one time to select it. In the lower right corner of the **Open** dialog box, click **Open**.

The name of your selected file displays above the Upload button.

15 To submit your file to **MyLab IT** for grading, click **Upload**, wait a moment for a green **Success!** message, and then in **step 4**, click the blue **Submit for Grading** button. Click **Close Assignment** to return to your list of **Course Materials**.

You have completed Project 10E **END**

MyLab IT Grader	Mastering Excel	Project 10F Beverage Supplies

Apply 10B skills from these Objectives:

4. Insert a Second Table into a Worksheet
5. Apply Conditional Formatting to Side-by-Side Tables
6. Create Custom Headers and Footers
7. Inspect a Workbook
8. Use Co-Authoring and Prepare a Final Workbook for Distribution

In the following Mastering Excel project, you will edit a worksheet for Pat Shepard, Vice President of Operations, detailing the current inventory of two beverage supply types—Beverage Supplies Staff and Beverage Supplies Guests. Your completed worksheet will look similar to Figure 10.55.

Project Files for MyLab IT Grader

1. In your **MyLab IT** course, locate and click **Excel 10F Beverage Supplies**, Download Materials, and then Download All Files.
2. Extract the zipped folder to your Excel Chapter 10 folder. Close the Grader download screens.
3. Take a moment to open the downloaded **Excel 10F Beverage Supplies_Instructions**; note any recent updates to the book.

Project Results

Figure 10.55

For Non-MyLab Submissions

For Project 10F, you will need:
e10F_Beverage_Supplies
e10F_Logo

In your Excel Chapter 10 folder, save your workbook as:
Lastname_Firstname_10F_Beverage_Supplies

After you have named and saved your workbook, on the next page, begin with Step 2.
After Step 14, submit your file as directed by your instructor.

(continues on next page)

Content-Based Assessments (Mastery and Transfer of Learning)

1 ▶ Navigate to your **Excel Chapter 10 folder**, and then double-click the Excel file you downloaded from **MyLab IT** that displays your name—**Student_Excel_10F_Beverage_Supplies**. If necessary, at the top, click **Enable Editing**.

2 ▶ On the **Beverage Supplies Inventory** worksheet, insert a table using the range **A7:E30**.

3 ▶ From the **Guests** worksheet, copy the range **A1:E20**, and then paste it into cell **F6** of the **Beverage Supplies Inventory** worksheet.

4 ▶ On the **Beverage Supplies Inventory** worksheet, format the data in the range **F7:J25** as a table, and then apply the **Medium 12** table style. Apply **AutoFit** to columns **H:I**.

5 ▶ Sort the **Beverage Supplies Type: Staff** table by **Item #**, using **Cell Values, A to Z**. Add a second level sort by **Purchase Price, Largest to Smallest**.

6 ▶ Using the same sort orders, sort the **Beverage Supplies Type: Guests** table.

7 ▶ Select the range **E8:E30**. Apply conditional formatting to the range using the **3 Arrows (Colored)** directional icon set.

8 ▶ Use **Quick Analysis** to apply the default conditional formatting icon set to the range **J8:J25**. (Mac users: Apply the 3 Arrows (Colored) directional icon set.)

9 ▶ In the range **C8:C30** create a new conditional formatting rule using the formula **=c8="Juice"** and setting the format to **Bold italic** with the **Red** font color. Click cell **A1**.

10 ▶ Delete the **Guests** worksheet.

11 ▶ From **Backstage** view, click the **Check Accessibility** command. On the **Information** worksheet, select the image in the lower left corner, and then edit the **Alt Text** by typing **Iced tea glasses** Close the **Accessibility** panes. Click cell **A1**. (Mac users: on the Review tab, click the Check Accessibility command.)

12 ▶ Display the **Beverage Supplies Inventory** worksheet, then right-click its **sheet tab** and click **Select All Sheets**. Group both worksheets, and then display the workbook in **Page Layout** view. In the middle section of the header, from the **Header & Footer Tools Design tab**, insert the picture **e10F_Logo**. In the right header section, type **Created by Pat Shepard** Move to the footer area and insert the **File Name** in the left section. Click any cell to close the **Footer** area, and then return to **Normal** view.

13 ▶ Press Ctrl + Home to move to cell **A1**. With your two worksheets still grouped, set the **Orientation** to **Landscape**, set the **Width** to **1 page**, the **Height** to **1 page**, and center horizontally on the page. Display the **document properties**. As the **Tags/Keywords**, type **beverage supplies** In the **Subject** box, type your course name and section number.

14 ▶ On the left, click **Print** to display the **Print Preview**. Scroll through the two worksheets. On the left, click **Save** to save your workbook and return to the workbook window. **Close** Excel.

15 ▶ In **MyLab IT**, in your **Course Materials**, locate and click the Grader Project **Excel 10F Beverage Supplies**. In **step 3**, under **Upload Completed Assignment**, click **Choose File**. In the **Open** dialog box, navigate to your **Excel** Chapter 10 **folder**, and then click your **Student_Excel_10F_Beverage_Supplies** file one time to select it. In the lower right corner of the **Open** dialog box, click **Open**.

The name of your selected file displays above the Upload button.

16 ▶ To submit your file to **MyLab IT** for grading, click **Upload**, wait a moment for a green **Success!** message, and then in **step 4**, click the blue **Submit for Grading** button. Click **Close Assignment** to return to your list of **Course Materials**.

You have completed Project 10F **END**

| **MyLab IT Grader** | **Mastering Excel** | **Project 10G Pharmacy Department** |

In the following Mastering Excel project, you will import data about Pharmacy suppliers. You will edit a worksheet for Pat Shepard, Vice President of Operations, detailing the current inventory of two pharmacy supply types—Hospital and Physician's Clinic. Your completed worksheet will look similar to Figure 10.56.

Apply 10A and 10B skills from these Objectives:

1. Get External Data into Excel
2. Clean Up and Manage Imported Data
3. Use Database Functions
4. Insert a Second Table into a Worksheet
5. Apply Conditional Formatting to Side-by-Side Tables
6. Create Custom Headers and Footers
7. Inspect a Workbook
8. Use Co-Authoring and Prepare a Final Workbook for Distribution

Project Files for MyLab IT Grader

1. In your **MyLab IT** course, locate and click **Excel 10G Pharmacy Supplies**, Download Materials, and then Download All Files.
2. Extract the zipped folder to your Excel Chapter 10 folder. Close the Grader download screens.
3. Take a moment to open the downloaded **Excel_10G_Pharmacy_Supplies_Instructions**; note any recent updates to the book.

Project Results

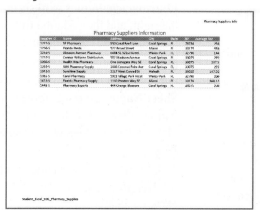

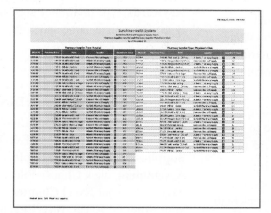

Figure 10.56

For Non-MyLab Submissions

For Project 10G, you will need:

e10G_Pharmacy_Suppliers (Access database)

e10G_Pharmacy_Supplies (Excel workbook)

e10G_Pharmacy_Suppliers_CSV_for_Mac_users (CSV file only for Mac users)

In your Excel Chapter 10 folder, save your workbook as:

Lastname_Firstname_10G_Pharmacy_Supplies

After you have named and saved your workbook, on the next page, begin with Step 2.

After Step 19, submit your file as directed by your instructor.

(continues on next page)

1 Navigate to your **Excel Chapter 10 folder**, and then double-click the Excel file you downloaded from **MyLab IT** that displays your name—**Student_Excel_10G_Pharmacy_Supplies**. If necessary, at the top, click **Enable Editing**.

2 Be sure the **Pharmacy Suppliers Info** worksheet is active. Click cell **A2**. From the **Data tab**, click **Get Data**, and then locate and click the command to get data **From Microsoft Access Database**.

In the **Import Data** dialog box, navigate to the files downloaded with this project in your **Excel Chapter 10 folder**. Click the Access file **e10G_Pharmacy_Suppliers**, and then click **Import**. (Mac users: use the file e10g_Pharmacy_Suppliers_CSV_for_Mac_users, select the imported data, and on the Insert tab, click Table. Apply Table Style, Medium 7.).

Select the **10G Pharmacy Suppliers** table, and then use the **Load To** command to import the data into the **Existing worksheet**. **Close** the **Queries & Connections** pane. Click cell **A1**.

3 Display the **Pharmacy Staff** worksheet. In cell **B18**, insert a **DAVERAGE** function using the range **A3:F16** as the database, that calculates the average **Hourly Wage** for pharmacists and using the criteria in the range **C18:C19**. Apply **Accounting Number Format** to your result in cell **B18**.

4 In cell **B21**, insert a **DSUM** function using the range **A3:F16** as the database, that calculates the **Wage per Shift** for pharmacy technicians using the criteria in cells **C21:D22**. Apply **Accounting Number Format** to your result in cell **B21**.

5 In cell **E18** type **Maximum Pharmacist Hourly Wage** and then use **Format Painter** to copy the format from cell **C18** to cell **E18**. Widen **column E** to **75** pixels.

6 In cell **E19**, begin the MAXIFS function by typing **=maxifs(** and then as the max range, select the range representing the *Hourly Wage* of the Pharmacy Staff. Type a comma, and then as the criteria range, select the range representing the *Status* of the Pharmacy Staff. Type a comma, and then as the criteria, click cell **C19**. Press **Enter**. Apply **Accounting Number Format** to your result.

7 Display the **Pharmacy Supplies Inventory** worksheet. Insert a table in the range **A7:E42**. Click cell **A1**.

8 Display the **Physician's Clinic** worksheet and copy the range **A1:E32**. Display the **Pharmacy Supplies Inventory** worksheet, and then paste the data into cell **F6**.

9 Insert a table in the range **F7:J37** and apply **Table Style Medium 7**. Apply **AutoFit** to **columns H:I**.

10 Sort both tables by **Model # A to Z** and then by **Purchase Price Largest to Smallest**.

11 Apply conditional formatting to the range **E8:E42** using the **3 Traffic Lights (Rimmed)** icon set.

12 Apply the same conditional formatting to the range **J8:J37**.

13 In the range **C8:C42** create a new conditional formatting rule using the formula **=c8="Pharmacy spill kit"** and set the format to **Bold Italic** with the **Red** font color.

14 Delete the **Physician's Clinic** worksheet.

15 Check the workbook for Accessibility. On the **Pharmacogenomics** worksheet, select the image on the right, and then add the following alt text: **Pharmacy supplies Close** the Accessibility panes.

16 Group the four worksheets. From **Page Layout** view, insert a header in the right section that displays the **Sheet Name**. Go to the footer, and then insert the **File Name** in the left section of the footer. Return to **Normal** view. Press **Ctrl** + **Home** to make cell **A1** the active cell.

17 Center the sheets horizontally on the page. Set the **Orientation** to **Landscape**. Set the **Width** to **1 page** and the **Height** to **1 page**.

18 Display the **document properties**. As the **Tags/Keywords**, type **pharmacy supplies** In the **Subject** box, type your course name and section number.

19 On the left, click **Print** to display the **Print Preview**. Scroll through the four worksheets. On the left, click **Save** to save your workbook and return to the workbook window. **Close** ☒ Excel.

20 In **MyLab IT**, in your **Course Materials**, locate and click the Grader Project **Excel 10G Pharmacy Supplies**. In **step 3**, under **Upload Completed Assignment**, click **Choose File**. In the **Open** dialog box, navigate to your **Excel Chapter 10 folder**, and then click your **Student_Excel_10G_Pharmacy_Supplies** file one time to select it. In the lower right corner of the **Open** dialog box, click **Open**.

The name of your selected file displays above the Upload button.

21 To submit your file to **MyLab IT** for grading, click **Upload**, wait a moment for a green **Success!** message, and then in **step 4**, click the blue **Submit for Grading** button. Click **Close Assignment** to return to your list of **Course Materials**.

You have completed Project 10G **END**

Content-Based Assessments (Mastery and Transfer of Learning)

GO! Fix It	**Project 10H Imaging Technicians**	IRC
GO! Make It	**Project 10I Snack Supplies**	IRC
GO! Solve It	**Project 10J Medical Imaging Suppliers**	IRC
GO! Solve It	**Project 10K Gift Shop Supplies**	

Project Files

For Project 10K, you will need the following file:

e10K_Gift_Shop

You will save your workbook as:

Lastname_Firstname_10K_Gift_Shop

Open the file **e10K_Gift_Shop** and save it as **Lastname_Firstname_10K_Gift_Shop** Insert a table to the Gift Shop Inventory worksheet for the range A7:E40. On the Clinic worksheet, remove duplicates, select and copy the remaining data, and then on the Gift Shop Inventory worksheet, paste it in the range beginning in cell F6. Insert a Table, and then apply Table Style Medium 13. AutoFit columns as necessary. Delete the Clinic worksheet. In each table's Quantity in Stock column, apply different conditional formatting icon sets. Convert each table to a Range. Insert the file name in the footer in the left section and the current date in the header right section. Set the orientation to landscape and center horizontally. Add appropriate information to the document properties including the tags **gift shop supplies, inventory** and submit as directed by your instructor.

		Performance Level		
		Exemplary	**Proficient**	**Developing**
Performance Criteria	**Remove duplicate data.**	All duplicate data was removed.	Some duplicate data was removed.	Duplicate data was not removed.
	Insert a Second Table in a Worksheet	A second table is inserted in a worksheet, and tables display side-by-side.	A second table is inserted in a worksheet, but tables do not display side-by-side.	A second table was not inserted in a worksheet.
	Delete the Clinic worksheet.	Clinic worksheet deleted.	N/A	Clinic worksheet was not deleted.
	Apply Conditional Formatting to Side-by-Side Tables	Conditional Formatting Icon Sets, applied to the Quantity in Stock columns.	Conditional Formatting Icon Sets, applied to one but not the other Quantity in Stock column.	Conditional Formatting was not applied to the Quantity in Stock columns.
	Convert a Table to a Range	The tables are converted to a range.	One but not the other table is converted to a range.	The tables are not converted to a range.
	Header and footer information inserted.	Header and footer correctly inserted.	Header and footer inserted but missing some information.	Header and footer not inserted.

You have completed Project 10K | END

Outcomes-Based Assessments (Critical Thinking)

Rubric

The following outcomes-based assessments are open-ended assessments. That is, there is no specific correct result; your result will depend on your approach to the information provided. Make Professional Quality your goal. Use the following scoring rubric to guide you in how to approach the problem and then to evaluate how well your approach solves the problem.

The *criteria*—Software Mastery, Content, Format and Layout, and Process— represent the knowledge and skills you have gained that you can apply to solving the problem. The *levels of performance*—Professional Quality, Approaching Professional Quality, or Needs Quality Improvements—help you and your instructor evaluate your result.

	Your completed project is of Professional Quality if you:	Your completed project is Approaching Professional Quality if you:	Your completed project Needs Quality Improvements if you:
1-Software Mastery	Choose and apply the most appropriate skills, tools, and features and identify efficient methods to solve the problem.	Choose and apply some appropriate skills, tools, and features, but not in the most efficient manner.	Choose inappropriate skills, tools, or features, or are inefficient in solving the problem.
2-Content	Construct a solution that is clear and well organized, contains content that is accurate, appropriate to the audience and purpose, and is complete. Provide a solution that contains no errors of spelling, grammar, or style.	Construct a solution in which some components are unclear, poorly organized, inconsistent, or incomplete. Misjudge the needs of the audience. Have some errors in spelling, grammar, or style, but the errors do not detract from comprehension.	Construct a solution that is unclear, incomplete, or poorly organized, contains some inaccurate or inappropriate content, and contains many errors of spelling, grammar, or style. Do not solve the problem.
3-Format and Layout	Format and arrange all elements to communicate information and ideas, clarify function, illustrate relationships, and indicate relative importance.	Apply appropriate format and layout features to some elements, but not others. Overuse features, causing minor distraction.	Apply format and layout that does not communicate information or ideas clearly. Do not use format and layout features to clarify function, illustrate relationships, or indicate relative importance. Use available features excessively, causing distraction.
4-Process	Use an organized approach that integrates planning, development, self-assessment, revision, and reflection.	Demonstrate an organized approach in some areas, but not others; or, use an insufficient process of organization throughout.	Do not use an organized approach to solve the problem.

Outcomes-Based Assessments (Critical Thinking)

Apply a combination of the 10A and 10B skills

GO! Think	Project 10L Facilities Pay

Project Files

For Project 10L, you will need the following file:

e10L_Facilities_Pay

You will save your workbook as:

Lastname_Firstname_10L_Facilities_Pay

Open the file e10L_Facilities_Pay, and then save it in your chapter folder as **Lastname_Firstname_10L_Facilities_Pay** In this project, you will use a worksheet that contains payroll information for the facilities staff. You will calculate the average pay and count how many employees have worked for the hospital for over five years.

In rows 26–27, enter the criteria and a DAVERAGE function to determine the average wage for housekeeping. Apply Currency Style to the result. In rows 29–30, enter the criteria and a DCOUNT function to count the number of employees hired prior to 1/1/2010.

Insert the file name in the left section of the footer and the current date in the right section of the header. Set orientation to landscape and center horizontally. Set width and height to 1 page. Add appropriate information to the document properties, including the tags **facilities pay** and submit as directed by your instructor.

	You have completed Project 10L	END

GO! Think	Project 10M Institutes of Health	IRC
You and GO!	Project 10N Budget	IRC

Appendix

MICROSOFT OFFICE SPECIALIST EXCEL 2019			
Obj Number	**Objective text**	**GO! Activity**	**Page Number**
2.2.3	Format cells by using Format Painter	3.14, 10.11	266, 697
2.2.4	Wrap text within cells	1.26, 2.25	147, 206
2.2.5	Apply number format	1.05, 1.09, 1.21	113,118, 140
2.2.6	Apply cell formats from the Format Cells dialog box	2.07, 8.01	182, 567
2.2.7	Apply cell styles	1.08, 1.09, 1.18, 1.21, 8.05	117, 118, 136, 140, 575
2.2.8	Clear cell formatting	2.23	204
2.3	**Define and reference named ranges**	5.19, 7.06, 7.07, 7.08, 8.16	403, 501, 506, 598
2.3.1	Define a named range		
2.3.2	Name a table	Online Supplemental	
2.4	**Summarize data visually**		
2.4.1	Insert Sparklines	1.13, 2.33, 6.01	126, 215, 429
2.4.2	Apply built-in conditional formatting	2.10, 8.17, 10.14	185, 600, 704
2.4.3	Remove conditional formatting	Online Supplemental	
3.0 Manage Tables and Table Data			
3.1	**Create and format tables**		
3.1.1	Create Excel tables from cell ranges	2.14, 10.12	190, 701
3.1.2	Apply table styles	2.14	190
3.1.3	Convert tables to cell ranges	10.03	684
3.2	**Modify Tables**		
3.2.1	Add or remove table rows and columns	10.03, 10.06	684, 688
3.2.2	Configure table style options	5.06	377
3.2.3	Insert and configure total rows	2.16	192
3.3	**Filter and sort table data**		
3.3.1	Filter records	2.16, 5.16, 5.17	192, 395, 397
3.3.2	Sort data by multiple columns	2.15, 5.14, 10.13	191, 391, 702
4.0 Perform Operations by using Formulas and Functions			
4.1	**Insert references**		
4.1.1	Insert relative, absolute, and mixed references	1.07, 1.22, 2.31, 7.11, 8.13	116, 142, 213, 513, 594
4.1.2	Reference named ranges and named tables in formulas	7.09, 8.16	508, 598
4.2	**Calculate and transform data**		
4.2.1	Perform calculations by using the AVERAGE(), MAX(), MIN(), and SUM() functions	1.06, 2.03, 2.05, 7.09	114, 177, 180, 508
4.2.2	Count cells by using the COUNT(), COUNTA(), and COUNTBLANK() functions	Online Supplemental	
4.2.3	Perform conditional operations by using the IF() function	2.09	184

MICROSOFT OFFICE SPECIALIST EXCEL 2019			
Obj Number	**Objective text**	**GO! Activity**	**Page Number**
4.3	**Format and modify text**		
4.3.1	Format text by using RIGHT(), LEFT(), and MID() functions	10.07	690
4.3.2	Format text by using UPPER(), LOWER(), and LEN() functions	10.07	690
4.3.3	Format text by using the CONCAT() and TEXTJOIN() functions	10.07	690
5.0 Manage Charts			
5.1	**Create charts**		
5.1.1	Create charts	1.11, 3.02, 6.02, 6.08, 8.06	120, 250, 431, 440, 577
5.1.2	Create chart sheets	3.02, 6.02, 6.09, 8.03	250, 431, 441, 572
5.2	**Modify charts**		
5.2.1	Add data series to charts	3.18, 8.03	273, 572
5.2.2	Switch between rows and columns in source data	1.11, 6.03	120, 435
5.2.3	Add and modify chart elements	1.12, 6.02, 6.04, 6.05, 6.07, 6.09, 6.10, 6.11, 6.12	123, 431, 437, 437, 439, 441, 442, 443, 444
5.3	**Format charts**		
5.3.1	Apply chart layouts	1.12, 3.04, 8.06	123, 252, 577
5.3.2	Apply chart styles	4.11, 6.02	324, 431
5.3.3	Add alternative text to charts for accessibility	Office Features 1.19	138

MICROSOFT OFFICE EXPERT EXCEL 2019			
Obj Number	**Objective text**	**GO! Activity**	**Page Number**
1.0 Manage Documents			
1.1	**Manage Workbook Options and Settings**		
1.1.1	Copy macros between workbooks	Online Supplemental	
1.1.2	Reference data in other workbooks	Online Supplemental	
1.1.3	Enable macros in a workbook	9.02	630
1.1.4	Manage workbook versions	Online Supplemental	
1.2	**Prepare workbooks for collaboration**		
1.2.1	Restrict editing	6.24	462
1.2.2	Protect worksheets and cell ranges	6.24	462
1.2.3	Protect workbook structure	6.24, 9.12, 10.20	462, 654, 715
1.2.4	Configure formula calculation options	Online Supplemental	
1.2.5	Manage comments	Online Supplemental	

MICROSOFT OFFICE EXPERT EXCEL 2019			
Obj Number	**Objective text**	**GO! Activity**	**Page Number**
1.3	**Use and configure language options**		
1.3.1	Configure editing and display languages	Online Supplemental	
1.3.2	Use language-specific features	Online Supplemental	
2.0 Manage and Format Data			
2.1	**Fill cells based on existing data**		
2.1.1	Fill cells by using Flash Fill	2.01, 10.06	175, 688
2.1.2	Fill cells by using advanced Fill Series options	Online Supplemental	
2.2	**Format and validate data**		
2.2.1	Create custom number formats	8.01	567
2.2.2	Configure data validation	7.12, 7.17	517, 531
2.2.3	Group and ungroup data	Online Supplemental	
2.2.4	Calculate data by inserting subtotals and totals	5.20	404
2.2.5	Remove duplicate records	10.05	688
2.3	**Apply advanced conditional formatting and filtering**		
2.3.1	Create custom conditional formatting rules	10.14	704
2.3.2	Create conditional formatting rules that use formulas	10.14	704
2.3.3	Manage conditional formatting rules	10.14	704
3.0 Create Advanced Formulas and Macros			
3.1	**Perform logical operations in formulas**		
3.1.1	Perform logical operations by using nested functions including the IF( ), IFS( ), SWITCH( ), SUMIF( ), AVERAGEIF( ), COUNTIF( ), SUMIFS( ), AVERAGEIFS( ), COUNTIFS( ), MAXIFS( ), MINIFS( ), AND( ), OR( ), and NOT( ) functions	2.34, 8.13, 8.14, 8.15, 8.17, 8.18, 8.19, 10.11	215, 594, 595, 597, 600, 601, 603, 597
3.2	**Look up data by using functions**		
3.2.1	Look up data by using the VLOOKUP( ), HLOOKUP( ), MATCH ( ), and INDEX( ) functions	7.11, 7.19	513, 536
3.3	**Use advanced date and time functions**		
3.3.1	Reference date and time by using the NOW( ) and TODAY ( ) functions	2.12	188
3.3.2	Calculate dates by using the WEEKDAY( ) and WORKDAY() functions	Online Supplemental	
3.4	**Perform data analysis**		
3.4.1	Summarize data from multiple ranges by using the Consolidate feature	Online Supplemental	
3.4.2	Perform what-if analysis by using Goal Seek and Scenario Manager	3.11, 7.02, 7.03, 8.10, 8.11, 8.12	259, 494,495, 590, 591, 592
3.4.3	Forecast data by using the AND( ), IF( ), and NPER( ) functions	7.01, 7.05, 8.16	491, 498, 598
3.4.4	Calculate financial data by using the PMT( ) function	7.01	491

MICROSOFT OFFICE EXPERT EXCEL 2019			
Obj Number	**Objective text**	**GO! Activity**	**Page Number**
3.5	**Troubleshoot formulas**		
3.5.1	Trace precedence and dependence	7.13, 7.14	520, 526
3.5.2	Monitor cells and formulas by using the Watch Window	7.18	532
3.5.3	Validate formulas by using error checking rules	7.15	527
3.5.4	Evaluate formulas	7.16	529
3.6	**Create and modify simple macros**		
3.6.1	Record simple macros	9.04	633
3.6.2	Name simple macros	9.04	633
3.6.3	Edit simple macros	9.07	638
4.0 Manage Advanced Charts and Tables			
4.1	**Create and modify advanced charts**		
4.1.1	Create and modify dual axis charts	6.12, 8.03	444, 572
4.1.2	Create and modify charts including Box & Whisker, Combo, Funnel, Histogram, Map, Sunburst, and Waterfall charts	3.22, 6.15, 6.16	281, 448, 449
4.2	**Create and modify PivotTables**		
4.2.1	Create PivotTables	4.01, 4.15	307, 334
4.2.2	Modify field selections and options	4.02	310
4.2.3	Create slicers	4.03	313
4.2.4	Group PivotTable data	4.05	317
4.2.5	Add calculated fields	4.08	321
4.2.6	Format data	4.09	322
4.3	**Create and modify PivotCharts**		
4.3.1	Create PivotCharts	4.11, 4.16	324, 335
4.3.2	Manipulate options in existing PivotCharts	4.12	325
4.3.3	Apply styles to PivotCharts	4.17	337
4.3.4	Drill down into PivotChart details	4.12	325

Glossary

3-D The shortened term for *three-dimensional*, which refers to an image that appears to have all three spatial dimensions—length, width, and depth.

Absolute cell reference A cell reference that refers to cells by their fixed position in a worksheet; an absolute cell reference remains the same when the formula is copied.

Accessibility Checker An Excel feature that finds any potential accessibility issues and creates a report so that you can resolve the issues to make your file easier for those with disabilities to use.

Accounting Number Format The Excel number format that applies a thousand comma separator where appropriate, inserts a fixed U.S. dollar sign aligned at the left edge of the cell, applies two decimal places, and leaves a small amount of space at the right edge of the cell to accommodate a parenthesis for negative numbers.

Active area The area of the worksheet that contains data or has contained data.

Active cell The cell, surrounded by a black border, ready to receive data or be affected by the next Excel command.

ActiveX control A graphic object, such as a check box or button that you place on a form to display or enter data, perform an action, or make the form easier to read. When the person filling in the form clicks the ActiveX control, VBA code runs that automates a task or offers options.

Add-in Optional command or feature that is not immediately available; you must first install and/ or activate it to use it.

Advanced Filter A filter that can specify three or more criteria for a particular column, apply complex criteria to two or more columns, or specify computed criteria.

Alt text A shortened version of the term alternative text, which is text added to images and other objects that provides information to understand the image or object.

Alternative text Text added to images and other objects that provides information to understand the image or object.

And comparison operator The comparison operator that requires each and every one of the comparison criteria to be true.

AND function A logical function that can be used to develop compound logical tests using up to 255 arguments. The function returns a result of TRUE if ALL of the conditions are met.

Arguments The values that an Excel function uses to perform calculations or operations.

Arithmetic operators The symbols +, -, *, /, %, and ^ used to denote addition, subtraction (or negation), multiplication, division, percentage, and exponentiation in an Excel formula.

Arrange All The command that tiles all open program windows on the screen.

Ascending The term that refers to the arrangement of text that is sorted alphabetically from A to Z, numbers sorted from lowest to highest, or dates and times sorted from earliest to latest.

Associated PivotTable report The PivotTable report in a workbook that is graphically represented in a PivotChart.

Auditing The process of examining a worksheet for errors in formulas.

Auto Fill An Excel feature that generates and extends values into adjacent cells based on the values of selected cells.

AutoCalculate A feature that displays three calculations in the status bar by default—Average, Count, and Sum—when you select a range of numerical data.

AutoComplete A feature that speeds your typing and lessens the likelihood of errors; if the first few characters you type in a cell match an existing entry in the column, Excel fills in the remaining characters for you.

AutoFilter menu A drop-down menu from which you can filter a column by a list of values, by a format, or by criteria.

AutoFit An Excel feature that adjusts the width of a column to fit the cell content of the widest cell in the column.

AutoSum A button that provides quick access to the SUM function.

AVERAGE function An Excel function that adds a group of values, and then divides the result by the number of values in the group.

AVERAGEIFS function A statistical function that enables you to specify multiple criteria when computing an average.

Axis A line that serves as a frame of reference for measurement and that borders the chart plot area.

Base The starting point when you divide the amount of increase by it to calculate the rate of increase.

Bevel A shape effect that uses shading and shadows to make the edges of a shape appear to be curved or angled.

Break-even point The point at which a company starts to make a profit.

Category axis The area along the bottom of a chart that identifies the categories of data; also referred to as the x-axis.

Category labels The labels that display along the bottom of a chart to identify the categories of data; Excel uses the row titles as the category names.

Category labels The labels that display along the bottom of a chart to identify the categories of data.

Cell The intersection of a column and a row.

Cell address Another name for a cell reference.

Cell content Anything typed into a cell.

Cell reference The identification of a specific cell by its intersecting column letter and row number.

Cell style A defined set of formatting characteristics, such as font, font size, font color, cell borders, and cell shading.

Chart The graphic representation of data in a worksheet; data presented as a chart is usually easier to understand than a table of numbers.

Chart area The entire chart and all of its elements.

Chart elements Objects that make up a chart.

Chart Elements button A button that enables you to add, remove, or change chart elements such as the title, legend, gridlines, and data labels.

Chart Filters button A button that enables you to change which data displays in the chart.

Chart layout The combination of chart elements that can be displayed in a chart such as a title, legend, labels for the columns, and the table of charted cells.

Chart sheet A workbook sheet that contains only a chart.

Chart style The overall visual look of a chart in terms of its graphic effects, colors, and backgrounds; for example, you can have flat or beveled columns, colors that are solid or transparent, and backgrounds that are dark or light.

Chart Styles button A button that enables you to set a style and color scheme for your chart.

Chart Styles gallery A group of predesigned chart styles that you can apply to an Excel chart.

Chart types Various chart formats used in a way that is meaningful to the reader; common examples are column charts, pie charts, and line charts.

Check box A type of ActiveX control that the person filling in the form can select to indicate a choice.

Clear Filter A button that removes a filter.

Co-authoring The process by which you and your colleagues can open and work on the same Excel workbook and see each other's changes.

Column A vertical group of cells in a worksheet.

Column chart A chart in which the data is arranged in vertical columns and that is useful for showing data changes over a period of time or for illustrating comparisons among items.

Column heading The letter that displays at the top of a vertical group of cells in a worksheet; beginning with the first letter of the alphabet, a unique letter or combination of letters identifies each column.

Columns area An area to position fields that you want to display as columns in the PivotTable report. Field names placed here become column titles, and the data is grouped in columns by these titles.

Comma delimited file A file type that saves the contents of the cells by placing commas between them and an end-of-paragraph mark at the end of each row; also referred to as a CSV (comma separated values) file.

Comma Style The Excel number format that inserts thousand comma separators where appropriate and applies two decimal places; also leaves space at the right to accommodate a parenthesis when negative numbers are present.

Comparison operators Symbols that evaluate each value to determine if it is the same (=), greater than (>), less than (<), or in between a range of values as specified by the criteria.

Compatibility Checker An Excel feature that finds any potential compatibility issues and creates a report so that you can resolve the issues.

Compatibility Mode A mode where the workbook is in Excel 97-2003 file format (.xls) instead of the newer file format (.xlsx).

Compound criteria The use of two or more criteria on the same row—all conditions must be met for the records to be included in the results.

Compound filter A filter that uses more than one condition—and one that uses comparison operators.

Concatenate A text function used to join up to 255 strings of characters.

Conditional format A format that changes the appearance of a cell—for example, by adding cell shading or font color—based on a condition; if the condition is true, the cell is formatted based on that condition, and if the condition is false, the cell is *not* formatted.

Constant value Numbers, text, dates, or times of day that you type into a cell.

Constraint In Solver, a condition or restriction that must be met.

Constraint cell In Solver, a cell that contains a value that limits or restricts the outcome.

Context sensitive A command associated with the currently selected or active object; often activated by right-clicking a screen item.

COUNT function A statistical function that counts the number of cells in a range that contains numbers.

COUNTIF function A statistical function that counts the number of cells within a range that meet the given condition and that has two arguments—the range of cells to check and the criteria.

COUNTIFS function A logical function that counts the cells that meet specific criteria in multiple ranges.

Criteria Conditions that you specify in a logical function or filter.

Criteria range An area on your worksheet where you define the criteria for the filter, and that indicates how the displayed records are filtered.

CSV (comma separated values) file A file type in which the cells in each row are separated by commas and an end-of-paragraph mark at the end of each row; also referred to as a comma delimited file.

Custom filter A filter with which you can apply complex criteria to a single column.

Custom list A sort order that you can define.

Cycle A category of SmartArt graphics that illustrates a continual process.

Data Text or numbers in a cell, or, facts about people, events, things, or ideas.

Data bar A cell format consisting of a shaded bar that provides a visual cue to the reader about the value of a cell relative to other cells; the length of the bar represents the value in the cell—a longer bar represents a higher value and a shorter bar represents s lower value.

Data connection A link to external data that automatically updates an Excel workbook from the original data whenever the original data source gets new information.

Data labels Labels that display the value, percentage, and/or category of each particular data point and can contain one or more of the choices listed—Series name, Category name, Value, or Percentage.

Data marker A column, bar, area, dot, pie slice, or other symbol in a chart that represents a single data point; related data points form a data series.

Data Model A method of incorporating data from multiple, related tables into an Excel worksheet.

Data point A value that originates in a worksheet cell and that is represented in a chart by a data marker.

Data series Related data points represented by data markers; each data series has a unique color or pattern represented in the chart legend.

Data table A range of cells that shows how changing certain values in your formulas affect the results of those formulas and that makes it easy to calculate multiple versions in one operation.

Data transformation Using Excel tools to modify the arrangement of the data you brought into Excel from another source to make the data more useful.

Data validation A technique by which you can control the type of data or the values that are entered into a cell by limiting the acceptable values to a defined list.

Database An organized collection of facts related to a specific topic or purpose.

DAVERAGE function A function that determines an average in a database that is limited by criteria set for one or more cells.

DCOUNT function A function that counts the number of occurrences of a specified condition in a database.

Decision variable In Solver, cell in which the value will change to achieve the desired results.

Defined name A word or string of characters in Excel that represents a cell, a range of cells, a formula, or a constant value; also referred to as simply a *name*.

Delimited A text file in which the text is separated by commas or tabs.

Dependent cells Cells that contain formulas that refer to other cells.

Descending The term that refers to the arrangement of text that is sorted alphabetically from Z to A, numbers sorted from highest to lowest, or dates and times sorted from latest to earliest.

Design Mode An Excel feature in which you can add and modify ActiveX controls.

Detail data The subtotaled rows that are totaled and summarized; typically adjacent to and either above or to the left of the summary data.

Detail sheets The worksheets that contain the details of the information summarized on a summary sheet.

Digital signature An electronic, encryption-based, secure stamp of authentication on a macro or document.

Displayed value The data that displays in a cell.

Document Inspector An Excel feature that can find and remove hidden properties and personal information in a workbook.

Drag and drop The action of moving a selection by dragging it to a new location.

DSUM function A function that sums a column of values in a database that is limited by criteria set for one or more cells.

Dual-axis chart A chart that has one series plotted on a secondary axis. Useful when comparing data series that use different scales or different types of measurements.

Embed The action of inserting something created in one program into another program.

Embedded chart A chart that is inserted into the same worksheet that contains the data used to create the chart.

Encryption The process by which a file is encoded so that it cannot be opened without the proper password.

Enterprise fund A municipal government fund that reports income and expenditures related to municipal services for which a fee is charged in exchange for goods or services.

Error Checking command A command that checks for common errors that occur in formulas.

Error value The result of a formula that Excel cannot evaluate correctly.

Event The action that causes a program or macro to run, such as clicking a button or a command or pressing a combination of keys.

Excel pointer An Excel window element with which you can display the location of the pointer.

Excel table A series of rows and columns that contains related data that is managed independently from the data in other rows and columns in the worksheet.

Expand Formula Bar button An Excel window element with which you can increase the height of the Formula Bar to display lengthy cell content.

Expand horizontal scroll bar button An Excel window element with which you can increase the width of the horizontal scroll bar.

Explode The action of pulling out one or more pie slices from a pie chart for emphasis.

Extensible Markup Language (XML) A language that structures data in text files so that it can be read by other systems, regardless of the hardware platform or operating system.

Extract area The location to which you copy records when extracting filtered rows.

Extract The process of pulling out multiple sets of data for comparison purposes.

Field A specific type of data such as name, employee number, or social security number that is stored in columns.

Field button A button on a PivotChart with an arrow to choose a filter, and thus change the data that is displayed in the chart.

Field names The column titles from source data that form the categories of data for a PivotTable.

Field section The upper portion of the PivotTable Fields pane containing the fields—column titles—from your source data; use this area to add fields to and remove fields from the PivotTable.

Fill handle The small black square in the lower right corner of a selected cell.

Filter The process of displaying only a portion of the data based on matching a specific value to show only the data that meets the criteria that you specify.

Filtering A process in which only the rows that meet the criteria display; rows that do not meet the criteria are hidden.

Filtering button A button on a slicer which you use to select the item by which to filter.

Filtering controls The arrows that display in the column titles of Excel data when the data is converted to a table and than enable you to sort and filter the data.

Filters area An area in the lower portion of the PivotTable Fields pane to position fields by which you want to filter the PivotTable report, enabling you to display a subset of data in the PivotTable report.

Financial functions Prebuilt formulas that perform common business calculations such as calculating a loan payment on a vehicle or calculating how much to save each month to buy something; financial functions commonly involve a period of time such as months or years.

Find A command that locates and selects specific text or formatting.

Find and replace A command that searches the cells in a worksheet—or in a selected range—for matches and then replaces each match with a replacement value of your choice.

Fixed expense Expense that remains the same each month regardless of the amount of activity.

Flash Fill An Excel feature that predicts how to alter data based upon the pattern you enter into the cell at the beginning of the column; the data must be in the adjacent column.

Forecast A prediction of the future, often based on past performances.

Form An Excel worksheet or object that contains fields and controls that enable a user to easily enter or edit data.

Form control A graphic object that does not require VBA code. A Form control is compatible with versions of Excel that do not support ActiveX.

Format Changing the appearance of cells and worksheet elements to make a worksheet attractive and easy to read.

Formula An equation that performs mathematical calculations on values in a worksheet.

Formula Auditing Tools and commands accessible from the Formulas tab that help you check your worksheet for errors.

Formula AutoComplete An Excel feature which, after typing an = (equal sign) and the beginning letter or letters of a function name, displays a list of function names that match the typed letter(s).

Formula Bar An element in the Excel window that displays the value or formula contained in the active cell; here you can also enter or edit values or formulas.

Freeze Panes A command that enables you to select one or more rows or columns and freeze (lock) them into place so that they remain on the screen while you scroll; the locked rows and columns become separate panes.

Function A predefined formula—a formula that Excel has already built for you—that performs calculations by using specific values in a particular order or structure.

Fund A sum of money set aside for a specific purpose.

Funnel chart A type of chart that shows values across the stages in a process.

Future value (Fv) The value at the end of the time period in an Excel function; the cash balance you want to attain after the last payment is made—usually zero for loans.

General format The default format that Excel applies to numbers; this format has no specific characteristics—whatever you type in the cell will display, with the exception that trailing zeros to the right of a decimal point will not display.

General fund The term used to describe money set aside for the normal operating activities of a government entity such as a city.

Get & Transform A group of commands that enables you to bring data from an Access database, from the Web, from a text file, from an XML file, and from many other sources, into Excel in a manner that lets you transform—modify—the data.

Go To A command that moves to a specific cell or range of cells that you specify.

Go To Special A command that moves to cells that have special characteristics, for example, to cells that are blank or to cells that contain constants, as opposed to formulas.

Goal Seek A what-if analysis tool that finds the input needed in one cell to arrive at the desired result in another cell.

Goal Seek One of Excel's What-If Analysis tools that provides a method to find a specific value for a cell by adjusting the value of one other cell—find the right input when you know the result you want.

Gridlines Lines in the plot area that aid the eye in determining the plotted values.

Hierarchy A category of SmartArt graphics used to create an organization chart or show a decision tree.

HLOOKUP An Excel function that looks up values that are displayed horizontally in a row.

Horizontal Category axis (x-axis) The area along the bottom of a chart that identifies the categories of data; also referred to as the x-axis.

HTML (Hypertext Markup Language) A language web browsers can interpret.

Hyperlink Text or graphics that, when clicked, take you to another location in the worksheet, to another file, or to a webpage on the Internet or on your organization's intranet.

Icon set A set of three, four, or five small graphic images that make your data visually easier to interpret.

IF function A function that uses a logical test to check whether a condition is met, and then returns one value if true, and another value if false.

IFS function A function that checks whether one or more conditions—logical tests—are met, and then returns a value corresponding to the first TRUE condition.

INDEX function An Excel function that finds a value within a table or range based on a relative row and column

Information Data that has been organized in a useful manner.

Integer A whole number.

Interest The amount charged for the use of borrowed money.

Interval The number of cells to include in a moving average.

Label Another name for a text value, and that usually provides information about number values.

Labels Column and row headings that describe the values and help the reader understand a chart.

Layout section The lower portion of the PivotTable Fields pane containing the four areas for layout; use this area to rearrange and reposition fields in the PivotTable.

LEFT A text function that returns the specified number of character from the beginning (left) of a string of characters.

Left alignment The cell format in which characters align at the left edge of the cell; this is the default for text entries and is an example of formatting information stored in a cell.

Legend A chart element that identifies the patterns or colors that are assigned to the categories in the chart.

Lettered column headings The area along the top edge of a worksheet that identifies each column with a unique letter or combination of letters.

Line chart A chart type that is useful to display trends over time; time displays along the bottom axis and the data point values are connected with a line.

List A series of rows that contains related data with column titles in the first row.

Locked [cells] In a protected worksheet, data cannot be inserted, modified, deleted, or formatted in these cells.

Logical function A function that tests for specific conditions.

Logical functions A group of functions that test for specific conditions and that typically use conditional tests to determine whether specified conditions are true or false.

Logical test Any value or expression that can be evaluated as being true or false.

Lookup functions A group of Excel functions that look up a value in a defined range of cells located in another part of the workbook to find a corresponding value.

LOWER A text function that changes the case of the characters in a string, making all characters lowercase.

Macro An action or a set of actions with which you can automate tasks by grouping a series of commands into a single command.

Macro virus Unauthorized programming code in a macro that erases or damages files.

Major sort A term sometimes used to refer to the first sort level in the Sort dialog box.

Major unit The value in a chart's value axis that determines the spacing between tick marks and between the gridlines in the plot area.

Major unit value A number that determines the spacing between tick marks and between the gridlines in the plot area.

Map chart A type of chart that compares values and shows categories across geographical regions; for example, across countries, states, counties, and regions.

Mark as Final A command that prevents additional changes to the file and disables typing and editing commands.

MATCH function An Excel function that finds the *position* of an item in a range of cells instead of the item itself; by providing search parameters, the MATCH function indicates *where* in the list you can find what you are looking for.

Matrix A category of SmartArt graphics used to show how parts relate to a whole.

MAX function An Excel function that determines the largest value in a selected range of values.

MAXIFS function An Excel function that returns the maximum value among cells specified by a given set of conditions or criteria.

MEDIAN function An Excel function that finds the middle value that has as many values above it in the group as are below it; it differs from AVERAGE in that the result is not affected as much by a single value that is greatly different from the others.

Merge & Center A command that joins selected cells in an Excel worksheet into one larger cell and centers the contents in the merged cell.

Microsoft Access A database program used to manage database files.

MID A text function that extracts a series of characters from a text string given the location of the beginning character.

MIN function An Excel function that determines the smallest value in a selected range of values.

MINIFS function An Excel function that returns the minimum value among cells specified by a given set of conditions or criteria.

Module The place where the Visual Basic for Applications (VBA) programming code is stored.

Moving average A sequence of averages computed from parts of a data series.

Name A word or string of characters in Excel that represents a cell, a range of cells, a formula, or a constant value; also referred to as *a defined name*.

Name Box An element of the Excel window that displays the name of the selected cell, table, chart, or object.

Navigate The process of moving within a worksheet or workbook.

Navigator window The window that displays the table or tables from the data source selected using the Get & Transform commands.

Nested function A function that is contained inside another function. The inner function is evaluated first and the result becomes the argument for the outer function.

Normal view A screen view that maximizes the number of cells visible on your screen and keeps the column letters and row numbers close to the columns and rows.

NOT function A logical function that takes only one argument and is used to test one condition. If the condition is true, the function returns the logical opposite FALSE. If the condition is false, then TRUE is returned.

NOW function An Excel function that retrieves the date and time from your computer's calendar and clock and inserts the information into the selected cell.

Nper The abbreviation for *number of time periods* in various Excel functions.

Number format A specific way in which Excel displays numbers in a cell.

Number values Constant values consisting of only numbers.

Numbered row headings The area along the left edge of a worksheet that identifies each row with a unique number.

Objective cell In Solver, a cell that contains a formula for the results you are trying to determine.

One-variable Data table A data table that changes the value in only one cell.

Operators The symbols with which you can specify the type of calculation you want to perform in an Excel formula.

Or comparison operator The comparison operator that requires only one of the two comparison criteria that you specify to be true.

OR function A logical function that can be used to develop compound logical tests using up to 255 arguments. The function returns a value of TRUE if ANY of the conditions are met.

Order of operations The mathematical rules for performing multiple calculations within a formula.

Organization chart A type of graphic that is useful to depict reporting relationships within an organization.

Orientation A feature with which you can rotate text diagonally or vertically in a cell and is useful when you need to label a narrow column.

Pane A portion of a worksheet window bounded by and separated from other portions by vertical and horizontal bars.

Password An optional element of a template added to prevent someone from disabling a worksheet's protection.

Paste The action of placing cell contents that have been copied or moved to the Clipboard into another location.

Paste area The target destination for data that has been cut or copied using the Office Clipboard.

Paste Options gallery A gallery of buttons that provides a Live Preview of all the Paste options available in the current context.

PDF (Portable Document Format) A file format developed by Adobe Systems that creates a representation of electronic paper that displays your data on the screen as it would look when printed, but that cannot be easily changed.

Percent for new value = base percent + percent of increase The formula for calculating a percentage by which a value increases by adding the base percentage—usually 100%—to the percent increase.

Percentage rate of increase The percent by which one number increases over another number.

Picture element A point of light measured in dots per square inch on a screen; 64 pixels equals 8.43 characters, which is the average number of characters that will fit in a cell in an Excel worksheet using the default font.

Picture A category of SmartArt graphics that is used to display pictures in a diagram.

Pie chart A chart that shows the relationship of each part to a whole.

PivotChart A graphical representation of the data in a PivotTable report.

PivotTable Fields pane A window that lists at the top, all of the fields—column titles—from the source data for use in the PivotTable and at the bottom, an area in which you can arrange the fields in the PivotTable.

PivotTable An interactive Excel report that summarizes and analyzes large amounts of data.

Pixel The abbreviated name for a picture element.

Plot area The area bounded by the axes of a chart, including all the data series.

PMT function An Excel function that calculates the payment for a loan based on constant payments and a constant interest rate.

Point and click method The technique of constructing a formula by pointing to and then clicking cells; this method is convenient when the referenced cells are not adjacent to one another.

Precedent cells Cells that are referred to by a formula in another cell.

Present value (Pv) The total amount that a series of future payments is worth now; also known as the *principal*.

Primary key The field used to uniquely identify a record in an Access table.

Principal The total amount that a series of future payments is worth now; also known as the *Present value (Pv)*.

Print Titles An Excel command that enables you to specify rows and columns to repeat on each printed page.

Procedure A unit of computer code that performs an action.

PROPER A text function that capitalizes the first letter of each word.

Property A characteristic of an object that can be changed.

Query A process of restricting records through the use of criteria conditions that will display records that will answer a question about the data.

Quick Analysis Tool A tool that displays in the lower right corner of a selected range with which you can analyze your data by using Excel tools such as charts, color-coding, and formulas.

Range Two or more selected cells on a worksheet that are adjacent or nonadjacent; because the range is treated as a single unit, you can make the same changes or combination of changes to more than one cell at a time.

Range finder An Excel feature that outlines cells in color to indicate which cells are used in a formula; useful for verifying which cells are referenced in a formula.

Rate In the Excel PMT function, the term used to indicate the interest rate for a loan.

Rate = amount of increase/base The mathematical formula to calculate a rate of increase.

Recommended Charts An Excel feature that displays a customized set of charts that, according to Excel's calculations, will best fit your data based on the range of data that you select.

Record All the categories of data pertaining to one person, place, thing, event, or idea.

Record Macro The Excel command that records your actions in Visual Basic for Applications (VBA).

Refresh The command to update a PivotTable to reflect the new data.

Relationship An association between tables that share a common field.

Relative cell reference In a formula, the address of a cell based on the relative positions of the cell that contains the formula and the cell referred to in the formula.

RIGHT A text function that returns the specified number of characters from the end (right) of a string of characters.

Rounding A procedure in which you determine which digit at the right of the number will be the last digit displayed and then increase it by one if the next digit to its right is 5, 6, 7, 8, or 9.

Row A horizontal group of cells in a worksheet.

Row heading The numbers along the left side of an Excel worksheet that designate the row numbers.

Rows area An area to position fields that you want to display as rows in the PivotTable report. Field names placed here become row titles, and the data is grouped by these row titles.

Scale to Fit Excel commands that enable you to stretch or shrink the width, height, or both, of printed output to fit a maximum number of pages.

Scaling The group of commands by which you can reduce the horizontal and vertical size of the printed data by a percentage or by the number of pages that you specify.

Scenario Manager A what-if analysis tool that compares alternatives.

Scenario A set of values that Excel saves and can substitute automatically in your worksheet.

Scope The location within which a defined name is recognized without qualification—usually either to a specific worksheet or to the entire workbook.

Select All box A box in the upper left corner of the worksheet grid that, when clicked, selects all the cells in a worksheet.

Series A group of values that come one after another in succession; for example, January, February, March, and so on.

Sheet tab scrolling buttons Buttons to the left of the sheet tabs used to display Excel sheet tabs that are not in view; used when there are more sheet tabs than will display in the space provided.

Sheet tabs The labels along the lower border of the Excel window that identify each worksheet.

Show Formulas A command that displays the formula in each cell instead of the resulting value.

Slicer header The top of a slicer that indicates the category of the slicer items.

Slicer Easy-to-use filtering control with buttons that enable you to drill down through large amounts of data.

Solver A what-if analysis tool with which you can find an optimal (maximum or minimum) value for a formula in one cell—referred to as the objective cell—subject to constraints, or limits, on the values of other formula cells on a worksheet.

Sort The process of arranging data in a specific order based on the value in each field.

Sort dialog box A dialog box in which you can sort data based on several criteria at once, and that enables a sort by more than one column or row.

Source data The data for a PivotTable, formatted in columns and rows, which can be located in an Excel worksheet or an external source.

Sparkline A tiny chart in the background of a cell that gives a visual trend summary alongside your data; makes a pattern more obvious.

Split The command that enables you to view separate parts of the same worksheet on your screen; splits the window into multiple resizable panes to view distant parts of the worksheet at one time.

Spreadsheet Another name for a worksheet.

Statistical functions Excel functions, including the AVERAGE, MEDIAN, MIN, and MAX functions, which are useful to analyze a group of measurements.

Status bar The area along the lower edge of the Excel window that displays, on the left side, the current cell mode, page number, and worksheet information; on the right side, when numerical data is selected, common calculations such as Sum and Average display.

Sub Short for a sub procedure.

Sub procedure A unit of computer code that performs an action.

Subtotal command The command that totals several rows of related data together by automatically inserting subtotals and totals for the selected cells.

SUM function A predefined formula that adds all the numbers in a selected range of cells.

SUMIF function A logical function that contains one logic test—it will add values in a specified range that meet certain conditions or criteria.

SUMIFS function A logical function that will add values in multiple ranges that meet multiple criteria.

Summary sheet A worksheet where totals from other worksheets are displayed and summarized.

Switch Row/Column A charting command to swap the data over the axis—data being charted on the vertical axis will move to the horizontal axis and vice versa.

Syntax The arrangement of the arguments in a function.

Tab delimited text file A file type in which cells are separated by tabs; this type of file can be readily exchanged with various database programs.

Table array A defined range of cells, arranged in a column or a row, used in a VLOOKUP or HLOOKUP function.

Table Data stored in a format of rows and columns.

Text function A function that can be used to combine or separate data, change case, and apply formatting to a string of characters.

Text values Constant values consisting of only text, and which usually provides information about number values; also referred to as labels.

Theme A predefined set of colors, fonts, lines, and fill effects that coordinate.

Trace Dependents command A command that displays arrows that indicate what cells are affected by the value of the currently selected cell.

Trace Error command A tool that helps locate and resolve an error by tracing the selected error value.

Trace Precedents command A command that displays arrows to indicate what cells affect the value of the cell that is selected.

Tracer arrow An indicator that shows the relationship between the active cell and its related cell.

Transpose To switch the data in rows and columns.

TRIM A text function that removes extra blank spaces from a string of characters.

Two-variable Data table A data table that changes the values in two cells.

Type argument An optional argument in the PMT function that assumes that the payment will be made at the end of each time period.

Underlying formula The formula entered in a cell and visible only on the Formula Bar.

Underlying value The data that displays in the Formula Bar.

UPPER A text function that changes the case of the characters in a string, making all characters uppercase.

Validation list A list of values that are acceptable for a group of cells; only values on the list are valid and any value *not* on the list is considered invalid.

Value Another name for a constant value.

Value after increase = base x percent for new value The formula for calculating the value after an increase by multiplying the original value—the base—by the percent for new value (see the *Percent for new value* formula).

Value axis A numerical scale on the left side of a chart that shows the range of numbers for the data points; also referred to as the y-axis.

Values area An area to position fields that contain data that is summarized in a PivotTable report or PivotChart report. The data placed here is usually numeric or financial in nature and the data is summarized—summed. You can also perform other basic calculations such as finding the average, the minimum, or the maximum.

Variable cell In Solver, a cell in which the value will change to achieve the desired results.

Variable expense Expense that varies depending on the amount of sales.

VBA The abbreviation for the Visual Basic for Applications programming language.

VBA construct An instruction that enables a macro to perform multiple operations on a single object.

Visual Basic Editor The window in which you can view and edit Visual Basic code.

Visual Basic for Applications The programming language used to write computer programs in the Microsoft Windows environment.

VLOOKUP An Excel function that looks up values that are displayed vertically in a column.

Volatile A term used to describe an Excel function that is subject to change each time the workbook is reopened; for example, the NOW function updates itself to the current date and time each time the workbook is opened.

Watch Window A window that displays the results of specified cells.

What-If Analysis The process of changing the values in cells to see how those changes affect the outcome of formulas in a worksheet.

Wildcard A character, for example the asterisk or question mark, used to search a field when you are uncertain of the exact value or when you want to widen the search to include more records.

Workbook An Excel file that contains one or more worksheets.

Worksheet The primary document that you use in Excel to work with and store data, and which is formatted as a pattern of uniformly spaced horizontal and vertical lines.

Worksheet grid area A part of the Excel window that displays the columns and rows that intersect to form the worksheet's cells.

X-axis Another name for the horizontal (category) axis.

.xlsx file name extension The default file format used by Excel to save an Excel workbook.

Y-axis Another name for the vertical (value) axis.

Index

Extensible Markup Language (XML), 684
external data, 331–333
Extract All, 11
extract area, 403
Extract tab, 11
extracting
    with File Explorer, 73–74
    zipped files, 11–14, 65–66
extracting, 10, 403

F

Few, Stephen, 101
field
    adding, to PivotTable, 310–312
    defining, 391
    in Microsoft Access, 331
    as vertical column, 679
field buttons, 324
field names, 307
Field section, 309–310
File Explorer
    copying and moving files by snapping
        windows in, 92–93
    copying files in, 89–90
    displaying locations, folders, and files
        with, 74–78
    extracting zipped files with, 73–74
    navigating with, 71–73
    OneDrive and, 54
    parts of window, 56–57
    ribbons in, 57
    searching, pinning, sorting, and filtering
        in, 84–85
    window, 56–57, 73
    window parts, 73
    zipped folders in, 65
File Explorer, 11, 52, 55
file lists
    All Files type in, 82
    quick access, 71
file lists, 56, 58, 64, 73, 76, 87–88
file name extensions, 82
file names, 37, 64
file properties, 76
File tab, 4, 6, 8
files
    compressed, 10
    copying, 89–90
        from removable storage, 85–86
        by snapping windows, 92–93
    creating and saving, 59–65
    creating folders for storing, 54–59
    defining, 54
    deleting, 87, 94
    displaying with File Explorer, 74–78
    Excel, 385–389
    moving, 85–86, 90–91
    opening, 80–83
    renaming, 87–88
    saving after naming, 9
    saving as templates, 459

    selecting, 91
    Word, 80–83
    XPS, 41
    zipped, 11–14, 65–66, 73–74
files, 6
Fill Effects dialog box, 16
fill handles
    Auto Fill with, 110
    copying formulas with, 116–117
Fill Series, 110
fills
    defining, 16
    gradient, 16
filtered lists, 85
filtering
    with advanced criteria, 399–402
    by custom criteria, using AutoFilter,
        397–399
    defining, 395
    Excel tables, 192–193
    in File Explorer, 84–85
    by format and values, using AutoFilter,
        395–397
    a PivotTable, 313–316
    by search box, 316–317
filtering buttons, 314
filtering controls, 702
filters
    applying to Excel tables, 192–193
    clearing, 193, 316–317
    custom and advanced, 395–404
Filters area, 310
financial function
    defining, 491
    PMT, 491–493
financial numbers, formatting, 118–120
Find and Replace feature, 187
Find command, 369
Firefox browser, 11, 65
Fit All Columns on One Page, 195–196
fixed expenses, 576
Flash Fill, 175–176, 688–689
folder structure, 70
folder windows, 72
folders
    creating, 87–88
        for file storage, 7–10
        new, 54–59
    defining, 54
    displaying with File Explorer, 74–78
    Documents, 82, 86–87
    parent, 57
    personal, 86
    renaming, 87–88
    subfolders, 70, 75
    zipped, 65
folders, 6
Font gallery, 28
fonts
    axis, 278–279
    Calibri Light, 28
    Cambria, 27
    chart title formatting, 252

    colors, 27–30
    formatting text with, 27–30
    sans serif, 28
    serif, 28
    sizes, 28
    styles, 27–30
    themes, 28
footers
    adding file name to, 37
    custom, 218, 706–709
    defining, 37
    inserting, 37–38
    repeating, 217–219
    in worksheets, 127–128
forecast, 573–575
form, 632
Form control, 643
format, filtering by, 395–397
Format Chart Area pane, 275–276
Format Data Labels pane, 253–254
Format Data Series pane, 254–257
Format Painter, 30–32, 266, 281
formatting
    axes, 273–275
    axis titles, 436–437
    cell styles, 118
    cells, 117–120, 145
    charts
        area, 258, 276–277
        elements, 252–254
        floors and chart walls, 438–439
        titles, 252, 436
    clearing from cells, 204–205
    conditional, 185–186, 199, 703–706
    data series, 442–443
        with shadow effects, 256
        with 3-D effects, 254–255
    dates, 202–204
    defining, 15
    exploding and coloring pie chart slices,
        256–257
    financial numbers, 118–120
    with Format Painter, 30–32
    funnel charts, 447–448
    grouped worksheets, 207–211
    with individual commands, 120
    line chart fonts, 278–279
    multiple worksheets, 217–219
    numbers, 113
    Paste Special and, 269
    pie charts, 252–258
    PivotTable Report, 322
    plot area gridlines, 278–279
    plot areas and data series, 442–443
    shadow effects, 256
    sparklines, 126–127, 429–430
    templates, 453–454
    text, 27–32
    3-D Pie PivotChart, 335–338
    3-D effects, 254–255
    worksheets, 146–150 (*See also*
        worksheets)
formatting marks, 12

Formula Auditing, 520
Formula Auditing group, 130–131
Formula AutoComplete, 264
Formula Bar, 109–110, 115–116, 136, 145, 265
formulas
  absolute cell references and copying, 142–144
  audit worksheet, 520–525
  complex, 597–604
  constructing, 114–116
  copying, 116–117, 142–144
  defining, 520
  displaying, 130–131
  on grouped worksheets, 207–210
  managing and using, in conditional formatting rules, 704–706
  mathematical operations with, 139–144
  parentheses in, 264–265
  point and click method for constructing, 115
  printing, 131–132
  referring to cells, 213
  template, 454–456
  underlying, 115
  using defined names in, 508–509
formulas, 108
free-form snips, 62
Freeze Panes command, 189, 369
freezing
  columns, 189
  panes, 188–189
frequent folders area, 56
full-screen snips, 62
Function Arguments dialog box, 178
functions. (*See also* database functions; financial function; lookup functions
  AVERAGE, 177–179, 198
  AVERAGEIFS function, 600–602
  CONCATENATE, 690
  COUNT, 183
  COUNTIF, 183, 198, 594
  COUNTIFS, 594, 596–597
  Date & Time, 188
  DAVERAGE, 692–694
  DCOUNT, 695–697
  defining, 114, 175, 691
  AND function, 597–599
  Google Sheets, 198
  IF, 184–185, 198
  IFS, 215–217, 602–604
  INDEX, 535–539
  Left and Right, 690
  logical, 183 (*See also* logical functions)
  LOWER, 690
  MATCH, 535–539
  MAX, 180
  MAXIFS, 697–699
  MEDIAN, 179–180
  MID, 690
  MIN, 180
  MINIFS, 697–699
  nested, 599–600

NOT function, 597
NOW, 188
OR function, 597
PROPER, 690
statistical, 175
SUM, 114–116, 177–179, 198, 210–211
SUMIF, 594–595
SUMIFS, 594–596
Text, 690–691
TRANSPOSE, 570
TRIM, 690
UPPER, 690
volatile, 188
funds, 249
funnel charts, 278, 280–281, 447–448
Future value (Fv), 491, 493

G

galleries, 18
general formats, 113
general funds, 249
Get External Data, 679
Get & Transform, 680
Go To command, 371–372
Go To Special command, 369–370
Goal Seek
  defining, 493
  using to find increased payment period, 495–496
  using to produce desired result, 494–495
Goal Seek, 259–260
Google Sheets
  functions, 198
  inventory valuation reports using, 151–152
  line charts in, 283
  pie charts, 262
  summarizing inventory lists, 198–199
Google Sheets, 133–134, 221–222
gradient fills, 16
graphical user interface (GUI), 47
graphics, 32
gridlines, 433
group names, 6, 12
grouped worksheets
  formatting, 211
  formatting and constructing formulas on, 207–210
  multiple totals on, 210–211
grouping, 404–406
groups, 19
GUI. *See* graphical user interface

H

handles, 434
hard disk drives, 54, 85
Header & Footer tab, 128
headers and footers, custom, 706–709
headings. *See also* column headings
  in File Explorer window, 73
  row, 108, 146

Help buttons, 56
Help features, 41–44
Help panes, 42
Help & Support group, 43
hiding, 328–329, 370–371
  rows and columns, 681–683
  worksheets, 208, 681–683
hierarchies, 70, 444
Highlight Cells Rules, 186
HLOOKUP, 512
Home tab, 4
Horizontal Category axis (x-axis), 433
HTML. *See* Hypertext Markup Language
hyperlinks
  defining, 379
  inserting, in worksheets, 382–383
  modifying, 384–385
Hypertext Markup Language (HTML), 385–387

I

icon sets, 704
icons, 47
IF function, 184–185, 198
IFS function, 215–217, 602–604
Illustrations group, 39
image, 456–457
importing data
  into Excel
    from Access database, 679–681
    from delimited Text File, 685–687
    from XML file, 684–685
income, 576–577
increased payment period, 495–496
indentation, 681–683
INDEX functions
  defining, 535
  using, 536–539
Info tab, 8, 38
information, 691
initial settings, restoring, 656
input devices, 47
Insert Chart dialog box, 121–123
Insert tab, Illustrations group, 39
inserting
  ActiveX controls, 643–646
  bookmarks, 39
  charts, 120–123
  columns, 146–147
  footers, 37–38
  hyperlinks, in worksheets, 382–383
  image, 456–457
  new data, into named ranges, 505–506
  rows and row headings, 146
  saved files, into presentations, 66
  second table, into worksheets, 701–703
  shape containing text, 600–602
  3D models, 39
  trendline, 443–444
  VLOOKUP function, 514–517
  worksheets, 212